BRYMAN'S SOCIAL RESEARCH METHODS

SIXTH EDITION

TOM **CLARK** | LIAM **FOSTER** | LUKE **SLOAN** | ALAN **BRYMAN**

Editorial advisor: Elena Vacchelli

OXFORD
UNIVERSITY PRESS

Great Clarendon Street, Oxford, OX2 6DP,
United Kingdom

Oxford University Press is a department of the University of Oxford.
It furthers the University's objective of excellence in research, scholarship,
and education by publishing worldwide. Oxford is a registered trade mark of
Oxford University Press in the UK and in certain other countries

Third edition 2008
Fourth edition 2012
Fifth edition 2016

Impression: 1

Published in the United States of America by Oxford University Press
198 Madison Avenue, New York, NY 10016, United States of America

British Library Cataloguing in Publication Data
Data available

Library of Congress Control Number: 2021930836

ISBN 978–0–19–879605–3

Printed and bound in Great Britain by Bell and Bain Ltd, Glasgow

Screenshots and screen captures are taken from IBM SPSS® Statistics Version 26.0 for Mac; NVivo® Version 12 for Mac; R Version 4.0.0 for Mac; Stata® Version 15 for Mac; and Microsoft Excel® 2016 for Windows.

This edition is dedicated to the memory of Professor Alan Bryman (1947–2017).

Hundreds of thousands of students across six continents have been fortunate enough to learn from Alan's publications. Few contemporary UK academics have had such a profound effect on learning. At Oxford University Press we are incredibly proud of Alan's significant achievements over the many years we worked with him. We thank him for everything he has done for research methods as a discipline, and for his tireless dedication to the pursuit of shining the light of understanding into the dark corners of students' minds. It was a real pleasure to work with him.

BRIEF CONTENTS

DETAILED CONTENTS

ABOUT THIS BOOK

The focus of the book

Alan Bryman originally wrote this book, and we have updated it, with two main groups of readers in mind. The first are undergraduates in social science subjects such as sociology, social policy, criminology, human geography, politics, and education who take a research methods module as part of their course. The second group comprises undergraduates and postgraduates on these courses who carry out a research project or dissertation as part of their studies, usually towards the end of their programme of study.

As well as providing you with practical advice on doing research, this book explores the nature of social research and the key arguments and debates that surround our methodological choices. It covers both the theory and the practice of a wide range of research methods, including key research strategies, common research designs, important methods of data collection and analysis, and ethical considerations. The book will be invaluable to both groups of readers.

Why it is important to study research methods

No professional turns up to work without the skills, knowledge, and instruments that they need in order to do their job properly, and social research is no different. If you want to take on the vital job of investigating the social world in all its fascinating (and often messy) complexity then you need the right tools, and studying research methods is the way to get them.

Studying research methods is partly about acquiring the *practical skills* that will allow you to carry out your own research—how best to design a questionnaire, observe people or settings, analyse documents, and so on. So this book will enable you to learn about the practices to follow when implementing particular data collection methods and approaches to analysing data, and the many pitfalls to be avoided. But studying research methods is also about gaining an appreciation of the *wider issues* that impact on the practice of doing social research. Crucially, knowledge of research methods will help you develop the critical awareness that allows you to understand not only *how* research is conducted but *why*, and with what assumptions.

Essentially, studying research methods sensitizes you to the choices that are available to social researchers. This knowledge and awareness will empower you to understand and critically evaluate the work that you encounter in books, in journals, and on your module or course, and it will also help you make the most appropriate choices for your own project.

Thinking beyond university, a training in research methods gives you transferable skills that are highly valued by employers. Knowing how to sample, how to design a questionnaire, how to conduct semi-structured interviews or focus groups, how to harness and analyse large quantities of data, and so on will be relevant in many spheres, and being able to interrogate evidence and reflect on practice are key skills in all areas of work.

Finally, studying research methods is important because it is what unites us as social scientists. You will have chosen to study social science because you are fascinated by how people relate to each other individually and in groups—how institutions shape us and how we shape institutions; how opinions and attitudes differ by demographic groups; and how ideas, norms, and practices change over time. Every social scientist has their own specific interests, driven by curiosity, personal experience, or a sense of social justice—our own interests range widely, from social media (Luke), to ageing (Liam), to the sociology of evil (Tom)—but we are all united by our commitment to understanding the social world through empirical inquiry. Research methods is the common language (albeit with some slightly different dialects) that allows us to work together to explore and try to address social issues.

The structure of the book

Social research has many different traditions, one of the most fundamental of which is the distinction between quantitative and qualitative research. Throughout his career Alan Bryman was steadfast in his belief that research methods need to be tailored to the problem that they are intended to address, and that the strict division between quantitative and qualitative research is not always helpful. Indeed, this was one of the reasons he was such an advocate for mixed methods approaches in research. This 'problem-based' approach to research methods is one that Liam, Luke, and Tom also very much agree on. All methods present opportunities and challenges; the key is to understand what each one offers and to reflect on and attempt to mitigate its shortcomings.

However, we are also experienced enough to know that having some degree of separation can aid the learning process, particularly where that process actually involves *doing* social research. It is for this pedagogical reason that we continue to use the distinction between quantitative and qualitative to help structure the book, and the way in which we approach issues and methods. We remain, and always will, agnostic on which method is 'better' or 'best' in absolute terms, because the answer will always depend entirely on what you are trying to achieve in your project.

The book is divided into four parts.

Part One comprises six scene-setting chapters. It deals with basic ideas about the nature of social research. In particular, the first three chapters provide the basic building blocks for the rest of the book.

- Chapter 1 outlines some of the *main stages* to consider when doing most kinds of social research, providing an overview of topics and areas that are addressed in much greater detail later in the book.
- Chapter 2 examines the nature of the relationship between *theory and research*, and the degree to which a natural science approach is an appropriate framework for studying society. Here, we set out the distinction between quantitative and qualitative research for the first time.
- In Chapter 3 we introduce the idea of a *research design*—the basic framework within which social research is carried out. We consider cross-sectional and longitudinal designs, case study research, experimental research, and comparative design.
- Chapter 4 takes you through the main steps involved in *planning* a research project and offers advice on how to manage this process. It includes a discussion of *research questions*.
- Chapter 5 introduces the main steps in conducting a *literature review*—part of a research project in which you evaluate the existing literature relating to your area of interest.
- Chapter 6 considers the ways in which *ethical issues* affect researchers and their practice, as well as the kinds of principles that are involved.

Part Two contains nine chapters exploring aspects of quantitative research. These include three chapters (9–11) that are largely devoted to aspects of social survey research.

- Chapter 7 explores the *nature of quantitative research*. It provides key context for the later chapters in this section.
- Chapter 8 deals with *sampling* issues, including how to select a sample and the considerations involved in assessing what we can infer from different kinds of sample.
- Chapter 9 considers the kind of *interviewing* that takes place in survey research—that is, structured interviewing.
- Chapter 10 covers the *design of questionnaires*. We explore how to devise self-completion questionnaires, such as those that people might fill out online or by post.
- Chapter 11 examines ways of *asking questions* and designing answers when preparing questionnaires and structured interviews.
- Chapter 12 focuses on *structured observation*, which is a method of data collection that is used for the systematic observation of behaviour.
- Chapter 13 covers *quantitative content analysis*. This is a method that provides a rigorous framework for analysing a wide range of documents, from written information to visual materials.
- Chapter 14 looks at *secondary data analysis*—that is, analysing existing data that has already been collected (by other researchers and by official bodies). It includes a focus on 'Big Data' and social media.
- Chapter 15 presents a range of basic tools and techniques that can be used for *analysing quantitative data*. We take a non-technical approach, with an emphasis on how to choose a method of analysis and how to interpret the findings, but this chapter is supplemented by extensive **online resources** on how you can use software packages to conduct quantitative data analysis. We have video tutorials and quick reference guides for the popular packages SPSS®, R, and Stata®, worksheets on using Microsoft Excel® for data analysis, and example data sets for you to use when practising.

Part Three contains eight chapters on aspects of qualitative research.

- Chapter 16 gives an overview of the *nature of qualitative research*, providing the context for the other chapters in this part of the book.
- Chapter 17 examines the main *sampling* strategies employed in qualitative research. As you will see, the principles involved are different from those usually used by quantitative researchers (covered in Chapter 8).
- Chapter 18 discusses *ethnography and participant observation*. These two terms, often used interchangeably, both refer to the researcher becoming immersed in a social setting.
- Chapter 19 deals with the kinds of *interviews* that qualitative researchers conduct, which are usually semi-structured or unstructured interviews.
- Chapter 20 explores the *focus group*, a method where groups of individuals are interviewed about a specific topic.
- Chapter 21 examines two approaches to *qualitative language analysis*: conversation analysis and discourse analysis.
- Chapter 22 explores the use of *documents as data* in qualitative research.
- Chapter 23 introduces some of the main approaches to *analysing qualitative data*. As with Chapter 15, this chapter is supplemented by **online resources** to support you in using software (the popular package NVivo) to conduct qualitative data analysis—though, as we discuss in Chapter 23, you should carefully consider whether this is the best approach for your project.

You will notice that certain topics recur across Parts Two and Three: sampling, interviewing, observation, documents, and data analysis. However, it will become clear that quantitative and qualitative researchers often approach these issues in different ways.

Part Four contains two chapters, one looking beyond the quantitative/qualitative divide and the other on how we conclude the research process.

- Chapter 24 looks at some of the ways in which the distinction between quantitative and qualitative research is less fixed than is sometimes supposed. It presents some of the ways in which—and reasons why—quantitative and qualitative research can be combined to produce what is known as *mixed methods research*.
- Chapter 25 provides guidance on writing up research, a key element of the research process.

How to use the book

Our experience as lecturers suggests that students will use this book in many different ways. For some, it will be a reference book that aids them throughout their programme, some will dip in and out of it as required for their research methods module and/or student research project, while others might use specific discussions associated with a particular method as a platform for their own study.

How we recommend that you use this book will therefore depend on what you are using it for, but the 'Guide to using this book', which appears later on in this introductory section, provides a good starting point for all readers. This will give you an overview of the main features and resources that we have provided within and alongside the text, and how they might help you achieve your aims.

Many of the features and resources will be equally useful for everyone—such as the 'Chapter guides', which outline the areas covered in each chapter, and the 'Research in focus' boxes, which illustrate how the methods or issues that we are discussing turn up within real studies. However, some features and resources may be particularly useful for readers at certain stages in their studies, or those with a particular aim in mind. For example, if you are using the book in the context of a research methods module, the 'Thinking deeply' boxes and many of the end-of-chapter review questions (and their accompanying answers and audio discussions) will help you to reflect on the issues in more depth. This is exactly what you will be required to do for your essays and assignments. If, however, you are searching for information and guidance to help you conduct your own student research project then 'Tips and skills' and 'Learn from experience' boxes, as well as our 'Student researcher's toolkit', will provide practical and student-focused tips, advice, and materials.

However you use this book (and however many times during the course of your studies and/or career), we hope that you find it as invaluable a guide to the essentials of social research as we found its earlier editions. Whatever your focus or stage, we recommend making full use of both the core chapter content and the online resources, including the self-test questions, the flashcard glossary provided for every chapter, and the 'Research process in practice' simulation. We also suggest that before you begin reading, you watch our videos about the impact of Covid-19 on social research. The pandemic is still underway at the time of writing but has already had a significant effect on the social world and therefore also on social research, so our reflections are intended to highlight some considerations to keep in mind as you approach the book's content and accompanying resources.

ABOUT THE AUTHORS

Tom Clark is a Lecturer in Research Methods at the University of Sheffield, UK. He is interested in all aspects of methods and methodology, particularly with respect to learning and teaching. He is the co-author of *How to do your Social Research Project or Dissertation* (Oxford University Press, 2019), with Liam Foster and Alan Bryman. His other interests have variously focused on the sociology of evil, student experiences of higher education, and football fandom. Tom's work has been published in a wide variety of journals, including *Sociology*, *Qualitative Research*, *Social Policy and Administration*, *Teaching in Higher Education*, *Journal of Education and Work*, and *Qualitative Social Work*.

Liam Foster is a Senior Lecturer in Social Policy and Social Work at the University of Sheffield, UK, who specializes in pensions and theories of ageing. Liam also has a longstanding interest in methods and has published widely in this area, including *Beginning Statistics for Social Scientists* (Sage, 2015), with Ian Diamond and Julie Jefferies, and *How to do your Social Research Project or Dissertation* (Oxford University Press, 2019), with Tom Clark and Alan Bryman. He has been an invited speaker at the UK's Department for Education and Department for Work and Pensions, the European Parliament in Brussels, the House of Lords, and the UN in New York, as a world-leading expert on ageing. Liam is a member of the UK Social Policy Association Executive Committee. He is also the former managing editor, with Majella Kilkey, of *Social Policy and Society*. Liam's work has appeared in journals including *Ageing and Society*, *Critical Social Policy*, *The Gerontologist*, *Journal of Social Policy*, *Policy and Politics*, and *Social Policy and Administration*.

Luke Sloan is Professor, Deputy Director of the Social Data Science Lab, and Director of Learning and Teaching at the School of Social Sciences at Cardiff University, UK. Luke's internationally recognized work focuses on exploring how social media data, specifically from Twitter, can be used for social-scientific research. He is co-editor of the *SAGE Handbook of Social Media Research Methods* (Sage, 2017), with Anabel Quan-Haase, and has published widely on how Twitter can help us understand social phenomena and the ethics of using this data for research. His work has appeared in journals including *Sociology*, *Social Media + Society*, *British Journal of Criminology*, *Electoral Studies*, *PLoS ONE*, and *Journal of Empirical Research on Human Research Ethics*.

Alan Bryman was Professor of Organizational and Social Research at the University of Leicester from 2005 to 2017. Prior to this he was Professor of Social Research at Loughborough University for 31 years.

His main research interests were in leadership, especially in higher education; research methods (particularly mixed methods research); and the 'Disneyization' and 'McDonaldization' of modern society. In 2003–4 he completed a project on the issue of how quantitative and qualitative research are combined in the social sciences, as part of the Research Methods Programme of the UK's Economic and Social Research Council (ESRC). He contributed articles to a range of academic journals, including *Journal of Management Studies*, *Human Relations*, *International Journal of Social Research Methodology*, *Leadership Quarterly*, and *American Behavioral Scientist*. He was a member of the ESRC's Research Grants Board and conducted research into effective leadership in higher education, a project funded by the Leadership Foundation for Higher Education.

Alan published widely in the field of social research. Among his writings were *Quantitative Data Analysis with SPSS 17, 18 and 19: A Guide for Social Scientists* (Routledge, 2011), with Duncan Cramer; *Social Research Methods* (Oxford University Press, 2008); *The SAGE Encyclopedia of Social Science Research Methods* (Sage, 2004), with Michael Lewis-Beck and Tim Futing Liao; *The Disneyization of Society* (Sage, 2004); *Handbook of Data Analysis* (Sage, 2004), with Melissa Hardy; *Understanding Research for Social Policy and Practice* (Policy Press, 2004), with Saul Becker; and the *SAGE Handbook of Organizational Research Methods*, with David Buchanan (Sage, 2009). He edited the Understanding Social Research series for the Open University Press.

 **www.oup.com/he/srm6e**

Access the **online resources** to watch the 'Meet the authors' video in which Tom, Liam, and Luke introduce themselves and discuss their work on this book.

GUIDE TO USING THIS BOOK

The sixth edition of *Bryman's Social Research Methods* provides a rich multi-media experience in which the text's unrivalled coverage is supplemented by resources that clarify, consolidate, and bring research methods to life. Outlined here are the key features and resources that we have included in the book and its accompanying **online resources** to help you understand each topic and, importantly, help you to use this knowledge to evaluate existing research and conduct your own.

MASTER THE ESSENTIALS

Placed at the start of each chapter, the **Chapter guide** grounds you in each topic, outlining the issues to be discussed and the knowledge and skills you will gain. It helps you navigate the chapters and provides benchmarks against which you can measure your progress and understanding. As you read, **Key concept** boxes provide clear, concise explanations of crucial terms and processes, and concluding lists of **Key points** sum up the essential ideas to take away.

CONSOLIDATE YOUR UNDERSTANDING

A total of over 300 **self-test questions**, hosted online but mapped to each section of the book, provide extensive opportunities to check your understanding. Each chapter's **flashcard glossary** and concluding **review questions** (with notes on their answers provided online) offer further ways to test your knowledge of both the specific and the broader issues associated with the topic.

LEARN FROM REAL RESEARCH

Countless examples of real-world studies bridge the gap between theory and practice and provide an invaluable window into the fascinating issues explored in social science. **Research in focus** boxes illustrate how professional researchers use the various methods, and the challenges and opportunities they encounter 'in the field', while **Learn from experience** boxes and their accompanying audio and video resources show how these ideas translate into the context of real student research projects.

TAKE YOUR LEARNING FURTHER

Thinking deeply boxes provide extended discussions of important issues, highlighting complexities and nuance to help you take your learning further. The authors' audio **discussions of key issues** and video **reflections on the impact of Covid-19 on social research** will also broaden your understanding and increase your appreciation of the wider issues and assumptions affecting social research.

PUT YOUR KNOWLEDGE INTO PRACTICE

Tips and skills boxes outline key practical considerations and skills for each method, and the **Student researcher's toolkit** online provides checklists, templates, and examples to help you put this knowledge into practice in your student research project. We also address common questions in the **toolkit FAQs**. The **'Research process in practice' simulation** allows you to gain experience of the full process—from choosing a research design to disseminating your findings—without real-world consequences if things don't work out quite as they should.

DELVE INTO YOUR DATA

Our online guidance on using the popular data analysis software packages **IBM SPSS®**, **R**, **Stata®**, and **NVivo®**—consisting of **video tutorials**, plus written versions with helpful screenshots, and **quick reference guides**—will help you get to grips with using these programs within your own research. We provide **quantitative data sets** (in SPSS and Excel formats) that you can use when practising with the programs. If you prefer to learn new tricks within a more familiar program, we also supply **worksheets on using Microsoft Excel®** for data analysis.

LEARN FROM EXPERIENCE

THE *SOCIAL RESEARCH METHODS* GRADUATE PANEL

To become an effective researcher, it is important to learn from the research process. As a reader of this edition, you can benefit from the experiences of 13 recent graduates who studied a variety of social science subjects at institutions across the UK and Europe—and, in some cases, have gone on to conduct postgraduate research. Our panel share their research methods insights, successes, and 'I wish I'd known . . . ' moments throughout this book, in the 'Learn from experience' boxes that appear in every chapter. Their reflections illustrate how the methods and issues that we discuss actually appear 'in the field', particularly in the context of student research, and will help you carry out successful research of your own. We are extremely grateful to the panel for their insights and generosity.

You can read about the panellists' backgrounds and research experiences below, and visit the **online resources** *to hear them expand on their comments in video and audio clips.*

Reni Adebayo studied Politics and International Relations at the University of Bath, UK, graduating in 2019. Her final year research project focused on the International Criminal Court and its alleged bias against African countries. Though initially daunted by research methods she gained confidence and skills, taking a mixed methods approach—which included hypothesis-testing and a comparison of two case studies—and using secondary data that she sourced online. She used SPSS in her analysis. Reni has used her research skills repeatedly since graduating; she conducted research for clients while interning at KPMG Nigeria and often analyses quantitative data within her current role at a New York tech startup.

Sarah Akhtar Baz graduated from the University of Sheffield, UK, in 2016 with a BA in Social Policy and Sociology. She continued her studies at Sheffield through an MA in Social Research, which led directly into her current PhD project at the same university. For her undergraduate research, which explored the role of social capital in empowering popular spaces, Sarah's main research method was semi-structured interviews. For her PhD on the lived experiences of South Asian Muslim lone mothers, intersectionality, and the role played by South Asian women's organizations in their lives, she is using both semi-structured interviews and extended participant observation. Her research is grounded in Black feminist methodological approaches.

Starr Campagnaro completed a BA in Anthropology at the University of Guelph, Canada, in 2014, and then gained an MSc in International and Comparative Education from Stockholm University, Sweden, in 2017. For the latter, her research project explored international and national (Canadian) ethical policies concerning higher education internationalization and compared international and domestic student experiences of one such policy within a particular Canadian educational faculty. Starr's qualitative research used a comparative case study design and she employed purposive and snowball sampling. She collected data through semi-structured interviews and documents and carried out an applied thematic analysis using the software package NVivo. Starr now works as a freelance editor to assist academics and ESL graduate students.

Ben Childs initially studied Product Design at the University of Huddersfield, UK, and then spent over 20 years working in the digital sector before completing an MA in Digital Media and Society at the University of Sheffield, UK, in 2019. Ben wanted to explore how data visualization could improve understanding of a process known as 'datafication' and used a mixed methods approach to analyse qualitative and quantitative data generated through an online survey. He drew on his expertise in digital design when developing his survey and recruited participants by engaging with digital networks, including Twitter users. Ben has now returned to the digital sector, where his work often takes a research-based approach.

Grace Davies completed her undergraduate degree in Education Studies and English Literature at Bath Spa University, UK, graduating in 2018. For her dissertation, she explored how disability is constructed in education policy in a post-conflict environment, with reference to Rwanda. She carried out critical discourse analysis on two documents—a government policy and an NGO policy—which allowed her to investigate the underlying meanings and implications in policymaking and the ways in which power is constructed through discourse. She is now studying for an MA in Education (Policy and International Development) at the University of Bristol, UK, and hopes to pursue a career in the field of research methods.

Minke Hajer completed a BA and MA in Sociology at the University of Amsterdam in the Netherlands, graduating in 2015. Her master's degree research focused on the citizenship struggles of undocumented migrants living in Amsterdam. Her main methods were (and continue to be, in her PhD studies) participant observation combined with interviews, but she has also used digital research methods to study the presence of irregular migrants and their social movements on social media. Minke is currently studying for a joint PhD in Sociology at the University of Amsterdam and the University of Milan, Italy, and is conducting an ethnography of 'irregular' migrants in Amsterdam and Turin.

Scarlett Hunt completed her bachelor's degree in Sociology at Staffordshire University, UK, in 2019, and her MRes in Social Science Research Methods at Keele University, UK, in 2020. For her undergraduate research project she examined the relationship between social media and the wellbeing of young people, employing methods including purposive sampling, self-completion questionnaires, and focus groups. Her postgraduate research also explored issues of wellbeing, this time in the context of post-university transitions. She has experience in using the data analysis software packages SPSS and NVivo and is the author of this book's resources on the latter. She is currently working at a UK high school as an inclusion support assistant.

Laura Keesman studied Social Work at Amsterdam University of Applied Sciences, the Netherlands, graduating in 2011. Her research at undergraduate level was qualitative, exploring the issue of violence against social workers, drawing on her own experience as a former social worker and focusing particularly on bodies and emotions in tense and threatening situations. She used snowball sampling and conducted semi-structured interviews. She continued her investigation of this issue through her Sociology master's thesis and is now studying violence against police officers as part of her PhD in Cultural Sociology at the University of Amsterdam, using a combination of ethnographic fieldwork, interviewing, and video elicitation methods.

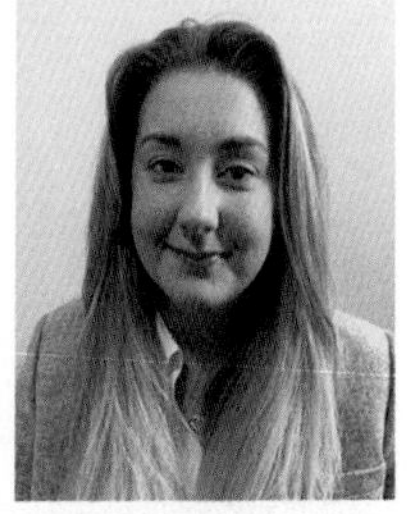

Jodie Luker did her undergraduate degree at Cardiff University, UK, graduating in 2018 with a BSc in Social Analytics. Her dissertation involved a quantitative analysis—mainly sentiment analysis—of over two million tweets to investigate Twitter as a platform for attitudes toward the LGBT+ community. She has remained at Cardiff, and her MSc project explored sexual prejudice in Europe through a secondary data analysis of European data sets. Currently she is studying for a PhD exploring the prevalence and harm(s) of online hate toward LGB+ individuals. She has extensive experience of using SPSS, R, and Stata, and is the author of our resources on these software packages.

Barbara Mirković studied for a BA and an MA in Psychology at the Catholic University of Croatia before moving to the National University of Ireland Galway for her PhD studies in Child and Youth Research. For her master's degree, she explored the roles and impact of key non-parental adults upon positive youth development. She collected data from high school students through self-completion questionnaires containing both closed and open questions. She used SPSS to analyse the data. Her PhD research is a mixed methods study (involving semi-structured interviews then the creation and validation of a scale) comparing similar issues for youth from both Ireland and Croatia.

Brendan Munhall completed an MA in International and Comparative Education at Stockholm University, Sweden, graduating in 2017. His research involved conducting semi-structured interviews with parents at Swedish refugee camps about their experiences of enrolling their children in primary school. He took a grounded theory approach. His current PhD (also at Stockholm University) also explores the challenges of navigating Sweden's education system but focuses on the experiences of recently migrated students as they transition to upper high school. He has used both purposive sampling and snowball sampling to establish a large sample, and has significant experience in using qualitative data analysis software.

Zvi Oduba completed his BSocSc in Sociology at the University of Manchester, UK, in 2019. His dissertation, titled 'Why can't iSleep?', examined the impact of screen time on the sleep duration of adolescents by analysing secondary data from the Youth Risk Behaviour Surveillance System—a large-scale cross-sectional survey of American high school students—from a sociological perspective. He used SPSS to perform univariate, bivariate, and regression analysis on 10 years' worth of data to explore the association between screen time and sleep duration. Since graduating, he has been an active alumnus of the university's Q-Step Centre and works as an analyst for the Greater Manchester Combined Authority.

Simon White completed a BA in Criminology at the University of the West of England, UK, as a mature student, graduating in 2017. Prior to this he spent 20 years working. Simon's undergraduate research used semi-structured interviews to investigate police officers' perceptions of how differences in social class affect the legitimacy of the police. For his MSc in Social Research Methods at Cardiff University, UK, he explored gender differences in the fear of crime in online and offline spaces, using statistical analysis to compare Big Data from Twitter to data from the Crime Survey for England and Wales. This forms the basis for his PhD studies at Cardiff.

WHAT DOES A GLOBAL PANDEMIC MEAN FOR SOCIAL RESEARCH?

A MESSAGE FROM THE AUTHORS

We provided the information and guidance in this edition with 'normal' social interactions in mind. However, December 2019 marked the start of a global pandemic that brought unprecedented and rapid changes to all aspects of social life and turned 'normal' on its head.

Whatever your social science discipline and your research topic, it is likely that it will have been touched by the Covid-19 pandemic, with new issues revealed and existing issues highlighted or exacerbated. There has never been such a need for social research as a tool to accurately and transparently observe, record, and report on behaviours, attitudes, and beliefs. As social researchers, we can help answer the many new questions that emerge during (and following) a time of crisis and ensure that all sectors of society have a voice.

At the time of going to press the pandemic is ongoing and it is far too early for us to predict its longer-term impact for social research and social research methods. Instead of providing written advice based on guesswork, then, we will be sharing our reflections on this theme via videos within our **online resources**. We will publish new videos regularly to respond to the latest developments as we continue to live through what is likely to be an ever-evolving 'new normal'.

We strongly encourage you to watch our latest videos before beginning to use this book, and to frequently check for updates so that you can read the guidance contained in each chapter with the latest developments in mind.

RESOURCES FOR LECTURERS

www.oup.com/he/srm6e

Bryman's Social Research Methods offers a complete package of information and resources to support your teaching of research methods. The text's crystal-clear theoretical explanations are complemented by countless real-world examples from both professional and student research, practical tips and tools for conducting research, and numerous interactive activities that will engage and inspire your students.

Adopting lecturers can access the following **online resources**:

- 250 test bank questions to check your students' understanding of each topic
- customizable PowerPoint presentations relating to each topic
- a seminar outline for each topic
- 75 exam or coursework-based questions for use in, or as starting points for, your assessments
- downloadable versions of the figures included in the book, for use in your teaching

NEW TO THIS EDITION

- The book has been thoroughly but sensitively updated by three new authors. Tom Clark, Liam Foster, and Luke Sloan bring specialist expertise in a variety of areas, including social media research, and have worked closely with students and lecturers to build on Alan Bryman's impressive legacy.
- All content has been extensively streamlined so that the sixth edition provides even more focused coverage than before of the key aspects of social research. As part of this, the previous edition's two chapters relating to mixed methods research have been combined into a single, highly engaging chapter.
- The authors have made adjustments throughout to aid navigation and improve clarity, including breaking down complex discussions into manageable parts and adopting a more straightforward writing style. Vocabulary is simpler and jargon has been removed, making the content easier for every reader to follow, but particularly those for whom English is not a first language.
- New material on recent developments within social research—including social media research, Big Data, and the use of technology to assist with data collection and analysis—has been embedded throughout, and the numerous examples of real research have been thoroughly updated to reflect contemporary methods and concerns.
- Coverage—including citations and real research examples—has been broadened to better reflect the concerns and contexts of the book's geographically diverse, multi-disciplinary readership.
- Material on feminist perspectives has been updated and relocated within the book. The core content now appears in Chapters 2, 6, 7, and 16, situating feminist ideas among the grounding principles of research; this allows for a briefer discussion elsewhere in relation to specific methods and approaches. The coverage has been broadened to explore intersectionality, positionality, and the 'insider/outsider' debate.
- New 'Learn from experience' boxes provide insights and advice on conducting a student research project from a diverse panel of recent social science graduates. These candid accounts will inspire readers, helping them to emulate successful approaches and avoid common pitfalls.
- Expanded digital resources now include a 'Research process in practice' simulation, answers to the end-of-chapter questions, and videos from the 'Learn from experience' graduate panel. They also include extensive video and textual resources to support students in using key data analysis software packages (SPSS®, NVivo®, R, and Stata®, as well as Microsoft Excel®), replacing the previous edition's two chapters on this aspect of research methods.

ACKNOWLEDGEMENTS

Social Research Methods is one of the many contributions Alan Bryman made to the social sciences. We, the book's current authors, all used copies of earlier editions as undergraduate or postgraduate students to help us study research methods at university. Subsequently, as teachers of research methods, we have all recommended it to our own students as an excellent resource to explore the subject. 'Bryman' was, and still is, a cornerstone textbook of many undergraduate experiences.

Given the way Alan's work had inspired us throughout our time at university and beyond (Tom and Liam were fortunate enough to have met and worked with him on several occasions), we were all extremely saddened to hear about his passing—and in many ways, we will always be indebted to him for helping us to develop the skills necessary for us to do our jobs today. So, we all experienced a strange combination of great regret and some honour when Oxford University Press told us that he had recommended our involvement in the new edition of this text. As such, our first acknowledgement must go to Alan Bryman, who has been such a great influence on many students and lecturers, ourselves included. In updating the text, we have tried very hard to be true to its original aims and Alan's interests, and we very much hope that he would have been pleased with the sixth edition of *Bryman's Social Research Methods*—the title of which has been changed to ensure that its association with his name continues.

This edition has also benefited from the contributions of students and colleagues at the University of Sheffield, Cardiff University, and countless other people. We thank them for their many comments, criticisms, and constructive suggestions about how to improve the teaching of social research methods. In particular, Luke would like to thank his colleagues Malcolm Williams, Matthew Williams, Anabel Quan-Haase, and Dhiraj Murthy for their support. Liam would like to thank Clive Norris, Dave Phillips, Alan Walker, and Lorna Warren for their contribution to his knowledge of methods and the social sciences. Tom remains thankful to Richard Jenkins, Susie Molyneux-Hodgson, Clive Norris, and Paul Knepper for all of their help, advice, and guidance over the years.

This edition of the book has also involved important contributions from numerous reviewers, and we are particularly grateful to Elena Vacchelli, who provided comments across the book in her capacity as editorial advisor, and Emma Uprichard, who assisted with Chapter 24 on mixed methods and also advised on Chapter 2. Their insightful comments and recommendations proved invaluable. Our 'Learn from experience' panel have provided a rich array of diverse and instructive reflections about their experiences of conducting social research. The online resources, which are such a valuable accompaniment to the book, have been further developed and expanded for this sixth edition. We are particularly grateful to Charlotte Brookfield (author of our core resources and consultant on the data analysis software guidance), Jodie Luker (author of our SPSS, R, and Stata resources), and Scarlett Hunt (author of our NVivo resources) for their excellent contributions.

We also owe a huge thanks to Emily Spicer, Jonathan Crowe, and Sarah Iles at Oxford University Press for their patience, feedback, and guidance throughout the process of developing and writing this book.

But more than anyone else, we owe a huge debt of gratitude to Livy Watson, our Development Editor for the sixth edition. She has given so much time, effort, enthusiasm, and good humour, and we very much appreciate her involvement—without her, this book would simply not have been possible. Indeed, the process of writing has been particularly challenging as much of our work on the book took place during the Covid-19 pandemic. But without any doubt, it is a stronger book because of her hard work and assistance—thank you Livy.

Finally, thanks go to our families for their support and encouragement (and patience!) throughout. In particular, Liam thanks Cassie and Chloe. Luke thanks Sarah for her amazing understanding and steadfast support, and Tilly (5) and Izzy (2) for keeping him on track by providing all the right distractions at (mostly) the right times. Tom thanks Lydia and Betsy-Lou for their smiles and support, and Arfur C. Whiskerson for his unending ability to press all the secret buttons on the keyboard.

The publishers would like to acknowledge everybody who kindly granted us permission to reproduce images, figures, and quotations throughout this text. Every effort was made to trace copyright holders, but we would be pleased to make suitable arrangements to clear permission for material reproduced in this book with any copyright holders whom it has not been possible to contact.

SHAPED BY YOUR FEEDBACK

OUR ACADEMIC ADVISORS

The authors and Oxford University Press would like to thank the many members of the academic community whose generous and insightful feedback has helped to shape this edition.

Dr Robert Ackrill
Nottingham Trent University

Dr Bernadine Brady
National University of Ireland, Galway

Dr Milena Büchs
University of Leeds

Dr Weifeng Chen
Brunel University London

Dr Yekaterina Chzhen
Trinity College Dublin

Dr Roxanne Connelly
University of Edinburgh

Dr Teresa Crew
Bangor University

Dr Neli Demireva
University of Essex

Dr Federico Farini
University of Northampton

Dr Sharif Haider
The Open University

Professor Meeri Hellstén
Stockholm University

Dr Katherine Hubbard
University of Surrey

Dr Lyn Johnstone
Royal Holloway, University of London

Dr Justin Kotzé
Teesside University

Dr Sung-Hee Lee
University of Derby

Dr Tim Mickler
Leiden University

Dr Gerben Moerman
University of Amsterdam

Dr Jasper Muis
Vrije Universiteit Amsterdam

Dr Stefanie Reissner
Newcastle University

Dr Chloe Shu-Hua Yeh
Bath Spa University

Dr Sebastiaan Steenman
Utrecht University

Dr Thomas Stubbs
Royal Holloway, University of London

Professor Laura Valadez-Martinez
Loughborough University

Dr Anja van der Voort
Leiden University

Professor Athina Vlachantoni
University of Southampton

Dr Aigul Zabirova
United Arab Emirates University

Dr Sotirios Zartaloudis
University of Birmingham

Dr Anna Zoli
University of Brighton

ABBREVIATIONS

AoIR	Association of Internet Researchers
ASA	American Sociological Association
BHPS	British Household Panel Survey
BPS	British Psychological Society
BSA	British Social Attitudes [survey]
BSA	British Sociological Association
CA	conversation analysis
CACA	computer-assisted content analysis
CAPI	computer-assisted personal interviewing
CAQDAS	computer-assisted/aided qualitative data analysis software
CATI	computer-assisted telephone interviewing
CCTV	closed-circuit television
CDA	critical discourse analysis
CSEW	Crime Survey for England and Wales
CV	curriculum vitae (also known as a resumé)
DA	discourse analysis
doi	digital object identifier
ECA	ethnographic content analysis
EPPI	Evidence for Policy and Practice Information and Coordinating Centre
ESRC	Economic and Social Research Council
FIAC	Flanders Interaction Analysis Categories
FMD	foot-and-mouth disease
GDPR	General Data Protection Regulation (European Union)
GESIS	Gesellschaft Sozialwissenschaftlicher Infrastruktureinrichtungen eV (German Social Science Infrastructure Services)
HETUS	Harmonized European Time Use Studies
KWIC	key-word-in-context
LFS	Labour Force Survey
NCDS	National Child Development Study
NHS	National Health Service (UK)
NS-SEC	National Statistics Socio-Economic Classification
ONS	Office for National Statistics (ONS)
RCT	randomized controlled trial
RDD	random digit dialling
REC	research ethics committee
SE	standard error [of the mean]
SPSS	Statistical Package for the Social Sciences
SRA	Social Research Association
SSCI	Social Sciences Citation Index
TB	tuberculosis
UKDA	UK Data Archive
WI	Women's Institute
WoS	Web of Science

PART ONE

THE RESEARCH PROCESS

In Part One of this book we lay the groundwork for the more specialized chapters in Parts Two, Three, and Four. In Chapter 1, we outline what social research is and how we go about doing it, as well as discussing some of its main elements. Chapters 2 and 3 focus on two ideas that we will come back to throughout this book—the idea of **research strategy** and the idea of **research design**—and outline considerations that affect how we practice social research. We will identify two research strategies: **quantitative** and **qualitative research**. Chapter 3 outlines the different research designs that are used in social research. In Chapters 4 and 5 we provide advice on some of the issues you will need to consider if you have to prepare a dissertation based on a relatively small-scale research project. Chapter 4 deals with planning and formulating **research questions**, including the principles and considerations that need to be taken into account when designing a small-scale research project, while Chapter 5 is about how to conduct a **literature review**. In Chapter 6 we discuss ethical and political aspects of social research and address some of the key challenges presented by new forms of data such as social media.

CHAPTER 1

THE NATURE AND PROCESS OF SOCIAL RESEARCH

CHAPTER GUIDE

This chapter is an introduction to the fundamental considerations we must work through when we conduct social research. We will cover much of this material in detail later in the book, so think of this as a simple outline of what social research involves. In this chapter we will discuss

- what we mean by 'social research' and the reasons why we conduct it;
- the context of social research methods—in terms of theory and its role in research, existing knowledge, views about how knowledge should be produced and on the nature of the social world, and values, ethics, and political considerations;
- the key stages of a social research project, including the literature review, formulating concepts and theories, devising research questions, sampling, data collection, data analysis, and writing up findings;
- the messy, non-linear nature of social research, and the fact that this is not unusual or something to be worried about.

1.1 Introduction

This book is about the ways in which social researchers investigate the social world. This means that it explores the approaches social researchers take at every stage of conducting research—from formulating research objectives, choosing research methods, and securing research participants; to collecting, analysing, and interpreting data; to disseminating findings to others. There are many reasons why social scientists need to understand social research methods, but two stand out.

First, this understanding should help you avoid some of the errors and difficulties that can arise when conducting social research, such as forgetting to match research methods to the research questions being asked, asking ambiguous questions in interviews or surveys, or engaging in ethically questionable practices. If you are expected to conduct a research project as part of your course, an education in research methods will not only help ensure that you follow the correct procedures; it will also ensure that you are aware of the full range of methods and approaches available to you and can choose those that are best suited to your project.

The second reason it is important to learn about social research methods is because this will help you understand the research methods used in the published work of others. All social science degree courses involve reading a lot of published research in the areas being studied, and having a good knowledge of the research process and some familiarity with potential pitfalls will help you gain much more from this activity.

1.2 Social research: what is it and why do it?

Having established *why* it is important to learn about social research methods, let's begin with the basics: what is 'social research' and why do people do it?

What is 'social research'?

In this book we use the term 'social research' to mean *academic* research conducted by social scientists from a broad range of disciplines such as sociology, anthropology, education, human geography, social policy, politics, and criminology. Social research can be motivated by developments and changes in society, such as the rise in social media use or attitudes towards migration, but it explores these topics using the ideas and intellectual traditions of the social sciences. In this sense, social research is essential for generating new knowledge and expanding our understanding of contemporary social life. There are lots of examples of social research throughout this book encompassing a wide range of methods and topics, including everything from a content analysis of how radio and TV programmes depict gender (Sink and Mastro 2017), to whether Twitter can help us to explain crime rates (Williams et al. 2017a).

This book is about the **research methods** (see Key concept 1.1)—that is, the tools and techniques—that social scientists use to explore such topics, and we aim to give you the tools and knowledge to enable you to conduct a social research project of your own. You should feel excited at the prospect of conducting your own research. We have supervised many student research projects over the years and have seen how exhilarating it is for students to find out something new and to add something to our current understanding of social life. If you are conducting a social research project, then this may be the first time that you have been given the autonomy to choose what you want to study and how. This might feel daunting at first, but throughout this book we will do our best to guide you through the necessary decisions and provide you with the tools and knowledge you will need to succeed. Conducting your own project provides you with a rare opportunity to direct your own learning and, in our experience, the process of taking ownership of your own project is transformative.

Why do social research?

We conduct social research because social life is fascinating! Think of the complexity of society, or of how groups and individuals behave and how this is shaped by institutions, or how institutions are shaped by people. Think how quickly things shift and how the digital revolution is changing the way we communicate. People are constantly interacting, negotiating, and thriving (or not) in the social world. Who is going to make sense of all this frenetic activity if not you, a social researcher?

KEY CONCEPT 1.1
Research methods

A research method is a tool, such as a survey, an interview, or a **focus group**, that a researcher uses to explore an area of interest by gathering information (data) that they then analyse. In this book, we discuss a wide variety of different research methods, each of which has strengths and weaknesses, and which can be used alone or in conjunction with each other (as we explore further in Chapter 24). It is important to be aware of the difference between a 'research method' and a 'methodology': the latter is broader and refers to the overall approach being taken in the research project and the reasoning behind your choices of this approach and the methods involved. For example, when writing up a piece of research you will justify your choice of *methods* in your *methodology* section.

In a very real sense, conducting social research is a way of searching for answers. We may, for example, notice a gap in the academic literature or an inconsistency between previous studies and have questions about why the gap or inconsistency exists, how the findings generated might apply to another group or in another setting, and/or whether the findings are representative. Or we may wonder why aspects of social life are the way they are, such as why many forms of work are still gendered. For example, why do so few men work in preschool education? These kinds of observations and circumstances often act as starting points for social research in which we identify a puzzle that intrigues us and draws us in. Another common stimulus for research is when a development in society prompts questions. For example, we might observe the increasingly widespread use of social media on portable devices and want to study the extent to which it has affected the nature and quality of interaction in social life. There are many different reasons why people conduct social research of the kind we discuss in this book, but these usually come back to the fact that there is an aspect of our understanding of what goes on in society that is unresolved.

This is why studying methods is so important. Methods courses equip you with the tools you will need in order to investigate the social world. Without these tools you are constrained by what others have found, but with them you can contribute new findings and knowledge to important topics and debates. Our panellists give their views on how to make the most of your research methods modules in Learn from experience 1.1.

LEARN FROM EXPERIENCE 1.1
Getting the most from a research methods module

The authors of this book have taught research methods for years, and we know that these modules are not always the most popular—some students even seem apprehensive about studying them. However, our experience is that once students are on the course they see the real value of research methods training, as several of our panellists comment on below.

> Research methods doesn't initially sound like something that is particularly engaging or requires discussion. I presumed we would just be learning the quantitative and qualitative methods and how to use them, but I discovered that there is much to debate and discuss within this subject. My modules were not just about rote learning of methodology; they asked me to think critically—particularly in regards to research ethics. My advice would be to go into a research methods module prepared to think critically about each method, not just taking them at face value, but really thinking about the impact of carrying out research on the participants you intend to study, and to start thinking early about the kind of research you would like to carry out, even if this is only a rough idea.
>
> Grace

1

There is always a big fuss among students about research methods modules and this makes a lot of people scared of what these modules bring. But I found that changing my perspective of them truly helped. They are like an instruction sheet of how to do research and that's it! Methodology is here to help us clarify what we want to do in our research and how to do it in the best possible way.

Barbara

I would advise students starting research methods modules to make the most of the opportunity to explore and experiment with different research methods, thinking about which you would enjoy doing the most when conducting your own undergraduate research project.

Sarah

Research methods stem from what research questions we ask. I wish I had used my research methods module as an opportunity to start thinking earlier about what I wanted to investigate, and then the methods I would use, rather than trying to fit the method I liked around my subject of interest. I'm not saying that we don't ask certain questions that may elicit specific methods (everyone has their strengths), but we should always use the best option—whether that be quantitative, qualitative, or mixed methods.

Jodie

Access the **online resources** to hear Reni's video reflections on this theme.

You can read about our panellists' backgrounds and research experiences on page xxvi.

1.3 The context of social research methods

Social research and its associated methods do not take place in a vacuum. They are inseparable from a variety of contextual factors:

- theory, and researchers' viewpoints on its role in research;
- the existing research literature;
- epistemological and ontological questions;
- values, ethics, and politics.

We will discuss these ideas in much more detail as we move through Part One, but here we briefly outline each one.

Theory and its role in research

We noted in the Introduction to this chapter (Section 1.1) that academic social research involves exploring topics using the ideas and intellectual traditions of the social sciences. When we say 'ideas and intellectual traditions', we are mainly talking about *theories*. A **theory** is a group of ideas that aims to explain something, in this case the social world. Theories have a significant influence on the research topic being investigated, both in terms of what is studied and how findings are interpreted. For example, if a researcher were interested in the impact of the use of online social media on sociability, it is quite likely that they would take into account the dominant theories at that time regarding how technology is used and its impact. As well as influencing social research, theories can themselves be influenced by it, because the findings of a study add to the knowledge base to which the theory relates.

Not only theory itself but also a researcher's *views* about the nature of the theory–research relationship can have implications for research. Some people think that theory should be addressed at the beginning of a research project. At this stage, a researcher might engage in some theoretical reflections, through which, if they are carrying out **quantitative research**, they formulate and then test a **hypothesis**. In **qualitative research**, it is more common to refer to exploring a 'research question' rather than using the language of hypothesis and testing. Others view theory as an outcome of the research process—as something that is formulated after research has been carried out, and developed through or in response to it. This difference has implications for research: the first approach implies that a set of theoretical ideas drive the collection and analysis of data, whereas the second suggests a more open-ended strategy in which theoretical ideas emerge out of the data. In reality, views on the role of theory in relation to research are rarely as simple and neatly contrasting as this account suggests, but they do differ from researcher to researcher.

The relationship between theory and research is a major focus of **Chapter 2**.

Existing knowledge: the literature

The existing knowledge about the area in which a researcher is interested also forms an important part of the background against which social research takes place. This means that when planning to conduct research, you must be familiar with the literature on the topic you are investigating so that you can build on it and avoid repeating work that has already been done. We return to this idea in Section 1.4 in the subsection 'Literature review'.

Reviewing the literature is the subject of **Chapter 5** and we also discuss it in other chapters, including in **Chapter 25**, which covers the writing up of a literature review as part of a research write-up.

Epistemological and ontological questions

Our assumptions and views about how knowledge should be produced and about the nature of the social world heavily influence the research process.

Views about how knowledge should be produced are known as epistemological positions. They raise questions about how the social world should be studied and whether the scientific approach advocated by some researchers (involving formulating a hypothesis and then testing it using precise measurement techniques) is the right one for social research. Some researchers favour interpretivist approaches, arguing that people and social institutions are very different from the subject matter studied by natural scientists and so social research needs a different approach: one that is more sensitive to the particular qualities of people and their social institutions.

Our views about the nature of the social world, and social phenomena (meaning observed facts, events, or situations), are known as ontological positions. Some writers believe that the social world should be viewed as external to social actors and something over which we have no control. It is simply there, acting upon and influencing behaviour, beliefs, and values. They might view the culture of an organization as a set of values and behavioural expectations that exert a powerful influence over those who work in the organization and into which new recruits have to be socialized. But the alternative view is that the social world is in a constant process of reformulation and reassessment. Considered through this perspective, an organization's culture is continually shaped and reshaped by the practices and behaviour of members of the organization. These considerations are essentially about whether social phenomena are relatively inert and beyond our influence, or are very much a product of social interaction.

The stance a researcher takes on both epistemological and ontological issues has implications for the ways in which social research is conducted.

Epistemological and ontological issues are a major focus of **Chapter 2**.

Values, ethics, and politics

The values of the research community have significant implications for research. Ethical issues have always been central in social research, but they have become even more important as new sources of data (such as social media) become available for studying the social world. Researchers usually have to go through a process of ethical clearance before conducting a social research project. Certain kinds of research require careful planning and consideration of ethical implications (such as research involving children or vulnerable adults), and these kinds of processes make it less likely that researchers will transgress ethical principles.

Another way in which the values of the research community can affect research is that in certain fields, such as in social policy, there is a strong view that those being researched should be involved in the research process. For example, when social researchers conduct research on service users, it is often suggested that the users of those services should be involved in formulating research questions and instruments such as questionnaires. Such views are not universally held (for a discussion, see Becker et al. 2010) but they form a consideration that researchers in some fields feel compelled to consider when contemplating certain kinds of investigation. In recent years there has been an increasing tendency to validate research participants as 'knowers' and, by questioning power imbalances between researchers and research participants, to consider social research as an outcome of a collaboration between all the parties involved. In some cases, authors define this process as 'co-production' (Olesen and Nordentoft 2013; Beresford 2019).

It is also important to be aware that social research operates within a wider political context. This includes the governmental type of politics (for example, much social research is funded by government bodies, and these tend to reflect the orientation of the government of the day, so certain research issues are likely to receive more financial support than others), but also 'politics' in the broader, non-party-political sense of the word—referring to issues of power and status. These political factors can include those associated with conducting research in teams, or of trying to gain and retain access to a research setting (for example an organization). The political context may also inform our training and personal values, which shape how we approach social research and can influence the research areas we are interested in, the research questions we pose, and the methods we use to investigate them.

We address ethical and political issues in **Chapter 6** and touch on them in several other chapters.

It is impossible to arrive at a complete list of the contextual factors that influence social research, but our brief discussion should have made it clear that social research and research method choices are closely related to, and strongly influenced by, the wider context.

1.4 The main elements of social research

In this section we will introduce the main stages of most research projects. We will not attempt to set them out in a particular order, as the order in which things happen varies according to different research strategies and approaches. All we want to do here is to introduce the elements that are common to most types of social research. We have touched on some of them in Section 1.3 and will discuss all of them in more detail in later chapters. We will summarize the full list of components in Table 1.1 later in the chapter.

Literature review

As we noted in Section 1.3, the existing literature is an important element in any research project. When we have identified a topic or issue that interests us, we need to explore what has already been written about it in order to determine

- what is already known about the topic;
- what concepts and theories have been applied to the topic;
- what research methods have been applied to the topic;
- what controversies exist about the topic and how it is studied;
- what contradictions of evidence (if any) exist;
- who the key contributors are to research on the topic;
- what the implications of the literature are for our own research.

Many topics have already been extensively researched, so it is unlikely that you will be able to read *all* the relevant literature on the topic you wish to investigate, especially within the time constraints of a student project. What is crucial is that you read the key books and articles relating to your topic and familiarize yourself with the views and work of the main figures who have written in this area. As we suggest in Chapter 5, it is crucial that you are aware of what is already known about the topic, so that you cannot be accused of not having thought carefully about how your research relates to the work of others.

You then share this knowledge with your future readers (including the person(s) who will be assessing and grading your work, if you are doing a student project) by writing a **literature review**. The key thing to note about this element of the research process—a point we make multiple times in Chapter 5 because it is so important—is that it is not simply a summary of the literature: it must be critical rather than simply descriptive. This does not necessarily mean that you need to be negative about the papers you read, but it does mean that you need to assess the significance of each piece of work and show how it fits into the narrative that you want to construct about the literature. If you do this, then the literature review becomes a very useful way to demonstrate the credibility of your research and the contribution it makes.

Reviewing the literature is the main focus of **Chapter 5**.

Concepts and theories

Concepts are the way that we make sense of the social world. They are labels that we give to aspects of the social world that seem to have common features that strike us as significant. The social sciences have a strong tradition of concepts, many of which have become part of the language of everyday life. One of the reasons it is so important to be familiar with the existing literature is that it reveals the main concepts that past researchers have used and how useful or limited those concepts have been in helping to answer the main questions about the topic. Concepts such as bureaucracy, power, social control, status, hegemony, and alienation are very much part of the theoretical body of work that generations of social scientists have constructed. Concepts are a key ingredient of theories.

We discuss the role of concepts further in **Chapter 7**.

Concepts serve several purposes in social research. First, they are important to how we organize our research interests and signal them to intended audiences (see Learn from experience 1.2). Second, they help us to reflect on and be more disciplined about what we want to investigate, as well as helping us organize our research findings. In section 1.3 we noted that the relationship between theory and research can be seen as involving a choice between theories driving the research process in all its phases, and theories as a product of the research process. These two perspectives on the role of theory in research are known as **deductive** and **inductive** approaches.

We expand on the contrast between inductive and deductive approaches to theory and research in **Chapter 2**.

This apparent contrast between views about theory in research has implications for concepts. Concepts can be seen as something we start out with, representing key areas around which data are collected. In other words, we might collect data in order to explore a concept, or more likely several concepts and how they are connected. The alternative view is that concepts are outcomes of research. According to this view, concepts help us to reflect on and organize the data that we collect. However, we have noted that the line between these views is not as clear as some writers might suggest, and it is important to be aware that these are not mutually exclusive positions. In practice, researchers often start out with some key concepts that help them to orient themselves within their subject matter, but they then revise these concepts as a result of collecting and interpreting data, or produce new concepts through their reflections during the analysis phase.

LEARN FROM EXPERIENCE 1.2
Identifying concepts

Identifying, clarifying, and defining concepts is an important part of the social research process. In her dissertation on the International Criminal Court (ICC) and its alleged bias against African countries, Reni identified several concepts that were important to her work and used them to help guide her reading and structure her analysis:

> On the Word document I was working on I wrote down a checklist of concepts that I needed to address within my literature review and then later in my analysis; these included statism, self-help, and survival. I identified these concepts using literature from the International Relations school of realism (the three 'Ss' of realism—statism, self-help, and survival—are widely referred to in realist literature).
>
> In the introduction of my dissertation, I identified all of the concepts I would be addressing and explained their role in answering my research question. I used these concepts as a lens through which to understand the interaction between the ICC and individual states. It was very important to refer back to these concepts continuously throughout my work. I tried to link at least one of the concepts to my analysis in each subsection, and this kept me accountable by making sure that my arguments were relevant and situated within the current literature. I used concepts as a signposting tool to organize my arguments. Because I had listed all of the relevant concepts, my introduction, which linked my arguments to concepts throughout the dissertation, made clear the relevance of my arguments to my thesis and the research question.
>
> Reni

As Reni observes, providing clearly defined concepts linked to previous research can help with structuring and writing up your work.

You can read about our panellists' backgrounds and research experiences on page xxvi.

1

Research questions

We have touched on **research questions** several times in this chapter, and you may have already realized that they are a key element of research. Research questions are explicit statements of what you intend to find out about. Most people start with a general idea of what they are interested in researching, and the exercise of developing research questions forces us to narrow down our broad area of interest to the thing(s) that we really want to find out and to express this much more precisely and rigorously—as we can see in Learn from experience 1.3.

Despite the importance of research questions, not all research starts with one, particularly if it is exploratory in nature (the researcher is working inductively to understand a particular phenomenon). This is a valid approach to social enquiry and you may encounter it in your reading, including when you look up some of the studies featured in this book, but it is important to be aware of the risks of this approach. Having no research questions or badly formulated research questions *can* lead to low-quality research. If you do not specify clear research questions, there is a *greater* risk that your research will be unfocused and that you will be unsure what your research is about and what you are collecting data for.

The advantages of research questions are that they will

- guide your literature search;
- guide your decisions about the kind of **research design** to use;
- guide your decisions about what data to collect and from whom;
- guide the analysis of your data;
- guide the writing up of your data;
- stop you from going off in unnecessary directions; and
- provide your readers with a clear sense of what your research is about.

It is important to note that although research questions will help to guide you in your search for literature to review, it is also possible, indeed likely, that reading the literature will prompt you to revise your research questions or come up with some new ones. For this reason, research questions and the literature relating to them are likely to be intertwined in the early stages of a research project. In our experience of supervising student research projects, it is a good idea to start with a question, but to be open to adapting and shaping it as you review the literature. Remember that when you begin your research you won't necessarily be familiar with the wider literature on

LEARN FROM EXPERIENCE 1.3
Generating and changing research questions

No one expects you to begin a research project with a perfectly crafted research question, and it's normal for questions to change over time as you read around the topic and narrow down the focus of your project. During her research on the role of social capital in empowering popular spaces, Sarah found herself refining her questions as the study progressed:

> Formulating research questions can be one of the most difficult stages of the research process, and they can change over time. You may begin with a set of research questions developed from your own research interests, which shift and are remodelled as you develop your literature review and analyse your findings. For example, in my undergraduate project I started off with broader research questions such as 'How is social capital utilized in the participation process to create more empowerment?' This later developed into the more specific research question of 'What is the role of bonding, bridging, and linking social capital in empowerment?'
>
> Sarah

Sarah's experience is a common one, and it should be seen as a good thing. This question could be even further refined by adding additional context. Reframing your ideas as your understanding develops is exactly what you should be doing, and reading widely will help you with this.

You can read about our panellists' backgrounds and research experiences on page xxvi.

a topic, and you might come across something that completely changes how you think about the problem.

We discuss research questions, and the process of formulating them, in **Chapter 4**.

The nature of the research question will determine how you proceed with your investigation and what research design you use. If you are looking at the impact of an intervention, then you might consider conducting an **experiment**; if you are interested in social change over time, then a **longitudinal** design might be appropriate. Research questions that are concerned with particular communities, organizations, or groups might use a **case study** design, while describing current attitudes or behaviours at a single point in time could use a **cross-sectional design**. Or maybe there is a **comparative** element that is integral to your question? You will need to become familiar with the many implications associated with different research designs and how the different designs lend themselves to different types of research question.

We discuss research designs in **Chapter 3**.

Sampling

In social research we are rarely able to interview, observe, or send questionnaires to all the individuals who are appropriate to our research. Equally, we are unlikely to be able to analyse the content of all publications or social media posts relating to the topic that interests us. Time and cost issues always limit the number of cases we can include in our research, so we nearly always have to study a **sample** of the wider group.

As we will see in later chapters, there are a number of different principles behind **sampling**. Many people associate sampling with quantitative research, such as the **survey** method, and with the search for **representative samples**. This is the approach behind the opinion polls we often see in the news, where researchers cannot survey everyone and so they aim to secure a sample that represents a wider **population** by effectively replicating it in miniature. If news media sources could not claim that the samples they used in their opinion polls were representative, the findings that they report (for example, about the public's views on particular political parties) would be problematic.

We discuss sampling for quantitative research in **Chapter 8**.

However, this is a simplistic view of sampling: sampling principles do not only apply to survey research, and many forms of social research do not prioritize representative samples. Sampling applies to a variety of types of investigation, for example when selecting the news articles you want to analyse (for a **content analysis**) or the case study you want to research (probably only one or two). With the latter type of research the goal is to understand the selected case or cases in depth, so it is crucial that the right one(s) are selected. Both the case or cases *and* the individuals who are members of the case study context have to be selected according to criteria relevant to the research. In Part Three we will discuss sampling principles for qualitative research that are based not on representativeness but on the idea that samples should be selected on the basis of whether they are appropriate for the purposes of the investigation.

We discuss sampling for qualitative research in **Chapter 18**.

Whatever **research strategy** you choose, sampling is a key consideration and an important stage of any investigation.

Data collection

To many people, data collection is the key point of any research project, so it is not surprising that we probably spend more words and pages discussing this stage in the research process than any other. Some of the methods of data collection we cover, such as interviewing and questionnaires, may be more familiar to you than others.

Some methods involve quite a structured approach to data collection—that is, the researcher establishes roughly what they want to find out about in advance and designs the research collection tool accordingly. The **self-completion questionnaire** is an example of this approach. Here, the researcher establishes what they need to know to answer their research questions and designs a questionnaire that will allow them to collect data to answer those questions. The **structured interview**—the kind of interview used in survey investigations—is designed in a similar way. We discuss these methods, which align with the deductive approach to the relationship between theory and research (see the section titled 'Concepts and theories' earlier in this chapter), in Part Two of the book.

Other methods of data collection are more flexible. In Part Three, we will discuss research methods that emphasize a more open-ended view of the research process, so that there is less restriction on the kinds of things that can be investigated. Researchers use data-collection methods such as **participant observation** and **semi-structured interviewing** so that they can keep an open mind about the data they want to collect and can allow concepts and theories to emerge out of the data. This is an inductive approach to theorizing and conceptualization. This research usually still aims to answer research questions, but these may not be explicitly stated.

Data analysis

At its most basic level, data analysis involves applying statistical techniques to data that have been collected. However, many types of data are not suitable for statistical analysis, and even when they are, researchers may want to take alternative approaches.

We discuss quantitative data analysis in **Chapter 15**.

We discuss qualitative data analysis in **Chapter 23**.

Our basic definition also does not acknowledge the fact that there are multiple aspects to data analysis: *managing* the raw data, *making sense* of the data, and *interpreting* the data.

Managing data involves checking it to establish whether there are any obvious flaws. For example, qualitative interviews are usually audio-recorded and then transcribed. The researcher needs to be alert to possible hearing mistakes that might affect the meaning of people's replies, so that the data is made as accurate and high-quality as possible before it is introduced into a software program. For quantitative studies, survey data will need to be managed and either inputted (paper surveys) or downloaded (online surveys) into specialist analysis software such as SPSS, Excel, or R.

In qualitative data analysis, making sense of the data often involves identifying themes within it. This is done by breaking down the data into component parts and giving those parts labels—in other words, **coding** it. The analyst then searches for instances of these sequences of coded **text** within and across cases and also for links between different **codes**. For quantitative data, the researcher has to choose how to make sense of anomalies in the data such as missing responses to questions.

For both qualitative and quantitative studies, the researcher interprets the data by trying to link the analysis of it with the research questions, as well as with the relevant background literature. Essentially, data analysis is about *data reduction*. It involves reducing the large body of information that the researcher has gathered so that they can make sense of it. Unless the amount of data collected is reduced—for example, by producing tables or averages in the case of quantitative data, and by grouping textual material into categories in the case of qualitative data—it is more or less impossible to interpret the material.

Another thing to bear in mind is that data analysis can refer to analysing either primary or secondary data. With primary analysis, the researchers who were responsible for collecting the data conduct the analysis. With **secondary analysis**, the data is already collected and available. Researchers who work in universities are encouraged to store their data in archives, and this allows others to analyse it, sometimes to answer different research questions from the ones that were originally asked. Given the time and cost involved in conducting most social research, it is sensible to use existing data where possible and appropriate. Conducting secondary analysis might allow you to explore the research questions in which you are interested without having to go through the time-consuming and lengthy process of having to collect primary data.

We discuss secondary analysis in **Chapters 14** and **22**.

Writing up

Research is no use to anyone if it is not written up. We conduct research so that it can be shared with others, allowing them to read what we have done, respond to it, and maybe even build their own work upon ours.

We focus on writing up in **Chapter 25**.

The ways in which social researchers write up their work will vary according to the different styles of doing research, especially depending on whether the research adopted a quantitative, qualitative, or mixed methods approach. However, most dissertations, theses, and research articles will include the following elements.

- *Introduction*. This outlines the research area and its significance. It may also introduce the research questions.
- *Literature review*. This sets out what is already known about the research area and examines it critically.
- *Research methods*. The researcher presents the research methods that they used (sampling strategy, methods of data collection, methods of data analysis) and justifies the choice of methods.

TABLE 1.1
Stages in the research process and where to find them in this book

Stage	Description of stage	Where to find in this book
Literature review	A critical examination of existing research that relates to the phenomena of interest, and of relevant theoretical ideas.	We cover reviewing the literature in detail in Chapter 5, and we pay particular attention to writing up literature reviews in Chapter 25.
Concepts and theories	The ideas that drive the research process and that help researchers interpret their findings. In the course of the study, the findings also contribute to the ideas that the researchers are examining.	We cover theories in Chapter 2, and we go into greater depth about concepts in Chapters 7 and 16.
Research question(s)	A question or questions providing an explicit statement of what the researcher wants to know about.	We cover research questions in Chapter 4. You will also come across them in many examples throughout this book.
Sampling cases	The selection of cases (often people, but not always) that are relevant to the research questions.	We cover sampling for quantitative studies in Chapter 8, and for qualitative studies in Chapter 17.
Data collection	Gathering data from the sample with the aim of providing answers to the research questions.	In Chapter 3 we cover research design, a precursor to selecting your method of data collection. Quantitative methods of data collection are covered in Chapters 9 to 14, and qualitative methods in Chapters 18 to 22. We discuss data collection for **mixed methods research** in Chapter 24.
Data analysis	The management, analysis, and interpretation of the data.	We cover quantitative data analysis in Chapter 15 and qualitative data analysis in Chapter 23. You will find video tutorials on using data analysis software packages (**SPSS**, **R**, **Stata**, and **NVivo**) in our **online resources**.
Writing up	Dissemination of the research and its findings.	Writing up quantitative, qualitative, and mixed methods research is covered in Chapter 25. You will also see plenty of instances of writing up in the examples used throughout this book.

- *Results*. The researcher presents their findings.
- *Discussion*. This examines the implications of the findings in relation to the literature and the research questions.
- *Conclusion*. This emphasizes the significance of the research.

Table 1.1 summarizes the seven elements of the research process that we have examined and where in this book you can find information about each stage. If you are preparing to conduct your own research investigations, you might find this table a useful guide to the book's content as it relates to the main steps in conducting research.

You will notice that Table 1.1 doesn't show a discrete stage for ethical considerations, and that is because we must consider and reflect on ethics, alongside our values and politics, throughout the research process. We will cover ethical aspects of social research in Chapter 6.

1.5 The messiness of social research

In this book we want to give you a clear and unintimidating picture of social research, and to convey the possibilities and satisfaction it can bring. However, we also want to emphasize that social research is often a lot less smooth than it appears when it is set out in books. In practice, research involves many false starts, mistakes, and enforced changes to research plans. Throughout the book we highlight issues that may potentially arise and we suggest ways to avoid them, but we cannot hope to cover them all—largely because many of them are one-off events and so are almost impossible to anticipate.

We know that research can get messy by reading candid, confessional accounts of the research process that have been written (for example the contributors to Hammond 1964; Bell and Newby 1977; Bryman 1988b; Townsend and Burgess 2009; Streiner and Sidani 2010).

So why do many reports imply that the process is smooth? One reason is that research does often involve only minor problems and proceeds roughly according to plan. However, the main reason is that although social researchers are usually **reflexive** about the limitations of their studies (acknowledging, for example, that some respondent or participant groups were excluded or could not be accessed), an academic paper is a report on what has been achieved rather than all of the things that did not go according to plan. These researchers are not being deceptive; it is simply that accounts of findings and how they were produced tend to follow an unspoken template that emphasizes some aspects of the research process and not others. Research reports usually display the elements we discussed in Section 1.4 in a straightforward way, using standard methodological terminology and focusing on the specific findings presented in the write-up, and do not discuss the ups and downs of the project. This tendency is not unique to *social* research: in Chapter 21 we look at a study of how researchers in the natural sciences present and discuss their work, which shows that they also tend to omit some core aspects of the production of 'findings' from the written account (Gilbert and Mulkay 1984).

So does acknowledging the messiness of social research devalue it? In a very interesting blog post (which you might want to read in its entirety), Tarr (2013) suggests:

> Good social scientific practice should be about acknowledging the weaknesses of the methods used: not to reward sloppiness, but to highlight what really goes on; to reassure novice researchers that real world research often *is* messy; or to improve on current methods and find ways to do things better. Better in this case does not necessarily mean less subjective, but it does mean more transparent, and usually more rigorous. The publication of mistakes is a necessary part of this process.
>
> (https://blogs.lse.ac.uk/impactofsocialsciences/2013/03/13/overly-honest-social-science/)

When writing up your own social research project you should reflect on any challenges you faced and any limitations of your study. By setting out what you planned to do, what actually happened, and any limitations arising from the change in plan, you are demonstrating to the reader that you understand the implications of changes of direction to your own work. In our experience of supervising (and marking) many student projects over the years, we have always been pleased to see students reflecting on what they could have done better or what they would do if developing their research further. No one expects a student project to be perfect—but we do want to see that you understand whether certain aspects *could* have been better.

There are two key points to take away from this chapter. The first is that social research encompasses a variety of methodological traditions that are not always in agreement with each other. This is an important and healthy trait: it encourages us to justify our decisions and think carefully about what it is we are trying to find out. An additional consideration is that the dividing lines between these traditions, such as between quantitative and qualitative research strategies, are often less clear-cut than they seem (an issue explored further in Chapter 24).

The second point is that the social world itself is wonderfully complex and messy, and this is precisely why it is so interesting to research. In the next 24 chapters we will guide you through the differing views on how things should be done and the principles of doing them, giving you a grounding in the theoretical knowledge that underpins research, as well as a road map for your research journeys.

KEY POINTS

- Social research methods provide us with the framework and tools we need to investigate and study the vast array of fascinating and complex phenomena in society in a rigorous way.
- Social research and social research methods are inseparable from wider contextual factors. They are not practised in a vacuum.
- Social research practice varies across projects, institutions, and academic disciplines, but there are some elements that are common to all or at least most forms of social research. These include: literature reviews; concepts and theories; research questions; sampling of cases; data collection; data analysis; and write-ups of research findings.

- Attention to these elements, particularly to the ideas and intellectual traditions of the social sciences (their theories and concepts), is what distinguishes academic social research from other kinds of social research.
- We can propose some general principles for conducting social research, but part of the excitement of investigating the social world is that it is complicated and things do not always go to plan. We must be prepared, as social researchers, to reflect and modify our ideas and rise to the challenge.

QUESTIONS FOR REVIEW

1. What is distinctive about academic social research, as opposed to other forms of social research?
2. Why do we do social research? What might motivate someone to undertake a social research project?
3. What are the main factors that influence social research and the ways in which social research methods are implemented? Can you think of any that we have not touched on?
4. Why is a literature review important when conducting research?
5. What role do concepts and theories play in the process of doing social research?
6. Why are researchers encouraged to specify their research questions?
7. Why do researchers need to sample? Why is it important for them to outline the principles that lie beneath their sampling choices?
8. Outline one or two factors that might affect a researcher's choice of data-collection instrument.
9. How might you structure the report of the findings of a project that you conducted?
10. If research does not always go according to plan, why should we bother with methodological principles at all?

ONLINE RESOURCES

www.oup.com/he/srm6e

You can find our notes on the answers to these questions within this chapter's **online resources**, together with:

- *audio/video comments* on this topic from our 'Learn from experience' panellists;
- *self-test questions* for further knowledge-checking; and
- a *flashcard glossary* to help you recall key terms.

CHAPTER

2

SOCIAL RESEARCH STRATEGIES

QUANTITATIVE RESEARCH AND QUALITATIVE RESEARCH

CHAPTER GUIDE

In this chapter we introduce the idea of *research strategies* to demonstrate the various considerations that guide our overall approach to social research. We will look at

- the relationship between theory and research, in particular whether theory guides research or is an outcome of research;
- *epistemological* issues—that is, issues to do with what is regarded as appropriate knowledge about the social world;
- *ontological* issues—that is, issues to do with whether the social world is seen as something external to people or as something that we are in the process of creating;
- the ways in which these issues relate to the widely used distinction in the social sciences between two types of research strategy, *quantitative* research and *qualitative* research;
- the impact of *values* and *practical issues* on the social research process.

2.1 Introduction

As this is a social **research methods** textbook, you might reasonably expect us to focus on the range of methods available to social scientists, how to choose between them, and how to apply them. But the practice of social research does not exist in a bubble, sealed off from other aspects of the social sciences, and it is influenced by the intellectual positions of its practitioners. Social research methods are not completely dependent on the views and preferences of the researcher employing them, but they are not neutral tools either: they are closely tied to various different ideas about the nature of social reality and how it should be studied. Research methods and practice are also connected with the wider social-scientific enterprise, in that researchers collect data in relation to something, and that 'something' is often a **theory**—an idea about how or why things happen in a certain way (we will discuss theories in Section 2.2).

This is not to suggest that social research is entirely driven by theoretical concerns. For example, Luke, one of this book's authors, used data from the 2015 British Social Attitudes Survey to understand the demographic characteristics of British Twitter users (Sloan 2017). The purpose of Luke's research was simply to describe who was using the platform in terms of their age, sex, and social class. Other research is entirely about fact-finding, such as national censuses (also discussed in Key concept 2.1). Sometimes, research exercises are motivated by a concern about a pressing social problem, such as Benson and Lewis's (2019) study of how (in their words) 'British People of Colour' currently living in the remaining 27 European Union countries are making sense of Brexit. Research may also be done on a topic because a specific opportunity arises. Williams and Burnap (2016) studied the occurrence of cyberhate (hatred expressed through digital means) on social media following the Woolwich terrorist attack in London in 2013. The authors were influenced by Cohen's (1972) work on the idea of action, reaction, and amplification. Yet another stimulus for research can be personal experiences. For example, Atkinson's (2006) motivation for conducting a study of Welsh National Opera was partly to do with a long-standing enthusiasm developed from when he first began going to the opera as a child. Personal experiences are often a strong influence for students conducting social research, as you can see in Learn from experience 2.1.

LEARN FROM EXPERIENCE 2.1
Personal experience as a basis for research

Conducting a research project is a significant undertaking, so it's not surprising that many of us choose to investigate topics that are of personal interest. This is often what motivates us and keeps us engaged in our work, as several of our panellists observe.

> My personal work experiences as a former social worker has helped tremendously in choosing a topic for my undergraduate research into violent interactions. While working as a social worker I experienced client violence myself and became interested in the phenomenon of client aggression in social work settings, and violence in general.
>
> Laura

> As a member of the LGBT+ community, I am sad to say I have experienced my fair share of prejudice. Therefore, it is no surprise that my interest in prejudice eventually combined with my own experiences and translated into my research, right through from my undergraduate to my PhD.
>
> Jodie

> My postgraduate research project focuses on the lived experiences of Pakistani and Bangladeshi Muslim lone mothers. Feminist research values acknowledge that research is inherently political; researchers' personal beliefs and values can influence the research process. My own personal experience of being brought up in a lone mother family influenced my choice in this topic as well as an interest in challenging negative stereotypes of Pakistani and Bangladeshi Muslim women (particularly migrants).
>
> Sarah

You can read about our panellists' backgrounds and research experiences on page xxvi.

Although, as we can see, there are many motivations for conducting research in the social sciences, theory is often a significant factor and studies make the most significant contribution to existing knowledge when they are viewed in relation to theoretical concerns. It is therefore important that we reflect on the link between theory and research, and specifically the philosophical assumptions we make about the roles of theory and data—in other words, what can be known and how we can know it. This will inform our **research design**, the formulation of our **research questions**, and whether we collect qualitative or quantitative data (or indeed both), which we will discuss in Section 2.5.

2.2 Theory and research

Characterizing the link between theory and research is not straightforward, for two main reasons. First, there is the question of what type of theory we are talking about. Second, there is the question of whether we collect data in order to test theories (a **deductive** approach) or to build theories (an **inductive** approach). Theory is important because it provides a background and justification for the research being conducted, but it also provides a framework within which social phenomena can be understood and research findings can be interpreted. In this section, we will consider the main types of and approaches to using theory in order to better understand the link between it and research.

What type of theory?

The term 'theory' is used in many different ways, but its most common meaning is as an explanation for particular events or patterns that have been noticed (often called 'observed regularities')—for example, why sufferers of schizophrenia are more likely to come from working-class than middle-class backgrounds, or why women typically earn less than men in the workplace. But discussions of social theory tend not to address this type of theory, instead focusing on theories with a higher level of abstraction. Examples of such theories include structural **functionalism**, **symbolic interactionism**, **critical** theory, poststructuralism, structuration theory, and so on. In dividing types of theory into these two categories, we have made a distinction between what Merton (1967) called *theories of the middle range*, which attempt to understand and explain a particular aspect of the social world, and *grand theories*, which operate at a more abstract level.

According to Merton, grand theories do not contain many clues as to how researchers might use them to guide or influence the collection of empirical evidence. They are so abstract that it is difficult to make the necessary links with the real world to test an aspect of a theory or draw an inference from it that could be tested. Merton argues that grand theories are therefore of limited use in connection with social research, and it is true to say that it is not usually grand theory that guides social researchers. Middle-range theories are much more likely to be the focus of empirical enquiry. Unlike grand ones, they operate in a limited domain, whether that is youth crime or 'bad' behaviour (known as juvenile delinquency), voting behaviour, educational attainment, or ethnic relations. They vary in terms of how widely they can be applied. An example is *labelling theory*, a middle-range theory in the sociology of deviance. *Deviance* is behaviour that is not in line with societal norms, and sociologists have tried to understand deviance in terms of societal reactions to deviation. Labelling theory proposes that the very act of labelling someone as 'deviant' can result in them acting in a deviant way. This theory can be applied to a variety of different forms of deviance, including crime and mental illness. In contrast, Cloward and Ohlin's (1960) *differential association theory* was formulated specifically in connection with juvenile delinquency, and this remained its main focus. Whether their application is very specific or more broad, middle-range theories represent attempts to understand and explain a limited aspect of social life.

But even the grand/middle-range distinction does not entirely address the deceptively simple question of what we mean by 'theory', because the term is often used to refer to existing background literature (see Chapter 5) in an area of social enquiry. In many cases, the background literature relating to a topic acts as the equivalent of a theory. For example, Cohen's (2010) mixed methods study of hairstylists' relationship with their clients drew on Hochschild's book *The Managed Heart* (1983), in which the term 'emotional labour' was first used. The literature on emotional labour forms the background of Cohen's study and plays a key role in their interpretation of the findings. As we will see in Chapter 5, background literature often plays an important role in setting the agenda for a research project: a researcher may identify a gap in the literature that needs filling; they may notice

KEY CONCEPT 2.1
What is empiricism?

The term 'empiricism' is used in a number of different ways, but two stand out. First, it is used to mean a general approach to the study of reality that suggests that only knowledge gained through experience and the senses is acceptable. In other words, this position means that ideas must be subjected to rigorous testing before they can be considered 'knowledge'. The second meaning is related to this and refers to a belief that gaining 'facts' is a legitimate goal in its own right. It is this second meaning that is sometimes referred to as 'naive empiricism'. However, no one would dispute the importance of non-theoretical data collection projects such as a national **census**, in which vital descriptive information is collected from the **population**. Being able to understand how a population ages or how ethnic composition changes over time is important to government agencies and social researchers alike.

inconsistency between findings in similar studies that mean further investigation is needed; or they may disagree with a particular methodological approach and try to tackle the issue from a different angle.

Social scientists are sometimes sceptical of research that has no obvious connections with theory, and such research is often dismissed as naive **empiricism** (see Key concept 2.1). It would be harsh and inaccurate to give this label to the many studies that use relevant background literature as theory. In these studies, research is conditioned by and directed towards research questions that come from an examination of the literature, with the data collection and analysis focused on addressing a research issue or problem that has been identified at the outset. The literature acts as a substitute for theory; theory lies within the literature.

Regardless of the nature of the relationship between theory and a piece of research, we must also ask ourselves what role theory plays and what the relationship is between theory and data. Up to this point, we have discussed the role of theory within social science research as though theory always guides and influences the collection and analysis of data—in other words, as if research is always done in order to answer questions posed by theoretical considerations. But theory can also emerge *after* the collection and analysis of some or all of the data associated with a project. This leads us to the second significant factor that affects the relationship between theory and research: whether we are referring to deductive or inductive theory.

Deductive and inductive theory

As we have noted, researchers take different approaches to using theory. They may use theory as a basis for their research, taking what is known as a deductive approach, or it may emerge following their research, known as an inductive approach. We will consider the former first, since most views of the relationship between theory and social research are associated with this approach.

The deductive approach

In this approach, the researcher draws on what is known about a particular domain and on relevant theoretical ideas in order to deduce (come up with) a **hypothesis** (or hypotheses): a speculation that they can test empirically. Embedded within the hypothesis will be **concepts** that will need to be translated into researchable entities (often referred to as **variables**). Developing hypotheses and ensuring that they can be tested also involves considering how data can be collected on each of the concepts that make up the hypothesis. (It is worth noting that deductive approaches are more commonly used in quantitative research; the language of hypotheses, variables and testing does not usually apply to qualitative research.)

This view of the role that theory plays within research is what Merton had in mind when he identified middle-range theories, arguing that they are 'principally used in sociology to guide empirical inquiry' (Merton 1967: 39). As shown in Figure 2.1, which sets out the sequence of events for a deductive research project, theory and the hypothesis deduced from it come first, and they drive the process of gathering data, as was the case in Röder and Mühlau's (2014) study—see Research in focus 2.1. The last step in this process, revision of theory, involves a movement that goes in the opposite direction from **deduction**—it involves **induction**, as the researcher reflects on the implications of their findings for the theory that prompted the whole exercise. The new findings are fed back into the existing body of knowledge in the area being studied.

2

For example, the findings of a study involving Twitter data by Williams et al. (2017a) built upon the knowledge base relating to the 'broken windows' theory (Wilson and Kelling 1982), which suggests that visible evidence of low-level crime, such as broken windows, encourages more crime. In the study conducted by Williams and colleagues, tweets containing certain terms relating to low-level disorder were found to be associated with rates of recorded crime, offering an insight into how the theory manifests in social media:

> The association of the measure [tweets containing 'broken windows' indicators] with a range [of] crime types can be explained in several ways. It is possible that tweeters sense degradation in the local area, and this is associated with increased crime rates. If this is the case, then it would suggest further support for the broken windows thesis, that is, if we accept the proxy measure of broken windows via social media. This argument certainly seems to hold for residents in low-crime areas in relation to certain offences. But the argument does not hold for high-crime areas. This can be explained in terms of differences in disposition to report local issues of crime and disorder, a pattern found in offline settings.
>
> (Williams et al. 2017a: 334)

FIGURE 2.1
The process of deduction

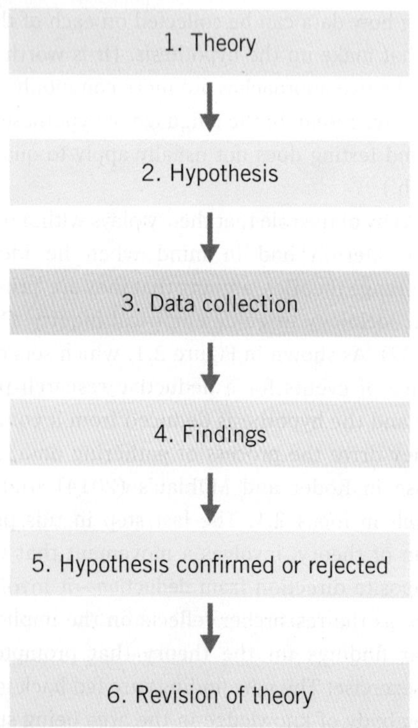

However, while there is undoubtedly an element of induction in the steps outlined in Figure 2.1, the approach is usually depicted as mainly deductive.

It is important to bear in mind that not every deductive research project follows this exact sequence. As we have discussed previously, 'theory' can refer to the literature on a certain topic, in the form of the knowledge gained from books and articles. Even when the research does stem from more specific theory or theories (such as the broken windows theory), explicit hypotheses are not always deduced from them in the way that Röder and Mühlau (2014) did in Research in focus 2.1. A researcher's view of the theory or literature may also change when they analyse the collected data. New theoretical ideas or findings may be published by others before the researcher has generated their findings, or the relevance of a set of data for a certain theory may become apparent only *after* the data have been collected.

These variations on the process may seem surprising and confusing. There is a logic to the idea of developing theories and then testing them, and we often apply this in everyday contexts. Generally, we think of theories as things that can be revealing but that need to be tested before they can be considered valid or useful. But in practice, the use of theory varies from study to study, so while the process of deduction outlined in Figure 2.1 does undoubtedly occur, it is best considered as a general perspective on the link between theory and research.

The inductive approach

Some researchers choose to disregard the sequence outlined in Figure 2.1 and adopt an *inductive* approach. Here, theory is the *outcome* of research and is formed by drawing generalizable inferences out of observations. In this way, induction represents an alternative strategy for linking theory and research—Figure 2.2 sums up the key difference between induction and deduction. However, just as deduction involves an element of induction, the inductive process is likely to involve a degree of deduction. Once the researcher has carried out some theoretical reflection on a set of data, they may want to collect further data in order to establish the conditions in which a theory will and will not hold. This is often called an *iterative* strategy and it involves moving back and forth between data and theory.

Research in focus 2.2 provides a useful example of an inductive approach, for two reasons: the clear theoretical significance of its findings, and the fact that it was based on qualitative data. The theoretical significance of the O'Reilly et al. (2012) study is related to the fact that it used a **grounded theory** approach in analysing data and

RESEARCH IN FOCUS 2.1
A deductive study

Röder and Mühlau (2014) note that egalitarian attitudes towards gender (i.e. whether people are treated the same, with the same rights and opportunities, whatever their gender) vary a great deal between nations. They focus especially on what happens when migrants move from a country in which egalitarian attitudes are weak to one where they are strong and often actively promoted, a scenario that they suggest is common. They also note that there is relatively little research on gender-egalitarian values among migrants, but they review the studies that do exist. Their review of the literature leads them to propose five hypotheses, such as:

> (H2) (a) Second-generation migrants have a more egalitarian-gender ideology than the first generation; and (b) the gender relations of the origin country exert less influence on the gender attitudes for second-generation immigrants than for first-generation immigrants.
>
> (Röder and Mühlau 2014: 903)

This hypothesis is made up of three main concepts: second-generation immigrants; gender-egalitarian attitudes; and gender relations of the origin country (i.e. the country from which an immigrant has emigrated).

In order to test the hypotheses, the authors used data from the European Social Survey (ESS), which is conducted by **structured interview** every two years and collects data from samples in all European Union countries and several other European countries (**www.europeansocialsurvey.org**, accessed 1 August 2019). Röder and Mühlau developed ways to measure each concept in the hypothesis quoted above.

- *Second-generation immigrants*—the authors had to be clear about what they meant by this term, so they defined it as someone who was born in the country in which they now live but who has one or both parents who were born abroad.
- *Gender-egalitarian attitudes*—this concept was measured using answers to two questions in the ESS **questionnaire**. Both questions take the form of statements with which respondents are asked to give their level of agreement on a five-point **scale**, with 'strongly agree' at one end and 'strongly disagree' at the other (a style of questioning known as a **Likert scale**—see Key concept 7.2). The two statements are: 'When jobs are scarce, men should have more right to a job than women' and 'A woman should be prepared to cut down on her paid work for the sake of her family'.
- *Gender relations of the origin country*—to measure this concept, the researchers compiled an index that was based on information for each country about female representation on parliaments; female representation in managerial and professional posts; and the earnings difference between men and women.

The hypotheses were broadly confirmed by the research, and the authors conclude that 'gender ideology is affected by an intergenerational acculturation process' (Röder and Mühlau 2014: 915). This study is a good example of the deductive process: hypotheses were deduced from existing theory and then tested.

generating theory. This approach, which we will consider further in Chapter 23, was first outlined by Glaser and Strauss (1967) and is seen as especially strong in terms of generating theories out of data. O'Reilly et al.'s use of it sets their study apart from other studies which are supposedly inductive but, although they generate interesting findings and provide insightful empirical **generalizations**, their theoretical significance is not entirely clear.

The fact that this study was based on qualitative data is significant because, in much the same way that the deductive strategy is associated with quantitative research, an inductive strategy linking data and theory is usually associated with qualitative research. O'Reilly and colleagues used qualitative data in the form of the researchers' **field notes** from observations and the respondents' detailed answers to the questions posed in in-depth, **semi-structured interviews**. However, as we will see, it would be simplistic to say that the inductive strategy is always associated with qualitative research: some qualitative research does not generate theory, and theory is often used as a background to qualitative investigations.

FIGURE 2.2
Deductive and inductive approaches to the relationship between theory and research

Deductive approach

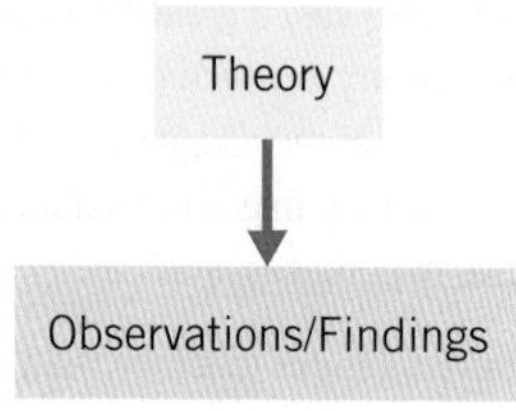

Inductive approach

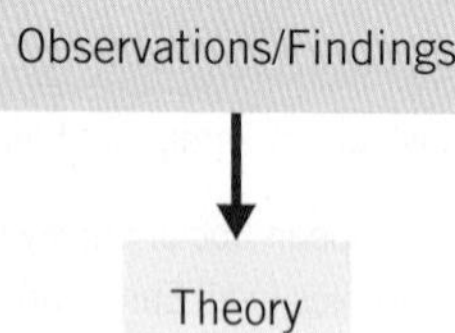

Considering deduction and induction together

It is useful to think of the relationship between theory and research in terms of deductive and inductive strategies, but it will be becoming clear to you that these distinctions are not as straightforward as they are sometimes presented. It is best to think of deductive and inductive strategies as tendencies rather than as fixed distinctions. There is actually a third approach called **abductive reasoning**, which has become increasingly popular because it proposes a way of addressing the limitations of both deductive and inductive approaches. For example, the deductive approach is in favour of a strict process of theory testing using hypotheses, but it doesn't address how researchers should select a theory in the first place. Inductive reasoning is also criticized because empirical data does not inevitably allow researchers to build theory. Abductive reasoning starts with an observation (which could be a puzzle or something unexpected) and tries to explain it using the most likely explanation, switching back and forth from the puzzle to the social

RESEARCH IN FOCUS 2.2
An inductive study

O'Reilly et al. (2012) discuss how one of their study's authors, Kelley O'Reilly, analysed her qualitative data on interactions between customers and front-line employees. Her initial data were collected at a site in the USA that sold products through a variety of channels, including in-store, over the phone, and online. Around 50 per cent of her interviews, and a large amount of observation, came from this site. She refers to her research as the 'Silo Study' because the idea of front-line employees working in *service silos* (i.e. separate areas from which they could not easily break out) became a key idea when she analysed her findings. The idea that people work in silos (for example, because they are unwilling to share information with each other) may seem inevitable and like common sense, but O'Reilly noticed that the theoretical construct of the silo had a different meaning in this context because the areas had been strategically created by senior managers. Service silos were meant to act as mechanisms of control by constraining what front-line employees could do, and they were introduced in response to the management's recognition that its existing arrangements could not cope with the volume of activity. The silo approach had implications for the quality of employees' relations with customers. In O'Reilly's dissertation (2010), on which the article is based, the impact of the service silo strategy on relations with customers is summed up when she asks one of her participants how he would return a product. His reply is deeply sarcastic:

> Well I can't really return that defective product for you Mrs. Customer ... I know it is only 69 cents, but I can't walk to the shelf and get you one that works. I am going to give you a sticker and you've got to go to a separate line, because the company doesn't trust me to make 69 cent decisions.
>
> (quoted in O'Reilly 2010: 116)

As O'Reilly (2010) notes, the participant's reply draws attention to his lack of empowerment to deal with the issue himself, even though the monetary amount involved is trivial.

In this study, the inductive nature of the relationship between theory and research can be seen in the way that O'Reilly's theoretical idea (the idea of the 'service silo' as a purposely designed managerial control strategy) comes *from* her data rather than being formed before she had collected her data.

world and the literature, in a process known as dialectical shuttling (Atkinson et al. 2003). Moving back and forth may not be distinct stages of the research process itself; rather, the researcher is thinking about data and theory at the same time (Schwartz-Shea and Yannow 2012). **Abduction** acknowledges that the conclusions arising from an observation are plausible, but not completely certain. It can also be thought of as *inference to the best explanation*—for example, you start with an observation or set of observations, such as smoke in your kitchen, and reason that the most likely explanation is that you have burnt the dinner you had in the oven. There could be other reasons for having smoke in your kitchen (perhaps someone left a window open, and smoke from an outside fire has entered the room), so you cannot be certain of the source of the smoke based on the initial observation alone, but the simplest and most probable explanation is that it is coming from the remains of your meal.

2.3 Epistemological considerations

We now move on to considering the **epistemological** issues associated with social research, in other words, the question of what is (or should be) seen as acceptable knowledge in a discipline. In the social sciences, a central issue is whether the social world can and should be studied according to the same principles, procedures, and ethos as the natural sciences. The argument that social sciences should imitate the natural sciences in this way is associated with an epistemological position known as **positivism** (see Key concept 2.2).

Positivism

The doctrine of positivism is difficult to pin down and outline neatly because people use it in different ways. For some writers, it is a descriptive **category**—one that describes a philosophical position that can be seen in research—though there are still disagreements about what it involves. For others, it is a negative term used to describe crude and often superficial practices of data collection.

There is a link between the five principles in Key concept 2.2 and some of the points that we have considered about the relationship between theory and research. For example, positivism involves elements of both a deductive approach (principle 2) and an inductive approach (principle 3). Also, positivism draws quite a sharp distinction between theory and research, the role of research being to test theories and to provide material for the development of 'laws'. But this implies that it is

KEY CONCEPT 2.2
What is positivism?

Positivism is an epistemological position that argues for the use of natural science methods to study social reality and beyond. The term stretches beyond this principle, and different authors describe its elements in varying ways. Generally, positivism stands by the following principles:

1. Only phenomena, and therefore knowledge confirmed by the senses, can genuinely be considered as knowledge (a principle known as phenomenalism).
2. The purpose of theory is to generate hypotheses that can be tested so that they enable explanations of laws—patterns and regularities—to be assessed (the principle of deductivism).
3. Knowledge is reached by gathering together facts that provide the basis for laws (the principle of inductivism).
4. Science must (and presumably can) be conducted in a way that is 'value-free': in other words, that is objective.
5. There is a clear distinction between scientific statements and normative statements—judgements about what is 'good' or 'bad'—and a true scientist should only make the former. This last principle is implied by the first one because we cannot establish the truth—or otherwise—of normative statements by using the senses.

possible to collect observations in a way that is not influenced by pre-existing theories. The fact that theoretical terms are only considered scientific if they can be directly observed implies that observation has greater epistemological status than theory.

We should note that it is a mistake to treat positivism as another word for science and the scientific. In fact, philosophers of science, as well as of the social sciences, have various views about how best to characterize scientific practice, and since the early 1960s there has been a movement away from viewing science in purely positivist terms. It is a fact that some writers and traditions reject the idea of studying social reality using principles of the natural sciences, but it is not always clear whether they are criticizing the application of a general natural-scientific approach or of positivism in particular. For example, **realism**—see Key concept 2.3—is another philosophical position that provides an account of the nature of scientific practice. There is a long-standing argument about the appropriateness of the natural science model for studying society, but as the model is often described in a way that tends to have largely positivist overtones, it would seem that positivism is the focus of attention rather than other accounts of scientific practice (such as **critical realism**—again, see Key concept 2.3).

Interpretivism

Interpretivism (see Key concept 2.4) is an epistemology that contrasts with positivism. It is a wide-ranging term that incorporates a number of different perspectives and approaches. This includes hermeneutics, phenomenology, Weber's concept of *Verstehen*, and symbolic interactionism. What these traditions share is the view that the social world cannot be studied using a scientific model. This is because the subject matter of the social sciences—people and their institutions—is fundamentally different from that of the natural sciences. The logic of social science research is, therefore, also different, and the methods used in social science research need to reflect the distinctiveness of human consciousness and experience.

Hermeneutics and 'Verstehen'

One of the key influences on interpretivism is **hermeneutics**. This is a term that originated in theology and is used in the social sciences to mean the theory

KEY CONCEPT 2.3
What is realism?

Realism shares two features with positivism: a belief that the natural and the social sciences can and should apply the same kinds of approach to the collection of data and to explanation, and a commitment to the view that there is an external reality on which scientists should focus (in other words, there is a reality that is separate from our descriptions of it). There are two main forms of realism: empirical and critical.

- *Empirical realism* is what people usually mean when they talk about 'realism' in a general way. This view simply asserts that reality can be understood through the use of appropriate methods. This version of realism is sometimes referred to as *naive realism* to reflect the fact that realists often assume that there is a perfect (or at least very close) correspondence between reality and the term used to describe it. Researchers have criticized the approach on the grounds that it 'fails to recognise that there are enduring structures and generative mechanisms underlying and producing observable phenomena and events' and is therefore 'superficial' (Bhaskar 1989: 2).
- *Critical realism* is a specific form of realism that aims to recognize the reality of the natural order and the events and discourses of the social world. It argues that

  > we will only be able to understand—and so change—the social world if we identify the structures at work that generate those events and discourses. . . . These structures are not spontaneously apparent in the observable pattern of events; they can only be identified through the practical and theoretical work of the social sciences.
  >
  > (Bhaskar 1989: 2)

  This implies two things. The first is that a positivist conceptualization of reality does not directly reflect that reality; rather, it is simply a way of knowing it. The second is that critical realists are happy to include in their explanations theoretical ideas that are not directly observable.

KEY CONCEPT 2.4
What is interpretivism?

Interpretivism is the term often used to describe an alternative to the positivist epistemology that has dominated the social sciences for decades. It is based on the view that there are fundamental differences between people and the objects of the natural sciences. Therefore, social scientists need distinct research methods that respect the differences between the natural world and the human one. These methods require the researcher to grasp the subjective experience of social action, what these experiences mean in practice, how those experiences and meanings are understood by others, and why they are interpreted in such ways. Interpretivism has been influenced by a number of intellectual traditions, including Weber's idea of *Verstehen*; the hermeneutic–phenomenological tradition; and symbolic interactionism.

and method associated with the experience of human action. At its most fundamental level, hermeneutics is concerned with interpretation and understanding, and how history, culture, and language shape those two key aspects of the human world (Mason and May 2019). Rather than seeing individuals as passive vessels who are subject to powerful, but unseen, social forces that are acting upon them, hermeneutics emphasizes the situated nature of human understanding and interaction. This contrast, between *explaining* social action through law-like generalizations and *understanding* human experience, is reflected in debates that have been around since long before the modern social sciences. We can, for example, see it in Max Weber's (1864–1920) idea of *Verstehen*, which very broadly means 'understanding'.

For Weber, the point of the social sciences is to understand how people see and act in the human world *and* to examine the social conditions that are necessary for such views and actions to emerge. Weber described sociology as a 'science which attempts the interpretive understanding of social action in order to arrive at a **causal** explanation of its course and effects' (1947/1922: 88). The crucial point here is that the task of 'causal explanation' is undertaken with reference to the 'interpretive understanding of social action', rather than to those external forces that tacitly act upon individuals. So, whereas Émile Durkheim chose to highlight that rates of suicide were higher where social integration and moral integration within a society were low (Durkheim 1952/1897), Jack D. Douglas—who was very much working in the Weberian tradition—viewed things differently. He demonstrated that not only is the recording of a suicide dependent on a coroner's interpretation, the situated meanings of suicide are quite different to the abstractions that might place its causes in broader social structures, as Durkheim did (Douglas 1967). This requires an examination of the different factors that influence when and where particular interpretations of human action—like the category of suicide—are developed and maintained.

Phenomenology

Another key intellectual tradition that has been responsible for the anti-positivist interpretivist position is **phenomenology**. This is a philosophical approach that focuses on how individuals make sense of the world around them and how, in particular, the philosopher is able to overcome their own preconceptions to better understand the phenomena that are associated with human consciousness. Phenomenological ideas were first applied to the social sciences by Alfred Schutz (1899–1959), whose work did not come to the notice of most English-speaking social scientists until his major writings were translated from German in the 1960s, over two decades after they had been written. His work was heavily influenced by Weber's concept of *Verstehen*, as well as by phenomenological philosophers such as Edmund Husserl (1859–1938). Schutz's position is captured in the following passage.

> The world of nature as explored by the natural scientist does not 'mean' anything to molecules, atoms and electrons. But the observational field of the social scientist—social reality—has a specific meaning and relevance structure for the beings living, acting, and thinking within it. By a series of common-sense constructs they have pre-selected and pre-interpreted this world which they experience as the reality of their daily lives. It is these thought objects of theirs which determine their behaviour by motivating it. The thought objects constructed by the social scientist, in order to grasp this social reality, have to be founded upon the thought objects constructed by the common-sense thinking of [people], living their daily life within the social world.
>
> (Schutz 1962: 59)

There are two important points to note about this quotation. First, Schutz asserts that there is a fundamental difference between the subject matter of the natural sciences and the social sciences, so we need an epistemology that reflects and capitalizes upon that difference. The fundamental difference, he suggests, is that social reality has a meaning for human beings and therefore human action is meaningful—that is, people act on the basis of the meanings that they attribute to their acts and to the acts of others. This leads us to the second point Schutz makes: that it is a social scientist's job to gain access to people's 'common-sense thinking' and use this to interpret their actions and social world from their point of view. This is the feature that social scientists identifying with phenomenology tend to emphasize. In the words of the authors of a research methods text whose approach is described as phenomenological: 'The phenomenologist views human behavior . . . as a product of how people interpret the world. . . . In order to grasp the meanings of a person's behavior, *the phenomenologist attempts to see things from that person's point of view*' (Bogdan and Taylor 1975: 13–14; emphasis in original).

In this account of *Verstehen* and phenomenology, we have skated over some complex issues. In particular, Weber's examination of *Verstehen* is far more complex than our discussion might suggest, in both theory and practice (Bauman 1978). There is also disagreement over what is and what is not a genuinely phenomenological approach to the social sciences (Heap and Roth 1973). However, similarity among the traditions of hermeneutics, phenomenology, and the *Verstehen* approach has contributed to the school of thought that is often called interpretivism (for example, J. A. Hughes 1990). Not only do these traditions reject positivism and the application of natural-science methodology to social science, they all also emphasize the idea that social action is meaningful to those involved and therefore needs to be interpreted from their point of view.

Symbolic interactionism

Verstehen and the hermeneutic–phenomenological tradition were not the only intellectual influences on interpretivism. Many writers see the theoretical tradition in sociology known as **symbolic interactionism**, often associated with George Herbert Mead (1863–1931), as a further influence. Symbolic interactionists argue that an individual is continually interpreting the symbolic meaning of their environment (which includes the actions of others) and acts on the basis of this meaning/these meanings. Again, the case for linking this tradition to interpretivism is not entirely straightforward and there has been some debate over the implications of its ideas for empirical research. One particular point of contention has been the claim that our idea of self emerges through an appreciation of how others see us. However, symbolic interactionism is generally seen as holding similar views to the hermeneutic–phenomenological tradition and is taken to be broadly interpretative in approach. This tendency is mainly down to Herbert Blumer, a student of Mead's who acted as his mentor's spokesperson and interpreter (Hammersley 1989; R. Collins 1994). He came up with the term 'symbolic interaction' and also wrote about Mead's writings in a way that gave them clear interpretative overtones. Blumer's claim that 'the position of symbolic interaction requires the student to catch the process of interpretation through which [actors] construct their actions' (1962: 188) clearly reveals a focus for research: the symbols through which people understand and experience interaction.

Although symbolic interactionism and the hermeneutic–phenomenological tradition share an opposition to positivism and an interpretative stance, they should not be seen as closely linked. Symbolic interactionism is a type of social theory with distinctive epistemological implications that help to focus research interest, whereas the hermeneutic–phenomenological tradition is best thought of as an epistemological approach in its own right. Weber's concept of *Verstehen*, however, is probably best seen as an all-encompassing aim for interpretative social research.

The process of interpretation

Taking an interpretative stance can mean that the researcher comes up with surprising findings, or at least findings that appear surprising outside the particular social context being studied. Research in focus 2.3 provides an example of this possibility and shows how, when the social scientist adopts an interpretative position, he or she does not simply reveal *how* members of a social group interpret the world around them. Instead, the social scientist will aim to place the interpretations they have gained into a social-scientific frame. This means that there is a double interpretation going on: the researcher provides an interpretation of others' interpretations. This process of interpretation between the context of those researched and the context of the researcher is sometimes referred to as the double hermeneutic. It is significant because it draws attention to the fact that researchers who are operating within the interpretivist tradition need to examine their preconceptions about research design, data collection, and the interpretation of that data. Decisions and preferences that could otherwise remain implicit need to be made explicit so that they can be examined with greater critical awareness. This attempt to reflect on the process of

RESEARCH IN FOCUS 2.3
Interpretivism in practice

In addition to conducting **participant observation** on an international 'pay to play' billiard league that lasted three years, O'Boyle (2019) conducted 60 semi-structured interviews with poolplayers who deliberately lost matches. These players would cheat in local league matches in order to lower their overall ranking so that they would not need as many points to win playoff and tournament matches, where the rewards were much higher. However, O'Boyle found that while the players he identified as having a ranking much lower than their skill level did admit to losing on purpose, they variously attempted to rationalize their behaviour as a legitimate strategy for winning. Not only did they suggest that other team members relied on their low ranking, they also claimed that no one got hurt; that the system of ranking required cheating; that everyone cheated; and that they had been told to cheat. For example, one suggested that '[i]f my league operator tried to stop cheating, things would be different, but she doesn't, so I have no choice but to cheat', with another highlighting '[p]layers talk about cheating all the time, so if I don't cheat too, I won't be able to win' (O'Boyle 2019: 1027). Knowing that their behaviour was wrong, the players neutralized the stigma that we might usually associate with cheating by interpreting their actions as appropriate and justifiable given the nature and structure of the league. These justifications allowed them to continue to acquire an unfair advantage against others for their own gain while not threatening their self-images as 'good' players. As O'Boyle highlights (2019: 1028), '[m]ost went to great lengths to illustrate a reasonable cause behind their cheating behaviour'.

knowledge-making is often called *reflexivity*, which we will discuss further in Section 2.6 and in Chapter 16.

Building on the idea of the double hermeneutic, we could even say that there is a third level of interpretation occurring, because the researcher's interpretations have to be further interpreted in terms of the concepts, theories, and literature of a discipline. Taking the example in Research in focus 2.3, O'Boyle's (2019) attempts to categorize how cheating poolplayers rationalize their behaviour is his interpretation of his interviewees' interpretations. He then had the additional job of placing his findings into a social-scientific frame, which he did by relating their justifications of cheating to discussions in criminology that concern the 'techniques of neutralization' that members of criminal and deviant groups use to retain a positive self-image.

In this section we have outlined how epistemological considerations are related to research practice. In particular, we have examined the question of whether a natural science approach, and in particular a positivist one, can supply legitimate knowledge of the social world. Through our discussion of interpretivism, we have also outlined what an alternative to positivism and the scientific method might look like and what it might involve. However, the types of knowledge that we choose to value are also underpinned by particular beliefs about the nature of the human world. It is these *ontological* issues that we will now consider.

2.4 Ontological considerations

Ontology is the study of being, and social ontology is about the nature of social entities, for example organizations or culture. Ontology matters because if, as social researchers, we are interested in understanding reality, our ontological stance will determine how we define that reality. The key question for social scientists is whether social entities can and should be considered as

1. objective entities that exist separately to social actors (people), or
2. social constructions that have been and continue to be built up from the perceptions and actions of social actors.

These two positions are referred to respectively as **objectivism** and **constructionism** (sometimes called constructivism). We can see their differences by using them as lenses through which to consider two of the most common and central terms in social science—'organization' and 'culture'.

KEY CONCEPT 2.5
What is objectivism?

Objectivism is an ontological position that claims that social phenomena, their meanings, and the categories that we use in everyday discourse have an existence that is independent of, or separate from, social actors.

Objectivism

Objectivism is an ontological position that implies that social phenomena confront us as external facts that are beyond our reach or influence (see Key concept 2.5).

We can discuss organization or *an* organization as a tangible object. It has rules and regulations. It adopts standardized procedures for getting things done. People are appointed to different jobs or roles within a division of labour. There is a hierarchy. It has a mission statement. And so on. These features, and whether they are present at all, will vary from organization to organization. By thinking in these terms, we are suggesting that an organization has a reality that is external to the individuals who inhabit it. The organization also represents a social order, in that it exerts pressure on individuals to conform to its requirements. People learn and apply the rules and regulations. They follow the standardized procedures. They do the jobs to which they are appointed. They are told what to do and tell others what to do. They learn and apply the values in the mission statement. If they do not do these things, they may be reprimanded or even dismissed from the organization. The organization is therefore a constraining force that acts on and inhibits the behaviour of its members.

We can say the same of culture. Cultures and subcultures can be seen as repositories of widely shared values and customs into which people are socialized so that they can function as good citizens or as full participants. Cultures and subcultures constrain us because we internalize their beliefs and values (for example, gendered roles in the workplace and the home).

In the case of both organizations and cultures, the social entity in question comes across as something external to the actor and as having an almost tangible reality of its own. It has the characteristics of an object and of having an objective reality. These are the classic objectivist ways of conceptualizing organizations and cultures.

Constructionism

We come to the alternative ontological position—*constructionism* (Key concept 2.6). This position challenges the suggestion that categories such as organizations and cultures are pre-given, external realities that social actors have no way of influencing.

KEY CONCEPT 2.6
What is constructionism?

Constructionism (often referred to as constructivism) is an ontological position that asserts that social phenomena and their meanings are continually being created by social actors. It implies that social phenomena are not only produced through social interaction but are in a constant state of revision. In recent years, the term has also been used to include the idea that researchers' own accounts of the social world are constructions. In other words, the researcher always presents a specific version of social reality, rather than one that we could see as definitive, meaning that knowledge is not seen as fixed. Both meanings are antithetical (opposite) to *objectivism* (see Key concept 2.5), but the second meaning is also antithetical to *realism* (see Key concept 2.3). We could think of the first, original meaning as describing constructionism in relation to the social world; the second meaning describes constructionism in relation to the nature of knowledge of the social world (and indeed the natural world).

These versions of constructionism are usually linked, and the second idea is increasingly incorporated into the first, but in this book we use the term in relation to the original meaning. We discuss constructionism as an ontological position in relation to social objects and categories—that is, one that views them as socially constructed.

As we did with objectivism, we may apply the term 'constructionism' to the study of organizations and cultures. Let us take organizations first. Strauss et al. (1973), drawing on insights from symbolic interactionism, carried out research in a psychiatric hospital and proposed that it was best thought of as a 'negotiated order'. Instead of taking the view that order in organizations is a pre-existing characteristic, the authors argue that it is worked at. Rules were far less extensive and less rigorously imposed than might be supposed from the classic account of organizations—Strauss and colleagues refer to the rules as 'much less like commands, and much more like general understandings' (1973: 308). Because the doctors, nurses, and other workers were constrained by relatively few fixed rules, the social order of the hospital was the product of agreed patterns of action that were themselves the products of negotiations between the different parties involved. The social order was in a constant state of change because the hospital was

> a place where numerous agreements are continually being terminated or forgotten, but also as continually being established, renewed, reviewed, revoked, revised. . . . In any pragmatic sense, this is the hospital at the moment: this is its social order.
>
> (Strauss et al. 1973: 316–17)

The authors argue that if we focus on the formal **properties** of organizations (rules, organizational charts, regulations, roles), we tend to neglect the degree to which order in these entities have to be accomplished in everyday interaction—though this is not to say that the formal properties have *no* element of constraint on individual action.

We can make much the same point about the idea of culture. Instead of seeing culture as an external reality that acts on and constrains people, we can take it to be an emergent reality in a continuous state of construction and reconstruction. Becker (1982), for example, has suggested that

> people create culture continuously. . . . No set of cultural understandings . . . provides a perfectly applicable solution to any problem people have to solve in the course of their day, and they therefore must remake those solutions, adapt their understandings to the new situation in the light of what is different about it.
>
> (Becker 1982: 521)

Like Strauss et al. (1973), Becker does also recognize that culture has a reality that 'persists and antedates [pre-exists] the participation of particular people' and shapes their perspectives, but it is not a fixed, objective reality that possesses only a sense of constraint: it acts as a point of reference but is always in the process of being formed.

Neither Strauss et al.'s nor Becker's work pushes the constructionist argument to the extreme: the writers admit to the pre-existence of their objects of interest (organizations and culture, respectively). However, they do stress the active role of individuals in the construction of social reality. Constructionism essentially invites the researcher to consider the ways in which social reality is an ongoing creation of social actors rather than something external to actors and that totally constrains them.

Constructionism also suggests that the categories people use to understand the world around them are in fact social products. They are not external to us; their meaning is constructed in and through interaction. So a category such as 'masculinity' is not treated as a distinct entity, but as something whose meaning is built up during interaction. That meaning is likely to be temporary, as it will vary depending on both time and place. This kind of stance often involves looking at the language used to present categories in particular ways. We can see this tendency particularly clearly in **discourse analysis**, which we will discuss in Chapter 21. As Potter (1996: 98) observes: 'The world . . . is *constituted* in one way or another as people talk it, write it and argue it.' This sense of constructionism is the opposite of realism (see Key concept 2.3).

While constructionism, as an ontological standpoint, argues that the categories we use in the social world are social products, often created through discourse, this is not to say that such constructions are meaningless. In fact, it is quite the opposite. One prominent ontological standpoint that is closely linked to constructionist approaches is **intersectionality** theory (Windsong 2016). This theory, which stems from **feminism**, specifically the work of Crenshaw (1989), centres on the idea that every person occupies positions within numerous social categories and that these categories cannot be considered in isolation from each other. Not only are the social categories we individually embody important, but we have multiple social categories and these interact and intersect in meaningful ways. Despite Black feminists' development of this theory in the late 1980s and 1990s onwards, it has only recently gained greater traction and has now become widespread in the social sciences as a way to 'account for multiple grounds of identity when considering how the social world is constructed' (Crenshaw 1991: 1245). We outline intersectionality theory—including the ways in which some intersectional approaches seek to *de*construct social categories—in Key concept 2.7.

KEY CONCEPT 2.7
What is intersectionality?

Intersectionality is the idea that we all occupy positions within different social categories, including gender, social class, sexuality, and race, and these cannot be understood in isolation—they can all influence an individual's experience. Intersectionality theory takes the view that if we want to fully understand any social category we must recognize how one social characteristic is experienced differently depending on how it intersects with other characteristics. For example, someone's experience will not only be shaped by the fact that they are a woman; it may also be affected by the fact that they are working class, mixed race, and attracted to women, and how these positions combine and intersect.

The term 'intersectionality' is attributed to the feminist American academic Kimberlé Crenshaw (1989), but in fact this kind of thinking was around before Crenshaw's work was published. Black women, in particular, have long argued that it is important to deconstruct the category 'women' and to recognize that social class and 'race' produce both commonalities and differences between women (Phoenix 2006). Today, the term 'intersectionality' is widely used across the social sciences, but especially in gender studies, as a tool for recognizing and analysing how intersecting social factors produce varying experiences of the social world. The main concern of intersectionality is to achieve 'a complete and substantive transformation of all the relationships of power, structures of subordination, and systems of domination which disadvantage people on the basis of their multiple group identities' (Atrey 2019: 53).

As a significant theoretical contribution to social science and beyond, intersectionality is not associated with specific methods. According to Phoenix (2006) and Prins (2006), intersectionality can be associated with a wide range of approaches rather than with only one type of epistemology or methodology, because its major focus is on ontology—that is, beliefs about the nature of the social world. The methodological thinking behind intersectionality has been developed by Leslie McCall (2005), who summarizes the three main methods used to study it. The approaches she identifies are not exhaustive, can overlap, and do not reflect the wide range of interdisciplinary methodologies that are now used, but they have helped to develop thinking around the concept and give us a sense of the ways in which it can be applied in practice.

- *Intra-categorical complexity* is 'the approach that has inaugurated the study of intersectionality' and the one that is most focused on categories. It critically interrogates the ways in which social categories are created by the making and defining of boundaries, but also recognizes that such categories may represent 'stable and even durable relationships' (McCall 2005: 174) at any point in time. One example is Wingfield's (2009) study of the experience of minority men in nursing. Earlier research had shown that men tend to ride a 'glass escalator' in women-dominated fields (meaning they are fast-tracked to more advanced positions), but Wingfield's study showed that this does not happen in the same way for Black men. In this case, race and gender intersect to limit the upwards mobility of minority men. The intra-categorical approach tends to focus on specific intersections in order to analyse the complexity of lived experiences, and it usually concentrates on those that have often been neglected or ignored (Phoenix 2006).
- *Inter-categorical complexity* is the relational approach to intersectionality and it focuses on how different positions or statuses meet. McCall (2005) observes that gender is always already 'raced' while race is already 'gendered', so these cannot be separated in practice. By comparing the experiences of these related categories, it is possible to identify patterns of resonance and difference between them. This approach is sometimes more empirical and this allows disadvantage and privilege to be included within the analysis. In particular, it means that whiteness comes under the analytical framework as being strongly related to privileged. While this approach studies relationships *between* categories, it is often associated with quantitative research; its intersectional focus means that it does not reduce categories to the extent of ignoring intersections and varied experiences.
- *Anti-categorical complexity* is a postmodern critique of categories, where categories and intersections are deconstructed and seen as unstable, not fixed, and impossible to separate (that is, they are mutually constitutive). This approach rejects the language of intersections, seeking to understand them in a

dynamically, contextually, and historically grounded way. Categories are seen as artificial constructs where interactions and structures are considered simultaneously.

As we have noted, McCall's categories are not exhaustive and do not capture all the types of intersectional research being conducted today. It is also important to be aware that despite the term's popularity in the social sciences, especially within feminist research scholarship, it has been subject to some criticism. Intersectionality has, as Atrey (2019) summarizes, been criticized for not providing a clear methodological strategy and giving little guidance on how the concept can be used 'as a critical theory or as an instrument of social change'. However, for the most part, this is arguably the result of misinterpretation of the original theory and poor application of it on to existing methodological understandings.

Ontology and social research

We cannot separate questions of social ontology from those about conducting social research. Ontological assumptions and commitments feed into the ways in which research questions are formulated and research is carried out. For example, if a research question (see Chapter 4) is formulated in a way that suggests organizations and cultures are objective social entities that act on individuals, the researcher is likely to emphasize the formal properties of organizations or the beliefs and values of members of the culture. If the research question implies that organization and culture should not be seen as objective categories, the researcher will probably emphasize the active involvement of people in reality construction. The researcher's ontological assumptions will usually influence their choice of research design and the methods they use to collect data.

2.5 Research strategy: quantitative and qualitative research

Writers on methodological issues often find it helpful to distinguish between **quantitative research** and **qualitative research**. This distinction is not universally accepted: while some see it as fundamental, others suggest it is no longer useful or even that it is 'false' (Layder 1993: 110). However, it continues to be widely used. You will probably find that your research methods classes are split according to the quantitative/qualitative 'divide', and you might have noticed that it also forms the structure for this book. We use it because it represents a useful way of classifying different methods of social research and a starting point for discussing a range of related issues.

At first, it might seem as though the main difference between quantitative and qualitative research is that quantitative researchers use measurement and qualitative researchers do not (in other words, the former involves *quantifying* things), but many writers have suggested that the differences go further and deeper. For example, many researchers see quantitative and qualitative approaches as having different epistemological foundations. If we think about the areas that we have discussed in this chapter—the connection between theory and research, epistemological considerations, and ontological considerations—then quantitative and qualitative research form two distinct clusters of research strategy. By a **research strategy**, we simply mean a general approach to conducting social research.

A very simple summary of quantitative research would be that it

- emphasizes quantification in the collection and analysis of data;
- involves a deductive approach to the relationship between theory and research, with an emphasis on testing theories;
- has incorporated the practices and norms of the natural-scientific model and of positivism in particular; and
- views social reality as an external, objective reality.

If we were to summarize qualitative research in the same broad, simple way, we would describe it as a research strategy that

- usually emphasizes words rather than quantification in the collection and analysis of data;

- emphasizes an inductive approach to the relationship between theory and research, focusing on generating theories;
- has rejected the practices and norms of the natural-scientific model, and of positivism in particular, preferring to emphasize how individuals interpret their social world; and
- views social reality as the constantly shifting creation of individual social actors.

We set out some key distinctions between quantitative and qualitative strategies in Table 2.1.

TABLE 2.1
Stereotypical ways of differentiating quantitative and qualitative research strategies

	Quantitative	Qualitative
Typical role of theory in relation to research	Deductive; testing of theory	Inductive; generation of theory
Epistemological orientation	Natural science model, in particular positivism	Interpretivism
Ontological orientation	Objectivism	Constructionism

While these lists and Table 2.1 provide a neat and, we hope, useful overview, you will have noticed that we introduced them as 'very simple summaries'. This is because the quantitative/qualitative distinction is not quite as straightforward as it might seem. We outline the nature of quantitative and then qualitative research in more detail in Chapters 7 and 16, but for now it is important to appreciate that although quantitative and qualitative approaches can be broadly distinguished in terms of their epistemological and ontological foundations and tendencies, we need to be careful about seeing them as exact opposites. For one thing, studies with the broad characteristics of one research strategy often have some characteristics of the other. For example, in the Williams et al. (2017a) study we discussed previously, a quantitative strategy was used, but the measurement of low-level disorder terms ('broken windows' indicators) began with the authors taking textual data (tweets) and **coding** it into a simple binary measure that reflected whether a tweet contained a 'broken windows' **indicator** or not. The process through which this happened was rigorous, but the fact remains that the authors started with what would typically be defined as qualitative data and transformed it into a quantifiable measure.

Many writers also argue that the two strategies can be usefully combined within a **mixed methods research** project. We explore this type of research in Chapter 24, but the study described in Research in focus 2.4 will give you a sense of what it involves, as well as showing you why we should avoid drawing a hard line between quantitative and qualitative research. The approaches of these two strategies might at first seem incompatible, but this study demonstrates that they can be usefully combined.

RESEARCH IN FOCUS 2.4
Mixed methods research

Gallaher and WrinklerPrins (2016) provide an accessible and clear **case study** of a mixed methods project into livelihoods and urban agriculture in Kibera, a division of Nairobi Area, Kenya. The study reflects the potential for mixed methods studies to use qualitative and quantitative data and become greater than the sum of their parts. The authors were particularly interested in food security and the use of 'sack gardening' (a productive form of container gardening). They collected data using

- 31 semi-structured interviews (a technique we will discuss in Chapter 19)
- 306 household surveys
- 7 **focus groups**
- 50 soil, plant, and water samples
- 2 feedback workshops

Gallaher and WrinklerPrins explain how, when the research was originally conceived, the strategy was a linear one that started with a survey, moved on to semi-structured interviews, and ended with the collection of samples from

soil, plants, and water. The researchers describe how, once they were in the field, the project adapted to become more iterative: interviews informed the creation and design of the survey, and both interview and survey data informed later focus-group discussions. As the authors point out, this change had a significant impact on their study:

> by using qualitative interviews first to inform the construction of a quantitative survey instrument, our survey was more targeted and better reflected the reality of urban agriculture in Kibera as described by the farmers we interviewed . . . This improved the overall quality of our survey data, and gave a voice to the population being studied in a way that is often overlooked when conducting household surveys.
>
> Gallaher and WrinklerPrins (2016:90)

Clearly there can be significant advantages to combining qualitative and quantitative methods in this way, and we return to this idea in Chapter 24.

2.6 Further influences on how we conduct social research

In addition to understanding how theory, epistemology, and ontology relate to conducting social research, we also need to consider the impact of *values* and of *practical considerations*.

Values

Values reflect the personal beliefs or the feelings of a researcher, and there are different views about the extent to which they should influence research—and whether we can control this at all. These views can be summarized as

- the value-free approach;
- the reflexive approach;
- the conscious partiality approach.

The value-free approach

The French sociologist Émile Durkheim (1858–1917) argued for a value-free approach, stating that because (in his opinion) social facts should be treated as things, all 'preconceptions must be eradicated' (Durkheim 1938/1895: 31). As values are a form of preconception, he was effectively saying that researchers should suppress them when conducting research. Phenomenology (see 'Phenomenology' in Section 2.3) is another research tradition that, in its most basic form, promotes the idea of value-free research. Because this approach tends to focus on the experience of research participants, it advocates using *epoche* (or 'bracketing'), which is when the researcher makes a conscious attempt to set aside their own experiences and values in order to carry out the research from a neutral and value-free scientific position. These positions might seem logical: we might think that social scientists should be value-free and objective because research that simply reflects the personal biases of the researcher(s) cannot be considered valid and scientific. However, there is a growing recognition, even within phenomenology, that it is not possible to completely 'eradicate' our values.

The reflexive approach

Researchers who take the position that research cannot be value-free exercise **reflexivity**, a concept we will explore further in Chapter 16 (see Key concept 16.6). This involves trying to identify and recognize the impact of their social location—that is, their gender, age, sexual orientation, ethnicity, education, background, and so on—on the kind of data that they produce and analyse during their research process. These researchers argue that our values, preferences, and inclinations can exert an influence at many stages in the process of social research, including

- choice of research area;
- formulation of research questions;
- choice of method;
- formulation of research design and data-collection techniques;
- implementation of data collection;

- analysis of data;
- interpretation of data;
- conclusions.

The researcher's values can also intrude into their work if they develop an affection or sympathy for the people being studied. As we will explore in Chapter 18, this is quite a common issue for researchers working within a qualitative research strategy, particularly when they use participant observation or very intensive interviewing, and they can find it difficult to disentangle their stance as social scientists from their subjects' perspective(s). This possibility might be exacerbated by the tendency that Becker (1967) identified for sociologists in particular to be sympathetic to 'underdog' groups (more marginalized groups). However, having a fixed set of values and beliefs can also be a barrier to understanding the people we study. Turnbull (1973) studied an African tribe known as the Ik and perceived them as a loveless (and for him unlovable) tribe that left its young and very old to die. Turnbull identified the conditions that had led to this culture but he was very honest about his strong disapproval for what he witnessed. This reaction was the result of his Western values about the family, and it is likely, as he acknowledged, that these values influenced his perception of what he witnessed. He wrote (Turnbull 1973: 13): 'the reader is entitled to know something of the aims, expectations, hopes and attitudes that the writer brought to the field with him, for these will surely influence not only how he sees things but even what he sees.'

The reflexive approach has become increasingly widespread in social research. Today, researchers often warn readers about the ways in which their identity and social position might have influenced their findings, and students conducting a research project are often encouraged to reflect on their positions as researchers and the assumptions and values they carry.

The conscious partiality approach

The third approach to the issue of values influencing research is to argue for *conscious partiality*—in other words, research that is knowingly and even deliberately influenced by values. Mies has argued that in feminist research the 'postulate of *value free research*, of neutrality and indifference towards the research objects, has to be replaced by *conscious partiality*, which is achieved through partial identification with the research objects' (Mies 1993: 68; emphases in original). So while reflexive approaches acknowledge the potential influence of values (both the researcher's and the research participants') and other factors, those in favour of conscious partiality see this influence as not just inevitable but welcome (as, for example, in Learn from experience 2.2). If a researcher identifies with and adopts a particular theoretical framework, for example feminist, Marxist, or postcolonial, they are practising conscious partiality: they will develop their research according to the values and interpretations of that framework. With a feminist approach, the research process and findings would be likely to highlight the disadvantages experienced by women and other marginalized groups as a result of patriarchal society (as we will see, the definition of 'feminism' is broader than it used to be); with a Marxist approach, the impact of class division and capitalism on socioeconomic inequality would probably be an important influence; and a postcolonial approach would be critical of the way in which knowledge production over the centuries has been shaped by intrinsically value-laden, Western-centric, and ethnocentric approaches (as we saw in the Turnbull example in the previous section on the reflexive approach).

These approaches generally follow historical shifts in understanding social research, and a school of thought known as feminist science studies was influential in recognizing the impact the researcher has on the studies they produce. The influence of the researcher's values and social position, alongside other social categories, are unavoidable. The recognition that research cannot be produced without involving human researchers with particular values has increased in recent decades, yet this is often not as explicit in quantitative research approaches. Qualitative approaches tend to recognize this positioning to a greater extent, and this explicit recognition and reflexivity is often favoured by feminist researchers. As we will see in later chapters (especially in Section 7.7 under the subheading 'The feminist critique'), feminist researchers traditionally (though less so in recent years) lean towards qualitative approaches because they see them as more compatible with and adaptable to their values. We return to feminism and some associated theoretical approaches in Section 6.6, at which point we will see that adhering to ethical principles or standards is another way in which values influence how we conduct social research.

In summary, social researchers take various different positions in relation to values and value-free research, but you will see as you progress through this book that there is an increasing awareness of the limits to objectivity, and today, views like Durkheim's are rare. Quantitative researchers sometimes write in a way that suggests objectivity (Letherby et al. 2012), but we simply do not know the extent to which they believe that this is achievable, or even possible.

LEARN FROM EXPERIENCE 2.2
Values in social research

Sarah clearly identifies how her values are integral to how she is conducting her current research project.

In my current, postgraduate study of Pakistani and Bangladeshi Muslim lone mothers' lived experiences I have employed standpoint Black feminism research values as part of the research process. Research on lone motherhood overwhelmingly focuses on the experiences of white women, so in my study I have tried to bring forward and emphasize the voices of other women who are often marginalized, challenging the view of such groups as being 'other' and instead assuming that they are entirely knowable (Bhabha 2003). Much like Mirza (1998) states, my research commits to: 'doing non-hierarchical, reciprocal, negotiated, emancipatory and subjective research which would be both about the South Asian women, for the South Asian women, and conducted from within the South Asian women's perspectives' (Mirza 1998: 81). I have given my participants space to discuss their own perspectives, positionings, and subjective experiences on their own terms.

This approach has also prompted me to reflect on my own positionality and identity as a young British Pakistani woman and how this has influenced the research process. I have reflected on both my insider status (in relation to Pakistani women) and outsider status (in relation to Bangladeshi women, my age etc.) and I have employed reflexivity, which is another practice of feminist researchers. Altogether, these values influence the conclusions I draw about my data as well as my view of research as a tool for social justice.

Sarah

Access the **online resources** to hear Sarah's video reflections on this theme.

You can read about our panellists' backgrounds and research experiences on page xxvi.

References:

Bhabha, H. K. (2003). 'Democracy De-realized', *Diogenes*, 50(1): 27–35.

Mirza, H. S. (1998). 'Race, Gender and IQ: The Social Consequence of Pseudo-scientific Discourse', *Race, Ethnicity and Education*, 1(1): 109–26.

Practical considerations

We should not forget about the importance and significance of *practical issues* in decisions about how social research should be carried out. There are three key areas to consider:

1. the nature of your research question(s);
2. whether much research has previously been done on your research topic;
3. the nature of the topic and/or the people being investigated.

Your choice of research strategy, design, or method must be tailored to the research question(s) you are investigating. If you are interested in exploring the relative importance of different causes of a social phenomenon, it is quite likely that a quantitative strategy (discussed in Chapter 7) will fit your needs. If, however, you are interested in the views of members of a certain social group, it may be preferable to use a qualitative research strategy that is sensitive to how participants interpret their social world.

If you are interested in a topic on which little or no research has been done in the past, a quantitative research approach may be difficult because you will not be able to draw on much existing literature and you may have difficulty in identifying the important concepts that you need to measure. In this case, a more exploratory stance may be best, and you might want to use a qualitative approach (discussed in Chapter 16) because this strategy is usually associated with generating rather than testing theory (see Table 2.1) and its equally structured but more iterative process might be more suitable for your topic.

The nature of the topic and/or of the people you intend to investigate also matters when you are planning your research. If you need to engage with individuals or groups involved in activities that are illegal or not socially acceptable, such as football hooliganism (Pearson 2009; Poulton 2012), drug dealing (Goffman 2014; P. A. Adler 1985), or the trade in human organs (Scheper-Hughes 2004), it is very unlikely that **survey research** (as described in Chapters 9 and 10) would allow you to gain the confidence of participants or achieve the necessary rapport. It would also be extremely difficult to envisage and plan such research. The same principle may apply if you plan to engage with marginalized groups or individuals. It is not surprising that researchers in these kinds of areas have tended to use qualitative approaches, which usually offer more of an opportunity to gain the confidence of the subjects of the investigation to the extent that they feel comfortable disclosing sensitive data about themselves. In some rare cases researchers have chosen to carry out **covert research** and not reveal their identities, though this comes with ethical dilemmas of the kind we will discuss in Chapter 6. In contrast, it seems unlikely that the hypothesis described in Research in focus 2.1—Röder and Mühlau's (2014) research on gender-egalitarian values among migrants—could have been tested with a qualitative method such as participant observation.

While practical considerations may seem dull compared with the philosophical debates surrounding epistemology and ontology, they are important. All social research involves a compromise between the ideal and the feasible, and there are many circumstances in which the nature of the topic or of the participants in an investigation and the constraints on a researcher (such as available time and budget) will have a significant impact on decisions about how best to proceed.

KEY POINTS

- Quantitative and qualitative research represent different approaches to social investigation, and they carry with them important epistemological and ontological considerations.
- Typically, theory can be seen either as something that comes before and prompts research (as in quantitative research) or as something that emerges out of research (as in qualitative research).
- Epistemological considerations are important when considering research strategy. To a large extent, they revolve around whether to use a natural science model (in particular positivism) or interpretivism.
- Ontological considerations about objectivism vs constructionism are also important in informing social research strategies.
- Values can intrude into the research process and can affect research findings, but there are different views as to how researchers should deal with this (whether to reject, reflect on, or embrace values).
- Practical considerations are also important factors in decisions about research methods.

QUESTIONS FOR REVIEW

1. If you had to conduct some social research now, what would the topic be, and what factors would have influenced your choice of topic? How important was theory in your consideration?
2. Outline, using examples of your own, the difference between grand and middle-range theory.
3. What are the differences between inductive and deductive theory, and why is the distinction important?
4. What is meant by each of the following terms: positivism; realism; and interpretivism? Why is it important to understand each of them?

5. What are the implications of epistemological considerations for research practice?
6. What are the main differences between epistemological and ontological considerations?
7. What is meant by the terms objectivism and constructionism?
8. Which theoretical ideas have been particularly instrumental in the development of qualitative research?
9. Outline the main differences between quantitative and qualitative research in terms of: the relationship between theory and data; epistemological considerations; and ontological considerations.
10. To what extent is quantitative research only concerned with testing theories and qualitative research only concerned with generating theories?
11. What are some of the main influences on decisions about how to conduct social research?

ONLINE RESOURCES

www.oup.com/he/srm6e

You can find our notes on the answers to these questions within this chapter's **online resources**, together with:

- *audio/video comments* on this topic from our 'Learn from experience' panellists;
- *self-test questions* for further knowledge-checking; and
- a *flashcard glossary* to help you recall key terms.

CHAPTER

3

RESEARCH DESIGNS

CHAPTER GUIDE

In this chapter, we discuss frameworks for collecting and analysing data in order to answer a certain question or questions. These frameworks are known as research designs. A research design also relates to the criteria we employ when evaluating the quality of social research. In this chapter we cover the following topics:

- reliability, replication, and validity, and their importance as criteria for assessing the quality of social research;
- the suggestion that such quality criteria are mainly relevant to quantitative research, along with the proposition that a different set of criteria should be employed for qualitative research;

- five prominent research designs, each of which we consider in terms of the criteria for evaluating research findings—the experimental design, the cross-sectional design, the longitudinal design, the case study design, and the comparative design;
- the relationship between research strategy and research design.

3.1 Introduction

In the previous chapter, we introduced the idea of *research strategy* as a broad orientation to social research, presenting quantitative and **qualitative research** as different research strategies. However, the decision to adopt a particular strategy will not get you far along the road of doing a piece of research. You will need to make two other key 'top-level' choices (along with many tactical decisions about how the research will be carried out and the data analysed): which *research design* and which *research method* to use. At first these two terms may seem to mean the same thing, but there is an important distinction between them. The terms are summarized in Key concepts 3.1 and 3.2.

Research methods can be associated with different kinds of research design. A research design represents a structure that guides the execution of a research method and the analysis of the data that emerges, but the two terms are often confused. For example, one of the research designs covered in this chapter—the **case study**—is often wrongly referred to as a *method*. A case study involves detailed exploration of a specific case, which could be a community, organization, or person, but you cannot gain data simply by selecting an organization and deciding to study it intensively. Do you observe? Do you conduct interviews? Do you examine documents? Do you administer **questionnaires**? You could use any or all of these methods, but the crucial point is that choosing a case study design will not, in its own right, provide you with data.

In this chapter, we will examine five different research designs: **experimental** design and its variants, including **quasi-experiments**; **cross-sectional** or **survey**

KEY CONCEPT 3.1
What is a research design?

A **research design** provides a framework for the collection and analysis of data. Our choice of research design reflects the priority and importance we attach to one or more **dimensions** of the research process:

- expressing **causal** connections between **variables** (an attribute or characteristic that can vary—see Key concept 3.3);
- generalizing to larger groups of individuals than those actually forming part of the investigation;
- understanding behaviour and the meaning of that behaviour in its specific social context;
- having a temporal (that is, over time) appreciation of social phenomena (observed facts or situations) and the connections between them.

KEY CONCEPT 3.2
What is a research method?

A **research method** is simply a technique for collecting data. It can involve a specific instrument, such as a **self-completion questionnaire** or a structured **interview schedule** (a list of prepared questions); or **participant observation**, whereby the researcher listens to and watches others; or the analysis of documents or existing data.

design; longitudinal design; case study design; and comparative design. However, before we discuss the natures of, and differences between, these designs, let's consider some recurring issues around the *quality* of social research—issues that are relevant across the various research designs.

3.2 Quality criteria in social research

Three of the most prominent criteria for evaluating social research are reliability, replication, and validity. We will consider these terms in much greater detail in later chapters, but in the meantime it will be helpful to have a basic understanding of each one.

Reliability

Reliability is concerned with whether we would get the same results from a study if we repeated it under the same conditions. The term is commonly used when considering whether the measures that we devise for concepts in the social sciences (such as poverty, racial prejudice, relationship quality, religious orthodoxy) are consistent. In Chapter 7 we will look at the idea of reliability in greater detail, particularly the different conceptualizations of it. Reliability is a particular concern for quantitative research, as the quantitative researcher is likely to be concerned with whether a measure is stable or not. For example, if IQ test scores, which were designed as measures of intelligence, were found to fluctuate within individuals, so that a person's IQ score was wildly different when the test was administered on two or more occasions, we would consider the IQ test an unreliable measure—we could not have faith in its consistency.

Replication

The idea of reliability is very close to another criterion of research—replication, and more especially replicability. Sometimes researchers choose to replicate (reproduce) previous studies. There are various reasons for doing so, such as a feeling that the original results do not match other existing evidence, or to see whether findings are consistent over time or between different groups. In order for replication to take place, a study must be capable of replication—it must be replic*able*. If we want to replicate a study, then we need to know exactly how it was designed, who was involved, what data was collected, and how it was analysed. So for a study to be replicable, a researcher must pay close attention to reporting their methodological choices when writing up.

Replication in social research is actually quite rare. When Michael Burawoy (1979) found that by accident he was conducting case study research in a US factory that had been studied three decades earlier by another researcher (Donald Roy), he thought about treating his own investigation as a replication. However, the low status of replication in academic life persuaded him to resist this option. He writes: 'I knew that to replicate Roy's study would not earn me a dissertation let alone a job. . . . [In] academia the real reward comes not from replication but from originality!' (Burawoy 2003: 650). Nonetheless, an investigation's replicability is highly valued by many social researchers working within a quantitative research tradition. It would not be unusual for a student preparing a dissertation to take a classic study and seek to replicate it with a new group of people or organizations, or to see if something that was found years ago is still the case today. We would not expect attitudes towards technology, immigration, or education, for example, to be the same as 10 years ago. See Research in focus 7.1 for an example of a replication study.

Validity

A further criterion of quality, and in many ways the most important, is validity. Validity is concerned with the integrity of the conclusions generated from a piece of research. We will examine this concept in greater detail in Section 7.6 and Section 16.6 for quantitative and qualitative research, respectively, but in the meantime it is important to be aware of the main facets of validity.

- Measurement validity relates primarily to quantitative research and how we measure social-scientific concepts. It is to do with whether a measure for assessing a concept really does reflect that concept—for example, whether an IQ test really does measure variations in intelligence. If the measure does not reflect the concept, the study's findings will be questionable. Measurement validity is related to reliability: if a measure of a concept is unstable—it fluctuates, and so is unreliable—it simply cannot be providing a valid measure of the concept in question.

- **Internal validity** relates mainly to the issue of **causality**, which we will consider in detail in Chapter 7. Internal validity is concerned with whether a conclusion that proposes a causal **relationship** between two or more variables—that claims that *x* causes *y*—is convincing. In discussing causality, we often refer to the factor that has a causal impact as the **independent variable** and the effect as the **dependent variable** (see Key concept 3.3). Internal validity raises the question: how confident can we be that the independent variable really is responsible, at least in part, for the variation that we identify in the dependent variable?
- **External validity** refers to whether the results of a study can be generalized beyond the specific research context. If the research is not externally valid, it will apply only to the group of participants or respondents involved in that research. If it is externally valid, we would expect it to apply more generally to the wider groups of people who are represented by the individuals involved. This context highlights the crucial issue of how people are selected to participate in research. This is one of the main reasons why quantitative researchers are so keen to generate **representative samples** (see Chapter 8).
- **Ecological validity** is concerned with whether social-scientific findings are applicable to people's everyday, natural social settings. The more a social scientist intervenes in natural settings or creates unnatural ones in order to conduct their research (such as using a laboratory, or a special room to carry out interviews), the more likely it is that the results are influenced by the data-collection method(s) and analytic tools. The findings that emerge from a study using questionnaires, for example, may have measurement validity, a reasonable level of internal validity, and external validity, but the unnaturalness of having to answer a questionnaire could mean that the findings have limited ecological validity.
- **Inferential validity**, sometimes neglected, concerns whether the inferences that researchers have made, and the conclusions that they have drawn, are warranted by the research and its findings. This consideration is often connected with the research design that the researchers used and the ways they interpreted its findings. For example, if a researcher infers cause and effect and we want to examine the validity of this conclusion, we might look at whether the research design is one that allows such an inference to be made. As we will see later, it is risky and often simply wrong to infer causality from research that is based on a cross-sectional design.

KEY CONCEPT 3.3
What is a variable?

A variable is simply an attribute on which cases vary. For example, in a data set of university students we could have variables concerning sex, age, ethnicity, educational attainment, nationality, and so on. 'Cases' can obviously be people, but they can also include things such as households, cities, organizations, schools, and nations.

If an attribute does not vary among the cases you are studying, it is a **constant**. For example, if everyone in your sample lives in the UK, then this would be a constant. Another example would be if you were conducting a survey of social media usage and found that everyone in your study used Facebook. Such observations provide important context for a study, but because they don't vary between study participants, they are rarely used for analysis.

There are different ways of classifying variables, but the most basic distinction is between *independent variables* and *dependent variables*. The former are considered to have an influence on the latter. In this sense there is a *direction* of influence. For example, your sex (independent) might have an impact upon your hourly wage (dependent)—but it would never be the case that your hourly wage would affect your sex. In addition, it is important to distinguish between variables—whether independent or dependent—in terms of their measurement **properties** (this is an important issue in the context of quantitative data analysis). See Chapter 15 for an explanation of the distinction between **interval/ratio variables**, **ordinal variables**, **nominal variables**, and **dichotomous variables**; see Table 15.1 for brief descriptions of them.

3

The relationship between quality criteria and research strategy

So far our discussion of quality criteria has been geared mainly to quantitative rather than to qualitative research.

- Both reliability and measurement validity are essentially concerned with the adequacy of measures, which is most obviously a concern in quantitative research.
- Internal validity is concerned with the soundness of findings that specify a causal connection, an issue that commonly concerns quantitative researchers.
- External validity *may* be relevant to qualitative research (see Chapter 16), but the question of whether research participants are representative of their **population** has a more obvious application to quantitative research, which is preoccupied with **sampling** procedures that maximize the opportunity for generating a representative sample.
- Ecological validity, with its focus on the naturalness of the research approach, is the criterion with most relevance to both qualitative and quantitative research.

Some writers have tried to apply the concepts of reliability and validity to qualitative research (e.g. LeCompte and Goetz 1982; Peräkylä 1997). Kirk and Miller (1986) are among them, but have very slightly changed the sense in which the terms are used. Qualitative researchers sometimes suggest that the studies they produce should be judged or evaluated by different criteria from those used in relation to quantitative research. Lincoln and Guba (1985), for example, propose **trustworthiness** as a criterion of how good a qualitative study is. Each aspect of trustworthiness has a parallel with quantitative research criteria.

- *Credibility*, which parallels internal validity—that is, how believable are the findings?
- *Transferability*, which parallels external validity—that is, do the findings apply to other contexts?
- *Dependability*, which parallels reliability—that is, are the findings likely to apply at other times?
- *Confirmability*, which parallels objectivity, a criterion discussed in Section 2.6—that is, has the investigator allowed their values to intrude to a high degree?

We return to the issue of applying quality criteria to qualitative research in Chapter 16.

Although the idea of ecological validity was, like reliability and measurement validity, formulated largely in the context of quantitative research, qualitative research tends to perform quite well against this criterion. Qualitative research often involves a *naturalistic* stance, meaning that the researcher seeks to collect data in naturally occurring situations and environments as opposed to fabricated, artificial ones. Ecological validity probably applies particularly well to ethnographic research, in which participant observation is a key element of data collection, but some suggest that it also applies to the sort of interview approach typically used by qualitative researchers, which is less directive than the kind of interviewing used in quantitative research.

We have spent some time discussing these issues in social research because some of them will emerge in the context of research designs, which we will discuss in the next section; but in a number of ways they also represent background considerations for many other issues that we will examine later in the book.

In the next sections we will look in detail at the five research designs: experimental design, **cross-sectional design**, longitudinal design, case study design, and comparative design. Some of these designs have variants that you should be aware of, and these are discussed in the relevant subsections. Your choice of design will depend on your research question, but also on the resources and time you have available, as discussed in Learn from experience 3.1.

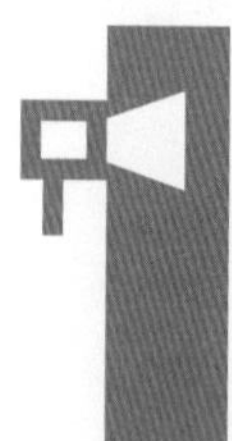

LEARN FROM EXPERIENCE 3.1
Choosing a research design

We would always advise staring with a **research question**, and then considering which research design is the most appropriate for answering it. However, sometimes you will find that the ideal design for your project is not feasible due to the length of time it would require or because of the lack of resources you have available. Scarlett reflects on this further:

> Research designs are very dependent on the topic you want to look into. For example, if you're interested in comparing drug use in one society to drug use in another society, a comparative study design might be

the most appropriate. If you're interested in seeing how effective rehabilitation programmes are on an individual over a two-year period, a longitudinal study design could be used. As you are likely to be completing this project for your undergraduate dissertation research project, it is also important to acknowledge the resources you have available to you and how likely it is that you will be able to conduct such research in the time you are given.

Scarlett

Once you've decided on a research design, you will have to justify this choice in your methodology chapter. This will give you the opportunity to explain how the design relates to the research question or why you might not have been able to go with the most effective design due to time and resource constraints.

 Access the **online resources** to hear Scarlett's video reflections on this theme.

You can read about our panellists' backgrounds and research experiences on page xxvi.

3.3 Experimental design

Experimental designs can be approximately grouped into 'classical experiments' and those that have only some experimental characteristics, which we can call 'quasi-experiments'. They can be either *field* experiments or *laboratory* experiments. Field experiments take place in real-life settings, such as in classrooms and organizations, or as a result of reforms or new policies having been implemented. Laboratory experiments take place in a laboratory or contrived setting. As you might expect, field experiments are more often relevant for social researchers.

Features of the classical experimental design

True classical **experiments** (as opposed to studies that have only some experimental characteristics, which we consider in 'Quasi-experiments') are quite unusual in sociology, but they are used in social psychology, organization studies, and politics, while researchers in social policy sometimes use them in order to assess the impact of new reforms or policies. Experimental research is often held up as a benchmark because it is a design that allows us to have considerable confidence in the robustness and trustworthiness of causal findings, and a true experiment is often used as a standard against which to assess non-experimental research. In other words, true experiments tend to be very strong in terms of internal validity.

If true experiments are so strong in this respect, why don't social researchers make more use of them? The reason is simple: to conduct a true experiment, you need to *manipulate* the independent variable in order to determine whether it does have an influence on the dependent variable, and this is very difficult and sometimes impossible to do outside of controlled settings. In a true experiment, participants are likely to be allocated to one of two or more **experimental groups**, each of which represents different types or levels of the independent variable. The researcher can then establish how far differences between the groups are responsible for variations in the level of the dependent variable. Manipulation essentially involves intervening in a situation and establishing the impact of the manipulation on participants. However, the vast majority of independent variables that social researchers are concerned with cannot be manipulated. For example, if we are interested in the effects of gender on language use on Twitter, we cannot *manipulate* peoples' gender. If we are interested in the effects of variations in social class on social and political attitudes toward migration, we cannot assign people to different social class groupings. Research in focus 3.1 describes a well-known piece of experimental research that illustrates the nature of manipulation and the idea of a field experiment.

The 'classical' experimental design is also often referred to as the *randomized experiment* or **randomized controlled trial** (RCT). We can see this in action in the Rosenthal and Jacobson study in the way that two groups

3

RESEARCH IN FOCUS 3.1
A field experiment

Although it is ethically very questionable (for reasons we consider in more depth in Chapter 6, Sections 6.3 and 6.4), Rosenthal and Jacobson's (1968) study of whether school teachers' expectations of their students' abilities influence the latter's performance is a useful example of manipulation and how a field experiment design can be used within social research.

The researchers looked into this question as part of a programme of research into the impact of self-fulfilling prophecies (for example, where someone's beliefs or expectations about someone else influence how the latter behaves), conducting research in a lower-social-class area in the USA where a high number of children came from minority group backgrounds. In the spring of 1964, all the students completed a test that was portrayed as a means of identifying 'spurters'—that is, students who were likely to excel academically—but which was actually an IQ test. At the beginning of the next academic year, the teachers were told the names of the students who had supposedly been identified as spurters, but in fact were simply 20 per cent of the schoolchildren, chosen at random. The disguised IQ test was readministered eight months after the original one, and the authors were able to compare the differences between the spurters and the other students in terms of changes in various measures of academic performance, such as IQ scores, reading ability, and intellectual curiosity.

This study's design makes it a field experiment because it takes place in a real-life setting, and the manipulation here is the act of separating the students into two groups, making teacher expectations the independent variable. As there was no evidence to suggest that there was any difference in ability between the students who had been identified as spurters and the rest, any indications that the spurters differed from their peers in the second test could be attributed to the fact that the teachers had been led to expect the former would perform better. The findings show that differences in ability between the spurters and their peers did in fact exist, but these differences tended to be concentrated in the first two or three years of schooling. In other words, the evidence for a teacher expectancy effect was patchy. Nonetheless, this remains an influential experiment that is widely believed to provide firm evidence of a teacher expectancy effect.

For a useful brief review of some subsequent related studies and reflections on Rosenthal and Jacobson's study, see Hammersley (2011: 106–9).

are established, with the 'spurters' forming what is known as the *experimental group* or *treatment group* and the other students forming a *control group*. The experimental group receives the *experimental treatment*—teacher expectancies—but the **control group** does not receive an experimental treatment. The dependent variable—student performance—is measured before (T_1—the first time) and after (T_2—the second time) the experimental manipulation, so that a before-and-after analysis can be conducted (see Figure 3.1). The researchers' use of **random assignment** to create the experimental and control groups meant they were able to feel confident that the only difference between the two groups was the fact that teachers expected the spurters to do better at school than the others. They could then also be confident that, if they did establish a difference in performance between the two groups, it was due to the experimental manipulation alone.

So how do classical experiments perform when we apply quality criteria? Let's consider the internal, external, and ecological validity of these designs and their replicability, before looking briefly at the benefits and limitations of laboratory experiments, which are widely used in areas such as social psychology.

Classical experimental design and validity

Internal validity of an experiment

A true experiment must be able to control for the possibility that there could be rival explanations for a causal finding—in the example of Research in focus 3.1, the researchers had to be confident that teacher expectancies really do have an impact on student performance. We might then be in a position to take the view that such a study is internally valid. By setting up a control

3

FIGURE 3.1
Classical experimental design

T₁		T₂
Measurement of dependent variable	**Control group** No treatment	Measurement of dependent variable
Measurement of dependent variable	**Experimental group** Treatment	Measurement of dependent variable

group *and* using random assignment to sort subjects into the experimental and control groups, we can eliminate threats to internal validity.

Campbell (1957) and Cook and Campbell (1979) list a number of threats to internal validity that are applicable to the Rosenthal and Jacobson (1968) study.

- *History*. Events within the environment other than the manipulation could have caused the result—in this case, something other than teacher expectancies might have caused the spurters' scores to rise. One such event could be if the school's head teacher had taken action to raise standards in the school since the first test. If there were no control group, we could not be sure whether it was the teachers' expectancies or the head teacher's actions that were producing the increase in spurters' grades. If there is a control group, we could say that history would have an effect on the control-group participants too, meaning that differences between the experimental and control groups could be attributed to the impact of teacher expectancies alone.
- *Testing*. Subjects may become more experienced at taking a test or may become sensitized to the aims of the experiment as a result of the pre-test. If we have a control group, they would also experience the same effect, so we can be confident that these factors are not responsible for any difference in levels of the dependent variable between the experimental and control groups.
- *Instrumentation*. Changes in the way a test is administered could account for an increase (or decrease) in scores between the pre-test and post-test—for example, if slight changes to a test had been introduced. Again, if there is a control group, we can assume that a change in testing would have affected the control group as well.
- *Mortality*. There is an unavoidable problem of attrition in many studies that span a long period of time, in that participants may drop out. In this case, students may leave the area or move to a different school. However, because this problem is likely to afflict the control group too, it does not pose a threat to the validity of the researchers' conclusions about the impact of teacher expectancies.
- *Maturation*. Quite simply, people change, and the ways in which they change may have implications for the dependent variable. The students identified as spurters might have improved anyway, regardless of the effect of teacher expectancies. But again, maturation should affect the control group subjects as well, allowing us to discount this possibility.
- *Selection*. If there are differences between the two groups (for example if one group was genuinely of higher ability than the other), the variations between them could be attributed to pre-existing differences in their membership. However, if researchers use a random process of assignment to the experimental and control groups, this possibility can be discounted.
- *Ambiguity about the direction of causal influence*. The very idea of an independent variable and dependent variable assumes a direction of causality. However, there may be occasions when the temporal sequence (the order in which things happen) in a study is unclear, so that it is not possible to establish which variable affects the other. In the Rosenthal and Jacobson study, however, the direction of causal influence is clear because the creation of teacher expectancies preceded the improvements in students' academic achievement in the earlier years of school.

Having a control group and using random assignment allows us to be much more confident in our causal findings, but it's important to be aware that even if research is considered internally valid, questions can still be raised about it. When we evaluate a quantitative research study, we can apply further criteria. First, there is the question of measurement validity. In the case of the Rosenthal and Jacobson study, we might ask whether academic performance has been adequately measured. Scores for reading ability seem to possess **face validity**, in the sense that they appear to show a correspondence with what they are measuring. However, given that there is considerable controversy surrounding IQ tests and what they measure (Kamin 1974), we might feel uneasy about how far gains in IQ test scores can be regarded as indicative of academic performance. Similarly, to take another of the authors' measures—intellectual curiosity—how confident can we be that this too is a valid measure of academic performance? Does it really measure what it is supposed to measure? The second question relating to measurement validity is whether the experimental manipulation really worked. In other words, did the random identification of some schoolchildren as spurters adequately create the conditions for researchers to examine the self-fulfilling prophecy? This very much relies on the teachers being tricked by the procedure, but it is possible that they were not all equally duped. If so, this would undermine the manipulation.

External validity of an experiment

Campbell (1957) and Cook and Campbell (1979) also consider threats to the external validity and therefore the **generalizability** of an investigation. They identify the following five major threats:

- *Interaction of selection and treatment*. To what social and psychological groups can a finding be generalized? Can it be generalized to a wide variety of individuals who might be differentiated by ethnicity, social class, region, gender, and type of personality? In the Rosenthal and Jacobson study, the students were largely from lower-social-class groups and a large proportion were from ethnic minorities. This might be considered a limitation to the generalizability of the findings (as well as adding to the numerous ethical issues raised by this study).
- *Interaction of setting and treatment*. How confident can we be that the results of a study can be applied to other settings? In the Rosenthal and Jacobson study, are the findings generalizable to other schools? There is also the wider issue of how confident we can be that the operation of self-fulfilling prophecies can be identified in non-educational settings. In fact, Rosenthal and others have been able to demonstrate the role and significance of the self-fulfilling prophecy in a wide variety of different contexts (Rosnow and Rosenthal 1997), though this does not answer the question of whether these specific findings can be generalized. One reason we might be uneasy about Rosenthal and Jacobson's findings is that they were given a great deal of freedom for conducting their investigation (which perhaps goes some way to explaining the ethical issues). The high level of cooperation from the school authorities was very unusual and may suggest that the school was not typical (though whether there is such a thing as a 'typical school' is questionable).
- *Interaction of history and treatment*. Can the findings be generalized to the past and to the future? Rosenthal and Jacobson conducted their research over 50 years ago. How confident can we be that the findings would apply today? Also, their investigation was conducted at a particular point in the school academic year. Would the results have been the same if the research had been conducted at another point in the year?
- *Interaction effects of pre-testing*. As we noted in the previous subsection on the internal validity of an experiment, pre-testing participants may sensitize them to the experimental treatment. This means that the findings may not be generalizable to groups that have not been pre-tested, because in the real world people are rarely pre-tested in this way. The findings may therefore be partly determined by the experimental treatment and partly by how far pre-test sensitization influenced the way that participants responded to the treatment. In the Rosenthal and Jacobson research all students were pre-tested at the end of the previous academic year.
- *Reactive effects of experimental arrangements*. People are often aware of the fact that they are participating in an experiment. Their awareness may influence how they respond to the experimental treatment and may therefore affect the generalizability of the findings. Since Rosenthal and Jacobson's subjects do not seem to have been aware of the fact that they were participating in an experiment, this problem is unlikely to have arisen. The issue of **reactivity**, and its potentially damaging effects on validity, is a recurring theme in relation to many methods of social research.

Ecological validity of an experiment

Are the findings ecologically valid—that is, are they applicable to people's everyday, natural social settings? The fact that the Rosenthal and Jacobson study is a field experiment rather than a laboratory experiment seems to enhance its ecological validity, as does the fact that the students and teachers seem to have had little if any appreciation of the fact that they were participating in an experiment. However, this is another aspect of the research that raises significant ethical concerns: deception seems to have been a significant and probably necessary feature of the investigation (see the discussion of deception in Section 6.4), and the ethical issues that we have highlighted throughout our discussion of this study are in many ways another dimension of its validity.

A further factor that might be seen to challenge the study's ecological validity is the researchers' intensive use of various instruments to measure academic performance, as the testing procedure itself could be viewed as an unnatural intervention. Because this study was conducted in a school the use of tests may not have been unnatural, but the issue of how data-collection instruments can affect ecological validity is relevant to most quantitative research.

Replicability of an experiment

What about replicability? The authors clearly lay out the procedures and measures they used for their study and, if you were to carry out a replication, theoretically you would be able to obtain any further information you needed from the authors (although as time passes this might become more difficult). So from an operational point of view the research is replicable, although the ethical issues concerning deception and treating the two groups of students differently based on random assignment would need to be resolved. Clairborn (1969) conducted one of the earliest replications and followed a procedure that was very similar to Rosenthal and Jacobson's, but the study was carried out in three middle-class, suburban schools, and the timing of the creation of teacher expectancies was different from that in the original Rosenthal and Jacobson study. Clairborn failed to replicate Rosenthal and Jacobson's findings. This failure to replicate casts doubt on the external validity of the original research and suggests that the interactions between *selection*, *setting*, and *history* in the treatment may have played a part in the differences between the two sets of results.

The laboratory experiment

Although field experiments are more common than laboratory experiments in social research overall, areas such as social psychology often involve laboratory experiments: an example is outlined in Research in focus 3.2. One of the main advantages of this type of experiment is that the researcher has greater influence over the experimental arrangements. For example, it is easier to assign subjects randomly to different experimental conditions in the laboratory than in an ongoing, real-life organization. This means the researcher has a higher level of control, which is likely to enhance the internal validity of the study. Laboratory experiments are also likely to be easier to replicate, because they do not involve reproducing a particular real-world environment.

Although they give the researcher considerably more control, laboratory experiments do suffer from a number of limitations. First, their external validity is often difficult to establish. There is likely to be interaction of setting and treatment, since the setting of the laboratory is likely to be unrelated to real-world experiences and contexts, and there is also likely to be an interaction of *selection* and treatment. Second, the ecological validity of the study may be poor, because we do not know how well the findings will apply to everyday life. However, while the study may lack what is often called *mundane realism*, it may still enjoy *experimental realism* (Aronson and Carlsmith 1968), meaning that the subjects are very involved in the experiment and take it seriously.

In the case of the study described in Research in focus 3.2, there will not have been a problem of interaction effects of pre-testing because, as in many experiments, there was no pre-testing. However, it is quite feasible that **reactive effects** may have been set in motion by the experimental arrangements. The main potential threats to the validity of this experiment include the following:

- the subjects were students, who are not representative of the general population, so their responses to the experimental treatment may have been distinctive;
- the students were recruited in a non-random way; and
- the students were given incentives to participate, which might be another way in which they differ from others, since not everyone is equally likely to accept inducements.

Quasi-experiments

A number of writers (such as Shadish et al. 2002) have highlighted the possibilities offered by the many varieties of quasi-experiments—that is, studies that have some characteristics of experimental designs but do not fulfil all the internal validity requirements. Quasi-experiments are often characterized by the lack of random assignment of participants to the experimental and control groups because of practical difficulties associated with implementing this—as, for example, in Research in focus 3.3.

RESEARCH IN FOCUS 3.2
A laboratory experiment

Blommaert and colleagues (2014) conducted a laboratory experiment to explore the part played by ethnic discrimination in job recruitment. They recruited 272 students in Utrecht in the Netherlands as participants and asked them to assess CVs. We would consider this to be a laboratory experiment because the setting was contrived: the participants were not real employers or personnel managers assessing real CVs; they were just asked to act as if they were.

Each participant was given two fictitious job descriptions and two sets of 24 fictitious CVs. One job was a customer advisor in a bank, requiring an intermediate or higher vocational qualification; the other was a recruiter in a human resource management firm, requiring a higher vocational qualification or a degree. For each job, participants had to rate each candidate's CV in terms of suitability and to select three applicants whom they would invite for a job interview. The authors write that within each set of CVs, 'there were sixteen [CVs] in which ethnicity, gender, level of education and work experience were varied systematically' (Blommaert et al. 2014: 737). Within these 16 CVs, there were eight native Dutch applicants and a corresponding set of eight non-native Dutch applicants with exactly the same mixes of education, gender, and work experience. Around half of the participants were told that the non-native Dutch applicants were Moroccan-Dutch, and the rest were told the applicants were Turkish-Dutch.

The researchers found that ethnic discrimination was a factor in the participants' ratings of the suitability of applicants for the jobs. Native Dutch applicants were typically viewed as more suitable than the Moroccan-Dutch or the Turkish-Dutch applicants, although ethnicity was not regarded as the most important factor in judging suitability: gender, education, and work experience emerged as more important factors. The same findings emerged when participants were choosing which applicants to invite for a job interview, suggesting again that ethnic discrimination had an impact but that it was less important than the applicants' gender, educational level, and work experience. Adjusting several independent variables in the artificial CVs—namely ethnicity, gender, educational level, and work experience—meant that the authors could establish the relative causal impact of these variables on the two dependent variables (suitability rating and invitation for interview). By contriving a controlled setting (rather than doing the experiment in the field) the authors could assert that any changes in the dependent variable were a result of only the factors that they chose to vary.

RESEARCH IN FOCUS 3.3
A quasi-experiment

Williams and colleagues (2016) used a quasi-experiment to explore attitudes towards quantitative research methods among second-year undergraduate students. All students in the study had to take a compulsory research methods module that covered both quantitative and qualitative data analysis, but the authors also designed an optional module based on the substantive topic of 'Migration, Race, and Ethnic Relations' in which they embedded quantitative content. Williams and colleagues were interested in whether embedding quantitative content in a substantive module would change student attitudes towards quantitative methods. As it is not possible or desirable to randomize the students' choices of modules, those who took the experimental module were *not randomly assigned*—meaning that there might have been something different about the students who opted for the embedded module. Instead, the authors tested for differences in experiences, attitudes, and attainment between both groups of students to see if there were any significant selection effects. While they found a handful of differences between the groups, 93 of the **items** on which they tested showed no difference, demonstrating that there was a great deal of similarity between those who took the embedded module and those who did not. So any changes in attitudes as a result of being on the experimental module were unlikely to have been a result of pre-existing differences between the groups.

Another form of quasi-experiment occurs in the case of 'natural experiments', where there is manipulation of a social setting but this occurs as part of a naturally-occurring attempt to alter social arrangements. In these circumstances, it is simply not possible to assign subjects randomly to experimental and control groups.

The absence of random assignment in such research casts some doubt on its internal validity, since the groups may not be equivalent to start with, but the results of such studies are still compelling because they are not artificial interventions in social life and their ecological validity appears strong. Most writers on quasi-experimentation discount natural experiments in which there is no control group or basis for comparison (Cook and Campbell 1979), but occasionally we come across a single-group natural experiment that is particularly striking, such as the St Helena study described in Research in focus 3.4. Experimental designs and more especially quasi-experimental designs have been particularly prominent in **evaluation research** studies (see Key concept 3.4).

The significance of experimental design

As we discussed at the start of this section on experiments, the main reason for using the experiment as a research design is because it is often considered a standard against which quantitative research is judged. This

RESEARCH IN FOCUS 3.4
A natural experiment

The effects of TV and video violence on children is one of the most contested areas of social research and causes much media outcry. The island of St Helena in the South Atlantic provided a fascinating laboratory in which to examine the various claims when TV was introduced to the island for the first time in the mid-1990s. This quasi-experiment can be considered a natural experiment because the change to the social setting was not instigated by the researchers. The researchers studied a single group, monitoring the TV viewing habits and behaviour of a large sample of schoolchildren and analysing 900 minutes of video footage of the children playing during school breaks, diaries kept by around 300 of the children, and ratings by teachers. The study found no evidence to suggest that the introduction of TV had led to an increase in antisocial behaviour (e.g. Charlton et al. 1998, Charlton et al. 1999) and the project leader Tony Charlton, a British psychologist, was quoted in *The Times* as saying: 'The argument that watching violent television turns youngsters to violence is not borne out . . . The children have been watching the same amounts of violence, and in many cases the same programmes, as British children. But they have not gone out and copied what they have seen on TV' (Midgley 1998: 5). A report of the findings in *The Times* in April 1998 found that 'the shared experience of watching television made them less likely to tease each other and to fight, and more likely to enjoy books' (Frean 1998: 7).

KEY CONCEPT 3.4
What is evaluation research?

Evaluation research, as its name implies, involves evaluating the effects of occurrences such as social and organizational programmes or interventions. The key question that these studies typically ask is: has the intervention (for example, a new policy initiative, a funded project, an educational strategy, or an organizational change) achieved its anticipated goals? A typical design may have one group that is exposed to the treatment (that is, the new initiative), and a control group that is not. Since it is often neither possible nor ethical to assign research participants randomly to the two groups, such studies are usually quasi-experimental. The use of experimental design principles is fairly entrenched in evaluation research, but other approaches have emerged in recent years, including approaches based on qualitative research. While there are differences of opinion about how qualitative evaluation should be carried out, most researchers recognize the importance of gaining an in-depth understanding of the context in which an intervention occurs, the diverse viewpoints of the stakeholders, and the range of outcomes of the intervention (Greene 1994, 2000).

is largely because a true experiment will dispel doubts about internal validity and allows the researcher to clearly determine causality—a key concern for quantitative research. As we will see in Section 3.4 on cross-sectional design, this form of design, often associated with survey research, is often seen as limited because of the difficulty in clearly establishing causality when using it.

However, before we explore such issues, let's briefly reflect on an important general lesson that experiments teach us. A central feature of any experiment is the fact that it involves a *comparison*: at the very least it involves comparing results obtained by an experimental group with those produced by a control group. In the case of the Blommaert et al. (2014) experiment in Research in focus 3.2, there is no control group: the research involves comparing the effects of two different types of ethnicity (native Dutch versus non-native Dutch) in relation to job recruitment. The advantage of carrying out any kind of comparison is that we gain a better understanding of the phenomenon that we are interested in when we compare it with something else similar. The case for arguing that non-native ethnic groups are discriminated against when they are seeking jobs is much more persuasive when we view their experiences in relation to the experiences of native applicants. While experimental design is typically associated with quantitative research, the potential for comparison is a more general lesson that goes beyond matters of both research strategy and research design, and we will discuss this further in 'Comparative design'.

3.4 Cross-sectional design

The cross-sectional design is often called a survey design, but the idea of the survey is so closely connected in most people's minds with questionnaires and **structured interviewing** that it is best to use the more generic term *cross-sectional design*. While it is true that the research methods associated with surveys are often used within cross-sectional research, so too are many other research methods, including **structured observation**, **content analysis**, **official statistics**, and **diaries**. We cover all these methods in later chapters; here we will just look at the basic structure of the cross-sectional design.

Features of the cross-sectional design

The cross-sectional design is briefly defined in Key concept 3.5, but it is worth unpicking some of its key elements further.

KEY CONCEPT 3.5
What is a cross-sectional research design?

A cross-sectional design involves collecting data on a sample of cases and at a single point in time. It is this use of a sample of cases that gives the design its name—the cases are a cross-section of the relevant group(s). The researcher collects a body of quantitative or quantifiable data in connection with two or more variables (there are usually many more than two), which they can then examine to detect patterns of association. A simple example would be that if you wanted to know whether there was an association between age and voting intention, you would select a sample of people who could vote and ask them what their age is and who they are going to vote for. In a cross-sectional design you would do this only once, to get a picture of voter intentions at the time you asked the question. This snapshot wouldn't tell you whether their voting intentions change as they age. Learn from experience 3.2 gives another example of a cross-sectional study, in this case investigating the association between screen time and sleep duration.

This is in contrast to longitudinal designs (see Section 3.5), in which you could take multiple snapshots over a period of time. This information would help you draw conclusions about how people arrived at their voting intention and how this changes over time.

3

The key feature of the cross-sectional design is its use of a sample of cases (as discussed in Learn from experience 3.2). This is because researchers using this design are interested in variations among people, families, organizations, nation-states, or whatever, and they can only establish variation by examining more than one case. They will usually select not just two, but quite a large number of cases, as this means they are more likely to find variation in all the variables that they are interested in and they can make finer distinctions between cases; also, they will often need large numbers to fulfil the requirements of their chosen sampling procedure (see Chapter 8).

Another feature of this design is that it involves collecting data on the variables of interest more or less simultaneously. When a person completes a questionnaire, which may contain 50 or more variables, the answers are supplied at essentially the same time. This is different from an experimental design, where a participant in the experimental group is pre-tested (T_1), then exposed to the experimental treatment, and then post-tested (T_2). The different phases might be separated by days, weeks, months, or even years. In the case of the Rosenthal and Jacobson (1968) study (Research in focus 3.1), eight months separated the pre- and post-testing of the schoolchildren. By contrast, the cross-sectional research design involves collecting data on a series of variables (Obs_1 Obs_2 Obs_3 Obs_4 Obs_5 . . . Obs_n with 'Obs' meaning 'observation') at a single point in time, T_1. The effect is to create what Marsh (1982) referred to as a 'rectangle' of data that comprises variables Obs_1 to Obs_n and cases $Case_1$ to $Case_n$, as in Figure 3.2a. For each case (which may be a person, household, city, nation, etc.) data are available for each of the variables, Obs_1 to Obs_n, all of which will have been collected at T_1. Each **cell** in the matrix will have data in it. In Figure 3.2b we've given an example of this data format with some actual data values in recording the case number, sex, age, employment status, and mode of work (full time or part time). You can see how each variable has its own column, and each row represents an individual respondent.

The body of data collected through a cross-sectional design is quantitative or quantifiable because the researcher needs a systematic and standardized method in order to gauge, establish, and ultimately examine variation between cases. One of the most important advantages of quantification is that it provides the researcher with a consistent benchmark (we consider the advantages of quantification and of measurement in more detail in Chapter 7).

The final stage of the cross-sectional design involves looking for patterns of association. With this design, the researcher can only identify relationships between variables. There is no time-ordering to the variables, because the data are collected more or less simultaneously, and we do not (because we cannot) manipulate any of the variables, which creates the problem we described in the section on 'Internal validity of an experiment' as 'ambiguity about the direction of causal influence'. If we discover a relationship between two variables, such as social media usage and mental health, we cannot be certain whether this implies a causal relationship, because the features of an experimental design are not present. All that we can say is that the variables are related. This is not to say that it is impossible to draw causal inferences from

LEARN FROM EXPERIENCE 3.2

Using a cross-sectional design

Cross-sectional designs are common in student dissertations. Many such projects are concerned with the association between variables, such as Zvi's study of the relationship between screen time and adolescents sleep duration in which he conducted a **secondary analysis** of the Youth Risk Behaviour Surveillance System survey (YRBSS).

> The YRBSS is administered by the Centre for Disease Control, the largest public health body in the United States. The survey aims to produce a nationally representative sample of 9th- to 12th-grade students in high schools in the USA and its purpose is to determine the prevalence of health risk behaviours in American adolescents. The survey is cross-sectional, which means it simply provides a snapshot of students at a certain point in time, rather than following the same students over a period of time. Cross-sectional data was suitable for my dissertation as I was mostly concerned with looking at the prevalence of certain behaviours, such as screen time and sleep duration.
>
> Zvi

You can read about our panellists' backgrounds and research experiences on page xxvi.

3

FIGURE 3.2
(a) The data rectangle in cross-sectional research (b) An example of cross-sectional data

(a)

	Obs_1	Obs_2	Obs_3	Obs_4	. . .	Obs_n
$Case_1$						
$Case_2$						
$Case_3$						
$Case_4$						
$Case_5$						
. . .						
$Case_n$						

(b)

Case number:	Sex	Age	Employment Status	Full Time or Part Time
1	Female	34	Employed	PT
2	Female	32	Employed	FT
3	Male	28	Unemployed	N/A
4	Female	33	Employed	FT
5	Male	42	Unemployed	N/A
...	...	...	...	...

research based on a cross-sectional design. As we will see in Chapter 15, there are a number of ways in which we might be able to draw certain causal inferences, but these inferences rarely have the certainty status of causal findings deriving from an experimental design. As a result, cross-sectional research lacks the internal validity that is found in most experimental research (as you can see from the example in Research in focus 3.5).

RESEARCH IN FOCUS 3.5
Causality and the cross-sectional research design

Bengtsson and colleagues' (2013) report on some of the findings of a cross-sectional survey reveal the difficulties in identifying the direction of cause and effect in this kind of study.

Using a **postal questionnaire**, the researchers collected data on class position and ideological orientation (political stance) from a representative sample of the Swedish population. Although they collected data on 2,374 individuals, the authors were especially interested in the significance of work-related variables for ideological orientations and therefore analysed only the data from 1,289 members of their sample who were employed at the time. The authors note:

> As survey data are cross-sectional, the directions of the relationships have been assumed on theoretical grounds. . . . We therefore cannot exclude reverse causality, i.e. that ideological orientations affect occupational choices, and thus, class position. However, most research assumes the same direction of the relationships as we do, although there are exceptions.
>
> (Bengtsson et al. 2013: 704)

It is clear that there is some ambiguity about the direction of causal influence in this kind of study, though the authors give theoretical reasons to try to justify their assumptions about the direction of cause and effect.

In this book, we will only use the term 'survey' for research that uses a cross-sectional research design and that collects data by structured interview or by questionnaire (covered in Chapters 9 and 10 respectively). This will allow us to keep a firm grip on the conventional understanding of a survey and also to recognize that the cross-sectional research design has a wider relevance—it is not necessarily associated with collecting data by questionnaire or by structured interview.

Reliability, replicability, and validity

How does cross-sectional research measure up with the criteria for evaluating quantitative research: reliability, replicability, and validity?

- The issues of reliability and measurement validity largely relate to the quality of the *measures* used to get at the concepts that the researcher is interested in; they do not really relate to a research design. In order to address questions of the quality of measures, we would need to consider some of the issues outlined in Chapter 7.
- Replicability is likely to be present in most cross-sectional research as long as the researcher spells out the procedures they used for selecting respondents, designing measures of concepts, administering research instruments (such as structured interviews or self-completion questionnaires), and analysing data. Most reports of quantitative research based on cross-sectional research designs contain this information.

Turning to validity:

- Internal validity tends to be weak. As we saw in the section on 'Features of the cross-sectional design', cross-sectional research produces associations, rather than findings that let the researcher make unambiguous causal inferences. It is possible to make causal inferences from cross-sectional data (and we will discuss these processes in Chapter 15), but they are usually considered to lack the internal validity of those deriving from experimental designs.
- External validity is strong when, as in the study described in Research in focus 3.5, the sample from which data are collected has been randomly selected. When non-random methods of sampling are used, external validity is questionable. We will consider sampling issues in survey research in Chapter 8.
- Ecological validity is likely not to be strong because much cross-sectional research makes considerable use of research instruments, such as self-completion questionnaires and structured **observation schedules**, and these instruments disrupt what Cicourel (1982) calls the 'natural habitat'.

Non-manipulable variables

As we noted in 'Features of the classical experimental design', in most social research it is not possible to manipulate the variables that we are interested in: they are **non-manipulable variables**. This is why quantitative researchers tend to use cross-sectional research designs rather than experimental ones. Researchers need to be cautious and refer to relationships rather than causality; they might also argue on theoretical grounds that a variable is more likely to be an independent than a dependent variable (see Research in focus 3.5 for an example).

Some variables, such as our ethnicity, age, and social backgrounds, are not only 'givens' that cannot be manipulated in the way necessary for a true experimental design, but are also extremely unlikely to be dependent variables. They will almost inevitably be independent variables, so we are on pretty safe ground if we infer causal direction when these variables are involved in research showing relationships between them and other variables. However, there are also many variables that we *could* manipulate but that we cannot manipulate due to ethical and practical constraints, and such constraints lead to doubt about the direction of causal inference.

The very fact that we can regard certain variables as 'givens' provides us with a clue as to how we can make causal inferences in cross-sectional research. Many of the variables that we are interested in can be *assumed* to be temporally prior to other variables: that is, they are characteristics that are established and fixed *before* other variables. For example, we can assume that, if we find a relationship between ethnicity and alcohol consumption, the former is more likely to be the independent variable because it is temporally prior to alcohol consumption. In other words, while we cannot manipulate ethnic status, we can draw causal inferences from cross-sectional data about it.

Cross-sectional design and research strategy

Our discussion of the cross-sectional design has shown it in the context of quantitative research, and in evaluating the design we drew on criteria associated with the quantitative research strategy. However, it is important to note that qualitative research often involves a form of cross-sectional design, for example when a researcher

3

RESEARCH IN FOCUS 3.6
Qualitative research within a cross-sectional design

Bisdee and colleagues' (2013) study is an interesting example of how cross-sectional design principles can apply within the qualitative research tradition. The researchers were looking at the connection between gender and the management of household money among older couples. They write that they were especially interested in the extent to which ageing influences the roles of men and women in relation to the management of money and the different responses of women to their situation. The authors carried out **semi-structured interviews** with 45 heterosexual couples who were initially interviewed together and then interviewed separately and simultaneously. Couples were identified through a **maximum variation sampling** approach (see Chapter 17, Section 17.3 for an explanation of this term) 'so as to include a range in terms of age, health . . ., ethnicity, social grade, income level and marital history' (Bisdee et al. 2013: 164). The interviews were recorded and transcribed, yielding a large amount of qualitative data.

employs semi-structured interviewing with a number of people. See Research in focus 3.6 for an example of this kind of study.

While clearly sitting within the qualitative research tradition, the study described in Research in focus 3.6 has many research design similarities with cross-sectional studies within a quantitative research tradition. The Bisdee et al. (2013) research was not preoccupied with criteria of quantitative research such as internal and external validity, replicability, or measurement validity. In fact, it could be argued that the conversational interview style made the study more ecologically valid than research using more formal instruments of data collection such as questionnaires.

It is also striking that the study was concerned with the factors that *influence* couples' management of household finances (such as the development of health problems), because the very idea of an 'influence' suggests that qualitative researchers are interested in investigating causes and effects, albeit not in the context of the language of variables used in quantitative research, and with more of an emphasis on revealing the *experience* of something like the management of household finances than is usually the case in the quantitative tradition. However, the main point of discussing this example here is its similarities to the cross-sectional design in quantitative research. It involved interviewing quite a large number of people at a single point in time. Just as with many quantitative studies using a cross-sectional design, examining early influences on people's past and current behaviour is based on their retrospective accounts of factors that influenced them in the past.

3.5 Longitudinal designs

The longitudinal design is a distinct form of research design that involves collecting data from participants more than once (hence the use of the syllable 'long' to represent that this happens over a period of time rather than a single time point). Because of the time and cost it involves, it is not very widely used in social research. It is usually an extension of survey research and is based on a self-completion questionnaire or structured interview research within a cross-sectional design. This means that in terms of reliability, replication, and validity, the longitudinal design is similar to cross-sectional research. However, a longitudinal design can offer some insight into the time order of variables, so it may allow stronger causal inferences to be made.

Features of longitudinal designs

There are two main types of longitudinal design: the *panel study* and the *cohort study*.

Panel studies

For panel studies, a sample, often a randomly selected national one, is the focus of data collection on at least two (and often more) occasions. Data may be collected from different types of case within a panel study framework: people, households, organizations, schools, and so on. The Understanding Society survey is an example of this kind of study (see Research in focus 3.7).

RESEARCH IN FOCUS 3.7
A panel study longitudinal design

Understanding Society, the UK Household Longitudinal Study, began in 1991 as the British Household Panel Survey (BHPS), when a national representative sample of 10,264 individuals in 5,538 households were interviewed for the first time in connection with six main areas:

- household organization;
- labour market behaviour;
- income and wealth;
- housing;
- health; and
- socio-economic values.

BHPS participants were then interviewed annually, meaning that researchers have been able to highlight areas of social change. For example, Laurie and Gershuny (2000) show that there have been changes in the ways that couples manage their money. Over a relatively short five-year period (1991–5), there was a small decline in the proportion of men having a final say in financial decisions and a corresponding small increase in those reporting equal say, although interestingly these trends refer to all the replies from partners—around a quarter of partners give different answers about who has the final say!

The BHPS was replaced in 2009 by Understanding Society: The UK Household Longitudinal Study, which is based on a panel of about 40,000 UK households. It uses similar procedures to the BHPS: eligible adults are interviewed annually face-to-face or by telephone using computer-assisted interviewing. See **www.understandingsociety.ac.uk/about#part2** (accessed 9 May 2019). The size and nature of the study means that a range of populations and phenomena can be studied. For example, Longhi (2020) used six waves of Understanding Society data, from 2009 to 2015, to look at ethnic differentials in unemployment in the UK. The study investigates how individual and job characteristics contribute to job losses and job finding. At the very start of her paper, Longhi identifies the weakness of cross-sectional data in this area:

> Cross-sectional evidence can only confirm the higher proportion of unemployed among ethnic minorities compared to the white British majority; because of lack of longitudinal data, however, it is still unclear how transitions into and out of unemployment contribute to the stock of unemployment for ethnic minorities, and how these dynamics compare to those of the white British majority.
>
> Longhi (2020: 879)

Cohort studies

In a cohort study, either an entire cohort of people or a **random sample** of them is selected as the focus of data collection. The cohort is made up of people who share a certain characteristic (which differentiates it from a panel study), such as all being born in the same week, or who all have a certain experience, such as being unemployed or getting married on a certain day or in the same week. The National Child Development Study (NCDS) and Millennium Cohort Study are both examples of cohort studies (see Research in focus 3.8).

Having considered examples of active panel and cohort longitudinal studies, you might be thinking of other studies you know that would fall into one of these categories. It is worth being aware that large-scale surveys that are carried out on a regular basis on samples of the population, such as the British Social Attitudes survey and the Crime Survey for England and Wales (see Table 14.1), are not truly longitudinal designs because they do not involve the same people being interviewed on each occasion. They are perhaps better thought of as involving a repeated cross-sectional design or trend design, where samples are selected on each of several occasions. They are able to track change, but they cannot address the issue of the direction of cause and effect because the samples are always different.

3

RESEARCH IN FOCUS 3.8
A cohort study longitudinal design

There are numerous examples of cohort study longitudinal designs.

The National Child Development Study (NCDS) is based on all 17,415 children born in Great Britain in the week of 3–9 March 1958. The study was initially motivated by a concern over levels of perinatal mortality and was not originally planned as a longitudinal study, but the data collected reflect a much wider range of issues than this focus implies. Data were collected on the children and their families when the children were age 7. The children and their families were followed up in 1965, 1969, 1974, 1981, 1991, 1999/2000, 2004/5, 2008/9, and 2013; the participants were surveyed in 2020 (when respondents were aged 62) to examine the impact of the Covid-19 pandemic on their lives. Data have been collected in relation to a number of areas, including physical and mental health; family; parenting; occupation and income; and housing and environment. For further information, see Fox and Fogelman (1990); Hodges (1998); and **https://cls.ucl.ac.uk/cls-studies/1958-national-child-development-study/** (accessed 12 February 2021).

The Millennium Cohort Study (MCS) began in 2000–1 based on a sample of all children born in England and Wales over a twelve-month period from 1 September 2000 and all children born in Scotland and Northern Ireland from 1 December 2000 (approx. 19,000 participants). The sample were followed up in 2004, 2006, 2008, 2012, 2015, and 2018. For further information, see **https://cls.ucl.ac.uk/cls-studies/millennium-cohort-study/** (accessed 9 May 2019).

Growing Up in Ireland began in 2006 with the aim of informing government policy around young people, families, and children. The study follows two cohorts of children who were aged 9 years (Child Cohort) and 9 months (Infant Cohort) when the study started, and participants are currently around 22 and 12 years old respectively. Data collection for the Child Cohort started in 2008 with 8,500 children, who were followed up at 13, 17/18, and 20 years old. The Infant Cohort started data collection in 2008 with more than 11,000 participants and families, followed up at ages 3, 5, 7/8, and 9 years. For the Infant Cohort, different information was collected at different waves from a range of people including parents, carers, partners not living in the household, and educational professionals. For further information see **www.growingup.ie/about-growing-up-in-ireland/** (accessed 12 February 2021).

Comparing panel and cohort studies

Panel and cohort studies share similar features. They have a similar design structure. Figure 3.3a illustrates that data are collected in at least two waves on the same variables on the same people. In Figure 3.3b we've provided a simple example of recording employment status at three time points (in a real longitudinal study you would have many more variables at each time point). Both panel and cohort studies are concerned with exploring social change and with improving the understanding of causal influences over time. The latter means that longitudinal designs are better able to deal with the problem of 'ambiguity about the direction of causal influence' than cross-sectional designs. Because we can identify certain potentially independent variables in an earlier survey (at T_1), we are in a better position to infer that alleged effects that we identify through later surveys (at T_2 or later) have occurred *after* those independent variables. This does not deal with the entire problem of the ambiguity of causal influence, but it at least addresses the problem of knowing which variable came first. In all other respects, the points we have discussed in relation to cross-sectional designs are the same as those for longitudinal designs.

Panel and cohort designs differ in important respects too. A panel study, such as the Understanding Society study, that takes place over many years can distinguish between age effects (the impact of the ageing process on individuals) and cohort effects (effects due to being born at a similar time), because its members will have been born at different times. A cohort study based on date of birth (such as the Millennium Cohort Study), however, can only distinguish ageing effects, since all members of the sample will have been born at more or less the same time. Another difference is that a panel study, especially one that operates at the household level, needs rules to inform how to handle new entrants to the panel—for example, new additions to

FIGURE 3.3
(a) The longitudinal design (b) An example of longitudinal data

(a)

T_1	...	T_n
Obs_1		Obs_1
Obs_2		Obs_2
Obs_3		Obs_3
Obs_4		Obs_4
Obs_5		Obs_5
...		...
Obs_n		Obs_n

(b)

Case number:	Sex	Employment Status at T_1	Employment Status at T_2	Employment Status at T_3
1	Female	Employed	Unemployed	Unemployed
2	Female	Employed	Employed	Employed
3	Male	Unemployed	Unemployed	Employed
4	Female	Employed	Employed	Unemployed
5	Male	Unemployed	Unemployed	Unemployed
...	...	...	...	...

households (perhaps as a result of marriage or elderly relatives moving in) and exits from households (perhaps as a result of marriage break-up or children leaving home).

Reliability, replicability, and validity

How does **longitudinal research** measure up with the criteria for evaluating quantitative research: reliability, replicability, and validity?

As with cross-sectional research, reliability and measurement validity are related to the quality of the measures used to get at concepts and they do not relate directly to research design. As for replicability, certainly the write-up should include information on sampling and the design and contents of the data-collection instruments, but it would be hard to replicate longitudinal research simply because of the scale and costs of running a project over time. Longitudinal designs can have good internal validity because they allow things to be placed in time order. The external validity of longitudinal research is similar to that of cross-sectional studies, although the issue of attrition over time can mean that panel and cohort studies can become less representative with each wave (see the discussion of attrition in the next subsection) and researchers need to consider and, where possible, correct for this. Finally, while ecological validity may be weakened through the disruptive effect of data-collection instruments, a repeated cycle of data-collection for panel and cohort study participants might in itself normalize the data-collection process.

Problems associated with longitudinal designs

Longitudinal designs go some way to helping address the problem of ambiguity about the direction of causal inference and they can produce some very interesting findings, but they are also associated with various problems. The time and cost they involve are the main reasons for this design not being widely used in social research, but other issues shared by both panel and cohort studies include

- the problem of sample attrition (drop out);
- a lack of guidelines as to when data should next be collected;
- the accusation that many longitudinal studies are poorly thought out, resulting in lots of data being collected with little planning;
- evidence that a 'panel conditioning' effect can occur as a result of continued participation in a longitudinal study and can alter how respondents behave.

Sample attrition is inevitable in long-running studies and occurs through death, moving, and subjects choosing to withdraw at later stages of the research. Lynn and Borkowska (2018) observe that 70 per cent of the initial sample from the BHPS were still involved in the study after 12 years, reducing to 40 per cent after 24 years. This is considered a low rate of attrition, given the length of the study period. In 1981 the National Child Development Study managed to secure data from 12,537 members of the original 17,414 cohort, which is quite an achievement bearing in mind that 23 years would have elapsed since the birth of the children. In 1991 data were elicited from 11,407 members.

The main problem with attrition is that those who leave the study may differ in some important respects from those who remain (that is, drop-out is not random), so that those who are left do not form a representative group. There is some evidence from panel studies that the problem of attrition declines with time (Berthoud 2000); in other words, those who do not drop out after the first wave or two of data collection tend to stay on the panel.

3

Longitudinal designs and research strategy

As with cross-sectional designs, it is easy to associate longitudinal designs almost exclusively with quantitative research. However, qualitative research sometimes incorporates elements of a longitudinal design, for example when interviews are carried out on more than one occasion to assess change. See Research in focus 3.9 for an example of this.

Most longitudinal studies will be planned from the outset in such a way that sample members can be followed up at a later date. However, occasionally the idea of conducting a longitudinal study only occurs to the re-

RESEARCH IN FOCUS 3.9
Qualitative longitudinal research

Qualitative longitudinal research (often abbreviated to QLL) that involves repeat qualitative interviews with research participants has become more common since the early 2000s, and the 'Timescapes' project is a good example of one such study. This major UK project began life in February 2007 and concluded in 2012. The aim was to interview and re-interview people on several occasions to capture social changes and shifts in people's life courses and in their thoughts and feelings. It comprised seven relatively independent projects, through which the researchers aimed to track the lives of around 400 people.

One of the projects is entitled 'Masculinities, Identities and Risk: Transition in the Lives of Men as Fathers' and aimed to get a sense of how masculine identities change in the wake of first-time fatherhood. This particular study built on research that originally began in Norfolk in 1999, well before the Timescapes project. Researchers interviewed 30 fathers in 2000–1. Each man was interviewed three times, with one interview before the child's birth and two interviews after the birth. This group of men was then followed up in 2008. Researchers conducted a further set of interviews with 18 men from south Wales in 2008–9, with the same pattern of one interview before and two interviews after birth. In the course of the interviews, the researchers used photographs of families and men with their children to stimulate participants' reflections on fatherhood (the use of photographs in interviews is explored in Chapters 19 and 20). The materials are available for secondary analysis through an online archive (**https://timescapes-archive.leeds.ac.uk/**).

'Bringing Up a Family: Making Ends Meet' is a qualitative longitudinal study that was still ongoing at the time of writing. It focuses on the experiences of families below the minimum income standard. The researchers talked to 30 families in 2015 (Hill et al. 2016) and contacted the families again in 2016 to see if any of them would participate in a follow-up exercise—26 agreed in principle, and in the event 18 in-depth interviews took place in 2017 (Hill and Davis 2018). The researchers conducted a third phase in 2020.

Sources:

The Guardian, 20 October 2009: **www.guardian.co.uk/education/2009/oct/20/timescapes-leeds-research-memories?INTCMP=SRCH**.

Timescapes website: **www.timescapes.leeds.ac.uk**.

For information on the masculinities project, see **www.timescapes.leeds.ac.uk/research/masculinities-fatherhood-risk/index.html**.

For some methodological reflections on the Timescapes project, see **www.timescapes.leeds.ac.uk/resources/publications.html**.

Bringing Up a Family: Making Ends Meet website: **www.lboro.ac.uk/research/crsp/currentresearch/bringing-up-a-family/**

All the above websites were accessed 21 February 2021.

searchers some time after they have collected the first set of data. In such cases, if there are good records it may be possible to follow up sample members for a second wave of data collection or even for further waves.

3.6 Case study design

The basic case study design involves detailed and intensive analysis of a single case. As Stake (1995) observes, case study research is concerned with the complexity and particular nature of the case in question. Some of the best-known studies in sociology are based on this kind of design. Some examples follow.

- Research may focus on a single community, such as Whyte's (1955) study of Cornerville in Boston; Gans's (1962) study of the East End of Boston; Stacey's (1960) research on Banbury; O'Reilly's (2000) and Benson's (2011) research on communities of expatriate Britons living on the Costa del Sol in Spain and rural France, respectively; and Banks's (2012, 2014) covert ethnography of an online gambling community. More recent examples include Bock's (2018) study about a confined community in the Harz Mountains in Germany during the refugee crisis in 2015–2016, and Lafleur and Mescoli's (2018) ethnographic study of Italian migrants in Belgium.
- The research subject may be a single school, as in studies by Ball (1981) on Beachside Comprehensive, by Burgess (1983) on Bishop McGregor, and by Khan (2011, 2014) of an elite school in the USA.
- The case may be a single family, such as O. Lewis's (1961) study of the Sánchez family or Brannen and Nilsen's (2006) investigation of a family of low-skilled British men, which contained four generations, in order to uncover changes in 'fathering' over time.
- Researchers may examine a single organization, as in studies of single factories by Burawoy (1979) and Cavendish (1982), of pilferage in a single location (Ditton 1977), of a single police service (Holdaway 1982, 1983), of a restaurant (Demetry 2013), of a single call centre (Callaghan and Thompson 2002; Nyberg 2009), of a single opera company (Atkinson 2006), or of a single voluntary sector organization (Askins 2016).
- The case may be a person, like the famous study of Stanley, the 'jack-roller' (Shaw 1930); such studies are often characterized as using the life history method or another biographical research approach (see Section 19.6 on life history and oral history interviewing). A more recent example is Zempi's (2017) autoethnography of victimization while wearing the Muslim veil (niqab) in public.
- Researchers may study a single event, such as the Cuban Missile Crisis (Allison 1971), the events surrounding the media reporting of a specific news topic (Deacon, Fenton, and Bryman 1999), a Balinese cockfight (Geertz 1973b), or a disaster incident (Vaughan 1996, 2004).

Features of the case study design

To understand the elements of a case study design, we first need to look at what 'case' means in this context. The most common use of the term 'case' associates the case study with a location, such as a community or organization. The emphasis tends to be upon intensive examination of the setting. There is a tendency to associate case studies with qualitative research, but although they do tend to use qualitative methods, such as participant observation and unstructured interviewing, to generate an intensive, detailed examination of a case, case studies often involve *both* quantitative and qualitative research (mixed methods research, discussed in Chapter 24). In some instances, when an investigation is based exclusively upon quantitative research, it can be difficult to determine whether it is a case study or a cross-sectional research design. The same point can often be made about case studies based on qualitative research. The crucial issue is to be clear about what the unit of analysis is.

For example, let's say that the research is carried out in a single location, which could be an organization or community. Sometimes, research is carried out in a single location but the location itself is not part of the object of analysis—it simply acts as a backdrop to the data collection. When this occurs, the sample from which the data were collected is the object of interest and the location is of little significance. On other occasions, the location is either primarily or at least to a significant extent the object of interest. In Research in focus 3.10 we can compare

RESEARCH IN FOCUS 3.10
Location and case studies

Sometimes the location in which a case study is based is important, and other times it is simply part of the background. For example, Uekusa's (2019) ethnographic study of fluid power dynamics among surfers (and how capital is used to catch the best waves) was based in a surf spot in California, but the location itself is not the object of study. Any surf spot where there were plenty of surfers of mixed ability could have been used.

In contrast, Guschwan's (2017) ethnography of ultrà football fandom could hypothetically have taken place anywhere in the world, but the author was specifically interested in understanding hard-core Italian fandom in Rome. As Guschwan says: 'My goal was to get to the heart of football fandom in Rome, plain and simple' (2017: 977).

two studies, one where the location certainly provides background but is not central to the research, and another where location is central.

With a case study, the case is an object of interest in its own right, and the researcher aims to provide an in-depth examination of it. If we did not draw this kind of distinction, almost any kind of research could be construed as a case study: research based on a national, random sample of the population of Great Britain would have to be considered a case study of Great Britain! What distinguishes a case study is that the researcher is usually trying to reveal the unique features of the case, whereas in the previous example Great Britain is just the area where the population of interest are. This is known as an *idiographic* approach. Research designs like the cross-sectional design are known as *nomothetic*, in that they are concerned with generating statements that apply regardless of time and place. However, in rare cases an investigation may have elements of both.

Types of case

It is useful to consider a distinction between different types of case that is sometimes made by writers. Yin (2009) distinguishes five types.

- The *critical case*. Here, the researcher has a well-developed **theory**, and they choose a case on the grounds that it will allow a better understanding of the circumstances in which the **hypothesis** will and will not hold. The classic study by Festinger et al. (1956) of a religious cult whose members believed that the end of the world was about to happen is an example. The fact that the event did not happen by the appointed day allowed the researchers to test the authors' propositions about how people respond to thwarted expectations.
- The *extreme* or *unique case*. The unique or extreme case is, as Yin observes, a common focus in clinical studies. Margaret Mead's (1928) well-known study of growing up in Samoa was motivated by her belief that the country represented a unique case. She argued that, unlike most other societies, Samoan youth do not suffer a period of anxiety and stress in adolescence. The factors associated with this relatively trouble-free period in their lives were of interest to her, since they might contain lessons for Western youth.
- The *representative* or *typical case*. We prefer to call this an *exemplifying* case, because ideas of representativeness and typicality can sometimes lead to confusion. With this kind of case, 'the objective is to capture the circumstances and conditions of an everyday or commonplace situation' (Yin 2009: 48). A case might therefore be chosen not necessarily because it is extreme or unusual, but because it epitomizes a broader **category** that it is a member of, or because it will provide a suitable context for certain research questions to be answered. An example of the first situation is Lynd and Lynd's (1929, 1937) classic community study of Muncie, Indiana, in the USA, which they called 'Middletown' precisely because it seemed to typify American life at the time.
- The *revelatory case*. The basis for the revelatory case exists 'when an investigator has an opportunity to observe and analyse a phenomenon previously inaccessible to scientific investigation' (Yin 2009: 48). As examples, Yin cites Whyte's (1955) study of Cornerville, and Liebow's (1967) research on unemployed Black men.

- The *longitudinal case*. Yin suggests that a case might be chosen because it gives the researcher the opportunity to investigate on two or more occasions. However, many case studies comprise a longitudinal element, so it is more likely that a case will be chosen not only because it can be studied over time but also because it is appropriate to the research questions on one of the other four grounds.

Any case study can involve a combination of these elements, which we can best view as rationales for choosing particular cases. For example, Margaret Mead's (1928) study of growing up in Samoa has been depicted above as an extreme case, but it also has elements of a critical case because she felt that it had the potential to demonstrate that young people's responses to entering their teenage years are not determined by nature alone. She used growing up in Samoa as a critical case to demonstrate that culture has an important role in the development of humans, which contributed to the general debate around nature versus nurture.

It may be that it is only at a very late stage that the uniqueness and significance of a case becomes apparent (Radley and Chamberlain 2001). Flyvbjerg (2003) provides an example of this. He shows how he undertook a study of urban politics and planning in Aalborg, Denmark, thinking it was a critical case. After conducting his fieldwork for a while, he found that it was in fact an extreme case. He writes as follows:

> Initially, I conceived of Aalborg as a 'most likely' critical case in the following manner: if rationality and urban planning were weak in the face of power in Aalborg, then, most likely, they would be weak anywhere, at least in Denmark, because in Aalborg the rational paradigm of planning stood stronger than anywhere else. Eventually, I realized that this logic was flawed, because my research [on] local relations of power showed that one of the most influential 'faces of power' in Aalborg, the Chamber of Industry and Commerce, was substantially stronger than their equivalents elsewhere. Therefore, instead of a critical case, unwittingly I ended up with an extreme case in the sense that both rationality and power were unusually strong in Aalborg, and my case study became a study of what happens when strong rationality meets strong power in the area of urban politics and planning. But this selection of Aalborg as an extreme case happened to me, I did not deliberately choose it.
>
> (Flyvbjerg 2003: 426)

As Flyvbjerg's account clearly shows, we may not always appreciate the nature and significance of a 'case' until we have subjected it to detailed scrutiny.

Longitudinal research and the case study

Case study research often includes a longitudinal element, in that the researcher is often a participant in an organization or a member of a community for many months or years in order to conduct an in-depth examination. Alternatively, they may conduct interviews with individuals over a lengthy period. The researcher may be able to inject an additional longitudinal element by analysing archival information and by retrospective interviewing.

Another way that researchers may include a longitudinal element is when they return at a later stage to a case that has previously been studied. A particularly interesting instance of this is the Middletown study mentioned under 'Types of cases'. The town was originally studied by Lynd and Lynd in 1924–5 (Lynd and Lynd 1929) and they restudied it to discern trends and changes in 1935 (Lynd and Lynd 1937). In 1977 the community was studied yet again by different researchers (Bahr et al. 1983), using the same research instruments with minor changes.

Reliability, replicability, and validity

How well does the case study stand up to quality criteria? This depends in large part on how far a researcher feels that validity (in its various forms), reliability, and replicability are appropriate for evaluating case study research. Some writers on case study research, such as Yin (2009), argue that they are appropriate criteria and suggest ways that case study research can be developed to enhance its ability to meet the criteria; for others, including Stake (1995), they are barely mentioned, if at all. Qualitative researchers tend to play down or ignore the importance of these factors, whereas quantitative researchers depict them as more significant.

Having said this, the external validity or generalizability of case study research has provoked a lot of discussion. A common criticism is that a single case cannot possibly be sufficiently representative that it might produce findings that can be applied more generally to other cases—for example, how could the findings from a single opera company (Atkinson 2006) be generalizable to all opera companies? However, advocates of case study research argue that the evidence they present is not limited by the fact that it has restricted external validity because the case study design does not aim to produce generalizable findings. This position is very different from that taken by practitioners of survey research: because they want to be able to generalize their findings to larger populations, they frequently use random sampling to enhance the representativeness of their samples and therefore the external validity of their findings. It is not possible to identify typical cases that represent a certain class of objects, whether it is factories, mass-media reporting, police services, or communities—in other words, researchers do not think that a case study is a sample of one—but case study researchers tend to argue that they aim to generate an *intensive examination* of a single case, and that in relation to this they can engage in a theoretical analysis.

The main concern here is the quality of the theoretical reasoning that the case study researcher engages in. How well do the data support the researcher's theoretical arguments? Is the theoretical analysis incisive? For example, does it demonstrate connections between different conceptual ideas that the researcher has developed out of the data? The crucial quality-related question is therefore not whether the findings can be generalized to a wider universe but how well the researcher generates theory out of the findings. This view of generalization is called 'analytic generalization' by Yin (2009) and 'theoretical generalization' by Mitchell (1983), and it places case study research firmly in the inductive tradition (where theory is generated out of research). However, a case study design is not necessarily associated with an inductive approach. Case studies can be associated with both theory generation *and* theory testing and, as Williams (2000) has argued, case study researchers are often in a position to generalize by drawing on findings from comparable cases investigated by others. We will return to this topic in Chapter 17.

3.7 Comparative design

We need to distinguish one more kind of design: comparative design. This design involves studying two contrasting cases using more or less identical methods and it implies that we can understand social phenomena better when they are compared in relation to two or more meaningfully contrasting cases or situations.

Features of the comparative design

The comparative design can be used in the context of either quantitative or qualitative research.

One of the most obvious forms of such research is in cross-cultural or cross-national research. In a useful definition, Hantrais (1996) has suggested that such research occurs

> when individuals or teams set out to examine particular issues or phenomena in two or more countries with the express intention of comparing their manifestations in different socio-cultural settings (institutions, customs, traditions, value systems, lifestyles, language, thought patterns), using the same research instruments either to carry out secondary analysis of national data or to conduct new empirical work. The aim may be to seek explanations for similarities and differences, to generalise from them or to gain a greater awareness and a deeper understanding of social reality in different national contexts.
>
> (Hantrais 1996: **https://sru.soc.surrey.ac.uk/SRU13.html**, accessed 1 March 2021)

The research by Röder and Mühlau (2014) described in Research in focus 2.1 is an example of cross-cultural research that involves a secondary analysis of survey evidence collected in 27 nations. Röder and Mühlau used data from the European Social Survey (**www.europeansocialsurvey.org/**); there are a range of data sets that facilitate such research, including the Eurobarometer (**https://ec.europa.eu/COMMFrontOffice/publicopinion/index.cfm**) and the World Values Survey (**www.worldvaluessurvey.org/wvs.jsp**—all links accessed 18 September 2019).

Cross-cultural research is not without problems, such as

- gaining and managing funding;
- ensuring, when existing data such as official statistics or survey evidence are submitted to a secondary analysis, that the data are comparable in terms of categories and data-collection methods;
- ensuring that samples of respondents or organizations are equivalent; and
- ensuring, when new data are being collected, that the need to translate data-collection instruments written in another language (for example, questions in interview schedules) does not undermine genuine comparability.

This last problem raises the further difficulty that, even when translation is carried out competently, there could still be insensitivity to specific national and cultural contexts.

Despite these potential issues, a major benefit of cross-cultural research is that it helps mitigate the fact that social science findings are often, if not always, culturally specific. For example, Crompton and Birkelund (2000) conducted research using semi-structured interviewing with comparable samples of male and female bank managers in Norway and Britain. They found that, in spite of more family-friendly policies in Norway, bank managers in both countries struggle to manage career and domestic life. It might have been assumed that the presence of family-friendly policies would ease these pressures, but cross-cultural research of this kind shows how easy it is to make such a mistaken inference. In the field of criminology, Williams (2016) used the Special Eurobarometer 390 to investigate incidences of online identity theft across Europe. While he was interested in individual level factors to see what the common predictors of being a victim might be, he also modelled country-level factors to control for the impact of national practices and security frameworks. This allowed him to identify how country-level differences moderated the effect of individual-level factors on the incidence of victimization.

Comparative research is not solely concerned with comparisons between nations; its logic can be applied to a variety of situations. The Social Change and Economic Life Initiative involved identical studies (mainly involving survey research) in six contrasting labour markets, which were chosen to reflect different patterns of economic change in the early to mid-1980s and in the then recent past. By choosing meaningful contrasts, the researchers could portray the significance of the different patterns for a variety of experiences of both employers and employees (Penn, Rose, and Rubery 1994). Such designs are not without problems: the differences that we observe between contrasting cases may not be due exclusively to the distinguishing features of the cases. It is important to exercise some caution when explaining contrasts between cases in terms of differences between them.

Reliability, replicability, and validity

In terms of issues of reliability, validity, replicability, and generalizability, the comparative study is no different from the cross-sectional design. The comparative design is essentially two or more cross-sectional studies carried out at more or less the same point in time.

The multiple-case study

The comparative design can be applied in relation to a qualitative research strategy. When this occurs, it takes the form of a **multiple-case study** (see Research in focus 3.11). In recent years, a number of writers have argued for a greater use of case study research that includes more than one case. Essentially, a multiple-case (or multi-case) study occurs whenever the number of cases examined exceeds one. The main argument in favour of the multiple-case study is that it improves theory building. By comparing two or more cases, the researcher is in a better position to establish the circumstances in which a theory will or will not hold (Eisenhardt 1989; Yin 2017), and the comparison may itself suggest concepts that are relevant to an emerging theory.

RESEARCH IN FOCUS 3.11
A multiple-case study based on difference between cases

In their study of the factors that contribute to the sense of 'place' and belonging among middle-class residents in two London neighbourhoods, Benson and Jackson (2013) adopted a multiple-case study approach that relied on differences between the cases.

The authors describe one neighbourhood as an inner urban neighbourhood and the other as a commuter belt village. The two neighbourhoods differed particularly in terms of the extent to which white British residents predominated and in levels of owner occupation (and, by implication, rented accommodation). The authors conducted semi-structured interviews with samples of middle-class residents and derived conclusions from a comparison of the two environments. For example, they write: 'The comparison of the discursive practices of place-making in two very different neighbourhoods has demonstrated that middle-class place-attachments need to be understood within the context of circulating representations of place' (Benson and Jackson 2013: 806). This kind of conclusion demonstrates the value of being able to forge a comparison through a multiple-case study approach. The comparison allows the distinctive and common features of cases to be drawn out.

3

The multiple-case study can also play a crucial role in relation to understanding causality, particularly for those working in the critical realist tradition. This is a rather different idea of causality from the one we outlined earlier in 'Validity'. When we discuss the independent and dependent variables that exist in experiments, there is an underlying sense of cause and effect. This type of causality is often referred to as 'successionist' because it involves an effect following on from a cause in succession.

On the other hand, the type of causality that can be inferred from a multiple-case study is more 'generative'. **Critical realism** (see Key concept 2.3) seeks out generative mechanisms that are responsible for patterns they observe in the social world and attempts to examine how they operate in particular contexts. In other words, it focuses on the causes and effects produced by distinctly social structures, rather than separating variables from the complexities of everyday reality. Critical realist writers see multiple-case studies as having an important role for research because the intensive nature of case studies enhances the researcher's sensitivity to factors that lie behind observed patterns (Ackroyd 2009). The multiple-case study offers an even greater opportunity to do this because the researcher can examine how generative causal mechanisms operate across different or similar contexts. Where findings do vary across specific contexts, then generative causal inferences can be made.

While she does not identify her approach as critical realism, Antonucci's (2016) study entitled 'Student Lives in Crisis: Deepening Inequality in Times of Austerity' is a good example of how multiple-case studies can uncover more nuanced findings than their single case counterparts. Antonucci was interested in how the financial support that is offered to students in higher education influenced the students' experiences of inequality. She conducted her research in six cities across three different countries—Sweden, England, and Italy—and used a mixed method design to collect survey and semi-structured interview data in each location. Given the different welfare context of each country, Antonucci might have theorized that experiences of inequality during university would vary by country. However, she discovered marked similarities across her cases. She explains this finding by highlighting that the general policy movement towards privatizing risk in neoliberal economies (for example individuals funding their studies themselves, via student loans, rather than being funded by the taxpayer) had resulted in five 'ideal types' of experience, each of which was dependent on socio-economic circumstance. Through the use of a multiple-case study, Antonucci was able to show how variation in experience across the countries was much less than we might otherwise expect because the five ideal types of experience she found were better understood through a generative causal mechanism (the privatization of risk) and through the significance of context (relative inequality).

Cases for a multiple-case study can be chosen either because of their differences or because of their similarities. Research in focus 3.11 provides an example where researchers used contrasting features both as a means of selecting cases and as a means of forging comparisons that allowed the researcher to demonstrate the implications for the data of the contrasting features. Research in focus 3.12 is an example of a study where the researcher

RESEARCH IN FOCUS 3.12
A multiple-case study based on similarity between cases

Kellogg (2009, 2011) used a multiple-case study design based on similarity between cases to assess the introduction of a new patient safety programme (involving a reduction in the number of hours worked by surgical residents—surgeons who are still in training) in US hospitals.

Initially, Kellogg studied two hospitals (2009), but she carried out further fieldwork in a third as well (2011). The hospitals (referred to as Advent, Bayshore, and Calhoun) were selected in large part because of their similarity, and Kellogg presents a table showing the dimensions on which they were similar (Kellogg 2011: 39–40). She found that the outcomes of the change differed between the three hospitals, which allowed her to examine the kinds of factors responsible for the differences in outcome in spite of the similarities between the hospitals. For example, Kellogg shows that the change 'ultimately failed' at Bayshore and Calhoun but that at Advent, 'reformers were victorious' (Kellogg 2011: 169). Because the three hospitals were similar at the outset, the differences in outcome could not be attributed to pre-existing characteristics. Kellogg draws attention to the ways in which forces for reform and forces for retaining as much of the status quo as possible produced different outcomes at the three hospitals.

selected cases on the basis of their similarity. The advantage of this strategy is that the researcher is able to say that any differences that are found between the cases in terms of the main focus of the research are likely to be due to the factors that the researcher reveals as important rather than to differences between the cases at the outset. This is, in a sense, a more open-ended approach to selecting cases than selecting them in terms of pre-existing characteristics (as in the studies in Research in focus 3.11). Selecting in terms of pre-existing difference means that the researcher is suggesting that they expect one or more factors to be significant for the focus of the research (for example place-making or feelings of deprivation), meaning that the researcher must have a rationale for the criteria they employ.

Not all writers are convinced about the merits of multiple-case study research. Dyer and Wilkins (1991), for example, argue that it tends to mean that the researcher pays less attention to the specific context and more to the contrasts between the cases. The need to forge comparisons can also mean that the researcher needs to develop an explicit focus at the outset, whereas critics of the multiple-case study argue that it may often be preferable to adopt a more open-ended approach. These concerns about retaining contextual insight and a rather more unstructured research approach are very much associated with the goals of qualitative research (see Chapter 16).

Essentially, a comparative design allows the distinguishing characteristics of two or more cases to act as a springboard for theoretical reflections about contrasting findings. This design is something of a hybrid, in that in quantitative research it is often an extension of a cross-sectional design and in qualitative research it is often an extension of a case study design. It even exhibits features that are similar to experiments and quasi-experiments, which also rely on forging a comparison.

3.8 Bringing research strategy and research design together

Finally, we can bring together the two research strategies we covered in Chapter 2 with the research designs we have considered in this chapter. Table 3.1 shows the typical form associated with each combination of research strategy and research design, together with a number of examples, some of which we will cover in later chapters.

TABLE 3.1
Research strategy and research design

Research design	Research strategy	
	Quantitative	Qualitative
Experimental	*Typical form*: in this design, most researchers use quantitative comparisons between experimental and control groups with regard to the dependent variable.	*No typical form.* However, Bryman (1988a: 151–2) notes a study in which qualitative data on schoolchildren were collected within a quasi-experimental research design (Hall and Guthrie 1981).
Cross-sectional	*Typical form*: survey research or structured observation on a sample at a single point in time, or content analysis on a sample of documents relating to a single time period.	*Typical form*: qualitative interviews or **focus groups** at a single point in time, or **qualitative content analysis** of a set of documents relating to a single period.
Longitudinal	*Typical form*: survey research on a sample on more than one occasion, as in panel and cohort studies, or content analysis of documents relating to more than one time period.	*Typical form*: ethnographic research over a very long period, qualitative interviewing on more than one occasion, or qualitative content analysis of documents relating to different time periods; researchers seek to track change over time.
Case study	*Typical form*: survey research on a single case that aims to reveal important features about its nature.	*Typical form*: the intensive study by ethnography or qualitative interviewing of a single case, which may be an organization, life, family, or community.
Comparative	*Typical form*: survey research making a direct comparison between two or more cases, as in cross-cultural research.	*Typical form*: ethnographic or qualitative interview research comparing two or more cases.

Table 3.1 also refers to research methods that we will explore in later chapters. The Glossary will give you a quick reference to terms used that are not yet familiar to you.

Strictly speaking, Table 3.1 should have a third column for mixed methods research (see Chapter 24), as an approach that combines both quantitative and qualitative research; but the resulting table would be too complicated, because mixed methods research can involve the combined use of different research *designs* (for example, a cross-sectional design and a multiple-case study) as well as methods. However, the quantitative and qualitative components of some of the mixed methods studies discussed in this book *are* included in the table.

The distinctions are not always perfect. In particular, in some qualitative research it is not obvious whether a study is an example of a longitudinal design or a case study design. Some studies cross the two types: for example, life history studies that concentrate on a specific issue over time (e.g. Deacon, Fenton, and Bryman 1999), and ethnography that charts change in a single case. It is probably best to think of these kinds of studies as longitudinal case studies rather than as belonging to one category of research design. You should also note that there is no typical form in the 'qualitative research strategy' / 'experimental research design' cell of the table. This is because qualitative research in the context of true experiments is very unusual. However, as noted in the table, Bryman (1988a) refers to a qualitative study by Hall and Guthrie (1981) that employed a quasi-experimental design.

One more important consideration when you come to choose a research design is what is possible given the amount of time that you have and the resources available. It is therefore essential to plan your research project, create timelines, and make sure that you can achieve what you set out to do. This is what we will cover in the next chapter.

KEY POINTS

- There is an important distinction between a research method and a research design.
- You need to become thoroughly familiar with the meaning of the technical terms used as criteria for evaluating research—reliability, validity, and replicability—and the types of validity: measurement, internal, external, ecological, and inferential.
- You also need to become familiar with the differences between the five major research designs covered: experimental, cross-sectional, longitudinal, case study, and comparative. In this context, it is important to realize that the term 'experiment', which is often used loosely in everyday speech, has a specific technical meaning.
- There are various potential threats to internal validity in non-experimental research.
- Although the case study is often thought to be a single type of research design, it in fact has several forms. It is also important to be aware of the issues surrounding the nature of case study evidence in relation to quality criteria such as external validity (generalizability).

QUESTIONS FOR REVIEW

1. In terms of the definitions used in this book, what are the main differences between each of the following: a research method; a research strategy; and a research design?
2. What are the differences between reliability and validity and why are these important criteria for the evaluation of social research?
3. Outline the meaning of each of the following: measurement validity; internal validity; external validity; ecological validity; inferential validity.

4. What alternative criteria to reliability and validity have qualitative researchers suggested when assessing the quality of investigations?
5. What are the main research designs that have been outlined in this chapter?
6. How far do you agree with the view that the main importance of the experimental design for the social researcher is that it represents a model of how to infer causal connections between variables?
7. Following on from the previous question, if experimental design is so useful and important, why is it not used more?
8. What is a quasi-experiment?
9. In what ways does the survey exemplify the cross-sectional research design?
10. Why might a longitudinal research design be superior to a cross-sectional one?
11. What are the main differences between panel and cohort designs in longitudinal research?
12. What is a case study?
13. What are some of the principles by which cases might be selected?
14. Why might comparative research yield important insights?

ONLINE RESOURCES

www.oup.com/he/srm6e

You can find our notes on the answers to these questions within this chapter's **online resources**, together with:

- *audio/video comments* on this topic from our 'Learn from experience' panellists;
- *self-test questions* for further knowledge-checking;
- a *flashcard glossary* to help you recall key terms; and
- a *Student Researcher's Toolkit* containing practical materials and resources to help you conduct your own research project.

CHAPTER

4

PLANNING A RESEARCH PROJECT AND FORMULATING RESEARCH QUESTIONS

CHAPTER GUIDE

In this chapter we walk through some of the issues that you will need to consider when planning a dissertation based upon a relatively small-scale research project. We provide advice on

- understanding what your institution expects from you in this context;
- working effectively with your supervisor;
- managing the timing and resources for your project;
- generating research questions—explicit statements about what it is that you intend to investigate;
- writing a research proposal—an outline of what your research is about and how you intend to conduct it;
- preparing to conduct your research.

4.1 Introduction

In this chapter we provide advice on carrying out your own small-scale research project—we're thinking here of the increasingly common requirement for undergraduate and postgraduate social science students to conduct and write up an independent research project (often called a dissertation) of around 10,000 to 15,000 words. This advice will be particularly useful for students who are conducting projects with a component of empirical research, in which they either collect new data or conduct a **secondary analysis** of existing data.

A successful project always starts with the researcher having a clear idea of the amount of time and resources available and what questions they are going to pose. Your project is likely to be accepted and given backing by your supervisor and other academic staff if you have written a clear, realistic, and well-thought-through proposal, and your research is more likely to produce reliable, replicable, and valid results (as we discussed in Chapter 3) if it is well conducted. We will therefore cover all these aspects here to help you get the most from your research project.

4.2 Preparing for your project

You will probably have an idea of what topic you want to research quite a while before you actually start your dissertation, but it is all too easy to get carried away with an idea without first checking that it is appropriate and researchable. Unfortunately, most of us do not operate in a world of limitless resources with no word counts, no time constraints, and extensive financial resources. These restrictions impact upon what we can and can't research, and we need to take them into account before we begin any research project. This is not to say that you can't be ambitious, but you do need to be realistic. Understanding what resources are available to you and how much time you have is a key part of this, and this is where supervisors are incredibly important. They will know what is and isn't possible and will guide their students through the research process. If your supervisor tells you that a topic is not suitable or feasible, then you really must not be upset by this. Their job is to make sure that you can complete your project and make a success of it.

In the following section we outline some of the main points that you should consider as you begin to plan your project. We discuss what is expected of you and how your supervisor can support you. We also suggest some strategies for planning and managing your time and for considering what resources are available to you.

What does your institution expect from you?

Your institution or department will have specific requirements relating to your dissertation's contents and format. These are likely to include such things as the form of binding; how it is to be presented; whether an abstract is required; how big the page margins should be; the format for referencing; the maximum number of words; the structure of the dissertation; how much advice you can get from your supervisor; how many **research questions** you should have; whether or not a proposal is required; how to gain ethical clearance; plagiarism; deadlines; how much (if any) financial assistance you can expect; and so on.

Our advice here is simple: *follow the requirements, instructions, and information you are given.* If anything in this book conflicts with your institution's guidelines and requirements, ignore this book! We very much hope this kind of conflict will not occur often, but if it does, you should follow your institution's guidelines.

Working with your supervisor

Most institutions allocate students to dissertation supervisors. Institutions vary in what can be expected of supervisors: in other words, in what kinds of assistance, and how much, supervisors will give to students allocated to them. Equally, students vary in how frequently they ask to see their supervisors and how they make use of them. We would strongly encourage you to use your supervisor to the fullest extent that you are allowed, and to follow the pointers that your supervisor gives you.

Your supervisor will be someone who is extremely familiar with the research process and who will be able to provide you with help and feedback at all stages of your research, subject to your institution's regulations. If your supervisor is critical of aspects of your project—your research questions, your **interview schedule**, written drafts of your dissertation, or whatever—try to respond positively.

Follow the suggestions that they provide, since there will be reasons for this feedback and it will be accompanied by constructive suggestions for revision. It is not a personal attack. Supervisors regularly have to go through the same process themselves when they submit an article to a peer-refereed journal, apply for a research grant, or give a conference paper, so they know how it feels. Respond to their suggestions positively and be glad that you are being given the opportunity to address problems in your work before it is marked.

It is also worth being aware that students who get stuck at the start of their dissertations, or who get behind with their work, sometimes respond to the situation by avoiding their supervisors. As a result, they don't get help to move forward and get caught in a vicious cycle that results in their work being neglected and potentially rushed at the end. Try to avoid this situation by confronting the fact that you are experiencing difficulties in beginning your work or are getting behind, and approach your supervisor for advice.

See Learn from experience 4.1 for our panel's tips on making the best use of your supervisor's support.

Working with the time and resources available

All research is constrained by time and resources. There is no point in working on research questions and plans

LEARN FROM EXPERIENCE 4.1
How to work productively with your dissertation supervisor

Supervising a student dissertation is an incredibly rewarding experience for academics. When supervisions work well, there is a free exchange of ideas, frequent and constructive feedback, and a highly productive and trusting relationship in which supervisors and students learn from each other. We (the authors) have supervised many dissertations over the years, and we genuinely do enjoy doing it.

Our panellists share their hints and tips below on how to get the best out of your supervisory relationship.

It is often helpful to send your supervisor a list of questions you have a few days before your meeting. That will help you put into words what you want to get from the meeting, and also give them a chance to think about the best way to guide you to the answers. Even if they don't have the time to prepare, you will come more prepared, which is often even more important.

Barbara

It is important to note that like each of us, each supervisor is also different. My best advice is: find what works for you personally but also for them. A few ideas that have made my relationship with my supervisor so fruitful are: set your own goals; be organized; find out what works for them. Build a working relationship so that you know not only their expectations, but also what you expect of them—for example, how long it would take them to get back to you with comments on your work. Take control—your supervisor may be quite relaxed, but you may want more structure. It is your project, after all—it's OK if you don't follow every bit of their advice. Ask questions. Meet and communicate regularly. Especially if you are struggling—don't leave it.

Jodie

My supervisors have been very useful in keeping me grounded and realistic. I tend to be overly ambitious in my research plans, but they have always told me when I am being unrealistic while suggesting more achievable targets. Maybe I have been really lucky with my supervisors, but it is more likely that as I have demonstrated that I want to learn and work hard, this leads them to be extra helpful.

Simon

My advice is, first, to listen closely to what your supervisor says. The advice they give comes from years of experience, and they know methodology, research traditions, and the ins and outs of the academic profession. Second, consider how you can combine their advice with your research topic. Remember that this is your study, and your passion in the subject is what drives you to do the best work that you can do. By combining your own passion with the expertise of your supervisors, you will be able to complete a piece of work that you can be proud of.

Brendan

Make sure to provide your supervisor with work to give feedback on, during regular set meetings—otherwise they cannot steer you in the right direction. I would also advise students to voice what they think is most interesting about their research ideas and data. Supervisors usually get excited about something when you are excited about it. So, be proactive and tell your supervisor what you want to know more about, what is a mystery to you, and why this is the case.

Laura

 Access the **online resources** to hear our panellists' video reflections on this theme.

You can read about our panellists' backgrounds and research experiences on page xxvi.

4

that cannot be carried through because of time pressure or because of the costs involved.

Managing your time

If you are to conduct effective research within the time available, you need to begin by working out a timetable—preferably in conversation with your supervisor—that sets out the different stages of your research (including the literature review and writing up) and the dates by which you should start and finish them (see Tips and skills 4.1). Some stages are likely to be ongoing—for example, searching the literature for new references (a process that will be covered in Chapter 5)—but that should not stop you from developing a timetable. Be careful not to underestimate the time you will need for certain stages. Sometimes, for example, your project will involve securing access to an organization in order to study some aspect of it, and students often underestimate the time it can take to arrange this. For his research on commercial cleaning, Shaun Ryan (2009) spent nearly two years trying to secure access to a suitable firm. Even if an organization wants to give you access to data, delays can occur. When Facebook wanted to make available a database of 38 million links (URLs) on civic discourse, it took around 20 months for the data to be properly anonymized and made available (Mervis 2020)! Our panel share their thoughts on managing your time in Learn from experience 4.2.

TIPS AND SKILLS 4.1
Drawing up a timetable

Assuming that you begin your project around the start of October and submit it around the end of April, this gives you approximately 30 weeks. In reality you will have less than that because you'll want to take some time off in December, and then you will have to factor in other assessment deadlines. You can start to see how easy it would be to lose track of time, and this is why drawing up a timetable should be an essential part of planning a research project.

The purpose of a timetable is not to provide fixed deadlines for the completion of particular tasks (although some people do work best to deadlines); rather, it is a baseline against which you can measure your progress. It also forces you to think about the order in which key things needs to happen and how long some tasks might take. For example, you can't start collecting data until you receive ethical clearance, and that can't happen until you've written a research proposal and/or completed an ethics form. In our example (Figure 4.1) we have left a four-week gap between submitting your ideas to the ethics committee and receiving ethical clearance from them.

How you write up a timetable is up to you, but we have found Gantt charts to be particularly useful: we have provided a simple example for a typical dissertation project in Figure 4.1. Gantt charts are easy to create (we designed this one in Excel) and easy to understand, and they can be as detailed and intricate as you like. For example, in our Gantt chart we have blocked out two weeks for a holiday in December. You may also decide with your supervisor that you will need to meet more frequently at the start of the project. In addition to listing the tasks relating to your research project, you could include deadlines for other key assessments within your course.

FIGURE 4.1

Gantt charts such as this are a useful way of planning your time when completing a research project

TASK	1	2	3	4	5	6	7	8	9	10	11	12	13	14	15	16	17	18	19	20	21	22	23	24	25	26	27	28	29	30
Meet Supervisor																														
Write Research Proposal/Ethics																														
Literature Review (ongoing)																														
Draft Methodology																														
Data Collection																														
Analysis and Draft Results																														
Draft Discussion and Conclusion																														
Final Draft of Everything																														

(The week numbers 1–30 are printed under the heading WEEK.)

LEARN FROM EXPERIENCE 4.2

Managing your time

Time management is a crucial skill to master when you're conducting a research project, and everyone has their own strategies and approaches to make sure that they get all the work done. Our panellists share some of their hints and tips below.

> It sounds like a cliché, but—find a system that works for you, and then stick to it. If you are someone who works more effectively in the morning, then get up and work for a period of time and then go and relax—that is important. Personally, I can't work without a certain amount of pressure, so I often did things in a shorter amount of time than my friends, and often late at night. This is because I have always felt most productive during this time and I find that I write better the less time I have to 'faff' around.
>
> To work out how much time is needed for each phase of research, I create a visual plan (for example, a Gantt chart). I always work backwards from my deadline, leaving two to four days for editing and one day for printing and submission. I always set deadlines to submit chapters to my supervisor for comments. Throughout my research projects, right from undergraduate to postgraduate level, I have found that no matter what you do, something will always throw your plan off slightly. Therefore, when planning I recommend accounting for a couple of extra days here or there. Otherwise, you may find yourself very stressed when you're behind schedule. Lastly, never underestimate how long it takes to format your document.
>
> Jodie

I recommend making a timetable of each stage of the research project—for an undergraduate project I'd recommend allowing two months to write the literature review and two months for data collection. This can be used as a guide. It's a good idea to leave plenty of time for writing the literature review, the methodology chapter, and the findings chapter. It is also very important to leave time (two to three weeks) to write the conclusion, as unlike an essay it cannot be left to the very end! In my experience it is particularly important to leave plenty of time for the data-collection phase of the research project. This phase can be unpredictable at times and, in the case of conducting interviews, you may find that they have to be rearranged. You also need to dedicate ample time before the data-collection phase for recruiting participants.

Sarah

I treated my undergrad studies as a full-time job. I worked from 9 to 5 Monday to Friday and this was really effective for me. I made a Gantt chart (which I reviewed regularly) to try and plan my time, and I left a clear month at the end as a contingency, which really helped. The whole process took a lot longer than I expected, and I used most of my month's contingency, but I still had enough time to revise for my exams and complete all my other coursework.

Simon

Research moves slowly, and it's important to realize this when planning your study. When I was organizing my data collection, I was surprised by how many people I needed to get permission from to prepare and conduct my interviews. What I initially thought would take a few weeks actually took a few months. Luckily, I started early so had plenty of time to finish.

Brendan

I think coming up with a rough time plan and deadlines for each chapter is super-helpful. Having several months can feel like you have ages, but it goes really quickly and you may have to pause your research for other assignments, so it's a good idea to plan long-term how you will complete your research project, so that you don't end up rushing in the final weeks. Proofreading, organizing, and formatting my dissertation took far longer than I expected. I would recommend leaving at least a week just to do this.

Grace

My dissertation supervisor strongly advised us to keep to a dissertation timetable. In all honesty, like most of my peers, I found that I had over- and underestimated certain parts of the dissertation. The literature review was definitely the phase that I underestimated. My best piece of advice would be to do as much of the literature review as possible during, if not before, the Christmas period. For me, going home during the Christmas period gave me at least two weeks of uninterrupted reading time (aside from the celebrations, of course) to do the literature review. Admittedly, you're not going to use everything you've collected in your literature review, but it's easy to overlook that one of the key functions of the literature review is to expand your knowledge on the subject area.

Zvi

Access the **online resources** to hear our panellists' video reflections on this theme.

You can read about our panellists' backgrounds and research experiences on page xxvi.

Managing your resources

It is very important that you find out early on what, if any, resources will be available for carrying out your research. For example, will you receive help from your institution with such things as access to an online survey platform, travel costs, photocopying, postage, stationery, and so on? Will the institution be able to loan you any equipment you need, for example recording and **transcription** devices to help you with interviewing? Has your institution got the software you will need for processing your data, such as **SPSS** or a qualitative data analysis package such as **NVivo**? (Visit our **online resources** for guidance on using these packages.) This kind of information will help you to work out whether your research design and methods are financially feasible and practical.

Throughout this section, including in the tips from our panel, you will have seen a clear message emerging: you must allow sufficient time for the various stages of the research process. Students often underestimate the time it will take to secure access to participants, analyse data, and write up findings. Another time-related issue, as illustrated in Tips and skills 4.1, is that it can take a long time to receive clearance from research ethics committees to conduct your investigation. (We discuss ethical issues in detail in Chapter 6.) However, one final point needs to be made: even with a really well-planned project, unexpected problems can mess up your timetable. For example, McDonald, Townsend, and Waterhouse (2009) report that they successfully negotiated access to the Australian organizations that were involved in a number of research projects in which the researchers were engaged. However, changes to personnel meant that those who had agreed to give them access (often called 'gatekeepers' in the research methods literature) left or moved on, so that the researchers had to forge new relationships and effectively had to renegotiate the terms of their investigations, which considerably slowed down the progress of their research. Such disruptions to research are impossible to predict. It is important not only to realize that they can occur but also to introduce a little flexibility into your research timetable so that you can absorb their impact. Most importantly, if this happens to you, then you should contact your supervisor as soon as possible for advice.

4.3 Starting your project

It is likely that your course leaders and supervisors will ask you to start thinking about what you want to research a while before you are actually due to start work on your dissertation. It is worth giving yourself quite a lot of time to consider your options. As you are studying various subjects, you should begin to think about whether there are any topics that interest you and might provide you with a researchable area. In this section, we return to the topic of research questions and explore where they might come from and how to assess their suitability. At this point it is important to acknowledge that not all projects necessarily require a research question up-front, and some supervisors might prefer to think in terms of research aims and objectives. For the purposes of this chapter, though, we will assume that you are required to pose research questions (this is often the case when submitting an initial proposal, even if your ideas then change as your project develops). We also discuss the importance of the research proposal and identify what you need to consider when preparing to conduct your research, as it is always beneficial to anticipate what might happen later in your project.

Formulating suitable research questions

Many students want to conduct research into areas that are of personal interest to them. This is not a bad thing at all and, as we noted in Chapter 2, many social researchers start from this point as well (see also Lofland and Lofland 1995: 11–14). However, even when considering an area about which you are naturally curious, you must still develop research questions relating to this area. This advice applies to qualitative as well as quantitative research. As we explained in Chapter 2 and will discuss in detail in Chapter 16, qualitative research tends to be more open-ended than quantitative research, and in Chapter 18 we refer to some notable studies that appear not to have been driven by specific research questions. However, very open-ended research is risky and can lead to confusion about your focus; there is a growing tendency for qualitative researchers to advocate a more focused approach (see, for example, Hammersley and Atkinson 1995: 24–9). So, unless your supervisor advises you otherwise, we would strongly suggest that you formulate some research questions, even if they turn out to be less specific than the kinds we often find in quantitative research. In other words, what is it about your area of interest that you want to know? Throughout this chapter we will assume that you are going to ask more than one research question, but it is perfectly acceptable to only ask one. You should talk to your supervisor about how many research questions are appropriate for your project.

Sources of research questions

When selecting research questions we usually start out with a general research area that interests us. It may originate from any of the following sources.

- *Personal interest/experience*. Your interest in theme parks could be traced back to a visit to Disney World in Orlando in 2018, or your interest in social media may have begun when you noticed that men and women seem to post about different things.

- *Theory*. You might be interested in testing or exploring aspects of how masculinity manifests online, or in the implications of a certain theoretical perspective for the use of technologies in everyday life.
- *The research literature*. Studies relating to a research area such as modern consumerism might stimulate your interest in the nature of the shopping experience in contemporary society, or you might want to know more about recent work on social class (see, for example, Savage et al. 2013).
- *Replication*. Relating to the previous point, it is perfectly legitimate to take a research question from the literature and to replicate it in your own work. Such studies are very valuable for checking whether findings are the same over time, between different groups of people, or in different countries (for a discussion, see Freese and Peterson 2017).
- *Puzzles*. An example of this would be how Curtice (2016) used data from the British Social Attitudes Survey 2015 to assess which considerations matter more, economic or cultural, in shaping attitudes towards the European Union in Britain. Previous research indicated that both were salient, but which is more important?
- *New developments in society*. An example of this is the work of Booker, Kelly, and Sacker (2018), who looked at the impact of social media interaction on wellbeing and how the effects may differ by gender.
- *Social problems*. An example is Black et al.'s study of how media reports about migration impacted the willingness of asylum-seekers and refugees to access healthcare (2018).

These sources of interest are not mutually exclusive; studies can be motivated by more than one of these kinds of sources.

Types of research questions

Research questions can generally be categorized into two types, those that seek to *describe* and those that seek to *explain*. White (2017: 57) suggests that the two groups can be thought of as relating to the 'Journalistic Six':

- *descriptive questions* are typically concerned with what, where, when, who, and how;
- *explanatory questions* are typically concerned with why and how.

So if you have a research question, you should find that it falls under one of these categories (with the exception of 'how' questions, which can be descriptive or explanatory). It is important to note that one type of research question is not, in itself, better or more important than the other—they are just different. Sometimes a phenomenon needs to be adequately *described* before it can be explored (see Research in focus 4.1). For example, if you are looking into the gender pay gap, it is really important to be able to describe *what* the pay gap is between men and women; if you are talking about increasing crime rates, you need to be able to describe *where* crime rates have increased over time. It is equally interesting and important to understand *why* the gender pay gap exists and *how* it could be eliminated, or *why* crime rates have increased in an area and *how* this has impacted upon residents.

RESEARCH IN FOCUS 4.1
The value of descriptive research questions

Description and descriptive research questions can be extremely important, both in their own right and as a foundation for further exploratory work. For example, if we want to understand how useful the social media platform Twitter is as a source of data for investigating the social world, then we need to know who uses it (also known as the *population* of users). Luke, one of this book's authors, set out to do this in Great Britain by using survey data to *describe* the proportion of men and women, the age distribution, and the social class according to the NS-SEC (the UK's National Statistics Socio-economic Classification system) of Twitter users (Sloan 2017). In his paper, the first research question relating to this aim was as follows:

> RQ1) To what extent are certain demographic characteristics associated with Twitter use for GB users? (2017: 2)

The author finds that, compared to the general population data, men are disproportionately more likely to be using Twitter then women, Twitter users show a younger age distribution, and certain NS-SEC groups are disproportionately present (typically respondents from managerial, administrative, and professional occupations).

4

However, the author is very clear that he is not providing answers on *why* these patterns occur:

> What this article is unable to answer is why differences in Twitter use are associated with the demographic characteristics. While we have offered some thoughts on the motivations for Twitter use and crafting of a virtual identity (boyd, 2006; Caspi and Gorsky, 2006; Joinson, 2003; Turkle 1995), much more research is needed to investigate the mechanisms through which these associations manifest.
>
> (2017: 9)

Despite this, by *describing* what is going on he is providing other researchers with a foundation from which to continue the important research of understanding why things are the way they are:

> It is our sincere hope that by describing the UK Twitter population, we have provided a foundation for further work to build upon.
>
> (2017: 9)

So description is important, and often precedes exploratory work. In some cases, *describing* a poorly understood phenomenon is an essential first step for researching an area.

Evaluating research questions

As we have seen, in research we often start out with a general research area that interests us, but this area may have to be narrowed down so that we can develop a tighter focus. In making this movement from research areas to specific research questions we have to recognize several points.

- We cannot answer all the research questions that occur to us. This is not just to do with the constraints of time and the cost of doing research. It is very much to do with the fact that we must keep a clear focus, so that our research questions relate to each other and form a coherent set of issues.
- We therefore have to select a shortlist from the possible research questions that we initially arrive at.
- In making a selection, we should be guided by the principle that the research questions we choose must relate to one another. If they do not, our research will probably lack focus and we may not make as clear a contribution to our discipline's understanding as we would have been able to do if our research questions had been connected to each other.

When evaluating possible research questions for your dissertation or project, bear in mind that effective questions should have the following characteristics.

- They should be *clear*, in the sense of being understandable.
- They should be *researchable*—that is, they should allow you to do research in relation to them. This means that they should not be formulated in terms that are so abstract that they cannot be converted into researchable points. (Examples of over-abstract questions: how do people feel about politics, or diets, or social media?)
- They should have some *connection(s) with established theory and research*. This means that you should develop your questions with reference to existing literature, which will give you an idea of how your research questions should be approached. Even if you find a topic that has not been addressed by many social scientists, it is unlikely that there will be no relevant literature at all (for example, there may be some on related or parallel topics).
- They should be *linked to each other*. Choosing unrelated research questions will prevent you from developing a clear argument in your dissertation.
- They should be *neither too broad nor too narrow*. If they are too broad, you would need huge resources to study them; if they are too narrow, this would prevent you from making a reasonably significant contribution to your area of study.

Try to apply these criteria to your own research questions and improve them accordingly (for an example, see Thinking deeply 4.1).

If you are stuck about how to formulate research questions, then you are not alone. It is difficult to shape a really good question, and often your question will change as you learn more about your topic (as we hear in Learn from experience 4.3). You might want to look at journal articles or past dissertations to see how other researchers have formulated them. When doing this, you will see that it is essential for research questions to be *justified*. You need to show how your research questions came about, and why they are important. Our list

THINKING DEEPLY 4.1

Evaluating research questions

While your supervisor will work with you to define your research question(s), you should not solely rely on them to evaluate your questions. You can assess your own research questions using the list of criteria above, and this will save you a lot of time at the start of your project by helping you fine-tune your ideas. Developing these skills will also help you to evaluate how effective others' research questions are.

Let's consider how the research questions posed in Luke's study of Twitter usage (Sloan 2017—see Research in focus 4.1) stand up to scrutiny by these standards. Before we evaluate them using the criteria above it is important to note that the study had two research questions, one of which we did not list in Research in focus 4.1 because it is a repeat example of a descriptive question. The two research questions were:

RQ1) To what extent are certain demographic characteristics associated with Twitter use for GB users?

RQ2) To what extent do the survey data confirm or challenge the demographic picture of Twitter users using computational methods that derive information from profile metadata?

The second question aims to compare what the survey data found about Twitter usage based on sex, age, and class against previous attempts to classify user demographics using data from a Twitter account itself (metadata such as first names and profile data).

Technical language aside, the research questions do seem to be *clear* and understandable, although perhaps the author could have replaced 'demographic' with the more specific terms 'sex', 'age', and 'class'. They are *researchable* as demonstrated by the research in the paper itself, and this is because they are clear questions that identify a **population** of interest for which we have information on Twitter use and demographics. They are *connected to established work*: there is existing research around the difficulties created by not knowing who uses social media. The questions also identify the need for a survey to verify (the author refers to *ground truth*) what the demographic profile of users is and to evaluate the quality of previous proxy measures. They are *linked to each other*, in that the first question describes patterns of use by sex, age, and class, while the second then compares these findings to previous research. They are not *too broad* (for example, unresearchable due to resource constraints) or *too narrow* (for example, too specialist to be of use to other researchers).

While these research questions seem to perform favourably against the evaluation criteria, remember that this is a finished product—the end of a long journey. As the author of this paper, and one of the authors of this textbook, Luke can confirm that he had many false starts during this project and it took quite a while to arrive at the research questions presented here. So don't be disheartened if you're not coming up with well-crafted research questions at the very start of your project!

LEARN FROM EXPERIENCE 4.3

Formulating research questions

Formulating good research questions is a journey. It's very rare for anyone, student or experienced academic, to start with a research question that doesn't change as a project progresses or as we learn something new from our wider reading, as our panellists observe below.

> I have always found formulating research questions tricky. Being able to formulate something that is specific enough, that isn't so broad that you have too much to answer, but equally not too narrow, can be challenging. All I can say is keep returning to them. Ask friends, family, supervisors what they think and what they require. Edit the questions. Leave them. Then return to them with fresh perspective.
>
> Jodie

4

Your research questions are what drive your research, so it's important that they are clear and focused. I found that my initial questions were very general and not as clear as they should be. After repeated revisions, I settled on these three questions that built upon each other: 1) What information do asylum-seeking parents report receiving about the Swedish compulsory school system? 2) What strategies do asylum-seeking parents use for finding information and participating within the Swedish compulsory education system? 3) What barriers do asylum-seeking parents identify in the process of enrolment and participation of their children in the compulsory Swedish school system?

Brendan

In my undergraduate study of violent interactions encountered by social workers, I started with an overall question of 'How do social workers experience violence on the spot?', but this was too broad. To make research questions more focused I'd suggest thinking, for instance, of specifics in terms of time, situation, or place. In my case, my original question evolved into 'How do social workers of the Salvation Army speak of (emotional) experience of verbal and (threatening) physical violence within the homeless shelters of Amsterdam?' This question is much more specific about what type of social workers I want to know about, what kind of violent situations I am interested in, and where such situations take place.

Laura

One of the most difficult things about formulating a research question is making sure the questions actually seek to explore the thing you want to explore. It sounds simple but it's actually quite difficult. I wanted to look at whether screen time affected a person's sleep, which is in itself a question: 'Does screen time affect a person's sleep?' But when you break it down, you actually need to conceptualize what screen time is and what sleep is in order to effectively answer the question. I had to decide: what did I really mean by screen time? The actual time someone spent looking at a screen? What type of screen—TV, tablet, smartphone? Did it matter what they did on the screen? Did it matter when they used the screen? And then there was sleep. What about sleep was I exactly going to measure? Sleep quantity? Sleep quality? Time spent in bed? Time taken to wake up in the morning?

Zvi

Access the **online resources** to hear our panellists' video reflections on this theme.

You can read about our panellists' backgrounds and research experiences on page xxvi.

of possible sources of research questions may be helpful, but in order to justify your choice of research questions, you will have to demonstrate the link between them and a body of existing literature. Remember that research questions should, as we have just noted, have some connection(s) with established theory and research, but in addition to *seeing* that the questions *have* a connection, you will have to *demonstrate* that connection.

Writing your research proposal

In preparation for any social research project, you may be asked to write a short proposal outlining what your research will be about and how you intend to conduct it. This is a useful exercise that will naturally prompt you to consider many of the issues we will cover in the next section, 'Preparing to conduct your research'.

In addition to outlining your topic area, your research questions, and your proposed research design and methods, your proposal will need to demonstrate that you have some knowledge of the relevant literature—for example, by identifying several key authors or significant research studies. Often, your course leaders will use this information as the basis for allocating you to a supervisor who is knowledgeable in your research area or who has experience with your proposed research approach. The proposal is also a useful starting point for discussion of your project with your supervisor. If you have drawn up a timetable (see the discussion of 'Managing your time' in Section 4.2), it can provide a template for planning regular meetings with your supervisor to review your progress.

When writing a research proposal, you should consider several issues.

- **Your research topic or research objective(s)**
  - What is it/are they?
  - Why is it/are they important?
- **Your research question(s)**
  - What it is/are they?
- **The relevant academic literature**
  - What does the literature have to say about your research topic or objective(s) and your research question(s)?
- **Your research methods**
  - How are you going to collect data relevant to your research question(s)? In other words, what research methods are you intending to use?
  - Why are these research methods or sources the appropriate ones for your research question(s)?
- **The people and organizations involved**
  - Who will your research participants be, and how will they be selected?
  - If the research will rely on documents, what kinds of documents will be the focus of your attention, and how will you select them?
  - If your research requires you to secure access to organizations, have you done so? If you have not, what obstacles do you anticipate?
- **The resources you need**
  - What resources will you need to conduct your research (for example, travel costs, recording and transcription equipment, photocopying, access to an online survey platform)?
  - How will those resources be funded?
- **The timings**
  - What is your timetable for the different stages of the project (see Tips and skills 4.1)?
- **Potential problems in carrying out your research**
  - What problems do you anticipate in doing the research (for example, gaining access to organizations)?
  - What are the possible ethical problems associated with your research?
- **How you'll find answers to your research questions**
  - How will you analyse your data?

You can see how, by answering these questions, writing a proposal will get you started and help you to set realistic objectives for your research project. In some institutions, the research proposal may form part (even if only a small one) of the overall assessment of the dissertation or report that is produced out of the research. While the research proposal is a working document, and the ideas that you set out in it can be refined and developed as your research progresses, it is important to be aware that if you keep changing your mind about your area of research and your research design, you will use up valuable time needed to complete the project within the deadline.

Your research proposal may also be part of the process for gaining ethical clearance (see Chapter 6). Once ethical clearance has been granted, there may be a limit to how much you can change your ideas without seeking new approval from your institution's ethics committee.

4

Preparing to conduct your research

Do not begin your data collection until you have identified your research questions reasonably clearly. Design your data-collection instruments with these research questions in mind. If you do not do this, there is a risk that your results will not allow you to address the research questions. If at all possible, it is a good idea to conduct a small **pilot** study to check how well your data-collection instruments work (see Chapter 11, Section 11.6, for advice on survey piloting).

You will also need to think about access and **sampling** issues, which we discuss in depth in Chapters 8 and 17. If your research requires you to gain access to or the cooperation of one or more closed settings, such as an organization, you need to confirm at the earliest opportunity that you have the necessary permission to conduct your work. You also need to think about how you will go about gaining access to people. These issues lead you into sampling considerations, such as the following:

- Who do you need to study in order to investigate your research questions?
- How easily can you gain access to a list of every person/household/organization who is eligible to participate in your study (a **sampling frame**)?
- What kind of sampling strategy will you employ (for example, **probability sampling**, **quota sampling**, **theoretical sampling**, **convenience sampling**—all of which are covered in Chapters 8 and 17)?
- Can you justify your choice of sampling method?

4.4 Doing your research and analysing your results

Since doing your research and analysing your results are the main focus of this book as a whole, we will not go into great detail here about these stages of the process. However, experience has taught us that the following hints and tips will help your project to run smoothly.

1. **Remember to always back up your data**, whether these are field notes or survey data sets. Data loss is one of the most significant risks in any social research project. Also be aware of any data security and storage requirements that your institution mandates, such as only storing non-anonymized data on an encrypted drive.
2. **Keep good records of what you do.** This might include keeping a research diary (see Key concept 10.1) and/or keeping good records of who within an organization you have spoken to, or who has responded to your questionnaire survey, so that you know who should be sent reminders. If participant observation is a component of your research, remember to keep detailed field notes and not to rely on your memory (see Chapter 18, Section 18.4, for a discussion of writing up such observations).
3. **Keep returning to your research questions.** It is very easy to get distracted from what you are researching either during the data collection or analysis phases. You should generally keep your research questions at the forefront of your mind at all times and always ask yourself whether what you're doing is relevant.
4. **Familiarize yourself with any devices, software, or equipment you need.** This applies both to those you are using to collect your data, such as phone apps and/or audio-recorders for interviewing, and to any data analysis software you will need to use (see the guides to using SPSS and NVivo in this book's **online resources**). Make sure you are comfortable with them all (the process of developing familiarity will also help you to establish whether you definitely need them) and check that they are in good working order. This includes checking that you have enough memory on your phone or the device and that it is fully charged.
5. **Do not wait until all your data have been collected to begin coding.** This applies to both quantitative and qualitative research. If you are conducting a paper questionnaire survey, begin coding your data and entering them into your data analysis package after you have received your first few completed questionnaires. The same point applies to qualitative data, such as interview transcripts—it is actually a specific recommendation of the proponents of grounded theory that data collection and data analysis should be intertwined (see Chapter 23, Section 23.4, for a description and discussion of grounded theory).
6. **Remember that transcribing recorded interviews takes a long time.** Allow at least six hours' transcription for every one hour of recorded interview talk, at least in the early stages of transcription.
7. **Never take risks with your personal safety.** Ethical research is not just about avoiding harm to participants, and some institutions have specific policies for lone researchers. Carefully consider any risks in your project and think about how they can be reduced (or preferably removed). For example, could your interviews be conducted in a public place such as a quiet coffee shop? Could you pair up with another researcher during your data collection?

In addition to this list, we asked our panellists for their top hints and tips for a successful research project. You can read what they said in Learn from experience 4.4.

LEARN FROM EXPERIENCE 4.4
Hints and tips for a successful research project

Our panellists have lots of hints and tips that will help you succeed in your research project, ranging from the importance of taking breaks to the value of seeking feedback from your friends.

> Find a balance that works for you—it's your personal project, after all—but make sure you are in control. Be strict with yourself about when you work, but make time to have breaks too. I also found creating a

mind map really useful at the start of my undergraduate dissertation, as I had never done a project of that size before. The mind map really helped me see how everything all linked together and where certain elements fitted best.

Jodie

Start early. Please. And don't be worried if your research design is radically different from the designs of your peers. All research questions are different so they all require different research methods.

Reni

Planning to speak with your supervisor after you submit each draft can alleviate the worries you may have about the quality of your work. And if you feel lost or overwhelmed, take a break, reach out to a friend, go for a walk. I often gained perspective on tricky elements of my research when brainstorming casually away from the computer. By giving your brain a rest, you will be able to return to your schedule refreshed and more productive.

Starr

I found that getting another student's perspective on your work can be really helpful, as it's easy to get vacuumed in your own thoughts and you can often overlook new ways of looking at your research questions or problems.

Zvi

You can read about our panellists' backgrounds and research experiences on page xxvi.

The final thing to consider is that social research is often more complicated in reality than it may appear when studying it from a distance in the classroom, or indeed from a textbook such as this! There is often not a single best solution, so it's important that you think critically at all times and keep in touch with your supervisor throughout the whole project.

KEY POINTS

- Follow the dissertation guidelines provided by your institution.
- Thinking about your research subject can be time-consuming, so allow plenty of time for this aspect of the dissertation process.
- Use your supervisor to the fullest extent allowed, and follow the advice they offer.
- Plan your time carefully, and be realistic about what you can achieve in the time available.
- Formulate some research questions to express what it is about your area of interest that you want to know.
- Writing a research proposal is a good way of getting started on your research project and will encourage you to set realistic objectives.
- Consider issues of access and sampling at an early stage.
- If possible, test your research methods by conducting a pilot study.
- Keep good records of what you do in your research as you go along.
- Don't wait until all your data have been collected before you start coding.

QUESTIONS FOR REVIEW

4

1. Why is it important to devise a timetable for your research project?
2. Why are research questions necessary?
3. What are the main useful sources of research questions?
4. What are the main types of research questions?
5. What criteria can we use to evaluate research questions?
6. What is the purpose of a research proposal, and how can it be useful?

ONLINE RESOURCES

www.oup.com/he/srm6e

You can find our notes on the answers to these questions within this chapter's **online resources**, together with:

- *audio/video comments* on this topic from our 'Learn from experience' panellists;
- *audio discussion from the authors* on the main sources of research questions (review question 3);
- *self-test questions* for further knowledge-checking;
- a *flashcard glossary* to help you recall key terms; and
- a *Student Researcher's Toolkit* containing practical materials and resources to help you conduct your own research project.

CHAPTER 5

REVIEWING THE LITERATURE

CHAPTER GUIDE

In this chapter we discuss the process and considerations involved in writing a literature review, which forms an important part of a research project or dissertation. We look at:

- narrative and systematic reviews
- how to search the existing literature
- how to correctly reference your work
- what plagiarism is and how to avoid it

5.1 Introduction

5

Once you have identified your research questions (see Chapter 4), the next step in any research project is to search the existing literature and write a literature review. In a research context, 'the literature' means existing research on a topic and 'review' means a critical evaluation of it. We conduct literature reviews to establish what is already known about a topic and, usually, to provide a background and justification for the investigation that we want to undertake.

There are two kinds of literature review: the narrative review and the systematic review. Narrative reviews are the traditional kind of literature review and they generally lead directly into a research project, whereas systematic reviews tend to be stand-alone (not a preface to research)—although their results may act as a springboard for research. We will discuss both types of review in the following sections, but will focus mainly on narrative reviews since it will nearly always be this type that people mean when they refer to 'doing your literature review' in the context of a student research project or dissertation. You might conduct a systematic review at some stage, and it is worth being aware that some of the processes involved can also be used within narrative reviews, but the narrative type will be your main concern as a student researcher.

5.2 Narrative reviews

What is a narrative review?

Most literature reviews take the form of narrative reviews (see Key concept 5.1), which aim to arrive at an overview of a topic or subject by conducting a reasonably comprehensive assessment and critical interpretation of the relevant literature, usually as a preface to conducting research in the area. This often involves examining and outlining the theory and research relating to your field of interest, and using this to frame and justify your research question(s). In Chapter 2 we discussed the relationship between theory and research and noted that the term 'theory' does not always relate to grand theories but can also mean the background literature on a topic. You may well find that some of the articles you read will use the subheading 'Theoretical Background' rather than 'Narrative Review' or, more commonly, 'Literature Review'.

When we look at the example of a narrative review in Research in focus 5.1 and at examples of written-up research in Chapter 25, we will see that researchers review the literature relating to their area of interest as a way of establishing why they are conducting the research and what its contribution is likely to be. Compared to systematic reviews, narrative reviews can sometimes seem a little unstructured and difficult to reproduce, leading some social scientists—usually those who endorse systematic reviews—to question how comprehensive they are and how their authors have decided what evidence to include. It is worth being aware of these criticisms, but they are often aimed at poorly conducted literature reviews that are not representative of all non-systematic reviews. As we will see in Section 5.3, systematic reviews are not always appropriate for social science research projects.

KEY CONCEPT 5.1
What is a narrative review?

A narrative review is the most common type of literature review that you will see in the social sciences. Whereas a systematic review (see Section 5.3) follows specific formal protocols and aims to gather and summarize *all* related research in a particular area, a narrative review summarizes the key work(s) selected by the author. This does not mean that it is not comprehensive—but it is the author who decides what to include and exclude, rather than an external set of criteria.

RESEARCH IN FOCUS 5.1
A narrative review

Let's have a look at how a narrative review can be used to provide a background for an empirical study. Williams et al. (2017a) set out to critically examine the advantages and disadvantages of using '**Big Data**' to study crime and disorder. Specifically, they investigated whether Twitter posts associated with disorder are related to actual recorded crime rates: is there a relationship between people tweeting about low-level disorder and actual occurrences of offline crime? We suggest that you look up this article and refer to it as you read our comments: **https://academic.oup.com/bjc/article/57/2/320/2623946**.

It's important to note, first of all, that the authors do not jump straight into the problem. They have carefully structured the article using subheadings, beginning in the introduction with a broad conceptualization of the topic and narrowing in on the specifics of the project. In the introduction section, titled 'Social Media Communications as a Source of Data for Criminology', the authors begin by talking broadly about the emergence of social media following the digital revolution, drawing on existing literature and theory to position Twitter users as 'sensors' for things that happen offline:

> In our exploratory study with big data, we make the assumption that each Twitter user is a *sensor* of offline phenomena. In the vein of Raudenbush and Sampson (1999), we consider these sensors, or nodes for systematic social observation, as part of a wide sensor-net covering *ecological zones* (in our case London boroughs). These sensors observe natural phenomenon—the sights, sounds and feel of the streets (Abbott 1997).
>
> (Williams et al. 2017a: 321)

Having positioned their research in the introduction, they then move on to set out the problem of how to approach 'Big Data' in the context of criminological research, in the section titled 'The Challenges of Big Social Data for Criminology: The 6 Vs' (volume, variety, velocity, veracity, virtue, and value). They point out a gap in the literature, thus justifying their own study:

> Criminology faces the challenge of how increasingly ubiquitous digital devices and the data they produce are reassembling its research methods apparatus. The exponential growth of social media uptake and the availability of vast amounts of information from these networks have created fundamental methodological and technical challenges. However, aside from recent papers by Chan and Bennet-Moses (2015) and Williams and Burnap (2015), big 'social' data have received little attention amongst criminologists, leaving the question of how as a discipline we respond to it largely unexplored.
>
> (Williams et al. 2017a: 322)

Following a series of insights into the difficulties and opportunities that 'Big Data' may provide, the next section is titled 'Big Data and Crime Estimation'. The authors discuss two studies in which social media data has been used for crime estimation, but note that their key limitation is that they were not concerned with the text of the tweets, again identifying a gap in the literature that their study will address; as they point out:

> The content of tweets may be relevant to the estimation of crime patterns, and simple geolocation data fail to relate to any possible theoretical explanation aside from routine activities.
>
> (Williams et al. 2017a: 324)

They follow this with an example of a study in which the content of tweets was used, but again, they criticize the methodology used with reference to another piece of published work:

> Although it is the first study to examine tweet content, Gerber's use of LDA [the abbreviation for a statistical model called Latent Dirichlet Allocation] is problematic given that it is an unsupervised method, meaning correlations between word clusters and crimes are not driven by prior theoretical insight (Chan and Bennett-Moses 2015).
>
> (Williams et al. 2017a: 324)

5

The authors conclude with a section on 'Broken Windows and Big Data', in which they briefly outline the 'broken windows' theory referring to the traditional literature: the idea that 'visible signs of neighbourhood degeneration are causally linked to crime' (2017a: 324), citing work published by Wilson and Kelling in 1982. They cite two more recent pieces of work, from 2015, to demonstrate that the theory is still relevant. To link all this back to Big Data, they discuss two studies in which a measure of physical disorder was constructed and validated using data from Boston, concluding that:

> Their findings revealed that (1) administrative records, collected for the purposes other than research, could be used to reliably construct measures of broken windows, and (2) these measures were significantly associated with levels of crime and disorder. These represent the first studies of broken windows using administrative 'big data', and the authors conclude: 'Going further, there are private databases, such as Twitter, cell phone records, and Flickr photo collections that are also geocoded and might be equally informative in building innovative measures of urban social processes. These various resources could be used to develop new versions of traditionally popular measures, like we have done here, or to explore new ones that have not been previously accessible' (O'Brien et al. 2015: 35). This paper takes on this task by testing three hypotheses.
>
> (Williams et al. 2017a: 325)

The main points to note about this literature review are as follows.

- It locates the study within existing conceptual and theoretical frameworks (sensors, broken windows theory, and the role of Big Data in criminological research).
- The authors are always progressing an argument and making the case for their research, developing ideas from other studies and linking them to their own work.
- Following on from the previous point, the review is more than a list of studies—it is *critical*, particularly where it identifies a gap in the literature or a deficiency in previous research.
- The review is structured with sub-headings around a number of themes.
- Immediately after the literature review, the authors present their hypotheses and identify the hypotheses' relationship with the literature.

There are many ways to write and structure a narrative review, and this is only one example. However, all well-written narrative reviews should result in the same outcome: by the end of the review, the reader understands the current state of research in the area, where the gaps are, and how this study links to existing theories and **concepts**. Most importantly, the reader can clearly see the argument that the authors are making to justify their research (even though they may disagree with the argument the authors are making!).

Why conduct a narrative review?

Why review the existing literature? A narrative literature review is almost certain to be a compulsory part of your research project, but you should not think of it as just a necessary formality. There are many reasons why it is in your interests to conduct a review (see Learn from experience 5.1). The most obvious reason is to establish what is already known about your area of interest, so that you do not simply repeat something that has already been done—in other words, so that you use the opportunity to *add* to the conversation and do not state something that is already known as though it is a new idea. A good literature review will demonstrate that you have engaged in scholarly practice based on your reading and understanding of other researchers' work and that you are knowledgeable in your chosen area. Using the existing literature on a topic is also a way of developing an argument about the significance of your research and where it leads. This means not simply reproducing the theories and opinions of others, but being able to interpret what they have written, possibly by using their ideas to support a particular viewpoint or argument. For **quantitative research**, a literature review can be used to help develop hypotheses about the **relationship** between two **variables** (such as gender and pay, or social class and educational attainment).

Essentially, a literature review provides a solid foundation for a research project by allowing you to get a clear

LEARN FROM EXPERIENCE 5.1

Why doing a literature review is important

Reviewing the literature is one of the first things you will do in a social research project. It is crucial because through wider reading we familiarize ourselves with our area of interest and learn what others have done. Jodie reflects on the importance of a literature review for her own work:

> A literature review is essential, as by reviewing what others have done and where the gaps are, it helps you identify where your study fits within the academic field and how it will offer something different. Your study may be attempting to fill some gaps, or to build upon other studies' findings. A literature review is crucial in situating your work and communicating the purpose of your research to others, and it also directly feeds into your research questions, in that it can inspire a new approach or avenue of investigation.
>
> Jodie

While it is often not essential that an undergraduate research project generates new knowledge, you may find that a review of the literature identifies some gaps in knowledge that your project can address, as Zvi and Scarlett reflect below.

> The literature I found really helped me to identify gaps in research and areas that are either over- or under-explored. For example, during my search of articles looking at the effect of screen time on children's sleep, I found that while the effect of the amount of time exposed to screens was well covered, there had been far less exploration of which activities on screens seem to be the most problematic, or whether the night-time use of screens was more problematic than screen time overall. It's only through an extensive literature review that you can begin to pick up on and highlight these subtle differences.
>
> Zvi

> When conducting a literature review for my project on the impact of social media on the mental wellbeing of young people, I found that while there was a lot of media coverage of the issue, there was little academic research that used a qualitative approach to look at the topic in-depth. I found that a lot of the research pertaining to the topic was survey-based and did not analyse the thoughts and opinions held by young people themselves. This then provided me with the justification and rationale for my project. I was not simply conducting a project that had already been done, but contributing to an underdeveloped area of research.
>
> Scarlett

 Access the **online resources** to hear our panellists' video reflections on this theme.

You can read about our panellists' backgrounds and research experiences on *page xxvi*.

picture of the existing discussion about your chosen area (what is already known about it; relevant concepts and theories; the **research methods** and designs used for studying it; associated controversies, inconsistencies, and unanswered research questions) and to see how this relates to your research question(s) as they stand. Researchers often revise and refine their research questions during, or as a result of, their literature review, to make sure that their study represents a meaningful contribution to the area.

We can summarize the many benefits of writing a literature review as follows.

- To establish what is already known in connection with your research area, so that you cannot be accused of reinventing the wheel.
- To give the person reading and assessing your work some background information about the area you are researching, in case they are not familiar with it.
- To learn from other researchers' mistakes and avoid making the same ones.
- To learn about different theoretical and methodological approaches to your research area.

5

- To help you develop an analytic framework.
- To give you new ideas about
  - variables that you could include in your research, and
  - further research questions that you could explore.
- To help you interpret your findings, and give you a way to present and frame them (in relation to what has already been said).
- To provide a platform for you to explain why your research will be significant—what it will add to the existing conversation.

Getting the most from your reading

Since quite a lot of time during the early stages of your research project will be taken up with reading the existing literature in order to write your review, it is important to prepare yourself for this stage. Getting the most out of your reading involves two main skills: effective note-taking, and reading actively and critically.

When we say 'effective note-taking', we mean taking notes about the material you read that are detailed and accurate, and that include the relevant publication details—see Section 5.5 (on referencing your work) for more details. This may seem time-consuming, but it is well worth the effort in the long run. It is extremely frustrating to find later on that you forgot to record the volume number of an article that you read, or the relevant page number within a book or article, and to have to go looking for it again in order to include it in your bibliography or reference list.

Turning to the second skill, it is very important that you do not simply read and summarize the literature, but approach it actively and critically. This does not necessarily mean simply criticizing the work of others. It means moving beyond straightforward description and asking questions about the significance of the work, such as: How does the **item** relate to others you have read? Are there any apparent strengths and deficiencies—perhaps in terms of methodology or in terms of the credibility of the conclusions drawn? What theoretical ideas have influenced the item you are reading? What are the implications of the author's ideas and/or findings? What was the author's objective in conducting the research? What are the main conclusions, and are they justified on the basis of the data provided in the item? What assumptions does the author make? Remember that your search for relevant literature should be guided by your research questions, but at the same time you should use your review of the literature to show why your research questions are important. For example, if one of your arguments in developing your research questions is that, although a lot of research has been done on a broad issue (such as the increase in social media use), little or no research has been done on a certain aspect of that issue (such as how an increase in social media use might impact on mental health), then the literature review is the part of your project where you can justify this claim. Alternatively, it might be that there are two competing positions, one that indicates a **positive relationship** between social media and mental health and another that indicates a **negative relationship**, and you are going to investigate which one provides a better understanding.

We provide some top tips for conducting a literature review in Tips and skills 5.1, but essentially, there are three important things to remember when it comes to making good use of the literature.

1. The literature review is an ongoing process, not a stage that can be ticked off the list and forgotten. You will want to return to the literature when you discuss your findings and in your conclusion, as this allows you to demonstrate the significance of your research, and you should keep reading relevant literature throughout your project (see the Gantt chart in Tips and skills 4.1). If you have written the literature review before beginning your data collection, you should treat this version as a draft—you may want to make substantial changes to it as you get close to completing your project.
2. Be selective in what you include in the final version of your written review. Trying to force everything you have read into your review (because you have put so much time and hard work into uncovering and reading the material) is not a good strategy. The written review should help you to develop and present your argument, and your argument will be clearest if you only refer to relevant material.
3. Try to *use* the literature to benefit your work (and make it clear in your write-up that you have done so—see Chapter 25), rather than just summarizing and being led by it. Aside from the fact that a simple summary is boring to read, it also does not tell the reader what your thoughts were about the literature, how it fits into your research project, or how it relates to your research questions.

TIPS AND SKILLS 5.1

Tips for conducting a literature review

Here are our top tips for conducting a narrative literature review.

- Try to be reasonably comprehensive in your coverage. At the very least, you should cover the most important readings relating to your area (your supervisor can advise on this).
- Consider dividing the review up into themes or sub-themes that will help to provide structure (see Research in focus 5.1 for an example).
- Try to be balanced in the way you present the literature. Do not give some authors or research more attention than others unless you want to make a particular point about their work, for example that you are going to try to reproduce their methods in a different context.
- Aim to comment on each item in your review and show how it relates to other items—avoid just describing its content and presenting the review as a series of points so that it looks more like a set of notes (A says this, B notes that, C says something else, D says something else again, etc.). Develop an argument about the items you include.
- Build up an argument by creating a 'story' about the literature. This means asking yourself: What key point or points do I want to get across about the literature as a whole? You will do this most effectively if you use your own words and avoid quoting too much. Put your own imprint on the literature.
- Don't be afraid to criticize the literature where appropriate. This is part of developing a critical stance, though it is not the only way. Another way is to show how the work of the authors you review has made a distinctive contribution to the field.
- Try to come up with a conclusion about the literature; tell your readers what you think your review demonstrates. If you want to show that there is a gap in the literature, or that there is an inconsistency, or that existing research has been dominated by a particular approach, you need to make that point very clear.

5.3 Systematic reviews

What is a systematic review?

As the name suggests, this more systematic approach to reviewing the literature involves adopting a defined set of procedures (see Key concept 5.2). It has gained interest for two main reasons. First, it is sometimes suggested (see, for example, Tranfield et al. 2003) that many literature reviews 'lack thoroughness' and reflect the biases of the researcher, and advocates of systematic reviews suggest that adopting explicit procedures makes such biases less likely to interfere. Second, in fields such as medicine, there is a history of evidence-based solutions to illnesses and developments of treatments. In the medical context, systematic reviews of the literature are often seen as an accompaniment to evidence-based approaches, as the aim of the review is to provide advice for clinicians and practitioners based on all available evidence. Such reviews are considered to be valuable for practitioners and decision-makers, particularly in areas where there is conflicting evidence concerning treatments (as often occurs in the case of medicine).

However, supporters of systematic reviews acknowledge that, unlike in medical science, where systematic reviews are common and often highly regarded, in social-scientific fields there is often no consensus about the key research questions because of the number of different theoretical approaches. Having said that, there are examples of systematic reviews in the social sciences concerned with the efficacy of certain policies and initiatives, for example the study by Piza et al. (2019) cited in Key concept 5.2. If you were conducting research in the area of surveillance and crime prevention, this review would be a great place to start. You can also read about how one of our panellists conducted a systematic review as part of their own research project in Learn from experience 5.2.

KEY CONCEPT 5.2
What is a systematic review?

The systematic review has been defined as 'a replicable, scientific and transparent process . . . that aims to minimize bias through exhaustive literature searches of published and unpublished studies and by providing an audit trail [a record] of the reviewer's decisions, procedures and conclusions' (Tranfield et al. 2003: 209).

This type of review is often contrasted with the traditional narrative review. Its supporters suggest that systematic reviews are more likely to generate unbiased and comprehensive accounts of the literature, especially in fields in which the aim is to understand whether a particular intervention has particular benefits (for example, whether a certain medicine helps to cure an illness or its symptoms), than those using the traditional review, which can be portrayed as random and less organized.

A systematic review that includes only quantitative studies and tries to summarize those studies quantitatively is a **meta-analysis** (see Chapter 14, Section 14.3), for example Piza et al.'s (2019) updated systematic review of the impact of CCTV surveillance on crime. Over recent years, there have been efforts to develop systematic review procedures for **qualitative research** studies, especially in the social sciences. **Meta-ethnography** (see Chapter 23, Section 23.8) is one such approach, but several different methods are in use, none of them historically widespread (Mays et al. 2005).

LEARN FROM EXPERIENCE 5.2
Conducting a systematic review

Most student research projects in the social sciences use narrative reviews, but a systematic review of an area can really strengthen your work and demonstrate a transparent, methodological, and comprehensive approach to reviewing the literature. Starr conducted a systematic review for her postgraduate project on refugee experiences of integration within Western higher education institutions:

> The objective was to gain a comprehensive understanding of my research topic through the available literature, to evidence gaps in the research and evaluate its comparative value. The element of comparison was a course requirement because my field is international and comparative education. Structuring a systematic literature review gave me a sense of confidence that I had a reliable overview of my topic. In the process, I solidified the key concepts necessary for my research, which I used as search terms in databases, branching searches of bibliographic sources, and Google queries. I was then able to define the different ways these concepts have been interpreted in the literature. In addition, I became comfortable managing large numbers of articles using the databases available through my university to conduct advanced searches using my defined terms. After completing my systematic review, I tailored my research question to fill a noticeable gap in the existing literature, and I was able to provide strong evidence of this gap.
>
> Starr

You can read about our panellists' backgrounds and research experiences on page xxvi.

Systematic review has attracted a great deal of attention in recent years, so it is worth exploring its main steps. Accounts of the systematic review process vary slightly, but they tend to involve the following steps in roughly this order.

1. Define the purpose and scope of the review.
2. Seek out studies relevant to the scope and purpose of the review.
3. Assess the relevance of each study for the research question(s).

4. Assess the quality of the studies from Step 3.
5. Extract the results of each study and synthesize the results.

Considering these in more detail, a systematic review needs an explicit statement of its purpose (in the form of, or leading to, a research question) so that the researcher can make consistent decisions about key issues, such as what kinds of research need to be searched for and what kinds of **samples** the research should relate to. It is often argued that, for a systematic review, the researcher and their team should assemble a panel to advise them on the precise formulation of the research question(s) to be examined (see Chapter 4) and also to help with suggestions for keywords for Step 2 (keywords are the search terms that you use to find relevant literature, and we discuss them in Section 5.4 under 'Keywords and defining search parameters').

For Step 2, the reviewer (the person conducting the systematic review) should seek out studies relevant to the research question(s). The search will be based on keywords and terms relevant to the purpose defined in Step 1. The reviewer must describe the search strategy in terms that allow it to be replicated by other researchers. The reviewer has to consider which kinds of publication should be incorporated. It is tempting to only search for research published in articles in peer-reviewed journals, because they are relatively easy to find online using keywords, but this would mean ignoring other valuable sources of evidence. The reviewer also needs to consider studies reported in books, in articles in non-peer-reviewed journals, and in what is often called 'grey literature' (for example, conference papers and reports by various organizations).

These searches will produce a huge number of possible readings for inclusion in the review, so at Step 3, the reviewer will reduce the list, often significantly, to a more manageable number by examining the abstracts of articles, and often articles themselves, in order to establish whether they are relevant. For example, in the research we discuss in Research in focus 5.2, Step 2 identified 7,048 reports, and the application of Step 3 reduced this number to 135.

RESEARCH IN FOCUS 5.2
A systematic review

Shepherd et al. (2006) published an account of the procedures they used to examine the barriers to healthy eating, and factors that encourage healthy eating, among young people aged 11–16 years. Table 5.1 sets out the main steps in doing a systematic review, as outlined in this chapter, and notes the corresponding procedures and practices in the review by Shepherd et al. These authors used methods for systematic review that have been developed by the Evidence for Policy and Practice Information and Coordinating Centre at the Institute of Education, University of London, which has a very comprehensive website outlining its approach and main methods, and providing full reports of many of the systematic reviews its members have conducted (**http://eppi.ioe.ac.uk/cms/Default.aspx?tabid=53&language=en-US**, accessed 25 July 2019). We suggest that you look up the Shepherd et al. article and refer to it as you read our comments: **https://academic.oup.com/bjc/article/57/2/320/2623946**.

One notable aspect of the summary in Table 5.1 is that the researchers separated out two types of study: intervention studies (studies that aimed to facilitate healthy eating, for example by training parents in nutrition and evaluating the outcomes of such an intervention) and non-intervention studies (studies where people were assessed in their existing state, for example a cohort or an interview study). This meant that the researchers could present a summary account of the findings and assess the quality of the studies before synthesizing the findings of both groups. This is not the case with every systematic review, but it was necessary here because the authors applied different quality criteria depending on the type of study. In the case of the non-intervention studies, each one was assessed on whether it met the following seven criteria:

1. an explicit theoretical framework and/or literature review;
2. a clear statement of the aims and objectives of the research;
3. a clear account of the context within which the research was conducted;
4. a clear account of the nature of the sample and how it was formed;

5. a clear description of methods of data collection and analysis;
6. 'analysis of the data by more than one researcher' (Shepherd et al. 2006: 242);
7. sufficient information provided to allow the reader to see how the conclusions were derived from the data.

You can see from the information in the table that this set of criteria, and a corresponding set for the intervention studies, reduced their numbers considerably.

In their synthesis of their review findings, the authors report that the non-intervention studies identified several barriers to, and facilitators of, healthy eating. For example, they write: 'Facilitating factors included information about nutritional content of foods/better labeling, parents and family members being supportive, healthy eating to improve or maintain one's personal appearance, will-power and better availability/lower pricing of healthy snacks' (Shepherd et al. 2006: 255). The authors linked such findings with intervention studies, arguing that 'juxtaposing barriers and facilitators alongside effectiveness studies allowed us to examine the extent to which the needs of young people had been adequately addressed by evaluated interventions' (Shepherd et al. 2006: 255).

TABLE 5.1

Steps in systematic review using the example of Shepherd et al.'s review of barriers to, and facilitators of, healthy eating among young people (Shepherd et al. 2006)

Steps in systematic review	Corresponding practices in Shepherd et al. (2006)
1. Define the purpose and scope of the review	Review question: 'What is known about the barriers to, and facilitators of, healthy eating among young people?' (Shepherd et al. 2006: 243).
2. Seek out studies relevant to the scope and purpose of the review	The authors used a combination of terms to do with healthy eating (e.g. 'nutrition'), health promotion or the causes of health or ill-health (e.g. 'at-risk populations'), and young people (e.g. 'teenager'). In order for a study to be included in the review, it had to be about 'the barriers to, and facilitators of, healthy eating among young people' and to have been conducted in the UK, in English. The authors included both intervention studies (also known as outcome evaluations, i.e. evaluating the outcome of an intervention) and non-intervention studies (e.g. cohort or case control studies, or interview studies). They formulated guidelines separately for these two types of study. Shepherd et al. searched several online bibliographical databases for the studies, including SSCI and PsycINFO. They also searched lists of references and other sources.
3. Assess the relevance of each study for the research question(s)	The authors gradually trimmed an initial 7,048 references down to 135 reports, relating to 116 studies. Of those studies, 75 were intervention studies, 32 were non-intervention studies, and 9 were prior systematic reviews. Once the full set of inclusion criteria were applied, only 22 intervention studies and 8 non-intervention studies met the criteria for what the authors refer to as 'in-depth systematic review' (Shepherd et al. 2006: 242).
4. Assess the studies from Step 3	Two researchers entered data for each study into a database, summarized the findings from each one, and assessed its methodological quality. They used separate quality criteria for intervention and non-intervention studies. The application of the 8 criteria for intervention studies resulted in just 7 being regarded as 'methodologically sound' and the results of just these 7 studies are the focus of the authors' summary.
5. Analyse each study and synthesize the results	Shepherd et al. conducted two separate syntheses of findings for the intervention and non-intervention studies and a third synthesis for the two types jointly. The authors say of the third synthesis: 'a [table] was constructed which laid out the barriers and facilitators identified by young people [in the non-intervention studies] alongside descriptions of the interventions included in the in-depth systematic review of outcome evaluations. The matrix was stratified by four analytical themes to characterize the levels at which the barriers and facilitators appeared to be operating: the school, family and friends, the self and practical and material resources' (Shepherd et al. 2006: 241).

Step 4 involves assessing the quality of the selected studies, an aspect of research that we cover in relation to quantitative and qualitative research in Chapters 7 and 16, respectively. The reviewer needs to decide on a set of quality criteria, such as whether an appropriate **research design** and research methods were used and whether they were effectively implemented (you can find checklists for assessing quality, but note that it is important to use criteria that are appropriate for the kinds of research you are examining). Sometimes, systematic reviewers will exclude studies that fail to meet the minimum criteria, but this can mean that the review is conducted on an extremely small sample. Alternatively, reviewers will categorize studies in terms of the extent to which they meet the quality criteria and may take this into account when synthesizing the research.

The fifth and final step involves recording important information such as the date when the research was conducted; location; sample size; data collection methods; and the main findings. The reviewer then produces a synthesis of the results. If the findings of a group of studies are quantitative in character, the reviewer may conduct a meta-analysis (see Chapter 14). This involves producing summary statistics from the quantitative data supplied with each study. For other kinds of systematic review, such as those based on qualitative research or where there is a combination of both quantitative and qualitative studies, systematic reviewers try to establish a 'narrative synthesis' to 'tell the story' of the research. This uses a narrative to bring together the key findings relating to the research question, often accompanied by simple statistical summaries, for example the percentage of studies that examined a certain issue or that adopted a particular perspective. One advantage of a narrative synthesis is that it can be used as a platform for reviewing and summarizing both quantitative and qualitative studies. In contrast, synthesis techniques such as meta-analysis and meta-ethnography can mainly be used for summarizing quantitative and qualitative studies, respectively (see Chapters 14 and 23).

Evaluating the systematic review

So how useful is the systematic review process? Tranfield et al. (2003) suggest that the process provides a more reliable foundation on which to design research because it is based on a comprehensive understanding of what we know about a subject. This means that the process does not only benefit practitioners: it can help researchers summarize findings. Supporters of the systematic review also recommend the approach for its transparency, because the grounds on which studies were selected and how they were analysed are clearly detailed and can be replicated.

It has sometimes been suggested that the systematic review approach is not useful for all areas of literature, because studies are not always concerned with whether a certain **independent variable** produces certain kinds of effects. Meta-analysis of quantitative studies requires this kind of research question, but qualitative studies and indeed some sorts of quantitative investigation are not necessarily in this format. The perception that systematic reviews have limited relevance may have emerged because many early systematic reviews were of the 'what works?' or 'does X work?' kind, and involved assessing and reviewing the literature relating to various kinds of intervention. In more recent years, though, a wider range of research questions have been subjected to systematic review and the process has been used for both qualitative studies and quantitative non-intervention studies. For example, Rees et al. (2013) conducted a systematic review of the evidence about the perceptions of young people aged 12–18 years concerning obesity, body size and shape, and weight. None of the research questions were expressed in terms of causes and effects; instead they were about perceptions, such as 'What are young people's views about influences on body size?' (Rees et al. 2013: 16).

A further criticism is that the systematic review approach can make the process of reviewing the literature very bureaucratic (overly concerned with procedure and following set rules), because it is more concerned with the technical aspects of how the review is conducted than with the analytical interpretations it generates. We can see this in the way that systematic reviews include extensive descriptions of search terms used, how potential candidates for inclusion in the review were sieved, which databases were used, etc. A final potential limitation is that the systematic review approach assumes that we can make objective judgements about the quality of an article. In relation to qualitative research in particular, there is little consensus on how the studies should be assessed (see Chapter 16).

5

5.4 Searching the existing literature

To conduct an effective search of the existing literature, you first need to carefully read some books, journals, and reports in your area of interest. You might well have in mind a few initial references when beginning your project: these may come from recommended reading in course modules, or from textbooks. However, this is only a starting point: you will find that the bibliographies provided at the end of textbook chapters or articles will usually provide you with many more relevant references that you can follow up. To really understand what literature is already out there, you will need to conduct a thorough search of online databases using keywords that help to define the boundaries of your chosen area of research (see 'Keywords and defining search parameters' later in this section). We will now explore what online databases are and how they work, followed by a more detailed look at how to use keywords to help you find relevant literature.

Online databases

Online databases allow you to search a vast repository of academic sources by keyword, author, and often also by date of publication. Many of these databases integrate with referencing software (see Tips and skills 5.3) so that you can easily import long lists of bibliographic information, which will save you a lot of time if your literature review is extensive. Online databases will often give you full electronic access to an article in PDF format, meaning that you don't have to physically visit the library. Having said that, you will find that not all sources are available through this service, particularly older work. If you're unsure of what is and isn't available or you can't find what you are looking for, then you should ask your subject librarian for help—after all, that's what they are there for (see Learn from experience 5.3).

LEARN FROM EXPERIENCE 5.3
Ask a librarian

By the time you come to work on your own research project you will have had some experience of searching and reviewing the literature, but conducting your own project from scratch and identifying the right sources independently can be daunting. So ask for help! No one expects you to do a research project on your own, and as a student you have access to a wide range of experts who can support you, including librarians who are experts in searching and accessing literature. Our panellists can't recommend getting help from librarians strongly enough, as Scarlett and Starr discuss below.

> You may feel embarrassed to ask, but librarians are there to help you access the books and online resources you need, and they will always be happy to show you the ropes. By asking the librarian's advice, I learnt how to properly search for resources online, which it turns out does not simply involve typing something in and hoping for the best! As my research project was looking at young people's mental wellbeing and the impact of social media, I wanted to find resources that included research which combined both of these topics. I found that when I was searching for such resources, the results were varied and it felt as though I was searching for two separate things. It was only when I asked the librarian that I realized what I was doing wrong. The librarian explained to me the importance of using Boolean operators when searching for literature. To find the resources I wanted, I simply needed to search 'young people's mental wellbeing AND social media' in order to bring up results that included both of these two topics. If I was interested in just young people's mental wellbeing without the topic of social media, I could search for 'young people's mental wellbeing NOT social media', which would remove all the sources that included social media. Lastly, if I was interested in young people's mental wellbeing and social media as two separate topics, I could search for 'young people's mental wellbeing OR social media', which would bring up results for the two topics separately.
>
> Scarlett

> Librarians are amazing! They are there to help you navigate the resources available at your university—don't be shy. At Stockholm University, I often ordered books through the interlibrary loan service as a way

of accessing electronic and physical copies of books that were catalogued in libraries in other areas of Sweden. Additionally, the librarians were very efficient in ordering new books that I requested for my research. I did most of my interaction with librarians online, because the library website made it easy to chat about and order resources quickly and easily. My advice is that before you begin your project, you should talk to a librarian and explore the library website as well as the databases available to you, so that you feel equipped at the start of your research schedule.

Starr

 Access the **online resources** to hear our panellists' video reflections on this theme.

You can read about our panellists' backgrounds and research experiences on page xxvi.

Perhaps the most commonly used and comprehensive online database is Web of Science (WoS), formerly known as Web of Knowledge. WoS contains academic sources from over 250 disciplines and contains journal articles, reviews, and the proceedings of conferences and other events. If your library has a subscription then you can access it here: **https://login.webofknowledge.com**. Although the search tools might seem daunting at first, they are intuitive. The following tips should get you started.

- After you have logged in you will see the 'Basic Search' tab. You can use this to specify topics, titles, authors, and editors that you're interested in. By selecting 'Add row', you can refine your search in several ways, for example by specifying that you want to find articles containing the words 'migration' but not the word 'bird'. Alternatively, you could search for the keyword 'migration' and the author 'Bloggs J'.
- The 'Timespan' option allows you to specify how far back you want the search to go. This may or may not be relevant depending on how recent (or not) your area of interest is. You can choose to search in a custom time range if none of the other options are appropriate (note that WoS goes back as far as 1900!).
- The 'Cited Reference Search' function is very useful if you have already found a key piece of work. It allows you to search for work that has cited a particular article, so you can see how the key piece of literature you have identified has been used by other authors.

To make the most of these tools you will need to become comfortable using search functions such as AND, OR, and NOT. The technical term for these functions is Boolean operators, but despite the formal-sounding name (they are named after a nineteenth-century mathematician called George Boole), the concept is quite simple and you are likely to use them every day for searching online. As an example, let's assume that you are researching hate crime on Twitter. Searching 'hate crime on Twitter' may return some results, but it is likely that many studies concerned with this topic did not use that exact phrasing. Here are three different ways that you might specify a search using Boolean logic.

- You could search 'hate crime' AND 'Twitter' meaning that only articles containing both those words, but not necessarily in that order, would be returned.
- If you were interested in multiple social media platforms, you could amend your search to include 'Twitter' OR 'Facebook' OR 'YouTube'.
- If you wanted to search all social media platforms apart from YouTube, you could amend your search to 'social media' NOT 'YouTube'.

The way in which you add together multiple conditions on WoS depends on whether you're using the 'Basic Search' or the 'Advanced Search', and for some more detailed queries the latter might be the only option. If you need help with searching, then you should ask a librarian or your supervisor (as our panellists advise in Learn from experience 5.3).

There is a current trend in academia to move away from publishing in journals that require you to have a subscription to access their content. Increasingly, you will find that articles are available freely online, either through a university's repositories or on journal websites themselves. These publications are referred to as 'open access' and can generally be found using search engines such as Google Scholar (see Tips and skills 5.2).

Researchers may also upload their publications to websites designed to promote the sharing of published work, such as ResearchGate, which boasts over 118 million publications (**www.researchgate.net/search**), and Academia.edu, which has over 100 million researchers on its platform (**www.academia.edu/**).

Another powerful repository that your institution might subscribe to is Nexis (**www.nexis.com/**)—this is a database of newspapers from around the world that you can search by headline and timespan. While media reports should be treated as secondary to academic literature, they can be useful in providing context for your study, and Nexis may be an important source of data for projects carrying out **content analysis** (see Chapter 13).

You may also benefit from accessing non-academic sources from a wide range of governmental, charity, and third sector organizations—the kind of content we referred to earlier as grey literature. Depending on who has published them, these documents may or may not be subject to the same rigorous reviewing process as academic journal articles, but they are often important for policy research and can set the tone for public debates. For example, any study on the persecution of sexual minorities should consider the wide range of reports published by charities such as Stonewall. These types of sources can be found using publicly available search engines such as Google.

At this point we should offer a word of warning about using Google and other search engines for research. Online search engines are very useful for researching all sorts of things. There is a huge amount of varied, freely available information about social research online that can be quickly and easily accessed without the need for university agreements. However, the quantity of information available can cause problems as it can be very difficult to differentiate what is useful and reliable from that which is too simplistic, too commercially oriented, too highly opinionated, or just not academic enough—or simply misleading and incorrect. So it is important to be selective in how you use information you find online and to evaluate your sources critically.

Remember that anyone can put information on the internet, so, when looking at websites, you need to evaluate whether the information you have found is useful. Consider:

TIPS AND SKILLS 5.2
Using online information

A searching tool

Google's academic search engine, Google Scholar, can be accessed from the Google home page and is a simple way to search broadly for academic literature. Searches are focused on peer-reviewed papers, theses, books, abstracts, and articles, from academic publishers, professional societies, preprint repositories, universities, and other scholarly organizations. Google Scholar also tells you how often an item has been cited by other people. This can be very useful in assessing the importance of an idea or a particular scholarly writer. See **http://scholar.google.com**.

Current affairs

For case study analyses and keeping up to date on current social issues, the BBC News website is reasonably well balanced and quite analytical: **www.bbc.co.uk**.

Statistics on social trends

Many national governments make a huge amount of data about social trends available online, from reports on the educational background of young offenders to the number of premises per square kilometre licensed to sell alcohol: for example, the UK's **www.statistics.gov.uk**.

European statistics relating to specific countries, industries, and sectors can be found on the Eurostat pages of Europa, the portal to the European Union website: **https://ec.europa.eu/eurostat**.

- The author—who is the author of the site, and what is their motive for publishing?
- The location—where is the site located? The URL can help you here. Is it an academic site (.ac.uk in the UK or .edu in the US—although not all research institutions across the globe use these) or a government site (.gov), a non-commercial organization (.org), or a commercial one (.com or .co)?
- Currency—how recently was the site updated? Many sites will give you a 'last updated' date, but you can get clues as to whether a page is being well maintained by whether the links are up to date and by its general appearance.

Try to confine your literature search to reliable websites, such as those mentioned in this chapter. For more on this issue, see Tips and skills 5.2. If you're in any doubt about the scale of the problems associated with internet-based information, Wikipedia keeps a log of the hoaxes that have been discovered (Wikipedia defines a hoax as a 'clear and deliberate attempt to deceptively present false information as fact') here: **https://en.wikipedia.org/wiki/Wikipedia:List_of_hoaxes_on_Wikipedia** (accessed 20 March 2021). When you consider the fact that a hoax is only identified when someone choses to challenge it, and that there are over 5.8 million articles on English language Wikipedia alone (Wikipedia n.d., b), the need to be critical and question the authenticity of online content becomes clear. Even Wikipedia point out that 'many hoaxes remain undiscovered' (Wikipedia n.d., a).

Keywords and defining search parameters

Typing in the title of your project, or a sentence or long phrase, as your search term might be a good place to start, but often it is not a good idea because unless someone has written something with the same title, you are unlikely to find very much! So before searching any database, you will need to identify some keywords that can be entered into the search engines and that will allow you to find suitable references (see the example we gave previously of hate speech on Twitter). Journal articles often include lists of keywords at the beginning, which might provide a useful starting point. It is a good idea to glance through articles you have identified to check that they are relevant. Titles are a good place to start, but the abstract (or, for a report, the executive summary) should give you a full outline of what the research is about, and will often also tell you what the authors did and what they found. When you find two or three articles that are relevant to your research and that have lists of keywords, it might be useful to use some of these keywords (the ones that are most relevant to your research) for searching for other articles. You will also need to think of alternative or related terms for the ones used and try to match your language to that of the source you are searching. Often this will help you to refine your ideas (for example, *deprivation* and *poverty* are not the same thing). Be prepared to experiment and to amend your keywords as your research progresses; you may find as you search the literature that there are other ways of describing your subject. You should also become familiar with 'operators' such as AND, OR, and NOT, as discussed earlier.

In some areas of research, there are a huge number of relevant references. If this is the case for your chosen area, try to identify the major pieces of research and work outwards from there. Make sure that you move on to the next stage of your research in accordance with your timetable, so that you set a firm time limit on your initial searches, as otherwise you could keep searching indefinitely. This does not mean that you no longer need to search for relevant literature (as we noted in 'Getting the most from your reading', your review will be ongoing), but you may need to force yourself to move on. Ask for your supervisor's advice on how much more you need to search the literature. Figure 5.1 outlines one way of searching the literature. The most important thing to remember—as shown in Steps 2a, 2b, and 2c in the figure—is to keep a good record of the process so that you can keep track of what you have done. Also, when you give your supervisor drafts of your literature review, make sure you include all the references and their details so that they can assess the coverage and quality of your review.

At each stage, keep a record of what you have done and your reasons for certain decisions. This will be useful in helping you remember how you proceeded and for when you write up a description and justification of your literature search strategy, which can form part of your methods section. When making notes on literature that you read, you should make notes on the content of the research and the method that the researchers used, as well as on its relevance to your own work, and keep thinking about how each item will contribute to your critical review of the literature.

5

FIGURE 5.1
One way of searching the literature

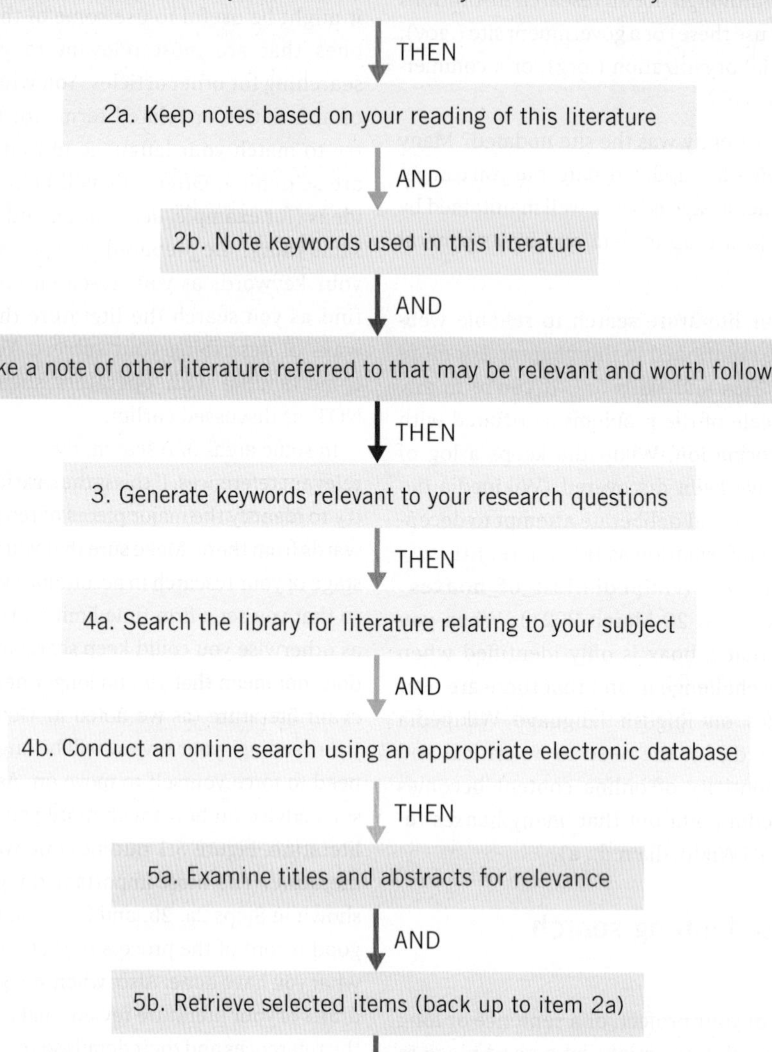
1. Read books or articles known to you or recommended by others related to your research questions
THEN
2a. Keep notes based on your reading of this literature
AND
2b. Note keywords used in this literature
AND
2c. Make a note of other literature referred to that may be relevant and worth following up
THEN
3. Generate keywords relevant to your research questions
THEN
4a. Search the library for literature relating to your subject
AND
4b. Conduct an online search using an appropriate electronic database
THEN
5a. Examine titles and abstracts for relevance
AND
5b. Retrieve selected items (back up to item 2a)
AND
5c. Check regularly for new publications

5.5 Referencing your work

Referencing (or 'citing') other people's work is an important academic convention, and one with which you will probably already be familiar from the rest of your studies. Including frequent and accurate references shows that you are aware of the historical development of your subject and that you recognize that your own research builds on existing work. In the context of your whole dissertation or student research project, referencing will generally show your understanding of methodological considerations and help to reinforce your argument, but in the literature review specifically, referencing is vital in demonstrating your knowledge and understanding of the subject.

A key skill in writing your literature review (as we noted in 'Getting the most from your reading') is keeping a record of what you have read, including all the bibliographic details about each article or book that will go into your bibliography or list of references (they are different things: see Key concept 5.3). For larger research projects it can be useful to use notecards or software packages that are designed specifically for this purpose, such as EndNote or Reference Manager (see Tips and skills 5.3), but for a small research project you could simply keep a digital record of all the items that you have read in a (carefully saved and backed up) Word document or Excel spreadsheet. Although you may not include all of these items in your final reference list, the important thing is that you keep your bibliographic records up to date and do not leave this task until the end of the writing-up process, when you will probably be under significant time pressure.

Methods of referencing

Your institution will probably have its own guidelines as to which style of referencing you should use in your dissertation, and if it does you should definitely follow them. The punctuation and style of references—such as where to place a comma, or whether to capitalize a title in full or just the first word—varies considerably from source to source. For example, in some books and journals using Harvard referencing (discussed below), the surname of the author is separated from the date in the text with a comma—for example (Name, 1999)—but in others, such as this book, there is no comma. The important thing is to follow the advice of your institution. Technical issues aside, we will now look in detail at the two main methods used for referencing: the *Harvard system* and the use of *footnotes and endnotes.*

The Harvard system

Following this widely-used system means that whenever you paraphrase the argument or ideas of an author or authors in your writing, you add parentheses (curved

KEY CONCEPT 5.3

What are the bibliography and reference list?

Students often get confused between the terms 'bibliography' and 'reference list', so they are worth clarifying here. A reference list should contain only the readings that are cited in your work. In contrast, a bibliography would include all of the readings that you have cited *plus* any other reading that you did around the topic.

TIPS AND SKILLS 5.3

Using bibliographic software

EndNote and Reference Manager are two of the leading software tools used for publishing and managing bibliographies, and your university may have a site licence for one of these packages. They are used by academic researchers and students, and they effectively allow you to compile your own personal reference database. The bibliographic records you collect can then be automatically formatted to suit different requirements—for example, to comply with the referencing requirements of your institution. Other advantages to using these tools are that they allow you to export references directly from databases such as WoS (as discussed in Section 5.4 under 'Online databases'), and they have search options that can help you locate particular references.

In the long run, using these tools can save you time and effort and reduce the possibility of errors, but it might not be worth learning how to use them just for the purposes of a student dissertation. On the other hand, if knowledge of the software may be useful to you in the longer term—for example, if you are thinking of going on to pursue an academic career, or to work in a field where research skills are valued—then it may be worth familiarizing yourself with one of the packages.

brackets, as used here) immediately after, which contain the surname of the author(s) and the year of publication (see Tips and skills 5.4). If you are quoting the author(s), you put quotation marks around the quoted text, and after the year of publication you include the page number where the quotation is from. All books, articles, and other sources that you have cited in the text are then given in a list of references at the end of the dissertation, ordered alphabetically by author surname. This is by far the most

common referencing system in social research and the one that is followed in this book. It is, therefore, the style that we would encourage you to use if your university does not require you to follow its own guidelines.

Footnotes and endnotes

This approach involves the use of superscript numbers (for example [1, 2, 3...]) in the text that refer to a note at the bottom of the page or the end of the text where the reference is given in full, together with the page number if it is a direct quotation (see Tips and skills 5.4). If a source is cited more than once, an abbreviated version of the reference is given in any subsequent citation, which is why this is often called the short-title system. As well as being used to refer to sources, footnotes and endnotes are often used to provide additional detail, including comments from the writer about the source being cited.

One of the advantages of the footnote or numeric method is that it can be less distracting to the reader in terms of the flow of the text than the Harvard method, where long strings of references can sometimes make a sentence or a paragraph difficult to follow. Software such as Word make it relatively simple to insert notes, and many students find that this is a convenient way of referencing their work. However, it can be difficult to use well,

TIPS AND SKILLS 5.4
The Harvard system and the note system: approaches to referencing

The examples below show some fictitious examples of referencing in published work that demonstrate how the two different reference systems are used. Bear in mind that it is essential when preparing your own referencing, both in the text and in the bibliography or list of references, that you *follow the conventions and style that are recommended by your institution for preparing an essay, dissertation, or thesis.*

Harvard system

	Reference in the text	Reference in the bibliography, list of references, or footnote/endnote
Reference to a book	As Name and Other (2021) argue, the line between migration and tourism is becoming increasingly blurred.	Name, A., and Other, S. (2021). *Title of Book in Italics.* Place of Publication: Publisher.
Reference to a direct quotation from a source	However, research on tourism was found to be very relevant to an understanding of migrants' experiences 'because the motivations of tourists and migrants are increasingly similar' (Name and Other 2021: 123).	Name, A., and Other, S. (2021). *Title of Book in Italics.* Place of Publication: Publisher.

5

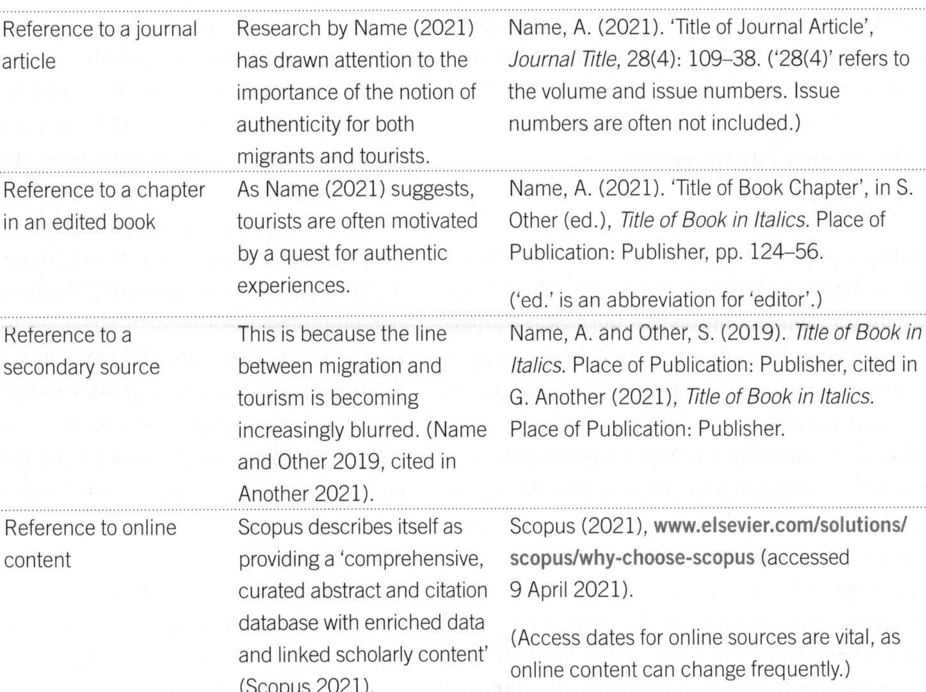

Reference to a journal article	Research by Name (2021) has drawn attention to the importance of the notion of authenticity for both migrants and tourists.	Name, A. (2021). 'Title of Journal Article', *Journal Title*, 28(4): 109–38. ('28(4)' refers to the volume and issue numbers. Issue numbers are often not included.)
Reference to a chapter in an edited book	As Name (2021) suggests, tourists are often motivated by a quest for authentic experiences.	Name, A. (2021). 'Title of Book Chapter', in S. Other (ed.), *Title of Book in Italics.* Place of Publication: Publisher, pp. 124–56. ('ed.' is an abbreviation for 'editor'.)
Reference to a secondary source	This is because the line between migration and tourism is becoming increasingly blurred. (Name and Other 2019, cited in Another 2021).	Name, A. and Other, S. (2019). *Title of Book in Italics.* Place of Publication: Publisher, cited in G. Another (2021), *Title of Book in Italics.* Place of Publication: Publisher.
Reference to online content	Scopus describes itself as providing a 'comprehensive, curated abstract and citation database with enriched data and linked scholarly content' (Scopus 2021).	Scopus (2021), **www.elsevier.com/solutions/scopus/why-choose-scopus** (accessed 9 April 2021). (Access dates for online sources are vital, as online content can change frequently.)

Note system

	Reference in the text	Reference in the bibliography, list of references, or footnote/endnote
Reference to a book	On the other hand, research by Name and Other[3] has drawn attention to the influence of intrinsic factors on employee motivation.	[3] A. Name and S. Other, *Title of Book in Italics.* Place of Publication, Publisher (2021), pp. 170–77.
Reference to online content	Scopus describes itself as providing a 'comprehensive, curated abstract and citation database with enriched data and linked scholarly content'.[39]	[39] Scopus, **www.elsevier.com/en-gb/solutions/scopus** (2021) (accessed 9 April 2021).

and people are sometimes unsure whether or not also to include a separate bibliography or reference list. As not having a bibliography or list of references is a potential disadvantage to this style of referencing, your institution might recommend that you do not use it.

The role of the bibliography or reference list

What makes a good bibliography or list of references? You might initially think that length is a good measure, because a longer bibliography containing more references might imply that the author has done a very comprehensive search of the literature. This is true up to a point, but it is also important for the bibliography to be selectively focused—it should not include everything that has ever been written about a subject but instead should reflect the author's informed judgement of the importance and suitability of sources. One useful indicator of quality is the reputation of the journal in which an article is published, but you should not rely on this exclusively: there might be relevant articles in lesser-status journals. It is important to be aware of these judgements of quality and to ask for your supervisor's advice in making them.

Another important feature of a good bibliography relates to secondary referencing. This is when you refer to an article or book that has been cited in another source, such as a textbook, and you do not, or cannot, access the original article or book from which it was taken. It is not a good idea to rely heavily on secondary references because you are dependent upon the interpretation of the original text that is offered by the authors of the secondary text. This may be adequate for some parts of your literature review, but there is always the potential for different interpretations of the original text, and this potential increases the further you are from the original source. So it is wise to be cautious about using secondary references, and it's best to go back to the original source if you can, particularly if it is an important one for your subject. Thinking deeply 5.1 gives an example of how an author's work can be referenced in ways that involve reinterpretation and misinterpretation long after the date of publication.

A further feature of a good reference list is that each item listed should be mentioned within the main text, and integrated into it in a way that shows you have read it in detail and understood its implications. This is much more impressive than if a reference is inserted in a way

THINKING DEEPLY 5.1
The problem of using secondary literature sources

We have noted that it is important to be careful when using second-hand accounts of theories or findings as they can be misleadingly represented in publications—though hopefully not in this book! Misinterpreting the work of others is not a new phenomenon, and it can be tempting with older studies to rely on the interpretation of others rather than seeking out the original source. An interesting case is the 'Affluent Worker' research that is described in Research in focus 7.2. This research entailed a survey in the 1960s of predominantly affluent workers in three firms in Luton. It is regarded as a classic of British sociology. Platt, one of the authors of the books that were published from this research, conducted a search for books and articles that discussed the study's findings. Platt (1984) showed that several authors misinterpreted the findings. Examples of such misinterpretation were the following assertions.

- *The study was based on just car workers.* It was not—only one of the three companies was a car firm.
- *The study was based on just semi-skilled or mass-production workers.* It was not—there were a variety of skill levels and technological forms among the manual sample.
- *The research 'found' instrumentalism*—that is, an instrumental orientation to work. This is misleading—instrumentalism was an inference about the data, not a finding as such.

The point is that sometimes authors misinterpret the work of others, so it is always a good idea to go back to the original source if you can. If you can't find the original source, then at least make sure that you reference it as a secondary source (see Tips and skills 5.4).

that does not closely relate to what is being said in the text, or add anything to the discussion.

In summary, then, a good bibliography or list of references

1. is reasonably long but also selective, including high-quality and genuinely relevant sources;
2. includes mainly primary sources, only using secondary references when it has not been possible to access the original source;
3. includes references that are mentioned in, and well integrated with, the main text.

5.6 Avoiding plagiarism

An issue to bear in mind when writing up your literature review is the need to avoid plagiarizing the work that you are reading. In this section, we look at what plagiarism is, why it is to be avoided, and how you can ensure that you avoid it.

What is plagiarism?

To plagiarize is defined in *The Concise Oxford Dictionary* as to 'take and use another person's (thoughts, writings, inventions . . .) as one's own'. Plagiarism does not just relate to the literature you read in the course of preparing an essay or report. Taking large amounts of unattributed material from essays written by others or from websites is also plagiarism. It is also possible to self-plagiarize—this is when a person lifts material that they have previously written and passes it off as new work.

There is a widespread view that plagiarism among students is more prevalent than in previous decades and still increasing, though whether this is in fact the case is difficult to establish for certain. Generally, it is difficult to establish how widespread student plagiarism is, and estimates of its prevalence vary significantly. In a study of two assignments for a business course at a New Zealand university, Walker (2010) found that just over one-quarter of the total number of assignments revealed some level of plagiarism. He also found that the level of plagiarism declined between the first and second assignments, suggesting that students were less inclined to plagiarize when they had been notified of the marker's comments on the first assignment. The widely accepted view is that the apparent increase in plagiarism is a result of the fact that nearly all students now have easy access to online content, meaning that they can copy and paste text from websites, e-journal articles, e-books, online essays sold commercially, and numerous other sources.

Why is it important to avoid plagiarism?

In academic circles, plagiarism is often viewed as morally wrong—it is seen as a form of cheating that is as bad as actions like making up research findings. This is because academic practice places a high value on the originality of the work that is presented, whatever its format. Your tutor will usually be able to tell if large chunks of your essay or report have been lifted from another source and just punctuated by some of your own words. In fact, this change in style can be a giveaway—the shift is often very obvious and prompts the tutor to consider whether some or much of the assignment you submitted has been plagiarized. And it is worth noting that even if you acknowledge the sources of quotations, your tutor is unlikely to be impressed by over-reliance on quotations that are just connected by linking sentences, as this makes it hard to establish what your own thoughts are on the issue. You should try to express your ideas in your own words, and you should properly acknowledge ideas that are not your own.

The final reason you should avoid plagiarizing at all costs is because when found in student work (and indeed the work of professional academics) it is nearly always punished, which could involve having a mark set to zero or, in extreme cases, being disqualified from all future assessments. Universities are so concerned about the growth in the number of plagiarism cases that come before examination boards that they now make heavy use of plagiarism detection software, which compares the content of student work with existing information online and in its database (for example, Turnitin UK: www.turnitin.com/, accessed 28 February 2019). This means that, as several writers (e.g. McKeever 2006) have observed, the internet is a facilitator of plagiarism but also provides a way to detect it. Even well-known search engines like Google can be used to detect student plagiarism by searching for unique strings of words.

How can you avoid plagiarism?

We have established that plagiarism is to be avoided at all costs, but how can you do this?

First, do not 'lift' large sections of text from other sources without making it clear that they are in fact quotations. This makes it clear that the text in question is not your own work but that you are making a point by quoting someone. It is easy to get this wrong. In June 2006 it was reported that a plagiarism expert at the London School of Economics had been accused of plagiarism contained in a paper he published on plagiarism! A paragraph was found that copied a published source by someone else word for word, and had not been acknowledged properly as being from another source. The accused person claimed that this was due to a formatting error. It is common practice in academic publications to indent a large section of material that is being quoted, like this:

> First, do not 'lift' large sections of text from other sources without making it clear that they are in fact quotations. This makes it clear that the text in question is not your own work but that you are making a point by quoting someone. It is easy to get this wrong. In June 2006 it was reported that a plagiarism expert at the London School of Economics had been accused of plagiarism contained in a paper he published on plagiarism! A paragraph was found that copied a published source by someone else word for word, and had not been acknowledged properly as being from another source. The accused person claimed that this was due to a formatting error.
>
> (Author 2021: p. XX)

In the 2006 incident, the lack of indentation meant that the paragraph in question looked as though it was the author's own work. While it may be that this is a case of 'unintentional plagiarism' (Park 2003), distinguishing the intentional from the unintentional is not easy. Either way, the credibility and possibly the integrity of the author may be undermined. It is also important to realize that, for many if not most institutions, copying large portions of text and changing a few words will also be regarded as plagiarism.

The second way that you can avoid plagiarizing is to ensure that you do not present other people's ideas as though they are your own. This means always acknowledging the source of any ideas you include that are not your own. It was this aspect of plagiarism that led to the author of *The Da Vinci Code* (2003), Dan Brown, being accused of plagiarism. His accusers did not suggest that he had taken large chunks of text from other works and presented it as his own. Instead, they accused him of lifting ideas from a non-fiction book they had written (*The Holy Blood and the Holy Grail*). However, Dan Brown *did* acknowledge his use of their historical work on the grail myth, though only in a general way in a list of acknowledgements, and Brown's accusers lost their case (fortunately for their readers, novelists do not need to continuously reference ideas that they use in their fictional work).

The best way to ensure that you do not accidentally or deliberately plagiarize in your dissertation or research project, both in the literature review and elsewhere, is to find and read through any guidelines on the matter that are published by your university and possibly also your department. Research in an Australian university revealed that only half of the students in the study had read the university's misconduct policy and that those who had read it had a better understanding of plagiarism (Gullifer and Tyson 2014).

One final point to note is that plagiarism is like a moving target. What it is, how it should be defined, how it can be detected, how it should be penalized: all these issues and others are in a state of flux. It is very much a shifting situation because of the changing ways in which research can be conducted and assessed. The penalties can be severe and, when students are presented with evidence of their plagiarism, it can be profoundly embarrassing and distressing for them to be caught out. The message is simple: make sure that you know exactly what plagiarism is and how it is defined at your institution, so that you do not inadvertently do this in your work.

KEY POINTS

- Writing a literature review is a means of reviewing the main ideas and research relating to your chosen area of interest.
- A competent literature review confirms you as someone who is knowledgeable in the subject area.

- Much of the work of writing a literature review involves reading the work of other researchers in your subject area; taking effective notes and reading actively and critically are key skills that will help you get the most from this exercise.
- Narrative review is a more traditional approach that has advantages of flexibility. It is the main type of literature review used in the social sciences.
- Systematic review is a method that is gaining in popularity in social research as a way of enhancing the reliability of literature searching and review.

QUESTIONS FOR REVIEW

1. How would you define a narrative literature review?
2. What are the main reasons for writing a narrative literature review?
3. How can you ensure that you get the most from your reading?
4. What are the main advantages and disadvantages associated with systematic review?
5. What type of research questions is systematic review most suited to addressing?
6. What are the main ways of finding existing literature on your subject?
7. What is a keyword, and how is it useful in searching the literature?
8. Why is it important to reference your work?
9. What are the main referencing styles used in academic work, and which of these does your institution prefer?
10. What is the role of the bibliography or reference list, and what makes a good one?
11. What is plagiarism?
12. Why is plagiarism taken so seriously by researchers?
13. How can you avoid plagiarizing?

ONLINE RESOURCES

www.oup.com/he/srm6e

You can find our notes on the answers to these questions within this chapter's **online resources**, together with:

- *audio/video comments* on this topic from our 'Learn from experience' panellists;
- *audio discussion from the authors* on the main ways of finding existing literature on your subject (review question 6);
- *self-test questions* for further knowledge-checking;
- a *flashcard glossary* to help you recall key terms; and
- a *Student Researcher's Toolkit* containing practical materials and resources to help you conduct your own research project.

CHAPTER

6

ETHICS AND POLITICS IN SOCIAL RESEARCH

CHAPTER GUIDE

Ethical concerns are an essential part of the research process, and principles of good ethical practice guide decisions on what is and is not acceptable behaviour for researchers. In this chapter we cover

- existing codes of ethics that you can read and reference;
- some famous (even infamous) examples of studies with unethical conduct, and the difficulty in writing about ethics;
- key stances (viewpoints) that can be taken on ethics;
- the four key ethical principles: avoiding harm to participants and researchers, ensuring informed consent, protecting privacy, and avoiding deception;

- some of the difficulties associated with ethical decision-making;
- additional considerations for different types of data, specifically secondary data, data gained through online studies, and visual data;
- some of the main political dimensions of research, from gaining access to research situations to publishing your findings.

6.1 Introduction

In this chapter we introduce the issues and debates about ethics with which all social researchers should engage. As we noted in the Chapter guide, ethical concerns are an essential part of the research process: if you are writing a proposal for a final-year project, then you will almost certainly have to highlight the ethical issues that your investigation may encounter. The increasing use of online data, such as social media, in social-scientific research has particular ethical implications that we will discuss.

We are not going to try to resolve the ethical issues that we present here because ethics are complicated, and some of the stances you could take (such as situation ethics, discussed in Section 6.3) do not provide researchers with clear direction. However, we will provide enough of an outline of the ethical principles involved in social research to give you the awareness and knowledge that you will need in order to make informed decisions about your own work. In social research, ethical considerations revolve around issues like these:

- How should we treat the people with whom we conduct research?
- Are there activities in which we should or should not engage with those we are studying?

You can see that the focus is on the principles that guide the relationship between researchers (us) and those who are being researched (participants). In addition to such ethical issues, we also need to consider how the politics of research (by which we mean how power is exercised, rather than party politics and governance) can impact upon how we think about, design, conduct, and share our research. We discuss these issues in Section 6.6.

6.2 Existing ethical guidance

Before we go any further in discussing ethical issues and debates, it is important to be aware of the formal guidance on ethics that is available to you as a social researcher. This comes in two main forms: codes of practice issued by professional bodies, and guidance provided by your university, both in written form (guidelines) and through ethics committees.

Guidance from professional associations

Professional associations, such as the British Sociological Association (BSA) and the Social Research Association (SRA), have formulated publicly available codes of ethics. These resources can be very useful because they discuss what is considered best practice among a community of scholars. While they might not always tell us exactly what to do (as decisions can depend on context), they often help us to identify where ethical issues may emerge. We will refer to the BSA's and SRA's codes on several occasions in this chapter.

These are some of the most useful codes of ethics:

- British Sociological Association (BSA), *Statement of Ethical Practice*: **www.britsoc.co.uk/media/24310/bsa_statement_of_ethical_practice.pdf.**
- Social Research Association (SRA), *Ethical Guidelines*: **https://the-sra.org.uk/common/Uploaded%20files/ethical%20guidelines%202003.pdf.**
- British Psychological Society (BPS), *Code of Ethics and Conduct*: **www.bps.org.uk/news-and-policy/bps-code-ethics-and-conduct.**

- American Sociological Association (ASA), *Code of Ethics*: www.asanet.org/sites/default/files/asa_code_of_ethics-june2018.pdf.
- Economic and Social Research Council (ESRC), *Framework for Research Ethics*: https://esrc.ukri.org/files/funding/guidance-for-applicants/esrc-framework-for-research-ethics-2015/.

Another useful resource is the *Global Code of Conduct for Research in Resource-Poor Settings* (www.globalcodeofconduct.org/, accessed 18 June 2020), which focuses on fairness, respect, care, and honesty in research between high-income and low-income settings. This code explicitly acknowledges the power relationships between the researcher and the researched.

Although these frameworks remain important sources of ethical guidance, the recent increase in the use of online data, particularly social media data, for social research presents new ethical challenges—especially because in this context the data is *naturally occurring* (Edwards et al. 2013) and not generated as part of a research project. We will keep returning throughout this chapter to the distinctive challenges that these data present, but for now we would highlight that specific ethical principles for digital research have been developed and you can access a range of case studies that exemplify how this type of research raises particular ethical issues. The following resources are publicly available:

- Association of Internet Researchers (AoIR), *Internet Research: Ethical Guidelines 3.0*: https://aoir.org/reports/ethics3.pdf.
- BSA, *Ethical Guidelines and Collated Resources for Digital Research*: www.britsoc.co.uk/media/24309/bsa_statement_of_ethical_practice_annexe.pdf.
- *Social Media Research: A Guide to Ethics*: www.gla.ac.uk/media/Media_487729_smxx.pdf.

All the above statements were accessed on 22 January 2021.

There is also a growing body of academic work looking specifically at ethical issues in social media research (for example, Williams et al. 2017b; Woodfield 2018; Sloan et al. 2019). The key point is that the field is under development, as our ethical thinking (what we *should* do) catches up with our technical ability (what we *can* do).

Guidance from your institution

In addition to being familiar with the codes of practice produced by professional associations such as the BSA, the ASA, and the SRA, you should be familiar with the ethical guidelines of your university or college. Most higher education organizations have ethics committees that issue guidelines about ethical research, providing indications of what practices are considered to be ethically unacceptable (see Learn from experience 6.1). These guidelines are often based on or influenced by the codes developed by professional associations. The ethics committee and the guidelines it produces are there to protect research participants from unethical and potentially harmful research practices. However, they also exist to protect institutions and researchers. They aim to help researchers avoid behaving in ethically unacceptable ways that might rebound on their university or college (ethically inappropriate behaviour can give rise to legal action against the institution or to negative publicity), or that could damage the researcher's own reputation and/or put them in a vulnerable position.

LEARN FROM EXPERIENCE 6.1
The role of ethics committees

Ethics committees are not a barrier to be overcome: they are an essential part of a social research project in which experts will review your ideas and the safeguards you have put in place. It is not unusual for ethical reviews to make recommendations that strengthen your project, as discussed by Sarah.

> A central concern that arose from the ethical review for my postgraduate project was the length of my information sheets. There was too much information for participants to process, and it was difficult to shorten the information sheets while retaining all the important ethical information. One useful piece of advice I received was to create a diagram that explained the research process in an easy format accessible to participants with English-language-skill barriers. I followed this advice and created a picture diagram that explained what my observations and interviews involved. I used this alongside the information sheet to explain the project to these participants.
>
> Sarah

You are more likely to receive ethical clearance if you put the time and effort into filling out the paperwork carefully and comprehensively. You will have to consider a wide range of issues, from GDPR and data security through to avoiding harm to participants or yourself. It is a good strategy to work through these issues with your supervisor, as Brendan and Scarlett reflect below.

My current doctoral study includes children, so a caring and ethical approach is important. Additionally, new privacy standards in the European Union (GDPR) require detailed data storage procedures. The ethical proposal had to be detailed and comprehensive to satisfy a number of detailed requirements. Many of the questions were hard for me to answer, so I worked closely with my supervisor, drawing on his experience, to pre-empt any criticism of my study. We were detailed and as transparent as possible. After a request for minor revisions, the proposal was accepted and I was able to start the interview process.

Brendan

As my research project involved vulnerable participants (young people under the age of 16) and required participants to talk about a sensitive topic (mental wellbeing), I had to go through the full ethical review process. Completing an ethics form is more of a practical piece of work than an academic one. It's hard work, and can sometimes be just as lengthy as your dissertation! It involves justifying your research project and identifying the ways you will minimize any ethical issues that may arise. My supervisor was extremely helpful when it came to filling out my ethics form; she was happy to offer feedback and sat down with me to identify the potential ethical issues that might arise. I submitted two draft ethics forms to my supervisor before it got sent off to the ethics committee, so do not expect to get it right the first time! Completing a full ethical review form enabled me to think differently about research and has helped me now, during my masters' degree, to identify the different kind of issues that may arise during research.

Scarlett

Access the **online resources** to hear our panellists' video reflections on this theme.

You can read about our panellists' backgrounds and research experiences on page xxvi.

6

As a student researcher, it might be that your only contact with your institution's ethics committee is reading and adhering to the ethical guidelines it produces. Often, however, you will need to submit your proposed research to the committee to be assessed. One of the main approaches used by ethics committees is to ask researchers to indicate whether their research involves procedures or activities that may be ethically problematic. This process usually involves completing a form to show that you have considered potential ethical issues that might arise. This form is likely to ask questions such as 'Will there be any potential harm, discomfort, or physical or psychological risks for research participants?' and the researcher needs to answer 'Yes' or 'No'. If there is a possibility that you may engage in such a practice, the proposed research is then 'flagged' for full scrutiny by the ethics committee. In such an instance, the researcher has to provide a full account of the research and the rationale for using the ethically dubious practice(s). In such cases it may take longer than you expect to receive ethical approval and the committee may come back to you several times for more information. This is why you should always plan your project with enough time to gain ethical clearance (see Chapter 4, Section 4.2 and Tips and skills 4.1).

6.3 Thinking about ethics in social research

When thinking about ethics in social research, we need to consider that writers take different stances over ethical issues, and that the prominence of these issues has changed over time. Our ethical frameworks also develop as new opportunities for social research become available to us, for example with the availability of social media data.

6

The difficulties of discussing ethics

Discussions about ethics in social research can be frustrating for four reasons.

1. Writers often differ quite widely from each other over ethical issues and questions. In other words, they differ over what is and is not ethically acceptable and take different stances (see Section 6.3 under 'Stances on ethics').
2. Compared to the limited attention given to ethical issues in social research during the 1960s, today ethics are central to discussions within social research. Some of the studies we will discuss in this chapter would never be conducted now. The message to take from this is that ethical norms can, and do, change over time.
3. Ethical issues in social research are usually not as extreme as the most-discussed cases might suggest. We often return to the same well-known, even notorious, examples of ethical transgression when discussing these kinds of debates. They include Humphreys' 'tearoom trade' study (1970) (see Research in focus 6.1); Milgram's obedience study (1963) (see Research in focus 6.2); the study of a religious cult by a group of covert researchers (Festinger et al. 1956); the use of pseudo-patients in the study of mental hospitals (Rosenhan 1973); and Rosenthal and Jacobson's (1968) field experiment to study teacher expectations in the classroom (see Research in focus 3.1). You may well have discussed these studies in class, as they are often used to demonstrate violations of key ethical principles. The problem with these examples is that they are extreme cases and do not accurately reflect the kinds of issues that most researchers need to consider. We keep talking about them mainly because it is very difficult, even impossible, to find such clear-cut cases of bad ethical practice in more recent years, but the reality is that most ethical issues you will encounter are more subtle and nuanced.
4. Related to this last point is the fact that these extreme cases of ethical violation tend to be associated with particular **research methods**—notably covert observation and the use of deception in **experiments**. The problem with associating particular studies and methods with ethical issues is that it implies that some methods are unlikely to bring up ethical concerns. However, it would be wrong to assume that methods such as **questionnaires** or overt observation are immune from ethical problems, especially because ethical problems often arise from the questions that are being asked. For example, conducting questionnaire or overt **observation research** with children will raise a lot of ethical issues that may not arise when the research is on adults.

RESEARCH IN FOCUS 6.1
An example of ethical transgression

An investigation that has achieved particular notoriety because of its ethics (or lack of them) is Humphreys' (1970) study of sexual encounters between men in public toilet facilities (known in the USA as the 'tearoom trade') in an unidentified American city. At that time, homosexuality was highly stigmatized. Humphreys' research interest was in impersonal sex and, in order to shed light on this area, he took on the role of 'watchqueen'—a term used at that time to describe someone who watched out for possible intruders while men met each other and engaged in sexual encounters in public toilet facilities. As a result of his involvement in these social scenes, Humphreys was able to collect the details of active participants' car licence numbers. He was then able to track down their names and addresses and ended up with a sample of 100 active tearoom-trade participants. After waiting a year and changing his appearance so he wouldn't be recognized, he then conducted an interview survey of a **sample** of those who had been identified, posing as a health service interviewer. The **interview schedule** was concerned with health issues and included some questions about marital sex (some of the men were married to women—at that time, neither same-sex domestic partnerships nor same-sex marriages were permitted in the USA).

Through his conduct in this study, Humphreys covertly observed his participants, who had not given their consent because they did not realize that they were being researched. By linking these private and largely anonymous sexual encounters with named individuals he potentially put his participants at risk, as homosexuality was highly stigmatized at the time. He also put himself at risk, both by participating in a highly stigmatized activity and by risking backlash from the men he observed should they discover his secret role as a researcher.

RESEARCH IN FOCUS 6.2

An example of ethical transgression

Milgram (1963) was interested in the circumstances associated with the use of brutality in Nazi concentration camps of the Second World War. In particular, he was interested in the processes whereby a person can be induced to cause extreme harm to another person by being ordered to do so. To investigate this issue, Milgram devised a laboratory experiment. He recruited volunteers to act out the role of teachers who punished learners (who were accomplices of the experimenter) by submitting them to electric shocks when they gave incorrect answers to questions. The shocks were not, of course, real, but the teachers/volunteers were not aware of this. The researcher asked the teacher/volunteer to gradually increase the level of electric shock with successive incorrect answers, until the teacher/volunteer refused to administer more shocks. Actors had been trained to respond to the rising level of supposed electric shock with simulated but appropriate howls of pain. In the room was a further accomplice of Milgram's who encouraged the teacher/volunteer to continue to administer shocks, suggesting that it was part of the study's requirements to continue and that they were not causing permanent harm, in spite of the increasingly shrill cries of pain. Milgram's study shows that people can be induced to cause very considerable pain to others, so he saw it as helping to explain the circumstances leading to the horrors of the concentration camps.

Despite the ethical violations in the obedience study, this work was replicated later by Burger (2009) to test whether the findings were still the same 45 years later (he found that obedience rates were only slightly lower). How could this be possible given the ethical controversies that Milgram's original study created? Burger (2009) discusses the substantial extra safeguards he introduced in this study.

1) He screened out any participants who might be negatively impacted by the experience.
2) The researcher informed participants multiple times that they could withdraw from the study at any time and still receive their $50 incentive.
3) Participants (with consent) were administered a small electric shock so that they knew what it would feel like (but only at low voltages).
4) Within seconds of a participant ending the exercise, the person they were supposed to be administering electric shocks to walked into their room to reassure them that no shocks had been given.
5) The experimenter overseeing the experiment was a trained clinical psychologist who was observing for signs of excessive stress and would end the experiment if needed.

By putting these measures in place, Burger was able to receive ethical clearance from his institution for the replication study, even though deception was part of the research.

6

Stances on ethics

Those writing about the ethics of social research can be characterized in terms of the stance (viewpoint) they take on the issue. The five stances we identify below are universalism, situation ethics, ethical transgression is widespread, 'anything goes' (more or less), and deontological versus consequentialist ethics.

Universalism

A universalist stance takes the view that ethical rules should never be broken. Violations of ethical principles are wrong in a moral sense and are damaging to social research. This kind of stance can be seen in the writings of Erikson (1967), Dingwall (1980), and Bulmer (1982). Bulmer does, however, point to some forms of what appears to be disguised observation that he suggests may be acceptable. One is retrospective covert observation, which is when a researcher writes up their experiences in social settings in which they participated but not as a researcher. An example would be Van Maanen (1991b), who wrote up his experiences as a ride operator in Disneyland many years after he had been employed there in vacation jobs. Even a universalist such as Erikson (1967: 372) recognizes that it 'would be absurd . . . to insist as a point of ethics that sociologists should always introduce themselves as investigators everywhere they go and should inform every person who figures in their thinking exactly what their research is all about'.

Situation ethics

Situation ethics can be seen as contrasting with the universalist stance. Goode (1996) has argued for deception to be considered on a case-by-case basis. In other words, he argues for what Fletcher (1966: 31) has called a 'situation ethics', or more specifically 'principled relativism'. This argument can be represented in two ways.

1. *The end justifies the means*. Some writers argue that, unless there is some breaking of ethical rules, we will never know about certain social phenomena. Nigel Fielding (1982) essentially argues for this position in relation to his research on the National Front, an extreme right-wing British political party that was politically influential in the 1970s. Without some kind of covert observation, this important movement and its appeal could not have been studied. Similarly, for their covert participant observation study of websites supportive of individuals with eating disorders (known as 'pro-ana' websites—see Research in focus 18.6), Brotsky and Giles (2007: 96) argue that deception was justified, 'given the charges laid against the pro-ana community (that they are effectively sanctioning self-starvation), and the potential benefit of our findings to the eating disorders clinical field'.
2. *No choice*. Proponents of situation ethics often suggest that sometimes we have no choice but to mislead if we want to investigate the issues in which we are interested. This view can be seen in the writings of Holdaway (1982) and Homan and Bulmer (1982). For example, Brotsky and Giles (2007: 96) write: 'it was felt highly unlikely that access would be granted to a researcher openly disclosing the purpose of her study'.

Situational ethics is often advocated as a stance from which to conduct social media research because it is not always possible or practical to seek **informed consent** for participation in a study. This might be because of the number of participants: for example, it would not be unusual for a study of Twitter to include millions of participants. There is also some acknowledgement that a situational approach can enable innovation in relatively new areas of research (see the BSA's *Ethical Guidelines and Collated Resources for Digital Research*: www.britsoc.co.uk/media/24309/bsa_statement_of_ethical_practice_annexe.pdf, accessed 20 August 2019).

Ethical transgression is widespread

Those who take this stance point out that almost all research involves elements that are in some way ethically questionable. This could be seen to occur whenever participants are not given all the details on a piece of research, or when there is variation in the amount of knowledge people have about the research. Punch (1994: 91), for example, observes that 'some dissimulation [hiding information] is intrinsic to social life and, therefore, to fieldwork'. He quotes Gans (1962: 44) in support of this point: 'If the researcher is completely honest with people about [the researcher's] activities, they will try to hide actions and attitudes they consider undesirable, and so will be dishonest. Consequently, the researcher must be dishonest to get honest data.'

'Anything goes' (more or less)

The writers who are associated with arguments relating to situation ethics and a recognition that ethical transgressions are widespread are not arguing that 'anything goes' in terms of research ethics; rather, they are arguing for a certain amount of flexibility in ethical decision-making. However, Douglas (1976) has argued that the kinds of deception in which social researchers engage are trivial compared to deceptions perpetrated by powerful institutions in modern society (such as the mass media, the police, and industry). His book sets out various tactics for deceiving people in order to gain their trust and encourage them to reveal themselves to the researcher. Very few researchers support this view, though Denzin (1968) comes close when he suggests that social researchers are entitled to study anyone in any setting provided the work has a 'scientific' purpose, does not harm participants, and does not deliberately damage the discipline.

Deontological versus consequentialist ethics

Another distinction that has attracted interest in recent years is between deontological and consequentialist ethics. Deontological ethics considers certain acts as wrong (or good) in and of themselves. Consequentialist ethics looks at the consequences of an act for guidance as to whether it is right or wrong. In the context of ethical issues in social research, deontological arguments tend to prevail. For example, deceiving research participants or not providing them with the opportunity to give informed consent is usually seen as ethically wrong. Consequentialist arguments do sometimes surface, however. For example, sometimes researchers argue that an activity like covert observation is wrong because it can harm the reputation of the profession of social research or of an organization, meaning that other social researchers would be adversely affected by the decision to engage in covert observation.

6.4 Ethical principles for conducting social research

So how does all of this translate into practice? In this section, we consider ethical principles for social research, the difficulties involved in ethical decision-making, and ethical issues relating to some particular types of data (online and visual data).

Discussions about ethical principles in social research, and perhaps more specifically about violations of them, have been usefully broken down by Diener and Crandall (1978) into four main areas:

1. whether there is *harm to participants*;
2. whether there is a *lack of informed consent*;
3. whether there is an *invasion of privacy*;
4. whether *deception* is involved.

We will look at each of these in turn, but we must keep in mind that the four principles often overlap. For example, it is difficult to imagine how the principle of informed consent could be built into an investigation in which research participants were deceived. However, there is no doubt that these four areas provide a useful classification of ethical principles for social research.

Avoidance of harm for participants

Research that is likely to harm participants is seen by most people as unacceptable. But what is harm? Harm can include physical harm; harm to participants' development; loss of self-esteem; stress; and 'inducing subjects to perform reprehensible acts', as Diener and Crandall (1978: 19) put it. In several of the studies discussed in this book, there has been real or potential harm to participants.

- In the Rosenthal and Jacobson (1968) study (Research in focus 3.1), it is possible that the pupils who had not been identified as 'spurters' (children who would excel in their studies) were adversely affected in terms of their intellectual development by the spurters receiving more attention from teachers. This research also involved socially and economically disadvantaged groups who did not explicitly give their consent.
- In the Festinger et al. (1956) study of a religious cult (mentioned in Chapter 3), it is quite likely that the fact that the researchers joined the group at a crucial time—close to what group members believed to be the end of the world—fuelled the delusions of group members as they perceived more and more people to be anticipating the end of the world.
- Many of the participants in Humphreys' (1970) research (see Research in focus 6.1) were married men who are likely to have been fearful of having their same-sex encounters revealed. It is conceivable that his methods could have resulted in some of them becoming identified.
- Many of the participants in the Milgram (1963) experiment on obedience to authority (Research in focus 6.2) experienced high levels of stress and anxiety as a consequence of being induced to administer electric shocks. It could also be argued that Milgram's observers were 'inducing subjects to perform reprehensible acts', even if the recipients of the shocks were not actually hurt.

For social media research, the discussions about causing harm to participants can be very complex: boyd (2014) discusses how the information that people put online is often intended for a specific audience (such as friends and family), even if it is technically public. Think of some of the opinions you have voiced on social media with your friends—would you feel harmed if they were available to the public at large and, for example, quoted in a national newspaper's report on some research findings? Even for very public data, such as open accounts on Twitter, replicating a tweet when writing up your work can expose the content to a new audience, which may ultimately cause harm to the content producer (see Research in focus 6.3 and Learn from experience 6.2).

The BSA *Statement of Ethical Practice* (see Section 6.2) instructs researchers to 'anticipate, and to guard against, consequences for research participants which can be predicted to be harmful' and 'to consider carefully the possibility that the research experience may be a disturbing one'. Similar sentiments are expressed by the SRA's *Ethical Guidelines* (see Section 6.2), for example, when it advocates that the 'social researcher should try to minimize disturbance both to subjects themselves and to the subjects' relationships with their environment'.

A key component to protecting participants from harm is maintaining the confidentiality and security of records, meaning that you should keep the identities and records of individuals confidential. This also means that you

RESEARCH IN FOCUS 6.3
Quoting tweets in research

Williams et al. (2017b) discuss in some detail the complexities around using Twitter data for social science research, focusing particularly on whether it is ethical to quote tweets when writing up research. On the face of it, Twitter is a public platform and (unless your account is locked) your tweets are freely and publicly available for everyone to see. But what if you say something that is later taken out of context? What if you see a tweet that

FIGURE 6.1
Williams et al.'s (2017b) decision flow chart for the publication of Twitter communications

Tweet is from
Public Figure Account
Organizational Account
Private Individual Account
Tweet is from an individual org. member
No
Yes
Member tweets in private capacity
No
Yes
Is the user identifiable as vulnerable?
No
Yes
Seek Opt-In Consent from user, guardian or proxy
Is the content sensitive?
No
Yes
Seek Opt-In Consent from user
Is tweet deleted at time of research/writing?
Seek Opt-Out Consent
No
Yes
Is account deleted at time of writing?
Was reply received?
Yes
No
No
Yes
Can you find ex-user contact details?
Has time to reply window expired?
No
Yes
No
Yes
Was consent received?
Yes
No
Publish
DO NOT PUBLISH

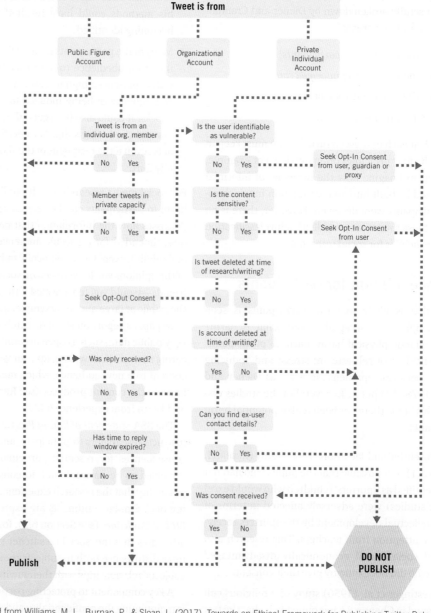

Adapted from Williams, M. L., Burnap, P., & Sloan, L. (2017). Towards an Ethical Framework for Publishing Twitter Data in Social Research: Taking into Account Users' Views, Online Context and Algorithmic Estimation. *Sociology*, 51(6), 1149–1168.

contains hateful content or incriminates the participant in some way (for example, underage drinking, illegal drug use)? What if the tweeter realizes this and has actually deleted the tweet from their account, but you collected the data before the deletion? By replicating this tweet in your write-up you are drawing attention to an individual who could be at increased risk of harm because you have bypassed their right to delete (by immortalizing their comment in your work) and exposed their views to a new audience in a different context.

All of this makes social research using Twitter data challenging, particularly when working on sensitive topics and for qualitative work where quoting data is an essential part of the write-up. Rather than relying solely on a situational ethics approach where a researcher must make their own judgement, Williams et al. (2017b) suggest a rules-based opt-in or opt-out system depending on who (or what) is tweeting, the nature of the content, and whether the tweet has been deleted. Wrapped up in this is the issue of informed consent (see Section 6.4 under 'Informed consent') and what this means for publicly available data. This is only one way of thinking about quoting tweets, but the flow diagram the authors provide (Figure 6.1) is a useful framework for considering the potential for harm.

LEARN FROM EXPERIENCE 6.2
Using Twitter data

Simon used Twitter data in his research project and wanted to reproduce tweets in the write-up of his work. He discusses the complexities of reproducing tweets and explains why, in the end, he opted for a bricolage approach ('bricolage' meaning construction using whatever diverse materials are available).

> I have been using Twitter to study sociological phenomena and this has brought to the fore some problems relating to consent. It would be useful for me to simply reproduce tweets and use them in my research. This is legal and is permitted by the Twitter Terms of Service, but whether this is *ethical* is another question.
>
> Firstly, tweets are publicly accessible. If I were to use one verbatim, then it would be possible to identify the original author, meaning that anyone could find out who it was. This could potentially cause the author harm. Secondly, even though the Terms of Service inform the user that their data is publicly accessible, they probably don't understand the implications of this. Again, this creates the potential for harm. So the right thing for me to do is to seek consent, but this isn't so straightforward either. I could Direct Message them but in order to do this I need them to follow me, which is highly unlikely. So the only option left is for me to tweet at them. This is then a publicly available item which could be seen by their friends or colleagues, and consent should be a matter they can decide on without public scrutiny.
>
> The solution I've adopted to this dilemma is to use a bricolage approach. I change portions of the original tweet while maintaining the original intent of the text and use this new version as an 'exemplar' of a tweet that supports (or contradicts) my hypothesis. By using this I approach I properly protect my participants.
>
> Simon

You can read about our panellists' backgrounds and research experiences on page xxvi.

must take care, when presenting your findings, to ensure that individuals stay anonymous (that is, not identified or identifiable). In **quantitative research**, it is relatively easy to make records anonymous and to report findings in a way that does not allow individuals to be identified. However, this is often less easy with **qualitative research**, and researchers have to take particular care with regard to the possible identification of people and places. The use of pseudonyms (fake names) is common, but this may not completely eliminate the possibility of identification. This issue raises particular problems with regard to the **secondary analysis** of qualitative data (see Chapter 23), since it is very difficult—though by no means impossible—to present **field notes** and interview **transcripts** in a way that will prevent people and places from being identified. The Humphreys and Watson (2009) study that we discuss in Chapter 18 details how the researchers were so concerned with protecting the anonymity of their participants (because they were asking participants to share views on their employer) that they went beyond using pseudonyms; they used the name 'Charity' to refer to a composite person who represented several participants with similar views.

The need for confidentiality can present dilemmas for researchers. Westmarland (2001) has discussed the dilemmas she faced when observing violence by the police towards people being held in custody. She argues that, while a certain level of violence might be considered acceptable (to protect the officers themselves and the public), there is an issue of deciding at what point it is no longer acceptable and the researcher needs to inform on those involved. Such a level of violence may also be consistent with the police's occupational culture. The problem for an **ethnographer** in this position is compounded by the fact that reporting the violence might result in the researcher losing credibility among officers, the investigation ending early, or the researcher (and potentially other researchers) being unable to gain access in the future. This kind of consideration also brings in career issues for the researcher, an element of ethics that connects with political issues and that we discuss in Section 6.6.

The issue of confidentiality is clearly a very important one. Israel and Hay (2004) treat it as a separate principle of ethics in its own right. As they observe, if researchers do not observe the confidentiality of what is said to them, 'who would talk to them in the future?' (Israel and Hay 2004: 94). So quite aside from the intrinsic wrongness of not keeping information and identities confidential (a deontological argument), this kind of ethical transgression could also harm generations of future researchers (a consequentialist argument). The issue has been

TIPS AND SKILLS 6.1
General Data Protection Regulation (GDPR)

On 25 May 2018 the UK Data Protection Act 1998 (DPA) was replaced with GDPR—a European Union framework for governing how personal and sensitive data should be collected, used, and stored. Essentially, GDPR requires personal data to be

a) processed lawfully, fairly, and transparently

b) collected for specified, explicit, and legitimate purposes

c) accurate and kept up to date

d) not kept longer than necessary in a form that allows identification of individuals

e) processed in an appropriately secure manner

It is notable that Article 5 of GDPR does make allowances for 'purposes in the public interest, scientific or historic research purposes or statistical purposes', which would include academic research. These allowances relate to purpose (b) and length of time (d) (**https://ico.org.uk/media/for-organisations/data-protection-reform/overview-of-the-gdpr-1-13.pdf**, accessed 20 August 2019).

There are very few instances where a social research project would not involve collecting personal and/or sensitive data on individuals, so it is important that you engage with your supervisor when designing your research project to make sure that you are observing these rules. In particular, you will need to consider issues around data security (using encrypted devices) and your duty regarding the archiving of identifiable data.

GDPR also includes the right to be forgotten—that is, the right for an individual to ask for their data to be deleted. However, this obligation does not apply in certain circumstances, for example if the data is being retained for reasons of public interest including statistical, scientific, or historical research or public health (**https://ec.europa.eu/info/law/law-topic/data-protection/reform/rules-business-and-organisations/dealing-citizens/do-we-always-have-delete-personal-data-if-person-asks_en**, accessed 16 April 2020). Note that de-personalized (anonymized) data can be retained, not least because you should not be able to identify the individual requesting their data to be removed if the anonymization has been done properly.

particularly prominent in discussions of research ethics—and legality—in recent years, with the introduction of the European Union's GDPR legislation in 2018 (see Tips and skills 6.1).

One of the problems with the harm-to-participants principle is that it is not always possible to identify whether harm is likely—though this should not be taken to mean that there is no point trying to protect participants from harm. When discussing this issue, Kimmel (1988) provides the example of the Cambridge–Summerville Youth Study in 1939. For this study, an experiment was conducted on 506 boys aged 5–13 who either were identified as likely to become delinquent or were average in this regard. The boys were equally divided in terms of this characteristic. They were randomly assigned either to an **experimental group**, in which they received preventative counselling, or to a no-treatment **control group**. In the mid-1970s the records were re-examined and were quite shocking: 'Treated subjects were more likely than controls to evidence signs of alcoholism and serious mental illness, died at a younger age, suffered from more stress-related diseases, tended to be employed in lower-prestige occupations, and were more likely to commit second crimes' (Kimmel 1988: 19). In other words, the treatment brought about a series of negative consequences for the group.

This is an extreme example and relates to experimental research, which is not a **research design** that is often used in social research (see Chapter 3), but it does illustrate the difficulty of anticipating harm to respondents and the possibility of your research having unintended consequences. Section 11.1 of the ASA *Code of Ethics* suggests that if there is more than 'minimal risk for research participants', then informed consent, the focus of a later subsection of this chapter, is essential.

Avoidance of harm for researchers

Another aspect of the principle that research should avoid inflicting harm is that there may be the potential for harm to the researcher—an issue that we introduced in Chapter 4, Section 4.4. In other words, you may be asked by your ethics committee to consider the possibility of physical or emotional harm to you, or to other researchers, through exposure to a fieldwork setting. Even if such a consideration is not included in an ethics form, it is something that you should consider very seriously. The study by Humphreys that we discussed in Research in focus 6.1 could have resulted in considerable harm for the researcher, both through engaging in stigmatized activity and by acting covertly. A student project is unlikely to involve covert observation like the Humphreys study, but in relation to the nature of the activity, our experience is that students are often interested in researching illicit behaviours such as violence in the night-time economy, drug use, or sexual crimes. Trying to observe these phenomena or ask participants about them can put the researcher in a compromised position, as a witness of illegal acts or as a confidant with whom participants discuss their illicit activity. This puts tremendous pressure on the researcher and raises important questions about how far confidentiality can be maintained. This is not to say that these important topics shouldn't be researched, but you must give proper thought to the risks that you might personally experience.

Another key consideration is how your own characteristics may impact upon interactions with your research participants. In Learn from experience 6.3 Minke discusses how factors such as the gender of the researcher can create uncomfortable situations that need to be carefully managed, and we might also reflect on other demographic characteristics that could increase the risk of harm. For example, researchers from minority backgrounds could be at significant risk when researching racist movements and interacting with participants who hold intolerant views. This raises some very pertinent questions about who can conduct research with particular groups, and how our integral qualities may affect our experiences and ultimately our safety in certain research settings.

Another risk that comes from conducting research is lone working. This refers to being in the field and collecting data on your own. Some institutions have specific policies on lone working, such as making sure that such activity takes place in a public place, ensuring that a colleague knows where you are and what you are doing, and carrying a mobile phone on you at all times. Even so, you should remember that being a researcher does not automatically protect you from harm. Something as simple as conducting a face-to-face survey in a public place could put you at risk, depending on who you approach (or who approaches you) to respond and how they react. None of this means that lone working is impossible, but you must think through the implications of this and how you can reduce the risks. Most of the time you can find a friend to come along with you, and then you can accompany them when they do their fieldwork.

Informed consent

The issue of informed consent is in many respects the area within social research ethics that is most hotly debated. Much of the discussion tends to focus on what is called

LEARN FROM EXPERIENCE 6.3
The risk of harm to researchers

Unfortunately, the qualities and characteristics that are inherent to us can sometimes increase the risk of harm, and they can strain or complicate the relationship between researchers and participants. Minke's research brought her into contact with a largely male group of participants and some of her interactions had to be navigated with great care:

> One issue that I encountered during fieldwork, during both my PhD and my master's, was the position of the young female researcher in a male-dominated research field. In my case, my presence as a young female in squats inhabited by many young men resulted in (unwanted) attention from respondents, and some respondents 'confusing' interviews with a romantic date, and there were therefore difficulties treading the fine line between creating 'rapport' and creating false expectations. I recently began to speak about this with fellow PhD students only to find out that many others had to deal with this issue as well. However, this issue is something that is hardly spoken about, even though more and more social science students are female.
>
> Minke

As researchers we must always be conscious of how we are perceived, and take great care to maintain rapport with our participants while ensuring that both sides understand the professional boundaries.

You can read about our panellists' backgrounds and research experiences on page xxvi.

6

disguised or covert observation (in this book we use the latter term), which can involve either covert **participant observation** (see Chapter 18, Section 18.3), or simple or **contrived observation** (see Key concept 14.2) in which the researcher's true identity is unknown. The principle of informed consent means that prospective research participants should be given as much information as might be needed in order to make an informed decision about whether or not they want to participate in a study. Covert observation violates this principle because participants are not given the opportunity to refuse to cooperate. They are involved, whether they like it or not.

Lack of informed consent is a feature of the research described in Research in focus 6.1 and 6.2 and a key concern in Research in focus 6.3. In Humphreys' research, informed consent is absent because the men for whom he acted as a watchqueen were not given the opportunity to refuse participation in his investigation. Similar points can be made about several other studies we discuss in this book, such as Festinger et al. (1956), Winlow et al. (2001), Brotsky and Giles (2007), Pearson (2009), Sallaz (2009), and Lloyd (2012). You may also remember the media coverage of the study by Kramer et al. (2014) in which researchers experimented with reducing positive and negative content from the newsfeeds of Facebook users. As the authors point out, this 'was consistent with Facebook's Data Use Policy, to which all users agree prior to creating an account on Facebook, constituting informed consent for this research' (Kramer et al. 2014: 8789), but participants were not given the opportunity to opt out, and the research thus violated a key principle of informed consent within social science ethical frameworks.

The principle of informed consent also means that, even when people know they are being asked to participate in research, they should be fully informed about the research process. The SRA *Ethical Guidelines* suggest:

> Inquiries involving human subjects should be based as far as practicable on the freely given informed consent of subjects. Even if participation is required by law, it should still be as informed as possible. In voluntary inquiries, subjects should not be under the impression that they are required to participate. They should be aware of their entitlement to refuse at any stage for whatever reason and to withdraw data just supplied. Information that would be likely to affect a subject's willingness to participate should not be deliberately withheld, since this would remove from subjects an important means of protecting their own interests.

Similarly, the BSA *Statement* says:

> As far as possible participation in sociological research should be based on the freely given informed consent of those studied. This implies a responsibility on the sociologist to explain in appropriate detail, and in terms

> meaningful to participants, what the research is about, who is undertaking and financing it, why it is being undertaken, and how it is to be distributed and used.

So although Milgram's experimental subjects were volunteers and therefore knew they were going to participate in research, there is a lack of informed consent because they were not given full information about the nature of the research and its possible implications for them.

However, as Homan (1991: 73) has observed, implementing the principle of informed consent 'is easier said than done'. Two major points stand out here.

First, it is extremely difficult to give prospective participants absolutely all the information that they might need in order to make an informed decision about their involvement. In fact, relatively minor transgressions probably pervade most social research, such as deliberately underestimating the amount of time that an interview or questionnaire is likely to take so that people are not put off being interviewed or completing the questionnaire, and not giving absolutely all the details about the research for fear of contaminating people's answers to questions.

Second, some researchers are likely to come into contact with a wide variety of people, and ensuring that absolutely everyone has the opportunity to give informed consent is not practicable because it would be extremely disruptive in everyday contexts. This is a common problem for ethnographers, who are likely to come across people in the course of their research who are part of the social setting but will only be briefly, lightly involved in the research so are not given the opportunity to provide informed consent.

Although there is widespread condemnation of violations of informed consent and covert observation is particularly likely to be accused of this type of unethical practice, studies using this method still appear (e.g. Brotsky and Giles 2007; Pearson 2009). What is interesting in this context is that the BSA *Statement* does not quite rule out **covert research**, leaving scope for ethical covert observation. The phrase 'as far as possible' regarding informed consent in the above quotation from the *Statement* does this, but the BSA goes even further in relation to covert research:

> There are serious ethical and legal issues in the use of covert research but the use of covert methods may be justified in certain circumstances. For example, difficulties arise when research participants change their behaviour because they know they are being studied. Researchers may also face problems when access to spheres of social life is closed to social scientists by powerful or secretive interests . . . However, covert methods violate the principles of informed consent and may invade the privacy of those being studied. Covert researchers might need to take into account the emerging legal frameworks surrounding the right to privacy. Participant or non-participant observation in non-public spaces or experimental manipulation of research participants without their knowledge should be resorted to only where it is impossible to use other methods to obtain essential data.

While this statement does not support the lack of informed consent that is automatically associated with covert research, it is not explicitly disapproving either. It acknowledges that covert methods jeopardize the principle of informed consent as well as the privacy principle (see the next subsection, 'Privacy'), but suggests that covert research can be used 'where it is impossible to use other methods to obtain essential data'—an example might be if the researcher could not otherwise gain access to the setting. Clearly, the difficulty here is how a researcher decides whether it is impossible to obtain the data other than by covert work. The guidance also highlights the importance of anonymity when informed consent cannot be gained and suggests that 'ideally' researchers should try to gain consent after the research has been conducted.

For online research the picture is even more complex. In the ESRC's *Framework for Research Ethics* it is acknowledged that

> Internet research can take place in a range of settings, for example email, chat rooms, web pages, social media and various forms of 'instant messaging'. These can pose specific ethical dilemmas. For example, what constitutes 'privacy' in an online environment? How easy is it to get informed consent from the participants in the community being researched? What does informed consent entail in that context? How certain is the researcher that they can establish the 'real' identity of the participants? When is deception or covert observation justifiable? How are issues of identifiability addressed?

For online settings, and in particular social media platforms, there is often friction between what researchers *can* do (dictated by the Terms of Service or End-User Licensing Agreement that a user signs up to) and what we *should* do (our own ethical duty as researchers). Beninger et al. (2014) reflect on the difficulty participants in their study had in understanding the terms and conditions of online platforms:

> [Participants] reported difficulty in staying up to date with 'constantly changing' terms and conditions of websites such as Twitter and Facebook. The frequency of websites

6

> updating, and the density of content, of terms and conditions was viewed as a barrier to [participants'] understanding [of] how the site they use works. In fact, *people admitted to not reading the terms* but instead accepting them in order to progress with using the platform.
>
> (Beninger et al. 2014: 14; emphasis added)

This study raises the question of whether accepting a set of terms and conditions counts as informed consent. Certainly based on these findings we would find it difficult to justify that most users made an 'informed' decision. However, there is some evidence that people are becoming more aware of the need to understand what they are signing up to. Williams et al. (2017b) found that 94 per cent of respondents in their study knew that Twitter had terms of service, just under two-thirds had read them partly or completely, and 76 per cent understood that their data would be accessible to third parties as a condition of their using Twitter. However, around 80 per cent agreed with the statement that they would expect to be asked for their consent for academic outputs to quote their tweets. It is this gap between what people sign up to and what they expect that led the authors of this study to design the flow-chart for quoting tweets (see Figure 6.1) as a way of deciding when informed consent is needed (that is, when there is a risk of harm to the participant).

Beyond online research, it is standard practice for researchers to obtain the informed consent of research participants by getting them to sign an informed consent form. For online surveys, this often involves respondents having to tick a box to confirm that they have read about and understood the project, with the tick box acting as a proxy for a signature. The advantage of informed consent forms is that they give respondents the opportunity to be fully informed of the nature of the research and the implications of their participation from the very beginning. The other benefit is that the researcher has a signed record of consent if any concerns are later raised by participants or others. However, being asked to sign a form may prompt rather than address prospective participants' concerns, so that they end up declining to be involved. Also, the direction of qualitative studies can be more flexible and spontaneous than that of quantitative ones, so it may be difficult to be specific about the nature of the research and implications of participation. Tips and skills 6.2 and 6.3 show the kinds of features you might want to take into account when seeking participants' informed consent. You will find very useful advice on information sheets, consent forms, and other aspects of ethical research practice at two sites: **www.ukdataservice.ac.uk/manage-data/legal-ethical/consent-data-sharing/consent-forms** and **www.cessda.eu/Training/Training-Resources/Library/Data-Management-Expert-Guide/5.-Protect/Informed-consent** (both accessed 20 August 2019).

Privacy

This third area of ethical concern relates to our duty to protect the privacy of participants. The right to privacy is an important principle for many of us, and violations of that right in the name of research are not seen as acceptable. Privacy is very much linked to the idea of informed consent because—to the degree that participants give informed consent on the basis of a detailed understanding of what participation is likely to involve—the participant in a sense acknowledges that they have surrendered their

TIPS AND SKILLS 6.2
A sample informed consent form

The sample informed consent form presented in Figure 6.2 is a template provided by the UK Data Service (UKDS). It was designed with GDPR in mind and covers the all the standard requirements of a consent form plus important issues such as how your data might be archived and used by future researchers. Note that there are questions on anonymity, quoting, and copyright, and that Section 3 on the second page of the form (titled 'Future use and reuse of information by others') should only be added if you are gaining consent in order to legally process personal data. If your data is anonymized or you are using pseudonyms then you do not need to gain consent in the manner shown in Section 3 of the form, and this could be stated in your information sheet (see Tips and skills 6.3).

The grey boxes on the form give more information on what aspects of your study need to be included. The UKDS also encourages researchers to check whether their institution has a similar template, and whether specific things need to be incorporated into the generic example given in Figure 6.2.

FIGURE 6.2
The informed consent form provided by the UK Data Service (UKDS)

Notes

1. Black text forms the standard content of a consent form
2. [Insert specific information in the highlighted square brackets]
3. Text notes in the grey boxes provide guidance only and are to be removed in the final consent form
4. Blue text indicates optional statements to add

Informed Consent for [name of study]

Please tick the appropriate boxes	**Yes**	**No**
1. Taking part in the study		
I have read and understood the study information dated [DD/MM/YYYY], or it has been read to me. I have been able to ask questions about the study and my questions have been answered to my satisfaction.	☐	☐
I consent voluntarily to be a participant in this study and understand that I can refuse to answer questions and I can withdraw from the study at any time, without having to give a reason.	☐	☐
I understand that taking part in the study involves [...].	☐	☐

Describe in a few words how information is captured, using the same terms as you used in the information sheet, for example: an audio-recorded interview, a video-recorded focus group, a survey questionnaire completed by the enumerator, an experiment, etc.].

For interviews, focus groups and observations, specify how the information is recorded (audio, video, written notes).

For questionnaires, specify whether participant or enumerator completes the form.

For audio or video recordings, indicate whether these will be transcribed as text, and whether the recording will be destroyed.

If there is a potential risk of participating in the study, then provide an additional statement: I understand that taking part in the study has [.......................................] as potential risk.	☐	☐
2. Use of the information in the study		
I understand that information I provide will be used for [..].	☐	☐

List the planned outputs, e.g. reports, publications, website, video channel etc., using the same terms as you used in the study information sheet.
Consider whether knowledge sharing and benefits sharing needs to be considered, e.g. for indigenous knowledge.

I understand that personal information collected about me that can identify me, such as my name or where I live, will not be shared beyond the study team.	☐	☐

At times this should be restricted to the researcher only.

INFORMED CONSENT FORM TEMPLATE PRODUCED BY UK DATA SERVICE

6

If you want to use quotes in research outputs, add: I agree that my information can be quoted in research outputs.	☐	☐
If you want to use named quotes, add: I agree that my real name can be used for quotes.	☐	☐
If written information is provided by the participant (e.g. diary), add: I agree to joint copyright of the [specify the data] to [name of researcher].	☐	☐

3. Future use and reuse of the information by others

I give permission for the [specify the data] that I provide to be deposited in [name of data repository] so it can be used for future research and learning.	☐	☐

> Specify in which form the data will be deposited, e.g. de-identified (anonymised) transcripts, audio recording, survey database, etc.; and if needed repeat the statement for each form of data you plan to deposit.
>
> Specify whether deposited data will be de-identified (anonymised), and how. Make sure to describe this in detail in the information sheet.
>
> Specify whether use or access restrictions will apply to the data in future, e.g. exclude commercial use, apply safeguarded access, etc.; and discuss these restrictions with the repository in advance.

4. Signatures

____________________ ____________________ ____________

Name of participant [IN CAPITALS] Signature Date

For participants unable to sign their name, mark the box instead of signing ☐

I have witnessed the accurate reading of the consent form with the potential participant and the individual has had the opportunity to ask questions. I confirm that the individual has given consent freely.

____________________ ____________________ ____________

Name of witness [IN CAPITALS] Signature Date

I have accurately read out the information sheet to the potential participant and, to the best of my ability, ensured that the participant understands to what they are freely consenting.

____________________ ____________________ ____________

Name of researcher [IN CAPITALS] Signature Date

5. Study contact details for further information

[Name, phone number, email address]

Source: Informed consent form (template): Addressing future reuse of research data, UK Data Service (UKDS), 2018. Copyright UK Data Service (UKDS). Reprinted with permission.

TIPS AND SKILLS 6.3

Designing a study information sheet

The UK Data Service (UKDS) also provides extensive advice on how to put together a study information sheet (**https://ukdataservice.ac.uk/media/622375/ukdamodelconsent.docx**, accessed 24 January 2020), and this is replicated below. You will notice that, in addition to ensuring that your research is ethical, there are legal considerations including specific responsibilities under GDPR. You should work closely with your supervisor when designing this form, especially as you might find that an informed consent form (with an accompanying information sheet) is a required part of applying for ethical clearance.

The informed consent form should be accompanied by an information sheet that describes:

1. **General information about the research and the collected research data**
   - Purpose of the research
   - Type of research intervention, e.g. questionnaire, interview, etc.
   - Voluntary nature of participation
   - Benefits and risks of participating
   - Procedures for withdrawal from the study
   - Usage of the data during research, dissemination and storage, including how the information will be shared with participants and any access and benefits-sharing that may be applicable (e.g. traditional knowledge under the Nagoya protocol)
   - Future publishing, archiving and reuse of the data, explaining to participants the benefits of data sharing and indicating whether research data will be deposited in a recognised repository, naming the organisation responsible for the repository (e.g. UK Data Service, your institutional repository, etc.)
   - Contact details of the researcher, as well as their organisation, funding source, how to file a complaint.
2. **Additional information if personal information is collected from participants** (for example their name, where they live, information that can disclose their identity)
   - How personal information will be processed and stored and for how long (e.g. signed consent forms, names or email addresses in online surveys, people's visuals in video recordings)
   - Procedures for maintaining confidentiality of information about the participant and information that the participant shares
   - Procedures for ensuring ethical use of the data: procedures for safeguarding personal information, maintaining confidentiality and de-identifying (anonymizing) data, especially in relation to data archiving and reuse.
3. **General Data Protection Regulation considerations**
   - Researchers undertaking research within or outside the EU, and where personal data will be stored within the EU, need to comply with the requirements of the GDPR from 25 May 2018
   - Researchers will need to identify for which of the six lawful reasons[1] personal data will be processed; this will inform what the **information sheet** and the **informed consent form** should include
   - If the reason is **consent**, it needs to be **freely given**, **informed**, **unambiguous**, **specific** and **affirmative**; participants need to be able to withdraw their consent for the processing of personal data (this will not affect the lawfulness of the processing up to that point)
   - The **information sheet** should also contain some specific information including:
     - The contact details of the Data Controller (the entity that determines the reason for processing personal data, this can be a responsible person within the researcher's organisation or the researcher), and the organisation's dedicated Data Protection Officer

- Who will receive or have access to the personal data, including information on any safeguards if the personal data is to be transferred outside the EU
- A clear statement on the right of the participant to request access to their personal data and the correction (rectification) of removal (erasure) of such personal data
- A reminder that the participants have the right to lodge a complaint with the Information Commissioner's Office (ICO)
- The period of retention for holding the data or the criteria used to determine this. (If data are to be archived for reuse, then the retention period should be indefinite)

[1] https://ico.org.uk/for-organisations/guide-to-the-general-data-protection-regulation-gdpr/lawful-basis-for-processing/

right to privacy for that limited time. The BSA *Statement* makes a direct link between informed consent and privacy in the passage we quoted in 'Informed consent': 'covert methods violate the principles of informed consent and may invade the privacy of those being studied.' Of course, the research participant does not *completely* give up their right to privacy by providing informed consent. For example, when people agree to be interviewed, they will often refuse to answer certain questions for a variety of reasons. Often, these refusals will be because they feel the questions reach into private areas that respondents do not want to make public, regardless of the fact that the interview will be conducted in private. Examples might be questions about income, religious beliefs, or sexual activities.

Covert methods are usually considered to be violations of the privacy principle because participants are not being given the opportunity to refuse invasions of their privacy. This kind of method also means that participants might reveal beliefs or information that they would not have revealed if they had known they were speaking to, or in front of, a researcher. The issue of privacy is linked to issues of anonymity and confidentiality in the research process (see Learn from experience 6.4), an area that we have touched on in 'Avoidance of harm for participants'.

Issues of anonymity and confidentiality in relation to recording information and maintaining records come up in all methods of social research. In other words, while covert research might pose particular problems regarding the invasion of privacy, other methods of social research

LEARN FROM EXPERIENCE 6.4
Anonymity and confidentiality

If you promise anonymity and/or confidentiality to participants, then you need the right processes in place to ensure that you are able to deliver on this. In her project on exploring the lived experiences of Pakistani Muslim lone mothers, Sarah had to think extensively about how to present her data while maintaining confidentiality and anonymity.

> I have promised confidentiality and anonymity to the subjects of my current, postgraduate research project during the informed consent process. I think this is particularly essential in my case due to the sensitivity of my topic—lone motherhood is often taboo, and some lone mothers have experienced domestic abuse. I have told participants that I will achieve this by not naming the organization and city in which the research took place and by assigning pseudonyms. However, I've also had to promise further anonymity, including not going into too much detail about participants' major life events and omitting identifiable details of both the organization and the participants. It is also important to note that the extent to which an organization can be fully anonymized is debatable, especially as I want to present findings on the work done to support lone mothers. It will be a difficult task to strike this balance.
>
> Sarah

Scarlett also promised anonymity and confidentiality to participants in her project on social media and its impact on young people's wellbeing, and she explains here that this had implications for how she shared her data with

her supervisor. Scarlett also reflects on when confidentiality and anonymity might be violated, either by participants themselves or because of the risk of harm to a participant.

> As my research involved young participants under the age of 16 and was focused on the topic of mental wellbeing, I promised my participants anonymity and confidentiality. I achieved anonymity and confidentiality through the use of pseudonyms (during both the focus group and the transcription process) and by storing the raw data in a secure, safe place that only I had access to. My supervisor had access to the data I had collected (transcripts), but this was still anonymized and I kept and later destroyed any documents that included participants' identities, such as consent forms. However, I made sure to remind participants that while I, as the researcher, could ensure anonymity and confidentiality, it was out of my hands if members of the focus group repeated things that were said by other participants to anyone outside the focus group. I also informed participants that due to the nature of the topic, I had the right to break confidentiality and anonymity if I felt that any participant was at risk of harm.
>
> Scarlett

You can read about our panellists' backgrounds and research experiences on page xxvi.

are not immune from difficulties in connection with anonymity and confidentiality. As we discussed in 'Avoidance of harm for participants', for online data this relates to the inherent searchability of quotes even if a pseudonym has been used, and the fact that sometimes anonymizing is against the original platform's term of service. The Twitter developer terms state that for displaying a tweet offline (that is, in print) you must always display the relevant username (and other things) and you must never modify the tweet text (Twitter 2019). It is also a common mistake for students to promise anonymity when it is not actually possible. Perhaps the most common example of this is when an online survey is presented as anonymous with no explicit individual identifiers, but the researcher requests an email address from the participant to enter them into a prize draw for taking part. Because the email address is unique and is stored in the same file as the rest of the **survey** data, the response is no longer anonymous.

Deception

Deception occurs when researchers represent their work as something other than what it is. Milgram's experiment (see Research in focus 6.2) undoubtedly involved deception. Participants were led to believe that they were administering real electric shocks. Deception in various degrees is probably quite widespread in experimental research, because researchers often want to limit participants' understanding of what the research is about so that they respond more naturally to the experimental treatment.

However, deception is certainly not confined to experimental methods in social psychology. Goode (1996), for example, placed four fake and slightly different dating advertisements in personal columns. He received nearly 1,000 replies and conducted a **content analysis** of them. Several of the studies referred to in this book involve deception: Rosenthal and Jacobson (1968) deceived teachers into believing that particular children in their charge were likely to excel at school, when they had in fact been randomly selected; Festinger et al. (1956) made cult members believe that they were in fact real converts; Rosenhan's (1973) associates deceived admissions staff at mental hospitals by pretending that they were mentally ill; and Brotsky (Brotsky and Giles 2007) posed as an anorexic and posted messages onto a 'pro-ana' website on that basis.

The ethical objection to deception is based on two key points. First, it is not a nice thing to do. While the SRA *Guidelines* recognize that minor deception is widespread in social interaction, we can agree that it is not desirable. Second, there is the question of professional self-interest. If social researchers became known as people who pry and deceive as a standard part of their profession, the image of our work would be adversely affected and we might find it difficult to gain financial support and the cooperation of future prospective research participants. As the SRA *Guidelines* puts it:

> It remains the duty of social researchers and their collaborators . . . not to pursue methods of inquiry that are likely to infringe human values and sensibilities. To do so, whatever the methodological advantages, would be to endanger the reputation of social research and the mutual trust between social researchers and society which is a prerequisite for much research.

THINKING DEEPLY 6.1
The role of deception in research

One of the authors of this book remembers being subjected to deception as an undergraduate, as part of a psychology study, and this story will probably be familiar to anyone who has helped out a final year psychology student as a participant in an experiment. The scenario was as follows. He was taken to a lab environment with a computer and asked to perform tasks that involved memorizing things. He was then asked to listen to some classical music. Following this, he was given another memory exercise. Then the experiment ended.

We can read between the lines and work out that this experiment was probably testing the impact of classical music on short-term memory, but this did not become clear until after the experiment had ended. The participant was deceived through not having been informed about the aims of the study at the start. The question is—if he had known what the study was trying to measure, would this have impacted upon his performance in the memory test?

In this example, deception was used to avoid prompting an 'unnatural response' in a laboratory setting. In laboratory experiments it is inevitable that participants' behaviour will be affected by the fact that they know they are being observed, but knowing what the experiment was trying to achieve could have had an even greater effect on the participant's behaviour. Gunderman and Kane (2013) discuss an example of a student who took part in an experiment. The student was asked to discuss a short article with a partner, and the partner expressed a racist sentiment. The experiment carried on and it was not until afterwards that the student was informed that the experiment was on contemporary racism. In such a situation it is likely that informing the participant beforehand of the nature of the experiment would have impacted on their behaviour, but is this ethical? Was any harm done to the participant through their involvement in this study? What if the participant had demonstrated support for the racist sentiment and then had the debrief—would they have felt that they had been tricked into revealing something that they did not want others to know?

Source: Gunderman and Kane (2013), **www.theatlantic.com/health/archive/2013/04/a-study-in-deception-psychologys-sickness/274739/** (accessed 24 January 2020).

Similarly, Erikson (1967: 369) has argued that covert observation 'is liable to damage the reputation of sociology in the larger society and close off promising areas of research for future investigators'.

One of the main problems with adhering to this ethical principle is that deception is, as some writers observe, widespread in social research (see Section 6.3 under 'Ethical transgression is widespread'). It is rarely possible to give participants a totally complete account of what your research is about. As we explore in Thinking deeply 6.1, sometimes research requires an element of deception. As Punch (1979) found in an incident we will refer to in Chapter 18 (see Section 18.3 under 'Active or passive?'), when a police officer he was working with told a suspect that Punch was a detective, Punch could hardly announce to the suspect that he was not in fact a police officer and give a full account of his research. Despite taking a stance that is predominantly universalist in terms of ethics, Bulmer (1982) recognizes that there are bound to be instances like this and considers them justifiable. However, it is very difficult to know where the line should be drawn.

6.5 The difficulties of ethical decision-making

Ethical dilemmas

We have outlined four key ethical principles, but it will be clear by now that adhering to these principles in practice is not as simple as it might at first seem (for example, see Learn from experience 6.5). This comes back to the wide variety of stances on what it means to be ethical or unethical in a research context.

We can see the difficulty of drawing a line between ethical and unethical practices in a number of different social research contexts. Here are some examples.

- Some members of a social setting may be aware of the researcher's status and the nature of their investigation.
- Manuals about interviewing are full of advice about how to encourage interviewees to open up about themselves.
- Interviewers often deliberately underestimate how long an interview will take.
- Researchers interviewing members of the same social or demographic group as themselves (sometimes referred to as insiders) may use this to probe into the lives of their participants and encourage them to reveal inner thoughts and feelings.
- In ethnographic research, **research questions** are either loose or not specified, so that it is doubtful whether ethnographers in particular are able to inform others accurately about the nature of their research.
- Some interviewees may find the questions we ask unsettling or may find the opinionated, forthright atmosphere of a **focus group** discussion stressful, especially if they inadvertently reveal more than they might have intended.
- Researchers making use of social media data can find it difficult to decide what is in the public or private domain and to accurately assess what is sensitive, when consent to quote data should be sought, and what the extent of harms could be for unaware participants.

There are, in other words, many ways in which social researchers might, perhaps accidentally, deceive or fail to gain informed consent. Of course, these kinds of ethical violations are a long way from the deceptions perpetrated in the research summarized in Research in focus 6.1 and 6.2, but they do point to the difficulty of arriving at ethically informed decisions in practice. Ethical codes give advice on which practices are clearly inappropriate (though sometimes leaving some room for manoeuvre, as we have seen), but they provide less guidance on marginal areas of ethical decision-making. Indeed, guidelines may even be used by research participants *against* the researcher when they try to limit the boundaries of an interviewer or fieldworker's investigation (Punch 1994).

We also need to recognize that there is sometimes a clash between the ethically desirable and the practical. For example, we have discussed that some researchers secure the informed consent of research participants by asking them to sign a consent form. However, we also know that asking people to sign such a form can reduce their willingness to be involved in **survey research**. For example, one study from the USA showed that 13 per cent of respondents were willing to participate in a study but not if they were required to sign a consent form (Singer 2003). This has led Groves et al. (2009) to recommend that for survey research the interviewer should ask the participant for their informed consent by speaking with them, and then sign the form on their behalf. However,

LEARN FROM EXPERIENCE 6.5
Dealing with ethical dilemmas

Sometimes, despite our best efforts to prepare, an ethical issue that we did not anticipate will arise. Sarah discusses an ethically difficult situation that occurred while she was in the field.

> In conducting my postgraduate research project with lone mothers, I encountered an ethical dilemma due to my dual identity/positionality as both a researcher and a volunteer (I volunteered at the organization specifically for this research project). A lone mother I was interviewing was contemplating withdrawing from the study. She seemed quite hesitant to do so, saying she thought that if she withdrew from the study, I would not support her as a volunteer. I had to reassure her that this was not the case; I would support her either way. Consequently, she decided to withdraw during the interview. I have found that ethical practices have to be embedded throughout the research process and go beyond the informed consent stage.
>
> Sarah

The important lesson to take from this is that ethics is not something that is dealt with at the start of a project, it is a live issue that we must always pay attention to and monitor.

You can read about our panellists' backgrounds and research experiences on page xxvi.

many surveys are now conducted online and gaining written or spoken consent is not possible. In this situation, it is important that you introduce the survey, setting out its aims and objectives, and that you record consent by asking participants to tick a box confirming that they understand the terms under which they are contributing and want to continue.

We saw in Learn from experience 6.1 that the kinds of participants that a study involves, and the extent of their vulnerability, can have implications for ethical decision-making. This is particularly true for studies involving children (as Scarlett's project did), and we explore the particular considerations for this type of research in Thinking deeply 6.2. Similarly, the nature of the *data* we are using can further complicate ethical decision-making. The key ethical principles we have discussed so far relate to primary data that is collected by a researcher from first-hand sources, such as data from surveys or **semi-structured interviews**, but secondary data, online data, and visual data pose different sets of ethical questions, as we will discuss in the sections that follow.

Ethical issues for secondary data

Secondary data projects use data that has already been collected. It is common to use secondary data in quantitative research, and we discuss this in detail in Chapter 14. It is also possible to conduct a secondary analysis of qualitative data. If someone else has collected the data you need to answer your research questions, then using this can save a lot of time. Gathering primary data is resource-intensive and time-consuming, particularly for representative surveys or when conducting interviews or focus groups, so reusing the data that others have collected can be a sensible decision. However, there are still ethical issues with the use of secondary data even though you did not collect it yourself.

If the data is available through a website, such as the UK Data Archive, then the researcher who deposited the data will have gained the right permissions to share their data with other researchers (see Tips and skills 6.2 for an example of how this consent can be recorded). But there are often data security requirements for using such data: these may include registering why you want to use the data, agreeing to delete it by a certain date, and, depending on how sensitive the data is, undergoing special training or gaining approved researcher status and maintaining strict data access controls (such as keeping the data on an encrypted device). One important thing to think about, if you are using this type of data for a dissertation, is that if you are granted a licence to use this data the licence is applicable only to you. If you think that you will need help from your supervisor when analysing this data, then they should also apply for access to it.

Ethical issues for online data

It is important to remember that online data does not just refer to social media; it covers a whole host of sources including blogs, discussion groups, email, hyperlinks, chatrooms, comment threads, instant messaging, and newsgroups. As well as this range of data types we have a variety of platforms, all with different purposes and terms of service, including Facebook, Instagram, Reddit, Twitter, YouTube, VK, and so on. To add to the complexity, different platforms have completely different operating frameworks—consider how different communication between friends is on WhatsApp and Snapchat compared

THINKING DEEPLY 6.2
Ethical concerns when conducting research with children

Conducting research with children generates some particular additional ethical concerns. You need to consider their capacity to consent, which may involve asking parents or carers to give permission on their behalf.

GDPR also places an emphasis on the right to be forgotten (the right to erasure) in relation to data provided by children (or people who are now adults but who *generated* the data when they were children), particularly in online environments. Organizations have to pay special attention to requests to remove personal data that was collected when the individual was a child.

The particular difficulty for social researchers investigating online environments is that it is not always possible to identify the age of participants. Using Twitter as a simple example, a user may give their age on their profile or they may not. Even if they do, it might not be accurate.

to Facebook. Some of this data may be public (Twitter), some private (WhatsApp), and other data may sit somewhere in the middle (Facebook), and we know from earlier in this chapter that users' expectations of privacy often differ hugely from the actual terms that they have signed up to. None of this necessarily prevents you from researching users on these platforms, but you will need to know very early on in your research project whether the ideas that you have are possible and whether you can actually access the data that you need to answer your research questions. So where to begin?

A good place to start is to consider the ethical expectations established by the platform. For instance, is there a posted site policy that notifies users that the site is public and specifies the limits to their privacy? Or are there mechanisms that users can use to change their default settings and indicate that their exchanges are private? The more that the platform is acknowledged to be public, the less obligation there is on the researcher to protect the confidentiality and anonymity of individuals using it, or to try to get their informed consent. Another issue is that often there will be a lot of people involved in the relevant posts or discussions (imagine a tweet or Facebook post with 100+ replies), making it difficult if not impossible to seek informed consent from all of the people who have contributed. The AoIR provides a useful graphic that captures the range of considerations for researchers conducting research online or using online data (**https://aoir.org/aoir_ethics_graphic_2016/**, accessed 21 August 2019). As stated at the top of the chart, 'while not intended to provide answers, it promotes consideration of a range of issues and questions that may become relevant in the course of any internet related research.' The good thing about the AoIR guidelines is that they encourage us to ask 'problem questions' about ethical research practice online and to seek some answers. This helps us to reflect on the implications of our research in greater depth.

Other than these helpful guidelines, it is surprisingly hard to find clear, directive guidance on conducting ethical online research. Halford (2018) identifies five factors (which she refers to as 'disruptions') that make the data generated through online research different from other data in terms of ethical considerations. Halford discusses these factors in the context of social media research, but they actually apply to most online research settings.

1. Online data are already created. Traditionally, social researchers have *generated new data* that specifically addresses their research questions. Even where secondary data analysis has taken place, the data is usually from another research study. In contrast, online data exists independently of research. We do not know who has generated it, so typical ethical practice of ensuring that consent is given before data collection is simply not possible. The implications of this are extensive.
2. Online data are beyond our control. In a typical survey, interview, or focus group study we could promise that participants' data would be kept confidential. We can secure it either physically, in locked rooms or cabinets, or digitally on encrypted hardware. We do not have similar control over online data—much of which is publicly observable, or at least observable to many outside of the research team. This is why anonymization of online data is so difficult.
3. Online data are not finite. This means that they are not fixed or permanent. A participant normally has the right to withdraw in a traditional social research project, but what does withdrawal mean for someone who has deleted a post on Reddit? What if they edit a post? How can we abide by the GDPR principle of keeping personal data accurate and up to date in this context?
4. Our assumptions about scale and granularity do not apply to online data. The sheer volume of data available to us means that it is difficult to have any relationship with participants (Halford even questions whether 'participant' is an appropriate term in this context). Ethical practice is often discussed in terms of the individual, but what is the relationship between a 'like' on Facebook and the individual who clicked the 'like' button?
5. Online data are attracting interest from across disciplines. Social research is no longer the exclusive domain of social scientists, with our ethical frameworks and well-tested methodological tools. Although social research is catching up with the ethical issues surrounding online data, other subject fields are making extensive use of online data and they may have very different ethical outlooks concerning what is public data and how it should be treated.

Halford's list is one way of thinking about the difficulties of dealing with this type of data, and there are no doubt many more. We can react to these difficulties in one of two ways. The first is to decide that it's all too complicated and messy, and to turn our backs on online data. The second is to embrace the complexities, reflect on our practice, and forge a way forward. As Woodfield and Iphofen (2018: 7) say: 'These challenges are hard things to tackle, but they also give us great opportunities to push the boundaries of our practice as social scientists.'

Ethical issues for visual data

Research methods using visual media such as photos have become increasingly popular, and these too raise particular ethical issues. An example is the rise of visual ethnography (see Chapter 18, Section 18.5, under 'Visual ethnography'). It is clearly best practice to get the informed consent of those who appear in photos, but it may not be possible to do this for absolutely everyone who appears. Some people may be in the background and may have moved away before the researcher can ask them to provide their informed consent. Also, the significance of a photo may only become clear when the researcher is analysing the visual and non-visual data, and by then it may not be possible to obtain informed consent from those affected. One solution is to 'pixelate' people's faces so that they cannot be identified.

A further potential ethical dilemma arises in relation to a **category** of visual research known as **photo-elicitation**, which sometimes takes the form of getting research participants to take their own photos and then encouraging them to discuss the images (see Chapter 18: Section 18.5, under 'Visual ethnography', and Research in focus 18.10). As Clark (2013) notes, the problem here is that, in a sense, it is the research *participant* who needs to secure informed consent when people appear in their photos. He notes that one of the areas of ethical anxiety for the participants in one of his research projects was how Clark and his co-researchers intended to use the images that were taken. Some participants were very cautious and either declined to take any photos or took photos but limited Clark and his co-researchers' access to them. As Clark observes, when consent was negotiated by participants, there is uncertainty about what exactly the implications are for how such photos can be used in research.

Social media clearly provides a rich, voluminous, and easily accessible source of visual data. Hand (2017: 217) observes that 'many of the problems faced by social media researchers—how to assess meaning, how to develop critique, how to identify continuity and discontinuity—are paralleled with those interpreting visual culture (Banks 2008, Heywood and Dandywell 2012, Jencks 1995).' However, the ethical difficulties with using this data and reproducing it in publications should be clear from our discussion in this section (see under 'Ethical issues for online data')—so we recommend that you proceed with caution.

6.6 Politics in social research

Ethics are not the only way in which wider issues impact upon social research. In this final section we will consider the ways in which politics (in the sense of status, power dynamics, and the use of power rather than of political parties and governance) plays an important role in all stages of social research—sometimes interlinking with discussions of ethics and bringing up potential ethical concerns.

In Chapter 2 (Section 2.6, under 'Values'), we noted that values intrude into all phases of the research process—from the choice of a research area to the formulation of conclusions. This means that as social researchers we never conduct an investigation in a moral vacuum: we are influenced by a whole range of presuppositions that in turn have implications for our projects. This view is now widely accepted among social researchers, including by proponents of quantitative research, an approach that has sometimes been presented as committed to objectivity (e.g. Lincoln and Guba 1985). In reality, many quantitative researchers do not see total objectivity as possible or even desirable, and today you rarely hear anyone claim that social research can be conducted in a wholly objective, value-neutral way. In fact, some writers on social research advocate what is known as 'conscious partiality', a term introduced by Mies (1993: 68). This refers to the idea that researchers should partially identify with those they are studying, and it differs from straightforward empathy or subjectivity in that Mies says the researcher should be conscious that they are taking a side and try to correct any distorted perceptions (both of the research participants and of the researcher).

In this section we will consider the many ways in which social research can be affected by politics, covering themes of taking sides (we mentioned above that the 'conscious partiality' stance involves taking sides to some degree, and being aware of this fact); the funding of research; gaining access to a research setting; working with and within the setting; working in a team; publishing findings; and claims of expertise in certain research methods.

Taking sides in research

As we anticipated in Chapter 2, in the context of how researchers' values can orient and shape their research, social researchers are sometimes put in the position where their politics and ideas about the world mean that they take sides, which can shape their methods and approaches. This might occur involuntarily (for example because they have developed empathy for those they are studying during the course of an ethnography—see Chapter 18) or deliberately, because it is their political or ideological standpoint that has motivated their research and they intend to use it to raise awareness or understanding of a group or phenomenon and/or to bring about some form of social change. After all, researchers usually research an area that is of interest to them and something they care about, so they are often invested to some degree, no matter what research method they use. Some writers have argued that the process of taking sides is widespread in sociology (see Thinking deeply 6.3), and this issue has been discussed in different ways within contemporary methodological debates. Feminist research (that is, research adopting the philosophical perspective of **feminism**) has developed the idea of **positionality** to make the research process more transparent and ethical by acknowledging the power relations that are inevitably embedded in research (and which Sarah discussed in Learn from experience 2.2). Relatedly, discussion has emerged within the social sciences around the researcher's position as an 'insider' or 'outsider' to the field, and these ideas have been extensively discussed in recent methodological literature. We will now go on to discuss both positionality and the insider/outsider perspective.

THINKING DEEPLY 6.3
Taking sides in social research: the Becker–Gouldner dispute

In the late 1960s there was an interesting dispute between two leading sociologists: Howard S. Becker (born in 1928) and Alvin Gouldner (1920–80). Their debate raised a number of issues concerning the role of values and politics in research. The issue of taking sides in research is a particularly interesting aspect of their dispute.

Becker (1967) argued that it is not possible to do research that is unaffected by our personal sympathies. When we conduct research, we are often doing so in the context of hierarchical relationships (police–criminal, managers–workers, warders–prisoners, doctors–patients, teachers–students). Becker felt that in the context of these relationships it is difficult not to take sides; instead, the bigger dilemma is deciding which side we are on. Becker recognized that within the field in which he conducted his research at the time—the sociology of deviance—many practitioners were sympathetic towards the underdog (the less privileged person or group) in these hierarchical relationships. At the very least, sociologists of deviance are likely to try to express or represent the viewpoints of criminals, prisoners, mental patients, and others, even if they do not go so far as to identify with them. Becker argued that when they do this, they are more likely to be accused of bias, because they are giving credibility to people or groups who/that are rejected and even hated by society. Why is a study stressing the underdog's perspective more likely to be regarded as biased? Becker gave two possible reasons: because members of the higher group are seen as having an exclusive right to define the way things are in their sphere, and because they are seen as having a more complete picture. In other words, credibility is not equally distributed in society.

Gouldner (1968) argued that Becker exaggerated the issues he described in that not all research involves taking sides. He also argued that it was a mistake to think that, simply because the researcher takes the point of view of a section of society seriously, they necessarily sympathize with that group.

Other voices have contributed to the debate in more recent years. Liebling (2001) has used prison research in the UK to show that not only is it possible to appreciate the value of different perspectives, it is also possible to do this without angering either side too much—in her case, prison officials and prisoners. However, when a researcher believes that a particular group is subject to repeated injustices, we can see that they often do favour a particular perspective. Goffman (2014) used information from a variety of sources (such as parole officers) for her ethnography of Black men who were on the run from the law in Philadelphia, but she admits to taking the

perspective of the men and their families. At times, this stance turns into a tangible anger when she describes what she sees as the underhand actions of the police and the pressures they pile on the women in the men's lives in order to find and prosecute them. Although we might agree with Liebling that it is possible to see and represent more than one viewpoint, it is perhaps not surprising that Goffman 'took the perspective of 6th street residents' (2014: xiv), given that while at the house of one of her informants in the course of her research, she was subject to the same aggressive physical treatment as her subjects:

> The door busting open brought me fully awake. . . . Two officers came through the door, both of them white, in SWAT gear, with guns strapped to the sides of their legs. The first officer pointed a gun at me. . . . The second officer in pulled me out of the cushions and, gripping my wrists, brought me up off the couch and onto the floor, so that my shoulders and spine hit first and my legs came down after. . . . I wondered if he'd broken my nose or cheek. . . . His boot pressed into my back, right at the spot where it had hit the floor, and I cried for him to stop. He put my wrists in plastic cuffs behind my back. . . . My shoulder throbbed, and the handcuffs pinched.
>
> (Goffman 2014: 61)

The positionality debate

The positionality debate is rooted in feminist research, a branch of research that we first discussed in Section 2.6 under 'Values', and to which we will return throughout the book, especially in Chapters 7 and 16 (in the context of its compatibility with quantitative and qualitative research strategies). Feminist research emerged during the 1970s and 1980s as a reaction against the androcentric (focused on men and the masculine point of view) bias in science, and initially its aim was to introduce women into the predominantly male samples that were used for social research and to ask different questions in order to account for women's different life experiences. In the 1980s, the feminist critique evolved to focus on developing new ways of generating knowledge, questioning and disrupting the dominant ways of thinking of that time. The first step in the development of this critique was the emergence of **standpoint** theories (Harding 1986; Hartsock 1983; Haraway 2003; Sandoval 2000), which came from socialist feminism and questioned power relations and their gendered nature. These theories considered the main systems of oppression for women to be patriarchy and capitalism.

Researchers arrived at the idea of positionality through the criticisms that were made of standpoint theories: they argued that by focusing on patriarchy and capitalism, these theories did not pay enough attention to equally oppressive systems and issues such as racism, white supremacy, and colonialism (Collins 1990). An awareness developed of the importance of situating knowledge production in women's experiences, and asking whose experiences are included and whose are left out, laying the foundations for postcolonial feminism (Collins 1990; Mohanty 1984; bell hooks 1989; Anzaldúa 1987). In this context, Haraway (2003) used the phrase 'situated knowledges' (note the use of the plural, implying that there are multiple realities) to highlight that research processes always involve positionality because both researchers and research participants occupy particular positions (such as gender, ethnicity, class) that need to be acknowledged. Similar ideas also shape **intersectionality** theory: the idea that every person occupies positions within different social categories (including gender, social class, sexuality, and race) and that these intersect to shape our experiences (see Key concept 2.7). Haraway and other writers also defined a feminist version of objectivity that reinforced the idea that research cannot be neutral and value-free: knowledge and truth are always partial and cannot be separated from the lived experience of the researched.

When considered in light of these ideas, ethical social research takes on a new meaning. It becomes about translating this specificity (the idea that knowledge is always associated with the positions of the researchers and the researched) into research findings that can truly represent these experiences. Positionality means acknowledging that experience captured by research is subjective, power-imbued, and relational (Hesse-Biber 2013), so values, biases, and politics cannot be ignored. By redefining experience, feminist research has led to new social research methods being developed, such as the use of creative and participatory methods. One example is Vacchelli's use of collage in a study with migrant women (Vacchelli 2018), in which the researcher questioned her own positionality alongside that of the research participants when deciding to deviate from standard qualitative research practices to reflect participants' specific subject positions.

Being an insider/outsider

Ideas about whether a researcher is an 'insider' or an 'outsider', and the impact of their position, have become key to discussions about ethical research in recent years, with new approaches being devised to try to overcome the issues raised by this dichotomy. The 'insider' position was first defined by Merton (1972) as when a researcher has cultural, linguistic, ethnic, religious, and/or national continuity with the group studied. In a similar way, professionals who decide to carry out research in their workplace could be defined as research insiders. By extension, an outsider is a researcher without these elements of continuity with the group being studied. The positions were initially seen as opposites, but by the 1990s, there had been a shift towards considering them as a continuum (Surra and Ridley 1991). Writers highlighted the contextual and fluid nature of this position, in that anyone could be considered an insider for certain aspects of their identity and not for others (Christensen and Dahl 1997). They also acknowledged that the insider position is the result of a constant negotiation between the researcher and the actors involved in the field (Andrade 2000; Nowicka and Ryan 2015).

In qualitative research, the position of insider has been seen as privileged, in that it allows researchers to benefit from additional levels of participant trust and openness. However, it has also been noted that when researchers are insiders, both participants and researchers might assume certain shared understandings without questioning them sufficiently (Chavez 2008; Ryan 2015). The position of outsider is less controversial: in quantitative research in particular, researchers with this status are often seen as better placed as they benefit from a certain degree of distance and can collect data beyond the realm of their personal experience. But even outsider researchers cannot be assumed to be neutral and objective: 'being an outsider does not create immunity to the influence of personal perspectives' (Dwyer and Buckle 2009: 59).

An applied example of the insider/outsider research debate is Ryan et al.'s (2011) investigation of studying Muslim communities as non-Muslim researchers, in which they considered issues of trust and access when academics work with community organizations. Given the complexity of this study, in terms of the number of identities and positionings involved, including religion, ethnicity, gender, and age, the researchers decided to use 'community' or 'peer' researchers to carry out fieldwork—this is a method for studying hard-to-reach groups that is sometimes used by researchers working with local communities and organizations. Peer researchers are members of the community who have similar ethnic, religious, or linguistic backgrounds to the research participants and are then 'matched' to the target community. Ryan et al. (2011) compared the barriers experienced by outsider academic researchers in negotiating trust to the peer researchers' advantages in accessing informants in the community, while at the same time warning against the risks of assuming that using insiders as researchers is always a successful strategy. The researchers also highlight the risks of seeing one community as representing all communities of the same religious group.

In summary, we can see that 'taking sides' is not just about preferences, sympathies, or political views: it also involves considering different subject positions in research, taking into account not just identity traits such as gender, age, ethnicity, class, sexuality, disability etc. (as well as how these traits interact) but also the position of the researcher in relation to the target group.

6

Funding of research

Research funding is unlikely to be an issue for undergraduates conducting a research project, but for postgraduates it may be applicable. Either way, funding is important to consider: journals often require researchers to declare who funded their work, and you may be reading papers and/or reports that have been funded by external organizations. Much social research is funded by such organizations as firms and government departments, which often have a vested interest in the outcomes of the research. The very fact that some research is funded while other research is not suggests that political issues may be involved, in that organizations are likely to want to invest in studies that will be useful to them and supportive of their operations and worldviews. Such organizations are often proactive, in that they may contact researchers about carrying out an investigation or call for researchers to tender bids for an investigation in a certain area. When social researchers participate in these kinds of exercises, they are entering a political arena because they are having to tailor their research concerns and even research questions to a body that defines, or at least influences, those research concerns and research questions.

When bodies such as government departments (for example, the Home Office in the UK) decide whether to provide funding for a research project, they are going to be influenced by how relevant the study seems to be to their work and by their understanding of their department's concerns. Discussing research in the field of crime, Hughes (2000) observes that an investigation of gun crimes among Britain's 'underclass' is more likely to receive funding than one that looks into state-related wrongdoings. Morgan (2000) points out that research funded by the UK Home Office is usually empirical; adopts quantitative research methods; is concerned with the costs and benefits of a policy or innovation; is short-termist (the cost–benefit analysis is usually concerned with immediate impacts rather than longer-term ones); and is uncritical (it does not probe government policy; it just considers the effectiveness of ways of implementing policy). There is also the fact that many agencies restrict what researchers are able to publish about their findings by insisting on seeing drafts of all proposed publications. Even bodies such as the ESRC, the UK's major funder of social research, increasingly shape their research programmes around what are seen as areas of concern in society and try to involve non-academics as evaluators of, and audiences for, research. This is because the ESRC is itself involved in a political process of trying to secure a continuous stream of funding from government, so needs to be able to demonstrate the relevance of its work.

Gaining access

Gaining access to a research setting, for example an organization, is also a political process, as we discuss further in Chapter 18 (Section 18.3, under 'Gaining access to a research setting'). Access is usually mediated by **gatekeepers**, who are concerned about the researcher's motives: what the organization can gain from the investigation, and what it will lose by participating in the research in terms of staff time and other costs, and potential risks to its image. Often, gatekeepers will try to influence how the investigation takes place in terms of the kinds of questions the researcher can ask, who can and cannot be the focus of study, the amount of time to be spent with each research participant, the interpretation of findings, and the form of any report to the organization itself. Reiner (2000) suggests that the police, for example, are usually concerned about how they are going to be represented in publications in case they are portrayed unfavourably to agencies to which they are accountable. Singh and Wassenaar observe that 'ethical dilemmas can occur if the gatekeeper is coercive in influencing participant involvement in the research' (2016: 43). Companies are also concerned about how they are going to be represented. All of this means that gaining access is almost always a matter of negotiation, so it inevitably turns into a political process. The results of this negotiation are often referred to as 'the research bargain'.

Working with and within a research setting

Getting permission to enter a setting is only the first stage in gaining access to the people or situations that are of interest to a researcher. Once in the organization, researchers often find that they have to constantly negotiate and renegotiate what is and is not allowed because there are several layers of gatekeepers, or the gatekeepers change during the course of the project (for example, if the original gatekeeper moves to a new job), so issues of access become an ongoing feature of research. For example, for their research on cargo vessels Sampson and Thomas (2003: 171) sought initial access through ship-owning or managing companies, but found that 'the *key* gatekeeper is invariably the captain'. Captains varied in the degree of willingness to accommodate the researchers' investigative and other needs, and their chief officers, who represented a further layer of access, were frequently delegated responsibility for dealing with the fieldworkers. These officers also varied a great deal, with the researchers quoting one case in which the chief officer wanted to call a meeting about how the interviews should be conducted whereas another officer gave a much freer rein. Researchers also need to continually work to win and retain the trust of those they are studying. Researchers are often treated with suspicion and are presented with more reserved speech and behaviour because people are uncertain about their motives—for example, employees may suspect that researchers are really working for management.

In short, researchers cannot assume that just because gatekeepers have given them access to the setting, their dealings with the people they are studying will be straightforward from that point on. Some participants will obstruct the research process, perhaps because they are suspicious or because they doubt the usefulness of social research. Researchers may also find themselves caught up in the internal politics of organizations, and groups within an organization may even try to use research projects to help convey their particular viewpoint or advance a particular cause.

Working in a team

When researchers work in teams, politics may be an influencing factor, owing to team members' different career (and other) objectives and different perceptions of their contributions. These kinds of issues are unlikely to affect most undergraduate or postgraduate research projects, but they are worth bearing in mind given that team-based assignments are becoming increasingly popular. Another way in which working with other researchers connected to your institution might influence social research is that supervisors of postgraduate research and undergraduate dissertations may be evaluated in terms of the number of postgraduate students they guide through to completion of a project, or in terms of the quality of the undergraduate dissertations for which they were responsible. These kinds of wider political processes could be relevant to many of this book's readers.

Publishing findings

Research can be affected by pressure to restrict the publication of findings. Steele et al. (2019) investigated agreements between researchers and the Coca-Cola Company. Although the content of the contracts varied, generally they found that Coca-Cola reserved the right to review and feedback on research before it is submitted for publication, but that researchers had the right to not accept any suggested changes. The primary concern for the authors was the presence of early termination clauses, meaning that Coca-Cola could stop funding a project before it had ended:

> Although not all agreements we reviewed allow for full recall of research documents and materials, we identified several agreements that in effect allow Coca-Cola to terminate a study, if the findings are unfavourable to Coca-Cola.
>
> (Steele et al. 2019: 282)

The authors observe that they did not find any evidence of Coca-Cola blocking the publication of negative research findings, but that these provisions might influence the conclusions that researchers draw from their work.

Method and expertise

The final way in which research can be influenced by political factors is through what Savage (2010) calls the politics of *method*. He argues that the social sciences, especially sociology, emerged as credible disciplines in the UK because their practitioners claimed to have expertise in using particular research methods in a neutral and broadly 'scientific' manner to explore the social world. Early researchers' use of sampling techniques, questionnaires, and interviewing was associated with this drive to be taken seriously as an academic discipline that offered a different expertise compared to the discipline of economics. The early UK sociologists were not claiming that they were the *only* professionals to use these research methods (market researchers, for example, were well-known practitioners), but that they could use them to uncover and explore 'the social', a domain that either had not previously been addressed by other academics or had been addressed in a loose and fairly unsystematic manner. This was a political battle for what Savage refers to as 'jurisdiction', and sociology largely emerged as a winner.

Savage argues (see also Savage and Burrows 2007) that this jurisdiction is under threat because others now use the methods over which sociologists claimed special expertise, and new kinds of data about social issues (such as social media) are emerging that sociologists play little or no role in curating. The field of research methods has become an arena in which many groups and individuals claim to have methodological expertise that allows them to understand the social world. It is therefore important that, as social researchers, we both continue the tradition of rigorous empirical enquiry and engage in new and innovative methodological debates. This may mean rethinking what skills and competencies should be part of the social scientist's toolkit in the twenty-first century and committing to developing new expertise in emerging areas, such as the use of social media data in social research.

KEY POINTS

- A number of ethical concerns can arise in the context of collecting and analysing data for social research, particularly in terms of the relations between researchers and research participants. The rights of research participants are the main focus of ethical principles, but issues of professional self-interest—and the interests of the researcher's institution—are also of concern.
- The codes and guidelines of professional associations provide some guidance, and it is important to be familiar with at least one of these codes of practice. Researchers also need to be familiar with the

guidelines provided by bodies within their institution, often called ethics committees, and with the process and requirements for submitting proposals to this body.

- The guidelines of professional associations are not always clear or definitive, and they often imply that researchers need to exercise some autonomy with regard to ethical issues. It is a good idea to check with your supervisor about any potential ethical concerns for your project, especially if the professional guidance is ambiguous.
- The main areas of ethical concern in social research relate to harm to participants or researchers; lack of informed consent; invasion of privacy; and deception.
- Covert observation and certain notorious studies have been particular focuses of concern, but the ethical concerns involved in most research projects are usually much less extreme than in these examples, and more nuanced.
- The boundaries between ethical and unethical practices are not always clear-cut, and writers on social research ethics have adopted several different stances in relation to the issue. Among these are universalism; situation ethics; the idea that ethical transgression is widespread; the 'anything goes' approach; and arguments for deontological versus consequentialist ethics.
- Projects using online data, particularly from social media, and/or visual data require special consideration.
- There are political **dimensions** to the research process that can affect research practice, findings, and how the findings are used. These dimensions are to do with power balances and how power is exercised at different stages of an investigation, and they often relate to the influence of values.

QUESTIONS FOR REVIEW

1. Why are ethical issues important in relation to conducting social research?
2. Outline the different stances on ethics in social research.
3. In what ways could participants be harmed through taking part in research?
4. What are some of the difficulties researchers might encounter when trying to ensure that no harm will come to their participants?
5. Why is the issue of informed consent the subject of such debate?
6. What are the main difficulties in securing informed consent from participants?
7. Why is the privacy principle important?
8. Why is it important to avoid deception?
9. How helpful are notorious research examples such as Milgram's electric shock experiments and Humphreys' study in helping us understand how ethical principles operate in social research?
10. How easy is it to conduct ethical research?
11. Read one of the professional codes of practice that we refer to in this chapter. How effective is it in helping researchers avoid ethical transgressions?
12. Why might traditional frameworks of ethical conduct not be suitable for guiding online research?
13. What are the key considerations for the ethical use of visual data?

14. What do we meant when we say that politics plays a role in social research?
15. In what ways does politics manifest itself in social research?

ONLINE RESOURCES

www.oup.com/he/srm6e

You can find our notes on the answers to these questions within this chapter's **online resources**, together with:

- *audio/video comments* on this topic from our 'Learn from experience' panellists;
- *audio discussion from the authors* on the importance of ethical issues in relation to conducting social research (review question 1);
- *self-test questions* for further knowledge-checking;
- a *flashcard glossary* to help you recall key terms; and
- a *Student Researcher's Toolkit* containing practical materials and resources to help you conduct your own research project.

PART TWO

QUANTITATIVE RESEARCH

In Part Two of this book we focus on quantitative research, beginning with its features and the different approaches you can use before moving on to consider the practical issues of collecting and analysing quantitative data.

We set the scene in Chapter 7 by exploring the main features of this research strategy. Then, in the following four chapters, we deal with survey research. In Chapter 8 we discuss the ways in which we select samples of people to participate in survey research. Chapter 9 focuses on the structured interview, one of the most frequently used methods of data collection in quantitative research. Chapter 10 is concerned with another common method of gathering data through survey research—questionnaires that people complete themselves. Chapter 11 provides guidelines on how to ask questions for structured interviews and for questionnaires.

We then move on from survey research to other quantitative research methods. In Chapter 12 we consider structured observation, a method that provides a systematic approach to the observation of people and events. We address content analysis in Chapter 13, showing how it can be used to systematically analyse a wide variety of documents and texts. Chapter 14 discusses how you can conduct research using existing data: official statistics as well as data collected by other researchers.

In Chapter 15, the final chapter of Part Two, we present some of the main tools you can use to analyse the quantitative data you have collected.

The information in Chapter 15 is supplemented by additional materials to support you in analysing quantitative data. Visit the **online resources** for written and video tutorials on using three popular statistical software packages (SPSS, R, and Stata) as well as guidance on using Microsoft Excel for data analysis.

CHAPTER 7

THE NATURE OF QUANTITATIVE RESEARCH

CHAPTER GUIDE

In this chapter we discuss the characteristics of quantitative research, showing what quantitative research typically involves, but also noting that there can be variations from this. In this chapter we explore

- the main features of quantitative research—measurement, causality, generalization, and replication;
- the main steps of quantitative research, which is often presented as a linear succession of stages;
- the importance of concepts in quantitative research and how to develop measures for concepts, including the idea of an *indicator*, used for measuring a concept when there is no direct measure;
- the procedures for checking the reliability and validity of the measurement process;
- some criticisms of quantitative research;
- gaps between the theory of quantitative research and the way it is actually carried out in practice.

7.1 Introduction

In Chapter 2 we noted that the two main social research strategies are qualitative and **quantitative research**—or sometimes a mixture of the two. Each of these strategies has distinctive features, preoccupations, and associated **research methods** and practices. In this chapter we will provide an overview of quantitative research, taking you through some defining features of the strategy, the main preoccupations of quantitative researchers, the steps involved in conducting this type of research, and how its quality can be evaluated. To gain a similar overview of **qualitative research**, you should read Chapter 16, and for an introduction to **mixed methods research** (which involves the use of both quantitative and qualitative elements in the same study), you should read Chapter 24.

7.2 What is quantitative research?

Quantitative research was the dominant strategy for conducting social research until the mid-1970s, since when qualitative research has been increasingly used. Despite this shift, quantitative methods still play an important role in social research, including student social research (see Learn from experience 7.1). In practice, both strategies have much to offer, with the type of strategy chosen also depending on the aims of the research. When we discussed quantitative research as a distinctive **research strategy** in Chapter 2, we broadly described it as involving the collection of numerical data and being characterized by the following key features:

- it takes a **deductive** view of the relationship between **theory** and research, meaning that theory comes first, driving the research, rather than emerging out of it;
- it has a preference for the natural science approach (and **positivism** in particular);
- it has an **objectivist** conception of social reality, implying that social phenomena and their meanings have an existence that is independent of social actors.

Most definitions of quantitative research refer to its focus on numbers, and the term 'quantitative' itself makes it tempting to assume that its focus on the quantification of aspects of social life is the only thing that distinguishes it from qualitative research. In fact, its distinctive **epistemological** position (belief about acceptable forms of knowledge) and **ontological** position (belief about the nature of reality, particularly social entities) suggest that there is much more to it than the presence of numbers, as will become clear as you read this chapter.

There are very few **texts** on quantitative research in the social sciences that outline all the key stages and approaches common to quantitative studies. Some of the texts that cover a wide variety of quantitative approaches also consider qualitative methods (as we do in this book), such as *Social Research Methods: Qualitative and Quantitative Approaches* (Neuman 2013). However, there are a number of excellent texts that focus on particular elements of quantitative social research, such as surveys or statistics. For surveys, see *Designing Surveys: A Guide to Decisions and Procedures* (Blair et al. 2014) and *Surveys in Social Research* (De Vaus 2013). Texts on statistics in the social sciences include *Beginning Statistics for Social Scientists* (Foster et al. 2014), *An Introduction to Secondary Data Analysis* (MacInnes 2017), and *Critical Statistics: Seeing Beyond the Headlines* (De Vries 2018). Also useful are the *SAGE Handbook of Quantitative Methodology for the Social Sciences* (Kaplan 2004) and the *Sage Quantitative Research Methods* series (Vogt 2011). There are a number of extremely useful journals that cover aspects of quantitative research methods, such as *Social Science Research*, *International Journal of Social Research Methodology*, and *Sociological Research Online*.

The main methods of data collection associated with quantitative research are

- **questionnaires** and surveys;
- quantitative content analysis, which evaluates documents and texts;
- secondary data analysis, which evaluates data already collected by others;
- **structured observation**, which involves systematically observing and recording behaviour.

LEARN FROM EXPERIENCE 7.1

Perceptions of quantitative research

Some students entering social science programmes have little experience of mathematical probability and statistics. Researchers have found that many students expect an emphasis on qualitative data, and simply don't expect, or want, to encounter statistics (Williams et al. 2016). This can lead to 'maths anxiety' among students (British Academy 2015; Clark and Foster 2017; Foster and Gunn 2017; MacInnes 2017). However, Zvi, who produced a quantitative dissertation on the relationship between screen time and sleep time among adolescents, indicated the need to be open-minded about the possibilities that quantitative research presents.

> I think many of my cohort, including myself, were quite surprised to learn that quantitative research methods were compulsory as part of our Sociology course at university. I was definitely intimidated at the thought of quantitative research, much more than qualitative research, because I had not formally studied maths or statistics since I was 16. Even though I thought I was good at maths, it was definitely something I couldn't wait to drop after I finished school! This was a preconception that many of my friends also had—that quantitative meant maths—whereas in reality this is quite far from the truth. My advice would be to remain open-minded about the use of quantitative methods as a social science student because, as I learned, it can be very useful in answering sociological enquiry. Also, don't be intimidated by the word 'quantitative' and don't assume that you have to be 'good' at maths or statistics, because often you just need to be able to understand why a method is useful or how a calculation works in practice, rather than being able to recite the mathematical formula!
>
> Zvi

 Access the **online resources** to hear Zvi's video reflections on this theme.

You can read about our panellists' backgrounds and research experiences on page xxvi.

7

While these are the core data-collection methods, so they are the ones that we focus on here, you should be aware that quantitative methods are continually evolving with new methods being regularly developed. It is also worth noting that researchers are not limited to one approach, and that studies often use more than one method—this is called **multi-method research**. Technological innovations have affected the kinds of quantitative analysis that we can conduct and have led to the development of software that enables more sophisticated forms of statistical analysis (MacInnes 2017). We discuss some of these software packages in Chapter 15. The use of **self-completion questionnaires** has also been affected by increased technological advances (see Chapter 10). For example, there are now a large number of software packages that can help you produce surveys, collect data, and analyse the data collected. While these tools still need the researcher's input and expertise, they can certainly simplify the quantitative research process.

Quantitative researchers have been presented with new possibilities for secondary data analysis by the emergence of what is known as **Big Data** (see Key concept 14.4). This usually refers to sources of data that are so large that they are difficult to process and analyse through conventional methods. The term 'Big Data' may also refer to predictive analytics, or other advanced data analytics, not just to the size of the data. In quantitative social research, the main Big Data used has been social media content: especially from Twitter and Facebook, but also Instagram and other platforms. In Chapter 13 we provide examples of how social scientists have used quantitative content analysis to evaluate Big Data drawn from social media. Overall, while the standard quantitative methods remain popular (though, as we will see in Chapter 12, structured observation is less frequently used), it is evident that the possibilities presented by Big Data and technological developments are transforming the quantitative research landscape.

7.3 The main preoccupations of quantitative researchers

Both quantitative and qualitative research can be seen as exhibiting sets of distinctive and contrasting preoccupations. These preoccupations reflect epistemologically grounded beliefs about what constitutes acceptable knowledge. In this section, we will examine four preoccupations of quantitative research: measurement, causality, generalization, and replication.

Measurement

The most obvious preoccupation in quantitative research is with measurement, which is seen to be beneficial for a number of reasons. We will come back to measurement, and the reasons it is so important to quantitative researchers, in detail in Section 7.5.

Causality

In most quantitative research, explanation is a key focus. Quantitative researchers are rarely focused on just describing *how* things are; they want to say *why* things are the way they are. For example, if a researcher was studying racial prejudice, they would generally want to go further than describing how much prejudice exists in a certain group of individuals, or what proportion of people in a sample are prejudiced. They would probably want to examine the *causes* of variation in racial prejudice, perhaps explaining it in terms of personal characteristics (such as levels of authoritarianism) or social characteristics (such as education or social mobility). The idea of 'independent' and 'dependent' variables reflects this tendency to think in terms of causes and effects. Staying with our example of racial prejudice, we could consider the concept of *racial prejudice* as the dependent variable, which can be explained by *authoritarianism*, an independent variable that has a causal influence upon prejudice.

When we use an experimental design (see Chapter 3, Section 3.3), the independent variable is the variable that is manipulated, and the direction of causal influence is clear: the researcher manipulates the independent variable and then observes any subsequent change in the dependent variable. However, with a cross-sectional design (see Chapter 3, Section 3.4), the kind most often used in survey research, the direction of causal influence can be less obvious as the data are simultaneously collected—we cannot say for sure that an independent variable precedes the dependent one. If we want to talk about independent and dependent variables in the context of cross-sectional designs, we must *infer* that one causes the other, like in the example of authoritarianism and racial prejudice. To do this we need to draw on common sense or theoretical ideas, and there is always the risk that the inference will be wrong.

This preoccupation with causality reflects concerns about internal validity, which we discussed in Chapter 3 (Section 3.2), noting that a criterion of good quantitative research is the extent to which we can be confident about the causal inferences. This means that research that has the characteristics of an experimental design is often more highly valued than cross-sectional research, because there is greater confidence in the causal findings. The rise of longitudinal research, such as the UK's *Understanding Society* study (as described in Research in focus 3.7) and the *Our Future* study (also known as the Second Longitudinal Study of Young People in England), is partly because it is easier to make causal inferences using longitudinal data.

Generalization

A key concern of quantitative researchers is whether they can generalize their findings beyond the context of their study—in other words, whether their research has sufficient external validity (another term we discussed in Chapter 3). As we touched on in Chapter 1 and will discuss in more detail in Chapter 8, it is rarely possible to assess, survey, or interview whole populations, organizations, or sets of documentation for a study, so we usually have to use a smaller sample taken from the larger group (the population). If we want to be able to say that our results can be generalized beyond the cases (for example, the people) that make up the sample, then it needs to be as representative of the larger group as possible. The main way researchers seek to generate a representative group is through probability sampling, which uses random selection to create the sample. This largely eliminates bias from the process of selection, but even this method does not guarantee sample representativeness because, as we will see in Chapter 8, it can be affected by other factors.

Strictly speaking, we cannot generalize beyond the population of which the sample is intended to be representative. If the members of the population from which a sample is taken are all inhabitants of a town, city, or region, or all members of an organization, we can only generalize to the inhabitants or members of that town, city, region, or organization. Despite this, it can be tempting to forget or sidestep the limits to generalizability and see findings as having a broader reach, so that if the sample were selected from a large city such as Birmingham, the findings would be relevant to similar cities. This is not good practice, and you should avoid making inferences beyond the population from which you selected your sample.

Generalization is a key concern across quantitative research—and it is this aspect of the strategy that often makes it attractive to student researchers (see Learn from experience 7.2)—but the focus on generalizability or external validity is particularly strong among quantitative researchers using cross-sectional and longitudinal designs. There is also a focus on generalizability among experimental researchers, as we noted in our discussion of external validity in Chapter 3, but users of this **research design** usually give greater attention to issues of internal validity.

Replication

The final quantitative research preoccupation we need to consider is that of replication. Again, we can draw parallels with the natural sciences, which are often shown as aiming to reduce the contaminating influence of the scientist's biases and values to a bare minimum. If biases and lack of objectivity were widespread, the natural sciences' claim to provide a definitive picture of the world would be undermined. In order to minimize the influence of these potential problems, scientists may seek to replicate (to reproduce) each other's experiments. If the findings repeatedly couldn't be replicated, serious questions would be raised about their validity. As a result, scientists are often very explicit about their procedures so that their experiments can be replicated. Quantitative researchers in the social sciences also regard the ability to replicate as an important part of their activity. It is therefore often seen as important that researchers clearly present their procedures so they can be replicated by others, even if the research does not end up being replicated.

In fact, replication is not a common activity in the natural or social sciences. Even where it is done, it is often difficult to ensure that the conditions in a replication are precisely the same as those in an original study. However, the example described in Research in focus 7.1, which is a replication *and extension* of several previous studies, shows how important this type of approach can be.

7

LEARN FROM EXPERIENCE 7.2
Generalizability in a student project

Many of our panellists cite generalizability as a key advantage of quantitative research.

> The main aspect of quantitative research that made it attractive to me was its level of generalizability. I really liked the idea of being able to generalize the findings from my research to a much wider population. The data I used came from a sample of 80,000 school-aged children in the United States. The sample was representative in terms of gender, age, and ethnicity. Weights could also be applied to counteract the effect of oversampling, for example of some ethnic minority groups (*see Chapter 8 for more information about weighting*). With this in mind, I could ensure that the findings from my research could be generalized to a much wider population.
>
> Zvi

> By defining and collecting key demographic information about participants I was able to generalize how my sample might be representative (or not) of a wider population.
>
> Jodie

However, as Simon notes, it is important to think critically about the data you use and to consider what limitations to generalizability may also exist.

I investigated the fear of crime using the social media platform Twitter. I chose a quantitative approach as I wanted to see if there were similarities to the Crime Survey for England and Wales (CSEW), which is a quantitative survey. I collected around 4 million tweets and identified relevant cases. I conducted some statistical analysis to identify whether my results were significant. By showing that my Twitter sample had similar patterns to those collected from an established and respected data source (the CSEW), I was able to argue that my results were generalizable to the population. There was a caveat to that because I used Twitter, where the active population is relatively young, which means my results only applied to this age group.

Simon

 Access the **online resources** to hear Zvi's video reflections on this theme.

You can read about our panellists' backgrounds and research experiences on page xxvi.

RESEARCH IN FOCUS 7.1

Replicating (and extending) an existing study

Although it is perhaps more common to replicate studies conducted by other researchers, Brewster and Lynn (2014) conducted what they refer to as a 'replication, extension, and exploration of consumer racial discrimination in tipping' (tipping in the sense of giving restaurant serving staff a small amount of money as a token of appreciation), focusing mainly on replicating a study in which Lynn had been involved (Lynn et al. 2008).

The earlier study demonstrated that Black restaurant servers received lower tips than white servers, and Brewster and Lynn argued that their replication was important because there were limitations in one of the measures used in the original study (a measure of service quality). They also positioned their research as an extension of the earlier investigation by using a more robust measure of 'service skills'. They predicted that this new variable might provide a potential *explanation* (remember that this is important for quantitative researchers) for the ethnicity-tipping relationship: if Black servers are found to receive lower tips, it could be that this is because their service skills tend to be poorer, resulting in diners giving them less financial recognition for their work.

The replication was conducted in a northern city in the USA, whereas the original study had been conducted in a southern city. If Brewster and Lynn's findings had been different from those of the original study, this could have been attributed to differences in the location of the research or differences in the way the data were collected, but the findings of the earlier study were successfully replicated. White servers were shown to receive superior tips to Black servers, so Brewster and Lynn were able to draw attention to the apparent robustness of the relationship between race and tipping.

7.4 The main steps in quantitative research

Figure 7.1 shows the main steps in quantitative research. While the process is rarely this linear, the diagram represents a useful starting point for understanding the main steps in quantitative research and the links between them. We covered some of these steps in Chapters 1, 2, and 3.

The fact that we start by using existing literature and theory (Step 1) signifies that there is a largely deductive approach to the relationship between theory and research. Outlines of the main steps of quantitative research, including Figure 7.1, commonly suggest that **research questions** and a **hypothesis** (see Key concept 7.1) are *deduced* from the theory and tested (Steps 2 and 3)—a process known as **deductivism**. However, in quantitative research, including some published research

FIGURE 7.1
The process of quantitative research

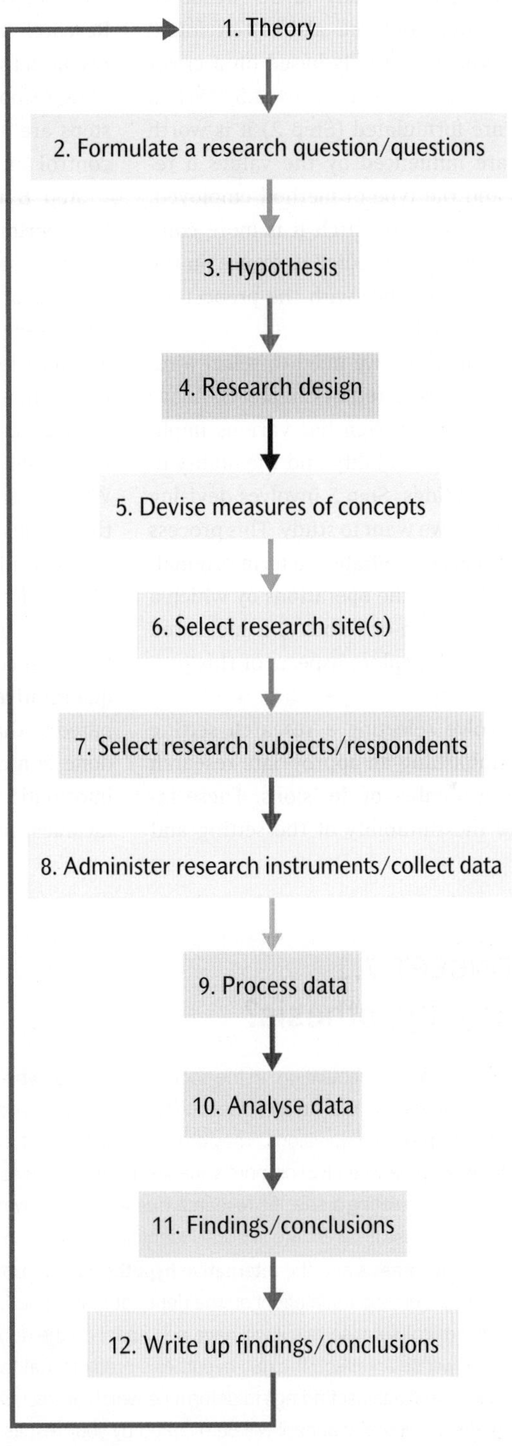

articles, it is worth noting that research questions and hypotheses are not always specified and it may be that researchers only loosely use theory to inform data collection. Hypotheses are most likely to be presented in experimental research, but are also often found in survey research, which is usually based on a cross-sectional design (see Research in focus 3.5). When research questions are formulated (Step 2) it is worth noting that these are influenced by the values a researcher possesses and the type of method employed. For example, in quantitative research it is more common to refer to terms such as 'predict' or 'cause' in the research questions in accordance with the preoccupations of quantitative research.

Step 4 is the point at which we need to select a research design, a topic we explored in Chapter 3. As we saw, the choice of research design has various implications, such as for external validity and the ability to attribute causality to findings. Step 5 involves devising measures of the concepts we want to study. This process is often referred to as **operationalization**, a term originally used in physics to refer to the operations by which a concept (such as temperature or velocity) is measured (Bridgman 1927). We will explore aspects of this process in this chapter.

Steps 6 and 7 involve selecting a research setting and participants. Establishing an appropriate research setting may involve a number of decisions. These include issues around the suitability of the setting and establishing whether it is accessible to the researcher. A number of issues need considering in your choice of participants, as your sample needs to be as representative of your population as possible (see Chapter 8). Research in focus 7.2 provides a couple of examples of research that involved selecting research sites and sampling respondents. In experimental research, these two steps are also likely to include assigning subjects into control and test groups.

Step 8 involves administering the research tools. In experimental research, this is likely to include pre-testing subjects, changing the independent variable (the factor that is thought to be the cause of the outcome—see Key concept 3.3) for the **experimental group**, and post-testing respondents. In cross-sectional survey research, it will involve interviewing the sample using a structured **interview schedule** (see Chapter 9) or distributing a self-completion questionnaire (see Chapter 10). When using structured observation (see Chapter 12), this means observing the setting and the behaviour of people and then assigning categories to each element of behaviour.

Step 9 simply refers to the fact that, once information has been collected, it needs transforming into 'data'. In quantitative research, this is likely to mean that it is prepared so that it can be quantified. Sometimes this can be done in a relatively straightforward way—for example, information relating to such things as people's ages, incomes, number of years spent at school, and so on.

KEY CONCEPT 7.1

What is a hypothesis?

A hypothesis is informed speculation. In the social sciences, a hypothesis is usually based on knowledge of the existing research literature. Blaikie and Priest (2019: 78) refer to hypotheses as 'tentative answers to "why" and, sometimes, "how" research questions. They are our best guess at the answers.' Testing hypotheses about the possible **relationship** between two or more variables is often seen as a key part of quantitative research. This normally involves articulating a specific research question where two (or more) answers are possible. In hypothesis testing, these answers are explicitly identified before data collection takes place and are typically labelled the **null hypothesis** and the **alternative hypothesis**. For example, you might predict that the independent variable will have a demonstrable effect on the dependent variable (see Key concept 3.3 for a definition of a variable), or you might surmise that it will have no impact on the dependent variable. The alternative hypothesis states that there will be an effect; the null hypothesis predicts that there will be none. The research will enable the question to be 'tested' against findings to determine which answer can be shown to be true or false. The hypothesis that you choose to accept will be dictated by your results. If there is no demonstrable effect, the alternative hypothesis is rejected and the null hypothesis accepted, whereas if there is a demonstrable effect the alternative hypothesis is accepted and the null hypothesis rejected.

RESEARCH IN FOCUS 7.2
Selecting research sites and sampling respondents

Vancea et al. (2019) conducted secondary research using representative cross-sectional survey data to explore whether there is evidence that young people in different countries are less satisfied with their lives when they are unemployed or working in precarious conditions. The researchers selected their research site(s) by choosing five European countries (Denmark, the UK, Germany, Spain, and the Czech Republic) corresponding to five different welfare state regimes with different labour market policies and levels of social protection, as defined in welfare regime theories. Once the sites had been selected, the researchers considered the participants to include. They selected a sample of young adults in each of the countries who were economically active or unemployed and also explored their employment conditions. This enabled Vancea and colleagues to explore differences in how the life satisfaction of unemployed and precariously employed young people varied across welfare states with different regimes.

Goldthorpe et al.'s (1968: 2–5) well-known study *The Affluent Worker* is a classic example of selecting a research site and participants in primary research. It involved two decisions about a research site. First, the researchers needed a suitable community to test the 'embourgeoisement' thesis (the idea that affluent workers were becoming more middle-class in their attitudes and lifestyles), which resulted in Luton being selected. Then a sample of 'affluent workers' was identified, in the form of employees from three of Luton's leading employers. The researchers' selection was also influenced by the fact that they wanted the firms selected to cover a range of production technologies, because of evidence at that time that technologies affected workers' attitudes and behaviour. Industrial workers were then sampled according to selected criteria associated with the researchers' interests in embourgeoisement and with the implications of technology for work attitudes and behaviour.

For other variables, quantification will require *coding* of the information—transforming it into numbers to enable the quantitative analysis of the data. For example, leisure activities or type of accommodation would require you to **code** the different responses, turning the categories of the variables into numeric form. If you plan to carry out the data analysis using a software package, you will need to code the data according to the software's specifications.

The preparation of the data is followed by Step 10—the analysis. This involves testing for relationships between variables, and interpreting and presenting the results of the analysis. It is at this stage that the 'findings' emerge (Step 11). It is important to consider the connections between the findings that emerge and the research questions, hypotheses, and/or theories that were developed. For example, what are the implications of the findings for the theoretical ideas that informed the research?

Finally, the research must be written up—Step 12. This involves more than relaying to others what has been found. The writing must *convince* readers that the conclusions are important and the findings robust. Once the findings have been published, they become part of the body of knowledge (or 'theory'). This means there is a feedback loop from Step 12 back up to Step 1.

The presence of both deduction (Steps 2 and 3) and **induction** (the feedback loop) in the process of quantitative research reveals its positivist foundations, and this influence is also visible in the emphasis on translating concepts into measures (Step 5). This idea is central to quantitative research and is characteristic of the principles of phenomenalism (see Chapter 2), which is also a feature of positivism.

Given the importance of translating concepts into measures, we will now consider this phase of the process (Step 5 in Figure 7.1) in more detail. In Section 7.5 we will discuss concepts and their measurement—what it means to devise a 'concept', why we measure it, and how we measure it—before moving on in Section 7.6, 'Reliability and validity of measures', to consider the two main ways through which we can evaluate the quality of the measures we devise.

7.5 Concepts and their measurement

We saw in Sections 7.3 and 7.4 that measurement is a key preoccupation for quantitative research. Let's consider this further, beginning by exploring concepts—the things that quantitative researchers seek to investigate.

What is a concept?

Concepts are the building blocks of theory and the points around which social research is conducted. Just think of the numerous concepts that we touch on in relation to the research examples we cite in this book:

> social capital, ethnic discrimination, gender values, ideological orientation, poverty, social class, job search methods, emotional labour, negotiated order, culture, academic achievement, teacher expectations, abusive supervision cultural capital.

Each concept represents a label that we give to elements of the social world that seem to have common features. De Vaus (2013: 41) states that concepts 'are summaries of a whole set of behaviours, attitudes and characteristics which we see as having something in common'. For example, with the concept of social mobility, we notice that some people improve their socioeconomic position relative to their parents, others stay roughly the same, while others are 'downwardly mobile', moving to a lower social class. These considerations have led to the concept of social mobility.

If a concept is employed in quantitative research, a measure needs to be developed for it so that it can be quantified. These concepts can take the form of independent or dependent variables (see Key concept 3.3). In other words, concepts may provide an explanation of a certain aspect of the social world, or they may stand for things we want to explain. A concept such as social mobility may be used in either capacity: as a possible explanation of certain attitudes (are there differences between the downwardly mobile and others in terms of their political dispositions or social attitudes?) or as something to be explained (what are the causes of variation in social mobility?). Equally, we might be interested in exploring changes in amounts of social mobility over time or between countries. We do not investigate such issues in isolation from theory. We formulate theories to help us understand why, for example, rates of social mobility vary between countries or over time. This will in turn generate new concepts—in our social mobility example, we will probably come up with new concepts as we try to explain the variation in rates.

Why measure?

There are three main reasons for the focus on measurement in quantitative research. These can be summarized as follows.

1. Measurement allows us to identify *fine differences* between people's characteristics.
2. Measurement gives us a *consistent device* for identifying such differences.
3. Measurement provides the basis for *more precise estimates of the degree of relationship between concepts*.

To expand on the first of these reasons, without measurement we can often distinguish extreme categories in our research, but measurement allows us to go a step further. It means, for example, that rather than just identifying clear variations in levels of job satisfaction between people who love or who hate their work we can differentiate between smaller, less extreme variations in job satisfaction.

The consistency that measurement provides relates to both our ability to be consistent over time and our ability to be consistent with other researchers. A measure should not be influenced by the timing of its administration or by the person who administers it. Measurement readings are bound to be influenced over time by social change, but a measure should generate results that are consistent other than when they vary as a result of natural changes. (Whether a measure actually possesses this quality is associated with the issue of ***reliability***, which we touched on in Chapter 3 and will examine again in Section 7.6.) Measurement can also enable us to be consistent with other researchers, meaning that our research helps to build up a single body of knowledge relating to a certain concept or concepts.

An example of a way measurement can provide the basis for more precise estimates of the degree of relationship between concepts is through **correlation** analysis, which seeks to assess the strength and direction of the relationship between variables, a term we will be examining in Chapter 15. If we measure both job satisfaction and things that it might be related to, such as stress-related illness, we can produce more precise estimates of how closely they are related than if we had not proceeded in this way.

How do we measure?

Devising indicators

In order to provide a measure of a concept (often referred to as an **operational definition**, a term deriving from the idea of operationalization), we need to have an **indicator** or indicators that will accurately represent the concept. So there are differences between indicators and measures.

Measures refer to things or quantities that can be relatively unambiguously counted, such as income, age, number of children, or number of years spent at school. Measures, in other words, are quantities. If we are interested in some of the causes of variation in personal income, the latter can be quantified in a reasonably direct way.

We use *indicators* to tap concepts that are less directly quantifiable. If we are interested in the causes in variation in job satisfaction, we will need indicators that will stand for the concept of job satisfaction (which may be about satisfaction with working conditions, for example). These indicators will allow job satisfaction to be measured, and we can treat the resulting quantifiable information as if it were a measure. A further example of the use of indicators can be found in a study involving Twitter data by Williams et al. (2017a), which we referred to in Chapter 2. This quantitative research used the 'broken windows' theory (Wilson and Kelling 1982), which suggests that visible evidence of low-level crime, such as broken windows, encourages more crime. To do this, tweets were classified as containing 'broken windows' indicators including vandalism, graffiti, and unsocial behaviour.

There are a number of ways in which we can devise indicators.

- We may use a question (or series of questions) that is part of a structured interview schedule or self-completion questionnaire. The question(s) could be concerned with the respondents' report of an attitude (for example, job satisfaction), their social situation (for example, poverty), or their behaviour (for example, leisure pursuits).
- We can record individuals' behaviour using a structured **observation schedule**: for example, pupil behaviour in a classroom.
- We may use **official statistics**: for example, Home Office crime statistics measuring criminal behaviour.
- We can examine media content using **content analysis**: for example, to examine depictions of gender on primetime television (Sink and Mastro 2017).

Indicators can be derived from a variety of different sources and methods. The researcher may have to consider whether one indicator of a concept will suffice. Rather than relying on a single indicator of a concept, they may prefer to ask a number of questions (in the course of a structured interview or a self-completion questionnaire, for example) that tap into a certain concept.

Using multiple-indicator measures

In much quantitative research there is a tendency to rely on a single indicator of a concept, and for many purposes this is adequate. However, as we have noted, some researchers decide that a single indicator will not suffice for their research and opt to use a number of indicators that tap into a certain concept. This is known as a **multiple-indicator measure** of a concept. Research in focus 7.3 is an example of one of the most common kinds of multiple-indicator measures for investigating attitudes, known as the **Likert scale**. We consider this method in detail in Key concept 7.2.

A researcher's reasons for using a multiple-indicator measure are likely to include one or more of the following:

- a single indicator may incorrectly classify individuals;
- a single question may be too general or too limited in scope;
- multiple questions allow researchers to make much finer distinctions.

Let's consider each of these reasons. A single indicator can result in incorrect classification due to the wording of the question or to misunderstanding. This kind of error can still happen within a multiple-indicator study, but if there are a number of indicators and some people are misclassified through a particular question it will be possible to offset the effects of that misclassification.

The fact that a single question may need to be very general could mean that it is not able to accurately reflect participants' responses. Alternatively, the indicator may be able to cover only one aspect of the concept, meaning that the researcher misses out on a lot of relevant information. For example, if you were interested in job satisfaction, would it be sufficient to ask people how satisfied they were with their pay? Most people would argue that there is more to job satisfaction than satisfaction with pay. Multiple questions would allow you to explore a wider range of aspects of this concept, such as people's satisfaction with conditions and with the work itself.

RESEARCH IN FOCUS 7.3
A multiple-indicator measure of a concept

Sturgis et al. (2014a) examined whether ethnic diversity in London neighbourhoods had an impact on their social cohesion. They measured social cohesion by giving respondents three statements and asking them to indicate their level of agreement or disagreement with each statement on a five-point scale running from 'Yes, I strongly agree' to 'No, I strongly disagree'. There was a middle point on the scale that allowed for a neutral response. This approach to investigating a cluster of attitudes is known as a Likert scale. The three statements were as follows.

1. People in this area can be trusted.
2. People act with courtesy to each other in public space in this area.
3. You can see from the public space here in the area that people take pride in their environment.

KEY CONCEPT 7.2
What is a Likert scale?

The Likert scale, named after Rensis Likert (1903–1981) who developed the method, is a **multiple-indicator** or **multiple-item measure** of a set of attitudes relating to a particular area, used to measure intensity of feelings. It usually comprises a series of statements (known as **items**) that focus on an issue or theme. Respondents are asked to indicate their level of agreement with the statement. This is usually through a five-item scale going from 'strongly agree' to 'strongly disagree', but seven-item scales and other formats can be used. There is usually a middle position of 'neither agree nor disagree' or 'undecided' that indicates neutrality on the issue.

Each item on the scale is assigned a number, allowing the respondent's replies to be given a score, and then the scores for each item are aggregated (a combined calculation of the different elements) to reach an overall score. Since the scale measures intensity, it is normally structured so that a high level of intensity of feelings receives a high score in each indicator (for example, on a five-item scale, a score of 5 for very strong positive feelings about an issue and a score of 1 for very negative feelings). Variations on the typical format are scales referring to frequency (for example, 'never' through to 'always' or 'very often') and evaluation (for example, 'very poor' through to 'very good').

There are points to bear in mind when constructing a Likert scale. The items

- must all relate to the same object (job, organization, ethnic groups, unemployment, sentencing of offenders, etc.), and
- must be interrelated (see the discussion of **internal reliability** in this chapter and Key concept 7.3).

Relying on answers to a single question can limit the precision and accuracy of our findings. If we ask respondents to indicate the frequency with which something happens using a scale of 1 to 5 (for example 1 = rarely; 5 = very often), then all we can do is assess the respondents on this limited 1-to-5 scale. However, if we use a multiple-indicator measure that asks nine questions of this kind, the range increases to 9 (9 × 1) to 45 (9 × 5). This will allow us to make more precise distinctions between respondents.

Research in focus 7.4 provides a further example of research using Likert scales. Thinking deeply 7.1 considers the design of Likert scales in a UK secondary data set, the British Social Attitudes survey. You can also find a Likert scale from the National Student Survey in Figure 10.1.

Dimensions of concepts

One further approach to measurement is to consider the possibility that the concept in which you are interested is made up of different **dimensions**. This view is particularly associated with Lazarsfeld (1958). The idea is that when the researcher seeks to develop a measure of a

RESEARCH IN FOCUS 7.4
Likert scales

Prada et al. (2018) used a survey containing Likert scales to explore attitudes towards and motives for using emojis and emoticons (emojis being actual pictures; emoticons being keyboard characters, such as punctuation marks, which are put together to form an image or facial expression). The survey was conducted in Portugal and aimed to examine how these attitudes and motives differed according to age and gender. Initially, participants were asked to report how often they use emojis and emoticons (separately) in their text-based modes of communication (their computer or smartphone, for example) using a seven-point Likert scale (from 1 = Never to 7 = Always). Then, they were asked to indicate their general attitude towards the use of emojis and emoticons separately, using a set of six bipolar items (1 = Useful to 7 = Useless; 1 = Uninteresting to 7 = Interesting; 1 = Fun to 7 = Boring; 1 = Hard to 7 = Easy; 1 = Informal to 7 = Formal; 1 = Good to 7 = Bad). The items regarding how useful, fun, informal, and good emoji/emoticon use is seen to be were reverse-coded, so that higher ratings indicated more positive attitudes. The researchers found that all the ratings were higher among younger rather than older participants. Results also showed that women reported using emojis (but not emoticons) more frequently than men and also expressed more positive attitudes towards their usage than men.

THINKING DEEPLY 7.1
Using a Likert scale in a secondary data set

The British Social Attitudes survey (BSA) has used Likert scales in the form of attitude scales for a number of years. The surveys comprise a number of statements to which the respondent is invited to 'agree strongly', 'agree', 'neither agree nor disagree', 'disagree', or 'disagree strongly'. For example, since 1986 the BSA surveys have included two attitude scales aiming to measure respondents' position on certain underlying value dimensions: left–right (political leaning) and libertarian–authoritarian ('libertarianism' is concerned with the belief that personal freedom should be maximized, while 'authoritarianism' is associated with the belief that authority should be obeyed).

Since 1987 (except in 1990 and updated from 2000 to 2001), a similar scale on 'welfarism' has also been included in the BSA. The current version of the scale is shown below. A useful way of summarizing the information from a number of questions of this sort is to construct an additive index. This approach relies on the assumption that there is an underlying—'latent'—attitudinal dimension characterizing the answers to all the questions within each scale. If so, scores on the index are likely to be a more reliable indication of the underlying attitude than the answers to any single question. The items on the welfarism scale are:

The welfare state encourages people to stop helping each other.

The government should spend more money on welfare benefits for the poor, even if it leads to higher taxes.

Around here, most unemployed people could find a job if they really wanted one.

Many people who get social security don't really deserve any help.

Most people on the dole are fiddling in one way or another.

If welfare benefits weren't so generous, people would learn to stand on their own two feet.

Cutting welfare benefits would damage too many people's lives.

The creation of the welfare state is one of Britain's proudest achievements.

The indices for the scale are formed by scoring the leftmost, most pro-welfare position as 1, and the rightmost, most anti-welfare position as 5. The 'neither agree nor disagree' option is scored as 3. The scores to all the questions in each scale are added and then divided by the number of items in the scale, giving indices ranging from 1 (most pro-welfare) to 5 (most anti-welfare).

See **http://www.bsa.natcen.ac.uk/media/39290/7_bsa36_technical-details.pdf** (accessed 20 March 2021).

RESEARCH IN FOCUS 7.5
Specifying dimensions of a concept

Eschleman et al. (2014) conducted a study that was concerned with the relationship between abusive supervision and counterproductive work behaviour (CWB). This latter variable was conceptualized as being made up of two dimensions: forms of CWB directed at the supervisor and forms of CWB directed at the organization. Nine Likert scale items were used to measure the former and ten items to measure the latter. Each item was presented as a statement about behaviour, and the respondent indicated the frequency with which they engaged in that behaviour on a five-point scale going from 'rarely' to 'very often'. Representative items of the two dimensions are 'Made fun of your supervisor at work' and 'Put little effort into your work'.

concept, the different aspects or components of that concept should be considered. The dimensions of a concept are identified with reference to the theory and research associated with it. We can find examples of this kind of approach in Seeman's (1959) assertion that there are five dimensions of alienation: powerlessness, meaninglessness, normlessness, isolation, and self-estrangement. People scoring high on one dimension may not necessarily score high on other dimensions, so for each respondent you end up with a multidimensional 'profile'. Research in focus 7.5 demonstrates the use of dimensions in connection with the concept of counterproductive work behaviour.

As mentioned, quantitative research studies employ single- and multiple-indicator measures of concepts, and sometimes a mix of the two. All these approaches can be perfectly adequate. What is crucial is whether measures are reliable and whether they are valid representations of the concepts. It is to this issue that we will now turn.

7.6 Reliability and validity of measures

Although the terms 'reliability' and 'validity' seem to be almost synonymous, they have quite different meanings in relation to the evaluation of measures of concepts, as we saw in Chapter 3 (Section 3.2). In this section we will recap the points we covered in Chapter 3 but explore these two key research terms in more detail.

Reliability

As Key concept 7.3 suggests, reliability is concerned with the consistency of measures. In this way, it can mean much the same as it does in a non-research methods context. If you have not put on any weight and you weigh exactly the same weight each time you step on your weighing scales, you would say your weighing scales are reliable: their performance does not fluctuate over time and is consistent in its measurement. We use the term in a similar way in social research. Key concept 7.3 outlines three different factors associated with the term—stability, internal reliability, and **inter-rater reliability**—which will we now elaborate on in turn.

Stability

Reliability is about the stability of measurement over a variety of conditions in which the same results should be obtained. The most obvious way of testing for the stability of a measure is the *test–retest* method. This involves administering the test or measure on one occasion and then re-administering it to the same sample on another occasion.

We should expect to find a high correlation (a measure of the strength of the relationship between two variables) between the observations made on the first and second occasions. (We will cover correlation in Chapter 15 when we discuss quantitative data analysis.) Let's imagine that we develop a multiple-indicator measure that is supposed to tap 'preoccupation with social media' (the extent to which social media infiltrate participants' social worlds and thinking). We would administer the measure to a sample of respondents and re-administer it some time later. If the correlation is low, the measure would appear to be unstable, implying that respondents' answers cannot be relied upon as indicators of what we want to measure.

KEY CONCEPT 7.3
What is reliability?

Reliability refers to the consistency of a measure of a concept. When considering whether a measure is reliable, you should always take the following three factors into account.

- *Stability.* Often referred to as test–retest reliability, it involves asking whether a measure is stable over time. This means that, if we administer a measure to a group and then re-administer it, there should be little variation over time in the results obtained.
- *Internal reliability.* The key issue here is whether the indicators that make up the **scale** or **index** are consistent—whether respondents' scores on any one indicator tend to be related to their scores on the other indicators.
- *Inter-rater reliability.* Subjective judgement is involved in activities such as recording observations or translating data into categories. Where more than one 'rater' is involved in these activities, it is important to ensure there is consistency in their decisions.

However, there are a number of problems with this approach to evaluating reliability. Respondents' answers at the first point that the test is administered, or that measurement occurs, may influence how they reply at the second point the test is administered or measurement occurs, resulting in greater consistency between observations made on the first and second occasion than is in fact the case. So if someone responds positively to a question about a particular political party at the first time period, but they now feel more negatively, they may feel they cannot be too negative in their response at the second time period as it will contradict their initial response and they may not want to appear as though they change their mind easily. Second, events may intervene between the first and second points that the test is administered or measurement occurs that influence the degree of consistency. For example, if a long span of time has passed, technological changes and other developments could influence preoccupation with social media.

There are no clear solutions to these problems, other than to introduce a complex research design that turns the examination of reliability into a major project in its own right. Perhaps for these reasons, many if not most social research studies do not appear to carry out tests of stability. Longitudinal research (research where data is collected on a sample on at least two occasions) is often undertaken precisely in order to identify social change and its correlates.

Internal reliability

This meaning of reliability applies to multiple-indicator measures (such as those examined in Research in focus 7.3). When you have a multiple-item measure where each respondent's answers to each question are aggregated to form an overall score, there is always the possibility that the indicators do not relate to the same thing. We need to be sure that all our indicators—in this case, regarding 'preoccupation with social media'—are related to each other. If they are not, some of the items may be indicative of something else, which would make our data on this specific concept less reliable.

Inter-rater reliability

The idea of inter-rater reliability is briefly outlined in Key concept 7.3. It is concerned with the consistency of observations and ways of recording data across the people who are involved (the 'raters'), in studies where there is more than one. We will briefly touch on the issues involved in later chapters, but they can get rather complex. Gwet (2014) provides a very detailed treatment of the issues and appropriate techniques for dealing with them. For now, simply think of inter-rater reliability in terms of exams and graders. In order to grade an exam reliably the grades of two or multiple examiners can be compared: if they show great agreement on the same exams, inter-rater reliability is higher than if they give different grades.

Validity

Measurement validity is concerned with whether a measure of a concept really measures that concept (see Key concept 7.4). When we discussed the reliability of weighing scales earlier, it is worth noting that they could have been consistent in their measurement, but they may always over-report weight by 2 kilograms. So these particular scales might be *reliable* in that they are consistent, but they are not *valid* because they do not correspond to the accepted conventions of measuring weight. When people argue about whether a person's IQ score really measures or reflects that person's level of intelligence, they are raising questions about the measurement validity of the IQ test in relation to the concept of intelligence. Whenever we debate whether formal exams provide an accurate measure of academic ability, we are also raising questions about measurement validity.

Social science writers distinguish between a number of ways of assessing the validity of a measure of a concept. Let's walk through these different ways of testing measurement validity.

Face validity

At the very minimum, a researcher developing a new measure should establish that it has **face validity**—that is, that the measure apparently reflects the content of the concept explored. Face validity might be identified by asking other people, preferably with experience or expertise in the field, whether the measure appropriately represents the concept that is the focus of attention. Establishing face validity is an intuitive process.

Criterion validity: concurrent and predictive validity

The researcher might also seek to assess the **concurrent validity** of the measure—'concurrent' means existing at the same time, or overlapping. This, along with predictive validity, is often termed a form of **criterion validity**, and it allows us to assess how well one measure predicts an outcome for another measure.

To conduct this assessment, the researcher employs a *criterion* on which cases (for example, people) are known to differ and that is relevant to the concept in question. A suitable criterion if we were testing the validity of a new way of measuring job satisfaction (to continue this example) might be absenteeism, because some people are more often absent from work (other than through illness) than others. To establish the concurrent validity of a measure of job satisfaction, we might look at the extent to which people who are satisfied with their jobs are less likely to be absent from work than those who are not satisfied. If we find a lack of correspondence, such as there being no difference in levels of job satisfaction among different levels of absenteeism, there would be doubt as to whether our measure, absenteeism, is really capturing job satisfaction. Research in focus 7.6 provides an example of concurrent validity.

KEY CONCEPT 7.4
What is validity?

Validity refers to whether an indicator (or set of indicators) that is devised to represent a concept really does measure that concept. We will explore a variety of ways of establishing validity: face validity; criterion validity, comprising concurrent and predictive validity; construct validity; and convergent validity. Here the term *validity* is used as a shorthand for *measurement validity*, referred to in Chapter 3. This form of validity should be distinguished from the other terms introduced in Chapter 3 in relation to research design: internal validity, external validity, and **ecological validity**.

RESEARCH IN FOCUS 7.6
Concurrent validity

The Gambling Commission (2017) in the UK has identified challenges in measuring gambling behaviour because self-reported gambling expenditure tends to be inconsistent with actual revenue that accrues from gambling. Wood and Williams (2007) approached this challenge by using 12 different ways to ask a large **random sample** of residents in Ontario, Canada how much they had spent on gambling in the last month.

The researchers noted that even slight variations in question wording could result in respondents giving very different estimates of expenditure (a concern that relates to issues we will discuss in Chapter 11, when we cover asking questions). However, some questions produced answers that were more consistent with an estimate of gambling expenditure per person in Ontario (obtained from actual gambling revenues in Ontario), which acted as the concurrent validity criterion. The authors recommend the following question on the basis of its performance in the validity test and its face validity:

> Roughly how much money do you spend on [specific gambling activity] in a typical month? What we mean here is how much you are ahead or behind, or your net win or loss in a typical month.
>
> (Wood and Williams 2007: 68)

The respondents' estimates of their gambling expenditure on each of several gambling activities have to be aggregated in order to achieve a total figure. Research in focus 10.1 is a further example of testing for concurrent validity.

RESEARCH IN FOCUS 7.7
Predictive validity

In the USA, Messing et al. (2017) carried out a study that evaluated the predictive validity of a set of 11 questions known as the Lethality Screen. This is a tool used by first responders (such as the police) to predict risks of severe violence/homicide, or 'intimate partner violence' (IPV), to a victim–survivor of violence.

The researchers recruited 254 participants into the study at the scenes of police-involved IPV incidents in one southwestern state. The participants, all reported victims of IPV, each took part in two structured telephone interviews approximately seven months apart. The researchers asked participants the Lethality Screen questions, and they then classified participants' partners as 'high danger' or 'not high danger' on the basis of the resulting score. Predictive validity allowed researchers to test whether the measure (the Lethality Screen) was correctly identifying cases and non-cases—that is, whether people were being correctly classified as likely or not likely to be 'revictimized by near lethal, severe, repeat violence, or abuse on follow-up'—by exploring their circumstances seven months later (Messing et al. 2017: 213). Future levels of victimization were therefore the criterion used to test the measure's validity.

The researchers found that the Lethality Screen had a considerable positive predictive value (people expected to be revictimized who are revictimized) of 92 to 93 per cent and a high negative predictive value (people expected not to be revictimized who are indeed not revictimized) of 93 to 96 per cent for near lethal and severe violence. This indicated the usefulness of the Lethality Screen in predicting IPV.

Another possible test for the validity of a new measure is **predictive validity**, in which the researcher uses a *future* criterion measure, rather than a current one as is the case for concurrent validity. With predictive validity, future levels of absenteeism would be used as the criterion against which the validity of a new measure of job satisfaction would be examined. Research in focus 7.7 provides an example of testing for predictive validity.

Construct validity

Construct validity is an approach that evaluates a measure by how well the measure conforms to theoretical expectations. This means that the researcher is encouraged to deduce hypotheses from a theory that is relevant to the concept. For example, drawing upon ideas about the impact of technology on experience of work, the researcher might anticipate that those people who are satisfied with their work are less likely to work on routine jobs, while those who are not satisfied are more likely to work on routine jobs. To investigate this theoretical deduction, we could examine the relationship between job satisfaction and job routine. However, if there did not appear to be a relationship between job satisfaction and job routine this would not necessarily suggest that your measure was invalid, highlighting the challenges of construct validity. First, either the theory or the deduction that comes from it might be misguided. Second, the measure of job routine could be an invalid measure of that concept. De Vaus (2013) asks how we know whether it is your theory that may be wrong or the measurement of the concepts that may be invalid? In practice, construct validity is rarely considered.

Convergent validity

Convergent validity involves comparing a measure to other measures of the same concept that have been developed through different methods—the fact that converging means different things coming together might help you to remember this term. To establish convergent validity, you need to show that the measures employed are related to each other. In addition to using a test of concurrent validity for their research on gambling expenditure (see Research in focus 7.6), Wood and Williams (2007) used a **diary** to estimate gambling expenditure for a subsample (a sample within a sample) of their respondents that could then be compared to questionnaire estimates. Respondents began the diary shortly after answering the survey question and continued completing it for a 30-day period. This allowed the researchers to compare what was actually spent in the month after the question was asked (assuming the diary estimates were correct!) with what respondents *thought* they spent on gambling.

An interesting instance of convergent *in*validity has been identified in relation to crime statistics. There are two main sources of national crime statistics in England and Wales, each using very different data-collection methods. The Crime Survey for England and Wales (CSEW), formerly known as the British Crime Survey, was devised, in part, to provide an alternative measure of levels of crime that would act as a way of checking the official statistics. Whereas the official statistics are informed by members of the British criminal justice system, mainly the police, as they carry out their law enforcement activities, the CSEW is (as the name suggests) a survey of a large sample of the English and Welsh public. A lack of convergent validity has been found between the two measures and in subsequent reporting of crime. While it can expose important issues, the convergent approach is not a perfect assessment of validity as it is not possible to establish which measure represents the more accurate picture.

Before we move on to reflect on reliability and validity more generally, read Research in focus 7.8 for a brief account of some ways in which reliability and validity were assessed as part of a study.

RESEARCH IN FOCUS 7.8
Assessing reliability and validity

Chin et al. (2002) provided a useful example of a piece of research that involved a combination of the tools and tests we have discussed so far in this chapter: a multiple-indicator measure and an assessment of the measure's reliability and validity.

In this study, researchers developed a 33-item Likert scale (see Key concept 7.2) to measure pro- and anti-vegetarian attitudes. (You may also be interested to look up a more recent study published by Judge and Wilson in 2018, where the same scale was used to create a measure of attitudes towards vegans.) The 33 items—developed following a **literature review**, examination of other relevant attitude scales, and discussions within the research team—were statements to which the respondent was asked to indicate strength of agreement or disagreement on a seven-point scale. Sample items included the following:

1. Behaviours: 'Vegetarians preach too much about their beliefs and eating habits.'
2. Beliefs: 'Vegetarians are overly concerned with animal rights.'
3. Health and mental: 'Vegetarians are overly concerned about gaining weight.'
4. Treatment: 'It's O.K. to tease someone for being a vegetarian.'

The researchers tested the scale for reliability and validity with a sample of university undergraduates in the USA. Some items from the scale showed poor internal consistency with the other items (i.e. they affected the measure's internal reliability) so they were dropped. Without them, the researchers considered the scale internally reliable. They also tested the scale's construct validity by asking the students to complete other scales that the researchers predicted would be associated with pro- or anti-vegetarian attitudes, but it was found to have questionable construct validity. The authors' hypothesis that people with authoritarian attitudes would be more likely to be anti-vegetarians was confirmed (although the relationship between these two variables was very weak), but attitudes towards vegetarianism were not found to be related to political conservatism, as the authors had predicted.

Reflections on reliability and validity

There are a number of different ways of evaluating the measures that are used to capture concepts. In quantitative research it is important that measures are valid and reliable. When new measures are developed, these should be tested for both validity and reliability. In practice, this often involves fairly straightforward but limited steps to ensure that a measure is reliable and/or valid, such as testing for internal reliability when a multiple-indicator measure has been devised (as in Research in focus 7.8) and examining face validity.

Although reliability and validity can be easily distinguished in terms of the analysis they involve, they are related because validity presumes reliability: if your measure is not reliable, it cannot be valid. This point can be made with respect to each of the three criteria of reliability that we have discussed:

- If the measure is not *stable* over time, it cannot be providing a valid measure; the measure cannot be tapping the concept it is supposed to be measuring if the measure fluctuates, and if the measure fluctuates, it may be measuring different things on different occasions.
- If a measure lacks *internal reliability*, it means that a multiple-indicator measure is actually measuring two or more different things, so the measure cannot be valid.
- If there is a lack of *inter-rater consistency*, it means that observers do not agree on the meaning of what they are observing, which in turn means that a measure cannot be valid.

7.7 The critique of quantitative research

Quantitative research has been the focus of considerable criticism, particularly from qualitative researchers. It is criticized generally as a research strategy as well as for its epistemological and ontological foundations and the specific methods and research designs with which it is associated.

The four most common criticisms of quantitative approaches to research are as follows.

1. Researchers treat people and social institutions in the same way as 'the world of nature'.
2. The measurement process involves an artificial sense of precision and accuracy.
3. The reliance on instruments and procedures limits the connection between research and everyday life.
4. The analysis of relationships between variables creates a static view of social life as if it were independent of people's lives.

We will consider each one in turn, before considering the **feminist** critique of quantitative research.

Treating the social world the same as 'the world of nature'

The phrase 'the world of nature' comes from Schutz (1962) and the specific quotation from which it has been taken can be found in Chapter 2 in the section on '**Interpretivism**' (Section 2.3). Schutz and other phenomenologists criticize social scientists who employ a natural science model and treat the social world as if it were no different from the natural order, despite the differences. As we discussed in Chapter 2, this, in its most extreme form, could mean ignoring the fact that people interpret the world around them, whereas this capacity for self-reflection cannot be found among the objects of the natural sciences ('molecules, atoms, and electrons', as Schutz put it). In practice, a recognition that people interpret the world around them should be a key focus of all research in the social sciences, not just qualitative research.

An artificial measurement process

There are a number of aspects to this criticism. It has been argued that the connection between measures developed by social scientists and the concepts they are supposed to reveal is assumed rather than real. The measurement process may be seen as flawed in that it presumes that respondents interpret the key terms in questions similarly. However, this is not necessarily the case. One response to this problem is to use questions with fixed-choice answers, but this approach then provides 'a solution to the problem of meaning by simply ignoring it' (Cicourel 1964: 108).

Limited connection to everyday life

This issue relates to the question of ecological validity that we raised in Chapter 3. Many methods of quantitative research rely on administering research instruments to participants (such as structured interviews and self-completion questionnaires) or on controlling situations to determine their effects (as in experiments). However, as Cicourel (1982) asks, how do we know if survey respondents have the necessary knowledge to answer a question, or whether they are similar in their sense of the topic being important to them in their everyday lives? So, if respondents answer questions designed to measure racial prejudice, are they aware of what it is and what its manifestations are, and can we be sure that it is of equal concern to them in the ways in which it connects with everyday life? Also, how well do their answers relate to their everyday lives? People may answer a question designed to measure racial prejudice, but respondents' actual behaviour may differ from their answers (see Research in focus 12.2 for a further discussion of this issue).

A static view of social life

Blumer (1956: 685) argued that studies that aim to bring out the relationships between variables omit 'the process of interpretation or definition that goes on in human groups'. This means that we do not know how an apparent relationship between variables has been produced by the people on whom the research was conducted. This criticism links to the first and third criticisms—that quantitative research ignores the meaning of events to individuals and that we do not know how such findings connect to everyday contexts—but adds a further element: that it creates a sense of a static social world that is separate from the individuals who make it up. Quantitative research is seen as carrying an objectivist ontology that reifies the social world.

These criticisms promote the case for a qualitative research strategy characterized by a combination of an interpretivist epistemological orientation (an emphasis on meaning from the individual's point of view) and a **constructionist** ontology (an emphasis on viewing the social world as the product of individuals rather than as something beyond them).

The feminist critique

You may be able to make some guesses as to the criticisms that feminist researchers—and those identifying with associated approaches and theories, such as post-colonial theory—make of quantitative research from your reading of the sections on 'Values' in Chapter 2 (Section 2.6) and 'Taking sides in research' in Chapter 6 (Section 6.6). Feminist researchers have traditionally tended to favour qualitative research because they have seen quantitative approaches as conflicting with feminism's values. On the other hand, some feminist researchers have also deliberately used quantitative methods: because quantitative methods were viewed by mainstream (sometimes called 'malestream') academia as more robust and 'objective', these researchers believed using them would be a more convincing way of getting their feminist research out there. However, several feminist social researchers in the early 1980s, such as Oakley (1981), argued that quantitative research was closely linked to male values of control (control of the research subject/respondent and of the research context and situation) and tended to be an unequal, 'extractive' (Hesse-Biber 2013) relationship between researcher and subjects of research: the researcher extracts information and gives nothing in return.

Another reason why feminist research tends to lean towards qualitative approaches is that quantitative research is thought to downplay the study of the role of the body and sensory experience as a way to capture reality. Traditionally, women and the feminine have been associated with the body, the sensorial, and the instinctive/irrational while men and the masculine have been linked to the mind and rationality. Feminist researchers have argued that these kinds of dichotomies (ideas that are positioned as completely separate and opposite) are rarely neutral; such researchers have worked over the years to dismantle these dichotomies and to highlight the power relations they imply. Inspired by the work of the French philosopher Maurice Merleau-Ponty (1969, 2002), feminist research raises questions about, first, the idea that the scientific method is the only legitimate way to understand the world, and second, the body–mind dichotomy that the natural science model suggests. Researchers identifying with this approach try to demonstrate that experience and perception are the basis of both subjectivity and objectivity, arguing that the mind is not superior and that knowledge can be accessed through the body, which in turn shapes experience.

It is worth noting that standard textbook advice of the kind we provide in Chapter 9 implies that in quantitative research, while rapport is useful to someone carrying out a structured interview (in encouraging interviewee participation, for example), they should take care not to become too familiar. This, and the risk that the respondent's subsequent answers may be biased, means that the interviewer should not engage too far with questions asked by respondents (for example, about the research or the topic of the research). This is perfectly valid and appropriate advice from the perspective of traditional quantitative methods such as structured interviewing (discussed in Chapter 9), with its quest for standardization and for valid and reliable data. However, the feminist perspective sees this strategy as almost exploitative, which is exactly the kind of relationship that feminist social science tries to resist and avoid. The type of rapport encouraged in quantitative research is seen as creating a distance between the researcher and the research participant that adds to the distance already created by the hierarchical relationship between them. This distance is considered incompatible with the feminist research ethos, which advocates deep exploration and transparency of research relationships in the field in order to produce ethical, more balanced, and less biased research findings.

For these reasons, quantitative research has traditionally been seen as less compatible with the values of feminism; qualitative research has been seen as more adaptable to those values. The kinds of critique we have just summarized led to a period in which many feminist social researchers gravitated towards qualitative research, showing a preference for methods such as **semi-structured interviewing**, ethnography-informed **unstructured interviewing**, and **focus groups**. We will consider these methods in later chapters. However, as we noted in Chapter 2 (Section 2.6 on 'Values'), particularly in more recent years feminist writers have acknowledged that quantitative research can be useful and acceptable, particularly when combined with qualitative research (Oakley 1998; Hughes and Cohen 2013). Today, many feminist researchers make use of quantitative and mixed methods research strategies to help them achieve their goals. This is about ensuring that the data-collection method will enable the researcher to address their research questions. For example, Walby and Towers (2017) have shown that surveys of violence against women that are dedicated to uncovering such violence (as opposed to general crime surveys such as the Crime Survey for England and Wales) reveal higher levels of violence than are often thought to occur, due to the anonymity of the survey format. By paying attention to issues such as greater privacy in the interview and special training in sensitive interviewing, dedicated surveys in some countries have been extremely revealing about the causes and incidence of violence against women. This kind of research, which is based on structured interviewing, would not seem to be inconsistent with the goals of most feminist researchers and indeed may be of considerable use for many researchers.

7.8 From theory to practice

One of the problems with characterizing any research strategy, research design, or research method is that we tend to outline an ideal-typical approach. In reality the strategy, design, or method may not be reflected in its entirety in research practice. This means that a model of the process of quantitative research, such as that provided in Figure 7.1, should be thought of as a general *tendency* rather than as a definitive description of quantitative research. In practice, differences may be associated with pragmatic concerns such as time, cost, and feasibility, all of which need consideration when we conduct social research. In this section, we will consider a few examples of gaps that can arise between 'good practice' and actual research.

Reverse operationism

One example of the gap between the ideal type and actual research practice is something called 'reverse operationism' (Bryman 1988a: 28). The model of the process of quantitative research in Figure 7.1 implies that concepts are specified and that measures and indicators are then devised for them. This is the basis of the idea of **operationism** or **operationalism** (introduced in Section 7.4), which implies a deductive view of research. However, the view of research presented in Figure 7.1 neglects the more inductive elements that are often involved in measurement. For example, sometimes measures are developed that in turn lead to conceptualization.

Reliability and validity testing

The gap between the ideal type and actual research practice can also arise because researchers do not report all of the recommended practices. While researchers may put a lot of time and effort into articulating the ways in which the reliability and validity of measures should be determined, they may not follow or present these procedures. Writers of social research rarely report tests of the stability of their measures and even more rarely report evidence of validity. The reasons why the procedures for determining stability and validity are rarely used are, almost certainly, the cost and time that they would probably involve. Researchers tend to be more concerned with substantive issues than with detailed considerations of measurement quality.

The fact that some researchers do not thoroughly assess the quality of their measurements does not mean that you should or can neglect this phase in your own work. We note this tendency simply in order to draw your attention to some of the ways in which practices we might describe are not always followed, and to suggest why this might be the case.

Sampling

We can make a similar observation about sampling, which we cover in Chapter 8. As we will see, good practice here is strongly associated with *random* or *probability sampling*. However, much research (by necessity) is based on **non-probability samples**—that is, samples that have not been selected in terms of the principles of probability sampling. Sometimes this is due to the difficulty of obtaining **probability samples**, or because of the time and cost involved. And sometimes the opportunity to study a certain group presents itself and is too good an opportunity to miss. Again, it is important to be aware of these facts but they do not give us licence to ignore the principles of sampling that we examine in Chapter 8, especially since they have implications for the kind of statistical analysis that we can employ (see Chapter 15).

KEY POINTS

- Quantitative research can be characterized as a linear series of steps moving from theory to conclusions, but in practice, the process described in Figure 7.1 is an ideal type and there are many possible departures from it.
- The measurement process in quantitative research involves the search for indicators.
- Establishing the reliability and validity of measures is important for assessing their quality.
- Quantitative research can be characterized as having certain preoccupations, the most central of which are measurement, causality, generalization, and replication.
- Quantitative research has been subjected to many criticisms by qualitative researchers. These criticisms tend to be associated with the view that a natural science model is not appropriate for studying the social world.

QUESTIONS FOR REVIEW

1. What are the main steps in quantitative research?
2. To what extent do the main steps follow a strict sequence?
3. Do the steps suggest a deductive or inductive approach to the relationship between theory and research?
4. Why is measurement important for the quantitative researcher?
5. What is the difference between a measure and an indicator?
6. Why might multiple-indicator approaches to the measurement of concepts be preferable to those that rely on a single indicator?
7. What are the main ways of thinking about the reliability of the measurement process? Is one form of reliability the most important?
8. 'Whereas validity presupposes reliability, reliability does not presuppose validity.' Discuss.
9. What are the main criteria for evaluating measurement validity?
10. Outline the main preoccupations of quantitative researchers. What reasons can you give for these?

11. Why is replication often an important preoccupation among quantitative researchers, in spite of the tendency for replications in social research to be fairly rare?
12. 'The crucial problem with quantitative research is the failure of its practitioners to address adequately the issue of meaning.' Discuss.
13. How central is quantitative researchers' adoption of a natural science model of conducting research to the critique by qualitative researchers of quantitative research?
14. Why do social researchers sometimes not test the validity and/or reliability of measures that they employ?

ONLINE RESOURCES

www.oup.com/he/srm6e

You can find our notes on the answers to these questions within this chapter's **online resources**, together with:

- *audio/video comments* on this topic from our 'Learn from experience' panellists;
- *audio discussion from the authors* on the main preoccupations of quantitative researchers and the reasons for their prominence (review question 10);
- *self-test questions* for further knowledge-checking; and
- a *flashcard glossary* to help you recall key terms.

CHAPTER

8

SAMPLING IN QUANTITATIVE RESEARCH

CHAPTER GUIDE

In this chapter and the three that follow it, we consider principles and practices associated with social survey research. In this chapter our focus is sampling, and we explore

- the role of sampling in the overall process of doing survey research;
- the related ideas of generalizability (also known as external validity) and a representative sample (which allows the researcher to generalize findings from a sample to a population);
- probability samples, using a random selection process;
- the main types of probability sample: the simple random sample, the systematic sample, the stratified random sample, and the multi-stage cluster sample;
- different types of non-probability sample, including convenience sampling, snowball sampling, and quota sampling (widely used in market research and opinion polls);
- the main issues involved in deciding on sample size;
- some of the issues raised by sampling for online surveys;
- the limits to generalization that go with sampling issues;
- potential sources of error in survey research.

8.1 Introduction

In this chapter we will explore the role of sampling in relation to conducting a survey. Sampling, which we define in detail in the next section, is about the process of selecting individuals to participate in our research. Although sampling is also applicable to other approaches to quantitative research (for example, sampling techniques are also relevant to selecting documents for content analysis—see Chapter 13) and is also required in qualitative research (see Chapter 17), sampling principles are most commonly used in relation to surveys. In view of this, in this chapter we focus on sampling as the process of selecting participants who we want to ask questions of, by interview or questionnaire.

It is important to understand where sampling fits in the process of undertaking survey research. Figure 8.1 outlines the main steps involved in doing survey research, including the role and place of sampling in this process. You can see that there are a number of steps involved in carrying out survey research. This chapter focuses on those steps that are involved with sampling. The sampling steps are shown in **bold** in the flow diagram. The other steps are discussed in detail in other parts of the book. The flow diagram shows that surveys begin with identifying the issues to be researched, and that these are gradually narrowed down so that you formulate research questions, as a result of reviewing relevant literature (see Chapters 1, 4, and 5). The researcher can then begin planning the fieldwork. In practice, decisions about sampling and the data-collection method(s) overlap, but they are presented in Figure 8.1 as part of a sequence. They are also affected by ethical considerations linked to access to data, including data protection regulations (see Chapter 6). You will find out more about the data-collection aspects of conducting a survey in Chapters 9, 10, and 11, while Chapter 15 deals with the analysis of data. When you have read these chapters, you will have a clear idea of the importance of sampling for the whole research process.

FIGURE 8.1
Steps in conducting a social survey, with steps involved with sampling shown in bold

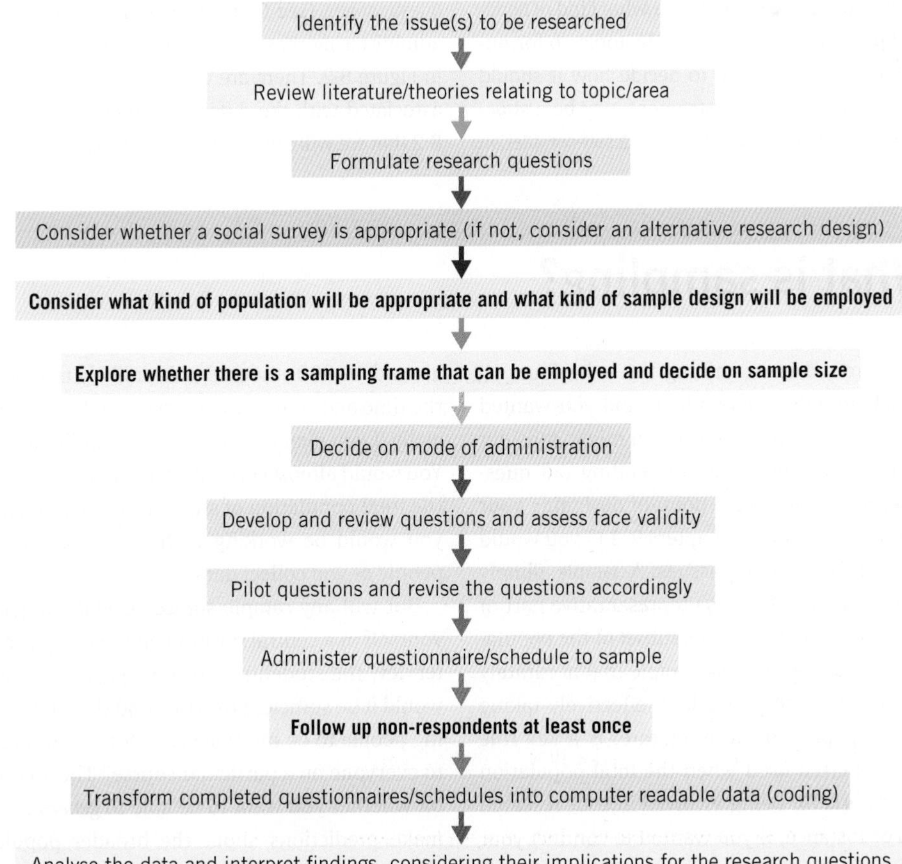

FIGURE 8.2
Main modes of administration of a survey

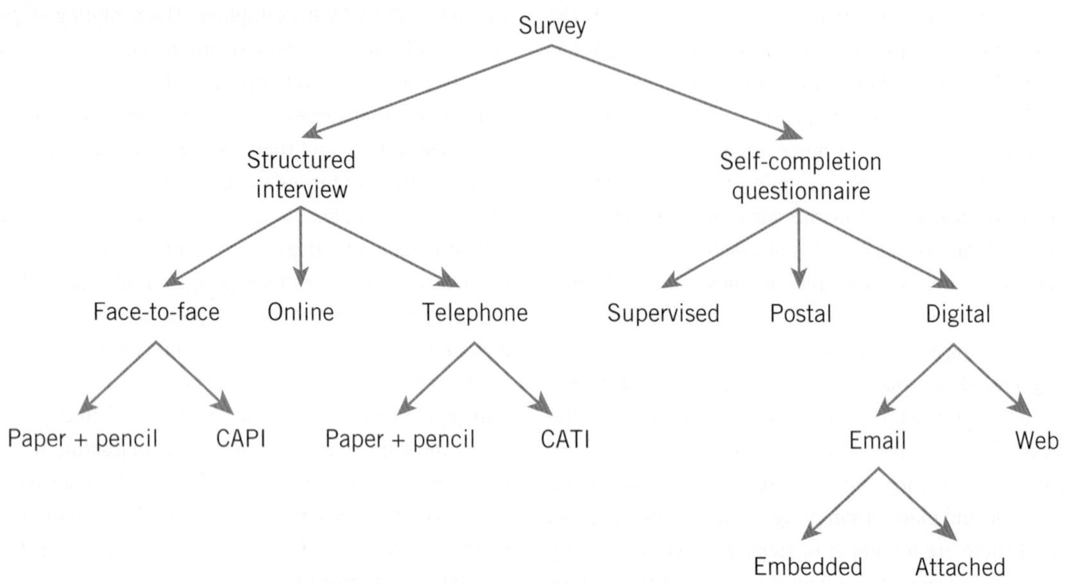

Notes: CAPI is computer-assisted personal interviewing; CATI is computer-assisted telephone interviewing.

The survey researcher needs to decide what kind of **population** is suited to their investigation of the topic, to formulate a 'research instrument', and to decide how it should be administered. The research instrument may be a **structured interview** schedule (see Chapter 9) or a **self-completion questionnaire** (see Chapter 10). There are several ways of administering these instruments, including those outlined in Figure 8.2. There are various strengths and weaknesses associated with the different approaches shown in Figure 8.2 that we will point out in the forthcoming chapters.

8.2 What is sampling?

If you were interested in examining the behaviour, attitudes, or backgrounds of individuals and you wanted to gather new data for this purpose, you might consider conducting structured interviews or sending out questionnaires. Before getting to the point of designing your interviews or questionnaires (Chapters 9–11) you would need to consider the sampling issues. A **sample**, simply defined, is a smaller and (ideally) representative part of a bigger whole or population. It is a subset of the population. Identifying a representative sample that accurately reflects the population to be studied, effectively taking the form of the population in miniature, is a key role of sampling. It is often used when the total population that fits your criteria for being involved in your research is too large. For instance, if you wanted to conduct your research with university students and your university has around 10,000 students, it is unlikely that you will have the time and resources to survey all these students, especially if you planned to do this by conducting interviews. You would almost certainly need to sample students from the total population of students at the university, so that you would be working with a manageable number of people as you collect data.

But will any sample suffice? Could you simply locate yourself in a central position on the campus and then interview the students who come past you? Alternatively, would it be sufficient to go around the student union asking people to be interviewed? Or to send questionnaires to everyone on a particular course? The answer depends on whether you want to be able to *generalize* (that is, to make predictions about the broader population from your sample) your findings to the entire student body in the university. In order to be able to generalize your findings from your sample to the population from which it was selected, the sample must be representative. See Key concept 8.1 for an explanation of this and of the other key terms concerning sampling.

If you do want to generalize, it is unlikely that any of the three strategies proposed (standing somewhere central on campus; going around the student union; sending a questionnaire to everyone on a course) would provide a *representative sample* of all students in the university. The reasons for this include the following.

- The first two approaches depend heavily upon the availability of students during the time that you carry out the research. Not all students are likely to be equally available at one time, so the sample will not reflect unavailable students, who may differ from available students—for example, if you stood in the middle of your campus on a Wednesday afternoon, when most sports team practices tended to be scheduled, your sample would not reflect the views of students on sports teams.
- The first two approaches also depend on the students going to your location(s). Not all students will pass the place you choose to stand, or will go to the student union, or they may vary greatly in the frequency with which they do so. Their movements are likely to be affected by such things as the location of their accommodation or departments, or their social habits. By focusing on these locations you would miss out on students who do not go there.
- Your decisions about which people to approach may be influenced by your own judgements and feelings: for example, how cooperative you think they are likely to be, or by how comfortable you feel about interviewing students of a different gender from your own.
- The problem with the third strategy is that students on one course are, by definition, taking the same subject as each other and so will not be representative of all students in the university. For example, they may have particular experiences based on levels of contact hours, which may differ on the whole from students on other courses.

With all three sampling approaches, your decisions about whom to sample would be influenced too much by personal judgements, by prospective respondents' availability, or by your implicit criteria for inclusion. It does not only mean that you miss out on interviewing students in some categories, but that these students could also have

KEY CONCEPT 8.1

Basic terms and concepts in sampling

- *Population*: the overall **units** from which the sample is to be selected. We say 'units' because it is not necessarily people who are being sampled—the researcher may want to sample from nations, cities, regions, firms, etc. Sinyor et al. (2015), for example, studied a random sample of suicide notes. Their population, therefore, was a population of the total number of suicide notes. So it is important to note that 'population' has a much broader meaning than the everyday use of the term, which tends to be associated with a city or nation's entire population and refers only to people.
- *Sample*: the segment of the population selected for investigation. The method of selection may be based on a probability or a non-probability approach (see Sections 8.4 and 8.5).
- ***Sampling frame***: the listing of all units in the population from which the sample will be selected. It defines eligibility for inclusion in your sample and identifies those features from which you can select your sample. The sampling frame should, as closely as possible, reflect the target population.
- *Representative sample*: a sample that reflects the population accurately so that it is effectively the population in miniature, with the same characteristics.
- ***Sampling bias***: a distortion in the representativeness of the sample that arises when some members of the population (or more precisely members of the sampling frame) stand little or no chance of being selected for inclusion in the sample.
- ***Probability sample***: a sample created using random selection so that each unit in the population has a known chance of being selected. It is generally assumed that this method is more likely to result in a representative sample. The aim of probability sampling is to limit sampling error (defined below).
- ***Non-probability sample***: a sample not selected using a random selection method. This implies that some units in the population are more likely to be selected than others.

- *Sampling error*: error in the research findings due to the difference between a sample and the population from which it is selected, even though a probability sample has been selected. 'Error' here does not imply carelessness, but is a result of the method used to select the sample.
- ***Non-sampling error***: error in the research findings due to the differences between the population and the sample that arise either from deficiencies in the sampling approach, such as an inadequate sampling frame or **non-response**, or from problems such as poor question wording, poor interviewing, or flawed processing of data.
- *Non-response*: a source of non-sampling error that is particularly likely to happen when individual people are being sampled. It occurs whenever some members of the sample refuse to cooperate, cannot be contacted, or cannot supply the required data (for example, because of mental incapacity).
- ***Census***: the enumeration (setting out all **items** one by one) of an entire population. If data are collected in relation to all units in a population, rather than a sample of units, the data are treated as census data. (The phrase '*the* census' usually refers to the complete enumeration of all members of the population of a nation-state—that is, a national census—but in a statistical context, like the term 'population', the idea of a 'census' has a broader meaning.)

features or opinions on your topic of research that are different from those of the students that you do question. Such limitations mean that your sample will be *biased*. A biased sample is one that does not accurately represent the population from which it was selected. Sampling bias will occur if some members of the population have little or no chance of being selected for inclusion in the sample. As far as possible, you should remove bias from the process of selecting your sample. It is incredibly difficult to remove bias altogether and to derive a truly representative sample, but you should always take steps to minimize bias.

Sampling is not only a consideration when working with primary data (that the researcher collects). When working with secondary data (data that has been collected by other researchers in the ways we will discuss in Chapter 14), you also need to consider sampling and how the sample has been derived from the population, including the potential implications for your own use of the data. You also need to be able to identify your sample from the data set, thinking carefully about the various issues, such as sample size, that we address in this chapter.

There are two potential sources of bias (see Key concept 8.1 for explanations of the terms mentioned here).

1. *If a non-probability or non-random sampling method is used.* If the method used to select the sample is not random, it is likely that human judgement will affect the selection process, making some members of the population more likely to be selected. This source of bias can be eliminated through the use of probability/random sampling.
2. *If the sampling frame is inadequate.* If the sampling frame is not comprehensive or is inaccurate, the sample that is used cannot represent the population, even if researchers use a random/probability sampling method.

Non-response, where some sample members refuse to participate or cannot be contacted, can also lead to a sample that is unrepresentative. The problem with this is that those who agree to participate may differ in various ways from those who do not agree to participate, and some of the differences may be significant to the research question. If the data are available, it may be possible to check how far, when there is non-response, the resulting sample differs from the population. It is often possible to do this in terms of characteristics such as gender or age.

One example of a sample that could be considered problematic because of non-response is the data provided by the Higher Education Statistics Agency (HESA) about higher education in the UK. This covers matters such as who is studying at universities, where they are from, and what their progression rates are (into employment, further study etc.). The data plays an important role in helping us to understand higher education in the United Kingdom (see **www.hesa.ac.uk/data-and-analysis/students**, accessed 28 March 2019). Potential students use the data to make choices about their studies, and governments use it to develop and review policies. However, there are challenges in relation to the collection of the data, particularly the data about progression rates. Universities are required to submit information to HESA about former students' employment status at a set time following completion of the course, but some former students do not provide universities with up-to-date contact details, and others fail to respond to requests for the information. This non-response may lead to a situation where students with particular employment circumstances may

TIPS AND SKILLS 8.1
Weighting

If a sample is biased, we cannot use it to generalize to the population without making statistical adjustments, called weighting, during the data analysis stage of a survey study. While, ideally, a sample is a miniature version of the population, this is often not the case, especially as a result of non-response. This may result in some groups being over- or under-represented. Self-selection can also take place, especially in online surveys. A technique that is often applied to try to correct this issue is weighting, in which each respondent in the survey is assigned an adjustment weight. Those who are under-represented get a weight larger than 1, while those in over-represented groups get a weight smaller than 1. This approach could be used if people of a particular gender group or ethnicity were disproportionately represented in a sample compared to the whole population. It is worth noting that with many forms of software used for the analysis of secondary data (see Chapter 15), it is possible to simply click a button to enable you to work with weighted data, meaning that the software works out the weighting for you.

be less likely to respond. This may include those who are no longer in the country. As such, we need to be cautious in how we interpret the data.

In some cases, high levels of non-response may lead to a survey's results not being published. This may be as a result of concerns about low numbers of participants and whether the findings can be generalized to a wider population. For instance, for data to be published from the National Student Survey (a survey conducted with final-year undergraduate students in the UK about the quality of their courses), the survey must achieve at least 10 student responses per course and a response rate of 50 per cent for the survey as a whole.

In some cases, researchers may use **weighting**, a form of statistical adjustment, in order to address issues of a bias. They make these adjustments to survey data after it has been collected in order to improve the accuracy of the data. The aim is to correct for unequal probabilities of selection that can occur during sampling or to try to help compensate for survey non-response. We discuss this idea in Tips and skills 8.1.

8.3 Sampling error

In order to better understand the implications of sampling error for achieving a representative sample, let's look at Figures 8.3–8.7. Imagine that we have a population of 200 people and want a sample of 50. Also imagine that one of the **variables** we are interested in is whether people watch soap operas, and that the whole population is equally divided between those who do and those who do not. This split is represented by the vertical line that divides the population in the figures into two halves (see Figure 8.3).

If the sample is representative, we would expect our sample of 50 to be equally split in terms of this variable (see Figure 8.4, where the outlined section represents the sample). If there is a small amount of sampling error, so that we have one person too many who does not watch soap operas and one too few who does, it will look like Figure 8.5. Figure 8.6 shows a more serious degree of over-representation within the sample of people who do

FIGURE 8.3
Soap opera watching behaviour in a population of 200

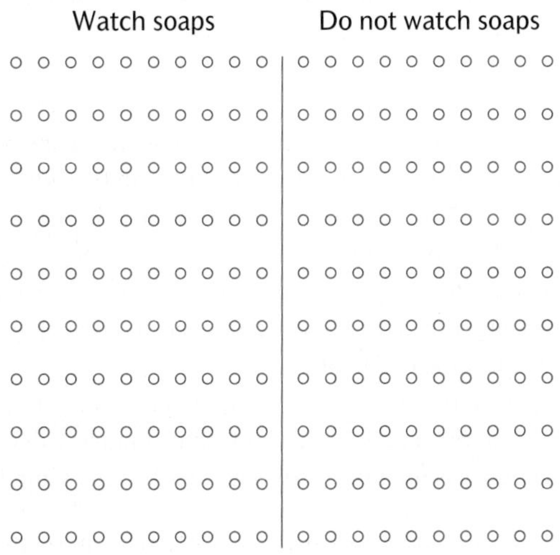

FIGURE 8.4
A sample with no sampling error

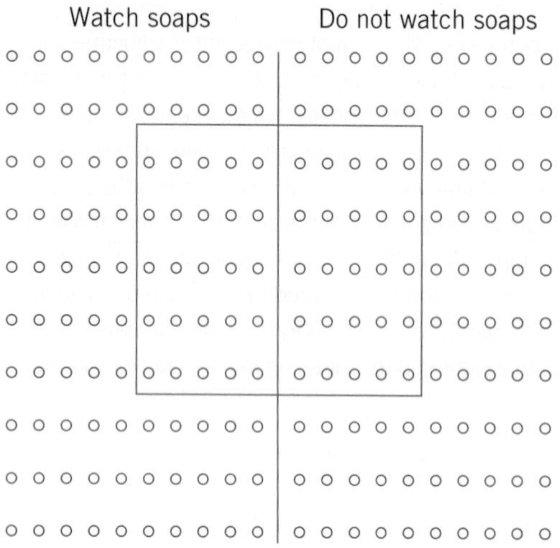

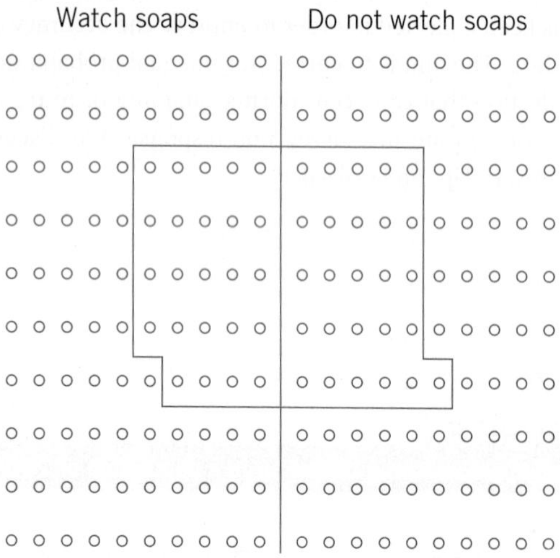

FIGURE 8.6
A sample with some sampling error

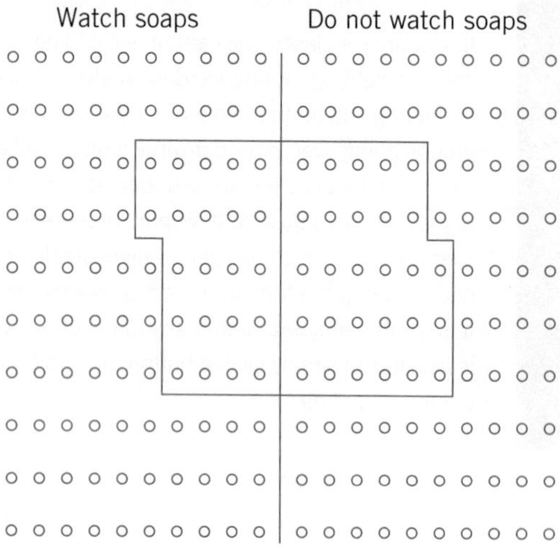

8

FIGURE 8.5
A sample with very little sampling error

FIGURE 8.7
A sample with a lot of sampling error

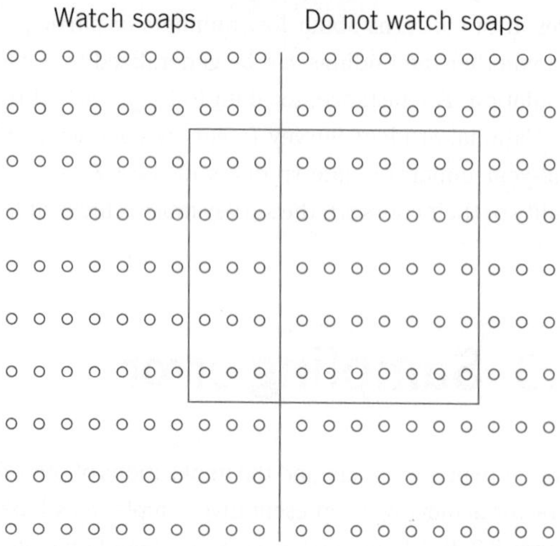

not watch soaps. This time there are three too many people who do not watch them and three too few who do. In Figure 8.7 we have a considerable over-representation of people who do not watch soaps, because there are 35 people in the sample who do not watch them, which is much larger than the 25 who should be in the sample if it is to reflect the population.

Probability sampling does not eliminate sampling error. Even with a well-crafted probability sample, a degree of sampling error is likely. However, probability sampling stands a better chance than non-probability sampling of reducing sampling error so that it does not end up looking like Figure 8.7. Probability sampling also allows the researcher to use statistical tests that enable inferences to be made about the population from which the sample was selected. (The term **inferential statistics**, discussed in Chapter 15, refers to the tests used to infer—in other words, draw conclusions about—qualities of a population from data about a sample drawn randomly from that population.) For example, Foster et al. (2014), providing an example of inferential statistics, state that if we asked 200 people who they were going to vote for on the day before a local election, we could try to predict or infer which party would win the election. It is for these reasons that we will spend quite a bit of time considering probability sampling in this chapter. The process of using a **test of statistical significance** to generalize from a sample to a population is known as **statistical inference**.

8.4 Probability sampling

Types of probability sample

Imagine that we are interested in levels of alcohol consumption among university students and that we want to examine the variables that relate to differences in levels of drinking. We might decide to conduct our research in a single university. This means that our population will be all students in that university, which means that we will only be able to generalize our findings to students of that university. We cannot assume that levels of alcohol consumption, and the variables that correlate with them, will be the same in other universities. We might decide only to research full-time students, with part-time students excluded. Imagine that there are 9,000 full-time students in the university.

There are four main types of probability sample that we could use to select participants:

1. simple random sample;
2. systematic sample;
3. stratified random sampling;
4. multi-stage cluster sampling.

We will consider each one and discuss how it could be used in this research scenario.

Simple random sample

The **simple random sample** is the most basic form of probability sample. It is a sample in which each unit (or person, in this case) has been selected entirely by chance and each unit has a known and equal probability of being selected.

Applying this to our scenario, if we decide that we have enough money to interview 450 students at the university, the probability of each student being included in this sample is

$$\frac{450}{9{,}000}, \text{ i.e. 1 in 20}$$

This is known as the *sampling fraction* and it is usually abbreviated to

$$\frac{n}{N}$$

where n is the sample size and N is the population size. If we wanted to devise a simple random sample of the population, the steps would be as follows.

1. Define the population. This is our N, and in this case it is 9,000 full-time students.
2. Devise a comprehensive sampling frame. The university keeps records of all students, and we can use these to exclude those who do not meet our inclusion criteria—that is, part-time students.
3. Decide your sample size (n). We have the means and funds to include 450 students.
4. List all the students in the population (your sampling frame) and assign them consecutive numbers from 1 to N. In our case, this will be 1 to 9,000.
5. Using a table of random numbers, or a digital tool that can generate random numbers, select n (450) different random numbers that lie between 1 and N (9,000).
6. The students to which the n (450) random numbers refer become the sample.

There are two points worth noticing about this process. First, there is almost no opportunity for human bias, such as selecting people who look friendly. The selection of whom to interview is mechanical. Second, the process is not dependent on the students' availability.

Step 5 mentions that you could use a table to generate a list of random numbers (these tables have traditionally been included in the appendices of many statistics books), but the easiest and quickest way to do this is to use an online tool (see Tips and skills 8.2), or generate a list of random numbers using Microsoft Excel, IBM **SPSS**, or another statistical package.

This type of probability sample is widely used as it is reliable and fairly straightforward, but in some circumstances, researchers may instead use a *systematic sampling* procedure.

8

TIPS AND SKILLS 8.2
Generating random numbers

This website provides an online random number generator that is very easy to use: **www.psychicscience.org/random.aspx** (accessed 27 March 2019).

If we want to select 450 cases from a population of 9,000, we specify 450 after 'Generate', the digit 1 after 'random integers between', and then 9,000 after 'and'. We would also need to specify 'Unique Values' from a drop-down menu, so that no random number is selected more than once. We would then simply click on GO. The 450 random numbers appear in a box below OUTPUT, and we can copy and paste them into a document.

Systematic sample

The **systematic sample** is a variation on the simple random sample. Here, you select units directly from the sampling frame—without using a table of random numbers.

We know that our chosen sample size means we are selecting 1 student from every 20 students. With a systematic sample, we would pick a random number between 1 and 20 (including those numbers) to use as a starting point, and then progress through the list of units in intervals of 20. So if we started with the number 16, the sixteenth student on our sampling frame is the first in our sample and after this we select every twentieth student on the list. So the sequence will go:

16, 36, 56, 76, 96, 116, etc.

This approach removes the need to assign numbers to students' names and then look up names of the students whose numbers have been drawn by the random selection process. It is important to ensure, however, that there is no inherent ordering of the sampling frame (for example, if the first 120 students were those studying a particular course), since this could bias the resulting sample. If there is some ordering to the list, rearrange it.

Stratified random sampling

A **stratified random sample** is one in which units are selected at random from a population that has been categorized (put into 'strata'). We might want to use this kind of sample if, in our study of university students, we want our sample to include a proportional representation of the different faculties that students are attached to. The kind of discipline a student is studying may influence the attitudinal features that are relevant to the study of drinking. So, if there are 1,800 students in the humanities faculty, using our sampling fraction of 1 in 20, we would want to have 90 humanities students in our sample. Generating a simple random sample or a systematic sample *might* result in such a representation, but because of sampling error, it is more likely that there will be a difference, with the sample including, for example, 85 (too few) or 93 (too many) students from this faculty.

Because the university will hold information about what faculty the student is a member of, it will be possible to ensure that students are accurately represented in terms of their faculty membership. This means stratifying the population by a criterion (in this case, faculty membership) and selecting units from within each stratum using either simple random sampling or systematic sampling. If there are five faculties, we would have five strata, and we would select one-twentieth (as we know that a 450-student sample means we are selecting 1 in every 20 students) of the numbers of students in each stratum, as shown in the right-most column of Table 8.1. The middle column of Table 8.1 shows what the outcome of using a simple random sample in this scenario could be—it could result in a distribution of students across faculties that does not accurately reflect the population, for example with higher numbers of pure science than engineering students included in the sample, despite the engineering faculty representing a bigger proportion of the overall population.

Using stratified random sampling means that the sample will be distributed in the same way as the population in terms of the stratifying criterion. If you use a simple random or systematic sampling approach, you *may* end up with a distribution like that of the stratified sample, but it is unlikely. Two points are relevant here. First, you can conduct stratified sampling sensibly only when it is relatively easy to identify and allocate units to strata. You might also be interested in stratifying your sample according to the nationality of the students, but this would only be possible if you had access to this information. Second, you can use more than one stratifying criterion. You could stratify by both faculty and gender or by both faculty and whether students are undergraduates or postgraduates.

TABLE 8.1
The advantages of stratified sampling

Faculty	Population	Possible outcome of a simple random or systematic sample	Stratified sample (1/20th of the total population)
Humanities	1,800	85	90
Social sciences	1,200	70	60
Pure sciences	2,000	120	100
Applied sciences	1,800	84	90
Engineering	2,200	91	110
Total	9,000	450	450

Multi-stage cluster sampling

In our example, the students to be interviewed are located in a single university so it will not involve a lot of travel. However, imagine that we wanted a *national* sample of UK students. In this case, interviewers would have to travel around the UK to interview the sampled students, adding to the time and cost of doing the research. This kind of problem occurs whenever the aim is to interview a sample drawn from a widely dispersed population, such as a national population. Zhang et al. (2020: 558) state that 'fielding opinion polls on high-quality probability samples entail substantial costs that limit the scale and breadth of research activity'. One way of dealing with this potential problem is to use the fourth type of probability sample: **cluster sampling**. With cluster sampling, the primary sampling unit is not all the units of the population to be sampled but groupings of those units (themselves selected using probability sampling), which are known as 'clusters'. The researcher then samples units from these clusters. Research in focus 8.1 provides an example of a study featuring a multi-stage cluster sample.

Let's consider a variation on our example where this method might be useful. Imagine that we want a nationally representative sample of 5,000 students. Using simple random or systematic sampling would result in a widely dispersed sample, so one solution might be to sample universities, and then students from each of the sampled universities. A probability sampling method would need to be used at each stage. For instance, we might randomly sample 10 universities from the entire population of universities, producing 10 clusters, and we would then interview 500 randomly selected students at each of the 10 universities.

Now imagine that the result of sampling 10 UK universities gives the following list:

- Glasgow Caledonian
- Edinburgh
- Teesside
- Sheffield
- Swansea
- Leeds Beckett
- University of Ulster
- University College London
- Southampton
- Loughborough

This list is fine, but interviewers will still have to do a lot of travelling, since the 10 universities are quite a long way from each other. One solution is likely to be that we group all UK universities by regions and to sample randomly two regions. We might then sample five universities from each of the two lists of universities, and then 500 students from each of the 10 total universities. So, there would be three separate stages, each one involving a round of probability sampling:

1. Group UK universities by standard region and sample two regions;
2. Sample five universities from each of the two regions;
3. Sample 500 students from each of the 10 universities.

In a sense, cluster sampling is always a multi-stage approach, because you always sample clusters first, and then sample something else—either further clusters or population units.

Many examples of multi-stage cluster sampling use stratification. If we were conducting our research in the UK we might, for example, want to stratify universities in terms of whether they are 'old' or 'new' universities (the latter, which are also called 'post-1992' universities, gained university status after a change in the law). In each of the two regions, we would group universities along the old/new university criterion and then select two or three universities from each of the two strata per region. If we

RESEARCH IN FOCUS 8.1
An example of a multi-stage cluster sample

Savage (2016) has written about the dramatic revival of interest in social class in the UK over recent decades. One of the classic studies in this area was conducted by Marshall and colleagues (1988). For their study of social class in modern Britain, Marshall et al. designed a sample 'to achieve 2,000 interviews with a random selection of men aged 16–64 and women aged 16–59 who were not in full-time education' (1988: 288). They present their sampling strategy as involving three stages: sampling parliamentary constituencies, sampling polling districts, and sampling individuals. (In a way, there are actually five stages, because they sampled addresses from polling districts and then individuals from each address, but Marshall et al. only highlight three.) The stages were conducted as follows:

1. Sampling parliamentary constituencies
   - Parliamentary constituencies were ordered by standard region (there are 11).
   - Constituencies were allocated to one of three population density bands within standard regions.
   - These subgroups were reordered by political party voted to represent the constituency at the previous general election.
   - These subgroups were listed in ascending order of percentage in owner-occupation.
   - 100 parliamentary constituencies were sampled.

This meant that parliamentary constituencies were stratified in terms of four variables: standard region; population density; political party voted for in last election; and percentage of owner-occupation.

2. Sampling polling districts
   - Two polling districts were chosen from each sampled constituency.
3. Sampling individuals
   - Nineteen addresses from each sampled polling district were systematically sampled.
   - One person at each address was chosen according to a number of predefined rules.

While this approach is beyond the capacities of people undertaking small scale research projects, it provides an indication of the possibilities presented by a multi-clustering approach.

were conducting our research in another country, such as Germany, we might instead want to stratify universities in terms of whether they are *technische Universitäten* (universities of technology): universities that have official university status, but that usually focus on engineering and the natural sciences rather than covering a more extensive range of academic disciplines.

Even when we use a very rigorous sampling strategy, it is impossible to completely avoid sampling error. In the selection of the students, it may be that certain types of students are still likely to be under-represented, for example those with poor attendance, which might be associated with challenging personal circumstances, caring responsibilities, or work commitments. It is also worth pointing out that certain categories of students may be under-represented simply by chance.

The qualities of a probability sample

Probability sampling allows us to make inferences (that is, **generalizations**) from information about a random sample to the population from which it was taken. However, we do not treat the population data and the sample data as the same. Let's take the example of our investigation (considered in 'Types of probability sample') into the level of alcohol consumption at university, using a sample of 450 students. If we gather information about how many units of alcohol the group of students consumed in the previous seven days, we can calculate the **mean** (or the **arithmetic mean**), which is the simple average—so the total number of units consumed by all students in the sample, divided by the number of students in the sample, 450. We can use the mean number of units consumed by the sample to estimate the population mean, but with known margins of error. The 'margin of error' is basically a statistic expressing the amount of random sampling error there is in a survey's results.

In order to address this point we need to use some basic statistical ideas. These are presented in Tips and skills 8.3, which you do not need to read if you only require a broad idea of sampling procedures.

TIPS AND SKILLS 8.3

Generalizing from a random sample to the population

Being able to generalize from a random sample to the population is a useful skill to develop if you want to improve your knowledge of sampling. In this box, we use our university student example (introduced in 'Types of probability sample') to take you through the process.

Let's say that the sample mean is 9.7 units of alcohol consumed—in other words, the average amount of alcohol that an individual student in the sample group consumed in the previous seven days. A crucial consideration here is: even if we have used probability sampling, how confident can we be that this mean level of alcohol consumption is likely to be found in the whole population? If we take an infinite number of different samples from a population, the sample mean will vary in relation to the population mean. This variation will take the form of a bell-shaped curve known as a **normal distribution** (see Figure 8.8). The normal distribution is the most important statistical distribution. Most of the observations are concentrated around the middle, with some values on either side. Data on heights or weights usually follow a normal distribution, because most people are around the average height, for example, but there are a few particularly short and particularly tall individuals in the population. The sample means cluster at or around the population mean. Half the sample means will be at or below the population mean; the other half will be at or above the population mean. As we move to the left (sample means that are at or lower than the population mean) or the right (sample means that are at or higher than the population mean), the curve tails off, implying that fewer and fewer samples generate means that are a long way from the population mean.

The variation of sample means around the population mean is known as the **sampling error** and is measured using a statistic known as the **standard error of the mean** (SE). This is an estimate of the amount that a sample mean is likely to differ from the population mean. It is worth noting that the standard error is actually inversely proportional to the size of the sample—basically, the larger the sample size is, the smaller the standard error is

FIGURE 8.8
The distribution of sample means

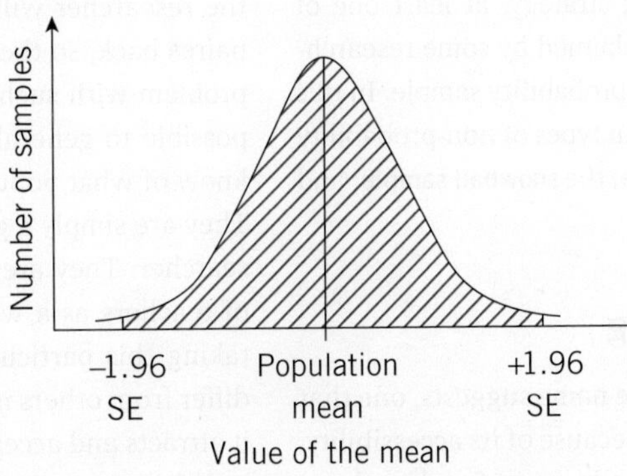

Notes: 95 per cent of sample means will lie within the shaded area. SE = standard error of the mean.

8

likely to be, as the statistic will approach the actual value of the population. It is logical that having a greater amount of data tends to lead to less variation (and more precision) in your findings.

Sampling theory tells us that 68 per cent of all sample means will lie between plus or minus 1.00 standard errors from the population mean and that 95 per cent of all sample means will lie between +1.96 or −1.96 standard errors from the population mean. It is this second calculation that is crucial, because it is at least implicitly used by survey researchers when they report their statistical findings. They usually employ 1.96 standard errors as the crucial criterion in how confident they can be in their findings. Basically, the criterion implies that you can be 95 per cent certain that the population mean lies within +1.96 or −1.96 sampling errors from the sample mean.

If a sample has been selected according to probability sampling principles, we know that we can be 95 per cent certain that the population mean will lie between the sample mean, +1.96 or −1.96 multiplied by the standard error of the mean. This is known as the **confidence interval**. If the mean level of alcohol consumption over the previous seven days in our sample of 450 students is 9.7 units, and the standard error of the mean is 1.3, we can be 95 per cent certain that the population mean will lie between

$9.7 + (1.96 \times 1.3)$

and

$9.7 - (1.96 \times 1.3)$

In other words, it would be between 12.248 and 7.152.

If the standard error was smaller, the range of possible values of the population mean would be narrower; if the standard error was larger, the range of possible values of the population mean would be wider.

If we had selected a stratified sample, the standard error of the mean would be smaller; this is because the variation between strata is essentially eliminated because the population will be accurately represented in the sample in terms of the stratification criterion or criteria we employed. This demonstrates how stratification provides an extra element of precision in the probability sampling process, as it eliminates a possible source of sampling error.

8.5 Types of non-probability sampling

The term 'non-probability sampling' is used to capture all forms of sampling that are not conducted using the principles of probability sampling. It covers a wide range of different types of sampling strategy, at least one of which—the **quota sample**—is claimed by some researchers to be almost as precise as a probability sample. In this section we will cover three main types of non-probability sample: the **convenience sample**; the **snowball sample**; and the quota sample.

Convenience sampling

A convenience sample is, as the name suggests, one that is available to the researcher because of its accessibility. Imagine that a researcher who lectures for the education faculty at a university is interested in the kinds of qualities that teachers look for in their head teachers. The researcher might administer a questionnaire to several classes of students, all of whom are teachers taking a part-time master's degree in education. It is likely that the researcher will receive almost all of the questionnaires back, so there will be a good response rate. The problem with such a sampling strategy is that it is impossible to generalize the findings because we do not know of what population this sample is representative. They are simply a group of teachers available to the researcher. They are almost certainly not representative of teachers as a whole, especially given that they are taking this particular degree programme (which may differ from others in terms of, for example, the students it attracts and accepts).

Although researchers may be discouraged from using convenience sampling (see Rivera 2019), this doesn't mean that convenience samples should never be used, particularly as they can be a useful way of accessing hard-to-reach populations. If the researcher is developing a series of questions designed to measure a certain area, for example the leadership preferences of teachers, it is extremely useful to **pilot** such a research instrument before using it in an investigation. Administering it to a group that is not a part of the main study may be a useful way of carrying out some preliminary analysis. For this kind of purpose, a convenience sample may be acceptable even if not ideal. A second context where convenience sampling may be useful is when there is a rare chance to gather data from a sample to which you have easy access and this represents too good an opportunity to miss. For instance, if an employee of a pension provider offered to send an online questionnaire out on your behalf to a large sample of people who were contributing to pensions, asking about their savings habits, this might be too good an opportunity to miss, even if you also want to explore the savings habits of those not contributing to a pension. The data will not provide definitive findings, because of the problem of generalization, but it could provide a springboard for further research or help you identify links with existing findings in this area.

It is also important to recognize that social research is frequently based on convenience sampling, and if the approach is clearly justified and limitations acknowledged this can be totally appropriate. Probability sampling requires a lot of preparation, so social researchers frequently avoid it because of the difficulty and costs involved. Research in focus 8.2 provides an example of a social research study that used convenience sampling.

Snowball sampling

In certain respects, snowball sampling is a form of convenience sample, but with this approach to sampling, the researcher makes initial contact with a small group of people who are relevant to the research topic and then uses them to establish contacts with others. The problem with snowball sampling is that it is unlikely that the sample will be representative of the population. Usually, snowball sampling is not used within a quantitative research strategy, but within a qualitative one. There is less concern about **external validity** and the ability to generalize within a qualitative research strategy as there would be in a quantitative research one (see Chapter 17). In qualitative research, the approach to sampling is more likely to be guided by a preference for what is known as **purposive sampling** (this involves selecting people who 'best fit' the requirements of the study, according to predefined characteristics) than by the kind of statistical sampling that we have focused on within this chapter (purposive sampling is discussed in detail in Section 17.3). There is a much better 'fit' between snowball sampling and the purposive sampling strategy of qualitative research than with the statistical sampling approach of quantitative research. This does not mean that snowball sampling is irrelevant to

8

RESEARCH IN FOCUS 8.2
A convenience sample

Ibrahim (2018) used convenience sampling in their study of the emerging social work profession in the Middle East and North Africa region, examining the effectiveness of social work education programmes at Arab universities. In doing so they raised questions about the ability of social work academic programmes in Arab universities to address societal issues. They used convenience sampling to select the universities and research participants, due to having relatively easy access to these groups.

At the time of the research, there was no available official information that identified all of the education institutions with social work departments or programmes in the Arab world, so the researcher's academic relations with colleagues were important in identifying and approaching participants. A sample of full-time faculty members of social work departments at 22 Arab universities in 8 Arab countries (out of 22 states in the Arab world) completed the questionnaire, namely Palestine, Jordan, Saudi Arabia, Oman, Yemen, Egypt, Libya, and Morocco. Ibrahim (2018: 83) stated that 'convenience sampling is appropriate for studies that examine hard-to-reach populations, such as the present case although this may present issues of selectivity and thus poses a limitation to this study'.

Importantly, the researcher highlighted the limitations of the convenience sampling in this research, including its implications for their findings. This is something you should consider if undertaking this form of sampling.

quantitative research: when the researcher needs to focus upon or reflect relationships between people, tracing connections through snowball sampling may be a better approach than conventional probability sampling (Coleman 1958). In Learn from experience 8.1, Scarlett explains how she used purposive sampling in a student project.

Quota sampling

Quota sampling is fairly rare in academic social research but is used intensively in market research and political opinion polling. Quota sampling aims to produce a sample that reflects a population in terms of the relative proportions of people in different categories, such as gender, ethnicity, age groups, socio-economic groups, and region of residence, and combinations of these categories. This might sound similar to a stratified sample, but in quota sampling, the sampling of individuals is not carried out randomly: the final selection of people is left to the interviewer. Quota sampling is especially useful if it is not possible for you to obtain a probability sample, but you are still trying to create a sample that is as representative as possible of the population you are studying (Sharma 2017). It is a form of purposive sampling procedure where cases/participants are sampled in a strategic way (see Key concept 17.1).

Once the researcher has decided on the categories they want to use and the number of people they need from each **category** (known as quotas or quota controls), they select people for inclusion in the sample who fit these categories. As in stratified sampling, the population might be divided into categories of, for example, gender, social class, age, and ethnicity. Researchers might use census data to establish the size of each of these categories in the overall population, so that they can ensure their sample reflects these proportions—for example, if Afro-Caribbean people make up 20 per cent of the population, 20 per cent of the people the researchers interview should be from this category. Researchers are often looking for individuals who fit several categories. They might know, for example, that if their sample is to reflect the population, they need to find and interview five Asian, 25- to 34-year-old, lower-middle-class females living in a particular location. The researcher usually asks people who are available to them about their characteristics in order to determine whether they fit a particular category. Once they have enough people from a category (or a combination of categories) to fill the necessary quota, they no longer need to find participants from this group. Foster and Heneghan (2018) used quota sampling when exploring young women's pension planning. They did this to ensure that their sample represented a mixture of ages and incomes, occupations, public/private sector

LEARN FROM EXPERIENCE 8.1
Purposive sampling

Scarlett used purposive sampling to identify the most appropriate participants for her research project, which focused on the effect of social media on mental wellbeing among secondary school students. Scarlett used this sampling method to address ethical concerns that might have occurred had she not chosen her sample carefully.

> For my project, I wanted to employ a random sampling technique—this way, the students in the project would be selected entirely at random and there would be no influence of bias. Students at the school were given an information sheet which contained information about the project, what participation would include, and where responses would go. Students were then asked to let their teacher know if they wanted to take part, and the teacher would select participants at random. However, as my project was focused on young people's mental wellbeing, the teacher selected students who they felt were more suitable to take part in the project. This meant that they did not select pupils who had poor mental wellbeing, as taking part in the study would perhaps pose a risk of psychological harm. Therefore, a purposive sampling technique was employed.

Scarlett

 Access the **online resources** to hear Scarlett's video reflections on this theme.

You can read about our panellists' backgrounds and research experiences on page xxvi.

employment, ethnicities, marital statuses, and whether women had children.

You will have gathered that with this type of sampling, the choice of respondents is left to the researcher as long as all quotas are filled, usually within a certain time period. If you have ever been approached on the street by someone with a clipboard or tablet and been questioned about your age, occupation, etc., before being asked a series of questions about something, you have almost certainly come across an interviewer with a quota sample to fill. Sometimes, they will decide not to interview you because you do not meet the criteria needed to fill a quota.

There are a number of criticisms of quota samples.

- The fact that the choice of respondent is left to the researcher means that a quota sample cannot be representative. It might accurately reflect the population in terms of characteristics defined by the quotas, but researchers' decisions about people to approach could be influenced by perceptions of how friendly or approachable they seem.
- People who are in the researcher's area at the times they conduct interviews may not be typical. There is a risk, for example, that people in full-time paid work may be under-represented, meaning that those included in the sample are not typical.
- The researcher is likely to make judgements about certain characteristics, such as age, when deciding whether to approach a person, and those judgements will sometimes be incorrect. A researcher might not approach someone who is eligible to be interviewed (because a quota that they fit is not yet filled) because they think the person looks older than the maximum age for the quota they are trying to fill. This introduces a possible element of bias.
- We cannot calculate a standard error of the mean from a quota sample because the non-random method of selection makes it impossible to calculate the **range** of possible values of a population.

All these criticisms make quota sampling seem like a bad choice, and as we have noted, it does not tend to be popular with academic researchers. It does have some arguments in its favour, however. They are as follows.

- The method is cheaper and quicker than an interview survey on a similar-sized probability sample, as interviewers do not have to spend a lot of time travelling between interviews.
- Interviewers do not have to keep following up with people who were not available when first approached.
- As there is no need for this kind of follow-up, a quota sample is easier to manage. There is no need to keep track of people who need to be recontacted or of refusals.
- A quota sample is quicker to assemble than a probability sample. Researchers might need to know about the impact of a sudden event and a quota sample will be much faster, or they might want to survey reactions to, or behaviour within, a situation that is changing rapidly.
- Like convenience sampling, quota sampling is useful for conducting development work on new measures or on research instruments. It can also be useful in exploratory work to generate new theoretical ideas.
- Although the standard error of the mean should not be computed for a quota sample, it frequently is. As Moser and Kalton (1971) observe, some writers argue that the use of a non-random method in quota sampling should not prevent the researcher doing this calculation because its significance as a source of error is small compared to other errors that can arise in surveys (see Figure 8.9; see also Kalton 2019).

Quota samples do, however, result in biases more often than random samples (Yang and Banamah 2013; Tyrer and Heyman 2016). They under-represent people in lower social strata, those employed in the private sector and manufacturing, and those at the extremes of income, and they over-represent women in households with children and from larger households. But probability samples are often biased too—under-representing men and those in employment (Marsh and Scarbrough 1990; Butcher 1994; Rada and Martín 2014).

An issue that has not been given much attention is whether quota samples produce different findings from probability samples. Yang and Banamah (2013) selected a probability sample and a quota sample from the membership of a university student society. For the quota sample, gender and educational level (master's degree, PhD, etc.) were used as quotas. In the case of the probability sample, 22.5 per cent responded more or less immediately, increasing to 42.5 per cent after a first reminder, and to 67.5 per cent after a second and final reminder. The questionnaire had only a small number of questions, which covered issues such as religious participation, personal friendships, and mutual trust among members. The researchers found that there were only statistically significant differences between the findings from the two samples when findings from the quota sample were compared to the findings after the second reminder.

8

There were few, if any, statistically significant differences between the findings from the two samples when the quota sample was compared with the findings from those who had replied immediately or those who replied after one reminder. Yang and Banamah propose that this suggests that when a probability sample generates a low response rate, it is likely that it does not have a great advantage over an equivalent quota sample.

8.6 Sample size

One of the most common questions that comes up in relation to research methods is how large a sample needs to be. As Reni's comments illustrate in Learn from experience 8.2, this decision is not straightforward and there is no one definitive answer. Decisions about sample size usually represent a compromise between constraints of time and cost and the need for precision, and such decisions depend on a variety of considerations that we will now address.

Absolute and relative sample size

An important consideration is that it is the *absolute* size of a sample that is important rather than its *relative* size. This means that a national probability sample of 1,000 individuals in the UK has as much validity as a national probability sample of 1,000 individuals in the USA, even though the USA has a much larger population. It also means that increasing the size of a sample increases its precision because, as we noted in Tips and skills 8.3, the 95 per cent confidence interval narrows. However, a large sample cannot *guarantee* precision; increasing the size of a sample just increases the *likely* precision of a sample. This means that as sample size increases, sampling error decreases: see Tips and skills 8.4.

An important consideration in deciding about sample size should therefore be how much sampling error you are prepared to tolerate. The less sampling error you are prepared to accept, the larger a sample will need to be. Fowler (2013) warns against simply accepting this criterion, arguing that in practice researchers do not base their decisions about sample size on a single estimate of a variable. Most survey research aims to generate a collection of estimates of the variables that make up the research instrument used. Fowler also observes that survey researchers are not often in a position to specify an ideal level of precision in advance. In fact, Greenland et al. (2016: 338) state that 'many decisions surrounding analysis choices have been made after the data were collected'. Since sampling error is only one part of any error involved in an estimate, the idea of using an ideal level of

LEARN FROM EXPERIENCE 8.2
Choosing your sample size

The process of choosing an appropriate sample for your student project is not always a straightforward one, and it has implications for your analysis. Reni, whose research focused on the International Criminal Court and its alleged bias against African countries, found these challenges in her work and identified the addition of another research method as one solution to the issue (you can read more about Reni's choice of method in Learn from experience 24.1). In other cases, slightly adapting your focus or using incentives to increase your sample size may also be effective. Whichever approach you take, it is important to point out any limitations when presenting your work, as Reni acknowledges.

> The main challenge I faced when formulating my methodology was choosing the 'right' sample size for my research question. At first, my sample size was too large and difficult to analyse. Then, it was too small and I had to account for this small sample size when presenting my conclusions. The truth is I was dealing with a rather awkward set of constraints. At first, my question was too broad and, as a result, so was my sample size. As I made my question a bit narrower, however, I realized that only a small sample size of cases suited the criteria for the hypothesis I was attempting to test. My advice to

students working with a small sample size would be to consider conducting more than one form of data analysis. Also, remember to acknowledge the sample size as a potential limitation on the accuracy of your study.

Reni

 Access the **online resources** to hear Reni's video reflections on this theme.

You can read about our panellists' backgrounds and research experiences on page xxvi.

TIPS AND SKILLS 8.4
Sample size and probability sampling

As we have discussed, the issue of sample size is one of the most important concerns for researchers, as bigger samples mean more accurate data. However, when doing research projects, students in particular have limited resources. Some departments may give guidelines about whether they expect samples of a minimum size. If not, you may need to conduct a mini-survey to maximize the number of interviews you can conduct or the number of online surveys you can send out, given the amount of time and resources available.

It is also true that in most student research projects, a truly random approach to sample selection may not be possible (as Scarlett discovered—see Learn from experience 8.1). The crucial point is to be clear about what you have done and to justify it. This includes explaining the difficulties you would have encountered in generating a random sample and why you could not include any more cases in your sample. Importantly, you must not make claims about your sample that are unsustainable. Do not claim that it is representative or that you have a random sample when this is clearly not the case (people will be more inclined to accept an awareness of the limits of your sample than claims about a sample that are false), but do make sure you state the positive features of your sample as well as being honest about its limitations.

precision to determine sample size is unrealistic. Instead, when researchers consider this idea, it is usually in a general rather than a calculated way.

Time and cost

Time and cost considerations are very relevant to decisions about sample size, and need to be weighed up against likely gains in precision if you increase your sample size. The gains in precision are noticeable as the sample size climbs from low figures of 50, 100, 150, and so on upwards, but after a certain point, often in the region of 1,000, the increases in precision (and the extent to which the standard error of the mean declines) slow down and become less obvious. This slow-down may affect decisions about the sample size, as it may not be worth significantly increasing the time and cost involved for only very small gains in precision.

Non-response

The problem of non-response, which we briefly considered in Section 8.2, is also important in relation to sample size. Most sample surveys attract a certain amount of non-response. It is likely that only some members of a sample will be contactable and that out of those who are contactable, some will refuse to participate. We saw this in the HESA example regarding the collection of student employment data (discussed in Section 8.2). This lack of response from people (units) is actually called '**unit non-response**' to distinguish it from **item non-response**, which is when people (units) agree to participate but fail, either deliberately or accidentally, to answer specific *items* (questions) on a questionnaire. Here we are using the term 'non-response' to refer to unit non-response. If our aim is to ensure as far as possible that 450 students are interviewed and we think that there may be a 20 per cent rate of non-response, then it might be sensible to sample 550–60 individuals, as approximately 90 will be non-respondents.

The issue of non-response, and in particular of refusal to participate, is significant: some researchers have suggested that response rates to surveys (response rates are defined in Key concept 8.2) are declining in many countries (see Groves et al. 2009). Research in focus 8.3 provides an example of a study that was biased because of the high non-response rate. Kibuchi et al. (2018: 4) state that 'low and declining response rates pose an existential threat to conventional approaches to data collection in survey research'. This could be associated with general data overload and fatigue. This has led to considerable thought about ways to minimize non-response rates (see Research in focus 8.4).

An important question concerning non-response is: how far should researchers go to increase their response rates? In Chapter 10, we will discuss a number of steps to improve response rates to postal and online questionnaires, which are particularly prone to poor response rates. Sending a reminder or second request to respondents who do not initially respond to a postal or online questionnaire is not too time-consuming and involves little or no extra cost, and it usually results in an improved response rate. See Learn from experience 8.3 for Scarlett's tips on mitigating the issue of non-response in a student project.

The efficacy of this technique was evident in a national online survey by Meterko et al. (2015) of healthcare leaders in the USA, which achieved a 95 per cent response rate. Researchers achieved this high response

KEY CONCEPT 8.2
What is a response rate?

When a survey is conducted, some people who are in the sample will always refuse to participate (referred to as non-response). The response rate is in effect the percentage of a sample that agrees to participate. However, the calculation is a little more complicated than this, first because not everyone who replies should be included (for example, if a respondent does not answer a large number of questions or if it is clear that they have not taken the survey seriously, it is better not to use their survey), and second, it may be that not everyone in a sample turns out to be an appropriate respondent or can be contacted. The response rate is therefo number of usable questionnaires

$$\frac{\text{number of usable questionnaires}}{\text{total sample} - \text{unsuitable or uncontactable members of the sample}} \times 100$$

RESEARCH IN FOCUS 8.3
The problem of non-response

Numerous studies have reported struggling with increasing non-response rates over recent years (for example Brick and Williams 2013; Meyer et al. 2015; Fosnacht et al. 2017), but the issue has been present for some time and was very clearly demonstrated in a December 2006 an article in *The Times*, which reported that a study of the weight of British children had been held back because many families declined to participate.

The study was commissioned by the Department of Health and found that among those aged 10 or 11, 14 per cent were overweight and 17 per cent were obese. However, *The Times* writer notes that a report compiled by the Department of Health on the research suggests that such figures are 'likely systematically to underestimate the prevalence of overweight and obesity'. The reason for this bias is that parents were able to refuse to let their children participate, and those whose children were heavier were more likely to refuse. As a result, the sample was biased towards those who were less heavy. The authors of the report made these observations about bias because they noted that more children were recorded as obese in areas where there was a higher response rate.

Source: **www.thetimes.co.uk/tto/news/uk/article1949951.ece** (accessed 30 March 2019)

LEARN FROM EXPERIENCE 8.3
Dealing with non-response

Non-response among participants can be problematic in student projects. This led Scarlett, whose dissertation research included a questionnaire focusing on the impact of social media on mental wellbeing, to develop strategies for dealing with these issues.

> When I conducted an online survey, I faced the issue of gaining a low response rate. This can be disheartening and can pose an issue in regard to inputting and analysing data. My tips for a low response rate would be to advertise your research as much as possible (perhaps using online or paper fliers) or ask your peers to spread the word. On the other hand, it might be that you're facing a low response rate because your survey is too long or your questions are too wordy. Talk to your lecturer about it and ask for some advice—they will be happy to help!
>
> Scarlett

 Access the **online resources** to hear Scarlett's video reflections on this theme.

You can read about our panellists' backgrounds and research experiences on page xxvi.

rate after four follow-ups of non-respondents. Of the healthcare leaders who participated, 29.7 per cent did so initially, 19.5 per cent after the first follow-up, 11.9 per cent after the second, 10.2 per cent after the third, and 28.8 per cent after the fourth. The researchers found no statistical difference between respondents when comparing data from the five waves of surveys in terms of 'demographic characteristics, missing data, and distribution of responses across categories' (Meterko et al. 2015: 141). In other words, boosting the response rate at each stage did nothing to enhance the quality or nature of the data, which differed very little after the initial contact, when the response rate was under 30 per cent, and after four follow-ups, when the response rate was 95 per cent. Their findings indicate that data from surveys with relatively low response rates, and therefore small sample sizes, should not be automatically dismissed. This is in contrast to Banamah and Yang's (2013) study, where the number of reminders sent had a statistically significant effect on the findings after the second reminder.

However, good response rates are important in securing a reasonable size of sample, and boosting response rates to interview-based surveys can prove more challenging. One approach to increase response rates, shown in Research in focus 8.4, involves using incentives to encourage participation in interview surveys (and these can also be used with other forms of survey research). Kibuchi et al. (2018) claim that evidence demonstrates that monetary incentives have a robust, positive effect on the probability of survey cooperation.

There is wide variation in the response rates that social scientists achieve when they conduct surveys. It is difficult to arrive at a clear answer as to what a minimum or reasonable response rate should be. What researchers might consider to be a reasonable response rate will vary according to the type of sample and the topics covered by the interview or questionnaire. While you should obviously do your best (within the constraints of cost, time, etc.) to maximize your response rate, when you present your research it is also important to be open about the limitations of a low response rate in terms of the likelihood that your findings will be biased.

Heterogeneity of the population

Yet another consideration for sample size is the homogeneity (similarity) and heterogeneity (diversity) of the population from which the sample is taken. When a population is very heterogeneous, such as a whole country or city, a larger sample will be needed to reflect the varied population. When it is relatively homogeneous, such as a population of students or of members of a certain occupation, the amount of variation is less and therefore the sample can be smaller. So the greater the heterogeneity of a population, the larger a sample will need to be. Of course this depends on what you are attempting to measure.

RESEARCH IN FOCUS 8.4
Incentivizing interview survey responses

Kibuchi et al. (2018) used data from three different UK face-to-face interview surveys to explore the role of financial incentives on survey response rates. These were the 2015 National Survey for Wales Field Test (NSW2015), the 2016 National Survey for Wales Incentive Experiment (NSW2016), and Wave 1 of the UK Household Longitudinal Study Innovation Panel (UKHLS-IP).

The researchers used stratified random sampling in each survey, selecting addresses from the Postcode Address File, which contains all UK postcodes. The two Welsh surveys randomly selected one eligible adult in each household (aged 16 and over), while the UKHLS-IP attempted to interview all eligible adults (aged 18 and over) in the household. NSW2015 randomly allocated 50 per cent of addresses to receive no incentive and 50 per cent to receive £10, while the NSW2016 also used this approach but with an incentive of £5. The UKHSL-IP randomly allocated one-third of addresses a £10 incentive and the remainder £5. The incentives provided in all of the surveys were dependent on the respondent(s) completing the questionnaire.

The findings showed that the response rates were higher when incentives were applied in all three surveys, with the UKHLS-IP and NSW2016 having cooperative rates of 2 percentage points higher and the NSW2015 a rate of 5 percentage points higher for the incentivized households. Thus it was evident that the incentives had a small effect on responses.

While financial incentives are not always encouraged by universities and may not be economically feasible, they can have an impact on the response rate.

Kind of analysis

Finally, when deciding on sample size researchers should bear in mind the *kind of analysis* they intend to undertake. The more comparisons they want to make between groups, or the more subgroups the research involves, the larger the size should be. If you plan to use a specific statistical technique it is important to ensure your data fulfils the necessary requirements to allow you to be confident in your conclusions (see Chapter 15 for further discussion).

8.7 Sampling issues in online surveys

Online surveys have expanded dramatically over recent decades. We consider them further in Chapter 10, but it is important to reflect on how the discussions so far in this chapter apply to online surveys, as well as the particular challenges they present in the context of sampling—for example, the fact that not everyone in any nation is online and has the technical ability to handle online questionnaires. Other features of online communications present issues for researchers.

- Many people have more than one email address (meaning it is important to ensure the same individual doesn't respond to the same survey more than once).
- A household's internet-enabled devices might be used by multiple people (ensuring that the appropriate person responds is important in this context).
- Internet users have traditionally been seen as a biased sample of the population, in that they have tended to be better educated, wealthier, younger, and not representative in ethnic terms (Couper 2000; Hargittai and Karaoglu 2018). It is apparent that there are still differences in terms of internet use and age (Hargittai and Karaoglu 2018).
- There are very few sampling frames of the general online population and most of them are likely to be expensive to acquire, since they are controlled by internet service providers or may be confidential.

These issues complicate the possibilities of conducting online surveys using probability sampling principles and should be carefully considered, but this is still a particularly useful way of accessing a sample.

It is worth remembering that the sampling challenges presented by online surveys apply differently to different groups. When thinking about our imaginary survey of student drinking habits (see Section 8.4 under 'Types of probability sample'), the fact that all UK students are provided with university email addresses and have access to university desktops or laptops (and, most likely, their own as well) mean that online surveys could be a particularly effective way of accessing this sample. In these circumstances, surveys can employ the same sort of probability sampling procedures we have previously outlined. Tourangeau et al. (2013: 13) note that there are several forms of probability sample usable for online surveys but suggest that most do not use this method. One of the most common forms of online survey that is based on probability sampling is the pre-recruited online panel. These tend to be groups of individuals who have agreed in advance to participate in a series of surveys. An example is Germany's GESIS panel, a probability-based mixed mode access panel ('mixed mode' means that it combined more than one method of administering the surveys). The panel was first surveyed in 2014 and comprised around 4,900 panel members. Initially, the researchers selected a random sample of the German population aged 18–70 and interviewed all who were prepared to be interviewed, using computer-assisted personal interviewing (CAPI), to establish their willingness to be involved in the panel. In 2018 the panel comprised 4,400 members, of whom roughly two-thirds were online participants. This fall in the number of participants was related to attrition, as people dropped out of the survey either because they no longer wanted to be involved or because they were not in a position to complete the survey (www.gesis.org/en/gesis-panel/gesis-panel-home/general-overview/, accessed 30 March 2019).

Using pre-recruited panels to complete more than one survey has the speed advantages of online surveys but eliminate the often lengthy recruitment process involved in surveys where people have not previously been recruited. However, pre-recruited panels are not without potential limitations. In particular, Fricker (2008: 2004) notes that 'researchers should be aware that long-term panel participants may respond differently to surveys and survey questions than first-time participants (called "panel conditioning" or "time-in-sample bias")'. In addition, if there is significant loss of potential respondents during the recruitment and participation stages, this can lead to non-response issues.

Hewson and Laurent (2008) suggest that when there is no sampling frame, the best way to generate an appropriate sample is to put an invitation to answer a questionnaire on a relevant message board, email it to suitable mailing lists, or share it on websites and social media. This will result in a sample of unknown representativeness, and it is impossible to know the response rate to the questionnaire because the size of the population is also unknown. However, if representativeness is not a significant concern for the researcher, the fact that it is possible to target groups that have a specific interest or form of behaviour makes these methods an attractive means of contacting sample members. They are also more cost-effective for projects with considerable financial restrictions than other methods, such as in-person surveys and postal questionnaires. It is also possible to embed videos and links in online questionnaires, so that participants can easily access more information related to an online survey. In addition, text-to-speech software can be used to make the research more inclusive.

8

Social media channels, such as Facebook, are now often used to access research participants (Kamp et al. 2019), particularly in the UK and the USA. In 2018, nearly 68 per cent of adults reported having a Facebook profile in the USA, and 74 per cent of these users stated that they accessed their profile at least once per day (Pew Research Center 2019). Samples recruited through Facebook include parent caregivers of children and teenagers with cancer (Akard et al. 2015), long-term smokers (Carter-Harris et al. 2016), and family caregivers (Herbell and Zauszniewski 2018). Although larger-scale studies with infrastructure and big budgets are more likely to be able to use targeted advertising (for example, by location and age group) to try to make their samples fulfil certain quotas, in student projects Facebook tends to represent a form of convenience sampling, particularly if the researcher approaches their own Facebook contacts to administer a questionnaire. It can be a form of snowball sampling, given that if people interact with a Facebook post on a publicly-accessible page or group, this post will be visible to their friends and contacts too—and they may also share the information with them directly. Whitaker et al. (2017) conducted a systematic review of Facebook recruitment and found that its advantages, compared with more traditional methods, included reduced costs, shorter recruitment periods, and improved participant selection from hard-to-reach populations. However, they also identified disadvantages, such as the fact that participants need internet access to participate, and they highlighted an over-representation of young white women.

A further issue to note about online surveys in relation to sampling error is the matter of non-response (see Key concept 8.2). There is evidence that online surveys typically generate lower response rates than postal questionnaire surveys (Converse et al. 2008; Pedersen and Nielsen 2016). A **meta-analysis** of 45 **experimental** comparisons of online surveys and other modes of survey administration (with email surveys included in the 'other survey modes' group) found that the former achieved on average an 11 per cent lower response rate (Manfreda et al. 2008). Research in focus 8.5 also shows variations between response rates depending on how the survey is administered.

You can boost response rates in online surveys by following three simple strategies.

1. Contact potential respondents before sending them a questionnaire.
2. Follow up non-respondents at least once (as with postal surveys).
3. Provide incentives to enhance the number of responses (Pedersen and Neilsen 2016). This could include access to your findings, vouchers, a prize draw, or charitable donations (though please check what your university or research organization allows you to use).

In relation to the first point, it is important to be aware that this is regarded as basic etiquette when conducting online surveys. Bosnjak et al. (2008) found that response rates to an online panel survey could be increased by pre-notifying prospective participants. They found that pre-notifications sent by text message were more effective than email but that a combination of both was more effective than text messages alone. However, pre-notification by letter has been shown to be even more effective than email (Tourangeau et al. 2013: 44).

Another factor that may affect response rates is how far the topic is interesting or relevant to the sample. During the 2008 US presidential campaign, Baumgartner and Morris (2010) conducted an online survey of students, examining the influence of social networking sites as sources of news upon students' engagement with the democratic process. The researchers achieved a respectable response rate of 37.9 per cent. Although they found little evidence of social networking sites having an impact on the students' political engagement, these platforms play a significant role in young people's lives, and the fact that the survey was about them may have helped the response rate.

The length of time needed to complete an online survey (or any survey for that matter) can influence response and completion rates (Clark et al. 2019). Crawford et al. (2001) report the results of a survey of students at the University of Michigan that experimented with a number of possible influences on the response rate. Students in the sample were initially sent an email inviting them to visit the website, which allowed access, via a password, to the questionnaire. Some of those emailed were led to expect that the questionnaire would take 8–10 minutes to complete (in fact, it would take considerably longer); others were led to expect that it would take 20 minutes. Those led to believe it would take longer were less likely to accept the invitation, resulting in a lower response rate for this group. However, Crawford et al. also found that those respondents who were led to believe that it would take only 8–10 minutes were *more* likely to give up on the questionnaire part of the way through, resulting in unusable partially completed questionnaires. We recommend piloting your questionnaire to get a clear sense of how long it will take and being honest about the likely time it will take to complete. Crawford et al. also found that respondents were most likely to abandon their questionnaires part way through when in the middle of

RESEARCH IN FOCUS 8.5
Response rates in postal and online surveys

Sebo et al. (2017) conducted a study to determine through a randomized design whether online surveys are feasible in primary medical care. They administered questionnaires to general medical practitioners (GPs) and assessed the GPs' participation rates, response times, and completeness of data using two different modes of questionnaire delivery: postal and online. They conducted this randomized trial in Western Switzerland (cantons of Geneva and Vaud) and France (regions of Alsace and Pays de la Loire) in 2015, as part of a study of GPs' preventive medicine practices. They found that in a random selection of community-based GPs (1,000 GPs in Switzerland and 2,400 GPs in France) where participants were randomly allocated to receive a questionnaire about preventive care activities either by post ($n = 700$ in Switzerland, $n = 400$ in France) or by email ($n = 300$ in Switzerland, $n = 2{,}000$ in France), differences in response rates were apparent. They found that the participation rate in the group who received the questionnaire via email was more than four times lower, but the response time was much shorter.

completing a series of open-ended questions, suggesting that it is best to minimize the number of these questions in self-completion questionnaires.

If respondents can see a progress indicator (a diagrammatic representation of how far the respondent has progressed through the questionnaire), this can reduce the number of people who abandon a questionnaire mid-way through (Couper et al. 2001). Couper et al. also found that it took less time for respondents to complete related items (for example, a series of Likert scale items) when they appeared on a screen together than when they appeared singly. An example of a Likert scale using related items can be found in Thinking deeply 7.1, which presents the welfarism scale.

Increasingly, mixed mode surveys have become standard practice among many survey researchers in both academic and commercial fields (De Leeuw and Hox 2015). There are a variety of reasons for this trend, some of which we will touch upon in Chapters 9 and 10, but one of the main reasons is that declining response rates have led to concerns about how well samples cover the populations they are meant to reflect. Giving potential respondents more than one way of completing the survey increases the likelihood of a reasonable response rate. Online surveys occupy an increasingly significant role here, in that they increase the range of opportunities to administer surveys to respondents, such as through the use of small, easily portable internet-enabled devices, including mobile phones and tablets.

8.8 Limits to generalization

Regardless of the methods of data collection and sampling that you use, you can only generalize your study's findings to the population from which your sample was taken. It is easy to think that findings from a study have some kind of broader applicability. If we return to our imaginary study of drinking habits among students at a university (see Section 8.4 under 'Types of probability sample'), we could only generalize our findings to that university. We would need to be very cautious about generalizing to students at other universities, as there are many factors that may affect the drinking habits of students at other universities—for example a higher (or lower) concentration of pubs near the university, more (or fewer) bars on campus, more (or less) of a culture of drinking at the university, or a higher (or lower) proportion of students with disposable income. Another generalizability issue that is rarely discussed (and one that is almost impossible to assess) is whether there is a time limit on the findings generated. To take a simple example: no one would be prepared to assume that the findings of a study in 1980 of university students' budgeting and personal finance habits would apply to students in the early twenty-first century. Quite apart from changes that might have occurred naturally, the changes to the student grant system has changed the ways students finance their education, including perhaps a greater reliance on part-time work and on parents, and the use of loans (Hordosy and Clark 2019). There are an increasing number of budgeting apps available, which could have an effect on students' financial habits. Many of the studies we examine in this book might also produce different findings if they were replicated several years later, particularly those using online surveys, given the pace of digital advances. To sum up, you need to be aware that research findings may be temporally specific.

8.9 Error in survey research and the role of sampling

We have seen that sampling is a key area where 'error' can occur in survey research. We can think of 'error' as being made up of three main factors (Figure 8.9), one of which relates to sampling procedures.

1. *Sampling error*. (See Key concept 8.1 for a definition.) This kind of error arises because it is extremely unlikely that any sample will be a truly representative sample of a population, even with probability sampling.

2. *Data-collection error*. This source of error relates to the design of the data-collection instruments and includes poor question wording in self-completion questionnaires or structured interviews; poor interviewing techniques; and flaws in the use of research instruments.
3. *Data-processing error.* This arises from issues in the way data is managed, in particular errors in the ways that answers are inputted and **coded**.

The second and third sources of error relate to factors that are not associated with sampling and instead relate much more closely to concerns about the validity of measurement, which we considered in Chapter 7. In Chapters 9–11, we will consider the steps that you can take to keep these sources of error to a minimum in survey research.

FIGURE 8.9
Three sources of error in social survey research

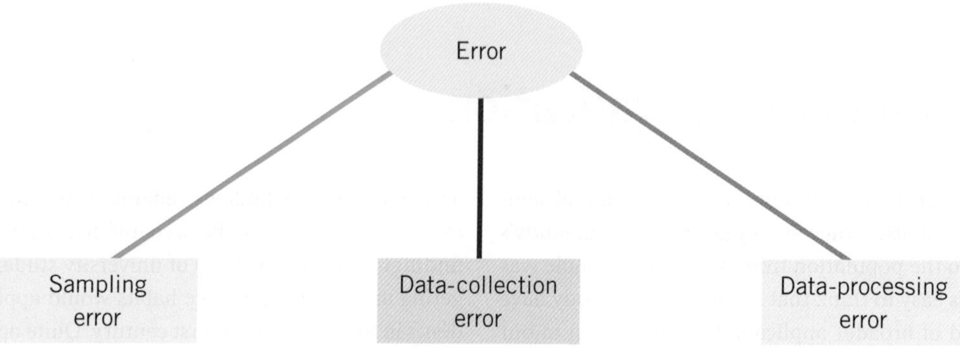

KEY POINTS

- Probability sampling is a mechanism for reducing bias in the selection of samples.
- It is important to become familiar with key technical terms in the literature on sampling, such as representative sample, random sample, probability sample, sampling frame, non-response, population, sampling error.
- Randomly selected samples are important because they allow generalizations to the population.
- Sampling error decreases as sample size increases.
- Quota samples can provide reasonable alternatives to random samples, but they have some limitations.
- Convenience samples may provide interesting data and be helpful in the development phases of a project, but the approach has considerable limitations in terms of generalizability.
- Most of the considerations involved in more traditional methods of survey sampling also apply to sampling for online surveys.

QUESTIONS FOR REVIEW

1. What do each of the following terms mean? Population; probability sampling; non-probability sampling; sampling frame; representative sample; sampling and non-sampling error.
2. What are the goals of sampling?
3. What are the main areas of potential bias in sampling?
4. What is the significance of sampling error for achieving a representative sample?
5. What is probability sampling and why is it important?
6. What are the main types of probability sample?
7. If you were conducting an interview survey of around 500 people in Manchester, what type of probability sample would you choose and why?
8. A researcher positions herself on a street corner and asks 1 in every 5 people who walk by whether they are prepared to be interviewed. She continues doing this until she has a sample of 250. How likely is she to achieve a representative sample of the population she wants to study?
9. When devising a probability sample, what factors would you take into account in deciding how large your sample should be?
10. What is non-response, and why is it important to the question of whether you will end up with a representative sample?
11. Are non-probability samples useless?
12. In what circumstances might you use snowball sampling?
13. Are response rates in online surveys worse or better than in other forms of survey?
14. What are the advantages of online surveys over other forms of survey?
15. 'The problem of generalization to a population is not just to do with whether the sample is representative.' Discuss.

ONLINE RESOURCES

www.oup.com/he/srm6e

You can find our notes on the answers to these questions within this chapter's **online resources**, together with:

- *audio/video comments* on this topic from our 'Learn from experience' panellists;
- *self-test questions* for further knowledge-checking;
- a *flashcard glossary* to help you recall key terms; and
- a *Student Researcher's Toolkit* containing practical materials and resources to help you conduct your own research project.

CHAPTER

9

STRUCTURED INTERVIEWING

CHAPTER GUIDE

The next stage of the survey research process, after sampling considerations (see Figure 8.1), involves planning and administering your survey, including deciding whether to administer the questionnaire via interview or to rely on self-completion. In this chapter we will consider the first of these options, the structured interview. We look at

- the reasons why structured interviews are a common method in survey research, including the importance of measurement standardization;
- the different contexts of interviewing, such as using more than one interviewee and whether the interview is conducted in person or by telephone;
- the preparation you need before you begin interviewing, including recruiting interviewees, becoming familiar with your interview schedule, the wording of questions and the order in which you present them, and the training and supervision needed when working with other interviewers;

- the various requirements of structured interviewing, including establishing rapport with the interviewee, asking questions as they appear on the interview schedule, recording exactly what is said by interviewees, making sure there are clear instructions about recording answers, and planning how you will end each interview;
- problems with structured interviewing, including the influence of the interviewer on respondents and the possibility of systematic bias in answers (known as response sets).

9.1 Introduction

Interviews are used regularly in many aspects of social life. They can take the form of job interviews, university entrance interviews, media interviews, or appraisal interviews. There are also research interviews, which are the kind of interview that we will cover in this and other chapters (including Chapters 19 and 20).

Research interviews are about gaining information from the interviewee and they are conducted with varying degrees of formality or explicitness. When conducting research interviews, the interviewer elicits various kinds of information from the interviewee (or *respondent*), on such topics as their own behaviour or that of others; attitudes; norms; beliefs; and values.

Interviews are popular data-collection strategies in both quantitative and **qualitative research** and there are many different types. In quantitative social science research, the most common type is the structured interview.

9

9.2 The structured interview

Structured interviews, in which the questions and procedures are standardized so as to minimize differences between them (see Key concept 9.1), are one of the two main ways of administering a survey—the other being **self-completion questionnaires** (see Figure 8.2, which provides a useful background to this chapter and to Chapter 10). In this section we consider the advantages offered by this type of interview, and the other types of interview used in social research.

Advantages of the structured interview

One of the key reasons **survey** researchers use structured interviews is that they promote standardization of *both* the asking of questions *and* the recording of answers, and this standardization provides a way of reducing the possibility of error. There are a number of common sources of error in **survey research**. We have discussed sampling error in Chapter 8. The other main sources of error in survey research include the following:

- a poorly worded question;
- the way the question is asked by the interviewer;
- misunderstanding on the part of the interviewee;
- memory problems on the part of the interviewee;
- the way in which the interviewee's answers are recorded by the interviewer; and
- the way the information is processed, either when answers are **coded** or data typed up.

Although structured interviewing cannot eradicate all these sources of error (for example, it cannot ensure that interviewees remember things accurately), it can limit the potential for many of these errors by reducing error due to variation in the asking of questions, by providing greater accuracy in processing respondents' answers, and by making that processing easier. Let's consider these effects in a little more detail.

Reducing error due to interviewer variability

Structured interviewing is concerned with standardizing both the asking of questions and the recording of answers, limiting the potential for error to be introduced as a result of interviewer variability.

Interviewer variability, which is associated with errors in the way the question is asked and the way the information is recorded, can occur in two ways. *Intra-interviewer variability* occurs when a single interviewer is inconsistent

KEY CONCEPT 9.1
What is a structured interview?

A structured interview, sometimes called a **standardized interview**, is the main form of interviewing used in **quantitative research** and involves using an **interview schedule**—a collection of questions designed to be asked by an interviewer. The aim is for all interviewees to be given the same context of questioning, meaning that each respondent receives exactly the same interview stimulus as any other. In structured interviewing you need to make sure that interviewees' replies can be effectively aggregated (collated together for analysis), and for this to be possible, their replies must be given in response to identical cues. The interview questions need to use exactly the same words in the same order. Questions are usually very specific, and they often offer the interviewee a fixed range of answers from which to choose (this type of question is often called a **closed-ended question**—or a *closed*, ***pre-coded***, or *fixed-choice* question).

9

in the way they ask questions and/or record answers. When there is more than one interviewer, there may be *inter-interviewer variability*, whereby interviewers are inconsistent with each other in the ways they ask questions and/or record answers. The standardization that is key to structured interviewing can minimize both forms of variability. Standardization is so significant to this method that some writers prefer to call structured interviews *standardized interviews* (e.g. Oppenheim 2008; Schaeffer 2017) or *standardized survey interviews* (e.g. Fowler and Mangione 1990).

So why is it so important to minimize interviewer variability? We have already shown how variability may exist in social research. For example, in Section 8.4 we discussed the potential variability of our findings on students' alcohol consumption as a result of the choices we might make of the types of universities we include in our **sample**. It is important not to add further variability as a result of the interview process. We can think of the answers to a question as constituting the values that a **variable** takes, but these values are likely to show some variation. Most variables contain an element of error, so it is helpful to think of variation as being made up of two components: true variation and variation due to error.

The researcher's aim is to minimize the error component, as error reduces the **validity** of a measure. (If the error component is quite high, validity will be compromised.) If researchers can standardize their approach so that variation they find is likely to be true variation between interviewees, and not variation due to the way questions were asked or answers recorded, their measure's validity will be high.

Thinking back to the question on alcohol consumption among students that we discussed in Section 8.4, while there will undoubtedly be variation in the number of alcohol units students are consuming, the researchers wanted to be able to say that this was true variation and not caused by error introduced in the research process. This error could, as we have discussed, be associated with interviewer variability, but it could also be a result of inaccurate classification or the way the sample was selected. Again, the standardization of structured interviewing can help us here.

Accuracy and ease of data processing

The other major advantage of structured interviews, and a way in which they help limit potential error, is the fact that they make data processing accurate and easy. Like self-completion questionnaires (see Chapter 10), most structured interviews contain mainly closed-ended questions. These involve the interviewer providing respondents with two or more possible answers and asking them to select which one(s) apply. Ideally, this will simply involve the interviewer placing a tick in a box or circling the answer(s) selected by a respondent, or using a similar procedure. This leads to much more accurate data as it reduces the potential for interviewer variability: there is no issue of the interviewer not writing everything down or misinterpreting the reply given. If the interviewer is asking an *open* or **open-ended question** they might not write down everything that the respondent says, might embellish the answer (to fit with their ideal findings), or might misinterpret it.

As we will see in Chapter 11, closed-ended questions in survey research produce data that is not only accurate but easy to process. When asking open-ended questions, we need to code the answers in order to quantitatively analyse the data. This is time-consuming, particularly where there are a large number of open-ended questions and/or respondents, and it is quite likely that another source of error will be introduced as a result of variability in the coding of answers (see Smyth and Olson 2015). When asking open-ended questions, the interviewer is supposed to write down as much of what is said as possible. The researcher then has to categorize all the answers, so that they can aggregate each person's answer with other respondents' answers to the same question. They then have to allocate a number to each category of answer so that they can enter the answers into a software program and analyse them quantitatively. We will examine this coding process in detail in Chapter 11.

There are other ways in which coding can introduce error. The variation that the researcher observes will not reflect the true variation in responses if the rules for assigning answers to categories, collectively known as the coding frame, are flawed, and even if these rules are sound, there is a risk of variability in the *ways* in which answers are categorized. As with interviewing, this variability comes in two forms: *intra-rater variability*, whereby the researcher applies the coding inconsistently in terms of the rules for assigning answers to categories, and *inter-rater variability*, where if more than one person is conducting the coding, they differ from each other in the way they apply the rules for assigning answers to categories.

Closed-ended questions do not have this problem because respondents allocate *themselves* to categories. Coding is then a simple process of attaching a different number to each category of answer and entering these into a database. This type of question is often referred to as pre-coded, because researchers usually make decisions about the coding of answers when they are designing the schedule, before asking any respondents questions. It is, of course, important to note that a closed-ended question does not automatically provide a valid measure: it will not be valid if some respondents misunderstand any of the terms in the alternative answers, or if the answers do not adequately cover the range of possible replies (an issue that we will return to in Chapter 11).

Other types of interview

Structured interviewing is not the only type of interviewing, but it is the main type that you are likely to come across in survey research. As we noted in Key concept 9.1, the structured or standardized interview is the main quantitative approach to interviewing. There are, however, a number of qualitative forms of interviewing, such as the unstructured interview, the semi-structured interview, and other types of in-depth interviewing, which we will cover when we discuss qualitative methods in Chapters 19 and 20. These approaches are rarely used in quantitative research because of the type of data that they generate, although occasionally surveys might include open-ended questions. As we will see in Chapter 11, unstructured or semi-structured interviews can play a useful role in providing researchers with the information they need in order to develop closed-ended questions.

9

9.3 Interview contexts

Usually in interviews an interviewer is positioned in front of a respondent, asking them a series of questions and writing down the answers. However, there can be exceptions across all types of interview.

In person, video interview, or telephone?

Interviews can be conducted by telephone or video call rather than face-to-face. Telephone interviewing is quite common in market research, where it usually takes the form of computer-assisted telephone interviewing (CATI; see the discussion of computer-assisted interviewing later in this subsection). It is less common in social research but still used. There are several advantages to conducting interviews by phone rather than face-to-face, and many of these advantages also apply to video interviews, which are hybrids of face-to-face and telephone interviews. Video conferencing platforms such as Zoom and Apple's FaceTime are widely used by qualitative researchers conducting semi-structured interviews (see Chapter 19).

The main advantages of these methods over face-to-face interviews are the following.

- *They are cheaper and quicker.* Interviewers do not have to spend time and money travelling between respondents, especially if the sample is geographically dispersed. CATI and CAPI (computer-assisted personal interviewing, 'personal' meaning face-to-face or by video) have enhanced the general efficiency of interviewing.
- *They are easier to supervise.* It is easier to check that interviewers' approaches are not likely to introduce

bias by, for example, rephrasing questions or making inappropriate use of probes (see Section 9.5): *probes* are stimuli that the interviewer uses to gain further information from the interviewee when their response either fails to answer the question or does not answer it in enough detail.

- *Respondents' answers are less likely to be affected by the interviewer.* In face-to-face interviews, respondents' replies are likely to be affected by characteristics of the interviewer (for example, class, ethnicity) and by their presence (the interviewees may reply in ways they feel will be seen as desirable by interviewers)—ideas we will discuss further in Section 9.7. In telephone interviewing the respondent cannot see the interviewer's personal characteristics, and in both telephone and video interviewing, the fact that the interviewer is remote may reduce the likelihood of respondents' answers being affected by their presence.

However, telephone and video interviewing also suffer from certain limitations when compared to the face-to-face interview. These include the following.

- *Potential for* **sampling bias**. Some people do not own a telephone or a device that permits video calls, or are not contactable by those means, so cannot be interviewed. This might seem like a fast-disappearing problem in today's hyper-connected world, but the potential for sampling bias still exists as it is most likely to be poorer households who cannot be reached by these methods.
- *Accessibility issues*. Respondents with hearing impairments are likely to find telephone interviewing much more difficult than personal interviewing. They might find video interviewing easier, as this can allow for lip-reading, but this depends heavily on having high visual and audio quality and a speedy internet connection.
- *Restrictions on interview length*. Respondents are unlikely to want to be interviewed by telephone or video for more than 20–25 minutes, whereas personal interviews can be much longer. Irvine (2011) found that differences in length between face-to-face interviews and telephone interviews are associated with less respondent speech in telephone interviews.
- *Potentially lower response rates*. Although it is unclear whether response rates (see Key concept 8.2) are lower with surveys by telephone interview than with surveys by face-to-face interview, there seems to be a general belief that telephone interviews achieve slightly lower rates than face-to-face interviews (Shuy 2002; Frey 2004; Mahfoud et al. 2015). There is no consistent evidence that the use of CAPI adversely affects response rates compared with face-to-face interviews (Bianchi et al. 2016; Watson and Wilkins 2011).
- *Difficulties asking about sensitive issues*. Telephone interviews may work less well than face-to-face interviews when they include questions about sensitive issues, such as drug and alcohol use, income, tax returns, or health (Groves et al. 2009), although other researchers have pointed out that they can be useful in increasing anonymity (Vogl 2013). The latter point would clearly not apply to video interviews, though the remoteness of the interviewer might make the interviewee feel more comfortable discussing such issues.
- *Missed opportunities to collect additional data*. In telephone interviews the researcher cannot see the respondent, so a lot of identifiable information is left uncollected unless the researcher asks about it (Oltmann 2016). Sometimes, face-to-face interviewers may be asked to collect subsidiary information in connection with their visits (for example, whether a house is dilapidated). Such information cannot be collected in telephone interviews.
- *Inability of the interviewer to respond to physical cues*. Telephone interviewers cannot observe their interviewee. This means that they cannot respond to visual signs of confusion or unease that might prompt a face-to-face interviewer to restate the question or attempt to clarify the meaning (though this has to be handled in a standardized way as far as possible). Video interviewing has the advantage here, but observation will be limited to what is 'in shot' (probably just the respondent's head and shoulders), and visual or audio delay might make this tricky.
- *Call screening and declines in the use of telephone landlines*. These changes have made it more difficult to conduct telephone surveys, especially where researchers don't have access to respondent telephone numbers. Call screening is available on both landlines and mobile phones. Research suggests considerable differences in demographic characteristics, attitudes, and behaviours between those who live in households without access to a mobile phone and those who do (Badcock et al. 2017). Since lists of mobile phone users are unlikely to be available in the way that telephone directories are, researchers seeking to interview by mobile phone and without access to contact details are likely to use **random digit dialling (RDD)**. Research in focus 9.1 explores two studies on whether conducting a survey via a landline or mobile has implications for the data collected.

- *Difficulties checking the respondent's identity.* Often, specific individuals in households or firms are the targets of an interview (individuals who match your sample characteristics). It is usually more difficult to establish by telephone interview whether the correct person is replying. Obviously, this is easier by video.
- *Difficulties using visual aids.* In telephone interviewing it is not possible to use visual aids such as show cards (see the discussion of 'Prompting' in Section 9.5), from which respondents might be asked to select their replies, or diagrams or photos. This is possible via video if visual quality is good and/or you are using software that allows participants to share a file or their screen, but it is still more difficult to manage than in person.

Overall, there is some evidence to suggest that the quality of data from telephone interviews is inferior to that of comparable face-to-face interviews. A series of **experiments** reported by Holbrook et al. (2003) on the mode of survey administration in the USA using long questionnaires found that respondents interviewed by telephone were more likely to engage in **satisficing** behaviour, such as expressing no opinion or 'don't know' (see Key concept 9.2 and Chapter 11 for more on this issue); to answer in the same way to a series of linked questions; to express socially desirable answers; to be apprehensive about the interview; and to be dissatisfied with the time taken by the interviews (even though they were invariably shorter than in the face-to-face mode). Also, telephone interviewees tended to be less engaged with the interview process (see West and Blom 2017). While these results should be viewed with caution, because these studies are affected by such factors as the use of a large questionnaire on a national sample, they are worth noting.

Computer-assisted interviewing

Researchers often use interviewing software to administer one of the interview methods we have discussed, especially commercial survey research organizations conducting market research and opinion polls. There are two main formats for computer-assisted interviewing, both of which we have touched on already: computer-assisted personal interviewing (CAPI) and computer-assisted telephone interviewing (CATI). A large percentage of telephone interviews are conducted with the help of software. Among commercial survey organizations, almost all telephone interviewing is of the CATI kind, but CAPI is increasingly widely used. The main reason for this increase is the growth in the number and quality of software packages that provide a platform for devising interview schedules; this makes them more suitable for use in face-to-face interviews. Many of the large data sets used for **secondary analysis** (we provide examples of these in Chapter 14) derive from computer-assisted interviewing studies carried out by commercial or large social research organizations.

9

RESEARCH IN FOCUS 9.1
Interviewing using mobile phones or landlines

Whether a telephone survey is conducted using a landline or mobile phone can have implications for the data collected. Let's explore these issues in two research studies.

ZuWallack (2009) reported the findings of some CATI projects conducted by mobile phone in the USA on health-related issues. The researchers found that many people hung up when contacted but that those respondents who persisted formed a useful complement to conventional landline telephone surveys because many of them were from groups often under-represented in such surveys, such as young adults and minorities who are less likely to have a landline.

Lynn and Kaminska (2012) examined findings from an experiment in Hungary comparing landline and mobile phone interviews and uncovered few significant differences in the findings. The authors were especially interested in whether interviewees were more likely to *satisfice* (see Key concept 9.2) in one telephone mode rather than the other. They examined several **indicators** of satisficing behaviour (for example, the likelihood of answering 'don't know') and found no statistically significant differences between landline and mobile phone interviews. They did, however, find some evidence of less social desirability bias (see Section 9.5) in mobile phone interviews than in landline ones, which they suggest may be due to interviewees' ability to choose where they are located while taking part in the interviews.

KEY CONCEPT 9.2
Satisficing in surveys

Drawing on Simon's (1960) notion of 'satisficing', Krosnick (1999) has argued that survey respondents sometimes satisfice rather than **optimizing**. Optimizing refers to trying to arrive at the best and most appropriate answer to a question (Zhang and Conrad 2018). Respondents sometimes satisfice instead, because of the effort required in optimizing their responses. They put less effort into answering the question so that 'Instead of generating the most accurate answers, respondents settle for merely satisfactory ones' (Krosnick 1999: 548). Examples of satisficing in answering survey questions include a tendency towards agreeing with statements ('yeasaying'—see the subsection on 'Acquiescence' in Section 9.7); opting for safe answers such as middle-points on answer scales (for example, 'don't know' or 'neither agree nor disagree'); and not considering the full range of answers offered to a closed-ended question (for example, tending to select the last one). Because of this, researchers want to keep to a minimum the amount of effort that respondents have to make to answer questions, so as to reduce the amount of satisficing.

With computer-assisted interviewing, the interview questions appear on the interviewer's screen. As interviewers ask each question, they type in the appropriate reply and proceed to the next question. This process has the great advantage that, when the interview uses **filter questions** (see Tips and skills 9.4) and certain questions may be skipped as a result of a person's reply, the software can be set up to 'jump' to the next relevant question. Computer-assisted interviewing enhances the researcher's control over the interview process and can improve standardization of the asking of questions and recording of answers.

One potential problem with both CAPI and CATI is 'miskeying', where the interviewer clicks on the wrong reply, although whether this is more likely to occur than when the interviewer is using pen and paper is unknown. There may also be times when researchers conduct qualitative interviews with some survey respondents, so that they can ask participants in the semi-structured interview phase about some of the answers they have given in the survey interview. Silva and Wright found in these circumstances that sometimes the participant had been recorded as giving an answer that was actually incorrect (Silva and Wright 2008). One possible reason for such errors is mis-keying by the interviewer: mistakes in typing in the answers. Other possibilities are that the interviewee misinterpreted the question or that the interviewer misinterpreted their response.

More than one interviewee

In a **focus group** (which we will cover in Chapter 20) there is more than one respondent, but this is not the only context where more than one person is interviewed. Heath et al. (2017), for example, interviewed not only individuals but also pairs of people about their experiences of living in shared accommodation. In some cases, they interviewed larger groups. However, it is unusual for researchers to use structured interviews in this kind of questioning because in survey interviews it is seen as advisable to avoid having others present during the interview. Research where more than one person is interviewed tends to be qualitative, though this is not always the case: Pahl's (1990) study of patterns of control of money among couples employed structured interviewing of couples and of husbands and wives separately. Some large-scale surveys, such as the Health Survey for England 2018 (**https://digital.nhs.uk/data-and-information/publications/statistical/health-survey-for-england/2018**, accessed 9 November 2020), also use structured interviewing with households, although in some cases researchers offer a self-completion booklet to individual family members, if they feel that it would be difficult to give honest answers to the questions face-to-face with other household members present.

In the next sections we will walk through the process of conducting structured interviews, looking at what is involved in preparing for, carrying out, and concluding an interview. You should note that the advice we give here relates specifically to conducting *structured* interviews. We discuss frameworks for carrying out qualitative interviewing (such as unstructured and semi-structured interviewing and the use of focus groups) in Chapters 19 and 20.

9.4 Preparing to conduct a structured interview

Thorough preparation is essential to conducting successful interviews and generating high-quality data. This includes knowing the interview schedule, giving clear instructions to any other interviewers who are involved, looking at question order, and considering whether there is a need for any training or supervision of interviewers. The researcher should also give careful thought in advance to the wording of interview questions, but we will focus on this aspect of interviewing in more detail in Chapter 11, because many of the rules of question-asking relate to self-completion questionnaire techniques, such as postal or email questionnaires, as well as to structured interviews.

Approaching interviewees

Approaching potential interviewees is a key part of the research process. If your approach lacks clarity about who you are, the research you are conducting, and why you are conducting it, you are likely to put off participants from being involved. You have already seen, in Chapter 8, some of the challenges involved in identifying an appropriate sample and difficulties regarding response rates. You will need to be polite, organized, and appreciative when you approach potential interviewees. We recommend that you consider Tips and skills 9.1.

Participating in research takes up respondents' valuable time, so it is important that you provide prospective respondents with a credible rationale for the research. This is particularly important at a time when there is some debate about the fact that response rates to survey research are declining (Groves et al. 2009). Interviewers have an important role to play in maximizing the response rate in surveys because they are the link between the research and the respondent.

The introductory rationale may be either spoken (such as when you 'cold call' respondents in their homes in person or by phone) or written (such as to alert respondents that someone will be contacting them in person or on the telephone to request an interview). Respondents will often encounter both forms of introduction to the research—for example, first in a letter or email and then explained by the interviewer on the day of the interview—and it is important that these accounts are consistent.

Introductions to research, which you will need to recap or summarize on the day of the interview, will usually contain the information outlined in Tips and skills 9.2. This introductory statement, which often comes in the form of an 'information sheet', is also important as part of good research practice and for receiving ethics approval (see Chapter 6 and Tips and skills 6.3).

Knowing the schedule

Before interviewing anybody, an interviewer should be fully clear about the schedule. Even if you are the only person conducting interviews, make sure you know your

9

TIPS AND SKILLS 9.1
Approaching potential interviewees

The following tips will help you recruit interviewees for your study.

- If recruiting by phone or by visiting residences, be prepared to keep calling back if potential interviewees are out or unavailable. Think about people's likely work and leisure habits and whether people living alone may be reluctant to answer the door when it is dark because of fear of crime.
- Be self-assured. You may get a better response if you presume that people will agree to be interviewed rather than that they will refuse.
- Let people know that you are a student or an academic researcher. In other words, make sure people know that you are not a salesperson. People are often suspicious when strangers say they would just like to ask a few questions.
- If recruiting in person, consider your appearance. Dress in a way that will be acceptable to a wide variety of people. (This may also help ensure that interviewees' responses are not influenced by your personal characteristics—see Section 9.3 under 'In person, video interview, or telephone?')
- Make it clear that you can be flexible. Say that you will be happy to find a time to suit the respondent.

TIPS AND SKILLS 9.2

Points to cover in an introductory statement

The main points that should be covered in an introductory statement to a prospective interviewee are the following.

- The identity of the person who is contacting the respondent.
- The person or organisation conducting the research—for example, a university, a market research agency.
- The source of any research funding—or, if you are a student doing an undergraduate or postgraduate dissertation or thesis as part of your degree programme, make this clear.
- What the research is about and why it is important, providing an indication of the kind of information that you will be collecting.
- Why you are selecting the respondent—such as whether they have been selected by a random process.

You should also highlight these points.

- Participation is voluntary.
- The respondent will not be identified or be identifiable in any way. You can usually show this by pointing out that you will anonymize the data when you enter them into the software and that you will conduct your data analysis at an aggregate level.
- Any information that the respondent provides will be confidential.
- The respondent will have an opportunity to ask any questions they may have. (Provide a contact number for respondents to call if they have any questions.)

These suggestions are also relevant to the covering letter and information that researchers provide in online surveys or with **postal questionnaires**, which we will discuss in Chapter 10.

9

schedule inside out. Interviewing can be stressful for interviewers and this is why preparation is so important. Standard interview procedures such as filter questions (see Tips and skills 9.4) can cause interviewers to get flustered and miss questions out or ask the wrong questions. You might find it useful to conduct a **pilot** of your survey to test your questions and gain some experience of the process—Barbara reflects on the value of pilots and holding 'mock interviews' in Learn from experience 9.1.

Question wording

It is crucial that each respondent is asked exactly the same questions in structured interviews because (as we saw in Section 9.2), variation in the ways a question is asked is a potential source of error in survey research. While structured interviews reduce the likelihood of this occurring, they cannot guarantee that it will not occur because there is always the possibility that interviewers will embellish or adapt a question when asking it. If you carefully consider question wording when preparing the interview, you can limit the chance of this happening.

You might ask: 'Does it really matter?' Do small variations in wording really make a big difference to people's replies? While the impact of variation in wording obviously differs in different contexts, experiments suggest that even minor variations in wording can have an impact on replies (Schuman and Presser 1981; Spratto and Bandalos 2020). Three experiments in England conducted by Social and Community Planning Research concluded that a considerable number of interview questions are affected by interviewer variability. The researchers estimated that, for about two-thirds of the questions that were considered, interviewers contributed to less than 2 per cent of the total variation in each question (Collins 1997). While this is a small amount of error, it may be a cause for concern for researchers. The key point here is the importance of making sure interviewers are asking questions exactly as they are written.

It is also important to make sure your questions are worded in a way that participants will easily understand. Scarlett and Barbara discuss the importance of clear wording in Learn from experience 9.2.

LEARN FROM EXPERIENCE 9.1

Piloting questions for a structured interview

One useful way to prepare for conducting a structured interview is to practise replicating the process by piloting the questions (see Chapter 11 for further details on piloting). Barbara, whose research focused on the role of important adults in positive youth development, used a mixed methods approach with both surveys and qualitative interviews. She found that conducting 'mock interviews' was an extremely helpful way of developing the skills she would need for conducting real structured interviews.

> My colleagues and I have sometimes practised our skills with 'mock interviews'. We would choose a random topic. One of us would be the interviewer, another the interviewee, and a third person would supervise the process and give comments to the interviewer. It would often help us to practise the phrases and to exercise active listening skills.
>
> Barbara

Access the **online resources** to hear Barbara's reflections on this theme.

You can read about our panellists' backgrounds and research experiences on page xxvi.

LEARN FROM EXPERIENCE 9.2

Question wording in structured interviews

Consistency and clarity in the way you ask questions is important for ensuring that the responses are not affected by variation in wording or by participants' confusion about the meaning of questions. Scarlett, who conducted research on the impact of social media on mental wellbeing, and Barbara, who focused on the role of important adults in positive youth development, both emphasize the importance of clarity of terminology when conducting structured interviews.

> It is important to be as clear as possible in the wording of your survey questions. Avoid long words, use of jargon, and lengthy questions as this can lead to a low response rate.
>
> Scarlett

> As a psychology student I started using wording that is not familiar to lay people. Words that I thought were clear, like 'resilience', 'self-esteem', or 'empathy', were not that clear to the high school students I was doing research with. That is why I started asking friends I know from that age group to give me feedback on the questions before the data collection.
>
> Barbara

You can read about our panellists' backgrounds and research experiences on page xxvi.

Question order

Keeping to the set order when asking questions is also important in surveys and requires careful planning. Varying the question order can result in questions being accidentally omitted, because the interviewer may forget to ask those that they have skipped during the interview. Varying the question order may have an impact on replies: if some respondents have been previously asked a certain question whereas others have not, this will have introduced variability in the asking of questions, which is a potential source of error. It is also worth noting that response quality tends to decrease as the survey progresses (Barge and Gehlbach 2012). You should bear this in mind when constructing your interview schedule, to ensure that you do not leave key questions until too late.

Quite a lot of research has been carried out on the general subject of question order, but with limited evidence of consistent effects on people's responses linked to asking questions at different points in a survey. Different effects have been shown on various occasions. A classic study in the USA found that people were less likely to say that their taxes were too high when they had been previously asked whether government spending ought to be increased in a number of areas (Schuman and Presser 1981: 32). The researchers felt that some people perceived an inconsistency between wanting more spending and lower taxes, and this led to them adjusting their answers. The same researchers' study on crime victimization in the USA also suggested that earlier questions may affect later ones (Schuman and Presser 1981: 45).

Mayhew (2000) provides an interesting example of the impact of question order in relation to the Crime Survey for England and Wales (CSEW), known at the time of Mayhew's research as the British Crime Survey. Each wave of the CSEW has included the question:

9

> Taking everything into account, would you say the police in this area do a good job or a poor job?

In 1988 this question mistakenly appeared twice for some respondents. For all respondents it appeared early on, but for around half it also appeared later on in the context of questions on contact with the police. Of those given the question twice, 66 per cent gave the same rating, but 22 per cent gave a more positive rating to the police and just 13 per cent gave a less favourable one the second time. Mayhew suggests that respondents became more sensitized to crime-related issues and more sympathetic to the pressures on the police as the survey progressed. More recently, Diersch and Walther (2016) also identified the impact of question order in responses to a survey by adolescents on environmental protection and sports activities (see Research in focus 9.2).

There are two general lessons to keep in mind when thinking about question order in a survey:

1. Interviewers should not vary question order (unless this is the subject of the study!);
2. You should be sensitive to the possible implications of the effect of early questions on answers to subsequent questions.

It is worth bearing the following rules in mind when deciding on question order.

- Early questions should be directly related to the topic of the research, which the respondent has already

RESEARCH IN FOCUS 9.2
The impact of survey question order

Diersch and Walther (2016) undertook a study investigating how variations in response format, answer scale frequency, and question order influence responses, and their findings are worth bearing in mind when developing an interview schedule.

The researchers examined the self-reports of two age groups of adolescents—the younger students were 11–13 years old and the older group 16–18 years old—based on the responses to a survey completed by 188 pupils from a German secondary school. They developed two versions of a questionnaire in which they varied four response options (open- vs. closed-response formats, frequency of answer scales, question order in attitude judgements, and question order of filter questions) within two different topics: environmental protection and sports activities. Each age group received one of the two questionnaire versions.

The results showed that cues related to certain question characteristics, response scales, and the order of questions influenced the self-reports of these age groups. The study also found that the answers of adolescents aged between 11 and 13 years were more likely to be affected by the question format and context than those of adolescents aged between 16 and 18 years, with younger adolescents generally agreeing more strongly with the attitude statements than older adolescents. Whether this might be due to satisficing or to a more positive attitude towards the topics is not entirely clear.

The researchers also found that closed-response formats tend to produce a greater variety of answers than open-response formats. Generating answers in an open-response format was harder than picking an answer from a list of possible answers. If an open-response format was presented, the respondents were more likely to skip the question completely.

been informed about. Personal questions about age, social background, and so on should ideally *not* be asked at the beginning of an interview (although there are some variations in views on this, with some researchers believing that straightforward questions are a good way of 'warming up' participants).

- Where possible, questions that are more likely to be of most relevance to respondents should be asked early in the schedule, in order to attract respondents' interest and attention.
- Sensitive questions or ones that might be a source of anxiety should be left till later in the survey.
- With a long survey, questions should be grouped into sections, as this allows a better flow than skipping between topics.
- Within each group of questions, general questions should come before specific ones—as shown in Tips and skills 9.3.
- It is sometimes recommended that questions dealing with opinions and attitudes should come before questions to do with behaviour and knowledge, because the latter type are considered to be less affected by question order.
- During an interview, the respondent sometimes provides an answer to a question that is going to be asked later in the interview. Because of the possibility of a question order effect, when the interviewer arrives at the question that appears already to have been answered, it should be repeated.

These rules may seem clear and easy to apply, but question order remains one of the more frustrating areas of structured interview and questionnaire design because the evidence regarding its implications is inconsistent.

Training and supervision

Training can be important when conducting interviews, although this is most common in contexts in which a researcher hires an interviewer to conduct interviews. Training is particularly important in research that involves several interviewers (see Research in focus 9.3 for an example of this kind of study), because—as we saw

TIPS AND SKILLS 9.3
Deciding on the best question order

As we have noted, general questions should usually come before specific ones in a survey. You can see this in action in the hypothetical example below from a survey about identity cards, a topic that has been controversial in the UK (Barnard-Wills 2016).

The question order is designed to first establish people's levels of knowledge of identity cards, before asking questions about them and distinguishing those who feel strongly about them from those who do not.

1. Have you heard of identity cards?

   Yes____ No ____ (If **No**, go to question 2)

   1a. What are your views about identity cards?

   1b. Do you favour or not favour identity cards?

   Favour ____ Not favour ____

   1c. Why do you favour (not favour) identity cards?

   1d. How strongly do you feel about this?

   Very strongly____

   Fairly strongly____

   Not at all strongly____

Although it is not associated with question order it is worth noting that question 1a is open-ended, so that the respondent's frame of reference can be established with respect to the topic, but it seems likely that if enough pilot research has been carried out, the researchers could devise a closed-ended question. This point applies equally to question 1c.

RESEARCH IN FOCUS 9.3
Training and briefing interviewers

Studies conducted by the Office for National Statistics (ONS) provide a good example of how to reduce the risk of error being introduced through poor interviewer technique, and/or through variation between techniques, through effective training and briefing.

The ONS is the UK's largest independent producer of **official statistics** and the recognized national statistical institute of the UK. They are responsible for collecting the data that we often use in secondary data analysis, such as the Crime Survey for England and Wales and the British Social Attitudes Survey (see Chapter 14), and all interviewers who work for the ONS are trained by the organization. They receive general training, which tends to cover broad areas such as interviewing skills, doorstep techniques, and use of the interview software. Each interviewer has a number of practice role-play interviews and is accompanied by a supervisor regularly during their first few months conducting structured interviews.

As well as this general training, interviewers will be required to attend some briefing sessions before starting work on any new survey. This includes an introduction to the survey and why it is important, questionnaire and sampling issues, a run-through of the questionnaire on the software, and some practice interview sessions. This training is provided by the research team who developed the survey. See **www.ukdataservice.ac.uk/media/262844/discover_surveyinterviewingfactsheet.pdf** (accessed 12 October 2019).

in Section 9.2—we need to avoid interviewer variability in the asking of questions. These situations are unlikely to be relevant to 'lone' researchers doing an undergraduate or master's dissertation, or an exercise for a **research methods** course, but interviewing on your own still involves some training. You need to train yourself to follow the procedures and advice provided in this chapter.

Whenever people other than the lead researcher are involved in interviewing, they will need training and supervision in the following areas:

- contacting prospective respondents and providing an introduction to the study;
- reading out questions as written and following instructions in the interview schedule;
- using appropriate styles of probing (which we will cover in Section 9.5);
- recording exactly what is said;
- using an interview style that does not bias respondents' answers.

The point about reading out questions as written and following instructions in the interview schedule is particularly important, especially with *filter questions* that require the interviewer to ask questions of some respondents but not others. For example, the question:

> For which political party did you vote at the last general election?

presumes that the respondent voted. The possibility that this is not in fact the case can be reflected in the fixed-choice answers that are provided, by providing a 'did not vote' option. A better solution is not to presume anything about voting behaviour but, instead, first to ask respondents whether they voted in the last general election and then to filter out those who did not vote. Then questions about political party voting can just be asked of those who voted. Tips and skills 9.4 provides a simple example in connection with an imaginary study of alcohol consumption. The key point here is that the interviewer must have clear instructions. Without such instructions, there is the risk that either the interviewer will ask respondents inappropriate questions (which can be irritating for them) or the interviewer will inadvertently fail to ask a question (which results in missing information). In Tips and skills 9.4, the contingent questions (1a and 1b) are indented and there is an arrow to indicate that a 'Yes' answer should be followed by question 1a and not question 2. These visual aids can help to reduce the likelihood of interviewers making errors.

The lead researcher can supervise interviewers in relation to all these issues by

- checking the response rates that individual interviewers achieve;
- recording at least a sample of interviews;

TIPS AND SKILLS 9.4

Instructions for interviewers in the use of a filter question

It is crucial that lead researchers give interviewers clear instructions on conducting the interviews, especially regarding the use of filter questions. The following example shows how you can include these instructions within questions.

1. Have you consumed any alcoholic drinks in the last twelve months?

No ____ (if **No** proceed to question 2)

Yes ____

1a. (*To be asked if interviewee replied* **Yes** *to question 1*)

Which of the following alcoholic drinks do you consume most frequently?

(Ask interviewee to choose the category that they drink most frequently and tick one category only.)

Beer ____

Spirits ____

Wine ____

Liqueurs ____

Other____ specify____________________

1b. How frequently do you consume alcoholic drinks?

(Ask interviewee to choose the category that comes closest to their current practice.)

Daily____

Most days____

Once or twice a week____

Once or twice a month____

A few times a year____

Once or twice a year____

2. (*To be asked if interviewee replied* **No** *to question 1*)

Have you ever consumed alcoholic drinks?

Yes ____

No ____

- examining completed schedules to see whether interviewers are leaving out any questions and if they are being completed properly;
- carrying out call-backs on a sample of respondents (usually around 10 per cent) to check that they were interviewed and to ask about the interviewers' conduct.

9.5 Conducting a structured interview

In the previous section we covered introducing your research to participants. Here, we will discuss building rapport with your respondents, asking questions (including how to use probes and prompts), and recording answers. Remember that even if you introduced the research when you initially approached respondents, you will need to recap this information in person before you begin the interview.

9

Building rapport

Building rapport with the respondent is important when interviewing, as it encourages the other person to want (or at least be prepared) to participate in and continue with the interview. However, while we recommend that interviewers are friendly with respondents and put them at ease, it is important not to go too far. Too much rapport could result in the interview going on too long and the respondent suddenly deciding that they are spending too much time on it. Also, a particularly friendly environment could also lead to the respondent answering questions in a way that is designed to please the interviewer. It could also result in the interviewer being more tempted to stray from the more formal structured schedule.

It is probably easier to achieve rapport in face-to-face interviews (and, to a slightly lesser extent, video interviews) than in telephone interviews, because in the latter the interviewer cannot offer visual cues of friendliness, such as smiling or maintaining good eye contact. These cues can be a great help in gaining and maintaining rapport.

Asking questions

Probing

Probing is a highly problematic area for researchers using structured interviews. Respondents often need help answering interview questions, perhaps because they do not understand the question and ask for further information, or because it is clear from what they say that they are struggling to understand the question. They may also provide an insufficiently complete answer and need to be probed for more information. The problem here is that the interviewer's intervention might influence the respondent, and the nature of interviewers' interventions may differ. Error could be introduced as a result of interviewer variability, meaning that a potential source of variability in respondents' replies will not reflect 'true' variation.

Generally, probing should be kept to a minimum (assuming it cannot be eliminated) as it dilutes the standardization of question-asking in structured interviewing and introduces error, but if you need to use it, keep the following rules in mind.

- If you need more information, usually in the context of an open-ended question, you can use standardized probes such as 'Could you say a little more about that?' or 'Are there any other reasons why you think that?' or simply 'Mmmm . . . ?'
- If you ask the respondent a closed-ended question and they reply in a way that does not allow you to select one of the pre-designed answers, you should repeat the fixed-choice alternatives and make it clear that the answer needs to be chosen from the ones that have been provided.
- If you need to know about something that requires quantification, such as the number of visits to banks in the last four weeks or the number of banks in which the respondent has accounts, but the respondent resists this by answering in general terms ('quite often' or 'I usually go to the bank every week'), you need to keep trying to get a number from the respondent. This will usually involve repeating the question. You should not try to guess a figure on the basis of the respondent's reply and then suggest that figure to them, as even if it is inaccurate they may be unwilling to disagree.

Prompting

Prompting occurs when the interviewer suggests a possible answer to a question to the respondent. Prompting should be the same with all respondents. All closed-ended questions involve standardized prompting, because the interviewer gives the respondent a list of possible answers to choose from. An unacceptable approach to prompting would be to ask an open-ended question and to suggest possible answers only to some respondents, such as those who seem to be struggling to think of a reply.

During face-to-face interviews, there are several circumstances when it is better to use 'show cards' rather than rely on reading out a series of fixed-choice alternatives. Show cards (sometimes called 'flash cards') display all the answers from which the respondent must choose, and the interviewer hands them to the respondent at different points during the interview. Three kinds of context in which it might be preferable to use show cards, rather than reading out the entire set of possible answers, are as follows.

- There may be a very long list of possible answers, for example if you ask each respondent which daily newspaper they read most often. To read out a list of newspapers would be tedious, and it would be better to give the respondent a list of newspapers from which to choose.
- Sometimes, during the course of interviews, it can be useful to present respondents with a group of questions that all have the same set of possible answers. An example of this strategy is Likert scaling (see Key concept 7.2),

as it would be dull to read out all possible answers for each item that comprises the scale. Where you are using a consistent scale (for example, the one shown in Tips and skills 9.5—Card 6), it can be helpful to give respondents a show card that applies to the entire batch of questions.

- You may find that some people are reluctant to provide personal details such as their age or income. One way of limiting the impact of such questioning is to present respondents with age or income bands with a letter or number attached to each band. They can then be asked to say which letter/number applies to them (see Tips and skills 9.5—Card 11). This will obviously not work if you need *exact* ages or incomes. You can also extend this approach to sensitive areas, such as number of sexual partners or sexual practices, for the same kinds of reason.

Recording answers

We have discussed concerns about consistency in asking questions, and interviewers also need to record answers carefully, with respondents' replies written down as exactly as possible. If interviewers do not do this, they will introduce error. These errors are less likely to take place when the interviewer simply has to allocate respondents' replies to a category, as in a closed-ended question, than when they are writing down answers to open-ended questions (Fowler and Mangione 1990). Where more than one interviewer is recording the answers to open-ended questions, this increases the likelihood of *inter-interviewer variability*, whereby interviewers are inconsistent with each other in the ways in which they record answers. If you record the structured interview, this makes it easier to revisit the respondent's replies and to ensure that you have transcribed them accurately. While you might not consider this necessary, especially if your structured interview only uses closed questions, it is certainly worth investigating where the responses deviate from this closed form (see Chapter 19 for further details on transcription). In Chapter 11 we explore in detail the process of recording answers and coding responses. We will focus on strategies to limit errors in this process and consider whether you should design codes before you begin collecting data, or after you have collected it.

9

TIPS AND SKILLS 9.5

Using prompts in a structured interview

You can use show cards to give respondents the possible answers to each question, or to the current batch of questions if you are using a consistent scale (such as a **Likert scale**, as here):

Card 6

Strongly agree
Agree
Undecided
Disagree
Strongly disagree

You can also use show cards to enable respondents to cite the number or letter of the band or category that applies to them:

Card 11

1. Below 20
2. 20–29
3. 30–39
4. 40–49
5. 50–59
6. 60–69
7. 70 and over

9.6 Ending a structured interview

The interviewer's work does not stop as soon as they have asked the last question. It is very important to thank respondents for giving up their time at the end of the interview process. The interviewer also needs to act and speak carefully following the interview in order to avoid introducing bias. This can occur because after an interview, respondents sometimes try to engage the interviewer in a discussion about the purpose of the interview and might communicate anything they are told to future respondents, which could bias the findings. Interviewers should be friendly and appreciative of the respondent's time but still firm and professional, and they should resist elaborating on the research beyond their standard statement.

9.7 Problems with structured interviewing

Despite their common use in social research, structured interviews are not without challenges. These are not necessarily unique to structured interviews, in that they can sometimes be attributed to related methods, such as self-completion questionnaires in survey research or even semi-structured interviewing in qualitative research. We will now discuss some of these limitations, including the characteristics of interviewers, **response sets** (specifically acquiescence and social desirability bias), and the problem of meaning. It is also worth noting the **feminist** critique of quantitative methods in Chapter 7. This highlights that the type of rapport that is encouraged in quantitative research may actually create distance between the researcher and research participant. This can have the effect of emphasizing the hierarchical relationship between them, and this may be at odds with the feminist research ethos, which advocates a deep exploration and transparency of the research relationships.

Characteristics of interviewers

As we touched on in Section 9.3 under 'In person, video interview or telephone?', there is evidence that interviewers' attributes can have an impact on respondents' replies, although the literature makes it difficult to generalize on this. This is partly because of the problem of disentangling the effects of interviewers' different attributes from each other (race, gender, socio-economic status); the interaction between the characteristics of interviewers and the characteristics of respondents; and the interaction between any effects observed and the topic of the interview. However, there is certainly some evidence that the characteristics of interviewers can affect respondent's replies.

Schuman and Presser (1981) cite a study that asked respondents to nominate two or three of their favourite actors or entertainers and found that respondents were much more likely to mention Black actors or entertainers when interviewed by Black interviewers than when interviewed by white ones. We consider a more recent study on the impact of interviewer characteristics in Research in focus 9.4.

It is important to recognize that the characteristics of interviewers almost certainly have an impact on respondents' replies, but also that the extent and nature of the impact are unclear and likely to vary from context to context.

Response sets

It has been suggested that structured interviews are particularly prone to the operation among respondents of what Webb et al. (1966: 19) call 'response sets', which they define as 'irrelevant but lawful sources of variance'. The idea is that people respond to the series of questions in a way that is consistent but that is irrelevant to the **concept** being measured. This form of response bias is especially relevant to **multiple-indicator measures** (see Chapter 7), where respondents reply to a series of related questions or items, of the kind found in a Likert scale (see Key concept 7.2).

Two of the most prominent types of response set are known as 'acquiescence' (also known as 'yeasaying' and 'naysaying') and **social desirability bias**.

Acquiescence

In this context, acquiescence is the tendency shown by some respondents to consistently agree or disagree with a set of questions or items. For instance, if a study used a

RESEARCH IN FOCUS 9.4
The impact of interviewer characteristics

The impact of interviewer characteristics on response rates and survey responses has been a topic of discussion in quantitative research for some time. Evidence suggests that interviewer characteristics have an effect on response rates (Schaeffer et al. 2010). Jæger's (2019) study explored these issues, producing some interesting findings that have significant implications for all kinds of interviewing, particularly those conducted via video link or face-to-face.

The study explored the effect of interviewer physical attractiveness on the likelihood that a respondent agrees to be interviewed and their interview responses. The researchers obtained information on the team of 93 interviewers from two sources: a questionnaire that they administered during interview training sessions and a set of physical attractiveness ratings carried out by a panel on the basis of a photo of each interviewer and a recording of each interviewer's voice. They also collected information on interviewers' body mass index (BMI) and height through self-reports. They drew potential interviewees from the Danish Longitudinal Survey of Youth–Children (DLSY–C), a long-running cohort study in Denmark.

The research showed that interviewers' characteristics, including their physical attractiveness, impacted on cooperation rates and survey responses in face-to-face interviews (including self-reports on physical appearance, weight, and health). They found that interviewers found to have more attractive faces according to these measures and a lower self-reported BMI achieved higher cooperation rates.

9

series of five Likert items with respondents being asked to indicate the degree to which the statement is true or false, and a respondent replied 'Definitely true' to all five very similar items, despite the fact that four of the five are in a positive direction and one is in a negative direction, this implies a form of acquiescence. One of the replies is inconsistent with the four other answers. One of the reasons why researchers who employ this kind of **multiple-item measure** use wordings that imply opposite stances (that is, some items implying a high level of clarity and others implying a low level of clarity) is to weed out respondents who appear to be replying within the framework of an acquiescence response set. Acquiescence is a form of satisficing behaviour in surveys (see Key concept 9.2).

Social desirability bias

Social desirability bias refers to evidence that some respondents' answers to questions are related to their perception of the social desirability of those answers. They are more likely to give an answer that they perceive to be socially desirable, which means that socially desirable forms of behaviour or attitudes tend to be over-reported and undesirable forms under-reported. For instance, people may over-report charitable behaviour as they may think it a socially desirable form of behaviour, but may under-report alcohol consumption, especially if is way in excess of recommended amounts (depending on the context). There is also evidence that the use of sensitive questions, which are often the context within which socially desirable responding occurs, can result in poorer response rates and **item non-response**: refusal to answer particular questions (Tourangeau and Yan 2007; Krumpal 2013).

There are several strategies for checking and reducing the risk of socially desirable responding. One is not to use interviewers, as there is some evidence that self-completion forms of answering are less prone to the problem (Tourangeau and Yan 2007; Yeager et al. 2011; Gnambs and Kaspar 2015). It is also possible to soften questions that are likely to produce social desirability bias, for example using 'forgiving' wording and phrases such as 'Everybody does it' (Näher and Krumpal 2012). Minson et al. (2018) conducted a study looking at undesirable work-related behaviours in the USA and found that 'negative assumption' questions that, in effect, presuppose a problem led to greater disclosure of undesirable work-related behaviours than when they asked 'positive assumption' questions that presuppose the absence of a problem, and general questions that do not reference a problem.

These forms of response error can represent sources of error in the measurement of concepts. It is difficult to know how common these effects are, and to some extent awareness of them has led to measures to limit their impact on data (such as by weeding out cases obviously affected by them, or by instructing interviewers to limit the possible impact of the social desirability effect by not becoming overly friendly with respondents and not being judgemental about their replies).

The problem of meaning

A critique of survey interview data and other similar techniques was developed by social scientists influenced by phenomenological and other **interpretivist** ideas of the kinds we touched on in Chapter 2 (Cicourel 1964, 1982; Filmer et al. 1972; Briggs 1986; Mishler 1986). This critique revolves around what is often referred to as the 'problem of meaning'. The key to this argument is the view that when humans communicate they do so in a way that not only draws on commonly held meanings but also simultaneously creates meanings. So 'meaning' is something that is worked at and achieved—it is not simply pre-given. In surveys there is an assumption that the interviewer and respondent share the same meanings of the terms employed in the interview questions and answers. The problem of meaning implies that interviewer and respondent may not be sharing the same meaning systems, and may imply different things in their use of words. This issue tends to be ignored in structured interview research.

KEY POINTS

- Structured interviews are used to standardize the asking of questions and often the recording of answers, in order to minimize interviewer-related error.
- Structured interviews can be administered in person, using a software package, or over the telephone.
- Structured interviews can be carried out using landlines, mobile phones, or video conferencing.
- It is important to keep to the same wording and order of questions when conducting survey research by structured interview.
- While there is some evidence that interviewers' characteristics can influence respondents' replies, the findings of experiments and studies on this are not totally conclusive.
- Response sets can be damaging to data collected from structured interviews, and researchers need to take steps to identify respondents exhibiting them.

QUESTIONS FOR REVIEW

1. Why is it important in interviewing for survey research to keep interviewer variability to a minimum?
2. How successful are structured interviews in reducing interviewer variability?
3. Why might a survey researcher prefer to use a structured rather than an unstructured interview approach for gathering data?
4. Why do structured interview schedules usually include mainly closed-ended questions?
5. Are there any circumstances in which it might be best to conduct structured interviews with more than one interviewer present?
6. 'Given the lower cost of telephone or video interviewing compared to face-to-face interviews, the former types are generally preferable.' Discuss.
7. 'The main reason for choosing computer-assisted interviewing over paper-and-pencil interviews is the greater ease with which filter questions can be asked and answered'. Discuss.

8. What might be the main reasons for choosing to interview members of a sample by mobile phone rather than by landlines?
9. To what extent is rapport an important part of structured interviewing?
10. How strong is the evidence that question order can significantly affect answers?
11. How strong is the evidence that interviewers' characteristics can significantly affect answers?
12. What is the difference between probing and prompting? How important are they and what are the potential dangers of their use?
13. What are response sets and why are they potentially important?

ONLINE RESOURCES

www.oup.com/he/srm6e

You can find our notes on the answers to these questions within this chapter's **online resources**, together with:

- *audio/video comments* on this topic from our 'Learn from experience' panellists;
- *audio discussion from the authors* on why some researchers prefer to use a structured rather than unstructured approach for gathering data (review question 3);
- *self-test questions* for further knowledge-checking;
- a *flashcard glossary* to help you recall key terms; and
- a *Student Researcher's Toolkit* containing practical materials and resources to help you conduct your own research project.

CHAPTER
10

SELF-COMPLETION QUESTIONNAIRES

CHAPTER GUIDE

Among the main instruments for gathering data using a survey design, along with structured interviews (covered in Chapter 9), are questionnaires that respondents complete themselves. In this chapter we will explore

- the advantages and disadvantages of questionnaires in comparison with structured interviews;
- how to address the potential problem of poor response rates, which is often a feature of email, online, and postal questionnaires;
- how to design questionnaires to make answering easier for respondents and less prone to error;
- some specific characteristics of email and online surveys and their relative advantages and disadvantages;
- the use of mixed modes in survey research;
- how to choose which mode would be best for your survey;
- the use of diaries as a form of self-completion questionnaire;
- a variation on the diary method known as experience or event sampling.

10.1 Introduction

In many ways, the bulk of Chapter 9 was about questionnaires, as the structured interview is essentially a form of questionnaire that is administered by an interviewer. However, there is a tendency to only use the term 'questionnaire' in contexts where a succession of questions, usually closed-ended questions, are completed by respondents themselves. In this chapter we will walk through the different forms or modes of self-completion questionnaire, discussing how we can use each type in social research. We touch on some elements of questionnaire design (we return to these considerations in Chapter 11 on 'Asking questions') and we also outline some of the differences between structured interviews, which are conducted in person, and the various forms of self-completion questionnaires.

10.2 Different forms of self-completion questionnaires

The self-completion questionnaire is sometimes referred to as a self-administered questionnaire. Either term is perfectly acceptable, but in this book we use the former. As the name suggests, this method involves respondents answering questions by completing a questionnaire themselves.

Self-completion questionnaires can be administered through different modes—online, by email, or by post. Email and online surveys are the most common method, mainly due to their convenience compared to postal questionnaires. Conducting surveys by email involves emailing a questionnaire to a respondent, whereas with online surveys, respondents are sent to a website where they can answer a questionnaire. These digital formats tend to be cheaper and quicker to administer than postal questionnaires, which involve posting a paper questionnaire to the respondent and usually asking them to return their completed questionnaire by post (although sometimes respondents may be asked to return their questionnaires to a certain location, such as a box in a school common room or in a supervisor's office in a firm). The term 'self-completion questionnaire' also covers other forms of administration, such as when a researcher hands out questionnaires to all students in a class and collects them back following completion. Two of this book's authors, Tom Clark and Liam Foster (2017), used this approach to evaluate the effect of changes to research methods teaching on student course satisfaction. Each year we asked the whole class to complete an anonymized evaluation form and put it in a designated box in the lecture theatre. (The lecturers left the room while students were filling in the form, so that their presence did not affect the responses.)

In this chapter, we will use the term 'self-completion questionnaire' when we make points that apply to all forms of self-completion questionnaire, but when a point refers specifically to a particular form, such as email, online, or postal questionnaires, we will specify this. There are some specific issues to bear in mind about email and online surveys, and given that these are the most common types of survey administration, we will consider those issues in detail in Section 10.5.

10.3 Comparing self-completion questionnaires with structured interviews

We have already pointed out that there are similarities between self-completion questionnaires and structured interviews, but the obvious difference between these methods is that an interviewer is present in structured interviews, whereas self-completion questionnaire respondents must read and answer the questions themselves. Because there is no interviewer administering the self-completion questionnaire, this research instrument has to be particularly easy to follow, with questions that are extremely clear and easy to answer. This means that in comparison to interviews, self-completion questionnaires tend to

- have fewer **open-ended questions**, since closed-ended ones tend to be easier to answer;
- have easy-to-follow designs, minimizing the risk that the respondent will fail to follow instructions or accidentally miss out questions;
- be shorter, in order to reduce the likelihood of 'respondent fatigue' leading to non-completion: it is easier for a respondent who becomes tired of answering questions to click the delete button or throw away a paper questionnaire than it is for a respondent to terminate an interview.

Advantages of self-completion questionnaires compared with structured interviews

Cheaper to administer

Self-completion questionnaires can be much cheaper to administer than structured interviews, especially when the **sample** is geographically dispersed and would involve considerable travel time and costs for interviewers. This is obviously less of an advantage compared to telephone interviews, because their costs are lower and travel time is minimal anyway, but even so, self-completion questionnaires are more cost-effective as they don't involve interviewers.

Quicker to administer

Administering self-completion questionnaires can involve distributing them in very large quantities at the same time. Once you have identified your sample, you could send out an almost unlimited number of email surveys or invitations to online surveys at once, or post out a batch of a thousand paper questionnaires. By contrast, even with a team of interviewers, it would take a long time to conduct personal interviews with such a large sample. However, it is important to bear in mind that the questionnaires will not all come back immediately, and researchers usually have to send out reminder emails, letters, and/or questionnaires to those who fail to return them initially.

Free from interviewer effects

As we saw in Chapter 9, various studies have demonstrated that characteristics of interviewers may affect the answers people give, and it has been suggested that characteristics such as ethnicity, gender, and the social background of interviewers may combine to bias the answers that respondents provide. The implications of this research are not clear so we should regard this advantage cautiously, but the fact that there is no interviewer present for a self-completion questionnaire means that there is no possibility of interviewer effects. Research in focus 10.1 describes a study looking at the truthfulness

RESEARCH IN FOCUS 10.1

Face-to-face interview or self-completion questionnaire: which is better at getting at the truth?

Preisendörfer and Wolter (2014) compared interviews and postal questionnaires to find out which was more likely to get people to admit to having a criminal conviction. The authors carried out two surveys: one used a face-to-face structured interview and the other a postal questionnaire. All the respondents had been identified as having been convicted of a (mainly minor) criminal offence some years before the survey was carried out. In both surveys, the question about criminality was one of many questions and was phrased as follows:

> Have you ever—by penalty order or in a court case—been convicted under criminal law of a minor or more serious offense? By 'convicted under criminal law' we mean that the issue was handled by a public prosecutor.
>
> (Preisendörfer and Wolter 2014: 138)

In all, 63 per cent of the sample answered truthfully, but postal questionnaire respondents were more likely to be truthful than interviewees—although the difference was not particularly high (67 per cent versus 58 per cent). This result indicates that self-completion questionnaires sent through the post may produce more willingness to give less socially desirable responses than face-to-face interviews. If you want to ask sensitive questions, it is worth bearing this in mind when you are deciding what type of survey to conduct.

of respondents' answers in interviews as compared to questionnaires.

One way in which interviewer presence can affect answers is that respondents may tend to exhibit social desirability bias (Gnambs and Kaspar 2015), meaning that they feel uneasy if their answers do not conform to norms or social expectations and may adjust them accordingly (Kaminska and Foulsham 2013). This effect is visible in the study we describe in Research in focus 10.1. Research by Sudman and Bradburn (1982) suggests that postal questionnaires work better than personal interviews when a question carries the possibility of such bias, and Zhang et al. (2017) found that online surveys have a similar effect, reducing social desirability bias compared with telephone and face-to-face interviews. Tourangeau et al. (2013) carried out a meta-analysis (see Chapter 14) of studies that compared telephone interviews with equivalent online questionnaires and found that respondents were more likely to report sensitive information in online questionnaires, implying that this method may be less prone to social desirability bias than interviews. These findings built on research that Tourangeau had previously summarized (Tourangeau and Smith 1996), which strongly suggested that respondents report more drug use and alcohol consumption and a higher number of sexual partners and abortions in self-completion questionnaires than in structured interviews.

Free from interviewer variability

Self-completion questionnaires do not suffer from the problem of interviewers asking questions in a different order or in different ways.

Convenient for respondents

Self-completion questionnaires are more convenient for respondents, because they can complete a questionnaire when they want and at their preferred speed.

Disadvantages of self-completion questionnaires compared with structured interviews

Researcher cannot prompt

If respondents are having difficulty answering a question, there is no interviewer to help them. This means it is particularly important that the questions asked in self-completion questionnaires are clear and unambiguous. The questionnaire also needs to be easy to complete, as respondents might accidentally miss out questions if the instructions are unclear.

Researcher cannot probe

Although probing is not always considered desirable (as we pointed out in Section 9.5), given that an interviewer's intervention may influence the respondent, it can be useful. Probing can be very important when open-ended questions are being asked, and interviewers are often trained to use this technique to get more information from respondents, especially in semi-structured and unstructured interviews. Probing is clearly not possible in self-completion questionnaires, but this is rarely an issue as the technique is most useful with open-ended questions, which are not often used in surveys.

Respondents may not want to answer questions that are not relevant to them

Respondents completing questionnaires are more likely than interviewees to become tired of answering questions that are not very relevant to them and that they see as boring. To avoid them abandoning the task altogether, it is important to ensure that most questions in a self-completion questionnaire are likely to be relevant to the respondent.

Other kinds of question are difficult to ask

We have noted that open-ended questions are not heavily used in self-completion questionnaires. This is because respondents frequently do not want to write a lot. Questions with complex structures, such as filters (discussed in Chapter 9), should also be avoided as far as possible, because respondents often find them difficult to follow—although well-constructed online surveys can resolve this issue by allowing respondents to 'jump' automatically to the next relevant question. Generally, a self-completion questionnaire should consist mainly of simple, closed-ended questions.

Questionnaire can be read as a whole

Unlike in an interview, a self-completion questionnaire respondent can choose to read all the questions before they begin, and this could lead to inconsistencies as none of the questions asked is truly independent of the others, leading to the potential problem of question order effects (see Chapter 9). Again, online surveys can help address this issue if they are designed so that the respondent can only view a small number of questions at a time.

Questionnaire may not be completed by the intended respondent

With online and postal questionnaires, you can never be sure whether the right person has answered the questionnaire. If a questionnaire is sent to a certain person in a household, someone else in the household may complete the questionnaire. Similarly, if a questionnaire is sent to a manager in a firm, they may delegate the task to someone else. Structured interviews avoid this issue when they are conducted in person, but not when administered by telephone, as again someone else could respond (leading to sampling issues; see Chapter 8 for a further discussion).

Olson and Smyth (2014) examined a household survey in the United States and found that 18 per cent of respondents were not the ones who were supposed to have completed the questionnaire. They found that the survey mode made a difference to the extent of this issue: 18.1 per cent of those households that received a postal questionnaire selected the wrong person, whereas this figure was 20.3 per cent among households that received an online version of the survey. In addition, among the households that were supposed to complete the questionnaire online but were then followed up by post, 14.4 per cent selected the wrong person, whereas among households contacted by post and then followed up online, the corresponding figure was 20.4 per cent. It is worth noting, though, that the reasons for the wrong person answering the questionnaire were not necessarily to do with households deliberately ignoring instructions; there may have been confusion about who was the correct person to nominate. However, these figures do indicate the problems with various forms of self-completion questionnaires in ensuring the correct person responds, in contrast to structured interviews.

Researcher cannot collect additional data

With a personal interview, interviewers might be collecting additional pieces of information about the respondent's home, school, firm, or whatever, but this is not possible with an online or postal questionnaire. On the other hand, if self-completion questionnaires are handed out in a school or firm, the researcher could still collect some additional data about the organization.

Number of questions must be limited

As we previously mentioned, the possibility of 'respondent fatigue' means that long questionnaires are usually best avoided. Including too many questions may mean that respondents leave questionnaires unfinished, that answers to later questions are inaccurate or incomplete because respondents are rushing to finish, or that fewer respondents take part in the first place because the questionnaire's length is off-putting.

Format may exclude some respondents

Respondents whose literacy is limited are likely to find it difficult to complete a questionnaire, as will those who are not confident speakers (or readers) of the language in which the study is being conducted—and of course those who do not speak the language at all will be completely excluded. Language barriers cannot be entirely overcome through the use of interviews, but they are likely to present more significant difficulties with self-completion questionnaires. It is possible to have questionnaires translated into relevant languages and responses translated back to the language of study for checking. This process occurs with the Eurobarometer surveys, which monitor the evolution of public opinion in all EU member states (**https://ec.europa.eu/echo/eurobarometer_en**, accessed 12 March 2020). The process involves developing equivalent basic bilingual questionnaires (English/French) and translating them into the other relevant languages. Proofreading and back-translation are performed by independent translators, followed by central checks.

Participants more likely to omit answers, leading to missing data

Partially answered surveys are more likely with self-completion questionnaires than in interviews, because of the lack of prompting or supervision. It is also easier for respondents to actively decide not to answer a question when on their own than when an interviewer is speaking with them, and questions that a respondent finds boring or irrelevant are especially likely to be skipped. If questions are not answered, this creates a problem of **missing data** for the **variables** that the researcher has created.

Response rates tend to be lower

Self-completion questionnaires usually result in lower response rates (see Key concept 8.2) than comparable interview-based studies (Mühlböck et al. 2017). The response rate is significant because there is likely to be a risk of bias, unless it can be proven that there are no differences between those who do and do not participate. If there are such differences, the findings relating to the sample will probably be affected, and if the response rate is low, it is likely that the risk of bias in the findings will be greater.

The lower the response rate, the more questions are likely to be raised about the representativeness of your sample and therefore the **external validity** of your findings. In a sense, this is likely to be an issue only with randomly selected samples; response rates are less of an issue for samples that are not selected on the basis of **probability sampling**, because these are not expected to be representative of the **population**.

There is considerable variation in what social scientists consider to be an acceptable response rate. Mellahi and Harris (2016) undertook a meta-analysis of academic articles published in management journals between 2009 and 2013. They found that among the 1,000 articles they reviewed there was considerable variation in response rates, which ranged from 1 per cent to 100 per cent with a **mean** of just under 45 per cent, despite much of the literature arguing for a response rate of at least 50 per cent: in other words, journals were usually willing to publish studies even when their response rates were considerably lower than 50 per cent. We are certainly not suggesting that response rates do not matter, but it is worth being aware that much academic research has a response rate below the recommended figures. The key point is to recognize and acknowledge the implications and possible limitations of a low response rate, and to do what you can to mitigate the issue—see Tips and skills 10.1 and Learn from experience 10.1.

TIPS AND SKILLS 10.1

Steps to improve response rates in self-completion questionnaires

Because of the tendency for online and postal questionnaire surveys to generate lower response rates than comparable structured interview surveys, with implications for the external validity of findings, a great deal of research has gone into ways of improving survey response. We suggest taking the following steps if you use one of these methods for your research project or dissertation.

- Write a good covering letter or email explaining the reasons for the research, why it is important, and why you have selected the respondent; mentioning sponsorship if any; and providing guarantees of confidentiality. You might find the advice in Tips and skills 9.2 useful here.
- If you are conducting a postal survey, make sure you include a stamped, addressed envelope, or at the very least return postage, with each questionnaire you send, to make it free and easy for the respondent to submit their answers.
- Follow up people who do not reply at first, possibly with two or three more emails or mailings. You could send reminder emails or letters to non-respondents about two weeks after the initial contact, or perhaps earlier if you are contacting them via email, reasserting the nature and aims of the survey and suggesting that the person contact a member of the research team, or you, if they have lost the original questionnaire and need a replacement copy. About two weeks after that, send all remaining non-respondents another letter or email along with a further copy of the questionnaire. You may even want to send out extra reminders depending on your response rate, as this tactic has been proven to have a positive effect on response rates (Jangi et al. 2018).
- Remember that shorter questionnaires tend to achieve better response rates than longer ones. It is difficult to specify when a questionnaire becomes 'too long', though, so this is not a clear-cut principle, and the effect of the length of questionnaires on response rates may depend on the relevance of the topic for respondents and the nature of the sample. Respondents may be highly tolerant of long questionnaires if they are on topics that interest them. Questionnaires measuring life satisfaction, for example, can result in response rates as high as 98 per cent (Diener et al. 2013).
- Provide clear instructions and an attractive layout. Dillman et al. (2014) recommend darker and/or larger print for questions and lighter and/or smaller print for closed-ended answers. Another aesthetic aspect is to ensure that your use of fonts, font size, and any symbols or embellishments is consistent. We will look at these issues further in Section 10.4.
- Begin with questions that are more likely to interest respondents, as with structured interviewing (see Section 9.4 under 'Question order').

- Use as few open-ended questions as possible, since people are often put off when they see that they will have to write a lot of text.
- A further step researchers can take to increase their survey response rate is to provide monetary incentives, but this is unusual in student research projects due to limited resources—and in fact, some university ethics do not allow the use of financial incentives in research. There is evidence suggesting that quite small amounts of money or vouchers have a positive impact on the response rate, but that larger amounts do not necessarily improve the response rate any further. In the case of online surveys, it is not uncommon to incentivize potential respondents with a *potential* reward—for example, telling them that they will be entered into a draw or lottery for a prize.

LEARN FROM EXPERIENCE 10.1

Avoiding a low response rate for self-completion questionnaires

As you can see from Tips and skills 10.1, there are a number of strategies researchers can employ to try and increase the response rate in self-completion questionnaires. Here, our panellists outline some of the different approaches they used that they believe worked well. For instance, Ben, whose research explored the challenges and opportunities for data visualization to improve understanding of datafication, discusses different ways he promoted his research, including its visibility. Scarlett, who focused on mental wellbeing and social media, emphasizes the idea of giving back to those you have researched, while Grace, who had used self-completion questionnaires in other work, discusses the length of the questionnaire as well as the possible use of incentives.

> I invested significant time on social media to engage mostly with two digital networks (Twitter generally, and a large specific online community related to my topic). With regard to the topic-related community, I was active in other discussions and visible in other ways so that I didn't seem to be just trying to generate survey engagement. Furthermore, I wrote a quite lengthy article on Medium that explained my research and the survey, as a means of enabling participants to fully understand the research before taking part. Both of these factors seemed to help the success of the survey.
>
> Ben

> When using self-completion questionnaires for my dissertation project, I received a high response rate. I believe this was because the questions were short and to the point. Participants are more inclined to take part in research if there is an incentive, but as our undergraduate dissertation projects are not funded, monetary incentives are not possible. For my project, I emphasized to participants that their responses were going to have an impact and make a difference. I explained to them that the project was partnered with local organizations who were interested in hearing what they had to say about social media and its impact upon their mental wellbeing. I think reiterating this to participants encouraged them to include as much information as they could.
>
> Scarlett

> It is common that people will not fill out questionnaires that are too time-consuming or offer no reward. Therefore, it is important to keep your questionnaire as short as you possibly can without compromising the data and, if possible, offer incentives for completing the questionnaire. This is difficult in the context of undergraduate research as you may not have access to money, but it is worth discussing possible incentives with your supervisor.
>
> Grace

 Access the **online resources** to hear Ben's video reflections on this theme.

You can read about our panellists' backgrounds and research experiences on page xxvi.

10.4 Designing a self-completion questionnaire

In this section we will discuss some important principles for designing self-completion questionnaires that apply to online, email, and postal questionnaires. We will go on to explore issues that specifically relate to the design of online surveys in Section 10.5.

Consider presentation and layout

It is important to consider the aesthetics of your questionnaire, because the attractiveness and clarity of its design can have a significant impact on the response rate you achieve and potentially the quality of the data you gain.

Researchers' fear of low response rates can mean that they try to make their questionnaire appear as short as possible, to avoid putting off prospective respondents, but this can make the questionnaire more cramped and less attractive. As Dillman et al. (2014) observe, an attractive layout is likely to enhance response rates, whereas the kinds of tactics that are sometimes used to make a questionnaire appear shorter than it really is—such as reducing margins and the space between questions—can do the opposite. Also, if questions are too close together, there is a risk that they will be accidentally omitted, creating the problem of **item non-response** resulting in missing data. This is not to say that you should leave lots of space, as this does not necessarily result in an attractive format and risks making the questionnaire look bulky, but there is a balance to be struck.

Making sure that your questionnaire has a clear and easy-to-follow layout also helps respondents in answering the questions that are relevant to them (Dillman et al. 2014). A variety of print styles (for example, different fonts, font sizes, and font styles—bold, italics, and capitals) can enhance the appearance *but must be used in a consistent way* to avoid confusing respondents. This means using one style for general instructions, one for headings, perhaps one for specific instructions (like 'Go to question 7'), one for questions, and one for closed-ended answers. Mixing styles, so that one style is sometimes used for both general instructions and questions, can be very confusing for respondents. It is also worth noting that respondents may complete your questionnaire on mobile phones or tablets, so you will need to consider how it will appear in different formats.

As part of your consideration of presentation and layout, you also need to think about whether you want to arrange the fixed answers of **closed-ended questions** vertically or horizontally—see the examples in Tips and skills 10.2. The length of the answers may mean that you have to arrange them vertically, and many researchers prefer to use this format whenever possible, because, in some cases where either arrangement is feasible, confusion can arise when a horizontal one is employed (Sudman and Bradburn 1982). De Bruijne and Wijnant (2014) examined the response effects of vertical or horizontal answer **scale** layout when using self-completion questionnaires on smartphones and found that the horizontal layout resulted in slightly more missing answers than the vertical layout. There is a risk that the respondent will put a tick in the wrong place in they are completing the questionnaire in a rush—for example, indicating Good when Fair was the intended response—and a vertical format more clearly distinguishes questions from answers. To some extent, you can avoid these potential problems through the sensible use of spacing and print variation, but you certainly need to consider them.

One of the advantages of using closed-ended questions is that you can pre-code them, so that if the data is collected on paper it is easy to enter into a data analysis software program (see Chapter 11 for more on this), or with an online survey it feeds automatically into the software program. Researchers need to put careful thought into how they will score each possible fixed answer when designing a self-completion questionnaire—see Tips and skills 10.2 and 10.3 for examples of how you might do this. Often, questionnaires on paper are arranged so that there are two columns on the right of each question: one for the column in which data relating to the question will appear in a data matrix, and the other for all the pre-codes. The latter allows researchers to assign the appropriate code to a respondent's answer by circling it, to speed up digital entry later.

Vertical alignments are probably easier to **code** in this way, especially when **pre-codes** appear on the questionnaire and it is completed by hand, but when there is a series of questions with identical answer formats, as in a **Likert scale**, a vertical format will take up too much space. One way of dealing with this issue is to use abbreviations with an accompanying explanation, as in Tips and skills 10.3, or to have a scale for each page if using an online survey. If you use a Likert scale, you might want to consider designing the questionnaire to include some items in which the question format is reversed (as in Tips and skills 10.3), in order to identify people who exhibit **response sets**, such as acquiescence (see Section 9.7), because their answers are unlikely to provide a valid assessment of whatever you are trying to measure.

TIPS AND SKILLS 10.2

Choosing between horizontal and vertical formats for closed-ended questions

As we have discussed, if you choose to use a self-completion questionnaire you are likely to use mainly closed-ended questions, so you will need to decide whether to arrange the fixed answers in a horizontal or vertical format—we have provided examples of both below. In making this decision you should consider the pros and cons of each arrangement (see Hu 2020 for further information). Make consistent use of whichever method you think is most likely to be clear to your respondents and produce high-quality data. You will also want to consider the **coding** of your data: in both these examples, you can see that the categories have numbers or codes associated with them.

Example of a horizontal format

What do you think of the Prime Minister's performance in his job since he took office?

(*Please tick the appropriate response*)

Very good ____ Good ____ Fair ____ Poor ____ Very poor ____

5 4 3 2 1

Example of a vertical format

What do you think of the Prime Minister's performance in his job since he took office?

(*Please tick the appropriate response*)

Very good	____	5
Good	____	4
Fair	____	3
Poor	____	2
Very poor	____	1

It is important to note that a Likert scale is never an individual **item**. Rather it is a set of Likert items that are forced-choice ordinal questions used to capture the intensity of survey responses. Historically a Likert item comprised five points or ordinal categories, worded 'Strongly approve', 'Approve', 'Undecided', 'Disapprove', 'Strongly disapprove' (Likert 1932), although other alternative wording may be used, including 'Agree' rather than 'Approve', or 'Neutral' or 'Neither agree nor disagree' rather than 'Undecided' (Derrick and White 2017). A Likert scale is formed by the summation of multiple Likert items that measure similar information, which usually requires the assignment of scores to the Likert ordinal **category** labels.

The National Student Survey (2020, **www.officeforstudents.org.uk/publications/the-national-student-survey-consistency-controversy-and-change/** accessed 13 March 2020) uses Likert items. For example, Figure 10.1 shows a Likert item exploring the **concept** of 'learning community'. Note that it includes important guidance on how the respondent should choose and mark their answer: 'Please show the extent of your agreement by selecting the box that reflects your current view of your course as a whole.'

Provide clear instructions about how to respond

You always need to be clear about how you want respondents to indicate their replies when answering

FIGURE 10.1

A Likert item exploring the concept of 'learning community' from the UK's National Student Survey

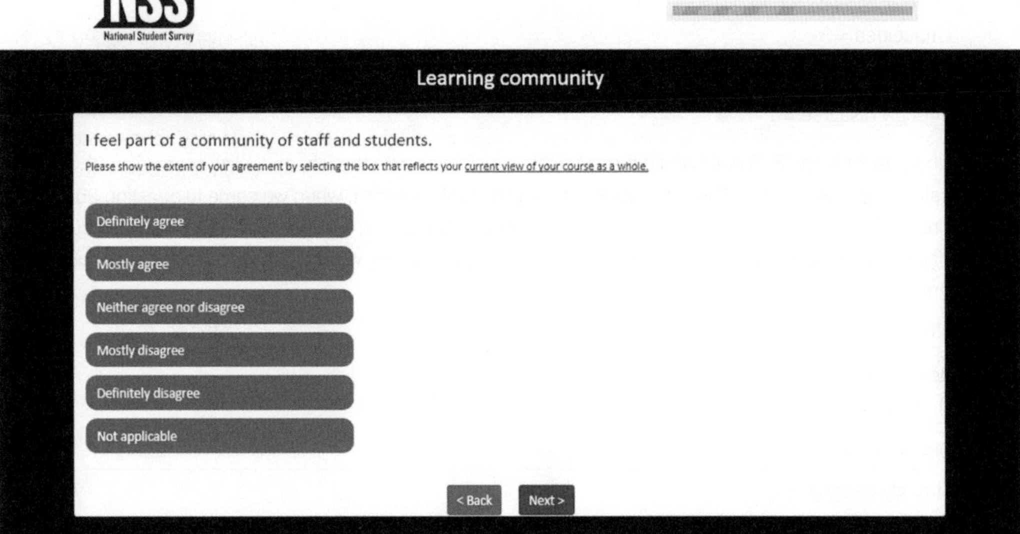

Source: Example NSS question, The National Student Survey: Consistency, controversy and change, Office for Students, 2020. © The Office for Students copyright 2020.

TIPS AND SKILLS 10.3

Designing a Likert scale for a self-completion questionnaire

When you ask a series of questions with the same fixed-answer format, as in a Likert scale, a vertical arrangement for answers can take up a lot of space unnecessarily. We can overcome this problem by using abbreviations that we explain before the series begins. In the classic example below, the four Likert items are taken from an 18-item Likert scale designed to measure job satisfaction (Brayfield and Rothe 1951).

In the next set of questions, you are presented with a statement. You are being asked to indicate your level of agreement or disagreement with each statement by indicating whether you: Strongly Agree (SA), Agree (A), are Undecided (U), Disagree (D), or Strongly Disagree (SD).

(*Please indicate your level of agreement by circling the appropriate response*)

23. My job is like a hobby to me.

SA A U D SD

24. My job is usually interesting enough to keep me from getting bored.

SA A U D SD

25. It seems that my friends are more interested in their jobs.

SA A U D SD

26. I enjoy my work more than my leisure time.

SA A U D SD

As we have noted, it is important to put some thought into how you will score items like these when you come to code responses. We might score question 23 as follows:

Strongly agree = 5

Agree = 4

Undecided = 3

Disagree = 2

Strongly disagree = 1

A high score for item 23 (5 or 4) would then indicate satisfaction with the job, and a low score (1 or 2) would indicate low job satisfaction. The same applies to question 24. However, when we come to question 25, the picture is different. Here, agreement indicates a *lack* of job satisfaction—it is *disagreement* that indicates job satisfaction. In the case of a reverse-format item such as question 25, we would have to reverse our coding system:

Strongly agree = 1

Agree = 2

Undecided = 3

Disagree = 4

Strongly disagree = 5

It is important to keep track of which answer is coded in which way to ensure that you analyse it properly later on.

Item 25 is the kind of item that we noted can be included to identify people who exhibit a *response set.* In this example, someone who agreed with all 18 items on the survey, despite some of them indicating job satisfaction and others indicating a *lack* of job satisfaction, would be exhibiting a response set and their responses would not provide a valid assessment of their job satisfaction. There are of course challenges with this kind of approach, and careful reading of the questions by participants is important here, as they may be more likely to misread the question when the direction is changed.

closed-ended questions. Are they supposed to place a tick next to, circle around, or line underneath the appropriate answer, or are they supposed to delete inappropriate answers? Also, in many cases the respondent may want to choose more than one answer—is this acceptable to you, and are your instructions clear in relation to this?

If you want the respondent to choose only one answer, you might want to include an instruction such as:

(*Please choose the* ***one*** *answer that best represents your views by placing a tick in the appropriate box.*)

If it is acceptable for the respondent to choose more than one category, you need to make this clear. For example:

(*Please choose* ***all*** *answers that represent your views by placing ticks in the appropriate boxes.*)

If you do not include such instructions, respondents are likely to make inappropriate selections or to be unsure about how to reply.

Keep question and answers together

You should never format a questionnaire so that a question and its answers are split across two separate pages. This increases the risk of the respondent forgetting to answer the question or providing an answer in the wrong group of closed-ended answers (this is especially likely when a series of questions with a common answer format is being used, as with a Likert scale).

Read Learn from experience 10.2 to hear how our panellists went about designing self-completion questionnaires.

LEARN FROM EXPERIENCE 10.2
Designing a self-completion questionnaire

Our panellists Ben and Scarlett reflected on the processes they used to design their self-completion questionnaires. It is obvious that clarity was a key consideration for both.

My design background provided me with expertise in how to create a successful survey experience. For instance, I created a common question schema that I adopted for every question and that was visually consistent for every question. This comprised: Question/statement—what I want to know (a maximum of one sentence, ideally on one line, bold text); Question rationale—why I was asking the question and why it helped the research (concise but clear, smaller grey text); Instruction—a few words, for example 'Select only one answer' (pink text); and Answer options—other/extra choices. I also adopted many other recognized techniques from literature on survey design (such as starting with more general questions and becoming more advanced or specific through the course of survey). I feel this question schema contributed to a good overall survey design and minimal cognitive effort for the participant.

Ben

Self-completion questionnaires need to be clear, concise, and to the point. Questions should be appropriately worded so that participants can understand them and so they are aware of what the questionnaire is asking of them. Ensure that the presentation of the questionnaire is simple; do not make anything too complicated by mixing up the responses to questions (for instance, tick boxes, Likert scales, and text boxes)—try to keep it as consistent as possible. Also, if you are asking participants to write things down, make sure that text boxes are large enough.

Scarlett

 Access the **online resources** to hear Ben's video reflections on this theme.

You can read about our panellists' backgrounds and research experiences on page xxvi.

10

10.5 Email and online surveys

Most of the issues we have discussed so far relate to both online and paper-based surveys. However, we now need to turn to a number of issues that relate particularly to digital surveys. As previously noted, there is a crucial distinction between surveys completed by email and surveys completed online. In the case of the former, the questionnaire is sent via email to a respondent, whereas with an online survey, the respondent is directed to a website in order to answer a questionnaire. Online surveys have increasingly become the preferred choice for researchers of all kinds, largely because of the growing number of useful online survey sites for designing these kinds of questionnaires.

Email surveys

It is important to distinguish between **embedded email surveys** and **attached email surveys**. With embedded questionnaires, questions are set out in the body of an email, although there may be an introduction to the questionnaire followed by some marking (for example a horizontal line) that separates the introduction from the questionnaire itself. Respondents have to click 'reply' and add their answers into the email below. They are often asked to indicate their replies using simple notations below each question, such as an '×'; or they may be asked to delete alternatives that do not apply; or when questions are open-ended, they may be asked to type in their answers. They then simply need to click 'send' to return their completed questionnaires. An attached questionnaire is similar in many respects, but the questionnaire arrives as an attachment to an email that introduces it. As with embedded questionnaires, respondents select their answers and/or type them into the document before returning it to the researcher, normally as an email attachment again.

Embedded questionnaires are easier for the respondent to access and return to the researcher, as they do not need to download email attachments. Sometimes, recipients' software may prevent them from reading attachments, and some respondents may refuse to open the attachment because of concerns about a virus. However, the formatting possible with most email software is more limited than formatting in a separate document, and if the questionnaire is embedded in an email, the alignment of questions and answers may be lost—this could be particularly problematic if answers are arranged horizontally and spaced using the tab key. The researcher loses some control over the presentation of the questionnaire.

Online surveys

You will almost certainly have had some personal experience with this type of self-completion questionnaire. With surveys in this format, prospective respondents are simply sent a URL through which they can access and complete the questionnaire online.

Online surveys have an important advantage over email surveys in that there is much more scope to customize their appearance, and many useful tools and types of functionality that can enhance their usability, not only for respondents but also for researchers when they come to collect and analyse the data. For example, to help respondents navigate the questionnaire, you can design it to skip automatically to the next appropriate question when there is a **filter question** (for example, 'if Yes go to question 12, if No go to question 14'), and you can choose to only display one question at a time to the respondent. It is also possible to dictate which questions must be answered and which are optional.

A major advantage of online surveys for researchers is that this format eliminates the challenge of coding a large number of responses, because it automatically downloads them into a database. There is no need to enter data into your software, and the coding of replies is required only for open-ended questions—and more advanced versions of some survey administration packages also offer some tools to help analyse these. These benefits not only save time but also reduce the likelihood of errors being introduced during the processing of data.

Figure 10.2 shows part of the questionnaire from a survey about gym use that we will examine in Chapter 15. Here, it is formatted as an online survey, but it has been answered in the same way as in Chapter 15, which presents it as a postal survey. As you can see, it includes some open-ended questions (for example question 2), where the respondent is invited to type directly into a boxed area. The researcher can set a character limit for these answers if they choose.

The huge number of online software packages available for designing and administering online surveys include Qualtrics, Survey Gizmo, Survey Monkey, and Google Forms. When choosing which online survey tool to use, it is important to consider data security and the legal requirements surrounding the collection and storage of data at your institution. For instance, there may be requirements regarding where data is stored, which may preclude the use of software packages based in particular countries. If you are in doubt, check with your institution or the organization approving your research project.

Figure 10.2 was created using Survey Monkey (**www.surveymonkey.com/**, accessed 5 December 2020). The questions in Figure 10.2 were created using the software's basic features, which are free of charge, but users need to pay to access more advanced features.

As we have seen, one potential issue with self-completion questionnaires compared to structured interviews is that researchers cannot know whether the intended respondent is actually the person who has completed the questionnaire, and studies have suggested this may be more of an issue with online than postal surveys (see Section 10.3 under the subheading 'Questionnaire may not be completed by the intended respondent'). You can minimize this risk, to an extent, by setting up a password system to filter out people whom you did not intend to include in your sample.

It is also worth noting that there can be technical issues with these forms of self-completion questionnaires. For instance, if respondents choose to complete the questionnaire in more than one sitting, previous answers may be lost, resulting in the questionnaire being incomplete or the respondent having to start again. These types of technical issues can mean that researchers receive, and have to respond to, a lot of queries.

FIGURE 10.2
Part of the gym survey in online survey format

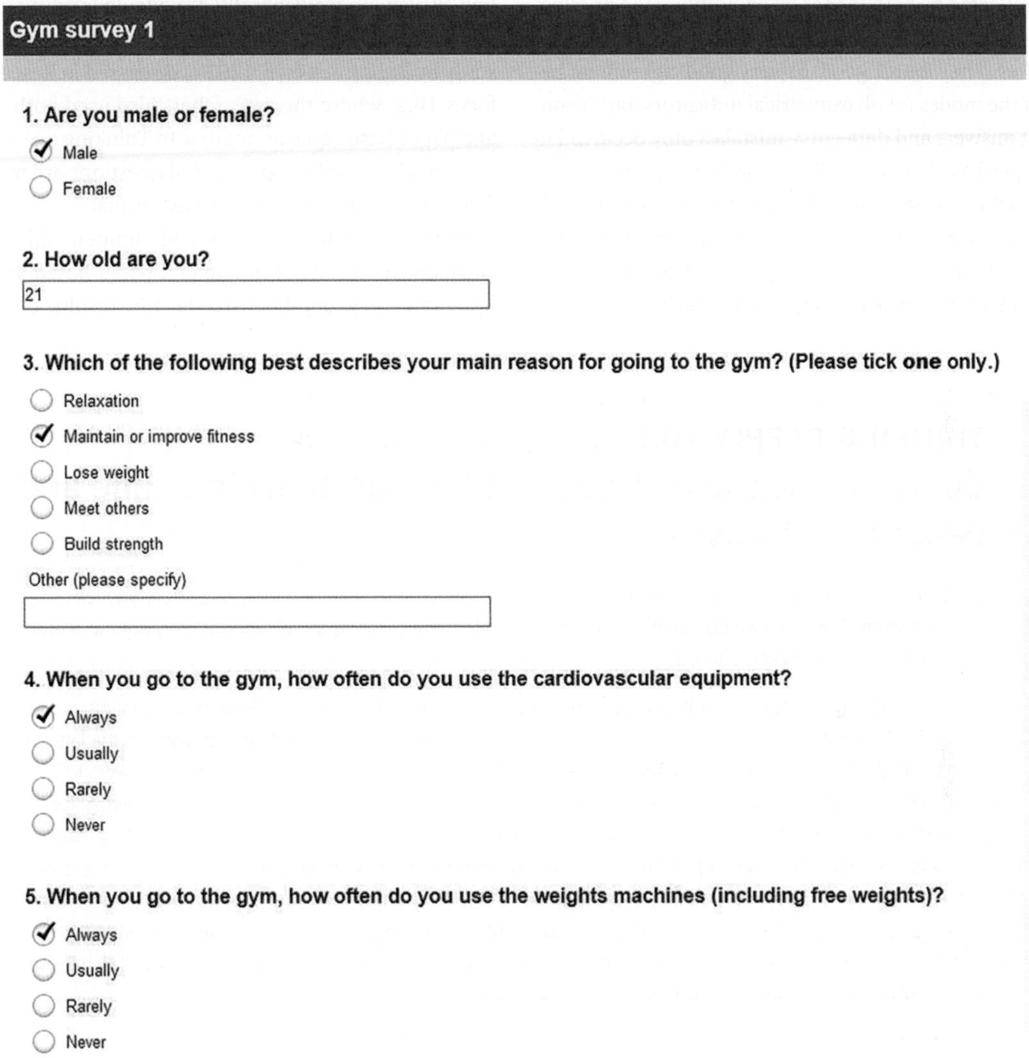

Gym survey 1

1. Are you male or female?

- ☑ Male
- ○ Female

2. How old are you?

21

3. Which of the following best describes your main reason for going to the gym? (Please tick one only.)

- ○ Relaxation
- ☑ Maintain or improve fitness
- ○ Lose weight
- ○ Meet others
- ○ Build strength

Other (please specify)

4. When you go to the gym, how often do you use the cardiovascular equipment?

- ☑ Always
- ○ Usually
- ○ Rarely
- ○ Never

5. When you go to the gym, how often do you use the weights machines (including free weights)?

- ☑ Always
- ○ Usually
- ○ Rarely
- ○ Never

10

10.6 Mixed modes of administering surveys

Now that we have an idea of what a self-completion questionnaire involves, and some of the advantages and disadvantages of its different forms, let's look at the results of studies that have experimented with different ways of administering surveys. **Mixed mode surveys** involve the use of two or more modes of administering a survey. These kinds of **experiments** are quite reassuring because they reveal that the differences between results from different types of delivery are often not that significant (Campbell et al. 2015). For example, a study of self-reported illicit drug use among a large sample of US university students who were randomly assigned either online or paper-based questionnaires found that the results of the two modes produced similar findings (McCabe 2004).

Braekman et al. (2018) explored the measurement effects between paper-based and online questionnaires for the Belgian Health Interview Survey, using a diverse range of health **indicators** related to general health, mental and psychosocial health, health behaviours, and prevention of ill health. They assessed the quality of the data they collected by both modes by quantifying the missing, 'don't know', and inconsistent values as well as data entry mistakes. They found 'good' to 'very good' agreement between the modes for all categorical indicators, but inconsistent answers and data entry mistakes only occurred in the paper-based mode. De Rada and Domínguez (2015), who studied citizens of Andalusia, Spain, who are residents of other countries, also found that there were more incomplete questions in the responses to a paper-based questionnaire than its online version. Their sample were given the option of answering by post or online. Braekman et al. (2018) found that missing values were no more common in the online mode, supporting the idea that online survey modes generally provide equal responses to paper-based modes. Similarities were also found in the study by Rübsamen et al. (2017) discussed in Research in focus 10.2, where the researchers also used both online and paper-based questionnaires. In Thinking deeply 10.1 we consider whether open-ended questions are more effective in an online or paper-based format.

Whereas studies have found limited differences between the results of online and paper-based surveys, the same may not be true for the results of online

THINKING DEEPLY 10.1
Comparing the use of open-ended questions in online and paper-based surveys

We have already established that open-ended questions should be used infrequently in self-completion questionnaires, but when we do use them, it is important to think carefully about whether they are more effective in an online or paper-based context.

Summarizing the results of several studies comparing the use of open-ended questions in both online and paper-based questionnaire surveys, Couper (2008) found that the former were at least as good as the latter in terms of both quantity and quality of answers. Smyth et al. (2009) reported that the quality of answers to open-ended questions in online surveys can be enhanced by increasing the size of the space available for answers; drawing attention to the flexible size of the box into which answers are typed; and providing instructions that both clarify what is expected and motivate the respondent (such as pointing out the importance of their replies). Blair et al. (2014) agree that the presentation of the different types of questions in online surveys can enhance response rates. Smyth et al. (2009) also observed that using open-ended questions in online questionnaires is easier for researchers as there is no need to transcribe people's sometimes illegible handwriting. **Transcription** can be an extremely time-consuming process.

RESEARCH IN FOCUS 10.2
Comparing the results from paper-and-pencil and online questionnaires

Rübsamen et al. (2017) compared response patterns in a population-based health survey using two survey designs: mixed-mode (giving respondents a choice between online questionnaires and paper-and-pencil) and online-only (without choice). The survey was conducted using a longitudinal panel, the Hygiene and Behaviour Infectious Diseases Study (HaBIDS), conducted in 2014/2015 in four regions in Lower Saxony, Germany. In two regions individuals could choose whether to use paper-and-pencil or online questionnaires, while in the other two regions individuals were not provided with a choice and were asked to complete online questionnaires. The researchers found that type of response did not differ between the online-only and the mixed-mode group. Both survey designs revealed similar response patterns, with only a few items answered differently, which was probably due to chance. Overall, Rübsamen et al. observed that online-only design does not strongly distort the results.

self-completion questionnaires compared with surveys conducted in person—in other words, structured interviews. In a study by Heerwegh and Loosveldt (2008) of attitudes towards immigrants that compared the results of online and face-to-face interviews (conducted in Belgian), online respondents were more likely to provide 'don't know' answers, less likely to differentiate on rating scales (this means they made less use of the full range of possible response options), and more likely to fail to reply to individual questions or items in rating scales. These findings suggest not only that the two modes can produce different kinds of response, but also that data quality may be poorer in the online mode.

However, don't let this put you off using self-completion questionnaires, whether in online or postal form. As we have discussed, they tend to be less time-consuming than structured interviews, and there is only limited evidence to suggest that the data produced is of lower quality. It is worth being aware of potential limitations, though, as it is with any form of data collection. One way to maximize the benefits of self-completion questionnaires and go some way to mitigating the risks of this method is to mix postal and online questionnaires, as some of the studies we have considered have done, and others have recommended (Van Selm and Jankowski 2006; Dillman et al. 2014; Rübsamen et al. 2017). There is, as we have seen, some evidence of differences in response between modes of survey administration, but mixing survey modes can offer greater coverage (for example, people who do not have internet access may be contactable by post) and better response rates (for example, people who do not want to complete and return a postal questionnaire may be more inclined to complete a questionnaire online).

However, Medway and Fulton (2012) conducted some research that highlights a potential challenge when using postal questionnaires that offer respondents the option of responding online. They conducted a meta-analysis of studies that examined the impact of offering an online option and found a clear tendency for such surveys to produce *lower* response rates than those that do not provide such an option. Explaining this possibly surprising finding, the authors suggested that the online option can increase the overall complexity of responding; introduces a break in the process of responding; and sometimes causes technical difficulties that result in respondents giving up (such as links being blocked). A clear covering letter can limit these challenges, drawing prospective respondents' attention to an online option and providing instructions for accessing it, so that those who prefer to work online are not put off responding.

Overall, it is difficult to provide a definitive verdict on whether online surveys, postal questionnaires, telephone interviews, or surveys conducted in person (in other words, structured interviews) are the most effective way of collecting survey data. When researchers have experimented with modes of administration, it has often proved difficult to separate out the effects of particular *formats* that researchers use from the effects of the modes themselves. If they had displayed online questions in a different way, their findings might have been different. However, it is important to bear in mind the practical implications of different modes and formats. As we noted in Thinking deeply 10.1 (in the context of open-ended questions) and as Barbara highlights in Learn from experience 10.3, handwritten results are less convenient as they need to be typed up for analysis.

LEARN FROM EXPERIENCE 10.3
Comparing the results from paper-and-pencil and online questionnaires

Barbara conducted research about the role of important adults for positive youth development among high school children and gave her participants the option of completing the questionnaire using paper-and-pencil or online. She reflected on the implications for analysing the data using the different approaches.

> When collecting data in high schools for my master's thesis I had printouts of questionnaires and a link for the questionnaire to be answered online. I presented both options to the students and found that many students preferred to do it on their phones or computers (if they were in the classroom with computers). That made it easier and quicker for me when putting the data into an electronic format (like Excel sheets or SPSS).
>
> Barbara

You can read about our panellists' backgrounds and research experiences on page xxvi.

10.7 Choosing which mode to use to administer your survey

Choosing which mode of survey administration to use can be a difficult decision. As we have previously stated, there is no doubt that technological advances have resulted in moves from postal questionnaires towards email or online surveys, while structured interviews remain popular. In this section, we explore the differences between these modes of administration. Tips and skills 10.4 summarizes the main factors to take into account when deciding which method of self-completion questionnaire to use, and Table 10.1 provides a reference point for comparing the different methods of administering a survey (online, email, postal, telephone, or surveys conducted in person—structured interviews). This provides a useful resource to help you choose your mode of administration.

TIPS AND SKILLS 10.4

Advantages and disadvantages of email and online surveys compared to postal questionnaire surveys

Here we will summarize the main advantages and disadvantages of email and online surveys compared to postal questionnaire surveys. Among the *advantages* are the following.

1. *Low cost, in terms of money and time.* Postal questionnaires involve postage fees, paper, envelopes, and a lot of preparation time (generating and printing address labels, sticking them on envelopes, and putting the questionnaire and covering letter into each). Online and email surveys may, however, involve start-up costs associated with the software needed to produce the questionnaire.
2. *Faster response.* Online and email surveys tend to be returned more quickly than postal questionnaires.
3. *Attractive and easy-to-use formats.* With online and email surveys, you can use a wide variety of stylistic formats, as well as features such as automatic skipping when using filter questions.
4. *Downloading of responses to a database.* Being able to immediately download questionnaire replies into a database can save time and energy.
5. *Fewer unanswered questions.* There is some evidence that online questionnaires are completed with fewer unanswered questions than postal questionnaires, resulting in less missing data, especially given that people can be compelled to answer questions before moving on.
6. *Better response to open-ended questions.* Although open-ended questions don't tend to be extensively used in any form of self-completion questionnaire, they are more likely to be answered online and in emails and to result in more detailed replies.
7. *Better data accuracy, especially in online surveys.* Data entry is automated so the researcher does not have to enter data into a spreadsheet or software package, which means errors in data entry are largely avoided.

Disadvantages of online and email surveys include the following.

1. *Low response rate.* Response rates to online and email surveys are usually lower than those for comparable postal questionnaire surveys.
2. *Restricted to online populations.* Only people who have access to the internet can reasonably be expected to participate in an online or email survey. Although most people have access to the internet, there is evidence that certain groups, including older people, are less likely to have access to it than other age groups. If online populations are the focus of interest, this disadvantage is unlikely to prove an obstacle.
3. *Confidentiality and anonymity issues.* It is normal for survey researchers to indicate that respondents' replies will be confidential and that they will be anonymous. The same suggestions can and should be made with

respect to online and email surveys. However, with email surveys, since the recipient must return the questionnaire either embedded within the message or as an attachment, respondents may be more cautious about whether their replies really are confidential and will be treated anonymously. In this respect, online surveys may have an advantage over email surveys.

4. *Multiple replies.* With online surveys, there is a risk that some people may, for whatever reason (for example, to sabotage the data or enter joke responses), complete the questionnaire more than once. For example, the Jedi **census** phenomenon is a grassroots movement that was initiated in 2001 for residents of a number of English-speaking countries, urging them to record their religion as 'Jedi' or 'Jedi Knight' (after the quasi-religious order of Jedi Knights in the fictional Star Wars universe) on the national census. In England and Wales 390,127 people (almost 0.8 per cent) stated their religion as Jedi on their 2001 census forms, surpassing Sikhism, Judaism, and Buddhism. In 2011 census figures, the number of Jedi had fallen to 176,632. There is less risk of this with email surveys.

Sources: Blair et al. (2014); Cobanoglu et al. (2001); Denscombe (2006); Dillman et al. (2014); Groves et al. (2009); Pedersen and Nielsen (2016); Sebo et al. (2017); Sheehan and Hoy (1999); **www.restore.ac.uk/orm/self-study.htm** (accessed 26 May 2019).

10

TABLE 10.1

The strengths of email and online surveys in relation to surveys conducted in person, by telephone interview, and by postal questionnaire

Issues to consider	Mode of survey administration				
	Structured in-person interview	Structured telephone interview	Postal questionnaire	Email	Online
Resource issues					
Is the cost of administration relatively low?	✓	✓✓	✓✓✓	✓✓✓	✓ (unless low-cost software available)
Is the speed of administration relatively fast?	✓	✓✓✓	✓✓✓	✓✓✓	✓✓✓
Is the cost of handling a dispersed sample relatively low?	✓ (✓✓ if clustered)	✓✓✓	✓✓✓	✓✓✓	✓✓✓
Can the researcher design a questionnaire without needing much technical expertise?	✓✓✓	✓✓✓	✓✓✓	✓✓	✓
Sampling-related issues					
Does the mode of administration tend to produce a good response rate?	✓✓✓	✓✓	✓	✓	✓
Can the researcher control who responds (so that the person targeted is the person who answers)?	✓✓✓	✓✓✓	✓✓	✓✓	✓✓
Is the mode of administration accessible to all sample members?	✓✓✓	✓✓	✓✓✓	✓ (because respondents need online access)	✓ (because respondents need online access)
Questionnaire issues					
Is it suitable for long questionnaires?	✓✓✓	✓✓	✓✓	✓✓	✓✓
Is it suitable for complex questions?	✓✓✓	✓	✓✓	✓✓	✓✓
Is it suitable for open questions?	✓✓✓	✓✓	✓	✓✓	✓✓

Continued

Issues to consider	Mode of survey administration				
	Structured in-person interview	Structured telephone interview	Postal questionnaire	Email	Online
Is it suitable for filter questions?	✓✓✓ (especially if CAPI used)	✓✓✓ (especially if CATI used)	✓	✓	✓✓✓ (if it allows jumping)
Does it allow control over the order in which questions are answered?	✓✓✓	✓✓✓	✓	✓	✓✓
Is it suitable for sensitive questions?	✓	✓✓	✓✓✓	✓✓✓	✓✓✓
Is it less likely to result in non-response to some questions?	✓✓✓	✓✓✓	✓✓	✓✓	✓✓
Does it allow the use of visual aids?	✓✓✓	✓	✓✓✓	✓✓	✓✓✓
Answering context issues					
Does it give respondents the opportunity to consult others for information?	✓✓	✓	✓✓✓	✓✓✓	✓✓✓
Does it minimize the impact of interviewers' characteristics (gender, class, ethnicity) where these are not relevant to the research aims?	✓	✓✓	✓✓✓	✓✓✓	✓✓✓
Does it minimize the impact of the social desirability effect?	✓	✓✓	✓✓✓	✓✓✓	✓✓✓
Does it allow control over the intrusion of others in answering questions?	✓✓✓	✓✓	✓	✓	✓
Does it minimize the need for respondents to have certain skills to answer questions?	✓✓✓	✓✓✓	✓✓	✓ (because of the need to have online skills)	✓ (because of the need to have online skills)
Does it enable respondents to be probed?	✓✓✓	✓✓✓	✓	✓✓	✓
Does it reduce the likelihood of data entry errors by the researcher?	✓	✓	✓✓	✓	✓✓✓

Notes: Number of ticks indicates the strength of the mode of administration of a questionnaire in relation to each issue. A single tick implies that the mode of administering a questionnaire does not fare well in terms of the issue in question. Two ticks implies that it is acceptable, and three ticks implies that it does very well. This table has been influenced by the authors' own experiences and the following sources.

Sources: Blair et al. (2014); Dillman et al. (2014); Groves et al. (2009); Sheehan and Hoy (1999); **www.restore.ac.uk/orm/self-study.htm** (accessed 26 May 2019).

10.8 Diaries as a form of self-completion questionnaire

A useful alternative to more traditional forms of self-completion questionnaires is the **diary**. Although this method is relatively rarely used, it can be particularly useful if you are interested in precise estimates of different kinds of behaviour. The term 'diary' has three different meanings in social research (see Key concept 10.1). It is the first of the three meanings—what Heather Elliott (1997) calls the 'researcher-driven diary'—that is relevant here, especially in the context of its use in relation to **quantitative research**. When used in this way, the researcher-driven diary functions in a similar way to the self-completion questionnaire. It could also be seen as an alternative method of data collection in the sense that the research participants observe and record their

KEY CONCEPT 10.1
The diary in social research

There are three main ways in which we use the term 'diary' in the context of social research:

1. the diary as a method of data collection;
2. the diary as a document;
3. the diary as a log of the researcher's activities.

When they want to use a diary as a method of data collection, the researcher devises a structure for the diary and then asks a sample of people to complete according to their instructions, so that they record what they do more or less at the same time as they engage with the relevant activities. Heather Elliott (1997) refers to this use of the diary as a 'researcher-driven diary'. Researchers can use these diaries for collecting quantitative and qualitative data, and can also supplement them with a personal interview where the diarist is asked follow-up questions, for example about what they meant by certain remarks.

Diaries can take the form of structured time-use diaries, such as those used by Gershuny and Sullivan (2014) in Research in focus 10.3, or by Anderson (2016), who used historical time diary data to explore the evolution of the temporal variation of 'doing the laundry' as an example of an energy-demanding activity over the previous 20 years in the UK. Such diaries are generally administered as part of a survey covering activities over a specified time period.

A diary written spontaneously by a diarist can be used as a document and source for analysis. Diaries in this sense are often used by historians but can be used by social researchers too. We will discuss diaries as documents further in Chapter 22.

Researchers sometimes keep a record of what they do at different stages as a memory aid. For example, the well-known social anthropologist Malinowski (1967) kept an infamous log of his activities ('infamous' because it revealed his distaste for the people he studied and his inappropriate involvement with females). This kind of diary has similarities with the writing of **field notes** by **ethnographers**, which we discuss in Chapter 18.

own behaviour. In many ways it can be thought of as the equivalent of **structured observation** (see Chapter 12) in that the person who completes the diary observes their own behaviour.

Corti (1993) distinguishes between 'structured diaries' and 'free-text diaries', both of which may be used by quantitative researchers. The research on gender and time use in Research in focus 10.3 by Gershuny and Sullivan (2014) is an example of the use of structured diaries. In this case, the researchers used a specific kind of diary often referred to as a 'time-use diary', as it is designed so that diarists can record the amount of time they spend engaged in certain activities—such as food preparation, childcare, self-care, eating, and so on—more or less at the exact time they complete each activity (Alaszewski 2018). Estimates of the amount of time spent on different activities in diaries are often seen as more accurate than questionnaire estimates, because the events are less subject to memory lapses or the tendency to round up or down (Fisher and Layte 2004). This was proven in a study of 30 households in Italy by Giordano et al. (2018), who were assessing the reliability of diaries and questionnaires as a method of quantifying household food waste. Initially, researchers asked participating households about their food waste quantities in a questionnaire and through self-completion diaries. Half of the households who filled in their diaries properly then had their household waste audited. In the audited subsample of households, food estimates were 334 grams per week based on questionnaires, 818 grams per week based on diaries, and 1,058 grams per week based on waste sorting, suggesting that questionnaires produced the least accurate estimates. A further concern about time use diaries is that they are arguably more intrusive than answering a questionnaire, and could also cause changes in behaviour.

Crook and Light (2002) employed time-use diaries with a free-text format, asking university students to keep a one-week diary of the different kinds of study and learning activity they engaged in at different times of the day. The diaries were divided into 15-minute intervals, so that all students had to indicate for each interval 'details of their activity, location, and any study resources that might be in use' (Crook and Light 2002: 162). The various activities were grouped into three types: classes, private study, and social study (study with a peer). The researchers were able to highlight differences in patterns and amounts of study typically undertaken during a day.

Using free-text recording of behaviour involves the same kinds of challenges as those associated with coding answers in structured-interview open-ended questions, including the time-consuming nature of coding and the risk of introducing error through this process (we discuss these issues in Chapter 11). The free-text approach is less likely to be problematic when diarists are clearly instructed about what is required and researchers have a focused idea of the kinds of behaviour they are interested in. It would be much

RESEARCH IN FOCUS 10.3
Using a diary as a method of data collection

Gershuny and Sullivan (2014) report the findings of a diary study that allowed them to examine the contributions to housework of all household members in four common household types: single mothers; couples with no children; non-parent non-partnered adults; and couples with children. They conducted an analysis of the 2000/1 UK Time Use Survey, which is part of the Eurostat Harmonised European Time Use Survey (see Research in focus 10.4) and identified differences between men and women in terms of the allocation of tasks, and also the contribution of others to the domestic division of labour. The study also showed that 'children, and particularly girls, contribute not insignificant amounts to household work' (Gershuny and Sullivan 2014: 23) and contained the suggestion that when there is an elderly adult, a considerable housework burden may fall on girls aged 13–17.

Mullan and Chatzitheochari (2019) used the UK 2000/1 Time Use Survey and 2014/15 Time Use Survey to study the impact of mobile digital devices on family time. They used matched diary data of parents and children to explore changes in different types of family time, including 'alone-together' time and its association with recent technological change. This provided the researchers with nationally representative evidence on the way mobile device use features in family life. The results show that children and parents used mobile devices during all aspects of family time in 2015. There was a significant increase of alone-together time, when parents and children were at the same location, but did not report being co-present with each other.

RESEARCH IN FOCUS 10.4
Using time-use diaries

Time-use diaries offer great opportunities for cross-cultural studies. The Harmonised European Time Use Surveys (HETUS) project coordinates time-use diary studies among a wide range of European nations (see Fisher and Layte 2004). The data-collection process involves sample members being asked to complete two diaries—one for a weekday and one on a weekend. The fieldwork covers a 12-month period and the variety of activities that take place over this period. Diarists complete the instruments themselves and write in their own words what they were doing during each ten-minute interval during the day. The information is later coded into 'clusters' of activities. Diarists also supply information about whether anyone else was present and the location of the activity. Figure 10.3 shows part of a sample one-day diary from the project. For more information about the HETUS project, see **https://ec.europa.eu/eurostat/web/time-use-surveys** (accessed 23 July 2020).

FIGURE 10.3
Sample diary entry for the Harmonised European Time Use Surveys project

Time	What were you doing? *Record your main activity for each 10-minute period from 07.00 to 10.00!* Only one main activity on each line! Distinguish between travel and the activity that is the reason for travelling.	*What else were you doing?* *Record your most important parallel activity.*	*Did you use a computer, smart device, internet, online tool, or similar technology or device for doing this?* Yes	*Where were you?* *Record the location or the mode of transport* e.g. at home, at friends' home, at school, at workplace, in restaurant, in shop, on foot, on bicycle, in car, on motorbike, on bus, …	*Were you alone or together with somebody you know? Mark "yes" by crossing*					
					Alone (or with unknown persons)	**With other household members**				**Other persons that you know**
						Partner	**Parent**	**Children** (up to 17 years)	**Other household member**	
07:00-07:10	*Woke up the childeren*		☐	*At home*	☐	☐	☐	☒	☐	☐
07:10-07:20	*Had breakfast*	*Talked with my family*	☐	↓	☐	☒	☐	☒	☐	☐
07:20-07:30	–"–	–"–	☐		☐	☒	☐	☒	☐	☐
07:30-07:40	*Cleared the table*	*Listened to the radio*	☒		☐	☒	☐	☐	☐	☐
07:40-07:50	*Helped the children dress*	*Talked with my children*	☐	↓	☐	☐	☐	☒	☐	☐
07:50-08:00	*Went to the day care centre*	–"–	☐	*On foot*	☐	☐	☐	☒	☐	☐
08:00-08:10	*Went to work*	*Read the newspaper*	☒	*Bus*	☒	☐	☐	☐	☐	☐
08:10-08:20	–"–	–"–	☒	–"–	☒	☐	☐	☐	☐	☐
08:20-08:30	*Work*		☐	*Workplace*	☒	☐	☐	☐	☐	☐
08:30-08:40	↓	*Meeting with boss*	☐	↓	☐	☐	☐	☐	☐	☒
08:40-08:50		–"–	☐		☐	☐	☐	☐	☐	☒
08:50-09:00		–"–	☐		☐	☐	☐	☐	☐	☒
09:00-09:10			☒		☒	☐	☐	☐	☐	☐
09:10-09:20			☒		☒	☐	☐	☐	☐	☐
09:20-09:30			☒		☒	☐	☐	☐	☐	☐
09:30-09:40			☒		☒	☐	☐	☐	☐	☐
09:40-09:50			☒		☒	☐	☐	☐	☐	☐
09:50-10:00	↓		☒	↓	☒	☐	☐	☐	☐	☐

Use an arrow, citation marks or the like to mark an activity that takes longer than 10 minutes

Source: Adult example, Eurostat (2019), Harmonised European Time Use Surveys (HETUS) 2018 Guidelines, 2019 edition, page 95. Reprinted with permission.

more difficult to code free-text entries relating to general types of behaviour of the kind studied by Gershuny and Sullivan (2014; see Research in focus 10.3). Structured diaries are particularly useful for examining cross-cultural differences in time use (see Research in focus 10.4).

The diary studies that we have discussed suggest the potential advantages of this method of data collection, as follows.

- When researchers need fairly precise estimates of the frequency and/or amount of time spent in different forms of behaviour, diaries may provide more valid and reliable data than questionnaires.
- Diaries are likely to perform better than questionnaires or interviews in gathering information about the sequencing of different types of behaviour.

These advantages could suggest that structured observation would be just as useful, but structured observation is probably less appropriate for producing data on behaviour that is personally sensitive, such as sexual behaviour.

On the other hand, diary studies can suffer from the following problems.

- They tend to be more expensive than personal interviews (because of the costs associated with recruiting diarists and checking that diaries are being properly completed).
- Diary studies can suffer from a process of attrition, as people decide they have had enough of the task of completing a diary.
- Diarists may become less diligent over time about their record keeping.
- Memory recall problems may affect the accuracy of data if the diarist does not record details quickly.

Despite these problems, the data resulting from diaries are likely to be more accurate than the equivalent data from interviews or questionnaires. See Tips and skills 10.5 for guidance on preparing a diary for use in data collection.

10

TIPS AND SKILLS 10.5

Preparing a diary as a mode of data collection

Corti (1993) recommends that a researcher preparing a diary should follow these guidelines:

- provide explicit instructions for diarists;
- be clear about the time periods within which behaviour is to be recorded—that is, a day, twenty-four hours, a week;
- provide a completed section of a diary as an example;
- provide checklists of items, events, or behaviour to help jog people's memory—but the list should not be too off-putting in length or complexity;
- include fixed blocks of time or columns showing when the designated activities start and finish.

10.9 Experience and event sampling

Experience sampling, also known as **event sampling**, is a variation on the diary method (so another alternative to self-completion questionnaires) that captures participants' feelings and emotional state or their behaviour at the point when they are prompted to complete the research instrument. It may also require reporting on situational aspects such as place, context, activities, and subjective conditions (Naab et al. 2019). It is basically a structured diary technique to study subjective experiences in life (Verhagen et al. 2016). The method allows researchers to gather something close to real-time data about the occurrence and possibly the intensity of the issue being asked about. Participants are usually prompted to complete the predetermined format, either at particular points in time (for example, at the end of the working day or after eating breakfast) or when particular things happen (for example, after receiving a phone call or after catching up on social media). Participants might also be prompted to complete the research instrument when a device they carry around emits a sound.

An experience sampling study of 82 Facebook users in the USA was conducted by Kross et al. (2013) to explore how far Facebook use influences subjective wellbeing. Initially, participants completed questionnaires asking about their satisfaction with life, depression, self-esteem, and uses of Facebook. Then, over a 14-day period, participants were sent text messages five times per day at random times. Each text message included a link to an online questionnaire that included five questions concerning how the respondent was feeling; level of worry; feeling of loneliness; extent of use of Facebook since previous text message; and level of face-to-face interaction since last text message. The authors found that Facebook use was associated with lower levels of two subjective wellbeing variables: how people feel from one moment to another and their levels of satisfaction with their lives.

The main advantages of the experience sampling method compared with traditional ways of using a self-completion questionnaire is that the data tends to be more immediate (because participants reply while going about their lives), less general (replies are based on feelings at that point, rather than over a period of time), and less prone to memory distortions, though the data share most of the limitations associated with using diaries. Experience sampling tends to be used more often than diaries for collecting data relating to participants' feelings and moods, whereas both methods are used for collecting information about behaviour.

The prevalence of smartphones today can make experience sampling easier to use, since they mean that participants are continually contactable and can be asked to complete and submit a research instrument on the go. For example, Hofmans et al. (2014) used smartphones to gather experience sampling data from 50 employees in a study of task characteristics and work effort. The employees were prompted with a beep, five times a day for five working days, to complete a small number of questions about their task at that time and their feelings about it. Although participants did not always respond to beeps, meaning there was an element of non-response, smartphones provided a convenient way of accessing this information.

KEY POINTS

- Many of the recommendations relating to self-completion questionnaires apply equally or almost equally to structured interviews, as both are ways of administering surveys.
- Closed-ended questions tend to be used in survey research, rather than open-ended ones. Coding is a particular challenge when dealing with answers to open-ended questions.
- Structured interviews and self-completion questionnaires have their own advantages and disadvantages, but a particular problem with questionnaires sent by post and, even more so, email and online questionnaires is that they tend to produce a low response rate. However, there are steps that researchers can take to boost response rates for self-completion questionnaires.
- Presentation of closed-ended questions and the general formatting and layout are important considerations when preparing a self-completion questionnaire.
- The researcher-driven diary is a possible alternative to using questionnaires and interviews when the research questions are very specifically concerned with aspects of people's behaviour.
- Experience and event sampling operate in similar ways to a diary and are valuable ways of collecting data on people's behaviour or subjective experiences.

QUESTIONS FOR REVIEW

1. Are the self-completion questionnaire and the online questionnaire the same thing?
2. Why are online questionnaires the most popular form of surveys used in social research projects?
3. 'The low response rates frequently achieved in research with email, online, and postal questionnaires mean that the structured interview is normally a more suitable choice.' Discuss.
4. What steps can be taken to boost self-completion questionnaire response rates?
5. Why are self-completion questionnaires usually made up mainly of closed-ended questions?
6. Why might a vertical format for presenting closed-ended questions be preferable to a horizontal format?
7. What is the significance of the distinction between email and online surveys?
8. What are the main kinds of diary used to collect social science data?
9. Are there any circumstances when the diary approach might be preferable to using a self-completion questionnaire?
10. Why might a researcher choose to employ more than one form of self-completion questionnaire?

ONLINE RESOURCES

www.oup.com/he/srm6e

You can find our notes on the answers to these questions within this chapter's **online resources**, together with:

- *audio/video comments* on this topic from our 'Learn from experience' panellists;
- *self-test questions* for further knowledge-checking;
- a *flashcard glossary* to help you recall key terms; and
- a *Student Researcher's Toolkit* containing practical materials and resources to help you conduct your own research project.

CHAPTER 11

ASKING QUESTIONS

CHAPTER GUIDE

In this chapter we discuss the considerations involved in asking the questions that are used in structured interviews (Chapter 9) and questionnaires (Chapter 10), continuing the focus upon survey research that we began in Chapter 8. In this chapter we explore

- the issues involved in deciding whether or when to use open- or closed-ended questions;
- the different kinds of question that we can ask in structured interviews and questionnaires;
- vignette questions, in which respondents are presented with a scenario and are asked to reflect on the scenario;
- rules to bear in mind when designing questions;
- the importance of piloting questions;
- the possibility of using questions from previous survey research.

11.1 Introduction

The way we ask questions in social survey instruments, such as structured interviews or self-completion questionnaires, affects the quality and usefulness of the data we gain. In the previous two chapters we have seen that there is much more to the design and administration of research instruments than how questions are phrased, but this is still a crucial concern for researchers designing and conducting a survey. In this chapter we will look at considerations and rules you should bear in mind when devising survey questions, focusing on the design and phrasing of questions, the types of question you could use, and the importance of testing (piloting) your questions. We will also discuss the option of reusing questions from existing research. It is important to recognize that much of the guidance provided in this chapter, in particular associated with open-ended questions, is also applicable to qualitative approaches to asking questions.

11.2 Question formats: open- or closed-ended?

One of the most significant considerations for many researchers when designing a survey question is whether to use an open or closed format, a distinction we first introduced in Section 9.2. This issue is relevant to designing both structured interview research and self-completion questionnaire research.

With an open-ended question, respondents are asked a question and can reply however they want. With a closed-ended question, they are presented with a set of fixed alternatives from which to choose an appropriate answer. All the questions in Tips and skills 9.3 are of the closed kind. So too are the Likert scale items in Research in focus 7.3 and Tips and skills 10.3; these form a particular kind of closed-ended question. It is important to be aware of the advantages and limitations of these two types of question format.

Open-ended questions

While open-ended questions have both advantages and disadvantages in survey research, the problems associated with processing their answers mean that researchers tend to favour closed-ended questions. Open-ended questions are more extensively used in qualitative forms of interviewing, as we show in Chapter 19, where researchers find them to be a particularly valuable approach to collecting data. Let's consider the pros and cons of this format.

Advantages

Open-ended questions have the following advantages over closed-ended ones.

- Respondents can answer in their own terms, rather than being forced to answer in the same terms as the response options.
- Open-ended questions allow for unusual responses, including replies that the survey researcher may not have considered and listed as fixed-choice alternatives. This may actually lead to a more accurate picture of respondents' attitudes or behaviour.
- They do not suggest answers to respondents, so researchers can assess respondents' levels of knowledge and understanding of issues.
- They are useful for exploring new areas or ones where the researcher has limited knowledge, as they enable respondents to highlight areas that they think are significant, rather than the researcher having to undertake the potentially time-consuming process of identifying fixed-choice alternatives.
- They are useful for generating possible answers to closed-ended questions that can then be used at a later stage of the research process (a point we return to in Research in focus 11.2).
- They can help with the inductive process of theory construction, which is typically not possible with closed-ended questions. This is one of the reasons they are often used in qualitative research.

Disadvantages

Open-ended questions present certain problems for survey researchers, mainly relating to the amount of effort and time they require from respondents and researchers, as well as the greater potential for variability.

- Open-ended questions are more time-consuming for both researcher and respondent. When structured interviews include open-ended questions, interviewees are likely to talk for longer than they would in response to a comparable closed-ended question, and when they are used in a self-completion questionnaire the respondent is likely to need to write more than for a closed-ended equivalent. Researchers do not use open-ended questions heavily in self-completion questionnaires partly because of concerns that the effort involved will put off respondents, leading to low response rates.
- Another reason that open-ended questions involve more time and effort than closed-ended formats is that their answers need to be coded. (**Coding**, which is outlined in Key concept 11.1, is likely to follow an identical process to that used in **content analysis**, discussed in Chapter 13, although it can use processes associated with qualitative approaches such as **thematic analysis**, as covered in Chapter 23.) In this time-consuming process, often known as post-coding, the researcher has to read through each answer, identify themes that can be used to form the basis for codes, code the data, and enter it into a software program. Post-coding is different from pre-coding, where the researcher designs a coding frame before they administer their survey instrument and often includes the pre-codes in the questionnaire, as shown in Tips and skills 11.1.
- In addition to being time-consuming, post-coding can also be unreliable, because it introduces the possibility of variability in the coding of answers and therefore of measurement error (and lack of **validity**). This is a form of data-processing error (discussed in Chapter 8: see Figure 8.9). Research in focus 11.1 describes the coding of open-ended questions, and Key concept 11.1 provides some guidance as to how to limit variability when coding.
- In research based on structured interviews, there is also the possibility of variability in how interviewers record answers, if they are taking written notes. However, many researchers address this issue by recording and **transcribing** the interviews. This can be done on a dedicated audio-recording device (see Chapter 19), but because almost all laptops or tablets have the built-in capability for digital recording, there is no real need for additional equipment (Singer and Couper 2017).

11

KEY CONCEPT 11.1
What is coding?

Coding is a key part of much **quantitative research**, given that many forms of data exist in an unstructured form, including answers to open-ended questions in interviews and questionnaires (see Chapters 9 and 10); newspaper articles (see Chapter 13); and behaviour in a school classroom (see Chapter 12). These types of data need to be coded in order to be quantified and analysed. This involves two main stages: categorizing the data (Research in focus 11.1 provides some examples of this process) and then assigning numbers to the categories created (effectively, tags that allow the material to be processed quantitatively).

When coding, we need to observe three basic principles (Bryman and Cramer 2011).

1. The categories that we generate must not overlap. If they do, we cannot apply the numbers that we assign to them to distinct categories. For example, imagine that you were interested in average daily levels of fruit and vegetable consumption, and you devised coding in which 1 means 1–2 fruits and vegetables per day, 2 means 3–4 fruits and vegetables, 3 means 5–6 fruits and vegetables, and 4 means 6 or more fruits and vegetables. This would be problematic, as someone who consumed, on average, 6 fruits and vegetables per day could be grouped in code 3 or 4.
2. The list of categories must be complete and cover all possibilities. If it is not, some material will not be able to be coded. This is why codes for the answers to open-ended questions sometimes include a **category** of 'other'.
3. There should be clear rules about how codes should be applied, to ensure that those doing the coding are consistent over time in how they assign the categories and, if more than one person is coding, are consistent with each other. Survey researchers may use a **coding frame** (often called a **coding manual** in content

analysis and **structured observation**) to describe the lists of codes that should be applied to unstructured data and the rules for their application.

Quantitative data are also sometimes *recoded*. For example, if we have data on the exact age of each person in a **sample**, we may want to group people into age bands (see Chapter 15).

Coding also occurs in qualitative research, although it is very different from that used in quantitative research: see Chapters 22 and 23.

RESEARCH IN FOCUS 11.1
Coding an open-ended question

Livingstone et al. (2014) describe a survey that they conducted on children's perceptions of internet risk. The survey was carried out using face-to-face interviews of over 25,000 European children aged 9 to 16 who used the internet. The schedule consisted of mainly closed-ended questions, but one question was open: 'What things on the internet would bother people of your age?'

Respondents wrote answers to this question on a piece of paper and placed it into an envelope that was then sealed. This question was asked before the other questions that focused on risk, so that the children's replies to the open-ended question were not affected by other questions that had been asked. Just over one-third of the sample identified one or more risks. Livingstone et al. developed a coding scheme based on a pilot analysis of the original comments, and the coding was carried out by native speakers. They coded up to three risks for each child, and each response was coded by two raters who coded independently of each other. They coded three main areas.

- The type of risk, of which three types were identified and coded: content risk (e.g. pornographic content); conduct risk from other young people (e.g. insults); and contact risk from adults (e.g. inappropriate contact from adults). Other risks, such as viruses and pop-ups, were also coded.
- The type of platform on which the risk might occur (e.g. email or a social media platform).
- Emotions (e.g. fear, annoyance, disgust).

Another example of coding an open-ended question can be found in Akerlof et al. (2013), whose survey included a closed-ended question that asked respondents whether they personally have experienced global warming. Those who believed they had experienced it were then asked an open-ended question: 'In what ways have you personally experienced global warming?' (Akerlof et al. 2013: 83–4). The authors then used a software program to search for words and phrases that recurred. They developed these into a **coding schedule** of 28 **variables** that was then used by three raters to code 30 answers as a pilot exercise.

Closed-ended questions

Having reflected on the advantages and disadvantages of open-ended questions, you can probably anticipate some of the pros and cons of using a closed-ended format. We consider them here.

Advantages

Closed-ended questions offer the following advantages to researchers.

- It is easy to process answers, as pre-codes are placed to the side of the fixed-choice answers and are either automatically entered into a software program (in the case of **online surveys**), or easily entered into one (with other forms of survey). See Tips and skills 11.1 for an example, which is based on Tips and skills 10.2.
- It is easier to compare answers. With post-coding for open-ended questions, it is always difficult to know

TIPS AND SKILLS 11.1

Processing a closed-ended question

This closed-ended question in vertical format was introduced in Tips and skills 10.2. It is useful because it highlights both how to set out a closed-ended question and how to follow the basic principles of coding set out in Key concept 11.1. In this example, the pre-codes are next to the fixed-choice answers. This makes the process of analysing the data straightforward.

What do you think of the Prime Minister's performance in his job since he took office?

(Please tick the appropriate response)

Very good	____	5
Good	✓	④
Fair	____	3
Poor	____	2
Very poor	____	1

how far respondents' answers that we have given a certain code are genuinely comparable.

- The fixed-answer options may clarify the meaning of a question for respondents.
- These questions are quicker and easier for interviewers and respondents to complete.
- They reduce the possibility of variability in the recording of answers (although there is still the potential problem that interviewers may have to *interpret* what is said to them in order to assign answers to a category).

Disadvantages

Closed-ended questions also have some disadvantages.

- There is a loss of spontaneity in respondents' answers. They may have an interesting response to a question that is not covered by the fixed answers provided. Solutions to this possible problem might include using an open-ended question, while designing the questions, to generate the categories (see Research in focus 11.2) and including a response category of 'Other' and allowing respondents to explain what they mean by using this category.
- It can be difficult to avoid overlapping fixed responses. It is important that the fixed-choice answers do not overlap because otherwise respondents will be unclear which option to choose and will select one at random or tick both answers. If a respondent selects more than one answer when only one is required, the researcher has to treat the respondent's answer as **missing data**, because they do not know which of the selected answers is the true response. This is a common mistake when using age bands. For example, if a respondent were 40 years old, would they select '30–40' or '40–50' if these were the fixed choices provided? It is important to avoid such overlap—in this example, using the categories '30–39' and '40–49' would avoid such issues.
- It is difficult to make fixed-choice answers exhaustive. Ideally the options should cater for all possible answers, but in practice this could result in excessively long lists of answer options. Again, a category of 'Other' may be helpful in allowing for a wide range of answers.
- There may be variation among respondents in how they interpret fixed-choice answers (for example, they may have different understandings of key terms that are used), potentially affecting validity.
- Closed-ended questions may irritate respondents if they are unable to find a category that they feel applies to them.
- Including a large number of closed-ended questions in an interview may make it difficult to establish rapport, because the exchange will have a more impersonal feel and the respondent and interviewer are less likely to engage with each other in a conversation (although remember that—as we saw in Section 9.5—there is debate about the role of rapport in structured interviewing).

RESEARCH IN FOCUS 11.2

A comparison of results for a closed-ended and an open-ended question

Schuman and Presser (1981) conducted an **experiment**, now seen as a classic study, to determine how far responses to closed-ended questions can be improved by initially asking the questions in an open-ended format and then developing categories of reply from respondents' answers. They asked a question about what people look for in work, using both an open and closed format, and found considerable disparities between the two sets of answers: 60 per cent of the categories revealed by the open-format categories could not be covered by the closed-format answers. They then revised the closed categories to reflect the answers they had received from people's open-ended answers and re-administered both the open-ended question and the revised closed-ended question to two large samples. The question and the answers they received are set out below.

> This next question is on the subject of work. People look for different things in a job. Which one of the following five things do you most prefer in a job? [closed-ended question]. What would you most prefer in a job? [open-ended question].

The revised survey showed a much higher proportion of the sample whose answers to the open-ended question corresponded to the closed-ended one. Schuman and Presser argue that the new closed-ended question was superior to its predecessor and to the open-ended question. It is still disconcerting that only 58 per cent of responses to the open-ended question could be subsumed under the same categories as those answering the closed one, and there were considerable differences with the distributions (for example, twice as many respondents answer in terms of a feeling of accomplishment with the closed format than with the open one). Overall, though, this experiment demonstrates the benefits of generating forced-choice answers from open-ended questions. This is a technique that you may want to consider in your own research projects.

Closed-ended format		Open-ended format	
Answer	%	Answer involving ...	%
Work that pays well	13.2	Pay	16.7
Work that gives a feeling of accomplishment	31.0	Feeling of accomplishment	14.5
Work where there is not too much supervision and you make most decisions yourself	11.7	Control of work	4.6
Work that is pleasant and people are nice to work with	19.8	Pleasant work	14.5
Work that is steady + little chance of being laid off	20.3	Security	7.6
	96% of sample		57.9% of sample
Other/DK/NA	4.0	Opportunity for promotion	1.0
		Short hours/lots of free time	1.6
		Working conditions	3.1
		Benefits	2.3
		Satisfaction/liking a job	15.6
		Other responses	18.3
	4.0% of sample		41.9% of sample

11

11.3 Types of questions

When you are using a structured interview or a self-completion questionnaire, you will probably be asking several different types of question. Some of the most common types of question are these:

- personal factual questions
- factual questions about others
- informant factual questions
- questions about attitudes
- questions about beliefs
- questions about normative standards and values
- questions about knowledge

We will consider each in turn.

Personal factual questions

These ask respondents to provide *personal information*—such as age, education, occupation, marital status, income, and so on—or ask about *behaviour*. These factual questions may rely on the respondents' memories, such as when asking how often they attend a religious gathering, how often they visit the cinema, or when they last ate out in a restaurant. Musa et al. (2015) undertook a survey with participants aged 65 or older in community dwellings that included personal factual questions regarding advance care planning (ACP). This is a process of assessment and dialogue with an individual to establish their needs and goals of care and to determine whether they want to express and document their preferences for future care and treatment, in case they later lose capacity to express such preferences. In total, participants completed 1,823 questionnaires, and the results showed that 17 per cent of respondents had prepared an ACP document.

Factual questions about others

These questions ask respondents for personal information about others, sometimes in combination with information about the respondent. For example, if you were asking about household income, you would want respondents to consider their own incomes in conjunction with those of their partners. Rosenfeld (2017) conducted longitudinal survey research on whether couples meeting online is a predictor of couple breakup. In doing so they asked respondents questions about themselves and how they met their partners, but also asked questions about their partners, such as the partner's gender, children, religion, region, and education.

Informant factual questions

Sometimes, we place people who complete surveys in the position of informants rather than of respondents providing information about themselves. For example, we might ask people about the size of the firm they work at, who owns it, and whether it makes use of certain technologies. It is also common for researchers to use informant factual questions that relate to behaviour. For example, in Research in focus 7.5, the survey asked respondents about the behaviour of their supervisor, such as whether the supervisor 'puts me down in front of others'.

Questions about attitudes

Social scientists often include questions about attitudes in survey research, and Likert scales (see Key concept 7.2) are a popular tool for this question type. Miske et al. (2019) looked at attitudes towards capital punishment in the USA using a survey made up of Likert scales. Among their 184 participants, they found that attitudes towards capital punishment were associated with more than just retributive motives and included factors such as deterrence. As Voas (2014) points out, attitudes, meaning 'an everyday judgement, a normative view of a specific matter' (2014: 2.1), are often confused with beliefs and values—the next question types we consider. We will reflect on why this can be problematic in a moment.

Questions about beliefs

These questions ask respondents about their beliefs, such as their religious and political beliefs or beliefs about particular events, for example climate change protests. In a survey about crime, you could ask respondents whether they believe that the incidence of certain crimes is increasing. Bansak et al. (2016) surveyed 18,000 eligible voters in 15 European countries to examine their beliefs about which types of asylum-seekers they were willing to accept in their countries. The researchers asked respondents to evaluate profiles of asylum-seekers that randomly varied on nine attributes. They found that voters believed applicants who will contribute to the recipient country's economy, who have suffered severe physical or mental distress as opposed to economic hardship, and who are Christian rather than Muslim, should receive greatest public support.

Questions about normative standards and values

Respondents may be asked to indicate what principles of behaviour influence them or they particularly value. This may relate to behaviour in a particular environment, such as the language a parent should use if they are assisting in a school (for example, when reading with children). Questions designed to show such norms of behaviour are likely to have considerable overlap with questions about attitudes and beliefs, given that norms and values can be construed as having elements of both.

Questions about knowledge

Questions can sometimes be used to 'test' respondents' knowledge in an area, for example on issues such as levels of environmental pollution, benefit levels, pay inequalities, or, in the case of Research in focus 11.3, financial literacy.

Choosing the right types of question

Most structured interviews and self-completion questionnaires comprise more than one, and often several, of the types of question listed above. It is important to bear in mind the distinction between the different types of question, for the following reasons.

- The distinctions force you to clarify in your own mind what you are asking about: for example, are you interested in asking just about factual personal information on the respondent alone, or factual questions about others too?
- It will help you to avoid asking questions in an inappropriate format. For example, a Likert scale is not a good choice if you are asking factual questions about behaviour.
- When building **scales** such as a Likert scale, do not mix different types of question. As we have noted, 'attitudes' and 'beliefs' sound similar, and you may be tempted to use the same format for mixing questions about them, but it is best to do this using separate scales for attitudes and beliefs. Mixing them means that the questions cannot really be measuring the same thing, and **measurement validity** will be threatened.

11

RESEARCH IN FOCUS 11.3
Using questions about knowledge

Anderson et al. (2017) conducted a study where they measured financial literacy among a sample of 5,814 LinkedIn members in the USA. One part of the survey involved respondents answering five questions associated with financial literacy that have been used in previous studies, including in the 2009 and 2012 US National Financial Capability Study (NFCS). These questions were designed to test the respondents' knowledge, for example:

1. *Compounding*. Suppose you had $100 in a savings account and the interest rate was 2% per year. After 5 years, how much do you think you would have in the account if you left the money to grow? Please select one.
   - More than $102
   - Exactly $102
   - Less than $102
   - Don't know
   - Prefer not to say

Anderson et al. asked additional questions in order to gauge respondents' perceptions of their own financial literacy. They were able to identify that, on average, financial literacy was low, especially given the demographics of the sample: fewer than two-thirds of chief financial officers, chief executive officers, and chief operating officers completed the test correctly.

11.4 Vignette questions

One way of asking mainly closed-ended questions to examine people's normative standards is to use the **vignette** technique. This technique, which researchers often use in experiments, involves presenting respondents with one or more scenarios and then asking them how they would respond in those circumstances. Research in focus 11.4 describes a vignette that was used in a classic study of family obligations.

RESEARCH IN FOCUS 11.4
Using a vignette

Finch (1987) used the vignette technique in her study of family obligations in Britain. She wanted to explore respondents' normative judgements about how family members should respond to relatives who are in need, and *who* they think should do the responding. Below are some extracts from one of the vignettes she used.

The researcher gave respondents the following vignette as a scenario:

> Jim and Margaret Robinson are a married couple in their early forties. Jim's parents, who live several hundred miles away, have had a serious car accident and they need long-term daily care and help. Jim is their only son. He and his wife both work for the Electricity Board and they could both get transfers so they could work near his parents.

The researcher then gave respondents a show card with these fixed-choice responses:

Card E

(a) From the card, what should Jim and Margaret do?

Move to live near Jim's parents

Have Jim's parents move to live with them

Give Jim's parents money to help them pay for daily care

Let Jim's parents make their own arrangements

Do something else (SPECIFY)

Don't know

(b) In fact, Jim and Margaret are prepared to move and live near Jim's parents, but teachers at their children's school say that moving might have a bad effect on their children's education. Both children will soon be taking O-levels [predecessors to the UK's current GCSE examinations, usually taken by 14- to 16-year-olds].

What should Jim and Margaret do? Should they move or should they stay?

Move

Stay

(c) Why do you think they should move/stay?

Probe fully verbatim

(d) Jim and Margaret do decide to go and live near Jim's parents. A year later Jim's mother dies and his father's condition gets worse so that he needs full-time care.

Should Jim or Margaret give up their jobs to take care of Jim's father? IF YES: Who should give up their job, Jim or Margaret?

Yes, Jim should give up his job

11

Yes, Margaret should give up her job

No, neither should give up their jobs

Don't know/Depends

(Finch 1987: 108)

This vignette has been designed to tease out respondents' norms in terms of family obligations in respect of several factors: the nature of the care (whether long- or short-term and whether it should entail direct involvement or just the provision of resources); the significance of geographical proximity; the dilemma of paid work and care; and the gender component of who should give up a job if the respondent saw that as the appropriate course of action. The questions present a gradual increase in the specificity of the situation facing Jim and Margaret and of the views of the respondent.

Many aspects of the issues being tapped by the series of questions shown in Research in focus 11.4 could also be accessed through attitude items, such as this:

When a working couple decides that one of them should care for parents, the wife should be the one to give up her job.

Strongly agree	____
Agree	____
Undecided	____
Disagree	____
Strongly disagree	____

However, the advantage of the vignette over an attitude question is that it anchors the choice in a realistic situation, requiring respondents to reflect on their responses. Finch (1987) also argues that, when the subject matter is a sensitive area (in this case, dealing with family relationships), there is the possibility that respondents may see the questions as threatening and they may feel that they are being judged on their replies. Finch argues that because vignette questions are about other (imaginary) people there is some distance between the questioning and the respondent, providing a less threatening context, even if respondents are still aware that their replies will at least in part be seen as reflecting on them.

Tuinman et al. (2018) conducted three experimental vignette studies in the Netherlands, whereby members of a dating website (324, in experiment 1) and college students (138 and 131, experiments 2 and 3 respectively) were randomly provided with a vignette of a person with or without a history of cancer (experiment 1 and 2), or a cancer survivor beyond or during active follow-up (experiment 3). Respondents were then asked to rate their interest in dating this fictitious person, and indicate their preferences about when they would want this disclosure to be made. Tuinman et al. were careful to embed the cancer information in a subtle way into the vignettes (rather than directly asking people about their interest in dating cancer survivors).

When designing questions using the vignette technique it is important to make sure that the scenarios are believable, so researchers must put considerable effort into constructing credible situations. Finch (1987) points to some further considerations in relation to this style of questioning, such as the fact that we don't know how far respondents are making assumptions about the characters in the scenario (for example their ethnicity) and what the significance of those assumptions might be for the validity and comparability of respondent's replies. It is also difficult to know how far people's answers reflect their own normative views or how they themselves would act when confronted with the kinds of choices revealed in the scenarios. Despite these reservations, the vignette technique is certainly worth considering when the research focus is an area that lends itself to this style of questioning.

11.5 Rules for designing questions

Over the years, numerous rules have been devised for 'dos' and 'don'ts' of asking questions in social science research. Despite the quantity of advice available, this aspect of research is one of the most common areas for making mistakes. There are three simple general principles we recommend thinking about as a starting point: bearing your research questions in mind at all times; thinking about exactly what you want to know; and thinking about how *you* would answer each question. Beyond those principles, the more specific rules we set out in this section will help you to avoid pitfalls.

General principles

Always bear in mind your research questions

When developing your self-completion questionnaire or structured interview schedule you should always be focused on trying to gain answers to your research questions. This principle has at least two implications. First, it means it is essential that you ask questions that relate to your research questions. Second, it means that there is little point in asking questions that do *not* relate to your research questions: aside from the fact that this will take up your time in coding and analysing non-essential information, your respondents will also waste time answering questions that are of little value to your research. It is also worth noting that the respondent may become suspicious if the questions you are asking do not appear to have a direct link to the research aims that you have described to them.

You also need to think about what forms of analysis you will use to address your research questions and what measurement levels you might need to use: we will discuss these issues further in Chapter 15.

What do you want to know?

It may sound obvious, but it's crucial that you decide exactly what it is you want to know and make sure your questions address this. Consider this question:

Do you have a car?

This question is ambiguous, as it is unclear what information the question is seeking to 'tap' (make use of). Is it car ownership? If so, the question is inadequate, largely because of the ambiguity of the word 'have'. The question could refer to personally owning a car; or having access to a car in a household; or 'having' a company car or a car for business use. So an answer of 'Yes' may or may not indicate car ownership. If you want to know whether your respondent owns a car, you should ask them directly about this. As another example, there is nothing wrong with the question:

How many children do you have?

However, if what you are trying to address is the standard of living of a person or household, you would want to know how many are living at home, so you might use a further question like 'How many of your children live at home with you?'

How would *you* answer it?

It is important to put yourself in the position of the respondent, asking yourself the question and trying to work out how *you* would reply. By doing this you should be able to identify ambiguity, such as that in the 'Do you have a car?' question, and gauge how effectively a question will tap into the relevant issue. Let's say that there is a follow-up question to the previous one:

Have you driven the car this week?

If you put yourself in the role of a respondent, it will be obvious to you that the phrase 'this week' is vague. Does it mean the last seven days, or does it mean the week in which the questioning takes place? This will, of course, be affected by such things as whether the question is being asked on a Monday or a Friday. This issue often arises partly because the person devising the question has not decided what the question is about, which shows us the importance of the previous principle: 'What do you want to know?' When respondents struggle to understand questions this can have several negative consequences for surveys (see Robinson and Leonard 2019), including respondents failing to complete the questionnaire or providing more 'nonsubstantive responses' (such as 'don't know') and middle alternative responses (such as 'neither agree nor disagree'), according to research by Lenzner (2012).

Taking account of these general principles, and the following dos and don'ts about asking questions, should help you to avoid the more obvious pitfalls.

DOs when designing questions

Make sure the respondent has the necessary knowledge

There is not much point asking respondents lots of questions about matters on which they have no knowledge. There is a limit to the data you could gain about the quality of public transport from respondents who never use it. While it might be useful to find out about why they don't use such services, the respondents wouldn't be able to answer questions about the comfort of the seats, conduct of the driver, etc. in the same way as people who regularly use public transport.

Make sure there is symmetry between a closed-ended question and its answers

When developing question, you need to make sure that their fixed-choice answers align with and accurately represent the questions. Thinking deeply 11.1 provides an example where the question and answers do not match. It is important to make sure the possible answers represent the potential responses to the question so that they address your questions appropriately.

Make sure the answers for a closed-ended question are balanced

A fairly common error when asking closed-ended questions is to provide answers that are not balanced. For example, imagine that a respondent is given this series of options:

Excellent ____

Good ____

Acceptable ____

Poor ____

In this case, the response choices are balanced towards a favourable response. Excellent and Good are both positive; Acceptable is a neutral or middle position; and Poor is a negative response, so the answers are loaded in favour of a positive rather than a negative reply. Another negative response choice (perhaps Very poor) is needed here.

Consider whether to use middle alternatives in attitude scales

One controversial aspect of asking closed questions is whether to offer a middle option in attitude rating scales and similar measuring devices, such as 'neither agree nor disagree', 'neither approve nor disapprove', and 'neither satisfied nor dissatisfied'. It is sometimes argued that

THINKING DEEPLY 11.1

Matching question and answers in closed-ended (and double-barrelled) questions

You have probably come across bad examples of survey questions in everyday life. Alan found a series of examples in a feedback questionnaire inserted into a novel by its publisher. The questionnaire included a series of Likert-style **items** regarding the book's quality and asked the respondents to indicate whether the attribute being asked about was: poor; acceptable; average; good; or excellent. However, in each case, the items were presented as questions, for example:

Was the writing elegant, seamless, imaginative?

The problem here is that an answer to this question would be 'Yes' or 'No'. At most, we might have gradations of Yes and No, such as: definitely; to a large extent; to some extent; not at all. 'Poor' or 'excellent' cannot be answers to this question. The questions should have been presented as statements, like this:

Please indicate the quality of the book in terms of each of the following criteria.

The elegance of the writing:

Poor ____

Acceptable ____

Average ____

Good ____

Excellent ____

Of course, we have changed the sense slightly here because a further problem with the question is that it is double-barrelled. In fact, it is 'treble-barrelled', because it is actually asking about *three* attributes of the writing in one question. This is problematic because the reader may have very different views about the three qualities—the writing may have been very imaginative but not, in their view, elegant.

The important point here is to think carefully about the connection between the question and the fixed-choice answers you provide, because a disjunction between the two could negatively affect the data you gain.

middle alternatives result in greater levels of **satisficing**, in that they give respondents an option to not give significant thought or attention to their answer (Alwin et al. 2018). On the other hand, *not* supplying a middle alternative may mean that some respondents have to select a response that is not accurate, for example selecting 'agree' when in fact they do not hold such an opinion. Not including a middle alternative could also result in greater **item non-response** and missing data (Revilla et al. 2014). Sudman and Bradburn (1982) suggested that including a middle alternative does not affect the ratio of agreement to disagreement compared to a question that excludes it. However, Sturgis et al. (2014b) were in favour of middle alternatives, finding that for the vast majority of respondents, selecting a middle alternative was actually to do with not having an opinion on the issue. We suggest it is probably best to include middle alternatives unless there is a very good reason for not including them.

There is a similar debate about offering 'don't know' alternatives (see Research in focus 11.5). A series of experiments conducted in the USA found that questions that appear later in a questionnaire are more likely to result in respondents selecting 'don't know' (Krosnick et al. 2002), implying that as respondents become increasingly tired or bored as the questioning proceeds, they are prone to satisfice. This indicates that you should carefully consider the 'don't know' option in designing your survey. In fact, this may be something you want to **pilot** in relation to your survey (see Section 11.6).

It may actually be possible to reduce the number of 'don't know' responses. De Leeuw and Hox (2015) refer to a study suggesting that gentle probes administered either in telephone interviews or in online questionnaires can reduce the number of 'don't know' answers, because when respondents elaborate on their reasons for choosing 'don't know' they provide a more substantive answer.

DON'Ts when designing questions

Avoid using ambiguous terms in questions

Avoid terms such as 'often' and 'regularly' as measures of frequency, because they are very ambiguous and respondents will operate with different frames of reference when employing them. (For example, one person may consider going to the gym 'often' to be going twice a week; another person may consider 'often' to be six days a week.) Sometimes you will not be able to avoid using them, but when there is an alternative that allows actual frequency to be measured, this is nearly always preferable. So, a question like this one suffers from the problem that, with the exception of 'not at all', the terms in the response categories are ambiguous:

How often do you usually visit the cinema?

Very often ____
Quite often ____
Not very often ____
Not at all ____

Instead, you should try to ask about actual frequency, such as:

How frequently do you usually visit the cinema?

(Please tick whichever category comes closest to the number of times you visit the cinema)

More than once a week ____
Once a week ____
2 or 3 times a month ____
Once a month ____
A few times a year ____
Once a year ____
Less than once a year ____

RESEARCH IN FOCUS 11.5

Providing 'don't know' options

A concern when measuring political knowledge is that respondents who say they don't know the answer to a survey question may actually have partial knowledge about the topic, and greater knowledge than respondents who answer incorrectly, but also less knowledge than those who answer correctly. Jessee (2017) tested this idea using survey questions and found that, contrary to previous claims that 'don't know' responses to political knowledge questions conceal a fair amount of hidden knowledge, these responses actually reflect less knowledge than both correct responses and also incorrect answers. They also showed that the meaning of 'don't know' responses did not vary strongly by respondent personality type.

Alternatively, you could simply ask respondents about the number of times they have visited the cinema in the previous four weeks.

Other ambiguous words include 'family', because people will have different ideas of who makes up their family. Some common words, such as 'dinner', mean different things to different people: for some, dinner is a midday snack, whereas for others it is a substantial evening meal. In such cases, you will need to define what you mean by the terms you use.

Avoid using long questions

It is generally thought that long questions are undesirable. In structured interviewing the interviewee can lose the thread of the question, and in self-completion questionnaires respondents may be tempted to skip long questions or not pay them close attention. However, Sudman and Bradburn (1982) have suggested that this advice applies better to attitude questions than to ones that ask about behaviour, arguing that when the focus is on behaviour, longer questions have some advantages in interviews—for example, they are more likely to prompt memory recall because of the time respondents have to take to complete the question. However, in general it is a good idea to keep questions short.

Avoid using double-barrelled questions

'Double-barrelled' questions ask about two things within one question, leaving respondents unsure about how to respond. Consider the question:

> How satisfied are you with pay and conditions in your job?

The problem here is obvious: the respondent may be satisfied with pay but not with conditions, or vice versa. Not only will the respondent be unclear about how to reply, but any answer they give is unlikely to be a good reflection of their level of satisfaction with both pay *and* conditions. Similarly:

> How frequently does your child help with cooking and cleaning?

suffers from the same problem. A child may be very helpful when it comes to cooking but totally uninvolved in cleaning, so any answer about how frequently they help with both activities will be ambiguous and create uncertainty for respondents and researchers.

The same rule applies to fixed-choice answers. In the study described in Research in focus 11.2, one of Schuman and Presser's (1981) answers (in response to what respondents look for in work) is:

> Work that is pleasant and people are nice to work with.

While there is likely to be a symmetry between the two ideas in this answer—pleasant work and nice people—there is not *necessarily* a correspondence between them. Pleasant work may be important for someone, but they may be relatively indifferent to how pleasant their co-workers are. You can see another example of a double-barrelled question in Thinking deeply 11.1.

Avoid using very general questions

It is easy to ask a very general question when in fact you want a response to a specific issue. The problem with very general questions is that they lack a frame of reference. Consider, for example:

> How satisfied are you with your job?

This question lacks specificity. Does it refer to pay, conditions, the nature of the work, or all of these? Respondents are likely to vary in their responses if it is possible to interpret the question in so many different ways.

Avoid using leading questions

Leading or loaded questions are ones that seem to lead the respondent in a particular direction. Questions such as 'Do you agree with the view that ... ?' fall into this class of question. This is because they suggest a particular reply to respondents. The respondents can, of course, rebut any implied answer, but they might feel pushed in a certain direction and this is clearly undesirable. We can see this in the following question:

> Would you agree to cutting taxes further even though welfare provision for the neediest sections of the population might be reduced?

This makes it difficult for some people to answer in terms of fiscal probability, bringing in an additional element associated with the neediest in society. In this instance, the mention of this group may make people feel as though they can't respond positively to the question even if they agree with the principle of cutting taxes, because they are concerned about being judged in relation to the second part of the question.

Avoid asking two questions in one

We have already discussed the need to avoid double-barrelled questions, where it is clear that the question has more than one element, but it is also important to avoid questions that are asking more than one question by implication. For example:

> Which political party did you vote for at the last general election?

The respondent may not have voted at the last election, so this question is effectively asking them another question as well. It would be better to ask two separate questions:

Did you vote at the last general election?

Yes ____

No ____

If Yes, which political party did you vote for?

Avoid using questions that include negatives

If you use questions containing 'not' or similar formulations, it is easy for respondents to miss this word out. If this occurs, they are likely to answer the question in the opposite way from the one you intended. Occasionally it is impossible to avoid negatives, but you should avoid as far as possible a question like the following:

Do you agree with the view that students should not have to take out loans to finance higher education?

11

It would be easy to misread this question as asking whether students *should* take out loans to finance higher education. Asking the question in a positive format (the question above but with the word 'not' removed) makes it much easier to respond. Questions with double negatives should be totally avoided, because knowing how to respond to them is difficult. An example of this kind of question might be:

Would you rather not use non-perishable foods?

It is quite difficult to establish what an answer of 'Yes' or 'No' would actually mean in response to this question.

One occasion when it might be difficult to avoid using questions with negatives is when designing Likert items, as you may want to identify respondents who exhibit **response sets** by reversing the direction of your question asking. As we explained in Chapter 9, this enables you to weed out those respondents who appear to be replying within the framework of an acquiescence response set.

Avoid using technical terms

We strongly recommend that you use simple, plain language and avoid jargon. Do not ask a question like this:

Do you sometimes feel alienated from work?

The problem here is that many respondents will not know what is meant by 'alienated', and even if they do understand it, they are likely to have different views of its meaning. Consider the following question:

The influence of the TUC on national politics has declined in recent years.

Strongly agree ____

Agree ____

Undecided ____

Disagree ____

Strongly disagree ____

Here, the problem is the use of the acronym TUC (the Trades Union Congress in the UK). You should avoid acronyms where possible because some people may not know what they stand for.

Avoid stretching respondents' memories too far

Do not rely too much on people's memories, as this can result in inaccurate results. For example, while it may be nice to have accurate replies to a question about the number of times respondents have visited the cinema in the previous 12 months, it is very unlikely that most people will remember events accurately over such a long period of time (except, perhaps, for those who have not gone at all or only once or twice in the previous 12 months). It may be better to use a time frame of just one month.

Avoid using 'tick all that apply' closed-ended questions

When asking a question that allows the respondent to select more than one answer sometimes researchers give an instruction that says something like 'Please tick all that apply'. There is some evidence to suggest that using fixed-choice answers instead, for example 'Yes' or 'No', tends to lead to fuller responses. An example might be a question asking which forms of exercise the respondent has engaged in during the previous six months. The question might look something like this:

Which of the following forms of exercise have you engaged in during the last six months?
(Please tick *all* that apply)

Going to a gym ☐

Sport ☐

Cycling on the road ☐

Jogging ☐

Long walks ☐

Other (please specify) ☐

An alternative way of asking a question like this is to use a conventional forced-choice format, such as:

Have you engaged in the following forms of exercise during the last six months?

	Yes	No
Going to a gym	☐	☐
Sport	☐	☐
Cycling on the road	☐	☐
Jogging	☐	☐
Long walks	☐	☐
Other (please specify)	☐	☐

Many people would assume that these two ways of asking questions are equivalent, but Smyth et al. (2006) have shown that the forced-choice format (the second example) results in more options being selected and, as a result, Dillman et al. (2014) advocate the use of the forced-choice format for this kind of question situation (also see Krosnick 2018).

Read Tips and skills 11.2 to make sure you avoid the most common mistakes when asking questions in your research project.

11

TIPS AND SKILLS 11.2

Avoiding common mistakes when asking questions

Over the years, we have read many projects and dissertations based on structured interviews and self-completion questionnaires, and the same mistakes tend to recur. You can avoid these in your research project by observing the following advice.

- Limit the number of open-ended questions you use. Including an excessive number of questions in this format is likely to reduce your response rate and make your analysis more difficult.
- Don't use excessive numbers of Yes/No questions, as not all potential responses fit into this format. Take this question:

  Are you satisfied with opportunities for promotion in the firm?

  Yes____

  No____
- This ignores the possibility that respondents will not simply feel satisfied or not satisfied. As people vary in the intensity of their feelings about such things, it would be worth rephrasing the question like this:

  How satisfied are you with opportunities for promotion in the firm?

  Very satisfied____

  Satisfied____

  Neither satisfied nor dissatisfied____

  Dissatisfied____

  Very dissatisfied____
- On self-completion questionnaires, provide clear instructions about how the questions should be answered, including specifying whether a tick, circle, or deletion (etc.) is required. If only one response is required, make sure you say so—for example, 'tick the *one* answer that comes closest to your view'.
- Be careful about letting respondents choose more than one answer. Although this can sometimes be unavoidable, questions that allow more than one reply are often more challenging to analyse.
- Formulate closed answers that are mutually exclusive and that include all categories. Avoid using questions like this:

  How many times per week do you typically use public transport?

  1–3 times____ 6–9 times____

  3–6 times____ More than 10 times____

Not only does the respondent not know where to answer if their answer is 3 or 6 times; there is also no answer for someone who would want to answer 10.

- Provide an appropriate time frame with questions. The question 'How much do you earn?' is problematic because it does not provide the respondent with a time frame. Is it per week, per month, or per year? Another problem is that respondents need to be told whether the figure required should be gross (that is, before deductions for tax, national insurance, etc.) or net (after deductions). Given the sensitivities surrounding a person's salary, it would be best not to ask the question this way anyway and instead to provide a set of income bands on a show card (for example, below £10,000; £10,000–£19,999; £20,000–£29,999; etc.).
- Use a format that makes it easy for respondents to answer and that reduces the likelihood of them making mistakes in answering.

11.6 Piloting and pre-testing questions

11

Before you administer a self-completion questionnaire or structured **interview schedule** to the respondents in your sample, it is always a good idea to conduct a pilot study. Piloting is not just about checking that your survey *questions* operate well; it also plays a role in testing whether the research instrument as a whole functions effectively. Pilots are particularly important in research that is based on self-completion questionnaires, because there will not be an interviewer present to clear up any confusion. When interviewing, persistent problems may emerge after a few interviews have been carried out, and you can then address the problems.

Reasons why you might want to conduct pilot studies in survey research include the following.

- You may be able to generate fixed-choice answers for your main study (if it will mainly consist of closed-ended questions) by asking open-ended questions in the pilot. This can also help you in the process of pre-coding your survey.
- You will gain experience and confidence in using an interview schedule.
- You will find out whether the instructions you have provided for interviewers, or to respondents completing a questionnaire, are clear and effective.
- You will have the opportunity to consider how well the questions flow and whether it is necessary to move some of them around to improve the flow.
- You may be able to identify any questions that are problematic:
  - questions that virtually everyone answers in the same way—if this occurs in a pilot, you may want to change your approach because the resulting data are unlikely to be of interest;
  - questions that make respondents feel uncomfortable in survey interviews;
  - questions that tend to make respondents lose interest at certain points;
  - questions that are difficult for respondents to understand (this is more likely to be revealed in an interview than in a self-completion questionnaire context) or are often not answered—this may be particularly useful when working with people from cultures other than your own, or for whom English is not their first language.

You should not carry out piloting on people who might be members of the sample that will be employed in your main study. If you are intending to use **probability sampling**, selecting a number of members of the **population** or sample in your pilot may affect the representativeness of any subsequent sample. If possible, it is best to find a small set of respondents who are comparable to members of the population from which you will take the sample for your main study. For example, if you were interested in doing a study of students from one university, you could use a small number of students from another university for your pilot. Hear about our panellists' experience of piloting questions for their projects in Learn from experience 11.1.

Researchers sometimes use *cognitive interviewing* when piloting in order to learn how people mentally process and respond to the survey questions. This tends to involve encouraging the pilot respondent to 'think out loud' while they consider the question (Padilla and Leighton 2017). It helps the researcher to understand whether

LEARN FROM EXPERIENCE 11.1
Piloting questions in student projects

Piloting the development of questions to be used in their projects was seen by our panellists as an important way of ensuring their questions were clear and the survey design was appropriate. This applied both to the quantitative approaches employed by Ben, who explored the challenges and opportunities for data visualisation to improve understanding of datafication, and Scarlett, who focused on the role of social media on mental wellbeing. It was also useful in Minke's development of open-ended questions in her qualitative research on claim-making by undocumented migrants in Amsterdam.

> I piloted my questions four times, initially with digital content experts who I had worked with, for sense checking and presentation for example, and then with participants with domain knowledge. The most tangible impact was that I added extra options for one of the demographic questions and for two of the quantitative multiple-choice questions.
>
> Ben

> I would encourage anyone who wants to use self-completion questionnaires for research purposes to pilot their questionnaire with peers. This means giving your questionnaire out to peers to gain feedback on your layout, questions, and length of the questionnaire. Doing this will enable you to ensure your questionnaire is created to the highest standard and will provide you with lots of useful data.
>
> Scarlett

> Piloting your questions is definitely a good idea. Sometimes social scientists forget that the social sciences have jargon too! Testing questions doesn't always have to be with someone in your intended research population, but can also be a family member or friend. They can easily tell you if they understand a question or not, and if they try to answer the question you can see whether they interpreted the question in the way you intended.
>
> Minke

 Access the **online resources** to hear our panellists' video reflections on this theme.

You can read about our panellists' backgrounds and research experiences on page xxvi.

the question is clear, whether there are particular challenges in relation to memory recall, whether there are issues around how sensitive a question is, and whether the response is in line with what they might have expected in terms of fulfilling the task requirement (Lavrakas 2008). For example, in order to answer the question 'In the previous year, how many days did you have off working for pay due to ill-health?' the respondent would have to recall information from the previous year, which may prove difficult, and there may be ambiguities regarding defining 'working for pay' and 'ill-health'. These difficulties would probably be revealed through cognitive interviewing and might lead the researcher to rephrase the question.

11.7 Using existing questions

We have spent this chapter discussing the considerations and rules for devising your own questions, but you should also think about using questions devised by other researchers for at least part of your questionnaire or interview schedule. While this may seem like stealing or copying, and it is certainly advisable to contact the relevant researcher(s) if you would like to use any questions they have devised, this is a common practice

11

TIPS AND SKILLS 11.3
Getting help in designing questions

When designing questions, try to put yourself in the position of someone who has been asked to answer the questions. This can be difficult, because some (if not all) of the questions may not apply to you—for example, if you are a young student doing a survey of retired people. However, try to think about how *you* would reply, concentrating not just on the questions themselves but also on the links between the questions. For example, do the filter questions work in the way you expect? Then try the questions out on some people you know, as you would in a pilot study. Ask them to be critical and to consider how well the questions connect to each other. If you are doing the research in the context of a dissertation, your supervisor may be able to look at your questions too.

As we have seen in this section, it is also a good idea to look at the questionnaires and structured interview schedules that other experienced researchers have devised. Even if they have not asked questions on your topic, the *way* they have asked the questions should help you see what to do and what to avoid when designing such instruments.

11

among researchers. As long as you make sure you properly attribute where the question has come from, you do not need to worry about issues of plagiarism. When you employ existing questions, it means that they have in a sense been piloted for you. If previous researchers did any **reliability** and validity testing, you will know about the measurement qualities of the existing questions. Using existing questions also means that you can draw comparisons with other research. This might allow you to indicate whether change has occurred or whether the findings apply to your sample. For example, if you are researching job satisfaction, using one of the standard job satisfaction scales would allow you to compare your findings with those of other researchers. Alternatively, using the same questions as another researcher may allow you to explore whether the location of your sample appears to make a difference to the findings. While you need to be cautious about inferring too much from comparisons between your own and other researchers' data, the findings can be illuminating. At the very least, examining questions that others have used might give you some ideas about how best to approach your own questions, even if you decide not to use them—see Tips and skills 11.3.

Examples of researchers who have used existing questions are Chin et al. (2002), whose study we discussed in Research in focus 7.8. These researchers developed a scale designed to measure attitudes to vegetarians and used several existing questions devised for measuring other **concepts** in which they were interested, such as measures of authoritarianism and political conservatism. If you would like to explore options for your research, the UK Data Archive (UKDA) has a very good 'Variable and question bank' that provides access to questionnaires from major surveys (including the **census**) and associated commentary to help with survey design. The bank presents questions in the context of the questionnaire in which they appeared, accompanied by technical details, and the search mechanism allows you to search for a particular questionnaire or to input keywords to find cases of the use of particular topics in questions. The bank is freely available and can be found at **http://discover.ukdataservice.ac.uk/variables** (accessed 9 May 2019).

KEY POINTS

- While open-ended questions undoubtedly have certain advantages, closed-ended questions are usually preferable for a survey, because of the ease of asking questions and recording and processing answers. This point applies particularly to self-completion questionnaires.
- Open-ended questions of the kind used in qualitative interviewing have a useful role in helping researchers formulate and pilot fixed-choice answers.

- Vignette questions are a useful way of examining people's normative standards.
- It is crucial to learn the rules of question-asking in order to avoid some of the more obvious pitfalls.
- Remember to always put yourself in the position of the respondent when formulating questions, to make sure that the questions function well and will enable you to generate data appropriate to your research questions.
- Piloting or pre-testing may clear up problems in question formulation.
- Existing questions can be useful as, in a way, they have been piloted for you.

QUESTIONS FOR REVIEW

1. What difficulties do open-ended questions present in survey research?
2. Why are closed-ended questions often preferred to open-ended questions in survey research?
3. What are the limitations of closed-ended questions?
4. How can closed-ended questions be improved?
5. What are the main types of question likely to be used in a structured interview or self-completion questionnaire?
6. What is wrong with each of the following questions?

   What is your annual salary?

   Below £10,000____

   £10,000–15,000____

   £15,000–20,000____

   £20,000–25,000____

   £25,000–30,000____

   £30,000–35,000____

   £35,000 and over____

   Do you ever feel alienated from your work?

   All the time____

   Often____

   Occasionally____

   Never____

   How satisfied are you with the provision of educational services and social services in your area?

   Very satisfied____

   Fairly satisfied____

   Neither satisfied nor dissatisfied____

   Fairly dissatisfied____

   Very dissatisfied____

   What is your marital status?

   Single____

   Married____

   Divorced____

7. In what circumstances are vignette questions appropriate?
8. Why is it important to pilot questions?
9. Why might it be useful to use questions devised by others?

ONLINE RESOURCES

www.oup.com/he/srm6e

You can find our notes on the answers to these questions within this chapter's **online resources**, together with:

- *audio/video comments* on this topic from our 'Learn from experience' panellists;
- *audio discussion from the authors* on the limitations of closed-ended questions (review question 3);
- *self-test questions* for further knowledge-checking;
- a *flashcard glossary* to help you recall key terms; and
- a *Student Researcher's Toolkit* containing practical materials and resources to help you conduct your own research project.

CHAPTER 12

STRUCTURED OBSERVATION

CHAPTER GUIDE

Structured observation is a method that is relatively little used in social research. It involves directly observing behaviour and recording that behaviour as data, in terms of categories that the researcher has devised before collecting the data. In this chapter we explore

- the potential value of structured observation for the study of behaviour;
- the different forms of observation in social research;
- how to devise an observation schedule;
- different strategies for observing behaviour in structured observation;
- sampling issues in structured observation research, which are not just about sampling people but also time and contexts;
- field stimulations (in which the researcher actively intervenes in social life and records what happens as a consequence of the intervention) as a form of structured observation;
- analysing the results of structured observation;
- the advantages of structured observation;
- the problems with structured observation, including issues of reliability and validity.

12.1 Introduction

Structured observation is a method for systematically observing the behaviour of individuals in terms of a schedule of categories—an **observation schedule**—where the researcher uses explicitly formulated rules for the observation and recording of behaviour. Unlike in **survey research**, which only allows you to *infer* behaviour, structured observation allows you to observe it directly.

In Chapters 8 to 11 we discussed how researchers can use surveys to collect data quantitatively, showing that while these methods are popular, they are not without limitations. We saw that one limitation with structured interviews and surveys is that researchers are not collecting data in naturally occurring situations. Structured observation represents a possible solution to this problem (Cohen et al. 2017).

12.2 Why observe behaviour?

Let's begin by considering why researchers want to observe people's behaviour. When people report their behaviour, they may report it inaccurately. Observing behaviour directly through an **observation research** method (see Key concept 12.1) such as structured observation (see Key concept 12.2), rather than relying on instruments of survey research such as **questionnaires** to get information, can provide a solution to that problem. We consider a classic example of the problem in Research in focus 12.1 and a more recent example in Research in focus 12.2, before reflecting on the potential reasons for inaccurate reporting of behaviour in Thinking deeply 12.1.

Much like interviewing (see Key concept 9.1), there are many different forms of observation research in the social sciences, both quantitative and qualitative (Marshall and Rossman 2016). Key concept 12.1 outlines the main forms researchers use. We discuss some qualitative approaches to observation research (**ethnography** and **participant observation**) in Chapter 18. These are unstructured forms of observation. Qualitative, unstructured approaches to observation, such as participant observation, tend to involve the researcher encountering the people and events studied with an open mind in terms of what events and behav-

RESEARCH IN FOCUS 12.1
The gap between stated and actual behaviour: a classic example

A study of racial prejudice conducted by LaPiere (1934) is one of the most infamous examples of the problems caused by the gap between what people say they do (or are likely to do) and their actual behaviour.

LaPiere spent two years travelling twice across the USA with a young Chinese student and his wife to observe whether hotels and restaurants refused entry to them. Of 66 hotels, one refused entry; of 184 restaurants and diners, none refused entry. (LaPiere tried to eliminate himself as a possible contaminating influence by ensuring that he was not involved in gaining access to the establishments.)

Six months later, LaPiere sent questionnaires to the hotels and restaurants they had visited. One of the questions he asked was: 'Will you accept members of the Chinese race as guests in your establishment?' Of the establishments that replied, 92 per cent of restaurants said 'No'; and 91 per cent of hotels said 'No'.

LaPiere's study clearly illustrates the fact that there can be a gap between reports of behaviour and actual behaviour. Research in focus 12.2 explores a more recent example of this phenomenon, a study that investigated the gap between stated and observed behaviour in terms of students using mobile devices during lectures.

RESEARCH IN FOCUS 12.2

The gap between stated and actual behaviour: a contemporary example

Abramova et al. (2017) conducted research that included a structured observation and questionnaires to explore the phenomenon of phubbing (the practice of ignoring companions in order to pay attention to a mobile device) among students, and the gap that may exist between reporting of behaviour and actual behaviour.

Part of the research involved conducting structured observations to assess the frequency of student phubbing activities during lectures. Researchers observed a **purposive sample** of students at one German university in 2016. At the onset, two observers took seats in the middle of the lecture hall and each selected three target seats while the lecture hall was still empty, in order to choose students without selection bias (choosing the person to the right if the selected seat stayed empty). They recorded several characteristics of each phubbing action, including start, end, and type (for example, browsing, texting), as well as the reaction of neighbours. At the end of the lecture, they asked the observed students to fill in a questionnaire about their own estimated smartphone use and some demographic information, allowing a comparison between self-assessment and the observations. The researchers conducted 60 observations (32 women and 28 men), generally over the entire lecture duration (the mean observation time accounted for 1 hour and 22 minutes).

The observations show that on average, students practiced phubbing activities about eight times during a lecture. As the observers were sitting almost directly behind the students, they could note the specific uses of the smartphone. The observers found that during lectures, 91.7 per cent of the students texted and 90.0 per cent browsed, with a typical student devoting around 16 minutes of their smartphone time to messaging. Browsing or social network activities accounted for longer time periods, at around 20 minutes.

After the observation, 56 of the monitored students filled out the questionnaire. Of these, 22 respondents (39.3 per cent) correctly estimated the time they phubbed during the lecture (being accurate to up to a five-minute difference), 21.4 per cent of respondents overestimated their phubbing behaviour, and the other 41.1 per cent underestimated their smartphone use, among which 14.3 per cent underestimated it by about 10–20 minutes. These represent considerable differences in self-reported and real behaviour, suggesting that if the researchers had been studying phubbing using only questionnaires, the data would have been potentially misleading.

THINKING DEEPLY 12.1

Why is there a difference between observed and stated behaviour?

If you do social research that uncovers differences between observed behaviour and stated behaviour, as in the examples in Research in focus 12.1 and 12.2, it is important not only to refer to these differences in your research conclusions, but also to reflect on why these differences might exist. For example, is it likely that certain behaviour is reported more frequently than it is observed because it is considered more desirable to respond in a particular way? This may be particularly likely if a survey or interview is not anonymous, in contrast with a structured observation conducted covertly. Differences in reported and observed behaviour could also be related to inaccurate memories, especially when respondents report the attitudes or behaviour a long time after the event.

KEY CONCEPT 12.1
Observation research

Observation research involves a researcher directly observing their subjects or participants in a natural setting. The most common forms of observational research in social science are as follows.

- *Structured observation* (also known as **systematic observation**) is a technique where the researcher follows set rules for observing and recording behaviour: see Key concept 12.2.
- *Participant observation* involves the observer immersing themselves in a social setting for a prolonged period of time and observing the behaviour of members of that setting (group, organization, community, etc.) in order to understand the meanings they attribute to their environment and behaviour. Participant observers vary considerably in how much they participate in the social settings in which they locate themselves. These observations are less structured than in structured observation, and are associated with **qualitative research**. See Key concept 18.1 for a definition of participant observation, and Chapter 18 in general for a detailed discussion.
- *Non-participant observation* describes a situation where the observer observes a social setting but is not participating in what is going on. Structured observers are usually non-participants, observing the social setting but rarely participating in what is happening. The term can also be used in connection with unstructured observation.
- *Unstructured observation*. This does not involve using an observation schedule to record behaviour. With this method, behaviour is recorded in as much detail as possible with the aim of developing a narrative account of that behaviour. Most participant observation is unstructured, but the term 'unstructured observation' tends to be used in connection with non-participant observation.
- *Simple observation and contrived observation*. Webb et al. (1966) write about forms of observation in which the observer is unobtrusive and is not observed by those being observed. With **simple observation**, the observer has no influence over the situation being observed; in the case of **contrived observation**, the observer actively alters the situation in order to observe the effects of an intervention. These two types of observation are forms of non-participant observation and can use either structured or unstructured observation.

12

iours might become relevant to their research area: an **inductive** approach. The kind of data that such research produces is normally not analysed statistically, and does not involve the process of counting numbers of events, as researchers do in the more structured forms of observation we will discuss in this chapter. In contrast, 'structured' approaches to observation involve a more **deductive** approach, with researchers largely deciding in advance what events and behaviours they are going to count.

12.3 Conducting structured observation

As we described in Section 12.1, structured observation is a type of observation research in which the researcher follows set rules for observing and recording behaviour—see Key concept 12.2 for a full definition. It can be an alternative or a useful addition to survey **research methods**, but it is not widely used in the social sciences and tends to be employed to study quite a narrow range of behaviour, such as that occurring in schools. In this section, we explore several important aspects of this method: devising and using an observation schedule, strategies for observing behaviour, and some particular **sampling** considerations.

KEY CONCEPT 12.2
What is structured observation?

Structured observation, also called *systematic observation,* is a technique that involves the researcher following explicitly formulated rules for the observation and recording of behaviour. The rules tell observers what they should be looking for and how they should record behaviour. Researchers observe each research participant for a predetermined period of time using the same rules.

Researchers articulate the rules to be followed in what is usually called an observation schedule, which is similar in many ways to a **structured interview** schedule with **closed-ended questions**. The aim of the observation schedule is to make sure that observers record each participant's behaviour systematically, so that they can then aggregate data on the behaviour of all those in the sample. The rules in an observation schedule need to be as specific as possible in order to direct observers to exactly what aspects of behaviour they are supposed to be looking for. The resulting data often looks similar to questionnaire data, as an observation generates information on different aspects of behaviour that can be treated as **variables**. Structured observation research is usually underpinned by a **cross-sectional research design** (see Key concept 3.5).

The observation schedule

The observation schedule (or *coding scheme*) specifies the categories of behaviour that researchers are to observe and how they should assign behaviour to those categories. A good illustration of this process of analysis is the Flanders Interaction Analysis Categories (FIAC), one of the best-known schedules for observing classrooms. This scheme was devised by Flanders (1970) in the USA but has been used fairly extensively in other countries. It involves an observer watching a classroom during a lesson and every three seconds allocating a **category** number to the type of activity that has taken place in that three-second period. (See Figure 12.1 for the different types of activity in the FIAC scheme.) So, every minute the observer writes down a total of 20 numbers, each of which relate directly to the coding scheme.

This tool allows researchers to explore a number of issues: for example, comparing teachers' styles, such as the relative emphasis on teachers doing the talking and pupils talking, or observing the amounts of silence or confusion that take place in their lessons. It also enables researchers to compare classes using these categories. This kind of structured observation, of which the schedule is a key part, produces data that can help enhance our understanding of what happens in the setting (in this case, lessons) and can be useful in developing further information about it (for example, which teaching styles seem most effective).

A scheme such as this could also be used in connection with higher education teaching, in particular in tutorials and seminars. If we imagine a scheme in which the focus is on the teacher, the categories might be:

Tutor

1. asking question addressed to group;
2. asking question addressed to individual;
3. responding to question asked by member of group;
4. responding to comment by member of group;
5. discussing topic;
6. making arrangements;
7. silence.

Student(s)

8. asking question;
9. responding to question from tutor;
10. responding to comment from tutor;
11. responding to question from another student;
12. responding to comment from another student;
13. talking about arrangements.

We might want to **code** what is happening every five seconds. The **coding** sheet for a five-minute period in the tutorial might look like Figure 12.2, where each **cell** in the grid represents a five-second interval so that a row consists of 12 five-second intervals—that is, a minute. The numbers in the cells are the codes used to represent the classification of behaviour, so the number 3 in the top left-hand cell refers to a tutor responding to a question asked by a member of the group. We might try to relate the amount of time that the tutor is engaged in each

12

FIGURE 12.1
Categories from the FIAC scheme for observing classrooms

Teacher talk	Response	**1 Accepts feeling** (e.g. accepts and clarifies an attitude or the feeling tone of a pupil)
		2 Praises or encourages
		3 Accepts or uses ideas of pupils
	Initiation	**4 Asks questions**
		5 Lecturing
		6 Giving direction
		7 Criticizing or justifying authority
Pupil talk		**8 Pupil talk—response**
		9 Pupil talk—initiation
Silence		**10 Silence or confusion**

FIGURE 12.2
A coding sheet for a hypothetical study of university tutorials

3	3	3	3	10	10	10	10	10	10	10	10
10	10	10	10	10	10	7	7	7	8	8	8
8	8	8	8	8	8	8	8	11	11	11	11
11	11	11	11	11	11	11	11	11	11	11	11
7	7	7	7	7	4	4	4	4	4	4	1

Note: Each cell represents a five-second interval and each row is one minute. The number in each cell is the code that represents a category of observed behaviour.

activity to such things as number of students in the group; layout of the room; subject discipline; gender of tutor; age of tutor; and so on. (There are similarities between this and the coding practices that we outline in Chapter 13 on **content analysis**.)

We saw in Chapter 9 that there are many considerations we must bear in mind when constructing an **interview schedule**. We need to devise observation schedules with similar care. Tips and skills 12.1 lists the main principles to keep in mind, Research in focus 12.3 provides an example of research using an observation schedule, and in Learn from experience 12.1 Barbara recounts how she learnt to develop a schedule. Whether you adhere to the principles in Tips and skills 12.1 could have a significant effect on the quality of the data you collect. For example, if an observer was using your schedule to record behaviour in a tutorial but your categories and guidelines did not cover the possibility of a student knocking on the tutor's door to ask them a quick question, the observer might be confused. They may not be sure whether this behaviour needed coding in terms of the 13 categories (which may not be exhaustive) or whether the coding should be temporarily suspended, and this confusion could result in problems with the data. The best approach here would probably be to include another category of behaviour called 'interruption'. It is often worth carrying out a certain amount of unstructured observation before constructing the observation schedule, and then

TIPS AND SKILLS 12.1

Devising an observation schedule

When devising an observation schedule, we recommend that you follow these principles.

- Make it clear to the observer exactly *who* or *what* (and possibly both) in the setting they are to observe and record. (For example, if people are the focus of attention, the observer needs to know precisely which people they are to observe.)
- Make it clear exactly which of the many *things* going on in the setting the observer is to record. Research in focus 12.3 describes the observation of individual children in a classroom using specified categories, modes, and time intervals.
- Use categories of behaviour that are both *mutually exclusive* (do not overlap) and *inclusive* (covering all likely types of behaviour)—principles we discuss further in the context of devising a **coding schedule** in Chapter 13.
- Devise recording systems that are *easy to operate*. This is crucial, as complex systems taking in large numbers of types of behaviour can make it confusing for the observer to choose the appropriate option and can lead to problems with the recording of information.
- Provide *clear guidance* for interpretation. Observation schedules sometimes require the observer to interpret what is going on, for example distinguishing between a student responding to a question raised by another student and discussing the tutorial topic. If interpretation is likely to be required, you need to provide clear guidelines for the observer.

RESEARCH IN FOCUS 12.3

Using an observation schedule

Blatchford et al. (2003) conducted structured observation research into the impact of class size on pupil behaviour, and their findings have been influential on debates in this area (Blatchford et al. 2016; Fredriksson et al. 2013; Solheim et al. 2017). They were interested in the possibility that, as class sizes increase, pupil inattentiveness also increases, resulting in difficult relationships between the children. The structured observational component of this research was based on children aged 4–5 years in large and small classes. The authors describe their approach:

> This involved direct, i.e. on-the-spot, observations of selected children in terms of previously developed categories and in terms of 5-minute observation sheets divided into continuous 10-second time samples. The schedule was child-based in the sense that one child at a time was observed. ... The schedule involved categories that provided a description of time spent in three 'social modes'—when with their teachers, other children and when not interacting. Within each of these three modes sub-categories covered work, procedural, social and off-task activity. ... The aim was to observe [six randomly chosen] children in each class five times per day, for 3 days. In the event the average number of completed observation sheets per child was 14. ... In terms of time there were 69 minutes of observation per child.
>
> (Blatchford et al. 2003: 21–2)

piloting your schedule so that you can anticipate possible problems arising from a lack of inclusiveness in your categories. You might choose to outline potential scenarios in your guidelines and explain how the observer should deal with them.

Strategies for observing behaviour

There are different ways of conceptualizing how behaviour should be recorded. These include recording in terms of incidents, or recording in either short or long periods of time.

LEARN FROM EXPERIENCE 12.1
Developing an observation schedule

Developing an observation schedule is part of the process of conducting a structured observation. Testing this out in order to ensure consistency is particularly important when more than one person will be collecting the data. Barbara reflects on this process in relation to one of her assignments.

> My colleagues and I had an assignment where we were required to observe dog owners' interactions in the city parks. We practiced developing the observation schedule by observing the same interaction in pairs and then commenting on the data collected. We compared several interactions and specifically agreed on the categories that would represent a certain behaviour.
>
> Barbara

Access the **online resources** to hear Barbara's reflections on this theme.

You can read about our panellists' backgrounds and research experiences on page xxvi.

Recording in terms of *incidents* means waiting for something to happen and then recording what follows from it. This is what LaPiere (1934) did (see Research in focus 12.1), in that he waited for the Chinese couple to try to negotiate entry to each hotel or restaurant and then recorded whether they were allowed entry.

We can observe and record in terms of *short periods* of time, such as in the research reported in Research in focus 12.3, where observers use '5-minute observation sheets'. Returning at structured intervals and conducting further structured observations (a form of **time sampling**) can also be useful, as it can help researchers to assess the **generalizability** of what goes on in the setting. For instance, if you were exploring managers' behaviour and they have a daily meeting at 10 a.m., you would need to make sure you didn't only conduct your structured observation at this time, as it would give the misleading impression that the managers' roles consisted solely of meetings.

Observing and recording observations for quite *long periods* of time involves the observer watching and recording more or less continuously for extended periods, as in the FIAC scheme (see earlier in this section under 'The observation schedule'). Martin and Bateson (2007) refer to this as **continuous recording**, whereby the observer observes for extended periods, thus allowing them to measure the frequency and duration of the types of behaviour that they are interested in. Martin and Bateson contrast this approach with time sampling, where observations take place at various different time periods (which may be random).

Sampling for an observation

Just like survey research, structured observation requires researchers to make decisions about sampling. However, with structured observation, sampling issues do not revolve solely around how to sample people.

Sampling people

You will be familiar with the considerations involved in sampling people from our discussions in Chapter 8. Many of the points we raised in that chapter about **probability sampling** apply to structured observation. This means that the observer will ideally want to sample on a random basis, as in the study by Blatchford et al. (see Research in focus 12.3), where the researchers randomly selected six students in each class but with the stipulation that three boys and three girls would be observed.

Sampling in terms of time

With time sampling, it is important to ensure that, if certain individuals are observed on more than one occasion (as is often necessary), they are not always observed at the same time of the day. This means that, if you are selecting particular individuals randomly to be observed for short periods on several different occasions, it is best if you randomly select the observation periods. For example, if you always observed pupils at the end of the day they might be tired, which could give a false impression of their overall behaviour. In the Blatchford et al. (2003) study (Research in focus 12.3), each child was observed at different times on three different days, meaning that the researchers' ratings of any child were unlikely to be distorted by unusual behaviour that the child might exhibit on just one or two occasions.

Other sampling considerations

The sampling procedures we have mentioned so far conform to probability sampling principles, because it is usually possible to construct a **sampling frame** from which researchers can randomly select individuals to observe. However, sometimes this is not possible. We cannot, for instance, use **random sampling** for studies in public areas because we cannot easily construct a sampling frame of people walking along a street. Similarly, we would struggle to construct a sampling frame of interactions—for example of meetings between social workers and their clients. The problem with doing structured observation research on a topic that involves these kinds of settings is that they do not lend themselves to specifying a sampling frame, and therefore the researcher cannot generate a probability sample.

Considerations relating to probability sampling mainly derive from researchers' concerns about the **external validity** (or generalizability) of findings. Probability sampling does not necessarily totally address these concerns. For example, if you are conducting a structured observation study over a relatively short period of time, there are likely to be issues around the representativeness of your findings. If you were conducting research in secondary schools, then observations towards the end of the school year, when examinations are likely to preoccupy both teachers and students, may give different results compared to observations conducted at a different point in the academic year. It is important to consider the timing of observation. Other important considerations include how you select the sites in which you are going to conduct structured observation. Can we presume that they are themselves representative? A random sampling procedure for selecting schools might help with this, but because it is often very challenging to secure access to settings such as schools and business organizations, it is likely that the organizations you do get access to will not be representative of the **population** of appropriate ones.

Martin and Bateson (2007) have identified the following types of sampling in structured observation:

- ***ad libitum* sampling**, whereby the observer records whatever is happening at the time;
- **focal sampling**, in which a researcher observes a specific individual for a set period of time and uses a schedule to record all examples of whatever forms of behaviour they are interested in;
- **scan sampling**, whereby the observer scans a whole group of individuals at regular intervals and records the behaviour of all of them at each interval—this sampling strategy allows only one or two types of behaviour to be observed and recorded; and
- **behaviour sampling**, whereby the observer watches a whole group and records who was involved in a particular kind of behaviour.

Most structured observation research seems to use the first two types: Flanders's FIAC scheme is an example of *ad libitum* sampling; the research by Blatchford et al. (2003; see Research in focus 12.3) and Abramova et al. (2017; see Research in focus 12.2) are illustrations of focal sampling.

12

12.4 Field stimulations as a form of structured observation

Before we conclude this chapter with an evaluation of structured observation, we will look briefly at the **field stimulation**, a term used by Salancik (1979) to describe a type of observation research that shares many of the characteristics of structured observation. It is worth being aware of this method because it has some advantages (discussed below) and you might come across it in your studies, but it has not been used extensively in social research (Hauser et al. 2017).

A field stimulation is a study in which the researcher directly intervenes in and/or manipulates a natural setting in order to observe what happens as a result. Unlike most structured observations, in a field stimulation participants do not know they are being studied. Although Salancik (1979) classifies field stimulations as a qualitative method, they may be better thought of as operating with a **quantitative research** strategy, because the researcher usually tries to quantify the outcomes they secure.

Research of this type, such as the study described in Research in focus 12.4, can result in interesting findings, and it gets around the problem of **reactivity** by not alerting research participants to the fact that they are

RESEARCH IN FOCUS 12.4
A field stimulation

An article was published in *The Times* (a daily national newspaper in the UK) on 10 May 2012 with the title 'Researchers Leave a Good Tip for Waitresses: Wear Red Lipstick'. The article reported on a field simulation conducted by Guégen and Jacob (2012) that suggested that if restaurant waitresses want to maximize their tips, they should wear red lipstick. In three French restaurants, the researchers randomly assigned diners to one of seven waitresses who had been made up so that the only feature distinguishing their makeup was whether they wore red, pink, brown, or no lipstick. The researchers observed each waitress for 40 observational periods, five days per week for eight weeks.

Guégen and Jacob found no differences in tips according to the waitresses' lipstick when the person paying the bill was female. However, when males were paying the bill, there was a statistically significant difference between the waitresses in terms of whether diners gave a tip and the amount of the tip. In the red lipstick condition, 50.6 per cent of male customers gave tips to the waitress, but in the pink, brown, and no lipstick conditions the figures were 39.7 per cent, 34.5 per cent, and 30.3 per cent. Also, waitresses with red lipstick received on average much larger tips than waitresses in the three other conditions. For example, waitresses in the red lipstick condition received tips that were 50 per cent larger than tips given to waitresses who wore no lipstick.

being observed. However, it sometimes raises ethical concerns, most often regarding the use of deception, as in the use of pseudo-patients in the study of mental hospitals (Rosenhan 1973). Also, it can be difficult for the researcher to use an observation schedule because referring to it excessively will reveal the observer as a researcher. Observers can usually only engage in limited coding.

12.5 Analysing structured observation data

The types of analysis that researchers use in structured observations depend on the research problem they are trying to address, the sample size, and the techniques that are appropriate for the type of data. In some cases, the analysis may take the form of **descriptive statistics** (see Chapter 15 for a detailed explanation of different forms of descriptive statistics), such as explaining the number of respondents who have been observed doing something that is found in your observation schedule. For example, Nosowska et al. (2014) conducted a structured observation of older people in public social spaces in six cities, each located in a different developing country (Syria, Jordan, Egypt, Thailand, Kenya, and Tanzania) and in one city in the United Kingdom (Sheffield). Employing a mixed method approach, they also conducted a content analysis of the representation of older people in newspaper pictures and on TV in the selected countries. They used descriptive statistics to report on the times and places older people were observed in public, also taking into account the gender of the participants. In total with regard to gender, they found that their observations consisted of 184 (59.4 per cent) men and 126 (40.6 per cent) women. In all cities in developing countries, they observed more men than women, whereas in the UK city (Sheffield) they observed more women than men in public. They also used descriptive statistics to look at the number of older people who were accompanied in public.

As well as describing and summarizing the data collected through structured observation it may be possible, depending on the sample size, to do additional analysis such as establishing whether there is a statistically significant **relationship** between particular variables (this process is described in Chapter 15). For example, Nosowska et al. (2014) did a statistical analysis of their structured observation data in order to explore whether there was a significant difference in whether older men were accompanied or alone in the different cities. They identified a statistically significant association, finding that Sheffield had the highest proportion of accompanied older men in the sample (42.0 per cent).

When analysing your data, it is important to be aware of any limitations with it. In Nosowska et al.'s study, a key limitation that the researchers highlighted was the difficulty of estimating age in their observations. People may look older or younger than they actually are. In this study, the observers recorded anyone appearing over the age of 60 as an older person. Estimates of age were further challenged by the distance between the researcher and the participant in the observations. A further issue is whether 60 was a suitable age at which to draw the boundary of old age, especially given the evident discrepancies in life expectancy across the sampled countries.

12.6 Evaluating structured observation

In laboratory **experiments** in fields such as social psychology, observation with varying degrees of structure is quite common, but, as we have noted, in social research structured observation has not been frequently used and has been quite controversial. We will spend the final section of this chapter evaluating the method, exploring the ways in which it can be valuable for researchers as well as some of the criticisms associated with it.

Advantages of structured observation

When overt behaviour is the focus of analysis and perhaps issues of meaning are less important, structured observation is almost certainly more accurate and effective than getting people to report on their behaviour through questionnaires. When comparing structured observations to interviews and questionnaires, McCall (1984: 277) has concluded that structured observation 'provides (*a*) more reliable information about events; (*b*) greater precision regarding their timing, duration, and frequency; (*c*) greater accuracy in the time ordering of variables; and (*d*) more accurate and economical reconstructions of large-scale social episodes'. Similar points have also been made by Ostrov and Hart (2013). Structured observation can also be used to explore differences between observed and stated behaviour.

Structured observation can work well (and perhaps best) when accompanied by other methods that complement it. For example, structured observation can rarely provide *reasons* for observed patterns of behaviour, so it can be useful to combine it with another method that *is* able to probe reasons. Abramova et al.'s research on phubbing (2017; see Research in focus 12.2) included structured observation as well as questionnaires. Blatchford (2005) reports that the data they collected through structured observation in the study described in Research in focus 12.3 were part of a wider study of the impact of variations in class size. The other methods they used were questionnaires administered to teachers each term to gauge their estimates of how they allocated time in classrooms between different activities; end-of-year questionnaires administered to teachers asking them about their experiences of the impact of class size; and case studies of small and large classes, which included structured observation of events and **semi-structured interviews** with teachers and the head teacher. In both studies, the researchers used structured observation in conjunction with other methods to gain a fuller picture of the people and issues in question.

Although, as we will see in the next section, there are some limitations and challenges associated with structured observation, it can be an effective method, especially when used in conjunction with other methods such as interviews and questionnaires. It is also true that if structured observation was more widely used it could perhaps be used more effectively, as reliable measures of the kind developed in areas such as education might emerge for other fields.

12

Challenges of structured observation

Like most research methods, structured observation suffers from a number of potential limitations, including issues relating to **reliability** and **validity**—problems that are acknowledged by McCall (1984: 277). Some of these issues are similar to those faced by researchers seeking to develop measures in social research in general (see Chapter 7) and in survey research in particular, but others are specific to structured observation and help explain its limited use in social research.

Structured observation cannot explore the reasons behind behaviour

Perhaps the main reason for the limited use of structured observation in social research is that because it concentrates upon directly observable behaviour, it is rarely able to get at the reasons and intentions behind behaviour. Sometimes, when intentions are of concern, observers impute them. In the FIAC scheme (see Figure 12.1), for example, the category 'teacher praises or encourages' means imputing a motive to something that the teacher says. Similarly, Blatchford et al. (2009: 668) report that in a study of the impact of teaching assistants on engagement in class, one of the categories of pupil behaviour they used was '*Individual off-task (passive)*: target child is disengaged during task activity, for example, day dreaming.' Essentially, the problem is that structured observation does not easily allow the observer to get to the *meaning* of behaviour.

One reason that social science researchers tend to favour interviews and questionnaires over structured observation, or use them alongside it, is that although these methods are limited in terms of their capacity to tap behaviour accurately, they can reveal information about attitudes and social backgrounds as well as behaviour. They are more flexible, allowing researchers to uncover a variety of factors that may be influencing behaviour (even if this is *reported* behaviour), such as social background. They can also ask questions about attitudes and investigate explanations that people give for their behaviour. As a result, they are able to gain information about factors that may lie behind the patterns of behaviour they uncover. It is also worth noting that not all settings or forms of behaviour are accessible to structured observation. This could include the observation of intimate behaviours, such as breastfeeding or condom use, or of confidential meetings or other restricted environments such as police stations or immigration detention centres (Halder et al. 2013).

Issues of reliability in structured observation

Researchers using structured observations are often concerned with *inter-observer consistency*. This involves how similarly two or more observers of the same behaviour are coding it on the observation schedule. Researchers also need to consider the degree of consistency in how each observer applies the observation schedule over time—*intra-observer consistency*. The procedures for assessing these aspects of reliability are broadly similar to those applied to the issue of inter-observer consistency.

Achieving reliability in structured observation is not always easy. This is a significant point, given that validity presupposes reliability (see Chapter 7). Reliability may be difficult to achieve because of the effects of such factors as observer fatigue and lapses in attention. However, this point should not be exaggerated: some researchers have been able to achieve high levels of reliability for many of their measures, and indeed two critics of structured observation have written that 'there is no doubt that observers can be trained to use complex coding schedules with considerable reliability' (Delamont and Hamilton 1984: 32).

Issues of validity in structured observation

Measurement validity relates to whether a measure is measuring what it is supposed to measure. The validity of any measure will be affected by two factors:

- whether the measure reflects the **concept** it has been designed to measure (see Chapter 7), and
- error that arises from the implementation of the measure in the research process (see Chapter 9).

The first of these considerations means that in structured observation, researchers need to attend to the same kinds of issues in terms of checking validity (assessing **face validity**, **concurrent validity**, and so on) that they would if conducting research based on interviews and questionnaires. The second aspect of validity—error in implementation—raises two questions in the context of structured observation:

- Is the observation schedule being administered as it is supposed to be?
- Do people change their behaviour because they know they are being observed?

When the schedule is correctly administered, it means that interviewers using a structured interview schedule are following the research instrument and its instructions exactly as they are supposed to. If there is variability between observers or over time, the measure will be unreliable and therefore cannot be valid. It is crucial to make sure that observers have as complete an understanding as possible of how they should implement the observation schedule. Remember that you can improve this by carefully considering the time points you use in relation to your sample.

The idea that people may change their behaviour because they know they are being observed is known as the **reactive effect** (Key concept 12.3). If people adjust the way they behave because they know they are being observed (perhaps because they want to be viewed in a favourable way by the observer), their behaviour would be atypical. This means we could not regard the results of structured observation research as necessarily indicative of what happens with no observer present. Of course, not all structured observation is known to the participants being observed, as was the case for the studies in Research in focus 12.1, 12.2, 12.3, and 12.4 (though this comes with

KEY CONCEPT 12.3
The reactive effect

Webb et al. (1966: 13) described the 'reactive measurement effect' as being when 'the research subject's knowledge that he is participating in a scholarly search may confound the investigator's data'. They identified four components of this effect.

1. *The guinea pig effect.* This refers to the subject's *awareness* of being tested. Examples include the research participant wanting to create a good impression or feeling prompted to behave in ways (or express attitudes) that they would not normally exhibit.
2. *Role selection.* Webb et al. argue that participants are often tempted to adopt a particular kind of role in research. For example, there is a well-known effect in experimental research (but which may have a broader applicability) whereby some individuals seek cues about the aims of the research and adjust what they say and do in line with their perceptions (which may of course be incorrect) of those aims.
3. *Measurement as a change agent.* The very fact of a researcher being in a context where they would not normally be could cause things to be different. For example, the fact that there is an observer sitting in the corner of a school classroom means that there is space and a chair being used that otherwise would be unoccupied, and this may influence behaviour.
4. ***Response sets.*** This is an issue that mainly relates to questionnaire and interview research and occurs when the respondent replies to a set of questions in a consistent but clearly inappropriate way. Examples of this kind of effect are measurement problems such as **social desirability bias** and acquiescence or 'yeasaying' (see Section 9.7).

Reactive effects are likely to occur in any research in which participants know that they are the focus of investigation. Webb et al. called for greater use of what they call unobtrusive measures or non-reactive methods, in which participants are not aware that they are involved in research (see Key concept 14.2 for more information).

12

ethical considerations). McCall (1984) points to evidence that a reactive effect occurs in structured observation, but also that, by and large, research participants become accustomed to being observed, so the researcher essentially becomes less intrusive the longer they are present.

Structured observation risks imposing an unhelpful framework

Similarly to the problem of the closed-ended question in questionnaires, there is a risk that the structured observation will, through the use of an observation schedule, impose a potentially inappropriate or irrelevant framework on the setting being observed, especially if the researchers do not know much about it. One solution to this challenge is to carry out a period of unstructured observation before undertaking the structured observation, in order to develop appropriate variables and categories.

Structured observation generates fragmented data

There is a tendency for structured observation to generate lots of fragments of data, creating the challenge of trying to piece them together to produce an overall picture, or trying to find general themes that link the fragments of data together. It can become difficult to see the bigger picture that lies behind the segments of behaviour that structured observation usually uncovers. It has been suggested, for example, that the fact that structured observation studies of managers often find little evidence of planning in their everyday work (e.g. Mintzberg 1973) is due to the tendency for the method to fragment a manager's activities into discrete parts. This means that something like planning, which may be an element in many managerial activities, becomes obscured from view (Snyder and Glueck 1980).

Structured observation neglects the context of behaviour

There are sometimes concerns that structured observation neglects the context within which behaviour takes place. For example, if you were observing teaching behaviour, you would develop categories and variables based on observations, but you would not know how the teacher's other characteristics and experiences may affect their teaching practice. Of course, the way to address this criticism would be to collect this kind of data, but structured observation researchers tend to concentrate on overt behaviour.

Structured observation can pose ethical challenges

As we showed in Chapter 6, all types of social research involve ethical considerations, and there are particular challenges associated with specific research methods. There are two key ethical considerations in structured observation:

- Is permission from anyone required in order to carry out the structured observation in the chosen setting?
- Is it necessary to let anyone know that they are being observed?

You may need to get permission to undertake the structured observation from someone in charge of the setting—as was the case in Blatchford et al.'s (2003) structured observations in classrooms (see Research in focus 12.3), where permission from the school was required.

These considerations also depend on whether the observation is conducted covertly or not. **Covert research**, which we discuss further in Chapter 18, presents particular ethical challenges as it does not involve seeking consent from participants. It could be considered a form of deception. This may also be problematic when you seek ethical approval for your project from your university or organization. It is also worth noting that it may not always be possible or appropriate to gain consent when planning to undertake a structured observation: for example, if you were going to conduct a study that involved observing and coding crowd behaviour or shoppers in a store. In these cases, it is important to explain your decision-making in your ethics application and to show how you have assessed whether your approach will cause potential risk or harm to participants, or to you as the researcher.

Our aim here is not to put you off from considering structured observation as an approach to research, but to make you aware of some of the challenging ethical considerations that you will need to explore.

KEY POINTS

- Structured observation is an approach to the study of behaviour that is an alternative to survey-based measures.
- It involves following explicit rules for the recording of behaviour.
- Structured observation has tended to be used in relation to quite a narrow range of behaviour, such as that occurring in schools.
- It shares with survey research problems concerning reliability, validity, and generalizability.
- Reactive effects have to be taken into account but should not be exaggerated.
- Field stimulations represent a form of structured observation but suffer from difficulties concerning ethics.
- Problems with structured observation revolve around the difficulty of attributing meaning to behaviour and employing a relevant framework for recording it.

QUESTIONS FOR REVIEW

1. What are the main characteristics of structured observation?
2. To what extent does structured observation provide a better approach to studying behaviour than questionnaires or structured interviews?
3. What is an observation schedule?
4. 'An observation schedule is much like a self-completion questionnaire or structured interview except that it does not involve asking questions.' Discuss.

5. Devise an observation schedule of your own for observing an area of social interaction in which you are regularly involved. Ask people with whom you normally interact in those situations how well they think it fits what goes on. Have you missed anything out?
6. What are the main ways in which behaviour can be recorded in structured observation?
7. Identify some of the main sampling strategies in structured observation.
8. How far do considerations of reliability and validity in structured observation mirror those that arise in relation to asking questions in structured interviews and self-completion questionnaires?
9. What is the reactive effect, and why might it be important in relation to structured observation research?
10. What are field stimulations, and what ethical concerns do they pose?
11. 'The main problem with structured observation is that it does not allow us access to the intentions that lie behind behaviour.' Discuss.
12. How far do you agree with the view that structured observation works best when used in conjunction with other research methods?

ONLINE RESOURCES

www.oup.com/he/srm6e

You can find our notes on the answers to these questions within this chapter's **online resources**, together with:

- *audio/video comments* on this topic from our 'Learn from experience' panellists;
- *self-test questions* for further knowledge-checking;
- a *flashcard glossary* to help you recall key terms; and
- a *Student Researcher's Toolkit* containing practical materials and resources to help you conduct your own research project.

CHAPTER 13

CONTENT ANALYSIS

CHAPTER GUIDE

Quantitative content analysis is a method of analysing documents and texts that aims to quantify content in terms of a particular range of categories in a way that is systematic and replicable. In this chapter we explore

- the kinds of research question that content analysis is suited to;
- how to sample the material you want to analyse;
- what kinds of features of documents or texts are counted;
- how to go about coding, which is the core of doing a content analysis;
- using online material as an object of content analysis;
- the content analysis of visual images;
- the advantages and disadvantages of content analysis.

13.1 Introduction

Content analysis is useful in exploring patterns and trends in relation to social research topics. Imagine that we are interested in the amount and nature of the interest shown by the mass media, such as newspapers, in a major news item—for example Facebook security, super-injunctions, or the resignation of a political party leader. We might want to ask questions like the following.

- When did news items on this topic first begin to appear?
- Which newspapers were fastest in generating an interest in the topic?
- Which newspapers have shown the greatest interest in the topic?
- At what point did media interest begin to decrease?
- Have journalists' stances on the topic changed?

Content analysis is a useful approach for analysing the data available to us in order to answer these kinds of research questions. It is also an important way of analysing data that may not be available in other forms. For instance, it is extremely unlikely that you would be able to interview the prime minister about environmental issues or get them to complete a questionnaire on the topic, but you could certainly conduct a content analysis of relevant speeches they have given.

Content analysis can be quantitative or qualitative. This chapter will predominantly focus on quantitative approaches to using content analysis, whereas Chapter 22 will discuss qualitative content analysis. Quantitative content analysis involves a process of counting the number of instances of particular categories or events (for example, certain words) occurring within the content being analysed. It is a very flexible method that we can apply to a variety of different media, whether printed or online, written or spoken, and involving words and/or images. In some respects it is not really a research method, in that it is an approach to analysing documents and texts rather than a way of generating data. However, it is usually treated as a research method because of its distinctive approach to analysis.

13.2 What is content analysis?

The best-known definition of content analysis (which we define more fully in Key concept 13.1) is probably this one:

> Content analysis is a research technique for the objective, systematic and quantitative description of the manifest content of communication.
>
> (Berelson 1952: 18)

Another well-known definition is this:

> Content analysis is any technique for making inferences by objectively and systematically identifying specified characteristics of messages.
>
> (Holsti 1969: 14)

These definitions might at first seem quite complicated, but essentially they highlight two key qualities of quantitative forms of content analysis: *objectivity* and being *systematic*. These elements are mainly about how to devise and apply rules for assigning raw material (such as newspaper stories) to categories. As with the use of observation schedules (Chapter 12), researchers using content analysis need to clearly specify the rules in advance and ensure that the procedures for applying them are transparent, so that personal biases intrude as little as possible. Being systematic means that researchers must apply the rules in a consistent way so that bias is suppressed. The idea is that if researchers adhere to these two qualities, anyone could follow the rules they devise and replicate the results. This enhances the reliability of the data. Krippendorff (2018: 6) has also emphasized the importance of transparency and being able to come up with the same results, saying that content analysis needs to 'explicate what we are doing and describe how we derive our judgements, so that others—especially our critics—can replicate our results or build on them'. In practice, the rules may reflect the interests and concerns of the researcher who developed them, and may be a product of subjective bias, but the key point is that once they are formulated, we should be able to *apply* the rules without the intrusion of bias.

Berelson's definition also makes reference to 'quantitative description'. Given that the aim of content analysis is to produce quantitative accounts of raw mate-

KEY CONCEPT 13.1
What is content analysis?

Quantitative content analysis is an approach to analysing documents and texts that aims to quantify content in terms of predetermined categories in a way that is systematic and replicable. Quantitative content analysis tends to be **deductive** in approach, associated with testing theories or hypotheses, with an emphasis on using predetermined categories in the analysis of data. Qualitative content analysis, on the other hand, tends to take an **inductive** approach. This relies on inductive reasoning, whereby themes emerge from the data being studied, through repeated examination and comparison. With qualitative content analysis it is also important to recognize the significance of the context in which an **item** being analysed (and the categories derived from it) appeared.

When we use the term 'content analysis' in this chapter we are referring to *quantitative* content analysis, as defined at the beginning of this Key concept, whereas Chapter 22 focuses on *qualitative* approaches to content analysis.

rial in terms of categories specified by a set of rules, it is firmly embedded in **quantitative research**. This element of quantification has the effect of adding to the systematic and objective nature of the process and its application of neutral rules. Returning to the example areas for content analysis that we listed in Section 13.1, the method's quantitative element would allow us to identify the period in which a topic, such as Facebook security, received the most media attention, and whether newspapers differed significantly in how they covered the issue.

It is worth noting two other elements in Berelson's definition, especially because they contrast with Holsti's. First, Berelson refers to 'manifest content', meaning that content analysis aims to uncover the *apparent* content of the item in question: what it is clearly about. Holsti refers to 'specified characteristics', which suggests that this method could be used to conduct an analysis in terms of what we might term *latent content*—that is, the meanings that lie beneath the indicators of content. To uncover latent content, we need to interpret underlying meanings. For example, Siegel et al. (2013) used content analysis to examine alcohol brand references in popular music in the USA in the years 2009 to 2011. In addition to the manifest content of brand references (brands and the types of alcohol referred to), they coded references to latent meaning, such as whether the brands and alcohol type were referred to in a positive, negative, or neutral context and whether references to the consequences of alcohol use were positive, negative, or neutral. Writers sometimes make a similar distinction between emphasizing the text (in particular, counting certain words) and *themes within* the text; the latter involves searching for certain ideas within the text (Beardsworth 1980; Krippendorff 2018). It is also worth noting that some academics question whether latent content can be suitably measured in quantitative content analysis (Ahuvia 2001), with latent constructs more likely to be associated with qualitative content analysis (see Neuendorf 2016 for further discussion). Some researchers have criticized the focus on the manifest/latent dichotomy, noting the often fuzzy distinction between them (Riffe et al. 2014).

A second element in Berelson's definition that is not included in Holsti's is the reference to 'communication'. Berelson's (1952) book was about communication research, a field that has focused particularly on newspapers, television, and other mass media. Holsti refers more generally to 'messages', again raising the prospect that content analysis can be used more widely, in this case beyond mass media and mass communications. It is evident within social research that content analysis is applicable to many different forms of unstructured information, such as **transcripts** of **semi-structured** and **unstructured interviews** or answers to **open-ended questions** in surveys, although other forms of analysis are often undertaken (see Riffe et al. 2014). Content analysis involves examining 'data, printed matter, images or sounds—text—in order to understand what they mean to people, what they enable or prevent, and what the information conveyed by them does' (Krippendorff 2018: 2). Here are a few examples to illustrate the diverse range of information on which content analysis has been constructed:

- newspaper coverage of the UK sugar tax debate (Buckton et al. 2018);
- online dog obituaries (to assess their usefulness as a source of information about human–animal bonds) (MacKay et al. 2016);

- radio and television programmes, such as the depictions of gender on primetime television (Sink and Mastro 2017);
- speeches, such as the Queen's Speech in the UK (John and Jennings 2010) and speeches in the European Parliament (Proksch and Slapin 2010);
- alcohol brand references in the lyrics of popular songs (Siegel et al. 2013);
- discrimination narratives taken from sex discrimination cases (Bobbitt-Zeher 2011);
- gender stereotypes in selfies uploaded on Instagram (Döring et al. 2016);
- published research on parenting and childhood obesity (Gicevic et al. 2016);
- types of meals in popular paintings (Wansink et al. 2016);
- accounts of bullying on websites and blogs (Davis et al. 2015);
- policy conditionality in the International Monetary Fund's loan agreements (Kentikelenis et al. 2016);
- levels of populism exhibited by political parties in Western Europe using press releases collected in the context of 11 national elections (Bernhard and Kriesi 2019).

These examples are diverse, but content analysis has traditionally been used to examine printed texts and documents, particularly in the mass media. However, there is no doubt that it is becoming more widely used in alternative media forms including social media. Furthermore, many forms of mass media are available digitally and can now be accessed and analysed this way. Content analysis is one of a number of approaches to examining texts that have been developed over the years.

13.3 Conducting content analysis

Now that we have outlined what content analysis is and what it entails, in this section we consider the main elements of conducting content analysis: determining research questions; selecting a sample; deciding what to count; and devising a coding scheme. These are important if you plan to use this form of analysis.

Determining the focus

As with most quantitative research, researchers must specify precise research questions before conducting their analysis, as these questions will guide the selection of data to be content analysed and inform the **coding schedule**. If you do not clearly articulate your research questions, there is a risk that you will analyse inappropriate sources of data or that your coding schedule will miss out key **dimensions** of the things you are interested in.

Most content analysis is likely to revolve around the questions of

- *who* (gets included);
- *what* (gets included);
- *where* (does the issue get included);
- *location* (of coverage within the items analysed);
- *how much* (gets included); and
- *why* (does the issue get included).

Much content analysis is also interested in omissions in coverage—so not just what gets reported but what *doesn't* get reported. Such omissions can help reveal what is and is not important in the area you are researching. For example, if you were undertaking a quantitative content analysis of government documents reviewing the use of community care provision and there was limited or no coverage of issues such as 'quality', 'choice', and 'service user satisfaction', this may be just as important as finding that there was considerable coverage of 'costs' and 'efficiencies'.

Another issue often considered in content analysis is how much the amount of coverage of an issue *changes over time*. This may be included in the form of a research question. This was a key element of the study described in Research in focus 13.1.

Selecting a sample

There are several phases involved in selecting a **sample** for content analysis: you need to sample both the media to be analysed and the dates or time period(s) in which you are interested. Here, we will focus on using sampling to analyse the mass media, as the basic principles of this process are relevant to content analysis more generally. However, remember that content analysis can be applied to many different kinds of document. In Chapter 8 we

13

RESEARCH IN FOCUS 13.1
Exploring coverage over time

Young and Dugas (2011) used content analysis to explore how climate change is being reported in two major national newspapers in Canada by examining the reporting in three time periods: 1988–9, 1998–9, and 2007–8. A key research question here related to changes over time in relation to newspaper coverage of climate change. The authors say that newspaper coverage is especially important for climate change as there is evidence that newspapers are the public's main source of information.

Young and Dugas searched a digital database of articles from the two newspapers using these keywords: 'climate change', 'global warming', 'greenhouse effect', and 'greenhouse gas'. Their content analysis produced some interesting findings: for example, claims that climate change is 'anthropogenically induced' (that is, caused by humans) declined substantially and progressively over the three time periods. They also show that some types of voice have become less prominent in terms of climate change, such as university-based experts and government employees; in contrast, representatives of industry associations and of environmental groups have become more prominent. More recently, Stoddart et al. (2016) built on this quantitative content analysis, asking the research question: 'What happened to the volume of climate change coverage during the period 1997–2010?' (2016: 219). They extended Young and Dugas's work by using a wider variety of themes and some more up-to-date reporting, and identified many similar trends.

considered the process of identifying a sample and the process of collecting data from a **representative sample**. These considerations are also worth thinking about when undertaking a quantitative content analysis.

13

Sampling media

Many studies of the mass media involve setting out a research problem in the form of 'the representation of *X* in *Y*'. The *X* could be trade unions, food scares, crime, drink driving, or social science research; the *Y* could be newspapers, TV, radio, podcasts, songs, tweets, blogs, or speeches. Once you have decided on broadly what **category** of material you will analyse (the *Y*), you need to think carefully about how you will select your sample within this material. For example, if you start by thinking that you want to analyse the mass media, you need to ask yourself which form of media will be your focus. If you intend to analyse newspapers, you need to consider whether you will include

- tabloids and/or broadsheets;
- weekday and/or weekend papers;
- national and/or local papers;
- paid-for and/or free newspapers.

And then, at a more granular level: Will you analyse all news items within your chosen papers, or only some? For example, would you include feature articles and letters to the editor, or only news items?

When conducting content analysis, researchers will usually choose one or possibly two forms of mass media and may sample within that type or types, although there are times when they examine multiple forms of mass media. For example, Stroobant et al. (2018) undertook a cross-sectional quantitative content analysis of health news items in the Dutch-speaking part of Belgium using a variety of different media—including newspapers, magazines, radio, television, and online health news websites—over a one-month period.

Sampling dates

Sometimes, the decision about which dates or time periods to sample is dictated by when a particular phenomenon occurred. For example, Bligh et al. (2004) were keen to explore Max Weber's (1947) suggestion that charismatic leadership is most likely to emerge during a period of crisis. By examining the **rhetoric** of President George W. Bush's speeches before and after the terrorist attacks on the World Trade Center, the Pentagon, and Flight 73 on 11 September 2001, the authors found not only that his speeches took on a more charismatic rhetoric compared to before the attacks, but also that the media portrayal of Bush tended to incorporate a more charismatic tone. In this case, the sample clearly needed to focus on the key date of 9/11 (11 September 2001, the date on which the coordinated attacks took place), though the researchers still needed to decide on the end date for their analysis. The last of the speeches they analysed was given on 11

March 2002, which raises the question of how long a charismatic style might be expected to continue following a crisis.

Similarly, Gunn and Naper (2016) performed a quantitative content analysis of tweets leading up to the US presidential election in 2012, drawing on 3,420 tweets posted during the US election campaign on the Twitter accounts of Democrat Barack Obama (who had been president since 2009) and Republican candidate Mitt Romney. In this case the end date of 6 November 2012 (the date of the election) was already set by the nature of the research topic; the researchers had to choose a start date, and they decided to include the entire campaign cycle, starting from 1 January 2012. In the UK, similar time-specific content analysis could be conducted in relation to Brexit or the Scottish referendum.

With a research question that involves researching an ongoing general phenomenon, such as the media representation of social science research or crime, the researcher has more choice over the dates to include. The principles of **probability sampling** that we outlined in Chapter 8 can easily be adapted for sampling dates. For example, Döring et al. (2016) took a **random sample** of 250 selfies portraying females and 250 selfies portraying males from images available on the photo sharing platform Instagram in April 2014. The selfies were identified using the internationally-used hashtags #selfie, #I, #me, #self, and #myself, with the researchers selecting every tenth picture displaying a male or female person until they reached the required sample size of 500.

One important factor to think about when sampling dates is whether you are focusing on an issue that involves conducting the content analysis as it happens, in which case you may begin at any time and the key decision becomes when to stop, or whether you need to select media from one or more time periods in the past.

Another consideration is making sure that your choice of dates or time periods (or other aspects associated with your choice of sample) does not mean that certain kinds of objects of analysis are over-represented in your sample. Random or **systematic sampling** will help prevent this issue, but sometimes you may need to take alternative steps. For example, in Research in focus 13.2 the authors write that because they 'wanted to avoid the overrepresentation of frequent and active Facebook users, for each profile the 20 last status updates were coded' (Beullens and Schepers 2013: 498). This kind of approach helps to ensure the sample is representative of the **population**.

RESEARCH IN FOCUS 13.2
Content analysis of social media

Beullens and Schepers' (2013) content analysis of 160 Belgian Facebook profiles is an interesting example of how this method can be used to analyse social media content. The study was driven by two research questions:

RQ1) How is alcohol use depicted on Facebook?

RQ2) How do peers react to alcohol-related content on Facebook?

The sample was created by producing a Facebook profile and sending friend requests to 166 college students who were informed that the researchers were looking for participants for their research. The authors chose to **code** the 20 most recent status updates rather than analysing activity within a set time frame, in order to avoid over-representing more frequent Facebook users in their sample. The researchers created a coding scheme that coded the sampled profiles and status updates at three levels: the profile (such as total number of photos); the personal/profile photos (all photos that included alcohol); and status updates (all text that included a reference to alcohol use). As an example of how coding worked at one of these levels, one of the **variables** at the second level, the personal/profile photos, was 'Evaluation of use'. Photos were coded according to whether they were in one of four categories.

(1) Positive: the picture shows alcohol use in a positive context (for example, a picture showing someone raising a glass with a smile on their face).

(2) Negative: the picture shows alcohol use in a negative context (for example, a picture showing someone looking disapprovingly at a drunk person).

(3) Neutral: the picture shows alcohol use in a neutral context (for example, a picture in which someone shows no explicit emotion on their face).

(4) Unknown: impossible to discern based on the picture (for example, a picture in which no face is shown).

In terms of the 'Evaluation of use' variable, Beullens and Schepers found that alcohol use was portrayed in a positive light in 72 per cent of photos and neutral in 23 per cent, while the remaining 5 per cent were either negative or unknown. This is perhaps unsurprising, given that photos are most frequently taken in positive contexts. Among the authors' other findings are that photos that portrayed alcohol use positively and that showed a brand logo were significantly more likely to receive Facebook 'likes' than others.

Deciding what to count

What should be counted in the course of a content analysis depends on the nature of the research questions under consideration. When conducting content analysis we need to think about different kinds of *units of analysis*. Common units of analysis include actors (people), words, subjects or themes, and dispositions. These are the types we consider in this section, but what you count for your own project will depend on the nature of your research questions.

Significant actors

The significant actors—in other words, the main figures—in any news item and their characteristics are often important items to code, particularly in the context of mass-media news reporting. You might record the following kinds of things.

- What kind of person has produced the item? (for example, a general or specialist news reporter)
- Who is or are the main focus of the item? (for example, a politician, expert, government spokesperson, or representative of an organization)
- Who provides alternative voices? (for example, a politician, expert, government spokesperson, representative of an organization, or person in the street)
- What was the context for the item? (for example, an interview, the release of a report, or an event such as an outbreak of hostilities or a minister's visit to a hospital)

The main reason researchers record such details is so that they can map the main figures involved in news reporting in an area, which could help reveal some of the mechanics involved in producing information for the public.

Words

Researchers undertaking content analysis sometimes count the frequency with which certain words occur. The use of some words rather than others can be significant, for example revealing a media tendency to sensationalize certain events. Bailey et al. (2014) examined the incidence of what they call 'epistemic markers' (words or expressions that imply uncertainty) in the media reporting of climate change. They compared two US newspapers with two Spanish newspapers for the years 2001 and 2007—chosen because these were years when reports from the Intergovernmental Panel on Climate Change (IPCC) were published. They searched the newspapers for various types of words and expressions, including the following.

- Activities leading to uncertain outcomes (for example, 'predicting', 'estimating')
- Quantitative indications of uncertainty (for example, 'probability', 'likelihood')
- Challenges to the IPCC and its reports (for example, 'challenge', 'debate')
- References to opponents of climate change ideas (for example, 'deniers')
- 'Modifiers' (for example, 'controversial').

While words alone *can* be interesting, when **coding** the articles 'context was always considered before a term was marked as "epistemic"' (Bailey et al. 2014: 202). Epistemic markers were found to be clearly more frequent in US than Spanish news items in both years, although their use increased from 2001 to 2007 in both countries. The authors point out that the latter is striking because scientific understanding of climate change and of the role of humans in connection with climate change strengthened during this period.

So how do we count words? Unlike many previous generations of researchers, we have the option to use **computer-assisted** (or automated) **content analysis (CACA)**. This software can count the frequency of words or phrases in a body of text (as in Research in focus 13.3) and offers considerable advantages over manual methods. These include the fact that it eliminates problems of human bias, cognitive limitations, and **inter-rater reliability** or **intra-rater reliability**; it allows key-word-in-context (KWIC) output to be easily generated (this can help with interpreting words and their frequencies); it can establish co-occurrences of words and phrases (the counting of paired data within a collection unit); and it can handle a lot of textual material very quickly. It does, however, have some limitations, such as its inability to handle nuances; the fact that it is difficult to give the software a sufficiently comprehensive list of words or phrases to search for; and the fact that relying on the software could lead to over-focusing on frequency and not paying enough attention to interpretation and meaning (Bligh and Kohles 2014).

Despite its limitations, CACA tools are increasingly used and widely available in different forms. You may have already used this software without realizing, by searching newspapers' websites or archives—we discuss this in Tips and skills 13.1. Researchers often use specialist CACA software for larger scale projects. Research in focus 13.3 provides an example of a study conducted using software called Wordsmith, and the Bligh et al. (2004) study we considered in the section 'Sampling dates' used a program called DICTION to examine whether there was a shift in the charismatic tone of President George W. Bush's speeches before and after the terrorist attacks of 9/11. This software can make use of pre-existing dictionaries that have already been set up, and it also allows users to create dictionaries for their own needs. You can find more information about DICTION at **www.dictionsoftware.com/diction-overview/** (accessed 5 June 2019).

Another kind of CACA is automated **sentiment analysis**. Greaves et al. (2014) used a combination of quantitative and qualitative content analysis to examine tweets aimed at NHS hospitals (we discuss this study in Chapter 22—see Section 22.6 under 'Social media'). Greaves et al. carried out most of the quantitative content analysis manually but also used automated sentiment analysis 'to produce an overall sentiment score for each tweet of positive, negative or neutral' (Greaves et al. 2014: 289). A useful program for doing sentiment analysis is SentiStrength (**http://sentistrength.wlv.ac.uk/**, accessed 7 March 2020), which aims to detect positive and negative sentiment in a given social web context (Thelwall 2017). Our panellist Jodie used sentiment analysis in her study of LGBT attitudes expressed on Twitter—see Learn from experience 13.1.

Although some of the software we have mentioned is not free, and your university may not have access to it, it is worth noting that often the companies that own the software offer free trials. Another way of trying CACA for free is to use **CAQDAS** software of the kind we demonstrate in our **online resources** to do some of the basic word counting and KWIC functions.

Subjects and themes

When conducting a content analysis a researcher will often want to code text in terms of subjects and themes. Essentially, what they are trying to do is to categorize the phenomenon or phenomena of interest. For example, in their content analysis of how social science research is reported in the British mass media, Fenton et al. (1998) wanted to classify the main social science disciplines in the research being reported into one of seven types: sociology; social policy; economics; psychology; business and management; political science; and interdisciplinary. On an even more basic level, researchers might categorize gender, as in Sink and Mastro's (2017) content analysis on the depictions of gender on primetime television and Döring et al.'s (2016) work on gender stereotypes in selfies uploaded on Instagram.

Buckton et al. (2018) conducted a quantitative content analysis on the media representation of sugar taxation. Their coding process involved reading the full text of

13

TIPS AND SKILLS 13.1
Counting words in digital news reports

The growing availability of printed news media in digital form, such as in online databases, makes it much easier to search for and count keywords and phrases in this kind of context. Most of the main UK newspapers and many overseas ones are available in digital formats either through their own websites or through websites such as British Media Online (**www.wrx.zen.co.uk/britnews.htm**, accessed 6 June 2019), or the British Newspaper Archive (**www.britishnewspaperarchive.co.uk/content/getting_started**, accessed 4 January 2020), which act as platforms for a number of different digital newspapers. The British Library Blog (**https://blogs.bl.uk/thenewsroom/2014/02/10-great-online-newspaper-archives.html**, accessed 4 January 2020) provides links to a variety of useful platforms for newspapers around the world. Universities usually provide access to databases of newspaper articles too: for example, Nexis (**https://advance.lexis.com/**, accessed 7 March 2020), which provides news information from a variety of sources, including UK national and regional newspapers, international newspapers, and foreign language news sources in Dutch, French, German, Arabic, Spanish, and Portuguese.

RESEARCH IN FOCUS 13.3
Digitized keyword analysis

Seale et al. (2006) used CACA software to examine all postings on a single day (20 April 2005) to the two most popular online support groups in the UK for people with breast and prostate cancer. They used a type of content analysis that they call **comparative keyword analysis**, and considered keywords to be words that occurred with unusual frequency compared with others in the data analysed. Seale and his colleagues were interested in comparing the keyword frequency in the breast cancer postings and the prostate cancer postings, searching for keywords using the specialist software Wordsmith: **www.lexically.net/wordsmith/** (accessed 6 June 2019).

Seale et al. (2006: 2582) then 'used this quantitative information to facilitate an interpretive, qualitative analysis focusing on the meanings of word clusters associated with keywords'. In effect, they used this quantitative analysis of words as a starting point for a more probing qualitative examination of the links between the words. In this case, the qualitative element complemented the quantitative component (see Chapter 24 for a further discussion of mixed methods approaches to social research). The researchers found that men with prostate cancer were more likely to use words associated with research (for example, 'study'), treatment (for example, 'radical prostatectomy'), and tests and diagnosis (for example, 'biopsy') compared to women discussing breast cancer. By contrast, women discussing breast cancer were more likely to use keywords associated with feelings (for example, 'scared') and people (for example, 'family'), and also to use 'superlatives' (for example, 'amazing').

LEARN FROM EXPERIENCE 13.1
Doing a sentiment analysis of Twitter data

13

Sentiment analysis can be used to analyse various forms of data including social media. Jodie explains how she used this approach to exploring Twitter as a platform for LGBT attitudes through the quantitative analysis of over 2 million tweets.

> In my undergraduate project, my research questions led me to investigate how attitudes toward the LGBT community and individuals manifest on Twitter and the extent to which this differed by gender. I chose to do sentiment analysis because the Collaborative Online Social Media Observatory (COSMOS) automatically assigns a sentiment score depending on the words included in the tweet text and, if identifiable, the gender of the Twitter user. Therefore, this seemed a natural analysis technique for the objectives of my research. In retrospect, it remains the most appropriate choice.
>
> Jodie

Access the **online resources** to hear Jodie's reflections on this theme.

You can read about our panellists' backgrounds and research experiences on page xxvi.

each newspaper article included in their study and, 'for each thematic code, recording whether the article overtly contained content relevant to that code'. They provided an example from a *Daily Mail* (29 May 2015) article that stated: 'The Scientific Advisory Committee on Nutrition last week called on the nation to halve the current recommended intake of sugar to seven teaspoons a day to tackle the growing obesity and diabetes crisis.' This was coded by the authors as associating sugar with both obesity and diabetes (either independently or through the link between obesity and diabetes).

Kentikelenis et al. (2016) used quantitative content analysis to explore countries' International Monetary Fund (IMF) loans between 1985 and 2014 and the conditions associated with these loans. In total, the researchers searched 4,590 loan-related documents to extract

55,465 conditions spread across 131 countries. The research consisted of a variety of documents including IMF staff reports, national governments' Letters of Intent, and accompanying Memoranda of Economic and Financial Policies, which specify conditionality. They were able to identify that the most recent data revealed a rising trend in measures associated with conditionality since 2008 (the time of the global financial crisis). Despite this increase in themes associated with conditionality, there has actually been a marked decline in the number of lending programmes.

While categorizations are often relatively straightforward, when the process of coding is thematic a more interpretative approach can be required. This means searching not just for manifest content but for latent content as well (see Section 13.2): in other words, probing beneath the surface in order to ask deeper questions about what is happening.

Dispositions

Researchers are likely to use another level of interpretation when they want to demonstrate a disposition (a particular value position or stance, whether positive or negative) in the texts being analysed. For example, a researcher might focus on establishing whether journalists reporting on an issue in the news media are positive about or hostile towards an aspect of it, such as their stances on the government's handling of a food scare crisis. In the case of the Buckton et al. (2018) study on the reporting of sugar taxation, each item was coded not only in terms of subjects and themes, but also whether it was positive or negative about sugar taxation. Similarly, when examining climate change reporting in US and Spanish newspapers (see Section 13.3 under 'Words'), Bailey et al. (2014) categorized the tone of epistemic markers as negative or as neutral. In some cases in content analysis a researcher might need to infer whether there is a judgemental stance in the item being coded, and if so, the nature of that judgement, if there is no clear indication of this kind of value position.

Another way of revealing dispositions in content analysis is to code ideologies, beliefs, or principles. For example, for her content analysis of discrimination narratives, Bobbitt-Zeher (2011) coded narratives in terms of whether there was evidence of gender stereotyping—in other words, beliefs about the characteristics and capabilities of a particular gender. In doing so, she used a distinction between descriptive and prescriptive stereotyping, with the former being 'expressions of how women in general are assumed to be and expressions indicating that women's traits are incompatible with a particular job', and the latter referring to 'expressions that a particular woman worker violates gender assumptions' (Bobbitt-Zeher 2011: 770). She found the former kind of stereotyping to be the more common: it was found in 44 per cent of narratives against 8 per cent for the other mode. In the remaining 48 per cent of narratives, no stereotyping was found in the majority (37 per cent) and the rest were categorized as 'other'.

Sink and Mastro (2017) also coded in terms of beliefs in their study of depictions of gender stereotyping in primetime television. They sampled from primetime programmes (shown between 8 and 11 p.m. PST) airing during a 10-week period across nine major US TV networks. This resulted in a final sample of 89 programmes that depicted 1,254 unique characters. Those undertaking the coding were instructed that coding decisions should be based on how the average American television viewer would perceive the characters' behaviour in terms of the conceptual definitions that the researchers provided in the **coding manual** (sometimes referred to as a codebook). They found that although some gender stereotypes seem to be declining, others—including dominant men and sexually provocative women—have persisted.

13

Devising a coding scheme

It is probably clear from our discussion so far that coding is a crucial stage in the process of doing a content analysis. We are now going to focus on this stage in more detail. There are two main elements to a content analysis coding scheme: devising a coding schedule and devising a coding manual. To illustrate these processes, imagine that you are interested in crime reporting in national newspapers in the UK. You choose to focus on the reporting of crimes that are subject to court proceedings and where the victim is a person rather than an organization. To simplify the issue, let's include only the following variables:

1. nature of offence;
2. gender of perpetrator;
3. social class of perpetrator;
4. age of perpetrator;
5. gender of victim;
6. social class of victim;
7. age of victim;
8. depiction of victim;
9. position of news item.

People conducting content analysis would normally be interested in a much larger number of variables than this, and may also want to collect and record the data in a way in which the details of more than one offender and more than one victim can be included. (This is because crimes often involve multiple perpetrators and/or victims, so the details of each of the key figures—age, gender, occupation, depiction of victim—would need to be recorded.) However, to keep our example simple, we will assume just one perpetrator and one victim in each crime report.

Coding schedule

A coding schedule is a form where all the data relating to an item being coded will be entered. Figure 13.1 shows what this might look like—in very simplified terms—for our example of analysing the reporting of crime. Each column in Figure 13.1 is a dimension that we are coding, with the column headings indicating the dimension names. The blank cells on the coding form are the places in which you would write codes. You would use one coding form for each media item that you coded. The codes could then be transferred to a digital data file and analysed with a software package like SPSS, R, or Stata (access the **online resources** for written and video tutorials and quick reference guides to support you in using each of these programs).

13

Coding manual

The coding schedule in Figure 13.1 is very bare and may not seem to provide much information about what should be entered or where. This is where the coding manual comes in, as it provides a statement of instructions to coders including all the possible categories for each dimension being coded. It will include the following elements:

- a list of all the dimensions;
- the different categories for each dimension;
- the numbers (that is, codes) that correspond to each category; and
- guidance on what each dimension means and any factors that should be taken into account in deciding which code to allocate to each dimension.

Figure 13.2 provides the coding manual corresponding to the coding schedule shown in Figure 13.1.

You can see that the coding manual includes the occupation of both the perpetrator and the victim. This list of categories uses Goldthorpe et al.'s UK social class categorization (1968) and is based on the important summary by Marshall et al. (1988: 22), but 'unemployed', 'retired', and 'housewife' have been added to reflect terms that might be used in newspapers, as well as the category of 'other'. These considerations were informed by the Office for National Statistics (2019a), which is a UK government department responsible for statistics related to the UK's economy, population, and society. The offences are categorized in terms of those used by the police, in accordance with the rules of the UK government's Home Office (a ministerial department responsible for immigration, security, and law and order), to record crimes that have been brought to their attention. We could use much finer distinctions, but if you were conducting this analysis for a small-scale student project and were not planning to examine a large sample of news items, it might be best to use these kinds of broad categories. (They also have the advantage of being comparable to the Home Office data, which could be illuminating.) The coding schedule and manual in Figures 13.1 and 13.2 would allow you to record two offences, as a single incident might involve more than one offence. If there were more than two, you would need to decide which additional offences were the most significant—you would need to treat the main offence mentioned in the article as the first one.

By providing coders with complete lists of all categories for each dimension they are coding and guidance about how to interpret the dimensions, the coding manual fulfils a crucial role in guiding how the schedule is completed. Even if you are a lone researcher, such as a student conducting a content analysis for a dissertation or thesis, it is important to spend ample time in setting out instructions about how you will code to ensure that you are consistent in your approach. While you may not face the problem of inter-rater reliability, the issue of intra-rater reliability is still significant in this context

FIGURE 13.1
Coding schedule

Case number	Day	Month	Year	Nature of offence I	Gender of perpetrator	Occupation of perpetrator	Age of perpetrator	Gender of victim	Occupation of victim	Age of victim	Depiction of victim	Nature of offence II	Position of news item

FIGURE 13.2
Coding manual

Nature of offence I

1. Violence against the person
2. Sexual offences
3. Robbery
4. Burglary in a dwelling
5. Burglary other than in a dwelling
6. Theft from a person
7. Theft of pedal cycle
8. Theft from shops
9. Theft from vehicle
10. Theft of motor vehicle
11. Vehicle interference and tampering
12. Other theft and handling stolen goods
13. Fraud and forgery
14. Criminal damage
15. Drug offences
16. Other notifiable offences

Gender of perpetrator

1. Male
2. Female
3. Unknown

Occupation of perpetrator

1. I Higher grade professionals, administrators, and officials; managers in large establishments; large proprietors
2. II Lower-grade professionals, administrators, and officials; higher-grade technicians; managers in small business and industrial establishments; supervisors of nonmanual employees
3. IIIa Routine nonmanual employees in administration and commerce
4. IIIb Personal service workers
5. IVa Small proprietors, artisans, etc., with employees
6. IVb Small proprietors, artisans, etc., without employees
7. IVc Farmers and smallholders; self-employed fishermen
8. V Lower-grade technicians, supervisors of manual workers
9. VI Skilled manual workers
10. VIIa Semi-skilled and unskilled manual workers (not in agriculture)
11. VIIb Agricultural workers
12. Unemployed
13. Retired
14. Housewife
15. Student
16. Other
17. Unknown

Age of perpetrator

Record age (–1 if unknown)

Gender of victim

1. Male
2. Female
3. Unknown
4. Organization (if victim is an organization as in fraud cases)

Occupation of victim

Same as for occupation of perpetrator

(if not applicable, code as 99)

Age of victim

Record age (–1 if unknown; –2 if not applicable)

Depiction of victim

1. Victim responsible for crime
2. Victim partly responsible for crime
3. Victim not at all responsible for crime
4. Not applicable

Nature of offence II (code if second offence mentioned in relation to the same incident; code 0 if no second offence)

Same as for Nature of offence I

Position of news item

1. Front page
2. Inside
3. Back page

(see Section 13.3 under 'Potential difficulties with devising coding schemes').

Let's apply this coding scheme and manual to two news items that you might be analysing: see Figures 13.3 and 13.4. Figure 13.3 is from a UK broadsheet newspaper, the *Sunday Times*, whereas Figure 13.4 is from a UK tabloid newspaper, the *Daily Star*. (Remember that when we discussed sampling—see

FIGURE 13.3
Reporting a crime in national newspapers I

THE SUNDAY TIMES

17.07.16 / 11

Josh Boswell and Leah Gavron

A COUPLE celebrating their 20th wedding anniversary are among more than 130,000 British tourists who have been left thousands of pounds out of pocket after a budget travel firm collapsed this weekend.

Lowcostholidays ceased trading abruptly on Friday evening, leaving 27,000 customers at resorts and 110,000 who had booked trips facing unpaid accommodation and travel bills, according to the firm's administrators.

Leah and Peter Norman had booked a three-week "dream holiday" for October through the travel operator to celebrate two decades of marriage. The couple from East Sussex said they were "gutted" by the firm's demise.

"We do not believe our travel insurance will cover the loss so it looks as though we've lost everything apart from the flights to Spain," Peter Norman said.

Wendy Maddison, from Yorkshire, had booked a £2,500 holiday to Tenerife for next month. She and her partner have recently separated and the holiday was to be their last together with their seven-year-old son.

Maddison said that if they still wanted to go ahead with the holiday it would now cost them an extra £1,300 to rebook the hotel and transfers.

"I'm upset, angry and frustrated that there is no one to speak [to], no help available to people whatsoever. I hope to go ahead for my little lad more than anything . . . I'm not optimistic though," she said.

Administrators Smith & Williamson said flights had already been paid for customers who were currently on holiday, but in many cases the hotel bills were not covered. As a result some tourists who booked through the firm face being stranded abroad after being asked to pay for their accommodation a second time.

Claire Price from Warrington, Cheshire, said she and other tourists at the Crete resort of Rethymnon are having to pay their hotel bills again or face being asked to leave.

David Early, a Glaswegian visiting Magaluf, Spain, with his girlfriend, had paid £800 for his hotel but was forced to leave this weekend when the owners demanded that he pay the bill again.

Kyle Hobbs from Swindon, Wiltshire, has also been left stranded: "We flew out yesterday on a delayed flight and arrived at the hotel only to be told that our booking had been cancelled while we were in the air. No one is answering any phones and our travel insurance was with Lowcostholidays as well. We're completely stuck. The travel company should not get away with it."

Eight teenagers from Nuneaton, Warwickshire, who had spent a total of £5,000 on a holiday to Malia in Crete before they go to university, face paying another £2,500 if they decide to go ahead with the trip. "We are gutted because now we have either lost our money or need to pay even more money to get a hotel," said Lewis Comins, 19.

The Association of British Travel Agents said "most travel insurance will not cover travel organiser failure" and advised customers to contact Citizens Advice and Trading Standards.

Lowcosttravelgroup, the parent company, was founded in 2004 by Paul Evans, who began his career as a resort manager for Club 18-30. He upset customers and regulators in 2013 by moving his company from the UK to Spain, taking it out of the Air Travel Organisers' Licensing scheme, which protects the customers of British package holiday operators.

Evans lives in Spain but still owns a £2m house in Fulham, west London.

Customers have left furious messages on the Lowcostholidays Facebook page underneath adverts for "60% off" deals posted just hours before the company went under.

Sales staff made redundant this weekend claimed that they were also kept in the dark by bosses and were still waiting to be paid six weeks of wages.

One Lowcostholidays salesman, who asked to remain anonymous, said he had been selling holidays costing thousands of pounds to customers as recently as Thursday: "We were summoned to a conference call . . . and told: that's it. We were kept completely in the dark . . . We've been screwed as much as customers."

A statement on the Lowcostholidays website expressed "deep regret" and blamed the "turbulent financial environment" for its collapse.

@joshtboswell

Peter and Leah Norman were due to celebrate their 20th wedding anniversary with a break booked through lowcostholidays. Wendy Maddison, above, had paid £2,500 for a trip to Tenerife

Thousands left stranded as holiday company goes bust

Paul Evans, the company's founder, and his £2m London home

Author's partner on murder charge

Robin Henry

THE partner of novelist Helen Bailey appeared in court yesterday charged with her murder.

Ian Stewart, 55, was charged after the body of the 51-year-old author was found in the garden of their home in Royston, Hertfordshire, on Thursday. A post-mortem will be carried out tomorrow.

Stewart appeared at Hatfield magistrates' court yesterday and was remanded in custody until tomorrow. He was arrested last week on suspicion of murder as specialist officers carried out searches of the £1.3m home and a holiday house in Broadstairs, Kent.

Bailey: vanished from home on April 11

Stewart has also been charged with perverting the course of justice by reporting Bailey as missing and hiding her body, and preventing a lawful burial.

Bailey vanished with her miniature dachshund on April 11 after apparently saying she needed some "time to herself". The dog's body was also found by police.

The author wrote the popular Electra Brown series of books and had written Planet Grief, a successful blog, after her husband drowned in Barbados in 2011 after 22 years together. She moved in with Stewart, a widower and father-of-two, in 2014.

Source: *Sunday Times*. 'Author's Partner on Murder Charge', 17 July 2016, p. 11. Reprinted with kind permission of the publisher: The Sun / News Licensing.

Section 13.3 under 'Selecting a sample'—we discussed the importance of being clear on not only what media form(s) you will be including in your analysis, newspapers in this example, but also what *types* of that media form you will look at, tabloid and broadsheet in this example.)

You would fill in the coding of the incidents on coding schedules like the one shown in Figure 13.1, and the data from each form would then be entered as a row of data in a computer program such as IBM SPSS.

The coding of the incident in Figure 13.3 would appear as in Figure 13.5; the data entered on the computer would appear as follows:

123 17 07 16 1 1 17 55 2 6 51 3 16 2

(Note that the news item in Figure 13.3 contains a second offence, which has been coded as 16 under 'Nature of offence II'.)

Figure 13.6 contains the form that would be completed for the item in Figure 13.4. The following row of data would be created:

301 08 11 18 1 1 1 −1 1 17 52 2 0 2

You would complete a form like this for each news item within the chosen period or periods of study.

Potential difficulties with devising coding schemes

There are several potential issues to be aware of when devising a content analysis coding scheme, and they are very similar to the kinds of considerations involved in

FIGURE 13.4

Reporting a crime in national newspapers II

10 DAILY STAR, Thursday, November 8, 2018

FOOTIE ACE NUTTED IN STORE BY LOVE RIVAL

YOU HAVE COT TO BE KIDDING

★ A BRITISH baby furniture firm has been slammed for creating a cot with a built-in iPad. Gary Taylor designed the £1,500 crib to help his nine-month-old daughter Graysie drift off to sleep.

But educational psychologist Dr Gary Allen said: "It won't be long before apps are developed simply to occupy a baby or child. It's outrageous."

★ Gary hit back: "It's not to sit your child in all day watching Peppa Pig. Some of the people hammering it have bought their child an iPad at four."

APPLE OF OUR EYE: Gary, wife Gemma and Graysie

COUPLE: Dorigo and Claire arrive at court

Star attacked after pair seen together

by MATT DRAKE

FORMER footballer Tony Dorigo was head-butted in a swanky department store by a jealous love rival.

Gareth Senior flew into a rage after spotting the star and his ex-girlfriend. He could be heard shouting: "I knew you were after her."

The IT manager started an 18-month relationship with Claire Joss in April 2016 after meeting her at work. But the relationship deteriorated after Senior introduced her to former Leeds United and England ace Mr Dorigo, 52.

JEALOUS: Senior

The couple split just before Christmas last year and Senior became suspicious they were together.

Then he saw the pair in the Victoria Gate store in Leeds.

Mr Dorigo said: "He was swearing and saying all sorts of things at this stage. I didn't really catch it all.

"He just headbutted me. I didn't really know what was going on. He caught me on my nose and top of the lip. I managed to move back or else my nose would have been broken."

Ms Joss said: "Gareth was shouting over the top of me. Words to the effect of he was going to kill Tony. Something along the lines of: 'I knew you were after her'."

Senior, of Churwell, Leeds, was convicted of actual bodily harm at Leeds magistrates.

He was fined £500 and ordered to pay £100 compensation.

news@dailystar.co.uk

Source: *Daily Star*. 'Footie Ace Nutted in Store by Love Rival', 8 November 2018, p. 10. Reprinted with kind permission of the publisher: *Daily Star*, 2018/Reach Licensing.

designing an **interview schedule** or **observation schedule** (see Chapters 9 and 12). You can avoid certain kinds of difficulties by making sure that your coding scheme has the following elements.

- *Discrete dimensions.* Make sure that your dimensions are entirely separate, with no conceptual or empirical overlap between them.
- *Mutually exclusive categories.* Make sure that there is no overlap in the categories you are using for each dimension, because if the categories are not mutually exclusive you will be unsure about how to code each item later on.
- *Exhaustive categories.* Make sure your list of categories is sufficiently comprehensive. When you are coding, all possible categories for each dimension should be available to you.
- *Clear instructions.* The instructions and coding manual should be very clear about how each dimension should be interpreted and what factors should be taken into account when assigning codes to each category. This means that instructions sometimes have to be very elaborate, but there should be little or no coder discretion in how codes are allocated to **units of analysis**.

FIGURE 13.5
Completed coding schedule for news item in Figure 13.3

Case number	Day	Month	Year	Nature of offence I	Gender of perpetrator	Occupation of perpetrator	Age of perpetrator	Gender of victim	Occupation of victim	Age of victim	Depiction of victim	Nature of offence II	Position of news item
123	17	07	16	1	1	17	55	2	6	51	3	16	2

FIGURE 13.6
Completed coding schedule for news item in Figure 13.4

Case number	Day	Month	Year	Nature of offence I	Gender of perpetrator	Occupation of perpetrator	Age of perpetrator	Gender of victim	Occupation of victim	Age of victim	Depiction of victim	Nature of offence II	Position of news item
301	08	11	18	1	1	1	–1	1	17	52	2	0	2

13

- *Clarity about the unit of analysis.* You need to be absolutely clear what constitutes the unit of analysis (see Section 13.3 under 'Deciding what to count'). For example, in our imaginary study of the media reporting of crime in the UK national press, more than one offence could be recorded per media item. You need to be clear about the distinction between the item being analysed (for example, a newspaper article—the unit of analysis) and the topic being coded (for example, an offence). Although you are likely to be interested in both, you still need to keep the distinction in mind, in order to avoid confusion.

To ensure that your coding scheme works well and avoids potential difficulties, we strongly recommend piloting early versions of it and your manual. Piloting is an important part of preparing to use many data-collection methods, and in this case it will help you identify difficulties in applying the coding scheme, such as uncertainty about which category to use when considering a certain dimension or discovering that there is no code to cover a particular case. It will also help you identify whether one category of a dimension tends to include an extremely large percentage of items. If this occurs, you might need to consider breaking that category down so that you can study the items in more detail.

You also need to consider the reliability of the coding when doing content analysis. We noted in 13.2 that content analysis involves devising clear rules and then applying them in a systematic way. This means that coding must be done consistently between coders (inter-rater reliability), and each coder must be consistent over time (intra-rater reliability). An important reason to **pilot** your coding scheme is to test for consistency between coders and, if time permits, consistency of coding over time. The process of assessing reliability is very similar to the process we briefly covered in the context of **structured observation**—see Section 12.6.

13.4 Content analysis of particular types of data

Having outlined the process of undertaking a quantitative content analysis, it is worth us giving more detailed consideration to how you might conduct content analysis on certain less traditional forms of data. In this section we look at applying the method to online data (websites, blogs, online forums, and social media) and visual materials. It is important to note that when considering your choice of data, you need to consider ethical issues. These include, among others, how the data was collected, whether the data can be reused, and, importantly, if consent has been provided to do so (see Chapters 6 and 14 for a further discussion of these ethical issues). We will touch on some of these issues in the following sections.

Content analysis of online data

Websites, social media posts, and similar virtual documents are sources of data in their own right and we can consider them as potential material for both quantitative and qualitative content analysis of the kind discussed in this chapter and Chapter 22. However, it would be wrong to treat all online data in the same way: it is important to distinguish content based on who has created it and what it has been created for.

In the following section we divide online material into four broad categories: websites, blogs, online forums, and social media. These are over-simplifications and some sources will sit between categories, but the broad principles of distinguishing between these four groups are important.

Websites

We have already shown how data used in more traditional content analysis is increasingly available through websites, including newspapers and policy documents. However, there are many examples of websites being the subject of content analysis. Websites are a rich source of data for social scientists, and indeed the study described in Research in focus 13.4 drew some interesting conclusions from a content analysis of school websites. There is a huge amount of publicly available data online (though, as we saw in Chapter 6, just because it is publicly available, this does not necessarily mean it can—ethically—be used in research), and like most documents, websites can be subjected to both qualitative and quantitative forms of analysis. However, there are a number of difficulties with using websites as sources of data in this way. For one thing, the four criteria for assessing the quality of documents (Scott 1990) that we discuss in Chapter 22 (see Section 22.2) can also be applied to websites. Scott's suggestions invite us to consider why a website is constructed. Why is it there at all? Is it there for commercial reasons? Does it have a particular purpose or motive? In other words, we should be no less sceptical about websites than about any other kind of document.

In addition to the issues that Scott's criteria raise, it is worth considering the following website-specific points.

- *Difficulties finding relevant websites.* Finding websites that relate to your research questions is likely to involve a lot of Google searching, and you need to bear in mind firstly that search engines may not give you access to the whole online world, and secondly that the sites they suggest could be a biased sample (for instance, they may be funded through advertising and may use

RESEARCH IN FOCUS 13.4

Conducting a content analysis of websites

Preventative health measures including the promotion of physical activity have become prominent in international policy discourse. However, in the USA, evidence suggests that most young people fail to meet recommended public health guidance for physical activity, and schools have been given a key role in assisting with addressing this problem. Kahan et al. (2019) decided to explore representations of physical activity on the websites of charter schools in the USA. School websites are the main way in which schools present themselves to the public and report on their activities. They offer public windows to share information about their programs, policies, and values. During spring 2018, the researchers completed a quantitative content analysis of specific information about physical activity on the websites of a representative sample of 759 US charter elementary schools. Nearly all schools (97 per cent) had a working website, but more than half (52 per cent) did not mention even one of five physical activity programs frequently offered at schools: physical education (PE), recess, intramurals, interscholastics, and physical activity clubs. PE, which represents a standard part of school curricula, was mentioned on only 34 per cent of the sites. Only 2 per cent of schools reported sufficient information to calculate the amount of PE, making it impossible to know whether sample schools provided sufficient PE to meet nationally recommended standards.

Overall, it was evident in the research that the school websites were neglected both as a way of identifying the importance of physical activity, and as an approach to letting students know about how and when to be active during school. However, although the quantitative content analysis showed the potential to generate data from schools in a cost-effective manner, the researchers found that the quantity and quality of data on physical activity programs on the websites was not sufficiently adequate to make widescale **generalizations**.

search engine optimization in order to appear higher up in the search rankings). There is also the fact that your search results will only be as good as the keywords that you enter. You need to try as many relevant keywords (and combinations of them—known as Boolean searches; see Chapter 5) as possible, and we suggest asking your supervisor or a librarian whether you are using the most appropriate ones.

- *Websites are constantly appearing and disappearing.* Researchers who base their investigations on websites have to accept that their analyses may be based on online data that no longer exists by the time the findings are published, and that new sites (which are perhaps more relevant to the research questions) may have appeared since they stopped collecting data.
- *Websites are continually changing.* Researchers might conduct an analysis on websites that are then thoroughly updated. This is why, when we reference a website in published work, we always include the exact date that the website was accessed (see Tips and skills 13.2).
- *There are multiple approaches to analysing websites.* Some draw on traditional ways of interpreting documents, such as **discourse analysis** and qualitative content analysis (see Chapter 21). Others have been developed specifically in relation to online material, such as the examination of hyperlinks between websites and their significance (Schneider and Foot 2004; Cowls and Bright 2017).

13

While the dynamic nature of websites makes it hard for other researchers to observe the original source on which a content analysis was conducted, it is not impossible. There is a concerted effort to archive historical internet pages and make them accessible for research purposes: for example, the Internet Archive provides access to over 411 billion web pages through its 'Wayback Machine' (**https://archive.org/web/**, accessed 28 February 2020).

Most researchers who use documents as the basis for their work have to confront the issue that it is difficult to determine the universe or population from which they are sampling. Therefore, the problems we have identified here and in Chapter 22 are not unique to websites. However, these problems are exacerbated by the fact that online content grows and changes so quickly—trying to study it is a bit like trying to hit a target that not only continually moves but is in a constant state of metamorphosis. Researchers need to be alert to the opportunities that online content offers, while remaining aware of the limitations of websites as material that can be analysed.

Blogs

Another type of online document that has been subjected to analysis is the blog. Blogs are a type of social media, but they tend to be presented as websites. In this sense they share many of the advantages and disadvantages of websites and we should ask the same questions of them: Why is it there? What is its purpose or motive? Blog content can also change, be edited, or be removed completely, and blogs are subject to the same difficulties as websites regarding their dynamic nature.

Boepple and Thompson (2014) conducted a quantitative content analysis of 21 'healthy living' blogs: that is, blogs in which the authors write about what they present as their healthy living regime. The blogs were sampled from those that had received a blogging award relating to health; of the blogs that had won an award, those with the largest numbers of page-views were selected. The authors coded information about the blogger and four categories of information:

TIPS AND SKILLS 13.2
Referring to websites

When referring to websites in academic work, you should include the date you consulted them—as we do throughout this book. This is a standard convention in academia, and it is very much associated with the fact that websites often disappear and frequently change. Citing the date on which you accessed the website may help to explain any discrepancies or 'page not found' errors if subsequent researchers want to follow up your findings, or even to check on them. This does mean, however, that you need to keep a running record of the dates you accessed the websites to which you refer. For example, if you wanted to refer to the Fawcett Society website, a charity campaigning for gender equality and women's rights at work, home, and public life, you would put the Fawcett Society (**www.fawcettsociety.org.uk/**, accessed [insert the date you access it]). This can be trickier with social media, but you should always include the source and the date you accessed it.

'appearance variables, thin appearance ideal variables, disordered food/nutrition variables and health variables' (Boepple and Thompson 2014: 364), as well as information in the 'About Me' sections of the blogs. The researchers found, for example, that five bloggers used very negative language about being fat or overweight and four expressed admiration for being thin. Boepple and Thompson draw the important conclusion that the blogs comprise messages that are 'potentially problematic' for anyone changing their behaviour on the basis of advice contained in them. As they put it: 'Much of the content emphasizes appearance, thin appearance ideals, and disordered messages about food/nutrition' (Boepple and Thompson 2014: 365).

Online forums

Online discussion forums have become a particularly fertile source of data for social scientists. They have proved especially interesting for researchers with interests in health and health-related issues (see Research in focus 13.3), but have been used for content analysis on a range of topics. Davis et al. (2015) conducted an analysis of postings that followed a blog post about a cyberbullying suicide by a 15-year-old named Amanda Todd. There were 1,094 comments, of which 482 contained stories about being bullied. Of the 482 stories, 12 per cent were about cyberbullying, 75 per cent about traditional bullying, and the rest comprised a mixture of both. Davis et al. analysed the stories for themes in terms of the reasons given for being bullied. The most common reason was to do with the victim's physical appearance. The researchers also coded the coping strategies developed by the victims and the perceived effectiveness of the strategies. The researchers say their findings imply that with both types of bullying the victims 'are often targeted because they do not conform in one way or another to mainstream norms and values' (2015: 371). Online forums can allow users to edit or delete their posts, so just like websites and blogs the content is dynamic. There are also ethical issues concerning whether data is public and whether presenting extracts of a blog in published work might cause harm to a participant (see Chapters 6 and 14 for further discussion of these ethical issues).

Social media

Much research has been conducted on the content produced on social networking platforms such as Facebook, Twitter, and Instagram. Quantitative analysis that has involved content analysis has used Twitter data to predict elections (Burnap et al. 2016) and crime patterns (Williams et al. 2017a) among other things. Social science students undertaking their final year dissertation or research project often focus on data from Twitter, Facebook, and Instagram to study a wide array of topics, from how masculinity and femininity are performed via profile pictures to gaining access to hard-to-reach populations through specialist groups. Learn from experience 13.2 gives an example: our panellist Simon's analysis of data from Twitter to investigate gender differences in the fear of crime.

The huge amount of data now available online, much of it produced by social networking sites, is known as '**Big Data**' (see Key concept 14.4). You may have seen or read some of the many books, articles, and videos in which people discuss how we can 'harness' this sea of information now available to us—which is, in its entirety, too large to process using normal data-processing methods. However, just because the data is there does not mean that it is available for researchers to use. We will not re-discuss here the points that we made in Section 6.5 (under 'Ethical issues for online data') concerning the ethics of using social media data for research and how users feel about it, but you should remember that there is an important distinction between content produced by organizations for public consumption and the user-generated content produced on social media in which the public/private boundaries are less clear. To take an example, is Facebook data in the public domain if you have to log in to the platform to access it?

In light of these concerns, there are several things that you should keep in mind when conducting a content analysis of social media data.

- *Public or private?* Be aware that privacy settings are highly individualized. For example, even if you can see the profile pictures of all of your friends on Facebook, this data might not be available to people *who are not friends of your friends*. This kind of data could not be considered to be in the public domain and you will need to seek **informed consent** (see Section 6.4 under 'Informed consent') from participants in order to use it in research.
- *Anonymity*. It is common for researchers working with textual data to reproduce extracts of the data to demonstrate a point relating to how they developed coding schemes—as we have seen in examples provided in this chapter. However, in these cases data from individuals is often anonymized. This presents challenges for using social media data, particularly that taken from Twitter, where a tweet can easily be traced back to an individual. The same can be said for image analysis from Facebook pages or Instagram posts.
- *Exposure*. It is important to be aware of the broad spectrum of opinion that comes from user-generated data. If

LEARN FROM EXPERIENCE 13.2

Doing a content analysis of Twitter data

Analysing social media can be a complicated process. Identifying a suitable sample is a key part of this, given the large amount of available data. Simon's postgraduate research focused on gender differences in the fear of crime in online and offline spaces and included the collection of Twitter data and the use of the Crime Survey for England and Wales.

> Conducting content analysis on Twitter data was no straightforward task. With a starting point of several million tweets that 'could' be relevant, it was necessary to filter these and identify only those that really related to what I wanted to study. This required a really good grasp of the phenomenon I needed to identify, which was the fear of crime. As I was matching the content to the Crime Survey for England and Wales, I could use this as a starting point for my filtering. Identifying my filtering terms was a laborious process. I had to test subsets of my data and constantly sense-check them to make sure I wasn't rejecting positive results. Slowly, I was able to build up a corpus of keywords that either included or rejected each individual tweet into an algorithm that I could apply to my data set. This was a great start—I could only take this approach so far, but it did allow me to reduce my data set to a manageable number. After this I adopted a much more traditional approach. I was able to identify differences in the content and group my data accordingly. For example, I could identify those who talked about personal experiences and those who tweeted more generally about how others should behave. The manual content analysis really allowed me to get to know my data and understand the subtle differences in it. This approach really worked for me. By doing this I was able to draw conclusions that had both a computational logic and a solid sociological foundation.
>
> Simon

You can read about our panellists' backgrounds and research experiences on page xxvi.

13

a user posts something xenophobic, misogynistic, or homophobic, then by reproducing this in your own work you are not only drawing attention to this individual and potentially causing them harm, but you are also creating a permanent record of their opinion that they can no longer remove. (As we saw in Section 6.4 under 'Informed consent', researchers must give participants the right at any stage to withdraw themselves and the data they have supplied from a study. Does immortalizing their social media opinion conflict with such a right?)

- *Replicability*. The terms of service of social media platforms vary greatly in what you can and cannot share with other people. If you want your work to be replicable and transparent, then you might consider how someone could access the same data that you did. With a website you provide a reference with a direct link to the source (see Tips and skills 13.2), but referencing social media data is much trickier.

Another challenge for the content analyst when faced with such data sources is how to reduce the population of tweets, images, or posts to a manageable size. We discuss this issue in Chapter 22 in the context of the qualitative content analysis of documents, but the suggestions there are relevant to quantitative content analysis too. Research in focus 13.5 provides an example of the process of reducing the sample size.

Social networking does not necessarily generate large populations of cases that have to be narrowed down through sampling. For example, Ledford and Anderson (2013) used content analysis to examine consumer responses to the way that the US drug company Novartis used Facebook to recall some batches of Excedrin, a headache medication. The company used the social media platform as a means of disseminating the recall, and the researchers examined Facebook posts to establish how consumers interacted as they sought information and support about what was happening. The researchers collected posts for the 10 days after the recall, producing 49 posts by the company and 655 posts by users. While this is a significant number of posts, the researchers chose to code all of them.

Content analysis of visual materials

Another data form that is increasingly used for content analysis and that brings up particular considerations for researchers is visual materials. We have already seen an example of this in research involving Facebook images by Beullens and Schepers (2013; see Research in focus 13.2). Visual content analysis is a useful approach to answering the questions of who or what is represented in visual data. Content analysis can be applied to various kinds of visual materials, including videos and vlogs or, in the case of Research in focus 13.6, paintings, and the principles we set out in earlier sections of this chapter in relation to textual forms can be applied to this kind of material too. The increasing use of smartphones and photo-based social media, such as Snapchat and Instagram, present possible sources of content that were not previously readily available. This means bearing in mind important considerations like the nature of the unit of analysis; sampling; reliability and **validity**; and deciding what it is you are going to be counting. Sampling decisions can be difficult, for instance, if there are different pictures of the same event. The choice of sample will depend on the amount of variation in the visual content. It is also important to note that analysis of visual content is extremely difficult without taking into account the context in which the data was produced. Bock et al. (2011) state that to understand the meaning of visual content, and be able to code and count it, it is also necessary to compile contextual information about the visual data.

To consider an example, Kapidzic and Herring (2015) undertook a content analysis using 400 photos on a chat site used by teenagers. One of their research questions was:

> RQ1: What differences, if any, are there in distance, behaviour, and dress in the profile pictures that male teens and female teens post for self-presentation?
>
> (Kapidzic and Herring 2015: 963)

Coding was done on all images in terms of distance (close, intermediate, or far); behaviour (looking away, which the authors call 'affiliation'; straight at camera, referred to as 'seduction'; down at camera, referred to as 'submission'; sideways at camera/head tilted, referred to as 'offer'; or other); and dress (fully dressed; revealingly dressed; partially dressed; or not applicable). When considering the behaviour variable they found particularly clear gender differences, with females being far more likely to look straight at the camera and males being more likely to look away, look down at the camera, or look sideways at the camera or with head tilted. They also identified differences regarding dress, with males more likely to be fully or partially dressed and females more likely to be revealingly dressed.

The Döring et al. (2016) study that we have considered in other contexts in this chapter used quantitative content analysis to examine a random sample of 500 selfies uploaded on Instagram (50 per cent representing females and 50 per cent males) and explore the degree of gender stereotyping. To code the images they used Goffman's (1979) and Kang's (1997) gender display categories (which include feminine touch, lying posture, withdrawing gaze, sparse clothing) in addition to three social media-related categories (kissing pout, muscle presentation, faceless portrayal) in order to measure the extent of gender stereotyping in the selfies. In line with the findings of Kapidzic and Herring (2015) the study revealed that the selfies were reproducing traditional gender stereotypes and that young females' selfies more often use 'social-media-specific gender expressions like the kissing pout, implying seduction/sexualization, and the faceless portrayal (implying focus on the body solely), while young males' selfies more often contain muscle presentation (implying strength)' (Döring et al. 2016: 961).

RESEARCH IN FOCUS 13.5
Content analysis of social media

An example is a content analysis by Humphreys et al. (2014) of the kinds of personal information disclosed on Twitter. The authors collected an initial sample of users and they then searched friends of this initial sample. They did this by taking the **median** number of friends of all users and searching for that median number of all members of the initial sample. They collected a second sample of tweets and in total collected 101,069 tweets. They then wanted to reduce these to a more manageable number through random sampling. Because they were also interested in how the tweets were submitted—whether through Twitter's website or app, or by text message—they took a random sample of 1,050 online and 1,050 text message tweets (though both figures declined slightly when non-English tweets were excluded). The authors found that not only do Twitter users share information about themselves, they often share information about others too. This included things like the activities people were engaged in, both at work and home, and, in some cases, the locations of these activities.

RESEARCH IN FOCUS 13.6
Content analysis of visual data

Wansink et al. (2016) conducted a content analysis of visual data to explore the frequency with which particular types of food are depicted in paintings and the extent to which this could give historical insight into family meals over the years and across countries.

The researchers initially examined 750 food-related paintings, but these were screened down to 140 paintings from Western Europe and the United States that depict small family meals, rather than bigger celebrations or banquets. The quantitative content analysis revealed that the most commonly eaten foods (such as chicken, eggs, and squash) were actually the least frequently shown in the paintings. Interestingly, the most aspirational foods, such as shellfish, were most often painted in countries that have the smallest coastlines (Germany), and more than half (51.4 per cent) of the paintings from the seafaring Netherlands actually contained non-indigenous tropical lemons. Wasnick et al. found that there was a tendency for paintings to feature meals with foods that were either aspirational to the family, aesthetically pleasing, or potentially technically difficult for the painter. They also found that food depictions in paintings should not be taken as indicative of what was actually served or eaten in that country at the time.

13.5 Evaluating content analysis

13

In this final section, we reflect on the advantages and disadvantages of content analysis as a method of conducting social research.

Advantages of content analysis

There are many advantages to conducting content analysis, which we will outline here.

- *It is very transparent*. The coding scheme and the sampling procedures can be clearly set out so that replications and follow-up studies can be conducted. It is this quality that has led to it being referred to as an objective method of analysis.
- *It can be longitudinal*. Several of the studies we have discussed allow the researcher to track changes in frequency over various different periods of time (Bligh et al. 2004; Young and Dugas 2011; Bailey et al. 2014; Gunn and Naper 2016; Stoddart et al. 2016).
- *It is highly flexible*. This method can be applied to a wide variety of unstructured textual information. We often associate content analysis with the analysis of mass-media outputs but, as we have seen throughout this chapter, it actually has a much broader applicability.
- *It allows researchers to gain access to hard-to-reach groups*. Content analysis provides a way to generate information about social groups to which it is difficult to gain access. For example, you are extremely unlikely to gain access to interview the prime minister or president, but you could analyse their speeches (like Bligh et al. 2004) or their tweets in the build-up to an election (like Gunn and Napier 2016).
- *It is unobtrusive*. Content analysis is often referred to as a form of **unobtrusive method**, a term devised by Webb et al. (1966), meaning that it does not involve the research participants having to take the researcher into account (see Key concept 14.2). Another, related, term often used to describe the method is non-reactive (see Key concepts 12.3 and 14.2).

It is worth noting that this last claim should be treated with a little caution. When we conduct content analysis with things like newspaper articles or television programmes, there is no **reactive effect** because newspaper articles are obviously not written in the knowledge that a content analysis may be carried out on them. However, if we are carrying out a content analysis on documents such as interview transcripts or **ethnographies** then even though the process of performing the content analysis does not *itself* introduce a reactive effect, the documents may have been at least partly influenced by such an effect.

The fact that content analysis is unobtrusive can be a significant advantage for many students as, if they are conducting research for a project or dissertation, content analysis does not usually require them to undergo the same level of ethical scrutiny that they would if using methods that involve research participants. We are certainly not suggesting that you should select research methods on the basis of whether they would require more attention to ethical issues, particularly given the arguments we put forward in Chapters 1 and 4 about the need to tailor research methods to research questions, and in Chapter 6 about the need to consider potential ethical issues for *all* methods, but such practical considerations are worth bearing in mind if you have a tight time frame in which to conduct your project.

Disadvantages of content analysis

Like all research techniques, content analysis suffers from certain limitations.

- *It depends on the quality of the documents/data.* A content analysis can only be as good as the documents you are working with (Krippendorff 2018). We suggest considering your data in the light of Scott's (1990) recommendations for assessing documents, in terms of such criteria as authenticity (is the document what it says it is?); credibility (could the contents of the document be distorted in some way?); and representativeness (are the documents you are examining representative of all possible relevant documents? If certain kinds of document are unavailable or no longer exist, generalizability will be jeopardized). These kinds of consideration are especially important when conducting a content analysis on documents such as letters. We will explore these issues in more detail in Chapter 22.
- *Coding manuals inevitably involve some interpretation.* It is almost impossible to devise coding manuals that do not involve some interpretation by those doing the coding. The fact that coders need to draw upon their everyday knowledge as participants in order to be able to code the material (Cicourel 1964; Garfinkel 1967; Riffe et al. 2014) means that there is the potential for misinterpretation.
- *The difficulty of imputing latent content.* Certain problems are likely to come up when researchers are aiming to impute latent rather than manifest content. As we saw in examples of this kind of analysis, such as Research in focus 13.2, there is greater potential for invalid interpretations.
- *The difficulty of answering 'why?' questions.* This can be problematic in content analysis because of the depth of the analysis it facilitates. For example, Beullens and Schepers (2013; see Research in focus 13.2) found that the presence of an alcohol brand logo in a photo made a difference to whether a posting received a 'like', but they were not able to understand why. The researchers (2013: 501) proposed a potential reason (that it is to do with 'a general positive attitude toward alcohol use'), but this is based on speculation; there is no further evidence. Sometimes, users of content analysis have used further data-collection methods to try to answer the 'why?' questions raised by their investigations. We noted in Research in focus 13.3 that Seale et al. (2006) used a quantitative content analysis of words as a starting point for a more probing qualitative examination of the links between words.
- *It is potentially atheoretical.* Content analytic studies are sometimes accused of being 'atheoretical', meaning that they do not have a strong theoretical basis. This is because the emphasis on measurement in content analysis can result in researchers focusing on what is measurable rather than on what is theoretically significant. This is not necessarily the case, though; a number of the examples we discuss in this chapter are certainly not atheoretical. Döring et al. (2016), for example, incorporated Goffman's (1979) and Kang's (1997) gender display categories when exploring the degree of gender stereotyping in selfies.

KEY POINTS

- Content analysis tends to be located within the quantitative research tradition of emphasizing measurement and specifying clear rules that emphasize reliability.
- Although it is traditionally associated with the analysis of mass-media content, content analysis is a very flexible method that can be applied to a wide range of sources, including online and visual materials.

- It is crucial to be clear about your research questions as a first step in content analysis so that you can be certain about your units of analysis and what exactly you are going to analyse.
- You also need to be clear about what you are going to count.
- Devising a coding schedule and coding manual are important stages in the preparation for a content analysis, and it is a good idea to pilot these tools.
- Content analysis tends to become more controversial when it is used to explore latent (rather than manifest) meaning and themes.

QUESTIONS FOR REVIEW

1. What kinds of documents and media can content analysis be applied to?
2. What is the difference between manifest and latent content? What are the implications of this distinction for content analysis?
3. Why are precise research questions especially important in content analysis?
4. What particular sampling issues does content analysis pose?
5. What kinds of things might be counted when doing a content analysis?
6. To what extent do you need to infer latent content when you go beyond counting words?
7. Why is coding so crucial in content analysis?
8. What is the difference between a coding schedule and a coding manual in content analysis?
9. What potential difficulties need to be considered when devising coding schedules and manuals for content analysis?
10. What particular difficulties are associated with conducting content analysis on websites compared to analysing offline or mass media sources of data?
11. Why is the use of social media in content analysis becoming increasingly frequent?
12. Do visual materials present special problems for content analysis?
13. 'One of the most significant advantages of content analysis is its immense flexibility, in that it can be applied to a wide variety of documents.' Discuss.
14. To what extent does the need for coders to interpret meaning undermine content analysis?
15. To what extent are content analysis studies atheoretical?

13

ONLINE RESOURCES

www.oup.com/he/srm6e

You can find our notes on the answers to these questions within this chapter's **online resources**, together with:

- *audio/video comments* on this topic from our 'Learn from experience' panellists;
- *self-test questions* for further knowledge-checking;
- a *flashcard glossary* to help you recall key terms; and
- a *Student Researcher's Toolkit* containing practical materials and resources to help you conduct your own research project.

CHAPTER 14

USING EXISTING DATA

CHAPTER GUIDE

In this chapter we explore the possibilities associated with analysing data that have been collected by others, a process known as secondary analysis.

This chapter explores

- the advantages and disadvantages of carrying out secondary analysis of data collected by other researchers, especially in the context of small-scale research projects;
- how to obtain such data sets;
- analysing data supplied in published or circulated outputs, for example journal articles;
- the reliability and validity of official statistics (statistics collected by government departments in the course of their work or specifically for statistical purposes);
- the growing recognition of the potential value of official statistics for social research;
- the idea that official statistics are a form of *unobtrusive method* (a method that is not associated with a reaction from those being studied to the fact that they are being researched);
- the limitations of official statistics for social research;
- the emerging possibilities associated with Big Data, in particular in the form of social media outputs.

14.1 Introduction

In most of the chapters in Part Two of this book we have focused on methods of collecting primary data, such as through a **questionnaire** survey or **structured observation**. These methods can be very time-consuming, raising the question of whether it might be possible to use existing data. To a certain extent, this is what **content analysis** (see Chapter 13) involves, as the data (newspaper articles, TV programmes, online material, etc.) already exist. In this chapter, we will examine four other ways in which researchers can use existing data:

1. *secondary analysis of data collected by other researchers* (see Key concept 14.1), emphasizing large, high-quality surveys that tend to operate on a continuous basis;
2. *meta-analysis*—the analysis of large numbers of published or otherwise-circulated quantitative studies;
3. *secondary analysis of data collected by government departments* (**official statistics**);
4. *analysis of Big Data*—the large volumes of data that are generated through media such as Facebook and Twitter.

14.2 Secondary analysis of other researchers' data

There are a number of good reasons why **secondary analysis** (see Key concept 14.1) should be considered a serious alternative to collecting new data. In this section we will outline the main advantages of this method of data collection, drawing on those identified by Dale et al. (1988) and built on by Johnston (2017), followed by its limitations, and we will then look at how you can access this kind of data.

14

In this section we will keep in mind the needs of a student conducting a small, individual research project as we consider the advantages and limitations of secondary analysis, but this emphasis does not mean that secondary analysis is only relevant to students. All researchers should consider secondary analysis. In fact, research funders often ask research grant applicants who propose collecting new data to demonstrate that relevant secondary data are not already available. The reason we emphasize the potential value of secondary analysis for students is because our teaching experience suggests that many students assume any research they conduct has to involve collecting primary data. If secondary analysis does not conflict with the guidelines you are given regarding the approach to data collection, then we recommend giving it serious consideration. Using existing data will give you more time to spend on analysing and interpreting the data, and it will almost certainly be of a higher quality than any data that you could produce with the time and resources available to you. There is also the fact that, as we will see in this section, you may be able to conduct analyses that would

KEY CONCEPT 14.1
What is secondary analysis?

Secondary analysis involves researchers analysing data that they probably were not involved in collecting, for purposes that may not have been envisaged by those responsible for the data collection. Secondary analysis can be used to analyse either quantitative or qualitative data, but we will focus on quantitative analysis in this chapter. We focus on qualitative uses of secondary data in Chapter 23.

It is worth being aware that the distinction between primary and secondary analysis is not always as clear as you might think. For example, if a researcher is involved in collecting **survey** data and analyses some of the data, with the analysis resulting in some publications, but some time later they decide to rework the data, it would be difficult to say whether the latter is primary or secondary analysis. Secondary analysis usually involves analysing data that others have collected, but, as this scenario suggests, this is not necessarily the case.

not be possible if you were relying on data you had collected yourself.

We will be mentioning several different surveys and data sources in the course of this section, and we will use acronyms (abbreviated names) for those we mention more than once. We will always provide the full name and the acronym the first time we mention it. You will find all of these acronyms listed in the abbreviations pages at the start of the book.

Advantages of secondary analysis

Secondary analysis offers numerous benefits to students carrying out a research project:

- it saves costs and time;
- the data tends to be of high quality;
- there are opportunities for longitudinal analysis, subgroup analysis, or cross-cultural analysis;
- the time saved can be spent on data analysis;
- reanalysis may suggest new interpretations;
- this method fulfils some wider obligations of social researchers.

Let's discuss each in turn.

Reduced costs and time

Secondary analysis saves researchers a lot of money and time. It allows them to access good-quality data, such as that available in the UK Data Archive (UKDA; see the later subsection 'Accessing data archives'), for a tiny fraction of the resources they would need to carry out their own data collection.

High-quality data

Many of the data sets that tend to be used for secondary analysis are of very high quality. This is due to several factors.

First, the sampling procedures were rigorous, in most cases resulting in samples that are as close to being representative as is likely to be possible. While the organizations responsible for these studies suffer the same problems of survey non-response as anybody else, they will usually have well-established procedures in place for following up with non-respondents, which keeps this problem to a minimum.

Second, the samples are often national samples. The geographical coverage and the sample size of such data sets are normally only achievable in well-funded research that attracts quite substantial resources. It would not be possible to achieve such extensive coverage in student projects.

The third factor affecting the quality of these data sets is that many of them have been generated by experienced and well-trained researchers. Some of the biggest data sets are collected by social research organizations that have developed structures and control procedures to check that the resulting data is of high quality. They include Understanding Society (USoc), which is the title for the UK Household Longitudinal Study (see Research in focus 14.1), and the British Social Attitudes Survey (BSA; see Research in focus 14.2). Eurostat is another high-quality source of data provided by the statistical office of the European Union (EU). It provides statistics at European level that enable comparisons between countries and regions. Overall there are hundreds of high-quality, publicly available, nationally representative surveys that can be used in social research.

While it is always important to consider ethical issues (see Sections 6.4 and 6.5), using secondary data may involve fewer ethical issues than primary research, particularly where robust data-collection procedures were in place and participants were given clear information about the reuse of data. This is normally the case with nationally representative surveys.

Opportunity for longitudinal analysis

We can use secondary analysis to carry out longitudinal research, which (as we noted in Chapter 3—see Section 3.5, 'Longitudinal designs') is otherwise quite rare in the social sciences because of the time and cost involved. Sometimes, as with the survey USoc, the original research used a panel design, allowing secondary analysts to chart trends and connections over time. Research in focus 14.1 describes a longitudinal study that used USoc. Some existing data sets were collected and analysed using a cross-sectional design, but there are obviously opportunities for longitudinal analysis as well. Also, with data sets such as the Crime Survey for England and Wales (CSEW) and the BSA (see Research in focus 14.2), similar data are collected over time, usually because interviewing involves questions being reused each year, so we can identify trends over time (such as changing opinions or behaviours). Sometimes different respondents are used from year to year, which makes it difficult to draw causal inferences, but it will still be possible to gauge trends. In the case of cohort studies (again, see Section 3.5, 'Longitudinal designs'), the data enables us to establish how members of a sample who were born around the same time are similar to or different from each other. For example, Janmaat and Keating (2019) used the BSA and

RESEARCH IN FOCUS 14.1

Secondary data analysis using a longitudinal survey

Thomas et al. (2018) used the longitudinal survey USoc, a large-scale representative panel survey with a core sample of around 40,000 households, to explore whether having children leads to changes in individual-level environmental attitudes and behaviours, potentially as a result of having greater consideration for future generations (what is sometimes called the 'legacy hypothesis').

This study primarily made use of two 'waves' of the survey: wave 1 (conducted from January 2009 to December 2010) and wave 4 (conducted from January 2012 to December 2013). In total, 40,172 individuals took part in wave 1 and, of these, 27,193 individuals (67.7 per cent) completed wave 1 through to wave 4. The survey included environment-related questions and a total of 1,656 respondents reported a newborn child during the different waves of the survey, which allowed Thomas and colleagues to investigate the legacy hypothesis longitudinally. The researchers assessed changes in three environmental attitude items and the frequency of 11 environmental behaviours for those who had newborn children in between the two waves of data collection. They found only small changes in individual-level environmental attitudes and behaviours following people having a new child. Contrary to the legacy hypothesis, all changes were negative, indicating environmental behaviours were actually performed less, with the only positive change observed among first-time parents who already had a high level of environmental concern, who had an increasing desire to act more sustainably.

Using secondary data allowed Thomas et al. to examine a much larger sample than would have been possible if they had collected the data themselves. Furthermore, collecting and analysing primary longitudinal data is extremely time-consuming, so using USoc enabled them to complete the study much more quickly than would otherwise have been the case.

the international World Values Survey, headquartered in Austria, to investigate whether cohorts' attitudes towards homosexuality and racial diversity have become more accepting over time.

Opportunity for subgroup analysis

When the data source features large samples, researchers have the opportunity to study what can often be very big subgroups. In most research involving primary data, small localized studies are the only way to study particular types of individuals because of the costs of doing otherwise. However, large data sets can often generate large, nationally representative samples of specialized categories of individuals, such as those with particular characteristics or views. For example, if you were interested in how much childcare grandparents are undertaking or wanted to look at self-employed workers' pension contributions, this would involve studying subgroups. Research in focus 14.2 demonstrates how researchers can use secondary data in this way.

RESEARCH IN FOCUS 14.2

Using a secondary data set to study subgroups

Luke, one of this book's authors, has conducted research on Twitter use (Sloan 2017) that is interesting in this context because he used secondary data to study subgroups. Luke used secondary data in the form of the 2011 census along with the BSA 2015 (where he was able to arrange for an additional question to be added) to explore Twitter use in the UK. Luke was interested in exploring who tweets, focusing specifically on particular subgroups in the form of three demographic characteristics—age, sex/gender, and class. Luke's findings suggest that Twitter users are not representative of the wider population, which creates an issue for researchers wanting to draw conclusions from the Big Data (see Section 14.5) that Twitter generates. Luke writes that there are a disproportionate number of male Twitter users, in relation to both the 2011 **census** and previous estimates; that Twitter users are mainly young, but that there are a greater number of older users than previously estimated; and that there are strong class effects associated with Twitter use.

Opportunity for cross-cultural analysis

A further benefit of using secondary data sets is that they can enable cross-cultural research. This type of research often appeals to social scientists because we are becoming increasingly aware of the processes associated with globalization and cultural differences. We are conscious that findings produced by research conducted in a particular country are not necessarily applicable to other countries. However, doing research in a different country presents considerable financial and practical issues, including the need to navigate potentially significant language and cultural differences.

Analysing comparable secondary data from two or more countries can be an effective way of avoiding many of these issues, but it is important to remember that the questions asked must be comparable. The research on egalitarian attitudes by Röder and Mühlau (2014) that we discussed in Research in focus 2.1 provides an example of the process of coordinating questions, which the authors describe as follows:

> Data were extracted from rounds 2 and 4 of the European Social Survey (ESS) collected in 2004 and 2008. These are two rounds for which measures of gender egalitarianism are included. The ESS is designed to allow cross-national analyses by ensuring that the questions are understood in the same way by respondents in different countries and languages, and is a high-quality data set where the sampling design approximates a simple random sample and has a relatively high response rate.
>
> (Röder and Mühlau 2014: 905)

Röder and Mühlau's results came from a secondary analysis of the data from 27 of the 33 nations involved in the research. Opportunities for undertaking such cross-cultural analysis seem to be increasing; for example, core questions used in the UK's Labour Force Survey (LFS, an annual study of people's employment circumstances) are also used in equivalent surveys conducted by EU member states and some other non-EU members.

In addition, statistics are available from the Global South that can be used in cross-cultural analysis, such as the Demographic and Health Surveys Program, run by the US Agency for International Development, which provides representative data on population, health, HIV, and nutrition through more than 400 surveys in over 90 countries. The Multiple Indicator Cluster Surveys are household surveys implemented by countries under the programme developed by the United Nations Children's Fund to provide internationally comparable data on the situation of children and women. This includes countries as diverse as Argentina, Bhutan, the Democratic Republic of the Congo, and Iraq.

More time for data analysis

Collecting data is usually a time-consuming process that can cut into the time available for analysing it. Students sometimes think of collecting the data as the difficult phase and analysing it as relatively straightforward, but this is rarely the case. Analysing your data is no easy matter; it involves a lot of thought and preparation, and you may need to learn unfamiliar data analysis techniques or use new software programs. Although secondary analysis tends to involve a lot of managing data—partly so that you can get to know the data and partly so that you can get it into the form(s) that you need (see the next section, 'Limitations of secondary analysis')—the fact that you are not collecting fresh data means that you can take a more considered approach to analysing the data than you might otherwise have been able to.

Possible new interpretations

Secondary data can be analysed in so many different ways that it is very unusual for researchers to run out of possible kinds of analysis. A secondary analyst might, for example, take one of the following approaches:

- consider the impact of a certain **variable** on the **relationships** between variables they are interested in, in a way that was not envisaged by the initial researchers;
- conduct further analysis of the data that could not have been considered by the original researchers, on the basis of new theoretical ideas;
- use an alternative method or technique of quantitative data analysis, which could lead to different interpretations of the data.

The wider obligations of the social researcher

A final, but important, advantage to using secondary data is that it helps researchers fulfil their wider obligations. Social research involves research participants giving up some of their time, usually for no reward. It is therefore reasonable for participants to expect that the data they help to generate will be used to its fullest extent. However, much social research is chronically under-analysed. Making data available for secondary analysis makes it more likely that fuller use will be made of data. It also helps to avoid research fatigue, where participants become less inclined to become involved in research or the quality of responses deteriorates due to the abundance of research taking place. There is also a potential ethical benefit of not collecting new data when existing data is already available.

Limitations of secondary analysis

Given the many benefits of secondary analysis that we have listed, this method might sound almost too good to be true. But as with all research methods, there are also limitations to consider, for example:

- the greater likelihood of a lack of familiarity with the data;
- the complexity of the data;
- the lack of control over data quality;
- the likely absence of key variables.

Lack of familiarity with data

When collecting your own data you are likely to be very familiar with its content, but with data collected by others, you have to allow for a period of familiarization. This involves getting to know the range of variables, the ways in which the variables have been coded, and various aspects of the organization of the data. While you have no control over the collection of the data, you still need to understand how it was collected and what it means. This process can be quite time-consuming and tricky with large, complex data sets, so you should not underestimate this.

Complexity of the data

Some of the best-known data sets that you can use for secondary analysis, such as USoc, are very big, with large numbers of both respondents and variables, which potentially presents problems with managing the information. Also, some of the most popular data sets for secondary analysis are known as *hierarchical* data sets (these include USoc), which means that the data are collected and presented at the level of both the household and the individual, as well as at other levels. Researchers therefore have to decide which level of analysis to employ. If you decide that individual-level data is most appropriate for your study, you will need to extract the individual-level data from the data set. It is worth noting that different data will apply to each level: at the household level, the USoc survey provides data on such variables as number of cars and number of children living at home, while at the individual level, it provides data on income and employment.

No control over data quality

While secondary analysis offers the opportunity to examine data of far higher quality than you are likely to be able to collect yourself, you should never assume this to be the case. In the case of large-scale data sets such as the CSEW (see Section 7.6), the BSA (see Research in focus 14.2), and USoc (see Research in focus 14.1), you can be reasonably sure of the quality as there is information available about their data-collection processes. With other data sets, however, you may need to be more cautious, although usually the archives that store the data will make some fundamental checks on quality.

Absence of key variables

Existing data will not necessarily meet all of your needs, because it may not have been collected to reflect the particular aspect of a topic that is of most interest to you. Secondary data will almost always have been collected by others for their own purposes, so it is not uncommon that one or more of the key variables for your project will not be present. Clearly, this is less likely to be an issue when examining primary data; it is most likely to arise when a new theory or area has emerged following data collection, which was not explored in the data. If this situation arises, you need to make a decision about whether to adapt your research focus in order to ensure that the necessary secondary data is available to answer your research questions, or whether, instead, you need to collect primary data that addresses your research focus. This is why it is a good idea to look at the variables that are included in secondary data sets before committing to their use.

Our panellists reflect on the advantages and disadvantages of secondary data in Learn from experience 14.1.

Accessing data archives

Having considered the advantages and limitations to analysing secondary data, how do you actually find this data so that you can use it, or consider using it?

Many government agencies, commercial organizations, and university researchers collect data that is stored in archives and made available for researchers to use, often for no cost. In the UK, the UKDA, based at the University of Essex, is likely to be your main source of access to quantitative data for secondary analysis (**www.ukdataservice.ac.uk/**, accessed 7 March 2020), and it provides a huge amount of data on different topics. The Consortium for European Social

LEARN FROM EXPERIENCE 14.1

Advantages and disadvantages of using secondary data

We have discussed some of the strengths and weaknesses of secondary data analysis. Here are explanations from three of our student panellists on how they considered these issues while carrying out their research: Jodie, whose postgraduate project focused on sexual prejudice in Europe using secondary data analysis of European data sets; Reni, who studied the International Criminal Court and its alleged bias against African countries; and Zvi, who focused on sleep patterns and screen time.

> Given that my MSc project was focused on how attitudes manifest in Europe, it was most suitable to conduct a secondary data analysis of highly reputable data for two reasons. The time, money, and effort that it would take to do something similar would be extremely problematic. The only limitation is that I was restricted by the fact that I did not design the survey, and therefore, I was unable to capture the concepts of interest in the exact way that I wanted. However, the measures that the survey utilized were perfectly sufficient.
>
> Jodie

> My dissertation relied entirely on secondary analysis of other researchers' data because there was no way of finding data relevant to my topic by myself. However, I made sure to only use data from credible sources such as official United Nations and Human Rights Watch reports. Most of the data was online, and a major challenge was the fact that a lot of gaps and uncertainty existed in the reported data. The advantage of using data from these sources was that I could answer my question using the same data that was used by the institution in my question (the International Criminal Court often works closely with the United Nations while investigating cases). It was difficult to ascertain the accuracy of the data because of chronic under-reporting and lack of official figures in cases concerning less developed countries. However, I made sure that I acknowledged any limitations and disadvantages in my methodology section.
>
> Reni

> One significant advantage of using secondary data is that you save a considerable amount of time in the data-collection phase of your project as this is already done for you. Moreover, you often don't have to go through the same ethics procedure as someone using qualitative methods as you don't come into direct contact with human subjects, as the ethics protocol would have been followed by those who conducted the survey.
>
> Zvi

 Access the **online resources** to hear our panellists' video reflections on this theme.

You can read about our panellists' backgrounds and research experiences on page xxvi.

14

Science Data Archives (**www.cessda.eu/**, accessed 8 February 2020) provides information on data archives from a number of EU member countries. Outside Europe and the UK, the US government provides access to their government data (**www.data.gov/**, accessed 7 March 2020) and the Australian Data Archive is a repository for lots of studies (**https://ada.edu.au/**, accessed 10 January 2020). You might also want to explore r3data.org, which is a global registry of research data repositories (**www.re3data.org/**, accessed 10 January 2020). These are just a few examples of data archives that are available to you, and it is worth noting that many of these archives hold data deriving from a wide range of studies, not only the very large ones, so you do not have to restrict yourself to the well-known secondary data sets. Simon and Zvi discuss ways of accessing secondary data in Learn from experience 14.2.

LEARN FROM EXPERIENCE 14.2
Accessing secondary data

There is an abundance of secondary data available to you as a social researcher. Sometimes students may be put off by the prospect of accessing secondary data but, as Simon and Zvi outline, it is generally a straightforward process that offers great potential.

In my comparative analysis, official statistics provided a benchmark to test my social media findings against. However, these had not been compiled in a way that usefully matched my Twitter data, so I went to the original secondary data and analysed it myself. This turned out to be a really straightforward process. The data was available using my institution's access to the UK Data Service website, and there were loads of data sets there that were easy to download. There were also some very useful guides to interpreting the data and the original questionnaires, both of which really helped when trying to get my head around the data. I used SPSS [see Chapter 15] to analyse the data because it was convenient, but I could have used other platforms. I was able to filter the variables in a way that was meaningful to my research and to conduct some statistical analysis on these. By going back to the original data used in the official statistics I was able to give my research added credibility. This really allowed me to demonstrate that the two data sources (the official statistics and Twitter data) could be meaningfully matched.

Simon

I would say to social science students to consider the use of survey data more often when given research tasks at university. The UK has a fantastic range of providers of great data, notably the Office for National Statistics and the UK Data Service, and most of their data is freely available to download. It is definitely worth, when considering a research project like a dissertation, seeing what data is already available on these sites. Just start with a few keywords and see what comes up. You will be surprised by just how many variables and measures are captured in some of these surveys. I think there is a misconception that using secondary data is somehow not as 'good' as collecting the data yourself, when this couldn't be further from the truth. When you think about it, if you get data from a reputable and trusted source such as the UK Data Service for example, these are large businesses with teams of people highly experienced in social research. The time and resources that would have been involved in their data collection would be much superior to anything you could achieve during your final-year research process.

Zvi

You can read about our panellists' backgrounds and research experiences on page xxvi.

14

Let's focus on the UK Data Archive in a little more detail to give you an idea of how it works. Everything in this archive is accessible to all academic researchers, including students, unless any specific data sets have had restrictions placed on them. The archives hold data on the UK census, from the Office for National Statistics (ONS), and they can be used to access data from other archives within Europe and beyond. The best way to find out about the data held in the archive is to examine its online catalogue, accessible via the UK Data Service catalogue search page: **http://ukdataservice.ac.uk/get-data.aspx** (accessed 11 December 2020).

If you wanted to know what information is available about housing in the archive, for example, you could search for any studies with 'housing' in the title by simply running a search for this keyword. On the day we conducted this search, it produced 1,180 studies (see Figure 14.1). You could then examine the documentation relating to any promising areas for analysis and you could even order the data set concerned. For each study included, there is

FIGURE 14.1
Results of a search of the UK Data Archive for the term 'housing' (accessed 11 December 2020)

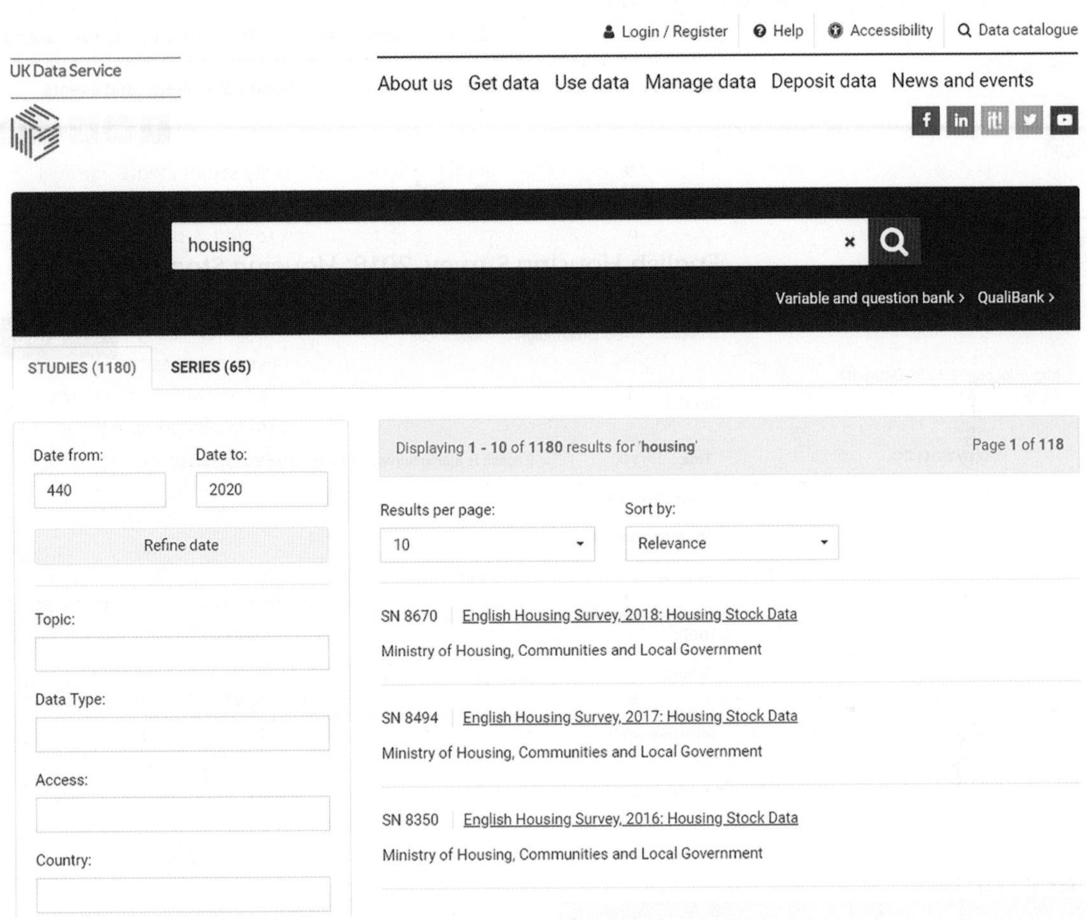

Source: Copyright UK Data Service (UKDS). Reprinted with permission.

usually a description of what it involved, along with a range of specific details: sponsors; sampling details; method of data collection; main topics of the survey; and information about publications deriving from the study. There will also be a note about whether there are special conditions relating to access. The first available data flagged up following our search was 'SN 8670 English Housing Survey, 2018: Housing Stock Data'. Figure 14.2 shows the information the archive provided when we clicked on this link to see more information. Clicking on the 'Documentation' tab brings up more detailed documentation about the data, including a user guide, and clicking on the 'Access data' tab allows us to do exactly that.

You will find information about searching for qualitative data in order to conduct a secondary analysis in Chapter 23. You can also search for qualitative data through the UK Data Service. A useful starting point for many, if not most, of the popular data sets that can be accessed through the UK Data Service can be found at **http://ukdataservice.ac.uk/get-data/key-data.aspx** (accessed 11 December 2020).

Table 14.1 lists several large data sets that are frequently used in social research, together with notes on the type of data they include and the topic(s) they cover. Further information about these data sets can be found via the UK Data Service.

FIGURE 14.2
Description and documentation for the chosen data (accessed 11 December 2020)

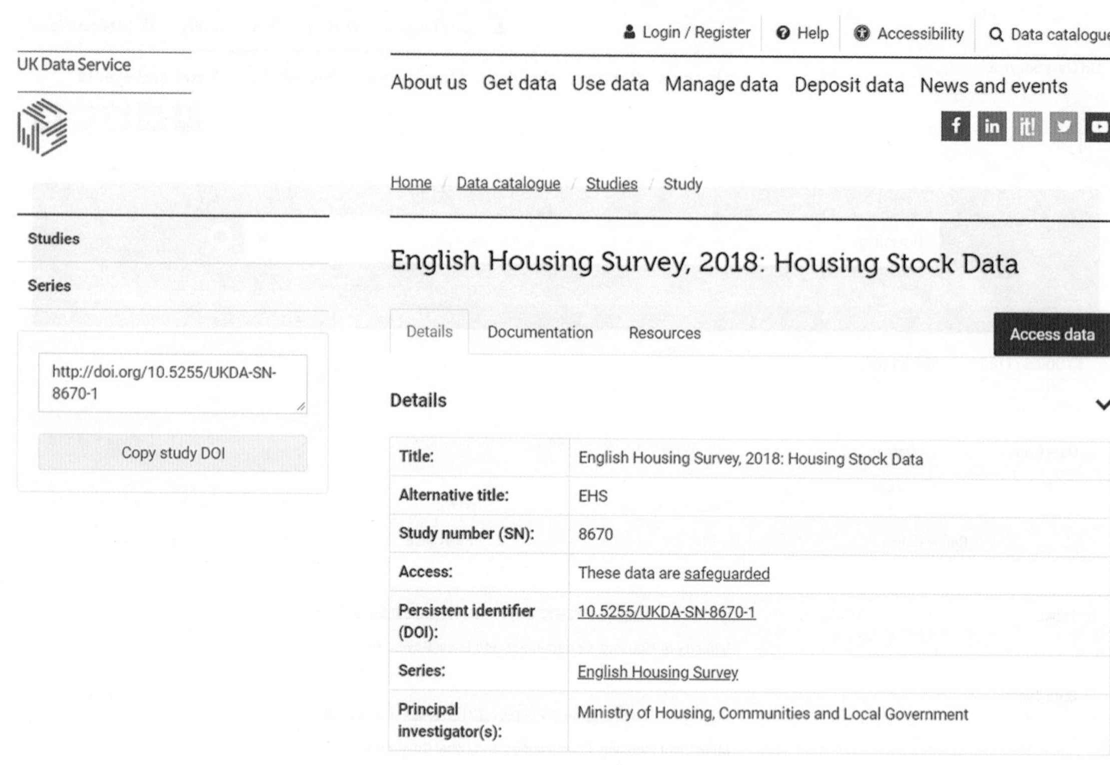

Source: Copyright UK Data Service (UKDS). Reprinted with permission.

14

TABLE 14.1
Large data sets that are suitable for secondary analysis

Title	Data set details	Topics covered
1970 British Cohort Study	An irregular survey of 17,200 people born in a single week in 1970. Data have since been collected at ages 5, 10, 16, 26, 30, 34, 38, and 42. Although this is a longitudinal survey, there is also an element of a cross-sectional design in that it is supplemented by a sample that includes immigrants who came to Britain before age 16 but were born in the same week. See **www.cls.ioe.ac.uk** (accessed 5 February 2020).	Health; physical development; economic and social circumstances; variety of attitudes.
Crime Survey for England and Wales (CSEW) (formerly the British Crime Survey)	An irregular survey of people selected using **random sampling** who are questioned by **structured interview**. It began in 1982 and was carried out in 1984, 1988, 1992, and then biennially between 1992 and 2000 and annually from 2001. For the 2018–19 survey, around 50,000 households were invited to participate. See **www.crimesurvey.co.uk/en/** (accessed 5 February 2020).	Experience of and attitudes to crime; fear of crime; perceived risk of crime.
Understanding Society: The UK Household Longitudinal Study (USoc) (formerly the British Household Panel Survey, BHPS)	A panel study that began as the BHPS in 1991 and was conducted annually by interview and questionnaire with a national **representative sample** of around 10,000 individuals in just over 5,000 households. The same individuals were interviewed each year. The BHPS was replaced in 2010–11 by USoc, which is based on a much larger panel of 40,000 households and includes the households that made up the BHPS. See **www.understandingsociety.ac.uk** (accessed 5 February 2020).	Household organization; labour market behaviour; income and wealth; housing; health; socio-economic values.

Continued

Title	Data set details	Topics covered
British Social Attitudes (BSA) Survey	A more or less annual survey conducted since 1983 using a multi-stage **stratified random sample** of over 3,000 respondents aged 18 and over. Each survey comprises an hour-long interview and a **self-completion questionnaire**. See **www.natcen.ac.uk/our-research/research/british-social-attitudes/** (accessed 5 February 2020).	Wide range of areas of social attitudes and behaviour. Some areas are core ones asked about annually; others are asked about irregularly.
European Social Survey (ESS)	A survey conducted every other year since 2001 across Europe, involving over 30 countries. Samples are selected randomly and face-to-face interviews are administered. See **www.europeansocialsurvey.org/about/index.html** (accessed 5 February 2020).	Attitudes, beliefs, and behaviour.
Labour Force Survey (LFS)	Biennial interviews, 1973–83, and annual interviews, 1984–91, comprising a quarterly survey of around 15,000 addresses per quarter and an additional survey in March–May. Since 1991 it has been a quarterly survey of around 40,000 addresses. Since 1998, core questions have also been administered in member states of the European Union. See **www.hse.gov.uk/statistics/lfs/about.htm** (accessed 5 February 2020).	Hours worked; job search methods; training; personal details such as nationality and gender.
Millennium Cohort Study	A study of 19,000 babies, and their families, born between 1 September 2000 and 31 August 2001 in England and Wales, and between 22 November 2000 and 11 January 2002 in Scotland and Northern Ireland. Data were collected by interview with parents when babies were 9 months and around 3 years old. Since then, surveys have been conducted at ages 5, 7, 11, 14, and 17 years old. See **www.cls.ioe.ac.uk** (accessed 5 February 2020).	Continuity and change in each child's family and its parenting environment; important aspects of the child's development.
National Child Development Study	Irregular but ongoing study of all 17,000 children born in Great Britain in the week of 3–9 March 1958. Since 1981 it has comprised both an interview and a questionnaire. There have been 10 waves of data collection: in 1965 (when members were aged 7 years), in 1969 (age 11), in 1974 (age 16), in 1981 (age 23), in 1991 (age 33), in 1999–2000 (age 41–2), in 2004 (age 46), in 2008–9 (age 50–1), in 2013 (age 55), and in 2020 (aged 62). See **www.cls.ioe.ac.uk** (accessed 5 February 2020).	Physical and mental health; family; parenting; occupation and income; housing and environment.
Opinions and Lifestyle Survey; formerly ONS Omnibus Survey and ONS Opinions Survey	This survey, run by the UK's ONS, involves interview data being collected 8 times a year following a period when data were collected monthly, and before that 8 times per year. The Opinions and Lifestyle Survey merges the ONS Opinions Survey and the LFS. See **https://beta.ukdataservice.ac.uk/datacatalogue/series/series?id=2000043** (accessed 5 February 2020).	Core questions each year about respondents, plus modules (asked on behalf of participating organizations) on topics that change annually concerning e.g. food safety; eating behaviour; personal finance; sports participation; management organization; employee representation.

14.3 Meta-analysis

We now turn to another way in which researchers can use existing data. **Meta-analysis** involves summarizing and comparing the results of a large number of quantitative studies on a particular topic and conducting various analytical tests to show whether or not a particular variable has an effect. This process corrects the various **sampling** and **non-sampling errors** that may arise in a single study, allowing researchers to estimate an overall effect. A meta-analysis lies between two kinds of activity that we cover in this book: doing a **literature review** of existing studies relating to the topic in which you are interested (see Chapter 5), and conducting a secondary analysis of other researchers' data (see Section 14.2). It differs from conducting a secondary analysis of other researchers' data in that in this context, you do not work on the raw data collected by the original researchers. Instead, you use the information given in the outputs of research in a certain area to help you estimate the effect of a variable you are interested in. With a meta-analysis, the researcher works on data supplied in articles and other outputs that have been shared or circulated, such as **correlation coefficients** (see Section 15.8).

Meta-analysis can be very effective—see Research in focus 14.3 for a good example—but its limitations include the fact that it relies on all the relevant information being available for each of the studies examined. This can sometimes rule it out as a data analysis method, because not every published paper will include all the same information relating to methods of study and sample size. Meta-analysis can also be affected by what is known as the **file drawer problem**, which occurs when a researcher conducting a study finds that the **independent variable** does not have the intended effect, which may lead to difficulty publishing their findings (Cooper 2016). As a result, the findings may simply be filed away in a drawer (or today, more likely a digital folder). If the file drawer problem is occurring in a field of research, the findings of a meta-analysis will be biased in favour of the independent variable having a certain effect, as some of the findings that contradict that effect will not be in the public domain. There may also be a bias against smaller studies because it is much easier to demonstrate a statistically significant effect when samples are large.

RESEARCH IN FOCUS 14.3
A meta-analysis

Badenes-Ribera et al. (2015) carried out meta-analysis to explore the prevalence of intimate partner violence (IPV) in self-identified lesbians and/or gay women in same-sex couples. The studies included in the analysis had to meet a number of criteria.

14

(1) They had to have been published between January 1990 and December 2013.
(2) They had to have been published in a peer-reviewed journal.
(3) They had to be original research.
(4) They had to be quantitative.
(5) The sample had to be made up, at least partly, of participants who self-identified as lesbians and/or gay women.
(6) The data on participants who self-identified as lesbians and/or gay women had to have been analysed separately from other data in the study.
(7) Participants who self-identified as lesbians and/or gay women had to have formed part of the general population from which the researchers selected their sample.
(8) The studies had to have measured IPV between people of the same sex.
(9) The studies had to have reported on the prevalence of IPV.
(10) The studies had to have a sample size equal to or greater than 30.
(11) The participants who self-identified as lesbians and/or gay women had to be 16 years old or more.

The researchers chose 14 US studies that met the inclusion criteria. All 14 studies used **non-probability sampling** methods. The researchers analysed the **mean** prevalence of victimization and of perpetration of IPV (the mean being the average: the sum of all of the values in a data set, divided by the number of values). The meta-analysis showed a mean prevalence of victimization in self-identified lesbians and/or gay women in same-sex couples, over the women's lifespans, of 48 per cent and a mean prevalence of perpetration of 43 per cent. It also showed a mean prevalence of victimization in the women's current relationships of 15 per cent. The high prevalence suggests that IPV prevention programmes need to be implemented among same-sex couples.

14.4 Official statistics

Official statistics represent an important way in which researchers can use existing data. In most countries, agencies of the state are required to keep a continuous record of their areas of activity (see **https://unstats.un.org/home/** for a list of national statistics agencies; accessed 10 February 2020). When these records are brought together, they form the official statistics in an area of activity. In the UK, the ONS is a useful resource through which you can access a wide variety of official UK statistics that can be used for research purposes (**www.statistics.gov.uk/default.asp**, accessed 5 February 2020). These include the statistics that the police compile from data that forms the crime rate (also known as 'notifiable crimes recorded by the police'), and data on unemployment based on those claiming unemployment related benefits (also known as the 'claimant count'). You will probably have seen these statistics cited in headlines in the mass media—for example, if there has been a sharp increase in the level of recorded crime or unemployment.

A range of administrative data is also available through various government departments. For example, in the UK, the Department for Education provides a range of data on such things as examination results, class sizes, and school finances. The Department of Health and Social Care provides information on the healthcare workforce, public health, social care, and social services for adults and children. The Department for Environment, Food and Rural Affairs provides statistics on the food sector, environment, sustainable development, and farm and sea fisheries. The Department for Work and Pensions has a variety of data on disability and carers, families and children, pensioners, and the working-age population. The Home Office provides data on crime, asylum-seekers, and immigration.

Official statistics have considerable potential value for social researchers, so it is important to appreciate their advantages, but also to be aware that they have some potential limitations that have made their use and analysis in social research controversial for many years.

Advantages of official statistics

Official statistics can be seen as having some advantages over other forms of quantitative data, such as data based on surveys.

- *Reduced time and cost*. The data have already been collected, which is likely to save a researcher considerable time and expense.
- *Potential for a complete picture*. The data may be based on an entire **population** rather than on samples, so it may be possible to obtain a complete picture.
- *Opportunities for cross-sectional analysis*. Researchers can often analyse this kind of data cross-sectionally, for example looking at crime rates (and the incidence of specific crimes) in terms of standard variables such as social class, income, ethnicity, age, gender, and region. This kind of analysis could help uncover the factors that are associated with crime or unemployment.
- *Opportunities for longitudinal analysis*. The data are often compiled over many years, making it possible to analyse longitudinally.
- *Opportunities for cross-cultural analysis*. Cross-cultural analysis is also a possibility, because researchers can compare official statistics from different countries for a specific area of activity. For example, one classic sociological study, Durkheim's *Suicide* (Durkheim 1952/1897), was the result of a comparative analysis of official statistics on suicide in several countries.
- *Lower risk of reactivity*. The people who are the source of the data are not being asked questions that are part of a research project, so there is very little risk of data being affected by **reactivity** (see Key concept 12.3).

14

This final point, that official statistics generate data 'without alerting the people under study' (Chambliss and Schutt 2019: 285), is one of the most compelling and commonly cited reasons for the continued use of official statistics. They can be considered a form of unobtrusive measure, although many writers prefer to use the term **unobtrusive method** (Lee 2000). We discuss this term in Key concept 14.2.

Limitations of official statistics

Earlier in this chapter (in Section 14.2) we outlined some limitations of the use of secondary data more generally:

- the greater likelihood of a lack of familiarity with the data;
- the complexity of the data;
- the lack of control over data quality;
- the likely absence of key variables.

KEY CONCEPT 14.2
What are unobtrusive methods?

'Unobtrusive method' is the term that most writers use to refer to the idea of an 'unobtrusive measure', which was introduced by Webb et al. (1966). (The preference for 'method' may be because 'measure' sounds like the term is only relevant for quantitative approaches, which is not the case.) In a highly influential book, Webb et al. argued that social researchers rely too heavily on measuring social phenomena using methods of data collection that are prone to reactivity. This means that when people know they are participating in a study (which is always the case when researchers collect data using methods such as structured interviewing and self-completion questionnaires), their replies or behaviour are likely to be influenced by this knowledge and therefore to be untypical. An unobtrusive method is 'any method of observation that directly removes the observer from the set of interactions or events being studied' (Denzin 1970), avoiding the problem of reactivity.

There are many non-reactive methods (Chambliss and Schutt 2019), but Webb et al. (1966) distinguished four main types.

1. *Physical traces.* These are the signs left behind by a group and include such things as graffiti and rubbish.
2. *Archive materials.* This **category** includes statistics collected by governmental and non-governmental organizations, diaries, the mass media, and historical records.
3. ***Simple observation.*** This refers to 'situations in which the observer has no control over the behaviour or sign in question, and plays an unobserved, passive, and nonintrusive role in the research situation' (Webb et al. 1966: 112).
4. *Contrived observation.* This is the same as simple observation, but the observer either actively varies the setting in some way (but without jeopardizing the unobtrusive quality of the observation) or uses hidden devices to record observations, such as video cameras.

Webb et al. (1966) were not arguing that unobtrusive methods should replace more conventional methods, but that social researchers should not rely almost exclusively on methods that were likely to be affected by reactivity. Webb et al. argued for greater **triangulation** (see Key concept 16.3) in social research, using both conventional (reactive) and unobtrusive (non-reactive) methods and evaluating the results together.

14

Official statistics fit clearly into the second of the four types of unobtrusive methods outlined here. Another research technique that would fall into category 2 is content analysis of media material (discussed in Chapter 13), if it is conducted in an unobtrusive way. Structured observation (see Chapter 12) will not usually fall into categories 3 or 4, because the observer is usually known to those being observed.

Although official statistics fit into Webb et al.'s category 2 of unobtrusive measures, note that the category (archive materials) also includes statistics generated by organizations that are not state agencies. Category 2 is a useful reminder of the amount of potentially interesting statistical data available to us, but social researchers do not often use unofficial existing statistical data (except that generated by other researchers, as discussed in Section 14.2).

It is worth noting that unobtrusive methods encapsulate several ways of thinking about the process of capturing data. First, many unobtrusive methods reveal sources of data (such as graffiti, diaries, media articles, and official statistics), and these sources need to be analysed in order to be considered interesting to a social-scientific audience. Second, although various kinds of documents can be called 'unobtrusive' sources of data, given that they have not been produced for a research project (and are therefore not reactive), we cannot assume that they are unproblematic. We need to remember that they are always produced for a purpose (even if not for research purposes), with a particular goal in mind. Third, some unobtrusive methods, such as simple and **contrived observation**, still involve methods of data collection with the researcher present at the time of the activities they are observing. These data have to be produced by the methods of data collection that researchers use. The data are not simply out there ready for our analysis in the way in which diaries or newspaper articles are (although even finding these sources can require a lot of detective work). This means that neither of the terms 'unobtrusive methods' or 'unobtrusive measures' captures the variety of forms very well.

Lee (2000) has developed a popular classification of unobtrusive methods that differs slightly from the one produced by Webb et al. (1966). Lee distinguishes the following kinds of data.

1. *Found data.* This corresponds more or less exactly to Webb et al.'s *physical traces.*
2. *Captured data.* This comprises both *simple observation* and *contrived observation* in Webb et al.'s list.
3. *Retrieved data: running records.* Records concerned with births, marriages, and deaths are prominent examples of this kind of method. They allow researchers to examine records over quite long periods and to explore changes. Lee also includes personal advertisements (such as marriage, dating, and job advertisements) in this category.
4. *Retrieved data: personal and episodic records.* Lee lists three kinds of data for this category: **personal documents** (letters, diaries, memoirs); visual images in the mass media (for example, newspaper photos and picture postcards); and 'documents produced through "institutional discovery" procedures' (Lee 2000: 87) (for example, reports of inquiries into the factors leading to a disaster).
5. *Records produced online.* Lee was thinking of email, message boards, and online forums, but we could add online messaging services, blogs, and tweets to this list.

We discuss many of these data types elsewhere in this book—for example, personal documents in Chapter 22 and digital communications (including 'Big Data') in Chapters 13 and 22—as well as in Section 14.5 of this chapter. Each of the types that Webb et al. and Lee distinguish has different advantages but also presents specific potential issues, including the reliability of the evidence and the ethical problems involved.

These limitations all potentially apply to the use of official statistics, depending on the types of data a researcher wants to use. While official statistics are often considered to have gone through rigorous collection procedures, they may also be misleading.

You might remember that in Section 7.4 we noted that there is a potential quality issue with existing statistics. The official statistics relating to an area of social life can be very misleading, because they are recording only the individuals who are processed by the agencies that have the responsibility for compiling the statistics. Crime and other forms of deviance have been a particular focus of attention and concern among critics of the use of official statistics, and we consider this issue in more depth in Thinking deeply 14.1, but this is not the only field in which you need to take care when interpreting this kind of data. For example, the 'claimant count' used for gaining a picture each month of the level of unemployment could misrepresent the 'real' level of unemployment. People who are unemployed but are not claiming benefits and those whose claims are rejected will not be counted in the statistics, while those who form part of the claimant count but who work in what is known as the 'informal' economy (and are not really unemployed) *will* be included in the unemployment statistics. It is important to think critically about official statistics you use and what they actually represent.

It is evident from Thinking deeply 14.1 that we need to think critically about what official statistics mean. It is important to consider both **reliability** and **validity** when working with official statistics. Reliability, and by extension validity, will be affected by changing definitions and policies regarding the area of interest. If we once again consider the collection of official statistics relating to crime, the following kinds of changes will probably take place over time and could affect the data.

- *Changes to policies or practices.* For example, in the crime context, changes to the policies of the UK Home Office or the police service may mean increasing resources are put into surveillance of a certain area of crime, such as drugs or drink driving. Or police officers may be more likely to charge people, rather than letting them off with a warning, during a crackdown (a series of particularly severe measures to reduce certain behaviour), resulting in more criminal charges being recorded.
- *Changes in definitions.* The behaviours that are viewed and defined as criminal, both by society and by the law, will vary over time. For instance, marital rape became legally defined as a criminal act in England and Wales in 1991, but between then and now there have also been substantial changes in how likely victims are to report crimes of sexual assault and proceed with a complaint (perhaps as a result of societal shifts or

THINKING DEEPLY 14.1
Can you trust official statistics?

It is important to think deeply about how your data is collected so that you are aware of any potential limitations with how the information is collected and recorded. Having a good understanding of your area of research will help you to identify these kinds of issues.

We have noted that one area of particular concern in relation to official statistics is crime rates, so let's reflect on why this might be. Figure 14.3 shows the steps involved before a crime is included in the official statistics. We can see that there are many stages that an offence must pass through before it contributes to the crime rate—we could see these as many opportunities for it to go unrecorded. To start with, an offence that is committed (step 1) usually becomes a candidate for inclusion in the crime rate as a result of one of two events: the crime is witnessed (or experienced) by a member of the public (step 2), or the crime is witnessed by a member of the police (step 5).

If we move through the steps from a crime being witnessed by a member of the public, a crime has to be *recognized* as a crime before someone will report it to the police (step 3). Even if it is recognized as a criminal offence, there are all kinds of reasons why the member of the public (even if they are a victim) may choose not to

FIGURE 14.3
The social construction of crime statistics: eight steps

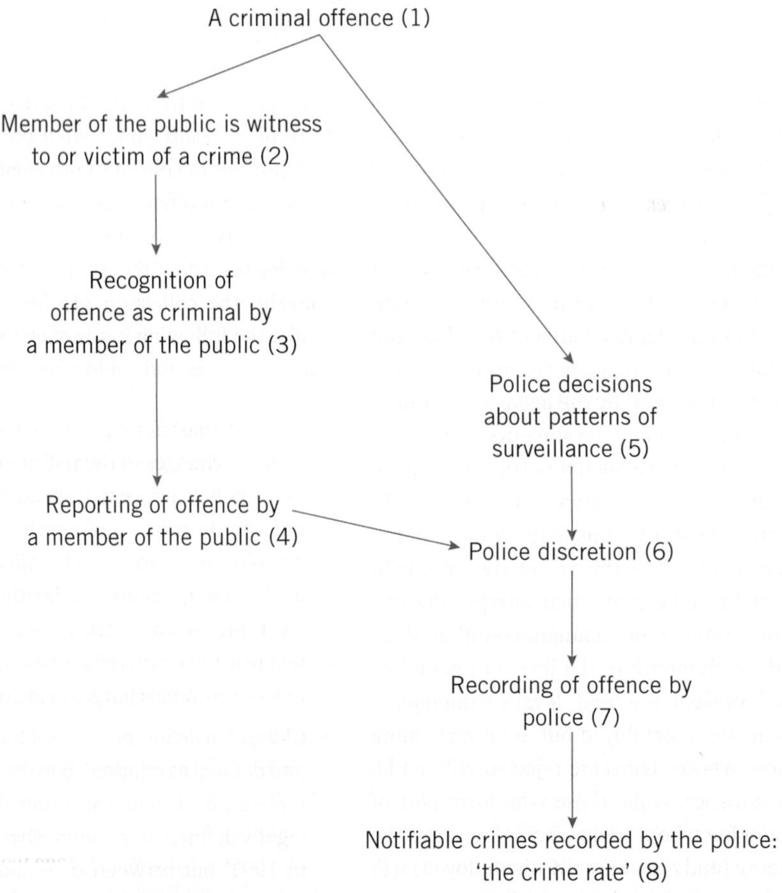

Source: adapted from a figure in Beardsworth et al. (n.d.)

14

report a crime to the police. This means that if a criminal act goes unnoticed, or is noticed but not recognized as criminal, or is noticed and recognized as criminal but not reported to the police, it will not enter the official statistics. Step 4 is the reporting of the crime to the police. Even then, the crime may not be entered into the crime statistics because the police have considerable discretion about whether they proceed with a criminal charge and may choose to let the person off with a warning (step 6). The factors that influence their decision might include the severity of the crime, the perpetrator's previous record, the perpetrator's demeanour or whether they seem to regret their actions, or the police's volume of work at the time (every criminal charge involves a lot of time-consuming paperwork). There are similar potential issues with offences that are observed by the police as a result of their patterns of surveillance (for example, patrolling areas). Whether the police happen to witness a crime is determined by decisions about how best to use police resources (step 5), and again, the crime may not become part of the crime rate because of the operation of police discretion.

All of this means that a substantial amount of crime goes unrecorded. This undercurrent of unrecorded crime is often referred to as 'the dark figure' (Coleman and Moynihan 1996), a term that has been used in relation to various areas of crime (Tcherni et al. 2016; Pezzella et al. 2019).

The User Guide to Crime Statistics for England and Wales (Office for National Statistics 2020) states that the CSEW (introduced in Table 14.1) 'is also a better indicator of long-term trends, for the crime types and population it covers, than police recorded crime because it is unaffected by changes in levels of reporting to the police or police recording practices'. In fact, the methodology and the crime types included in the main count of crime have remained comparable since the survey began in 1981. This indicates that official statistics may not always be the most effective form of statistics to use and that you need to think deeply about how secondary data has been collected.

social movements, for example the #metoo campaign against sexual harassment).

- *Changes in how phenomena are recorded*. For example, police officers might now classify multiple burglaries that take place in a block of flats on one day as a single incident, whereas they might previously have reported similar incidents as several burglaries.

The problems with official statistics also extend to the variables with which they are associated. To continue with our crime rate example, if we explore regional differences and find that the crime rate varies depending on the ethnic or social class composition of an area, this might at first seem to imply that ethnic status and social class are themselves related to crime. This assumption is problematic for a number of reasons. First, there is an analytic difficulty known as the **ecological fallacy** (see Key concept 14.3). Second, there is an issue of validity. There are many potential reasons for variations in reported crime between ethnic groups or social classes that are unrelated to whether these groups are more or less likely to commit crimes. The factors could include whether members of the public report crimes differently depending on the ethnic group or perceived social class of the perpetrator; whether police surveillance activities focus on areas with a high concentration of members of one ethnic group or class; whether police officers are more likely to exercise discretion when dealing with people of particular ethnic groups or social classes; and whether the police are less likely to uncover and investigate certain crimes that are related to ethnicity or class (for example, financially-motivated crimes committed by business and government professionals, known as 'white-collar crime'). In fact, in the past, evidence of institutional racism has been identified in the UK's police forces (MacPherson 1999).

These limitations should not lead you to rule out using official figures in your research project, given the many potential advantages associated with doing so, but you need to be aware of these potential issues with the reliability and validity of the data. While we have shown that these concerns are especially prominent in relation to official crime statistics, they are not limited to this area, as we saw in relation to official statistics regarding levels of employment. At the same time, it is important to recognize that issues of reliability and validity are not only relevant when using official statistics; they should be considered in any research project. When you come to write up your research (a stage we cover in Chapter 25), you should note any potential limitations of your data in your conclusion, and you should take them into account when making claims on the basis of your findings.

KEY CONCEPT 14.3
What is the ecological fallacy?

The ecological fallacy is the error of assuming that we can make inferences about individuals using findings relating to aggregated data (data based on combining several measurements). In this data, groups of observations are replaced with summary statistics that are based on those observations.

Harrison and McCaig (2015) have explored the idea of the ecological fallacy in relation to the link often made between 'low participation neighbourhoods' (LPNs) and universities, and the saying that 'you are where you live'—people tend to infer significant information about an individual or their family circumstances from the conditions around their home. LPNs have been defined, through the use of historic aggregated official data, as being neighbourhoods in which young people are less likely to go to university, and the term is increasingly used to refer to young people from disadvantaged backgrounds who could benefit from higher education but need support and/or incentives to do so. However, Harrison and McCaig examined a range of official data and found that the label may not be very diagnostically valuable. In fact, more disadvantaged families live outside these areas than within them, and they contain a higher-than-expected proportion of relatively advantaged families. The researchers argue that targeting LPNs leads to a slightly improved probability of '"finding" the "right" students, but [the term] does not have the predictive power that one might assume from their use by universities and governmental bodies' (Harrison and McCaig 2015: 811).

14.5 Big Data

A further form of existing data that can be used to undertake secondary analysis is **Big Data**. In many respects it is difficult to define and pin down what 'Big Data' means, especially because not only the information itself but also the *nature of* the information to which 'Big Data' refers is constantly changing as new developments occur. However, we attempt to define it in Key concept 14.4, and in this section we aim to give you a sense of the range of areas to which researchers have applied Big Data analyses. It is worth noting that new forms of analysis are developing rapidly and researchers often struggle to keep up with the possibilities that Big Data presents.

We note in Key concept 14.4 that social media is the main Big Data focus for social scientists, and Luke, one of our authors, has argued that the 'big' nature of the data that platforms like Twitter generate presents certain challenges for researchers (see Kitchin and McArdle 2016). The factors contributing to these challenges include the huge size of the data sets; the speed at which data are produced; and the variety of forms they can take (text, images, audio, videos, and hyperlinks) (Sloan 2017). Our student panellists discuss some of these challenges in Learn from experience 14.3.

Tinati et al. (2014) suggest that there has been a tendency for researchers using Big Data to reduce the data available in order to deal with its volume, resulting in smaller-scale analyses that do not take advantage of the full potential of the data. This reduction is usually achieved either by concentrating on a reduced sample of *users*, as in a study by Lieberman et al. (2013) of police departments' use of Facebook that focused on only the largest US police departments; or by taking a sample of *tweets or posts*, usually for content analysis, as in the study by Humphreys et al. (2014). Scourfield et al. (2019) emphasized the need for a clear time period in their study of media reporting of suicides, which compared the number and characteristics of reports on suicides and on road traffic accidents in young people during a six-month period (see Research in focus 14.4). Tinati et al. (2014: 665) argue that, to a certain extent, much Big Data research is 'methodologically limited because social scientists have approached Big Data with methods that cannot explore many of the particular qualities that make it so appealing to use: that is, the scale, proportionality, dynamism and relationality'.

There tends to be a distinction between two main ways of analysing Big Data, at least in the social media context. Studies either use the *content* of social media postings (which may or may not involve sampling), or they focus on revealing aspects of the *structure and process* of social media activity. The Big Data studies that we discuss in

KEY CONCEPT 14.4
What is Big Data?

'Big Data' is often used as a catch-all term, which can be problematic because the data it describes is highly heterogeneous. It is usually taken to refer to extremely large sources of data, so large that it is difficult to process and analyse using conventional methods. It can also refer to predictive analytics, or other forms of advanced data analytics, rather than just referring to the size of the data source. The term has been used in connection with things like the vast amounts of data that retailers collect about us and our spending habits when we use loyalty cards. Much of our lives now involve using digital technologies, so companies and platforms are able to monitor and log our activities in great detail. Because of this, there has been much talk in recent years of an 'explosion' of Big Data. This has resulted in Big Data analysis skills being in high demand with employers.

In addition to business transactions, Big Data can be generated by a variety of sources including social media (such as Twitter and Facebook, but including an expanding number of platforms), wearable technologies (such as Fitbits, which track activities such as the amount of steps people walk and the amount of sleep they have), mobile transactions, and automated cameras (Kitchin 2014). In the context of social research, the main Big Data information that has been used so far is social media, especially Twitter and Facebook, but also Instagram and other platforms. The studies we referred to in Chapter 13 by Humphreys et al. (2014; see Research in focus 13.5), who examined the personal information revealed on Twitter, and Greaves et al. (2014), who analysed the contents of tweets aimed at NHS hospitals (also discussed in Chapter 22: see Section 22.6 under 'Social media'), are examples of the use of Big Data by social scientists. Other examples include Brandtzaeg's (2017) use of a Big Data tool (Wisdom) to explore gender disparities in relation to Facebook liking practices concerning expressions of civic engagement in ten countries, and a study by Bharti et al. (2016) that analysed sarcastic sentiments in tweets.

LEARN FROM EXPERIENCE 14.3
Using Big Data in the form of Twitter

Two of our panellists, Simon and Jodie, used Big Data in the form of Twitter in their research projects and felt that it benefited their research in a number of ways. These included the amount of data available to them, its cost-effectiveness, and the ability to access hard-to-reach populations. Jodie also identified some of the challenges, including storage issues associated with the size of the data.

> In my BSc dissertation project, I collected Twitter data. I did this because my research objectives and research questions required it. I collected the data myself using the Collaborative Online Social Media Observatory (COSMOS)—a platform that assists social scientists with the collection and analysis of Twitter data. There were multiple issues and challenges that I faced. These included storing the data (the files were large, so they had to be externally stored, saved, and analysed); analysing the data, which could be slow due to its size and the computational power required; and deciding on the key terms and hashtags to use in collecting the data.
>
> However, utilizing Twitter's naturally occurring data had two distinguishing features that highlighted its potential for the research while subverting traditional research methods. The first incorporated the **concept** of 'locomotion', while the other takes advantage of the type of users present on the Twitter platform. As Twitter is locomotive, it is constantly flowing. This gives rise to a mass of valuable unique real-world data that elicits interesting findings in an online setting. Simultaneously, this data is from an abundance of users with unique voices, who partake in discussions and debate on a multitude of topics and respond to real-life events. It allows individuals (and corporations, charities, etc.) that are often hard to access through other methods to express themselves. Consequently, combining the methodological innovation of Twitter studies with the substantive area of the LGBT community had an incredible amount of potential for

my dissertation. It enabled me to investigate how gender impacts within the virtual world on a historically marginalized population: LGBT individuals.

Jodie

I collected vast amounts of Twitter data. By using an API (Application Programming Interface) I could collect my data for free. This was a simple process of identifying the keywords that I wanted and asking the platform to do this. I used the Collaborative Online Social Media Observatory (COSMOS), which gave me plenty of data. Overall, it was a really good way to collect data and I got masses of quality data easily and cheaply. Most importantly, by collecting data in this way I could be sure that it was not subject to any researcher biases—it was created completely independently and not influenced by anything that I had done.

Simon

Access the **online resources** to hear Jodie's reflections on this theme.

You can read about our panellists' backgrounds and research experiences on page xxvi.

Chapters 13 and 22 are mainly of the former type, while Research in focus 14.5, an example of social research using social media, provides an example of research measuring structure and process.

Big Data is an attractive source of material for social scientists because the sources are non-reactive: they have not been generated for research purposes. They offer opportunities for working on large amounts of data, although clearly this can be challenging too, particularly as unlike many large-scale secondary data sets, the data tends to require organizing. Research based on Big Data that focuses on the content of communication is certainly

RESEARCH IN FOCUS 14.4
Comparative approaches using Big Data

Scourfield et al. (2019) studied media reporting of suicides by comparing the number and characteristics of reports on suicides and on road traffic accidents (RTAs) in young people (aged 11–18) in newspapers and Twitter during a six-month period. Their research used the following definitions and parameters.

- A 'case' was defined as any death by suicide or RTA of a person aged 11–18 in England that was reported in a newspaper between 1 February 2014 and 31 July 2014.
- They studied reports on deaths that happened within the study period but also reports on the inquests into earlier deaths.
- They defined RTA deaths as any death apparently caused by a RTA, as long as it was not a suicide.

The researchers monitored the newspapers using sources such as the online service Nexis (UK) (see Chapter 13). For tweets, they used a database of all tweets worldwide that mentioned the name of the deceased (checking to ensure that they referred to the same individual). They then compared the number and characteristics of the Twitter and newspaper reporting of the cases.

Scourfield et al. found that there were more tweets than newspaper reports about young people's suicides. Twitter and newspaper reports were more strongly correlated for suicides than for RTAs, with recent suicides less likely to be reported in newspapers than recent deaths by RTA. Bullying-related suicides were found to be especially newsworthy. Scourfield et al. (2019: 519) concluded that 'there is potentially scope for the kind of media monitoring that some suicide prevention organizations (for example, the Samaritans in the UK) currently undertake to be extended to social media platforms such as Twitter, to ensure good quality reporting which contributes to reducing stigma and encouraging help-seeking'.

RESEARCH IN FOCUS 14.5
Big Data and tweeting

Tinati et al. (2014: 668) developed a tool 'that enables the metrics, dynamics and content of Twitter information flows and network formation to be explored in real-time or via historical data'. They focused in particular on the role of Twitter in political activism, collecting tweets relating to the protest against the increase of tuition fees in English universities using the hashtag #feesprotest. The collection comprised 12,831 tweets sent by 4,737 users in the period 8 October to 21 November 2011. The tool they developed allowed them to show the patterns of information flow both before and during the protest in terms of the numbers of retweeted messages, which reveal the most influential users and their location. The tool also enabled them to see changes in the popularity of users over time.

Tinati et al. were interested in content too, pointing out a shift in content from 'calls to participation' such as this:

> *[Wed 02 Nov 2011 20:40:49] "RT @michaeljohnroberts: There is a march of 10000 students to the city of London on November 15th come! #barricades #feesprotest"*
>
> (Tinati et al. 2014: 673)

—to emphasis on the police and intimations of heavy-handed tactics, such as this:

> *[Sat 05 Nov 2011 20:27:52] "RT @Witness: More disgusting police behaviour. We need to think about #feesprotest and how to defend ourselves. #abca"*
>
> (Tinati et al. 2014: 673)

They also show that there are individuals who, though not generators of content themselves, play a significant role in the flow of information by retweeting regularly.

an option for students and early-career researchers, but studies emphasizing the structure and process of social media communications can require quite specialist skills.

As we discussed in Chapter 6, the increasing use of Big Data means that questions about data protection, consent, and confidentiality are becoming increasingly important. The European General Data Protection Regulation (GDPR) plays a key role in relation to this, providing regulation regarding security and privacy. It is important, as it is with any form of research, to consider the ethical implications before using this type of data in your project.

KEY POINTS

- Secondary analysis of existing data gives researchers the opportunity to explore research questions that interest them without having to spend considerable time and money collecting data.
- Secondary analysis often allows researchers to use high-quality data sets that are based on large and reasonably representative samples.
- Analysing official statistics is often more controversial because of unease about the reliability and validity of certain types of official data, especially those relating to crime and deviance.
- Official statistics represent a form of unobtrusive method and enjoy certain advantages (especially lack of reactivity).
- Big Data, particularly that generated by social media, can be the focus of a secondary analysis but presents some challenges to researchers.

QUESTIONS FOR REVIEW

1. What is secondary analysis?
2. Outline the main advantages and limitations of secondary analysis of other researchers' data.
3. Examine recent issues of a sociology journal, such as *Sociology*. Locate an article that uses secondary analysis. How well do the advantages and limitations you outlined fit this article?
4. Does the possibility of conducting a secondary analysis apply only to quantitative data produced by other researchers?
5. For which kinds of studies is meta-analysis suitable?
6. Why have many social researchers been sceptical about the use of official statistics for research purposes, and how justified is their scepticism?
7. What reliability and validity issues do official statistics pose?
8. What are unobtrusive methods or measures? What is the chief advantage of such methods?
9. How might Big Data be of use to the social researcher?
10. How might you be able to use Big Data in a research project of your own?

ONLINE RESOURCES

www.oup.com/he/srm6e

You can find our notes on the answers to these questions within this chapter's **online resources**, together with:

- *audio/video comments* on this topic from our 'Learn from experience' panellists;
- *self-test questions* for further knowledge-checking;
- a *flashcard glossary* to help you recall key terms; and
- a *Student Researcher's Toolkit* containing practical materials and resources to help you conduct your own research project.

CHAPTER 15

QUANTITATIVE DATA ANALYSIS

CHAPTER GUIDE

In this chapter, we show you some of the most commonly used methods for analysing quantitative data. We explore the following topics:

- the importance of *not* leaving considerations of how you will analyse your quantitative data until after you have collected all your data;
- the distinctions between the different kinds of variable that can be generated in quantitative research;
- methods for analysing a single variable at a time (*univariate analysis*);
- methods for analysing relationships between two variables (*bivariate analysis*);
- methods for analysing relationships between three or more variables (*multivariate analysis*);
- the meaning of statistical significance and how to assess it.

15.1 Introduction

In this chapter, we will take you through some very basic techniques for analysing quantitative data. We will illustrate these methods using a small imaginary set of data based on attendance at a gym. This is approximately the amount of data that most students will analyse for their undergraduate dissertation or research project, but if you had access to suitable secondary data (see Chapter 14) you could analyse a larger sample. We recommend that in addition to reading this chapter you also visit our **online resources**, where you will find extensive guidance on how to implement these techniques using **SPSS**, **R**, or **Stata**, three of the most popular statistical software packages, or by using Microsoft Excel. While SPSS is commonly used and taught on many undergraduate courses, R is gaining prominence, so it is worth thinking carefully about which software package would be most suitable for your study—we discuss this in Thinking deeply 15.1.

In this chapter we will not be looking at the mathematical formulae that underpin the data analysis techniques, because the necessary calculations can easily be carried out by the software programs. Our intention here and in the associated digital resources is simply to give you a grounding in quantitative data analysis; if you want to use more advanced approaches, we recommend that you move on to more detailed books that focus specifically on this aspect of research (e.g. Bryman and Cramer 2011; MacInnes 2016).

THINKING DEEPLY 15.1
Choosing a software program

In this chapter we will use SPSS (**www.ibm.com/products/spss-statistics**) to analyse the imaginary data from our example small-scale research project. However, there are a number of statistical software packages available, all of which operate slightly differently. The most popular of these include

- STATA (**www.stata.com**)
- R (**www.r-project.org/**)
- **SAS** (**www.sas.com/en_gb/home.html**)

(accessed 30 May 2019)

Ozgur et al. (2017) state that SPSS provides the easiest-to-use and most intuitive interface. For example, menus and dialogue boxes make it possible to perform analyses without having to write command syntax. However, if you cannot access it through a university it can be expensive. R, on the other hand, is a free open-access package with no subscription fees or licence managers. Learning to use R can be time-consuming, which is also true of SAS. Although the base for R is very easy to install, users must download further packages to perform specific analyses, which can also take up time. STATA is more commonly used in econometrics. R offers more opportunities to modify and optimize graphs than SPSS, due to the wide range of packages that are available. As you can see, there are a number of advantages and disadvantages associated with the different software packages, and we recommend you explore these further to determine which of them might work best for your study.

It may be that you have had training, for example in a **research methods** module, that makes you more confident with particular software, or your decision may be limited by the fact that your organization or university only provides access to certain software. If you are interested in using one of these packages we recommend that you read the information on their websites (listed above) and discuss the options with your supervisor, if you have one. You might also find it useful to watch our introductory video tutorials for SPSS, R, and Stata, to get a sense of what each program looks like and involves: you will find them within our **online resources**.

15.2 Approaching quantitative data analysis

Before we begin to look at some of the techniques used in quantitative data analysis, there are a few general points we need to briefly discuss.

The first point is the importance of thinking about how you will analyse your data early on in the research process. One of the biggest mistakes people tend to make here is that they do not give any thought to how they will analyse their data until they have collected it, because they do not think the data analysis method will affect the data-collection process. This assumption is to an extent understandable, because quantitative data analysis can look like a distinct phase that occurs quite late in the process, after the data has been collected (see, for example, Figure 7.1, in which the analysis of quantitative data is shown as a late step—number 10—in **quantitative research**). However, it is important that you decide early in the process what techniques you will be applying—for example, when you are designing your **questionnaire**, **observation schedule**, or **coding frame**. There are two main reasons for this.

1. You cannot apply just any technique to any **variable**—your data analysis techniques have to be appropriate for the types of variables that you have created. This means that you must be familiar with the ways in which different types of variable are classified, which we will discuss in Section 15.4.
2. The size and nature of your **sample** are likely to affect the kind of techniques you can use. This will become evident in our discussion of statistical significance in Section 15.8.

So, you need to be aware that decisions that you make at quite an early stage in the research process, such as the kinds of data you plan to collect and the size of your sample, will have implications for the sorts of analysis that you will be able to conduct. The kinds of variables you employ and the types of analysis you conduct will also depend on the **research questions** you are trying to address in your project. So it is important to reflect on the research questions your project is addressing and to ensure that your analysis will be able to address these. The link between the research questions, the data collection, and the subsequent analysis is crucial to successfully undertaking social research. It is also important to check the level of analysis that your institution will expect of you in any research project you conduct.

LEARN FROM EXPERIENCE 15.1

Conducting univariate, bivariate, or multivariate analysis

The types of data you have collected, and what you want to find out, will dictate whether you conduct univariate, bivariate, or multivariate analysis. However, even if you plan to use multivariate data analysis, Jodie recommends that it is important to get to know your data, initially working with univariate analysis, before moving to bivariate and multivariate analysis.

> I always start with univariate analysis—simply to get a feel for my data, to realize how they are coded—which may lead to recoding or noticing that missing data has not been correctly accounted for. Bivariate analysis is the next natural step, prior to multivariate analysis, as this allows you to realize the nature of the relationship between your independent variables and your dependent variable—and its suitability to be included in the multivariate analysis (that is, if you find statistical significance). It is important to go through this process so that you really get to 'know' your data. Knowing how it is coded is vital in understanding what it is telling you.
>
> Jodie

 Access the **online resources** to hear Jodie's reflections on this theme.

You can read about our panellists' backgrounds and research experiences on page xxvi.

In some cases, you may want to describe the data using univariate analysis (exploring one variable), or bivariate analysis (looking at the interactions between two variables), or even multivariate analysis (analysing three or more variables simultaneously). You may want to use statistical tests such as those associated with associations and linear relationships. We will touch on these concepts later in the chapter. In Learn from experience 15.1 Jodie explains how she approaches these types of analysis.

It is also worth noting the difference between descriptive statistics, which are methods used to describe data and their characteristics, and inferential statistics, which involve making inferences (estimates or predictions) about what we don't know. For example, if you were investigating the number of visitors to a homeless shelter, you might produce a graph to explore how the number of visitors varied each day, calculating how many people visit on an average day and perhaps the proportion of visitors in different age ranges. These would all be *descriptive* data. You will encounter numerous forms of descriptive data in this chapter. Inferential statistics, on the other hand, are a powerful way to move beyond a random sample to suggest something greater about a population. To take the example used in Chapter 8, if we questioned 200 people about who they were going to vote for on the day prior to an election, we could attempt to predict which party would win the election (see Foster et al. 2014). We will explore some statistical tests that use inferential statistics in Section 15.8.

15.3 An example of a small research project

15

Our discussion of quantitative data analysis will centre on an imaginary piece of research on a scale that an undergraduate student could conduct for a dissertation. Our imaginary student is interested in the area of leisure in modern society and in particular, because she enjoys going to a gym, the ways in which these venues are used and people's reasons for joining them. She hypothesizes that they may be indicative of a 'civilizing process' and uses this theory as a framework for her findings (see Elias 2000; Rojek 1995; Wagg 2017). The student is also interested in issues relating to gender and body image and suspects that men and women will differ in their reasons for going to a gym and the kinds of activities they undertake when they are there. Suspecting that these factors will vary by age, she also intends to collect information on this.

The student secures the agreement of a gym close to her home and contacts a sample of its members by post (those who had agreed to be contacted). The gym has 1,200 members and she decides to take a simple random sample of 10 per cent of the membership (120 members). She sends out postal self-completion questionnaires to members of the sample, with a covering letter explaining that the gym supports her research and that it has been ethically approved through her university ethics procedure (see Section 6.2 under 'Guidance from your institution'). She would have preferred to contact the members of her sample online so that they could complete the questionnaire this way, but the gym was not willing to pass on members' email addresses. (It could easily have been the other way round and they might not have wanted to provide postal addresses, or they might have wanted to send out the questionnaire on the student's behalf.) However, she does offer participants the option of completing the questionnaire online, so that this is in effect a mixed mode survey (postal and online), although most of those replying opt to do so via post.

One thing she wants to know is how much time people are spending on each of three main types of activity in the gym: cardiovascular equipment, weights equipment, and exercises. She defines each of these carefully in the covering letter, asking members of the sample to keep a note of how long they are spending on each of the three activities on their next visit. They are then requested to return the questionnaires to her in a prepaid reply envelope or online. She ends up with a sample of 90 questionnaires—a response rate of 75 per cent. This is an impressive response rate, and above what you might usually expect to receive (see Section 8.45).

We present part of the student's four-page questionnaire in Figure 15.1, which has been completed by a respondent and coded by the student. You can see that many of the questions (1, and 3 to 8) are pre-coded, so when the student is preparing to process the data, she simply has to circle the code on the far right of the question under the column 'code'. The other questions request specific figures, so the student has to transfer the relevant figure to the code column. It is also worth

FIGURE 15.1
A completed and processed questionnaire from an imaginary student survey on gym-going

Question		Code
1. Are you male or female (please tick)?		
Male ✓ Female ___		①2
2. How old are you?		
_21_ years		_21_
3. Which of the following best describes your main reason for going to the gym? (please tick *one* only)		
Relaxation	___	1
Maintain or improve fitness	✓	②
Lose weight	___	3
Meet others	___	4
Build strength	___	5
Other (please specify)	___	6
4. When you go to the gym, how often do you use the cardiovascular equipment (treadmill, step machine, bike, rower)? (please tick)		
Always	✓	①
Usually	___	2
Rarely	___	3
Never	___	4
5. When you go to the gym, how often do you use the weights machines (including free weights)? (please tick)		
Always	✓	①
Usually	___	2
Rarely	___	3
Never	___	4
6. How frequently do you usually go to the gym? (please tick)		
Every Day	___	1
4–6 days a week	___	2
2 or 3 days a week	✓	③
Once a week	___	4
2 or 3 times a month	___	5
Once a month	___	6
Less than once a month	___	7
7. Are you usually accompanied when you go to the gym or do you usually go on your own? (please tick one only)		
On my own	✓	①
With a friend	___	2
With a partner/spouse	___	3
8. Do you have sources of regular exercise other than the gym?		
Yes ___ No ✓		1②
If you have answered ***No*** *to this question, please proceed to question* **9**		
8a If you have replied **Yes** to question **8**, please indicate the main source of regular exercise in the last six months from this list. (please tick one only)		⓪
Sport	___	1
Cycling on the road	___	2

(continued)

15

Continued

Jogging	___	3
Long walks	___	4
Other (please specify)	___	5

9. During your last visit to the gym, how many minutes did you spend on the cardiovascular equipment (treadmill, step machine, bike, rower)?

 _33_ minutes *33*

10. During your last visit to the gym, how many minutes did you spend on the weights machines (including free weights)?

 _17_ minutes *17*

11. During your last visit to the gym, how many minutes did you spend on other activities (e.g. stretching exercises)?

 _5_ minutes *5*

noting that questions 4 and 5 use terms like 'rarely' and 'usually'. Sometimes we cannot avoid using these terms, but remember (see Section 11.3, 'Types of questions') that when there is an alternative that allows actual frequency to be measured, this is nearly always preferable.

You can see the data for all 90 respondents in Figure 15.2, which presents the gym survey data. Each row represents a different respondent, and for the moment, each of the 12 questions (remember that question 8 has two parts to it) is labelled as a variable number (var00001, etc.), which is a default number assigned by SPSS. Each variable number corresponds to a question in the gym survey data (that is, var00001 is question 1, var00002 is question 2, etc.).

15

When conducting quantitative data analysis, you need to decide how you will deal with the issue of '**missing data**', which occurs when respondents fail to reply to a question—either by accident or because they do not want to answer it. Chapter 8 discusses the notion of non-response in relation to sampling, including some of the challenges this can present for the **generalizability** of the data. Chapters 9 and 10 then outline some of the techniques that researchers can employ to try and reduce the level of missing data. These include clear instructions, good question design and clarity, and consideration of the length of the data-collection tool.

If you are entering your own data you need to assign a particular code for missing data (which can be a different number for different questions) to make sure that the software registers the absence of a response so that you can take this into account during the analysis. (Where data has already been collected, as in a secondary data set, the missing values, like other variables, will already have been assigned a number—a code.)

There is some missing data among the responses shown in Figure 15.2.

- Respondent 24 has failed to answer question 2 about their age. This has been coded as a zero (0) so that the software registers it as missing data. It is worth noting that some researchers prefer to use alternatives to zero (0), including where zero could be a possible response rather than missing data. For example, you could use a symbol such as . or a figure such as −99 to represent missing data, which would avoid any potential confusion.
- Question 8a has a large number of zeros; this is because many people did not answer it because they were filtered out by the previous question (they do not have other sources of regular exercise). The absences here have been coded as zero, representing missing data, but in this case the failure to reply just indicates that the question was not applicable to these respondents.
- There are zeros for var00010, var00011, and var00012 but these do *not* denote missing data; here, they are showing that the respondent spends zero minutes on the activity in question. You can see that it is important to remember how each response to each particular variable is coded when it comes to the analysis.
- Everyone has answered questions 9, 10, and 11, so there are no missing data for these variables. If there had been missing data, the student would have needed to code the missing data with a number that could not also be a true figure. For example, she could use 99, as nobody has spent 99 minutes on these activities. This should be a number that is easy to remember and that could not be read by the software as anything other than missing data.

FIGURE 15.2
Data from an imaginary student survey on gym-going

var00001	var00002	var00003	var00004	var00005	var00006	var00007	var00008	var00009	var00010	var00011	var00012
1	21	2	1	1	3	1	2	0	33	17	5
2	44	1	3	1	4	3	1	2	10	23	10
2	19	3	1	2	2	1	1	1	27	18	12
2	27	3	2	1	2	1	2	0	30	17	3
1	57	2	1	3	2	3	1	4	22	0	15
2	27	3	1	1	3	1	1	3	34	17	0
1	39	5	2	1	5	1	1	5	17	48	10
2	36	3	1	2	2	2	1	1	25	18	7
1	37	2	1	1	3	1	2	0	34	15	0
2	51	2	2	2	4	3	2	0	16	18	11
1	24	5	2	1	3	1	1	1	0	42	16
2	29	2	1	2	3	1	2	0	34	22	12
1	20	5	1	1	2	1	2	0	22	31	7
2	22	2	1	3	4	2	1	3	37	14	12
2	46	3	1	1	5	2	2	0	26	9	4
2	41	3	1	2	2	3	1	4	22	7	10
1	25	5	1	1	3	1	1	1	21	29	4
2	46	3	1	2	4	2	1	4	18	8	11
1	30	3	1	1	5	1	2	0	23	9	6
1	25	5	2	1	3	1	1	1	23	19	0
2	24	2	1	1	3	2	1	2	20	7	6
2	39	1	2	3	5	1	2	0	17	0	9
1	44	3	1	1	3	2	1	2	22	8	5
1	0	1	2	2	4	2	1	4	15	10	4
2	18	3	1	2	3	1	2	1	18	7	10
1	41	3	1	1	3	1	2	0	34	10	4
2	38	2	1	2	5	3	1	2	24	14	10
1	25	2	1	1	2	1	2	0	48	22	7
1	41	5	2	1	3	1	1	2	17	27	0
2	30	3	1	1	2	2	2	0	32	13	10
2	29	3	1	3	2	1	2	0	31	0	7
2	42	1	2	2	4	2	1	4	17	14	6
1	31	2	1	1	2	1	2	0	49	21	2
2	25	3	1	1	2	3	2	0	30	17	15
1	46	3	1	1	3	1	1	3	32	10	5
1	24	5	2	1	4	1	1	2	0	36	11
2	34	3	1	1	3	2	1	4	27	14	12
2	50	2	1	2	2	3	2	0	28	8	6
1	28	5	1	1	3	2	1	1	26	22	8
2	30	3	1	1	2	1	1	4	21	9	12
1	27	2	1	1	2	1	1	3	64	15	8
2	27	2	1	2	4	2	1	4	22	10	7
1	36	5	1	1	3	2	2	0	21	24	0

(continued)

Continued

var00001	var00002	var00003	var00004	var00005	var00006	var00007	var00008	var00009	var00010	var00011	var00012
2	43	3	1	1	4	1	2	0	25	13	8
1	34	2	1	1	3	2	1	1	45	15	6
2	27	3	1	1	2	1	1	4	33	10	9
2	38	2	1	3	4	2	2	0	23	0	16
1	28	2	1	1	3	3	1	2	38	13	5
1	44	5	1	1	2	1	2	0	27	19	7
2	31	3	1	2	3	2	2	0	32	11	5
2	23	2	1	1	4	2	1	1	33	18	8
1	45	3	1	1	3	1	1	2	26	10	7
2	34	3	1	2	2	3	2	0	36	8	12
1	27	3	1	1	2	3	1	3	42	13	6
2	40	3	1	1	2	2	1	4	26	9	10
2	24	2	1	1	2	1	1	2	22	10	9
1	37	2	1	1	5	2	2	0	21	11	0
1	22	5	1	1	4	1	1	1	23	17	6
2	31	3	1	2	3	1	1	4	40	16	12
1	37	2	1	1	2	3	2	0	54	12	3
2	33	1	2	2	4	2	2	0	17	10	5
1	23	5	1	1	3	1	1	1	41	27	8
1	28	3	1	1	3	3	2	0	27	11	8
2	29	2	1	2	5	2	1	2	24	9	9
2	43	3	1	1	2	1	2	0	36	17	12
1	28	5	1	1	3	1	1	1	22	15	4
1	48	2	1	1	5	1	1	4	25	11	7
2	32	2	2	2	4	2	2	0	27	13	11
1	28	5	1	1	2	2	2	0	15	23	7
2	23	2	1	1	5	1	1	4	14	11	5
2	43	2	1	2	5	1	2	0	18	7	3
1	28	2	1	1	4	3	1	2	34	18	8
2	23	3	1	1	2	1	2	0	37	17	17
2	36	1	2	2	4	2	1	4	18	12	4
1	50	2	1	1	3	1	1	2	28	14	3
1	37	3	1	1	2	2	2	0	26	14	9
2	41	3	1	1	2	1	1	4	24	11	4
1	26	5	2	1	5	1	1	1	23	19	8
2	28	3	1	1	4	1	2	0	27	12	4
2	35	2	1	1	3	1	1	1	28	14	0
1	28	5	1	1	2	1	1	2	20	24	12
2	36	2	1	1	3	2	2	0	26	9	14
2	29	3	1	1	4	1	1	4	23	13	4
1	34	1	2	2	4	2	1	0	24	12	3
1	53	2	1	1	3	3	1	1	32	17	6
2	30	3	1	1	4	1	2	0	24	10	9
1	43	2	1	1	2	1	1	2	24	14	10
2	26	5	2	1	4	1	1	1	16	23	7
2	44	1	1	1	4	2	2	0	27	18	6
1	45	1	2	2	3	3	2	0	20	14	5

15.4 Types of variable

You may have noticed from looking at the questionnaire extract in Figure 15.1 that the kinds of information the student will receive varies between questions.

- Questions 2, 9, 10, and 11 require answers in terms of real numbers.
- Questions 1 and 8 produce either/or answers (male/female and yes/no, respectively) and are therefore in the form of dichotomies (though see Thinking deeply 15.2 for a reflection of whether gender should be seen as a dichotomous variable).
- The rest of the questions involve lists of categories, but there are differences between these too.
  - Questions 4, 5, and 6 have answers that are rank ordered. For example, in question 6 the **category** 'Every day' implies greater frequency than '4–6 days a week', which implies greater frequency than '2 or 3 days a week', and so on.
  - Questions 3, 7, and 8a have categories that cannot be ranked. For example, in question 3 we cannot say that 'relaxation' is *more of* something than 'maintain or improve fitness' or 'lose weight'.

So, because the type of information that the student receives varies between questions, in order to analyse her data she needs to classify the different types of variables according to **levels of measurement**. The four main types of variable are as follows.

- **Interval/ratio variables**. These are variables where the distances between the categories are identical across the **range** of categories. This applies to variables var00010, var00011, and var00012 in the student's data (produced by questions 9 to 11 in the questionnaire), as in each case, the distance between the categories is 1 minute. So, a person may spend 32 minutes on cardiovascular equipment, which is 1 minute more than someone who spends 31 minutes on this equipment. That difference is the same as the difference between someone who spends 8 minutes and another who spends 9 minutes on the equipment. Interval/ratio variables are viewed as the highest level of measurement because they allow you to conduct a wider variety of statistical analyses on them than with other types of variable. They also tend to enable more powerful analyses. We say 'interval/ratio variables' here as though these are alternative names for the same level of measurement, but there is actually a distinction between them, in that ratio variables are interval variables with a fixed zero point. In social research, many interval variables

15

THINKING DEEPLY 15.2
Is gender really a dichotomous variable?

This student project presents gender as a dichotomous variable—the questionnaire asks the respondent to say that they are either male or female. However, gender is in fact a social construction that relates to behaviours and attributes based on labels such as 'masculinity' and 'femininity'. Gender identity is therefore a personal perception and the gender category someone identifies with may not match the sex (male or female) they were assigned at birth. Gender is increasingly understood as not binary but existing on a spectrum, with a growing number of people describing themselves in their own terms rather than simply using the predefined categories of male and female.

In the UK, the Office for National Statistics (ONS 2019b) reports that most official data only include 'male' and 'female' options for what is sometimes termed 'sex' and sometimes 'gender'. The ONS does not currently collect data on wider gender identities in any social surveys. This student may have decided to only use the categories of 'male' and 'female' because they anticipated wanting to compare their findings to data from the ONS. However, as gender identity is increasingly recognized as subjective and often non-binary, there is a strong argument that in the future, data collection on gender needs to offer more options than simply 'male' or 'female'.

exhibit this quality (for example, income, age, number of employees, revenue).

- **Ordinal variables**. These are variables whose categories can be rank ordered (as in the case of interval/ratio variables) but where the distances between the categories are not equal across the range. In the case of question 6, the difference between the category 'every day' and '4–6 days a week' is not the same as the difference between '4–6 days a week' and '2 or 3 days a week', but we can say that 'every day' is more often than '4–6 days a week', which is more frequent than '2 or 3 days a week' (etc.). You should also bear in mind that often the process of grouping an interval/ratio variable such as var00002, which refers to people's ages, into categories (for example 20 and under; 21–30; 31–40; 41–50; 51 and over), you are transforming it into an ordinal variable.
- **Nominal variables**. These variables consist of categories that cannot be rank ordered. As we have noted, we cannot say in the case of question 3 that 'relaxation' is more of something than 'maintain or improve fitness' or 'lose weight'.
- **Dichotomous variables**. These are **categorical variables** containing data that only have two categories (for example, yes/no). Their position in relation to the other variables is slightly ambiguous as they only have one interval, meaning that they can be considered as having attributes of the other three types of variable. They look as though they are nominal variables, but because they only have one interval they are sometimes treated as ordinal variables. For most purposes, it is probably safest to treat them as if they were ordinary nominal variables. It has also been suggested that dichotomous variables, especially when they express a certain characteristic to be either present or not, can be compared with interval/ratio values.

In Table 15.1 we summarize these four main types of variable and provide examples of each one from the gym survey. You can see here that the variable name in the SPSS column is a shortened version of the full question—you need to devise suitable variable names so that you can easily recognize the variables. Figure 15.3 provides guidance about how to identify variables of each type.

There is considerable debate about the level of measurement associated with **multiple-indicator** (or multiple-item) **measures** of concepts, such as **Likert scales** (see Key concept 7.2). In many ways we can see them as ordinal variables, because whether the distances between the different **attributes** (or categories) of a variable measured using a Likert scale are equal depends on individual perception (Foster et al. 2014). However, many writers argue that we should treat them as though they are interval/ratio variables, because of the relatively large number of categories they generate. For a brief discussion of this issue, see Bryman and Cramer (2011) and Bors (2018), who distinguish between 'true' interval/ratio variables and those produced by multiple-indicator measures.

15

TABLE 15.1
Types of variable

Type	Description	Examples in gym study	Variable name in SPSS
Interval/ratio	Variables where the distances between the categories are identical across the range	var00002	age
		var00010	cardmins
		var00011	weimins
		var00012	othmins
Ordinal	Variables whose categories can be rank ordered but where the distances between the categories are not equal across the range	var00004	carduse
		var00005	weiuse
		var00006	frequent
Nominal	Variables whose categories cannot be rank ordered	var00003	reasons
		var00007	accomp
		var00009	exercise
Dichotomous	Variables containing data that have only two categories	var00001	gender
		var00008	othsourc

FIGURE 15.3
Deciding how to categorize a variable

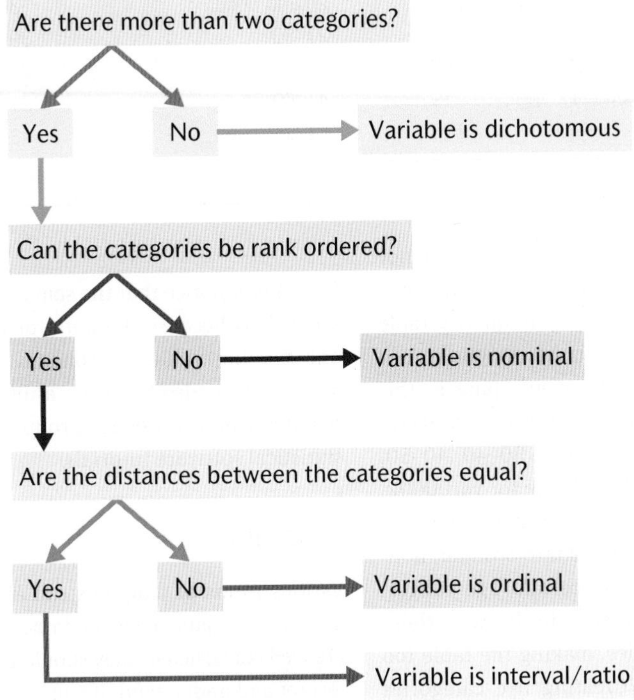
Are there more than two categories?
Yes
No
Variable is dichotomous
Can the categories be rank ordered?
Yes
No
Variable is nominal
Are the distances between the categories equal?
Yes
No
Variable is ordinal
Variable is interval/ratio

15.5 Univariate analysis

15

It is important to understand the difference between different types of analysis. In this section we focus on univariate analysis, which refers to the process of analysing one variable at a time and produces what are known as descriptive statistics—these are numerical representations or summaries of data, which help to give it meaning. We will outline the most commonly used approaches for this form of analysis, namely **frequency tables**, diagrams, **measures of central tendency**, and **measures of dispersion**. We will also take a brief look at the **boxplot**, a figure that provides an indication of both a measure of central tendency and a measure of dispersion.

Frequency tables

A frequency table shows how frequently particular values occur in a data set. For example, a frequency table can set out the number of people, and the percentage of people, belonging to each of the categories of a variable. As you can see from Table 15.2, a frequency table for var00003 presents the values associated with our variable simply and clearly. No one chose the possible choices 'meet others' and 'other', so we have not included these in the table. The values for the remaining options are shown under an *n* column, indicating the number of people who selected the option, and a % column, indicating the percentage of the sample that this figure represents. This format allows us to easily 'read' the data. We can see, for example, that 33 members of the sample are going to the gym to lose weight and that they represent 37 per cent (percentages are often rounded up and down in frequency tables) of the entire sample. If the sample is small enough, you could create a frequency table manually. However, you can access the statistical software tutorials on our **online resources** to learn how to use them to generate a frequency table.

TABLE 15.2
Frequency table showing reasons for visiting the gym

Reason	*n*	%
Relaxation	9	10
Maintain or improve fitness	31	34
Lose weight	33	37
Build strength	17	19
TOTAL	90	100

TABLE 15.3
Frequency table showing ages of gym members

Age	*n*	%
20 and under	3	3
21–30	39	44
31–40	23	26
41–50	21	24
51 and over	3	3
TOTAL	89	100

Nominal variables are often represented in frequency tables, but if we want to present an interval/ratio variable (for example people's ages) in a frequency table format, we need to group or recode the categories (see Learn from experience 15.2). When grouping in this way, it is important to make sure the categories you create do not overlap (for example: 20–30, 30–40, 40–50, etc.). Table 15.3 shows a frequency table for var00002, an interval/ratio variable, and you can see that the individual categories have been grouped into broader, non-overlapping categories indicating certain age ranges. If the student did not group the data in this way, there would be 34 different categories, making the table too big to work with effectively. Creating five categories makes it much easier to see the distribution of ages. (You might notice that the sample totals 89, rather than 90. This is because the data for this variable contains one missing value, respondent 24. The percentages are therefore also based on a total of 89.) We demonstrate the procedures for grouping respondents in our statistical software tutorials.

Diagrams

Various forms of diagrams can also be used to display quantitative data. Their main advantage is that, if they are well constructed, they should be relatively easy to interpret and understand. If you are working with nominal or ordinal variables, the **bar chart** and the **pie chart** are

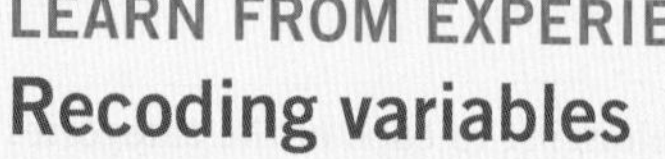

LEARN FROM EXPERIENCE 15.2
Recoding variables

Recoding variables can be an important part of ensuring that you can analyse the data using your chosen form of analysis. Our panellist Zvi, who focused on adolescents' sleep patterns and screen time, explains how he recoded the variable associated with sleep time on a typical school night in order to be able to conduct multivariate analysis (see Section 15.7). He referred to information about recommended sleep time to guide his decision-making. You should explain these kinds of decision-making processes in the methodology chapter of your research project.

> One of the conditions for logistic regression (a form of multivariate analysis) is that the dependent variable has to be binary—in other words, consist of only two outcomes. As I wanted to predict the chance of getting a good night's sleep, I first had to conceptualize what I meant by 'good night's sleep' using the data I had to hand. The data I used asked how many hours the respondent slept for on a typical school night and gave a selection of 1 hour, 2 hours, 3 hours etc. up to 10 hours or more. Therefore, in order to make this binary, I banded those 7 hours or less and 8 hours or more into a category each, based on the widely accepted medical recommendation that children should sleep for at least 8 hours a night. Recoding variables in SPSS is quite straightforward, so this wasn't an issue.
>
> Zvi

You can read about our panellists' backgrounds and research experiences on page xxvi.

two of the easiest diagrams to use (both are methods that you have probably come across before). This is because nominal and ordinal variables involve non-continuous data. With nominal data there are no mid-points between the categories: answers are either in one or the other, never between, so the categories are mutually exclusive and non-continuous. Similarly, the scaling of ordinal data is often difficult to determine and should also not be treated as continuous. By contrast, interval/ratio variables involve continuous data, and the **histogram** is commonly used to display data for such variables. These data are measured in numbers, and an observation may take any value on a continuous scale. For example, the question 'During your last visit to the gym, how many minutes did you spend on other activities (for example stretching exercises)?' could take a value of zero, or any other number depending on the length of time spent on other activities. For continuous variables the standard rules of arithmetic apply, so it makes sense to say that if you spend 20 minutes on other activities at the gym, this is twice the amount of someone who spends 10 minutes. There are also other forms of diagrams you might want to explore, such as the **infographic**.

Bar charts

The bar chart in Figure 15.4 uses the data shown in Table 15.2. Each bar represents the number of people within each category, and the relative height of the bars helps us see how the counts compare with each other. We noted above that bar charts are used for nominal and ordinal variables because they involve non-continuous, mutually exclusive data, and this characteristic is represented by the gaps between the bars of a bar chart.

We produced Figure 15.4 using SPSS. We demonstrate the procedures for generating a bar chart, using SPSS and the other main software packages, in our statistical software tutorials.

Pie charts

Another way of displaying nominal and ordinal data is through a pie chart, like the one in Figure 15.5 (which again uses the data from Table 15.2). Like the height of bars in a bar chart, this visual representation of the data shows the relative size of the different categories, bringing out the size of each 'slice' relative to the total sample. This diagram also provides the percentage that each slice represents of the whole sample. Pie charts are useful in helping an audience get a sense of the distribution of your data quickly, but in conveying these

FIGURE 15.4

Bar chart showing the main reasons for visiting the gym (SPSS output)

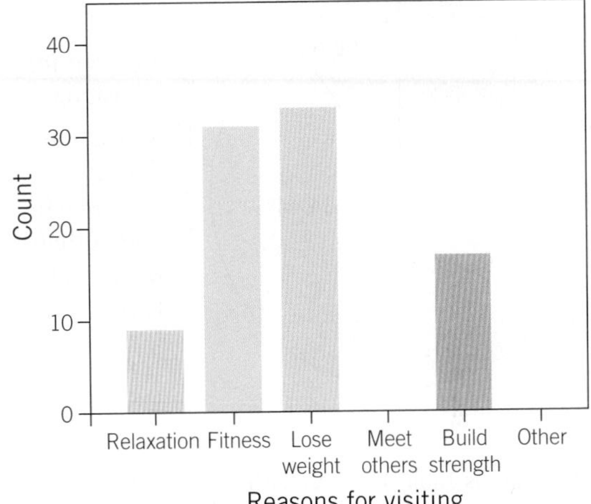

relative differences efficiently, they also have some limitations. These can mean some researchers prefer not to use them. It is harder to compare the size of slices in a pie chart than to compare the heights of bars, partly because of the way that the components are arranged and partly because angles are harder to compare than lengths. That is why we recommend providing the numbers too. You should do this either by clearly labelling each 'slice' of the pie or providing a separate key to show what the different colours/shadings in each 'slice' represent. This is particularly useful if you are dealing with lots of slices, or have some small frequencies (some slices might be too narrow to contain a number). If you are drawing more than one pie chart on the same subject (such as types of crimes in different regions), always use the same categories, presented in the same order, to help to avoid confusion. It is also best to use pie charts where there are not too many categories, as too many slices can make the chart difficult to read.

We demonstrate the procedures for generating a pie chart, using SPSS and the other software packages, in our statistical software tutorials.

Histograms

If you are displaying an interval/ratio variable, like var00002, you could use a histogram. Figure 15.6, which was also generated by SPSS, uses the same data and

FIGURE 15.5
Pie chart showing the main reasons for visiting the gym (SPSS output)

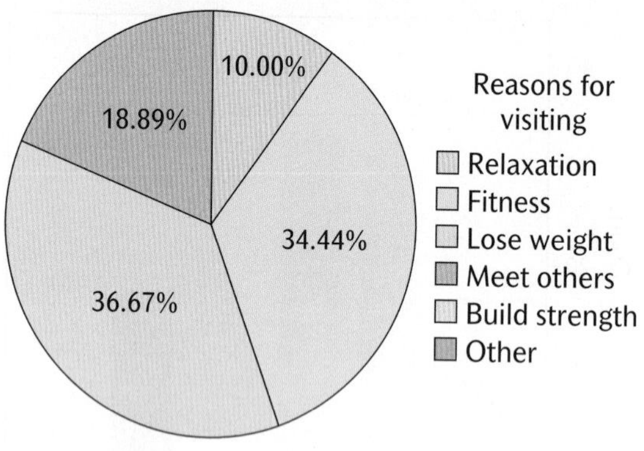

FIGURE 15.6
Histogram showing the ages of gym visitors (SPSS output)

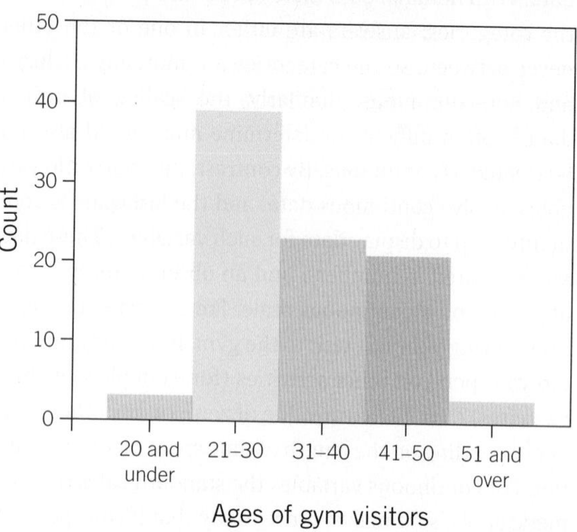

categories as Table 15.3. As with the bar chart, the bars show the relative size of each of the age bands. They provide a visual representation of how often different values occur, how much spread or variability there is among the values, and which values are most typical for the data. However, unlike on a bar chart, with a histogram there is no space between the bars. This is because histograms are produced for interval/ratio variables, where the data is continuous. We demonstrate the procedure for generating a histogram, using SPSS and the other main software packages, in our statistical software tutorials.

Infographics

There are an increasing number of ways of presenting data beyond the more traditional forms we have outlined so far. These different forms of infographics—the term refers to the fact that they combine 'information' and 'graphics'—aim to provide visual representations of information, data, or knowledge in a clear and quick way. They are not only used for univariate data; depending on the type of infographic, they can also be used to effectively represent bivariate analysis. Research in focus 15.1 provides an example of the visual representation of information about health inequalities and deprivation indicators, using a map of the number 83 bus route in Sheffield, UK.

Regardless of the form of presentation we use to display our data, it is important to present it clearly and

RESEARCH IN FOCUS 15.1
Presenting data in different ways

The Sheffield Fairness Commission was set up by the City Council of the English city of Sheffield in 2012 to explore inequalities in the city and how to tackle them. Figure 15.7, from the Sheffield Fairness Commission report *Making Sheffield Fairer*, (2013), is based on the 65-minute number 83 bus route and illustrates life expectancy and indices of multiple deprivation through the city.

It is well known that Sheffield is split in terms of health and wellbeing, with the people in the south-west of the city doing much better than those in the north east areas in terms of income levels, health, and educational achievement. The researchers used the 83 bus route to structure the data because it travels through both well-off and more deprived areas on its journey across the city. It starts in Millhouses, an area where female life expectancy is 86.3, but by the time it reaches Burngreave, female life expectancy has reduced to 76.9. This shows that a person born in Burngreave who remains in the area throughout their life can expect to live nearly 10 years less than a person living four miles away in Millhouses, because of socio-economic circumstances and the area in which they have lived. This diagram represents the data in a clear and interesting way.

FIGURE 15.7

Life expectancy and indices of multiple deprivation through the city of Sheffield, following the number 83 bus route

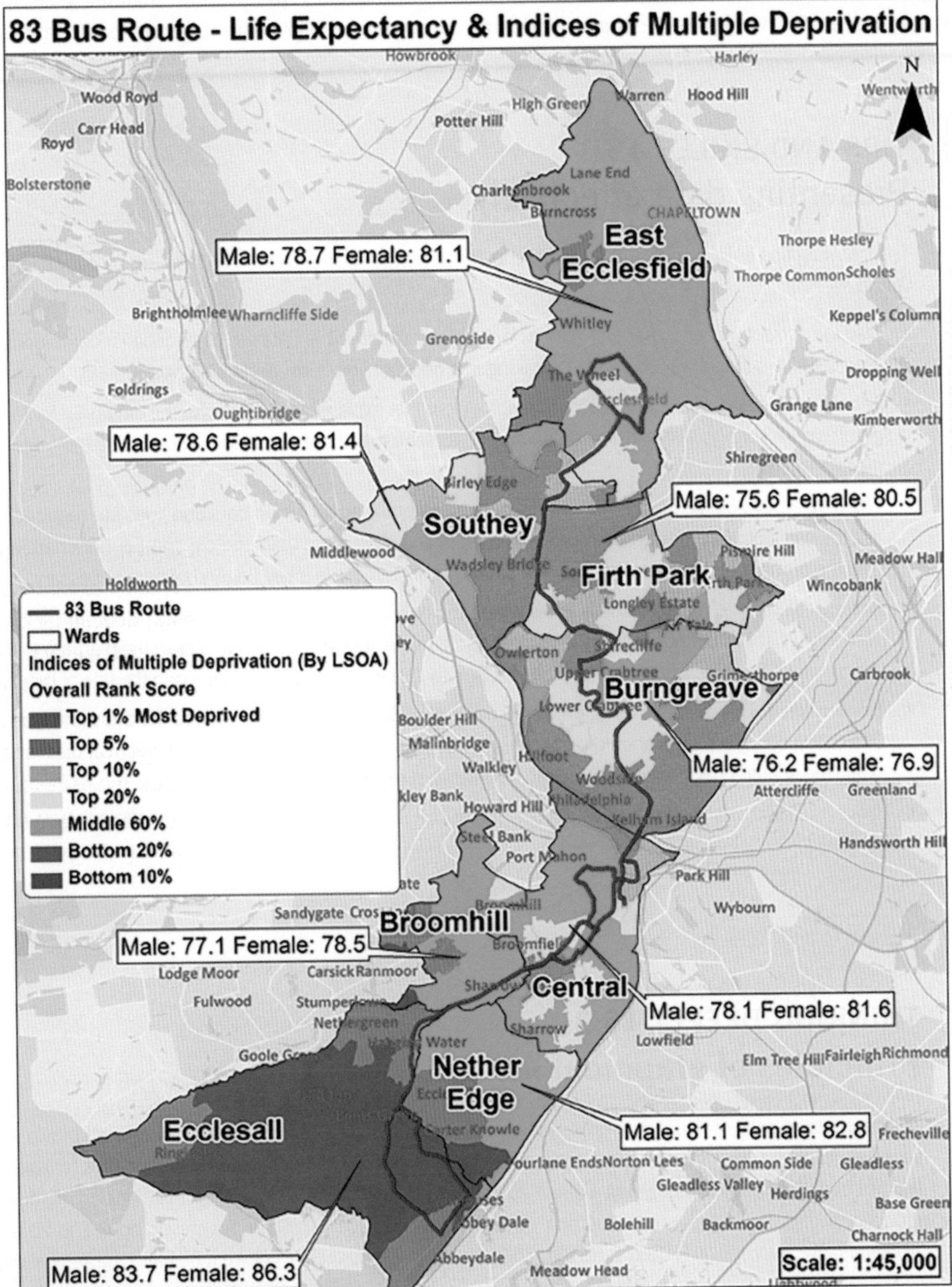

Source: Sheffield Fairness Commission Report, Sheffield City Council, 2013. Produced with kind permission of Ordnance Survey.

15

accurately. This can, in some cases, mean that the simpler the presentation is the better. Although the main purpose of a graph or table is to communicate your findings, this does not detract from the need for a well-designed, aesthetically pleasing presentation. You need to bear these points in mind when presenting your data analysis. In Tips and skills 15.1 we list some practical tips for presenting data in meaningful ways, based on Clark et al. (2019), and in Thinking deeply 15.3 we reflect on Tufte's (1983) six guiding principles for 'graphical integrity'. You can find more detailed information on infographics in Foster et al. (2014) and in the American Psychological Association's publication manual (see **https://www.apastyle.org/manual/**, accessed 7 March 2020).

TIPS AND SKILLS 15.1

Presenting data effectively

The following tips build on our authors Liam and Tom's work in Clark et al. (2019) and are useful when presenting your data.

- *Use the correct way of presenting your data.* Consider whether the data are categorical or continuous and then select a suitable way to present it, taking into account your aims and objectives.
- *Label the diagram clearly.* Give each diagram a clear title explaining what or who the data refer to. In any graph, make sure both the *X* (horizontal) and *Y* (vertical) axes have labels and also provide the units of measurement.
- *The diagram should be clear.* This means thinking carefully about which bars and lines are required. Always use the same colours for the same categories when you have more than one pie chart or bar chart, and try to limit the number of different shadings in a single graphic. Include a key (legend) where necessary.
- *Include the source.* You will usually know where the data came from (such as a secondary data set or your own survey). If you did not collect the data yourself, make sure you put a note below the diagram to this effect (for example, 'Source: British Social Attitudes Survey 2019') or include the source in the title of the diagram.
- *Be consistent.* This includes using the same number of decimal places throughout for the same type of data. One or two decimal places should be sufficient, but some disciplines may prefer no decimal places to be used at all. You should check your any guidance available in relation to this.
- *Totals and subtotals.* Include relevant totals and subtotals in the diagram, and check that they add up correctly.

THINKING DEEPLY 15.3

Principles of graphical integrity

The best-known critic of visual data presentation is Tufte. The bulk of his work is concerned with providing a series of negative and positive examples of ways of presenting data, extracting general principles (or rules of thumb) from them rather than giving a direct guide to practice: 'more akin to a reference book on ingredients than a cookbook for daily use in the kitchen' (Healy and Moody 2014: 109). In his classic book *The Visual Display of Quantitative Information* (1983) Tufte did, however, set out six principles of what he called 'graphical integrity'.

1. Representation of numbers should match the true proportions. This means that the size of the effect displayed in the graphic should be the same as the size of the effect present in the data.
2. Labelling should be clear and detailed. As a result all of the information required to understand a graphic should be easily available.

3. Design should not vary for some ulterior motive, show only data variation. For instance, if the space between gridlines does not represent the same period/distance for each data point, this is misleading.
4. To represent money, well known units are best. This will avoid a lack of clarity.
5. The number of dimensions represented should be the same as the number of dimensions in the data. This will serve to ensure consistency.
6. Representations should not imply unintended context. When viewing data presented in a graphic, seeing it should be able to answer the question: 'compared to what?'

Tufte (1983) warned against avoiding content-free decoration, including 'chartjunk', and emphasized a focus on the substance (contents) of the presentation. The graph should show the data, rather than the technical skills of the person creating it. These are all principles you should consider when working with representations of your data.

Measures of central tendency

Measures of central tendency play an important role in univariate statistics by providing, in one figure, a value that is typical for a **distribution of values**. In effect, we are trying to find an average for a distribution, but in quantitative data analysis, there are three different forms of average: the arithmetic mean, the median, and the mode. We describe the procedures for generating these measures, using SPSS and the other main software packages, in our statistical software tutorials.

Arithmetic mean

The **arithmetic mean** is simply the average as we understand it in everyday use—in other words, it is the number we get when we add together all the values in a distribution and then divide the total by the number of values. The arithmetic mean (or more simply 'the **mean**') for var00002 is 33.6, meaning that the average age of gym visitors is nearly 34 years. The mean should only be used in relation to interval/ratio variables, though it is not uncommon to see it being used for ordinal variables as well.

Median

The **median** is the mid-point in a distribution of values. Whereas the mean can be distorted by **outliers** (extreme values at either end of the distribution), the median is not affected in this way. We get the median by setting out all the values in a distribution from the smallest to the largest and then finding the middle point. So if there are 89 values, we would list them in this order and then treat the 45th value as the median. If there is an even number of values, say 90 values, we would calculate the median by taking the mean of the two middle numbers of the distribution—so the mean of the 45th and 46th numbers. In the case of var00002, the median is 31. This is slightly lower than the mean, partly because some respondents are considerably older (especially respondents 5 and 10) so their ages inflate the mean slightly. The median can be used in relation to both interval/ratio and ordinal variables.

Mode

The **mode** is the value that occurs most frequently in a distribution, and it can be used in relation to all types of variable. The mode for var00002 is 28.

Measures of dispersion

The amount of variation in a sample can be just as interesting as its typical value. It allows us to draw contrasts between comparable distributions of values. For example, is there more or less variability in the amount of time people are spending on cardiovascular equipment compared to weights machines? There are two main ways of measuring dispersion.

Range

The most obvious way of measuring dispersion is by using the range. This is simply the difference between the maximum and the minimum value in a distribution of values associated with an interval/ratio variable. In our gym study, the range is 64 minutes for the cardiovascular equipment and 48 minutes for the weights machines, suggesting that there is more variability in the amount of time spent on the former. However, like the mean, the range is influenced by outliers, such as respondent 60 in the case of var00010.

Standard deviation

The **standard deviation**, another way of measuring dispersion, is basically the average difference between individual values and the mean. The standard deviation for var00010 is 9.9 minutes and for var00011 it is 8 minutes, so not only is the average amount of time people are spending on the cardiovascular equipment higher than for the weights equipment: the standard deviation is greater too. The standard deviation is also affected by outliers, but unlike the range, a calculation of standard deviation reduces their impact because it divides by the number of values in the distribution. We describe the procedures for generating the standard deviation, using SPSS and the other main software packages, in our statistical software tutorials.

Boxplots: displaying both central tendency and dispersion

A popular type of figure for displaying interval/ratio variables is the boxplot, which is useful because it provides an indication of both central tendency (the median) and dispersion (the range). It is also helpful in indicating whether there are any outliers. Figure 15.8 is a boxplot for the total number of minutes that users spent in the gym on their last visit. There is an outlier—case number 41, who spent a total of 87 minutes in the gym. The box represents the middle 50 per cent of users, with the upper line of the box indicating the greatest use of the gym within the 50 per cent and the lower line of the box representing the least use of the gym within the 50 per cent. The line going across the box indicates the median. The line going upwards from the box goes up to the person whose use of the gym was greater than any other user, other than case number 41. The line going downwards from the box goes down to the person whose use of the gym was lower than that of any other user.

Boxplots vary in their shape depending on whether cases tend to be high or low in relation to the median. With Figure 15.8, the box and the median are closer to the bottom end of the distribution, suggesting less variation among gym users below the median. There is more variation above the median.

We describe the procedures for generating boxplots, using SPSS and the other main software packages, in our statistical software tutorials.

15

FIGURE 15.8

A boxplot for the number of minutes spent on the last visit to the gym

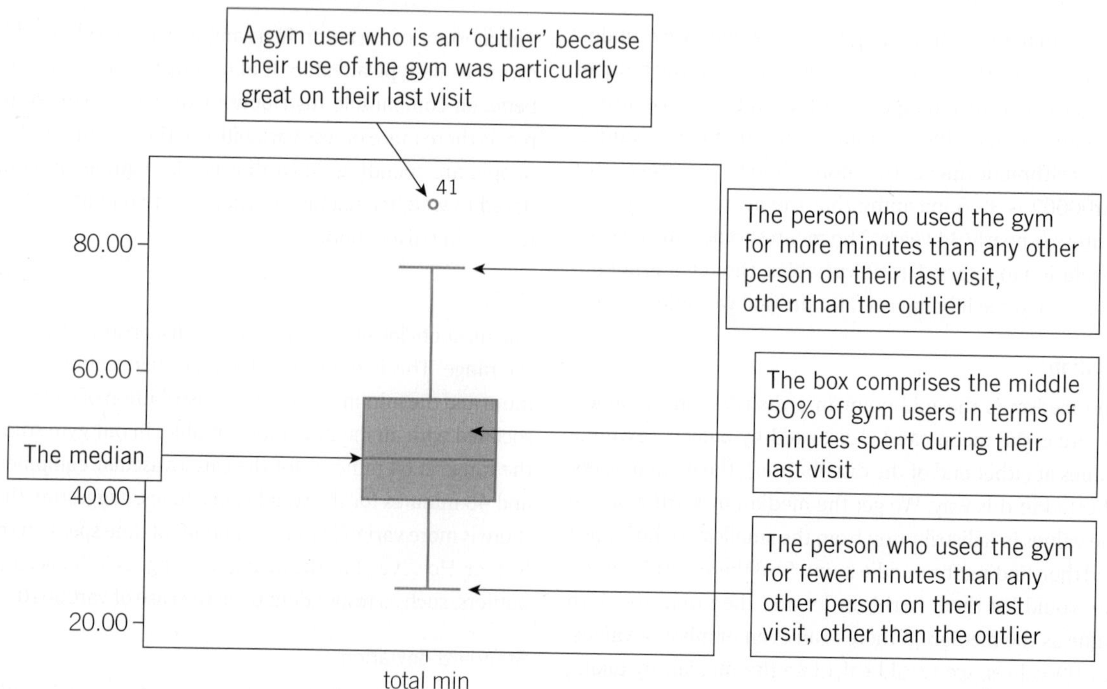

15.6 Bivariate analysis

Bivariate analysis involves analysing two variables at a time in order to uncover whether or not they are related. This means searching for evidence that the variation in one variable coincides with variation in another variable. A variety of techniques is available for examining **relationships**, and deciding which technique to use depends on the nature of the two variables being analysed. Table 15.4 sets out some of the main types of bivariate analysis you might use according to the types of variable involved. (The column titles relate to one variable, and the row titles relate to the other variable.) In this section we will cover each of the types of analysis shown in Table 15.4. There are also other forms of bivariate analysis you could consider, and in some cases, depending on the distribution of your data, these may even be more appropriate. We suggest you use a statistics book to explore the other possibilities (see Foster et al. 2014; Field 2017).

Relationships, not causality

It is important to remember that the various techniques for analysing relationships do exactly that: they simply uncover relationships. This means that they do not allow us to infer that one variable *causes* another (as we discussed in Chapter 3 in relation to the **cross-sectional design**). It can even be the case that what appears to be a **causal** influence working in one direction actually works in the other way. One of the most interesting examples of this problem of causal direction is a study by Sutton and Rafaeli (1988). The researchers expected to find a causal relationship between the display of positive emotions in retail outlets (for example, smiling or friendliness from checkout staff) and sales in those outlets, guessing that the former would exert a causal influence on the latter. It turned out that the relationship was actually the other way round: levels of retail sales had a causal influence on the display of positive emotions.

Sometimes, we may feel confident about inferring a causal direction when we identify a relationship between two variables—for example, if our findings show that age and voting behaviour are related. It is impossible that voting influences peoples' ages, so if our findings show that the two variables are related we can infer with complete confidence that age is the **independent variable**. When researchers analyse their data, they often draw inferences about causality based on their assumptions about the likely causal direction among related variables, as Sutton and Rafaeli (1988) did in their study. These inferences may be based on sound reasoning but they can only ever be inferences, as there is always the possibility that the real pattern of causal direction is the opposite to what we had anticipated. For

TABLE 15.4
Methods of bivariate analysis

Type of variable	Nominal	Ordinal	Interval/ratio	Dichotomous
Nominal	Contingency table + chi-square (χ^2) + Cramér's *V*	Contingency table + chi-square (χ^2) + Cramér's *V*	Contingency table + chi-square (χ^2) + Cramér's *V* If the interval/ratio variable can be identified as the dependent variable, compare means + eta	Contingency table + chi-square (χ^2) + Cramér's *V*
Ordinal	Contingency table + chi-square (χ^2) + Cramér's *V*	Spearman's rho (ρ)	Spearman's rho (ρ)	Spearman's rho (ρ)
Interval/ratio	Contingency table + chi-square (χ2) + Cramér's *V* If the interval/ratio variable can be identified as the dependent variable, compare means + eta	Spearman's rho (ρ)	Pearson's *r*	Spearman's rho (ρ)
Dichotomous	Contingency table + chi-square (χ^2) + Cramér's *V*	Spearman's rho (ρ)	Spearman's rho (ρ)	phi (φ)

example, you might hypothesize (see Key concept 7.1) that undertaking physical activity enhances people's mental wellbeing, so physical activity (the independent variable) positively affects mental wellbeing (the **dependent variable**). However, your research results might suggest that mental wellbeing actually influences whether people feel able to undertake physical activity, so you could argue that mental wellbeing (the independent variable) positively affects physical activity (the dependent variable). It is important to remember that the causal direction of the relationship between variables is not always straightforward.

We now move on to explore some of the methods of bivariate analysis outlined in Table 15.4, starting with the use of **contingency tables** before discussing **Pearson's r**, **Spearman's rho**, **phi**, and **Cramér's V**. We will conclude our discussion of bivariate analysis by looking briefly at how you can compare the means of two variables, through a test of association called **eta**.

Contingency tables

Contingency tables are widely used in social research and are sometimes referred to as cross-tabulations or cross-tabs, especially when using a software package. A contingency table is like a frequency table, but whereas a frequency table shows the distribution of a single variable, a contingency table allows us to simultaneously analyse two variables at the same time, so that we can see relationships between them. (The name comes from the fact that this method reveals how one variable is *contingent* on another.) Contingency tables are probably the most flexible of all of the methods of analysing relationships in that they can be used in relation to any pair of variables, though they are not the most efficient method for some pairs, which is why the method is not recommended in every **cell** in Table 15.4. Table 15.5 shows a contingency table for the relationship between gender and reasons for visiting the gym; the approach works well for dichotomous/nominal variables (though, as we discussed in Thinking deeply 15.2, gender is increasingly seen as non-dichotomous). If we wanted to present an interval/ratio variable in a contingency table format, we would need to group or recode the categories (as in our earlier example of the ages of people attending the gym).

It is normal for contingency tables to include percentages, since these make them easier to interpret. The percentages in Table 15.5 are *column percentages*—that is, they calculate the number in each cell as a percentage of the total number in that column. So, if we take the top left-hand cell, the three men who go to the gym for relaxation represent 7 per cent of all 42 men in the sample. In contingency tables the presumed independent variable (if one can be presumed) is often presented as the column variable and the presumed dependent variable as the row variable. This is why contingency tables usually provide column rather than row percentages. We describe the procedures for generating a contingency table, using SPSS and the other main software packages, in our statistical software tutorials.

TABLE 15.5

Contingency table showing the relationship between gender and reasons for visiting the gym

Reasons	Gender			
	Male		Female	
	No.	%	No.	%
Relaxation	3	7	6	13
Fitness	15	36	16	33
Lose weight	8	19	25	52
Build strength	16	38	1	2
TOTAL	42		48	

Note: $\chi^2 = 22.726$; $p < 0.0001$

The fact that gender is the column variable and the reason is the row variable in Table 15.5 tells us the student has presumed that gender influences reasons for going to the gym (which is logical, given that going to the gym seems unlikely to influence gender). We can see that her assumption was correct: the table reveals clear gender differences in reasons for visiting the gym, with females much more likely than men to be going to the gym to lose weight. Women are also somewhat more likely to be going to the gym for relaxation. In contrast, men are much more likely to be visiting the gym to build strength. There is little difference between men and women in terms of fitness as a reason.

Line graphs

A **line graph** is another way of presenting bivariate data. It is similar to a scatter diagram (which we explore shortly) but, importantly, the consecutive points are linked by a line that 'joins the dots'. A line graph is a useful way of visually representing bivariate data that is associated with interval/ratio variables. When constructing a line graph, you should usually place the independent variable on the horizontal axis and the dependent variable on the vertical axis. It is best to start at zero on the *Y* axis or, if this is not appropriate, at least make it clear to the reader that it does not start at zero by including a break at the bottom of the axis (see De Vries 2018 for further discussion).

Pearson's *r*

Pearson's *r* is a method for examining relationships between interval/ratio variables that focuses on the **coefficient**, a figure indicating the degree of **correlation** between variables (we do not discuss how to produce coefficients here, but these can be produced easily using software such as SPSS). This method works on the assumption that the relationship between the two variables is broadly *linear,* so before using it researchers need to plot out the values of their variables on a **scatter diagram** to check that they form something like a straight line (even if they are scattered, as in Figure 15.9). If they curve, the researcher will need to analyse the relationships using another method.

The main features of Pearson's *r* are as follows:

- the coefficient will almost certainly lie between 0 (zero or no relationship between the two variables) and 1 or −1 (a perfect relationship between the variables)—this indicates the *strength* of a relationship;
- the closer the coefficient is to 1 or −1, the stronger the relationship, and the closer it is to 0, the weaker the relationship;
- the coefficient will be either positive or negative—indicating the *direction* of a relationship.

We illustrate these features using Table 15.6, which shows imaginary data from five variables to show different types of relationship, and with the scatter diagrams in Figures 15.9 to 15.12, which look at the relationship between pairs of interval/ratio variables.

- Figure 15.9 shows a perfect **positive relationship** between variables 1 and 2. It would have a Pearson's *r* correlation of 1. This means that as one variable increases, the other variable increases by the same amount, and no other variable is related to either of them. If the correlation was below 1, it would mean that variable 1 is related to at least one other variable as well as to variable 2.
- Figure 15.10 shows a perfect **negative relationship** between variables 2 and 3. It would have a Pearson's *r* correlation of −1. This means that as one variable increases, the other variable decreases, and no other variable is related to either of them.
- Figure 15.11 shows that there is no relationship between variables 2 and 5. We can see this from the fact that there is no clear pattern to the markers in the scatter diagram. The correlation is virtually zero, at −0.041, meaning that the variation in each variable is associated with variables that are not present in this analysis.
- Figure 15.12 shows a strong positive relationship between variables 2 and 4. We can see this from the clear pattern to the variables. Here, the Pearson's *r* value is +0.88 (usually, positive correlations are presented without the + sign), meaning that the variation in the two variables is very closely connected, but that there is some influence of other variables in the extent to which they vary.

So what does Pearson's *r* tell us about the student's findings from the gym survey? The correlation between age (var00002) and the amount of time spent on weights equipment (var00011) is −0.27, implying a weak negative relationship. This suggests that the older a person is, the less likely they are to be spending much time on such equipment, but also that other variables clearly influence the amount of time people are spending on this activity.

If you square a value of Pearson's *r*, you can produce another useful statistic—the **coefficient of determination**. This figure expresses how much of the variation in one variable is due to the other variable. So if *r* is −0.27,

15

TABLE 15.6

Imaginary data from five variables to show different types of relationship

Variables

1	2	3	4	5
1	10	50	7	9
2	12	45	13	23
3	14	40	18	7
4	16	35	14	15
5	18	30	16	6
6	20	25	23	22
7	22	20	19	12
8	24	15	24	8
9	26	10	22	18
10	28	5	24	10

FIGURE 15.9
Scatter diagram showing a perfect positive relationship

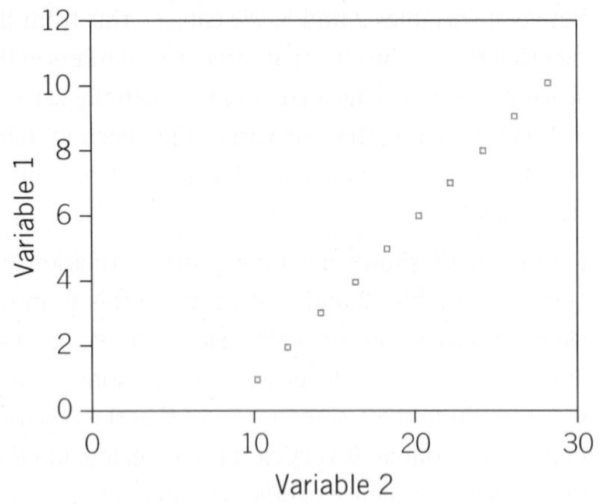

FIGURE 15.10
Scatter diagram showing a perfect negative relationship

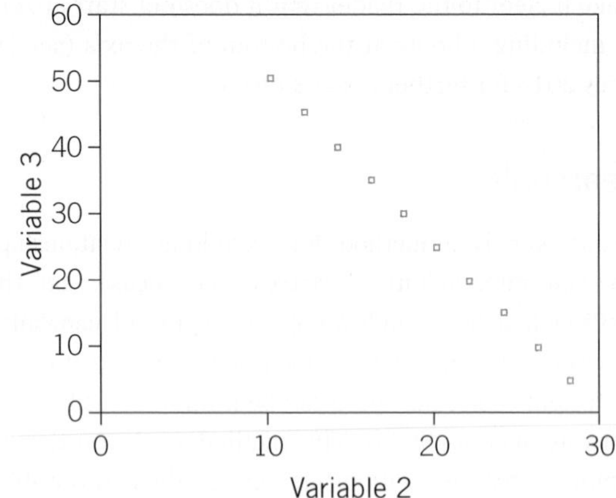

FIGURE 15.11
Scatter diagram showing two variables that are not related

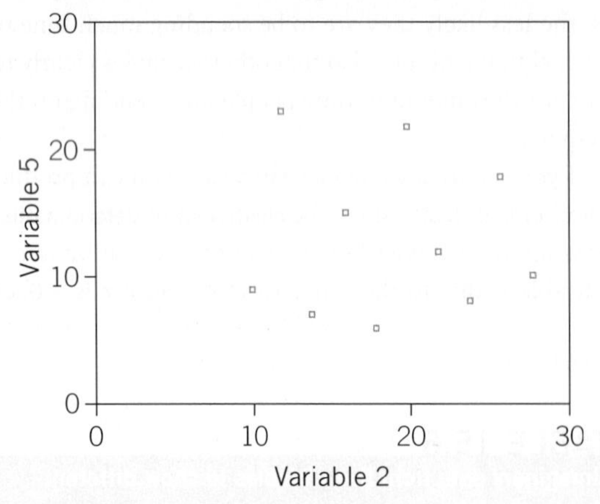

FIGURE 15.12
Scatter diagram showing a strong positive relationship

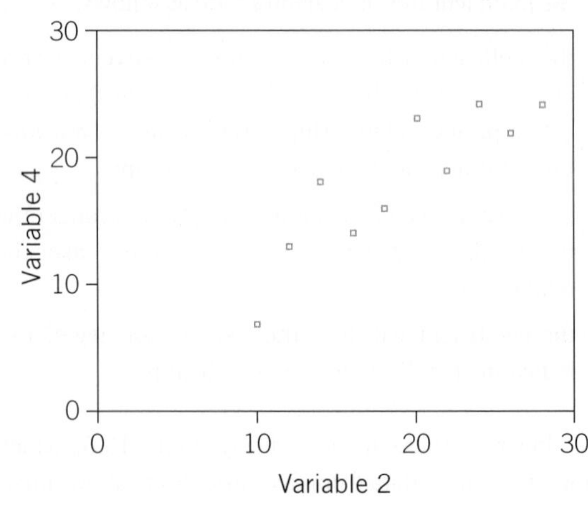

r^2 is 0.0729. We can then express this as a percentage by multiplying r^2 by 100. The result is 7 per cent, meaning that just 7 per cent of the variation in the use of cardiovascular equipment is accounted for by age. The coefficient of determination is a useful extra tool when interpreting correlation information.

We describe the procedures for using SPSS, and the other main software packages, to generate Pearson's *r* and scatter diagrams in our statistical software tutorials.

Spearman's rho

Spearman's rho, which is sometimes represented with the Greek letter ρ, is designed for use with pairs of ordinal variables, but as Table 15.4 suggests, it is also used when one variable is ordinal and the other is interval/ratio. It is exactly the same as Pearson's *r* in terms of the outcome of calculating it, in that the value of rho will be either positive or negative, varying between 0 and + or −1. If we look at the gym study, there are three ordinal variables: var00004, var00005, and var00006 (see Table 15.1). If we calculate the correlation between the first two variables using Spearman's rho, we find that the correlation between var00004 and var00005—frequency of use of the cardiovascular and weights equipment—is low, at 0.2. There is a slightly stronger relationship between var00006 (frequency of going to the gym) and var00010 (amount of time spent on the cardiovascular equipment), with rho at 0.4. In the latter pair, the second variable is an interval/ratio variable. When we want to calculate the correlation between an ordinal and an interval/ratio variable we cannot use Pearson's *r*, because for that method both must be interval/ratio levels of measurement, but we can use Spearman's rho (see Table 15.4). We describe the procedures for generating Spearman's rho, using SPSS and the other main software packages, in our statistical software tutorials.

Phi and Cramér's *V*

Phi (φ) and Cramér's *V* are two closely related statistics that are forms of bivariate analysis.

The phi coefficient is used for analysing the relationship between two dichotomous variables and, like Pearson's *r*, it results in a statistic that varies between 0 and + or −1. If we use it to analyse the correlation between var00001 (gender) and var00008 (whether people have other sources of regular exercise), the result is 0.24, implying that males are somewhat more likely than females to have other sources of regular exercise, though the relationship is weak.

Cramér's *V* uses a similar formula to phi and can be used with nominal variables (see Table 15.4). However, this statistic can only take on a positive value, so it can only give an indication of the *strength* of the relationship between two variables, not of the direction. If we use the analysis presented in Table 15.5, the value of Cramér's *V* is 0.50, suggesting a moderate relationship between the two variables. Cramér's *V* is usually reported along with a contingency table and a **chi-square test** (see Section 15.8), not on its own.

We describe the procedures for generating phi and Cramér's *V*, using SPSS and the other main software packages, in our statistical software tutorials.

Comparing means and eta

If we are examining the relationship between an interval/ratio variable and a nominal variable and we can relatively unambiguously identify the latter as the independent variable, it can be useful to compare the means of the interval/ratio variable for each subgroup of the nominal variable. As an example, consider Table 15.7, which presents the mean number of minutes spent on cardiovascular equipment (var00010) for each of the four categories of reasons for going to the gym (var00003). The means suggest that people who go to the gym for fitness or to lose weight are spending considerably more time on this equipment than people who attend the gym to relax or to build strength.

This procedure is often used alongside a test of association between variables called eta (η). This statistic expresses the level of association between the two variables and, like Cramér's *V*, it will always be positive. The level of eta for the data in Table 15.7 is 0.48, suggesting a moderate relationship between the two variables. Eta-squared (η^2) expresses the amount of variation in the interval/ratio variable that is due to the nominal variable, and in the case of this example, eta-squared is 22 per cent. Eta is a very flexible method for exploring the relationship between two variables, first because it can be employed when one variable is nominal and the other interval/ratio, and second because it does not assume that the relationship between variables is linear.

We describe the procedures for comparing means and for generating eta, using SPSS and the other main software packages, in our statistical software tutorials.

15

TABLE 15.7

Comparing subgroup means: time spent on cardiovascular equipment by reasons for going to the gym

Time	Reasons				
	Relaxation	Fitness	Lose weight	Build strength	Whole sample
Mean number of minutes spent on cardiovascular equipment	18.33	30.55	28.36	19.65	26.47
n	9	31	33	17	90

15.7 Multivariate analysis

Multivariate analysis involves analysing three or more variables simultaneously. These types of analysis allow researchers to control for lots of confounding factors, search for complex relationships, build multi-level models, and test theories and ideas with more detail. It is quite an advanced topic, so if you are thinking of undertaking multivariate analysis we recommend that you consult a textbook dedicated to quantitative data analysis for a more detailed critique of the various techniques (e.g. Bryman and Cramer 2011, Field 2017, or MacInnes 2016). There are three main contexts within which you might want to use multivariate analysis: when the relationship could be **spurious**; when there could be an intervening variable; and when a third variable could potentially moderate the relationship. We will discuss each of these in turn.

Could the relationship be spurious?

In order for us to establish that there is a relationship between two variables, there must not only be *evidence* that there is a relationship, but also the relationship must be shown to be *non-spurious*. A **spurious relationship** is when there appears to be a relationship between two variables, but the relationship is not real: it is being produced because each variable is itself related to a third variable. For example, if we find that there is a relationship between income and voting behaviour, we might want to ask: could the relationship be linked to age? The older someone is, the more they are likely to earn, and age is known to influence voting behaviour. If we found that in fact age was producing the apparent relationship between income and voting behaviour, we would conclude that the relationship is spurious—shown diagrammatically in Figure 15.13. In this case, the variable of age would be known as a **confounding variable**.

Another example of a spurious relationship can be found in Sweden, where data might suggest that there is a relationship between the number of storks in an area and the number of children born in the area. However, this interpretation is spurious as the finding is actually associated with a third confounding variable—that of whether the area is rural or urban. There are more storks in rural areas, where the birth rate is also higher (see Hoefnagels 2017).

FIGURE 15.13
A spurious relationship

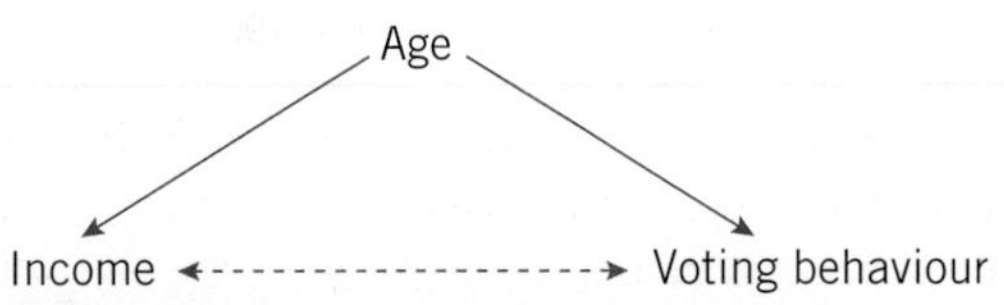

Could there be an intervening variable?

Let's say that we do not find that a relationship is spurious; we might want to know *why* there is a relationship between two variables. For example, it is well known that there is a relationship between people's incomes and their voting behaviour. The fact that political attitudes vary among people with different incomes may in fact have implications for their voting behaviour. We would then say that the political attitudes are an **intervening variable**:

income → political attitudes → voting behaviour

An intervening variable can help us answer questions about a bivariate relationship between variables. Since the impact of people's income on their voting behaviour is viewed as occurring via their political attitudes, it suggests that the relationship between the two variables is not a direct one. This is why intervening variables are sometimes called ***mediating variables***.

Could a third variable moderate the relationship?

We might be asking a question such as 'Does the relationship between two variables hold for men but not for women?' If it does, the relationship is said to be 'moderated' by gender. In the gym study, we might ask if the relationship between age and whether visitors have other sources of regular exercise (var00008) is moderated by gender. This would imply that, if we find a pattern relating age to other sources of exercise, this pattern will vary by gender. Table 15.8, which is a contingency table, shows the relationship between age and other sources of exercise, with age broken down into just three age

TABLE 15.8
Contingency table showing the relationship between age and whether or not gym visitors have other sources of regular exercise (percentage)

Other source of exercise	Age		
	30 and under	31–40	41 and over
Other source	64	43	58
No other source	36	57	42
n	42	23	24

15

TABLE 15.9

Contingency table showing the relationship between age and whether or not gym visitors have other sources of regular exercise for males and females (percentage)

Other source of exercise	Gender					
	Male			Female		
	Age			Age		
	30 and under	31–40	41 and over	30 and under	31–40	41 and over
Other source	70	33	75	59	50	42
No other source	30	67	25	41	50	58
n	20	9	12	22	14	12

bands to make it easier to read the table. The table suggests that the 31–40 age group is less likely to have other sources of regular exercise than the '30 and under' and '41 and over' age groups. However, Table 15.9, which breaks the relationship down by gender, gives us a different picture of the pattern for males and females. We can see that among males, the pattern shown in Table 15.8 is very pronounced, but women are less likely to have other sources of exercise as they get older. We could say that the relationship between age and other sources of exercise is likely to be a **moderated relationship** because it is moderated by gender.

Tables 15.8 and 15.9 illustrate how contingency tables can be used for multivariate analysis.

Multiple regression

A regression analysis examines whether one variable is related to another. For example, it could allow us to see whether 'years spent in education' are related to 'wealth' in later life. The statistic that is produced by the analysis essentially gives us a number between −1 and 1 that allows us to assess the direction and strength of that relationship. A multiple regression analysis—a form of multivariate analysis—is just an extension of this principle. In the social world, as we have shown, it is rare that just one thing is related to another. For example, there are many things in later life that may influence 'wealth', not just 'years in education'. 'General health', 'inheritance', and 'region' could all be factors that help to account for how wealthy someone is. So, by including other variables in our analysis, it is possible to account for more and more of the variation in our dependent variable, wealth. This helps us to produce more comprehensive descriptions of social patterns. Multiple regression also allows us to assess the relative influence of a group of variables (the independent variables) on our chosen target variable (the dependent variable). In essence, it allows us to see which variables are having more influence than others, and crucially, which of those variables make the most contribution. As a result of all of this, the technique is really useful for building 'models' of social behaviour.

There are many other techniques that can be used to undertake multivariate analysis: see Bryman and Cramer (2011), Bors (2018), and Tabachnick and Fidell (2018) for more information.

We describe the procedures for conducting a multivariate analysis, using SPSS and the other main software packages, in the statistical software tutorials within our **online resources**.

15.8 Statistical significance

Statistical significance and the various tests of statistical significance (see Key concept 15.1) are extremely useful in exploring how confident we can be that our results are generalizable to the population from which the sample was selected. Although the idea of statistical significance has received some criticism, these techniques are generally seen as allowing us to do two things:

1. establish how confident we can be in our findings;
2. establish the size of the risk we are taking in inferring that the finding exists in the population.

Tests of statistical significance are very useful in allowing us to explore confidence in our findings, but it is important to understand that we can only use them in relation

KEY CONCEPT 15.1
What is a test of statistical significance?

A **test of statistical significance** allows us to estimate how confident we can be that results deriving from a study based on a **probability sample** are generalizable to the population from which the sample was taken. When we examine statistical significance in terms of the relationship between two variables, it also tells us about the risk of concluding that there is a relationship in the population when in fact the relationship does not exist. This is very useful, but it is important to be aware that even if our analysis reveals a statistically significant finding, this does not mean that the finding is intrinsically interesting, as statistical significance is only about how *confident* researchers can be in their findings. In fact, Amrhein et al. (2019) draw on a collection of articles that question the use of statistical significance. They point out that factors including the study design, data quality, and understanding of underlying mechanisms are potentially more important than statistical measures.

to samples that have been selected *using probability sampling*. Inferring findings from a probability sample to the population from which it was selected produces inferential statistics (a form of **statistical inference**).

We will touch on some of the ways of testing statistical significance in this section but, much like with multivariate analysis, we would expect you to need to do some further reading of statistics books in order to use tests of statistical significance in your own research. It is also worth noting that the software packages that we introduced you to earlier in the chapter, such as SPSS, allow you to calculate statistical significance at a click. However, you still need to know which statistical tests are appropriate to use with your data, and how to interpret the findings those tests produce. The extent to which you deal with statistical significance depends on what you are trying to find out. For instance, if you are trying to establish causation (such as looking at whether older age causes lower levels of gym use), you would need to test whether there is a statistically significant relationship between the variables in order to do this. There is also the fact that some social science disciplines may expect you to use statistical tests in your quantitative analysis, whereas it may not be a requirement in others. This is something you will need to make sure you check before undertaking any quantitative project. In addition, it is also useful to consider the effect size (see Key concept 15.2).

We touched on the ideas behind statistical significance in Chapter 8 (see Tips and skills 8.3), when discussing the **standard error of the mean**—the amount that a sample mean is likely to differ from a population mean. In our gym example, we know that the mean age of the sampled members is 33.6. By using the concept of the standard error of the mean, we can calculate that we can be 95 per cent confident that the mean age of the population lies between 31.72 and 35.47 (within + or −1.96 sampling errors from the sample mean; see Foster et al. 2014 for further detail). The standard error of the mean gives

KEY CONCEPT 15.2
What is the effect size?

Determining the effect size enables us to establish how much is explained by the statistically significant difference. If only a small amount is explained, then it is possible that the finding is statistically significant but relatively unimportant for answering your research question. Effect size is basically a measure of how different two groups are from one another (Salkind and Fry 2019). Unlike significance tests, these indices are independent of sample size. Calculating the effect size, and interpreting what it means, adds another dimension to understanding significant outcomes. As with many other statistical techniques, there are a number of ways of calculating the effect size. With a *t*-test, for example, the appropriate effect size is known as Cohen's *d*, which is a standardized measure of the difference between two means (Jensen and Laurie 2016). It is possible to use Becker's website, **https://lbecker.uccs.edu/** (n.d., accessed 27 November 2020) to assist you in calculating Cohen's *d*.

us a sense of the degree of confidence we can have in a sample mean.

In the rest of this section, we will look at the tests that can be used to determine the degree of confidence we can have in our findings when we explore relationships between variables. All of the tests involve the same three stages.

1. *Set up a null hypothesis and an alternative hypothesis.* Remember from Section 7.4 that a **null hypothesis** states that two variables are *not* related in the population from which the sample was selected, for example, that there is *no* relationship between gender and visiting the gym, whereas an **alternative hypothesis** states that there *is* a relationship, for example between gender and visiting the gym.
2. *Establish the level of statistical significance that you find acceptable.* This is about measuring the degree of risk that your findings might lead you to reject the null hypothesis when you should support it (that is, the risk that you would find that there is a relationship in the population when in fact there is no relationship). We express the level of statistical significance (see Key concept 15.3) as a probability level—that is, the probability of rejecting the null hypothesis when you should be confirming it. The convention among most social researchers is that the maximum level of statistical significance that is acceptable is $p < 0.05$ (p means probability and $<$ means less than), which suggests that there are fewer than 5 chances in 100 that your sample will show a relationship when there is not one in the population. (Alternatively, some researchers may also deem something to be statistically significant if it is *equal to or less than* 0.05, which would be written like this: $p \leq 0.05$.) However, in other forms of research, including medical research, the maximum acceptable level of statistical significance is likely to be set at a higher level. For instance, medical researchers may require there to be fewer than 5 chances in 10,000, or indeed higher, that a sample will show a relationship when there is not one in the population, given the potential seriousness of medical errors.
3. *Determine the statistical significance of your findings.* This involves using a statistical test like chi-square (see 'The chi-square test' below) to find out whether or not they are statistically significant. If your findings are statistically significant at the 0.05 level—meaning that there are fewer than 5 in 100 chances that the relationship shown in your sample is not reflected in the population—you would reject the null hypothesis, because your analysis would imply that the results are unlikely to have occurred by chance.

Two types of error can occur when you infer statistical significance. These are known as Type I and Type II

15

KEY CONCEPT 15.3
What is the level of statistical significance?

The level of statistical significance is concerned with the level of risk you are prepared to take that you are inferring there is a relationship between two variables in the population from which your sample was taken when in fact there is not. The maximum level of risk that we conventionally take in social research is to say that there are up to 5 chances in 100 that we might falsely conclude that there is a relationship when in fact there is not one in the population from which the sample was taken. This significance level is shown by $p < 0.05$ (p means probability).

This means we are recognizing that if we drew 100 samples from a population, as many as 5 of them might falsely suggest that there is a relationship when there is not one in the population. Our sample *might* be one of those 5, but the risk is fairly small. If we instead use a higher significance level of $p < 0.1$, we accept a greater risk that our sample might suggest a relationship when there is not one in the population: a likelihood of 10 out of 100 when $p < 0.1$ rather than 5 out of 100 when $p < 0.05$. We would therefore be able to have greater confidence in our findings by using a significance level of $p < 0.05$. If we wanted to be even more confident, perhaps because of concerns about how our results might be used, we could use a stricter test such as the $p < 0.01$ level. This means that there is only a 1 in 100 probability that our results could be caused by chance (that is, due to sampling error). If the results of a test show that a relationship is statistically significant at the $p < 0.05$ level, but not the stricter $p < 0.01$ level, we would have to confirm the null hypothesis and conclude that there is no relationship between the variables.

errors. A Type I error is when you reject the null hypothesis when it should in fact be confirmed, meaning that your results have arisen by chance and you are falsely concluding that there is a relationship in the population when there is not one. A Type II error is when you accept the null hypothesis but you should reject it, meaning that you falsely conclude that there is not a relationship in the population. If we use a $p < 0.05$ level of significance we are more likely to make a Type I error than when using a $p < 0.01$ level of significance, because with 0.01 there is less chance of falsely rejecting the null hypothesis. However, in using a lower level of significance you increase the chance of making a Type II error because you are more likely to confirm the null hypothesis when the significance level is 0.01 (the chance is 1 in 100 when the significance level is 0.01 and 1 in 20 when it is 0.05). The risks of these errors occurring are shown in Figure 15.14.

The chi-square test

The chi-square (χ^2) test is a widely used statistical test in the social sciences and often in student projects—see Learn from experience 15.3. It is normally used when working with categorical data—that is, nominal and ordinal data—and can be used in both univariate and bivariate analysis. Although the chi-square test has many uses, it is worth noting that it does not tell us anything about the *strength* of the association between the variables—no matter how high the chi-square value, all it can tell us is that there is an association. This is why it is often used alongside other tests that can determine the strength of a relationship. For example, we have already mentioned that the Cramér's *V* value is usually reported along with a contingency table and a chi-square test.

We can apply the chi-square test to contingency tables like Table 15.5, which shows the relationship between gender and reasons for visiting the gym, in order to establish how confident we can be that there is a relationship between the two variables in the population. The test works by calculating an expected frequency or value for each cell in the table—that is the distribution of responses we would expect to see if the variables were not in any way related. We can calculate the chi-square value, which in Table 15.5 is 22.726, by working out the differences between the actual and expected values for each cell in the table and then adding together those differences (though in practice it is slightly more complicated than this—you can find further details about this process in Foster et al. 2014). The chi-square value means nothing on its own and can only be meaningfully interpreted in relation to its associated level of statistical significance. In this case we might choose to use $p < 0.0001$ (although you may choose a different p value depending on your research, as we have already discussed). This means that there is only 1 chance in 10,000 of falsely rejecting the null hypothesis (that is, inferring that there is a relationship in the population when there is no such relationship). Given this very low risk, you could be extremely confident that your sample does reflect a relationship between gender and reasons for visiting the gym among all gym members.

Whether or not a chi-square value achieves statistical significance depends not just on the figure produced but also on the number of categories of the two variables being analysed. The number of categories is governed by

FIGURE 15.14
Type I and Type II errors

p level	Error: Type I (risk of rejecting the null hypothesis when it should be confirmed)	Error: Type II (risk of confirming the null hypothesis when it should be rejected)
0.05	Greater risk	Lower risk
0.01	Lower risk	Greater risk

LEARN FROM EXPERIENCE 15.3

Working with statistical significance levels when conducting chi-square tests

To provide a clear picture of your findings, levels of statistical significance and how you represent them are important. Zvi, who studied the relationship between adolescents' sleep patterns and screen time, explained how he used levels of statistical significance when working with chi-square tests. This approach may be useful in thinking about your own approach to statistical significance.

> It is important to include the results from a chi-square test along with your findings, as they illustrate the statistical robustness of your study. That being said, there can be a lot of chi-square values to include if you are presenting the results from a multivariate regression analysis. I found that one way of tidying up these tables is to group the significance levels into 3 bands – ***$p < .001$, **$p < .01$ and *$p < .05$ – and to use an asterisk to indicate the significance level in the tables and in the main body of the report. So, for example, you might write 'the results from the regression indicate that the odds of someone with 3 hours screen time a day getting 8 hours or more sleep are 0.856* compared with someone with no screen time'.
>
> Zvi

Access the **online resources** to hear Zvi's video reflections on this theme.

You can read about our panellists' backgrounds and research experiences on page xxvi.

what is known as the 'degrees of freedom' associated with a table. The number of degrees of freedom is governed by this simple formula:

Number of degrees of freedom
= (number of columns – 1) × (number of rows – 1).

In the case of Table 15.5, gender has 2 columns and reasons for visiting the gym has 4 rows, so the calculation will be $(2 - 1) \times (4 - 1)$, which equals 3 (1 multiplied by 3). So we know that the degrees of freedom are 3. We can then use our chi-square figure (22.726) and degrees of freedom (3) to determine whether our chi-square figure is statistically significant at $p < 0.0001$, by using a predefined table developed by Karl Pearson (this process is explained in Foster et al. 2014). So the chi-square value that we arrive at is affected by the size of the table, and this is taken into account when deciding whether the chi-square value is statistically significant or not.

We describe the procedures for generating a chi-square value in conjunction with a contingency table, using SPSS and the other main software packages, in our statistical software tutorials.

Correlation and statistical significance

Examining the statistical significance of a **correlation coefficient**, which is based on a randomly selected sample, provides information about the likelihood that the coefficient will be found in the population from which the sample was taken. If, for example, we find a correlation of −0.62, we need to know how likely it is that a relationship of at least that size exists in the population. This tells us if the relationship could have arisen by chance.

If the correlation coefficient r is −0.62 and the significance level is $p < 0.05$, we can reject the null hypothesis that there is no relationship in the population. We can infer that there are only 5 chances in 100 that a correlation of at least −0.62 could have arisen by chance alone. We *could* have one of the 5 samples in 100 that shows a relationship when there is not one in the population, but the degree of risk is reasonably small. If, however, we used a significance level of $p < 0.1$, there could be as many as 10 chances in 100 that there is no correlation in the population. This would probably *not* be an acceptable level of risk for most purposes, as it would mean that in as many as 1 sample in 10 we might find a correlation of −0.62 or above, when there is not a correlation in the population. If we used a stricter significance level of $p < 0.001$, there is only 1 chance in 1,000 that there is no correlation existing in the population, so there would be a very low level of risk in inferring that the correlation in the sample also exists in the population.

Two factors affect whether a correlation coefficient is statistically significant or not:

1. the size of the computed coefficient; and
2. the size of the sample (the larger the sample, the more likely it is that a correlation coefficient will be found to be statistically significant).

Even though the correlation between age and the amount of time spent on weights machines in the gym survey was found to be just −0.27, which is a fairly weak relationship, it is statistically significant at the $p < 0.01$ level. This means that there is less than 1 chance in 100 that there is no relationship in the population. As the question of whether or not a correlation coefficient is statistically significant depends so much on the sample size, you should always examine *both* the correlation coefficient *and* the significance level, rather than examining one and ignoring the other.

This treatment of correlation and statistical significance applies to both Pearson's *r* and Spearman's rho. We can also apply a similar interpretation to phi and to Cramér's *V*. SPSS and other statistical packages automatically produce information regarding statistical significance when Pearson's *r*, Spearman's rho, phi, and Cramér's *V* are generated.

Comparing means and statistical significance

We can apply a further test of statistical significance to the comparison of means that we carried out in Table 15.7. This involves treating the total amount of variation in the dependent variable—the amount of time spent on cardiovascular equipment—as being made up of two types: variation *within* the four subgroups that make up the independent variable, and variation *between* them. The latter is often called the *explained variance* and the former the *error variance*. A test of statistical significance for the comparison of means involves relating the two types of variance to form what is known as the *F* statistic, which expresses the amount of explained variance in relation to the amount of error variance. In the case of the data in Table 15.7, the resulting *F* statistic is statistically significant at the $p < 0.001$ level. This finding suggests that there is only 1 chance in 1,000 that there is no relationship between the two variables among all gym members.

KEY POINTS

15

- You need to ensure that your data analysis will be able to address your research questions.
- You need to think about your data analysis before you begin designing your research instruments. Do not leave these considerations until your data have been collected.
- The different techniques of data analysis are suitable for different types of variable.
- To understand what kind of analysis you can use, you will need to know the difference between the four types of variable: nominal, ordinal, interval/ratio, and dichotomous variables.
- It is a good idea to familiarize yourself with software such as SPSS before you begin designing your research instruments, so that you are aware at an early stage of any difficulties you might have in presenting your data using such software.
- Make sure you are familiar with the techniques introduced in this chapter and when you can and cannot use them.
- Do not confuse the statistical significance of your findings with their substantive significance.

QUESTIONS FOR REVIEW

1. At what stage should you begin to think about the kinds of data analysis you need to conduct?
2. What are missing data and why do they occur?

3. What are the differences between the four types of variable outlined in this chapter: interval/ratio; ordinal; nominal; and dichotomous?
4. Why is it important that you can distinguish between the four types of variables?
5. Imagine that you administered the following four questions in a survey. What kind of variable would each question generate: dichotomous; nominal; ordinal; or interval/ratio?
   a. Do you enjoy going shopping?

Yes	___
No	___

   b. How many times have you shopped in the last month? Please write in the number of occasions below.
   c. For which kinds of items do you most enjoy shopping? Please tick one only.

Clothes (including shoes)	___
Food	___
Things for the house	___
Presents	___
Entertainment (games, toys, etc.)	___

   d. How important is it to you to buy clothes with designer labels?

Very important	___
Fairly important	___
Not very important	___
Not at all important	___

6. What is an outlier and why might it distort the mean and the range?
7. In conjunction with which measure of central tendency would you expect to report the standard deviation: the mean; the median; or the mode?
8. Can you infer causality from bivariate analysis?
9. Why are percentages crucial when presenting contingency tables?
10. In what circumstances would you use each of the following: Pearson's *r*; Spearman's rho; phi; Cramér's *V*; eta?
11. What is a spurious relationship?
12. What is an intervening variable?
13. What does it mean to say that a relationship between variables is moderated?
14. What does statistical significance mean, and how does it differ from substantive significance?
15. What is a significance level?
16. What does the chi-square test achieve?
17. What does it mean to say that a correlation of 0.42 is statistically significant at $p < 0.05$?

ONLINE RESOURCES

www.oup.com/he/srm6e

You can find our notes on the answers to these questions within this chapter's **online resources**, together with:

- *audio/video comments* on this topic from our 'Learn from experience' panellists;
- *video tutorials and quick reference guides on using SPSS, R, and Stata* to support you in using statistical software;
- *guidance on using Microsoft Excel for data analysis* to help you use this program in a quantitative research context;
- *example quantitative data sets* for data analysis practice;
- *self-test questions* for further knowledge-checking;
- a *flashcard glossary* to help you recall key terms; and
- a *Student Researcher's Toolkit* containing practical materials and resources to help you conduct your own research project.

PART THREE

QUALITATIVE RESEARCH

In Part Three of this book we consider **qualitative research**. We set the scene in Chapter 16 by introducing the main features of this **research strategy** before exploring, in Chapter 17, the distinctive approach that qualitative researchers take towards **sampling**. In Chapter 18 we deal with ethnography and participant observation, which are among the main ways of collecting qualitative data. In Chapters 19 and 20 we look at the kind of interviewing that qualitative researchers carry out. We begin with a general discussion of interviewing (Chapter 19) and then move on to cover focus groups (Chapter 20), a technique where the researcher invites a small group of people to discuss certain topics or personal experiences in an interactive way. In Chapter 21 we explore two approaches to studying language in social research: conversation analysis and discourse analysis. We then consider the types of documents that qualitative researchers tend to be concerned with, and the approaches used to examine them, in Chapter 22. This part of the book concludes with Chapter 23, in which we look at different approaches to qualitative data analysis and discuss some of the ways to carry it out.

The information in Chapter 23 is supplemented by additional materials to support you in analysing qualitative data. Visit the **online resources** for written and video tutorials and a quick reference guide on using the popular qualitative data analysis software package **NVivo**.

CHAPTER
16

THE NATURE OF QUALITATIVE RESEARCH

CHAPTER GUIDE

We first introduced qualitative research in Chapter 2. In this chapter we discuss the overall nature and main features of this research strategy. We will explore

- the main preoccupations of qualitative researchers;
- the main steps in qualitative research;
- the relationship between theory and research in qualitative research;
- the nature of concepts in qualitative research and their differences from concepts in quantitative research;
- ways of ensuring and assessing the quality of qualitative research;
- some common criticisms of qualitative research;
- the main differences between qualitative and quantitative research, and some similarities between them.

16.1 Introduction

Qualitative research is a type of **research strategy** that emphasizes words, images, and objects when collecting and analysing data. It is broadly inductivist, constructionist, and interpretivist, but it can take a wide variety of forms; qualitative researchers do not always subscribe to all three of these features. In this chapter, we will give you a sense of the breadth and variety of methods that researchers can use for qualitative purposes, and of its broad characteristics and preoccupations. Although we will make comparisons with **quantitative research** where relevant, it is important to appreciate and understand this strategy independently of quantitative research rather than seeing the two as a pair of opposites.

16.2 What is qualitative research?

Qualitative research aims to generate deep insights concerning particular topics, and it does this through a considered engagement with places and social actors. This might include people, communities, organizations, or institutions. Aside from its focus on words, images, and objects, the key features of qualitative research can be summarized as follows.

- It tends toward an **inductive** view of the relationship between theory and research, with the former generated out of the latter (though see the discussion in Section 2.2 on **abductive reasoning**, in which we qualify this view).
- It is broadly **interpretivist** in nature, meaning that it tries to generate an understanding of the social world by examining how its participants interpret it.
- It has an **ontological** position we can describe as **constructionist**, in that social **properties** are seen as outcomes of the interactions between individuals, rather than phenomena that are 'out there' and separate from those involved in constructing them.

There are many high-profile journals and texts dedicated to qualitative research. Key journals include *Qualitative Sociology*, *Qualitative Research*, *Ethnography*, and *Qualitative Inquiry*. There are also key textbooks, such as *An Introduction to Qualitative Research* (Flick 2018) and *Doing Qualitative Research* (Silverman 2017), and a very well regarded *Handbook of Qualitative Research* in several editions (Denzin and Lincoln 1994, 2000, 2005a, 2011). Many more books that explore its different facets are also available, for example the Sage Qualitative Research Methods series.

However, perhaps because of its wide-ranging nature, it is often difficult to describe 'qualitative research' with absolute precision. Bryman and Burgess (1999) suggest that there are three key reasons for this.

1. The term 'qualitative research' is sometimes taken to imply that it is a research strategy that does not involve any quantitative data. Many writers on qualitative research are critical of this emphasis because the absence of numbers is not the distinctive aspect of the strategy. As we will see in Chapter 23 on processing qualitative data, there are also ways of incorporating numerical elements into qualitative research.
2. There are different traditions and perspectives within qualitative research, and there is often significant variation between approaches. It is certainly not a unitary strategy.
3. Qualitative research is often discussed in terms of the ways in which it differs from quantitative research, which can mean that it is addressed in terms of what it is *not* rather than what it is.

Traditions and perspectives in qualitative research

Having a sense of the traditions and perspectives that have influenced qualitative research, and how it has developed over time, can help us appreciate why it can have such a broad definition. Denzin and Lincoln (2005b) have suggested that qualitative research has progressed through eight significant stages, which are briefly summarized in Table 16.1.

As with any timeline, Denzin and Lincoln's 'moments' have to be treated with some caution. First, they seem to

TABLE 16.1

Denzin and Lincoln's list of the eight 'moments' of qualitative research (2005b)

Early 1900s to 1945 (the end of the Second World War)	The traditional period	In-depth studies of 'slices of life' that portrayed those under investigation as strange or alien. Heavily positivist.
1945 to early 1970s	Modernist phase	Attempts to make qualitative research more rigorous and to reflect on the process of doing research. Tendency towards positivism remained.
1970 to 1986	Blurred genres	Various approaches and theoretical ideas explored as bases for qualitative inquiry. Continued tendency towards positivism, but an interpretivist consciousness emerges, influenced by Geertz's books *The Interpretation of Cultures* (1973) and *Local Knowledge* (1983).
Mid-1980s onwards	Crisis of representation	Following the publication of *Anthropology as Cultural Critique* (Marcus and Fischer 1986), *The Anthropology of Experience* (Turner and Bruner 1986) and *Writing Culture* (Clifford and Marcus 1986), this phase was characterized by an increase in self-awareness, including recognition that qualitative accounts of fieldwork are one way of representing reality and that all research is influenced by subjective locations.
Mid-1990s onwards	Postmodern period of experimental **ethnographic** writing	Heavily influenced by **postmodernism** (see Key concept 16.1). Recognition of the different ways in which research participants can be represented when writing up findings.
1995–2000	Postexperimental enquiry	Mainly associated with the emergence of AltaMira Press, a publisher of qualitative research that encouraged experimental and interdisciplinary writing.
2000–2004	The methodologically contested present	A period of considerable disagreement about how qualitative research should be conducted and the direction in which it should be heading. Denzin and Lincoln (2005b) date this period as ending in 2004 but it could be argued that this time of disagreement is ongoing.
2004 onwards	The fractured future	Lincoln and Denzin (2005: 1123) speculated that the future would hold 'randomized field trials' for one group of researchers and 'the pursuit of a socially and culturally responsive, communitarian, justice-oriented set of studies' for the other.

present the 'moments' as distinct, consecutive phases, where one moment led to another. The reality is that each 'moment' continued to develop and contemporary qualitative research is actually still composed of all of these traditions. Second, some phases are strongly associated with particular events—the arrival of a new publisher or new journals—which looks strange given that the earlier moments are each associated with several decades. There were certainly disagreements and agreements associated with qualitative research practice in the modernist phase, for example. Third, the eighth and final moment seems to be concerned with a rift in social research in general rather than within qualitative research specifically. Although it is probably possible to identify particular methodological preferences associated with different journals and disciplines, it is debatable whether this separation has happened in the way that is proposed here.

Perhaps the most obvious issue with Denzin and Lincoln's list is that it ends in the early 2000s and does not acknowledge the many new forms of and perspectives within modern qualitative research that have emerged since. We might summarize the more recent themes and 'movements' associated with qualitative research as follows.

- *An emphasis on the sensory*. While the sensory has been a part of the social sciences for a long time—as evident in Georg Simmel's (1908) work on odour, for example, or H. S. Becker's (1974) observation that many nineteenth-century issues of the *American Journal of Sociology* contained visual material—there has been a recent refocusing on the importance of the sensory in accessing and interpreting reality. This can be seen in Pink's work on sensory ethnography (Pink 2015) and research that has followed Kress and Leeuwen's exploration of multimodality (2001).
- *A questioning of normative* ***concepts*** *of identity and experience*. We introduced the idea of **intersectionality** in Chapter 2 (see Key concept 2.7), and it has become a key focus for some qualitative researchers. This has led to a renewed emphasis on how such positionality might intersect to produce particular experiences, and to reflections about who might be best positioned to access and research these areas. **Queer methodologies**, for example, have built on some of the ideas developed in **feminist** and postcolonial research, and further work within the field of gender and sexuality is taking into account all kinds of non-dominant identities and experiences (for example, those relating to ethnicity). Some of the more radical work in the area is distinctly postmodernist (see Key concept 16.1) in that subjectivities are seen to be fluid and constantly evolving, and researchers have questioned how data can be gathered in such an unstable reality (see, for example, Nash 2016).
- *The use of creative and participatory approaches*. **Creative research** and **participatory research** methods attempt to rebalance power relations in research by conducting studies 'by' or 'with' rather than 'on' participants. Although, again, participatory methods have been around for some time (see Reason and Rowan 1981, for example), they are now being used in an increasing number of areas and are often employed when working with vulnerable groups (see, for example, Vacchelli 2018). Creative methods include collage, storytelling, sandboxing, puppetry, drawing, theatre, and various other forms or artistic expression, as well as everyday activities such as walking (O'Neill and Roberts 2019). You will find examples of these approaches throughout this book (see, for example, Research in focus 18.10). Publications that include further discussion of their rationale and the methodologies involved are Mannay (2015), Kara (2015), Vacchelli (2018), and Erel et al. (2017).

As with Denzin and Lincoln's 'moments', we intend this description of recent developments to be instructive rather than definitive. Other interpretations of the history of qualitative research are possible, as are other descriptions of the notable features of current practice. In the future, it will be interesting to see how qualitative researchers respond to the opportunities presented by digital technology and **Big Data**. Without a doubt, there will always be a place for qualitative studies that have a small number of participants (sometimes referred to as 'small N research', N being sample size), but advances in computing processing power, the availability of 'big' qualitative data sets, and the accessibility of more user-friendly forms of **Computer Assisted Qualitative Data Analysis Software (CAQDAS)** have the potential to transform the scale of qualitative research. Again, computational social science is not particularly new, but as we will see across Part Three of this book, continuing advances in the digital realm are facilitating innovative approaches to the practice of qualitative research; interest is likely to grow as this technology continues to advance.

Data-collection methods in qualitative research

The main methods of data collection associated with qualitative research are

- ethnography/**participant observation**;
- qualitative interviewing;

KEY CONCEPT 16.1
What is postmodernism?

Postmodernism is extremely difficult to define with any certainty. Part of the problem is that it is at least two things.

1. It is an attempt to get to grips with the nature of an increasingly diverse society and culture.
2. It represents a way of thinking about and representing the nature of the social sciences and their claims to knowledge.

The latter point is perhaps more relevant for this book, and it has particular implications for the representation of social-scientific findings. This is because postmodernists tend to be deeply suspicious of the idea that it is possible to arrive at a definitive version of any reality. Reports of findings are viewed as *versions* of an external reality, so the key issue is the plausibility of those versions for the participants themselves rather than whether they are 'right' or 'wrong' in any absolute sense. This has probably had most influence in discussions about the nature of ethnographic writing and the fact that an ethnographer implicitly claims to have provided a definitive account of the group or society they are studying (see Section 18.4 on 'Writing ethnography' in Chapter 18).

For postmodernists, there is no objective reality 'out there', waiting to be revealed by social scientists. Any reality is always going to be accessed through narratives, whether these are research participants' own narratives, or the dominant narratives that emerge from things like policy documents and research write-ups. Postmodernist researchers aim to critique these representations, highlighting the power relations that are often contained within them. They focus on the language used in these discourses and the devices researchers use to imply that their findings are definitive (see Delamont and Atkinson 2004). Postmodernists also tend to emphasize the idea of **reflexivity** (see Key concept 16.6). This concept was developed within feminist research and highlights the significance of the researcher's influence on the research process, and the implications for the quality and depth of the findings presented in a research report (given that the researcher is always implicated in their findings).

- **focus groups**;
- the collection of **texts** and documents.

Because these are the core data-collection methods that qualitative researchers use—and are particularly appropriate for student projects—they are the ones that we outline here. But you should be aware that other, less widely used methods are available, and that studies can use more than one method—this is called a multi-method approach. Researchers in ethnography who use participant observation, for example, frequently also conduct qualitative interviews and collect documents. There has always been considerable variation in how data is collected in qualitative studies and, as we have outlined above, new ways of collecting and analysing data continue to be developed. Therefore, you should not see the methods and studies we describe under the heading 'qualitative research' as an exhaustive depiction of an approach that is both diverse and continuing to develop.

16.3 The main preoccupations of qualitative researchers

We noted in Chapter 7 that quantitative and qualitative research can be seen as having a set of distinctive and contrasting concerns. Their preoccupations reflect different beliefs about what kind of knowledge is acceptable. In Chapter 2, we suggested that whereas quantitative research is profoundly influenced by the natural sciences in terms of what should count as acceptable knowledge, qualitative researchers are more influenced by interpretivism (see Key concept 2.4). In this section we will consider the five common concerns of qualitative researchers:

- seeing through the eyes of those being studied;
- providing full descriptions and emphasizing context;
- the importance of process in social life;
- prioritizing flexibility;
- grounding concepts and theory in data.

Seeing through the eyes of the people being studied

Many qualitative researchers operate on the assumption that the subject matter of the social sciences is different from that of the natural sciences. The key difference is that the objects of analysis of the natural sciences (atoms, molecules, gases, chemicals, metals, and so on) cannot attribute meaning to events and to their environment, whereas people can and do. This argument is especially evident in the work of Schutz—see the passage quoted in Section 2.3 of Chapter 2.

Many qualitative researchers argue that we need a methodology for studying people that reflects this difference, and express a commitment to viewing the social world through the eyes of the people that they study. The **epistemology** underlying qualitative research has been expressed by the authors of one widely read text as having two central principles: '(1) . . . face-to-face interaction is the fullest condition of participating in the mind of another human being, and (2) . . . you must participate in the mind of another human being (in sociological terms, "take the role of the other") to acquire social knowledge' (Lofland and Lofland 1995: 16).

It is not surprising, therefore, that many researchers say that understanding and conveying the views of the people they study is the central focus for their research. We can see this tendency to try and see through the eyes of other people in a great number of studies. Here are some examples.

- Pearson conducted an ethnography of football fans and writes that he wanted 'to access the intersubjective "life-world" (Husserl 1931) of the supporter groups, spending time with them and trying to understand their behaviour, motivations and their interpretations of the world around them' (2012: 13).
- Benson writes that in her ethnographic study of British expatriates in rural France, she chose to emphasize the 'worldview' of her participants and to focus on 'understanding . . . their everyday lives in their own terms' (2011: 17).
- Nichols spent 18 months conducting an ethnography of 'lad culture' in a rugby club. This included visiting the club two nights a week, both on training days and match days, and taking a voluntary job behind the bar on other nights. This enabled her 'to gain insight and understanding of the interactions and practices associated with the rugby culture which may not have been possible through observations as an outsider alone' (2016: 76).
- In her study of masculinity and the personal lives of Muslim men, Britton sought to 'provide a valuable window on men's lives, enhancing understanding of changing gender and generational relations in Muslim families and shifting masculine roles and identities' (2018: 36–7).

The preference for seeing through the eyes of the people studied often goes along with the closely related goal of probing beneath surface appearances. In attempting to take the position of the people you are studying, you may find that they view things in a different way from what you might have expected. This stance is clear in Mason's (2018) study of Somali teenagers in the north of England, showing how 'swagger' plays an important role in affirming boundaries associated with place, race, and class. 'Swagger' is a particularly embodied subcultural style that incorporates clothing and bodily movement. It is often ascribed to teenagers or youth culture, particularly in the lower social classes, who may appear dressed in a somewhat showy way and to be exaggeratedly confident in their manner. It is also sometimes ascribed as a negative trait that is associated with criminality.

Reflecting these views, much academic research in this area has suggested that those people whose patterns of consumption are associated with swagger are seeking a way of avoiding the shame of poverty and attempting to 'fit in'. This implies that dressing in expensive clothes is a way of disguising poverty. However, following a three-year ethnographic study of youth clubs in an inner city area, Mason argues that 'swagger' plays an important part in the construction and negotiation of identity in racialized working-class cultures. Rather than passively consuming cultural products, Mason demonstrates how the people in his study used 'swagger' to actively produce and recode values in ways that allowed them to challenge their marginality. Swagger enabled them to make judgements about 'authentic' and 'non-authentic' forms of culture, and to make identifications with each other. This also allowed them to resist forms of middle-class appropriation and categorization. In demonstrating these things, Mason showed how seemingly mundane things like clothing are actually central to ongoing racial and class positioning.

The qualitative researcher's attempt to try to see through the eyes of their participants strongly resonates with the goals of interpretivism. However, this is not without practical problems, which include the risk of 'going native' and losing sight of what you are studying (see Key concept 18.3); the problem of how far the researcher should go, for example in participating in illegal or dangerous activities; and the possibility that the researcher will be able to see through the eyes of some of the people, but not others. We will address these and other practical difficulties in the chapters that follow.

It is worth being aware that because much qualitative research focuses on the perspectives of those being studied, many writers argue that the kind of reasoning required is not inductive (see Section 16.2) but **abductive** (e.g. Blaikie 2004; Charmaz 2006). Induction involves theory emerging out of research, whereas abduction involves the researcher grounding a theoretical understanding of the contexts and people they are studying in the language, meanings, and perspectives that form that worldview. So any theory that emerges from the research should be understandable to those people involved in the study. The crucial step in abduction is that, having described and understood the world from participants' perspectives, the researcher must come to a social-scientific account of the social world from those perspectives. They must not lose touch with the world as it is seen by those whose voices provided the data. At first this might look like inductive logic, and there is an element of induction in this process, but what distinguishes abduction is that the researcher grounds a theoretical account in the worldview of the people being researched.

The importance of context

Qualitative researchers are much more likely than quantitative researchers to provide a lot of descriptive detail when reporting their findings. This is not to say that description is their *only* focus. They also try to provide explanation, and the extent to which qualitative researchers ask 'why?' is often understated. For example, Skeggs has written that her first question for her research on young working-class women was 'why do women, who are clearly not just victims of some ideological conspiracy, consent to a system of class and gender oppression which appears to offer few rewards and little benefit?' (1997: 22; see Research in focus 18.12 for further details of this study). However, it is certainly true that many qualitative studies provide detailed descriptions of what goes on in the setting being investigated—what Geertz (1973a) called **thick descriptions**—and the researcher has to take care not to get too caught up in descriptive detail. Lofland and Lofland warn against 'descriptive excess' (1995: 164–5), where the amount of detail overwhelms or interferes with the analysis of data, and there is always a delicate balance to be struck in providing a detailed, but not too detailed, account of the context within which people's behaviour takes place. Qualitative researchers argue that we cannot understand the behaviour of members of a social group without appreciating the specific relations, networks, and environments in which they operate. When we know more about the social context, behaviour that could otherwise appear odd or irrational may make more sense.

The emphasis on context in qualitative research goes back to many of the classic studies in social anthropology. These studies often demonstrated how a particular practice, such as a magical ritual that may accompany the sowing of seeds, made little sense unless it was placed within the belief systems of that society. The tendency to provide a lot of description can also be seen as a manifestation of the **naturalism** that is central to much qualitative research and that places great value on detailed, rich descriptions of social settings.

Conducting qualitative research in more than one setting can also demonstrate the significance of context and the ways in which it influences behaviour and ways of thinking. Research in focus 16.1 is an example of a **multiple-case study** in which the importance of context is clear.

Emphasis on process

Qualitative research tends to view social life in terms of processes. This reveals itself in a number of different ways, including the way that qualitative researchers try to show how events and patterns unfold over time. As Pettigrew usefully puts it, process is 'a sequence of individual and collective events, actions, and activities unfolding over time in context' (1997: 338).

Ethnographic research is particularly associated with this emphasis (see Chapter 18), and ethnographers are typically immersed in a social setting for a long time—often years. This means that they are able to observe the ways in which events develop and/or the ways in which the different elements of a social system interconnect. These might be values, beliefs, behaviours, or collective affinities. Such findings can help us to see social life in terms of streams of interdependent events and elements (see Research in focus 16.2 for an example).

RESEARCH IN FOCUS 16.1
The importance of contextual understanding

Drawing on the strengths of **multi-sited ethnography**, Trouille and Tavory (2016) write about an ethnographic study of 'sociable' interactions in a Los Angeles public park, which was mostly frequented by working-class Latino men. In the initial phase of the ethnography Trouille simply spent time with the men in the park, often playing 'pick up' soccer with them, or observing the occasional fight. After two years, he began to accompany the men (the researchers use the term 'shadowing') in other sites, away from the park. This included their work environment, bars, restaurants, and other public settings. It also involved being with them when violent altercations occurred around their local areas.

In comparing the different sites of interaction, Trouille began to see the wider role that the park, and the people they met there, played within the fabric of their lives. Not only did the men develop employment opportunities in the park, they were also able to establish reputations and build trust within informal labour markets. These contacts were vital to them in making ends meet. However, what happened in the park also provided the events and tales that could be used within interactions elsewhere, whether it be to alleviate the day-to-day boredom of working life or as an opportunity to anticipate future entertainment.

The contextual nature of Trouille's ethnography revealed the importance of the park within the context of everyday life—and it was only by shadowing the men in these other arenas that Trouille was able to examine how they developed and maintained networks in the local area. Indeed, the shadowing technique that Trouille and Tavory developed allowed them to build what they term 'intersituational variation' into the ethnography. This enabled them to compare and contrast actors, acts, and actions across different contexts. The researchers suggest four specific advantages of this approach: it allows the ethnographer to empirically defend claims about what happens 'in context'; it deepens the ethnographer's ability to show how meanings can change according to context (and where they don't); it enables the ethnographer to examine the patterned ways in which meanings are constructed in relation to each other; and it helps the ethnographer make claims about how general conditions that they study (in this case poverty, racial segregation, and migration) can have an impact on different aspects of everyday life.

RESEARCH IN FOCUS 16.2
An emphasis on process and flexibility

Demetry's ethnography in 'the kitchen of a high-end restaurant' in the USA (2013: 583) reveals the qualitative researcher's focus on process and flexibility. For this study, she observed events in the restaurant's kitchen over a period of six months, spending four hours in the kitchen once or twice a week, at various different times. She also conducted interviews with staff at all levels.

Part of the way through Demetry's research there was a change of head chef. This resulted in a change of regime and a shift from an informal atmosphere of camaraderie to a more professional one with an emphasis on following regulations and being more businesslike. The change in management gave Demetry the opportunity to observe what she termed a 'natural ethnographic experiment'. She could see how time and space were organized in a different way under the two regimes, even though the physical space of the kitchen and the restaurant was unchanged.

This ethnographic case study provides interesting insights into the ways in which the change process is played out in work settings. Demetry was fortunate in being able to study a process because she was in the right place at the right time. However, she also wanted to highlight another kind of process, namely 'where reoccurring patterns of interaction within a group create culture' (2013: 581). The study also demonstrates the significance of flexibility in qualitative research, in that Demetry was able to capitalize on an event that happened to occur and to weave it into her ethnography.

This is not to say, however, that ethnographers are the only qualitative researchers who can explore process within social life. Researchers can also examine process through semi-structured and **unstructured interviewing**, by asking participants to reflect on the processes leading up to or following on from an event. For example, Krause and Kowalski (2013) were interested in the processes through which young adults aged 26 to 31 years acquire romantic or sexual partners in New York and Berlin. They did this by asking their interviewees how they got together with their current partners or most recent 'dates'. Interviewees were instructed to provide 'concrete stories in as much detail as possible' and the researchers probed for 'the details, turning points and key decisions' as well as 'other stories of courtship' (Krause and Kowalski 2013: 25). The researchers were able to build up accounts of the process of getting together and to compare results from the two cities. They found greater intentionality in the process of getting together in New York than in Berlin.

Flexibility

Many qualitative researchers are critical of approaches to research that involve imposing predetermined formats on the social world. This position is largely to do with their preference for seeing through the eyes of the people being studied. After all, if researchers use a structured method of data collection (such as a **structured interview** with **closed-ended questions**), they must have made decisions about what they expect to find, and about the nature of the social reality that they will encounter. This necessarily limits the degree to which the researcher can try to adopt the worldview of the people being studied. For example, Dacin, Munir, and Tracey explain that their investigation of dining rituals at Cambridge University, aiming to examine whether they help to perpetuate the British class system, 'allowed us to build our understanding of the properly contextualized experiences of those involved in the dining ritual, rather than imposing a particular framework upon them' (2010: 1399).

Consequently, most qualitative researchers prefer a research orientation that involves as little prior contamination of the social world as possible. Keeping some flexibility in the ways they collect data also makes it more likely that research participants' perspectives will be revealed. It means that the aspects of people's social worlds that are particularly important to them can emerge, regardless of whether or not it has occurred to the researcher to ask the 'right' question.

Within ethnographic approaches, the preference for a less structured approach to data collection often means that the investigator does not need to develop highly specific **research questions** in advance (see Thinking deeply 16.1). This allows researchers to submerge themselves in a social setting with a fairly general research focus in mind, and then gradually develop a narrower focus by making as many observations of that setting as possible. They can then formulate more specific research questions out of their collected data. We could say the same of many approaches to qualitative interviewing and even the use of documents.

Another advantage of taking a less structured approach is that it offers more scope for flexibility. The researcher can change direction in the course of their investigation much more easily than in quantitative research, which tends to have a built-in momentum once the data collection is under way. For example, if you receive hundreds of replies to your **online survey** but then realize there is something else that you would have liked to investigate, it will be difficult to do anything about it. Structured interviewing and **structured observation** can have some flexibility, but this is limited by the requirement to make interviews as comparable to each other as possible. Qualitative research is generally much more responsive to the needs of the field. O'Reilly (2000), for example, has written that because of unforeseen limitations, her research on the British on the Costa del Sol shifted in two ways over the duration of her participant observation: from focusing on the elderly to observing expatriates of all ages; and from focusing on permanent residents to also including those migrating in less permanent ways, such as tourism. Demetry's restaurant kitchen study (2013; see Research in focus 16.2) is another example of a shift in research due to circumstances that the researcher encountered as her study progressed.

Concepts and theory that are grounded in data

We noted in Section 16.2 (and mentioned earlier in this section) that one of the noteworthy features of qualitative research is its tendency to take an inductive view of the relationship between **theory** and research. Qualitative researchers usually develop concepts and theories using the data that are collected during the research project. This differs from quantitative research, where theoretical issues are usually seen as driving the formulation of research questions, which in turn shapes how data is collected and analysed. Findings then feed back into the relevant theory. This is something of a caricature, but it is true that within qualitative research, the relationship between theory and data *is* more nuanced and ambiguous. Theory can be both the starting point and the outcome of an investigation, rather than only something that precedes it. This explains the often dynamic nature of contemporary field research design in qualitative research (Silverman 2017).

We will further consider the relationship between theory and qualitative research in Section 16.4.

16.4 The main steps in qualitative research

Despite the variety in approaches associated with qualitative research, it is possible to identify the main steps that most of these studies involve. These are depicted in Figure 16.1. In order to help illustrate each step, we will use a study by Oncini (2018) that examined how parents, teachers, cooks, and children resist 'top-down' ideas—ideas that are initiated by higher authorities—about healthy meals and good nutrition in school canteens (the rooms where school pupils eat meals).

Step 1. General research question(s)

The starting point for Oncini's (2018) study is the growing public attention on both childhood obesity and healthy eating. As he suggests, these concerns are reflected in attempts by global institutions such as the World Health Organization to encourage healthy eating from an early age. Oncini also highlights how much of the research in the area has been quantitative, generally concentrating on the capacity for school meals and menus to improve children's eating habits. He points out that the school canteen 'is one of those settings where scientific knowledge and power strategically intertwine to accustom children to dietary standards' (2018: 645). However, Oncini also notes how little of the current literature has explored the phenomenon that school meals are subject to several forms of resistance from the very people the programmes are typically aimed at. As a result, Oncini formulated two main objectives of his fieldwork: first, to understand the practices that parents use to convey certain food preferences to their children, and second, to illuminate 'the role

FIGURE 16.1
An outline of the main steps of qualitative research

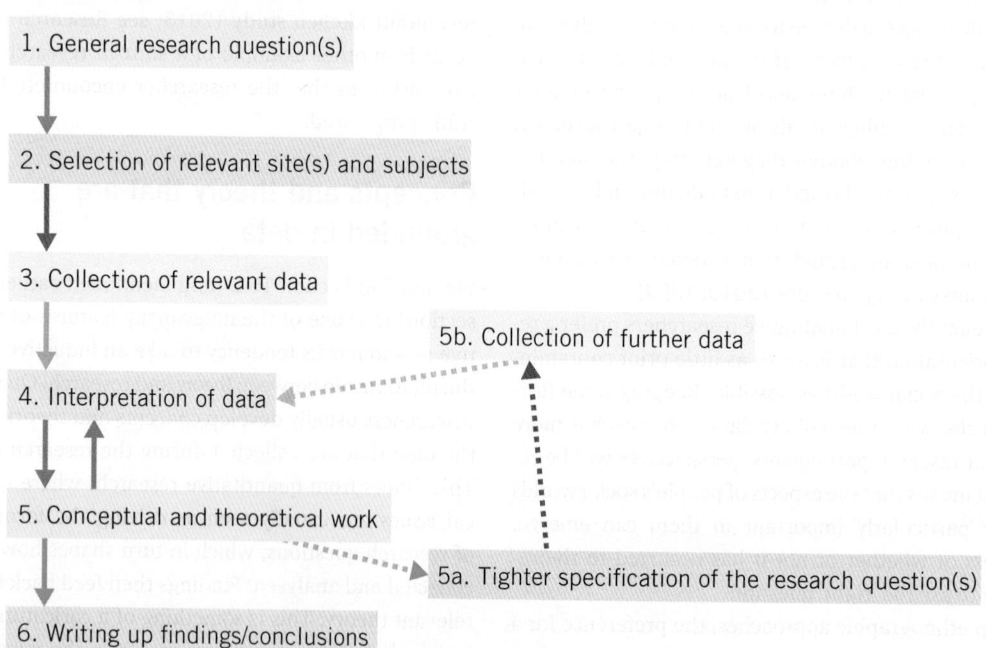

16

of the primary school in the construction and modification of such preferences, so as to highlight possible conflicts' (2018: 646).

Step 2. Selection of relevant site(s) and subjects

Oncini selected three full-time Italian primary schools where the vast majority of children ate school meals. He purposively sampled these schools according to their socio-economic background, the relative importance that each of the schools placed on providing a healthy diet for their children, and his own capacity to access the school.

Step 3. Collection of relevant data

Oncini describes his research as 'ethnographic', and states that he conducted fieldwork across two school years, spending around four months in total in each school and eating around 120 meals with the children. After conducting a short **pilot** study in which he spent a month in one school, he describes a number of different stages of fieldwork: talking with children as they ate their lunch; helping the canteen staff set up lunch tables and clean them away afterwards; formal interviews with nutritionists, medical doctors, and service providers who planned or implemented menus, as well as interviews with 44 primary caregivers and several focus groups with teachers; and analysis of **official documents** relating to the school's nutritional policy. Oncini's fieldwork produced three types of data: fieldnotes, interview **transcripts**, and secondary data. Using the **sensitizing concepts** (terms that point to what is relevant or important and are used to guide an investigation—see Section 16.4) that he had already identified in his **literature review**, he states: '[A]ll data were analysed thematically and coded in QDA miner [a data analysis software program]. . . . [I] categorized the material into different themes, distinguishing between the formal rules behind the making of the school meal, complementary pedagogies, actors involved, and reactions to the school meal' (2018: 648).

Step 4. Interpretation of data

One of the key findings to emerge from the data was the fact that the 'top-down' ideas about healthy eating, as expressed in menus that are prescriptively designed to satisfy the requirements of school meal policies, are not passively accepted and consumed (in every sense) in the school canteen. Instead, the canteen becomes a contested site in which 'the agency of the actors is always at play, to a lesser or greater extent, in any governmental intervention' (2018: 662). Parents might sneak food from home into their child's bag, cooks bend the rules to please their diners, children share food they do and do not like, and teachers mostly 'just want to get to the end of lunch as quickly as possible' (2018: 657).

Step 5. Conceptual and theoretical work

No new concepts seem to emerge from Oncini's research, but using the sensitizing concepts generated through his literature review—which are identified to be the frameworks of Foucault (1991; 1998; 2009) and de Certeau (1984)—enabled him to respond to the aims we outlined under Step 1. For example, he writes:

> These findings shed light on the complementary nature of power and resistance. Subjects, regardless of their age, are not inhibited by biopedagogies [methods of teaching about and regulating the body], but rather find their own way through them, and creatively mold their implementation . . . [However], Studies on biopedagogies at school often respond to this question by showing its undesirable outcomes or side effects. In this article, however, I take a different approach, and show how resistances to the top-down medical model on nutrition emerge from various sides, and are indeed an integral part of the model: in other words, resistance is always intrinsic to the exercise of power.
>
> (Oncini 2018: 663)

Steps 5a and 5b. Tighter specification of the research question(s) and collection of further data

We have noted that the relationship between theory and data is nuanced in qualitative research, and in some studies there can be an interplay between interpretation and theorizing on the one hand, and data collection on the other, with the researcher gradually reaching findings through repeated cycles of data collection and analysis. This is often referred to as an *iterative* approach. Oncini clearly followed this process, as he states: 'Data collection, data analysis, and literature review proceeded simultaneously as iterative processes' (2018: 648). Therefore it is highly likely that he was talking to, and interacting with, people in the light

THINKING DEEPLY 16.1
The role of research questions in qualitative research

There is quite a lot of variation in how explicitly qualitative researchers state research questions. Sometimes the research question is embedded within a general account of the researcher's approach and aims. Consider Brannen, O'Connell, and Mooney's study of how dual-earner families with young children integrate mealtimes and food preparation into their busy lives. They write:

> We sought to understand how employed parents (mothers) fitted food and eating into their working family lives and how habitual practices of eating together and eating meals were influenced by the timetables of other family members.
>
> (Brannen et al. 2013: 420)

In other studies, questions are explicitly listed as bullet points that emerge from a statement of the aims and objectives of the research. Hine was interested in the ways in which parents participated in discussions of headlice in an online parenting forum. She was specifically concerned with how parents explained their handling of headlice and the extent to which they drew on scientific understanding when providing justifications. She specified several research questions:

- What resources do participants in online discussions about headlice draw upon, and in particular what part does science play? What forms of authority are held to be convincing?
- What notions of risk do participants express, and how are these made accountable?
- How do the dynamics of advice-giving in this context relate to conventional notions of medical and scientific expertise and/or to new relations of expertise such as apomediation that may be occasioned by the internet? (Hine 2014: 578)

Research questions for qualitative research are formulated with reference to the relevant literature, but not everyone agrees that this must happen at the beginning of an investigation (as we indicated in Figure 16.1). Some supporters of **grounded theory** (see Key concept 16.2) advocate a more open-ended strategy—usually beginning with more of a 'blank slate'. This is because the aim of grounded theory—perhaps the most radical example of an inductive research approach—is to develop a theory through an iterative process of data collection and analysis. When working in this way, the literature becomes much more significant at later stages of the research process because it helps to inform the research questions and theoretical ideas as they emerge from the data.

of his emerging ideas about his data and the literature more generally. This pattern is common in qualitative research. We explore these ideas further in Thinking deeply 16.1 on the development of research questions in qualitative research.

Step 6. Writing up findings/ conclusions

There is no real difference between the significance of writing up in quantitative research and qualitative research, so we can make exactly the same points here as we made in relation to Step 12 in Figure 7.1. The writer has to convince an audience about the credibility and significance of the interpretations they offer. Researchers are not simple messengers for the things they see and the words they hear. The researcher has to make clear to the audience the importance and relevance of what they have seen and heard. Oncini does this by highlighting that his findings and chosen methods have implications for policies on school mealtimes:

> The advantage of ethnography, a method that entails long-term listening to the ways subjects make sense of their world, has offered me insight into the perspectives of actors at the intersection with food education policy. This study can hence suggest that the scientific eye that guides the implementation of school meal policies might benefit from alternative approaches involving children, cooks, teachers, and parents in the construction of the menu.
>
> (Oncini 2018: 664)

16.5 Theory and concepts in qualitative research

When writing about the research process, most qualitative researchers emphasize a preference for treating theory as something that informs and, at the same time, emerges out of data collection and analysis. In the case of grounded theory (see Key concept 16.2), theory emerges from an iterative process of data collection and analysis. Other examples of inductive approaches where theory is generated from the data include **thematic analysis** (see Chapter 23), **analytic induction** (Chapter 23), and some forms of **discourse analysis** (Chapter 21). Some researchers have also argued that qualitative research should be developed according to particular theoretical approaches that help to define elements of a study, including the research question(s) and the **research design**. Silverman (2014), in particular, has highlighted that qualitative researchers have become increasingly interested in the use of theories to shape the research and suggests that this is a reflection of the growing maturity of qualitative research. So, in Figure 16.1, the loop back from Step 5a, 'Tighter specification of the research question(s)', to Step 5b, 'Collection of further data', implies that a theoretical position might emerge in the course of research that prompts the researcher to collect further data to reflect emerging issues of interest that they had not initially foreseen.

Concepts and their measurement were a central feature of our discussion in Chapter 7 and—as we noted in Section 16.3—concepts are also very much part of the landscape in qualitative research. According to Blumer (1954), there are two types of concepts that can be used for qualitative purposes: definitive concepts and sensitizing concepts.

Definitive concepts are typified by the way in which a concept, once developed, becomes almost entirely defined by its **indicators**. Socio-economic class is an example of a definitive concept. It is often indicated through an assessment of wealth, employment, and culture. However, Blumer notes that this can constrain our understanding of the social world because the concept comes to be seen exclusively in terms of the indicators that have been developed for it. Subtle nuances in the form that the concept can assume are then ignored because definitive concepts are too focused on what is common to the phenomena, rather than with variety (Blumer 1954: 7).

Instead, qualitative researchers tend to prefer what Blumer refers to as sensitizing concepts. These provide a more general sense of what to look for and guide empirical work. They help researchers uncover the variety of ways in which something can exist and be seen, rather than imposing rigid measurements. We saw in Section 16.3 that Oncini (2018) used sensitizing concepts to guide his study of resistance to 'top-down' healthy eating ideas in school canteens, and you can see another example of a sensitizing concept in Research in focus 16.3.

16

KEY CONCEPT 16.2
What is grounded theory?

Strauss and Corbin define grounded theory as 'theory that was derived from data, systematically gathered and analysed through the research process. In this method, data collection, analysis, and eventual theory stand in close relationship to one another' (1998: 12). There are two central features of grounded theory:

1. theory develops out of data;
2. the approach is iterative (sometimes called recursive), meaning that data collection and analysis proceed in tandem, repeatedly referring back to each other.

Beyond this basic description, there is not much agreement on what constitutes grounded theory, not least because the two originators of the approach—Glaser and Strauss—eventually disagreed on its development. To some writers, it is a distinct method or approach to qualitative research in its own right; to others, it is not a conventional theory but an approach to the generation of theory out of data. We take the second view in this chapter. In discussions of grounded theory, 'data' is usually taken to refer to qualitative data, but researchers can use grounded theory in connection with other kinds of data too, and can also use it to generate concepts rather than theory as such (see Chapter 23).

RESEARCH IN FOCUS 16.3

The emergence of a sensitizing concept in qualitative research

Hochschild's (1983) idea of emotional labour—labour that 'requires one to induce or suppress feelings in order to sustain the outward countenance that produces the proper state of mind in others' (1983: 7)—has become a very influential concept in the sociology of work and in the developing area of the sociology of emotions. Emotional labour is essentially emotion work that is performed as part of one's paid employment. In order to develop the concept, Hochschild examined the emotional labour taken on by flight attendants. She gained access to Delta Airlines, a large American airline, and in the course of her investigations she

- watched sessions for training attendants and had many conversations with both trainees and experienced attendants during the sessions;
- interviewed various personnel, such as managers in various sections of the company and advertising agents;
- examined Delta advertisements spanning 30 years;
- observed the flight attendant recruitment process at Pan American Airways, because she had not been allowed to do this at Delta;
- conducted 'open-ended interviews lasting three to five hours each with thirty flight attendants in the San Francisco Bay Area' (Hochschild 1983: 15).

It is clear that Hochschild's concept of emotional labour began as a fairly imprecise idea that emerged out of a concern with emotion work but that she then gradually developed in order to address its wider significance. The concept has since been picked up and developed by other qualitative researchers in the sociology of work. For example, in their study of film sets, Watson et al. (2018) used it to examine how directors, cast, and crew engage in routine displays of emotional labour in order to stage particular atmospheres that are conducive to the nature of the scene being shot. Similarly, in their study of police control rooms, Lumsden and Black (2018) have demonstrated how staff who are responding to emergency calls use emotional labour to help manage the clash of expectations between the public and the police. The concept of emotional labour has even started to be used within public discourse to refer to emotions that are repressed in families, relationships, and social justice campaigns. A quick search for the term online will show you just how far it has travelled.

16

There are some problems with Blumer's (1954) distinction between definitive and sensitizing concepts. For example, it is not clear how far a very general formulation of a concept can be regarded as a useful guide to empirical enquiry (investigation based on observation or experience, not through logic or intuition). If it is too general, it will not provide a useful starting point because its guidelines are too broad; if it is too narrow, it is likely to repeat some of the difficulties Blumer (1954) identifies in relation to definitive concepts. However, his general view of concepts has attracted some support, because his preference for not imposing predetermined schemes on the social world resonates with the views of many qualitative researchers. As the example in Research in focus 16.1 suggests, the researcher frequently starts out with a broad outline of a concept, which they then revise and narrow during the course of data collection. Later researchers may take up and revise the concept as they use it in connection with different social contexts or in relation to different research questions.

16.6 Research quality and qualitative research

There has been some discussion among qualitative researchers about how relevant the criteria of **reliability** and **validity** are for qualitative purposes, and researchers have taken a number of different positions on these issues. It may be that these terms need to be redefined for use in qualitative contexts. For example, the idea of measurement validity, in its name, carries connotations of measurement. Because measurement is not a major preoccupation among qualitative researchers, it would seem that the issue of validity has limited relevance for these studies. It is for this reason that some researchers have suggested using an entirely different set of criteria for qualitative studies. In this section we consider:

- the use of reliability and validity in qualitative research;
- alternative criteria for evaluating qualitative research;
- methods of evaluating quality that sit between quantitative and qualitative research criteria.

The use of reliability and validity in qualitative research

Some researchers refer to reliability and validity within qualitative research with little change of meaning other than reducing the emphasis on measurement issues. Mason, for example, argues that reliability, validity, and generalizability (see Chapter 3) 'are different kinds of measures of the quality, rigour and wider potential of research, which are achieved according to certain methodological and disciplinary conventions and principles' (1996: 21). She sticks very closely to the meaning of these criteria as they are used in quantitative research, considering validity to refer to whether 'you are observing, identifying, or "measuring" what you say you are' (Mason 1996: 24).

Another option is to alter the emphasis of the terms associated with reliability and validity so that they resonate more strongly with the opportunities and constraints presented by qualitative research. LeCompte and Goetz (1982), for example, consider the terms in the following ways:

- External reliability is taken to refer to the degree to which a study can be replicated. This is a difficult criterion to meet in qualitative research because, as LeCompte and Goetz recognize, it is impossible to 'freeze' a social setting and the circumstances of an initial study to make it replicable in the sense we discussed in Chapter 7. However, they offer several strategies to try to address this issue. For example, they suggest that a qualitative researcher replicating ethnographic research needs to adopt a similar social role to that adopted by the original researcher. However, we saw in Chapters 2 and 6 that researchers are increasingly conscious of the impact of both their and their participants' values and social positions on the research process, and it may be impossible to reproduce specific characteristics of a project.
- Internal reliability is the extent to which, when there is more than one observer, members of the research team agree about what they see and hear. This is similar to inter-rater reliability (see Key concept 7.3).
- Internal validity refers to the correspondence between researchers' observations and the theoretical ideas they develop. LeCompte and Goetz see this as a strength of qualitative research, particularly ethnographic research, because this method involves participation in the social life of a group over a long period of time. This allows the researcher to develop deep analytical insights between concepts and observations.
- External validity is concerned with whether specific findings can be generalized across different social settings. LeCompte and Goetz suggest that, unlike internal validity, external validity is problematic for qualitative researchers because of their tendency to use ethnographic approaches, case studies, and relatively small samples compared to those used in quantitative research. There is also the fact that the aim of qualitative research is to reach a deep, highly contextual understanding of a social phenomenon. That said, it remains perfectly possible for qualitative research to be instructive about similar situations, even if not exhaustively so.

Alternative criteria for evaluating qualitative research

An alternative position is that qualitative studies should be judged or evaluated according to entirely different criteria from those used by quantitative researchers. In order to overcome what they see as the limitations created by using reliability and validity in a qualitative context, and as a way to acknowledge the specificities of qualitative research, writers have proposed alternative schemes of criteria.

Lincoln and Guba's criteria

Lincoln and Guba (1985) and Guba and Lincoln (1994) propose two main criteria for assessing a qualitative study: trustworthiness and authenticity.

Trustworthiness

Trustworthiness is made up of four criteria, each of which has something of an equivalent criterion in quantitative research:

1. *credibility*, which parallels internal validity;
2. *transferability*, which parallels external validity;

3. *dependability*, which parallels reliability;
4. *confirmability*, which parallels objectivity.

A major reason for Guba and Lincoln's unease about simply applying reliability and validity to qualitative research is that these criteria assume that it is possible to have a single, absolute account of social reality (an approach described in Chapter 2 as **realism**). Instead, Guba and Lincoln argue that there can be more than one account.

This emphasis on multiple accounts of social reality is especially clear in the criterion of *credibility*. After all, if there can be several possible accounts of an aspect of social reality, it is the credibility of the account that determines whether it is acceptable to others. There are a number of ways to establish credibility: making sure there is prolonged engagement 'in the field'; analysing negative (divergent) cases; and the **triangulation** of data, analysis, and findings (see Key concept 16.3; we also consider this process in Chapter 24). Triangulation may also include submitting research findings to the members of the social world who were studied so that they can confirm that the investigator has correctly understood what they saw and/or heard. This technique is often referred to as **respondent validation** or **member validation** (see Key concept 16.4 and Learn from experience 16.1).

The next sub-criterion of trustworthiness, proposed as a parallel to external validity, is *transferability*. Qualitative research often involves the intensive study

KEY CONCEPT 16.3
What is triangulation?

Triangulation refers to the use of more than one method or source of data to study social phenomena. The term has also been used more broadly to refer to an approach that uses 'multiple observers, theoretical perspectives, sources of data, and methodologies' (Denzin 1970: 310), but the emphasis tends to be on methods of investigation and sources of data. It involves cross-referencing one method or source of data with another to increase the researcher's field of vision and to cross-validate findings. Where a researcher finds correspondence among different methods or data sources, they can have greater confidence in those results. Because triangulation is able to operate within and across research strategies, some see it as a way to develop more robust and meaningful assessments of the social world (Webb et al. 1966; see Key concept 12.1).

Triangulation has traditionally been associated with quantitative research, but it can also take place as part of a qualitative research strategy. Ethnographers, for example, often check their observations with interview questions to determine whether they might have misunderstood what they had seen. This is a form of data triangulation where different forms of data are assessed in respect to each other to examine how they might, or might not, resonate with each other. Eaton (2018) reports that he investigated how narratives are used within the context of amateur ghost hunts by observing paranormal investigations, attending paranormal conventions, and conducting 48 interviews with participants. Increasingly, 'triangulation' is also used to refer to a process of cross-checking findings deriving from both quantitative and qualitative research (Moran-Ellis et al. 2006). We cover issues associated with **mixed methods research** in Chapter 24.

16

KEY CONCEPT 16.4
What is respondent validation?

The process of respondent validation, sometimes called participant validation or member checking, involves a researcher asking their participants to validate aspects of the research. The aim is to check that the researcher's findings and impressions are consistent with the views of those people the researcher was studying, and/or to identify and understand areas where the perspectives do not match up. Birt et al. (2016) identify several different forms of respondent validation.

- The researcher provides each research participant with an account of what they said in an interview and conversations, or of what the researcher observed by watching them in an observational study.

- The researcher feeds back to a group of people or an organization their impressions and findings in relation to that group or organization.
- The researcher disseminates some of their writings that are based on a study of that group or organization, for example as draft articles or book chapters.

Respondent validation has proved popular among qualitative researchers, who usually want to ensure that there is a good correspondence between their findings and the perspectives and experiences of their participants. However, respondent validation brings some practical difficulties.

- Telling participants what you have seen or observed may prompt defensive reactions and even censorship.
- Participants may be reluctant to be critical if they have developed relationships of 'fondness and mutual regard' with the researcher (Bloor 1997: 45).
- Participants may not be well placed to validate a researcher's analysis, since it is often intended for an academic audience and needs to be set into a social science framework if it is to be published.

It is also unclear what a researcher should do if participants disagree with their analysis or findings.

LEARN FROM EXPERIENCE 16.1
Using quality criteria in qualitative research

It is important to remember that quality criteria are meant to be used during the process of research. Here, Starr describes how she incorporated Lincoln and Guba's trustworthiness criteria in her research—and how that led to her seeking a form of respondent validation.

> To help me think about the quality of my research, I was guided by the Lincoln and Guba (1985) trustworthiness criteria described in Bryman (2012, 5th edn). These criteria—credibility, transferability, dependability, and confirmability—were useful because they do not assume objective truths about social reality, something that aligned with my qualitative strategy and interpretivist epistemology. Throughout the research process, I continuously referred back to these criteria to hold myself accountable and ensure that I was developing a social research project that was as transparent as possible.
>
> For example, to help determine the credibility of my research—whether or not my interpretations of the social world under study appropriately reflected the context—I turned to respondent validation. I offered the interview transcripts as well as the research findings to my informants for feedback and confirmation. The responses from my informants were positive, although it took some time before I heard back from them, which is always important to consider. My research depended upon a mutual understanding of concepts that included global sustainability, economic equity, social justice, intercultural awareness, and reciprocity. Through the analysis of informant descriptions of these and other concepts, I took steps to ensure that informants' subjective conceptual understandings resonated with those of the research.
>
> Starr

Access the **online resources** to hear Starr's video reflections on this theme.

You can read about our panellists' backgrounds and research experiences on page xxvi.

of a small group, where depth is emphasized rather than breadth. As a result, qualitative findings tend to stress the contextual uniqueness and significance of the particular social world being studied. For example, as we noted in Section 16.3 (under the subheading 'The importance of context'), ethnographers often aim to produce **thick description**, meaning rich accounts of the details of a culture. Lincoln and Guba argue that thick description provides others with a 'database' for making judgements about the possible transferability of findings to other settings.

Lincoln and Guba propose the idea of *dependability* as a parallel to reliability in quantitative research. They suggest that researchers should adopt an 'auditing' approach in order to establish the merit of research. This idea requires researchers to keep an **audit trail** of complete records for all phases of the research process, including problem formulation, selection of research participants, fieldwork notes, interview transcripts, data analysis decisions, and so on. Keeping these records allows peers to act as auditors, possibly during the course of the research and certainly at the end, checking how far appropriate research procedures have been followed. This would also include assessing the degree to which theoretical inferences can be justified. It must be said, however, that this idea of auditing has never really been explored in any detail and there are few studies that report using it to assess research quality.

The final criterion of Lincoln and Guba's definition of trustworthiness, *confirmability*, recognizes that complete objectivity is impossible but requires the researcher to show that they have acted in good faith. In other words, it should be clear that they have not overtly allowed personal values or theoretical inclinations to sway the conduct of the research and any findings deriving from it. Respondent validation or member checking (see Key concept 16.4) would be one way of assessing confirmability.

Authenticity

16

In addition to the four trustworthiness criteria, Lincoln and Guba suggest five criteria of authenticity. These criteria raise a wider set of issues concerning the broader political impact of research.

1. *Fairness*. Does the research fairly represent different viewpoints among members of the social setting?
2. *Ontological authenticity*. Does the research help members to arrive at a better understanding of their social environment?
3. *Educative authenticity*. Does the research help members appreciate the perspectives of other members of their social setting?
4. *Catalytic authenticity*. Has the research prompted members to engage in action to change their circumstances?
5. *Tactical authenticity*. Has the research empowered members to take the steps necessary for engaging in action?

The authenticity criteria are thought-provoking, but they have not been particularly influential. It is, however, true to say that they have certain points of affinity with **action research** (see Key concept 16.5), largely because the emphasis on practical outcomes differentiates this approach from most social research.

Tracy's criteria

Lincoln and Guba's criteria are some of the best-known alternatives to quantitative ideas of assessing research quality, but others have also suggested frameworks for assessing the quality of qualitative research. Tracy (2010), for example, provides eight 'big tent' criteria:

- *Worthy topic*: the topic of research is relevant, timely, significant, and of interest.
- *Rich rigour*: the study is sufficient, abundant, appropriate, and complex.
- *Sincerity*: the study demonstrates reflexivity and transparency. (See Key concept 16.6 on reflexivity.)
- *Credibility*: the research is characterized by thick description, triangulation, multivocality (multiple voices), and/or member reflections.
- *Resonance*: the research influences, impacts, or moves audiences.
- *Significant contribution*: the research makes a difference in some way to the knowledge base.
- *Ethics*: the researcher has given consideration to procedural, situational, and relational ethics and also to exiting ethics (connected with how the researcher leaves the group or setting).
- *Meaningful coherence*: the study achieves what it sets out to, uses methods that are appropriate to those goals, and meaningfully connects literature, methods, findings, and discussion with one another.

Between quantitative and qualitative research criteria

So far, we have considered arguments in favour of using quantitative research criteria to assess qualitative research, and arguments in favour of creating alternative criteria. Hammersley's (1992a) approach lies midway between these preferences. He sees validity as an important criterion but reformulates it, and also suggests *relevance* as an important criterion of qualitative research.

KEY CONCEPT 16.5
What is action research?

There is no single type of action research, but it can broadly be defined as an approach in which the action researcher and members of a social setting collaborate to diagnose a problem *and* develop a solution in a collaborative way through a set of processes that are initiated by the researcher.

It can take a variety of forms, from the action researcher being hired by a client to work on the diagnosis and solution of a problem, to working with a group of individuals who need to develop the capacity for independent action. In each case, the point of research engagement is the changing of social practices through a cycle of feedback and implementation where the investigator becomes part of the field of study.

A project conducted in Canada and described by Gibson (2004: 5) provides a useful example. The idea for the study, which looked at the social and cultural factors that have an impact on the prevention and treatment of tuberculosis (TB) among 'foreign-born and aboriginal populations', came from a nurse in a TB clinic who secured support from the groups most affected by the disease—so the study was initiated in a practical context in order to solve a specific problem. An advisory committee was formed, drawing its membership from the local community as well as from government and academic constituencies, and two representatives from each of ten distinct socio-cultural communities were recruited. These representatives acted as research associates, gathering and helping to analyse data once they had received training.

The study's findings revealed that, while the healthcare system dealt well with active TB cases, it was less effective in relation to prevention in communities at risk. They also revealed that health professionals often fail to identify TB because it is not prevalent in Western nations. The advisory group then produced a plan to disseminate its findings and developed other practical initiatives including 'an information video, a community education nurse position, and TB fact sheets in their various languages' (Gibson 2004: 5).

Action research is most common in fields such as business and management research, education, international development, and social care. Because of the distinctive social justice agenda that often characterizes action research, it is dismissed by some academics for lacking rigour and for being too partisan in approach (i.e. promoting a particular cause), but advocated by others because of its commitment to involving people in the process of change rather than imposing solutions on them.

KEY CONCEPT 16.6
What is reflexivity?

In both everyday language and academic discourse, reflexivity is the act of reflecting upon yourself and your experiences. Feminist research applied and developed the concept in the context of **research methods**. In an account of the research process, reflexivity involves explaining the position of the researcher in relation to the position of the researched (Al-Hindi and Kawabata 2002). Longhurst (2009) defines reflexivity as the practice of examining one's own 'embodied subjectivities' in order to gain new insights into research. In simple terms, this means being reflective about the implications of your methods, values, biases, and decisions (including your cultural, political, and social context) for the knowledge you generate. From a reflexive position, 'knowledge' is always a reflection of a researcher's location in time and social space.

There has been evidence of a growth in reflexivity in social research in recent years, with numerous 'confessional tales' emerging (see Section 18.4 on 'Writing ethnography' in Chapter 18) and a far greater awareness and acknowledgement of the role of the research participant as an integral part of the construction of knowledge. A reflexive approach can redress some of the imbalances in power dynamics between the researcher and the

researched (which, as we noted in Chapter 7, is one of the criticisms made of quantitative approaches) because it can help to avoid the researcher acting as someone who simply 'extracts' knowledge and then 'transmits' it to an audience. Instead, the researcher is thoroughly implicated in the construction of knowledge through the perspective they adopt and the decisions they make about how to represent it.

However, critics of reflexivity have argued that it is a slippery concept. Lynch (2000) observes that it is often assumed that a reflexive position is somehow superior to an unreflexive one, but the case for this dynamic is rarely made. He also points out that the term has different meanings, one of which is methodological reflexivity, which comes closest to the kind of reflexivity we refer to in this chapter. This meaning has a number of sub-meanings, three of which are especially prominent in methodological writings.

1. *Philosophical self-reflection*: an introspection involving 'an inward-looking, sometimes confessional and self-critical examination of one's own beliefs and assumptions' (Lynch 2000: 29).
2. *Methodological self-consciousness*: the researcher must become consciously aware of those beliefs and assumptions, examining how they might influence uncertainties in the research process, and looking at problems of access and **reactivity**.
3. *Methodological self-criticism*: this includes the confessional style of ethnographic writing (see Chapter 18) and the anti-objectivistic styles of discourse analysis (see Chapter 21), but Lynch notes that the need to be self-critical and reject particular ideas and approaches is also widespread in natural-scientific disciplines.

Reflexivity can be a useful tool to reflect on the research process, and researchers need to use their own discretion to assess when and how they should integrate reflexivity into their research findings and write-up. However, as Lynch's discussion implies, the term has to be used with a degree of caution.

Hammersley on validity

For Hammersley, validity means that an empirical account must be plausible and credible, and that it should take into account the amount and kind of evidence used to arrive at a set of findings. Hammersley's position is based on the realist idea that there is an external social reality that can be accessed by the researcher (see Key concept 2.3). However, he rejects the idea that such access is direct, and that the researcher can act as a mirror, reflecting the social world back to an audience. Instead, he argues that the researcher is always engaged in representations or constructions of that world. The plausibility and credibility of a researcher's 'truth claims' are therefore the main considerations in evaluating qualitative research. Hammersley's *subtle realist* position, as he calls it, means recognizing that we can never be absolutely certain about the truth of any account, since we have no way of gaining direct access to the reality on which it is based. Therefore, he argues, 'we must judge the validity of claims [about truth] on the basis of the adequacy of the evidence offered in support of them' (1992a: 69). This means that an account can be held to be 'valid or true if it represents accurately those features of the phenomena that it is intended to describe, explain or theorise' (1992a: 69).

Hammersley on relevance

Hammersley uses this term to refer to the importance of a topic within its substantive field, or its contribution to the literature in that field. This includes the question of whether research is responsive to the concerns of practitioners—that is, the people who are part of the social setting being investigated and who are likely to have a vested interest in the research question and the implications of findings deriving from it. In this way, his approach resonates with the kinds of considerations that are addressed by Guba and Lincoln's authenticity criteria (Lincoln and Guba 1985; Guba and Lincoln 1994). However, Hammersley recognizes that the kinds of research questions and findings that might be of interest to practitioners and researchers are likely to be different. Practitioners are likely to be interested in research that helps them to understand or address problems with which they are confronted, and these may not be central concerns for an academic researcher. However, there may be occasions when researchers can address both sets of interests, and they may even be able to use this as a way to secure access to the organizations in which they want to conduct research (see Chapter 18 for a further discussion of access issues).

Overview of the issue of quality criteria

Let's reflect on what we now know about the use of quality criteria within qualitative research. Most researchers recognize that it is not appropriate to simply apply the quantitative research criteria of reliability and validity to qualitative research, but there is little agreement about the extent to which these criteria should be completely overhauled. Nor do the three positions we have outlined—adapting quantitative research criteria, developing alternative criteria, and taking a middle approach (Hammersley's subtle realism)—represent the full range of possible criteria for assessing quality in qualitative research (Hammersley 1992a; Seale 1999; Flick 2014).

The differences between the three positions mainly reflect the extent to which the researcher accepts or rejects the realist position. Writers on qualitative research who apply the ideas of reliability and validity with little, if any, adaptation broadly position themselves as realists because their approach implies that qualitative researchers can capture social reality through their concepts and theories. Lincoln and Guba reject this view, arguing that qualitative researchers' concepts and theories are only representations and so there may be other equally credible representations of the same phenomena. If we imagine an axis with realism at one end and anti-realism at the other, Hammersley's position occupies a middle ground in that he acknowledges the existence of social phenomena that are part of an external reality but argues that it is impossible to reproduce that reality. Most qualitative researchers nowadays probably operate around this mid-point, though without necessarily endorsing Hammersley's views. They usually treat their accounts as one of a number of possible representations rather than as definitive versions of social reality. They also strengthen their accounts through some of the strategies advocated by Lincoln and Guba, such as thick descriptions, respondent validation exercises, and triangulation.

16.7 The critique of qualitative research

Just as a range of criticisms have been levelled at quantitative research, criticisms have also been made of qualitative research. The most common are that qualitative research is:

1. too subjective;
2. difficult to replicate;
3. difficult to generalize;
4. not sufficiently transparent.

Let's consider each criticism in turn.

Too subjective

Quantitative researchers sometimes criticize qualitative research for being impressionistic and subjective. This argument suggests that qualitative findings rely too much on the researcher's own, often unsystematic, views about what is significant and important, and also on the close personal relationships that the researcher develops with the people studied. As qualitative research tends to begin in a relatively open-ended way, with a gradual narrowing of focus, it is true that there are often few clues as to why one area was given further attention rather than another. In response, quantitative researchers may highlight how, in the stage of research when they are formulating questions or problems to be solved, they state their research focus explicitly in terms of the existing literature and key theoretical ideas.

Difficult to replicate

Although **replication** in the social sciences is not straightforward regardless of the research strategy (see Chapter 7), quantitative researchers often argue that the subjective tendencies of qualitative research are even more problematic because they pose difficulties for attempting to replicate this kind of study. The fact that the qualitative approach is usually flexible and reliant upon the researcher's ingenuity means that it is almost impossible to conduct a true replication. In qualitative research, the investigator is often the main instrument of data collection, so what is observed and heard, not to mention the focus of the data collection, is very much the product of their preferences.

So we can see that this criticism has several components.

- What qualitative researchers choose to emphasize while in the field is whatever strikes them as significant, whereas other researchers might focus on other issues.

16

- The responses of participants, or those being observed or interviewed, are likely to be affected by the characteristics of the researcher (personality, age, gender, and so on).
- Because of the unstructured nature of qualitative data, interpretation will be influenced by the subjective decisions of the researcher.

All of these things make it very difficult to replicate qualitative findings. This is reflected in the difficulties that ethnographers experience when they revisit topics, groups, or settings previously explored by another researcher. Indeed, these 're-studies' do not inspire confidence in the replicability of qualitative research (Bryman 1994).

Problems of generalization

It is often suggested that the findings of qualitative investigations have limited scope. When qualitative research is carried out with a small number of individuals and/or in a certain organization or locality, critics argue that it is not possible to know how the findings can be generalized to other settings. How can just one or two cases be representative of all cases? Can we treat Mason's research on the Somali teenagers who attended the youth clubs he studied as representative of all Somali teenagers or all youth clubs? Can Oncini's research on Italian school canteens be representative of schools and all school meals in another country, and is Demetry's (2013) study of a high-end restaurant in the USA as generalizable to all such establishments? Can we treat interviewees who have not been selected through **probability sampling** as representative?

The answer in all these cases is, of course, emphatically 'no'. A **case study** is not a sample of one drawn from a known **population**. Similarly, the people who are interviewed in qualitative research are not meant to be representative of a population, and in some cases it may be more or less impossible to calculate the population with any accuracy. Instead, the aim of much qualitative research is to generalize to theory rather than to populations. It is 'the cogency of the theoretical reasoning' (Mitchell 1983: 207)—in other words, the quality of the theoretical interferences drawn from the qualitative data—rather than statistical criteria that helps us decide whether qualitative research findings are generalizable. As we noted in Chapter 3, this view of generalization is called '**analytic generalization**' by Yin (2009) and 'theoretical generalization' by Mitchell (1983).

However, not all writers accept this view of generalization in qualitative research. Williams (2000: 215) has argued that, in many cases, qualitative researchers are actually in a position to produce what he calls **moderatum generalizations**—that is, ones in which aspects of the focus of enquiry (a group of drug users, a meeting such as a cosplay convention, or an event such as a strike) 'can be seen to be instances of a broader set of recognizable features'. Williams suggests that not only is it the case that qualitative researchers *can* make such generalizations, they often *do* make them. When forging such comparisons and linkages from one area to another, the researcher is engaging in moderatum generalization. Moderatum generalizations will always be limited and more tentative than statistical generalizations associated with probability sampling (see Chapter 8), but they do permit a small amount of generalization and help to counter the view that generalization beyond the immediate case is impossible in qualitative research.

Lack of transparency

The final common criticism made of qualitative research is that it can lack transparency, in that it is sometimes difficult to establish what the researcher actually *did* and how they arrived at the study's conclusions. A lack of transparency is symptomatic of problematic practice regardless of the research strategy, but qualitative research reports are sometimes unclear about how people were chosen for observation or interview—this can be in sharp contrast to the sometimes overly detailed accounts of sampling procedures in reports of quantitative research. But it does not seem fair to suggest that outlining the ways in which research participants are selected goes too far towards quantitative research criteria, since readers have a right to know how research participants were selected and why they were sampled in a particular way (see Chapter 18).

The process of qualitative data analysis can also be unclear in some studies (Bryman and Burgess 1994a). It is often not obvious how analysis was conducted—in other words, what the researcher was actually doing with the data and how they arrived at any associated conclusions. It is striking, for example, that in O'Cathain et al.'s (2008) study of quality issues in mixed methods research in the health services field, the qualitative methods were less likely to be described fully than the quantitative components—and sometimes were not described at all. Raskind et al.

(2019) have similarly reviewed a number of articles in the journal *Health Education and Behavior* to look at the analytic processes they describe. They found that nearly one-third of the articles they examined did not clearly describe the **coding** approach, and few discussed issues of trustworthiness or reflexivity—and of those that did, member checks, triangulation of methods, and peer debriefing were the most common procedures used.

16.8 From theory to practice

We used this heading in Chapter 7 in relation to quantitative research, but the relationship between theory and practice is less clear for qualitative research. This is because qualitative research is less influenced by strict guidelines about how to go about data collection and analysis. This picture might be changing, as there are a growing number of books aiming to provide clear recommendations about how qualitative research should be carried out, but—as you may have gathered from our discussion of the broad qualitative preoccupations (see Section 16.3)—there are a wide variety of practices associated with this strategy.

For example, qualitative studies vary widely in terms of the extent to which the research is guided by specific research questions or objectives from the start. Grounded theory practitioners sit at the extreme end of this spectrum, as they tend to advocate beginning with a 'blank slate'—that is, with no focus or specific aims. At the opposite end are studies that investigate a specific problem. Qualitative research need not begin with a general research question that is then narrowed down during data collection; it can start with a very, very particular goal in mind. And between these two extremes there are studies that are quite open-ended and relatively unfocused—though a more specific focus may emerge over time. Mason, for example, reports that his study of 'swagger' was 'taken from a broader ethnographic study that sought to investigate the everyday experiences of marginalized young people from minority ethnic backgrounds' (2018: 1121). The focus on swagger only emerged as the process of fieldwork progressed. This is in contrast to Oncini's (2018) study of Italian school canteens, which appears to have been specifically designed to examine how nutritional policy is received and negotiated within school settings—although the exact theoretical framework for the study emerged during the research process. See Research in focus 19.5 for another example of a qualitative study in which a more specific focus emerged over time.

Another way in which qualitative research in practice is sometimes said to differ from quantitative research is in the apparently flexible approach to collecting and analysing data. In comparison to a quantitative survey, for example, qualitative methods of data collection are much more open to negotiation. **Interview schedules** have to be responsive to the needs of a particular interview (see Chapter 19), while an ethnographic researcher will also often find themselves adapting to the needs of the field (see Chapter 18). In many cases, these processes will not be consistent or uniform, and will instead be based on the particular situation faced by the researcher. Similarly, how one qualitative researcher approaches thematic analysis might not be exactly the same as how another approaches it. This is unlike the statistical tests you might use in quantitative data analysis (see Chapter 15), where the underlying mechanisms remain relatively unchanged from one study to another.

However, as we have demonstrated throughout this chapter, qualitative research does need to be structured, rigorous, and transparent if it is to produce meaningful findings. Flexibility can also be a strength rather than a hindrance, as the flexible nature of qualitative research allows researchers to shape their methods around the needs of the social world under investigation, rather than forcing it into preconceived boxes (see Learn from experience 16.2). As we will see in Chapter 21, it is also true that data analysis techniques situated at the interface between quantitative and qualitative research, such as **conversation analysis**, require highly codified methods for analysing talk—these are extremely systematic in nature. The growing use of computer-assisted qualitative data analysis software (CAQDAS—for example **NVivo**) is also leading to greater transparency in the procedures used for analysing qualitative data, helping to make the process of qualitative data analysis much more intelligible to the broader social-scientific community.

LEARN FROM EXPERIENCE 16.2
Flexibility and qualitative research

Qualitative research tends to be described as inductive in nature, since it often has a very general research focus in the beginning and research questions are refined during the course of the research process. This means that researchers often have to be willing to adapt to the needs of the field and any associated data. Taking a flexible approach can be very useful in the early stages of research—as Laura explains:

> A key advantage of qualitative research is the flexible nature of the approach. Fieldwork experiences can help to inform the focus of the research and guide what data is seen as relevant. That way, researchers can always follow up on interesting leads, without abandoning the original aims of the research. I would advise students to take the flexible nature of qualitative research to heart and not to remain adamant about what you are, or are not, looking for. The goal is to learn and gain new information, and the qualitative approach provides enough room to change premeditated ideas that do not correspond with the field.
>
> Laura

 Access the **online resources** to hear Laura's video reflections on this theme.

You can read about our panellists' backgrounds and research experiences on page xxvi.

16.9 Comparing quantitative and qualitative research

16

When getting to grips with research methods, you may find it useful to draw comparisons between quantitative and qualitative research. This can help you to understand their broad tendencies and features. We will outline some of the main differences and similarities in this section, but like any typology they are broad generalizations and should not be viewed as clear, fixed distinctions, or as the only things you need to know about the two research strategies. There are many variations on these themes, and studies within a particular research strategy can differ widely from each other. It is also important to remember that quantitative and qualitative research are not so far apart that they cannot be combined (an idea we explore further in Chapter 24). But despite these caveats, there is enough consistency in the contrasts to allow us to highlight some useful distinctions.

Differences between quantitative and qualitative research

Several writers have explored the contrasts between quantitative and qualitative research by devising tables to demonstrate key contrasts between the strategies (e.g. Halfpenny 1979; Bryman 1988a; Hammersley 1992b). Table 16.2 is an attempt at drawing out the main contrasting features.

Most of these comparisons should make sense to you, having read the rest of this chapter, but we will unpick them briefly here.

- *Numbers vs Words*. Quantitative researchers are often portrayed as being preoccupied with the numerical measurement of social life, while qualitative researchers are seen as using and examining words to interpret meaning.
- *Point of view of the researcher vs Point of view of participants*. In quantitative research, the researcher is very much in control of the research process. They choose what to study and (usually in the form of highly structured research instruments) how to study it. In contrast, qualitative research centres on the perspective of those being studied—what they see as important and significant.
- *Researcher is distant vs Researcher is close*. Quantitative researchers are relatively uninvolved with their participants, and in some cases, as in research based on online questionnaires or with hired interviewers, they may have no contact with them at all. They may

TABLE 16.2
Some contrasts between the features of quantitative and qualitative research

Quantitative	Qualitative
Numbers	Words
Point of view of the researcher	Points of view of participants
Researcher is distant	Researcher is close
Theory and concepts are tested in research	Theory and concepts emerge from data
Static view of social life	Emphasis on process
Structured	Flexible
Aimed at generalization	Aimed at contextual understanding
Hard, reliable data	Rich, deep data
Macro	Micro
Behaviour	Meaning
Artificial settings	Either artificial or natural settings

consider it preferable not to have a relationship with participants, so that they can ensure they remain objective. By contrast, qualitative researchers aim for close involvement with the people being investigated in order to understand the world through their eyes.

- *Theory and concepts are tested in research vs Theory and concepts emerge from data*. Quantitative researchers typically use concepts to build research instruments, so theoretical work precedes data. In qualitative research, the concepts and any theoretical elaboration usually emerge out of data collection.
- *Static view vs Process*. Quantitative research is often said to present a static image of social reality, with its emphasis on **relationships** between **variables**. This is especially likely to be the case with research that incorporates cross-sectional designs. Qualitative research often focuses on unfolding events over time and the interconnections between the actions of participants of social settings.
- *Structured vs Flexible*. Quantitative research is usually highly structured, to allow the investigator to examine precise concepts. Qualitative research, on the other hand, is usually less structured and more flexible. The researcher has more freedom to respond to the needs of the field, and more capacity to develop concepts from data.
- *Generalization vs Contextual understanding*. Whereas quantitative researchers want their findings to be generalizable to the relevant population, qualitative researchers aim to understand behaviour, values, beliefs, and collective affinities in terms of the context in which the research is conducted.
- *Hard, reliable data vs Rich, deep data*. Quantitative data are often depicted as 'hard' in the sense of being robust and unambiguous, owing to the precision offered by measurement. Qualitative researchers claim, by contrast, that their contextual approach and their often prolonged involvement in a setting generate 'rich' data.
- *Macro vs Micro*. Quantitative researchers often aim to uncover large-scale social trends and connections between variables, whereas qualitative researchers are more likely to be concerned with small-scale aspects of social reality, such as interactions among individuals.
- *Behaviour vs Meaning*. It is sometimes suggested that quantitative researchers are concerned with people's behaviour, whereas qualitative researchers are concerned with the meaning and understanding of thought and actions.
- *Artificial settings vs Artificial or natural settings*. Whereas quantitative researchers conduct research in a contrived context, qualitative researchers sometimes investigate people in natural environments (most notably when carrying out participant observation or when working with secondary documents).

As we noted above, these contrasts are not clear-cut or definitive—they are simply broad tendencies and do not apply in every case. Qualitative research can be used to test theories, for example, and quantitative research can be much more exploratory than is often assumed. Indeed, our discussion of reverse operationism in Chapter 7 implies that research concepts often emerge out of quantitative data. It is tempting to draw neat and dichotomous contrasts (i.e. pairs of opposites), but in many instances this is not possible—for example, we cannot accurately say that quantitative research generally takes place in artificial settings and qualitative research in natural settings, because a lot of qualitative research involves interviewing: even if these interviews take place in the participant's home or workplace (and often they will not), interviews for the purposes of research are not a natural environment for most people.

Similarities between quantitative and qualitative research

Hardy and Bryman (2004) have also pointed out that although there clearly are differences between quantitative and qualitative research, there are also a number of similarities. They draw attention to the following points.

- *Both involve data reduction*. Although it might differ in form, both quantitative and qualitative researchers collect large amounts of data, which they have to reduce in order to produce findings. In quantitative research, the process of data reduction takes the form of statistical analysis—something like a **mean** or a **frequency table** (see Chapter 15). In qualitative data analysis (Chapter 23), researchers tend to develop concepts out of rich data.

- *Both involve answering research questions with evidence.* While the kinds of research questions they ask tend to be different (more specific in quantitative research, more open-ended in qualitative research), they both attempt to get answers about the nature of social reality. Both also require any arguments to be supported by evidence.
- *Both involve relating data analysis to the research literature.* Regardless of research strategy, researchers have to relate their findings to the wider literature and disciplines within which they are working. In other words, their findings take on greater significance when they are related to the wider body of work on the subject.
- *Both involve variation.* In different ways, quantitative and qualitative researchers seek to uncover and then represent variation. Both are keen to explore how people (or whatever the **unit of analysis is**) differ and to examine some of the factors connected to that variation (although, once again, the *form* that the variation takes differs).
- *Both treat frequency as a springboard for analysis.* In quantitative research, frequency is a core outcome of collecting data, as the investigator usually wants to reveal the relative frequency with which 'things' occur. In qualitative research, the frequency with which certain themes occur often acts as a catalyst for choosing which ones to emphasize when writing up findings. This is why terms such as 'often' or 'most' appear throughout research reports.
- *Both try to ensure that deliberate distortion does not occur.* Very few social researchers would argue that it is possible to be an entirely objective and dispassionate observer of social life, and sometimes they can be explicitly partisan (see Section 6.6). However, this does not necessarily imply that 'anything goes'. Both groups of researchers aim to avoid 'wilful bias' (Hammersley and Gomm 2000), or what Hardy and Bryman (2004: 7) call 'consciously motivated misrepresentation'.
- *Both argue for the importance of transparency.* Both quantitative and qualitative researchers try to be clear about their research procedures and how they arrived at their findings. This allows others to judge the quality and importance of their work. As we have seen, qualitative researchers have sometimes been criticized for a lack of clarity about how they conducted their investigations (Section 16.7), but increasingly transparency is expected if the research is to be published.
- *Both must address the question of error.* For quantitative researchers, error must be reduced as far as possible so that any variation uncovered is real and not the result of problems with how questions are asked or how research instruments are administered. In qualitative research, the investigator tries to reduce error by ensuring that, for example, there is a good fit between their concepts and the evidence that they have gathered.
- *Research methods should be appropriate to the research questions.* This point is not addressed by Hardy and Bryman (2004) directly, but it was certainly a core concern of Alan Bryman's 'problem-based approach' to research methods more generally. Indeed, Alan frequently made the argument that *the* overriding concern for the social researcher is to ensure that, when they specify research questions, the research methods that they employ are appropriate to that problem.

These points of similarity are quite general, but it is important to be aware that the two strategies cannot be portrayed as completely different. There are many differences between quantitative and qualitative research, but there are still some notable points of similarity.

16

KEY POINTS

- There is some disagreement over the precise definition of qualitative research, but we can identify features and steps that apply across qualitative studies, such as that it is generally inductive, interpretivist, and constructionist, and that most qualitative researchers have a preference for seeing through the eyes of research participants.
- Qualitative research encompasses a wide variety of different traditions and perspectives, which continue to evolve and expand. These include feminist research and its associated standpoints and theories.

- Qualitative research does not necessarily lend itself to a clear set of linear steps.
- It tends to be a more open-ended research strategy than is typically the case with quantitative research.
- Theories and concepts are viewed as outcomes of the research process.
- In assessing the quality of research, researchers are uneasy about simply applying criteria associated with quantitative research to qualitative research, particularly in the case of reliability and validity. Some writers prefer to adapt those criteria or develop alternative criteria.

QUESTIONS FOR REVIEW

1. What are some of the difficulties with providing a general account of the nature of qualitative research?
2. How compelling is Denzin and Lincoln's (2005b) marking-out of distinct 'moments' in the history of qualitative research?
3. What are some of the main research methods associated with qualitative research?
4. Does a research question in qualitative research have the same significance and characteristics as in quantitative research?
5. What is the difference between definitive concepts and sensitizing concepts?
6. How have some writers adapted the ideas of reliability and validity for qualitative research?
7. Why have some writers developed alternative criteria for evaluating qualitative research?
8. What is respondent validation?
9. What is triangulation?
10. 'The difference between quantitative and qualitative research revolves entirely around the concern with numbers in the former and with words in the latter.' How far do you agree with this statement?
11. Does it make sense to describe quantitative and qualitative research as being characterized by both differences *and* similarities?

ONLINE RESOURCES

www.oup.com/he/srm6e

You can find our notes on the answers to these questions within this chapter's **online resources**, together with:

- *audio/video comments* on this topic from our 'Learn from experience' panellists;
- *self-test questions* for further knowledge-checking; and
- a *flashcard glossary* to help you recall key terms.

CHAPTER

17

SAMPLING IN QUALITATIVE RESEARCH

CHAPTER GUIDE

In this chapter, we consider the main ways of sampling in qualitative research. We explore

- the different levels of sampling;
- purposive sampling and the reasons for its emphasis among many qualitative researchers;
- theoretical sampling, and the nature of theoretical saturation;
- the difference between theoretical and purposive sampling;
- the generic purposive sampling approach;
- the snowball sampling approach;
- issues around sample size;
- the sampling of contexts as well as people;
- the use of more than one sampling approach in qualitative research.

17.1 Introduction

Unlike in survey research, where there is an emphasis on probability sampling, discussions of sampling in qualitative research tend to revolve around the idea of purposive sampling. This is a form of non-probability sampling that involves strategically selecting information-rich units or cases (that is, those likely to provide a lot of relevant information), with direct reference to the aims of the research. 'Purposive' sampling has this name because it involves having specific reasons for selecting cases: people, organizations, documents, departments, and so on. The research questions should provide a guide as to which categories of people, places, and things should be the focus of attention, and the sampled units or cases should be information-rich so that the researcher can generate meaningful data about issues that are central to the aims and objectives of their research.

Although purposive sampling is a non-probability sampling approach, it is important to note that probability sampling (that is, sampling randomly—see Chapter 8) can also be used in qualitative research, although it is more likely to occur in interview-based rather than in ethnographic research. There is no obvious rule for when it might be appropriate to use probability sampling in a qualitative context, but it might be useful either if it is important to be able to generalize to a wider population, or if the research questions do not suggest that particular categories of unit should be sampled. That said, probability sampling remains relatively uncommon in qualitative research. In many cases, it is simply not feasible because of the constraints of fieldwork. It can also be difficult to map 'the population' from which a random sample might be taken—that is, to create a sampling frame. However, many qualitative researchers will still want to ensure that they gain access to as wide a range of individuals as possible, so they will need to use more purposive approaches.

In this chapter, we will treat purposive sampling as the master concept around which we can distinguish different sampling approaches in qualitative research. Before we go further, though, we first need to reflect on the main *levels* of sampling in qualitative research.

17.2 Levels of sampling

It is important to understand that sampling in qualitative research often involves two different levels. These levels are sometimes conflated in methodological accounts of research, which is problematic as it can obscure the justification for the choice of sample, and can also constrain any reflection about its potential limitations. The issue of levels is particularly relevant in research that is based on single-case study or multiple-case study designs (see Chapter 3), where the researcher must first select the case or cases for inclusion, and then the sample units within the case(s). Here, there are two clear levels of sampling: first the case or context, then the participants.

When sampling contexts or cases, qualitative researchers can draw from a number of principles of purposive sampling. We discussed the ideas behind these principles in Chapter 3, in connection with the different types of case that were introduced by Yin (2009). A useful example is a study by Abbas et al. (2016) of the ways in which sociology students learn about feminism, and how feminist knowledge can be used to tackle gender inequality. The authors selected four higher education institutions in England and then sampled groups of sociology students within each of those universities.

To sample *context*, the researchers selected four English sociology departments according to their position in UK university league tables, giving them fictional names in their report: '"Community" and "Diversity" were post-1992 universities, consistently rated in the lower quartile, and "Prestige" and "Selective" pre-1992 universities regularly ranked in the top quartile' (Abbas et al. 2016: 445). The four departments were purposively selected in respect to the researchers' focus on how feminist knowledge can be used to address issues of inequality. Each is an exemplifying case in its own right, since the four areas were chosen to represent specific types of university within England in terms of their history and typical students. We see here a common strategy when sampling for multiple-case studies: sampling for both heterogeneity (the different social mixes of the four universities) and homogeneity (all within England and therefore sharing a common regulatory framework).

In order to sample *participants*, the researchers then sought to generate a sample within each sociology department. Abbas et al. do not actually state how they selected students at the unit level, but do suggest that they used 'curricula documents, 98 first year interviews from across the four universities, interviews with 31 case-study students about their second and third year and, a gendered analysis of the videos of seminars in the first and second years' (Abbas et al. 2016: 445). Their sampling strategy allowed them to examine similarities and differences among students within each university *and* between universities.

Sampling areas, and then participants, is a common strategy in qualitative research. It can be seen in Swain's (2004) ethnographic study of friendship groups in schools. Swain was interested in the construction of masculinity in schools of contrasting socio-economic backgrounds. His research question implied that the performance of male behaviour draws upon the cultural resources that are available within a setting. Therefore, he needed to sample those schools where those resources might be different. Because friendship groups are places within which masculinity is performed, he then sampled units by drawing on nominated friendship groups. In this research, there were two levels of sampling—of contexts or cases (that is, the schools) and then of participants (that is, the students). See Research in focus 3.11 for a further example of sampling on two levels.

17.3 What is purposive sampling?

We have noted that most sampling in qualitative research involves purposive sampling (see Key concept 17.1) of some kind. The logic of this form of sampling is different from probability sampling, where selection is based on achieving the statistical representativeness that allows generalization from sample to population. Instead, purposive sampling requires the deliberate selection of information-rich units or cases on the basis that they allow the researcher to learn as much as possible about the phenomena of interest. What links the various kinds of purposive sampling is that they are all conducted with direct reference to the research questions. Researchers select cases and units of analysis precisely because they will allow the researchers to answer the research questions in a way that is as meaningful and informative as possible.

17

KEY CONCEPT 17.1
What is purposive sampling?

Purposive sampling is a form of non-probability sampling and does not aim to sample research participants on a randomized basis. Instead, the goal is to sample cases or participants in a strategic way, selecting participants on the basis of the kind of information they can provide, usually because they have the right kind of life experience for the research in question or because they are expert in a certain field. Very often, the researcher will also want to ensure that there is a good amount of variety in the resulting sample, so that sample members differ from each other in terms of key characteristics that are relevant to the research question. This allows them to identify similarities and differences across the sample.

Because it is a non-probability sampling approach, purposive sampling does not allow the researcher to statistically generalize to a population. Although a purposive sample is not a random sample, it is not a **convenience sample** either (see Chapter 8). A convenience sample is simply available by chance to the researcher, whereas in purposive sampling the researcher samples with their research goals in mind and selects units of analysis because of their relevance to the research questions. This means that the researcher needs to be clear about the criteria for inclusion or exclusion. Examples of purposive sampling in qualitative research are **theoretical sampling** and **snowball sampling**, which we will discuss in Section 17.4 (see also Research in focus 17.2 for an example of snowball sampling). In **quantitative research**, **quota sampling** (discussed in Chapter 8) is a form of purposive sampling procedure.

Writers such as Patton (2015) and Palys (2008) have identified a range of different types of purposive sampling.

1. *Extreme or deviant case sampling.* This involves sampling cases that are unusual or that demonstrate exceptional qualities. It allows researchers to investigate people, behaviours, or events that are particularly interesting because they are atypical and deviate from what might otherwise be expected.
2. *Typical case sampling.* Researchers select cases because they are typical in terms of their features and do not deviate from the norm. This is effectively the opposite of extreme or deviant case sampling.
3. *Critical case sampling.* Researchers choose cases because they display features that are central to the phenomenon of interest. These cases are those likely to reveal the most information with respect to the research questions. As suggested by Patton (1990: 174), the existence of a critical case is particularly likely where there is a statement to the effect of '"if it happens there, it will happen anywhere," or, vice versa, "if it doesn't happen there, it won't happen anywhere"'.
4. **Maximum variation sampling**. The logic of this strategy is to describe common features or themes that exist across a wide variety of contexts. Researchers identify characteristics that might reasonably be thought to influence data, and then select cases or units to ensure as wide a variation as possible in terms of those characteristics. This strategy is particularly effective in identifying both unique and shared features between units and across cases.
5. *Criterion sampling.* This involves sampling cases or units that meet a particular criterion. Researchers are likely to use this strategy if information they gain from an initial survey provides a basis for further qualitative investigation. They can also use particular incidents to identify cases: for example, in a study that looked at school children who are in danger of being excluded from school, they might select students based on whether they have been formally reported for truancy.
6. *Theoretical sampling.* This is where the selection of cases or units is driven and controlled by the emerging theory; we discuss this in Section 17.4 and Key concept 17.2.
7. *Snowball sampling.* This technique involves sampling a small group of people who are relevant to the research questions and relying on these participants to recommend or bring in other participants who have the required experience or characteristics. We discuss snowball sampling in Section 17.4, and there is an example in Research in focus 17.2.
8. *Opportunistic sampling.* This strategy capitalizes on the unpredictability of qualitative fieldwork and involves taking advantages of opportunities in the field. This is not the same as selecting whoever comes along on a 'first come, first served' basis. Instead, researchers purposively select information-rich cases or units as and when they become available, and only if they are able to provide data relevant to the research question.
9. *Stratified purposive sampling.* This strategy involves sampling particular sub-groups of interest and it is something of a step below maximum variation sampling (number 4 in this list) in that each stratum constitutes a fairly homogeneous group. The aim is to capture the major differences between those groups, rather than identify their similarities.

The first three purposive sampling approaches in the list are ones that are particularly likely to be employed in connection with the selection of cases or contexts. The others are likely to be used in connection with both the sampling of individuals and that of cases or contexts. Arguably the most commonly-used types from this list are theoretical sampling and snowball sampling, and we can add to these an approach that Alan Bryman has called 'generic purposive sampling'. This approach is relatively open-ended and emphasizes the generation of concepts and theories but does not have certain characteristics of theoretical sampling, such as its cyclical, iterative nature, and it can be used in conjunction with some of the other types. We consider all three types in Section 17.4.

17

As well as appreciating the different types of purposive sampling, it is useful to be aware of distinctions in the process through which purposive sampling is conducted. There are notable differences between **sequential sampling** and **non-sequential sampling** (Teddlie and Yu 2007), and between **a priori sampling** and **contingent sampling** (Hood 2007).

Teddlie and Yu (2007) saw sequential sampling as an evolving process, in that the researcher begins with an initial sample and gradually adds to the sample as required by the research questions. They select units according to their relevance, and they gradually add to the sample as the investigation evolves. Snowball strategies are an example of sequential sampling. By contrast, non-sequential approaches to sampling might be called 'fixed sampling strategies', because the sample is more or less established at the start of the research. The research

LEARN FROM EXPERIENCE 17.1
A priori sampling

In an a priori sampling project, the researcher selects participants according to particular pre-established criteria that do not change as the research progresses. This was the case for Brendan, who contacted a large number of schools to maximize the chances of gaining access to participants who met his requirements:

> I chose to use a purposive sampling method in my research because I was interested in a very specific group who could be considered 'hard to reach'. I emailed every primary school in Sweden's four largest cities to increase my chances of receiving responses that would match my requirements. I expected a very low response rate but was pleasantly surprised to find that a number of schools responded, even just to say that they would not be able to participate. I credit this success to a detailed letter I wrote to principals asking for their assistance, in which I promised to be considerate of their time. In the end, I had 11 schools that had students that satisfied my criteria, which meant that I had more than enough to interview.
>
> Brendan

You can read about our panellists' backgrounds and research experiences on page xxvi.

questions still guide the sampling approach, but the sample is predetermined before data collection.

Turning to the second distinction, Hood (2007) suggested that a purposive sampling approach is contingent when the *criteria* for selection evolve over the course of the research. The research questions again guide how participants are sampled, but the relevant sampling criteria shift as the research questions change or multiply. Theoretical sampling is a form of contingent sampling. By contrast, in an a priori sampling process the researcher establishes criteria for selecting participants at the outset of the research—as our panellist Brendan did in his project (see Learn from experience 17.1). The criteria will still reflect the requirements of the research questions, but they do not evolve as the research progresses.

17

17.4 Common forms of purposive sampling

In this section we consider the three most common forms of purposive sampling (listed in Section 17.3) in more detail. We will look in turn at theoretical sampling, generic purposive sampling, and then snowball sampling.

Theoretical sampling

Theoretical sampling was advocated by Glaser and Strauss (1967) and Strauss and Corbin (1998) in the context of an approach to qualitative data analysis that they developed known as **grounded theory** (see Key concept 16.2), but it can be adapted for use with other forms of analysis (see Chapter 23).

According to Glaser and Strauss (1967: 45), theoretical sampling 'is the process of data collection for generating theory whereby the analyst jointly collects, **codes**, and analyzes his data and decides what data to collect next and where to find them, in order to develop his theory as it emerges. The process of data collection is *controlled* by the emerging theory, whether substantive or formal.' A crucial characteristic of theoretical sampling is that it is an ongoing process rather than one that is fixed from the start. It is also important to realize that it is not just people who are the 'objects' of sampling. Theoretical sampling is defined as: 'Data gathering driven by concepts derived from the evolving theory and based on the concept of "making comparisons," whose purpose is to go to places, people, or events that will maximize opportunities to discover variations among concepts and to densify categories in terms of their properties and dimensions' (Strauss and Corbin 1998: 201).

For Charmaz (2000: 519), theoretical sampling is a 'defining property of grounded theory' and involves refining the theoretical categories that emerge in the course of collecting and analysing data, rather than simply boosting sample size. Glaser and Strauss suggest that probability sampling is not appropriate for qualitative research because it relies on statistical, rather than theoretical, criteria. As they put it: 'Theoretical sampling is done in order to discover categories and their properties and to suggest the interrelationships into a theory. Statistical sampling is done to obtain accurate evidence on distributions of people among categories to be used in descriptions and verifications' (Glaser and Strauss 1967: 62). Proponents of grounded theory often argue that there is a lot of redundancy in statistical sampling. For example, if you commit to interviewing a certain percentage of an organization's members you end up wasting time and resources because you could have confirmed the significance of a concept and/or its connections with other concepts by using a much smaller sample.

Instead, grounded theory advocates that you sample in terms of what is relevant to, and meaningful for, your theory. The approach is supposed to be an iterative one, with movement backwards and forwards between sampling and theoretical reflection until the researcher achieves theoretical saturation, as shown in Figure 17.1 and discussed in Key concept 17.2. As Charmaz (2006) puts it, theoretical saturation is achieved when new data no longer stimulate new theoretical understandings or new **dimensions** of the principal theoretical categories. In terms of the distinction proposed by Teddlie and Yu (2007), theoretical sampling is a sequential approach; in terms of Hood's (2007) distinction, it is a contingent sampling approach.

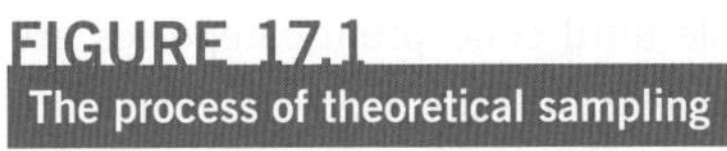
FIGURE 17.1
The process of theoretical sampling

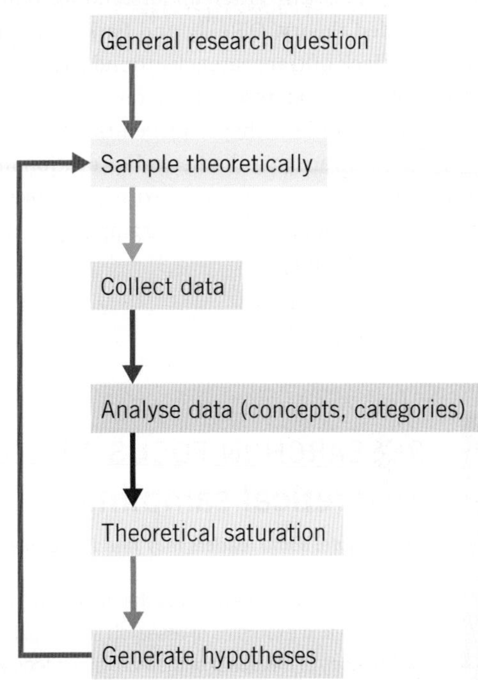

The main advantage of theoretical sampling is the emphasis it places on theoretical reflection, and using it to decide whether further data is needed. This places a premium on theorizing rather than the statistical adequacy of a sample. However, O'Reilly and Parker (2013) argue that the notion of theoretical saturation has become overused in qualitative research, often in ways that do not respect the true meaning of the term. They distinguish between **data saturation**, which is when sampling continues until no new data are generated, and **theoretical saturation**, which involves

KEY CONCEPT 17.2
What is theoretical saturation?

The key idea with theoretical sampling is that you continue sampling until a **category** has been saturated: 'This means, until (*a*) no new or relevant data seem to be emerging regarding a category, (*b*) the category is well developed in terms of its properties and dimensions demonstrating variation, and (*c*) the relationships among categories are well established and validated' (Strauss and Corbin 1998: 212). In the language of grounded theory, a category operates at a somewhat higher level of abstraction than a concept in that it may group together several concepts that have common features. Saturation is achieved when these categories are fully articulated. This does not mean that the researcher develops a sense of déjà vu when listening to what people say in interviews. Instead, it is reached when new data no longer offer new theoretical insights or suggest new dimensions of theoretical categories.

continuing to sample until conceptual categories are fully developed and relationships between them are accounted for. It is this latter understanding that is key to grounded theory. O'Reilly and Parker are also critical of the lack of transparency around the idea of saturation, noting that researchers rarely provide a clear explanation of how they achieved this. It is also important to be aware that theoretical saturation may be an unrealistic target in the context of **inductive** research, as the number of themes emerging from a data set is potentially limitless.

We will come across the ideas of theoretical sampling and theoretical saturation again when we consider grounded theory in more detail in Chapter 23.

Generic purposive sampling

Hood (2007: 152) has usefully pointed out that there is a tendency among many writers and researchers to 'identify all things qualitative with "grounded theory"'. This is particularly the case with theoretical sampling (see Research in focus 17.1), which is often treated as

RESEARCH IN FOCUS 17.1
Theoretical sampling

Please note: some readers may find this content, which relates to a study of bereaved parents, upsetting.

Butler et al. (2018) have noted that although theoretical sampling is a key part of grounded theory, it is often difficult to find examples of research that detail how the approach works in practice. Using their study of parental experiences of the death of their child in intensive care, they demonstrate how theoretical sampling can be directed toward three different data-collection techniques: sampling new research sites, adding new interview questions, and sampling for specific characteristics.

Their study began by interviewing five parents from an initial site. They analysed the interview **transcripts** using open, focused, and theoretical coding, **constant comparison**, and **memos** (notes of their ideas about and reactions to the data; see Research in focus 23.1). They then applied theoretical sampling to further develop the categories they had discovered. In the first instance they sought out two further research sites, and they then added a fourth toward the end of the project. Given that the concept of 'support' (the help offered to the parents by the hospital and other professionals) had emerged as a key consideration during the early phases of analysis, they specifically chose hospitals that provided the same level of care as the original site but that also offered support in the form of a family social worker. Interviewing participants from these two new sites, they continued to interview parents from the original site in order to use 'constant comparison and memoing to explore the concept of support across all sites' (Butler et al. 2018: 564).

At the same time as adding new research sites, their analysis was also revealing that judging healthcare providers was also important to participants. This was an unexpected finding. As a result, the researchers incorporated this into the **interview schedule** by noting that where a participant mentioned 'fantastic' staff, they would probe for examples of 'poor' staff too. This enabled them to develop the categories of 'good' and 'poor' healthcare professionals.

While there is no specific requirement within grounded theory for population representativeness, Butler et al.'s third type of theoretical sampling was used to identify new participant characteristics. During the process of data collection, they noticed that there were differences in responses from those parents where a child had died under the age of five, or where there was significant developmental delay, and from those where a previously healthy teenager had died. To explore these differences further, they deliberately sought out parents of primary- and secondary-school-aged children in later interviews.

Butler et al. (2018) highlight that there is no single correct way to approach theoretical sampling, but their multi-faceted approach does provide a helpful illustration of how researchers can make sampling decisions in relation to their emerging theory.

though it is the same thing as purposive sampling. In fact, as we saw in Section 17.3, theoretical sampling is just one form of purposive sampling. Hood also contrasts grounded theory with what she calls a 'generic inductive qualitative model', which is relatively open-ended and emphasizes the generation of concepts and theories but does not involve (among other things) the iterative style of grounded theory. Whereas theoretical sampling is a sequential process designed to develop theoretical categories, sampling in the generic inductive qualitative model is conducted purposively but not necessarily with reference to theory—the approach that Alan Bryman has called generic purposive sampling.

When using a generic purposive sampling approach, the researcher draws up criteria for the kinds of cases they will need to address the research questions. They then identify appropriate cases, and then sample units from within those cases. Generic purposive sampling can be used in conjunction with several of the sampling strategies identified in Key concept 17.1. It can be used in a sequential or a fixed way, and the criteria for selecting cases or individuals can be formed a priori or be contingent—or even a mixture of both. It would be possible, for example, to plan a priori criteria based on sampling from some initial socio-demographic characteristics such as gender, ethnicity, and age, and then develop more thematic criteria based on the emerging **properties** of the data.

When researchers sample contexts, as in the work of Swain (2004) and Abbas et al. (2016) (see Section 17.2), they often use some form of generic purposive sampling. In the case of the study by Abbas et al., each of the four sampled areas had to be English universities, but they also needed to vary in terms of type. The researchers specified these criteria at the outset of the project. In Swain's (2004) ethnographic research, the researcher selected three schools in order to reveal variation in terms of two criteria: type of school (state versus fee-paying) and the social characteristics of the pupils.

But generic purposive sampling can also be used to select participants. In a study by Jones et al. (2010) of people taking early retirement, the researchers generated their initial sample by searching the databases of several organizations for senior managers who had taken early retirement. Thus they established two criteria from the outset on an a priori basis—being a senior manager and an early retiree. Mason et al. (2020) similarly purposively sampled social work teams from six quite different local authorities (LAs: local government bodies) that had some responsibility for child welfare. They write: 'Case study sites were each embedded within host LAs. These sites formed the basis of comparative analysis across the host LAs and were selected according to their geographical size, population size, and level of deprivation'.

Sometimes, when conducting a mixed methods investigation involving both quantitative and qualitative research, the findings from a survey might be used as the basis for selecting a purposive sample. For example, in a study of social policy researchers in the UK, researchers conducted an **online survey** to gather respondents' views on a wide variety of issues concerning how the quality of social policy research might be assessed (Sempik et al. 2007; Bryman et al. 2008). They then asked respondents whether they would be prepared to be interviewed over the phone so that they could identify issues of interest and probe them more deeply. Of the 251 respondents who replied to the online **questionnaire**, 28 respondents were subsequently interviewed over the phone using a semi-structured approach. The researchers selected the interviewees to reflect a variety of orientations to social policy research and to the evaluation of research quality. For example, one criterion was related to their opinion about whether social policy research should contribute to policy and practice, or to knowledge, or to a combination of both. This sampling strategy allowed the researchers to select interviewees purposively in terms of criteria that were central to the main topic of the research—the appraisal of research quality.

Another example is the study by Brannen et al. (2013) that we discussed in Thinking deeply 16.1, which looked at the ways in which dual-earner families with young children integrate meal times and food preparation into their busy lives. The researchers selected interviewees by following up respondents to the UK's National Diet and Nutrition Survey (NDNS). The authors write:

> We selected households from NDNS according to a number of criteria: a range of households with higher and lower incomes, and a roughly equal distribution of children by gender and age.
>
> (Brannen et al. 2013: 420)

In this way, you can use quantitative data as a sampling frame to purposively select the people from whom you want to collect qualitative data.

17

Snowball sampling

Snowball sampling is a technique in which the researcher initially samples a small group of people who are relevant to the research questions, and those sampled then recommend other participants who have experiences or characteristics that are relevant to the research. These participants will then suggest others, and so on. Just like a snowball, the sample gradually increases in size as the research rolls along. Becker's (1963) study of marijuana users, detailed in Research in focus 17.2, used snowball sampling to very good effect, and Learn from experience 17.2 provides an example of its effective use within a student project.

Snowball sampling is also sometimes recommended when networks of individuals are the focus of attention (Coleman 1958). In Noy's studies of Israeli backpackers and male drivers (2008), for example, he observes that one advantage of the technique is that it is able simultaneously to capitalize on and to reveal the connectedness of individuals in networks. Snowball sampling was also employed in Alan Bryman's study of visitors to Disney theme parks (1999; see Chapter 19) and by Demetry in her ethnography of the restaurant business (2013; see Research in focus 16.2).

The sampling of informants in ethnographic research is sometimes a combination of opportunistic sampling and snowball sampling. Much of the time, ethnographers are forced to gather information from whatever sources are available to them. They can face opposition or indifference

RESEARCH IN FOCUS 17.2
A snowball sample

American sociologist Howard Becker's classic study of marijuana users is one example of a study that employed **snowball sampling.** It is still widely cited by sociologists and criminologists and is said to have had 'long-lasting impacts upon our collective understanding of how individuals become drug users' (Athey et al. 2017: 226). In the study, Becker (1963) describes how he used snowball sampling to generate a sample of marijuana users:

> I conducted fifty interviews with marijuana users. I had been a professional dance musician for some years when I conducted this study and my first interviews were with people I had met in the music business. I asked them to put me in contact with other users who would be willing to discuss their experiences with me. . . . Although in the end half of the fifty interviews were conducted with musicians, the other half covered a wide range of people, including laborers, machinists, and people in the professions.
>
> (Becker 1963: 45–6)

As Becker's study demonstrates, snowball sampling can be a valuable way of accessing participants, especially if they are hard to reach.

17

LEARN FROM EXPERIENCE 17.2
Snowball sampling for a student project

Where large numbers of potential participants are hard to identify and access, it can sometimes be a very useful to strategy to ask other people and groups to help identify them for you. Sarah used a snowballing approach in her research to gain access to participants.

> For my undergraduate dissertation, I used a snowball sampling technique to recruit participants from an anti-tree-felling campaign group. I first contacted the campaign headquarters by making an initial inquiry via their generic contact address. The individual who responded mentioned two public events organized by the campaign group, which I subsequently attended. At these events, I approached potential participants and some individuals suggested other people to contact. As I spoke to more and more people the 'snowball' got bigger and I was able to identify more potential participants.
>
> Sarah

 Access the **online resources** to hear Sarah's video reflections on this theme.

You can read about our panellists' backgrounds and research experiences on page xxvi.

RESEARCH IN FOCUS 17.3
Snowball sampling in qualitative research: A cautionary tale

Snowball sampling is generally understood to be a useful technique for getting access to individuals and groups who are hard to reach or where the topic of research is considered private or sensitive. It was partly due to these advantages that Waters (2015) chose to incorporate snowball sampling into her study of drug users over the age of 40. Broadly following the **open-ended questions** on drug use contained in the Crime Survey for England and Wales, Waters planned to interview users about drug careers over the life-course, including their reasons for using illegal drugs and their attitudes toward drug use in general. Contacting various friends, colleagues, and professionals she hoped to recruit a base of around six to ten participants, from which she could then snowball. Unfortunately, the first 24 months of the study only produced 9 interviews, and of those, only two led to a subsequent interview with another participant. This was in spite of participants referring to over 50 people in the course of the interviews who would have otherwise fitted the criteria. Waters proposes four reasons for what she refers to as her 'scrounging sample':

1. participants were being asked to talk about a topic that was usually kept hidden;
2. older people often have more to lose than younger participants, so the risks of participation are higher;
3. the age of the researcher, approximately half that of her interviewees, may have compromised perceptions of trustworthiness; and
4. older drug users might not be part of a well-defined social network.

This is not to say that snowball sampling should be dismissed, and there are many examples of it being used successfully—and sometimes it is actually the only sampling option.

to their research and are often relieved to gather information from whoever is prepared to divulge such details. For example, in her study of British expatriates in the rural Lot department of France, Benson (2011: 17) notes that although she was very occasionally able to approach Britons who she had overheard talking in restaurants, she soon realized that 'there were very few public places where the British in the Lot regularly congregated'. Fortunately, she encountered a family who were very cooperative and, in addition to acting as participants, introduced her to friends and acquaintances in the area. Over time, she was able to use her contacts with these initial participants to establish herself within the 'expat' community (Benson 2011: 17).

Similarly, Mawhinney and Rinke (2018) had some success in employing a snowball sample in their study of teachers who had left the profession, while also noting some constraints:

> We found that relying on our social networks to initiate the snowball sampling process enabled us to construct a geographically diverse sample of teacher leavers to inform our research question, a sample that otherwise might have been unavailable. However, imbalances inherent in our own identities and social networks translated across our sample, infusing implicit characteristics into the recruitment process.
>
> (Mawhinney and Rinke 2018: 9)

These examples point to some of the potential issues with relying on snowball sampling, which are further illustrated by Research in focus 17.3.

17.5 Key considerations for sampling in qualitative research

Having discussed the main types of purposive sampling, we now turn to some more general considerations in relation to sampling in qualitative research: sample size, the need to sample context as well as people, and the option to combine multiple sampling approaches.

Sample size

One of the problems commonly associated with qualitative sampling is knowing how extensive the sample needs to be at the start of the project. This is especially true if theoretical considerations are guiding selection, but it is also often the case that as an investigation proceeds, it becomes clear that more people and groups will need to be interviewed than were initially anticipated.

As a guiding principle, the broader the scope of the study and the more comparisons being made between groups, the larger the sample size should be (Warren 2002; Morse 2004). However, Warren (2002: 99) observes that, for a qualitative study based on interview data to be published, the minimum number of interviews required seems to be between 20 and 30, although some qualitative approaches can actually use less than this. This suggests that although there is an emphasis on the importance of sampling purposively in qualitative research, there are still minimum levels of acceptability of sample size. Unfortunately, the issue is not clear-cut: there are certainly exceptions to Warren's rule. Life story research, for example, is often based on very intensive interviews where there may be just one or two interviewees. Also, not all researchers agree with Warren's figure. Gerson and Horowitz (2002: 223) write that 'fewer than 60 interviews cannot support convincing conclusions and more than 150 produce too much material to analyse effectively and expeditiously'. Adler and Adler (2012), on the other hand, advise a **range** between 12 and 60 and a **mean** of 30.

Given these disparities, it is not surprising that when Mason (2010) examined the abstracts of doctoral theses resulting from interview-based qualitative research in Great Britain and Ireland, he found that the 560 studies used samples ranging in size from 1 to 95, with a mean of 31 and a **median** of 28. The difference between the mean and median suggests that the mean is being inflated by some rather large samples. Mason similarly refers to another study that reviewed 50 research articles based on grounded theory and found that sample sizes varied between 5 and 350.

All of this shows how difficult it can be to try to specify minimum requirements. The size of sample that is able to support convincing conclusions is likely to vary from situation to situation, and qualitative researchers have to recognize that they are engaged in a delicate balancing act:

> In general, sample sizes in qualitative research should not be so small as to make it difficult to achieve data saturation, theoretical saturation, or informational redundancy. At the same time, the sample should not be so large that it is difficult to undertake a deep, case-oriented analysis.
>
> (Onwuegbuzie and Collins 2007: 289)

Taking quite an innovative perspective, Malterud et al. (2015) suggest that 'information power' should be taken into account when making an assessment about sample sizes. They argue that the information power of a study will vary according to the aims of the study, the sample specificity, the use of established theory, the quality of dialogue, and the analysis strategy. A study will need the least amount of participants if the aims are narrow, the criteria for selecting participants are highly specific, the theoretical base is well established, the data is rich in detail, and there is in-depth analysis of narratives or discourses. On the other hand, a study will need a larger number of participants if the aims are broad, the criteria for choosing participants are less well defined, the research is not theoretically informed, the data is weak, and the analysis is exploratory. Malterud et al. did not intend their model to be a checklist to calculate the sample size; they simply advise that information power should be used to make informed decisions about the nature of the sample needed, according to the particular demands of the project.

However, if theoretical saturation is the criterion for sample size then there is no point specifying minimum or maximum sample sizes. Essentially, the criterion for sample size will be whatever it takes to achieve saturation. Even then, as several writers observe (e.g. Malsch and Salterio 2016; Dai et al. 2019), saturation is often *claimed* but not justified or explained (see Thinking deeply 17.1). If a researcher claims to have reached saturation with a relatively small sample size, their findings might be seen to lack integrity, so it can be advisable to increase sample size to boost credibility.

Drawing on several of these issues, Bryman (2012) suggested five considerations that should be taken into account when deciding how large a sample needs to be.

1. *Saturation*. If it is a consideration (as it is in many qualitative studies), this will necessarily be a factor in when researchers decide to stop collecting data. However, the researcher needs to be clear whether it is *theoretical* saturation or *data* saturation that is the criterion.

THINKING DEEPLY 17.1

Theoretical saturation and sample size

As we have noted, it is very difficult to know in advance how many interviews you need to conduct if you are using theoretical saturation as a principle for assessing whether a sample is adequate (see Key concept 17.2). There are also no clear criteria for deciding when theoretical saturation has been achieved. Let's take a closer, critical look at the actual numbers needed to achieve data saturation, using an empirical example to explore the issue.

In response to the problems associated with applying the concept of theoretical saturation in practice, Guest et al. (2006) conducted some **experiments** with data they had collected from 60 in-depth interviews with women in two West African countries. They analysed the process of what they call 'data saturation', which means the number of interviews 'needed to get a reliable sense of thematic exhaustion and variability within [their] data set' (Guest et al. 2006: 65).

Interestingly, they found that data saturation was generally achieved after only around 12 transcripts had been thematically analysed. They suggest that by the time 12 interviews had been examined, 92 per cent of the codes had been generated. Also, the codes generally did not require significant revision after 12 interviews, implying that they arrived at saturation of categories quite quickly. However, as the authors note, their sample was relatively homogeneous (women at high risk of contracting HIV) and the research was narrow in scope (studying how these women discuss sex), so it may be that saturation was achieved at an earlier point than might be the case for qualitative studies that draw upon more heterogeneous samples and/or have a broader scope. The experiment is still useful, though, in demonstrating how theoretical saturation can be achieved with quite small samples. Further work could undertake similar experiments with different samples and topics.

2. *The minimum requirements for an adequate sample* (though, as we have noted, there is little consensus as to what this figure might be).
3. *The style or theoretical underpinnings* of the research. Some approaches to enquiry, such as the life story method and **conversation analysis**, tend to be associated with smaller samples on which the researcher carries out an intensive analysis.
4. *The heterogeneity of the population* from which the sample is drawn. Researchers might need to secure a larger sample from a heterogeneous population in order to reflect its inherent variability.
5. *Research questions*. These vary in scope and specificity, and researchers might need larger samples to address questions that are broad and quite general.

These five factors are meant to provide some guidelines in deciding on a sample size. However, it is crucial to remember that researchers should always make a robust and rigorous justification for their sampling decisions, both in terms of the sampling approach and the resulting sample size. Rather than rely on others' ideas of suitable sample sizes in qualitative research, it is better to be clear and persuasive about the sampling method that you use, why you have used it, and why your sample size is appropriate.

The issue of **generalization** is also relevant when we consider sample size in qualitative research. Onwuegbuzie and Leech (2010) observe that two kinds of generalizations can be made from a qualitative study: **analytic generalization** and what they call '**case-to-case transfer**'. Analytic generalization is similar to theoretical generalization (Mitchell 1983) and involves comparing the results of a study with previously developed theory. The idea is that qualitative studies are generalizable to theoretical propositions rather than statistical populations. Case-to-case transfer refers to making generalizations from one case to another case that is broadly similar in nature. This is more or less the same as the notion of **moderatum generalization** (Williams 2000), which we referred to in Chapter 16. Onwuegbuzie and Leech analysed 125 empirical articles that had been published in the *Qualitative Report*, an academic journal that has been in publication since 1990. They found that 29.6 per cent of the articles contained generalizations that illegitimately went beyond the sample participants. In other words, just under one-third of articles made statements about a population beyond the study's participants. As the authors note, when this occurs there is an inconsistency between the design of the research and the interpretations that the researchers make about the resulting data. There is clearly a lesson here about the need to appreciate what you can and cannot infer from a sample of any kind.

Sampling contexts as well as people

Another dimension to sampling in qualitative research that is worth bearing in mind is the need to sample the different contexts within which interviewing or observation take place. Writing about ethnographic research, Hammersley and Atkinson (2019) suggest that we need to consider both time and context when sampling.

Attending to *time* means that the ethnographer must make sure that people or events are observed at different times of the day and different days of the week. To do otherwise risks drawing inferences about behaviour or events that are valid only for particular times or days. For several reasons it is impossible to be an ethnographer at all times of the day, but it is important that researchers make an effort to schedule ethnographic encounters at different times to try and ensure fuller coverage of the field.

It can also be important to sample in terms of *context*. People's behaviour is influenced by situational and environmental factors, so they need to be observed in a variety of locations. For example, one of the important features of football fandom is that it is not solely located within stadiums. In order to understand the culture and lives of football fans, researchers such as Millward (2009) and Pearson (2009; 2012) had to ensure that they interacted with supporters not just around the time of football matches, but also in a variety of contexts (such as pubs and general socializing). This also meant interacting with them at different times. Pearson (2012) contrasts his experiences as a participant observer of supporters of both Blackpool and Manchester United football clubs and notes that one significant difference was that he was not a Blackpool resident whereas he did live in the Manchester area. He writes:

> I was now able to gain data about their behaviour outside the immediacy of the football match. Living locally gave me access to a wider and more varied life-world of some of the individuals . . . This gave me a much better idea of how their behaviour around football changed from their behaviour in other contexts.
>
> (Pearson 2012: 31)

17

Using more than one sampling approach

Purposive sampling can often involve using more than one of the approaches we have outlined. For example, it is quite common for snowball sampling to be preceded by another form of purposive sampling. In effect, the process involves sampling initial participants without using a snowball approach and then using these initial contacts to broaden the sample through a snowballing method. For example, Vasquez and Wetzel (2009) report the results of a study of racial identities among two ethnic groups in the USA. When collecting data on one of these groups—a First Nation tribe, the Potawatomi—the researchers collected data from an initial group of interviewees who they selected because they held formal positions within Citizen Potawatomi Nation. After this, the researchers used snowball sampling to broaden out the scope of the research, interviewing 113 individuals. The researchers initially selected individuals because they occupied a position relevant to the investigation (a generic purposive sample of individuals who met a criterion), and then used this primary sample to suggest further relevant participants to expand the research (a snowballing approach).

Another way of using more than one sampling approach is when researchers appear to aim for an element of both purposiveness and representativeness in their approach. Butler and Robson (2001), for example, aimed to interview 75 'gentrifiers' in each of three London areas and used the electoral register to locate individuals who could be identified as appropriate to their research. They write: 'we believe that our respondents are largely representative of the middle-class populations in each of our areas' (Butler and Robson 2001: 2148). For a study of hair salons and barbers, Cohen (2010) constructed an initial sample by listing all salons in the city by postcode and interviewing at least one person in each establishment. There was then a second more purposive stage where Cohen used data from the survey to select interviewees from four categories of salon that were relevant to the research questions: 'salons containing chair-renting, chain-salons, barbershops, and salons with primarily ethnic minority clients' (Cohen 2010: 204).

In Butler and Robson's study, the purposive element lies mainly in the search for areas with appropriate characteristics; in Cohen's research, it is evident in the way she built on to the initial sample with additional interviewees who were likely to be relevant to the research questions. At the same time, however, there is a strong sense that the researchers wanted to generate a sample with at least an appearance of representativeness. This is an interesting development, not least because it raises an interesting question that may lie behind the use of representativeness in these studies. In purposive sampling, it is often the case that multiple individuals (or whatever the **unit of analysis** is) will be eligible for inclusion. So, how do you decide which one or ones to include? Sampling with the intention of achieving some representativeness, as these researchers appear to have done, may be one way of making such a decision.

KEY POINTS

- Purposive sampling is the fundamental principle for selecting units and/or cases in qualitative research.
- Purposive sampling places the research questions at the forefront of sampling considerations.
- Understanding and identifying the different levels of sampling is integral to qualitative research.
- It is important to distinguish between theoretical sampling and the generic purposive sampling approach, though they are sometimes treated synonymously.
- Snowball sampling can be a useful way to generate a sufficient sample starting with only a few individuals.
- Theoretical saturation is a useful principle for making decisions about sample size, but there is evidence that it is often claimed rather than demonstrated.
- There is considerable disagreement about what is an acceptable minimum sample size.
- It is important to consider sampling in relation to context, as well as people.
- Combining different approaches to qualitative sampling can be very effective in terms of scope and representativeness.

QUESTIONS FOR REVIEW

1. How does purposive sampling differ from probability sampling, and why do many qualitative researchers prefer to use the former?
2. Why might it be significant to distinguish between the different levels at which sampling can take place in a qualitative research project?
3. Why is theoretical sampling such an important part of grounded theory?
4. How does theoretical sampling differ from the generic purposive sampling approach?
5. Why is theoretical saturation such an important component of theoretical sampling?
6. What are the challenges you might face if you adopt snowball sampling?
7. Why do writers disagree on the minimum acceptable sample size in qualitative research?
8. To what extent does theoretical sampling help qualitative researchers make decisions about sample size?
9. Why might it be important to remember in purposive sampling that it is not just people who are candidates for consideration in sampling issues?
10. How might it be useful to select people purposively following a survey?

ONLINE RESOURCES

www.oup.com/he/srm6e

You can find our notes on the answers to these questions within this chapter's **online resources**, together with:

- *audio/video comments* on this topic from our 'Learn from experience' panellists;
- *audio discussion from the authors* on how purposive sampling differs from probability sampling and why many qualitative researchers prefer to use the former (review question 1);
- *self-test questions* for further knowledge-checking;
- a *flashcard glossary* to help you recall key terms; and
- a *Student Researcher's Toolkit* containing practical materials and resources to help you conduct your own research project.

CHAPTER
18
ETHNOGRAPHY AND PARTICIPANT OBSERVATION

CHAPTER GUIDE

Ethnography and participant observation are forms of data collection that involve the researcher immersing themselves in the day-to-day practices of the human world. In this chapter we explore

- the problems of gaining access to different settings, and how such problems might be negotiated;
- the issue of whether a covert role is practicable and acceptable;
- the concept of key informants;
- the different kinds of roles that ethnographers can adopt 'in the field';
- the uses of field notes in ethnography;
- issues involved in 'leaving the field' and ending your research;
- the use of online ethnography;
- the role of visual materials in ethnography;
- feminist ethnography;
- writing ethnography;
- the changing meanings of 'ethnography'.

18.1 Introduction

Discussions about the merits and limitations of participant observation have been a fairly standard ingredient in textbooks on social research for many years. From the 1970s, the term 'ethnography' was increasingly used to describe the practice of observing participants. Before that, 'ethnography' was primarily associated with anthropological research, whereby the investigator visits a (usually) foreign land, gains access to a group (for example, a tribe or village), and spends a considerable amount of time (often many years) with that group, with the aim of uncovering its culture and writing about it. However, ethnography now has a far broader relevance, and for our purposes **ethnography** and **participant observation** refer to much the same thing. As a method of collecting data it is widely used across the social sciences, and it continues to change shape along with the research landscape.

18.2 What are ethnography and participant observation?

In Key concept 18.1 we have attempted to provide a working definition of ethnography, which can be broadly summarized as the process of joining a group, watching what goes on, making extensive notes, and writing it all up. However, ethnography is nowhere near as straightforward as this implies. The diversity of experiences that confront ethnographers—and the variety of ways in which they deal with them—make it difficult to generalize about the ethnographic process or provide recommendations about research practice:

> Every field situation *is* different and initial luck in meeting good informants, being in the right place at the right time, and striking the right note in relationships may be just as important as skill in technique. Indeed, many successful episodes in the field do come about through good luck as much as through sophisticated planning, and many unsuccessful episodes are due as much to bad luck as to bad judgement.
>
> (Sarsby 1984: 96)

It is important to be aware of these factors, but ethnography *does* require forethought, awareness, and reflection. It is exactly these kinds of issues that we will consider in the rest of this chapter. We will also reflect on ways in which ethnographic research can be conducted on a smaller scale, to fit the shorter time frame of a student project—known as a micro-ethnography (see Key concept 18.2).

KEY CONCEPT 18.1
What are ethnography and participant observation?

As Hammersley (2018) has noted, the term 'ethnography' has acquired a range of meanings and can take many different forms. But one way of beginning to think about what ethnography might mean is to consider how it might be similar to, and different from, participant observation.

Both require the participant observer/ethnographer to immerse themselves in a group for an extended period of time. Both call for the observation of behaviour in naturalistic settings, with particular reference to the meanings people give to things. This involves listening to what is said in conversations between others, as well as asking questions 'in the field'. Some people may prefer to use the term 'ethnography' because 'participant observation' seems to imply just the observation of participants, but actually both participant observers and ethnographers usually gather further data through more formal interviews and by collecting documents. However, ethnography is sometimes taken to refer to a study in which participant observation is the prevalent **research method**, but there is a specific focus on the *culture* of the group in which the ethnographer is immersed. The term 'ethnography' has additional meaning in that it often refers to both a method of research *and* the written product of that research.

In this book, we take ethnography to include participant observation and also to include the idea of ethnography as a written product of ethnographic research. We consider ethnography to mean a research method in which the researcher

- is immersed in a social setting for an extended period of time;
- makes regular observations of the behaviour of members of that setting;
- listens to and engages in conversations;
- interviews key participants (often referred to as informants) on issues that are not directly amenable to observation, or that the ethnographer is unclear about (note that in-depth interviews are a separate thing to both participant observation and ethnography);
- collects documents about, or relevant to, the group;
- seeks to develop an understanding of the culture of the group and people's behaviour within the context of that culture; and
- writes up a detailed account of that setting.

Notice that these features of ethnographic research touch on several preoccupations of **qualitative research** (as we describe them in Section 16.3), including the preference for seeing through the eyes of the people being studied and for taking a naturalistic stance.

KEY CONCEPT 18.2
Micro-ethnography

If you are doing research for a dissertation or a small project it is unlikely that you will be able to conduct a full-scale ethnography. Ethnographic research usually involves long periods of time in the field in an organization, as part of a community, or in the company of a group. However, it may be possible to carry out a form of **micro-ethnography** (Wolcott 1990b). This involves focusing on a particular aspect of everyday or professional life. For example, if you are interested in call centres, you might focus on the way staff manage to interact with each other and discuss work problems in spite of continuously receiving calls and being monitored. You would only need to spend a relatively short period of time (from a couple of weeks to a few months) in the organization—on either a full-time or a part-time basis—to study such a tightly defined topic.

18

18.3 Doing ethnography

Let's move on to the ethnographic research process. In this section we will consider the issues involved in gaining access to a research setting, the role of the ethnographic researcher, the practice of taking **field notes**, and how to end an ethnographic study.

Gaining access to a research setting

One of the first—and also one of the most difficult—steps in conducting ethnographic research is gaining access to a social setting that is relevant to the research problem. But research sites have several dimensions that influence how they can be approached. One of these is whether the setting is relatively open or closed (Bell 1969). Hammersley and Atkinson (2019) make a similar distinction when they refer to public and non-public settings (see also Lofland and Lofland 1995). Closed, non-public settings usually require some form of permission to access them and are likely to be organizations of various kinds. This includes professional organizations, schools, religious movements, and so on. Open/public settings, on the other hand, can be freely accessed by anyone without the need for informal or formal permission. This might include parks, sporting matches, or community events.

Overt versus covert ethnography

Another issue to consider when doing ethnography is whether to conduct **overt research** or **covert research**. Adopting an *overt* strategy requires the researcher to be open about the fact that they are conducting research, whereas taking a *covert* position means not disclosing the fact that you are a researcher. The latter removes many of the problems associated with gaining access to a setting, as there is no need to negotiate access or to explain why you want to intrude into people's lives and make them objects of study.

Using this distinction in combination with the distinction between open and closed settings, Bell (1969) identifies four types of ethnographic approach. These are shown in Table 18.1.

There are three points to note about Bell's typology:

1. The distinction between an open/public setting and a closed one is not rigid.
2. There is also a lack of clarity in terms of what constitutes an overt or covert approach.
3. There tend to be more type 1 and 2 studies than type 3 and 4.

Let's consider these points in turn.

It can be hard to draw a clear distinction between an open/public setting and a closed one because some settings can have both qualities. Gaining access to open groups can have a near-formal quality, such as having to reassure a community leader about the aims of the research. In contrast, organizations that are usually closed can sometimes create contexts that have a public character, such as meetings arranged for members or prospective recruits by social organizations such as religious groups or political movements.

18

There are similarly blurred lines between overt and covert strategies. For example, an ethnographer may seek access through an overt route but might come into contact with many people who are not aware of the ethnographer's status as a researcher. Cassidy's (2014) ethnographic research in London betting shops was not covert, but she notes that 'it is possible that some of the people I observed in shops were unaware of the reason for my presence' (2014: 172). Another interesting case is a study by Glucksmann (1994), who in the 1970s left her academic post to work on a factory assembly line in order to explore the reasons why **feminism** appeared not to be relevant to working-class women. In a sense, she was a covert observer, but her motives for the research were primarily political, and she says that at the time she was undertaking the research she had no intention of writing the book that subsequently appeared and that was published under a pseudonym (Cavendish 1982). After the book's publication, it was treated as an example of ethnographic research. Was she an overt or a covert observer (or neither, or both)?

TABLE 18.1
Four forms of ethnography

	Open/public setting	Closed setting
Overt role	*Type 1*	*Type 2*
Covert role	*Type 3*	*Type 4*

We have said that studies of Types 1 and 2 tend to be more numerous than Types 3 and 4. This reflects the fact that ethnographers are far more likely to adopt an overt role than a covert one. For this reason, most of our discussion of access issues will focus on ethnographers aiming to employ an overt role, but it is worth our briefly reflecting on the value of the covert role in ethnography. The advantages of this strategy include the following.

- *The problem of securing access is greatly reduced*. Adopting a covert role largely removes the access problem, because the researcher does not have to seek permission to gain entry to a social setting or organization.
- ***Reactivity** is not a problem*. Using a covert role reduces reactivity (see Research in focus 12.4) because participants do not know the person conducting the study is a researcher. Therefore, they are less likely to adjust their behaviour because of the researcher's presence.

There are, however, many disadvantages to covert research.

- *The problem of taking notes*. As Ditton (1977; see Research in focus 18.1) discovered, it is difficult to take notes in circumstances where people do not realize you are conducting research. Notes are very important to an ethnographer and it can be risky to rely exclusively on memory. For his covert research on Blackpool Football Club supporters, Pearson writes that he tried to write up the bulk of his observations as soon as possible after a match but he acknowledges that 'much useful data was almost certainly forgotten' (2012: 28; see also Research in focus 18.2 for another example of difficulties with writing up while researching).
- *The problem of not being able to use other methods*. Ethnography often involves using several methods, but if the research is covert it is difficult to steer conversations in a certain direction for fear of detection, so more formal in-depth interviews are essentially impossible.

- *Anxiety*. The covert ethnographer is under constant threat of being discovered, and if they are found out, the whole research project may be jeopardized. Ethnography can be a stressful research method, and worries about detection can add to those anxieties.
- *Ethical problems*. Covert observation goes against a number of important ethical principles. It does not provide participants with the opportunity for **informed consent** (allowing them the chance to agree or disagree to participate on the basis of information supplied to them) and it necessarily requires deception. It can also be seen as a violation of the principle of privacy. This is potentially damaging to research participants; moreover, some writers, such as Warwick (1982), also take the view that covert approaches can harm the reputation of social research, particularly where researchers are identified by the public as snoopers or voyeurs. For these reasons, covert ethnography is not very common within student-led research. We consider ethical issues in greater detail in Chapter 6.

It is understandable that these disadvantages dissuade many ethnographers from taking a covert approach, but in some circumstances an overt approach may not be practical, such as if you were conducting an ethnography where large groups of people are present. In other circumstances the overt/covert distinction may be a matter of degree. While Mattley (2006) describes herself as having been a covert participant observer when she worked for and conducted ethnographic research on a sex fantasy phone line, she writes: 'I decided that I would be open about who I am, but not why I wanted to be hired' (2006: 144). Part of the way through the research, her supervisor suggested she should do a study of the callers. She asked the owner of the business about whether she could do this and he agreed, declining her offer to let him read anything she wanted to write about the work prior to publication. As he graphically put it: 'I hate to read that fucking stuff, I trust you, you won't fuck me over' (Mattley 2006: 146). However, with respect to her callers, Mattley was still a covert participant observer.

Access to closed settings

One of the key difficulties of doing research in closed or non-public settings is the issue of access. Van Maanen and Kolb (1985: 11) observe that 'gaining access to most organizations is not a matter to be taken lightly but one that involves some combination of strategic planning, hard work and dumb luck'. The researcher might

RESEARCH IN FOCUS 18.1
The difficulties of covert observation

Though it was conducted some time ago, Ditton's (1977) research on 'fiddling' (taking money dishonestly) in a bakery still provides an interesting and entertaining illustration of the difficulties associated with covert observation:

> Nevertheless, I *was* able to develop personal covert participant-observation skills. Right from the start, I found it impossible to keep everything that I wanted to remember in my head until the end of the working day. . . . and so had to take rough notes as I was going along. But I was stuck 'on the line', and had nowhere to retire to privately to jot things down. Eventually, the wheeze of using innocently provided lavatory cubicles occurred to me. Looking back, all my notes for that third summer were on Bronco toilet paper! Apart from the awkward tendency for pencilled notes to be self-erasing from hard toilet paper . . . my frequent requests for 'time out' after interesting happenings or conversations in the bakehouse and the amount of time I was spending in the lavatory began to get noticed. I had to pacify some genuinely concerned workmates, give up totally undercover operations, and 'come out' as an observer—albeit in a limited way. I eventually began to scribble notes more openly, but still not in front of people when they were talking. When questioned about this, as I was occasionally, I coyly said that I was writing things down that occurred to me about 'my studies'.
>
> (Ditton 1977: 5)

Although he still maintained some covert elements, Ditton was forced to move from covert to more overt observations because of the practical difficulties he encountered. In terms of the distinctions in Table 18.1, Ditton moved from a Type 4 to a Type 2 form of ethnography.

18

use several criteria to select a particular social setting as a site for ethnographic investigation, and they should determine these criteria based on the general research area in which they are interested. While there are no guarantees of instant success in terms of negotiating access, and rejection is a possibility that might require a rethink, it is crucial to be determined in your efforts if you want to study a specific organization or group. Sometimes sheer perseverance pays off. In his ethnography of Italian football supporters, known as the Ultrà, Guschwan used a number of strategies to access the people he was researching:

> Some of the work of ethnography is social 'grunt work' as one must keep showing up and pestering people in order to meet people and to expand one's social network. Some contacts lead nowhere. At other times, good timing and luck lead to productive contacts. The internet has made some networking easier. I gained entry into one fan group simply by responding to an advertisement on their website that invited anyone interested to meet them for a banquet.
>
> (Guschwan 2017: 983)

However, with many research questions, several potential research sites are likely to meet your criteria, so it is often a case of trying different tactics to secure access. These strategies might include the following.

- Using friends, contacts, colleagues, and academics to help you gain access. Provided that the organization is relevant to your **research question**, the route into it should not matter.
- Trying to get the support of someone within the organization who will act as your champion by vouching for you and the value of your research. These people are sometimes referred to in the literature as taking the role of 'sponsors' or 'advocates'.
- Getting access through top management or senior executives. Even though you may secure a certain level of agreement lower down the hierarchy, you will usually need clearance from the top management. Such senior people act as '**gatekeepers**'.
- Offering something in return (for example, a report). This strategy—often referred to as 'the research bargain'—carries risks in that it may turn you into a cheap consultant and may result in restrictions on your activities, such as insistence on seeing what you write. However, it helps to create a sense of being *trustworthy*. Some writers on research methodology do not recommend this approach, but it is common among researchers on formal organizations. Our panellist Sarah's voluntary work with the women she was studying is an example of this tactic—see Learn from experience 18.1.

18

LEARN FROM EXPERIENCE 18.1
The role of the 'research bargain' in securing access to a research setting

The 'research bargain' is sometimes used by ethnographers to help them better engage with the fieldwork site, but also to help give something back to the individuals, group, or community that are offering their time to the researcher. Sarah, for example, describes how she volunteered as a support worker to help those she was researching in her postgraduate project.

> In an effort to build rapport and get to know the barriers that Pakistani Muslim lone mothers experience in everyday life, I chose to take on an active role by supporting them as a volunteer support worker. After a few observation sessions, the lone mothers began to engage with me and we interacted with each other more and more. For example, on busy occasions I would help the key worker contact the services that their clients were required to engage with. But one difficulty in being such an active participant was that I often found myself more concerned with solving the task at hand (e.g. creating a CV), so it was difficult to fully concentrate on observing as a researcher. Balancing my role as a volunteer with my role of researcher needed careful reflection to ensure that I could do both effectively.
>
> Sarah

 Access the **online resources** to hear Sarah's video reflections on this theme.

You can read about our panellists' backgrounds and research experiences on page xxvi.

- Providing a clear explanation of your aims and methods and being prepared to deal with concerns. Suggest a meeting that will enable you to discuss any worries the people involved may have and to provide an explanation of what you intend to do in a manner that can be easily understood by others.
- Being prepared to negotiate—you will want complete access, but it is unlikely you will be given free rein to do exactly what you want.
- Trying to be reasonably honest about the amount of people's time you are likely to take up. This is a question you will almost certainly be asked if you are seeking access to commercial organizations, but it will come up for many not-for-profit ones too.

Access to open/public settings

Gaining access to public settings can also be problematic, and many of these difficulties are similar in nature to those involved in gaining access to closed settings. One is recognizing that open *physical* access to a research site is not the same as having *social* access to it. We can see an example of this in Whyte's (1955) classic **case study** *Street Corner Society*, when he was trying to make contacts during his early days in the field in Boston's North End. The following incident occurred in a hotel bar:

> I looked around me again and now noticed a [group consisting of] one man and two women. It occurred to me that here was a maldistribution of females which I might be able to rectify. I approached the group and opened with something like this: 'Pardon me. Would you mind if I join you?' There was a moment of silence while the man stared at me. He then offered to throw me downstairs. I assured him that this would not be necessary and demonstrated as much by walking right out of there without any assistance.
>
> (Whyte 1955: 289)

Whyte was able to enter the hotel as he pleased, but actually talking to and getting to know the other customers proved to be much more difficult. Hardie-Bick (2017) experienced similar issues with gaining meaningful access to a research setting that was seemingly open and just required 'turning up'—see Research in focus 18.2.

There are two common methods of gaining access to groups—via gatekeepers and via acquaintances who then act as sponsors or advocates for the research. Sometimes, ethnographers will be able to have social access facilitated by particular **key informants** who act as sponsor, gatekeeper, and participant. In Whyte's case, the role played by an informant known as 'Doc' has become the stuff of ethnographic legend. Doc immersed Whyte in the 'corner boy' culture by introducing him to key participants, involving him in special activities, and even helping him to collect and interpret data. This is why subsequent ethnographers are often tempted to seek out a Doc type of character when attempting to gain access to a group.

RESEARCH IN FOCUS 18.2
Access to open public settings

Hardie-Bick (2011; Hardie-Bick and Bonner 2016; Hardie-Bick and Scott 2017) carried out an ethnography in a relatively open and public research setting in order to 'explore the values, norms, behaviour and experiences that typify the social world of skydiving' (2017: 248). Over the course of 15 months of fieldwork at a parachute centre in the UK, he adopted both covert and overt strategies in order to collect his data. He states that '[t]o a certain extent gaining access to the local parachute centre was simply a matter of "turning up" and enrolling on one of the training courses. Nevertheless, access is rarely as straightforward as it may initially appear. Simply turning up was only the first stage of a complex and drawn-out process gaining access to this research setting' (2017: 249).

Enrolling on a training course, he initially planned to adopt a covert strategy because he did not want to be treated differently or cause unnecessary suspicion. However, this led to some difficulties. First, he was only able to access settings that his student status allowed. Secondly, he struggled to make good field notes as he had to store up memories and recall them later. Thirdly, he experienced constant low-level anxiety at the prospect of being discovered. After nine weeks, these stressors eventually led him to 'go overt'. Unfortunately, while some participants were enthusiastic, others then viewed him with suspicion. We can make three observations about Hardie-Bick's experiences: that open access isn't the same as social access; that there are various different ways to conduct ethnography in an open setting, depending on the circumstances of the setting and your relationship to those being observed; and that it can be possible to swap from covert to overt roles.

Another example of gaining access by gradually identifying gatekeepers is Ernst's (2014) ethnography of Los Caballeros Templarios (LCT), a group associated with organized crime in western Mexico. Ernst took a very flexible approach, actively seeking out people who were not involved with any illegal activity but could provide valuable information about the group. This approach eventually led to him meeting someone who was prepared to act as a gatekeeper and introduce him to members of LCT.

In seeking access to access to animal rights activists, Upton (2011) consciously used a gatekeeper strategy. He was able to gain access to monthly meetings of one group, and at his first meeting he met 'Emma' who he believed might be convinced to act as a gatekeeper. Although initially unenthusiastic about Upton's research, she did provide some contacts and as a result he was able to observe some protest demonstrations.

As we noted in 'Access to closed settings', ethnographers might also gain access by striking a research bargain, in other words by offering something in return or agreeing to do something in return. Sallaz (2009) managed to secure access to a casino in South Africa in part because the person who was acting as gatekeeper wanted him to be his 'eyes and ears' in the casino, though in fact Sallaz developed various ways of not meeting his 'obligations'.

'Hanging around' is another common strategy to gain access. It usually involves loitering in an area until you are noticed and gradually accepted into a group. This was roughly the approach Whyte (1955) took, which nearly led to the incident with a staircase. Wolf (1991) used a hanging-around strategy to access outlaw bikers in Canada. On one occasion he met a group of them at a motorcycle shop and expressed an interest in 'hanging around' with them, but he tried to move too quickly and his efforts to join the gang were rebuffed. His determination did eventually pay off, though, as he was approached by the leader of a biker group (Rebels MC) who acted as his sponsor. As a part of the process of gaining physical and social access, Wolf had to make sure that he was properly dressed. Attention to dress and general appearance can be a very important consideration when seeking access to either public or closed settings.

18

Ongoing access

As these examples suggest, gaining access to social settings is a crucial first step in ethnographic research. Without access, you simply cannot move forward with your research plans. However, the need to gain access does not stop when you have made contact and gained entry to the group. You still need access to *people*. As we have noted, physical access is not the same as social access, and there is a difference between being present and being accepted.

One potential issue is that people might have suspicions about you and your motives, and have concerns about what will happen to the information they give you. They may, for example, see you as an instrument of management or a local or government official. When Baird (2018) approached potential participants for his research on how Colombian gang members negotiate violence, he was quick to say 'Hey! I work at a University, not for the police or nothin' (2018: 343). You don't have to talk to me or if you don't want to talk to me, no sweat'. In her research on the British on the Costa del Sol, O'Reilly (2000) was similarly suspected of being from the UK's Department of Social Security and of being a tax inspector. People may also worry that you will report things they say or do to bosses, to colleagues, or to peers in other kinds of environment. Van Maanen (1991a) notes from his research on the police that if you conduct ethnographic research among officers, you are likely to observe activities that may be deeply discrediting and even illegal. Your credibility among police officers will be determined by your reactions to these situations and events.

If people have these worries, they may go along with your research to influence your findings, or in some cases actively work to sabotage your project by engaging in deception or misinformation, or not allowing you access to 'back regions' (Goffman 1956).

However, there are things that you can do to facilitate ongoing access.

- *Talk up your credentials*. Use your past work experience and your knowledge of the group, community, or organization to reassure people; familiarize yourself with their problems. If you are taking a covert approach, make sure you have thought about ways in which people's suspicions can be allayed. You will need a 'front', as Ditton (1977; Research in focus 18.1) had when referring to 'his studies'. Similarly, in his research on Columbian gangs, Baird (2018) simply said that he was doing research for a book.
- *Be discreet and open-minded*. Try not to make judgements when things are said to you about informal activities or about the organization; make sure information given to you does not get back to others, whether bosses or peers. For example, when researching gang members in a poor community, Horowitz (Gerson and Horowitz 2002) writes that she was frequently told 'confidential' stories that turned out to be fictional, to determine whether she could keep a secret.

- *Be prepared for checks of competence or credibility.* Upton (2011) was asked, in front of other animal rights protestors, where he stood on animal rights and animal testing. He answered that he was able to see both sides and admitted that he did believe in animal testing in medical experiments, explaining that a chemotherapy treatment that would have been tested on animals helped to prolong the life of his father, who was suffering from gallbladder cancer, by eight months. His frankness appears to have been reassuring and was almost certainly more effective than an insincere answer of support. O'Brien (2010) conducted participant observation research as a female bouncer in several clubs and felt that sometimes the male bouncers used 'overtly sexualized behaviour' towards her as a means of testing her suitability for the work.
- *Consider whether you need to find a role in the group.* If your research involves quite a lot of participant observation, the role will be part of your position in their world; otherwise, you will need to construct a 'front' using your clothing and your explanations about what you are doing there, and by helping out occasionally with work or offering advice. Be consistent—do not behave ambiguously or inconsistently.
- *Be prepared for changes in circumstances.* Guschwan (2017) found that when he tried to revisit one of the Ultrà groups that he was researching, they had simply vanished due to their alleged ties with the Mafia. This meant that he needed to find another site for his research.

Key informants

An ethnographer relies a lot on informants, but certain informants may become particularly important during the research process. These **key informants** often develop an appreciation of the research and direct the ethnographer to situations, events, or people likely to be helpful to the progress of the investigation. Whyte (1955), for example, reports that his key informant 'Doc' said to him: 'You tell me what you want to see, and we'll arrange it. When you want some information, I'll ask for it, and you listen. When you want to find out their philosophy of life, I'll start an argument and get it for you. If there's something else you want to get, I'll stage an act for you' (Whyte 1955: 292). Doc was also helpful in warning Whyte that he was asking too many questions, when he told him to 'go easy on that "who," "what," "why," "when," "where," stuff' (Whyte 1955: 303). Key informants can clearly be a big help to the ethnographer, but it is important to be aware of the risks of working with them. The ethnographer may develop an excessive reliance on the key informant, and might begin to see social reality through the eyes of the informant rather than through the eyes of members of the social setting.

Often, the ethnographer will not rely on a single person—they will come across many people who will act as informants. These informants will provide solicited or unsolicited accounts (Hammersley and Atkinson 2019). Solicited accounts can occur in two ways: by interview (see Chapter 19) or by casual questioning during conversations—though in ethnographic research the boundary between an interview and a conversation is not always clear-cut, as Burgess (1984) points out. When the ethnographer needs specific information about an issue that cannot easily be directly observed or that is not cropping up during 'natural' conversations, solicited accounts are likely to be the only way forward.

Some researchers prefer unsolicited accounts, because of their greater spontaneity and naturalism. Research participants often develop a sense of the kinds of events or encounters the ethnographer wants to see. Armstrong (1993) says that while he was doing research on the Blades, a group of supporters of Sheffield United Football Club who were engaged in hooligan activity, he would sometimes get tip-offs:

> 'We're all gonna' Leeds in a couple o' weeks. . . . four coaches, Pond Street, town centre. If you're serious about this study you'll be down there on one of 'em.' I often travelled on the same coach as Ray [an informant]; he would then sit with me at matches and in pubs and point out Blades, giving me background information. Sometimes he would start conversations with Blades about incidents which he knew I wanted to know about and afterwards would ask 'Did you get all that down then?' . . . There was never one particular informant; rather, there were many Blades I could ring up and meet at any time, who were part of the core and would always welcome a beer and a chat about 'It', or tell me who I 'ought to 'ave a word wi''.
>
> (Armstrong 1993: 24–5)

But again, there are downsides to such tip-offs. While unsolicited sources of information are attractive to ethnographers, as Hammersley and Atkinson (2019) observe, they may on occasion be staged for the benefit of the researcher.

The roles of the ethnographic researcher

Related to the issue of ongoing access (or relationships in the field, as it is sometimes called) is the kind of role the ethnographer adopts while in the field. This includes the extent to which they adopt a covert or overt strategy, and whether they are a passive observer or active participant.

Field roles

Researchers have identified a number of different roles that can be taken 'in the field' (Gold 1958; Gans 1968; Adler and Adler 1987). These classifications usually focus on the degree of involvement of the ethnographer in the social world they are researching. Table 18.2 attempts to summarize some of the underlying features of these classifications. It distinguishes six role types and is a reasonably exhaustive list. Most ethnographic roles can be more or less incorporated under one of these types. You will notice that roles involving higher levels of participation tend to rely more heavily on observation rather than interviewing and/or examining documents; those with lower levels of participation usually rely more on interviewing and/or documents and less on observation.

Each role carries its own advantages and risks. The roles of full member (covert and overt) and participating observer carry the risk that the researcher may over-identify with the group and 'go native' (see Key concept 18.3), but they offer the researcher the opportunity to get close to people and gain a more complete understanding of their culture and values. However, the role an ethnographer takes is not only a matter of choice—it might, for example, be determined by their own characteristics, knowledge, or abilities. Not everyone has the physical credentials to be a full member as a bouncer (Calvey 2019), a basketball player (Rogers 2019), or a fashion model (Mears 2011). Equally, it would have been very difficult for someone like Gusterson (1996; see Thinking deeply 18.4) to gain full-member access for his study of a nuclear weapons laboratory.

Ethnographers often move between roles at different times during the research process (see Research in focus 18.2). Skeggs (1994) appears to have begun her research as a participating observer. She was supplementing her research grant with some part-time teaching and gradually got to know her students—a group of young working-class women (eventually there were 83 of them) whom she realized were very relevant to the research project that she was planning.

> Over a period of three years [1980–83] I did the research by spending as much time as I could with the young women. . . . I traced the trajectories of the young women through the educational system and asked them for biographical details. . . . I also conducted formal and informal interviews and meetings with family members, friends, partners and college teachers. . . . Obviously, it was physically impossible to do intensive participant observation with all eighty-three of them all of the time, so during the three years, I concentrated on different groups at different times.
>
> (Skeggs 1994: 72, 73)

TABLE 18.2
Field roles and participation in ethnographic research

Type	Description of role
Covert full member	Full membership of group, but the researcher's status as a researcher is unknown. In closed settings such as organizations, the researcher works as a paid employee for the group. The researcher may already be employed in the organization or may get a job there in order to conduct the research. In open settings, such as communities, the researcher moves to the area for a significant length of time or, like Hardie-Bick (see Research in focus 18.2), uses a pre-existing identity as a means of becoming a full member for the purposes of research.
Overt full member	Full membership of group but the researcher's status as a researcher is known. In other respects, this is the same as a covert full member.
Participating observer	Researcher participates in group's core activities but not as a full member. In closed settings such as organizations the researcher works for the group, either on an occasional basis or as part of a research bargain to gain entry or acceptance; in open settings, the researcher is a regular in the vicinity and is generally involved in the main activities.
Partially participating observer	Same as participating observer, but observation is not necessarily the main data source. Interviews and documents can be as significant as the observation or even more so.
Minimally participating observer	Researcher observes but participates minimally in group's core activities. They interact with group members but observation may or may not be the main source of data. When it is not the main source of data, interviews and documents play a prominent role.
Non-participating observer with interaction	Researcher observes (sometimes minimally) but does not participate in group's core activities. Interaction with group members occurs, but often tends to be through interviews which, along with documents, are usually the main source of data.

KEY CONCEPT 18.3
What is 'going native'?

Sometimes ethnographers lose their sense of being a researcher and become wrapped up in the worldview of the people they are studying. This is often termed 'going native'. The problem is usually associated with prolonged immersion in the lives of the people ethnographers study and a general commitment to seeing the social world through their eyes.

This is a potential problem for several reasons, but especially because in losing sight of their position as an independent researcher, the ethnographer loses the ability to critically reflect on the collection and analysis of data. When Hobbs (1988: 6) writes in connection with his fieldwork on entrepreneurship in London's East End that he 'often had to remind [himself] that [he] was not in a pub to enjoy [himself] but to conduct an academic inquiry, and repeatedly woke up the following morning with an incredible hangover facing the dilemma of whether to bring it up or write it up', he may have been close to going native.

However, not all researchers see going native as a necessarily bad thing. Wacquant (2009), for example, who researched the world of boxing, describes his position as 'go native, but *go native armed*' (2009: 145). What he means by this is not losing one's perspective as (in his case) a sociologist and therefore making sure that he uses the discipline's full set of theoretical and methodological skills to study the field site. Wacquant refers to his awareness of *habitus*, a sociological term referring to the norms, values, attitudes, and behaviours of a particular social group:

> Go ahead, go native, but come back a sociologist. In my case, the concept of habitus served as both a bridge to enter the factory of pugilistic know-how and methodically parse the texture of the work(ing) world of the pugilist, and as a shield against the lure of the subjectivist rollover of social analysis into narcissistic story-telling.
>
> (Wacquant 2009: 145)

In other words, the ethnographer should immerse themselves in the world of their participants, without losing their sense of perspective. Wacquant actually took up amateur boxing to fully experience the world of the boxer, but always remained a sociologist.

Skeggs adds that the 'time spent doing the ethnography was so intense that the boundary between my life inside and outside the research dissolved' (1994: 73). After the initial study she 'followed the women's progress through further interviews in 1985, 1989 and 1992' (1994: 73). This suggests that she moved into something closer to the role of a non-participating observer with interaction.

Even if it were possible to adopt a single ethnographic role over the entire course of a project, this probably would not be desirable. It would limit the researcher's flexibility in handling situations and people, and there would be serious risks of excessive involvement or excessive detachment. The role an ethnographer adopts is also likely to have implications for their capacity to penetrate the surface layers of an organization. One of the strengths of organizational ethnography is that it offers the prospect of being able to find out what an organization is 'really' like, as opposed to how it formally depicts itself. For example, Humphreys conducted ethnographic research in the UK headquarters of a US bank to which he gave the pseudonym Credit Line (Humphreys and Watson 2009). He was aware of the firm's commitment to corporate social responsibility but became increasingly conscious that, although people working in the organization were publicly enthusiastic about its ethical stance, many were privately sceptical about the firm's actual commitment. For example, he quotes one employee (Charity) as saying:

> My problem is that, in this organization, corporate social responsibility is a sham—it's just rhetoric—I mean how can we call ourselves responsible when we give credit cards to poor people and charge them 30 per cent APR [annual percentage rate] just because they are high risk?
>
> (quoted in Humphreys and Watson 2009: 50)

For employees to share private views that reflect negatively on their organization, the ethnographer will probably need to become something of a confidant, so that organizational participants feel confident that what they say will not get back to senior managers.

Active or passive?

Whichever role(s) the ethnographer assumes, they need to consider the degree to which they should or can be an active or a passive participant (Van Maanen 1978). Even when the ethnographer is in a predominantly non-observing role, there may be some contexts in which either participation is unavoidable or they feel compelled to become involved in a limited way, meaning that they become a minimally participating observer (see Table 18.2). In many instances, the researcher has no choice as to the extent of their participation. If the researcher takes on the job of a bouncer, for example, they cannot opt to passively observe fights, as stopping them is likely to be a major part of their role (Calvey 2019). In contrast, researchers who do ethnographic research on the police are unlikely to be able to be active participants beyond offering fairly trivial assistance—unless they are an existing member of the police and a covert observer like Holdaway (1982), or take steps to become a police officer like Rubinstein (1973). Punch's field notes in connection with his research on the police in Amsterdam illustrate this kind of necessarily minimal participation:

> Tom wanted to move the cars which were blocking the narrow and busy street in front of the station, and said sternly to the suspect, but with a smile at me behind his back, 'You stay here with your hands up and don't try anything because this detective here [pointing at me] is keeping an eye on you.' I frowned authoritatively.
>
> (Punch 1979: 8)

Sometimes, ethnographers may feel they have no choice but to get involved, because a failure to participate actively might indicate a lack of commitment and lead to a loss of credibility among members of the social setting. For example, Baird's (2018) study of youth violence in Medellín, Colombia, relied on **semi-structured interviews** with gang members, but he found himself in situations where he felt as though he had to collude with gang members because he needed to retain access and he feared for his safety. Ryan (2009) conducted research on commercial cleaning in Australia and found that being prepared to help cleaners with some of their tasks helped to build up his credibility and made them more prepared to be interviewed by him. In the course of her study of a restaurant, Demetry (2013; see Research in focus 16.2) also found it difficult to find a suitable point at which to observe, partly because she would often get in the way of the various staff as they frantically moved around trying to satisfy diners' needs. She began to involve herself with the working practices of the restaurant and relayed messages, carried dishes, and even on one occasion assisted with meal preparation. Like Ryan, she suggests that this may have helped to establish rapport with her subjects.

However, participation in group activities can lead to dilemmas for ethnographers, especially when the activities in which they actively take part (or might do so) are illegal or dangerous (see Research in focus 18.3). Many writers argue against active participation in criminal or dangerous activities (Polsky 1967) and both Armstrong (1993) and Giulianotti (1995) refused to participate in fights while doing research into football hooliganism. On the other hand, Pearson (2012: 33) admits that he sometimes committed offences. There is a strong argument against conducting covert research on criminals or those involved in dangerous activities because it is much more difficult for someone in such a role not to participate.

One final point to make is that the roles that ethnographers take on will probably be influenced by emotions—

RESEARCH IN FOCUS 18.3
Active ethnography

In the context of his study of 'entrepreneurship' (a euphemism for several kinds of legal and illegal activity) among East Enders in London, Hobbs (1988) admits that he was an active participant to the extent of engaging in illegal activities:

> A refusal, or worse still an enquiry concerning the legal status of the 'parcel', would provoke an abrupt conclusion to the relationship. Consequently, I was willing to skirt the boundaries of criminality on several occasions, and I considered it crucial to be willingly involved in 'normal' business transactions, legal or otherwise. I was pursuing an interactive, inductive study of an entrepreneurial culture, and in order to do so I had to display entrepreneurial skills myself. . . . [My] status as an insider meant that I was afforded a great deal of trust by my informants, and I was allowed access to settings, detailed conversations, and information that might not otherwise have been available.
>
> (Hobbs 1988: 7, 15)

THINKING DEEPLY 18.1
Emotion and fieldwork

Fieldwork sites are not just places for data collection, they are emotional landscapes that both researcher and researched experience in a variety of ways. Researchers may experience enthusiasm at the start of the project; they may feel happiness when they successfully engage with the field, and frustration when they don't; they may develop affection for some of the actors in the field, and dislike for others; they may feel mentally and physically exhausted toward the end of the engagement; they may feel sadness (or happiness) at leaving it and its people. Conducting her research in a large London cemetery, Woodthorpe (2011) notes how her emotional reaction to the people she met there became a problem:

> Over time my reluctance to approach certain people became a great source of anxiety. Was I being methodical enough in how I asked visitors to participate? Was I skewing my sample with the people I felt confident in approaching? These uncertainties started to impact on fieldwork more generally, as I found myself gradually becoming more and more uneasy approaching and talking to visitors . . . On some days observing children's graves or witnessing parents around my age attend a grave would move me to tears and render me 'out of action' for some time (at best half an hour, at worst the rest of the day). On one occasion, I was so touched by a man's careful and concentrated nurturing of a flowerpot by a grave that I had to leave the cemetery for a short while.
>
> (Woodthorpe 2011: 104)

both their own and those of their participants—because emotions are implicitly intertwined with the research process. We discuss this idea further in Thinking deeply 18.1.

Taking field notes

Because of the frailties of human memory, ethnographers have to take notes based on their observations. These should be fairly detailed summaries of events and behaviour and the researcher's initial reflections on them. The notes need to specify key **dimensions** of whatever is observed or heard.

Strategies for taking field notes

There are five general principles to bear in mind when producing field notes.

1. *Speed is key.* Write down notes, however brief, as quickly as possible after seeing or hearing something interesting, so that you do not forget important details. Many people find it useful to record initial notes digitally, perhaps on their phone, but be aware that this will mean that you need to transcribe a lot of speech (although there are digital applications that transcribe speech—we discuss these in the context of interviewing in Section 19.4 and in Thinking deeply 19.1).
2. *Notes must be vivid, clear, and detailed.* You should not have to ask at a later date 'what did I mean by that?' Include such details as the location, who was involved, what prompted the exchange or activity, and the date and time of the day.
3. *Include your feelings about occasions and people.* These notes may be helpful for formulating a **reflexive** account of fieldwork. Czarniawska (2007) provides a lot of field notes in connection with a study in Warsaw of a company she calls Big City Management. She sought to shadow a finance director who was uncooperative, and her notes are revealing as much for the self-doubt and anxiety about her research skills as for the substantive findings she conveyed.
4. *Include your initial analysis.* Your initial analytic thoughts about what you have observed and heard are likely to be valuable, as they may act as a springboard for theoretical elaboration of the data.
5. *If in doubt, write it down!*

It is very useful to write your notes straight away—that is, as soon as something interesting happens. However, wandering around with a notebook and pencil in hand, continuously scribbling notes down, may make people self-conscious. It may be necessary, therefore, to take small amounts of time out of sight to quickly record events, though hopefully without generating the anxieties Ditton (1977) appears to have suffered from (see Research in focus 18.1).

Strategies for taking field notes are affected by the degree to which the ethnographer enters the field with clear research questions—and whatever you do write down needs to reflect your research focus in some way. As we discussed in Chapter 16, most qualitative research begins with general research questions, but there is considerable variation in how specific those questions are. Obviously, where the question is clearly defined from the outset, ethnographers have to align their observations with that research focus, but at the same time they need to maintain a fairly open mind so as to maintain the element of flexibility that is a strength of qualitative research (see Thinking deeply 18.2).

Reflecting on his ethnography of tattooists in the USA, Sanders (2009) writes that he was not motivated to conduct his study in order to answer a research question; instead, he writes, 'Concepts, theories, research questions, hypotheses, and other abstract intellectual scaffolding arise from the experiences I share with people in the field and the things they tell me' (Sanders 2009: 65). Similarly, Armstrong (1993: 12) writes of his research on football hooliganism that it 'began without a focus' and as a result he 'decided to record everything'. A typical Saturday would result in thirty pages of handwritten notes. Such detailed recording of open-ended observation usually cannot be maintained for long, because trying to record the details of absolutely everything is very time-consuming and can quickly produce an overwhelming amount of data. Usually the ethnographer will begin to narrow down the focus of their research and to match observations to the emerging research focus.

THINKING DEEPLY 18.2
Research questions in ethnographic research

As we noted in Chapter 16, research questions in qualitative research, and in ethnographic research in particular, are usually open-ended. This often means that field notes can begin in a very broad, all-encompassing manner, but get more and more refined during the ethnography and as the research questions come into focus. However, the extent to which this is the case varies considerably.

Anderson (2006) provides a fascinating account of the background to his participant observation research into the lives of Black street-corner men in Chicago in the 1970s (Anderson 1978). This study focused on the lives and habits of clients of 'Jelly's'—a drinking venue that acted as both a bar and a store for the sale of alcoholic drinks. Similarly to Sanders (2009) and Armstrong (1993), Anderson suggests that he 'had absolutely no idea where the research would lead' and had in mind 'no explicit sociological problem or question' (2006: 40). Indeed, he writes that 'this open-ended approach was a conscious act', arguing that to go in with a pre-designed set of issues 'could preclude certain lines of enquiry that might prove valuable later' (2006: 40). Gradually, the research questions emerged: 'Why did men really come to and return to Jelly's corner? What did they seek to gain? What was the nature of the social order there? What was the basis for their social ranking?' (2006: 46).

18 Anderson's open-ended strategy can be interestingly contrasted with Gambetta and Hamill's study of taxi drivers in New York and Belfast, which began with an explicit research question. They describe their data as 'of an ethnographic kind' (Gambetta and Hamill 2005: 18). The researchers were fundamentally interested in the sociological study of trust and sought to explore how taxi drivers establish whether prospective passengers that they might pick up are trustworthy. Taxi drivers are very vulnerable in many ways: the passenger may not pay, or worse may rob the driver, or even worse may rob and assault the driver. They are forced to make instant decisions about whether someone who hails them is trustworthy. Gambetta and Hamill's research question was: '*drivers screen passengers looking for reliable signs of trust- or distrust-warranting properties*, in the sense that they look for signs that are too costly for a mimic to fake but affordable for the genuine article' (Gambetta and Hamill 2005: 11; emphasis in original).

To investigate this explicit research question, Gambetta and Hamill (2005: 18) conducted 'partially structured interviews and participant observation with drivers, dispatchers, and passengers'. Unlike Anderson's strategy, which began open-ended and allowed research questions to emerge in the course of the study, Gambetta and Hamill collected their data to examine the **validity** of their research question, which they also refer to as a **hypothesis**. Their findings are presented in order to shed light on this research question, and new research questions do not appear to have emerged in the course of the study.

For most ethnographers, the main equipment they will need in the course of observation will be a notepad and a pen. However, improvements in voice recognition software and mobile technologies have made text and speech recording devices much more popular for producing field notes (see Learn from experience 18.2 and Section 19.4).

There are various applications with the capacity to automatically transcribe voice recording—and the technology is improving all the time. That said, all **transcription** requires close checking for transcription errors. It is also worth highlighting that how we speak is not the same as how we write, so some editing is always inevitable. Using recorders can also be more obtrusive than writing notes. Most ethnographers report that after a period of time they become less conspicuous to participants in social settings, who become familiar with their presence. While mobile phones are now ubiquitous, speaking into a recording device may remind participants of the ethnographer's status. Recording can also be compromised because of background noise. Photography can be a useful additional source of data and helps to stir the ethnographer's memory, but will not be possible in some kinds of research, for example studies of crime and deviance, and can raise ethical concerns—as we discuss in Chapter 6. All of this suggests that ethnographers need to be very flexible in the methods they use to take notes—as shown in Research in focus 18.4.

Types of field notes

Some writers have found it useful to classify the types of field notes that are generated in the process of conducting an ethnography. The following classification is based on the similar categories suggested by Adler and Adler (2009), Sanjek (1990), and Lofland and Lofland (1995).

- *Mental notes*—used when it is inappropriate to be seen taking notes (for example, during the coffee breaks Atkinson refers to in Research in focus 18.4).
- *Jotted notes* (also called *scratch notes*)—very brief notes written inconspicuously on pieces of paper, in small notebooks, or on a phone, that serve as a reminder about events that the researcher will write up later. Lofland and Lofland (1995: 90) refer to these as being made up of 'little phrases, quotes, key words, and the like', whereas Adler and Adler (2009: 227) highlight them as 'writing down the facts of what was happening'. These are equivalent to the 'rough notes and jottings' that Atkinson refers to in Research in focus 18.4.
- *Full field notes*—detailed notes (about events, people, conversations etc.), made as soon as possible, which will serve as the main data source. The researcher can record initial ideas about interpretation at this stage, as well as impressions and feelings (see the five principles in 'Strategies for taking field notes'). When Atkinson (in Research in focus 18.4) refers to notes in which he 'amplified and added to' the jottings made during the

LEARN FROM EXPERIENCE 18.2
Strategies for taking field notes

After a day in the field, writing up your field notes is often the last thing you want to think about. However, it is very important to write your field notes as soon as is possible so that you don't lose that all-important detail. Here, Minke talks about how she managed the process:

> Writing up field notes is a time-consuming process. During my research I often conducted observations that lasted the whole day, or that took place late at night. I often couldn't bring myself to write up notes after I arrived at home because the fieldwork process was so tiring. I therefore tried to use my phone to type notes on site, which is a lot faster than writing physical notes and left more time for observing or participating. After I left the observation site, I would then use the voice recorder to record my own detailed account of any interesting observations that needed further detail. This helped save time and improved the quality of my field notes.
>
> Minke

 Access the **online resources** to hear Minke's video reflections on this theme.

You can read about our panellists' backgrounds and research experiences on page xxvi.

18

RESEARCH IN FOCUS 18.4
Taking field notes

In the context of his research in a medical school, Atkinson (1981) provides an account that strongly implies that ethnographers need to be flexible in their note-taking tactics:

> I found that my strategies for observation and recording changed naturally as the nature of the social scene changed. Whenever possible I attempted to make rough notes and jottings of some sort whilst I was in the field. Such notes were then amplified and added to later in the day when I returned to the office. The quantity and type of on the spot recording varied across recurrent types of situation. During 'tutorials', when one of the doctors taught the group in a more or less formal manner, or when there was some group discussion . . . then it seemed entirely natural and appropriate to sit among the students with my notebook on my knee and take notes almost continuously. At the other extreme, I clearly did not sit with my notebook and pen whilst I was engaged in casual conversations with students over a cup of coffee. Whereas taking notes is a normal thing to do, taking notes during a coffee break chat is not normal practice. . . . Less clear cut was my approach to the observation and recording of bedside teaching. On the whole I tried to position myself at the back of the student group and make occasional jottings: main items of information on the patients, key technical terms, and brief notes on the shape of the session (for example, the sequence of topics covered, the students who were called on to perform, and so on).
>
> (Atkinson 1981: 131–2)

day, he was producing full field notes. You can see an example of a full field note in Research in focus 18.5.

- *Methodological notes.* Adler and Adler (2009) also use a separate file of notes in which they record observations about methodological decisions, experiences in the field, and 'barriers and breakthroughs'. This type of note is useful for recording the process of research and why the researcher made particular decisions.

Should the ethnographer be visible in field notes?

Field notes record a researcher's observations and experiences, so the ethnographer's presence in them is often clear. We see this in the field note in Research in focus 18.5, when the ethnographer—Demetry—is motioned to the dining table by the manager so that she can see the head chef at work. However, in the finished work—the ethnography in the sense of a written

RESEARCH IN FOCUS 18.5
Types of field note

18

We discussed Demetry's (2013) ethnographic research on a high-end restaurant in the United States in Research in focus 16.2, as an example of qualitative research's emphasis on process and flexibility. During the first day of her time at the restaurant, Demetry recorded the following full field note:

> The dining room of Tatin has an inviting atmosphere: one is greeted by beige and light-green color tones and a roaring fireplace. Soft lighting bathes the room, and classical music plays quietly in the background encouraging one to relax and unwind. Two swinging doors with glass window cut-outs lead to the kitchen. I walk into the kitchen to find the TOTAL opposite of the relaxing dining room ambiance. Rap music is blaring, and cooks in jeans and T-shirts are nodding their heads as they work separately at their stations. The manager motions me to the 'dining table'—a small nook across from the hotline set up similar to the tables on the other side of the swinging doors. Inside sits Matt, the head chef, typing on a white Mac laptop, surrounded by stacks of mail and clothing draped all over the table.
>
> (Demetry 2013: 586)

As Demetry points out, the field note brings out the informal kitchen ambience created by the head chef and the use that he made of music as a means of reinforcing that atmosphere.

account of a group and its culture—the ethnographer is often written out of the picture (Van Maanen 1988). This is because field notes are usually for personal consumption, at least initially (Coffey 1999). In contrast, the written ethnography is for public consumption and has to be presented as a definitive account of the social setting and culture in question. Allowing the ethnographer to be visible in the final publication risks making it seem like a cleverly constructed (and therefore potentially misleading) account rather than an authoritative record. We will address this issue in more detail in 18.4, Writing ethnography.

How comprehensive should field notes be?

There is an issue of how comprehensive an ethnographer's notes should aim to be. Wolfinger (2002) has observed that, if the ethnographer does not try to be comprehensive, their background expectations are likely to influence what they see as significant, and therefore what they do or do not record. In the case of the field note in Research in focus 18.5, the loud rap music seems to have had a considerable impact on Demetry's immediate impression of the restaurant's ambience, as she is clearly surprised by it.

Sometimes, field notes may seem to describe incidents so mundane that they seem barely worth recording. For example, the following field note is taken from Watts's (2008) study of train travel (social geographers and sociologists are increasingly interested in the idea of 'mobile ethnography' and the research methods that might be used to study people on the move). Watts travelled on the same train service once a week over three weeks:

> Nothing seems to happen. . . . I want to write that something happens. But nothing happens. A man reads a book, then reads a newspaper. A woman fidgets and sniffs. . . . A cloud catches me and I drift off, dreaming of my destination. . . . I am drifting into reverie, the flashing light, the tiredness, the endless munching of crisps from nearby, the reading, reading . . . the juddering, the rolling of the carriage, the white light of Cornwall. I am travelling outside the train, through the fields, as though the carriage were air on which I was carried, blown along.
>
> (Watts 2008: 713)

The sense of boredom is unmistakable and hardly seems worth recording. However, quite apart from providing insight into her own experience of train travel, Watts also reveals the tediousness of the experience of train travel for others. She reports some things that did happen but they are not striking or colourful. Ethnographers in such circumstances need to allow the dullness of the experience to come through, but must take care not to get so sucked into boredom that they lose sight of recording it in their field notes.

Bringing ethnographic research to an end

Knowing when and how to stop observation is not an easy or straightforward matter in ethnography. Because of its unstructured nature and the absence of specific hypotheses to be tested (other than those that might emerge during data collection and analysis), ethnographic research tends to lack an obvious end point. Reasons for the research ending at a certain point might include the following.

- The study may come to an almost natural end, such as when a strike that is being observed comes to a conclusion (though such natural endings are a fairly rare occurrence).
- The rhythms of the ethnographer's career or personal and family life may mean that they have to withdraw from the field. Perhaps they have reached the end of a period of sabbatical leave; or they need to submit a doctoral thesis by a certain date; or their research funding is drawing to a close.
- The ethnographer may simply feel that they have had enough. Ethnographic research can be highly stressful for many reasons: the nature of the topic, which may place the fieldworker in stressful situations (as in research on crime); the marginality of the researcher in the social setting and the need to constantly manage a front; and the prolonged absence from their normal life that is often necessary.
- The ethnographer may feel that the research questions on which they have decided to concentrate have been answered, so that there are no new data worth generating. Altheide's (1980: 310) decision to leave the various news organizations in which he had conducted ethnographic research was motivated by 'the recurrence of familiar situations and the feeling that little worthwhile was being revealed'. This is a form of **data saturation** (see Chapter 17).

Whatever the reason for bringing ethnographic research to a close, disengagement has to be *managed*. This means that promises must be kept: if you agreed to write a report to an organization as a condition of them giving you access to the site, you should not forget that promise. It also means that ethnographers must provide good explanations for their departure. Members of a social setting always know that the overt researcher is a temporary fixture, but over a long period of time, and especially if there was genuine participation in activities within that setting, people may forget that the ethnographer's presence is not permanent. Covert ethnographers will also need to make sure that they leave the field in an ethically appropriate manner. All goodbyes have to be carefully managed. Further, the ethnographer must not forget their *ethical* commitments, such as the need to ensure that persons and settings are anonymized—unless, of course, as sometimes happens, they have made an agreement with participants that they can disclose information about the social setting.

In his research on Credit Line bank, Humphreys went even further in his desire for organizational participants to remain anonymous (Humphreys and Watson 2009). He became aware that the gulf between the company's public position on corporate social responsibility and the private views of many staff presented him with an ethical dilemma. He clearly needed to protect their anonymity so that they would not get into trouble with the firm. We quoted the words of 'Charity' earlier, in 'The roles of the ethnographic researcher', but Charity is not a pseudonym for an individual (the usual tactic used by researchers to preserve the identity of their informants). Instead, 'Charity' is a composite person rather than a real individual. 'Her' views and words are those of several employees who expressed identical or similar positions.

18.4 Writing ethnography

As we have noted, the term 'ethnography' refers both to a method of social research and to the finished product of ethnographic research. In other words, it is both something that is carried out and something that you write up and read. Since the mid-1980s, the production of ethnographic texts has become a focus of interest in its own right and writers have discussed not just how ethnography is conducted in the field but also the **rhetorical** conventions that researchers can use to produce ethnographic texts: ways of making their written account, and their conclusions, convincing to the reader. Here we will discuss rhetorical considerations, and if you are writing up an ethnography or micro-ethnography for your student research project you should read this section in conjunction with Chapter 25.

Ethnographic texts are designed to convince readers of the *reality* of the events and situations described, and the plausibility of the ethnographer's explanations. The ethnographic text must not simply present a set of findings: it must provide an 'authoritative' account of the group or culture in question. In other words, the ethnographer must convince us that they arrived at an account of social reality that has strong claims to be considered truthful. This means that ethnographic texts make heavy use of stylistic and rhetorical devices that aim to persuade the reader to enter into a shared framework of facts and interpretations, observations and reflections.

To do this, the ethnographer's writing strategy is usually saturated with **realism**. This simply means that the researcher presents an authoritative, unemotional account that aims to represent an external, objective reality. However, not all ethnographic texts follow these conventions. Van Maanen (1988) identified three types of ethnographic writing.

1. ***Realist*** *tales*—confident, unemotional, and seemingly definitive third-person accounts of a culture and of the behaviour of members of that culture. This is the most common form of ethnographic writing.
2. *Confessional tales*—personalized accounts of research in which the ethnographer is fully implicated in the data-gathering and writing-up processes. These accounts of *doing* ethnography are open about the difficulties researchers encountered and are generally more concerned with detailing how research was carried out than with presenting findings. They have become more common since the 1970s and reflect a growing emphasis on **reflexivity**, particularly in qualitative research. Several of the examples we have discussed in this chapter are, or include, confessional tales (e.g. Baird 2018; Guschwan 2017; Wacquant 2004). Very often the confessional tale is told in one context (for example, the researcher might be invited to contribute a chapter to a book of similar tales), but the main findings are written up as realist tales.
3. *Impressionist tales*—accounts that place a heavy emphasis on 'words, metaphors, phrasings, and . . . the expansive recall of fieldwork experience' (Van Maanen 1988: 102). There is a heavy emphasis

on stories of dramatic events that provide 'a representational means of cracking open the culture and the fieldworker's way of knowing it' (Van Maanen 1988: 102).

However, Van Maanen (2011) subsequently revised his characterization of ethnographic writing in light of the fact that it is now much more common for confessional tales to be incorporated within standard ethnographies than to appear as distinct chapters or appendices. He also adjusted his categories to reflect emerging trends in ethnography.

1. *Structural tales*—accounts that link observation of everyday occurrences to 'macro' issues in society more widely. Burawoy's (1979) ethnography of a factory, which was heavily influenced by labour process theory, is an example, as is Sallaz's (2009) ethnography of casinos in Las Vegas and South Africa, in which he links his findings about the work conditions of casino workers to the wider regulatory environments operating in the two countries.
2. *Poststructural tales*—accounts that suggest that reality is a 'fragile social construction subject to numerous lines of sight and interpretation' (Van Maanen 2011: 248). This is done by exploring behind the scenes of an apparent reality and suggesting that things are not quite what they seem. Jackson's study (2020) of the policing of protests against fracking in England is one example of this approach. He specifically sought to explore the perspectives of those on the other side of policing—the protesters. Jackson argues that the views of those policed are often missing from studies of policing, and he attempts to document 'how policing is done, how it has changed, and how it could be done' (Jackson 2019: 169).
3. *Advocacy tales*—accounts that are profoundly motivated by a sense that something is wrong and that the ethnographer wants to reveal the issue for all to see. Examples are Gusterson's (1996) ethnography of a nuclear weapons laboratory, Khan's (2011) ethnography of an elite United States high school in which he shows how privilege and cultural capital are interlinked and are perpetuated over generations, and Goffman's (2014) account of the injustices faced by Black men in a deprived Philadelphia ghetto.

Elsewhere, Adler and Adler (2008) have provided a categorization of genres of ethnographic writing that builds, at least in part, on an earlier version of Van Maanen's (1988) categorization. They distinguish four genres.

1. *Classical ethnography*—realist tales that are accessible and aim to provide a persuasive account of a setting. The discussion of research methods often takes on the style of a confessional tale, and the **literature review** is often used to show a gap in previous research on the topic area. Garthwaite's (2016) study of volunteering in a food bank is one example of this type of ethnography, but there are many, many more.
2. *Mainstream ethnography*—also realist tales, but directed to a wider group of social scientists rather than just other qualitative researchers. This genre tends to be **deductive** in approach, and, although Adler and Adler do not put it this way, it has many of the features of a **positivist** style of representation. Mainstream ethnographies draw on an established literature and tend to be explicit about the research questions that drove the investigations. The research methods are laid out in a formal and specific way. Uekusa's (2019: 539) study of the relationship between power and surfing, with an explicit focus on 'what determines who gets the waves?', provides a good example, as does Maitlis and Lawrence's (2007) study of three British orchestras, which uses the literature on sensegiving in organizations—that is, how people give meaning to collective experience—as its *raison d'être*.
3. *Postmodern ethnography*—the ethnographer and writer is overtly part of the writing and may themselves be present within the data and findings. Postmodern ethnographies often take the form of auto-ethnographies (see Key concept 18.4), in which the text is heavily personalized and the overall approach intensely reflexive. Mears's (2011) ethnography of the world of the fashion model and Pheko's (2018) study of workplace bullying and mobbing have some of these features, though neither researcher would necessarily accept the label of 'postmodern'.
4. *Public ethnography*—a form of ethnography that has existed for decades and keeps a general audience in mind. It is usually written in an accessible style and is fairly light on the discussion of previous literature, and the presentation of the research methods is brief. Examples of this genre are Venkatesh's (2008) study of a Chicago gang, Khan's (2011) ethnography of an elite high school in the United States, Goffman's (2014) study of the experiences of Black men in a Philadelphia ghetto who are wanted for criminal offences, and Búriková and Miller's (2010) study of Slovak au pairs in London. Public ethnographies are more likely to be in book than article format.

KEY CONCEPT 18.4
What is auto-ethnography?

According to Ellis and Bochner (2000), the goal of auto-ethnography is to see the researcher as subject and to tell highly reflexive and personal narratives about everyday and professional life. It is '[an] autobiographical genre of writing and research that displays multiple layers of consciousness, connecting the personal to the cultural' (2000: 209). Often, autobiography, biography, poetry, art, and performance are also associated with auto-ethnographic practice. In some ways, the term is necessarily a little resistant to definition because it is an attempt to try to get away from modernistic concerns that reality is something essential, specific, and definite. Instead, it seeks to emphasize the diversity of personal experience and perspective.

We should note that any ethnography may well contain elements of more than one of these categories. Although Garthwaite's (2016) ethnography of food banks can be classified as a classical ethnography in Adler and Adler's scheme, it has elements of a postmodern ethnography in the way in which the author and researcher appears in the text on a number of occasions. These various ways of portraying modes of writing and representation in ethnography are therefore best thought of as tendencies within ethnographies rather than as definitive descriptions of them. However, the types of ethnography described in this section do have different styles and conventions and it is worth recognizing these when planning an ethnographic encounter and when writing one up.

18.5 Reflecting on ethnography

We have now considered how a researcher may conduct and write up an ethnography, but as we highlighted in sections 18.1 and 18.2, the term 'ethnography' is broad and constantly evolving. In this concluding section, we will reflect on the idea of the ethnography, considering newer forms of ethnography, whether there can be a feminist ethnography, and the changing nature of ethnography.

18

Newer forms of ethnography

As the social world we study changes, research methods must also adapt, and over recent years newer forms of ethnography have become very common: online and visual ethnography.

Online ethnography

Ethnography may not seem like an obvious method for collecting data on internet use. We tend to think of the ethnographer as someone who visits communities and organizations, and at first glance the internet may seem a placeless space. But in fact, as Hine (2000) has observed, thinking of the internet as a place—a cyberspace—actually allows us to conduct ethnographic studies of the online and virtual communities that exist in these digital worlds. In this way, our ideas of place that are closely tied to the physical world can be transferred into an online context.

Of course, the line between online and offline worlds is not clear-cut—and many studies involve both elements. Practitioners of what might be thought of as conventional ethnography increasingly have to take their participants' online interactions into account, making use of methods and sources of data associated with online ethnography. For example, Pearson (2012) found that numerous online football forums and message boards were relevant to his research, as they were places in which supporters discussed footballing issues and arranged to meet up. Similarly, in two separate conventional ethnographies of 'physical spaces' Hallett and Barber (2014: 314) found themselves increasingly '*pulled* into online spaces because that was where our participants were' (emphasis in original). In one of the studies—an ethnography of two men's hair salons—the authors had planned a conventional ethnography based on observations and interviews but had to turn to online reviews when one of the salons refused to allow clients to be interviewed. Similarly, researchers focusing on digital worlds also need to acknowledge these blurred lines: as both Hine (2008) and Garcia et al. (2009) observe, even the most committed internet user has a life beyond their device(s).

Studies of cyberspace invite us to consider not only the nature of online worlds as a domain for investigation, but also the nature and the adaptability of our research methods. One aspect of online ethnography that has been subject to considerable debate is the practice of 'lurking', meaning watching an online community, or reading its output, without participating or engaging with it. Members of these communities often dislike such behaviour, and if they detect it they may express their disapproval or even block the researcher's access to discussions and activities. Hine (2008) has also suggested that relying solely on lurking without participation risks missing out on understanding crucial experiential aspects of online communities. However, she was able to use a non-participative approach to an online community to good effect in her examination of the use of science in discussions of headlice in an online forum (Hine 2014). Hine gained permission from the administrators of the Mumsnet forum to examine discussion threads relating to headlice and their treatment, but she did not contact participants to the discussions or participate herself. Her study shows, among other things, that while scientific knowledge was often introduced into discussions, it was not privileged over personal experience and was sometimes given less credibility.

Online ethnographers sometimes lurk before conducting their fieldwork in order to gain an understanding of the setting prior to their participation—but even when ethnographers only lurk at the start, ethical issues still arise (see Chapter 6). The issue of whether to lurk or participate actually suggests a division between forms of documentary analysis and ethnographic study. The **thematic analysis** of postings without participation, as in Hine's study, suggests that this is a form of documentary qualitative analysis (like those we discuss in Chapter 22). On the other hand, the presence of participation, as in the thematic analysis of postings with participation outlined in Research in focus 18.6, suggests that this is a virtual or online ethnographic study. Research in focus 18.7 provides another example of an online ethnography that involved postings and participation.

Online ethnographies often involve looking at communities, and these studies generally take one of the four forms described in Thinking deeply 18.3. However, researchers often have little choice as to which type of study they adopt. For example, if a community is hostile to outsiders, a researcher may be more inclined to lurk or to participate covertly, as suggested by Brotsky and Giles (2007) in Research in focus 18.6.

The nature of the community being studied can also influence the approach taken. Kozinets, who developed the approach and term of **netnography** (see Key concept 18.5), draws a distinction between ethnographies of online communities and ethnographies of communities online (Kozinets 2010). The former involve the study of communities that have a largely online existence, such as his research

RESEARCH IN FOCUS 18.6

Covert participant observation in cyberspace

Brotsky and Giles (2007) report some findings and experiences relating to the first author's covert participation study of the 'pro-ana' community. This is a community of people who are supportive of eating disorders such as anorexia nervosa. She identified 12 pro-ana websites and obtained membership of the various discussion contexts each website hosted—forums, email discussion lists, chatrooms, and so on. Brotsky fabricated a plausible persona in terms of age, sex, height, eating disorder (anorexia), and weight (current, past, and intended). The authors write that Brotsky

> began by introducing herself as an authentic pro-ana sympathizer who was hoping to establish virtual relationships with like-minded individuals, and continued to participate as naturally as possible across the course of the investigation. As the investigation unfolded, connections were made and close relationships developed through ongoing conversations with participants. . . . [She] successfully acquired membership of 23 separate groups across 12 websites, including discussion forums, chatrooms, blog sub-communities, online journal/diary sites, and e-mail-group affiliations.
>
> (Brotsky and Giles 2007: 98)

Through this study, the authors were able to identify the sources of support offered within the communities and group identities (such as whether anorexia was viewed as a lifestyle or illness).

RESEARCH IN FOCUS 18.7
Participant observation in cyberspace

Underwood (2017) conducted participant observation research into the social lives of recreational bodybuilders who use image and performance enhancing drugs (IPEDs). Most IPED users are not professional athletes and are instead the non-competitive weightlifters you might come across in any gym. Such users are unlikely to belong to athletic federations and, given the illegal nature of IPEDs, are often not organized into visible communities. However, the internet provides an opportunity for them to connect with each other and there are now a number of online platforms where people interested in taking IPEDs can interact.

Conducting her online ethnography with one of these groups—the 'Zyzz' community—Underwood wanted to understand how IPEDs are experienced and acquire meaning within a community of recreational bodybuilders, and how recreational IPED use transforms users both physically and socially. To do this, she created a Facebook profile in which she would participate in the Zyzz community by authoring and responding to posts, and by posting selfies of herself flexing her muscles. Gradually, she amassed a following of what she refers to as 59 friends and 20 key cultural consultants, with whom she had in-depth interactions with via email and online platforms. She also engaged with various Zyzz websites, forums, and social media accounts to collect a corpus of data that was over a million words.

Analysing this material using **NVivo**, Underwood found that Zyzz fans saw the prohibition of IPEDs as dangerous because it constrained the level of good medical information about how to use them safely. They also contrasted their attempts at body modification with more invasive techniques such as plastic surgery and the dieting industry. Indeed, many argued that banning IPEDs was sexist because it prevented them from achieving the body image that they desired and from accessing the social benefits that being 'shredded' can bring. Through her work, Underwood was able to demonstrate how changes in the expectations of gender roles and the so-called crisis in masculinity was informing the use of IPEDs, but also how such usage was being normalized on online platforms.

THINKING DEEPLY 18.3
Types of online community study

Qualitative researchers tend to use four main types of online interaction study. All four involve a considerable degree of immersion in the postings, but Type 1 is the least likely to be viewed as a form of online ethnography, as the researcher is more of an external observer.

Type 1. Study of online communities only, with no participation

Usually involves examining blogs, discussion groups, electronic mailing lists, social media feeds, etc., without any participation or intervention on the part of the researcher. It generally takes the form of 'lurking' and analysis is conducted without the authors of the materials being aware of the researcher's presence.

Type 2. Study of online communities only, with some participation

Usually involves examining discussion groups, forums, electronic mailing lists, social media feeds etc., but with some participation or intervention on the part of the researcher. The researcher is not passive and intervenes (overtly or covertly) in the postings and discussions.

Type 3. Study of online communities plus online or offline interviews

Same as Type 2, but in addition the researcher interviews some of the people involved in the online interaction. The interviews may be online or offline.

Type 4. Study of online communities plus offline research methods (in addition to online or offline interviews)

Same as Type 3, but the researcher(s) also participate in the offline worlds of those being studied, such as attending gatherings, as well as conducting interviews (which may be online or offline). Clearly, this type of study is only possible where the community has a clear offline presence.

KEY CONCEPT 18.5
What is netnography?

One of the most significant approaches to conducting ethnographic research on online communities is netnography. Developed by Kozinets (2002, 2010), netnography is a form of ethnography because it involves the researcher's immersion in the online worlds under investigation. This means that it is an essentially naturalistic method that relies considerably on observation, but it is often supported by forms of online interview. It is best suited to examining communities that have an exclusively online existence, although it can play a role in relation to communities that have both an online and an offline existence. In studies of the latter, the offline element needs to be examined through a conventional ethnographic approach. In a sense, the term 'netnography' and its associated methods represent a very useful way to think about doing ethnography online. For example, Mkono and Markwell (2014) consider such terms as 'online ethnography', 'webnography', and 'virtual ethnography' to be synonyms for netnography.

An example of a netnography is Wu and Pearce's (2014) examination of new tourist markets in a digital era. They take the example of recreational vehicle tourists and examine Chinese tourists' experiences in Australia. The authors conducted a search for appropriate travel blogs posted on two sites (Qyer.com and Sina.com) in January 2013 and by focusing only on 'rich detailed blogs posted by mainland Chinese' they identified 37 blogs (Wu and Pearce 2014: 467). Because the blogs were open-access, the researchers did not seek permission from the bloggers to quote and process their words. They manually coded the blogs and developed themes to reveal the motivations for this form of tourism. They were also able to examine typical routes taken and calculate distances travelled, because routes were included in the blogs.

on online discussion forums of knowledgeable coffee enthusiasts (Kozinets 2002). Another example of a community with an exclusively online existence is Banks's (2012, 2014) covert online ethnography of the 'advantage play' subculture, whose participants use mathematical techniques to try to reduce the risks of gambling by taking advantage of technical weaknesses in gambling products. Banks became an advantage player and was a covert participant observer of an online forum for 18 months. The study shows how participants seek to manage risk, not just of losing money, but of being fleeced by gambling sites that take the gambler's stake but closes down its operations before paying out.

Visual ethnography

One of the most striking developments in qualitative research in recent years has been the growth of interest in the use of visual materials. Visual methods in social science are by no means new. Social anthropologists, for example, have long used photos to record the lives and cultures of the tribes and villages they study, and they often featured in late nineteenth- and early twentieth-century articles in the *American Journal of Sociology*. However, interest in the use of the visual then decreased from the First World War until the turn of the millennium. This is likely to have been, at least in part, due to a feeling that including photos was inconsistent with sociology's efforts to establish itself as a science. However, in recent years social research has made more use of visual materials: see, for example, Banks and Zeitlyn (2015), Rose (2016), and Pink (2020).

It is worth noting that although the term 'visual ethnography' is becoming increasingly popular (e.g. Pink 2020), it is sometimes used in a way that does not imply the kind of sustained immersion in a social setting that we have taken to be a key feature of ethnography. We can also make a distinction between the use of existing visual materials and those that are produced more or less exclusively for the purposes of research. In this chapter, we will focus on research-driven visual images; we will return to the examination of existing images in Chapter 22. Visual material can also be used in the kinds of interview we will discuss in Chapters 19 and 20.

Visual images that are research-driven may be taken either by the researcher or by research participants themselves. There are three main ways in which qualitative researchers use photos.

1. As a memory aid in the course of fieldwork, essentially contributing to the ethnographer's field notes. We touched on the practice already in 'Strategies for taking field notes'. This is how Alan Bryman (2004) used images in his work (see Research in focus 18.8).

RESEARCH IN FOCUS 18.8
Photos as a memory aid for field notes

In his book on Disneyization, the process by which the principles associated with the Disney theme parks have permeated many aspects of modern society and economy, Alan Bryman (2004) included several photos that he felt illustrated the Disneyization processes he was describing.

This was especially the case in a paper he wrote on the Disneyization of McDonald's (Bryman 2003). At one point in the paper he discusses the bizarre case of a McDonald's in Chicago that used a rock 'n' roll theme. He had visited Chicago a year before to give a talk at the American Sociological Association conference and took the opportunity to take some photos of the restaurant. Although he did not end up using the images in either the book or the article, he found them a very helpful reminder of the vivid detail of the restaurant. One of the images is presented here—Figure 18.1 shows the restaurant's exterior against the Chicago skyline.

FIGURE 18.1
Disneyization in pictures: a themed McDonald's

2. As a starting point for discussion with participants, a practice often referred to as ***photo-elicitation*** (see Research in focus 18.10 for an example).
3. As sources of data in their own right (see Research in focus 18.11).

It is worth elaborating slightly on the use of photo-elicitation, which applies to both images taken by the researcher and those taken by research participants. Images taken by researchers can be shown to participants to prompt discussion of certain issues, and images taken by participants allow researchers to learn about the participants' realities and to see through their eyes—a key feature of qualitative research. Pink (2004: 399) writes: 'By working with informants to produce images that are meaningful for them we can gain insights into their visual cultures and into what is important for them as individuals living in particular localities.' In their study of

18

African-Caribbean young people who had been excluded from school, Wright et al. (2010) aimed to understand how they managed their transition into adulthood. The researchers equipped the young people with disposable cameras and asked them to take photographs of family and friends who had been sources of support. The images tended to be of events and contexts that were significant to them in terms of the development of their personal identities. The authors argue that using photo-elicitation helped to empower these marginalized young people and to reduce some of the power distance between the researchers and their participants.

Pink (2013a) also draws attention to two ways in which researchers *think* about visual images in social research. She calls these realist and reflexive approaches (see Key concepts 2.3 'What is realism?' and 16.6 'What is reflexivity?'). The realist approach uses photos or video recordings to simply capture an event or setting (see Research in focus 18.9). This visual record then becomes a 'fact' for the ethnographer to interpret along with their other data. The image and what it represents are essentially unproblematic and act as a window on reality. Whether used to illustrate a study or as part of the researcher's notes, this has been the dominant frame within which visual resources have been produced and analysed.

In contrast, Pink draws attention to a position that she calls *reflexive*, which requires a sensitivity to the ways in which the researcher as a person has an impact on what a photo reveals. This means developing an awareness of the way that age, gender, and background influence what is captured by the research and how it is composed, and the influence that informants and others may have had in the resulting image or recording. The reflexive approach is often collaborative, in the sense that research participants may be involved in decisions about what photos should be taken and then how they should be interpreted. It also involves recognizing the fluid meaning of images: the idea that they can never be fixed and will always be viewed by different people in different ways. This was evident in Pink's (1997) research on Spanish bullfighters, where the images she took of bullfights were interpreted by enthusiasts in terms of the performative qualities of the bullfighter, but by UK viewers in terms of animal rights and cruelty. The study described in Research in focus 18.10 also took a reflexive approach, for example in that Warren (2018) gathered data not only on the experiences and views of her participants, but also on the reactions of members of the public to the images generated through the project.

The growing number of studies involving visual materials suggest that they have great potential for ethnographers and qualitative researchers more generally. However, their increasing popularity does not mean that visual methods should always be incorporated into an investigation. Their use must be relevant to the research questions being asked. For her research on the body work landscape in South Florida, Wolkowitz (2012; Research in focus 18.11) was interested in what she terms the growth of the 'body work economy'—that is, turning the body into an object to be worked on for profit. She recognizes that statistical data can document aspects of this process but argues that photos are better at demonstrating the clustering of body work establishments in the location. The photos also provide readers with the raw material to assess the researcher's inferences.

As sources of data, visual research methods require the researcher to 'read' images in a way that is sensitive to the context in which they were generated. Whether taking a realist or a reflexive approach, researchers need to recognize the potential for misinterpretation and have to carefully work with research participants and, where the researcher is the source of the images, recognize the significance of their own social position. In other words, a researcher analysing visual materials needs to be critical about the idea that a photo provides an unproblematic depiction of reality. For this reason, researchers will usually include non-visual research methods (such as interviews) in their investigations, but this can bring into question the relative significance of words and images in the analysis of data and the presentation of findings. It can be easy to slip into using visual elements as ancillary. At the same time, though, Pink (2004) reminds us that visual research methods are never purely visual. She highlights how they are usually accompanied by other (often traditional) research methods such as interviewing and observation (as in both Research in focus 18.10 and Research in focus 18.11), and further non-visual content in that words are the medium of expression for both the research participants and the researchers themselves.

A final important point to consider in relation to visual research methods is that they raise especially difficult issues of ethics, an area that we explored in Chapter 6. It is particularly important to clearly explain the dissemination strategy of the project and establish ownership of the photographs. In certain circumstances, copyright can be given to the researcher, but a researcher taking this option may need to seek legal advice as copyright legislation will vary according to location. In all

RESEARCH IN FOCUS 18.9
The realist approach to visual ethnography

Blauner's (1964) influential book on work in four different technological conditions provides an interesting example of how researchers have used photos in ethnographic studies. Blauner published the photos with detailed captions to tell readers what they were seeing in the images. This technique of presenting the photos as having clear, uncontested meanings is very much in line with the realist stance on visual images.

Figure 18.2 is very similar to* one of Blauner's examples that attempted to illustrate assembly-line work in the US car industry at that time. The photograph had the title 'Subdivided jobs and restricted freedom' and was accompanied by a description of employees' work with the following comment:

> These men perform the identical tasks shown above all day long and may fasten from eight hundred to one thousand wheels in eight hours. The movement of the cars along the conveyor belt determines the pace of their work and kept them close to their stations, virtually 'chained' to the assembly line.
>
> (Blauner 1964: 112)

FIGURE 18.2

In realist ethnographic research, photos like this one—which is similar to Blauner's (1964) images of assembly-line work in the US car industry—are published with detailed captions to tell readers what they are seeing

* We say that Figure 18.2 is 'very similar' to Blauner's image because it proved impossible to track the owner of the image. This experience demonstrates some of the difficulties with the use of photographs in general and of older ones in particular.

RESEARCH IN FOCUS 18.10

Using visual images to challenge representations of ageing

In her project, officially titled 'Representing self—representing ageing' but known more familiarly as the 'Look at Me!' project, Warren (2018) was interested in examining how older women challenge persistent media stereotyping of the ageing process. In addition to visiting a number of community groups, she recruited 'ordinary' women who self-defined as older and asked them to produce visual images that represented their feelings of the ageing process and how it was typically represented in the media. They worked alongside art therapists, professional photographers, and visual artists to produce photographs, sculptures, and artwork that represented their views—see Figure 18.3. Participants were also interviewed before and after the creative process to explore how they felt about the representation of ageing and their participation in the project, with some asked to keep photo-diaries to document their participation. The subsequent artwork was then publicly exhibited in three different locations, where the researcher gathered further qualitative survey data from visitors to assess how the artwork impacted the public. By using a range of different visual methods alongside more standard techniques, Warren was able to show the overshadowing power of visual images in shaping experiences of ageing, but also how older women empower themselves to challenge those stereotypical representations.

FIGURE 18.3

Warren's (2018) project made use of a variety of visual methods alongside more standard techniques

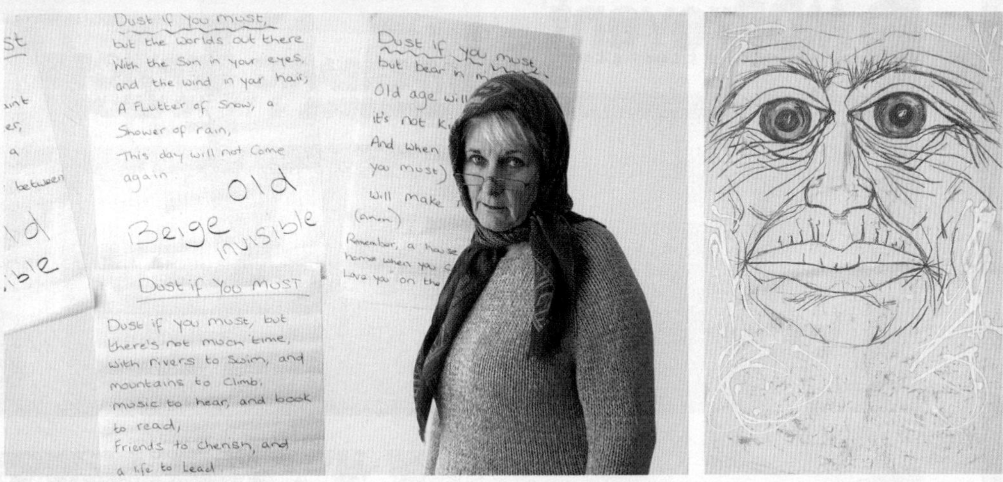

Source: 'Representing Self—Representing Ageing' project, funded by the New Dynamics of Ageing cross-council research programme (grant number: RES-356-25-0040).

RESEARCH IN FOCUS 18.11

Using photos where they will add value

Wolkowitz (2012) used photos in documenting the growth of what she calls the 'body work economy' in South Florida. Over several visits to the region, she took numerous photos and collected relevant photos taken by others relating to 'places where body work goes on' (2012: para. 3.5).

The process began as the equivalent of taking written notes to record observations, but Wolkowitz writes that she became increasingly aware of 'not only the ubiquity of body work enterprises as a feature of the landscape, but also their size, self-presentation (modest, grand, welcoming, forbidding), the apparent seamlessness of their integration into the consumer services sector, and the explicitness of their focus on the body' (Wolkowitz 2012:

para 3.5). Her photos, which she supplemented with interviews, show a variety of locations of different sizes and contexts (beauty service establishments, general medical facilities, specialist medical treatment centres, gyms, tattoo studios), some workers involved in the industries, and some of those targeted by the businesses. Figure 18.4 contains an example of the kinds of photos of medical establishments that featured in her research. Wolkowitz writes:

> While my photographs are intended to be mainly descriptive . . . none the less I recognise that landscape photography is as much about different ways of looking as picturing what is there, inviting the viewer to look in particular ways . . . this is exactly why photography is such a useful vehicle for problematising aspects of the taken-for-granted environment. However, visual sociology has recognised from its outset the dangers of misrepresenting an environment through the publication of selective images.
>
> Wolkowitz (2012: para 3.5)

Wolkowitz makes it clear why she chose to use photos, and how they are the most effective way of establishing 'a vivid picture of how body work as a social phenomenon is changing in its appearance and scale' (2012: para 7.2), how these establishments are clustered in the region, and how the body is being commodified in contemporary capitalism.

FIGURE 18.4

Using visual images in the study of the body landscape of South Florida

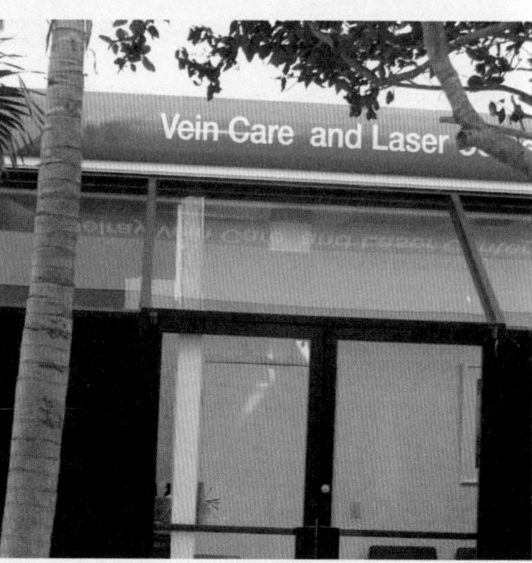

18

cases, participation should be based on the freely given, informed consent of those studied. Using visual materials is particularly sensitive in that the subjects who appear in them may have their images widely disseminated. It is important, therefore, to gain permission from those whose images appear and to ensure that they are fully aware of the implications of that agreement.

Can there be a feminist ethnography?

This heading is in fact the title of a widely cited article by Stacey (1988) that challenges the view that there can be a distinctively feminist ethnography that draws on the strengths of ethnography *and* is informed by feminist principles of the kind we outlined in Chapter 6 in our discussion of positionality.

Reinharz (1992) sees feminist ethnography as significant for three reasons. First, it documents women's lives and activities, which were previously seen as marginal and subsidiary to men's lives. Second, it understands women from their perspective, whereas male-led research tends 'to [trivialize] female activities and thoughts, or [interpret] them from the standpoint of the male researcher' (Reinharz 1992: 52). Finally, a deliberately feminist ethnography places women's lives within the context where they actually take place.

Similarly, Skeggs (2001: 430) has observed that ethnography, 'with its emphasis on experiences and the words, voice and lives of the participants', has been viewed by many feminist researchers as being well suited to the goals of feminism. Fish (2017) used participant observation to collect data on secure wards for women with learning disabilities because it helped her conduct her research in a more inclusive manner:

> The ethnographic method I used was informed by feminist and disability studies principles. Both of these research traditions privilege the voices of marginalised groups and identify structural and societal barriers as the sources of inequality.
>
> (Fish 2017: 9)

A significant question for feminist researchers is whether the research allows for a non-exploitative relationship between researcher and researched. One of the main elements of feminist research practice is that the researcher does not treat the relationship as a one-way process of extracting information from others, but provides something in return.

Skeggs's (1994; 1997) account of her ethnographic research on young women represents an attempt to carry out research in a non-exploitative manner (see Research in focus 18.12). However, Stacey (1988) argues that the

RESEARCH IN FOCUS 18.12
A feminist ethnography

Set in the north-west of England, Skeggs's (1997) classic study of 83 white working-class women was based on research conducted over a total period of 12 years including three years' full-time, in-the-field participant observation. It began when the women enrolled on a 'caring' course at a local college, and it follows their trajectories through the labour market, education, and the family.

The elements of a distinctively feminist ethnography can be seen in the following comments.

- This ethnography was 'politically motivated to provide space for the articulations and experiences of the marginalized' (Skeggs 1997: 23).
- The 'study was concerned to show how young women's experience of structure (their class and gender positioning) and institutions (education and the media) framed and informed their responses and how this process informed constructions of their own subjectivity' (Skeggs 1994: 74). This comment, like the previous one, reflects the commitment to documenting women's lives and allowing their experiences to come through, while also pointing to the significance of the understanding of women in context, to which Reinharz (1992) refers.

Skeggs also feels that the relationship with the women was not an exploitative one. For example, she writes that the research enabled the women's 'sense of self-worth' to be 'enhanced by being given the opportunity to be valued, knowledgeable and interesting' (Skeggs 1994: 81). She also claims she was able to 'provide a mouthpiece against injustices' and to listen 'to disclosures of violence, child abuse and sexual harassment' (Skeggs 1994: 81).

various situations she encountered as a feminist ethnographer placed her

> in situations of inauthenticity, dissimilitude, and potential, perhaps inevitable betrayal, situations that I now believe are inherent in fieldwork method. For no matter how welcome, even enjoyable the fieldworker's presence may appear to 'natives', fieldwork represents an intrusion and intervention into a system of relationships, a system of relationships that the researcher is far freer to leave.
>
> (Stacey 1988: 23)

Stacey also argues that, when the research is written up, it is the feminist ethnographer's interpretations and judgements that come through and that have authority. Skeggs responds to this criticism by acknowledging that in the case of her study, her academic career was undoubtedly enhanced by the research, but her participants were not in any way victims. Instead, she argues:

> The young women were not prepared to be exploited; just as they were able to resist most things which did not promise economic or cultural reward, they were able to resist me.... They enjoyed the research. It provided resources for developing a sense of their self-worth. More importantly, the feminism of the research has provided a framework which they use to explain that their individual problems are part of a wider structure and not their personal fault.
>
> (Skeggs 1994: 88)

Similarly, Reinharz (1992: 74–5) argues that, although ethnographic fieldwork relationships may sometimes *seem* manipulative, there is often an underlying reciprocity. The researcher may offer help or advice to their research participants, or they may be giving a public platform to normally marginalized voices (although the ethnographer is always the mouthpiece for such voices, so may present them in a certain way). There is also the fact that if we abandon feminist ethnography on the grounds that the ethnographer cannot fulfil all possible obligations at once, this would lead to all research being abandoned, feminist or otherwise.

18

Another crucial element of feminist research is transparency in the ethnographer's dealings with the women she studies and transparency in her account of the research process. These are great strengths of Skeggs's work.

It is clear that the question of whether there is or can be a feminist ethnography is a matter of ongoing debate.

The changing nature of ethnography

Ethnography has been in a state of continuous change since the end of the twentieth century. The newer forms of ethnography, such as visual ethnography and virtual/online ethnography, and the growing interest in alternative forms of writing ethnography suggest that this is a vibrant and flexible arena. However, some are concerned that the term 'ethnography' is used too loosely and that while many studies might be ethnographic in nature, they are obviously not ethnographies in the traditional sense of involving a period of prolonged participant observation in a social setting (see Thinking deeply 18.4).

Hammersley (2018) identifies five challenges to the practice of, and justification for, ethnography.

1. There is a growing demand for research to be accountable in terms of public impact and engagement, and of knowledge transfer. The work required to do this is effectively being squeezed from time spent in the field as researchers turn to more cost-efficient forms of data collection. Funding bodies are also increasingly operating on shorter time scales that are not well suited to ethnography.
2. The lure of '**Big Data**' in the form of large quantitative surveys, data science, and mixed methods make traditional ethnography look particularly costly by comparison.
3. Increasing demands on academics in terms of teaching and administration, as well as the plethora of activities associated with research, make it difficult to do ethnographic research thoroughly. Zickar and Carter, for example, have noted: 'The time commitment of traditional ethnographic research is intense and would require a reorganization of academic rewards and tenure policies given that ethnographic research often does not get published until 7 to 10 years after the original fieldwork began' (Zickar and Carter 2010: 312). As a result, qualitative researchers are increasingly likely to conduct something closer to what Wolcott (1990b) calls 'micro-ethnographies' (see Key concept 18.2), or adapt their methods accordingly (see Thinking deeply 18.4).
4. Hammersley argues that as society becomes more saturated with research—and more people become wary of involvement as a result—gaining access is increasingly difficult (Clark 2008). This is especially the case in public organizations such as schools, hospitals, and social services, where resources can be scarce.
5. The increasing requirements of ethical review boards are not well suited to ethnography. This is partly because the focus of ethnographic work often changes over time, but also due to the problems associated with gaining informed consent in the field.

Hammersley also notes that the term ethnography has acquired a range of different meanings, some of which are widely divergent from each other. In fact, he goes on to identify 41 qualifying adjectives that have been used

THINKING DEEPLY 18.4
When is a study ethnographic?

There is some debate about when it is appropriate to refer to a qualitative investigation as an ethnography. Ethnography almost seems to be a matter of degree. For such writers as Emerson (1987) and Wolcott (1990b), some immersion in the field is the defining feature of ethnography, with Emerson arguing (as we have noted) that too often, ethnographers do not spend enough time in the field—and our account of ethnography in Key concept 18.1 specifically requires immersion in a social setting.

However, ethnographers are rarely just participant observers, in that they almost always conduct interviews or examine documents, and this raises the question of when it is appropriate to call a qualitative study an ethnography. There may also be circumstances when the requirement of immersion needs to be relaxed. One of the most striking examples of this is Gusterson's (1996: ix) 'ethnographic study of a nuclear weapons laboratory' in the USA. Because of the top-secret nature of the work being conducted here and its sheer scale, traditional participant observation in the sense of prolonged immersion in the field was not possible. Gusterson (1996: 32) writes: 'I decided to mix formal interviews and the collection of documentary sources with a strategy of participant observation adapted to the demands and limitations of my own fieldwork situation. . . . I relied less on participant observation than most anthropologists in the field.' However, he did seek out as many employees as he could, and he lived in the community in which the laboratory was located and was able to participate in many of their core activities.

While a study like this does not seem to have the characteristics of a conventional ethnography of a workplace—because this option was not available to the researcher—Gusterson's determination to live in the community and to use interviews to see the development of nuclear weapons through the eyes of those who worked there gives the investigation significant rigour. The study underlines the idea that whether a qualitative study is ethnographic is a matter of degree.

in conjunction with the term 'ethnography'. Among them are collaborative ethnography, Marxist ethnography, militant ethnography, corporate ethnography, literary ethnography, postmodern ethnography, race ethnography, and slow ethnography. Given both the growing diversity of forms and modes of ethnography and the wider use of the term 'ethnography' (with prolonged participant observation no longer seen as an essential characteristic), it may be that the term is losing its original meaning.

All of this leads Hammersley to conclude that the current environment represents something of a challenging future for ethnographic work. However, rather than arguing for a reformulation of the term that would specifically identify the appropriate theoretical and value commitments that are essential to ethnography, he suggests an alternative position that conceives it simply as a **research strategy**. This enables researchers to adopt a range of different positions and approaches, while retaining a basic set of meaningful principles that are not based on personal commitments or judgements. In these terms, and just as has been outlined in this chapter, ethnography is just one set of methods among others, with the choice of method made on the basis of which is most appropriate for answering the particular research questions being addressed (Hammersley 2018: 7).

KEY POINTS

- The term 'ethnography' refers to both a method and the written product of research based on that method.
- The ethnographer is typically a participant observer who also uses non-observational methods and sources such as interviewing and documents.
- The ethnographer may adopt an overt or covert role, but the latter carries ethical difficulties.
- The method of access to a social setting will depend in part on whether it is a public or closed one.

- Key informants often play an important role, but the ethnographer needs to take care that the informant's impact on the direction of research is not excessive.
- There are several ways of classifying the kinds of role that the ethnographer may assume. These roles are not necessarily mutually exclusive.
- Field notes are important for prompting the ethnographer's memory and form much of the data for subsequent analysis.
- The consideration of different ways of writing up ethnographic research has become a topic of interest in its own right.
- There has been growing interest in the use of online ethnography, which involves studying both communities that solely exist online, and communities mainly existing offline but that also interact online.
- Visual materials such as photos and video have attracted considerable interest among ethnographers in recent years, not just as another method of data collection but as objects of interest in their own right.
- Feminist ethnography has become a popular approach to collecting data from a feminist standpoint, though there have been debates about whether there really can be a feminist ethnography.
- The nature of ethnography and what is taken to be an ethnography has changed over the years.

QUESTIONS FOR REVIEW

1. Is it possible to distinguish ethnography and participant observation?
2. How does participant observation differ from structured observation?
3. What issues does a researcher need to consider when doing covert ethnography?
4. Is access to closed settings necessarily more difficult to achieve than to open settings?
5. Does the problem of access finish once the researcher has achieved access to a chosen setting?
6. What might be the role of key informants in ethnographic research? Is there anything to be concerned about when using them?
7. Why might it be useful to classify participant observer roles in ethnography?
8. What is meant by 'going native'?
9. Should ethnographers be active or passive in the settings in which they conduct research?
10. Why are field notes important for ethnographers?
11. How do you decide when to complete the data-collection phase in ethnographic research?
12. To what extent is a feminist ethnography possible?
13. Are ethnographies of online worlds really ethnographic?
14. What kinds of roles can visual materials play in ethnography?
15. What forms of ethnographic writing other than realist tales can be found?
16. To what extent is ethnography changing?

ONLINE RESOURCES

www.oup.com/he/srm6e

You can find our notes on the answers to these questions within this chapter's **online resources**, together with:

- *audio/video comments* on this topic from our 'Learn from experience' panellists;
- *audio discussion from the authors* on whether access to closed settings is necessarily more difficult to achieve than open settings (review question 4);
- *self-test questions* for further knowledge-checking;
- a *flashcard glossary* to help you recall key terms; and
- a *Student Researcher's Toolkit* containing practical materials and resources to help you conduct your own research project.

CHAPTER 19

INTERVIEWING IN QUALITATIVE RESEARCH

CHAPTER GUIDE

In this chapter, we focus on two forms of individual interviews in qualitative research: semi-structured and unstructured interviews. We will explore

- the differences between structured interviewing and qualitative interviewing;
- the main characteristics of semi-structured and unstructured interviewing, as well as the differing degrees of structure that lie between the extremes;
- how to devise and use an interview guide for semi-structured interviewing;
- the different kinds of questions that you can ask in an interview guide;
- practical preparations for interviewing;
- methods of qualitative interviewing, including how you can conduct interviews online;
- the importance of recording and transcribing qualitative interviews;
- life history and oral history interviewing;
- the significance of qualitative interviewing in feminist research;
- the advantages and disadvantages of qualitative interviewing compared to participant observation.

19.1 Introduction

The interview is probably the most widely used method in qualitative research, largely because of the flexibility it offers, and the term 'qualitative interview' is often used very broadly to capture the range of different ways in which researchers talk to their participants. We outlined several different types of interview in Chapter 9 and saw that with the exception of the structured interview (or the *standardized interview*), which was our main focus in Chapter 9, these types are mainly qualitative in nature. We will examine the focus group and group interviewing in Chapter 20, but in this chapter we will explore the forms of individual interview that are primarily associated with qualitative research. The two main approaches that we will consider are the semi-structured interview and the unstructured interview.

19.2 The qualitative interview

Let's begin by looking at how qualitative interviewing differs from structured interviewing, and then at the main features of semi-structured and unstructured interviews.

Qualitative interviews vs structured interviews

Qualitative interviewing is usually very different from interviewing in quantitative research, in the following ways.

- The qualitative interview process is flexible and dynamic in nature. In quantitative research, the interview is designed to maximize the reliability and validity of measurement of key concepts because the researcher is investigating a clearly specified set of variables. In qualitative interviewing, the researcher's ideas are often more malleable, with much more room for the interviewee to shape the focus and direction of the interview.
- There is a greater interest in the interviewee's point of view. In quantitative research, the interview reflects the researcher's specific concerns, which participants are asked to quantify and rate within closed-question-type scales. Qualitative interviewers tend to be more interested in how the interviewee thinks and feels about the issues being explored, so they use more of an open-question format.
- Researchers often encourage spontaneous discussion in qualitative interviewing, as it gives insight into what the interviewee sees as relevant and important. Researchers usually discourage spontaneous discussion in quantitative research, as it is thought to constrain reliability.
- Interviewers can depart significantly from the interview guide. They can adjust emphases to address issues that emerge (see Research in focus 19.3 for an example), ask new questions that follow up interviewees' replies, vary the order of questions, and even alter the wording of questions. In quantitative interviewing, researchers usually avoid such changes because they will compromise the standardization of the interview process and therefore the reliability and validity of measurement.
- The researcher wants rich, detailed answers. Although this can mean that interviews are time-consuming to transcribe, code, and analyse, the material better reflects the depth of participants' views. In contrast, quantitative interviews are often designed to generate answers that can be coded and processed quickly.
- Researchers may interview the same people on more than one occasion (see Research in focus 19.3 for an example). In structured interviewing, unless the research is longitudinal, each person will only be interviewed on one occasion.

Types of qualitative interview

The characteristics listed above might suggest that all qualitative interviewing takes a similar form, but in fact it varies considerably depending on the approach taken by the interviewer. We mentioned in Section 19.1 that there are two main types of qualitative interviews: semi-structured and unstructured interviews.

In a *semi-structured interview*, the researcher has a list of questions to be asked, often referred to as an interview guide or interview schedule. The questions need to be framed in

RESEARCH IN FOCUS 19.1
Semi-structured interviewing

Twine (2017) was interested in investigating veganism as a practice and its increasing visibility in society. His research involved 40 semi-structured interviews in three UK cities (Manchester, Glasgow, and Lancaster). He writes:

> Participants were recruited initially through an advert in the *Vegan Society* magazine, through local vegan organisations and word of mouth. Once momentum was reached the sample was simple to obtain via the snowball technique. The interviews were semi-structured and open. First participants were asked to narrate their own story of transition. Second, participants were asked about their everyday doing of veganism. Finally, participants were asked a set of questions about transition and relationships . . . Interviews lasted between 40 and 75 minutes and took place either at the participant's home, my home, in my office or in a vegan friendly cafe.
>
> (Twine 2017: 171)

an open way that allows and encourages the interviewee to articulate a fairly detailed response. This is the most challenging aspect of developing an effective semi-structured interview schedule. The interviewer doesn't have to ask the questions exactly in the way outlined on the guide, and in some circumstances they can ask questions that were not planned as they pick up on interviewees' replies. The interviewee has some freedom in how they reply, as they are usually being asked to tell a story based on their own life experience or in their professional capacity as experts in a given field. Questions also need to be designed in a way that accommodates a different question order, in case, in the flow of answering, the participant anticipates some of the questions in the interview guide. However, it remains important that the interviewer asks all the questions on the guide and uses similar wording to what is in the guide, as this will be beneficial to the analysis and enable comparability between different respondents' answers, especially where there are a large number of interviewees. You can see these characteristics in the study we describe in Research in focus 19.1.

In an *unstructured interview*, a type common in **ethnographic** research, the researcher uses little more than a brief set of prompts to deal with a certain range of topics and the interviewee is relatively unconstrained in terms of the discussion. The interviewer may just ask a single question, to which the interviewee can respond freely, with the interviewer simply responding to points that seem worth following up. Unstructured interviewing tends to be very similar in character to a conversation (Burgess 1984), as you can see from Research in focus 19.2.

In keeping with the key preoccupations of qualitative researchers (see Section 16.3), in both unstructured and semi-structured interviewing the process is *flexible*—as illustrated by Research in focus 19.3. There is also an emphasis on exploring what the interviewee views as important in explaining and understanding events, patterns, and forms of behaviour.

RESEARCH IN FOCUS 19.2
Unstructured interviewing

Rayburn and Guittar (2013) describe how they carried out interviews with homeless people in Orlando, Florida, to gain an understanding of how they cope with the stigma associated with their situation. They describe their interviewing approach, which was broadly unstructured, as follows.

> During the interviews, participants discussed any aspects of their lives they wanted, for as long as they wanted. Although we prepared guiding questions, we tried not to lead participants in any particular direction during the interview. The main aim of interviews and focus groups was to generally inquire about sobriety, homelessness, and what it was like to live at a facility for homeless people, and through this, themes of stigma management emerged.
>
> (Rayburn and Guittar 2013: 164)

RESEARCH IN FOCUS 19.3
Flexibility in semi-structured interviewing

Mazmanian, Orlikowski, and Yates (2013) used semi-structured interviews to study the use of mobile email devices (for example phones, tablets, and laptops) by knowledge professionals: people whose work involves producing or analysing information or ideas. They conducted two rounds of interviews with 48 participants. The interviews were 'open-ended conversations covering a broad and evolving set of questions' (2013: 1340). The authors write:

> As interesting themes emerged in one interview, we incorporated these into our conversations in subsequent interviews. We began our interviews by asking participants to describe their jobs and organizational positions, as well as the nature of their work and communication practices. We then asked participants to describe in detail their activities during the prior day, from waking up to going to sleep. We were specifically interested in where, when, and why they engaged with their mobile email device to get their work done. This chronological narrative provided a structure to the interview, but we encouraged elaborations and digressions as people recounted and reflected on their communicative choices, actions, experiences, and outcomes.
>
> (Mazmanian et al. 2013: 1340)

We can see two forms of flexibility in this process. First, the interview would often take its lead from participants in that their 'elaborations and digressions' were followed through. Second, the interview evolved as the research progressed: the researchers brought 'interesting themes' that emerged in early interviews into later interviews. The evolving nature of the interview is also clear in the researchers' discussion of some of the questions asked:

> As it became clear that participants—although predominantly positive about their choice to use the mobile email devices—were also claiming a sense of compulsion to use them, we began to probe more deeply for these tensions. For example, we asked questions such as 'When you receive a message, how soon do you feel you have to respond? Why?' and 'Would you ever come to work without checking your emails from home? Why/why not?'
>
> (Mazmanian et al. 2013: 1340–1)

As the analysis developed and the researchers defined more specific **research questions**, they subsequently re-interviewed a sub-sample of these participants using a more structured instrument.

Semi-structured and unstructured interviews should not be considered as polar opposites, and there is quite a lot of variability between them, but most qualitative interviews can be broadly categorized as one type or the other. In both types of interview the interviewer does not follow a fixed schedule, and the process of data collection is much more dynamic than in quantitative interviewing.

Now that we have considered the characteristics of qualitative interviews, we can explore how they are conducted. In the next sections we walk through the various stages of qualitative interviewing, from preparation to carrying out the interview and then concluding it.

19.3 Preparing to conduct a qualitative interview

Even though qualitative interviews do not follow a fixed structure, they still require careful preparation. Researchers have to choose the type of interview (semi-structured or unstructured) they want to use, prepare questions, and consider some important practical matters in advance.

Semi-structured or unstructured interview?

Choosing whether to take a semi-structured or unstructured approach will depend on a number of things. These include your methodological framework, research questions, and any associated techniques of analysis.

- Researchers who are concerned that even the most basic interview guide will prevent them from gaining genuine access to the worldviews of their interviewees are likely to favour an unstructured interview.
- If the researcher is beginning the investigation with a fairly clear focus, rather than a very general idea of wanting to do research on a topic, they are likely to use semi-structured interviews because this type allows them to address more specific issues.
- If more than one person is going to carry out the fieldwork, semi-structured interviewing is likely to be preferable because it helps to ensure some consistency in interviewing style. (See Research in focus 19.2 and 19.3 for examples.)
- If the project involves multiple-case-study research (see Section 3.6), semi-structured interviews are again likely to be preferable because they ensure some cross-case comparability.

Preparing an interview guide

If you are preparing for a semi-structured interview, you will need to put together an interview guide. This is much less specific than a structured interview schedule (as described in Section 9.2), and usually refers to a list of issues that the researcher wants to address. It is crucial that the questioning allows interviewers to gain research participants' perspectives on their social world, so there must be flexibility in how the interviews are conducted. However, any questions and accompanying prompts must also be meaningful in relation to your research focus and any associated theoretical framework. This often means that something of a balance is needed and it can take a few attempts before you get it right. But whatever you do include in your interview guide, you must make sure that your participants can understand your questions from their perspective. Using theory-laden terms is not likely to be particularly helpful unless the participant understands what they mean. Figure 19.1 summarizes the main steps involved in formulating questions for an interview guide in qualitative research, and we provide some advice on drawing up your guide in Tips and skills 19.1.

19

FIGURE 19.1
Formulating questions for an interview guide

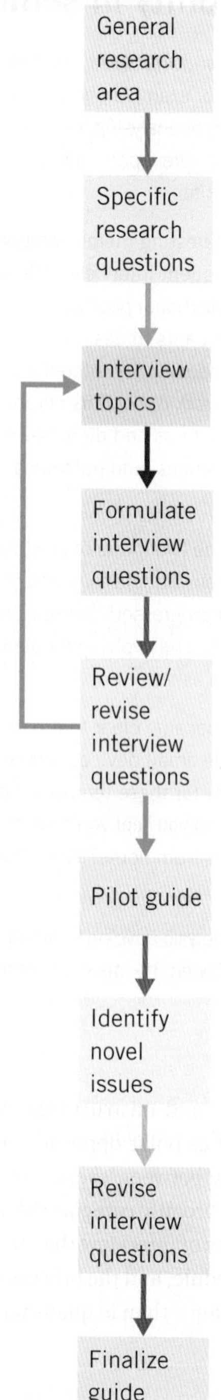

In preparing for any kind of qualitative interview, Lofland and Lofland (1995: 78) suggest asking yourself the question 'Just what about this thing is puzzling me?' You can apply this to each of the research questions you have generated, or you could use it to help you generate some

TIPS AND SKILLS 19.1
Preparing an interview guide

When preparing your interview guide, you should keep these points in mind.

- Create a certain amount of order in terms of the topic areas, so that your questions about them flow reasonably well, but be prepared to change the order of questions during the actual interview.
- Formulate interview questions or topics in a way that will help you to answer your research questions (but try not to make them too specific).
- Try to use language that will be comprehensible and relevant to the people you are interviewing.
- As in quantitative research, avoid asking leading questions: questions that could steer your interviewee towards answering in a particular way.
- Remember to ask for relevant contextual information of both a general kind (name, age, gender, etc.) and a specific kind (position in company, number of years employed, number of years involved in a group, etc.), because this information is useful for contextualizing people's answers.

research questions. Lofland and Lofland suggest that your curiosity might be stimulated by various activities: initial thoughts in different contexts, which you should write down as quickly as possible; discussions with colleagues, friends, and relatives; and, of course, the existing literature on the topic. You should not formulate such a specific research question (or questions) that you close off the possibility of exploring other areas of enquiry that might come up as you collect fieldwork data. Gradually, an order and structure will begin to emerge in your thinking around your research question(s), and this will form the basis for your interview guide.

Another question to ask yourself when drawing up an interview guide is 'What do I need to know in order to answer each of the research questions I'm interested in?' This means thinking about what the interviewee is likely to see as important in relation to each of your topic areas. Your questioning must cover the areas necessary to address your research questions but from the perspective of your interviewees. The experiential focus of a qualitative interview might include one or more of the following:

- values—of interviewee, of group, of organization;
- beliefs—of interviewee, of others, of group;
- behaviour—of interviewee, of others;
- formal and informal roles—of interviewee, of others;
- relationships—of interviewee, of others;
- places and locales;
- emotions—particularly of the interviewee, but also possibly of others;
- encounters;
- stories.

After you have developed your interview guide, you should reflect on the questions to make sure they really do cover the range of issues that you need to address. Indeed, although flexibility is a key characteristic of qualitative interviews, you still need to give some thought to *how* you will gather information about the phenomena you are interested in—in other words, the types of questions you will ask.

The types of questions that researchers ask in qualitative interviews vary considerably between and within studies. Kvale (1996) has identified nine different categories of question. Most semi-structured interviews will contain almost all of these types (see Research in focus 19.4), but interviews that rely only on lists of topics are likely to follow a looser format. Whichever method you are using, being familiar with these formats will help you to be flexible and effective in your interviewing as you will be able to draw on a variety of techniques to gather the richest possible data.

The nine types of question Kvale (1996) identifies are as follows.

1. *Introducing questions*: 'Please tell me about when your interest in *X* first began.' 'Have you ever . . . ?' 'Why did you go to . . . ?'
2. *Follow-up questions*: getting the interviewee to elaborate their answer, such as 'What do you mean by that?' or even 'Yeeees?' See Research in focus 19.4 for an example when the interviewer's simple interjection—

19

RESEARCH IN FOCUS 19.4

Using different question types in a semi-structured interview

The following exchange between the interviewer (*Int*) and interviewee (*R*) is taken from a study by Jones et al. (2010) that examined people who had taken early retirement. It is an interesting example of how interviewers can encourage people to expand on their original answers.

Int Yes, would you ever consider going back to work?

R Not at the moment, well I suppose it depended what was on offer, the big problem is, I did actually consider, or I considered and was considered for a directorship at Lloyds Insurance Company, so I went down and spoke to them, and I said to Diane [wife] before I went, it's like two days every month, you know you get paid thirty thousand a year, which is very nice, but it's two days every month and you've got to be there, which means if we went away for five weeks, we're sort of knackered and you've got to build all your holidays around it, so anyway went for the interview, I didn't get it but on the other hand I wasn't that enthusiastic about it.

Int No.

R But if I could actually do something I don't know, fundraising or something like that, and got paid for it, I wouldn't mind doing that, on my own terms and when it suits me, but I don't think I'd want to go back full time or consultancy.

(Jones et al. 2010: 111)

The striking feature of this exchange is the way in which the interviewer's simple interjection—'No'—draws out a further set of reflections that qualify the interviewee's previous remark. It acts as what Kvale calls a follow-up question. In the following exchange, there is an interesting use of a probing question:

R I'd like to find out what we want to do. I think the hardest thing we've got is both of us don't know what we want.

Int Uh huh. But I mean, you have been retired for ten years, haven't you?

R Ten years, yeah but we still don't know what we want to do. We're drifting, I suppose—nicely, no problems on that, but we haven't got anything . . . we keep on saying, we've got the money, what do we want to spend it on? We don't know. It's always been that we don't know what we want to do; we don't know whether we want to buy a house. We do look at them and say we don't want another house. We don't really want another car—can't be bothered about that. I should give my car away! And things like that, so . . . no, we don't know what we want to do.

(Jones et al. 2010: 113)

The interviewer is clearly paying close attention to what is being said because they pick up on the respondent's claimed lack of post-retirement direction and seek clarification of the interviewee's reply. There is a risk that the interviewer could be viewed as being judgemental (the subtext of their question could be seen as 'How on earth can you not have decided what you want to be doing with your retirement after ten years?') but the interviewer handles the comment skilfully and, as it happens, productively, in that the interviewee expands significantly on their earlier answer.

'No'—invites further information. Kvale suggests that repeating significant words in an answer can stimulate further explanation.

3. *Probing questions*: following up what has been said through direct questioning, such as 'Could you say some more about that?' 'You said earlier that you prefer not to *X*. Could you say what kinds of things have put you off *X*?' 'In what ways do you find *X* disturbing?' In Research in focus 19.4 the interviewer asks, 'Uh huh. But I mean, you have been retired for ten years, haven't you?' In effect, the interviewer is trying to get the interviewee to explain how he could have been retired for ten years and yet still not know what his plans were.

4. *Specifying questions*: 'What did you do then?' 'How did *X* react to what you said?' 'What effect did *X* have on you?' In Research in focus 19.3, the question

'When you receive a message, how soon do you feel you have to respond? Why?' is of this type.

5. *Direct questions*: 'Do you find it easy to keep smiling when serving customers?' 'Are you happy with the way you and your husband decide how money should be spent?' These kinds of questions are perhaps best left until towards the end of the interview, so that they do not influence the direction of the interview too much. In Research in focus 19.3, the question 'Would you ever come to work without checking your emails from home? Why/why not?' is of this type. A further example is in Research in focus 19.4, where the interviewer asks, 'would you ever consider going back to work?'
6. *Indirect questions*: like their direct counterparts, these questions are also framed around specific issues, but are perhaps more nuanced. 'What do most people round here think of the ways that management treats its staff?', perhaps followed up by 'Is that the way you feel too?', could be one example. These questions allow the researcher to gain some insight into the individual's own view.
7. *Structuring questions*: 'I would now like to move on to a different topic, is that OK?'
8. *Silence*: allowing pauses signals that you want to give the interviewee the opportunity to reflect on and expand an answer.
9. *Interpreting questions*: 'Do you mean that your leadership role has had to change from one of encouraging others to a more directive one?' 'Is it fair to say that what you are suggesting is that you don't mind being friendly towards customers most of the time, but when they are unpleasant or demanding you find it more difficult?'

The kind of questions asked in qualitative interviewing also vary in terms of the stage of the interview. Charmaz (2002) distinguishes between three types of questions:

- *Initial open-ended questions*: 'What events led to . . . ?' 'What was your life like prior to . . . ?' 'How far is this organization typical of others you have worked in?'
- *Intermediate questions*: 'How did you feel about . . . when you first learned about it?' 'What immediate impacts did . . . have on your life?' 'What do you like most/least about working in this organization?'
- *Ending questions*: 'How far have your views about . . . changed?' 'What advice would you give now to someone who finds that they must get experience . . . ?' 'If you had your time again, would you choose to work for this organization?'

Most questions are likely to be of the intermediate type, and in practice there is also likely to be overlap between the three types, but this idea of ordering questions is useful to bear in mind because it can help you to consider the flow of the interview.

Practical preparations

As well as preparing an interview guide, you will also need to consider some practical issues that can influence the direction and flow of the interview.

- Make sure you are familiar with the setting in which the interviewee works or lives. This will help you to understand what the interviewee is saying in their own terms.
- Try to show the interviewee that you have a compelling reason for wanting to examine the topic that you are addressing: why it is important, why you selected them to be interviewed, and so on.
- Get hold of a good-quality recording device and microphone. Qualitative researchers nearly always record and then transcribe their interviews (see 'Recording and transcription'). A good microphone is important, because many interviews are let down by poor recording. Make sure you are familiar with how to use the equipment before beginning your interviews.
- Try to ensure that the interview takes place somewhere quiet, so that there is little chance of background noise affecting the quality of the recording. The setting should also be private so interviewees do not have to worry about being overheard.

19.4 Conducting a qualitative interview

While interviewing might appear to be little more than a list of questions—a sort of guided conversation—conducting an effective interview actually requires quite a high degree of skill. In this section we will consider some of the issues that can impact on the interview. We will explore the qualities that make an interviewer effective, how you should use the interview guide you have drawn up, the different methods of interviewing, and how to record and transcribe the interview.

Qualities of an effective interviewer

The more effective you are as an interviewer, the richer the data you will collect. Kvale (1996) has listed a number of qualities that make a successful interviewer (see Tips and skills 19.2). What underpins a lot of the qualities he specifies is that the interviewer must be a good *listener*, which means being active and alert in the interview. An inability to listen may mean failing to pick up on a really important point or asking a pointless question later in the interview, which could irritate the interviewee. Kvale's list is also underpinned by a need for the interviewer to be *flexible* and *non-judgemental* as far as possible. Generally, they should try not to indicate agreement or disagreement with the interviewee, even if the interviewee seeks a response to their views, as this may distort later answers.

The balance between being active but not too intrusive is difficult to strike, and an interviewer must be very responsive to not only what the interviewee is saying (or not saying), but also what they are doing. Something like body language may indicate that the interviewee is becoming anxious about a line of questioning. An ethically sensitive interviewer will not want to place undue pressure on the person they are talking to and will need to be prepared to cut short a line of questioning if it is clearly a source of concern.

Although interviewing can produce extremely rich data, it is very demanding, and students who are new to

TIPS AND SKILLS 19.2
Criteria of a successful interviewer

Kvale (1996) has proposed a very useful list of 10 qualities that make a successful interviewer, and these are well worth bearing in mind when you conduct your interviews. A successful interviewer should have the following traits.

1. *Knowledgeable*: is thoroughly familiar with the focus of the interview; **pilot** interviews can be useful in developing this knowledge.
2. *Structuring*: states the purpose for the interview; begins and closes it appropriately; asks whether the interviewee has questions.
3. *Clear*: asks simple, easy, short questions; uses as little jargon as possible.
4. *Gentle*: allows people to finish what they are saying; gives them time to think; tolerates pauses.
5. *Sensitive*: listens attentively to what is said and how it is said; is empathetic in dealing with the interviewee.
6. *Open*: responds to what is important to the interviewee and is flexible.
7. *Steering*: knows what they want to find out and is able to direct the flow of the conversation accordingly. The interviewer can do this by following the interview guide, but they will often need to have the presence of mind to steer the conversation if it goes off-topic.
8. *Critical*: is prepared to challenge what the interviewee says—for example, dealing with inconsistencies in the interviewee's replies.
9. *Remembering*: relates what the interviewee says to what they previously said.
10. *Interpreting*: clarifies and extends meanings of interviewees' statements, but without imposing meaning on them.

To Kvale's list we would add the following.

- *Balanced*: does not talk too much, which may make the interviewee passive, and does not talk too little, which may result in the interviewee feeling that they are not talking along the right lines.
- *Ethically sensitive*: is sensitive to the ethical dimension of interviewing, ensuring that the interviewee appreciates what the research is about and its purposes, and understands that their answers will be treated confidentially.

the method sometimes do not fully appreciate the personal issues involved. It is worth conducting some pilot interviews, not just to test how well the interview flows but also to develop experience of interviewing (see Tips and skills 19.3). Pilot interviews are a sort of practice run where you try out your planned interview guide with a participant to see how well it works. This process will help you to identify any problems with your interview preparations. It might result in you restructuring your interview guide so that it flows better, or altering specific questions so that they are easier for the interviewee to interpret. Piloting will also help you to familiarize yourself with the process of interviewing and help you become more comfortable in working with silences! Follow your reading of Tips and skills 19.3 with Learn from experience 19.1, in which our panellist Simon reflects on how he approached interviewing for the first time and what he learned from the experience.

Using an interview guide

When it comes to using an interview guide, flexibility is often key. Indeed, one of the big advantages of taking a semi-structured approach is that it allows the interviewer to shape the questions around the needs of the interviewee. This might mean slightly diverging from the questions in the interview guide, or changing the order of the questions if the participant anticipates one of the questions before it has been asked. The dynamic nature of semi-structured interviewing allows researchers to depart from their interview guide where necessary in order to get the best data from each interviewee.

Research in focus 19.5 is a short transcript from an interview with visitors to Disney theme parks by this book's original author, Alan Bryman (1999). It provides a useful example of how an interviewer needs to keep flexibility in mind when conducting an interview. Alan conducted

TIPS AND SKILLS 19.3
Interviewing for the first time

The prospect of doing your first interview can be daunting, and it is easy to make some mistakes when you first begin interviewing. A study of American postgraduates' experiences of an interview training course showed that novice interviewers face five challenges that are worth bearing in mind when approaching your first interview(s) (Roulston et al. 2003).

1. *Unexpected interviewee behaviour or environmental problems.* Roulston et al.'s novice interviewers were easily discomfited by responses or behaviour from interviewees, and by problems of noise nearby. When you go into the interview, bear in mind that things may not go according to plan. Interviewees sometimes say things that are surprising—some like to startle or even shock interviewers—and there can be many distractions around where the interview takes place. You clearly cannot plan for or control all of these things, but you can bear in mind that they might happen and try to limit their impact on you and on the course of the interview.
2. *Intrusion of own biases and expectations.* When they read transcripts of their interviews, some of the students were surprised by how their own biases and expectations were evident in the ways they asked questions and followed up on replies.
3. *Maintaining focus in asking questions.* Students reported that they sometimes had difficulty probing answers, asking follow-up questions, and clarifying questions in a way that did not lose sight of the research topic and what the questions were getting at.
4. *Dealing with sensitive issues.* Some students asked questions that caused interviewees to become upset, and this often had a negative impact on the course of the interview. However, most students felt that they coped reasonably well with such emotionally charged situations.
5. *Transcription.* Many reported finding **transcription** difficult and time-consuming—more so than they had imagined.

There are, of course, many other possible issues that affect first-time interviewers. Many do not go away either, no matter how experienced you become. It is difficult to know how to deal with some of these issues, but it is worth being aware that they can arise and that they may have the biggest impact when you are new to interviewing.

LEARN FROM EXPERIENCE 19.1

Learning how to interview

Qualitative interviewing is a skill—and although the idea of 'a guided conversation' sounds easy to do, it is often much harder to achieve in practice. Not only do you have to ask and reformulate questions, you also need to listen closely to the answers and think about how those responses relate to other questions in the interview guide. This is all complicated further by the fact that interviewees can respond quite differently to the same set of questions—as Simon discovered:

> I thought interviews would be really easy—you just sit down and read out questions, right? Well, it wasn't really that straightforward for me. My first interview was great. I was ready, and the person was really invested in what I was doing so we had a great interview. But others were much more difficult. Some people were obviously busy and didn't necessarily have time to talk, whereas others were quite sceptical of me. Those interviews were much more difficult. It was really hard to find the right balance of professionalism and friendliness that got people to trust me. I'm not sure I ever mastered that; rapport was a lot more important than I had thought.
>
> Simon

You can read about our panellists' backgrounds and research experiences on page xxvi.

RESEARCH IN FOCUS 19.5

Encouraging interviewees to expand on responses in a semi-structured interview

Alan Bryman was interested in how some of the business practices of Disney had influenced society more generally, and he interviewed visitors to Disney theme parks to find out how they interpreted their experiences (Bryman 1999). The following extract, which is taken from an interview with a couple in their 60s who had visited Walt Disney World in Orlando, Florida, illustrates why the interviewer needs to keep flexibility in mind when conducting an interview.

Interviewer OK. What were your views or feelings about the presentation of different cultures, as shown in, for example, Jungle Cruise or It's a Small World at the Magic Kingdom or in World Showcase at Epcot?

Wife Well, I thought the different countries at Epcot were wonderful, but I need to say more than that, don't I?

19

Husband They were very good and some were better than others, but that was down to the host countries themselves really, as I suppose each of the countries represented would have been responsible for their own part, so that's nothing to do with Disney, I wouldn't have thought. I mean some of the landmarks were hard to recognize for what they were supposed to be, but some were very well done. Britain was OK, but there was only a pub and a Welsh shop there really, whereas some of the other pavilions, as I think they were called, were good ambassadors for the countries they represented. China, for example, had an excellent 360-degree film showing parts of China and I found that very interesting.

Interviewer Did you think there was anything lacking about the content?

Husband Well I did notice that there weren't many black people at World Showcase, particularly the American Adventure. Now whether we were there on an unusual day in that respect I don't know, but we saw plenty of black Americans in the Magic Kingdom and other places, but very few if any in that World Showcase. And there was certainly little mention of black history in the

American Adventure presentation, so maybe they felt alienated by that, I don't know, but they were noticeable by their absence.

Interviewer So did you think there were any special emphases?

Husband Well thinking about it now, because I hadn't really given this any consideration before you started asking about it, but thinking about it now, it was only really representative of the developed world, you know, Britain, America, Japan, world leaders many of them in technology, and there was nothing of the Third World there. Maybe that's their own fault, maybe they were asked to participate and didn't, but now that I think about it, that does come to me. What do you think, love?

Wife Well, like you, I hadn't thought of it like that before, but I agree with you.

this interview with a couple in their 60s who had visited Walt Disney World in Orlando, Florida, to investigate their interpretations of the theme park.

The sequence begins with the interviewer asking what would be considered a 'direct question' in terms of Kvale's (1996) nine types. The initial reply is very bland and does little more than reflect the interviewees' positive feelings about their visit to Disney World. The wife acknowledges this when she says 'but I need to say more than that, don't I?' Interviewees often know that they are expected to be expansive in their answers, and as this sequence occurred around halfway through the interview, the interviewees had realized by this point that more details were expected. There is a slight hint of embarrassment that the answer has been so brief and not very illuminating. The husband's answer is more expansive but not particularly enlightening, so the interviewer uses probing questions to gather more information.

The interviewer's first prompt ('Did you think there was anything lacking about the content?') produces a more interesting response from the husband: he begins to suggest that black people might be under-represented in attractions such as the American Adventure, a dramatic production that tells the story of America through a debate between two audio-animatronic figures—Mark Twain and Benjamin Franklin. The second prompt ('So did you think there were any special emphases?') produces further useful reflection, this time carrying the implication that 'Third World' (developing) countries are under-represented in World Showcase in the Epcot Centre (an area of the theme park that claims to provide a country-by-country world tour, showcasing national culture, history, architecture, cuisine etc.). The couple are clearly aware that it is the prompting that has led to these reflections when they say: 'Well thinking about it now, because I hadn't really given this any consideration before you started asking about it' and 'Well, like you, I hadn't thought of it like that before.' This is the whole point of prompting—to get the interviewee to think more about the topic and to give them the opportunity to provide a more detailed response. It is not a leading question, because the interviewer didn't ask 'Do you think that the Disney company fails to recognize the significance of black history (or ignores the developing world) in its presentation of different cultures?'

Being flexible when conducting qualitative interviews is not only about being responsive to what interviewees say to you and following up interesting points that they make. As we have noted, flexibility is also significant in such areas as varying the order of questions, following up leads, and clearing up inconsistencies in answers. It is important in other respects too, for example in coping with technical difficulties such as audio-recording equipment breakdown or managing refusals by interviewees to allow a recording to take place.

It is also common to find that as soon as researchers switch off their recording equipment, the interviewee continues to reflect on the topic of interest and sometimes will say more interesting things than in the interview. It is usually not feasible to begin recording again because it will disrupt the flow of the conversation and the interviewee is now tacitly speaking 'off-record', so if this happens, try to take some notes while the person is talking or as soon as possible after they leave. Such 'unsolicited accounts' can often be the source of revealing information or views (Hammersley and Atkinson 2019). This is certainly what Parker found when he conducted research on three British organizations—a National Health Service District Health Authority, a building society (a bank), and a manufacturing company—that relied mainly on semi-structured interviews: 'Indeed, some of the most valuable parts of the interview took place after the tape had been switched off, the closing intimacies of the conversation being prefixed with a silent or explicit "well, if you want to know what I really think . . . ". Needless to say, a visit to the toilet to write up as much as I could remember followed almost immediately' (Parker 2000: 236).

In terms of both ethics and good research practice, it will probably not be viable to quote this material verbatim in your analysis or your final report. However, it can help contextualize and develop your findings beyond the content of the interview itself. If you are uncertain about whether to include this material, it is a good idea to ask your interviewee whether they are happy for you to use anything they said 'off the record' to help inform your project.

Methods of interviewing

A 'standard' qualitative interview could be described as involving spoken questions and being conducted face-to-face, at a single location. Here, we discuss some alternative methods of conducting this kind of interview: using 'props' such as **vignettes** and visual media to provide a basis for discussions; using the mobile interview approach (conducting interviews on the move); and conducting the interview remotely, via telephone, email or online messaging, or video call.

Vignettes and photo-elicitation

Although there may be times when you want to ask fairly general questions, these are usually best avoided. Indeed, Mason (2002) suggests that when they are used, it often only leads interviewees to ask the interviewer to clarify what they meant. For example, the question 'How do you think you are affected by advertising?' is likely to be met with the response 'In what way?' Vignette questions can be a useful alternative, outlining a specific situation that can lead to a more focused discussion. Vignettes (which we cover in Section 11.4) are brief descriptions of an event or episode, and you can use them to ground interviewees' views and accounts of behaviour in particular situations (Barter and Renold 1999). Researchers usually devise them before the interview, and they can be read aloud to interviewees, or given to them in written format. In either case, the point is to present interviewees with concrete and realistic scenarios so that researchers can assess how certain contexts might affect behaviour. Research in focus 19.6 provides two examples of studies that made effective use of vignettes to facilitate questioning.

Another way to facilitate questioning in qualitative interviews is with photos. (We discussed the use of visual media with respect to visual ethnography in Chapter 18, but here we look at it in the specific context of interviewing.) Using photos to generate discussion in the context of a qualitative interview is often called **photo-elicitation**. This has been defined as 'the simple idea of inserting a photograph into a research interview' (Harper 2002: 13). In some cases, the photos might be part of the interviewee's collection (see Research in focus 19.7 for an example), while in others, researchers actually create the photos as a stimulus for questioning. In their study of how men's identities change after they have their first child, Henwood, Shirani, and Finn (2011) used some of the fathers' own photos but also presented them with historical photographs depicting fatherhood and

RESEARCH IN FOCUS 19.6
Studies using vignettes

Edmiston (2018) used vignettes in a study of attitudes toward welfare, inequality, and wealth redistribution. Having encouraged participants to reflect upon their material well-being and position, Edmiston presented them with a number of vignettes and used these as the bases for an applied discussion about structural inequality, individual agency, and welfare. Conducted with 28 materially deprived individuals and 22 affluent people, the structured conversation allowed him to explore understandings of inequality and welfare among those who are often absent from, or mischaracterized within, mainstream political and policy discourse.

Jenkins et al. (2010) also made use of the vignette technique with a sample of 78 drug users, some of whom were beginning drug treatment and some who were further through the rehabilitation process. Of the original sample, 59 were re-interviewed 12 weeks later and were asked to comment on the vignette in respect to the treatment they had received. This longitudinal element allowed the researchers to chart changes in the respondents' orientation to drugs over time. In fact, just over one-third of those interviewed a second time showed a marked change of perspective.

RESEARCH IN FOCUS 19.7
A photo-elicitation study

Twine (2006) discusses her use of photo-elicitation in interviews designed to explore racial consciousness in inter-racial families across several different countries. In one study, she interviewed 'white mothers of African-descent children' and used family photos to examine the practices through which cultural identity is generated, and how racial identities shift over time. Her interviews explored what was important to the interviewees about the photos. In combination with the interviews, the photos allowed Twine to reveal that the images of apparent familial and racial harmony masked an underlying opposition to the inter-racial partnership that was created. She found this opposition on both sides of the family. However, the use of both the photos and the interview generated an account in which these tensions were balanced by considerable harmony. Referring to the particular photo-elicitation interview that is the focus of her article, Twine (2006: 507) writes: 'photo-interview combined with my analysis of the photographs brought into sharp relief the emphasis that I had placed on conflicts, tensions and racial troubles while not considering the degree of social cohesion that existed.' Twine argues that the photos enabled the interviewees to reflect on the struggles of the past in relation to the present and to reframe their understanding of the significance of the photos. What emerges is a balanced account of harmony and disharmony and of change in relationships in connection with the life course.

masculinity. They used five images, going from the Victorian era through the 1950s and on to the present day. Interviewees were asked to discuss their reactions to the photos, considering what they represented and how it related to them. In this way, the researchers used historical photographs to explore contemporary perceptions of fatherhood and masculine identity.

Harper (2002) argues that using photos in interviews can serve several useful roles (and we could see these points as also applying to the use of vignettes).

- Images can help to ground the researcher's interview questions. The kinds of things that social researchers are interested in are often quite difficult for others to relate to. Using a photo can provide both parties with a meaningful context for discussion.
- Asking interviewees to engage visually with familiar settings and objects may help them to think in different ways about the things they take for granted.
- The use of photos may prompt the interviewee to remember people, events, or situations that they might otherwise have forgotten.

However, Harper also warns that using photos does not necessarily result in superior qualitative interviews. He cites a study he conducted of farmers in the USA through which he tried to understand their perspectives on a range of issues, including how they defined the land and the animals they nurtured and their views of changes in farming technology. Unfortunately, the photos he took 'did not evoke deep reflections on the issues I was interested in' and 'did not *break the frame* of farmers' normal views' (Harper 2002: 20; emphasis in original). He suggests that the photos may have been too familiar in appearance to the farmers, in that they possibly looked similar to images from farming magazines. When he subsequently took aerial photographs and incorporated historical ones, farmers were more reflective in their interviews. From a leading exponent of visual **research methods**, this example reminds us that there is no way of guaranteeing interesting data in qualitative investigations. It also suggests that researchers need to be prepared to **experiment** when things do not go quite according to plan.

The mobile interview approach

At the beginning of this century, the emergence of the so-called 'new mobilities' paradigm was meant to draw attention to the fact that people are increasingly on the move and that traditionally, the social sciences have used relatively static research methods (see, for example, Sheller and Urry 2006). As a result, there has been growing interest in focusing on and developing methods for studying people moving about the human world. This has resulted in approaches such as the mobile interview.

This method involves interviewing participants as they move around their environments. The 'walking interview' is one type of mobile interview. It was used by Clark and Emmel (2010: 1) as a 'way of understanding senses of places and neighbourhood attachment, and the extent to which social networks are contextualised and reproduced spatially'. Clark and Emmel argue that this kind of interview has a number of advantages over static interviews:

- it increases interviewees' control over the direction of the interview;
- it focuses more on what interviewees see as important to them in their neighbourhoods;
- it helps to connect experiences and contexts more closely, stimulating reflections on those connections;
- it can produce reflections that would not otherwise have arisen; and
- it is more closely related to people's everyday lives than static interviewing.

The idea is to get participants to reflect on the meaning of places to them. This might include their memories, which places they go to or do not go to, people they know in each location, or what they like or dislike about an area. In their study, Clark and Emmel used a digital recorder, but they note that a video recording might provide more detailed information as it can provide a more visually rich representation of any routes taken. However, as they point out, a video recording may make people too self-conscious and there would be significant ethical implications of videoing in public without their consent (see the discussion in Chapter 6 about the ethics of photographing or recording members of the public).

In addition to collecting observational data, Ferguson (2016) accompanied social workers on their way to their clients. He conducted interviews with them en route, either on foot or in the car, and made audio recordings of their conversations. Ferguson points out that these interviews provided him with information about the clients and their situation, about the social workers' plans for the meeting, about how they felt about the case at that particular time, and about how they were feeling at the point of arrival. He could then capture their thoughts afterwards about how the meeting had gone and their feelings about the clients. The car journey also gave social workers the chance to prepare themselves for what could sometimes be difficult meetings *and* allowed them to verbally articulate thoughts and feelings that they might not have otherwise expressed.

Mobile interviews, then, provide opportunities for social researchers to make use of the fact that their participants are often on the move and to reflect that movement in the kinds of data they collect. In both of the examples we have considered, the fact of movement allowed the researchers to collect data that probably would not have been accessible through conventional static methods.

Telephone interviewing

Telephone interviewing is quite common in **survey research** but has not been widely used in qualitative research. However, it can have certain benefits compared to face-to-face qualitative interviewing, many of which are similar to those we considered in the context of survey interviewing (Chapter 9). One benefit is, of course, cost: it will be much cheaper to conduct qualitative interviews by telephone. This method is likely to be especially useful for dispersed groups and when interviewer safety is a consideration. It can also be more effective to ask sensitive questions by telephone, as interviewees may be less anxious about answering when the interviewer is not physically present (see Drabble et al. 2016).

However, there is also evidence to suggest that whether researchers pose questions by telephone or in person—whichever 'interview mode' they use—makes little difference to the answers that respondents give (such differences are usually referred to as 'mode effects' in social science literature). Vogl (2013) compared qualitative data collected through telephone and face-to-face interviews. She conducted 112 semi-structured interviews with 56 children aged 5, 7, 9, and 11, interviewing each child once by telephone and once face-to-face. This allowed her to compare interview modes, and the results revealed very little difference between them. In their study of visitors' and correctional officers' views of visiting jail inmates in California, Sturges and Hanrahan (2004) drew similar conclusions. However, Irvine et al. (2013) conducted a small number of semi-structured interviews on the topic of mental health and employment. Some interviews were face-to-face and some were by telephone. Unlike Vogl and Sturges and Hanrahan, they found that interviewees tended to talk for longer in face-to-face interviews. Interestingly, they also found differences between the two modes in terms of the behaviour of the interviewer. For example, the interviewer was more likely in face-to-face interviews to give vocalized responses to show that they understood what was being said (such as 'yeah' and 'mm-hm'). They were also more likely not to finish their questions fully, or the questions were less likely to be grammatically correct. But overall, the studies of mode effects for telephone and face-to-face qualitative interviewing are fairly reassuring and suggest that we do not need to be too concerned about data quality being lower when interviews are conducted by telephone mode.

That said, telephone interviews do have some disadvantages for qualitative interviewing.

- They will not be appropriate for some groups of interviewees, such as those with no or limited access to a telephone.
- They are unlikely to work well with interviews that will last a long time, as it is much easier for the interviewee to end a telephone interview than one conducted in person. (This is more significant for qualitative than quantitative interviews, as they are often time-consuming for interviewees.)
- They prevent the interviewer from observing body language to see how interviewees respond physically to questions. As we noted earlier, in 'Qualities of an effective interviewer', body language is important because it reveals things like discomfort or confusion.
- There can be technical difficulties with recording telephone interviews. There are various devices and mobile phone apps that can do this, but, as always, you should check any permissions when downloading the app. If you are using a landline you will need access to special equipment, and there is always the possibility that the line will be poor.
- The interviewer cannot collect potentially useful observational material about such things as the setting (local area, type of building, whether lots of people are around, etc.).

Interviewing via email or online messaging

Another popular way to conduct qualitative interviews is via email or online messaging. This type of approach is useful where the participant needs to have more control over their participation. This may be because the interviewee is particularly busy, as is often the case in elite interviewing (interviewing individuals who are at the 'top' of a system, whether this is in politics, in an industry, or in terms of their social status), or where the content of the interview is particularly sensitive. It may also be due to the situational context—for example, the interviewee may have difficulty accessing possible locations for face-to-face interviewing and may have better access via an online environment. Not only do these advantages allow the researcher to access samples that may otherwise be hard to reach, it has the added bonus that responses are already typed up and there is no need to transcribe them (Gibson 2010).

Compared with a face-to-face approach, there is always a risk that the respondent will just drop out of the exchange because the interview can take place over quite a long period of time. However, it may also be the case that the greater amount of control the participant has in choosing when and how to respond can facilitate a relationship of mutual trust (Mason and Ide 2014). This can make it easier for respondents to maintain a longer-term commitment to the interview. It also makes it easier for the researcher to go back to their interviewees for further reflection, something that is difficult to do with the face-to-face interview (Gibson 2010). To facilitate this process of trust, Mann and Stewart (2000) suggest that it is important for interviewers to keep sending messages to respondents to reassure them that what they have written is helpful and significant.

When working in an asynchronous mode such as email (where questions and responses do not take place at the same time), another issue is whether to send all the questions at once or to interview on the basis of a single question followed by a reply. The problem with the former tactic is that respondents may read all the questions and then reply only to those that they feel interested in, or to which they feel they can make a genuine contribution. One question at a time is therefore likely to be more reliable. Bampton and Cowton (2002) report their experiences of conducting email interviews by sending questions in small batches. They argue that this approach took pressure off interviewees to reply quickly, gave them the opportunity to provide considered responses (although the authors recognize that there may have been a loss of spontaneity), and gave the interviewers more of an opportunity to respond to interviewees' answers.

There is evidence that prospective interviewees are more likely to agree to participate if researchers solicit their agreement prior to sending them the questions. This is also the case if the researcher uses some form of self-disclosure, such as directing the person they are contacting to the researcher's website, which contains personal information relevant to the research issue (Curasi 2001; O'Connor and Madge 2001). The argument for obtaining agreement from interviewees before sending them questions to be answered is that unsolicited emails can be seen as a nuisance or as spam.

Curasi (2001) conducted a study in which they contrasted 24 online interviews carried out through email correspondence (and therefore asynchronously) with 24 parallel face-to-face interviews. The interviews were about online shopping. She found the following features.

- Face-to-face interviewers are better able than online interviewers to maintain rapport with respondents (we discussed the importance of rapport in Chapter 9).
- Completing an online interview requires more commitment and motivation, but, because of this, replies

are often more detailed and considered than with face-to-face interviews.

- Online interviewers are less able to have an impact on whether the interview is successful or not because they are more remote. This means they are less able to adapt to any cues that might be inferred in a face-to-face interview.
- Online interviewees' answers tend to be more considered and grammatically correct because they have more time to think about their responses and can tidy them up before sending them. Whether this is a positive feature is debatable: there is the obvious advantage of a 'clean' transcript, but there may be some loss of spontaneity—this is what Gibson (2010) found when she compared email and face-to-face interviews.
- Follow-up probes can be carried out in online interviews, as well as in face-to-face ones.

On the other hand, Curasi also found that the interviews that produced the least detailed data were online interviews. This and the other differences could be to do with the fact that, whereas a qualitative face-to-face interview is *spoken*, the parallel online interview is *typed*. The significance of this difference in the nature of the respondent's mode of answering has not been fully appreciated. However, it could be that the immediacy of face-to-face interviews provides greater opportunity for the interviewer *and* interviewee to offer verbal and non-verbal cues that facilitate greater interaction and further information.

It is very clear from many of the discussions about interviews by email that a significant problem for many interviewers is keeping respondents involved in the interview when questions are being sent one or two at a time. Respondents tend to lose momentum or interest. However, Kivits (2005) has shown that regularly recontacting interviewees and adopting an accessible and understanding style can not only help to maintain momentum for many interviewees, but also bring some who have lost interest or forgotten to reply back into the research.

Evans, Elford, and Wiggins (2008) employed both face-to-face and **synchronous online interviews** in a study of gay men and HIV. They found that the online interviews lasted longer and produced considerably fewer words, and that there was considerably more variation in both interview length and number of words in the face-to-face context. James (2016) also notes that using email as a means of interviewing provides a way for people to participate in research that is important to them, and that some of these people might not have been able to do so if the researcher had to rely on face-to-face interviews.

Video call interviewing

Apps and software such as Microsoft Teams, Zoom, Google Hangouts, WhatsApp, and FaceTime are increasingly used to conduct interviews remotely via video calls. Researchers' reflections on their experiences of using video calls for interviewing have been broadly positive (see, for example, Iacono et al. 2016; Seitz 2015; Deakin and Wakefield 2014). The obvious advantage over telephone interviewing is that it allows interviewee and interviewer to see each other, like in a face-to-face interview, but there are other advantages too.

- Video call interviews are more flexible than face-to-face interviews, in that it is easier to accommodate last-minute changes to their day and time.
- There are obvious time and cost savings as there is no need for interviewer or interviewee to travel, which is a major advantage with geographically dispersed samples.
- The convenience of being interviewed by video call may encourage some people to agree to be interviewed when they might otherwise have declined.
- There are fewer concerns about the safety of interviewer and interviewee, particularly when the interview is being conducted at night.
- There seems to be little evidence that the interviewer's ability to build rapport is significantly lower via video call than in face-to-face interviews.

However, there are some limitations that are worth noting too.

- There are potential technological problems. Not everyone has a high-speed wifi connection or a device that is capable of video calling, and not everyone is familiar with the relevant platforms.
- The quality of the connection can fluctuate (and sometimes cut out altogether), which can interrupt the flow of the interview. Slight audio delays and breaking up of speech can also result in poor recordings of interviews, which can make them difficult to transcribe.
- Unlike in an email interview, the respondent's answers need to be transcribed, as in traditional qualitative interviewing. Some apps have a voice-transcription feature, but the quality can vary considerably.
- Although it is clearly helpful for interviewers and interviewees to be able to see each other, so that visual cues can be picked up, responses may be affected by visual characteristics of the interviewer, such as gender, age, and ethnic group.

- There is some evidence that prospective interviewees for this method are less reliable than face-to-face interviewees, in that they are more likely to drop out at the last moment.
- It can sometimes be harder to persuade people to agree to a video call than a telephone call. This was a finding of Weinmann et al.'s (2012) study of German youth.

Interviewing via video call clearly has great potential and some of the difficulties above are likely to become less pronounced as people get more familiar with the software and as software and wifi connections improve.

Recording and transcription

Most qualitative interviews are recorded. This is because it allows the researcher to have a more or less accurate account of what was said during the interview. 'Transcribing' refers to the process of transforming that spoken material into a written format. However, this process is not always as straightforward as you might imagine. How we speak is not the same as how we write, so we need to discuss the process of both recording and transcribing in a little more detail.

Why record and transcribe?

Recording and **transcribing** is essential for approaches that involve detailed attention to language, such as **conversation analysis** and **discourse analysis** (see Chapter 21), but researchers who use qualitative interviews and focus groups (see Chapter 20) also tend to follow this process. Generally, qualitative researchers are interested not just in *what* people say, but also in the *way* that they say it, and if they are going to factor this into their analysis they need to have access to a complete account of the series of exchanges in an interview.

Heritage (1984: 238) suggests that recording and transcribing interviews has the following advantages.

- It helps to correct the natural limitations of our memories and our interpretations of what people might have said in interviews.
- It allows more thorough examination of what people say.
- It allows repeated examinations of interviewees' answers.
- It means that the data can be scrutinized by other researchers, who can evaluate the analysis that is carried out by the original researchers (that is, a **secondary analysis**).
- It therefore helps to counter accusations that a researcher's analysis might have been influenced by their values or biases.
- It allows the data to be reused in other ways from those intended by the original researcher—for example, in the light of new theoretical ideas or analytic strategies.

We would add that recording and transcribing interview data also allows the interviewer to fully concentrate on the interview, making them more effective (see 'Qualities of an effective interviewer'). Even if they are a very quick writer or typist, being distracted by taking notes will prevent them being fully alert to what is being said—and not said—and responding accordingly (for example following up interesting points, prompting and probing where necessary, drawing attention to any inconsistencies in the interviewee's answers, and reading body language).

The process of recording and transcribing

Most qualitative interviews today are recorded digitally. These recordings can be backed up and played back as many times as necessary on any device with the appropriate software. Digital recordings are of high sound quality compared to previous non-digital methods, and they can also be enhanced to filter out background noise, making the discussion clearer and mistakes in transcription less likely. Researchers can set bookmarks or time markers so that they can easily navigate to specific segments that might be unclear, or particularly interesting, and play them repeatedly.

To facilitate the analysis, interview recordings are usually transcribed, a process that can be very time-consuming—as our panellist Scarlett cautions in Learn from experience 19.2. Although transcription *can* be assisted by voice recognition tools, the software is still far from perfect (as we consider in Thinking deeply 19.1) so the process is usually done manually, which involves listening to the recording and regularly pausing it to type up exactly what was said. It is best to allow around five to six hours for transcription of every hour of speech. You should also bear in mind that transcription produces vast numbers of words, which you will need to process when analysing the data. For example, Wright, Nyberg, and Grant (2012) report that the 36 semi-structured interviews they carried out with managers or external consultants with a responsibility for sustainability issues lasted between 50 and 120 minutes each and produced over 1,000 pages of transcript. Therefore, while transcription has the advantage of keeping the interviewee's (and interviewer's) words intact, it does so by accumulating a lot of text to be analysed. It is no wonder that writers includ-

LEARN FROM EXPERIENCE 19.2
Managing interview data

One of the advantages of qualitative research is the attention to detail that it allows. This is what provides the rich data. However, all of that detailed data needs transcribing and analysing. Evidently, this is going to take time, and students need to balance the demands of the project with other requirements of study or professional life. As Scarlett describes, all of this rich detail can mean that requirements about the length of written submission that might have initially seemed large can quickly become quite the opposite.

> While it may seem great to conduct lots of interviews for your research project, it is also important to keep in mind how much data you will have and how much transcribing you will need to do. Keep in mind how long your interviews are and how much data you really need; 10,000 words seems like a lot to write, but once you get started you often find that it is not enough!
>
> Scarlett

 Access the **online resources** to hear Scarlett's video reflections on this theme.

You can read about our panellists' backgrounds and research experiences on page xxvi.

THINKING DEEPLY 19.1
Using voice recognition software for transcription

One emerging advantage of digitally recording an interview is that it may be possible to use voice-recognition (voice-to-text) software to transcribe the interviews. This could represent a massive saving on time. The problem is that, although the software is improving all the time, it is not yet perfect. Speech-recognition tools often need to be 'trained' to recognize a voice, but an interview comprises at least two voices and a project will usually comprise many interviewees. This makes the process of 'training' difficult. Some researchers have tried to address this issue by using their own voice to speak back the recording into the microphone, so that their speech alone is processed by the software. They use a headset to listen to the recording and simultaneously speak what is said into the microphone. They will need to keep on stopping and starting the recording they are listening to. They are also likely to need to check that the transcription is accurate. However, there is widespread use of virtual assistants such as Siri and Alexa, and speech-recognition software is fast improving. Dragon is an effective piece of software, available as a desktop package and a mobile app, although it is not cheap. Free software is usually not so accurate, but it can be worth experimenting with. Options include Google Docs voice typing and Windows 10 speech recognition.

ing Lofland and Lofland (1995) advise that researchers should not leave the analysis of qualitative data until all the interviews have been completed and transcribed. Delaying may give the researcher the impression that they face a huge task. Making analysis an ongoing activity also allows the researcher to be more aware of emerging themes that they may want to ask about in a more direct way in later interviews (see Research in focus 19.3 for an example). Researchers who advocate approaches to qualitative data analysis such as **grounded theory** also recommend ongoing analysis (see Chapter 23).

When transcribing an interview, the written text must exactly reproduce what the interviewee said, word for word. For this reason, you should not guess or make up any parts of the interview that you cannot hear properly on the recording; instead indicate in your transcript that there is a missing word or phrase—for example, by using the convention {???}. This helps to give the reader confidence in your data-collection process.

Another issue is that people rarely speak in fully formed sentences. They often repeat themselves and they may have verbal 'tics' in the form of a word or phrase that they

TIPS AND SKILLS 19.4

Quoting from an interview transcript

When quoting from an interview transcript in the write up of your research, you should follow these conventions.

- Indicate text that is a direct quotation, either by using quotation marks or by consistently formatting it so that it stands out from the main text—for example, using indentation or a different font. This makes the difference obvious to the reader and enables you to differentiate between the data and your analysis of it.
- Indicate who is speaking in the quotation, either introducing the speaker before the quotation by saying something like 'As John put it', or 'Aunam explained her reasons for this', or by attributing the quotation to the interviewee immediately afterwards—for example, by writing their pseudonym or [Interviewee 1] in square brackets.
- To quote pieces of text together that are separated by other sentences or phrases in the transcript, use three consecutive dots to indicate the break point. For example (using the extract in Research in focus 19.5), 'Well thinking about it now . . . it was only really representative of the developed world'.
- If an interviewee omits a word from a sentence so that it is grammatically incorrect, or they refer to a subject in a way that does not make its meaning clear and readers will need more contextual information in order to understand the quotation, you can insert words within square brackets.
- One of the most difficult things about presenting interview data is that it can take some effort to make the text flow smoothly because of the switches between your 'voice' as the researcher, and the 'voices' of the interviewees. This can make the text seem quite fragmented. For this reason it is important to introduce direct quotations, then present them, and briefly explain in your own words how you have interpreted them. In this way, you can construct a narrative that guides the reader through your data and shows why you have chosen particular quotations to illustrate themes or **concepts**.

You might also like to read Thinking deeply 25.2 on how verbatim quotations are used in written research.

often use. So when it comes to writing up your research, you might want to edit out some of these instances for the sake of length and ease of understanding. However, you must not paraphrase the words of the speaker and present them as the actual words that were spoken, because this is misleading and someone reading your work might suspect that the interviewees did not really speak in such a fluent way and therefore question the accuracy of your findings. Tips and skills 19.4 sets out some conventions for quoting from an interview transcript that can help to overcome these problems.

Generally, the main challenges to bear in mind with recording and transcription are these.

- Consider the need for and cost of a good quality recording device. It is important to use a high-quality microphone so that the recording is easy to hear and transcribe.
- You will need to find a quiet (to limit background noise) but convenient venue for the interview.
- Digital audio files, for example .wav ones, are huge, so they require a lot of disk space for storage. It is also important to think about storage in relation to the ethical requirements of the research. This might mean paying particular attention to the anonymity of the transcripts, but also the security of any recording/transcription. Many word-processing packages have password protection capacity, as do many storage platforms, and you should use these where possible to provide multiple layers of encryption.
- There are competing formats for both digital files and voice-to-text software, which can cause compatibility problems.

It is also important to remember that using a recorder can disconcert respondents, who may become self-conscious or alarmed at the idea that their words will be preserved. While most people agree for the interview to be recorded, and anonymity can help in this respect, it is not uncommon for some to refuse.

Other reasons why it may not be possible to record an interview are because of issues with recording equipment, or because of the interview setting. Grazian (2003) conducted ethnographic research into the manufacture

THINKING DEEPLY 19.2
The usefulness of interview transcripts

Sometimes interviews, or at least portions of them, are not very useful or relevant. Gerson and Horowitz (2002: 211) observe that some qualitative interviews are 'uninspiring and uninteresting'. This might be because what interviewees say is not relevant to your research, or because they are not very forthcoming or cooperative. Shorter interviews are not necessarily less useful than longer ones, but they may be if their brevity is a product of interviewee non-cooperation or anxiety about being recorded.

It is worth assessing the value of each interview carefully, and considering whether it is worth the time (and/or the cost) of transcribing an interview that has produced very little significant information. It may be that, for some of your interviews, it would be better to listen to them closely first, perhaps twice, and then transcribe only the portions that you think are useful or relevant. However, the risks with this approach are that you may miss things or that you have to go back to the recordings at a later stage in your analysis to try and find something that only emerges as significant later on.

of authentic blues music in Chicago blues clubs, and although he initially tried to record interviews with musicians and members of the audience, he had to give up. He explained: 'I was observing settings where the combination of loud music and chattering customers made the level of background noise extremely high, and thus a recording device would have proved useless' (Grazian 2003: 246). If you are unable to record an interview for any of these reasons, it is usually best to still go ahead with it. Although the information might be more difficult to make sense of, it is better than having nothing.

One final point to make about recording and transcribing interviews is that you should think carefully about whether it is worth transcribing every part of every interview you conduct. We consider this further in Thinking deeply 19.2.

19.5 Ending a qualitative interview

Once you have gone through all of your interview topics and exhausted any other avenues of exploration, it is time to think about ending the interview. There are a number of ways to do this, but it is often a good idea to say something along the lines of 'Well, I think that's everything I wanted to talk about, is there anything that you'd like to ask me?' This allows the interviewee some space to clarify anything they might have said, as well as giving them the opportunity to ask about any part of the research that interests them. Then it is a good idea to remind them what will happen to their data and confirm whether they are happy to be contacted about the project in the future. Finally, thank them for their time.

19

It's also worth remembering that an audio transcript will also not tell you everything about an interview. So after an interview, try to make notes about:

- how the interview went (whether the interviewee was talkative, cooperative, nervous, etc.);
- where the interview took place;
- body language;
- any other feelings about the interview (did it open up new avenues of interest?);
- the setting (busy/quiet, many/few other people nearby, new/old building, use of digital devices).

This will help you remember the contextual detail of the interview when you conduct your analysis.

It is also worth reflecting how issues of your own identity might have influenced the direction and flow of the interview. What was the rapport like during the interview? What sort of role did you take during the interview—for example, a naïve student, expert, or friend—and how did this seem to impact on the discussion? How might characteristics of your identity such as gender, race, or class have enhanced or inhibited the conversation and what participants may have been willing to reveal? These things do not always matter, but in some contexts they can and they are worth reflecting upon because they can help you evaluate the research process.

19.6 Life history and oral history interviewing

There are two special forms of interviewing known as *life history* and *oral history* interviews. Both tend to be much more unstructured than semi-structured interviews. Indeed, when taking either of these approaches the interviewer purposely takes less control over the direction and focus of the interview. In some instances the researcher might encourage the interviewee to talk around some loose themes and to change direction as and when necessary; in others the content can be completely dependent on the interviewee. Both life history and oral history approaches are worth considering further, as they have been particularly popular with qualitative researchers.

Life history interviews

A **life history interview** is a kind of unstructured interview in which the subject is asked to look back in detail at their entire life course. This form of interview is generally associated with the **life history method** of research, in which interviews are often combined with **personal documents** such as diaries, photographs, and letters (of the kind discussed in Chapter 22). It is often considered to be a type of **biographical research**. The terms *life history* and *life story* are also sometimes used interchangeably, but R. L. Miller (2000: 19) suggests that the latter is an account someone gives about their life, whereas a life history combines a life story with other sources. Such research has been described as documenting 'the inner experience of individuals, how they interpret, understand, and define the world around them' (Faraday and Plummer 1979: 776). Thomas and Znaniecki, who were among the pioneers of the approach in their classic study in the 1910s of Polish immigrants to the USA, regarded it as 'the *perfect* type of sociological material' (quoted in Plummer 1983: 64). Their use of a solicited autobiography that was written for them by a Polish peasant is seen as a prime example of the method.

However, in spite of Thomas and Znaniecki's endorsement the approach did not become popular until the 1990s. This is probably because it relies on a sample of one and therefore is sometimes perceived to be of limited **generalizability**. However, the method has clear strengths for qualitative researchers. It has an unambiguous emphasis on the point of view of the life in question and a clear commitment to the processes of social life, showing how events unfold and interrelate in people's lives. Research in focus 19.8 discusses another example of the life history interview approach.

Laub and Sampson's (2004) research on the lives of 52 delinquents (people involved in criminal activity) provides another interesting example of this method. The researchers developed a form of life history calendar that provided their sample with a framework within which they could pinpoint major turning points in the individuals' lives, such as marriage, job change, and divorce. They write:

> Of particular interest were the questions regarding the participant's assessment of his own life, specifically whether he saw improvement or a worsening since childhood, adolescence, or young adulthood and the self-evaluation of turning points in one's own life course and the relationship to criminal activity and various life course transitions (for example, marriage, divorce, military service, residential change, and the like).... By drawing on the men's own words, narratives helped us unpack mechanisms that connect salient life events across the life course, especially regarding personal choice and situational context.
>
> (Laub and Sampson 2004: 93, 94)

Through collecting these data, the researchers gained a better understanding of how turning points in an individual's life can influence their likelihood of continued involvement in or desistance from crime. The age-graded theory of informal social control has become a key part of what is now known as 'life-course criminology' (Laub and Sampson 2019).

Plummer (2001) draws a useful distinction between three types of life story:

1. *Naturalistic life stories*. These are life stories that occur whenever people reminisce or write autobiographies or diaries, or when job applicants write letters of application and are interviewed.
2. *Researched life stories*. These are solicited by researchers with a social-scientific purpose in mind. Most research based on life history/story interviews is of this kind.
3. ***Reflexive** and recursive life stories*. These life stories recognize that the life story is always a construction in which the interviewer is implicated.

While the length of the typical life story interview does vary, Atkinson (2004) suggests that it usually comprises two or three sessions of between one hour and one-and-a-half hours each. He has drawn up a catalogue of question types (Atkinson 1998) that can be asked in the course of a life history interview.

- *Birth and family of origin*. For example: 'How would you describe your parents?'
- *Cultural settings and traditions*. For example: 'Was your family different from others in the neighbourhood?'

RESEARCH IN FOCUS 19.8
The life history interview approach

Winkle-Wagner et al. (2019) used the life history approach to explore the ways in which Black female alumnae who studied in predominantly white US colleges managed and resisted expectations and stereotypes that were placed upon them by peers and staff:

> We collected data through individual, face-to-face, life story interviews. Each woman completed one interview that lasted between 60 and 180 minutes. The interview protocol was open-ended, posing a guiding question: If your college experience was a book where important moments were chapters, how might your book begin? After this initial question, participants were encouraged to follow their own chronology to tell the story of their time in college and what important moments meant to them and their lives. Participants were asked follow-up questions, such as the role of their peers, families, professors, and administrators during college. They were also asked about their involvement in cocurricular activities and the community.
>
> (Winkle-Wagner et al. 2019: 414–15)

- *Social factors*. For example: 'What were some of your struggles as a child?'
- *Education*. For example: 'What are your best memories of school?'
- *Love and work*. For example: 'How did you end up in the type of work you do or did?'
- *Historical events or periods*. For example: 'Do you remember what you were doing on any of the really important days in our history?'
- *Retirement*. For example: 'What is the worst part of being retired?'
- *Inner life and spiritual awareness*. For example: 'What are the stresses of being an adult?'
- *Major life themes*. For example: 'What are the crucial decisions in your life?'
- *Vision of the future*. For example: 'Is your life fulfilled yet?'
- *Closure questions*. For example: 'Do you feel that you have given a fair picture of yourself?'

(Atkinson 1998: 43–53)

19

Oral history interviews

An **oral history interview** is usually more specific than a life story interview, in that the subject is asked to reflect upon specific events or periods in the past. The emphasis is more on these specific events than on the individual and their life. Like the life story interview, it is sometimes combined with other sources, such as documents. The main problem with the oral history interview (which it shares with the life history interview) is the possibility of bias as a result of memory lapses and distortions (Grele 1998). On the other hand, oral history testimonies have given voice to groups that are usually marginalized in historical research either because of their lack of power or because they are seen as unexceptional (Samuel 1976). Bloor (2002) has shown how oral history testimonies, collected in 1973 and 1974, of Welsh miners' experiences of pit life could be used to understand how they collectively tried to improve their health in the pits and to improve safety. Bloor drew lessons from these testimonies for social policies at the time he was writing.

19.7 Evaluating qualitative interviewing

In this final section we evaluate qualitative interviewing, mainly by comparing the merits and limitations of interviewing in qualitative research with those of **participant observation**. These are probably the two most prominent methods of data collection in qualitative research, so it is worth assessing their strengths.

Participant observation has a number of advantages over qualitative interviewing.

- *Seeing through others' eyes*. As participant observers are in much closer contact with people for a longer period of time, it could be argued that they are better able to understand the experiences of others. In research that relies on interviewing alone, contact with those being studied is likely to be briefer and less intensive (though qualitative interviews can last for hours and re-interviewing is not unusual). The extent to which interviews can truly reveal others' perspectives may also be hindered by the fact that the interview method tends to reproduce the problematic discourses and power relationships of wider society. This is a key concern for **feminist** researchers in particular, and some have suggested that the issue could be mitigated through principles such as 'sustained immersion' and 'active listening'—see Thinking deeply 19.3.
- *Learning the native language*. Becker and Geer (1957) argued that a participant observer is in the same position as a social anthropologist visiting another country, in that they have to learn the native language, including the 'argot' (special uses of words and slang), in order to understand the culture. This means that a participant observer can better understand the complexity of a society.
- *The taken-for-granted*. Interviews mainly rely on verbal behaviour, so things that interviewees see as normal and accept without questioning are not likely to surface, whereas these features of social life are likely to be revealed at some point during participant observation.

THINKING DEEPLY 19.3
Feminism, sustained immersion, and active listening

Semi-structured and unstructured interviewing are popular methods of data gathering within a feminist research framework. While it is useful to consider why this is the case, it can also be important to reflect on the implications of such approaches for qualitative interviewing more generally.

For Oakley (1981), the qualitative interview is a way of resolving the dilemmas that she encountered as a feminist interviewing other women. In her research on the transition to motherhood, she was often asked questions by her respondents and argues that it would be ethically indefensible for a feminist not to answer such inquiries. To achieve her goals for a more equal research relationship, it was essential that she was able to foster a sense of a give-and-take discussion.

Elsewhere, DeVault and Gross (2012) make it very clear that for feminist and other interviewers, debates about who can research what—and which researchers should interview which participants—raise important issues about power relationships within research and society more generally. However, they suggest that the most important question is how to organize interviews so as to produce more collaborative encounters, whatever the identities of the participants. They point toward the principle of 'sustained immersion'. This is the researcher's considered attempt to review material produced during interviews collaboratively with the research participants. This sort of reflexive interviewing is explicitly designed to acknowledge the ways in which interviews are always embedded in wider concerns of identity and power. This may mean, for example, that when white women interview Black women they have to address issues of race and ethnicity.

However, DeVault and Gross also emphasize the need for 'active listening' to avoid the risk of uncritically reproducing dominant discourses. This can be achieved through close attention to what is being asked and what said within an interview, and a detailed examination of interview text in respect to the structure of exchanges and the language used.

For Oakley and for DeVault and Gross, the purpose is to avoid simply extracting information from the participants in ways that reproduce problematic discourses of wider society. Indeed, while qualitative interviewing has become a very popular research method for feminist researchers because it can be shaped into a form that aligns with the principles of feminism, it is important to be aware of the questions raised in more general terms about the relationship between researchers and participants, and the conduct of qualitative research more generally.

- *Ability to observe behaviour.* Whereas interviewers have to rely on verbal reports of behaviour, participant observation allows researchers to observe it directly. However, not all behaviour will be accessible to participant observers (for example, the observer's gender could make it difficult to observe certain areas of behaviour) so they often need to interview in order to get information about difficult-to-access areas or types of behaviour.
- *Deviant and hidden activities.* Much of what we know about criminal and deviant subcultures has been uncovered through participant observation because people are often reluctant to talk about these activities in an interview. Ethnographers conducting participant observation are likely to be able to gradually infiltrate such social worlds.
- *Sensitivity to context.* A participant observer's extensive contact with a social setting allows them to fully map out the context of people's behaviour. They interact with people in a variety of different situations, and possibly roles, in order to identify links between behaviour and context.
- *Encountering the unexpected and being flexible.* The unstructured nature of participant observation means it is more likely to uncover unexpected topics or issues. The interview process is likely to involve some degree of structure that is mainly driven by the interviewer.
- *Naturalistic emphasis.* Participant observation has the potential to come closer to a naturalistic emphasis, because the researcher observes members of a social setting in their natural environments. Interviewing necessarily involves disrupting people's normal lives so cannot achieve this to the same extent.
- *Embodied nature of experience.* Participant observation requires a more embodied approach to collecting data than qualitative interviewing, 'embodied' meaning that the researcher becomes physically involved in what they are studying. This is more apparent in some studies than in others. A good example is Wacquant's (2004) research on boxing culture. After an initial period of research he realized that in order to understand the culture of the gym and the world of the boxer more generally, he would need to gain first-hand experience of what it was like to be a boxer. As a result, he actually became an amateur boxer, participating in shadow-boxing drills, sparring sessions, and even competitive fights. In this respect, the researcher's decision to become a boxer required an embodied approach to appreciate the rigours of the craft.

However, interviews do have some advantages over participant observation.

- *Investigation of issues that are resistant to observation.* There are a wide range of issues that are difficult or impossible to observe, so can only be investigated by asking people about them.
- *Reconstruction of events.* Qualitative research often involves reconstructing events by asking interviewees to reflect on how a situation was created. Depending on the type of research role taken, this is not always possible with participation observation.
- *Ethical considerations.* There are some areas that could theoretically be observed, but doing so would raise ethical considerations for researchers and those being researched. This is particularly the case with deviant sub-groups or where illegal activity is taking place. These kinds of concerns can be better negotiated in the context of an interview.
- *Less intrusive in people's lives.* Participant observation can be very intrusive in people's lives because an observer is likely to take up a lot more of their time than an interviewer. Qualitative interviews can be very long, and re-interviewing is not uncommon, but the impact on people's time will probably be less than having to take observers into account on a regular basis.
- ***Longitudinal research** is easier.* One of the advantages of participant observation is that it is inherently longitudinal, because the observer is present in a social setting for a period of time. But there are limits to the time that participant observers can spend away from their normal routines. It is easier to carry out interviewing within a longitudinal **research design** because repeat interviews can be easier to organize than repeat visits to participant observers' research settings, though the latter is not impossible.
- *Greater breadth of coverage.* In participant observation, the researcher is constrained to a fairly restricted range of people, incidents, and localities. Interviewing can allow access to a wider variety of people and situations.
- *Specific focus.* Qualitative interviewing could be seen as better suited to research that has a very specific focus, because the researcher can direct the interview at that focus and its associated research questions.

Many of these points can also be seen in the academic debates about the respective merits and problems of interview-based studies and ethnography—see Thinking deeply 19.4.

THINKING DEEPLY 19.4
A debate about ethnography and interviewing

Jerolmack and Khan (2014) write that research based on interviews and survey research suffers from what they call 'the attitudinal fallacy', which is when a researcher makes inappropriate inferences about behaviour from the verbal account(s) that they are given.

We discussed a related issue in Research in focus 12.2, namely the gap between what people say they do and what they actually do. Jerolmack and Khan group qualitative interviewing and survey research together as methods that only produce verbal accounts, but are simultaneously critical of putting qualitative interviewing and ethnography together because of the inconsistency between attitudes and behaviour. They note that whereas ethnography 'routinely attempts to explain' the relationship between what is said and what is done, studies using interviews 'regularly [disregard] the problem' (Jerolmack and Khan 2014: 180). Jerolmack and Khan are not saying that interview-based studies (and surveys) are worthless, but they do argue that inferences about situated behaviour are inappropriate because, unlike in ethnography, behaviour has not been directly studied. Of course, ethnographers also interview in the course of their work, but the difference is that ethnography 'prioritizes the observation of social action . . . within the real-world rather than a research context' (Jerolmack and Khan 2014: 202).

The journal in which this article was published invited several leading writers to comment on it, as well as a response by Jerolmack and Khan. These comments came from several different standpoints. Some suggested, for example, that the attitudinal fallacy problem is over-stated because research suggests that there is often a fairly good correspondence between accounts and actual behaviour. Others noted that not all potential sites of action can be easily observed (Cerulo 2014). In addition, Lamont and Swidler (2014), two leading qualitative researchers, have separately written an article defending the value of the interview against Jerolmack and Khan's arguments and other recent examples of what they call 'methodological tribalism'. They claim that it is too restrictive to focus on the issue of the correspondence between attitude and behaviour, and that we should focus instead on what qualitative interviews can be used for. They point to the fact that in interviews, researchers can do the following:

- draw 'comparison across contexts, situations, and kinds of people' (Lamont and Swidler 2014: 158), which allows them to develop an in-depth understanding and draw on a wide range of coverage to answer research questions;
- gather data about the emotional side of human experience that is not necessarily obvious from people's behaviour;
- invite people to reflect on their behaviour in a variety of situations, whereas there is limited scope to vary situational differences in ethnography.

So which method is best?

Becker and Geer (1957: 28) state that the 'most complete form of the sociological datum [the singular form of "data"] . . . is the form in which the participant observer gathers it'. Trow (1957: 33), however, argued that 'the problem under investigation properly dictates the methods of investigation'. In this book we take the latter view. We would suggest that every research method we discuss is appropriate for researching some issues and questions but not others. As we noted earlier, comparing interviewing and participant observation is in a sense an artificial exercise because the latter is usually carried out as part of ethnographic research, meaning that it is usually accompanied by interviewing as well as other methods. In other words, participant observers often support their observations with methods of data collection that allow them to access important areas that cannot easily be observed. However, the aim of this comparison is to give you an idea of the advantages and disadvantages of the two methods alone, as these are factors that you might want to take into account when deciding how to plan a study and even how to evaluate existing research.

KEY POINTS

- Interviewing in qualitative research is usually either unstructured or semi-structured.
- Interviewing may be the only method in an investigation or might be used as part of an ethnographic study, or used with another qualitative method.
- Qualitative interviewing is meant to be flexible and to seek out the worldviews of research participants.
- If an interview guide is used, it should not be too structured in its application and should allow some flexibility in the asking of questions.
- The qualitative interview should be recorded and then transcribed.
- Interviewing in qualitative research can take a variety of forms, such as life history and oral history interviewing.
- The qualitative interview has become an extremely popular method of data collection in feminist studies.
- Conducting personal interviews online is a viable alternative to face-to-face interviews in many instances.
- Whether to use participant observation or qualitative interviews depends in large part on their suitability for the research questions being addressed. However, participant observers always conduct some interviews in the course of their investigations.

QUESTIONS FOR REVIEW

1. Outline the main types of interview used by qualitative researchers.
2. How does qualitative interviewing differ from structured interviewing?
3. What are the differences between unstructured and semi-structured interviewing?
4. What are the differences between life history and oral history interviews?
5. What kinds of considerations do researchers need to bear in mind when preparing an interview guide?
6. What kinds of questions might be asked in an interview guide?
7. Why is it important to record and transcribe qualitative interviews?
8. What role might vignette questions play in qualitative interviewing?
9. To what extent can platforms such as Zoom, Google Hangouts, and FaceTime be used as an alternative to face-to-face personal interviews?
10. What are the main kinds of life history interview and what are their respective uses?
11. Why has the qualitative interview become such a prominent research method for feminist researchers?
12. What dilemmas might be posed for feminist researchers using qualitative interviewing?
13. Outline the relative advantages and disadvantages of qualitative interviewing and participant observation.
14. Does one method seem better aligned with the preoccupations of qualitative researchers than the other?

ONLINE RESOURCES

www.oup.com/he/srm6e

You can find our notes on the answers to these questions within this chapter's **online resources**, together with:

- *audio/video comments* on this topic from our 'Learn from experience' panellists;
- *audio discussion from the authors* on how qualitative interviewing differs from structured interviewing (review question 2);
- *self-test questions* for further knowledge-checking;
- a *flashcard glossary* to help you recall key terms; and
- a *Student Researcher's Toolkit* containing practical materials and resources to help you conduct your own research project.

CHAPTER

20

FOCUS GROUPS

CHAPTER GUIDE

The focus group method is a focused discussion with several people on a specific topic or issue that also has an interest in the dynamics of the group discussion. In this chapter we will explore

- reasons for preferring focus groups to individual interviews;
- how to plan and conduct focus groups, including deciding on the number and size of groups, how to select participants, how direct the questioning should be, and the recording and transcribing of group interactions;
- the interaction between participants in focus group discussions;
- conducting focus groups online;
- some practical difficulties with focus group sessions, such as potential loss of control over proceedings and potential unwanted group effects.

20.1 Introduction

We are used to thinking of interviews as one-on-one conversations between an interviewer and interviewee. Most textbooks reinforce this perception by concentrating on individual interviews. The **focus group** technique is a method of facilitating discussion on a particular topic or issue that involves more than one, usually at least four, interviewees. It might look something like a group interview, but we will see that there are a number of differences between focus groups and group interviews.

The focus group method has been gaining popularity in the social sciences since the 1980s, but it is by no means a new technique (Tadajewski 2016). It has been used for years in market research, where it is employed for purposes like testing responses to new products and advertising initiatives. In fact, there is a significant body of literature within market research which looks at the practices associated with focus group research and their implementation (e.g. Calder 1977). Most social science focus group researchers undertake their work within the traditions of **qualitative research**, meaning that they are explicitly concerned with revealing how the group participants view the social world in relation to their own life experiences. The researcher will therefore aim to provide a setting that allows participants to express their beliefs and perspectives. With this aim, the person who runs the focus group session—usually called the **moderator** or **facilitator**—is expected to guide the discussion but not to be too intrusive.

20.2 What is a focus group?

As we noted in Section 20.1, the focus group (see Key concept 20.1) has become a popular method within social science. Although it might initially sound like a group interview it differs from this method in a number of ways, including the following.

- Focus groups *are specifically designed to produce interaction between participants*. The aim of a group interview, on the other hand, is to prompt detailed responses from a wide group of people.
- Focus groups *are not used as a cost-saving measure*. Sometimes group interviews are carried out as a time-saving device to interview a number of individuals simultaneously. This is not a reason why researchers use focus groups; they will be more motivated by the group dynamics of focus groups and the kinds of data they generate (see the following two points).
- Researchers conducting focus groups *are interested in group dynamics*: the ways in which individuals discuss a certain issue *as members of a group*, rather than simply as individuals. In other words, the researcher will be interested in things like how people respond to each other's views and the interaction that takes place within the group.
- Focus groups *generate data at multiple levels*. Cyr (2016) argues that focus groups purposely aim to generate data in respect to the individual, the group, and the interaction that takes place. That is to say, data collection is specifically directed toward what people think and why, how that compares and contrasts with others, and how those views interact with one another. By contrast, group interviews are usually just an attempt to interview a number of individuals at the same time (see also Kidd and Parshall 2000).

KEY CONCEPT 20.1
What is the focus group method?

The focus group method is a form of group discussion in which there are several participants (in addition to the moderator/facilitator). There is an emphasis on a fairly tightly defined topic, and the researcher gives particular attention to the interactions that take place within the group. As such, the focus group contains elements of two methods: the group interview, in which several people discuss a number of topics; and what has been called a focused interview, where interviewees are selected because they 'are known to have been involved in a particular situation' (Merton et al. 1956: 3).

However, the distinction between the focus group method and the group interview is by no means clear-cut, and the terms are often used interchangeably. Nonetheless, the definition proposed in Key concept 20.1 provides a useful starting point.

There are many different reasons why researchers use focus groups. These reasons fall under three main categories:

- to explore how people construct meaning through social interactions;
- to make use of a group dynamic to obtain more interesting, nuanced, and realistic data;
- to give research participants more freedom than in a conventional, one-to-one interview.

Let's consider each reason in turn.

Exploring how people construct meaning through social interactions

The original idea for the focus group—the focused interview—was that people who were known to have had a certain experience could be interviewed in a relatively unstructured way about that experience. This approach was then adapted by researchers who were interested in examining the ways in which people develop understandings of particular topics by interacting with each other. In this respect researchers use focus groups both to explore how people construct *individual* meanings/understandings through their *interactions* with others, and also how people construct a collective understanding with a social *group*.

One of the best-known studies using the focus group method for this purpose is Morgan and Spanish's (1985) study of everyday understandings of who has heart attacks and why. The researchers' emphasis was on how people make sense of medical information and how it informs their understanding of health-related issues. Through the use of focus groups they found that social interaction influences particular health beliefs in relation to heart attacks.

It is a central idea of theoretical positions such as **symbolic interactionism** that people do not reach understandings and interpretations of social phenomena in isolation, but through interaction and discussion with others. Focus groups allow researchers to study the processes through which individuals collectively make sense of a phenomenon and construct meanings around it. The fact that focus group discussions reflect the ways in which meaning is constructed in everyday life means that this method can be seen as more naturalistic than individual interviews. In fact, focus groups are also widely used in media and cultural studies, mainly to explore 'audience reception'—how people respond to TV and radio programmes, films, newspaper articles, and so on (Schrøder 2019; Livingstone 2019; Fenton, Bryman, and Deacon 1998: Chapter 1). An influential study in this context was Morley's (1980) research on *Nationwide*, an early-evening British news programme that was popular in the 1970s. Morley organized focus groups made up of specific categories of people (for example, managers, trade unionists, students) and showed them recordings of the programme. He found that the different groups arrived at quite different interpretations of the programmes they had watched, suggesting that meaning comes not only from such programmes but also from the ways and contexts in which viewers watch and interpret them.

Using group dynamics to obtain better data

The interactive, fluid nature of focus group discussions, which do not follow the predictable question–answer pattern of an individual interview, can mean that researchers gain more nuanced and interesting accounts than they would through other methods. Our panellist Scarlett certainly found this to be the case in her research into young people and mental wellbeing—see Learn from experience 20.1. The fact that participants often prompt, probe, and challenge each other—sometimes more than an interviewer would feel able to do—allows researchers to develop an understanding not just of what people feel, but *why* they feel the way they do (Cyr 2016). Hearing other people's opinions may prompt participants to develop, qualify, or modify their original view, or to voice agreement with something that they probably would not have thought of on their own. These possibilities mean that focus groups can also be very helpful in gathering a range of views in relation to a particular issue.

A further benefit of group members probing and challenging each other is that the accounts they give may end up being more realistic and representative of what people actually think. In conventional one-to-one interviewing, interviewees are rarely challenged; they might say things that are inconsistent with earlier replies or that might not be true, but researchers will often be reluctant to point out these errors. In a focus group, the fact that people often argue and challenge each other's views means that all members are forced to think about their views carefully.

LEARN FROM EXPERIENCE 20.1

The effect of group dynamics on data

Scarlett used focus groups for her project on young people and mental wellbeing and found that the group dynamics meant that participants were readily forthcoming. Here, she suggests that this enhanced the quality of the data she gained:

> For my project on young people and mental wellbeing, I used focus groups to allow participants to share and discuss ideas with peers. The group setting provided a great dynamic and all students stated in the follow-up questionnaires that they found the interview 'fun' and 'interesting'. I think the 'group effect' enabled participants to really open up and they seemed to enjoy discussing the topics. Focus groups worked extremely well for me and provided me with lots of in-depth data about my topic.
>
> Scarlett

 Access the **online resources** to hear Scarlett's video reflections on this theme.

You can read about our panellists' backgrounds and research experiences on page xxvi.

Giving participants freedom to shape the discussion

Another reason for choosing the focus group method is that it is seen as giving more control to research participants, who can more easily highlight the issues that they see as important and significant. This is clearly an aim of individual interviews too, but because in a focus group the moderator has to give up a certain amount of control to the participants, there is more freedom for participants to shape the discussion. This is clearly an important consideration in the context of qualitative research, because the viewpoints of the people being studied are central to the aims of the approach. It can also mean that focus groups are useful ways to collect data on sensitive issues—see Research in focus 20.1.

The fact that focus groups give participants the capacity to shape the direction of the discussion is a key reason for its appeal to, and increasing use by, **feminist** researchers. Indeed, Walters (2020) argues that because the researcher has to relinquish control—and their position as 'expert'—to participants, the method can help to redress the hierarchical nature of the research relationship. Evidently, this resonates with the goal of reciprocity within feminist research. Other researchers also point toward the dialogic nature of focus group discussion, where participants are able to transform social knowledge when they talk and think together (Caretta and Vacchelli 2015). The contextual and non-hierarchical capacity of the focus group can facilitate diversity of opinion and reveal how collective sense is made (Merryweather 2010). Nevertheless, we should not imply that focus groups are inherently participatory. Gender, social status, and other **intersectional** dimensions of identity could mean that some people do not want to share their thoughts.

RESEARCH IN FOCUS 20.1

Researching sensitive issues using focus groups

It is often suggested that focus groups are a useful way to elicit data on sensitive issues, and there is some empirical evidence to support this view. Guest et al. (2017b) conducted a study that sought to compare the nature of the data that is generated by focus groups and by individual interviews. They spoke to 350 African-American men living in North Carolina about their health-seeking behaviour. They randomly allocated participants to a focus group or individual interview, where they were asked exactly the same questions. They found that while individual interviews were more effective at generating a broader range of material, several types of sensitive disclosures were more likely in the focus groups, and some sensitive material was revealed only in that context.

There is always a danger that some voices might prevail over others. On the opposite side, it is also worth highlighting that the general tendency for consensus within human interaction can also inhibit a healthy and constructive multivocality where diversity of opinions is stimulated (Merryweather 2010). So while focus group discussion can provide unique insight, and be very useful in addressing issues of power in the research relationship, we cannot take these things for granted.

20.3 Conducting focus groups

Given the larger number of people involved in a focus group compared to an interview, it is to be expected that there are several practical considerations involved in carrying one out successfully. In the first instance, if you are planning to conduct a focus group, you will need to consider the various points on preparing for and carrying out a qualitative interview that we discussed in Chapter 19 (see Section 19.3). But in this section, we will look at the considerations that are particular to focus groups:

- how many groups you should have;
- the size of those groups;
- the level of moderator involvement;
- how to select participants;
- how to ask questions;
- how to begin and end the discussion; and
- why and how you should record and transcribe focus group sessions.

Number of groups

As Guest et al. (2017a) highlight, there is little clear guidance about how many groups will be needed for a research study. It is unlikely that just one group will meet a researcher's needs because there is always the possibility that the responses are particular to that one group. This would make any qualitative assessment of **generalizability** impossible (see Section 16.7). Equally, there are strong arguments for saying that too many groups will be a waste of time. Calder (1977) suggests that when the moderator reaches the point when they can fairly accurately anticipate what the next group is going to say, there are probably enough groups. This is very similar to the idea of **data saturation** that we introduced in Chapter 17 (see Key concept 17.2), and can be seen in Research in focus 20.2. In other words, once new themes are no longer emerging there is not much point continuing with data collection. The problem, of course, is that

RESEARCH IN FOCUS 20.2
How many focus groups are enough?

As part of their study into the health-seeking behaviours of African-American men in North Carolina (see Research in focus 20.1), Guest et al. (2017b) also attempted to investigate the number of focus groups necessary to achieve data saturation.

After **coding** the focus group transcripts, the researchers documented the frequency of a total of 94 codes across a series of 40 transcripts and attempted to determine when 80 per cent and 90 per cent of all thematic codes had been identified. Almost two-thirds of the 94 codes were identified in the first focus group; 84 per cent were identified by the end of the third focus group; and 90 per cent were identified after six groups. Randomly ordering the transcripts, they repeated this process another 10 times and found the same pattern. When they combined these results, the mean number of focus groups required to reach 80 per cent was 2.7 (with a range of 2 to 3), and to reach 90 per cent the mean number of groups was 4.3 (with a range of 3 to 6). They then examined the relative importance of the 94 codes by dividing them into those that were high-, medium-, and low-frequency. All of the high- and medium-frequency codes that they developed during the analysis could be identified by the end of the third focus group. Again, this pattern repeated across the 10 randomly ordered transcriptions. These findings broadly correspond to those of other empirical studies that have tried to determine how many focus groups are needed to reach saturation (Morgan et al. 2002; Coenen et al. 2012).

you cannot be sure from the outset when this will happen. The number of focus groups you require will depend on the needs of the research questions and the data you collect, so it is probably best not to arrange a long series of focus groups in case not all of them are necessary. At the same time, you need to make sure that you have arranged enough groups for important themes to emerge.

Another important factor that may affect a researcher's decision about the number of groups they need is whether they feel that the range of views are likely to be affected by socio-demographic factors such as age, gender, and class. Many focus group researchers use stratifying criteria such as these to ensure that they assemble different groups that represent a wide variety of characteristics—for example, groups representing different age ranges. If this is the case, they might need more groups in order to reflect the criteria. So, for example, a project that was interested in audience responses to a party political broadcast would need to include people from across the totality of that audience. This would require a large number of groups to ensure that the research was as representative as possible. However, it may be that researchers do not anticipate high levels of diversity in connection with some more specific topics, in which case it might be unnecessarily time-consuming and expensive to assemble multiple groups. For example, a study that was interested in internet access for elderly women in deprived areas would be focused on one particular group who share similar demographic characteristics.

It is also worth noting that the more groups you have, the more complicated the analysis will be. For example, Skoglund (2019) reports that in her study of how kindergarten workers intervene in physical conflicts between children, 12 focus groups that were an hour in length with a total of 47 practitioners produced 240 pages of transcription.

Size of groups

How big should focus groups be? There is some variation in the composition of focus groups. Generally, the consensus is that there must be at least four members, with Morgan (1998a) suggesting that the typical group size is 6 to 10 members. One major problem for focus group practitioners is that sometimes people agree to participate but do not turn up on the day. It is almost impossible to control this other than by deliberately over-recruiting, a strategy that some writers do recommend (e.g. Wilkinson 1999: 188).

Setting aside the issue of 'no-shows', Morgan (1998a) recommends smaller groups if the participants are likely to have a lot to say on the research topic. This is likely to be the case where participants are very involved in or emotionally preoccupied with the topic. He also suggests that smaller groups are best when topics are controversial or complex, and/or when eliciting participants' personal accounts is a major goal. It follows, therefore, that Morgan recommends having larger groups when involvement with a topic is likely to be low, or when the researcher wants 'to hear numerous brief suggestions' (Morgan 1998a: 75). However, big groups might make people less likely to speak if they are discussing a topic about which they know little or have little experience. For example, big groups may be nearly silent on the topic of media representations of social science research, as most people are unlikely to have much interest in it or to have thought about it. This was the topic explored by Fenton, Bryman, and Deacon (1998)—see Research in focus 20.3 and 20.4.

Barbour (2007) suggests that a maximum group size of eight people works well for most purposes. She argues that larger groups will be less suited to exploring the topic and will constrain the capacity of the researcher to analyse the ways in which views are constructed in the course of sessions. She also suggests that larger groups can be more challenging for moderators in terms of responding to participants' remarks, and can pose difficulties at the analysis stage because it is harder to recognize the different voices in audio recordings (see Tips and skills 20.1). Peek and Fothergill (2009) confirm that in many contexts, smaller groups will be preferable. They report that in their study, focus groups that included between three and five participants 'ran more smoothly than the larger group interviews that we conducted' (Peek and Fothergill 2009: 37). By contrast, they found it much more difficult to manage larger focus groups of between six and 15 people, as it was harder to encourage less talkative members to speak up. In the smaller groups there also seemed to be more opportunity for disagreement and diversity of opinion, perhaps because there was less of a tendency for one person to dominate the discussion.

Level of moderator involvement

How involved should the moderator/facilitator be? In qualitative research, the aim is to elicit participants' perspectives. This means that the approach should not be intrusive and overly structured, so researchers tend to use a small number of very general questions to guide a focus group session. Moderators also tend to give participants quite a lot of freedom, allowing the discussion to range as widely as is necessary. If the discussion goes off at a total tangent they may need to refocus the participants' attention, but even then it is important to intervene carefully, because what appear to be digressions may in fact reveal something of interest to the participants and/or the researcher. As we saw in Section 20.2, one of the main reasons that researchers use this method is that focus groups give participants more control over the discussion. This means that the researcher is more likely to get access to what people see as important or interesting. However, too much irrelevant discussion may make a session unproductive. Much the same could also be said about managing consensus and difference. The moderator will need to develop a great detail of sensitivity in assessing when and where there appears to be surface agreement but underlying differences, and where there is genuine consensus.

Another situation in which the moderator may need to intervene and direct participants more firmly is when respondents have made specific points that could help respond to the research questions, but these points have not been picked up by other participants. We can see an example of this in Research in focus 20.3, an extract from a study in which Alan Bryman was involved.

The moderator in Research in focus 20.3 has to strike a balance between two positions: intervening to bring out important issues, particularly when group participants do not do so, *and* allowing the discussion to flow freely. In the extract in Research in focus 20.4, taken from the same study, the moderator clearly feels that it is best not to intervene and to allow the discussion to flow.

It is not easy to balance the needs for reengagement, realignment, and restraint, and both tactics—intervention and non-intervention—carry risks. The best advice is to intervene as little as possible, except when the group is struggling in its discussions or when it has not elaborated on something that seems significant for the research topic. Kandola (2012) recommends some useful tactics to keep the discussion flowing, which include acknowledging what has been said, summarizing and stimulating reflection on what has been said, and allowing enough time for participants to speak. She also suggests nodding to encourage participants to speak, but take care when using this technique as participants may interpret it as agreement. Expressing agreement—or disagreement—is one of the forms of intervention that Kandola advises that the moderator should avoid, along with expressing personal

RESEARCH IN FOCUS 20.3
Focus group moderator involvement

In the following extract from Fenton, Bryman, and Deacon's (1998) study of how people view media representations of social science research, three focus group participants engage in a discussion with only a little intervention or involvement on the part of the moderator. In this instance, the focus group was made up of a particular subsection of British society—women in private-sector employment who were educated up to age 16. They are talking about a news item that reported research on victims of crime but also included a number of detailed case studies of individual experiences of being a victim.

R1	That was easy and interesting.
[Moderator]	Why interesting? Why easy?
R2	Because it affects all of us.
R1	It was actually reading about what had happened to people. It wasn't all facts and figures. I know it was, but it has in the first sentence, where it says 'I turned the key and experienced a sinking feeling'. You can relate to that straight away. It's how you'd feel.
R3	She's in a flat [apartment] and she hears noises—it's something that everyone does. Being on their own and they hear a noise.

(Fenton, Bryman, and Deacon 1998: 129)

On this occasion, the moderator's brief intervention allows the discussion to bring out the kinds of attributes that the participants feel make a media item on this topic 'easy' and 'interesting'. We can see that the participants appreciate the media representation of social science research when it is described in a way that they can relate to, and that an important way that media can do this is to use people's personal experiences as a lens through which people can view the research.

RESEARCH IN FOCUS 20.4
No involvement from a focus group moderator

In the following extract from Fenton, Bryman, and Deacon (1998), three focus group participants begin to discuss the differences between the natural and the social sciences with no intervention or involvement on the part of the moderator. The group consists of men who have been in higher education and are in private-sector employment.

R1 Essentially with the pure sciences I get an end result. Whereas with the social sciences it's pretty vague because it's very, very subjective.

R2 I suppose for me the pure sciences seem to have more control of what they are looking at because they keep control of more. Because with social sciences there are many different aspects that could have an impact and you can't necessarily control them. So it seems more difficult to pin down and therefore to some extent controversial.

R3 Pure science is more credible because you've got control over test environments, you've got an ability to test and control factually the outcome and then establish relationships between different agents or whatever. I think in social science it's always subject to interpretation. . . . I think if you want to create an easy life and be unaccountable to anybody, to obtain funding and spend your time in a stress-free way then one of the best things to do is to work in funded research and one of the best areas to do it in is in social science.

(Fenton, Bryman, and Deacon 1998: 127)

It is interesting to see how a consensus about the social sciences builds up in this discussion, with a particular emphasis on the lack of control in social research and on what the participants see as the subjectivity of interpretation compared to the 'pure' sciences.

opinions and interrupting. She also warns moderators not to display physical responses like frowning, looking distracted, fidgeting, and shaking their head.

One of the challenges for focus group moderators is ensuring that there is a good level of participation among members. Expecting equal participation is unrealistic, but it is clearly best if all group members contribute to a reasonable degree. Kandola suggests writing comments that arise in the course of a discussion onto a flipchart, advising that as far as possible the moderator should use participants' own language to avoid imposing their own interpretation on the discussion. The researcher can then use this written material as a prompt to elicit discussion from those participants who, for whatever reason, have not contributed as much as other members of the group.

The role of moderator is not just about asking questions and ensuring that the discussion flows well. It is also to do with controlling events in the discussion. If participants begin to talk at the same time, as often happens when a discussion really 'takes off', it will make it hard for members to hear each others' points, as well as making the audio recording of the session impossible to interpret when **transcribing**. This means that the moderator has an important role in reminding participants to talk one at a time (see Research in focus 20.9 for an example).

In Learn from experience 20.2 our panellist Barbara explains that she found it helpful to involve a co-moderator when running a focus group, and Scarlett reflects on the impact that her identity as a researcher and moderator had on the discussion.

Selecting participants

Who should participate in a focus group? This will depend on the research question. Some projects will not require participants of a particular kind, so there is little if any restriction on who might be appropriate. However, this is a fairly unusual situation and normally some restriction is required. For example, for their research on people's knowledge about heart attacks, Morgan and Spanish (1985: 257) recruited participants in the 35–50 age range, because they 'would be likely to have more experience with informal discussions of our chosen topic', but excluded anyone who had had a heart attack or who was uneasy about discussing the topic. Research in focus 20.5 describes various recruitment strategies used by researchers.

LEARN FROM EXPERIENCE 20.2
Focus group moderation

Moderation is a crucial element of a focus group. Not only do you have to set and deliver the questions, you may also have to intervene to steer the discussion back on track or try to ensure that the voices of all participants get heard.

As a result, it can sometimes be very helpful to have a co-moderator who has a specific role. For instance, one person might manage formalities and the questions, while another is in charge of monitoring the progress of the discussion. This strategy worked well for Barbara, as she explains:

> Focus group research might benefit from a co-moderator. In my experience of running a focus group, it was a great help to have another colleague with me. I didn't have to worry about the practicalities around the individual needs of the participants, and I could focus more on the content and direction of the focus group.
>
> Barbara

The moderator role is also important because their identity and how they choose to present themselves can influence the group discussion. In some instances a moderator might decide to present themselves in a very formal and professional way, while sometimes it might be more effective to appear as an interested outsider. In this example, Scarlett describes how her own identity and knowledge of social media helped to facilitate discussion:

> I think my characteristics as a researcher helped the discussion. Many of the participants stated that because I was a young researcher who was also a student, they could relate to me on a peer level. They explained that older researchers might not always understand social media in the same way and it was nice to talk to someone who had experience of what they were saying.
>
> Scarlett

 Access the **online resources** to hear Barbara's reflections on this theme.

You can read about our panellists' backgrounds and research experiences on page xxvi.

RESEARCH IN FOCUS 20.5
Recruiting focus group participants

Peek and Fothergill (2009) outlined the strategies they used in recruiting participants for three studies they conducted in North America: with parents, children, and teachers in two urban day-care centres; with Muslim Americans following 9/11; and with children and young people after the Hurricane Katrina flooding of New Orleans. They used three approaches.

- *Researcher-driven recruitment*: the researcher, often with the support of an organization with an interest in the research, uses email, letters, flyers, phone calls, or social media to build interest in participation.
- *Key informant recruitment*: stakeholder organizations actively help to recruit participants. For example, in the Hurricane Katrina study, a schoolteacher helped the researchers make contact with 'middle school students'.
- *Spontaneous recruitment*: individuals volunteer to participate, having heard about the research through others or seen someone being interviewed.

Guest et al. (2017b: 9) seem to have used similar strategies to assemble the focus groups that formed part of their research on the health seeking behaviour of African-American men in North Carolina (Research in focus 20.1 and 20.2). To be eligible for the study, each participant had to be a (self-identified) African-American/Black man, aged 25–64, from the city of Durham, North Carolina, and they were recruited 'through Craigslist [a classified advertisements website], through flyers posted in public areas, and through peer recruitment'.

As we touched on earlier in 'Number of groups', researchers often aim to include a wide range of people in their focus groups, but organize them into separate groups in terms of stratifying criteria. These criteria might include age, gender, education, occupation, and having or not having had a certain experience—we saw examples of focus groups organized by gender, education level, and occupation in the Fenton, Bryman, and Deacon (1998) study featured in Research in focus 20.3 and 20.4. Once researchers have organized potential participants for each group, they can then select them randomly or through some kind of **snowball sampling** method. The aim of this kind of strategy is to establish whether there is any systematic variation in the ways in which different groups discuss a matter. An interesting example of this is van Bezouw et al.'s (2019) cross-national comparative study of political protest. The researchers used focus groups to examine how attitudes toward political protest and mass mobilization are influenced by peers, current events, and socio-cultural developments. However, in designing the study the researchers faced a problem: how could they standardize the focus groups so that they could make meaningful comparisons across the eight different (democratic) countries they were interested in?

> How do we maintain the richness of the data that focus groups provide without treating these insights as unique instances of political discussion? Our methodology is based around standardization of the design across countries. Standardization of the research design allows for interpreting differences in focus group discussions between countries as stemming from differences in attitudes, the political culture, the social context, and other influences than the research design itself . . . not only do the question items need to be understood the same by participants in different countries but the selection criteria and moderating style also need to be similar across countries in order to produce comparable data.
>
> (van Bezouw et al. 2019: 2721)

Van Bezouw et al. attempted to solve this tricky dilemma in a number of ways, one of which was to stratify the groups based on age and education level. They created four age groups (18–25, 26–40, 41–60, and 61+) and two groups based on level of education (low and high). They then placed participants in 'socially homogeneous but politically heterogeneous' groups (2019: 2724) based on a brief screening **questionnaire**, while also standardizing recruitment methods, the types of questions, and the moderating style.

A further issue to consider when designing focus groups is whether to select people who do not know each other or to use natural groupings (for example friends, co-workers, students on the same course). Some researchers prefer to exclude people who know each other because of concerns that pre-existing styles of interaction or status differences may contaminate the session. Not all writers accept this argument, and some prefer to select 'natural groups' whenever possible. These are groups that are comprised of people who already know each other, such as family, friends, or work colleagues. They have the distinct advantage of recreating familiar everyday social interactions. Piper (2015), for example, used groups made up of people who already socialized together for his research on how audiences receive, interpret, and respond to representations of lifestyle shown in images of a particular celebrity chef. The reason was that he wanted the discussions to be as natural as possible, and he felt that this quality would be enhanced by using existing friendship networks that paralleled everyday life. In her research on the relationship between masculinity and violence in young people's discussions about risk-taking, Ravn (2018: 295) conducted 13 focus groups with young people. Using an **informant-driven sampling** procedure, she deliberately assembled groups of participants 'who knew each other well and hung out regularly'. This was because it helped to ensure that the young people were at ease when speaking about issues that might be considered sensitive if discussed in front of strangers.

However, it is not always possible to recruit people entirely from natural groups because of difficulties in securing participation. In the context of their research on the representation of social science research, Fenton, Bryman, and Deacon (1998: 121; see Research in focus 20.3 and 20.4) report that they preferred to recruit 'naturally occurring groups' but 'this was not always achievable'. Morgan (1998a) suggests that one problem with using natural groups is that people who know each other well are likely to make certain assumptions when they discuss matters, and will feel that there are some things that do not need to be said out loud. He suggests that, if it is important for the researcher to bring out such assumptions, groups of strangers are likely to work better.

The issue of how to select participants also suggests another very particular problem for the focus group method—ethics, and more specifically confidentiality and anonymity. Evidently, if participants already know each other both confidentiality and anonymity are clearly compromised. But even if your group members are all strangers to one another, at the very least they will see each others' faces and perhaps even remember their names and/or what they said. So, in terms of the mechanics of participation, it is essential that researchers fully inform participants about the limits of confidentiality and anonymity, and make sure that they understand how this might differ from how you might use the data in any subsequent written report. At the beginning of any focus group, it can also be a very good idea to ask participants to ensure that anything that is said during the discussion is not repeated elsewhere.

Asking questions

Although participants have quite a lot of control over how focus group discussions unfold, the researcher needs to consider what sorts of topics they want addressed during a session, and how to ask the questions on those topics. These issues are similar to the considerations in qualitative interviewing about how unstructured an interview should be (see Chapter 19).

Some researchers prefer to use just one or two very general questions to stimulate discussion, with the moderator intervening as necessary. For example, in their research on knowledge about heart attacks, Morgan and Spanish (1985) asked participants to discuss just two topics. One topic was 'Who has heart attacks and why?'; here the moderator encouraged participants to talk about people they knew who had had heart attacks. The second topic was 'What causes and what prevents heart attacks?'

Other researchers prefer their focus group sessions to be more structured. An example of this is the research on political protest by van Bezouw et al. (2019). The researchers' comparative cross-national design meant that they wanted to ask the same questions in each country, and they wanted those questions to be understood in the same way by participants in each country. They achieved this by constructing six key points for discussion.

- Initially, moderators invited participants to introduce themselves and tell the group the first thing they thought of when they heard the word 'politics'. The authors argue that this forced each participant to make an early contribution to the discussion, while also helping to orientate them towards potential topics of interest.
- Questioning then moved on to a collective discussion on what five issues were most important for society. This helped to establish the key foci for discussion.
- The moderators then asked participants what could be done about those issues. In order to further stimulate focused discussion, they presented participants with pictures of institutionalized and non-institutionalized forms of political participation.
- This led to questions about why certain strategies were not used and why some people chose not to be politically active.
- The moderators then asked participants which institutions are best placed to listen to citizens and act on their behalf.
- Finally, they asked participants about what they thought of taking a more people-led approach to political decision-making.

While the research by van Bezouw et al. (2019) clearly contained quite a lot of specific areas, the questions themselves were fairly general and were designed to ensure that there was comparability between the focus group sessions across the eight countries. The researchers also made an effort to ensure that the moderating style was the same across the groups. In practice, this meant adopting a 'non-directive' stance, 'giving clear instructions to each moderator about the goals of the research and the necessity to avoid follow-up questions aside from clarification prompts' (van Bezouw et al. 2019: 2728). This approach to questioning, which is fairly common in focus group research, allowed the researchers to address the research questions and ensure comparability between sessions, and allowed participants to raise issues they saw as significant.

Another quite structured approach to focus group questioning was used in a cross-national study of young Europeans' 'orientations to the present and future, with respect to their "careers" as partners, parents and workers' (Smithson and Brannen 2002: 14). The countries involved were Ireland, Norway, Portugal, Sweden, and the UK. There were 312 participants, but the number of groups and the number of participants in them varied considerably by country. The researchers' relatively structured approach to questioning can be seen in the fact that there were 19 topic areas, each of which had several questions. For example, for the topic of 'jobs', the questions were these:

- What do you want from a job?
- What is important when you look for a job?
- Do you think it is important to support yourself?
- How do you expect to do that (job/state/spouse/other way)?
- Do you think it is different for women and men of your age?
- Do you expect to be in paid employment in five years' time/ten years' time?

(Brannen et al. 2002: 190)

As in van Bezouw et al.'s cross-national study, it seems likely that Brannen et al. chose this more structured approach to questioning in order to ensure comparability between the sessions conducted in different countries.

There is probably not a single best way to moderate a focus group, but most studies using this method seem to adopt 'middle ground' approaches similar to those used by Fenton, Bryman, and Deacon (see Research in focus 20.3 and 20.4). This style of questioning sits between the relatively open-ended approach used by Morgan and Spanish (1985) and the more structured one used by van Bezouw et al. (2019). It can also be seen in the way that Macnaghten and Jacobs (1997) used a 'topic guide' to group the issues to be covered into discrete areas of discussion. The following passage gives us a sense of the extent to which the questioning in their focus groups was structured. Here, a group of working women reveal a cynicism about governments and experts' accounts of environmental problems, preferring to rely on their own sensory experience (a tendency that could also be seen in most of the other groups). In this passage *F* is 'female'.

> *F* They only tell us what they want us to know. And that's just the end of that, so we are left with a fog in your brain, so you just think—what have I to worry about? I don't know what they're on about.
>
> *Mod* So why do Government only tell us what they want us to hear?
>
> *F* To keep your confidence going. (All together)
>
> *Mod* So if someone provides an indicator which says the economy is improving you won't believe it?
>
> *F* They've been saying it for about ten years, but where? I can't see anything!
>
> *F* Every time there's an election they say the economy is improving.
>
> (Macnaghten and Jacobs 1997: 18)

In this passage, the moderator emphasizes the topic to be addressed but also picks up on what the group says.

The style of questioning and moderating is likely to be affected by various factors, such as the nature of the research topic and levels of interest and/or knowledge among participants in the research. For example, if the topic is one that the researcher suspects participants already know a lot about, it may be easier to use a less structured approach, whereas if there is a low level of participant interest it will probably be best to use a somewhat more structured approach. Kandola (2012) recommends asking for examples and further elaboration to help stimulate further discussion. This allows key points to be expanded. The sensitivity of the topic may be a further consideration; if it is very sensitive, moderators may need to ask several **open-ended questions** as 'icebreakers' to help relax participants (see Research in focus 20.6). Even if they opt for a more structured approach to questioning, focus group researchers should be prepared to allow at least some discussion to depart from the topic guide, because this kind of debate might provide new and unexpected insights. A more structured approach to questioning might reduce the likelihood of such spontaneity, but it is unlikely to remove it altogether.

Beginning and finishing

As in the research by van Bezouw et al. (2019) (see 'Asking questions'), it is usually recommended that focus group sessions begin with an introduction. This might include these elements:

- the moderators introducing themselves and thanking people for coming;
- an outline of the goals of the research;
- an overview of key ethical issues, including **informed consent** and right to withdraw (see Chapter 6);
- the fact that the session will be recorded and the reasons for doing so;
- the format that the focus group will take; and
- the amount of time that the discussion will take.

It is also important to present some of the conventions of focus group participation, such as these:

- that only one person should speak at a time (perhaps explaining that when people speak over each other this causes problems with recording the discussion);
- that the researcher will treat all data confidentially and anonymize it; and
- that the session is open, and everyone's views are important.

During the introduction, focus group researchers often ask participants to fill in forms providing basic socio-demographic information about themselves, such as age, gender, occupation, and where they live. It is also a good idea for participants to introduce themselves and to write out their first names on a card or sticky label, so that everyone's name is visible.

At the end, moderators should thank the group members for their participation and explain very briefly what

RESEARCH IN FOCUS 20.6
Questioning in a focus group

Warr's (2005) study was concerned with ideas of intimacy among predominantly socio-economically disadvantaged people in New Zealand. Most of her participants were aged between 18 and 29 years. Her questioning strategy was to begin with what she calls an 'icebreaker', which involved asking participants about a popular movie that was on release at the time. This kind of opening question can be useful in stimulating participants' initial thoughts on the topic, and is particularly useful for a study relating to intimacy, given how often relationships are emphasized in movies. The researcher followed this icebreaker with some broader questions:

> 'How do you know when you've in love?' 'How do you know when someone is in love with you?' 'In getting to know people, who makes the first move?' and 'How do you learn about sex and love?' To conclude, I would request participants to imagine the future in terms of whether they expected to settle down with someone, get married, or have children. The theme list posed very broad questions for discussion so there was plenty of scope for participants to pursue the topics in undirected ways and to introduce other issues as required.
>
> (Warr 2005: 156)

Warr used a 'theme list' to direct the discussion (to a degree) and to keep it relevant to her research, but notes that she kept her questions broad in order to retain some spontaneity.

will happen to the data they have supplied. If they want to arrange a further session with the same group, they will need to take steps to coordinate this.

Recording and transcription

As with interviewing for qualitative research, a focus group session will be most useful for your project if you can record and later transcribe it. There are a number of reasons for this.

1. Focus groups are fast-paced. This makes it extremely difficult to keep exact notes of what people say and who says it. In an individual interview you might be able to ask the respondent to pause while you write something down, but it would be very disruptive to do this in an interview involving several people.
2. Recording and transcribing will ensure you have an accurate record of who expresses views within the group: for example, whether particular individuals seem to act as opinion leaders or dominate the discussion, and where the range of opinions within groups come from (does most of the range of opinion derive from just one or two people, or does it come from most of the people in the group?).
3. An accurate record will help to facilitate an analysis of how the group collectively constructs meaning. As we saw in Section 20.2, this is a major reason for conducting focus group research. It would be very difficult to do this by taking notes, because of the need to keep track of *who* says what. If this element is not recorded accurately, the dynamics of the focus group session would be lost.
4. Like all qualitative researchers, focus group practitioners are interested in not just what people say but *how* they say it. The nuances of their language will probably be lost if the researcher relies exclusively on notes.

However, transcribing focus group recordings is more complicated—and therefore more time-consuming—than transcribing traditional interview recordings. This is because you need to take account of *who* is talking in the session, as well as what is said. This is sometimes difficult as it is not always possible to distinguish different people's voices, and because people sometimes talk over each other. All of this means that it is extremely important to ensure that you equip yourself with a very high-quality microphone that is capable of picking up voices from many directions. Focus group transcripts always seem to have more missing bits, because of lack of audibility, than transcripts from conventional interviews. Tips and skills 20.1 lists some ways to make the process of recording and transcribing easier.

TIPS AND SKILLS 20.1

Running a focus group and thinking about transcription

There are a number of things that you can do within the focus groups to help with the process of recording and transcribing.

- Make sure the room in which the group takes place is relatively free from external noise. This will help to ensure that the recording is clear.
- Try to arrange the room so that it allows you to record the discussion as clearly as is possible. This might involve some **experimentation** to see what sort of setup works best, so allow enough time to enable you to do this.
- Provide clear instructions to participants about the nature of the discussion. Ask them not to talk over each other where possible—and be prepared to remind them during the interview if necessary.
- At the beginning of the discussion, go around the group and ask each participant to introduce themselves. Having this on the recording will help you to connect a voice to a name.
- Transcribing the focus group as soon as possible can help aid recall.
- Within the transcription, you can use a space between two brackets ( ) to denote where any spoken words are too unclear to transcribe.

20.4 Group interaction in focus group sessions

We saw in Section 20.2 that one of the distinguishing features of the focus group method, and a reason why many researchers choose it, is that it allows us to study the operation, forms, and impact of social interaction. But as a number of researchers have observed (e.g. Kitzinger 1994; Kidd and Parshall 2000; Cyr 2016), reports of focus group research often do not take into account patterns of interaction within the group. Wilkinson reviewed over 200 focus group studies published between 1946 and 1996. She concluded: 'Focus group data is most commonly presented as if it were one-to-one interview data, with interactions between group participants rarely reported, let alone analysed' (Wilkinson 1998: 112). Cyr (2016) similarly analysed a sample of 70 articles published in political science and sociology journals between the years 2004 to 2013 that had used focus groups. She found that very few went beyond the individual level of analysis to examine the interactions of the groups or how the participants constructed collective understandings. Here, we look at the main types of interaction that take place in focus groups and how researchers can capture these complex dynamics during data analysis.

Complementary and argumentative interactions

Kitzinger (1994) draws attention to two types of interaction in focus groups: complementary and argumentative. Complementary interactions reveal the consistent frameworks of understanding that resonate across participants' understandings of the social world. Argumentative interactions are, as the term suggests, interactions that expose different views among participants.

The discussion in Research in focus 20.4 provides an example of complementary interactions, as it illustrates that the participants share some views of the natural sciences and the social sciences—for example, they seem to agree that social science involves subjective interpretation and does not produce concrete results. These views emerge as a product of the interaction, with each participant building on the preceding remark. We can see a similar pattern in the following passage, which is taken from Rhodes and Tiernan's (2015) study of people who have operated as chief of staff to the prime minister of Australia. They conducted two focus groups with 11 people who had been employed in the role. During the sessions, the job of personal physician to the prime minister was explored by two participants:

Geoff Walsh: Paul [Keating] wasn't too fussy [about food], except when we went [on an overseas visit]. We had a doctor who travelled with us – the improbably named Dr Killer.

Grahame Morris: He is still the man.

20

Geoff Walsh: He hasn't lost a Prime Minister yet [laughs]. Anyway, Dr Killer went to inspect the kitchen before the state dinner. . . . He came back ashen-faced and said, 'There's a toilet in the middle of the kitchen. My advice is don't eat anything.' So Paul spent the night with the menu in front of him and basically dodging, because he had a view that you could pick up hepatitis or something. That would be the end of your career.

Grahame Morris: It's still the standard advice of Graham Killer now: anything that might have been near water, lettuce or anything, don't eat it. Brush your teeth out of bottled water or whiskey. So, he's still giving the same advice and he's still keeping PMs alive.

(Rhodes and Tiernan 2015: 128)

This sequence brings out a consensus around the question of how to manage the diet of the prime minister when visiting foreign countries. Geoff Walsh introduces the key character of Dr Killer, and Grahame Morris confirms that he is still operating in the role. Geoff Walsh then proceeds to outline a major role of the job with an amusing anecdote, and this is confirmed by Grahame Morris, who elaborates on Killer's advice.

Munday (2006) suggests that the way in which focus groups can highlight a consensus, as well as the mechanics of that consensus (how it was reached), makes this method a powerful tool for research into collective identity. She gives the example of her research on social movements and, in particular, a focus group with members of a Women's Institute (WI) in which she asked about the movie *Calendar Girls*, based on the nude calendar made by the members of the WI in Rylestone (a village in Yorkshire, England) some years previously. Munday writes that she asked the question because she felt it might encourage them to discuss the traditional image of WIs as old-fashioned and 'out of touch'. Instead, the women chose to discuss Rylestone WI and the impact that the calendar's notoriety had on its members. Later, the participants had the following interaction:

Alice It might appeal more to the younger ones than perhaps the older members don't you think? . . . Although I suppose they were middle-aged ladies themselves.

Jane Oh yes.

Mar Oh yes they were yes.

Jane They weren't slim and what have you.

Mary Oh no no.

Jane ()

Mary No they were quite well . . .

Jane They were.

Mary Weren't they?

June I mean it was very well done because you never saw anything you wouldn't want to.

(Munday 2006: 100)

Munday notes that the discussion of the movie did not revolve around dispelling the traditional image of WIs, but instead on dispelling a traditional image of older women, while at the same time recognizing that the women's respectability was not compromised. A sense of collective identity surrounding gender emerged that was different from how the researcher had anticipated the discussion would develop. This particular example demonstrates the potential of the focus group to reveal how collective ideas emerge within social interaction and how they are then subsequently reinforced by the group.

However, Kitzinger (1994) suggests that argumentative interactions in focus groups can be equally revealing. She suggests that moderators can play an important role in identifying differences of opinion and exploring with participants the factors that may lie behind them. Disagreement can give participants the opportunity to revise their opinions or to think more about the reasons why they hold the view that they do. In their study of experiences of the transition phases between junior and senior teams for Swedish ice hockey players, Pehrson et al. (2017) conducted a series of three focus groups with professional players and coaches. They wanted to see whether a model of transition that they had created from an earlier round of data collection would be validated by participants.

P7: I think everything can be faster than what it is here [duration of the phases]. If you get up to a senior team, I would say six months for this [orientation phase] and the rest of the season is the adaptation phase. Starting from the second year I think it should be the stabilization phase.

P6: I don't think it's realistic to become an established player after the first season. That would be really hard.

P7: If you have the skills, I think one should be able to be there.

P8: I'm thinking that all of us come from the major clubs and to get established in one of those clubs after the first season will be very hard.

P7: Well, yes. That would be really hard.

P5: So, most often it will take more time.

(Pehrson et al. 2017: 755)

After initially disagreeing about the length of time needed to make the transition to established player, the participants seek clarification about the context in which transition takes place, in this case 'major clubs'. They then reach an agreement that the original scenario is not feasible. Kitzinger (1994) argues that drawing attention to patterns of interaction within focus groups allows the researcher to determine how group participants view the relevant issues in their own terms. The way that participants pose questions and express agreement or disagreement with each other helps to draw out their own stances on the issues. Disagreements also mean that participants are forced to explain *why* they hold particular views.

Focus groups rarely consist of solely complementary or argumentative interactions; they often feature a mixture of the two. This contrast allows the researcher to see the tensions associated with people's private beliefs and wider public debates and expectations. This was particularly significant for Warr's (2005) study of intimacy because of the difficulties involved in resolving disagreements about what is and is not appropriate in matters of love and sex. These are particularly sensitive topics where individual views are likely to vary considerably. Indeed, like Kitzinger, Warr argues that focusing on areas of agreement and disagreement can be a useful starting point for interpreting and analysing the qualitative data that are produced in focus groups.

Analysing group interactions

While interaction and disagreements are distinctive characteristics of focus groups compared to individual interviews, they do also add a layer of complexity to the analysis of the data. There is actually very little agreement in the literature concerning the analysis of focus group data, particularly with respect to the social interaction that occurs. It is true enough to say that while most of the principles and approaches for data analysis that we will identify in Chapter 23 can be usefully applied to the transcription of a focus group, capturing group dynamics is much more difficult. Barbour (2014) recommends looking for patterns within focus group data that suggest particular interpretations are associated with individuals in different positions or with certain social characteristics. This might involve looking for intra-group (within a group) or inter-group (across different groups) patterns, depending on whether each group is made up of similar individuals, different individuals, or a mixture of both. Elsewhere, there are a number of very specific attempts to describe how the analysis of group dynamics might be conducted, but their usefulness will depend on the focus of the research project in question (see Onwuegbuzie et al. 2009; Farnsworth and Boon 2010; Halkier 2011).

However, Morgan (2010) questions the assumption that focus group data that emphasize group interaction are superior to those that do not. He argues that it depends what the researcher wants to demonstrate. Sometimes, quoting what individuals have said can be more effective than passages of interaction, if what the researcher wants to show is a position that is often repeated. Quoting sequences of interaction might be less effective in making the point and also uses up far more words, which may be a consideration when there is a tight word limit. But one situation in which Morgan feels that interaction should almost always be emphasized is when a new topic is introduced and this quickly stimulates a series of responses from a number of participants. Both the speed of responses and any emerging consensus or dispute in this situation mean that it is likely to be very significant to participants so it should be analysed in detail.

20.5 Online focus groups

Synchronous and asynchronous groups

As with qualitative interviews, there has been a growth in the use of online focus groups, and it is worth highlighting some key characteristics and issues associated with the method. In the first instance, there is a crucial distinction between **synchronous** and **asynchronous online focus groups**.

With synchronous groups, the focus group is in real time, so contributions are made more or less immediately after previous contributions among a group of participants, all of whom are simultaneously online. Contributions can be responded to as soon as they are typed (in an online chat space) or spoken (in a video or audio conference). In a way, this reflects the immediacy of offline focus groups. However, as Mann and Stewart (2000) observe, this can actually complicate the analysis because several participants can type in a response to a contribution at the same time. Therefore, normal turn-taking conventions do not necessarily operate as they would in offline environments. With asynchronous groups, the exchanges are not in real time. Group emails are a form of asynchronous communication that has been used to conduct online focus groups. The moderator can ask the focus group participants a question via email, and the participants reply to the moderator and the other group members at some time in the future. These kinds of groups get around the time-zone problem; are probably easier than synchronous groups for participants who are not skilled at using a keyboard; and allow participants to consider their answers in more detail and respond at the time that best suits them. However, there can be a higher risk of dropouts due to the repeated nature of the commitment.

Conducting an online focus group

The main practical difference between running a focus group online compared to face-to-face is that rather than choosing a suitable physical location in which to run a focus group session, the researcher needs to choose the digital 'place' or forum in which they would like to host the discussion. This might include, for example, email, an online platform (for example social media), a website, or piece of specialist software such as Google Meet or Zoom.

Many of the points we covered in Section 20.3 apply to conducting online focus groups too, but the following are worth in bearing in mind.

- *Size of groups*. For synchronous groups, the same kinds of restrictions on number of participants apply as for face-to-face sessions—Mann and Stewart (2000) suggest that if there are too many participants it can make it difficult for some people to contribute, and recommend groups of between six and eight participants. Also, moderating the session can be more difficult with large numbers. Asynchronous groups can be larger. However, Lijadi and van Schalkwyk (2015) note that large groups can present research management problems.
- *Selecting participants*. Researchers can select participants in much the same way as for face-to-face groups, but depending on how and where the session(s) will be hosted, researchers may first need to confirm that potential participants have access to the relevant software or are happy to install it.
- *Level of moderator involvement*. In synchronous groups, similar principles apply to those we have already discussed. In asynchronous groups, it will probably not be possible to have a moderator online at all times and extensive intervention may also be limited by the size of the group. This lack of continuous availability means that emails or postings may be sent and responded to without any ability of the moderator to intervene or participate. This feature may not be a problem, but could become so if offensive messages were being sent or if it meant that the discussion was going off at a complete tangent from which it would be difficult to redeem the situation.
- *Beginning and finishing*. Before starting the online focus group session, moderators should send out a welcome message introducing the research and laying out some rules for the ongoing discussion. There is evidence that participants respond more positively if the researchers take the time to develop rapport with participants (see, for example, Moore et al. 2015). This can be done in the opening message and accompanying introductions or by creating links to personal websites (as in Research in focus 20.8).
- *Recording and transcribing*. A major advantage of online focus groups in written format (that is, not using video calling) is that you will not need to transcribe the responses. With some platforms or forums researchers may need to manually copy and paste discussions into a separate document in order to record and save them safely, but most conferencing software will allow you to download a transcript following the session.

Research in focus 20.7 and 20.8 provide examples of asynchronous and synchronous online focus groups, respectively.

Advantages and disadvantages of online focus groups

Many of the advantages and disadvantages of online versus face-to-face focus groups are similar to those associated with online and face-to-face interviews, so these overarching points are summarized in Thinking deeply 20.1. Here, we reflect on some points that are particular to, or particularly relevant to, online focus groups.

Perhaps the most significant advantages of conducting focus groups online rather than face-to-face are the following.

- They present researchers with a greater opportunity to use a 'captive population' of people who are already communicating with each other. This is unlike face-to-face focus groups, where people are often (though not always) brought together for the purpose of the session (Stewart and Williams 2005).

20

RESEARCH IN FOCUS 20.7
An asynchronous online focus group

'Third culture kids' (TCKs) are children who are raised in a country that is not their parents' native country. This is often because their parents are working abroad. Their situation means that they are simultaneously part of three cultures: their country of origin; their host culture; and the global culture of an international settler. Given the displaced nature of this group, Lijadi and van Schalkwyk (2015) thought that an asynchronous focus group would be the best way to study how adults who were formerly TCKs experienced their developmental years.

The researchers set up a 'secret group' on Facebook and, following some preliminary exploration of associated groups, they recruited participants via snowball sampling. They posted in TCK groups asking for volunteers and further recommendations for people who satisfied the criteria of being 18 years or older and who lived in at least three cultures growing up. Thirty-five participants from seven continents volunteered for the study, with participants assigned to seven focus groups based on their age. The researchers provided participants with a list of housekeeping rules with respect to how to communicate, and online discussions took place over a minimum of eight days and a maximum of 18 days. Although the authors write that they found the process quite intense, the technique did allow them to collect robust data from a hard-to-reach **population**.

RESEARCH IN FOCUS 20.8
A synchronous online focus group

There is now a range of literature that has explored the use of text-based communication for the purposes of facilitating focus group participation, particularly with samples that are geographically distant (see Synnot et al. 2014, for example). However, recent developments in video conferencing software have enabled researchers to explore the potential for online focus groups in a way that is more closely aligned with traditional face-to-face methods.

Matthews et al. (2018), for example, used video-enabled online focus groups to examine the factors that were thought to influence the implementation of advanced practitioners in radiation therapy in Australia. Although the number of participants and groups was relatively small—four groups of two, and two groups of three—the researchers report that the study was broadly successful in that it brought a range of professionals together for participation in a manner that would have been geographically impossible in a physical sense, and very laborious if conducted via a textual format. A post-focus-group survey revealed that participants appreciated the enhanced accessibility provided by the software. Similarly, the stability and recording capability of the software was also broadly successful, and the researchers ensured the privacy of the data by downloading the focus group recordings to a standalone computer on completion. While they reported high attrition—although not above that expected for text-based online focus groups—the researchers judged the capacity of the moderator to be similar to that expected of a more traditional focus group (although they note that this may be more problematic when researching issues of a sensitive nature).

So, although the use of video-conferencing software for the purposes of 'face-to-face' focus groups is still evolving, there is some emerging evidence that it can be beneficial in certain contexts.

- They provide a way to address the logistical issues that are usually presented by participants living a long way apart, and can enable cross-cultural discussions at a relatively low cost.
- They allow participants to contribute to the discussion at a time and location that is convenient for them, making the exercise more accessible. For example, some people may find face-to-face discussions anxiety-provoking or

THINKING DEEPLY 20.1

Online versus face-to-face focus groups and qualitative interviews

Here is a summary of the main advantages and disadvantages of online focus groups and online one-to-one interviews compared to their face-to-face counterparts. We have combined our discussion of the two methods for this purpose because, as we have seen in this chapter and Chapter 19, most of the advantages and disadvantages apply equally well to both. (Points marked with an asterisk * do not apply, or are less likely to apply, to audiovisual interviews or focus groups.)

Advantages of online focus groups include the following.

- Online interviews and focus groups are relatively cost-effective compared to face-to-face equivalents.
- Participants who would otherwise normally be inaccessible (for example, because they live in another country) or hard to involve in research (for example, very senior executives; people with almost no time for participation) can be more easily recruited.
- Large numbers of possible participants can be accessed online.
- Participants can reread what they (and, in the case of focus groups, others) have previously written in their replies. This allows them to carefully consider their response.*
- Participants may be better able to fit their involvement with the research into their own time, especially as they do not have to spend time travelling to a venue to contribute to the discussion.
- There is often no need for transcription. This is a huge advantage because of the time and cost involved in getting recorded interview sessions transcribed.*
- The transcripts are more likely to be accurate, because issues of mistranslating do not arise. This is a particular advantage with focus group discussions, because in a recording of a face-to-face session it can be difficult to establish who is speaking and often it is impossible to distinguish what is said when participants speak at the same time.*
- Focus group participants can use pseudonyms to keep their identity hidden from others in the group and even the interviewer. This can make it easier for participants to discuss potentially embarrassing issues or to share potentially unpopular views. They may also feel more comfortable discussing sensitive issues generally in an online rather than face-to-face context.*
- Participants are less likely to be influenced by characteristics such as the age, ethnicity, or appearance (and possibly even gender if pseudonyms are used) of the interviewer/moderator and any other participants.* When interviewees and participants are online at home, they are essentially in something of an anonymous, safe, and non-threatening environment, which may be especially helpful to vulnerable groups. The experience may also feel—and be—safer for researchers than invading other people's homes or workplaces.

Among the disadvantages of online focus groups are the following.

- The evidence tends to show that face-to-face focus groups produce higher-quality data compared to online ones.
- Only people with access to online facilities and/or who find them relatively straightforward are likely to be able to participate. This means that those without access are likely to be excluded from the research.
- It can be more difficult for the interviewer/moderator to establish rapport and to engage with interviewees (though this may not matter when the topic is of interest to participants), and it can be difficult to retain rapport over time in asynchronous interviews.
- Probing is more difficult—though not impossible. Curasi (2001) reports some success in eliciting further information from respondents, but it is easier for interviewees to ignore or forget about the requests for further information or expansion on answers given.*

- Asynchronous interviews and focus groups may take a long time to complete, depending on participants' availability and cooperativeness, and (partly linked to this issue) there may be a greater tendency for participants to discontinue their involvement than is likely to be the case with face-to-face contexts.
- Responses have less spontaneity, because interviewees can reflect on their answers to a much greater extent than is possible in a face-to-face situation. However, this can also be seen as an advantage, because interviewees are likely to give more considered and perhaps consistent replies.*
- In online contexts, the researcher cannot be certain that the people who are interviewed are who they say they are (though this issue may apply to face-to-face interviews as well).*
- Turn-taking conventions between interviewer/moderator and interviewee/focus group participant are more likely to be disrupted.
- In synchronous focus groups, variations in keyboard skills may prevent participants from contributing equally.*
- Participating from home in online interviews and focus groups requires considerable commitment from interviewees and participants if they have to install software onto their computers and remain online for extended periods of time.
- Online connections may be lost, so participants need to know what to do if this occurs. Poor connection or loss of connection may disrupt the flow of a group discussion.
- Interviewers/moderators cannot take into account body language or other forms of non-verbal data that might suggest different reactions, for example confusion, or in the case of focus groups frustration at not being able to contribute to the discussion.*

Sources: Mann and Stewart (2000); Curasi (2001); Sweet (2001); Evans et al. (2008); Hewson and Laurent (2008); Williams et al. (2012); Tuttas (2014); and Abrams et al. (2015).

have trouble travelling to the venue. Asynchronous online focus groups are particularly useful in terms of improving accessibility. They allow people to participate who may struggle with the speed of a face-to-face or online synchronous discussion—especially, in the case of online synchronous sessions, if they are not skilled in using, or find it difficult to use, a keyboard.

- They have been shown to lead to increased participation and fewer socially desirable responses from participants compared with face-to-face discussions, particularly for sensitive issues or topics related to sexual health (Tates et al. 2009). Generally, they increase the chance of equal participation within a group, as shy or quiet participants may find it easier to voice opinions than in face-to-face contexts and overbearing participants are less likely to dominate.

However, online focus groups also have some notable disadvantages compared to face-to-face sessions.

- Online focus groups can help researchers get around the logistical and financial problem of geographical distance, but time zone differences can still cause problems in terms of continuous moderation. It can also be difficult to try to find a time to run a synchronous group session that is convenient for everyone (Stewart and Williams 2005).
- Focus group participants will need access to the software being used and so may have to install it onto their computers. Participants may not feel confident about using the software, and there may be compatibility problems with particular machines and operating systems.
- Selecting participants for online focus groups can be difficult because it often relies on participants having particular access to the necessary hardware and software. One possibility is to use questionnaires as a springboard for identifying possible participants who have access, while another possibility is to contact them by email.
- Asynchronous online focus group sessions can go on for a long time, perhaps for several days or even weeks, so it is more likely that participants will drop out of the study.
- Response rates may be lower than for face-to-face focus groups (Stewart and Williams 2005). It is relatively easy for the researcher to contact a large number of possible respondents using email, but the response rates of those wanting to participate in an online focus group have been found to be quite low.

Online focus groups that do not use video also do not allow researchers to gain non-verbal data, such as facial expression. Underhill and Olmstead (2003) compared data from synchronous online focus groups with parallel data from face-to-face groups and found little difference in terms of data quantity or quality. In contrast, Brüggen and Willems (2009) found that when they compared synchronous online focus group findings with those deriving from face-to-face ones in a market research area, the latter produced richer data. Abrams et al. (2015) compared the quality of data deriving from two face-to-face, two online audiovisual (using video calling applications), and two online text-only focus groups. They found that face-to-face focus groups produced considerably more topic-related data. Coders rated the data from the face-to-face and the online audiovisual face-to-face groups as superior to online text-only ones in terms of depth, with the latter groups also found to be inferior in terms of the numbers of words they produced.

The balance of evidence, then, still seems to favour the traditional face-to-face focus group, but the online audiovisual mode may prove to be a viable alternative in the future as more people become familiar with tools such as Zoom, and as their technology develops so that they become more effective and reliable for this purpose. Online focus groups are unlikely to replace their face-to-face counterparts, but they will probably be increasingly used for certain kinds of research topic and/or samples. As regards samples, dispersed or inaccessible people are especially relevant to online focus group research—as we have seen in examples like Lijadi and van Schalkwyk's (2015) study (Research in focus 20.7). Reisner et al. (2018) also highlight that the anonymity of the online setting also makes it easier to study hard-to-reach populations that are socially excluded, marginalized, or stigmatized. This includes 'those affected by HIV/AIDS, sexual and gender minority (lesbian, gay, bisexual, transgender, queer/questioning [LGBTQ]) youth and adults, sex workers, and people with criminal records' (Reisner et al. 2018: 1660).

20.6 Limitations of focus groups

Focus groups clearly have considerable potential for investigating research questions that are concerned with the processes through which meaning is collectively constructed. They allow participants' perspectives—an important feature of much qualitative research (see Chapter 16)—to be revealed in ways that are different from individual interviews. Given the more participant-led nature of a focus group, there is also the possibility to redress some of the unequal power dynamics that are inherent in the conventional research relationship. But, like all data-collection methods, the method has some limitations.

- *The researcher has less control than with an individual interview*. This is not necessarily a disadvantage as it means that emerging issues can be covered, and also means that participants have some 'ownership' of the interview and the research process more generally. However, researchers may find it hard to gauge the extent to which they should allow participants to 'take over' the running of a focus group. How involved should moderators be, how far should a set of prompts or questions influence the conduct of a focus group, and to what degree should control of a discussion be given to its participants? The line between control and spontaneity is particularly difficult to determine when the researcher is seeking answers to a fairly explicit set of research questions.
- *Focus group data are difficult to analyse*. The method can produce a huge amount of data very quickly, and developing a strategy of analysis that incorporates themes in both what people say and patterns of interaction is not easy. However, studies such as those by Morgan and Hoffman (2018) and Ravn (2018) demonstrate that examining group interactions can help show how issues of thematic interest arise in the course of discussion.
- *Focus groups are difficult to organize*. Not only do you have to secure the agreement of people to participate in your study, you also need to persuade them to turn up to a particular place at a particular time (even if this is a virtual space). Researchers sometimes offer small payments, such as vouchers, to induce participation, but some people will still not turn up. As a result, researchers often deliberately over-recruit for each session.
- *Focus group transcribing is time-consuming*. We saw in Chapter 19 that transcribing individual interviews is also time-consuming, but focus group transcription

is even more so. This is because of variations in voice pitch and the need to take account of who says what. For example, Bloor et al. (2001) suggest that a focus group session lasting one hour can take up to eight hours to transcribe, which is longer than it would take with a one-hour individual interview. Given the different voices present and the difficulty of getting very high quality recordings, the use of voice recognition software is very problematic.

- *The issue of overlapping speech is common*. There is a tendency for two or more participants to speak at the same time in focus groups, and it is very difficult to transcribe these parts of a discussion. Moderators can ask participants not to speak at the same time, but it is difficult to prevent this from occurring in spite of constant warnings (see Research in focus 20.9 for an example).
- *There are potential issues of group effects*. This includes the obvious problems of dealing with both reticent and dominant speakers. Krueger (1998: 59) suggests that the moderator should make clear to an overly-dominant speaker and other participants that other people's views are definitely required, for example by saying something like 'That's one point of view. Does anyone have another point of view?' Researchers also try to actively encourage quieter participants to say something. Another point worth noting about group effects is that, as the well-known Asch experiments showed, an emerging group view may mean that individual perspectives may be suppressed (Asch 1951). There is also evidence that as a group comes to share a certain point of view, its members come to think uncritically about it and develop almost irrational attachments to it (Janis 1982). We do not know how far group effects have an adverse impact on focus group findings, but we cannot entirely ignore them.
- *Participants may be influenced by the group's norms and expectations*. This is the idea that in group contexts, participants may be more prone to expressing culturally expected views than in individual interviews. Morgan (2002) cites a study in which group interviews

RESEARCH IN FOCUS 20.9

Dealing with participants speaking at the same time in a focus group

Taken from Silva and Wright (2005), this excerpt provides a good example of how moderators can attempt to prevent—or reduce the frequency of—participants talking at the same time, which makes it hard for the discussion to progress and causes major issues for transcribing. The researchers were investigating the extent to which the concept of 'cultural capital' can be used to explain the various experiences of social exclusion in the UK. The extract below is taken from a focus group conducted with unskilled and semi-skilled workers on the topic of museum visiting.

[All talking at once]

Stephanie Please, please, I know I'm being like a schoolteacher . . .

Bill No, no, we're all ears 'Miss'!

[General laughter]

Stephanie Will you all shut up!

Tel I don't think I would go to the [museum] in Swansea because it wouldn't be as good as the one in London. And please 'Miss' I need to piss.

Stephanie All right then but no running in the corridors and make sure you wash your hands afterwards.

[General laughter]

(Silva and Wright 2005: 7)

The moderator, Stephanie, has clearly had problems stopping this group talking at the same time. She cleverly turns it into a joke by likening herself to a schoolteacher, even telling them to shut up. The group seems to enter into the spirit of the joke but whether she was actually able to stop participants from talking over each other, thereby making the audio-recording and transcribing progress easier, is another question . . .

with boys discussing relationships with girls were compared with individual interviews with them on the same topic. In the latter they expressed a degree of sensitivity that was not present in the group context, where the views tended to be more macho. This suggests that in the group interviews, the boys were seeking to impress others and were being influenced by peer-group norms. This does not mean that group interview data is questionable, but it does highlight the difference between privately and publicly held views.

- *Some focus group situations may make participants uncomfortable*. This is a point made by Madriz (2000), who argues that in such circumstances individual interviews may be preferable. Situations in which participants might feel uneasy include when intimate details of private lives need to be revealed; when participants may not be comfortable in each other's presence (for example, bringing together people who are in a hierarchical relationship to each other); and when participants are likely to profoundly disagree with each other.

KEY POINTS

- The focus group method is an interview with several people on a specific topic or issue where the researcher also has some interest in the dynamics of the group discussion.
- The moderator generally tries to allow the discussion to unfold more freely than in a semi-structured interview. However, there may be contexts in which they need to ask fairly specific questions, especially when cross-group comparability is an issue.
- An important aspect of the focus group is the way in which participants collectively produce meanings.
- Focus group discussions need to be recorded and transcribed, and the latter is usually more difficult and time-consuming than with individual interviews.
- There are several issues to note concerning the recruitment of focus group participants—in particular, whether to use natural groupings and whether to employ stratifying criteria.
- Group interaction is an important component of discussions, although this element is often underemphasized in the literature.
- Focus groups can be, and increasingly are, carried out online but this poses some challenges.
- Some writers view focus groups as being well suited to a feminist standpoint and to interviewing marginalized groups.

QUESTIONS FOR REVIEW

1. Why might it be useful to distinguish between a focus group and a group interview?
2. What advantages might the focus group method offer compared to an individual qualitative interview?
3. How involved should the moderator of a focus group be in the discussion?
4. Why is it necessary to record and transcribe focus group sessions?
5. Are there any circumstances in which it might be a good idea to select participants who know each other?
6. What might be the advantages and disadvantages of using a topic guide in focus group sessions?

7. Why might it be important to treat group interaction as an important issue when analysing focus group data?
8. What is the significance of the distinction between synchronous and asynchronous online focus groups?
9. How different is the role of the moderator in online, compared to face-to-face, focus groups?
10. Does the potential for the loss of control over proceedings and for group effects to influence the discussion damage the potential usefulness of the focus group as a method?
11. How far do the problems of transcription and difficulty of data analysis undermine the potential of focus groups?
12. To what extent are focus groups a naturalistic approach to data collection?

ONLINE RESOURCES

www.oup.com/he/srm6e

You can find our notes on the answers to these questions within this chapter's **online resources**, together with:

- *audio/video comments* on this topic from our 'Learn from experience' panellists;
- *audio discussion from the authors* on why it is useful to distinguish between a focus group and a group interview (review question 1);
- *self-test questions* for further knowledge-checking;
- a *flashcard glossary* to help you recall key terms; and
- a *Student Researcher's Toolkit* containing practical materials and resources to help you conduct your own research project.

CHAPTER

21

LANGUAGE IN QUALITATIVE RESEARCH

CHAPTER GUIDE

In this chapter we consider two approaches to examining language: conversation analysis and discourse analysis. Both of these approaches make language itself the focus of interest; it is not simply seen as a resource through which research participants communicate with researchers. We explore

- the roots of conversation analysis in ethnomethodology;
- some of the rules and principles of conversation analysis;
- the main aims of discourse analysis;
- some of the analytic strategies of discourse analysis;
- features of a variant of discourse analysis called critical discourse analysis;
- points of difference between conversation analysis and discourse analysis.

21.1 Introduction

Language is a central component of social research. It is, after all, through language that we ask people questions in interviews and through language that they answer our questions. Understanding how language is used is an important aspect of all research, because knowing how words are used and the meanings of specific terms in the local language or dialect is often crucial in appreciating how the members of a group view the social world.

In this chapter, we will examine two approaches that treat language as the focus of study: **conversation analysis** (CA) and **discourse analysis** (DA), as well as a notable variant on the latter—**critical discourse analysis** (CDA). By 'approach' we simply mean a shared focus for study, a more or less common set of theoretical assumptions, and some accepted methods of data collection and analysis. What is most notable about these approaches is that they treat language as a topic in itself rather than a medium through which social research is conducted. The focus for analysis in CA is on the 'naturally occurring talk' that occurs within the contexts of everyday and professional life. DA is more flexible in terms of focus and methods. While CA and DA do not represent every possible way of studying language as a topic, they are two of the most prominent approaches within social research. We will discuss the characteristics, technical vocabulary, and techniques associated with each approach, evaluating each one and highlighting some of the main ways in which they align and differ.

21.2 Conversation analysis

In this section, we will explore what is meant by the term 'conversation analysis'. We will first introduce the approach and then examine the key principles that underpin it, and then provide an outline of how to do it by looking at some key terminology and the basic tools of the approach. Finally, we'll reflect on some of the challenges in doing conversation analysis.

What is conversation analysis?

In order to understand conversation analysis, we first need a basic understanding of **ethnomethodology**, the sociological position from which it emerged. Ethnomethodology was developed in the USA by Harold Garfinkel and Harvey Sacks, though CA is more associated with the latter. It focuses on 'practical, common-sense reasoning' in everyday life and takes the view that social life is an accomplishment. Social order is not a pre-existing force that restricts individual action, but something that is worked at and achieved through interaction. Despite what its name suggests, ethnomethodology is *not* a research methodology; it is the study of the ways in which social order is achieved in everyday life. As Garfinkel (1967) put it (in his own roundabout way):

> in contrast to certain versions of Durkheim that teach that the objective reality of social facts is sociology's fundamental principle, the lesson is taken instead, and used as a study policy, that the objective reality of social facts *as* an ongoing accomplishment of the concerted activities of daily life, with the ordinary, artful ways of that accomplishment being by members known, used, and taken for granted, is, for members doing sociology, a fundamental phenomenon.
>
> (Garfinkel 1967: vii)

Two ideas are particularly central to ethnomethodology and both are clearly expressed in CA: *indexicality* and ***reflexivity***. Indexicality refers to the meaning of an act in relation to the conversational context in which it is used—and 'acts' in CA are spoken words or utterances (tiny units of speech) including pauses and sounds. Reflexivity is the idea that spoken words do not just represent or reflect reality but *help to construct* the social world in which they are located. In these ways, ethnomethodology aligns well with two aspects of **qualitative research**—an emphasis on the contextual understanding of action (see Chapter 16) and an ontological position associated with **constructionism** (see Chapter 2).

In the years following its initial introduction into sociology, ethnomethodological research took two different directions. One involved drawing on traditional social **research methods**, particularly **ethnography**, though in a slightly altered form (e.g. Cicourel 1968). The other, which is mainly associated with Sacks and his fellow researchers (e.g. Sacks et al. 1974), involved conducting detailed analyses of talk in naturally occurring situations. The latter is often seen as the root of CA (see Key concept 21.1).

KEY CONCEPT 21.1
What is conversation analysis?

Conversation analysis (CA) is the detailed analysis of naturally occurring conversation—this is basically talk as it occurs in everyday life. The aim is usually to uncover the underlying structures of conversation and the ways that people achieve social order through interaction.

CA often begins with the researcher noticing something striking about the way that a speaker says something. This generates an emphasis on what that phrase might be 'doing' in the context of that conversation—that is, what functions it serves. Clayman and Gill (2004) give the example, which was first noticed by Sacks, of the way in which children often begin a question by saying 'You know what, Daddy [or whoever]?' when among adults. Conversation analysts would perform a detailed analysis of this phrase in the context of the interaction, and would be able to conclude that because this question always produces the reply 'What?', it allows the child to find a slot in a sequence of conversation or to begin such a sequence. The use of this strategy reflects children's desire to take part in conversations as legitimate participants and indeed to be able to initiate sequences of talk.

CA considers how talk is organized *in the context of interaction* so researchers emphasize the need to record and transcribe naturally occurring conversations. This allows them to perform an intensive analysis of the sequences of interaction that help to order everyday life. As such, CA is a multifaceted approach—part **theory**, part method of data acquisition, and part method of analysis.

CA is also concerned with how people produce social order through and in the course of natural social interaction; but it differs from ethnomethodology in that it takes conversation as the basic form through which that social order is achieved. In other words, conversation is the focus of analysis in CA, whereas ethnomethodologists take a broader view of what might be considered an 'act'. The element of indexicality is also clear, in that practitioners of CA argue that the meaning of words is contextually grounded, while its commitment to reflexivity is revealed in the view that talk constructs the social context within which it occurs.

Although we are discussing CA within Part Three of this book, it can be seen as having both 'qualitative' and 'quantitative' characteristics. CA is contextual and naturalistic, and it involves studying the social world in its own terms and without prior theoretical commitments, all of which align it with qualitative research strategies. However, it studies talk in interaction using what have been described as 'rigorous, systematic procedures' that can 'provide reproducible results' (Psathas 1995: 1). This framework resonates with the **quantitative research** commitment to **coding** procedures in a way that generates valid, reliable, and replicable findings, and explains why CA is sometimes described as having a **positivist** orientation.

Another way in which CA does not align with other qualitative research approaches is that it places a different emphasis on context. For CA practitioners, context refers to the specific here-and-now context of immediately preceding talk, whereas for most qualitative researchers it refers to wider concerns such as the culture of the group within which action occurs. Most qualitative researchers understand 'action' in terms of the values, beliefs, and typical modes of behaviour of the group in question—but attributing action in this way is exactly what CA practitioners are keen to avoid. It is no wonder, therefore, that writers such as Silverman, author of *Interpreting Qualitative Data* (2015), continue to find it difficult to fit CA into broad descriptions of the nature of qualitative research.

Principles of conversation analysis

Once conversation analysts have identified a focus for their analysis, they usually proceed on the basis of some fundamental principles. Heritage (1984, 1987) has suggested that there are three underlying assumptions of CA.

1. *Talk is structured*. Talk follows very particular conventions. Participants are implicitly aware of the rules that underpin these patterns. As a result, conversation analysts avoid inferring speakers' motivations from what they say or seeing their talk as a product of their personal characteristics. This kind of information is unnecessary for CA, because conversation analysts focus on the underlying structures of action, as revealed in talk.

2. *Talk is constructed contextually*. Action is revealed in talk. That is, words construct reality, not the other way around. Therefore we must analyse talk with reference to the context it takes place within—and when we examine what someone says, we must bear in mind the utterances that precede and follow it. In this way, conversation analysts see talk as exhibiting patterned sequences.
3. *Analysis is grounded in data*. Conversation analysts reject existing theoretical schemes and instead argue that we must induce, from the data, how talk constructs social order.

Heritage (1987: 258) has written: 'it is assumed that social actions work *in detail* and hence that the specific details of interaction cannot simply be ignored as insignificant without damaging the prospects for coherent and effective analyses.' This assumption explains CA's emphasis on the very specific details that actually help to constitute conversation, including what people say and how they say it, but also things like the lengths of pauses and the sounds that occur in all conversations.

Transcription and attention to detail

As the third assumption associated with CA might suggest, this approach requires the researcher to produce detailed **transcripts** of natural conversation. Consider the extract from a transcript in Research in focus 21.1, which contains some of the basic notational symbols used in CA (see Tips and skills 21.1 for explanations of some of these). You can see that this sequence is set out in much more detail than is usually the case when social researchers analyse talk—for example, in transcriptions from qualitative interviews. With CA, pauses and emphases are not incidental events with little relevance to what the speaker is trying to achieve; they are an essential ingredient of 'the specific details of interaction [that] cannot simply be ignored as insignificant', as Heritage put it (1987: 258). These tiny elements reveal the

RESEARCH IN FOCUS 21.1

Conversation analysis: a question and answer adjacency pair

Rowan (2016) used CA to analyse an online recording of a demonic deliverance ceremony (exorcism) performed at a Pentecostal church in London. She provides the following extract of an interaction between an evangelist (E), who is performing the ceremony, and a participant who is on the receiving end of it (P) (see Tips and skills 21.1 for explanations of the symbols used here).

1 *P: ↑.hhhh ↑hee:::*
2 *E: speak out ↑WHO:: ARE ↑YOU: [IN THIS BODY?]*
3 *P: [↑a::::::::::::::::::::::h] (0.6) ↑huh ↑huh ↑huh*
4 *↑huh ↑huh ↑huh (0.4) .hhhhh (↑I ↑↑want↑ destroy her)*
5 *E: HOW HAVE YOU DESTROYED HER LIFE [you demon]*
6 *P: [↑a::h ↑ha]*
7 *P: .hhh ↑↑u:::::h I para↑lysed ↑he:r I don't want her to*
8 *su↑ccee::d, ↑eh ↑.hh[h hhhhhh hu:::h hu:::h]*
9 *E: [speak louder (.) HOW HAVE] YOU DES↑TROYED*
10 *HER LIFE,*
11 *P: .hhh I ↑have ↑para↑↑lysed ↑he:r not to a↑chieve anything, .hhh*
12 *↑HHHH ↑.hhhhh HH*

Rowan argues that the evangelist's initial question (2) for the spirit/demon to identify itself is fundamental to the successful performance of the exorcism. Even though the participant's response does not specify the identity of the spirit/demon and instead articulates intended action (3–4), that is enough for the evangelist to determine that

they are addressing something demonic. This 'reality' is then twice reinforced by the suggestion that the spirit/demon has paralysed the participant from succeeding in life (6–8 and 11). Rowan draws two main inferences from this interaction.

First, giving an identity to a 'demon' is an integral part of performing a deliverance. Without it, the ceremony cannot proceed. The emphasis that the evangelist places on 'who' and 'you' in the initial 'who are you?' question highlights the implicit importance of identification.

Second, the successful categorization of 'demon' within the interaction provides an external explanation for negative life events. The link between identity and determination uncovered by the question-and-answer structure (an example of what is called an adjacency pair—see the next section on 'Basic tools of conversation analysis') then allows all those present at the ceremony to separate the participant from any negative experiences of the self *and* give outside agency to that adversity.

In other words, Rowan uses CA to uncover a conversational strategy that allows this group to construct a social reality. Through the question and answer pattern of identifying a 'demon' residing within a participant, the group are able to see the participant as separate from and not responsible for their actions—their behaviour is determined by something external with a will of its own. All of this particular reality is achieved through conversation.

TIPS AND SKILLS 21.1
Basic notational symbols in conversation analysis

Conversation analysis often uses the Jefferson system of transcription notation (2004). So when reading or using CA, you will need to be familiar with the symbols it uses to describe the detailed elements of conversation that are being transcribed. The main symbols are listed below, but you can find a full list of CA notation at **http://ca-tutorials.lboro.ac.uk/notation.htm** (accessed 3 February 2020).

.hh	h's preceded by a dot indicate an intake of breath. If no dot is present, it means breathing out.
We:ll	A colon indicates that the sound that occurs directly before the colon is prolonged. More than one colon means further prolongation, for example : : : :
(0.8)	A figure in brackets indicates the length of a period of silence, usually measured in tenths of one second. So (0.8) means eight-tenths of a second of silence.
you and knowing	An underline indicates an emphasis in the speaker's talk (in the extract in Research in focus 21.1 this is shown with capital letters).
(.)	Brackets around a full stop indicates a very slight pause.
↑↓	Arrows indicate a change of pitch in an upwards (↑) or downwards (↓) direction.
[	Square brackets indicate overlapping talk: that is, two or more speakers talk at the same time.
=	The equals sign refers to a continuation of talk.

underlying structures of conversation and how it constructs social order.

You will by now be getting a sense of the detailed work involved in conducting CA. Because of this, it is important to avoid the temptation to collect too much data for a project using this approach. Your time will be better spent analysing relatively small amounts of text in close detail.

Basic tools of conversation analysis

In addition to the notation symbols used in CA, we can also identify some recurring features of the ways in which it is organized. We can see these features as tools that we can apply to any sequence of conversation. We consider just a few examples in this section: turn-taking, adjacency pairs, preference organization, and repair mechanisms.

Turn-taking

One of the most basic ideas in CA is that people achieve order in everyday conversation through turn-taking. This is a particularly important tool of CA, because it illustrates that talk depends on shared codes. If these codes did not exist to indicate where utterances end, there would not be smooth transitions in conversation. Hutchby and Wooffitt (1998: 47) provide an overview of the basic codes that help to structure turn-taking:

(1) people take turns to speak;

(2) one speaker tends to talk at a time; and

(3) people take turns with as little gap or overlap between them as possible.

Adjacency pairs

One of the ways we can see turn-taking in operation is by examining adjacency pairs. This term relates to the tendency for turn-taking to involve two linked phases. This might take the form of a question followed by an answer (as in Research in focus 21.1); an invitation followed by a response (accept/decline); or a greeting followed by a returned greeting. The first phase always implies that the other part of the adjacency pair is expected—for example, that an invitation will be responded to. The second phase is interesting to conversation analysts not just because it involves a response being given in its own right, but because if the responder complies with the normative structure of the pairing, this suggests that they understand how they are supposed to respond to the initial phase. In this way, 'intersubjective understandings' are continuously reinforced through the successful and shared performance of adjacency pairs (Heritage 1987: 259–60).

Preference organization

The second phase in an adjacency pair does not *always* follow the first. It is always anticipated, but some responses are clearly preferential to others and sometimes people might fail to comply with the expected response. Conversation analysts call this process preference organization. A simple example of this in action occurs when someone makes a request. Accepting the invitation does not usually require justification, but it is generally expected that a refusal will need to be justified simply because an invitation has been made. This means that acceptance is the *preferred response* and the refusal with justification is the *dispreferred response* (otherwise why make the invitation at all!). Conversation analysts try to discover the preference structure of an adjacency pair by examining the responses to an initial statement.

Repair mechanisms

Often, things go 'wrong' in conversations: for example, when speakers don't follow turn-taking conventions so that there is overlapping of people talking, or when someone gives an inappropriate response, or no response, to an invitation. When these kinds of issues occur, people tend to use what conversation analysts call repair mechanisms to try to maintain the rules of turn-taking. Silverman (2015: 132) notes several examples, including the following:

- when someone starts to speak before someone else has finished, the initial speaker stops talking before completing their turn;
- when a change in an adjacency pair does not occur at an appropriate point (for example, when someone does not respond to a question), the speaker may speak again, perhaps reinforcing the need for the other person to speak (for example, by repeating the question).

You can clearly see repair mechanisms and preference organization (specifically a dispreferred response) in the extract in Research in focus 21.2.

Evaluating conversation analysis

This review of CA can only scratch the surface of the approach and its sophisticated method of studying talk in interaction. As we discuss in Thinking deeply 21.1, in recent years CA has been applied to online interactions and, as was the case in the example from Rowan (2016) in Research in focus 21.1, video recordings have also been used to extend its scope. Researchers have even used it in conjunction with eye-tracking software to examine how gaze is used within interactions (Kendrick and Holler 2017). But although CA has a lot of potential as an approach, inevitably, it has also some methodological weaknesses. These centre around its restrictive nature and what some see as the trivial focus of its analysis.

CA's restrictive nature

The first criticism made of CA relates to its emphasis on 'naturally occurring' talk, and on only analysing the particular sequences of talk that are of interest. Conversation analysts stress that we should not make inferences based on external information about the meanings of the talk being analysed, which, as we noted in our section on 'What is conversation analysis?' is a different approach from much qualitative research. Whereas many qualitative researchers say they aim to achieve understanding from the perspective of those being studied, conversation

RESEARCH IN FOCUS 21.2
Conversation analysis: preference organization

Clearly, the preference organization of adjacency pairings has implications for the structure of a conversation. We can see this in Hester's (2016) examination of the ways in which teenagers avoid telling their parents about their daily activities during family meals. The following data is taken from a conversation between a mother (J) and father (H) and their son (R) that occurred within the context of an evening family meal.

H: wha' – how what did you do in athletics today?
R: athletics
H: I knew you'd say that if I'd Jeezuz I should have put some
money on that then
J: huh- huh-huh
H: are you into having a conversation with me or are you gonna
be weird?
R: yeh
H: I mean I don't mind
J: he's being a bit Kevinish at the moment

H's initial utterance is a question that invites his son to tell a story about what he did in athletics that day. These kinds of invitations are common in the context of a family's mealtime talk, but as Hester notes, they often do not produce the preferred response. In this case, R 'fails' to produce both the story acceptance (accepting the invitation to tell a story) and therefore H's preferred way to continue the sequence. R declines the preferred response indirectly by answering the question in a way that is technically correct, but alternative—he just repeats information that H already knows. In doing so, he ignores the conventional requirements of the dispreferred response (saying 'I'm not going to tell you') that would otherwise need some justification. H then continues by highlighting the predictability of the response—'should have put money on that then'—and then asking a question. This presents R with a choice between 'having a conversation' and being 'weird'. This choice highlights both the original lack of the preferred response *and* the fact that R has breached linguistic convention by not complying with the requirements of an adjacency pair. Had he reproduced these norms he would have engaged in 'a normal conversation'. J then compares him with Kevin the Teenager, an uncooperative teenage boy from a popular TV programme. Hester notes:

> Russell's breaching, of adjacency pair organization and preference organization is both a source of irritation and an accountable matter. For his father, it is 'being weird', not 'being normal' and 'not having a normal conversation'; for his mother, it is burdensome and it is accountable as another instance of his being 'Kevinish'. Either way, it is achieved by the methodical production of the manipulation of the formal or generic structures of language which breaches his parents' expectations. However, in spite of this masterly manipulation of the formal or generic structures of language, its use does not prevent his parents from continuing to ask him about his day in athletics. In this way his breach fails as a [device] for avoiding telling [them] about his day.
>
> (Hester 2016: 64)

analysts do this only to the extent that participants' understanding can be revealed in the specific contexts of the talk being analysed. CA practitioners argue that importing elements that are not specifically grounded in what has just been said during a conversation risks implanting an understanding that is not grounded in participants' own terms (Schegloff 1997). However, this stipulation can be seen as restrictive and problematic.

When we take an interpretative approach to analysing social action there is always a risk of misunderstanding something. But when this kind of speculation is effectively forbidden, as it is with CA, we cannot go beyond the

THINKING DEEPLY 21.1
Online conversation analysis

Conversation analysis has traditionally been associated with the spoken word. However, there is increasing use of CA to study other mediums of communication, and researchers have developed digital forms of conversation analysis to examine online interaction. This 'digital CA' focuses on the content of computer-mediated interactions *and* the norms, dynamics, and practices that help to structure it and give it meaning. Paulus et al. (2016) note that these studies have taken a number of different forms:

- comparing face-to-face talk with online interaction;
- attempting to understand how online talk is coherent to participants;
- examining how participants deal with 'trouble' in online talk; and
- investigating how participants achieve social action in asynchronous environments.

However, this field is still in its infancy and a number of methodological issues still need to be addressed. The first issue relates to the fact that CA assumes linearity. That is to say, CA is usually concerned with how one utterance follows another and with the relationship between those utterances. Given the asynchronous or semi-synchronous nature of computer-mediated interaction, we cannot necessarily assume this in online environments where there is often sequential disruption, both in terms of time and because of interruptions from other people. Beyond the mechanics of actually accessing data, another issue is how specific technological platforms shape the nature and form of interaction. Interaction on Facebook, for example, will necessarily be different from interaction that takes place on Twitter. We might even question whether such 'interaction' can actually be considered to be conversation at all. Finally, there are also ethical concerns about using the conversations we might find online (see Chapter 6), and we need to consider whether there are substantive differences between public and private interactions.

detail of the specific interaction we are studying. When people interact with each other, much of their talk is informed by their mutual knowledge of contexts. However, CA cannot take any of this context into account if the people talking do not specifically speak about it. For this reason, CA is most useful for **research questions** that can be addressed by locating meaning in talk alone. Its restrictive nature is also problematic because conversation analysts do (necessarily) make pre-conceived inferences about the nature of talk. By transforming ordinary talk into the specialist language of CA they separate utterances from their lived experience. The use of technical tools such as adjacency pairs and preference organization also impose a very particular structure on that talk. You only need to look at the examples of transcription in Research in focus 21.1 and Research in focus 21.2 to get a sense of just how much CA transforms everyday utterances.

The trivial focus of analysis

The second methodological weakness involves what some see as CA's rather trivial focus of analysis—that is, its detailed focus on seemingly unimportant details. It can sometimes look as though CA practitioners select a piece of talk at random and over-theorize it, or that they 'cherry-pick' a sequence to fit a point they want to make. However, as Wilkinson and Kitzinger (2008) make clear, there are several steps involved in the process of CA. Analysts have to:

- become aware of a feature of conversations that appears striking;
- bring together possible examples of that conversational feature;
- uncover the most striking of these examples;
- perform a detailed analysis on the clearest examples;
- examine cases that are less clear; and
- conduct an analysis of deviant conversational cases (those that do not conform to expectation).

In other words, the examples of talk that appear in a research publication based on CA, and the points that researchers make about them, are actually the end product of a rigorous process of analysis.

Conversation analysts usually respond to such criticisms by highlighting that the shared linguistic competences that exist between participants and analysts are a starting point for a robust scientific enterprise—and CA does certainly reduce the risk of researchers making ungrounded speculations about what is happening in social interaction. Indeed, the approach has made significant contributions to our understanding of the accomplishment of social order, which is one of the classic concerns of social theory.

21.3 Discourse analysis

There are a number of different versions of discourse analysis (DA). In this section we define DA, discuss its main aims and the most common techniques used to achieve them, and then consider the critical variant of the approach.

What is discourse analysis?

Like CA, DA (defined in Key concept 21.2) is an approach to analysing language, and it incorporates insights from CA. Unlike CA, though, DA can be applied to forms of communication other than talk. It can be and has been applied to different forms of texts, including material such as newspaper articles, books, and films (see Tips and skills 21.2). In this respect, it is more flexible than CA. Another difference between the two approaches is that in DA there is much less of an emphasis on naturally occurring talk. This means that the 'talk' in research interviews, for example, can be a legitimate target for analysis.

DA is closely aligned to the work of continental philosophers such as Michel Foucault (1926–84). He used 'discourse' as a term to describe the way in which a particular set of linguistic categories relating to an object frame the way we understand that object. The discourse forms a particular version of understanding that actually comes to *constitute* the object. In other words, language structures reality, rather than simply reflecting it. For example, the discourse relating to mental illness helps to define our concepts of what mental illness is like, how it should be treated, and who is legitimately entitled to treat it—none of which is inevitable. **Foucauldian discourse analysis** focuses on how power is constructed through discourse, so in this example it would look at how the discourse on mental health becomes a framework through which practitioners working within the mental illness sphere can justify their power and their use of treatment regimes. In this way, a discourse is much more than an arrangement of words: it makes up the social world. Foucault took a broad historical approach to the study of discourse, and there are several different approaches that writers have labelled as DA (Potter 1997). The version of DA that is our focus in this section (see Key concept 21.1) has been described as having two distinctive features in terms of **epistemology** and **ontology** (Potter 1997).

21

KEY CONCEPT 21.2
What is discourse analysis?

DA is an approach to examining language that is, perhaps, more flexible than CA because it does not rely so heavily on complex transcription systems. The type of DA that is our focus in this section is the one that is associated with such writers as Gilbert and Mulkay (1984); Potter and Wetherell (1987, 1994); Billig (1992); and Potter (1997). This variant of analysis has been of particular interest to social scientists and can be applied to both naturally occurring and contrived forms of talk, as well as to texts.

According to Potter (1997: 146), DA 'emphasizes the way versions of the world, of society, events and inner psychological worlds are produced in discourse'. Language is depicted in discourse analysis not as a neutral device for imparting meaning, as it is in most quantitative and qualitative research methods, but as *constituting* or *producing* the social world. People seek to achieve things when they talk or when they write; DA is concerned with the strategies they use in trying to create these different kinds of effect. This version of DA is therefore action-oriented—that is, language is seen as a way of getting things done.

TIPS AND SKILLS 21.2
Using existing material for discourse analysis

Unlike CA, DA is not just limited to naturally occurring talk. It can be used with almost any type of discourse that is already within the public domain. Researchers commonly use DA to examine speeches, debates, and news items, but it can also be used in conjunction with newer forms of communication such as podcasts and YouTube videos. In many cases, these will be available digitally. The advantage of this for researchers, especially student researchers, is that you do not have to put a lot of time and effort into collecting data and you can give a greater amount of time to analysis. See Research in focus 21.4 for an example.

1. It is *anti-realist* in that it does not take the view that there is an external reality that researchers can discover and definitively portray. It therefore rejects the idea that any researcher can arrive at a privileged account of the social world. Some discourse analysts adopt a softer stance that acknowledges some sort of external reality, but most seem to be anti-realist in orientation.
2. It is *constructionist* (see Key concept 2.6) in that it gives attention to the versions of reality that members of a social setting reproduce. This emphasis implies that any discourse is just a selection from many possible representations, but by taking the form that it does, it helps to structure the nature of 'reality' and our understanding of it.

As we noted in Key concept 21.2, the version of DA in which we are interested is action-oriented. We can see this emphasis in three basic questions that are central to discourse analysis:

- What is this discourse doing?
- How is this discourse constructed to make this happen?
- What resources are available to perform this activity?

(Potter 2004: 609)

The action orientation of DA (What is this discourse *doing*?) is usefully revealed in another study that (like the one described in Research in focus 21.2) explores family mealtimes. In this instance, the focus is on how parents attempt to manage a child's 'problem' behaviour. Through an analysis of nearly 100 mealtimes across seven families, Potter and Hepburn (2019: 7) show that parents' rebukes perform certain actions.

- They aim to constrain ongoing problem behaviour, often by attempting to make children conform and/or regret their actions.
- They construct the child's behaviour as negative, often in an extreme or increasingly intense manner.
- They use direct commands such as 'no' or 'stop it'.
- The sequence of rebukes is important, as is the manner of delivery (increased volume/pitch, stretch, emphasis etc).
- They ascribe intention in that they frame the child as purposefully misbehaving, which is publicly presented as negative by the parent.

Performing a discourse analysis of these brief moments of conversation allows researchers to identify that the flow of discourse is directed towards achieving a number of objectives.

Like CA, DA also emphasizes the immediate contextual specifics of talk. As Potter (1997: 158) puts it, discourse analysts prefer to avoid making reference to what he calls 'ethnographic particulars' (essentially other techniques of data collection), and argues that they prefer 'to see things as things that are worked up, attended to and made relevant in interaction rather than being external determinants'. However, some DA practitioners show more willingness than conversation analysts to make reference to these 'ethnographic particulars'. For example, the research by O'Grady et al. (2014) that we describe in Research in focus 21.3 concentrates on short interactional sequences, but the authors add that DA 'was complemented by ethnographic approaches that included interviews at the clinical site and an extended interview with the participating surgeon, so as to bring the perspective of the medical profession to bear on our interpretation of the data' (O'Grady et al. 2014: 68). However, in the case of Potter and Hepburn's (2019) study of conversations during mealtimes, the researchers seem as keen as CA practitioners to keep the analysis located within ongoing conversational sequences.

An important difference between CA and DA is that discourse analysts tend to resist the idea of codifying

RESEARCH IN FOCUS 21.3
Discourse analysis: solving a problem

O'Grady et al. (2014) used DA to examine how trust was achieved in surgical consultations at a gastro-intestinal clinic in Australia. The focus of this particular paper was on a 56 year old woman who, accompanied by her niece, was seeking a second opinion after an inguinal hernia operation because the pain had worsened. (An inguinal hernia is when tissue bulges through a weak area in the abdominal wall.) The patient's confidence in the medical profession was low, and O'Grady et al. show how the doctor, through a variety of discursive moves, gradually tries to build up trust in him and in the process. This is reinforced towards the end of the consultation, when the doctor decides that the three of them will construct a letter to the referring doctor. Consider the following sequence, which addresses the patient's weight gain and in which the doctor is dictating the letter:

364 Doctor: As far as the weight gain's concerned (.) a::h (.) there's been an increase of (.) inverted commas (.) three dress sizes (.) close inverted commas (.) stop (.) new paragraph Mrs Bada a:hh looks (.) despairing (.) stop < That's a (.) an ex (.) an explanation isn't it>
365 Niece: Yeah.
366 Patient: (hhh hh)
367 Doctor: Um () very uncomfortable and er self-conscious about being inverted commas (.) seven months pregnant (.) close inverted commas
368 Niece: [chuckles].
369 Patient: [chuckles].

(O'Grady et al. 2014: 78)

O'Grady et al. point out that at turns 364 and 367, the doctor dictates the same words the patient and her niece had used. This, combined with the element of humour that he injects, reinforces that he has been listening and wants to reduce the patient's embarrassment about gaining weight. At the same time, the reference to looking 'despairing' introduces an element of empathy that reinforces that he takes the patient's concerns very seriously. As the authors argue, although trust was developed gradually in this encounter, the 'co-constructed consultation letter' is a 'final means to strengthen trust' (O'Grady et al. 2014: 79).

their practices and argue that this kind of codification is probably impossible. Instead, they prefer to see their style of research as an 'analytic mentality' and as 'a craft skill, more like bike riding or chicken sexing than following the recipe for a mild chicken rogan josh' (Potter 1997: 147–8). A useful way to think about this approach has been suggested by Gill (1996), who says that DA treats the way that something is said as 'a solution to a problem' (Widdicombe 1993: 97; quoted in Gill 1996: 146). She also suggests adopting a posture of 'sceptical reading' (Gill 2000). This means searching for a purpose behind the ways that something is said or presented. In doing this, discourse analysts need to remember that, as Gill (1996) suggests, what is said is always a way of *not* saying something else. In other words, noticing whether there is total silence on a topic, or whether an argument in a conversation or article is formulated in one way rather than in another way, is crucial to seeing discourse as a solution to a problem and as trying to achieve particular aims. Gill (2000) has proposed that DA has four main themes.

1. *Discourse is a topic*. Discourse is a focus of investigation in itself, not just a way of gaining access to aspects of social reality that lie behind it. This view contrasts with traditional research interviews, in which language is seen as a way of revealing what interviewees think about a topic or their behaviour and the reasons for that behaviour.
2. *Language is constructive*. Discourse is a way of constructing a particular view of social reality. The writer or speaker makes choices about the most appropriate way of presenting reality, and their decisions will reflect their stance on the issue(s).
3. *Discourse is a form of action*. Language is viewed 'as a practice in its own right' (Gill 2000: 175). It is a way of achieving acts, such as attributing blame, presenting yourself in a particular way, or making an argument heard. A

person's discourse is affected by the context that they are confronting. For example, your account of your reasons for wanting a job might vary depending whether you are talking to interviewers, members of your family, or friends. See Research in focus 21.4 for an example of discourse as a form of action.

4. *Discourse is rhetorically organized.* DA practitioners recognize that discourse is about 'establishing one version of the world in the face of competing versions' (Gill 2000: 176). In other words, they recognize that we want to persuade others when we present a version of events.

Aims of discourse analysis

Although we would reiterate Potter's (1997) point that DA 'is like riding a bicycle' because it is not prescriptive in terms of analytic procedure and that there are different forms of DA, it is possible to outline some general stages and tendencies.

We can summarize these general stages of DA as follows:

- Identifying a research question appropriate for DA
- Selecting data sources relevant to the research question
- Collecting and **transcribing** data
- Initial familiarization with the data
- Examination and identification of discourses within the data
- Contextualizing findings
- Writing up

This is meant as a very rough guide for the general research process and there will be variations on this theme. But it is true enough to say that there is a general process

RESEARCH IN FOCUS 21.4
Discourse analysis: Discourse as action

We have noted on several occasions that discourse is a form of action. The fact that it *does* things means that it can be considered performative—a term used in linguistics to mean utterances that are used to bring about a particular social action. For example, O'Reilly et al. (2009) conducted discourse analysis on the decision letters written by representatives of research ethics committees (RECs, discussed in Chapter 6) to researchers who apply for ethical clearance to conduct health-related research. The authors write: 'We argue that RECs use texts not only to [demonstrate] their own accountability, using a range of discursive devices to display the quality of their own work and the resulting decisions, but also to establish the accountability of applicants for the quality of their applications' (O'Reilly et al. 2009: 248). They suggest four ways in which accountability is performed in the letters.

1. Referring to the *process behind the decision.* The letters often drew attention to the rigorous discussion and thought that went into the REC's decision, with such wording as 'considered carefully' and 'discussed the protocol at great length'.
2. *Holding the applicants accountable.* The letters made it clear that, when ethical issues are raised about the application, it is the applicant who is accountable for the REC's decision, not the REC. This justifies the REC's decision and the demands for revision that it makes.
3. Reference to the REC's *specialist expertise.* The letters often drew attention to the specific expertise of particular REC members by highlighting their occupation and associated characteristics. This expertise was used to emphasize the committee's ability to judge the quality of the research application.
4. Reference to *external authorities.* Decisions were also justified by reference to an applicant's failure to conform to official guidelines. An example is this statement concerning an application that was given a provisional outcome but was later accepted: 'For the storage of samples, patient information sheets and consent forms should conform to the current MRC publication on Human Tissue and Biological Samples for use in Research—Operational and Ethical guidelines. These are available from the MRC website, **www.mrc.ac.uk**' (quoted in O'Reilly et al. 2009: 256).

This study shows that accountability is performed first in the sense that the REC accounts for its decision but also in the sense that it deflects blame for those decisions onto the applicants themselves.

that again starts with the identification of an appropriate research question; then you make a selection of sources that will help you respond to those questions; and then you analyse the discourse within that data—which you then write up.

In terms of that process of analysing discourse, Potter and Wetherell (1994) also suggest that there are two tendencies within the kind of DA work we discuss in this chapter (though they also acknowledge that the distinction is a little artificial). The first is the identification of 'the general resources that are used to construct discourse and enable the performance of particular actions' (1994: 48–9). These are sometimes referred to as **interpretative repertoires**. The second attempts to identify 'the detailed procedures through which versions are constructed and made to look factual' (1994: 49). In this section, we'll explore both of these aspects of DA.

Uncovering interpretative repertoires

To illustrate the idea of an 'interpretative repertoire', let's consider an influential study of scientists by Gilbert and Mulkay (1984). They focused on the field of bioenergetics and, in particular, the process through which scientists working in this area come to understand a mechanism they called 'oxidative phosphorylation'. The main source of Gilbert and Mulkay's data was interviews with 34 researchers in this field. The interviews lasted between two-and-a-half and three hours on average and were transcribed in full. The authors also drew on other sources of data, including letters written by leading authorities and the main articles and textbooks on the subject.

During their research, Gilbert and Mulkay noticed differences between the ways the scientists presented their work in formal contexts (scientific papers etc.) and informal contexts (including in interviews with the researchers). These went far beyond predictable differences in the tone of presentation, to the extent that there were also differences in how they described the emergence of their findings. In one example, Gilbert and Mulkay noted an instance in which a scientific paper portrayed a model as having emerged out of the data. This contrasted with what was suggested in the research interview, where a scientist described data as being in need of a different perspective so that the model could be reinterpreted. This prompted a new series of **experiments**. Similarly, Gilbert and Mulkay found that the scientific papers tended to imply that the procedures involved in the experimental methodology were neutral operations, mainly independent of the scientist, which could be replicated by anyone. In the research interviews, however, scientists emphasized the fact that the procedures involved practical skills, which are the product of experience, and required them to develop a 'feel' for experimental work. As one scientist put it:

> How could you write it up? It would be like trying to write a description of how to beat an egg. Or like trying to read a book on how to ski. You'd just get the wrong idea altogether. You've got to go and watch it, see it, do it. There's no substitute for it. These are *practical* skills. We all know that practical skills are not well taught by bits of paper.
>
> (Quoted in Gilbert and Mulkay 1984: 53; emphasis in original)

Gilbert and Mulkay argue that these differences in presentation are the result of the scientists using two different types of interpretative repertoire in their talk and writings for formal and informal contexts: **empiricist** repertoire and contingent repertoire. In the formal context of the scientific paper there is a mainly empiricist repertoire, identifiable because 'the texts of experimental papers display certain recurrent stylistic, grammatical, and lexical features which appear to be coherently related' (1984: 55–6). The researchers highlight:

- the emphasis placed on describing the procedural routines of experiments, so that the findings seem to be an inevitable, logical outcome of those experiments;
- the use of an impersonal writing style;
- the fact that the papers rarely mentioned the authors' role in producing the findings, or their theoretical commitments.

In contrast, in the *contingent repertoire* used in the research interviews, 'scientists presented their actions and beliefs as heavily dependent on speculative insights, prior intellectual commitments, personal characteristics, indescribable skills, social ties and group membership' (1984: 56). In other words, they were much less likely to present their findings as the inevitable outcome of their experiments and were much more likely to acknowledge their own role in producing the findings. Gilbert and Mulkay go further and show that the different repertoires are not only used in response to the setting; they are often used when scientists disagree with the positions of other scientists. In this context, scientists describe their own work within an empiricist repertoire and the other scientists' work within a contingent repertoire, presenting their own findings as being inevitable if proper procedures are followed and their competitors' errors as the product of prejudices, theoretical commitments, bias, and so on.

Producing 'facts'

The idea of the interpretative repertoire is interesting because it brings out the idea that belief and action take place within frameworks that guide and influence the writer or speaker. Similar frameworks are also used to convey supposedly factual knowledge. One area of social life where 'facts' are often constructed is in political discourse, which we can clearly see in Demasi's (2019) study of how politicians use factual claims and counterclaims in political debates that are broadcast on TV. We consider this study in Research in focus 21.5.

Discourse analysts study how otherwise taken-for-granted 'facts' are produced in discourse by looking for particular techniques and tendencies in the language

RESEARCH IN FOCUS 21.5
Discourse analysis: Producing 'facts'

Demasi (2019) used discourse analysis to study how politicians use 'facts' within the context of political debate. He focused on the apparent rise of 'post-truth politics' and the way that issues of 'fact' and 'truth' seemed to be a central component of debates in the UK about the European Union (EU) in the years 2012–2014, preceding its exit from the EU ('Brexit'). He studied eight separate recordings of debates on political TV programmes such as *Newsnight*, *Question Time*, *The Record Europe*, and two special-edition live TV debates on the EU. These were transcribed and then analysed. Demasi described the process of analysis as follows:

> moments of prominent disagreement were identified during the process of recording and initial transcription of the data. This is the first analytical step. These were chosen so that the argumentative dimension of political debates would be at the fore. Once enough extracts in which disagreements were prominent had been identified and transcribed in more detail, the focus shifted to looking at what these have in common with each other. The orientation to 'facts' and the way these are challenged stood out as prominent aspects of the collection. The analysis, generally speaking, draws inspiration from an amalgamation of literature relevant to [discursive psychology]. Specifically, Edwards and Potter (1992), Potter (1996), and literature on rhetorical psychology and epistemics have played a central part.
>
> (Demasi 2019: 7)

One of the debates Demasi studied took place in an episode of *The Record Europe*, a BBC political programme. Consider the transcript extract below, in which politician Nigel Farage (FAR) is arguing against the EU, and politicians Graham Watson (WAT) and Dan Jørgensen (absent in extract below) are arguing in favour.

1 FAR: but=y'know this argument about what it cost the British people .hh
2 whether we talk gross or net this year our net contribution to
3 the EU is gonno be <nine billion> pounds. and what people see
4 (.2) .h is (.) they see in their own lives at the moment y'know
5 the local gravedigger or sweep streete- being sAcked as a
6 result of local government (.) ah cUts and ↑what they see ↓here

(Approximately 70 lines of transcript omitted)

77 WAT: where Nigel's argument falls down is he's said it's terrible
78 that the UK is paying nine billion .h every every year to to- in
79 net to the European Union which will be the case next year. .h ↑but↓
80 what he doesn't point out is that we're paying sixty billion a
81 year for health .h we're paying a hundred and thirty two billion
82 a year for social security and b[enefits]
83 X: [(coughs)]

21

WAT: ↑for nine billion↓ it's all that's costing us we're ↑getting a
fantastic [deal↓ from the European] Union
FAR: [what are we ( ) about]
WAT: we're getting the solidarity of being part (.) of an association
of twenty seve[n nations]
FAR: [hehhehhehheh]
WAT: =we're getting the diplomatic clout that it gives us we're
getting the clout that it gives us in trade talks

Demasi (2019) argues that this sequence demonstrates the contrast between particularization and categorization (Billig 1996). The politicians are discussing the same figure—the £9 billion per year that the UK paid to the European Union—but they use discourse to present the meaning of the number in different ways. Farage attempts to highlight that the £9 billion is large and therefore problematic (particularization), whereas Watson aligns the figure with other governmental costs and, in turn, attempts to demonstrate how it is relatively small in that context (categorization). Farage does not attempt to challenge these 'facts', but he does resist the idea that the United Kingdom was 'getting a fantastic deal' (lines 86, 89). Thus the 'battle for primacy over epistemic domain of the EU remains a live, and unresolved issue in the debate' (Demasi 2019: 16).

under investigation and considering the roles they play. Here, we will consider two common foci: rhetorical devices and quantification rhetoric.

Rhetorical devices

The attention to the **rhetorical** detail demonstrated in Research in focus 21.5 requires a sensitivity to the ways in which arguments are constructed. Research in focus 21.6 also examines one rhetorical device—the extreme case formulation—that is often employed in making a persuasive argument. Rhetorical analysis examines techniques that are used in language in order to achieve a particular effect. It emphasizes the ways in which arguments are constructed (as demonstrated in Research in focus 21.5) either in speech or in written texts and the roles that various linguistic devices (such as metaphor, analogy, and irony) play in the formulation of arguments. O'Reilly et al. (2009) noted several rhetorical constructions in

RESEARCH IN FOCUS 21.6
Discourse analysis: rhetorical devices

One rhetorical device people use to present arguments is the *extreme case formulation*. This involves writers or speakers attempting to strengthen knowledge claims by taking them to their extremes. They will often use maximal or minimal **properties** like 'everyone', 'nobody', 'always', 'never', and 'completely'. An interesting use of the concept can be found in Taylor et al.'s (2018) study of talk about sunbed tanning in online discussion forums. Using a range of search terms entered in to the search engine Google, they identified threads from a variety of forums not directly concerned with sunbeds. The final data comprised 556 temporally asynchronous posts (posts that were not published at the same time) that allowed the researchers to explore the interactional work between sunbed users and non-users. They were specifically interested in how arguments unfolded, and how rhetorical devices were used to enhance or defend the sunbed-related position of the forum posters. Consider the following extract from the study:

> P1 I see the concern and risks and danger of them, but I only use them for 3 or 4 minutes every other week, I think they only become a massive risk when you use them as part of your life for example some people use them every week of every year and rely on them. I think along with most things in life, everything in moderation is fine!

P2 After using them for a short amount of time (twice a week for a few weeks in the rainy summer days) for two years, maybe less, I've noticed A LOT more moles, some [of] which are strange looking, so I dread to think what my skin would be like if I had carried on.

(Taylor et al. 2018: 529)

Taylor et al. highlight that the initial post begins with a rhetorical disclaimer that functions to both anticipate *and* deny that the writer is ignorant to the risks. The writer then uses an extreme case formulation to minimize the risk to themselves ('I only use them for . . . ') and maximize the level of use needed to invoke such a risk ('every week of every year'). Similarly, they disassociate excessive sunbed use from their own behaviour by alluding to the addictive behaviours of 'some people'. However, the second poster attempts to undermine the extreme case formulation by highlighting that sunbed use can be risky even after 'a short amount of time', using specific quantification to emphasize the relative briefness of their own sunbed use.

their study of the decision letters produced by RECs (see Research in focus 21.4). For example, third-person terms like 'the Committee' were used to give a sense of an authoritative and official judgement. The authors also note that the letters are rhetorically organized to negate alternative versions of ethical practice, thereby privileging the REC's decision.

Quantification rhetoric

Quantification rhetoric refers to the ways in which numerical and non-numerical statements are used to support or challenge arguments. The term draws attention to the importance of quantification in everyday life *and* the tendency for many social scientists to make use of this strategy themselves (John 1992). An early example of quantification rhetoric is described in Potter et al.'s study of a 1988 TV programme called *Cancer: Your Money or Your Life* (Potter et al. 1991; Potter and Wetherell 1994). The programme claimed to show that the huge amounts of money donated by the public to cancer charities were doing little to 'cure' the disease. Potter et al. collected a wide range of data, including a video recording of the programme; **participant observation** of the making of the programme; drafts of the script, shooting schedules, and recordings of editing sessions; the entire interview transcripts of the various people interviewed for the programme (such as cancer research specialists and heads of charities); research interviews with some of these people; and research interviews with some of the people involved in making the programme. As a part of their analysis, they focused on how numbers were used to legitimate and/or challenge particular knowledge claims.

One phrase that the authors highlight is: 'those three curable types are amongst the rarest cancers—they represent around 1 per cent of a quarter of a million cases of cancers diagnosed each year. Most deaths are caused by a small number of very common cancers' (Potter and Wetherell 1994: 53). They particularly note the '1 per cent of a quarter of a million' used to describe the advances that have been made in three relatively rare forms of cancer. Potter et al. note that this phrase incorporates two quantitative expressions that are designed to legitimate the argument that cancer research is relatively ineffective: the first is a relative expression (a percentage) and the second is an absolute frequency (quarter of a million). This change in the register of quantification is important because it allows the programme-makers to emphasize the low cure levels (just 1 per cent) compared with the large number of new cases of cancer. They could have pointed to the absolute number of people who are cured, but the impact would have been less. Also, the 1 per cent is not being contrasted with the actual figure of 243,000 but with the more approximate phrase 'a quarter of a million'. Not only does the latter citation allow the figure to increase by 7,000 in people's minds; a quarter of a million also *sounds* larger. This is a powerful use of quantification rhetoric. However, it is worth noting that the programme-makers were aware that they needed to be accountable for the position they took. Potter and Wetherell's (1994: 61) transcript of notes from an editing session suggest that the producers were keen to ensure that they provided a credible account and could defend their inference about the 1 per cent. Discourse analysts are often interested in this element of accountability, and finding it often involves examining the details through which accounts are constructed.

Another noteworthy point from the Potter et al. study is the researchers' suggestion that reading other discourse studies is itself an important activity. This helps to refine the analytic mentality needed for DA, and reading other studies can also provide insights that you could apply to your own data. For example, Potter and Wetherell (1994) indicate that they were influenced by a study of market traders by Pinch and Clark (1986). This research showed that traders often used a kind of quantification rhetoric (though Pinch and Clark did not use this term) to convey a sense of value. Potter et al. identified a similar device in their data, in that the large number of cancers and the long list of types were contrasted with the small number (three) of curable ones.

Critical discourse analysis

We will spend the final section of this chapter considering critical discourse analysis (CDA), a particular type of discourse analysis that aims to explore how language can be used to impose and maintain power and social inequalities in society. We defined it in more detail in Key concept 21.3, and one of our student panellists reflects on its importance in Learn from experience 21.1. Critical discourse analysts usually study a particular *discursive event* according to a 'three-dimensional' framework.

1. Examination of the actual content, structure, and meaning of the text under scrutiny (the *text dimension*).
2. Examination of the form of discursive interaction used to communicate meaning and beliefs (the *discursive practice dimension*).
3. Consideration of the social context in which the discursive event is taking place (the *social practice dimension*) (Grant et al. 2004: 11).

Another key concept within CDA is the idea of **intertextuality**. This draws attention to connections between texts, so that any text that is being examined is considered in the context of other related texts.

Like discourse analysts, CDA practitioners tend to want to analyse naturally occurring data. Phillips and Hardy propose several considerations for deciding how to select texts for analysis but the first—'What texts are the most important in constructing the object of analysis?' (2002: 75)—is probably the main and overriding consideration. CDA practitioners differ from many discourse analysts in that they are much more likely to take the context of discourse into account when conducting their analysis. Indeed, many see this as a crucial element of the approach. As Phillips and Hardy put it: 'if we are to understand discourses and their effects, we must also understand the context in which they arise' (2002: 4). The study described in Research in focus 21.7 provides an example of how CDA can be used.

Evaluating discourse analysis

As we have emphasized on several occasions, DA draws on insights from CA, particularly when analysing strings of talk, and both are interested in the ways in which interaction is realized in and through talk and/or text. Indeed, how intersubjective meaning is accomplished

KEY CONCEPT 21.3
What is critical discourse analysis?

Critical discourse analysis is strongly influenced by the work of Michel Foucault (e.g. 1977). The approach aims to examine how language is used to exercise power in society—in other words, how language constructs ideas and practice of discipline. CDA defines 'discourse' in broader terms than in the more detail-focused approaches taken by Potter et al., as this summary by Phillips and Hardy (2002) illustrates:

> We define a discourse as an interrelated set of texts, and the practices of their production, dissemination, and reception, that brings an object into being . . . In other words, social reality is produced and made real through discourses, and social interactions cannot be fully understood without reference to the discourses that give them meaning. As discourse analysts, then, our task is to explore the relationship between discourse and reality.
> (Phillips and Hardy 2002: 3)

CDA practitioners are more open than discourse analysts to the idea that there is a pre-existing material reality that restricts our ability to act as we choose. Discourses are seen as drawing on and influencing other discourses; so, for example, the discourse of globalization might affect discourses on new technology, free trade, and liberalism, or on corporate social responsibility. CDA involves exploring why some meanings become privileged or are accepted unquestioningly while others become marginalized, and the role of power in relation to these developments. In other words, discourse does not just provide an account of what goes on in society; it is also a *process* through which meaning is created and suppressed. CDA usually involves asking 'who uses language, how, why and when' (van Dijk 1997: 2), to which we could add: 'and to what effect?'

LEARN FROM EXPERIENCE 21.1
The importance of *critical* discourse analysis

Critical discourse analysis emphasizes the role that power has within texts and how particular ideologies are embedded within particular discourses. The 'critical' emphasis of CDA reveals an interest in how these ideas are often implicit rather than explicitly expressed. This relationship is explained by Grace, who used CDA to investigate the idea of 'development' in relation to Rwandan education programmes:

> My chosen method of discourse analysis was critical discourse analysis (CDA). I chose CDA because it emphasizes the relationship between the production of a text and societal power. CDA enabled me to look at the wider discourse that frames themes like 'development'. I was very focused on how larger powers employ such discourse and how this can filter down through society. I used Fairclough's (1995) three levels of analysis to examine the documents. This was really helpful in investigating latent meanings within the policy discourse that were not at first apparent when looking solely at each document in itself and enabled a broader scope for interpretation of the data.
>
> Grace

Reference

Fairclough, N. (1995). *Critical Discourse Analysis: The Critical Study of Language*. London: Longman.

 Access the **online resources** to hear Grace's video reflections on this theme.

You can read about our panellists' backgrounds and research experiences on page xxvi.

RESEARCH IN FOCUS 21.7
Critical discourse analysis

Mattsson et al. (2016) used CDA to examine how discourse on 'the War on Terror' has been incorporated into European education systems. They note that the European Commission devised a working group, the Radicalisation Awareness Network (RAN), to research and develop strategies of educational practice that would help prevent the radicalization of young people. These strategies were summarized in a document called 'Preventing Radicalization to Terrorism and Violent Extremism'. The authors' research questions provide a strong sense of the concerns of CDA practitioners, that is, how discourses help construct particular 'realities':

> (a). what discourses on radicalization and the War on terror emerge in [the document] (b). what discourses regarding educational practices and approaches emerge in [the document]; and (c). how do discourses on radicalization/War on terror and on educational practices/approaches relate to each other?
>
> (Mattsson et al. 2016: 253)

Their data comprised the introductory chapter from the document, and its Chapter 5, which detailed 19 different strategies of intervention and prevention. Adopting CDA as their theoretical and methodological basis, the authors analysed the documents with specific reference to Fairclough's (1995) three layers of CDA: text, discursive practice, and social practice. The first layer—text—refers to the descriptive content of the communication, that is, what the text says. The examination of discursive practice focuses on the interpretation of that text with respect to both production and reception, or what the text is constructed to mean. The final layer—social practice—considers how discursive practices are organized and reproduced within society. This is what the text actually achieves in practice.

By using this framework, the authors were able to develop an analytic mentality with which they aimed to 'discover the structure of and relation between the text, the discursive practice and, to some extent, the social practice' (Mattsson et al. 2016: 255).

Their research demonstrated how discourse about the War on Terror tends to individualize and decontextualize the tensions that contribute towards radicalization. This discourse then leads to educational policy that prioritizes controlling students (through surveillance, etc.) over developing their capacity to think critically about the nature of social inequality, difference, and conflict.

RESEARCH IN FOCUS 21.8
Ethnography and discourse analysis

Macgilchrist and Van Hout (2011) use the term 'ethnographic discourse analysis' to describe the analytical framework they developed, which draws on both ethnography and discourse analysis. They were interested in the role of press releases in journalistic writing, and their research began with a period of participant observation at the business news desk of a major Dutch-language newspaper. After attending a number of meetings where decisions about what news stories to cover were made, Van Hout (the fieldworker) began to investigate the process through which one particular story about the supply of gas to French consumers was developed. This involved ethnographic work to follow the development of the story; a discourse analysis of the text itself; and an examination of the keystroke logs and screen recording of the actual writing process. Finally, they conducted a 'reflexive discourse-based interview' with the journalist. This involved direct discussion of parts of the text and sections of the recording of the writing process.

The research demonstrated that hegemonic power must be performed. However, these performances do not only happen in large-scale political frames or on controversial topics; they are also visible in the everyday practices of people who are making knowledge claims. In developing their analytic framework, the authors were able to connect large scale analysis of the newsroom, while simultaneously focusing on the everyday practices that are necessary to maintain hegemony. They highlight that ethnography and discourse analysis 'share an epistemology which goes beyond post-positivist criteria for qualitative research, and attempts to find a vocabulary which does not require reference to intersubjectivity, inter-coder reliability or representativeness as a measure of quality' (Macgilchrist and Van Hout 2011: 50–1).

in sequences of interaction is a key feature of each approach. This is not always straightforward, and when you read articles based on DA, it sometimes seems as though the practitioners come very close to making speculations that do not seem to be directly visible in the sequences being analysed. However, this criticism could be largely addressed by combining discourse analysis and critical discourse analysis with ethnography, as some researchers have attempted to do—see, for example, the study by Macgilchrist and Van Hout (2011) described in Research in focus 21.8. In this example, the periods of ethnographic observation at least in part informed the discourse analytic interpretation of the sequences of recorded talk. Attention to ethnographic detail alerted the researchers to nuances and understandings that are not directly visible in the flow of discourse.

In some ways, DA takes a more flexible approach to language in social research than CA. This is because it is not only concerned with the analysis of naturally occurring talk—this is certainly the preference, but practitioners also use various kinds of documents and research interviews in their work. DA also allows its practitioners to incorporate into their analysis understandings of what is going on that are not evident in the exact or immediately preceding utterances being studied. It is this element that conversation analysts criticize, with Schegloff (1997: 183) writing about DA that: 'Discourse is too often made subservient to contexts not of its participants' making, but of its analysts' insistence.' But discourse analysts sometimes object to the contextual restrictions imposed by CA, because they mean that conversation analysts 'rarely raise their eyes from the next turn in the conversation, and, further, this is not an entire conversation or sizeable slice of social life but usually a tiny fragment' (Wetherell 1998: 402). Essentially, discourse analysts see phenomena that are very much part of the context within which talk occurs, whereas in CA they are seen as inadmissible evidence. This exposes a key dilemma for discourse analysts: they want to factor in a broader sense of context but also agree, to an extent, with CA's preference for excluding ethnographic particulars (Potter 1997). It is not clear just how far DA and CDA practitioners should go in including factors that are not embedded in the text or speech.

The anti-realist inclination of many DA practitioners has also been a source of controversy, because its emphasis on representational practices through discourses largely rules out the idea that there is a pre-existing material reality that restricts individual agency. Reality becomes little more than that which is constructed in and through discourse. Some social researchers and theorists feel that this lack of attention to everyday reality makes DA too abstract. For example, writing from a critical realist position (see Key concept 2.3), Reed (2000) has argued that discourses should be examined in relation to social structures, such as the power relationships that are responsible for generating those discourses, and on the ways in which discourses work through existing social structures. In this view, discourse is seen as a 'generative mechanism' rather than as a sphere that only refers to itself, and beyond which nothing significant exists. Reed (2000: 529) provides an interesting example of such an alternative view:

> Discourses—such as the quantitatively based discourses of financial audit, quality control and risk management—are now seen as the generative mechanisms through which new regulatory regimes 'carried out' by rising expert groups—such as accountants, engineers and scientists—become established and legitimated in modern societies. What they represent is less important than what they do in facilitating a radical re-ordering of pre-existing institutional structures in favour of social groups who benefit from the upward mobility which such innovative regulatory regimes facilitate.
>
> (Reed 2000: 529)

We can see that although many DA practitioners are anti-realist, it is possible to take an alternative, realist position in relation to discourse. This alternative position is perhaps closer to the classic concerns of the social sciences than an anti-realist stance.

21.4 Overview of language analysis in qualitative research

Many of the studies we have been discussing in this chapter refer to their analysis of language using the term 'discourse'. However, the extensive use of this term brings its own problems—particularly if you want to attempt discourse analysis in your own studies. So while conversation analysis does have a fairly explicit focus, **theory**, and method, how the term 'discourse' is used by researchers can vary considerably, and so can their approach to analysis. As Alvesson and Kärreman (2000) have noted, there is a danger that the term 'discourse analysis' is too broad to be meaningful, but authors use it as though there is a clear, broadly agreed-upon meaning. From reading just this chapter, it will be clear to you that it does not. As a result, 'discourse sometimes comes close to standing for everything, and thus nothing' (Alvesson and Kärreman 2000: 1128). However, the important thing to remember with respect to both conversation and discourse analysis is the emphasis they place on the role that language has in helping to construct the social world. The approaches we have examined in this chapter outline some tools through which you can explore language as a focus of attention in its own right.

KEY POINTS

- Approaches to CA and DA take the position that language is a focus of research interest and not just a medium through which research participants communicate with researchers.
- CA is a systematic approach to conversation that locates action in talk.

- In CA, talk is seen as being structured, in the sense that it follows rules.
- Practitioners of CA aim to make inferences about talk without allowing contextual factors that are not directly embedded in the talk to intrude into their analysis.
- DA shares many features with CA, but there are several different versions of it.
- DA can be applied to a wider variety of phenomena than CA, which focuses only on naturally occurring talk.
- DA practitioners are more willing to relate meaning in talk to contextual factors.

QUESTIONS FOR REVIEW

1. In what ways does the role of language in conversation and discourse analysis differ from the role it plays in most other research methods?
2. In what ways is conversation analysis fundamentally about the production of social order in interaction? (Related to this: why are audio-recording and transcription crucial in conversation analysis?)
3. What is meant by each of the following: turn-taking; adjacency pair; preference organization; repair mechanism?
4. How do the terms in the previous question relate to the production of social order?
5. Evaluate Schegloff's (1997) argument that conversation analysis removes the need to make potentially ungrounded assumptions about participants' motives.
6. What does it mean to say that discourse analysis is anti-realist and constructionist?
7. What is an interpretative repertoire?
8. What techniques are available to discourse analysts when they try to understand the ways in which facts are presented through discourse?
9. What is distinctive about critical discourse analysis?
10. What key questions might a critical discourse analysis practitioner ask when trying to uncover the meaning of discourses surrounding something like climate change?
11. Why is the idea of intertextuality important to critical discourse analysis practitioners?
12. What are the main points of difference between conversation analysis and discourse analysis?

ONLINE RESOURCES

www.oup.com/he/srm6e

You can find our notes on the answers to these questions within this chapter's **online resources**, together with:

- *audio/video comments* on this topic from our 'Learn from experience' panellists;
- *self-test questions* for further knowledge-checking;
- a *flashcard glossary* to help you recall key terms; and
- a *Student Researcher's Toolkit* containing practical materials and resources to help you conduct your own research project.

CHAPTER 22

DOCUMENTS AS SOURCES OF DATA

CHAPTER GUIDE

The term 'documents' covers many different kinds of data. In this chapter we aim to reflect that variability by examining a wide range of documentary sources that can be used in qualitative research and how they might be approached in terms of analysis. We will explore

- the criteria for evaluating documentary sources;
- personal documents in both written and visual form;
- official documents produced by the state;
- official documents from private sources;
- mass-media documents;
- digital media documents;
- the extent to which documents can be seen as reflecting reality;
- the use of qualitative content analysis and semiotics for analysing documents.

22.1 Introduction

This chapter will explore a fairly diverse set of data sources. This includes letters, diaries, autobiographies, newspapers, magazines, websites, blogs, and photos. The common factor is that these types of documents have not been produced at the request of a social researcher; they already exist 'out there', waiting to be assembled and analysed. This type of data might sound very appealing, especially if you are conducting student research, but it is important to be aware that using documents for the purpose of research is not necessarily any less time-consuming than using other forms of qualitative data. Documents are also not necessarily any easier to process or analyse for the purpose of data collection. In fact, the opposite can be true: the search for documents relevant to your research can be a frustrating and lengthy process, and once they have been collated it often takes considerable interpretative skill to analyse their meaning. Documents often exist and make sense in relation to other documents, and these chains of meaning often need attention in their own right.

22.2 The nature of 'documents'

The word 'document' can mean many different things in everyday language. In this chapter, we use 'documents' to refer to materials with the following qualities:

- they can be read (though the term 'read' has quite a loose meaning in the context of visual materials, such as photos);
- they have not been originally produced specifically for the purpose of social research;
- they have been preserved so that they become available for analysis; and
- they are relevant to the concerns of the social researcher.

We have already encountered some documents in this book. For example, content analysis (Chapter 13) is often carried out on documents such as news articles, and in Key concept 14.2 we noted that research on archive materials is a form of unobtrusive method. In this chapter we will focus on the use of documents in qualitative research, but if you have read Chapter 13 or 14 you will be familiar with the key advantage of using documents for both qualitative and quantitative research: they are not reactive. As the documents we refer to have not been created specifically for the purposes of social research, our techniques of data collection do not impact on the data, so there are fewer limits on the validity of our research.

In Chapter 13 we also introduced Scott's (1990) useful framework for thinking about the nature of documents and how we can assess their relative quality—and for the purposes of this chapter we will make frequent reference to both aspects of his framework. In the first instance, Scott distinguishes between personal documents and official documents and further classifies the latter as private and state official documents. Second, he provides four criteria for assessing the quality of documents (1990: 6).

1. *Authenticity*. Is the evidence genuine and of unquestionable origin?
2. *Credibility*. Is the evidence free from error and distortion?
3. *Representativeness*. Is the evidence typical of its kind, and if not, is the extent of its untypicality known?
4. *Meaning*. Is the evidence clear and comprehensible?

Taken together, this framework provides an extremely rigorous set of criteria against which we may assess documents.

22.3 Personal documents

In this section we will discuss the nature of what Scott called personal documents—documents that individuals produce in the course of their personal and professional lives—as well as some of the issues involved in using this kind of data. We will first consider written personal documents, and then their visual equivalents.

RESEARCH IN FOCUS 22.1
Using historical personal documents

Knepper (2018) provides an interesting account of the use of historical personal documents in his study of Cesare Lombroso (1807–36). Knepper argues that Lombroso occupies a somewhat strange position within the field of criminology. He is popularly positioned as both a central figure in the development of the scientific study of criminal behaviour *and* as someone with a flawed theory, methodology, and conclusion—for example, he is often perceived to have supported the idea that criminals had a different and more primitive genetic makeup, and even that they could be identified by their physical appearance. Despite Lombroso being widely considered 'the father of criminology', his ideas have now been discredited to the extent that they are often used as a starting critique for criminologists to justify their own projects.

Knepper used personal historical documents—Lombroso's original writings—to examine the wider context in which Lombroso was writing and consider how significant these factors might have been in influencing his ideas. In doing so, Knepper demonstrates that Lombroso's work, though undoubtedly problematic, was thoroughly embedded within the broader currents of thought at the time he was writing. He was neither a lone scholar nor the only person interested in such ideas.

Diaries, letters, and autobiographies

Diaries and letters (see Key concept 10.1) are heavily used by historians but tend to be given less attention by social researchers. When we do use them, social researchers often specifically elicit them from their authors—this is usually known as a research-driven **diary**, and it was this type of diary that we discussed in Section 10.8. However, the kinds of diary and letter that we consider in this chapter are ones that have *not* been solicited by a researcher: they existed before the researcher saw an opportunity to use them for the purposes of research. Research in focus 22.1 and 22.2 provide examples of the use of personal documents in social research in both historical and more contemporary contexts.

Personal documents exist in many forms, although their popularity among the public does change. For example, it is likely that the use of traditional letters for the purposes of social research will be fairly limited to a certain time period. The emergence of email and other forms of digital communication is likely to mean that the role of letters has been declining for some time and may continue to do so. However, many letters, other personal documents, and administrative correspondence are held in archives, so it is always worth investigating what personal documents could be available to you (see Key concept 22.1).

Whereas letters and emails are a form of communication with other people, diarists have traditionally written for themselves. Again, however, the popularity of such writing is subject to change, in terms of both format and audience. When written for wider consumption, diaries are difficult to distinguish from another kind of personal document—the autobiography—and where they are (re)presented in shorter forms online, they are referred to as blogs (or weblogs). And, of course, where these blogs take audiovisual form, they become vlogs (or video-weblogs).

All of these types of personal documents can also be created at the request of a researcher, and researchers have used diaries particularly in connection with the **life history method** (see Chapter 19). When we evaluate unsolicited personal documents, however, the *authenticity* criterion is clearly of considerable importance. Is the purported author of the letter or diary the real author?

This question has become increasingly problematic in relation to autobiographies in recent years as a result of the increasing use of 'ghost' writers by celebrities and public figures, but this form of document can still be useful for social research. Pasquandrea (2014) conducted a discursive analysis of the autobiographical writings of Louis Armstrong, the famous jazz trumpeter (1901–71). The written works included two autobiographies, an anthology of his writings, and a long interview with Armstrong. Pasquandrea shows that Armstrong presented the inability of some of his peers to read and write music in quite different ways, and suggested that he (Armstrong) did this in order to produce certain effects on the reader,

KEY CONCEPT 22.1
What is an archive?

An archive is simply a collection of documents, items, or objects that relate to specific topics—usually a person, an organization, or an event. In some instances, they are concerned with a single theme, while in others they can feature many different topics from many different places. Equally, archives can be very small or very large, and can exist in physical or digital form—and sometimes they are both. The UK's National Archives, for example, is the official archiver and publisher of the UK government and contains material collected over more than 1,000 years. Based in Richmond, West London, it contains both physical and digital records about a huge range of issues. It is freely accessible to the public. The Marx Memorial Library, on the other hand, has a range of collections that broadly relate to the history of socialism. This includes material relating to trade unionism, peace movements, and the Spanish Civil War. Based in Clerkenwell, London, it can be visited by appointment and has a fully searchable online catalogue.

But these are only two examples of what is a huge and expanding range of resources for social researchers. Many archives are associated with particular libraries, and both public and private organizations can also have repositories that hold archival material. Some, like the UK's National Archives, will be freely accessible whereas others will require some sort of prior agreement to gain access. What is contained within an archive can be equally varied—not just in terms of topics, but also in the medium. Newspapers and other printed records, personal documents, audiovisual material, and digitized material are all commonly held within archives.

There are, of course, some key methodological issues to think about when thinking about working with archival material.

- *Identification.* Which archive might hold material of interest to you, and how can you identify it?
- *Access.* Where is the archive, and how can you access it?
- *Selection.* What has been chosen for inclusion in the archive, and what might be left out?
- *Analysis.* How can you record your data, and what kinds of analysis will it allow you to conduct?

All archives are also different in terms of how you can search their collections, how you access the material, what has been selected for inclusion, and how you can work with the data you might find there. Therefore one of the first things that any researcher needs to find out, when physically entering an archive for the first time, is how that particular archive operates and the rules of what they are and are not allowed to do within that archive. In some cases cameras will be allowed, in others there will be print services (usually for a charge), and in some the only things you will be allowed to take into 'the reading room' are a pencil and some paper! All of this is vitally important because it will influence the types of things that you can do with the documents you find.

such as whether particular musicians were to be depicted in a positive or negative light. Sometimes he presented the inability to read or write music as a virtue, and at other times as a flaw. However, the issue of whether others influenced the writing process is relevant here too, as it is clear that the original draft of one of the autobiographies (which is preserved in an archive) was heavily edited.

We can see that authenticity is important, and we certainly should not assume it when analysing written personal documents. So how do personal documents perform when assessed against Scott's other criteria? Scott (1990) observes that there are at least two major concerns with respect to the *credibility* of personal documents: the *factual* accuracy of reports, and whether they do in fact report the true *feelings* of the writer. Tom, one of this book's authors, examined these issues in relation to an autobiographical letter by the serial killer Myra Hindley—see Research in focus 22.2.

Indeed, Scott recommends maintaining an attitude of healthy scepticism regarding the sincerity with which the writer reports their true feelings. Famous people may be fully aware that their letters or diaries will be of considerable interest to others and may, therefore, be conscious of the degree to which they really reveal themselves in their writings, or will actively try to project a certain 'front'—as was the case with Hindley.

Representativeness is clearly a major concern for documentary materials, particularly where issues of

RESEARCH IN FOCUS 22.2
Using contemporary personal documents

Tom, one of this book's authors, analysed the 'prison files' of the British serial killer Myra Hindley (Clark 2019). The files consist of a range of documents, including personal letters and request/complaint forms written by Hindley herself, as well as a variety of administrative documents relating to the negotiation and management of her sentence. Tom used this wealth of data to reconstruct the process of how an autobiographical letter about her life appeared in a UK newspaper. His analysis of the documents revealed that the letter, rather than depicting a straightforward and unproblematic version of history, was a product of a variety of sources and influences, including Hindley's high-profile advisors, her relationship with the press, and the requirements of her prison sentence. Tom (Clark 2019: 14) notes that 'the letter does not passively represent a reality that is independent of the narrator and her responses are not as definitive, inevitable, or even falsifiable as they might first appear.' While Hindley did write the autobiographical letter, Tom demonstrates that the narrative was shaped by 'a number of other structures and resources that were both implicitly and explicitly present in her local context and within society more generally'.

production and curation influence what material is created and kept. Historical letters, diaries, and autobiographies will usually have been written by the literate, who were often the middle and upper classes. Since boys were historically often more likely to receive an education than girls, this means that the voices of women have also tended to be under-represented in such documents. Wilson (2008), for example, demonstrates how the decommissioned prisons in Australia that had been converted into museums often inadvertently reproduced the dominant narratives of custodial staff, policymakers, and the media. Her research sought to examine the lost narratives of those who were 'othered' by both administrative procedures and the narratives that reproduced them.

Whether you find relevant documents that are available to you can be a question of how hard you look (see Learn from experience 22.1).

Historical documents can be biased in terms of authorship, but a further problem is the selective survival of documents such as letters: why do any survive at all, and what proportion are damaged, lost, or thrown away? We do not know why, for example, the letters of an American Civil War soldier called 'Charlie Mac' survived (whereas presumably those written by other soldiers did not), and we do not know whether we have the complete set (that is, whether some of his letters did not survive)—see Research in focus 22.3. The question of *meaning* can become problematic in this context, because damage to letters and diaries makes the data difficult to triangulate. Also, as Scott (1990) observes, letter-writers may leave much unsaid in their communications, because they share common, unrevealed values and assumptions with their recipients.

Visual objects

There is a growing interest in the visual within social research, as we highlighted in Chapter 16 and discussed in more depth in Chapter 18 (see Section 18.5 under 'Visual ethnography'). The photograph is the most obvious manifestation of this trend, in that photos are becoming objects of interest in their own right, rather than being thought of as incidental to the research process. But, as with the personal documents we discussed above, we need to make a distinction between visual objects that are created as part of fieldwork and those that already exist (see Chapter 18). Our focus here is on those visual objects, like photographs, that exist before the researcher uses them for the purposes of social research. (We will discuss TV and film as 'documents' in Section 22.5, 'Mass-media documents'.)

One of the ways in which existing photos may be of interest in social research is in terms of what they reveal about families. As Scott (1990) observes, many family photos are taken as a record of ceremonial occasions (weddings, christenings) and of recurring events such as religious festivals and annual holidays. Scott distinguishes between three types of home photo:

- *idealization*, which is a formal pose—for example, a wedding photo or a photo of a family in formal clothes;
- *natural portrayal*, which involves capturing actions as they happen, though there may be a contrived component to the photo; and
- *demystification*, which involves capturing an image of the subject in an untypical (and often embarrassing) situation.

LEARN FROM EXPERIENCE 22.1
Discovering documents

Discovering documents often requires both ingenuity and perseverance. Not only do you need to think about how certain **concepts** and ideas will be realized within public discourse and then coded into databases, you also have to think critically about what you might be *unable* to access. Starr reflects on the process of finding the documents for her study of refugee experiences at Western higher education institutions:

> I located my documents through online resources, such as web queries and library databases, as well as through the websites/databases of specified educational organizations. My search terms included 'ethics', 'values', 'principles', 'guidelines', 'internationalization', 'higher education', and 'students'. Where applicable, I also conducted further searches using references that I found within those initial documents.
>
> The main challenge of this process was defining and justifying which organizations to include, as well as modifying search terms to locate appropriate documents that explicitly discussed ethics and the student body. However, it must be noted that there was a wealth of data on this topic—in the form of private documents between internal members of the organizations—that I did not have access to. Ultimately, while I could understand the official perspectives of a number of international and Canadian organizations, I could not access more personal understandings without the need for additional interviews, which would have been challenging to schedule within the time frame of my research.
>
> Starr

 Access the **online resources** to hear Starr's video reflections on this theme.

You can read about our panellists' backgrounds and research experiences on page xxvi.

RESEARCH IN FOCUS 22.3
Comparing historical and contemporary personal written documents

It is tempting to think that the century-and-a-half that separates the military blog of a modern-day soldier and the letters and diary of a soldier in the American Civil War will mean that the two sets of documents are far apart in tone and content, but Shapiro and Humphreys (2013) found similarities as well as differences in their study of historical and contemporary personal documents on military experiences. They compare the blog of 'Dadmanly', who was in the US army for just over four years beginning in August 2004 and who served in Iraq for 18 months, with the letters and diaries of 'Charlie Mac', who joined the Union Army in 1862. The latter's writings continued until April 1865 and have been compiled in an anthology.

The researchers found clear differences between the two sets of documents, notably that Dadmanly knew his letters would be visible to a general audience, the vast majority of whom he would never know, whereas Charlie Mac wrote primarily to members of his large family. However, Mac does seem to have anticipated that his letters might be handed around to others and have a wider readership, and the researchers found a number of other common elements:

- both writers show a desire to reassure family and friends about their safety and wellbeing;
- both expressed opinions about the progress of their respective wars and offered political comments about them;

- both wrote in large part to maintain relationships with their families; and
- for both Dadmanly and Mac, writing was therapeutic in dealing with the personal experience of war.

Shapiro and Humphreys see this comparison as significant because it suggests that although the contexts of writing are very different in these two instances, the continuities between them suggest that we should be wary of assuming that new media formats necessarily imply changes in the content of communications.

It is important to be aware of these different types so that we are not exclusively concerned with the superficial appearance of the images and can probe beneath the surface. He writes:

> There is a great deal that photographs do not tell us about their world. Hirsch [1981: 42] argues, for example, that 'The prim poses and solemn faces which we associate with Victorian photography conceal the reality of child labour, women factory workers, whose long hours often brought about the neglect of their infants, nannies sedating their charges with rum, and mistresses diverting middle class fathers.'
>
> (Scott 1990: 195)

As Scott argues, this means not only that the photo must not be taken at face value when used as a research source, but also that we need to have considerable additional knowledge of the social context in order to probe beneath the surface. Given this, are photos any use to a researcher at all? We consider the role of photos within social research in Thinking deeply 22.1.

THINKING DEEPLY 22.1
What roles can photos play in social research?

Photos may have a variety of roles in relation to social research. While in Chapter 18 and this chapter we discuss them in relation to qualitative research, there is no reason why they cannot also be employed in quantitative research, and some researchers have used them in this connection—as we saw in Chapter 13. For example, photos could be the focus of content analysis or used as prompts in connection with **structured interviewing** or an experiment. However, the growing interest in photos and visual materials more generally has tended to come from qualitative researchers. There is an important distinction between the use of *extant* photos, which already exist and were not generated as part of the research, and *research-generated* photos that have been produced by the researcher or at the researcher's request. We can point to three prominent roles for photos in social research.

1. *Illustrative*: photos can simply illustrate points and therefore help to bring what might otherwise be quite a dry discussion of findings to life. They have seemed to play this kind of role in some classic anthropological reports of research findings, but more recently anthropologists have experimented with forms of **ethnography** in which photos have a more prominent position.
2. *As data*: we can view photos as data in their own right. When they are research-generated photos, they essentially become part of the researcher's **field notes** (see Research in focus 18.10 for an example). When they are extant photos, they become the main source of data about the field in which the researcher is interested—as in the studies by Blaikie (2001) and Stauff (2018) discussed in this chapter.
3. *As prompts*: we can use photos as prompts to encourage people to talk about what is represented in them. Both research-generated photos (see Research in focus 18.10) and extant photos can be used in this way. Sometimes, research participants might volunteer their photos for this kind of use.

The creation of substantial digital archives in recent decades has provided different kinds of uses for visual documents in social research. Müller (2017), for example, argues that when anthropological images are contained within an 'authoritative' digital archive this alters both the materiality of an image and its meaning altogether. As a democratized and accessible object, the digital image allows for endless numbers of reproductions and interpretations. There is no longer any sense of the image being an 'original' or 'copy', and the

process of digitization becomes a way of creating meaning and value. Müller uses the example of Purvajo-ni Aankh ('Through the Eye of the Ancestors')—an exhibition-cum-ancestral worship event held by the Adivasi Museum of Voice in Tejgadh, India, which used the digital archives of three European museums. The Adivasi Museum presented the images of the Adivasi people (the original tribal inhabitants of the country) in pre-independence India at this event and asked community members to integrate the images into ancestral worship and memory-making—which they did using their own histories and cultural practices. Müller demonstrates that while the active appropriation of digital copies does not necessarily challenge the documentary character of the original image, the idea that there is any authoritative meaning within the archive is undermined by the way the digitized images can be used and situated within different knowledge systems.

Scott sees the issue of *representativeness* as a particular issue of interest for researchers attempting to analyse photos. As he suggests, the photos that survive the passage of time—for example, in archives—are unlikely to be representative. They are likely to have been subject to all sorts of hazards, such as damage and selective retention. The other problem relates to the issue of what is *not* photographed, as implied by the quotation from Hirsch, and supported by Stauff's suggestion (2018; see Research in focus 22.4) that particular representations of competitive sports are given primacy. Indeed, a sensitivity to what is not photographed can reveal the 'mentality' of the person(s) behind the camera. This is the point that Stauff is making: the absence of photos depicting other experiences of competitive sports suggests something about how those capturing the competition think it should be viewed and interpreted (for example, victorious winner, gallant loser). It is as interesting and important to examine what is not represented in photographs as it is to study what does survive, because the former highlights how the selective survival of photos can help to construct a particular kind of reality: one favoured and encouraged by media outlets.

Another key problem for researchers wanting to use photos is recognizing the different ways in which the image may be understood. Blaikie (2001) found some fascinating photos in the local museums of the Northern Isles of Orkney and Shetland that derived from the work of local photographers and donated family albums. Blaikie (2001: 347) observes that in both the images themselves and the ways they are represented by the museums, the 'apparently raw "reality" of island culture has already been appropriated and ordered'. So, is the image of a crofter—an owner or tenant of a small farm—standing by his home suggestive of respectability or of poverty? And should we see the image as a social commentary on the photographer's part, or as a depiction of a disappearing way of life, or simply as an image with no particular subtext? Any or a combination of these different narratives may be applicable. These points might lead us to conclude that such photos have limited value as a form of document for the social researcher. However, while

RESEARCH IN FOCUS 22.4
Analysing the reality constructed by photos

Stauff (2018) analysed a range of sports photography from the 1930s to the 1960s to explore how competitive sport is organized and constructed on a publicly visible stage. Sport has a very visual culture, so individual images can powerfully frame and emphasize successful performance. Stauff's research demonstrates that images also highlight specific aspects of competition, revealing the way in which the media think that sports should be viewed—heroic winners and gallant losers. But he also notes that sports photos appear to deliberately draw attention to their own limitations *as images*—while they might suggest the adulation or anguish of competitors, they do not reveal the 'full story'. This suggests that further articulation and expertise is needed to interpret their meaning, which subtly legitimates the authority of any accompanying commentary.

The researcher therefore has to pay close attention to not only the content and the form of the image, but also the narratives that are reproduced around it. Photos might *appear* to capture real events but these visual performances can only be understood in relation to further context, embellishment, and explanation.

FIGURE 22.1

An image known as 'toffs and toughs' that is presumed to demonstrate Britain's class divides—does this photo tell the whole story?

Source: Jimmy Sime / Stringer / Hulton Archive via Getty Images.

acknowledging the diversity of interpretations that can be drawn from the images he examined, Blaikie argues that these photos provide a perspective on the emergence of modernity and the sense of loss of a past life, especially in terms of the ways in which they were organized by the museums. Coming to this kind of understanding requires a sensitivity to the contextual nature of images and the variety of interpretations that can be attributed to them.

A related issue is the tendency in everyday language to give photos special *credibility* (to return to Scott's criteria) and to assume that their meaning is transparent—we can see this in sayings like 'a picture is worth a thousand words' or 'the camera never lies'. Figure 22.1 is a good example of how photos can in fact be misleading. This photo was taken on 9 July 1937 outside Lord's cricket ground, London, on the opening day of the annual cricket match between two prestigious fee-paying schools, Eton and Harrow, and the image is widely seen as exemplifying the divided nature of Britain's class system. For example, in an article in *The Times* in 2015, the journalist Philip Collins wrote an article on the class-bound nature of Britain's education system. The middle portion of the photo is included (though not commented on at any point in the article) with the caption: 'The class-bound way we educate our children is economic suicide' (Collins 2015). The meaning and significance of the photo are treated as obvious and not requiring comment or elaboration. The photo is known as 'toffs and toughs' and widely presumed to show two Etonian boys in uniform standing outside Lord's, being looked on by three working-class 'toughs'. However, in an article originally published in *Intelligent Life* magazine in 2010 (but since taken down), Ian Jack explained that this widely held view is extremely misleading.

Aside from the fact that the two boys in top hats were from Harrow, not Eton, they had dressed for a special party that the parents of one of them were organizing following the cricket match. This was not their standard school uniform. The boys were waiting for a car to arrive to take them to the party and it was late, possibly accounting for them apparently ignoring the 'toughs' and staring into the distance—they were looking out for their transport. The smartly dressed boys were not in fact 'toffs' (aristocrats)—the father of one of them was a professional soldier. Nor were the three boys 'toughs'. They attended a local Church of England school and had been hanging around at Lord's trying to make some money by carrying bags or opening car doors (and had been successful in that respect). Also, as Jack notes, the trio are not unkempt—they are simply wearing open-necked shirts and informal clothes that were typical of working-class boys of their day. In contrast, the two Harrow pupils were in special clothes rather than what was typical uniform at the fee-paying schools of their day.

This story provides some insight into why we should adopt a questioning stance as to the credibility of photos. But it does not mean that existing images are useless for the purposes of social research. Indeed, many of the examples we have discussed, while noting the limitations of the photographic format, still successfully use them to illuminate social life.

22.4 Official documents

In this section we look at the other main **category** of documents that Scott (1990) identified: official documents. These are the administrative records associated with administrative bureaucracies and organizations. Scott divided this form of document into two further categories: documents deriving from the state, and documents deriving from private sources.

Official documents produced by the state

The state provides a lot of data that may be of interest for social research. Not only does it produce large volumes of statistical information (as we touched on in Chapter 14), it also generates textual material such as legislative documents and official reports, which, as Research in focus 22.5 demonstrates, can be a rich source of data for social scientists.

In terms of Scott's (1990) four criteria, materials produced by the state can certainly be seen as authentic and as having meaning, in the sense of being clear and comprehensible to the researcher. But are they credible and representative? The question of credibility raises the issue of whether the documentary source is biased in some way. This bias is not necessarily a bad thing in a social research context, particularly when working from an **interpretivist** standpoint. Thompson et al. (2013), for example, were interested in the documents they studied precisely *because* of the biases they reveal. But the issue does remind us that we need to be cautious in attempting to treat documents as simple depictions of reality. The issue of representativeness is similarly complex in that many documents are in a sense unique, and it is precisely their uniqueness that makes them interesting in their own right. There is also, of course, the question of whether the case itself is representative more generally, but in the context of qualitative research this is not a particularly helpful question because no qualitative case can be representative in a statistical sense. Instead, the priority is to develop a persuasive theoretical account, and then the researcher might examine that account in related or similar contexts.

Official documents from private sources

'Documents deriving from private sources' is a very broad category, encompassing many kinds of sources, but one type that is often used in social research is documents that are associated with organizations. Some of these are in the public domain, such as annual reports, mission statements, press releases, advertisements, and public relations materials (see Learn from experience 22.2). Other documents, however, might not be publicly accessible. These might include things like company newsletters, organizational charts, minutes of meetings, **memos**, internal and external correspondence, manuals for new recruits, and so on. These kinds of materials are often used by organizational ethnographers as part of their investigations, but the difficulty of gaining access to some organizations (a difficulty we discussed in Chapters 4 and 18) means that many researchers have to rely on documents that exist in the public domain alone. However, in some cases, it might be possible to use Freedom of Information laws to request particular material. In her study into algorithms used by government organizations, Fink (2018) compared

RESEARCH IN FOCUS 22.5
Using official documents produced by the state

Thompson et al. (2013) used UK government policy documents from 2002 to 2011 to show how east London was positioned as a problem area and how this narrative was deployed as a justification for locating the 2012 Olympic Games in London. The documents included:

- several House of Commons sources (the London Olympic Bid and a publication on the funding and legacy of the Olympic Games and the Paralympic Games);
- Department for Culture, Media, and Sport sources (such as a publication on making the most of the games and a framework for the evaluation of the games' impacts and legacy);
- a British Olympic Association publication on London;
- a statement on the Olympic legacy by the boroughs involved; and
- a spatial development strategy report by the Greater London Authority.

The authors quote from the House of Commons report on the funding and legacy of the games: 'Public money is being used to transform the Olympic Park, a contaminated wasteland, into a cleansed zone ready for development' (quoted in Thompson et al. 2013: 3.3). The depiction of the area as one of deprivation was coupled with a narrative in which community sport was in decline and where being out of work had become a way of life. The London 2012 Olympic Games were presented as fundamental to the transformation and regeneration of east London. Thompson et al. use their analysis of these documents to demonstrate how Olympic planners used neoliberal discourse to justify the massive investment involved.

a range of laws, regulations, advisory opinions, and court rulings about algorithms. To gain further information beyond what was publicly available, she made Freedom of Information Act requests to various US government agencies about their use of algorithms. The responses she received then formed part of her data.

In terms of Scott's four criteria, documents deriving from private sources are likely to be authentic and meaningful (in the sense of being clear and comprehensible to the researcher)—though this is not to suggest that the analyst should be complacent. Issues of credibility and representativeness are also always worth considering. People who write documents are likely to have a particular point of view that they want to get across. Natow's (2020) analysis of 120 peer-reviewed articles that reported findings from elite interviews illustrates this observation. Natow was interested in how researchers approached the problem of potential bias when conducting interviews with people in positions of power and authority. While researchers clearly adopted a range of different formats for triangulating data in order to mitigate potential issues of bias (see Key concept 16.3 on **triangulation**), she found that '[b]y far the most common technique of using multiple qualitative methodologies was to combine elite interviews with documentary analysis' (Natow 2020: 166). Natow's study highlights that, like all sources of data, documents cannot be seen as providing necessarily objective accounts. They have to be interrogated and examined in the context of other sources of data. Indeed, any difference in data that emerges between primary and secondary research methods can actually be used as a platform for developing insights into the processes and factors that lie behind the divergence. In this instance, the documents were interesting to researchers because they helped bring out the role and significance of subcultures within the organization.

Issues of representativeness, too, are often important in this context. In his study of how Alfred Hitchcock's reputation as a significant film-maker was created, Kapsis (1989) analysed a wide variety of documents relating to the Hollywood director. These included correspondence, speeches, and publicity files. Because Kapsis was interested in the role played by Hitchcock and others in the construction of his reputation as a significant film-maker, documents that might have been less than supportive of this reputation would be of considerable importance. The study described in Research in focus 22.6 demonstrates something similar: the findings tell us that the moon landings are remembered both nostalgically and with a

LEARN FROM EXPERIENCE 22.2

Recording the process of document discovery

Being clear about how you discover documents will help you and others to judge the transparency of your work. Indeed, when we assess a **literature review**, a record of the process of searching is often a key criterion of its quality, and much the same is also true when working with documents more broadly. Starr describes how she recorded her process of discovery:

> For my research I used public documents from private organizations. I would advise students to keep an organized record of their process of discovery, much like you might do with a literature search. Being transparent about how you located your documents—including the search terms, databases, and websites used—increases the transparency of your study. My research detailed the process of collecting documents and analysing them, with the bibliography listing all the documents included in the analysis. This was accompanied by a table in the appendix that demonstrated all the organizations sampled, with accompanying links to their websites.
>
> Starr

 Access the **online resources** to hear Starr's video reflections on this theme.

You can read about our panellists' backgrounds and research experiences on page xxvi.

RESEARCH IN FOCUS 22.6

Using official documents from private sources

Goodings et al. (2013) used official documents from private sources to explore how organizations construct versions of their own history that gain significance within cultural memory. They examined how the USA's National Aeronautical and Space Administration (NASA) 'constituted both its own past and future significance through the remediation and premediation of key images of the Apollo space programme' by examining visitor feedback relating to a special exhibition about the Apollo moon landings at the National Space Centre in the UK.

Visitors to this exhibition were encouraged to write 'memory cards', which were put up on a wall at the exhibition. Goodings et al. analysed over 400 cards, stating that they 'were looking at the internal structure of the brief accounts on the cards, what they defined as important and relevant, how they constructed a personal narrative, and the meanings that were accorded to the historical event' (Goodings et al. 2013: 271). The researchers produced a set of themes 'that loosely organised the accounts offered on individual cards' (Goodings et al. 2013: 271) and identified three broad narratives associated with remembering the moon landings:

- an association of the moon landings with the writer's sense of 'my generation';
- a recollection of watching the landings on television;
- the sense of a new future that was associated with the landing but which NASA actively managed.

recognition of disappointment about what followed, but there could be issues of representativeness: the narratives described may not apply to all visitors to the exhibition discussed in this research, and the researchers may not have had access to all the 'memory cards' that the visitors produced. Of course, there are also the unrecorded memories of those who never visited the exhibition at all.

22.5 Mass-media documents

Mass media—by which we mean newspapers, magazines, TV, and films—can provide useful sources for social research. We encountered these kinds of sources when we explored content analysis in Chapter 13, but it is also possible to examine them in a way that preserves their qualitative nature. This analysis usually involves searching for themes in these sources.

Vincent et al. (2010) conducted a textual analysis of English newspapers' narratives about the England football team's participation in the 2006 World Cup in Germany. They examined *The Times*, the *Daily Telegraph*, the *Daily Mail*, the *Daily Mirror*, and *The Sun*, as well as those newspapers' Sunday publications (which included the now defunct *News of the World*), for the duration of the competition. The authors propose that in contrast to the competition's official slogan of 'a time to make friends', the newspapers fuelled a patriotic fervour in which they drew on traditions and motifs from English history that were often invented. For example, they show how the idea of a 'lionheart spirit', associated with the famous lions on the England shirt and with King Richard I, known as 'the Lionheart', produced frequent allusions to lions and roaring. Examples included the *Daily Mirror*'s 'Let's Roar! The Hearts of Our Nation are with You' and *The Sun*'s 'England Lionheart Wayne Rooney is Fired Up and Ready to Roar.' An 'us and them' **rhetoric** was also projected by allusions to English fair play and the propensity of others to cheat (diving, feigning injury, etc.). The theme of fairness and xenophobia surfaced again when England were knocked out of the competition in a match against Portugal. The newspapers focused on Portugal's Cristiano Ronaldo (at that time also Rooney's Manchester United team-mate) for his role in getting Rooney sent off, and they also turned on the Swedish manager of the England team, Sven Göran Eriksson, in a way that highlighted his foreignness. These themes are evident in this quotation from the *Daily Mail*:

> The most disgracefully prepared team in England's World Cup history was managed by a money-grabbing charlatan . . . all Sven Göran Eriksson deserves is to go back up his fjord to the land of winter darkness, hammer throwers and sexual promiscuity from where he came. We've sold our birthright down the fjord to a nation of seven million skiers and hammer throwers who spend half their lives in darkness.
>
> (quoted in Vincent et al. 2010: 218)

This research demonstrated the propensity of newspapers to use themes of English identity, invented traditions, and the apparently problematic nature of globalization. It also showed that although these themes cropped up in all the newspapers that were included in the analysis, the more lurid xenophobic allusions tended to be found in the tabloids.

Returning to Scott's criteria, authenticity is sometimes difficult to establish in the case of mass-media outputs. The outputs can usually be verified as genuine, but the authorship of articles is often unclear, so that it can be difficult to know whether the account can be relied upon as being presented by someone in a position to provide an accurate version. Credibility is frequently an issue, but in fact, as the examples used in this section show, the aim of researchers' analysis is often to uncover error or distortion. Representativeness is rarely an issue for analyses of newspaper or magazine articles, because it is usually possible to identify the body of work from which a **sample** has been drawn. In terms of meaning, the evidence is usually clear and comprehensible, but understanding it may require the analyst to have considerable awareness of contextual factors. In his analysis of football fanzines, for example, Wagg (2010) had to be sensitive to the history of Manchester United and its significance for the club's supporters (see Research in focus 22.7).

RESEARCH IN FOCUS 22.7
Analysing mass media outputs: fanzines

Fanzines can provide interesting alternative insights, as they are often positioned by their contributors as providing an alternative worldview to mainstream commentators and media. Wagg (2010) notes that during Cristiano Ronaldo's time on the Manchester United football team in the years 2003–2009, he was widely seen as a very talented player, equivalent in footballing stature to Manchester United idols such as George Best. However, Wagg also observes that Ronaldo was not regarded with the same affection by *Red Issue*, a Manchester United fanzine,

one of whose contributors described him as a 'preening, perma-tanned, posturing, petulant prick' when he was close to a move to rival team Real Madrid in Spain (2010: 920). Wagg argues that the reason for this writer's displeasure was not just the nature of Ronaldo's participation—he secured a lucrative deal—but his failure to display the appropriate markers of being a Mancunian (a Manchester local) who inhabited a certain niche in terms of place and class. Wagg also shows that among Portuguese migrants living in the same area who followed Manchester United, the view of Ronaldo was more positive. Wagg attributes this stance to the fact that, like Ronaldo, they are trying to prosper in a global economy and want to take up the international opportunities it offers.

22.6 Digital media

Websites, online discussion groups, blogs, vlogs, email, and social networking sites are all potential sources of data for both quantitative and **qualitative content analysis**.

Websites

Nearly every organization now has a website through which they strive to present a particular image and share a considerable amount of information. This can make them valuable sources of data for social researchers. Sillince and Brown (2009) examined the websites of all English and Welsh police constabularies between October 2005 and March 2006 to explore how the constabularies constructed particular organizational identities. Their analysis revealed that organizational identity was constructed through three core themes:

1. the constabulary as effective or ineffective;
2. the constabulary as part of the community or as apart from the community;
3. the constabulary as progressive or not progressive.

Within each theme, Sillince and Brown identified distinctive rhetorical devices. With respect to the last theme, for example, they found that the identification of the constabulary as progressive was often placed within a wider narrative of improvement, where the past was represented as being less developed than the present. Interestingly, the researchers also found that organizational identity is not unitary but often displays conflicting or ambiguous features, and that it is used to support claims to legitimacy for both internal and external audiences.

22

Many other researchers have found websites to be useful sources of qualitative data—see Research in focus 22.8 for another example—but there are clearly difficulties with using this form of document, and it is again important to bear in mind Scott's four quality criteria. In particular, the criteria invite us to consider how a website is constructed. Why is it there at all? Is it there for commercial reasons? Is it trying to publicize a particular view or argument? In other words, we should be no less sceptical about websites than about any other kind of document.

Blogs and vlogs

Another kind of digital media document that has been subjected to analysis is the blog. We discuss one study that made use of this data source in Research in focus 22.9. Another interesting study that used blogs was conducted by Drdová and Saxonberg (2020). They were interested in how public representations of the sexual practices of bondage, discipline (or domination), sadism, and masochism (BDSM) in the novel/film *Fifty Shades of Grey* corresponded with the self-image of people who actually identified with BDSM subcultures, asking whether the 'public view [is] based on the self-image of BDSM subcultural members or is . . . a figment of the imagination of writers and journalists' (Drdová and Saxonberg 2020: 1). To explore the issue they examined the blogs and comments associated with chapter-by-chapter reviews of *Fifty Shades* that were written for members of the BDSM community. In contrast to the book/film, they found that the blogs did not associate BDSM activity with personal or psychological characteristics. Instead, bloggers highlighted how BDSM identities were relatively consistent over time and entirely voluntary. Similarly, any roles associated with BDSM were negotiated beforehand and not during engagement.

Chatrooms, forums, and online communities

Postings to chatrooms, forums, and online communities can also be a fertile source of data for researchers. Collectively, these are often referred to as studies of

RESEARCH IN FOCUS 22.8
Analysing digital media: websites

Brooks and Waters (2015) noted that the theme of internationalization is common in British higher education (HE), with its emphasis on maintaining a global reach and attracting students from overseas. They argue that a similar theme is present in certain schools where parents are concerned that their children acquire what the authors call 'global capital'. To investigate this further, they analysed websites, prospectuses, and other public documents relating to 30 'elite' secondary schools in England. The sample comprised 'influential' private schools, 'high-performing' private schools, and 'high-performing' state schools. The researchers analysed documents relating to 10 schools of each type, and describe their research as follows:

> We were interested to explore the extent to which certain themes were mentioned and/or represented (e.g. HE destinations outside the UK, international pupils, trips and expeditions abroad), and used a detailed grid to record this information. We also explored, in a more discursive manner, the way in which these various themes were constructed in the websites and elsewhere.
>
> (Brooks and Waters 2015)

The authors found that while internationalism was significant for the schools, it was less prominent than providing a strong sense of the 'Englishness' or 'Britishness' of the school, as demonstrated in the following quote taken from one school's website:

> While [Influential Private 10] provides a distinctively British education, our programmes include extensive international links with a group of schools around the world through which exchange of educational practice and ideas and cross-cultural encounter can be developed over the long term.
>
> (quoted in Brooks and Waters 2015)

This research then uses the documents (including a headmaster's blog for at least one of the schools) to reveal some interesting tensions in the ways in which elite schools represent themselves.

RESEARCH IN FOCUS 22.9
Analysing digital media: blogs

Snee (2013) was interested in how representations of cultural difference were portrayed in 'gap year' narratives. She sought out blogs containing the phrase 'gap year' using two blog search engines (Google Blog Search and Technorati) and also searched some websites that seemed to be associated with the blogs she uncovered. She selected blogs that fulfilled the following criteria.

- The author was from the UK.
- The author's gap year was taken overseas.
- The gap year was taken between school and university.
- The blog included more than a couple of posts.

Initially, she uncovered 700 blogs but narrowed the list down to a sample of 39 by seeking a balance in terms of both gender and the type of gap year. These blogs—specifically the written text, rather than the multimedia that they often contained—form her data, along with interviews with nine of the bloggers. The interviews indicated that bloggers wrote up their experiences in this format because it was more convenient than emailing updates to large numbers of people and as a way to keep 'a record of their travels' (Snee 2013: 147), suggesting that blogs are very much a modern form of public diary. Her **inductive** analysis of the blogs allowed her to identify four themes.

1. The bloggers drew on common representations of the exotic qualities of the places they visited in order to portray their destinations. For example: 'We sailed to White Haven Beach which is just like on the postcards; white sands and light blue sea' (Jo, quoted in Snee 2013: 149).

2. The bloggers often conveyed a sense of feeling out of place in these exotic locations. This arose either from an awareness of the bloggers' physical differences or from cultural factors. For example, one of the bloggers came to realize that by standing with her arms crossed in Uganda she had in fact been rude according to the local cultural traditions.
3. Through their interaction with local people and their physical environment, gap year bloggers often displayed a sensitivity to local customs and to the complexity of the locations in which they were travelling. For example, one blogger expressed his unease at the lack of respect shown by some tourists at Ayers Rock (Uluru) in Australia by clambering over it.
4. There was often a narrative of the danger, risk, and sometimes irritations associated with the local environment. There were complaints about the quality of driving in Delhi, lack of concern for safety in Ecuador, and comments about the frightening quality of Rio de Janeiro. These involved implicit and sometimes explicit comparisons with the UK.

As Snee notes, the themes deriving from the blogs reveal a tension:

> On one hand, there is a desire to learn about and understand the local, reflect on global issues and experience what places are 'really like' . . . On the other hand, established discourses are reproduced of an 'Other' that is exoticized, romanticized, or even criticized.
>
> (Snee 2013: 158)

These detailed observations give an indication of how rich a data source these types of document can be. Snee has produced a useful toolkit for doing analyses of blogs in collaboration with the ESRC National Centre for Research Methods: eprints.ncrm.ac.uk/1321/2/10-toolkit-blog-analysis.pdf (accessed 10 November 2020).

'online interaction' and sometimes, when it is appropriate, as studies of 'online communities'.

When researchers analyse postings to online discussion groups they need to decide whether they will do so with or without participating. When the 'documents' are publicly available it can be tempting for them to perform this analysis without participating or announcing their presence, but this can lead to being accused of 'lurking'. This practice is sometimes regarded as being ethically dubious because of the lack of **informed consent** (as we discussed in Chapter 6). Other researchers argue that traditional principles of ethical practice are sufficient in dealing with 'public' data such as that found in open forums.

When the researcher participates in the online discussions, their analysis of online documents comes closer to online ethnography. However, the generally nuanced nature of online data in terms of 'openness' and 'participation' makes any strict division between the two methods difficult to establish or maintain. When conducting a wider ethnography on how English working-class communities resolve conflict, Willis (2018) was invited by an informant to view a community-based Facebook newsfeed that had 3,000 members. This represented around 5 per cent of the community's **population**. She 'gratefully accepted the opportunity' but quickly realized this posed an ethical dilemma for her research: 'When is it justifiable for a researcher to use data without informed consent?' (Willis 2018: 2).

To answer this question, Willis makes a distinction between documentary research and human subject research. With the former, participants can be considered as public authors; with the latter, participants are human subjects. While Facebook newsfeeds are, more or less, publicly available and could be treated as documentary data, Willis argued that because she was already interacting with the community offline she was already interacting with the human subjects who produced it. However, she further notes that the newsfeed was part of her wider observational ethnography, where it was unfeasible to continuously gain informed consent. This also applied to the online data, and Willis therefore maintained that her study remained ethical.

22

Social media

Social media are another type of virtual document that can be used for the purposes of social research. Again, it is possible for social media accounts to be either personal or official, depending on the account that is posting the information. Unfortunately, one of the major advantages of this data is also one of its main drawbacks. The content can provide very rich data, but the vast quantity of material available can also make it difficult to construct an appropriate and manageable sample. However, we have already seen from the examples of quantitative content analysis we discussed in Chapter 13 (for example Research in focus 13.2) that this kind of investigation is certainly feasible. Another study we considered in Chapter 13 was that conducted by Greaves et al. (2014), which is of interest here too because the researchers used both quantitative and qualitative content analysis. Greaves et al. were interested in the frequency of tweets relating to acute NHS hospitals in England and also in their content, especially in relation to care quality. They write:

> We prospectively collected tweets aimed at NHS hospitals from the Twitter streaming application-programming interface (API) for a year. We identified tweets aimed at NHS hospitals by using 'mentions', where a tweet includes the '@username' of a Twitter user.
>
> (Greaves et al. 2014)

The authors searched hospital trust websites to determine which ones were on Twitter and found that 75 out of 166 had a Twitter presence. They also collected 198,499 tweets covering the period 17 April 2012 to 26 June 2013 and randomly selected 1,000 tweets for a quantitative content analysis and a more nuanced qualitative content analysis. It is worth further highlighting three methodological points about this study.

- In the interests of confidentiality, all of the quotations anonymized people, hospitals, and wards.
- Greaves et al. (2014) note that when compared to a study of reviews of hospital care posted on review websites, there was far more frequent mention of technical aspects of care. The researchers speculate that this may be due to the fact that tweets have to be brief (at that time, the maximum length was 140 characters). This suggests a possible limitation of using tweets as documents for the purposes of content analysis—their brevity can act as a constraint on what can be written and therefore on what can be inferred about their meaning. Irony or sarcasm, for example, can be very difficult to detect in tweets.
- The decision to sample randomly is a sensible way forward when the population of relevant tweets is so large (nearly 200,000). An alternative might be to use **purposive sampling**, but that would require reading through a huge number of tweets to establish whether they meet the criteria being employed. **Theoretical sampling** might be a better option, since the researcher would be able to stop reading the tweets once the saturation of theoretical categories had been achieved.

Research in focus 22.10 suggests another way of drawing a manageable sample of 'documents' from the wealth of data on Twitter, and Research in focus 22.14 demonstrates that Facebook can be subjected to the same kind of analysis.

RESEARCH IN FOCUS 22.10
Analysing digital media: social media

Schneider (2016) conducted qualitative content analysis on a number of tweets in order to explore how the Canadian Toronto police present themselves through Twitter. He went through a multi-stage process to identify tweets that would help him address his **research questions**.

1. He used search terms to identify appropriate Twitter accounts and tweets, generating 105,801 tweets.
2. He identified certain useful themes in these tweets, including that of 'police professionalism', using an ethnographic content analysis approach.
3. He used search terms to identify the tweets associated with the concepts he had developed, creating another data set. (The term 'professional', for example, produced 124 tweets.)
4. Given that many of the key terms Schneider wanted to develop (including 'professional') can mean different things, he then searched for tweets that related to their different facets. (For example, there were 34 tweets relating to the idea that police officers are apolitical enforcers of the law.)
5. Schneider continued this process for each of the key terms that he wanted to develop, selecting tweets using a theoretical sampling procedure—that is, on the basis of their theoretical relevance and with the goal of saturation in mind.

Schneider's techniques enabled him to narrow down the vast number of relevant tweets to a reasonably-sized sample that would be suitable for the kind of close scrutiny associated with qualitative forms of content analysis. One of Schneider's research questions was 'How does the use of Twitter contribute to the development and expansion of police presentational strategies?' Through his ethnographic content analysis, he showed that the officers used Twitter to present official accounts but often also about off-duty activities (such as attending a sporting event), giving an impression of being thoroughly engaged in police work and creating a form of organizational publicity that seeks to enhance the public's trust in the police.

22.7 Interpreting documents

We discuss the different ways of qualitatively interpreting documents in some depth in Chapter 23, but here we highlight an important consideration when analysing this form of data—the extent to which documents reflect reality—and briefly outline the main approaches researchers take to document analysis.

Do documents reflect reality?

The extent to which documents reflect reality is an ongoing issue, and it has implications for how we interpret documents. It is tempting to assume that documents reveal something about an underlying social reality (see Section 2.4 on **ontology**). This would mean, for example, that the documents that an organization generates (minutes of meetings, newsletters, mission statements, job descriptions, and so on) are representations of the reality of that organization. In other words, we might take the view that such documents tell us something about what goes on in that organization that will help us to uncover such things as its culture or its ethos. According to this view, documents are windows onto social and organizational realities. However, some writers have suggested that rather than viewing documents as ways of gaining access to an underlying reality, we should see them as a distinct level of 'reality' in their own right. Coffey (2014), for example, argues that documents should be examined in terms of both the context in which they were produced and their implied readership. When viewed in this way, documents are significant for what they were supposed to accomplish and who they are written for. Any document should also be seen as linked to other documents, because they will often refer to and/or be a response to other documents, and other documents form part of the context or background to the creation of the document. Atkinson refers to the interconnectedness of documents as **intertextuality**. The central message of Coffey's argument is that documents have a distinctive ontological status in that they form a separate reality, a 'documentary reality', and should not be taken to be 'transparent representations' of an underlying organizational or social reality. This position is broadly **constructionist**, but one that also recognizes that documents do have their own independent reality as objects (see Section 2.4).

Let's take the example of the minutes of a meeting in an organization. This is the kind of document that might interest a social scientist because, at a basic level, it is a record of such things as the issues raised at the meeting; the discussion of those issues; the views of the participants; and actions to be taken. It might reveal the culture of the organization, its preoccupations, and/or possible disputes among the meeting participants. However, the researcher has to remember that the minutes are likely to be written with external scrutiny in mind, as this form of document is produced not only for participants but also—and arguably more so—for other people. This might include, for example, members of other departments or organizations, or even the general public in the case of a public-sector organization. The awareness of the potential audience may mean that disagreements are suppressed in the meeting and/or within the minutes themselves. The agreed actions may also reflect the participants' desire to demonstrate that they are addressing important issues, rather than because the speakers have a genuine desire or intention to act on them. We noted that documents are always interconnected, and the minutes are likely to be connected either explicitly or implicitly to other documents generated by that organization—such as previous minutes, mission statements, job descriptions, organizational regulations. For these reasons, any minutes that are generated by organizations should be examined for the ways that their creators use language to convey certain messages.

All of this means that we need to recognize documents for what they are—namely, texts or images created with distinctive purposes in mind—and not as simply reflections of reality. So, if a researcher wants to use documents to help them understand aspects of an organization and its operations—in other words, to tell them something about an underlying reality—they are likely to need to strengthen their analysis by employing other sources of data regarding that reality and the contexts within which the documents are generated. These other sources will help the researcher develop a contextual understanding of the documents and their significance. We can see this with Tom's study of Myra Hindley's prison files (Clark 2019—see Research in focus 22.2). As Tom notes: 'Hindley's version of her life-history is not definitive, inevitable, or necessarily falsifiable' (Clark 2019: 13). The autobiographical letter had a life history of its own, and that history needs to be understood in relation to other documents that were generated by significant individuals, the general administration of her sentence, and the wider penal policy of the time.

It is important to remember that a document is rhetorically designed to 'do something'. Indeed, documents are often parts of chains of action that can be potential research topics in their own right. An example that is relevant here is Wästerfors and Åkerström's (2016) examination of institutional reports written by staff in a Swedish institution for 'troublesome boys'. The case files can be analysed for their meaning (as in Research in focus 22.2) but the researchers also suggest that these documents construct particular versions of reality. They write:

> The 'documentary reality' (Smith, 1974) of these case histories revealed a discourse in which staff members textually represented the boys by what we call (1) trouble zooming, (2) mood notes and (3) deflecting staff agency. Taken altogether, these techniques produce 'working versions' of the boys—unfinished portraits or running sketches—that serve as a resource so that staff can put characters and events into an institutionally preferred order.
>
> (Wästerfors and Åkerström 2016: 872)

The authors found that interpersonal troubles that occurred within everyday settings were emergent, negotiable, and contextual. However, those events were represented within the files using a set of discursive techniques that protected staff from social complexities and criticism. This was similar to the way that Vaughan (2006) found US Presidential Commission reports were written in a way that deflected blame from the president and from US foreign policy (see Research in focus 22.11). Wästerfors and Åkerström's (2016) approach is part of a shift in how documents are now regarded for research purposes. Many researchers continue to focus on content, but there is widespread awareness of the importance of being attuned to the significance of documents

RESEARCH IN FOCUS 22.11
Do documents reflect reality?

Vaughan (1996) wrote a highly regarded book on the accident that occurred in January 1986 when the *Challenger* space shuttle burst into flames just after its launch, killing the seven crew members on board. Vaughan had been interested in what she calls the 'dark side' of organizations and wanted to use this tragic incident as a **case study** for understanding the chain of individual and organizational factors that led to the decision being made to launch the shuttle in spite of evidence of possible problems.

Vaughan examined a wide range of data sources:

- a huge report written by the Presidential Commission that was appointed to investigate the *Challenger* accident;
- an archive of NASA documents;
- other investigations of the accident;
- transcripts of hearings in the US House of Representatives;
- transcripts of 160 interviews conducted by government investigators with people involved with *Challenger*;
- risk-assessment documents that Vaughan requested under the US Freedom of Information Act; and
- numerous interviews that Vaughan herself conducted (Vaughan 2004).

Vaughan (2006) points out that documents such as the Presidential Commission report can be extremely illuminating in terms of the kinds of issues that are emphasized and the ways in which the issues are framed. She went on to examine two further Commission reports on major incidents: the *Columbia* Accident Investigation Board report, which dealt with another space shuttle disaster that took place in February 2003; and the Commission report into the 9/11 terror attacks.

Vaughan shows that each report was shaped by a dominant frame, and these were an 'accident investigation frame'; a 'sociological frame'; and a 'historical/war frame', respectively (2006: 304). She notes that the 9/11 report attributed what she calls 'regulatory failure' as the cause of the attacks (2006: 300). This put the responsibility onto the agencies charged with upholding national security and meant that the president, and to some extent US foreign policy, were absolved of responsibility. Vaughan's examination of the documents implies that they can tell us about such things as how those responsible for producing official reports on major incidents construe the background and **causal** precedents of those incidents. The reports are interesting as much for where they show that responsibility does *not* lie, as for where they actively place responsibility.

in terms of the parts they play and are intended to play in organizations and social life in general.

Approaches to interpreting documents

Two common approaches for analysing documents within a qualitative or mixed methods strategy are qualitative content analysis and **semiotics**—although it is also worth highlighting that **discourse analysis** is also often used in conjunction with documents. We cover this approach in depth in Chapter 21, but Research in focus 22.12 provides an example of how researchers can use **critical discourse analysis** to interpret the kinds of document we have considered in this chapter.

Qualitative content analysis

Qualitative content analysis is probably the most prevalent approach to analysing documents. It involves searching for underlying themes in the materials being analysed and can be seen in several of the studies we have discussed in this chapter (see Snee 2013, Goodings et al. 2013, and Schneider 2016, for example). According to Schreier (2014), the method has three advantageous characteristics: it reduces data; it is relatively systematic; and it is flexible. It reduces data because it takes a large amount of qualitative material and attempts to identify core patterns of latent and manifest meaning; it is systematic because it follows a relatively transparent method of **coding** and categorizing data (often using a codebook); and it is flexible because it can operate inductively or **deductively**.

22

In qualitative content analysis, researchers usually illustrate the themes they identify with examples from the documents—for example, brief quotations from a news article or magazine. Snee identified four themes through her analysis of gap year blogs (see Research in focus 22.9). She arrived at these themes inductively and they reveal the main elements of **thematic analysis**, which we examine in Chapter 23. She illustrates the second of the four themes—that of 'feeling out of place'—using several quotations from blogs, one of which is striking because it describes an account of travelling in a Western country:

> We were slightly nervour [nervous] about travelling on teh [the] subway esp[ecially] later in the evening. However it wasnt [sic] too bad despite getting a few looks and for a whi;e [while] travelling in a carriage where we were the only white people out of 20 or so people (Hugo).
>
> (quoted in Snee 2013: 151)

Research in focus 22.13 provides another example of a qualitative content analysis that illustrates some of its typical components.

In their study of Facebook posts associated with the 2011 Vancouver riots (see Research in focus 22.14), Altheide and Schneider (2013) outlined a similar form of qualitative content analysis called **ethnographic content analysis** (ECA) that is particularly useful for analysing media content. Schneider and Altheide's approach differs from more quantitative content analyses (see Chapter 13 and Key concept 13.1), in that the researcher is constantly revising the themes or categories that they have distilled from the documents. As they put it:

> ECA follows a recursive and reflexive movement between concept development—sampling—data collection—data coding—data analysis—interpretation. The aim is to be systematic and analytic but not rigid. Categories and **variables** initially guide the study, but others are allowed and expected to emerge during the study, including an

RESEARCH IN FOCUS 22.12

Using critical discourse analysis to interpret digital media

Farkas et al. (2018) used critical discourse analysis to interpret racist discourses on fake Facebook pages that claimed to speak on behalf of Muslims in Denmark. They were interested in the ways in which disinformation around Muslim identities was disseminated through digital media. Critical discourse analysis was a suitable approach for interpreting these digital documents because of its capacity to provide insights into the way in which language produces and legitimates racism in digital environments. As Farkas et al. (2018: 468) observe, '[u]nderstanding racism relies on critically examining the articulation of antagonism: how the construction of "us" relies on the production of them'.

Focusing on 11 Facebook accounts—which involved looking at 77 posts, the 'about' sections, profile images and photos, as well as over 1,000 user comments and 'likes'—the researchers found that a variety of mechanisms are used to convey what they call a 'platformed antagonism'. This includes constructing the Muslim identity as a political identity and portraying Muslims as characteristically violent, exploitative, hypersexual, conspiratorial, and systematically organized—all of which is depicted as being in opposition to the Danish national character. The overall effect is to cultivate antagonism between different ethno-cultural identities.

RESEARCH IN FOCUS 22.13

Identifying themes in news articles

Wood et al. (2014) carried out a qualitative content analysis of articles that addressed the harms associated with alcohol consumption in seven UK and three Scottish national newspapers between January 2005 and May 2012, when legislation had just been passed to impose a minimum unit price on alcohol in Scotland. The authors searched two electronic databases—Nexis UK and Newsbank—using the search terms 'alcohol and/or pricing'. They excluded articles that did not make a reference to minimum unit pricing, which left 403 articles to be included in the analysis. The researchers describe their process as follows:

> To develop a coding frame, a random selection of 100 articles were read to identify key themes around alcohol and create thematic categories in the initial coding frame. Using the principles of grounded theory, further batches of 20 articles were read and coded until no new categories emerged. At this point we assessed we had reached 'saturation', having identified all relevant thematic categories . . . Coding of articles was conducted over a 10-week period by three coders . . . working together in close collaboration . . . checking and validating each others' coding . . . All text was re-read and re-coded to discover patterns and anomalous ideas.
>
> (Wood et al. 2014: 579–80)

Wood et al. identified five themes in the articles:

- the extent of harm on people other than drinkers themselves;
- harms being diffused throughout society;
- the economic cost to society at large;
- the harm associated with social disorder and crime; and
- the harm to families.

As Wood et al. observe, their qualitative content analysis reveals how the newspapers framed the debate about minimum unit pricing to the public. They show how the current emphasis on youth binge drinkers may actually serve to constrain a much needed population-based intervention because the focus ignores wider problems associated with alcohol abuse in other areas of society.

RESEARCH IN FOCUS 22.14
Using ethnographic content analysis to interpret social media content

Schneider and Trottier (2012) also conducted a related ethnographic content analysis of the role that Facebook played in the 2011 Vancouver riot, when the Stanley Cup ice hockey game on 15 June 2011 prompted a major public disturbance (see also Altheide and Schneider 2013: 105–14). The researchers examined a Facebook page of photos taken of the riot and 12,587 postings on the main 'wall' of the page. As with Schneider's (2016) Twitter study, all the postings were saved into a .pdf file (though you could use any text-based file). This helps ensure that the documents are preserved and enables them to be easily searched. One interesting theme that Schneider and Trottier (2012) identified was the role of Facebook itself in providing photos and accounts of the activities of rioters and their lack of awareness that their posts meant that they could be prosecuted. As one post put it:

> these people are so stupid!! LOL dont they realize everyone has cameras and will sell you out for a nickel!! AHAHAHAHAHAHAHAHAH!!! yea post those pics, people will recognize you, give your name . . . its gunna be a kina 'wheres waldo' game for locals to play. LETS SEE HOW MANY NAMES WE GET!! A photo says a million things but all the police want is a name.
>
> (quoted in Schneider and Trottier 2012: 65–6)

> orientation to *constant discovery* and *constant comparison* of relevant situations, settings, styles, images, meanings, and nuances.
>
> (Altheide and Schneider 2013: 26; emphases in original)

Altheide and Schneider (2013) write that ECA requires a researcher to go through the following steps:

1. generate a research question;
2. become familiar with the context within which the documents were/are generated;
3. become familiar with a small number of documents (6–10) and consider what the **unit of analysis** is (for example, whether it is articles or incidents, of which there may be several in an article);
4. generate some categories that will guide the collection of data and draft a protocol for collecting the data in terms of the generated categories—the protocol is very similar to the kind of instrument (**coding schedule**) used to conduct a quantitative content analysis (see Figure 13.1);
5. test the protocol by using it for collecting data from a number of documents;
6. revise the protocol and select further cases to sharpen it up;
7. establish a sampling strategy (Altheide and Schneider suggest that this will usually involve theoretical sampling);
8. collect data, which means filling the empty spaces in the protocol for the item under consideration (there will be a protocol for each case) with notes that address each area that needs to be addressed—the researcher is essentially summarizing each case in terms of the areas that the protocol needs to address;
9. conduct data analysis, which includes refining and developing categories;
10. make notes about extreme cases and differences between cases;
11. combine the summaries of cases, drawing attention to extremes and typical cases;
12. bring together findings and interpretation in the writing up.

We can see that ECA involves much more movement back and forth between conceptualization, data collection, analysis, and interpretation than is the case with the kind of content analysis we discussed in Chapter 13. It draws on some elements of **grounded theory**, most notably theoretical sampling, coding, and **constant comparison** (see Chapter 23). Whereas quantitative content analysis usually involves applying predefined categories to the sources, ECA employs some initial categorization but leaves scope to refine those categories and to generate new ones. The highly iterative nature of the ECA process is clear in Altheide and Schneider's (2013: 112) proposal that the goal is to keep searching with an open mind for 'emergent patterns' in the data, making notes as you go along on the key themes. As 'themes continue to emerge, the researcher can then move from open coding (e.g. "criminal") to more specific coding (e.g. activities, actions, etc.).' ECA also emphasizes the context within which documents are generated—so in order to study news reports on a certain issue, a researcher needs to have knowledge of the work of news organizations and journalists (Altheide and Schneider 2013).

Altheide and Schneider (2013) offer some useful advice on the practicalities of using the ECA approach, recommending that researchers do initial searches for key words and phrases in order to familiarize themselves with the data and get a sense of the frequency of key terms. They give an example of the protocol they created for the word 'criminal', which appeared 402 times in their document but in a variety of contrasting ways and contexts. Four interesting elements in the protocol are the following.

- The type of crime: this means indicating what crimes are identified in a post (e.g. arson, vandalism, breach of the peace).
- The theme: this takes the form of specifying whether the posting conveys the riot in a positive or negative light. For example, Altheide and Schneider note the contrasts between criminal or non-criminal and whether those involved were real sports fans or otherwise.
- The perspective: this includes such things as whether the posting is pro-authority and whether it reveals a strong regional identity (e.g. pro-Vancouver).
- The language: the researchers propose considering whether the discourse adopts a criminal justice stance.

The analysis allows the researchers to 'provide insight into everyday members' assumptions and expectations as they pertain to "law and order"' (Altheide and Schneider 2013: 111), such as whether the police and their activities are supported rather than the rioters, and beliefs about the criminal justice system.

Semiotics

Semiotics is generally known as the 'science of signs'. It is an approach to analysing symbols in everyday life and treats phenomena as texts, so it can be used in relation to not only documentary sources but all kinds of other data. Research in focus 22.15 is an example of a study from a semiotic perspective.

RESEARCH IN FOCUS 22.15
A semiotic analysis

Gottdiener (1982; 1997: 108–15) subjected Disneyland in Los Angeles, California, to a semiotic analysis. In so doing, he was treating Disneyland as a text (showing how broad the definition of 'text' is for this approach). One component of his analysis is the idea that Disneyland's meaning 'is revealed by its oppositions with the quotidian—the alienated everyday life of residents of L.A.' (1982: 148). He identifies through this principle nine *sign systems* that involve a contrast between the park and its surrounding environment: transportation; food; clothing; shelter; entertainment; social control; economics; politics; and family. The first of these sign systems—transportation—reveals a contrast between the Disneyland visitor as a pedestrian (walk in a group; a form of efficient mass transportation that is fun) and as a passenger (car is necessary; poor mass transportation; danger on the congested freeways). Another component of his study involves an analysis of the connotations of the different 'lands' that make up the park. He suggests that each land is associated as a signifier with signifiers of capitalism, as follows:

- Frontierland—predatory capital
- Adventureland—colonialism/imperialism
- Tomorrowland—state capital
- New Orleans—venture capital
- Main Street—family capital

(Gottdiener 1982: 156).

The main terms used in semiotics are:

- the **sign**—that is, something that stands for something else, and that is made up of the *signifier* and the *signified*;
- the *signifier* is the thing that points to an underlying meaning (the term *sign vehicle* is sometimes used instead);
- the *signified* is the idea or concept to which the signifier points;
- a **denotative** meaning is the manifest or more obvious meaning of a signifier, so indicates its function;
- a *sign-function* denotes the purpose of that meaning;
- a **connotative** meaning provides further social context in addition to the signifier's denotative meaning;
- *polysemy* refers to the fact that signs are always capable of being interpreted in many ways;
- the ***code*** is the generalized meaning that interested parties may try to instil in a sign (a code is sometimes also called a *sign system*).

A traffic light, for example, is made up of signs. The red light is a signifier because it points to an underlying, signified, meaning—stop. So the purpose of the denotative meaning of this particular sign is to induce an approaching driver to stop their vehicle. This is the sign-function. Particularly within contemporary Western contexts, the connotative meaning of red more generally is danger, and this is exactly why the colour is used in traffic lights. However, while road planners might instil a very rigid code into the sign system of a traffic light, in some contexts drivers may still choose to interpret that red light in different ways. Unfortunately, not everyone always stops at a red light. This is an example of polysemy.

Semiotics often aims to uncover the hidden meanings that lie within texts ('texts' being very broadly defined). Let's take as an example the resumé or curriculum vitae (CV) that you might use to gain employment. The typical CV contains features such as personal details; education; previous and current jobs; and administrative responsibilities and experience. We can treat the CV as a system of interlocking signifiers that signify, at the level of denotative meaning, a summary of the individual's experience. This is its sign-function. At the connotative level, however, it also serves an indication of an individual's value, particularly in connection with their potential employability. Each CV can be interpreted in many different ways and is therefore polysemic, but there is a code that means that certain attributes of CVs are seen as especially desirable, so these elements have more universally-attributed meanings. Job seekers are well aware of this latter point, so will usually devise their CVs to try to emphasize and amplify the desired qualities in accordance with the particular job they are applying for.

The main strength of semiotics is the way that it invites the analyst to try to see beyond and beneath the apparent ordinariness of everyday life and its manifestations. However, although writers will aim to provide a compelling explanation of the semiotics of the texts they analysed, the analysis provided can sometimes feel a little arbitrary. This sensation is probably unfair to the approach, because the results of a semiotic analysis are probably no more arbitrary than any interpretation of documentary materials or other data. In fact, proponents of semiotics could argue that a sense of arbitrariness in interpretation is inevitable, given that the principle of polysemy lies at the heart of semiotics.

22.8 An overview of documentary research

This chapter demonstrates the potential that documents can have as a form of qualitative data. Documents are particularly useful where the researcher would have little or no chance of being able to access the people, places, or organizations necessary to collect first-hand data for themselves. In part, this is why documents are particularly useful in historical contexts, but they can also be used to cross-reference different perspectives and triangulate data, or to explore how particular realities are created and communicated within everyday and professional life. As we have seen, documents can also take many different formats. These include personal letters, diaries, and photographs; organizational material such as minutes of meetings, policy reports, press releases, and advertisements; and visual material such as photos and video. Indeed, what can be taken to be a document for the purposes of qualitative research is actually very broad, and we have only reviewed a very small range of the documentary materials that can be used for qualitative purposes. These potentials are extended yet further when we consider documents such as websites, social media, and online forums. Interest in these areas is growing to include podcasts, vlogs, and certain forms of '**Big Data**'. Advances in digital document processing and Optical Character Recognition are being made all the time, and the processing hardware and software required is becoming more and more user-friendly. There is much potential for social research within these developments.

But regardless of their availability and usefulness, documents always require careful consideration. To this end, we have used Scott's criteria to demonstrate how all documents need to be approached with caution. This includes thinking carefully about issues of authenticity, credibility, representativeness, and meaning.

From the outset of any research project that incorporates documents it is also important to consider what type of data analysis you will employ, as this influences how the documents are to be approached and interpreted. We have introduced the more common varieties of documentary analysis—qualitative content analysis and semiotics—in this chapter, but other approaches such as discourse analysis, which we discussed in Chapter 21, are also compatible with documents.

A further consideration when working with documents is the ethical concerns attached to this type of research (see Chapter 6). When working in public archives, the ethics of documentary research are generally straightforward, in that the material is in the public domain already. However, it is still worth noting any guidance that the curators of the archive give on the ownership, publication rights, and confidentiality that apply to the archive's contents. Private archives, on the other hand—which could include family documents—will require greater attention to the requirements of the archive in question, and researchers have a responsibility to use material in a legal and ethical manner. Before you enter an archive it is worth discussing these points with the archive's owner or curators:

- how the material will be used—including whether images can be taken of any documents;
- whether it is either desirable or possible to anonymize data;
- the ownership and copyright of the material; and
- any rights of approval associated with publication of the material.

It is always useful to make sure that you explicitly reflect upon and, where appropriate, record your reflections on these issues when you write up your research.

The ethics of working with mass media documents are more nuanced, and it will be worth revisiting Chapter 6 to examine some of these issues in further depth (in particular Section 6.5 on ethical decision-making).

So, while documents are certainly not without limitations for the purposes of qualitative research, and working with them requires caution and some consideration of potential ethical concerns, they provide the social researcher with some fantastic opportunities to think creatively about data collection and analysis.

KEY POINTS

- Documents constitute a very varied set of data sources, which include personal documents, official documents from both the state and private sources, the mass media, visual objects, and online content such as blogs and social media.
- These materials can be the focus of both quantitative and qualitative enquiry, but in this chapter we have emphasized the latter.
- Documents of the kinds we have considered can be in printed, visual, digital, or indeed any other retrievable format.
- Criteria for evaluating the quality of documents (devised by Scott 1990) are authenticity, credibility, representativeness, and meaning. The relevance of these criteria varies according to the kind of document being assessed.
- There are several ways of analysing documents within qualitative research. In this chapter we have covered qualitative content analysis, semiotics and, very briefly, discourse analysis.

QUESTIONS FOR REVIEW

1. What do we mean by the term 'document'?
2. What are Scott's four criteria for assessing documents?
3. Outline the different kinds of personal documents and the main considerations or potential issues for each in terms of Scott's criteria.
4. What might be the role of personal documents in relation to the life history method?
5. What uses can family photos have in social research?
6. What potential do official documents deriving from the state have for social researchers, and how do they stand up in relation to Scott's criteria?
7. What kinds of documents might be considered official documents deriving from private sources, and how do they perform in relation to Scott's criteria?
8. What kinds of documents constitute mass-media outputs, and how do the main types of this form of document fare in terms of Scott's criteria?
9. Do online documents and other digital outputs raise particular problems in terms of Scott's criteria?
10. How do the different kinds of digital media documents differ from each other in terms of their potential for research and the challenges they pose?
11. In what sense—and to what extent—can documents provide evidence that social researchers can draw on as data?
12. How does qualitative content analysis differ from the kind of content analysis we discussed in Chapter 13?
13. What is a sign, and how central is it to semiotics?
14. What is the difference between denotative meaning and connotative meaning of a signifier?

ONLINE RESOURCES

www.oup.com/he/srm6e

You can find our notes on the answers to these questions within this chapter's **online resources**, together with:

- *audio/video comments* on this topic from our 'Learn from experience' panellists;
- *audio discussion from the authors* on Scott's criteria for assessing documents (review question 2);
- *self-test questions* for further knowledge-checking;
- a *flashcard glossary* to help you recall key terms; and
- a *Student Researcher's Toolkit* containing practical materials and resources to help you conduct your own research project.

CHAPTER

23

QUALITATIVE DATA ANALYSIS

CHAPTER GUIDE

In this chapter, we will examine some general approaches to qualitative data analysis and demonstrate the process of coding data in qualitative research, which is the main feature of many of these approaches. We will explore

- analytic induction as a general strategy of qualitative data analysis;
- grounded theory as an all-encompassing approach to qualitative research, including its main features, processes, and outcomes, along with some of the criticisms that are made of the approach;
- coding as a key process in qualitative data analysis, in terms of what it involves and some of the limitations of relying on the coding process;
- thematic analysis as a strategy for analysing qualitative data that is dependent on coding as a way of identifying themes in the data;
- narrative analysis as an alternative approach to data analysis that does not result in data fragmentation;
- synthesizing findings deriving from qualitative studies;
- computer-assisted analysis of qualitative data.

23.1 Introduction

One of the major strengths of qualitative research is the depth and richness of the data it produces (think of the reams of material you might collect from recordings of two or three focus groups), but these positive attributes also mean that it is not always straightforward to analyse. Miles (1979) described qualitative data as an 'attractive nuisance' for this reason. There is also the fact that there are many different ways of approaching qualitative analysis, and many writers would argue that fixed rules for analysis are not necessarily desirable (see Bryman and Burgess 1994b). But what qualitative research *does* provide are some broad orientations to data (see Okely 1994), and it is to discuss these that we have written this chapter. The chapter is also supplemented by video tutorials and guidance documents to support you in conducting qualitative data analysis using the software package NVivo, if you decide to use this tool after reading Section 23.9. (Note that NVivo will not be appropriate for every project.) These materials can be found within our **online resources**.

23.2 An overview of qualitative data analysis

The most frequently cited general strategies for doing qualitative data analysis are analytic induction, grounded theory, thematic analysis, and narrative analysis, so they are our focus in this chapter (for further coverage, see Miles et al. 2019). By 'general strategy' of qualitative data analysis, we simply mean an established set of principles and practices that guide the coding and analysis of data. As we will explain, one of the ways in which qualitative and quantitative data analysis differ is that you will almost always do quantitative analysis *after* you have collected your data (though, as we note in Section 15.2, it is crucial to give consideration to the analysis phase before collecting data). By contrast, approaches to qualitative analysis are often described as *iterative*—that is, there is a repetitive interplay between the collection and analysis of data. The qualitative researcher starts the analysis after *some* of the data have been collected, and this shapes the next steps in the data-collection process. Consequently, while approaches such as grounded theory, analytic induction, and narrative analysis are described as strategies of *analysis*, they can also be viewed as strategies for *collecting* data.

For this reason, we begin by considering analytic induction and grounded theory, as both of these strategies have implications for how data is collected. We then focus on the process of coding, which is central to grounded theory, before considering the other two general analysis strategies of thematic analysis and narrative analysis. In the final sections of this chapter we look at the process of synthesizing qualitative studies—ways of combining their findings in a systematic and rigorous way—and the use of CAQDAS, or computer-assisted qualitative data analysis software.

23.3 Analytic induction

Analytic induction is one of the most common general strategies for doing qualitative data analysis, and because it is an iterative approach we can also see it as a strategy for collecting data. We give a definition of analytic induction in Key concept 23.1, and we outline its main steps in Figure 23.1. As the figure shows, a researcher using an analytic induction approach begins with a rough specification of a research question, develops a hypothetical explanation of that problem, collects data on cases that will allow them to interrogate their hypothesis, and examines the cases. If the researcher encounters a case that is inconsistent with their hypothesis, they either *redefine* the hypothesis so as to exclude the deviant or negative case, or *reformulate* the hypothesis to account for it, after which they collect further data. If the researcher chooses the latter path and then finds another deviant case, they must choose again between reformulating or redefining their hypothesis.

FIGURE 23.1
The process of analytic induction

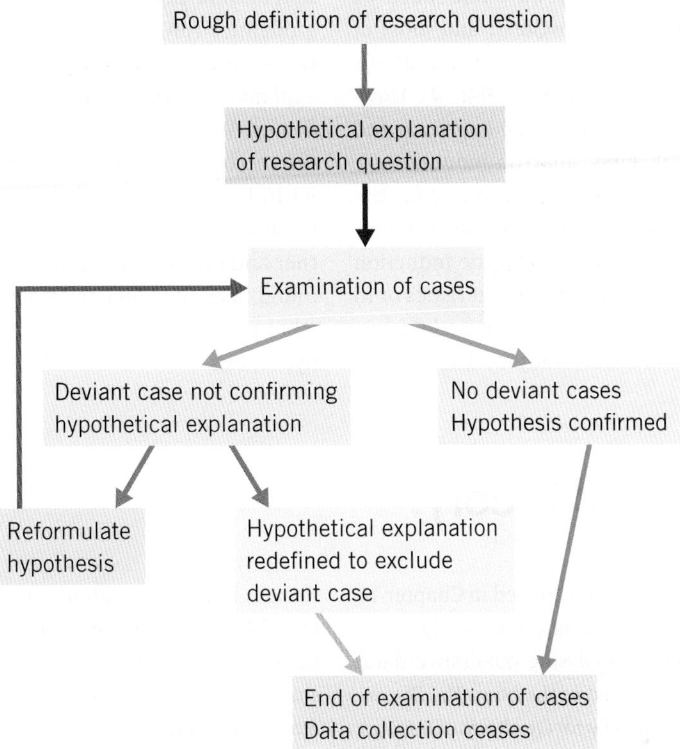

As this brief outline suggests, analytic induction is an extremely rigorous method of analysis, because encountering just one case that is inconsistent with a hypothesis is enough to mean that you need to either collect more data or redefine your hypothesis. Redefining the hypothetical explanation might sound like an easier option, but this is certainly not the case, as shown by Katz's (1982) study of lawyers working to help the poor in Chicago. Katz was interested in finding characteristics that distinguished those who remained in this line of work despite the lower pay and status associated with it. What made them different from those who moved on quickly to work in more lucrative areas of the legal profession? He writes that 'the definition of the explanandum [the phenomenon to be explained] was changed from staying two years, to desiring to stay two years, to desiring to stay in a frustrating place, to involvement in a frustrating place, to involvement in an insignificant status' (Katz 1982: 200). Each shift resulted in Katz having to reanalyse and reorganize his data.

KEY CONCEPT 23.1
What is analytic induction?

Analytic induction is an approach to analysing data in which the researcher seeks to explain phenomena by collecting data until they no longer find cases that are inconsistent with a hypothetical explanation of a phenomenon. First articulated by Florian Znaniecki in his book *The Method of Sociology* (1934), the approach aims to provide an exhaustive knowledge of the situation under study, so that any further research cannot reveal anything new. The logical structure offered by the process, argued Znaniecki, allows us to discover genuinely casual laws. While this promise initially proved attractive, the implicit **objectivist** assumptions contained within the approach have led to a decline in popularity and it is not widely seen today.

Although we can still find examples of qualitative research using this approach—particularly in the fields of education, health, and consumerism—the very specific requirements of analytic induction have not endeared the approach to qualitative researchers, and most of the examples that illustrate it come from the 1940s and early 1950s (Bryman and Burgess 1994a: 4). However, it is still worth being aware of the approach and of two problems with it. First, analytic induction often describes the conditions that are *sufficient* for the phenomenon to occur, but it rarely specifies the *necessary* conditions. This means that analytic induction may find out why people of certain characteristics or in certain circumstances become drug addicts (the focus of one major analytic induction study by Lindesmith, published in 1947), but it does not allow us to say why those particular people became addicts while others in the same situation with the same characteristics did not. Second, analytic induction does not provide useful guidelines (unlike grounded theory) as to how many cases are needed before the validity of the hypothetical explanation (whether reformulated or not) can be confirmed. When do you stop looking for cases that might refute your hypothesis or require you to reformulate it? In Katz's case (1982), we saw that because of the requirements of analytic induction, Katz moved further and further away from his original intention as he found cases that deviated from his initial hypothesis. At what point should he have stopped and redefined his hypothesis?

23.4 Grounded theory

Grounded theory, a concept we introduced in Chapter 16 (see Key concept 16.2), has become one of the most widely used frameworks for analysing qualitative data. The approach was first described in the book *The Discovery of Grounded Theory: Strategies for Qualitative Research* by Barney G. Glaser and Anselm L. Strauss (published in 1967), which must now be one of the most widely cited texts in the social sciences. However, providing a definitive account of the approach is not straightforward.

Following the publication of their initial text, Glaser and Strauss had something of a disagreement and began to develop different versions of grounded theory. Glaser felt that the approach to grounded theory that Strauss was promoting (most notably in Strauss 1987, and Strauss and Corbin 1990) was too prescriptive and put too much emphasis on the development of concepts rather than of theories (Glaser 1992). However, Strauss's writings became more prominent, and his version is largely the one that is followed today. There is, however, considerable controversy about what grounded theory should consist of and the processes that it should follow, and other approaches have subsequently been developed (see Bryant and Charmaz 2019, for example).

23

Some researchers have also highlighted that grounded theory is often very difficult to conduct in practice because of its all-encompassing nature. The approach has to be built in from the very beginning of a study rather than being imposed when data collection is complete. This means that while researchers often claim to have used 'grounded theory' in their studies, in some cases there is little clear evidence of the process that they followed (Bryman 1988a: 85, 91; Locke 1996; Bryant and Charmaz 2019). Sometimes researchers use the term simply to imply that they grounded their theory in data, making grounded theory more or less synonymous with an **inductive** approach. In other cases, researchers refer to having used grounded theory but seem to have only used one or two features of the approach (Locke 1996). We can't really consider such cases to be based on 'grounded theory' in the way that either Glaser or Strauss originally used the term (Walsh et al. 2015).

Against this background, and given the many facets of grounded theory, it can be tricky to identify what the approach is and what it is not. Here, we will simply outline its main features, looking at the tools of grounded theory and the coding and categorizing process it requires, before considering some of the general criticisms that researchers have made of this particular analytical strategy.

Tools of grounded theory

There are, perhaps, four main tools of grounded theory. We have already referred to some of these in previous chapters, so we will mention where you can find further information in this book.

- **Theoretical sampling**—the process by which a researcher selects cases based on the needs of emerging theory rather than on pre-specified criteria. (For more discussion of theoretical sampling, see Section 17.4.)

- **Coding**—a key process in grounded theory. The researcher breaks down the data into component parts, and gives them names or labels. They begin to do this soon after they begin collecting data. As Charmaz (2000: 515) puts it: 'We grounded theorists code our emerging data as we collect it. . . . Unlike **quantitative research** that requires data to fit into *preconceived* standardized codes, the researcher's interpretations of data shape his or her emergent codes in grounded theory' (emphasis in original). In grounded theory, the researcher identifies different types or levels of coding within the data and organizes them as the iterative process of data collection and analysis develops (see 'Coding in grounded theory' later in this chapter).
- **Theoretical saturation**—a process that relates to two phases in grounded theory: the collection of data and the coding of data. In the first instance, data collection reaches a point where new data are no longer helpful or have become repetitious: that is, the data you have already got meet your requirements. In the second, it is the codes or categories themselves that no longer help to elaborate the concepts that you have developed. (For further discussion of theoretical saturation, see Key concept 17.2.)
- **Constant comparison**—an aspect of grounded theory that was prominent in Glaser and Strauss (1967) and that practitioners often refer to as a significant phase. It is the process of maintaining a close connection between data and conceptualization, so ensuring that there is correspondence between codes, categories, and concepts. This procedure requires the researcher constantly to compare the phenomena that they are coding under a certain **category** so that a theoretical elaboration of that category can begin to emerge. Constant comparison also entails being sensitive to contrasts between the categories and concepts that are emerging. This often involves the nuanced examination of existing codes and categories for similarities and differences. It is this process that allows the researchers to elaborate theory.

A further, very practical tool that is important to the process of grounded theory is the **memo**. In simple terms, memos are researchers' notes about the process of analysis. Glaser and Strauss suggest writing memos after you have coded a few phenomena, to aid the process of constant comparison. Memos can take many forms and be used for many different purposes—as illustrated by Research in focus 23.1. A memo might include theoretical notes; explanations of incidents, codes, or possible relationships between concepts; reflective comments; ideas for further development; a point for thinking about **data saturation**; or simply a reminder to do something. Memos act as a record about the meanings of the terms the researcher is using and provide a way of crystallizing their ideas. In this way, memos help to build a secure platform on which the researcher can develop their emerging analysis.

RESEARCH IN FOCUS 23.1
Memos

Morris and Cravens Pickens (2017) made extensive use of memos in their study of the impact of 'unplugging' on individual and interpersonal wellbeing. Unplugging is essentially the act of purposely disconnecting from digital media and technology. Drawing on a total of 29 naturally-occurring blogs and articles written by people who described the process of disconnecting from digital media, the researchers followed Charmaz's **constructionist** (though she calls it constructivist) grounded theory to examine how people experienced 'unplugging' and what the consequences were. Using a hand-coding process (that is, not a computer platform), they used memos throughout the process of analysis. This initially meant recording their 'reactions to the data, questions or uncertainties about the data, ideas, and even conversations directed at the participants' (Morris and Cravens Pickens 2017: 268). However, as their analysis progressed, the nature and purpose of their memo-writing also helped to organize, structure, and explore the emerging theory:

> Using memos as a guide, the primary researcher began piecing different themes together under larger thematic codes such as 'recognising levels of use' and 'experiencing addiction symptoms' serving as sub-themes to the larger thematic code of realizing the dependence. This process continued until the researcher felt like the emergent themes were comprehensive.
>
> (Morris and Cravens Pickens 2017: 268–9)

Coding in grounded theory

Coding is a key process of grounded theory. It involves reviewing **transcripts** and/or **field notes** and giving labels (names) to component parts that seem to be of potential theoretical significance and/or that appear to be particularly important within the social worlds of those being studied. As Charmaz (1983: 186) puts it: 'Codes . . . serve as shorthand devices to *label, separate, compile,* and *organize* data' (emphases in original). Qualitative coding is a different process from coding quantitative data, such as **survey** data. With the latter, coding is a way of preparing data for quantitative data analysis, whereas in grounded theory—and in many approaches to qualitative data analysis—it is an important first step in the generation of theory. Coding in grounded theory is also more tentative than in quantitative contexts, where there is a tendency to think of data and codes as fixed. Instead, qualitative coding tends to be in a constant state of potential revision and fluidity. The data are treated as potential **indicators** of concepts, and the indicators are *constantly compared* (see the previous section on 'Tools of grounded theory') to see which concepts they best fit with. As Strauss put it: 'Many indicators (behavioral actions/events) are examined comparatively by the analyst who then "codes" them, naming them as indicators of a class of events/behavioral actions' (1987: 25).

Grounded theory practitioners tend to see coding as a progression through a series of stages. Two different ways of representing and classifying this progression have been developed: one by Strauss and Corbin (1990) and the other by Charmaz (2006; Thornberg and Charmaz 2014). Table 23.1 sets out the main stages of each approach, allowing you to see how they differ.

Let's consider the two approaches in turn. We can see that Strauss and Corbin (1990) distinguish between three types of coding practice: *open coding, axial coding,* and *selective coding*. Each relates to a different point in the development of categories in grounded theory. While the phase of open coding is relatively exploratory, the idea of axial coding it is sometimes seen as closing off the dynamic nature of qualitative data analysis and has been controversial because of this. Linvill and Warren (2020) provide a useful example of the move from open coding to axial coding in their analysis of tweets that appear to emanate from 'troll factories': large-scale and organized attempts to spread disinformation through bogus social media accounts. They looked at nearly 3 million tweets associated with 1,858 Twitter handles (accounts) and write:

> First, we engaged in a process of unrestricted open coding, examining, comparing, and conceptualizing the content. We considered elements of tweets including the hashtags

TABLE 23.1
Two approaches to developing concepts and theories in grounded theory

The Strauss and Corbin approach	The Charmaz approach
Open coding: 'the process of breaking down, examining, comparing, conceptualizing and categorizing data' (Strauss and Corbin 1990: 61). This process of coding produces concepts, which are later grouped and turned into categories.	*Initial coding*: 'When researchers conduct initial coding . . . , they compare data with data; stay close to and remain open to exploring what they interpret is happening in the data; construct and keep their codes short, simple, precise and active; and move quickly but carefully through the data' (Thornberg and Charmaz 2014: 156). This often involves assigning codes to each line of text.
Axial coding: 'a set of procedures whereby data are put back together in new ways after open coding, by making connections between categories' (Strauss and Corbin 1990: 96). This is done by linking codes to contexts, to consequences, to patterns of interaction, and to causes.	*Focused coding*: 'As a result of doing initial coding, the researcher will eventually "discover" the most significant or frequent initial codes that make the most analytical sense. In focused coding . . . , the researcher uses these codes, identified or constructed as focused codes, to sift through large amounts of data' (Thornberg and Charmaz 2014: 158). 'Focused coding requires decisions about which initial codes make the most analytic sense to categorize your data incisively and completely' (Charmaz 2006: 57–8).
Selective coding: 'the procedure of selecting the core category, systematically relating it to other categories, validating those relationships, and filling in categories that need further refinement and development' (Strauss and Corbin 1990: 116). A *core category* is the central issue or focus around which all other categories are integrated. This is the term Strauss and Corbin use to refer to the central idea that frames an analytical account of the phenomenon of interest.	*Theoretical coding*: 'theoretical codes specify possible relationships between categories you have developed through your focused coding . . . .Theoretical codes are integrative; they lend form to the focused codes you have collected . . . .these codes not only conceptualize how your substantive codes are related, but also move your analytic story in a theoretical direction' (Charmaz 2006: 63). At this stage, the researcher may incorporate ideas from the existing literature to enhance the story that they are developing.

employed by a handle, cultural references within tweets, as well as issues and candidates for which a handle advocated . . . We conducted axial coding to identify patterns and interpret emergent themes. Through axial coding, we identified links and relationships between codes and, through both inductive and deductive reasoning, built a frame to better understand the data. To verify the validity of results, near the end of axial coding, peer debriefing was conducted.

(Linvill and Warren 2020: 4)

It is useful to be aware of the distinction that Strauss and Corbin make between the three types of coding, especially since other researchers refer to them, as Linvill and Warren (2020) do. However, we should also note that in some descriptions of the process the authors seem to place far less emphasis upon the three types, to the extent that they have more recently referred mainly to open coding in their coding process (Corbin and Strauss 2015).

Like Strauss and Corbin, Charmaz (2006) also distinguishes between three main types of coding, and these can also be seen as different phases of coding: *initial coding*, *focused* or *selective coding*, and *theoretical coding*. Initial coding, which aims to provide initial impressions of the data, tends to be very detailed and can often involve a code per line of text. It is crucial that the researcher is open-minded at this stage and generates as many new ideas and codes as necessary to encapsulate the data. Focused coding involves identifying the most common codes and those that are seen as most revealing about the data. This means that the researcher will drop some of the initial codes. However, they may also generate new codes by combining initial codes. The researcher then re-explores and re-evaluates the data in terms of these selected codes. This means that Charmaz's approach is highly iterative: there is a constant cycle between data, coding, and concepts. The third stage, theoretical coding, occurs when the researcher brings together the codes produced in the previous stage to provide a theoretical understanding of the object of interest. These 'higher order' codes and categories balance out the data fragmentation associated with initial and focused coding, and this is the point at which the researcher attempts to build theoretical coherence and understanding of the data.

So, although there are differences in the way these researchers advise conducting the coding process in grounded theory, in both approaches there is agreement that it involves a movement from generating codes that stay close to the data to more selective and theoretically elaborate ways of conceptualizing the phenomena being studied.

Processes and outcomes of grounded theory

The different elements of grounded theory are sketched out in Figure 23.2, but in order to understand this representation you need to be familiar with the products of the different phases of coding. These are the items listed on the right-hand side of the diagram under the heading *Outcomes*. They are as follows.

- **Concepts**—labels given to discrete phenomena. Strauss and Corbin referred to them as the 'building blocks of theory' (1998: 101), and using their approach we would produce concepts through *open coding*.
- **Categories**—concepts that have been developed with the aim of representing real-world phenomena. As noted in Key concept 17.2, a category may cover two or more concepts. This means that categories are more abstract than concepts. A category may become a **core category** around which the other categories pivot. Another key term in relation to categories is **properties**—attributes or aspects of a category. Properties are often built from codes generated during the coding process.
- **Hypotheses**—initial hunches about relationships between concepts that can be explored through the process of theoretical sampling or further coding.
- **Theory**—according to Strauss and Corbin, 'a set of well-developed categories . . . that are systematically related through statements of relationship to form a theoretical framework that explains some relevant social . . . or other phenomenon' (1998: 22). Generally speaking, there are two types or levels of theory.
    - **Substantive theory** relates to theory in a certain empirical instance or substantive area, such as occupational socialization.
    - **Formal theory** is more abstract and can be applied to different substantive areas beyond the one being researched, suggesting that higher-level processes are at work. In fact, the process of generating formal theory usually requires the researcher to collect data from contrasting settings. Examples include socialization or 'Disneyization'. Alan Bryman explored the latter theory in some depth, building on his initial investigation of how the Disney organization constructed the biography of Walt Disney to resonate with the economic and cultural goals of their theme parks, and then going on to demonstrate how such processes are endemic across society (Bryman 1995; 2004).

With these definitions in mind, let's look at the diagram of grounded theory presented in Figure 23.2. It is worth remembering that all diagrams are simply representations, and this is particularly true in the case of grounded theory because the existence of multiple versions of the approach makes it difficult to provide a definitive outline. Some of the more constructionist grounded theorists would probably be uncomfortable with the use of the term 'hypotheses' in such a diagram. Also, it is difficult to visually present the iterative nature of grounded theory—in particular its commitment to the idea that data collection and analysis is dynamic and cyclical rather than being linear in nature. But we have tried to achieve this in Figure 23.2 by showing arrows pointing in both directions between some steps. This diagram implies that the researcher goes through the following process.

- The researcher begins with a general research question (step 1).
- They perform theoretical sampling of relevant people and/or incidents (step 2).
- They collect relevant data (step 3).
- They code the data (step 4), which may, at the level of open coding, generate concepts (step 4a).
- There is a constant movement backwards and forwards between the first four steps, so that early coding suggests that new data is needed, which means the researcher has to sample theoretically, and so on.
- The researcher's constant comparison of indicators and concepts (step 5) generates categories (step 5a). The important thing is to ensure that there is a fit between indicators and concepts.
- Categories become saturated during the coding process (step 6).
- The researcher explores relationships between categories (step 7), and hypotheses about connections between categories emerge (step 7a).
- The researcher collects further data via theoretical sampling (steps 8 and 9).
- Data collection is likely to be shaped by the theoretical saturation principle (step 10) and by testing the emerging hypotheses (step 11), which leads the researcher to come up with substantive theory (step 11a). (See Research in focus 23.2 for an illustration of this process.)
- The researcher explores their substantive theory using grounded theory processes to collect data in different settings from the one(s) in which they generated the theory (step 12), so that they can generate formal theory (step 12a). Step 12 is relatively unusual in grounded theory because researchers typically concentrate on a certain setting, although the investigation we describe in Research in focus 23.3 did examine other settings to explore the emerging concepts. Another way to generate formal theory is by using existing theory and doing research in comparable settings, which is an element of the study in Research in focus 23.2.

FIGURE 23.2
Processes and outcomes in grounded theory

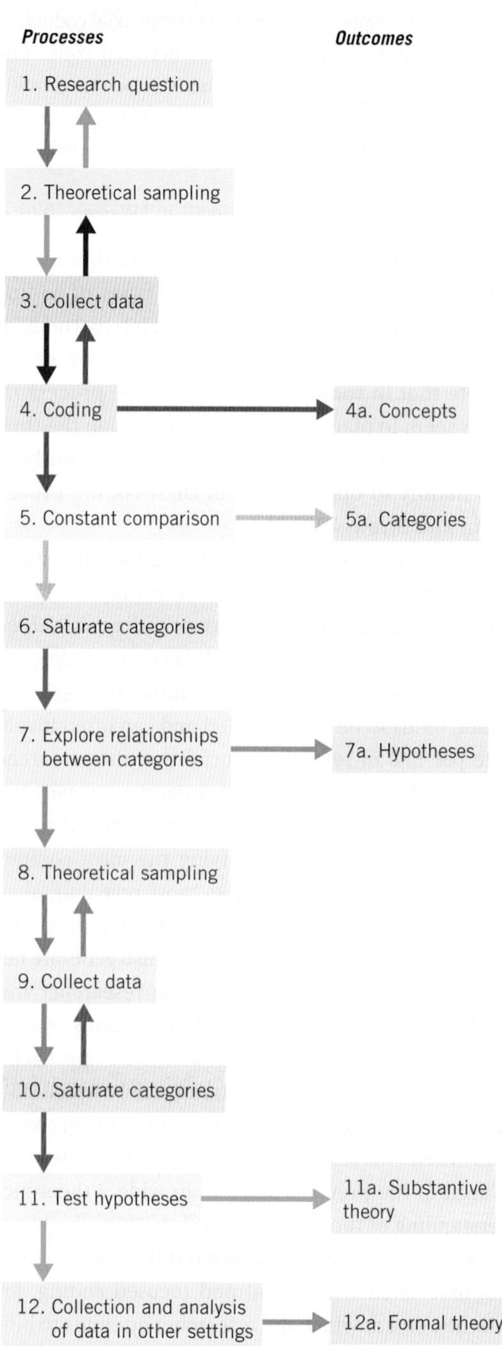

23

RESEARCH IN FOCUS 23.2
Grounded theory: an illustration of the process

Thornberg's (2018) study of school bullying exemplifies many features of grounded theory. Drawing on fieldwork conducted in three public primary schools in Sweden, he began his research with a focus on the social **dimensions** of bullying, and wanted to avoid reducing it to an individual and pathological psychological phenomenon.

Thornberg's data collection and analysis were guided by a constructionist approach to grounded theory, with the first step of initial coding involving open exploration of data, generating codes by constantly comparing data with data, and comparing codes with other emerging codes. Thornberg states that he was guided by a number of key questions, including 'What is happening in the data? What is going on? What are the main concerns faced by the participants in the action scene? What do the data suggest? What category does this incident indicate?' (Thornberg 2018: 147). He then used a phase of focused coding to sift through the data looking for more selective and conceptual codes. This allowed him to examine how codes were related to each other and to identify categories that helped him understand his data. During the analysis, he also used pre-existing theoretical concepts taken from the literature to further elaborate his grounded theory. He selected these according to their relevance to the data and emerging codes. Thornberg found that thinking of bullying as an individual phenomenon blinded educational professionals from seeing how it operated according to gender norms, heteronormativity, racism, and other oppressive mechanisms.

RESEARCH IN FOCUS 23.3
Grounded theory: collecting data in additional comparable sites

Goulding (2009) has discussed the way in which she implemented grounded theory in a study of how visitors experience museums, particularly 'living' museums that try to recreate the UK's industrial heritage. The approach she took was closer to Glaser's than to Strauss's version of grounded theory. Initially, she selected an open-air museum and interviewed the director. She then conducted observations of parties of visitors, noting how they handled the attractions and exhibits. While these relatively unstructured observations were illuminating in terms of how visitors responded to the attractions, they did not generate insights into visitors' motivations, so Goulding conducted interviews with visitors to shed light on such things as their expectations and their perceptions of the exhibits.

She conducted a line-by-line analysis of the interview transcripts, which generated a huge number of codes and words. She reduced this vast array of codes to themes that helped to understand her data, and this produced seven concepts, including the stimulation of nostalgia, the desire for education, and the experience of alienation in the present. Each of these concepts had distinctive properties or dimensions. For example, the stimulation of nostalgia was encapsulated in such things as a sense of retreat from the present and a 'rose-tinted' recollection of the past. However, Goulding felt that she had not saturated her concepts, so she collected new data in two new comparable but different sites. She took the same data-collection approach as with the original site, but the further data did not generate any new concepts. However, the new data did allow her to reinforce her concepts and to produce a categorization of three types of visitor to such museums: existential, purist, and social. For example, existential visitors tended to exhibit high levels of the stimulation of nostalgia (one of the seven concepts derived from the data), which could be seen from their position with regard to such codes as 'selective recall', 'rose-tinted remembrance', a 'rejection of the present', and an 'ability to distort the past'.

Out of the various elements of grounded theory depicted in Figure 23.2, concepts and categories are perhaps the most important. They are at the heart of this approach, and key processes such as coding, theoretical sampling, and theoretical saturation are designed to guide their generation. In fact, it is sometimes suggested that, as a strategy for qualitative data analysis, grounded theory works better for generating categories than for generating theory. This is perhaps because studies claiming to use the approach often generate grounded *concepts* rather than grounded theory.

Criticisms of grounded theory

Although it is popular, grounded theory is not without limitations. These can be summarized as follows.

- The need to be led by the emerging properties of the analysis can be problematic.
- There are practical difficulties with the approach.
- It is debatable whether grounded theory does actually produce theory.
- When describing grounded theory, its proponents are vague on some points, with inconsistent use of key terms.
- Grounded theory encourages fragmentation of data, which some feel can strip it of a sense of context and narrative.
- Generally, it can be difficult to characterize and to implement in practice.

A key criticism has centred around the first problem we've listed: being led by the emerging properties of the analysis. For instance, Bulmer (1979) has questioned whether researchers can suspend their awareness of relevant theories or concepts until quite a late stage in the process of analysis. On the one hand, being led by the emerging properties of the data means that the focus of the research is kept grounded, but on the other, it means that there is heavy reliance on the researcher being able to supress their own ideas about what data might mean. Social researchers are usually sensitive to the key foci and concepts within their chosen disciplines and it seems unlikely that this awareness can be put aside, especially because overcoming issues of subjectivity has long been shown to be problematic (Saldaña 2021). In other words, it is likely that what we 'see' when we conduct research is conditioned by many factors, one of which is what we already know about the social world being studied. Some writers actually take the view that it is desirable that researchers are sensitive to existing conceptualizations, so that their investigations are focused and can build upon the work of others. That said, more recent developments have also suggested that grounded theory could be usefully combined with more computational methods of analysis to help suppress researcher subjectivity—see Research in focus 23.4.

Related to this criticism is the fact that researchers are often required to articulate the implications of their planned investigation before data collection begins. For example, an academic making a bid for research funding or a student writing a dissertation proposal is usually required to demonstrate how their research will build upon what is already known. Researchers are also likely to have to demonstrate that they have a reasonably well defined research question. Both of these things are generally discouraged in grounded theory.

There are also some more practical difficulties with grounded theory. The time it takes to transcribe recordings of interviews, for example, can make it difficult for researchers to fulfil the requirements of both constant comparison and saturation. The time and effort it would take to achieve theoretical saturation would also make it unsuitable for most time-limited student projects. It is also debatable whether grounded theory really results in *theory*. As we have previously suggested, it provides a rigorous approach for generating concepts, but it is often difficult to see what theory, in the sense of an explanation of something, a researcher is putting forward. In many instances, researchers simply *organize* data into a series of related themes rather than examining them to reveal their underlying properties. Indeed, while the goal of grounded theory is the generation of formal theory, most applications of the approach are substantive in character. In other words, they are about the specific social phenomenon being researched and not the broader range of phenomena of which they are symptomatic (though, of course, they *may* have such broader applicability).

Perhaps because of the many subtle changes in its development, grounded theory is still vague on certain points. For example, while Strauss and Corbin (1998: 73) refer to theoretical sampling as 'sampling on the basis of emerging *concepts*' (emphasis added), Charmaz (2000: 519) writes that it is used to 'develop our emerging *categories*' (emphasis added). The term 'categories' is increasingly used rather than 'concepts', but such inconsistent use of key terms is not helpful to people trying to understand the overall process. Related to this point is the fact that grounded theory is very much associated with an approach to data analysis that invites researchers to fragment their data by coding it into discrete chunks. Some writers feel that this kind of fracturing reduces the sense of context and narrative flow (Coffey and Atkinson 1996).

More generally, the fact that there are different approaches to grounded theory means that it is not

RESEARCH IN FOCUS 23.4
Towards a computational grounded theory?

A key criticism of grounded theory has centred around the issue of the researcher needing to be led by the data and the emergent properties of the analysis. This puts a great deal of reliance on the researcher being able to supress their own preconceptions of what data might mean so that what emerges from the data is theory, rather than what the researcher wants to see. However, recent developments in the area have suggested that grounded theory could be usefully combined with more computational methods of analysis to help reduce subjectivity in the earlier parts of analysis. Nelson (2017), for example, has demonstrated how interpretive understanding of qualitative data could be enhanced with the processing power of computer-assisted analysis to come up with a fully reproducible computational grounded theory.

Drawing on a study that explored the development of the first- and second-wave **feminist** movements in Chicago and New York, Nelson suggests a three-step framework. The first is a pattern recognition phase that draws on unsupervised machine learning and automated word scores to identify novel patterns in large qualitative data sets. This essentially reduces large and often messy text into quantitative lists and networks of words. In the second phase—the pattern refinement step—the researcher returns to the data to confirm the viability of the initial findings, add interpretation, and modify or reject patterns where necessary. A final third phase of pattern confirmation then draws on computational processing power again to assess the patterns that the researcher has inductively adjusted.

While the methods suggested by Nelson and others are still being developed, often require knowledge of specialist computer packages, and are by no means without problems, they certainly seem to produce some interesting findings that are grounded in large data sets.

only—as we have noted—difficult to characterize, but also difficult to use in practice. This issue has been exacerbated by Charmaz's (2000) suggestion that most grounded theory is objectivist. She argues that the grounded theory associated with Glaser, Strauss, and Corbin aims to uncover a reality that is external to social actors. Instead, she offers an alternative, constructionist (though, as we have noted, she calls it constructivist) version that 'assumes that people create and maintain meaningful worlds through dialectical processes of conferring meaning on their realities and acting within them. . . . Thus, social reality does not exist independent of human action' (Charmaz 2000: 521). This position contrasts with earlier grounded theory texts that 'imply that categories and concepts inhere within the data, awaiting the researcher's discovery. . . . Instead, a constructivist approach recognizes that the categories, concepts, and theoretical level of an analysis emerge from the researcher's interaction within the field and questions about the data' (Charmaz 2000: 522). It is certainly fair to suggest that Glaser, Strauss, and Corbin seem to neglect the role of the researcher in generating knowledge, but it is not clear that they reject the idea that social reality exists independently of social actors. Strauss was, after all, the lead author of the study we discussed in Chapter 2 (see Section 2.4 under 'Constructionism') exploring the hospital as a negotiated order (Strauss et al. 1973).

Despite these issues, grounded theory is probably the most influential general strategy for conducting qualitative data analysis, and many of its core processes—such as coding, memos, and the very idea of allowing theoretical ideas to emerge out of your data—have been hugely influential.

23.5 Coding qualitative data

Coding is the starting point for most forms of qualitative data analysis (some writers prefer to call the process *indexing*). The coding process usually involves writing marginal memos alongside data (as shown in Table 23.2) and gradually refining those notes into codes, meaning that portions of transcripts can be seen as belonging to certain names or labels. The principles involved in the process have been well developed by writers on grounded theory and others. In this section we will look first at the practicalities of coding qualitative data—the main steps and considerations involved—and then at the problems associated with it.

How to code qualitative data

It is well worth carrying out your coding as soon as possible—ideally you should do it as you collect your data. This will help you develop a detailed understanding of your data and it can help with theoretical sampling. It may also prevent you feeling overwhelmed by a large amount of unstructured data, which can happen if you leave the analysis until you have collected all your data (see Learn from experience 23.1). At the very least, you should begin transcription at a relatively early stage and/or keep your field notes up to date.

The main steps to follow when coding qualitative data are as follows.

1. *Familiarize yourself with your data*. Start the coding process by reading through your initial data without taking any notes or considering an interpretation. When you've finished, write down a few general notes about what struck you as especially interesting, important, or significant.
2. *Re-read your data and write memos*. Read through your data again, but this time keep in mind the kinds of questions listed in Tips and skills 23.1 and begin to make memos about significant remarks or observations. Make as many as possible. Initially, they will be very basic—perhaps key words used by your

LEARN FROM EXPERIENCE 23.1
The relationship between data collection and analysis

Many qualitative approaches to data analysis encourage an iterative process of data collection and analysis. This means that analysis begins early in the qualitative research process and continues in parallel with data collection. This is particularly the case in **ethnography**, where the initial research focus is often quite general at the start and is refined as the researcher spends time in the field. Minke describes this process of familiarization and 'meaning-making':

> During my ethnographic study, the phases of fieldwork, analysis, and writing phase could not always be clearly distinguished. I made field notes of my observations and I conducted interviews that produced notes and transcriptions. These outputs functioned as a tangible product of the fieldwork. But my understanding of the research came through the *process* of doing fieldwork: by gradually accessing the experiences, lives, and meaning-making of the respondents. This process of sense-making also came to be part of the analysis.
>
> My field notes already contained many preliminary (theoretical) insights and ideas. This allowed for a constant comparison between theory and the emerging empirical data. I hand-coded field notes, transcribed interviews, and acquired documents. Initially, I kept the codes very broad, and then elaborated on them using mind maps in which the various aspects of the codes were expanded using my data. Participant observation provided me with the opportunity to easily go back and forth between fieldwork and analysis. It allowed me to ask certain questions to respondents, look for particular situations, and check preliminary insights with respondents. In Italy, for example, I often did this when people would give me a ride home or brought me to the tram or bus stop. I would casually share some things I observed and asked them how they thought I should interpret that, and/or asked if they agreed with my interpretation of it. Respondents showed remarkable interest and asked many questions. These conversations provided a very good opportunity to enhance my analysis and the findings from my project.

Minke

 Access the **online resources** to hear Minke's video reflections on this theme.

You can read about our panellists' backgrounds and research experiences on page xxvi.

respondents or names that you give to themes in the data. When you do this you are *coding*—generating an index of terms that will help you to interpret and theorize in relation to your data.

3. *Review your codes.* Begin to review your codes, possibly in relation to your transcripts. Consider the following.
   - Are you using two or more words or phrases to describe the same phenomenon? If so, remove one of them.
   - Do some of your codes relate to concepts and categories in the existing literature? If so, might it be sensible to use these instead?
   - Can you see any connections between the codes? Is there some evidence that respondents believe that one thing tends to be associated with or caused by something else? If so, how do you characterize and therefore code these connections?
4. *Consider more general theoretical ideas in relation to codes and data.* Try to outline connections between the concepts and categories you are developing. Consider in more detail how they relate to the existing literature. Develop hypotheses about the linkages you are making, and go back to your data to see if they can be confirmed.

Table 23.2 shows an example of coded text—this is the interview transcript segment we considered in Research in focus 19.5, taken from Alan Bryman's Disney study (Bryman 1999). You can see how the data was coded, the labels that Alan used to identify the codes, and how those codes fed into substantive categories (visitor's ethnicity feeding into ethnicity critique) or became categories in their own right (nationality critique).

You should remember when coding that any incident of data can, and sometimes should, be coded in more than one way. Don't worry about generating what seem to be too many codes—at least, not in the early stages of your analysis. Some codes will become and remain useful and others will not. The important thing is to be as inventive and imaginative as possible; you can focus on tidying things up later.

It is also important to keep coding in perspective. Coding is not your analysis—it is just *part* of your analysis, albeit an important part. Coding is a way of thinking about the meaning of your data and of reducing the vast amount of data that you have gathered (Huberman and Miles 1994). Once you have done your coding you will still need to interpret your findings, which means considering the significance of your coded material for the lives of the people you are studying, forging interconnections between codes, and reflecting on the overall importance of your findings for the research questions and the research literature that have driven your data collection.

Problems with coding qualitative data

The main problems associated with coding qualitative data are these:

- the process is laborious and time-consuming;
- fragmenting the data can mean that you lose valuable context;
- it can be difficult to reducing the codes you initially generate to a manageable number.

TIPS AND SKILLS 23.1
Developing codes

When developing your codes, here are some of the key questions you should be asking yourself as you read through your data (derived from Lofland and Lofland 1995).

- Of what general category is this item of data an instance?
- What does this item of data represent?
- What is this item of data about?
- Of what topic is this item of data an instance?
- What question about a topic does this item of data suggest?
- What is happening here?
- What are people doing?
- What do people say they are doing?
- What kind of event is going on?

TABLE 23.2
An example of coded text from Alan Bryman's Disney study (Bryman 1999)

Interviewer	OK. What were your views or feelings about the presentation of different cultures, as shown in, for example, Jungle Cruise or It's a Small World at the Magic Kingdom or in World Showcase at Epcot?		
Wife	Well, I thought the different countries at Epcot were wonderful, but I need to say more than that, don't I?	uncritical enthusiasm	
Husband	They were very good and some were better than others, but that was down to the host countries themselves really, as I suppose each of the countries represented would have been responsible for their own part, so that's nothing to do with Disney, I wouldn't have thought. I mean some of the landmarks were hard to recognize for what they were supposed to be, but some were very well done. Britain was OK, but there was only a pub and a Welsh shop there really, whereas some of the other pavilions, as I think they were called, were good ambassadors for the countries they represented. China, for example, had an excellent 360 degree film showing parts of China and I found that very interesting.	not critical of Disney content critique	aesthetic critique
Interviewer	Did you think there was anything lacking about the content?		
Husband	Well I did notice that there weren't many black people at World Showcase, particularly the American Adventure. Now whether we were there on an unusual day in that respect I don't know, but we saw plenty of black Americans in the Magic Kingdom and other places, but very few if any in that World Showcase. And there was certainly little mention of black history in the American Adventure presentation, so maybe they felt alienated by that, I don't know, but they were noticeable by their absence.	visitors' ethnicity	ethnicity critique
Interviewer	So did you think there were any special emphases?		
Husband	Well thinking about it now, because I hadn't really given this any consideration before you started asking about it, but thinking about it now, it was only really representative of the developed world, you know, Britain, America, Japan, world leaders many of them in technology, and there was nothing of the Third World there. Maybe that's their own fault, maybe they were asked to participate and didn't, but now that I think about it, that does come to me. What do you think, love?	nationality critique	
Wife	Well, like you, I hadn't thought of it like that before, but I agree with you.		

As we have seen, the coding process usually involves writing marginal memos alongside data and gradually refining those notes into codes. You can then identify portions of transcripts as belonging to certain names or labels (codes), and you will need to organize the data accordingly. This often requires cutting and pasting, previously in a literal sense (with scissors and glue) but now usually in word-processing packages. It can also be facilitated by CAQDAS (see Section 23.9), but in the context of a student research project you may decide that your data set is not large enough to make it worth learning how to use a CAQDAS program.

Aside from its time-consuming nature, one of the most commonly mentioned criticisms of the coding approach to qualitative data analysis is the problem of losing the context of what is said. By taking chunks of text out of the narrative within which they appeared, you can lose the meaning of what was being said or described. This results in the fragmentation of data—which means that the narrative flow of what people are saying or doing becomes obscured (Coffey and Atkinson 1996). There has been increased awareness of this issue since interest in narrative analysis began to grow in the late 1980s (see 'Narrative analysis'). Riessman (1993) became concerned about the fragmentation of data that results from coding themes when she came to analyse data she had collected through **structured interviews** on divorce and gender. She writes:

> Some [interviewees] developed long accounts of what had happened in their marriages to justify their divorces. I did not realize these were narratives until I struggled to code them. Applying traditional qualitative methods, I searched the texts for common thematic elements. But some individuals knotted together several themes into long accounts that had coherence and sequence, defying easy categorization. I found myself not wanting to fragment the long accounts into distinct thematic categories. There seemed to be a common structure beneath talk about a variety of topics. While I coded one interview, a respondent provided language for my trouble. As I have thought about it since, it was a 'click moment' in my biography as a narrative researcher.
>
> (Riessman 1993: vi)

Riessman's account is interesting because it suggests several possibilities: that coding fragments data; that some forms of data may not be suited to coding; and that researchers can turn narrative analysis on themselves, as what Riessman provides in this passage is precisely a narrative of her own research practice.

TIPS AND SKILLS 23.2

Getting to a manageable number of codes

If your initial coding of qualitative data produces a large number of codes, do not worry. You simply need to ask questions about what these codes have in common, so that they can be combined into higher-order and more abstract codes, and consider whether any seem to cover the same phenomena, meaning that you can discard the excess codes.

A further problem with the qualitative coding process is that it tends to generate a large and potentially overwhelming number of codes. The first stage of coding that Charmaz (2004) recommends, for example, involves 'line by line coding', whereby virtually every line in a transcript or other source of data is given a code. She argues that this process means that the qualitative researcher does not lose contact with their data and the perspectives and interpretations of those being studied. However, this process will almost certainly result in a huge number of codes, which need to be reduced to a more manageable number. Tips and skills 23.2 suggests some ways of doing this.

Whichever analytical strategy you employ, you should avoid simply saying: 'this is what my subjects said and did—isn't that interesting?' It may be interesting, but your work will only become significant when you theorize in relation to it. Sometimes, researchers are wary of this—they worry that, in the process of interpretation and theorizing, they may not do justice to what they have seen and heard, or that they may contaminate their subjects' words and behaviour. This is a risk, but it has to be balanced against the fact that your findings only gain significance when you have reflected on, interpreted, and theorized your data. You are not there just to describe it.

23.6 Thematic analysis

Another common approach to qualitative data analysis is thematic analysis. Unlike analytic induction and grounded theory, this is solely an approach for analysis and does not inform data collection as well. Thematic analysis also differs from strategies such as grounded theory or **critical discourse analysis** in that it does not have an identifiable heritage and has not been outlined in terms of a distinctive set of techniques. Indeed, the term is often used in quite an imprecise way, and we can identify a search for themes in many if not most approaches to qualitative data analysis, such as grounded theory, critical discourse analysis, **qualitative content analysis**, and narrative analysis. As you can see from Research in focus 23.5, studies can use or draw on a mixture of approaches. Also, for some writers a theme is more or less the same as a code, whereas for others it transcends any one code and is built of groups of codes. Key concept 23.2 provides some criteria for identifying what a theme is.

KEY CONCEPT 23.2

What is a theme?

There are a number of different versions of thematic analysis (e.g. Ryan and Bernard 2003; Braun and Clarke 2006), so it can be difficult to identify what actually constitutes a theme. Generally, we can say that a theme

- is a category of interest identified by the analyst;
- relates to the research focus (and quite possibly the research questions);
- builds on codes identified in transcripts and/or field notes;
- provides the researcher with the basis for a theoretical understanding of their data that can make a theoretical contribution to the literature relating to the research focus.

One increasingly popular form of thematic analysis has been proposed by Braun and Clarke (2006; Clarke and Braun 2013). This popularity is partly due to its theoretical and methodological transparency, but also because it is sympathetic to the emergent properties of the data and those themes of interest that are actively chosen by the researcher. This makes it particularly useful for dissertation research. Braun and Clarke's general method involves a six-stage process.

1. *Familiarization*. This involves **transcribing** interviews or focus groups; writing and reading fieldnotes; or examining documents and other material.
2. *Initial coding*. Thematic analysis follows the basic process of coding described above. The researcher can use 'open' coding to capture the emergent properties of the data, and then do more theoretical coding of concepts as they become relevant.
3. *Identifying themes*. Again, as in the general process of coding already outlined, the researcher needs to compare and contrast any emergent codes with both previous codes and any theoretical concepts of interest. This allows the analyst to elaborate the properties of any emergent themes and make interconnections between data.
4. *Reviewing themes*. The analyst further develops themes by combining them into high-order constructs and by identifying and then searching for sub-themes that help to further articulate their analysis.
5. *Defining themes*. The analyst then develops a narrative that describes the properties of those themes and sub-themes, demonstrating how they may, or may not be, related.
6. *Evidencing themes*. Finally, the analyst uses evidence from the codes that underpin themes to substantiate their analysis. This process also aims to link the theme to the wider literature.

As is the case with much qualitative analysis, Braun and Clarke highlight how these stages should be iterative in nature—analysts need to compare emergent codes, concepts, and themes with previous data. While the process of analysis can actually be left until after data collection is complete (unlike, for example, in grounded theory), we would suggest that it is often very helpful to begin analysis while still collecting data. This will enable your research to be responsive to the emergent needs of the field and the theoretical direction of your research focus.

The Framework approach to thematic analysis

Braun and Clarke's approach is not the only method of thematic analysis: 'Framework' is also a general strategy for carrying out a thematic analysis of qualitative data. This strategy was developed at the National Centre for Social Research in the UK and is described as a 'matrix based method for ordering and synthesising data' (Ritchie et al. 2003: 219).

The idea is that the researcher constructs an index of central themes and subthemes, which are then represented in a spreadsheet that displays cases and **variables**. The themes and subthemes are essentially recurring motifs that have been derived from a thorough reading and rereading of the transcripts or field notes that make up the data. The data is then analysed with reference to the spreadsheet, with any instances of data that correspond to relevant cases and variables inserted directly into the spreadsheet matrix.

Figure 23.3 is a matrix that draws on the coded text in Table 23.2 and that would be used for representing the data on the theme 'Ideological critique'. The four subthemes are presented, and the researcher would copy brief excerpts from the data into the appropriate **cell**. The data shown in two of the cells comes from Interviewee 4, and you can see that it also specifies where these quotes are located within the transcript (in response to Question 14). Ritchie et al. (2003) advise that, when inserting material into cells, the researcher should

1. indicate where in the transcript the fragment comes from;
2. keep the language of the research participant as far as possible;
3. try not to insert too much quoted material; and
4. use abbreviations so that cells do not become too full.

How to identify themes using the Framework approach

As its name implies, the Framework approach is meant to supply a framework for carrying out a thematic analysis of qualitative data, and it provides one way of managing themes and data. It does not tell the user how to *identify* the themes. Identifying themes is a stage or two further on from coding data in terms of initial or open codes (Braun and Clarke 2006). The researcher has to reflect on the initial codes that they have generated and try to gain a sense of the patterns

FIGURE 23.3
The Framework approach to thematic analysis

Theme: Ideological critique

	Class critique	Ethnicity critique	Gender critique	Nationality critique
Interviewee 1				
Interviewee 2				
Interviewee 3				
Interviewee 4		'saw plenty of black Americans' in MK 'but few if any in that World Showcase'. 'Little mention of black history' (Q14)		World Showcase 'only really representative of the developed world' (Q14)
Interviewee 5				

and connections between them. When searching for themes, Ryan and Bernard (2003) recommend looking for several elements.

- *Repetitions*: topics that recur again and again. For example, Green, Steinbach, and Datta (2012: 276) write that when they reviewed interview transcripts derived from their research on Londoners' transport choices, they 'were struck by the frequency of references to responsibilities and the moral significance of transport choices'.
- *Indigenous typologies or categories*: local expressions that are either unfamiliar to the researcher or used in an unfamiliar way.
- *Metaphors and analogies*: the ways in which participants represent their thoughts by comparing them to something else—Ryan and Bernard (2003) give the example of people describing their marriage as like 'the Rock of Gibraltar'.
- *Transitions*: the ways in which topics shift in transcripts and other materials.
- *Similarities and differences*: exploring how interviewees might discuss a topic in different ways or differ from each other in certain ways, or exploring whole texts such as transcripts and asking how they differ.
- *Linguistic connectors*: examining the use of such words as 'because' or 'since', because they point to causal connections in the minds of participants.
- *Missing data*: reflecting on what is *not* in the data by, for example, asking questions about what interviewees omit in their answers to questions.
- *Theory-related material*: using social-scientific concepts as starting points for themes.

Repetition is probably one of the most common ways of identifying themes. Repetition may refer to recurrence *within* a data source (for example, an interview transcript or document) or, as is more often the case, *across* data sources (for example, a collection of interview transcripts or documents). However, repetition in itself is not sufficient for something to be labelled a theme. It must be relevant to the investigation's research questions or research focus. In other words, just because a large number of people who have been interviewed say almost the same thing, this does not necessarily mean that it should be considered a theme for the purposes of research.

Bazeley (2013) is cautious about thematic analysis, arguing that researchers who claim to have used it are often vague about how themes were 'identified' or how they 'emerged' from the data. She argues that it is important not just to specify themes that have been

RESEARCH IN FOCUS 23.5
A thematic analysis

Grogan et al. (2013) were interested in how women relate to their clothes and their body image. They accompanied 20 women aged between 18 and 45 on shopping trips in which they were looking for a dress. The researchers audio-recorded their comments as they tried on the dresses and as they chose the one they eventually purchased. They also body-scanned and photographed each participant. They used the resulting images as visual aids in **semi-structured interviews** that they carried out after the fitting to understand each participant's feelings about the dress and how it fitted them.

The researchers write that they carried out a thematic analysis of transcripts but that this was 'broadly informed' by grounded theory procedures. This involved

- carrying out line-by-line coding 'to identify initial categories' (2013: 383);
- using axial coding whereby the researchers 'combined similar and related categories and investigated the relationships between them' (2013: 383);
- using selective coding 'to confirm and verify the categories and to make changes where necessary' (2013: 383).

The researchers performed this sequence on 11 of the transcripts and used the resulting codes to create a model of the main themes and sub-themes and their interconnections. The researchers then checked this model against the remaining nine transcripts after discussion among the research team. The model comprises four themes: functional aspects of clothes fit; body confidence and clothes fit; clothes dimensions and size coding; and the slim hourglass ideal. Each theme was made up of sub-themes; for example, the theme 'functional aspects of clothes fit' had three dimensions.

- *Clothes should emphasise most attractive features.* For example, one participant, Ellie, said while trying on dresses that she prefers 'something that pulls in at the waist' (quoted in Grogan et al. 2013: 383).
- *Clothes should hide disliked parts of the body.* For example, Mary said of her chosen dress that she liked it 'Because it's a bit flattering for my tummy, otherwise it would stick out a bit, so I think it's good' (quoted in Grogan et al. 2013: 384).
- *Clothes should not expose breasts, thighs, or underwear.* An example is Anna, who said while trying on her dress: 'My boobs [breasts] weren't on show, my bra wasn't on show, and my bum [buttocks] wasn't, you know, my bum and my tum [stomach] were fairly covered up' (quoted in Grogan et al. 2013: 384—text in square brackets is in the original).

In their discussion of their findings, the researchers systematically relate the findings to existing research on body image.

identified but to justify *why* they are important and significant. As we noted in Section 23.4 in relation to coding, researchers cannot simply present the themes accompanied by some illustrative quotations. They need to go further by showing how the themes are significant: for example how they relate to other themes, what their implications are, and how they relate to other literature. The researcher also needs to present the process through which they identified their themes—as Grogan et al. (2013) did in their study of how women relate to their clothes and their body image (see Research in focus 23.5). Having an **audit trail** of key decisions relating to coding, theme identification, and conceptualization, as well as an evidence base for those decisions, is likely to help you justify how you arrived at your chosen themes.

Thematic analysis as the basis for a generic approach to qualitative data analysis

In much the same way that there is a generic **purposive sampling** approach that goes beyond the minor differences between the specific purposive sampling strategies (see Chapter 17), we can also identify a generic approach to qualitative data analysis. The account we set out here mainly draws on thematic analysis as the guiding set of principles (especially Braun and Clarke 2006; Clarke and

Braun 2013), but it also incorporates insights from other writers, most notably Attride-Stirling (2001), Gioia et al. (2012), Ritchie et al. (2003), and Thomas (2006).

The process of analysis is as follows.

1. *Read through at least a sample of the materials to be analysed.* Initially, the researcher needs to become very familiar with the data they have collected (which may be transcripts, field notes, documents, or media). This is a crucial first step.
2. *Begin coding the materials.* The researcher develops their thinking about the data. The coding that takes place at this stage is likely to be at the level of open coding or initial coding, which will probably result in a large number of codes. The researcher gives names or labels to what are usually quite small portions of text.
3. *Elaborate codes into themes.* The researcher next tries to reduce the number of codes by searching for common elements between them so that key codes can be raised to the level of higher-order codes or themes. At this stage, it is a good idea to begin writing summaries (in the form of memos) of what is meant by the codes/themes. The researcher provides names for the codes and themes.
4. *Evaluate the higher-order codes or themes.* For some writers this stage means seeking to combine the codes from Stage 3 into even higher-order codes, but it also might involve searching for sub-themes or dimensions among the codes. The course they choose to take is likely to depend on the level of abstraction of the codes and themes that they developed at Stage 3. Again, writing memos is likely to have an important role.

4a. *Give names or labels to the themes and their sub-themes (if there are any).* This stage involves developing names that adequately reflect the codes that underpin them. The researcher needs to ensure that the names successfully capture large portions of the data and provide genuine insight into the data. The names can at this stage be considered *concepts*.

5. *Examine possible links and connections between concepts and/or how the concepts vary in terms of features of the cases.* The researcher might want to consider whether the concepts are related in a sequence (for example in terms of the order in which they happen), or to examine whether the intensity of some of the concepts varies in terms of what is known about the cases that produced the data (such as women versus men, or mature students versus younger students). Some writers suggest that networks of themes and sub-themes can be constructed to portray the interconnections (Attride-Stirling 2001; Grogan et al. 2013). You could, for instance, think about how you could use a spider diagram or a flow chart to represent your data.
6. *Write up the insights from the previous stages to provide a compelling narrative about the data.* Remember, the themes that you derive are not intrinsically interesting and important. You have to *explain why* they are interesting and important. We consider this in more detail in Chapter 25 on writing up, but you should try to draw inferences about the themes' interconnections with each other and their implications, and it is crucial that you tie your themes to your research question(s) and to the literature that relates to your research focus. You also need to justify how you arrived at the themes and provide a transparent account of the process of reading through transcripts, documents, etc. and the ways in which you identified themes as you coded the data.

Although we have numbered these stages, they do not necessarily follow a strict sequence. In qualitative data analysis there is a constant interplay between conceptualization and reviewing the data. It is a dynamic process rather than a linear one. However, the stages should give you a rough sense of the main elements in thematic analysis and an indication of how they interconnect.

23.7 Narrative analysis

Narrative analysis is an approach to gathering and analysing data that is sensitive to the sense of temporal sequence that people use to tell stories about everyday life. In this section we will look firstly at what narrative analysis is and what it involves before considering some of the criticisms made of the approach.

Features of narrative analysis

Narrative analysis has a different emphasis from the one on coding that we see in both grounded theory and thematic analysis. With narrative analysis, the focus of attention shifts from 'What actually happened?' to

'How do people make sense of what happened?' The last point can be expanded to 'How do people make sense of what happened and with what consequence?', because stories are nearly always told with a purpose in mind—there is an intended effect. Proponents of this strategy argue that most approaches to collecting and analysing data neglect the fact that people see their lives in terms of continuity, and in neglecting this, researchers underestimate the importance of the perspective of the people they are studying. Narrative analysis has mainly been applied as part of the **life history method** (see Chapter 19), but its use can be much broader than this. Mishler (1986: 77), for example, has argued for greater interest in 'elicited personal narratives'. In his view, shared by many others, the answers that people provide within qualitative interviews can be seen as stories that are potential raw material for a narrative analysis. In other words, narrative analysis relates not just to the whole life span but also to accounts of episodes and to the interconnections between them.

For example, in her account of her 'click moment' as a **narrative researcher** (quoted in 'Problems with coding'), Riessman describes how she applied narrative analysis to conventional interview transcript material and then began to uncover the stories her interviewees were telling her. In this case, Riessman was applying a narrative approach to materials that had been gathered in a conventional way for conventional purposes.

Other researchers start out with the intention of conducting a narrative analysis and deliberately ask people to recount stories (e.g. R. L. Miller 2000). Riessman (2004) suggests that a request such as 'Tell me what happened', followed up with 'And then what happened?', is much more likely to provide a narrative account than 'When did *X* happen?' While some narrative researchers prefer to just start people off by asking them to tell their story about an event, Riessman argues that researchers usually need to keep asking follow-up questions to stimulate the flow of details and impressions. For example, in her study of divorce, she often asked 'Can you remember a time when . . . ?' and then followed it up with 'What happened that makes you remember that particular moment in your marriage?'

23

We can see that there are two distinct ways of thinking about narrative analysis: for some researchers it is an approach to analysing different kinds of data; for others, it also involves deliberately trying to stimulate the telling of stories. Coffey and Atkinson (1996) argue that a narrative should be viewed in terms of the functions that it serves for the teller. The aim of narrative interviews, therefore, is to elicit interviewees' reconstructed accounts of connections between events, *and* between events and contexts. This involves examining both the forms *and* the functions of a narrative. Indeed, Miller (2000) suggests that narrative interviews used in the life story method or within **biographical research** are far more interested in eliciting the interviewee's perspective, as revealed in the telling of the story of their life, than with the facts of that life. The interviewer is very much a part of the process in that, for the interviewee, they are fully implicated in the construction of the story. Research in focus 23.6 demonstrates the potential of narrative analysis beyond the life story context, showing the approach being used to explore competing narratives about a particular event—in this case, the collapse of a school–university partnership. Both Research in focus 23.6 and Research in focus 23.7 also demonstrate that, as Riessman (2008) observes, narratives can relate to a specific event as well as to quite long periods of time.

Narrative analysis, then, is an approach to analysing qualitative data that emphasizes the stories that people tell to explain events. But although narrative analysis often involves qualitative interviewing (as in Research in focus 23.7), it would be wrong to view it only in these terms. We can use the approach in relation to documents too, and it provides a potential strategy for analysing these kinds of sources in addition to the strategies we covered in Chapter 22. For example, McKernan (2015; 2018) conducted a narrative analysis of posts that were made to NeoGAF—the most popular video game discussion forum in the USA—about the racial imagery contained within the horror survival video game *Resident Evil 5*. McKernan (2015) used two central dimensions of narrative to analyse the **rhetoric** contained within these online documents: character and plot. In terms of character, McKernan was interested in the figures occupying prominent positions within the narrative and how people posting in the forum portray them. He was particularly interested in how the forum contributors understood racial identity, given that the game was set in Africa. In terms of plot, he looked at the overarching story being told through the evaluations of character and identified two key reactions: on the one hand, denial and hypersensitivity, and on the other, the identification of racism and the dangers of denial. In these respects, McKernan locates the debate in wider socio-political narratives and aesthetics that seek to deny or highlight problematic representations of race in cultural objects. This study demonstrates that narrative analysis has considerable value beyond interviewing.

RESEARCH IN FOCUS 23.6
Narrative analysis of reactions to a specific event

Phelps Moultrie et al. (2017: 6) examined the competing narratives involved in the aftermath of 'a disturbing interaction' between a white male teacher and a first-grade Black student within the context of a partnership between urban schools and a local university in the USA. The incident in question involved a physical altercation between the teacher and student, and the student being accused of impeding the progress of other students in the class. Using theoretical tools associated with critical race theory and organizational narratives, Phelps Moultrie et al. set out to explore how certain narratives gain legitimacy within organizational structures.

The altercation produced at least three contrasting narratives: the teacher's narrative; the school principal's reaction; and the institutional response (that of the university). So while the teacher blamed the parents and highlighted the impact of repeat offenders on the progress of others and on his own evaluations, the principal—a career educator and African-American woman—reflected on a continuing negative discourse that positioned the children as a problem, 'with clear notes of deficit thinking, victim-blaming, and racism' (Phelps Moultrie et al. 2017: 13). Given the situation, the principal believed that the teacher would have to resign. However, framed by an overarching narrative that was promoting the 'successful' partnership between urban schools and the local university, the institutional response was to exclude the school from the programme because it was 'too overburdened' by a changing demographic in which Black and Latin-American students were becoming the majority. This, the partnership suggested, had produced 'a lot of problems' that were not compatible with the aims of the programme—which was to develop schools that had 'gifted' students, effectively meaning (according to the authors) schools with 'a white and more affluent student population' (Phelps Moultrie et al. 2017: 14). The principal was subsequently directed to treat the incident as a lone incident.

So, in terms of the contrasting narratives of what went wrong, the teacher blamed the students and their parents for the students' poor progress; the principal reflected on the difficulties of getting qualified and experienced staff; and, ultimately, the partnership evaded the problem by excluding the school. By taking a narrative approach, the researchers were able to document the process by which 'organizational practices conceal, recast, and reconstruct structural racism across schools' (Phelps Moultrie et al. 2017: 17).

Criticisms of narrative analysis

As an approach to analysing qualitative data, narrative analysis has not gone without critique. Atkinson and Delamont (2006), for example, have highlighted that some researchers have treated narrative representations as relatively unproblematic accounts of everyday and professional life. They note that while narratives are important social phenomena, they cannot be understood without looking at the forms and functions that they take within naturally-occurring settings. Rather than being critical of narrative inquiry itself, Atkinson and Delamont aim to highlight the fact that narratives 'do not speak for themselves'. Like the various types of documents we discussed in Chapter 22 (see Section 22.5), narratives do not exist in a social vacuum, and biographical material cannot provide a privileged way of accessing personal experience and understanding because the retelling is necessarily dependent on the context within which the teller performs the narrative (Atkinson and Delamont 2006: 166). Narratives are no more authentic than other modes of representation, and researchers need to remember to treat narrative as performance.

Another issue is that narrative analysis has splintered into a number of different approaches, so there is no single, widely accepted method that new researchers can follow. For example, Phoenix et al. (2010) draw a distinction between analyses that focus on the content and structure of stories and analyses that emphasize how the stories are conveyed. The latter involve focusing on such things as stories as performances, or the rhetorical devices that are used to convey them. As Riessman (2008: 11) has observed: 'Narrative analysis refers to a family of methods for interpreting texts that have in common a storied form. As in all families, there is conflict and disagreement among those holding different perspectives.' The fact that there are different ways of practising narrative analysis is not a criticism of the approach itself, but it does suggest that students interested in applying it to their data will need to do quite a lot of groundwork to identify what kind of narrative analysis they will be conducting.

RESEARCH IN FOCUS 23.7
Narrative analysis using qualitative interviewing

Carson et al. (2017) note that most narratives of giving birth within the public domain reflect the interests and experiences of middle-class, adult women. This ignores the experiences of early-age mothers, who are often subject to the broader stigma associated with childbearing at 'too early' an age. In order to try and understand how such experiences might be narrated within the wider life-course, Carson et al. interviewed 81 mothers between 15 and 24 years in age. Participants were recruited from a number of different school and community programmes in two metropolitan regions of Canada: British Columbia and Greater Vancouver. The semi-structured interview covered a range of topics that included 'preparations for labour, experiences during labour and birth, and perceptions about others who figured in their stories about giving birth' (Carson et al. 2017: 819).

To facilitate the analysis, Carson et al. drew on a narrative approach described by Cortazzi (2001). This involved examining the participants' narratives in order to identify how the story-tellers understood their narratives. The researchers paid attention to

- the description of events (who, what, where);
- the feelings and reactions that the narrator gives to those events;
- the form that the narrative takes; and
- how the narrator tries to evaluate the events they describe.

Carson et al. (2017: 819) also extended their analytic approach to include 'other characteristics in the stories such as voice, verb tense, points that are emphasized or downplayed, and aspects that may appear contradictory to one another'.

According to Carson et al., three major themes emerged from their analysis. Firstly, the narratives they analysed highlighted the importance of the birth narrative in respect to the identity of 'motherhood':

> Forming an identity as a capable, competent, and mature person emerged as a central theme across the interviews. Constituting oneself as mother and managing the life transitions that accompany that experience were discussed in great detail. Mothers concentrated primarily on establishing themselves as a person 'fit' to be a mother. Stories that emphasised previous experience in caring for children featured strongly.
>
> (Carson et al. 2017: 820)

Secondly, the narratives emphasized both the labour of childbirth and the general desire for a natural birth as key points of reference. Descriptions of stoicism, calmness, and rationality in the face of pain appeared to be highly valued by young mothers and served to legitimize their status as a mother, and they valued the idea of a medication-free birth—as this mother suggested:

> [T]here's 10 centimetres of dilation. You're supposed to dilate one centimetre an hour. So that's pretty much what happened. [Laughs] I, like, had the, like, textbook-perfect birth and didn't have to, like, get an epidural or anything, which I was happy about 'cause I didn't want to use very much medication.
>
> (quoted in Carson et al. 2017: 822–3)

Finally, the narratives demonstrated how the mothers negotiated the social spaces within which childbirth occurred. For some, this involved actively managing who was present during the birth, while for others it meant explaining how they retained a sense of control of those spaces despite decisions being taken for them. What each of the mothers did do was to demonstrate resilience and confidence in negotiating potentially challenging circumstances.

Using narrative analysis enabled the researchers to illustrate how the retelling of birth stories allows young mothers to resist broader social and cultural stigmatizing forces. They are shown as creating narratives that emphasize capability, competence, and maturity, and reinforce the construction of positive identity.

23.8 Synthesizing qualitative studies

We have now looked at the various ways of analysing qualitative data, but as we have seen in other chapters (for example Chapter 14), not all research projects make use of primary data. There is continuing interest among qualitative researchers in how to synthesize qualitative studies—that is, how to combine the findings of existing studies in a systematic and rigorous way. This is particularly the case in disciplines linked to health sciences: organizations such as the Cochrane Collaboration—a network of researchers with interests in medical evidence—are at the forefront of establishing both quantitative and qualitative methods that can provide accessible and credible information to support informed decision-making in health settings. Going beyond more commonplace notions of the **literature review** (see Section 5.3), we use 'synthesis' here to refer to the process of combining the results of a series of related studies in order to produce more powerful conclusions, often associated with 'what works' in a given area. The aims of such a synthesis are similar to the aims of a **meta-analysis** of quantitative studies (see Section 14.3). Synthesizing qualitative evidence provides a rigorous way for researchers to gain a sense of what is known in a particular domain, and it can therefore help to move future research forward.

However, the methods researchers have used for integrating qualitative evidence are not particularly consistent: there are several different approaches (Paterson 2012; Timulak 2014). Noyes et al. (2017), for example, note that there are at least 30 different methods for qualitative evidence synthesis, although they also highlight that approaches to mixed methods evidence are still in their infancy (see Heyvaert et al. 2016 for an overview of current techniques). Methods for qualitative synthesis include meta-narrative, critical interpretative synthesis, ecological **triangulation**, meta-studies, and textual narrative synthesis. Many of these approaches are quite technical and it is not possible for us to cover all of them in this book. We will, though, briefly discuss two of the more prominent approaches—**meta-ethnography** and **thematic synthesis**.

Meta-ethnography

Meta-ethnography, introduced by Noblit and Hare in 1988, was one of the first types of evidence synthesis developed specifically for qualitative research, and it remains popular in healthcare research. Its aim is to achieve an interpretative synthesis of qualitative research (see Research in focus 23.8) and other secondary sources. Like meta-analysis in quantitative research, we can use it to synthesize and analyse information about a phenomenon that has already been extensively studied. But this is where the similarity with quantitative analysis ends, because meta-ethnography 'refers not to developing overarching **generalizations** but, rather, translations of qualitative studies into one another' (Noblit and Hare 1988: 25). Noblit and Hare base their approach on the idea that all social science explanation is comparative, involving the researcher in a process of translating existing studies into their own worldview.

Meta-ethnography involves seven phases that overlap and repeat as the synthesis progresses.

1. *Getting started.* This happens when the researcher identifies an intellectual interest that relates to the types of interpretative evidence that qualitative research produces.
2. *Deciding what is relevant to the initial interest.* Meta-ethnographies are not necessarily concerned with developing an exhaustive list of studies that might be included in a review. Instead, the researcher's main aim is to determine which existing accounts are likely to be credible and interesting to their intended audience.
3. *Reading the studies.* The researcher reads the studies in detail and repeatedly, without moving on to analyse their characteristics.
4. *Determining how the studies are related.* This stage involves the researcher 'putting together' the various studies by determining the relationships between them and the metaphors used within them.
5. *Translating the studies into one another.* The researcher is now concerned with interpreting the meaning of studies in relation to each other. Are they directly comparable or 'reciprocal' translations? Can the concepts used by one study be translated into the concepts used by others? Do they stand in opposition to each other as 'refutational' translations, or do they, when taken together, represent a line of argument that is neither 'reciprocal' nor 'refutational'?
6. *Synthesizing translations.* The researcher compares the different translations and shows how they relate to each other. This may involve grouping them into different types.

RESEARCH IN FOCUS 23.8
A meta-ethnography

Sleijpen et al. (2016) conducted a meta-ethnography to examine the contextual factors that contribute to the ways adolescent refugees cope with adversity and how they develop strategies of resilience. They searched for relevant studies on five electronic databases (CINAHL, Embase, Pilots, PsycINFO, and Pubmed), as well as manually searching reference lists of any articles that matched their search criteria. Their criteria stipulated that articles must be written in English; published in a peer-reviewed journal; qualitative or mixed method in design; include participants aged 10 to 20 years; and focus on refugees and asylum-seekers. Their search produced 26 studies that matched the criteria. The studies used a variety of data-collection methods, including interviews, **focus groups**, observations, and visual methods.

Sleijpen et al. used the process outlined by Noblit and Hare to guide their synthesis. They reported six sources of resilience emerging from their analysis: social support, acculturation strategies, education, religion, avoidance, and hope. Collectively, the results demonstrated that the experiences of young refugees could be quite variable, but also showed 'the universality of the resilience-promoting processes' (Sleijpen et al. 2016: 158).

7. *Expressing the synthesis.* This involves the researcher translating the synthesis into a form that can be understood by the audience for which it is intended.

A central concern of this approach is the interpretations and explanations that existing studies offer, rather than the data that these studies produced. Meta-ethnography translates the interpretations of one study into the interpretations of another one. Although the name of the approach implies that it is to do with synthesizing ethnographic studies, it is usually applied to groups of studies that are qualitative in character, not just ethnographies.

Cahill et al. (2018: 130) conducted an interesting meta-ethnography on several meta-ethnographies that 'described an evaluation or critique of meta-ethnography as a research method'. They identified 10 studies in the literature that matched their inclusion criteria. After synthesizing these studies, they found that there was often considerable variation in how researchers had implemented Noblit and Hare's stages. One of their conclusions was that collaborative work is extremely important for conducting meta-ethnography, because it allows different interpretations of studies to surface, and researchers can then debate and reconcile them. This feature might make it less feasible for a student dissertation, although your supervisor could provide valuable input on selecting studies for inclusion and on the interpretative process.

23

Thematic synthesis

Thematic synthesis essentially applies thematic analysis, which we discussed in Section 23.6, to existing studies in a particular domain. Although thematic synthesis tends to be used for synthesizing qualitative studies, it can include quantitative studies too (Kavanagh et al. 2012). However, to simplify this discussion, we will focus here on its use in qualitative synthesis.

To conduct a thematic synthesis of qualitative studies, the researcher has to specify a clear research question. This is often called the 'review question'. They then have to search for studies that meet the criteria implied by that question, and assess the quality of those studies. This stage of evaluation can also involve excluding studies that do not pass the researcher's quality criteria, but in some cases researchers include all the eligible studies in their evaluation and just take the quality assessment into account when presenting their synthesis. Once the researcher has decided on the final group of studies to be synthesized, the process has three main stages (Thomas and Harden 2008; Thomas, Harden, and Newman 2012).

1. *Coding the text in the studies.* The very first thing to do is to identify what each study's findings are, which is not as straightforward as it might seem. This might mean referring to what the participants in each of the studies said or to the researchers' inferences and conclusions. Once you have determined the findings, you can begin coding. As with thematic analysis, this initial coding stage usually involves line-by-line coding. The reviewers examine each line of text for what it is saying and label what they see as its significance for the research question. They may construct codes from quotations from interview transcripts or quotations from researchers' presentations of their findings.

RESEARCH IN FOCUS 23.9
A thematic synthesis

Williams et al. (2020) conducted a thematic synthesis of qualitative studies investigating the psychosocial impacts of miscarriage on men. They initially identified 16,088 studies that matched their search criteria, reducing this number to 467 studies after screening them for eligibility, and again to 27 after assessing their quality. This represented the views of 231 men whose partners had miscarried. The researchers' approach corresponds quite well to the three stages outlined by Thomas and Harden (2008):

1. *Coding the text in the studies.* The authors report that '[t]exts were coded to represent meanings inherent in the original manuscripts rather than to fit any pre-determined model(s), until all data were coded' (Williams et al. 2020: 134).
2. *Generating descriptive themes.* The authors discussed the codes to identify similarities, differences, and any connections between them. Where the authors recognized codes or concepts that resonated across the studies but that were not necessarily expressed with the same terms, they combined these to produce 'parent codes'.
3. *Generating analytic themes.* The researchers then further refined these 'parent codes' into subthemes, taking care to retain any data that contradicted the emerging synthesis. They then devised **operational definitions** of the resulting codes and themes to identify relevant latent assumptions, contextual factors, and relationships associated with them. At the last stage, the researchers produced four analytic themes: secondary status in comparison with the female partner; uncertain transition to parenthood; gender roles and coping responses; and the ambiguous entitlement to healthcare.

This study provides an explicit application of thematic synthesis to a body of literature. At the same time, it provides a good illustration of thematic analysis itself.

2. *Generating descriptive themes.* The researcher then organizes the many line-by-line codes into higher-order themes by combining them together. Thomas et al. (2012) say that some thematic syntheses will stop at this stage if the results have provided adequate answers to the review question. Other syntheses, however, will progress to the next stage.
3. *Generating analytic themes.* This stage, if it occurs, involves drawing together the themes generated at the previous stage into what Thomas et al. call 'new conceptualisations and explanations'. These higher-order themes will often transcend the codes and descriptive themes contained in the original studies.

Thematic synthesis is strongest when it provides compelling answers to the review question through descriptive or, more likely, analytic themes. As Thomas and Harden (2008) make clear, generating analytic themes is controversial because it is so reliant on the impressions and ingenuity of the researcher, but if the researcher performing the thematic synthesis does not make this leap, their synthesis risks simply descriptively synthesizing studies without offering many new insights.

Research in focus 23.9 provides an example of a thematic synthesis examining studies of men's experiences of miscarriage.

23.9 Computer-assisted qualitative data analysis software (CAQDAS)

One of the most notable shifts within qualitative research in recent years has been the ongoing development of digital platforms that can help facilitate the analysis of qualitative data. In this section we will look at the increasing use of CAQDAS and what it does, and then we will evaluate it, considering both some of the criticisms that are made of it and the benefits it can offer. We will conclude by considering whether it could help you with your project.

If you are considering using or planning to use CAQDAS in your project, visit this book's **online resources** to explore our video tutorials and quick reference guide for the popular program NVivo.

The increasing use of CAQDAS

Ever since the term 'computer-assisted qualitative data analysis software', and its abbreviation CAQDAS, were coined by Lee and Fielding in 1991, both the number of programs that support qualitative analysis and the numbers of people using them have grown rapidly. Woods et al. (2016) conducted an analysis on 763 empirical articles between 1994 and 2013 reporting on research that used CAQDAS programs. They found that the number of articles reporting CAQDAS use is increasing each year, particularly in the health sciences, and that it is being used in conjunction with a variety of **research designs** and data-collection methods. This includes interviews, focus groups, documents, field notes, and open-ended surveys.

Most of the best-known CAQDAS programs are variations on the 'code-and-retrieve' theme—although there are a number of newer platforms that perform much more specific tasks. In a review of the history of CAQDAS platforms, Davidson et al. (2016) suggest that there have been both homogenizing and diversifying tendencies. So, while there are a growing number of programs available, most qualitative researchers will be familiar with just one package. According to the CAQDAS Networking Project at the University of Survey (**www.surrey.ac.uk/computer-assisted-qualitative-data-analysis/about**), most CAQDAS packages have some, but not all, of the following features:

- content searching tools
- linking tools
- coding tools
- query tools
- writing and annotation tools
- mapping or networking tools

At its most basic, CAQDAS usually allows the analyst to code text on a computer, write memos, and then use the computer's processing power to quickly label, sort, and retrieve the coded text. This means that you can retrieve any sequences of text under specific codes (or combination of codes). Essentially, the computer does the manual tasks associated with the coding process, including marking different sequences of text in terms of codes (coding) and collecting together all sequences of text that have been coded in a particular way (retrieving). There is no need for the scissors-and-glue methods used by previous generations of researchers, or even for using the cut-and-paste functions in word-processing software (although such software can still be useful: see Learn from experience 23.2). While the researcher must still interpret their data, the computer takes over some of the more laborious and time-consuming elements of organizing what are often large, messy collections of material. In some packages, like NVivo (see our video tutorials on this program within this book's **online resources**), the term **node** is used in the process of coding and retrieving text: see Key concept 23.3.

Evaluating CAQDAS

CAQDAS differs from quantitative data analysis software mainly in terms of the types of data it can help to process and the forms of analysis it can support. Some writers have commented that CAQDAS does not *and cannot* help with decisions about the coding of textual materials or about the interpretation of findings (Woods et al. 2016), but this is not unique to qualitative data analysis software. In quantitative research, the investigator sets out the crucial concepts and ideas in advance rather than generating them out of their data.

KEY CONCEPT 23.3
What is a node?

NVivo uses the term 'node' to refer to a collection of material relating to a specific theme, place, person, or issue. Nodes are, therefore, the means by which coding is undertaken. When a document has been coded, the node will contain all the coded passages of text in which the code appears. Once established, nodes can be changed, deleted, and even linked to other nodes.

LEARN FROM EXPERIENCE 23.2

Adapting word-processing packages for analysis

The entry costs of CAQDAS and the time-limited nature of a student project can mean that it is simply not worth it for a student to get to grips with new software. However, it is possible to adapt word-processing applications to help organize your data. Sarah describes how she used one such program to facilitate her analysis:

> For my postgraduate research project I analysed my data using Microsoft Word and created codes. I created individual Word documents for some of the key themes, which had lots of data with imported quotes from transcripts. I read through the responses adding notes. As my main interview sample was relatively small (16) I found this manageable (although time-consuming), and found that it made it easier to analyse key themes because I did not have to jump between each interview schedule. I also found significant wider themes that reoccurred across the developed themes. In the initial stage of analysis, I sent a practice analysis document to my supervisors. We discussed emerging themes and findings reflecting analysis of the interview transcript. It can also be useful to highlight codes using different colours.
>
> Sarah

 Access the **online resources** to hear Sarah's video reflections on this theme.

You can read about our panellists' backgrounds and research experiences on page xxvi.

Also, this comment seems to imply that the use of quantitative data analysis software such as **SPSS** is purely mechanical, which is not true: once the analyses have been conducted, the researcher still has to interpret them. In fact, both the choice of variables and the techniques of analysis are areas that require a considerable amount of interpretative expertise. Both forms of software require creativity.

However, unlike quantitative data analysis, in which the use of computer software is both widely accepted and in many cases a necessity, CAQDAS is by no means universally embraced by all qualitative researchers. Here, we consider the concerns that people have raised about its use, and then the benefits it can offer researchers.

Potential problems with using CAQDAS

A number of issues with the use of CAQDAS have been raised over the years, which we can summarize as follows.

- Qualitative research could become overwhelmed by quantification and a 'new orthodoxy'.
- The code-and-retrieve process could result in fragmentation of data and a resulting loss of narrative flow and valuable context.
- There are practical issues, including the time it takes to learn how to use a new program and difficulties with collaborating with other researchers.

Taking the first point, some writers are concerned that the ease with which coded text can be counted means that there will be an irresistible temptation to quantify findings in the form of measures such as 'code frequency' (see O'Kane et al. 2019, for example). The fear is that qualitative research will then be colonized by the reliability and validity criteria of quantitative research (Pratt 2008). That said, this issue has been repeatedly raised since the initial development of the software, and over 30 years later there is little evidence of qualitative research being overwhelmed by quantification.

Similarly, some time ago Coffey, Holbrook, and Atkinson (1994) argued that the style of qualitative data analysis tacitly incorporated into CAQDAS platforms (including NVivo) could result in a new, but perhaps unacknowledged, orthodoxy emerging. They argued that this problem could arise because these programs presume a certain style of analysis—one based on coding and retrieving text—that owes a great deal to grounded theory. Again, however, there is little evidence that such an orthodoxy has actually emerged in the way Coffey et al. feared it might (see Davidson et al. 2016).

In respect to the second point, it has also long been suggested that the code-and-retrieve process that underpins many CAQDAS platforms can result in the fragmentation of data (Weaver and Atkinson 1994). As a result, the narrative flow of interview transcripts and events recorded in field notes may be lost. This is something that is a standard difficulty for qualitative researchers, regardless of the software they use, but the problem when using CAQDAS packages is that researchers might not be fully aware of just how much the narratives have become fragmented in the code-and-retrieve process. It is certainly the case that the process of coding text into chunks that are then retrieved and put together into groups of related fragments does risk decontextualizing data. It is very easy for the coding process to produce collections of reorganized fragments. An awareness of context is crucial for many qualitative researchers so the prospect of losing this detail is likely to be problematic *if left unchecked*.

It is worth noting that the point about decontextualization is particularly important for the analysis of transcripts from focus groups. As Catterall and Maclaran (1997) have argued, CAQDAS might not be particularly suitable for this kind of data because it is difficult for the code-and-retrieve process to record and assess the dynamic interactions between participants—and interaction is, in part, what defines a focus group. The researcher can overcome this by using research memos, notes, and observations—which are themselves then included in the analytic process—but the researcher does need to pay deliberate attention to these things, record them, and include them in their analysis. However, while there are some rather mechanical and unreflective uses of CAQDAS within the literature that might lend some support to these critiques, nearly three decades later there is remarkable variation in the use of CAQDAS. For example, Le Blanc (2017) demonstrates how this software can be used within a postmodern theoretical perspective to challenge metanarratives. Working within perhaps a more conservative **epistemology**, Jackson et al. (2018) have also questioned the extent to which CAQDAS necessarily distances the researcher from their data. They use the metaphor of the zombie to express how standard critiques of CAQDAS that suggest it leads to distance, standardization, mechanization, and quantification are historical artefacts reproduced in textbooks rather than useful descriptions of the evolution of the software. While the issues raised are possible problems, they are neither inevitable nor a very accurate description of present practice.

23 However, it is important to be aware that there are also some more practical issues associated with using CAQDAS. Many of the coding and retrieval features can also be achieved through word-processing or spreadsheet software (Stanley and Temple 1995; La Pelle 2004; Mason et al. 2018). The big advantage of using software such as Microsoft Word, Excel, or Google Sheets is that they are unlikely to require researchers to spend a long time familiarizing themselves with new software—and some CAQDAS packages are not very straightforward or intuitive to use. Historically, there have also been concerns that researchers working in teams may experience difficulties in coordinating the coding of text when multiple people are involved in the analysis (Sprokkereef et al. 1995). However, advances in 'cloud technology' have made these difficulties easier to overcome, particularly where packages are more accessible.

Benefits of CAQDAS

Despite these criticisms, several writers have enthusiastically highlighted the benefits of using CAQDAS. These can be summarized as follows.

- CAQDAS makes coding and retrieval quicker and more efficient.
- It can help highlight connections between codes.
- Newer features can assist with the analysis of newer forms of data.
- It can enhance the overall research process.
- It allows researchers to easily include some elements of quantification in their findings.
- It could increase the rigour of qualitative analysis.

Most obviously, CAQDAS can make the coding and retrieval process faster and more efficient. This is particularly the case when dealing with large amounts of data. CAQDAS platforms can also invite researchers to think about codes in terms of 'trees' of interrelated ideas, which can prompt further consideration about possible connections between codes. It has also provided new opportunities for analysis. Woods et al. (2016), for example, note that many new features have been added to CAQDAS platforms in recent years, and that although they might not always be available, these functions can support the analysis of multimedia data, social media data, geodata, and survey data sets.

A standard critique of the presentation of qualitative research results has been that it tends towards anecdotalism—that is, it uses quotations from interview transcripts or field notes but with little sense of the prevalence of the phenomenon they are supposed to exemplify (see Silverman 1985, for example). CAQDAS allows researchers to easily count such things as how frequently a form of behaviour occurred or a viewpoint was expressed in interviews. While—as we have seen—some qualitative researchers see risks in this opportunity for quantification of findings, the capacity for counting does allow researchers to be more specific when using phrases such as 'the majority of participants said' or 'many people in the sample suggested'.

Paulus, Lester, and Britt (2013) analysed a number of textbooks on qualitative research and note that sometimes the attitude to CAQDAS is overly cautious, emphasizing its limitations rather than its advantages. They suggest that this cautionary approach is based on an outdated understanding of what the software can and cannot do, and they urge researchers to embrace the advantages of this technology. They also note that some textbook authors, usually writing within a more **positivist** frame, have suggested that CAQDAS actually increases the rigour of qualitative data analysis.

Should you use CAQDAS?

So, will using CAQDAS benefit your research? Although it has many benefits, the answer is not an automatic 'Yes'. If you have a very small data set, it is probably not worth your time and trouble to navigate your way around unfamiliar software. On the other hand, if you are working with a particularly large data set or you think you may use the software again in the future, for example in postgraduate studies, then it might be worth making the effort to learn how to use it. Also, regardless of whether you use the particular program again, learning new software provides you with useful skills that might be transferable on a future occasion.

If you do not have easy access to CAQDAS, the commercial CAQDAS packages may be too expensive for you to buy as an individual. However, a quick online search should reveal some platforms that are free of charge. These free platforms can be useful for basic tasks, but remember that the maintenance of free software can be limited, as can its functionality.

Overall, investing a little time and effort in learning the software is worthwhile, but you need to bear in mind some of the factors we have mentioned in deciding whether or not it would be useful for your project. If you are unsure, we recommend talking to your supervisor or an experienced colleague, but you may also find it helpful to watch the first of our six video tutorials on NVivo (available within our **online resources**) in which our panellist Scarlett (an experienced user of the program) provides a useful overview and demonstrates the program's basic features.

KEY POINTS

- Collecting qualitative data often leaves researchers with a large volume of information to analyse.
- Qualitative data analysis is not governed by fixed rules in the same way as quantitative data analysis.
- There are different approaches to qualitative data analysis, of which grounded theory is probably the most prominent.
- The process of data analysis can influence the process of data collection.
- Coding is a key process in most qualitative data analysis strategies, but it is sometimes accused of fragmenting and decontextualizing text.
- Narrative analysis is an approach that emphasizes the stories that people tell in the course of interviews and other interactions with the qualitative researcher. It has become a distinct strategy in its own right for analysing (and collecting) qualitative data.
- Approaches are being developed to allow researchers to synthesize qualitative studies. The main ones for our purposes are meta-ethnography and thematic synthesis.
- CAQDAS packages are now an important tool in the analysis of a variety of qualitative data.

QUESTIONS FOR REVIEW

1. What are the main ingredients of analytic induction?
2. What makes it a rigorous method?

3. What are the key processes of grounded theory?
4. What is the role of coding in grounded theory, and what are the different types of coding?
5. What are some of the main criticisms of grounded theory?
6. What are the main steps in coding?
7. To what extent does coding result in excessive fragmentation of data?
8. Is there a codified scheme for conducting thematic analysis?
9. How does the Framework approach help with a thematic analysis?
10. What are the main ways of identifying themes in qualitative data?
11. To what extent does narrative analysis provide an alternative to data fragmentation?
12. How does the emphasis on stories in narrative analysis provide a distinctive approach to the analysis of qualitative data?
13. Can narrative analysis be applied to all kinds of qualitative interview?
14. To what extent does thematic synthesis involve applying the principles of thematic analysis?
15. What are the advantages of using CAQDAS in qualitative research?

ONLINE RESOURCES

www.oup.com/he/srm6e

You can find our notes on the answers to these questions within this chapter's **online resources**, together with:

- *audio/video comments* on this topic from our 'Learn from experience' panellists;
- *guidance on using NVivo* in the form of written and video tutorials plus a quick reference guide;
- *self-test questions* for further knowledge-checking;
- a *flashcard glossary* to help you recall key terms; and
- a *Student Researcher's Toolkit* containing practical materials and resources to help you conduct your own research project.

PART FOUR

MIXED METHODS RESEARCH AND WRITING UP

In Part Four we will explore areas that transcend the quantitative/qualitative distinction. Chapter 24 invites you to consider how useful this distinction is and discusses the possibilities of mixed methods, in which qualitative and quantitative strategies are combined. In Chapter 25 we turn our attention to writing up social research and explore the features of good writing in quantitative, qualitative, and mixed methods research.

These chapters draw together certain issues from previous parts of the book. They also address others that have been raised already but that, this time, we discuss in greater depth.

CHAPTER 24

MIXED METHODS RESEARCH

CHAPTER GUIDE

In Parts Two and Three we discussed the methods and considerations associated with quantitative and qualitative research, respectively. Here, we consider the two strategies together. This chapter explores

- the reasons why some researchers choose to 'mix methods', using quantitative and qualitative methods together;
- the theoretical and philosophical debates that mixed methods research prompts us to consider, and the ways in which the quantitative/qualitative 'divide' can break down;
- the main classifications and types of mixed methods research designs, and why it is important to understand these key considerations for conducting effective mixed methods research;
- further issues around the added value and practicalities of mixed methods projects.

24.1 Introduction

So far, we have looked at individual methods or single 'families' of methodological approaches. In this chapter, we expand on the single method research design by looking at approaches that use more than one method. The technique of using multiple methods together has been around for centuries. Historians, for example, have been doing what is effectively mixed methods research (see Key concept 24.1) since the late nineteenth century, without labelling it as such. Throughout that long history, various terms have been used to indicate the different methodological combinations. As with so much of the terminology of social research methods, the very term 'mixed methods' can mean different things to different people. A lot of the time, 'mixed methods' is used to mean any combination of more than one method within a particular design (an approach that is also described as multi-method research), but increasingly the term is used as shorthand for research that combines methods from both quantitative and qualitative research strategies within a single project.

In this chapter we use the term in the latter way—to refer to research that involves both quantitative and qualitative methods. We explore some of the reasons for and against using multiple methods together, the theoretical and philosophical issues that this approach prompts us to consider, and the forms that mixed methods research can take. We conclude by looking at the characteristics of good mixed methods research, which are important for understanding and evaluating existing research but which we should also bear in mind when using, or considering using, this strategy.

24.2 Why mix methods?

Mixed methods research (see Key concept 24.1) has grown significantly in popularity since the first edition of this book in 2001 and is now a widely used and accepted approach to conducting social research. There are whole books about this approach, including a specialist handbook (Tashakkori and Teddlie 2010) and extensive guides on how to design and conduct such studies (Creswell and Plano Clark 2018; Fetters 2020), and specialist journals, such as the *Journal of Mixed Methods Research*, publish papers covering a wide range of topics. A glance at some of the recent work in that journal shows that mixed methods studies cover topics as important and diverse as vaping culture on social media (Colditz et al. 2019), gender-based violence at Spanish universities (Puigvert et al. 2019), and child welfare inequalities (Mason et al. 2020).

So why do researchers opt to mix methods? There are number of reasons why we might want to combine quantitative and qualitative methods in a single research design. Mostly, the idea is that the different methods complement one another, as the strengths of qualitative methods are brought together with the strengths of quantitative methods. Nowadays, it may seem obvious why different methods might be brought together. But in some areas, especially where quantitative methods dominate, the idea of 'needing' qualitative methods is still quite novel. Conversely, in spaces where qualitative methods dominate, it is still relatively new to bring in quantitative methods.

Increasingly, though, researchers accept that combining quantitative and qualitative approaches can potentially add value to a study. In examining the different ways that researchers had actually combined the methods in practice, Alan Bryman (2006a) found that they gave many different reasons why quantitative and qualitative methods might be combined. The complete list is provided in Thinking deeply 24.1, but here we will focus on the ones that are cited most frequently or that we think are the most relevant for students working on social research projects. These reasons are triangulation, completeness, sampling, and enhancement.

Triangulation

We first came across the idea of triangulation in Key concept 16.3. When applied to mixed methods research, triangulation refers to the practice of cross-checking results that we have gained using a method associated with one research strategy against the results we have gained using a method associated with the other research strategy. It is an adaptation of the argument by such writers as Webb et al. (1966) that we can increase

KEY CONCEPT 24.1
What is mixed methods research?

The terms *mixed methods*, *multi-method*, and *multi-modal* are often used interchangeably in relation to research approaches. Increasingly, though, 'mixed methods' describes a study that employs both quantitative and qualitative methods as part of a single research strategy. For example, a researcher may use both a **questionnaire** and **focus groups** within the same study. For some, mixed methods only refers to the use of *primary* quantitative and qualitative methods in the same study. In other words, a study that uses *secondary* quantitative data (instead of actually conducting, for example, a **survey** as part of the actual study) would not be considered 'mixed methods'. As is often the case with methodological **concepts** and terms, there is a range of perspectives on what must be involved when a study uses 'mixed methods'. The important thing is that 'mixed methods' generally refers to studies that use both quantitative and qualitative approaches within a single research design.

THINKING DEEPLY 24.1
The added value of mixed methods

Drawing on a content analysis of articles from mixed methods research, Bryman (2006a) identified a number of different ways in which researchers suggested that bringing together quantitative and qualitative approaches added value to their research.

1. *Triangulation or greater validity*—researchers combine quantitative and qualitative research to triangulate findings in order to mutually corroborate them (that is, the findings confirm and support each other).
2. *Offset*—combining research methods associated with both quantitative and qualitative strategies allows the researcher to offset their weaknesses and draw on the strengths of both.
3. *Completeness*—the researcher can produce a fuller account of the area in which they are interested if they use both quantitative and qualitative research.
4. *Process*—**quantitative research** provides an account of structures in social life, but qualitative research provides a sense of process.
5. *Different research questions*—quantitative and qualitative research strategies can each answer different research questions.
6. *Explanation*—researchers can use one of the two research methods to help explain findings generated by the other.
7. *Unexpected results*—sometimes either quantitative or qualitative research methods generate surprising results that we can understand using the other strategy.
8. *Instrument development*—researchers can use qualitative research to develop instruments for quantitative research methods, for example questionnaire and scale **items**, so that they can construct better-worded questions or more comprehensive closed answers.
9. ***Sampling***—one approach can allow researchers to sample respondents or cases for the other approach.
10. *Credibility*—using both approaches can enhance the integrity of findings.
11. *Context*—researchers use qualitative research to provide contextual understanding, which they can then use in conjunction with **generalizable**, externally valid findings or broad **relationships** among **variables** that they have uncovered through, for example, a survey.
12. *Illustration*—researchers use qualitative data to illustrate 'dry' quantitative findings, providing further information and helping to bring them to life.

13. *Utility or improving the usefulness of findings*— combining the two approaches will be more useful to practitioners and others. (This advantage is more likely to be prominent in research with an applied focus.)
14. *Confirm and discover*—researchers use qualitative data to generate hypotheses and then use quantitative research to test them within a single project.
15. *Diversity of views*—this covers two slightly different rationales: combining researchers' and participants' perspectives through quantitative and qualitative research, respectively; and uncovering relationships between variables through quantitative research while also revealing meanings among research participants through qualitative research.
16. *Enhancement or building upon quantitative/qualitative findings*—making more of, or enhancing, either quantitative or qualitative findings by gathering data using a qualitative or quantitative research approach.
17. *Other/unclear.*
18. *Not stated.*

confidence in the findings from a study using a quantitative research strategy by using more than one way of measuring a concept. Usually, researchers conducting a triangulation exercise compare quantitative and qualitative findings. McCrudden and McTigue (2019) did this in their study of high school students' belief bias (the tendency to believe things that fit with our own values, prior beliefs, and prior knowledge) relating to climate change. The authors present an integrated results matrix in which they displayed quantitative and qualitative results side by side. They summarize the separate strands and show how the quantitative and qualitative findings support each other. For example, they show that students in a survey who did not rate the strength of arguments differently based on their own beliefs also exhibited this tendency in the qualitative phase of the research, in that they were able to independently assess the quality of the arguments presented. Research in focus 24.1 provides two further examples of studies that used mixed methods in order to employ a triangulation approach, as well as for completeness (see the next section). A researcher might plan a triangulation exercise from the start of a project, or they might decide to conduct it only when the data have been collected.

Completeness

Often, a researcher undertakes mixed methods research because they believe that using both quantitative and qualitative methods will give them a more complete answer to their **research question** or set of research questions. This rationale implies that the gaps left by methods associated with one research strategy can be filled by methods associated with the other strategy. A common example is when researchers conducting an **ethnography** use **structured interviewing** or a **self-completion questionnaire** to gather more data because they cannot access everything they need to know about through **participant observation**. So, they employ different methods in order to gain a more complete empirical description of what they are researching. Similarly, researchers might need to use alternative methods because qualitative interviewing can leave some questions unanswered (for example, systematic information about the social backgrounds of people in a particular setting), or because of the difficulty of gaining access to certain groups of people.

Grogan et al. (2013; see Research in focus 23.5) administered a questionnaire to participants in their study of dress fit and body image, using the quantitative evidence it generated to help them understand their qualitative findings and gain a more complete picture. For example, one of the themes they derived from the qualitative research was that clothes should hide disliked parts of the body, and the questionnaire data allowed the authors to infer that this theme was most likely to be expressed by the women who were least satisfied with their body image (as indicated by the questionnaire). The three women who had the highest satisfaction scores tended to be less concerned about this theme. However, the person with the highest body satisfaction score also expressed a concern about her 'tum', so even when someone is broadly satisfied with their body image, there can still be a lingering concern. The quantitative evidence therefore provided valuable contextual information that helped with the understanding of the qualitative findings and provided a more complete picture.

While the studies we describe in Research in focus 24.1 used mixed methods for completeness as well as

RESEARCH IN FOCUS 24.1
Mixed methods for triangulation and completeness

A good example of a study using mixed methods to triangulate data as well as to ensure completeness (also discussed in this chapter) is the research conducted by Grassian (2020) on the dietary behaviours of people involved in meat-reduction and pro-vegan campaigns in the UK. Grassian employed a **longitudinal** design and used mixed methods to triangulate the data and provide a more complete picture of why and how people choose to eat and not eat what they do, especially when it comes to changing diets. The idea behind the longitudinal element was to capture not only the dietary changes across an individual's life, but also the interactive ways that dietary change (for example, eating less meat) can itself influence a person's perception of other behaviours (for example veganism). In other words, he was interested in examining the feed-forward and feedback loops that take place with seemingly 'small steps' in dietary change, such as eating a bit less meat.

Grassian administered an online longitudinal quantitative survey to 1,539 participants over 12 months, and conducted five focus groups (33 individuals in total) whose members were involved in a pro-vegan campaign. They used the quantitative data to access perceptions and self-reported dietary behaviours and included questions about the barriers to dietary change. They used the qualitative focus groups as a secondary method to 'enrich and triangulate survey data through the emergence of specific experiences and areas of conflicting opinion' (Grassian 2020: 5).

Overall, the study concluded that campaigns that aimed to promote small, gradual changes in dietary behaviour (such as reducing red meat consumption) had the most chance of resulting in sustainable change in the long run.

Please note: some readers may find the following content, which relates to a study of campus sexual assault, upsetting.

Another example of a study using mixed methods for both triangulation and completion is Shah and Gu's (2020) exploration of concerns about sexual assault on campus at a US university. They used a variety of data, including logs of reported incidents from the university's police department; publicly available annual reports of the university's multi-campus crime statistics; and an **online survey** with multiple-choice and **open-ended questions** that all 8,770 students were invited to complete anonymously. The researchers triangulated the different data sources to provide completeness in understanding the reported incidence of sexual assault on campus as well as students' perceptions and concerns about campus sexual assault. The triangulated data helped the researchers identify policy gaps and draw up a plan of actions and recommendations to monitor the situation and improve victim support.

triangulation, Research in focus 24.2 provides an example of a study where the researchers implied multiple reasons for using mixed methods but 'completeness' was the main rationale they stated.

Sampling

Another common use of mixed methods is when researchers employ quantitative strategies to select people who they then study qualitatively (for example through unstructured or **semi-structured interviews**). In Fenton et al.'s (1998) interesting study of how social science research is reported in the British mass media, the researchers used a (quantitative) **content analysis** of media content as a source of data in its own right but also as a way for the researchers to identify journalists who had reported relevant research, who they could interview using a semi-structured approach—in other words, they used their content analysis to help with **purposive sampling** for qualitative interviewing. Another example of mixed methods within the study is the way that the researchers first conducted a survey of social scientists' views about media coverage and their practices, and then used the survey replies to identify two groups of social scientists—those with particularly high and those with low levels of media coverage of their research—who they then interviewed using a semi-structured approach.

There are many other examples of quantitative data being used to purposively sample participants for qualitative research. We consider one in Research in focus 24.3, and

RESEARCH IN FOCUS 24.2
Mixed methods for completeness and sampling

Though it was conducted some years ago, Poortinga et al.'s (2004) mixed methods study of the foot-and-mouth disease (FMD) outbreak in the UK in 2001 remains an excellent example of the multiple reasons why researchers might use mixed methods. Their main rationale for this approach was completeness, in that they felt that mixed methods would generate a more comprehensive picture than using a single research strategy. Their use of a survey also allowed the researchers to select focus group participants using purposive sampling, so in terms of Alan Bryman's categories (see Thinking deeply 24.1) the reasons for their approach were both completeness and sampling. In all, we can identify six reasons for Poortinga et al.'s use of mixed methods.

1. *Illustration.* The authors write that they used focus group data 'to illustrate the findings of the questionnaire' (Poortinga et al. 2004: 77).
2. *Completeness.* They write that the focus groups 'provided valuable additional information, especially on the reasons, rationalizations and arguments behind people's understanding of the FMD issue' (2004: 86).
3. *Triangulation.* Focus group findings 'reinforce' questionnaire findings (for example, that not many people were worried about the health impacts on people) and reveal concern about government policies in the handling of FMD rather than about the disease itself.
4. *Explanation.* The authors suggest that in the English town Bude, the high trust ratings of local sources of information and the low trust ratings of government 'may well be a judgement of where these sources are thought to stand in this debate. . . . the focus groups suggested that trust judgements might reflect the extent to which sources are believed to protect people and their interests' (2004: 88).
5. *Sampling.* As we have noted, the survey allowed the researchers to use purposive sampling to select focus group participants.
6. *Enhancement.* This occurs on several occasions in this study, including through the triangulation exercise (see point 3), as the qualitative findings enhanced the quantitative ones by clarifying the nature of the concern about the disease. See this chapter's section on 'Enhancement' for more on this aspect.

RESEARCH IN FOCUS 24.3
Mixed methods for sampling and enhancement

In their study on how Covid-19 affected anxiety levels in children and adolescents with severe obesity in the Netherlands, Abawi et al. (2020) used both qualitative and quantitative methods. The different methods helped them to sample participants as well as to gain a more enhanced picture of how children and adolescents with severe obesity were experiencing lockdown and perceiving Covid-19. In their study, they contacted 90 families with children who were currently receiving treatment at Obesity Center CGG (a unit of the Erasmus MC Sophia Children's Hospital), a national referral centre for obesity. Of those 90 families, 75 took part in telephone interviews; and of those who took part in the qualitative phase, 40 also completed the quantitative Pediatric Quality of Life inventory (PedsQL), which they had also completed prior to the pandemic as part of being under treatment.

In this study, qualitative interviews allowed the researchers to explore what was behind Covid-19-related anxiety and also what could potentially be done to ease this anxiety. The quantitative data also allowed them to understand the participants' quality of life both before and during the pandemic. The researchers concluded that healthcare professionals should give support and intervene on Covid-19-related anxiety for children and young people with severe obesity.

others include the McCrudden and McTigue (2019) study of belief bias about climate change that we discussed earlier in the chapter, which used an explanatory sequential design (an approach we will discuss in Section 24.4). Following the quantitative data-collection phase, in which respondents were asked to rate the strength of arguments that were in line with or contrary to their own beliefs about climate change, the researchers purposively sampled to create two groups of four respondents—one group with low belief bias, and another with high belief bias. In another example, Jamieson (2000) reports that in her study of criminal offending she administered a self-completion questionnaire to a sample of young men and asked them whether they had been convicted of any criminal offences. On the basis of their replies, she selected equal numbers of young men from three categories to question using a qualitative interview: those who had not offended; those who had offended but not recently; and persistent offenders.

Enhancement

Researchers may use mixed methods to try to enhance or expand on the findings they have generated through one research strategy by gathering data using the other strategy. This is quite a common use of mixed methods and is often an implicit aspect of mixed methods designs. In Bickerstaff et al.'s (2008) study of people's views of nuclear power, radioactive waste, and the measures being taken to address climate change, for example, survey evidence suggested that respondents were more likely to see the causes of climate change (car use, energy use, etc.) as beneficial to themselves and to society than the causes of radioactive waste (for example, nuclear power production). The focus group data then enhanced the **causal** inferences that the researchers drew from the surveys. For example, when talking about energy-consuming aspects of modern life, such as transport and heating, focus group participants tended to emphasize the benefits rather than the risks. They saw the negative effects on the environment as unavoidable features of modernity. Research in focus 24.4 describes another study in which researchers used mixed methods for enhancement purposes.

It should by now be clear that there are numerous reasons why researchers might choose to use mixed methods. If you are considering conducting mixed methods research of your own, we strongly encourage you to look up the original studies we have mentioned in order to better understand how mixed method approaches can be beneficial, and how they can help with issues such as instrument development and explanation. You do not

RESEARCH IN FOCUS 24.4
Mixed methods for enhancement

We can see how findings from one methodological approach can be used to enhance the findings from another in Li et al.'s (2020) mixed methods study of whether parents' nonstandard work schedules were linked to lower social and emotional wellbeing in children. The aim of the study was to examine the daily life of the families from the parents' perspective, and the researchers particularly wanted to explore the impact of parents' nonstandard work schedules on social and emotional wellbeing in children aged from 8 to 16.

Li et al. (2020) used both quantitative and qualitative methods and, in particular, they used longitudinal data to gain an in-depth picture of how parental work schedules affected the wellbeing of their children over time as the children were getting older. They used longitudinal quantitative data on six waves of the German Family Panel Study (2011–2016) alongside qualitative interviews with participating families. As they explain, taking the quantitative and qualitative findings together allowed them to gain a better understanding of the important and nuanced role that stress played in linking parental work schedules to children's social and emotional wellbeing. They go on to suggest that it is not simply a matter of parental work schedules having an impact on children's wellbeing; they also affect other aspects of the family context, for example income and parental mental wellbeing. Indeed, they go to suggest that in some families, stress caused by work patterns could be mitigated and somewhat offset by other things such as the other parent's work schedule, support from grandparents, and so on.

As Li et al. sum up, 'the advantage of [combining] quantitative and qualitative approaches is that the quantitative and qualitative arms of the study can inform and enrich one another in terms of both theories guiding the analytical design, statistical modeling and sampling for the qualitative component and the interpretation of the results' (2020: 348–9).

LEARN FROM EXPERIENCE 24.1
The value of mixed methods research

Mixing quantitative and qualitative approaches can allow you to address the weaknesses that either approach would have in isolation, potentially making for a better research project. Reni used a mixed methods approach in her study into whether the International Criminal Court is biased against African countries, and we can see that her motivation best aligns with the **category** of reason that Alan described (see Thinking deeply 24.1) as 'offsetting'.

> I felt that my questions could not be sufficiently addressed with solely the use of either quantitative or qualitative methods, so I used both. I chose this approach because my qualitative methods made up for the weaknesses of my quantitative methods and vice versa. I used both numbers and facts from case studies to illustrate my thesis statement. It largely benefited my project by strengthening my argument through answers informed by a variety of methods. My experiences have taught me that elements of quantitative and qualitative research often complement each other. I would recommend that students compare and contrast quantitative and qualitative research with a view towards using the strengths of each type of research to make up for the shortcomings of the other.
>
> Reni

Access the **online resources** to hear Reni's video reflections on this theme.

You can read about our panellists' backgrounds and research experiences on page xxvi.

necessarily need to refer to or think about your approach using the exact labels that Bryman provides (see Thinking deeply 24.1), but you should be clear in your mind about why you are using mixed methods—how this approach will help you answer your research question(s)—and you should explain this rationale in your write-up (see Chapter 25, Section 25.3). In Learn from experience 24.1, Reni reflects on why she used mixed methods for her student research project.

24.3 How definitive is the quantitative/qualitative divide?

You will have noticed that up to this chapter, this book has been structured around the distinction between quantitative and qualitative research. This distinction is there mainly for historical reasons, which are largely rooted in **epistemological** assumptions (that is, ideas about what constitutes valid knowledge) of what is involved in the different methodological traditions. As we have seen, there are a huge number of research methods, and thinking of them as belonging to two broad groups can also be a useful way of organizing the different approaches, even though it is a crude way of grouping them. However, the distinction between quantitative and qualitative methods is not as robust as it may at first appear. More worryingly, this categorization tends to set one group 'against' the other, and this can be highly problematic. Research methods, and approaches to social research in general, are much more flexible than the qualitative/quantitative distinction suggests. Indeed, while there are many differences between the qualitative and quantitative research strategies, research can be—and increasingly is—conducted that goes beyond this distinction. Jodie reflects on the quantitative/qualitative 'divide' in Learn from experience 24.2.

In this section, we consider the main debates about research methods and epistemological and **ontological** positions, and we then explore the supposed 'divide' between quantitative and qualitative research from four different angles.

LEARN FROM EXPERIENCE 24.2

Comparing and contrasting quantitative and qualitative methods

To what extent is it helpful to compare and contrast quantitative and qualitative methods, and to see them as divided? Jodie comments:

> It is important to compare and contrast quantitative and qualitative research to recognize, acknowledge and understand the benefits and limitations of both approaches. It also provides a platform to see how they can complement each other, or fill in gaps that are perhaps missing from certain approaches. In my experience, the 'divide' is not clear-cut. Think of a survey: it could be solely qualitative or quantitative, or even both. It depends on the questions that we ask and how we analyse them. This ultimately depends on what we want to investigate and how we then go about it.
>
> Jodie

Jodie makes two very important points here. The first is that we can think of qualitative and quantitative methods not as incompatible, but as complementary. The second is that a particular method is not inherently qualitative or quantitative, a point that Ben expands upon:

> I would argue that the survey method should not be categorized purely as a quantitative method. In my project I wanted and planned to collect both structured data (quant) and insights (qual) from my participants in one survey. I designed the survey deliberately to 'build' towards the two open questions at the end. The survey was split into three sections whereby the initial compulsory closed demographics questions could be answered swiftly, followed by compulsory closed questions on the topic and finally optional open questions on the topic allowing for more detail. From my perspective as the researcher, it didn't feel strange or unexpected to analyse both types of data within the one data set.
>
> Ben

You can read about our panellists' backgrounds and research experiences on page xxvi.

Epistemological and ontological positions

To those new to, or outside of, social research, combining quantitative and qualitative methods may appear unproblematic. But there are longstanding and ongoing debates about the extent to which combining quantitative and qualitative methods is or is not a contentious matter. Some even go as far as saying that they cannot be combined, whereas others argue that they can. At the crux of the debates is the question of whether quantitative and qualitative methods are fundamentally different in their philosophical underpinnings. But note that pointing out this difference also assumes that certain research methods are connected with particular epistemological and ontological standpoints in the first place. So, there are a number of 'tangled ties' that come about when thinking about using quantitative and qualitative methods together that are important to know about, if only so that you are aware of the kinds of scholarly debates that researchers engage in about mixed methods research.

Essentially, the quantitative/qualitative divide is a complicated matter for two main reasons. These can be summed up as the 'paradigm' argument and the 'embedded methods' argument.

The paradigm argument

The extent to which philosophical perspectives necessarily underpin particular methods is a thorny matter, but it is one that drives much of the 'war of methods'. If we think of quantitative and qualitative research as **paradigms** (see Key concept 24.2) in which epistemological assumptions, values, and methods are inextricably bound together, then we quickly get into a situation where quantitative and qualitative methods are incompatible (see, for example, Guba 1985; Morgan 1998b). So, with this view, a researcher who takes the **positivist** perspective and assumes that only things that can be measured are worth knowing will have difficulty understanding why or how we might want to speak to small non-random sample of individuals, let alone in an unstructured way, such as via a semi-structured or

KEY CONCEPT 24.2
What is a paradigm?

Kuhn's (1970) highly influential use of the term 'paradigm' comes from his analysis of revolutions in science. A paradigm is 'a cluster of beliefs and dictates which for scientists in a particular discipline influence what should be studied, how research should be done, [and] how results should be interpreted' (Bryman 1988a: 4). Kuhn presented the natural sciences as going through periods of revolution, so that normal science (science carried out in terms of the dominant paradigm) is increasingly challenged by anomalies that are inconsistent with the assumptions and established findings in the discipline at that time. The growth in anomalies eventually gives way to a crisis in the discipline, which brings about a revolution. The period of revolution is resolved when a new paradigm emerges as the dominant one and a new period of normal science sets in. An important feature of paradigms is that they are *incommensurable*—that is, they are inconsistent with each other because their assumptions and methods are different. Disciplines in which no paradigm has emerged as dominant, such as the social sciences, are seen as pre-paradigmatic, in that they feature competing paradigms. The term 'paradigm' is widely used in the social sciences (see, for example, Ritzer 1975; Guba 1985), but it is worth noting that it can be problematic because it is not very specific: Masterman (1970) identified 21 different uses of 'paradigm' by Kuhn.

unstructured interview. On the other hand, those coming from a strong **interpretivist** tradition may equally disregard survey data because they assume that it cannot capture or convey the meanings that individuals give to their world and experiences—an element that they consider to be core to understanding the social world.

The problem with the paradigm argument is that it depends on claims about the interconnectedness of method and epistemology that cannot—in the case of social research—be demonstrated. There is also the fact that while some *argue* that paradigms are incommensurable (cannot be judged by the same standards), for example as Kuhn asserts (1970; see Key concept 24.2), it is certainly not clear that quantitative and qualitative research are in fact paradigms.

The embedded methods argument

Some writers have suggested that research methods themselves are inevitably rooted in certain epistemological and ontological commitments, meaning that if, for example, you use a self-completion questionnaire you are selecting a natural science model and an **objectivist** worldview. Similarly, using participant observation is often taken to imply a commitment to interpretivism and **constructionism**. We can see these views in comments such as this:

> the choice and adequacy of a method embodies a variety of assumptions regarding the nature of knowledge and the methods through which that knowledge can be obtained, as well as a set of root assumptions about the nature of the phenomena to be investigated.
>
> (Morgan and Smircich 1980: 491)

We can think of the 'embedded methods' argument as being strongly based on philosophical and methodological stereotypes, where quantitative methods tend to be associated with positivism and qualitative methods with interpretivism. But just as with all stereotypes, this way of putting approaches in boxes is widely contested. In social science research, many increasingly see it as outdated. Not only are there a number of other philosophical perspectives—for example **realism**, **feminism**, and **pragmatism**—that are used in studies with a single method design as well as in mixed methods social science; there are also many variations within any particular philosophical perspective.

Rather than sitting within or outside of a particular philosophical stance and representing a series of discrete, fixed viewpoints on what the world is or is not, each of which has implications about the ways through which we can (or cannot) know the world, epistemological and ontological perspectives are much more like a spectrum of positions. For example, the term 'positivist' has to be treated carefully—an argument made by Platt (1981). Although it does refer to a distinctive kind of scientific enquiry, it is often also used in a polemical way—that is, critiquing and attempting to undermine others' work or approaches. When used in this way, 'positivist' is rarely helpful, because the term is usually a negative characterization of someone else's work. So, the boundaries between what may seem like a 'paradigm' are blurrier than may first appear. This does not mean that anything goes. But it does mean that there are some schools of thought that would argue that certain strands of, say, positivism are much more similar to, say, interpretivism than people often assume.

If we accept that there is no perfect link between research method and matters of epistemology and ontology, the claim that a method inherently or necessarily indicates certain wider assumptions about knowledge and the nature of social reality becomes less convincing. In fact, research methods are much more 'free-floating' in terms of epistemology and ontology than we might think. This is particularly clear in studies of social research. For example, Platt's (1986) historical research on US sociology has suggested that the connection that is often made between **functionalism** (which itself is often associated with positivism) and the social survey is greatly exaggerated. Her research suggested that 'the two originated independently, and that leading functionalists had no special propensity to use surveys and leading surveyors no special propensity for functionalism' (Platt 1986: 527).

Platt's general conclusion from her research on the use of research methods in US sociology between 1920 and 1960 is very revealing. She states:

> research methods may on the level of theory, when theory is consciously involved at all, reflect intellectual *bricolage* or *post hoc* justifications rather than the consistent working through of carefully chosen fundamental assumptions. Frequently methodological choices are steered by quite other considerations, some of a highly practical nature, and there are independent methodological traditions with their own channels of transmission. . . . In many cases general theoretical/methodological stances are just stances: slogans, hopes, aspirations, not guidelines with clear implications that are followed in practice.
>
> (Platt 1996: 275)

Platt's references to 'intellectual *bricolage*' ('bricolage' meaning construction using whatever diverse materials are available) and '*post hoc* justifications' suggest that choices of research methods are influenced by numerous factors rather than being mainly dictated by how neatly they align with the researcher's theoretical/methodological viewpoint—which, as Platt notes, is often not a fixed stance anyway. Her conclusion suggests that the idea that research methods are inevitably associated with certain assumptions about knowledge and social reality has to be questioned. When we examine how research methods are used in practice, the connections between methods and standpoints are not absolute.

Although in an ideal world it may be both useful and interesting to think of the extent to which methods and philosophical positions necessarily dictate one another, in practice social research can often be a lot more pragmatic. Indeed, in some instances, the practicalities of actually *doing* research become a key, if not the main, driving factor as to how researchers conduct mixed methods work. For example, a researcher might prefer to conduct a study of refugee populations using **probability sampling**, because of their theoretical standpoint, but they may be forced to use snowball sampling because the refugee population is difficult to reach. These very practical considerations in the way that methods do and do not get combined together are less commonly discussed. But increasingly, especially as more studies make use of social media data, we see that access to data and considerations of what is or is not publicly available strongly influence which data, and which methods, get used in a study.

Having considered the connections between research methods and epistemological and ontological considerations, we can so far draw the following conclusions:

- there are differences between quantitative and qualitative research in terms of their epistemological and ontological commitments, *but*
- the connection between research strategy, on the one hand, and epistemological and ontological commitments, on the other, is not deterministic—that is, one does not dictate the other. There is a *tendency* for quantitative and qualitative research to be associated with the epistemological and ontological positions we outlined in Chapter 2, but the connections are not perfect.

All that said, even after philosophical considerations have been expressed and reconciled, there are still some important differences between the different methodological approaches between quantitative and qualitative methods that we need to acknowledge when we consider mixed methods designs. After all, mixed methods designs are one context in which quantification is incorporated into qualitative methods (and vice versa). Once again, though, when we start to look more closely at quantitative and qualitative approaches side by side, what first appears to be a 'hard division' between them becomes increasingly blurred.

The 'divisions' between quantitative and qualitative research

We can look at the supposed divisions between quantitative and qualitative research from four angles:

- numbers vs words;
- the qualitative characteristics in quantitative research;

- the quantitative characteristics of qualitative research, that is, quasi-quantification; and
- the ways in which some digital data, such as social media and other related **Big Data**, are neither purely quantitative nor qualitative and are increasingly seen as 'hybrid'.

Let's consider each angle in turn.

Numbers vs words

The 'numbers vs words' contrast is probably the one that most people would cite first if asked to think about the differences between quantitative and qualitative research. After all, it relates to the terms 'quantitative' and 'qualitative' themselves, which seem to imply the presence and absence of numbers. However, in reality the line is often blurred.

Quantitative researchers do often focus on words: they take words and quantify them in some way. In Chapter 2 we discussed how Williams et al. (2017a) took textual data from Twitter and converted it into a quantitative measure for the criminological concept of 'broken windows'. It is also not unusual for a survey with fixed-response items to include an option for respondents to provide an open text response. In Learn from experience 24.2 Ben describes having taken this approach, and a larger-scale example is the National Student Survey in the UK (**www.thestudentsurvey.com/**, accessed 22 October 2020), which has both scale measures and open-text responses. Those analysing this kind of data often count the number of times that certain themes appear in order to identify those that are common to many respondents. It is important to note that this process of quantification gives us a measure of how *prevalent* something is, but it rarely captures the *importance* of an issue for an individual. Something is both lost and gained by quantifying data in this way.

'Qualitative' characteristics in quantitative research

Just as quantitative elements can appear in qualitative research, quantitative research can exhibit characteristics and standpoints that are more often associated with qualitative approaches. Qualitative research might seem to be the research strategy best suited to studying meaning, and some of its supporters would claim that only qualitative methods allow us to view the world through the eyes of the people we are studying. We can see this in Platell et al.'s (2020) mixed methods study (see Research in focus 24.7), where researchers used qualitative interviews with health professionals and young people to compare their perceptions of barriers to young people accessing mental health services. What was important for the researchers was to understand how barriers to access *appeared* to young people and how they *experienced* barriers, rather than whether or not the barriers were 'real' in terms of the bureaucratic processes that young people encountered.

However, it is also possible to understand individuals' perceptions of meaning and their interpretations through quantitative surveys. Indeed, qualitative aspects of everyday life and experiences are an intrinsic part of many quantitative surveys. As Platt (1981: 87) observes, we often capture and study attitudes in social surveys using structured interviews and questionnaires. Likewise, Marsh (1982) points out that the practice in much survey research of asking respondents the reasons for their actions indicates that quantitative researchers are often interested in uncovering issues of meaning. Connelly et al. (2016) provide an excellent discussion around the complexities of measuring ethnicity in survey research, which is of course not an attitude, but may often be subjective. Similarly, in addition to Platell et al.'s (2020) qualitative interviews with health workers and young people regarding access to mental health services, they also used an online quantitative survey 'to identify and elucidate perceptions of the barriers and potential benefits associated with mental health help-seeking in adolescents who have not accessed or fully engaged with mental health services' (2020: 2). So, the argument that qualitative methods are 'better' than quantitative methods at capturing individuals' experiences does not always hold up.

Quasi-quantification

Another angle from which to consider the 'divide' is the fact that numbers are not completely absent from qualitative research. Qualitative researchers engage in what we could call 'quasi-quantification' through the use of terms like 'many', 'frequently', 'rarely', 'often', and 'some'. If they are making these kinds of references to quantity, the qualitative researcher will have some idea of the relative frequency of the phenomena being referred to. However, as expressions of quantities they are imprecise, and it is often difficult to work out why they are used at all. One alternative is for qualitative researchers to engage in a limited amount of quantification when it is appropriate, for example when an expression of quantity would strengthen their argument. Silverman (1984; 1985) quantified some of the data he gained from observing doctor–patient interactions in the UK National Health Service and private oncology clinics in order to bring out the differences between the two types of clinic. This quantification allowed him to show that patients in private clinics could exert more influence over what went on in the consultations, and he argues that some quantification of findings from qualitative research can help to uncover the generality of the phenomena being described. However, it is important to note Silverman's warning that such quantification should reflect research participants' own ways of understanding their social world (in keeping with the preoccupations of qualitative research—see Section 16.3).

Digital data as hybrid

When you think about what data actually are, it becomes even more difficult to always divide them neatly according to whether they are only 'qualitative' or only 'quantitative'. To an archaeologist, pieces of pottery become data—items to be classified, measured, and recorded carefully for further exploration. For us as social scientists, the digitization of information has radically transformed the kinds of data we can use to better understand the social world. Increasingly, in a world where Big Data and algorithms pervade all areas of everyday life, social science itself is changing. Instead of thinking of data as 'quantitative' or 'qualitative', in the current digital era we can think of data—and Big Data in particular—in terms of the 'four Vs': its volume, variety, veracity, and velocity. YouTube and social media data are streamed in 'real time', involve numbers that are automatically logged in terms of their metrics (for example the number of 'likes'), and also involve words (for example comments, or the number of words in a tweet on Twitter). As the world changes, so too do the data that constitute it. On the one hand, we can think of these new kinds of digital data as 'hybrid' forms of data—data that are neither purely qualitative nor purely quantitative. On the other hand, the methods that people use to collect them and make sense of them are increasingly mathematical, computational, and quantitative. These new kinds of 'hybrid' data arguably mess up the quant/qual divide all over again, albeit in a contemporary context.

24.4 Types of mixed methods research

As interest in mixed methods research has grown, various typologies have emerged as researchers have attempted to identify common types of mixed methods designs. Understanding these typologies is important not only because they will help you reflect on and engage with existing research, but also because increasingly there is an expectation that in their write-ups, mixed methods researchers will explain the type of design they have employed.

One approach to classifying mixed methods studies focuses on their purposes and the roles that the quantitative and qualitative components play (see also Bryman 2006a; 2008b). However, another approach is to classify mixed methods studies in terms of two criteria (e.g. Morgan 1998b).

- *The priority decision*. To what extent is a qualitative or quantitative method the main data-gathering tool, or do they have equal weight?
- *The sequence decision*. Which method comes first? In other words, does the qualitative method come before the quantitative one or vice versa, or is the data collection associated with each method concurrent (that is, collected at more or less the same time)?

These criteria produce nine possible types of design, as shown in Figure 24.1. Here, capital letters indicate priority and lower-case letters indicate a more minor role—for example, QUAL indicates that the qualitative component was the main data-collection approach. Arrows refer to the sequence—for example, QUAN→qual means quantitative data was the main, and first, data collection approach and that the qualitative data were collected afterwards and have a subsidiary role in the study. The order matters where we need to know if one phase influenced or was used to inform the other. The + simply means that the quantitative and qualitative data were collected more or less concurrently. One difficulty with this way of classifying mixed methods studies is that it is not always easy to assess priority and sequence when reading the report of a study. However, it does provide a useful way of thinking about how mixed methods studies are designed, as well as the relationship between components that might work best for your project.

Classifying designs by priority and sequence gives us a way of distinguishing between the overarching strategies that underpin different mixed methods studies and the relationship between their component parts. Writers on mixed methods research have drawn on these distinctions to identify the main types of design that are employed. The typology developed by Creswell and Plano Clark (2011; 2018) is probably the most commonly used. They identify three core designs—the convergent design, the explanatory sequential design, and the exploratory sequential design—which we summarize diagrammatically in Figure 24.2. Let's examine each of these.

The convergent design

The **convergent design** (sometimes also referred to as the 'concurrent' design or the 'concurrent triangulation' design) involves *collecting quantitative and qualitative data*

FIGURE 24.1
Classifying mixed methods research in terms of priority and sequence

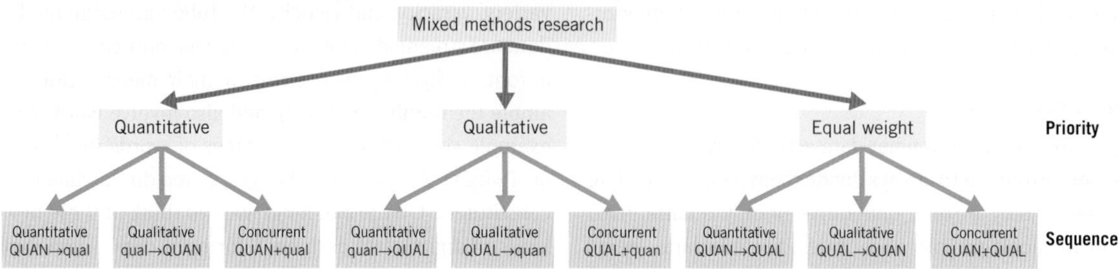

Note: Capitals and lower case indicate priority; arrows indicate sequence; + indicates concurrent.

FIGURE 24.2
Three core mixed methods designs

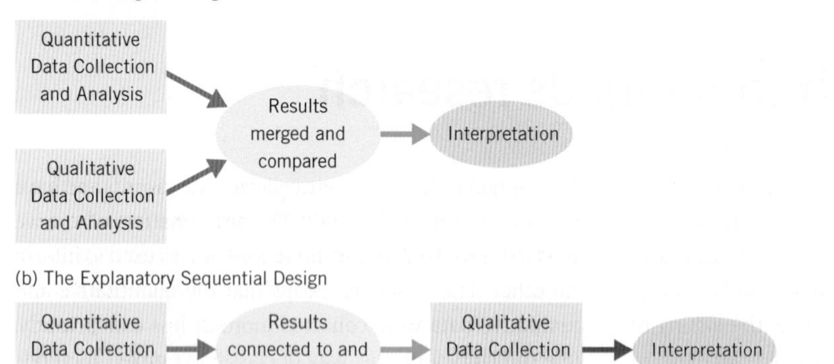

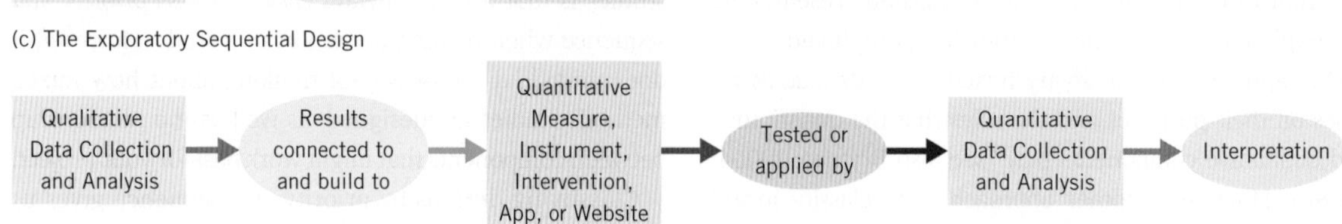

Source: Reproduced from Creswell, J. and Plano Clark, V. (2018). *Designing and Conducting Mixed Methods Research*, 3rd edn. London: SAGE.

simultaneously, or implies that the sequence in which the data are collected does not matter, because one will not influence the other. These data usually have equal priority. The researchers then compare the resulting analyses and/or merge them to form an integrated analysis. This kind of design tends to be associated with *triangulation* exercises, in which (as we discussed in Section 24.2) the researcher aims to compare two sets of findings, as well as with situations in which the researcher aims to *offset* the weaknesses of both quantitative and qualitative research by capitalizing on the strengths of both. For example, Bregoli (2013) was interested in whether the strength of a tourist destination brand is stronger when stakeholders in that brand co-ordinate their brand activities. She collected quantitative data through an online questionnaire that she sent to stakeholders in tourism organizations in Edinburgh, and qualitative data from semi-structured interviews with representatives of tourism organizations and from documents. She writes: 'Results were merged by comparing them and were interpreted and discussed by stating the degree to which they converged, diverged, or related' (Bregoli 2013: 216).

The explanatory sequential design

The **explanatory sequential design** involves *first collecting and analysing quantitative data, and then collecting and*

RESEARCH IN FOCUS 24.5
Explanatory sequential mixed method design

In their cross-cultural comparative study of youth drinking in the USA and Italy, Aresi et al. (2020) used a sequential explanatory mixed method design. In the first phase, they used a secondary quantitative analysis data set to identify subgroups of drinkers from samples of 424 (61.3 per cent female) Italian and 323 US college students (57.3 per cent female). In the second phase, they went on to use focus groups with 41 Italian and 47 US young people.

The quantitative phase allowed them to obtain an overview of the different groups of drinkers. Here, they found that drinkers across the two countries could be thought of as belonging to one of four groups: current non-drinkers, weekend non-risky drinkers, weekend risky drinkers, and daily drinkers. In contrast, the qualitative phase allowed the researchers to construct narratives about the kinds of factors that helped to explain those differences, for example gender, and societal beliefs and norms in the USA and Italy. They organized the qualitative data into three main themes: first experiences with alcohol; views about alcoholic drinking and food; and how participants responded to the four types of drinkers that the researchers identified in the quantitative part of the study.

This mixed methods study found that, even though there were similar kinds of drinking behaviours in the USA and Italy, there were important differences in how predictable the drinking was and how childhood experiences with drink influenced drinking behaviour later in life.

analysing qualitative data in order to elaborate or explain the quantitative findings. Researchers might use this approach when they feel that the broad patterns of relationships that they have uncovered through quantitative research require an explanation that the quantitative data on their own are unable to supply, or when they need further insight into their quantitative findings. Although the quantitative element comes first in the sequence, it does not necessarily have *priority* within this design, as the explanation or elaboration provided by the qualitative findings may be especially significant for the study's research questions. The study by McCrudden and McTigue (2019) into belief bias among high school students regarding climate change (which we first discussed in Section 24.2) began with the collection of quantitative data, and then the researchers followed up with a purposively selected sample of respondents who took part in interviews in which they were prompted to explain their responses. A study by Aresi et al. (2020) on youth drinking provides another example of the use of this design—see Research in focus 24.5.

The exploratory sequential design

The **exploratory sequential design** involves *first collecting qualitative data and then collecting quantitative data*. It is associated with investigations in which the researcher wants to generate hypotheses, which they can then test using quantitative research. It is also associated with investigations in which the aim is to develop research instruments such as questionnaire questions, which the researcher can then use in a quantitative investigation. This design can also use quantitative research to follow up qualitative findings in order to assess their scope and generalizability. The qualitative element does not always have priority in this design. Alatinga and Williams (2019) used the exploratory sequential design when trying to identify which very poor households in Ghana should be exempt from paying insurance premiums. They began by conducting 24 focus groups that identified who the very poor were and what characterizes them, and used this qualitative data to build a survey, which they then distributed to 417 households. Research in focus 24.6 provides a further example of a study using this design.

From these brief descriptions of the main types of mixed methods design, it is worth noting two further points. Firstly, while we can think of the convergent, explanatory sequential, and exploratory sequential types as—broadly speaking—among the most common mixed methods designs, these kinds of typologies are only ever a guide. Sometimes, a project may incorporate elements of more than one of these designs, as in Platell et al.'s (2020) study—see Research in focus 24.7. This project mainly used sequential mixed methods but also elements of concurrent mixed methods. The key idea is that it can be useful to think of the mixed methods research process as one that may involve a set of methodological activities that are more or less sequential, concurrent, exploratory,

RESEARCH IN FOCUS 24.6

A mixed methods exploratory sequential design

Faulk and Crist (2020) carried out a mixed methods exploratory sequential study on library communication with students and faculties. The study was conducted in response to a 2017 report that stressed the importance of communicating the library's contributions if the library is to have a meaningful impact on academic success. Faulk and Crist developed **vignettes** based on different library communication scenarios that the researchers had witnessed, and they used these vignettes to trigger conversations in a series of **asynchronous online focus groups**. They used the results from these focus groups to inform the design of a questionnaire that they then used to 'generalize these findings into a quantitative strand' (2020: 364). Their study is a good example of one method feeding into another method, using findings from both methods to learn something more about how communication between the library and students and faculty could be improved.

RESEARCH IN FOCUS 24.7

A study using both sequential and concurrent mixed methods

Platell et al. (2020) conducted a sequential mixed methods study, comprising three phases, to understand why many young people fail to seek help and access mental health services even when they want help, know that they may need help, and also know that services are available precisely to support them.

The three phases were as follows.

- Phase 1: face-to-face semi-structured interviews with mental health professionals and clinicians providing services to adolescents.
- Phase 2: an **online survey** with adolescents aged 14–18 years who had intended to seek help but did not.
- Phase 3: interviews with adolescents aged 14–18 years who were currently using a mental health service or had previously used a mental health service in the past 24 months.

The researchers gave equal **weighting** to the qualitative and quantitative results. They integrated the findings of all three phases, and write:

> By collecting data from mental health professionals first, Phase 1 results could then be directly used to inform the development of the survey questions and interview guide used in Phases 2 and 3 on adolescent 'real-world' experiences. Phases 2 and 3 were then undertaken concurrently (QUAL (QUAN + QUAL)). Phase 1 data was also used for comparative purposes to enable the authors to determine whether professionals' perceptions corresponded with adolescent real-world experiences.
>
> (Platell et al. 2020: 2)

Once the researchers had analysed the data from the different phases separately, they integrated them by drawing out themes, using **thematic analysis**, that bridged the different phases together. For example, they grouped **indicators** of 'facilitators' or 'barriers' to accessing mental health services. This process of integration through narrative allowed the researchers to identify key components that both hindered and facilitated adolescents seeking help for mental health issues (such as being 'put off' by something a mental health service worker might have unintentionally said, or by the triage process at the entry point for accessing help). Platell et al. sum up the benefits of conducting a mixed methods study as follows:

> One of the major strengths of this research was the use of a mixed methods approach. This allowed us to capture a more integrated picture of the factors contributing to adolescent mental health service access. A mixed methods approach provided flexibility in the selection of data collection methods deemed most appropriate for each population, and allowed us to draw on the complementary strengths of both qualitative and quantitative techniques.
>
> (Platell et al. 2020: 8)

or explanatory. Being clear about the actual research process is also useful when you come to write up mixed methods research, as this will ensure that you provide transparency to those reading about your research.

Secondly, it should be clear by now that the choice of design is closely bound up with the researcher's anticipated use(s) of a mixed methods approach. As we discuss further in Section 24.5, many things come together to shape the design that is ultimately selected—the amount of time available, how doable it is to actually collect the different data, and so on. It is not that there is a 'best' design—an explanatory sequential design is not always better than a convergent one, for example. You might ask yourself what the 'best' design might be in an ideal world, but the reality is that we never do research in an ideal world. We always need to make compromises. What makes a design 'better'—or more accurately, more appropriate—than another one depends on many interrelated factors. In the next section, we explore the kinds of questions we need to ask when it comes to evaluating a mixed methods project and conducting one of your own.

24.5 Conducting mixed methods research

We have covered a lot of ground in this chapter with the aim of introducing you to the key issues and debates involved in conducting mixed methods research. Several of our 'Learn from experience' graduates have successfully conducted mixed methods research (see Learn from experience 24.1 and 24.2), but is this a good approach to take for your research project? If so, what considerations should you bear in mind? What makes a mixed methods project good or bad? What does the researcher need to communicate clearly to readers when presenting a mixed methods project? We address these questions in what follows. As we will see, many of the criteria for choosing to conduct a mixed methods project and subsequently evaluating its quality are similar to those we would use for single-method or single-strategy studies. But there are also some that are particular to mixed methods approaches.

We will now list five factors you will want to take into account when evaluating or considering mixed methods research. The reflections we list are influenced by writings about indicators of quality in mixed methods research (for example Bryman et al. 2008; Bryman 2014; O'Cathain et al. 2008), but they can also act as practical guidance to students and researchers thinking about doing mixed methods research for the first time. This is not an exhaustive list of all possible quality criteria or considerations that can or have been applied to mixed methods research (such as the list in O'Cathain 2010), but rather a summary of the main considerations that come up in discussions of this approach. It is important to note that each item on the list interrelates with the others. Overall, the decision to conduct a mixed methods project and your ability to deliver high quality research depends on all of these issues and how they work together as a whole. For this reason, we have not ranked the five items in order of importance; they are simply a set of interdependent issues that you should consider if you are thinking about doing a mixed methods project. If you do decide to use mixed methods, then you will need to explicitly address each of these issues when you write up your research. The issues are:

- the *added value* of doing mixed methods
- whether the *research design* is appropriate for the research questions
- how the *data will be integrated*
- whether the *ethical procedures* are thorough for both methods
- whether the *project is doable* within the time frame

Let's consider each point in turn.

What is the added value of using mixed methods?

We have seen that there can be many advantages to using both qualitative and quantitative methods. Therefore, a mixed methods approach is certainly worth considering for any project, but it is important to realize that it is not necessarily 'better'. It is tempting to assume that more findings, and more varied findings, such as those that mixed methods can generate, are inevitably 'a good thing' and improve the quality of a study. Indeed, social scientists sometimes display such a view (Bryman 2006b). However, mixed methods designs are not fundamentally superior to single-method or single-strategy research, and it is not always sensible to do more simply because you can. Simple research designs can be very powerful if done well. In some instances, using a single method may even be viewed more favourably, say in an application for research funding, than a mixed methods design, because the simpler research design could seem more achievable within the permitted time frame. So, the benefits of doing a mixed methods project need to clearly outweigh the costs (financially, but also in a broader sense) that it will involve.

Is the research design appropriate for the research question(s)?

Mixed methods research must be appropriate to, and thoroughly integrated with, the research questions. Again, this is the same as for single-method or single-strategy research. There is no point collecting more data on the assumption that 'more is better', especially given that using multiple methods is likely to be more expensive and time-consuming than relying on just one. Mixed methods research, like single-method research, must be competently designed and conducted. Poorly designed research will result in poor findings, no matter how many methods are used. As we consider further in Chapter 25 on writing up, good quality mixed methods research should give the reader a clear sense of the relationship between the research questions and the research methods, and also a sense of what the use of two or more methods, rather than one, was meant to achieve in terms of the overall project.

How will the data be integrated?

It is important that from the start of your mixed methods research you give careful thought to how the quantitative and qualitative components relate to each other, not only at the point of data collection but in the analysis as well. You should be clear about how you will *integrate* the data. In your write-up you should clearly state and explain these integration strategies, and discuss the sets of findings together, otherwise—as Alan Bryman noted (2006a)—the project cannot really be considered a mixed methods study at all. You should also consider whether you have the skills needed to do every aspect of the research. For example, are you confident that you can design a meaningful set of interviews alongside a questionnaire, implement these data-collection tools effectively, analyse both sets of data properly, and integrate the data and findings in a sensible way? Consider this further in Thinking deeply 24.2.

Data integration can produce results that are inconsistent across methods, and can even 'mess up' what you think you are studying (Uprichard and Dawney 2019). For example, in their study of media reporting of social science research, Fenton et al. (1998) found an inconsistency between some of the quantitative and qualitative data: the quantitative methods suggested that journalists' reporting of social science research reflected approaches and values that were mainly aligned with those of social scientists, but the qualitative findings suggested greater conflict. But these kinds of inconsistencies are not necessarily a

THINKING DEEPLY 24.2
Data integration in mixed methods research

Data integration in mixed methods research is increasingly at the heart of methodological debates about such research, because the **validity** and **reliability** of the findings tend to rest on how the data do or do not come together. Questions raised include whether the data *can* come together; if so, what that involves; and what it means to 'integrate data' in the first place. If we think of data as depicting something about the world we are studying, then does it really matter that the data from one method may show something different from another method's data? Surely the whole point of using mixed methods is because we want to have the possibility of quantitative and qualitative methods revealing different things about what we are studying? The early philosophical debates about whether or not qualitative and quantitative methods are epistemologically equivalent are reflected in modern discussions about how to deal with what researchers may see as more or less opposing sets of data, depending on the researchers' particular standpoints. While there are no set rules about what data integration must involve, there have been many different attempts to provide students and researchers with a set of guidelines or systematic typologies.

problem—the important thing is to make it clear in your write-up that you have attempted to bring the different data together, and to acknowledge any challenges involved in doing that. Fenton et al. (1998) dealt with the inconsistency in their data by re-examining it, rather than deciding that one set of findings provided a more accurate view.

Are the ethical procedures thorough for both methods?

Like any good-quality piece of research, a good mixed methods study must be ethically conducted from start to finish (see Chapter 6 on ethics), including how the work is written up and published. For most projects you will need to gain ethical approval before you begin, but remember that if you are using a sequential mixed methods design, you may know some elements of the project better than others; indeed, some elements of the research design (for example the questionnaire or interview questions) may only come to be designed *after* the research has begun. Ethical committees generally require a significant amount of detail in order to approve the whole project. So, it is not uncommon for an ethical panel to approve a mixed methods project in principle, so it can start with this or that method, but also insist that the researcher applies for further approval later on. For example, a panel may approve the use of interviews and a survey in principle, but because the researchers will only finalize the survey questions *after* they have analysed the interview data, the panel may ask for the researchers to apply for further approval for the survey component of the project. So, if you are using a sequential mixed methods design you may need to factor in extra time for a multi-stage ethical approval process—which brings us to the consideration of timing.

Is the project doable within the time frame?

When deciding whether to adopt a mixed methods approach, you need to consider the time and resources (including financial resources) you have available, and both are likely to be more limited for a small-scale student project. You will need to think through the order of actions. For example, a concurrent design, where both qualitative and quantitative approaches take place in parallel to one another, might be preferable to a sequential design as it could save time. But are you sure you can actually do both at the same time? Likewise, you may need to allow a significant amount of time for ethical approval, as we have just mentioned; for the data analysis stage, especially if you have less experience with analysing one type of data; and for writing up.

Mixed methods projects do tend to need more time than projects that only use one single method, but much depends on the research questions, the size of the samples, the skillset and experience of the researcher, and so on. Having enough time to do a particular project may seem like an obvious issue to consider, but it is often one of the more challenging aspects to get right ahead of any project, because so many different things can happen during the course of the research. Yet whether findings are seen to be valid, meaningful and worthwhile is just as likely to be assessed in the context of the time frame of the project as in relation to the questions that are being explored.

Further considerations

In addition to the five considerations we have just looked at, you might find it useful to refer to the A–Z list of questions in Tips and skills 24.1 as a checklist for evaluating existing mixed methods research and/or devising your own mixed methods study (Sammons and Davis 2017). None of the points we have raised so far are intended to put you off using mixed methods. Instead, they are there to help you think carefully about whether the approach is right for you and your project. Each project is unique and will require a bespoke approach. This is the case for all research, not just mixed methods projects. The trick is to weigh up the pros and cons and make careful, realistic assessments, rather than becoming set on a particular approach and forging ahead without thinking through the potential implications. The other important thing—and again, this applies to all research—is to make sure that all this careful thought is evident in your write-up. This means stating the type of mixed methods design you used (see Section 24.4 and Figure 24.2) and providing a sufficiently detailed account of aspects such as sampling, the design and administration of your research instruments, and the analysis of data for *both* the quantitative and the qualitative components of the study. (Often researchers provide more detail on one element or too little detail on both.) You should explain and clearly justify the decisions you made in connection with these issues. We discuss the particular considerations for writing up a mixed methods study—including making sure that your overall rationale for mixing methods is clear—in Chapter 25, where we will walk through an example.

TIPS AND SKILLS 24.1
A–Z for evaluating mixed methods studies

Sammons and Davis (2017) provide a list of interrelated questions they recommend to those who may be new to mixed methods ('MM') research as a way of evaluating MM studies. These questions are also useful prompts for thinking about and planning your own mixed methods project.

A. What was the overall purpose of this study (aims/objectives)?

B. What are the quantitative research questions?

C. What are the qualitative research questions?

D. How are the quantitative and qualitative questions linked?

E. What is the sample for the quantitative component of the study? How was it selected?

F. What is the sample for the qualitative component of the study? How was it selected?

G. What is the overall **sampling frame** and how are the qualitative and quantitative samples linked/related?

H. What are the quantitative data collection instruments/sources?

I. What are the qualitative data collection instruments/sources?

J. What are the joint quantitative/qualitative data collection instruments/sources (if any)?

K. What kinds of quantitative analyses strategies are used and how have they addressed the quantitative research questions?

L. What are the qualitative analyses strategies [. . .] used and how have they addressed the qualitative research questions?

M. What are the 'points of interface' linking the qualitative and quantitative data analyses?

N. What is the priority accorded to the qualitative and quantitative components of the study?

O. How were concerns about the quality of the quantitative data addressed (for example, reliability, validity, generalizability)?

P. How were concerns about the quality of the qualitative data addressed (for example, **trustworthiness** of findings)?

Q. What attempts were made to link or integrate the qualitative and quantitative components of the study?

R. How far do the quantitative and qualitative findings align? What efforts were made to reconcile/explain any differences in the findings of the qualitative and quantitative components of the study?

S. Are there any examples of any quantitizing of qualitative data?

T. Are there any examples of any qualitizing of quantitative data?

U. How rigorous is the description of the research design and methods?

V. Have the authors used a diagram to illustrate the MM design and the way different components are linked?

W. Do the researchers make an explicit case for adopting a MM design?

X. What is the philosophical position underpinning the research and how does it link with the research aims and purposes?

Y. Do the researchers make new knowledge claims that are based on the integration and synthesis of qualitative and quantitative data and findings?

Z. Is there evidence that the MM design has produced findings/added new knowledge that is more than the 'sum' of the quantitative and qualitative parts?

Source: Sammons, P., and Davis, S. (2017). 'Mixed Methods Approaches and their Application in Educational Research', in D. Wyse, N. Selwyn, and E. Smith (eds), *The BERA/SAGE Handbook of Educational Research*, vol. 2. London: SAGE.

KEY POINTS

- There are differences between quantitative and qualitative research, but it is important not to exaggerate the contrasts. Each strategy can exhibit characteristics that are usually associated with the other.
- While there has been a growth in the popularity of mixed methods research, not all writers support its use. Objections to mixed methods research tend to be on the grounds that quantitative and qualitative research cannot be combined because they are inherently linked to particular epistemological and ontological positions.
- However, the connections between research methods and epistemological and ontological positions are not deterministic. Qualitative research sometimes exhibits features normally associated with a natural science model, for example, and quantitative research sometimes aims to engage with an interpretivist stance.
- Research methods are more autonomous in relation to epistemological commitments than is often appreciated.
- There are several different ways of combining quantitative and qualitative research and of representing and rationalizing mixed methods research.
- Mixed methods research is not necessarily superior to single-method research, and there are important criteria to consider to ensure that it is of good quality.
- Mixed methods can be an effective approach for student research projects, but it requires careful thought, and there are important considerations that are specific to mixed methods and that you will need to bear in mind at all stages of the research process, especially in terms of the analysis and writing up.

QUESTIONS FOR REVIEW

1. What is mixed methods research?
2. What is the logic of triangulation?
3. What are the main reasons why researchers conduct mixed methods research?
4. Why might it be useful to distinguish between quantitative and qualitative approaches?
5. What is the nature of the link between research methods and epistemology?
6. To what extent can some quantitative research be seen as exhibiting characteristics of interpretivism?
7. Outline some of the ways in which the quantitative/qualitative contrast may not be as clear-cut as is often supposed.
8. To what extent is quantification a feature of qualitative research?
9. What, if anything, is lost when qualitative data are quantified?
10. How are priority and sequence significant as ways of classifying mixed methods research?
11. What are the main ways in which quantitative and qualitative research have been combined?
12. Traditionally, qualitative research has been presented as helping researchers to prepare for quantitative research. To what extent do the different forms of mixed methods research reflect this view?
13. Is mixed methods research necessarily superior to single-method research?
14. Are there any quality considerations that apply specifically to mixed methods research? If so, what are they?

ONLINE RESOURCES

www.oup.com/he/srm6e

You can find our notes on the answers to these questions within this chapter's **online resources**, together with:

- *audio/video comments* on this topic from our 'Learn from experience' panellists;
- *self-test questions* for further knowledge-checking;
- a *flashcard glossary* to help you recall key terms; and
- a *Student Researcher's Toolkit* containing practical materials and resources to help you conduct your own research project.

CHAPTER
25
WRITING UP SOCIAL RESEARCH

CHAPTER GUIDE

Our focus in the rest of this book has been on planning for a social research project, obtaining the data, and analysing the data. But the work does not end there: everything now needs to be written up. In this chapter we look at

- the principles of good practice when writing up your research;
- how you can structure your write-up;
- examples of how to write up quantitative, qualitative, and mixed methods research.

25.1 Introduction

Planning and successfully carrying out a social research project is quite an achievement. Whether you have completed a quantitative, qualitative, or mixed methods project, you will have put a lot of thought and work into designing and implementing it. Beginner researchers can sometimes fall into the trap of thinking of writing up as 'the easy bit'. While writing up does not have to be a painful process—in fact, it can be very enjoyable!—it is crucial that you do not underestimate the task and that you spend enough time and thought on this phase to do justice to your work. Obvious though this may sound, you have to write up your project in order to convey your findings to an audience, and no matter how well you have planned and conducted the research, it will only have an impact (and receive a high mark, if it is a student project) if your readers can understand exactly what you did and why, and are convinced by the knowledge claims you are making.

In this chapter we will discuss some principles of good practice that you can develop and incorporate into your own write-up of your research project or dissertation. We will cover the main ingredients of a successful write-up and the overall structure to follow, before looking at the specific considerations and structures for writing up quantitative, qualitative, and **mixed methods research** projects, which we will illustrate through three examples. You should finish this chapter with a clearer idea of what writing up involves, and a variety of tips that you can put into practice and templates that you can use as a starting point. We advise reading this chapter and beginning to think about the writing up phase sooner rather than later, so that you know what is involved and can get started in good time, increasing the chances of it being an enjoyable and ultimately successful part of your research.

25.2 Tips for a successful write-up

Your research write-up is likely to be a different kind of academic piece from those that you have produced before, as much of your written work so far has probably been shorter coursework assessments or exam answers. Many of your existing academic writing skills will be useful here—for example planning the content to be included, using a clear structure, following certain conventions, and writing clearly and persuasively—but you will need to take some extra factors and elements into account. You will be most likely to produce a successful write-up if you focus on the following elements, each of which we will discuss.

- Start early
- Structure your writing
- Be persuasive
- Signpost your work
- Justify your decisions
- Maintain an argument
- Get to know your institution's writing conventions and expectations
- Avoid discriminatory language
- Get feedback
- Fulfil your obligations

We explore these ideas in more detail in this section, but we do not provide detailed examples from real research—we do this in Section 25.4, in the context of different research strategies (quantitative, qualitative, and mixed methods research).

One very general point that we want to emphasize is that if you *enjoy* your research, this can have a big impact on the quality and persuasiveness of your write-up, as well as helping you stay motivated during this phase of the project. Our panellists discuss this in Learn from experience 25.1.

Start early

Students sometimes underestimate the amount of time it will take to write up their research and delay starting this phase until after data collection. Clearly, you cannot write up your findings until you know what they are, but there are good reasons for starting to think about writing up early on, and even drafting parts of the write-up. For example, although your **literature review** can be iterative and you will probably revise it throughout your project, it is a really good idea to produce an early draft while you are doing your initial reading. You might also be able to produce a draft of the methodology section, as you will

LEARN FROM EXPERIENCE 25.1

Enjoying your research

Having the freedom and autonomy to choose your own area of investigation and design your own research project should be exciting, and having enthusiasm and a genuine interest in a topic can keep you motivated over a substantial period of time. Interest and enthusiasm were certainly important to our panellists.

> I think interest and enthusiasm are absolutely key! You will be working on the project over several months, so in order to motivate yourself for such a long period you must be invested, otherwise your work will suffer, because the energy and enthusiasm for your project inevitably dictates how much effort you put in. This is especially obvious during the writing up phase. I was absolutely fascinated by my research project and I think if you go into it with the mindset that it is your personal project then it will be a very enjoyable and rewarding experience.
>
> Grace

> Enjoying my research is so important for me. My passion, and my goals to influence change and contribute to knowledge, all drive my motivation. If you don't have a genuine interest or enthusiasm for your work you may find it very difficult to write it up.
>
> Jodie

However, as Simon reflects, we sometimes have to ensure that our enthusiasm and interest in a topic does not cloud our judgement.

> When I was an undergrad researching the police, I found it really difficult to remain objective. I knew what I wanted to prove and I kind of set out to do so. Good supervision kept me in line. I was challenged regularly about assumptions I was making in my research and my write-up, and was asked to back them up with academic literature. This really helped me to put my feelings to one side.
>
> Simon

You can read about our panellists' backgrounds and research experiences on page xxvi.

have decided what methods you are going to use quite early in the project, before you begin to gather data.

There is another, entirely practical, reason why we recommend starting to write sooner rather than later: many people find it difficult to get started with writing up and will procrastinate. This can result in the writing being left until the last minute and therefore being rushed. As we noted in Section 25.1, how you represent your findings and conclusions is a crucial part of the research process, so you must allow enough time to do justice to the significant time and effort you will have put into your project. In Learn from experience 25.2, our graduates share their experiences and advice on getting started with your writing.

Structure your writing

A clear, logical structure is an essential aspect of most academic writing. In your essays, for example, you will have structured your writing so that you begin with an introduction; build up your argument step by step, providing evidence to back up your assertions; and then end with a conclusion. Similar principles apply when writing up a research project, but here a clear structure is even more important for two reasons. First, there is likely to be much more content involved. Dissertations are often around 10,000 to 15,000 words long, so their content needs to be organized into sections, often called chapters, which can also have subsections. Second, a research write-up has to adhere to a more rigid framework than most essays. It needs to include certain components, clearly titled, and these should appear in a particular order. This might sound restrictive, but in fact, having this kind of framework to follow will help you write about your project clearly and succinctly. It also makes it easier to assess what needs to be done (so that you can plan your time accordingly), break the task into manageable chunks, and keep track of your progress.

We recommend familiarizing yourself with the structure of a social research write-up as early as possible, so that none of its components take you by surprise and so that you can start drafting some elements early on (see 'Start early'). We walk through the typical components of an undergraduate dissertation, and the order in which they should usually be presented, in Section 25.3.

LEARN FROM EXPERIENCE 25.2

Getting started with writing

It's fair to say that starting to write up your research can be hard. Even when you have plenty to say, getting everything down in a structured, well-argued, and logical manner can be tricky. All of us (including the authors of this book) have at some point delayed starting to write something new or stared at a blank page for hours on end, just waiting for inspiration to come. So how to get over this? Our panellists share their advice.

> Start writing when you feel ready. Don't rush it and be patient. Writer's block is real—we all suffer from it at times. But when some inspiration comes just go with it, no matter what—make sure you get it down on the page. Then edit, then take a break, then edit some more. Repeat. I have always found plans and rough drafts really useful and valuable, but everyone needs to find what works for them. That also goes for what order to write in. My usual journey for writing an academic project starts with the introduction [although many researchers leave writing the introduction until the end of the write-up process, as we will discuss], followed by a bit of the literature review (so that I can place my work), then I write my methods completely, revisit my literature review, write my results, analysis and discussion—revisit my literature review. Then I finally write my conclusion—while revisiting my introduction. Then I do a final edit of the whole piece. Learning what time of day (or night) you write best is unbelievably rewarding, but that said, sometimes it's good to mix up your work routine as it can inspire a boost in your productivity.
>
> Jodie

> I started writing early on in my fieldwork, first by extending my field notes through describing situations and what I thought made these situations interesting, and later by writing preliminary versions of possible chapters, which forced me to formulate my thoughts. This helped me because once I finished my fieldwork and my supervisor wanted me to submit my work, I already had a lot of material I could use.
>
> Minke

> I found writing rough drafts to be an important part of the process. I was required to submit these to my supervisor, which was hugely beneficial. She would often recommend additional literature I should pursue to strengthen particular points, or would recommend researchers to look into. Setting the goal of submitting a draft a week helped to keep me on track, even if at times the drafts were not as well written as I would have liked—that's part of the beauty of drafts. Students often have different writing styles, but I recommend writing freely and editing later because there is a good chance you'll feel less inhibited.
>
> Starr

> I found it useful to be flexible about the order in which I wrote. For example, I often found myself writing my introduction last, as it was clear that the direction of my project had changed slightly as it progressed. I also found that setting a target of 5 or 6 hours of writing a day during the day time worked well for me, rather than working later in the day or aiming to do a 12 hour day—but this was down to personal preference.
>
> Zvi

 Access the **online resources** to hear our panellists' video reflections on this theme.

You can read about our panellists' backgrounds and research experiences on page xxvi.

Be persuasive

This point is crucial. Writing up your research is not simply a matter of reporting your findings and drawing some conclusions. Your write-up will contain many other features, such as references to the literature on which you drew, and explanations of how you did your research and conducted your analysis. But above all, you must be *persuasive*. Simply saying 'This is what I found; isn't it interesting?' is not enough. You must convince your readers that your findings and conclusion are significant and that they are plausible, and this cannot be achieved with lifeless, uncertain-sounding writing. You can use some of

KEY CONCEPT 25.1
What is rhetoric?

Rhetoric is the art of persuasion through effective speaking or writing. We often hear the term used in a negative context (for example, assertions made by politicians can be criticized as 'mere rhetoric' and sometimes people talk about the opposition of 'rhetoric and reality'), but rhetoric is an essential ingredient of writing. It is a fundamental part of writing up social research, because it helps us to convince others about the credibility of our knowledge claims (an idea that we also consider in Chapter 21, in the context of **discourse analysis**).

the same **rhetorical** strategies (see Key concept 25.1) employed by social researchers to persuade readers of the value of their work, and if you start writing early, you can develop your style throughout your project.

Signpost your work

Academic writing tends to provide lots of 'signposts'. You will notice, when reading the example journal articles we discuss in Section 25.4, that authors will generally tell you what they are going to do at the start. We often use signposts in this book—for example, at the beginning of this section we summarized the ideas that will be covered here. Students often worry that this will sound too obvious and/or that they will give away 'spoilers', but signposts will help the reader follow your argument. We often advise students to tell the reader what you are going to do, do the thing, and then tell the reader what you did. This is not 'dumbing down' your work—it is making it clearer.

Justify your decisions

Academic writing requires you to justify your key decisions and assertions. For example, you may select a certain theoretical perspective as your starting point, but you need to justify why that is an appropriate **theory**. Similarly, you should not simply assert your **research questions** and the focus of your research—you need to demonstrate *why* those research questions and the focus of your research are important and significant, and this means justifying them. You also need to justify your choices of methods, including your **research design**, your **sampling** approach, your data-collection methods, and your approach to data analysis. Referencing the literature (see Chapter 5) is an important way of justifying these kinds of decisions.

Maintain an argument

A research write-up should be organized around an argument that links all aspects of the research process and runs through all its stages: problem formulation; literature review; choice and implementation of **research methods**; discussion; and conclusion (see Figure 25.1 for an illustration of this). Too often, students make a series of points without explaining what each point contributes to the overall argument that they are trying to present. If you do this, you are very vulnerable to the 'So what?' question.

An argument will naturally emerge if you think about what your claim to knowledge is and try to organize your writing to support and enhance that claim. Consider the *story* you want to tell about your research and your findings, and the key point or message that you want your readers to take away when they finish reading your work. Try to avoid tangents and irrelevant material that may mean that your readers lose track of your argument. One way to give readers a clearer sense of an argument is to provide some signposts of where you intend to go in your dissertation and why. (See 'Signpost your work' earlier in this section.)

Get to know your institution's writing conventions and expectations

Make sure you are familiar with the writing conventions required by your department or institution. One of these is whether it is acceptable to use the word 'I' (the first person singular). In this book we write in the first person plural ('We will discuss'), using a relatively informal style to invite you into and help you understand the subject, but sometimes you will need to write in the third person—as in the phrases included in Figure 25.1. For example:

- 'a questionnaire was administered' rather than 'I administered a questionnaire'
- 'it will be argued that' rather than 'I will argue'
- 'it has been shown that' rather than 'I have shown that'
- 'a thematic analysis was carried out' rather than 'I carried out a thematic analysis'

As Billig (2013) observes, third-person writing helps to convey a sense of objectivity, but it also means that the

FIGURE 25.1
The role of an argument in a dissertation

Dissertation chapter		Commonly used phrases in formulating an argument
Introduction		This dissertation is concerned with. . . This dissertation will explore/examine. . . There has been a growth of interest in X to which this dissertation will make a contribution. The growing adoption of . . . has attracted a lot of interest in the mass media but there is a dearth of research into its actual use.
Literature review		X has attracted a great deal of interest in recent years. In particular, [name1 year] has argued/suggested/noted. . . According to [name2 year] the concept of Y can be usefully employed to illuminate X because. . . Recent research on X has shown that. . . . . .although the findings are somewhat inconsistent. Therefore, much of the existing research suggests. . . By contrast, [name3 year] found/argued/suggested. . . One area of controversy in the literature about X revolves around the question of. . . This dissertation will build on [name3]'s suggestion that. . . In exploring this issue, the following research questions are proposed:. . .
Research methods	A	Research method1 was employed to answer the research questions because/in order to. . . The sampling approach entailed a purposive sampling approach because. . . The research followed [name3]'s approach to studying X by. . . Questionnaires were administered by postal mail in order to. . . A mixed methods approach was taken so that it would be possible to. . .
Results/ findings	R G U M	In exploring the research questions, three main themes were identified. . . The findings suggest that. . . Interviewees differed in their perspectives on X in two key respects. . . As Table 7 shows, women were more likely than men to. . . No statistically significant relationship between variable4 and variable15 was uncovered (see Table 4) which suggests that. . . This theme is exemplified by Interviewee23's comment that. . . By contrast, Interviewee12 pointed out that. . .
Discussion	E N T	The aim of this study was to. . . The findings reported in Table 4 failed to provide empirical support for Hypothesis 2 in that. . . The thematic analysis strongly suggests that the concept of Y is very significant for an understanding of. . . The findings provide clear evidence that [name2]'s concept of Y can be usefully employed to extend our understanding of X because. . . Overall, these findings confirm/fail to provide support for the suggestion that. . . Four main themes relating to the research questions emerged. These themes have implications for the investigation of X. . . The themes derived from the semi-structured interviews helped to explain the correlation between variable4 and variable9 by suggesting that. . .
Conclusion		In conclusion, these findings suggest that [name2]'s concept of Y can provide a useful springboard for the investigation of X because. . . A key finding of this research for [name2]'s Z theory is that. . . The failure to confirm Hypothesis 2 implies that [name3]'s concept of Y is of questionable utility, since it would be expected that. . . The concepts that have been used to research X have been shown to be of some utility but the results are somewhat mixed in that. . . Through this research it has been demonstrated that. . . The main contribution(s) of this research is (are). . . Taking a mixed methods approach proved beneficial because. . . The implications of these findings for the study of X are that. . . In conclusion, it is proposed that future research should concentrate on/not rely so much on. . . On the basis of the findings generated by this study, it is concluded that. . . One limitation of this study is that. . .

X refers to a topic or area (e.g. mobile phones, recycling)
Y refers to a concept (e.g. cultural capital, quasi-subject)
Z refers to a theory (e.g. actor network theory, risk society)

researcher disappears from the text. Third-person writing can also lead to very long-winded and passive sentences. Sometimes the preference for writing in the first or third person is connected to disciplinary or methodological positions, so our advice is always to check with your supervisor.

You should also consider what your institution expects of you depending on the level that you are writing at. Their expectations and assessment criteria will differ depending on whether you are working on an undergraduate, master's, or doctoral programme. For example, originality is essential for a PhD—it is expected that you will make a meaningful contribution to your discipline. At master's and undergraduate level you may find there is less consensus between institutions and countries about issues such as **replication**, originality, maximum word counts, and how much space you need to dedicate to particular parts of your work when writing up.

Avoid discriminatory language

Your writing should avoid language that discriminates against, or risks causing offence to, groups of people or individuals. Make sure that you are sensitive and respectful of equality and diversity issues such as sex, gender, race, ethnicity, disability, sexuality, and so on. The British Sociological Association provides some very good advice, both general and more specific, about the use of non-disablist language and how to refer to sex and gender, and ethnicity and race, which can be found at **www.britsoc.co.uk/equality-diversity/** (accessed 1 October 2019).

One point to note in this context is that using 'his/her' formulations in order to avoid sexist language can lead to long and complex-sounding sentences. The easiest way of dealing with this is to use 'they' or 'them'. Consider, for example: 'I wanted to give each respondent the opportunity to complete the questionnaire in his or her own time and in a location that was convenient for him or her.' This sentence is grammatically correct, but it would be clearer and easier to read if phrased using 'their' and 'them' as singular forms: 'I wanted to give each respondent the opportunity to complete the questionnaire in their own time and in a location that was convenient for them.' The use of 'their' is also more gender-inclusive as it avoids the false dichotomy between male and female (which excludes non-binary individuals—see Thinking deeply 15.2).

Get feedback

In Chapter 4 we recommended that you make the most of your supervisor when planning your research project (see Section 4.2 under 'Working with your supervisor'). The same ideas apply in this closing phase of the project: try to get as much feedback on your writing as possible and make sure that you respond positively to the points people make about your drafts. Your supervisor is likely to be your main source of feedback, but what supervisors are allowed to comment on varies between institutions. Give your supervisor the maximum amount of draft content that regulations will allow. Give them plenty of time to provide feedback: other students will want your supervisor to comment on their work too, and if the supervisor feels rushed, their comments may be less helpful. You could also ask others on your degree programme to read your drafts and comment on them, including to help you with proofreading (see Tips and skills 25.1). They may ask you to do the same. Your friends' comments may be very useful, but your supervisor's comments are the main ones you should seek out.

When you receive feedback, it is important to remember that your supervisor wants you to do the best project

TIPS AND SKILLS 25.1
Proofreading your dissertation

Before submitting your dissertation, make sure that you check it for spelling and for grammatical and punctuation errors. You should read it closely, perhaps even only spending an hour at a time doing this and giving yourself lots of breaks, so that you can maintain concentration. Sometimes when proofreading your own work you start to follow the flow of the text, or you see what you intended to say, rather than reading it closely. For this reason, it may be useful to ask someone else (a friend, coursemate, or family member) to have a look in case there are errors that you have missed. As well as being an important presentational issue, errors will affect how easily people can read and understand your work, and therefore its overall quality. One effective technique is to read your work out loud. This often highlights grammatical and structural problems that are not immediately obvious when reading in your head.

that you can. If they have suggested lots of changes, you should not take this as a personal attack. Academia works on the basis of peer review and (as we noted in Chapter 4) your supervisors will receive comments on their own work when submitting it for publication. By allowing others to interrogate our writing we make our work stronger. However, if you do not understand the feedback you have been given then you should always ask for clarification.

Fulfil your obligations

Remember to fulfil any obligations that you entered into throughout the research process. These might include providing a copy of your dissertation to participants and/or organizations, and maintaining the confidentiality of information that your participants supplied and the anonymity of your informants and other research participants.

25.3 How to structure your write-up

In Section 25.2 (under 'Structure your writing') we discussed the importance of structuring your write-up carefully. Here, we walk through the typical components of an undergraduate dissertation, in the order in which they are usually required to appear (summarized in Figure 25.2). The information in this section is intended only to give you a *basic overview* of the typical components—and the order of these components—in a social research project or dissertation. You will not necessarily write the sections in the order they appear below (for example, we discuss later how the introduction is normally one of the last things that you write); you will probably draft and revisit some sections, such as your literature review, as your project progresses; and the structure you use may vary slightly according to the **research strategy** you have used—in Section 25.4 we look in more detail at the specific requirements for quantitative, qualitative, and mixed methods research. Exact requirements regarding the structure of a research write-up can also vary between institutions and disciplines, so we recommend checking with your supervisor and your institution's guidance before planning your write-up or drafting any content.

Remember that whatever structure you use, there is a risk that by separating everything into sections, you will fail to integrate the ideas and themes that you have developed throughout your work. To address this, you should keep coming back to the literature and your research questions at key points in your write-up—as our panellists discuss in Learn from experience 25.3.

FIGURE 25.2
A typical structure of a social research dissertation

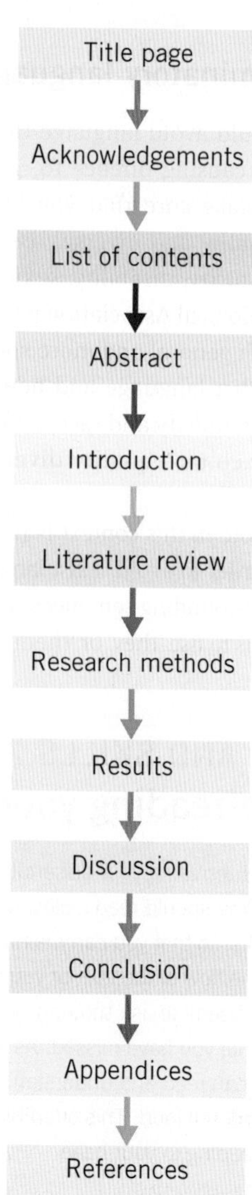

Title page

Your write-up should always begin with a title page, and you should check your institution's rules about what information to enter here.

LEARN FROM EXPERIENCE 25.3

Using your research questions, theory, and the literature in writing up

We spend a lot of time talking about how you should shape your research questions by consulting the literature and existing theory, but of course these three things should be woven into your write-up throughout. As supervisors, we think of this as 'closing the loop': referring back to existing theory and literature to demonstrate how your work contributes to the area of interest. Our panellists discuss below how they made sure that their findings fed into this loop, and how keeping an eye on research questions, theory, and literature can help to keep you on track with writing up.

Research questions, theory, and literature are key and I structured my work around them. Research questions were presented in my introduction, with the theory and literature that influenced and guided my project presented in my literature review. These were then synthesized against my findings in my results and discussion chapter. I would relate my results back to the existing literature and theory by identifying whether they challenged or supported what is already known, and I then explained the implications of this.

Jodie

When writing up my undergraduate dissertation I used my theoretical framework of social capital, in that I presented how my findings illustrated the **relationship** between social capital and empowerment. However, a significant theme from my findings was the internal feelings of empowerment that participants felt in being involved in a campaign group. This is something I did not initially fully consider in the literature review, but as it was a significant theme it was important to include it in my write-up. This demonstrates how conducting research can create new knowledge that is lacking in the existing literature.

Sarah

My research questions, theory, and literature were essential elements for completing my thesis. Without my research questions, I would have struggled with writing up a focused discussion and my reader would have had trouble making sense of the outcomes of my research. Without theory, I would not have been able to generalize my findings to the contemporary frameworks guiding the discussion on ethical internationalization. And without the literature that I reviewed, I would not have had a solid knowledge base to build any of the sections of my thesis, nor would I have had references to support my claims.

Starr

I think it is extremely important to relate your research findings back to the literature you have discussed in previous chapters. This is so that you can use your findings to confirm or question previous ideas relating to your topic. It allows you to demonstrate what your research has proved, why it is important, and what new knowledge it has contributed towards. If your findings contradict a lot of what has been stated in your literature review, use them to suggest what more can be done and what further research needs to be conducted in order to confirm your ideas.

Scarlett

 Access the **online resources** to hear our panellists' video reflections on this theme.

You can read about our panellists' backgrounds and research experiences on page xxvi.

Acknowledgements

The acknowledgements give you the opportunity to thank various people for the help they gave you in the course of your research project. For example, you might want to acknowledge **gatekeepers** who gave you access to an organization (see Chapter 6), people who have read your drafts and provided you with feedback, and/or your supervisor for their advice. The acknowledgements section is generally quite short, but it serves an important purpose in thanking people for their support.

List of contents

Your institution may have recommendations or rules about the form that the list of contents should take—for example, its level of detail regarding chapter headings and titles for subsections. This guidance might also tell you how to present lists of tables and figures. If you look at the start of this book you'll see that we present two lists of contents—one brief and one detailed. You will not have to present two versions in your work, but you can see that when all the subheadings are included in the detailed version the list of contents can become very long. If you are not sure how to proceed, then check with your supervisor.

Abstract

An abstract is a brief summary of your dissertation. Not all institutions require this component, so do check whether it is definitely required for your write-up. Journal articles usually have abstracts, so if you do need to provide one there are many examples that you can draw on for guidance.

Introduction

The introduction is where you set out the context of your research and get the reader's attention. A good introduction will set the tone for the rest of the work. You should explain what you are writing about and why it is important, and you should outline your research questions, aims, and/or objectives. In explaining these, you can express them in a fairly open-ended way if your dissertation is based on **qualitative research**, but you will need to identify them clearly. Describing your research aims as totally open-ended can mean that your write-up lacks focus. You might also indicate—in quite general terms—the theoretical approach or perspective you will be taking and why.

When explaining what you are writing about and why, it is not enough to say that you have a long-standing personal interest in the topic: you need to show its importance within the field. Quoting other sources can help to demonstrate the importance of an issue. For example, a project on the gender pay gap might quote recent studies that demonstrate the difference in hourly wages, or a project on hate crime might quote police figures showing a recent rise in this type of offence.

The hardest part of the introduction is often writing the opening sentence. In *Writing for Social Scientists* (1986), Becker advises strongly against opening sentences that he describes as 'vacuous' and 'evasive'. He gives the example of 'This study deals with the problem of careers', and adds that this kind of sentence uses 'a typical evasive maneuver, pointing to something without saying anything, or anything much, about it. *What* about careers?' (Becker 1986: 51). He suggests that this kind of evasiveness often occurs because of concerns about revealing what is coming up. In fact, he argues, it is much better to give readers a quick and clear indication of what you are going to present to them and where it is going. This last point is crucial. The introduction should be one of the last things you write, so that you can write it with the benefit of knowing what you did and what you found. You should use this knowledge to tell the reader what you are going to cover in your dissertation.

Literature review

We provide detailed advice on how to go about writing your literature review in Chapter 5. While you will have listed your research questions or aims in your introduction, this chapter of your dissertation is where you demonstrate their relationship with the existing literature. One important thing to consider is that you should avoid using long quotes from other sources where possible. Try to paraphrase the work of others or, if you're referencing a more general point, use multiple references to support your argument. If you're unsure of how to do this, have a look at the literature reviews we discuss later, in Section 25.4, to see how other authors *make the literature work for them*.

Research methods

We use the term 'research methods' to refer to a chapter of the write-up in which you need to outline a number of issues and elements:

- your research design
- your sampling approach
- how you achieved access to participants (if relevant)
- the procedures you used (for example, if you sent out invitations for an online questionnaire, did you follow up non-respondents?)
- the nature of your data-collection tool (for example, questionnaire, **interview schedule**, **participant observation** role, **observation schedule**, coding frame)

- problems of non-response
- note-taking
- any issues of ongoing access and cooperation
- coding
- how you proceeded with your data analysis
- ethical considerations

When discussing each of these issues, you should describe and justify the choices you made, such as why you used an online questionnaire rather than a structured interview approach, why you focused upon a particular population for sampling purposes, or why a particular case was appropriate for your case study. You will usually need to provide a copy of your data-collection tool in an appendix, but in the research methods section of your write-up you should comment on things such as your style of questioning or observation and why you asked the things you did.

It is important to ensure that you provide a full account of your research method. Writing about management and about criminal justice respectively, Zhang and Shaw (2012) and Fox and Jennings (2014) have noted that methods sections are often incomplete in articles that are submitted to journals. Zhang and Shaw (2012) write that when writing the methods section it is important to remember what they call the 'three Cs': completeness; clarity (transparency about what you did and how you went about it); and credibility (justifying your methodological decisions). The reader should not be left guessing what your sampling approach is or suddenly wonder how you obtained data about a particular issue.

This chapter is also where you will discuss the ethical issues around your project. When discussing ethics you should do more than just report that your project received ethical clearance. You should highlight any ethical difficulties or complexities, such as whether your research participants are from a vulnerable population or whether there is any risk of harm to either your participants or yourself. If your study required informed consent from participants, then you should explain how you obtained this—you may even include your informed consent protocol in an appendix (discussed later in this section). You may also discuss any appropriate data security measures that you took, such as using encrypted devices and/or anonymizing participants' responses.

You should also remember that methodological choices are informed decisions that you need to justify through reference to the academic literature. We have read countless student projects in which the literature reviews are very effective and well referenced, but the methods chapters barely reference any literature. This can be a significant weakness in student work because it demonstrates a lack of consideration when designing a study. In this textbook we cite many writers on the advantages and disadvantages of particular research designs and data-collection approaches. Remember to look up their work and reference it!

Results

It is in the results chapter of your write-up that you will present most of your findings. If you intend to have a separate 'Discussion' chapter, you will probably want to present the findings in the results section quite simply, with little commentary on their implications or reference to literature. However, if you will not have a separate 'Discussion' chapter, you will need to use the results section not only to set out your findings but also to reflect on their significance: for your own research questions/aims, and in relation to the existing literature in your area of study. Our panellists reflect on their decisions to have separate or combined results and discussions chapters in Learn from experience 25.4.

Whichever approach you take, we recommend keeping the following points in mind.

- *Remember not to include* ***all*** *your results.* You should only present and discuss the findings that relate to and help to answer your research questions. This can be difficult, and you might need to seek guidance from your supervisor on how to identify what is important and what can be left out, but when writing up results it is important to focus on *quality*, not *quantity*. Learn from experience 25.5 shows how some of our student panellists handled these choices. You can use an appendix (see 'Appendices') to help with this.
- *Point the reader to what is important in your data and analysis.* Rather than simply summarizing what a table, graph, or piece of data shows (or presenting it with no commentary at all), you should direct the reader to the component or components of it that are particularly striking in terms of your research questions or aims. Ask yourself what story you want the table to convey, and tell that story to your readers.
- *Vary the method of presenting quantitative findings.* This might involve setting out results using a mixture of diagrams and tables. (But remember that in Chapter 15 we discussed the importance of using the methods of analysis that are appropriate for different types of variable.)

LEARN FROM EXPERIENCE 25.4

Results and discussion—integrated or separate?

When we asked our panellists about their experiences of writing up their results and discussion sections, we received lots of observations and thoughts that demonstrate why it's so difficult to give guidance in this area. You should make your decision in the context of your own project, and in consultation with your supervisor, but some of the points our panellists make might help you to think about which approach will fit your project best.

> In my BSc dissertation, I wrote my results and discussion simultaneously. This approach seemed most appropriate for me to link back to previous literature while also presenting my findings. However, in my MSc thesis, I wrote my results and discussion separately. I decided on this approach during writing as the complexity of the analysis, combined with multiple topics, made for a complicated and overwhelming read. It was much clearer to separate the results and analysis from the discussion. For me, the key thing is clarity: you should write in whichever way is most likely to allow the reader to completely understand what you are attempting to communicate.
>
> Jodie

> I have always taken the approach of integrating my results and discussions section. The main reason for this is because I feel it can save a lot of words from the word count (which it is good to keep an eye on throughout writing) and I think it's best to integrate the discussion rather than returning to it separately. In my view, it disrupts the flow of writing and the structure of the dissertation.
>
> Sarah

> On the advice of my supervisor, I chose to separate my results and discussion. In the chapter on my results, I focused on describing the themes I'd analysed in both the documents and interviews, providing examples of how these themes were discussed by organizations/informants, and addressing the objectives of my research. In my discussion chapter, I focused on answering my research questions and relating the results to theory. I chose to organize my thesis in this way because it helped to clearly demarcate the perspectives of my documents and informants from my own theoretical interpretation and discussion in the final chapter (a disadvantage of integrating the two). To connect the two sections, I did my best to label subsections clearly throughout both chapters so that I could refer my reader to ideas that were previously discussed, using numbered section markers, so that I did not have to repeat ideas.
>
> Starr

> I integrated my findings and discussion chapter as I felt that separating them would have increased my word count. I structured my findings and discussion chapter into subsections relating to the key themes I had identified through analysis. I began each point by stating what the findings evidenced, then backed this up with quotes from the focus groups, and then went on to relate this back to the literature and whether this confirmed or questioned the ideas discussed in the literature review.
>
> Scarlett

> I decided to separate my results from my discussions and this was also the recommendation of my dissertation supervisor. I felt it was best to separate them because I wanted the empirical findings to remain just that—the findings—and for the discussion section to provide my own interpretation and analysis of the results. I also found it easier to write in this way.
>
> Zvi

You can read about our panellists' backgrounds and research experiences on page xxvi.

It is worth noting that the first point above (the importance of not including *all* your results) is particularly relevant for qualitative research. As one experienced qualitative researcher has put it: 'The major problem we face in qualitative inquiry is not to get data, but to get rid of it!' (Wolcott 1990a: 18). Wolcott goes on to say that the 'critical task in qualitative research is not to accumulate all the data you can, but to "can" [get rid of]

LEARN FROM EXPERIENCE 25.5

Choosing what to write up

You can't write up everything, and you shouldn't. Reporting everything you have found, whether your project is quantitative or qualitative, will take up too much space and give the impression that you are not able to identify what is important in your data. You need to be selective, but that's not to say that this is going to be easy. As our panellists discuss below, you will have to think very carefully about what to include and what to put to one side.

Choosing what to write up, and what not to, was one of the most difficult aspects of my project. It was a bit like decluttering a closet; I constantly had to ask myself 'Do I love this piece?' 'Does this piece fit (here)?' 'Can this piece be useful somewhere else?' If the answer is 'No', then be ruthless and cut it.

Minke

For me, deciding what to write up was about finding the signal in the noise by consulting my research question during the writing process. I would recommend that students revisit their research question(s) throughout their project to check that they are not going off track. This will help to filter out which data and which parts of the data are relevant to the question(s). Don't be alarmed if you find yourself deleting entire paragraphs after re-reading the question(s).

Reni

After identifying the main themes from my data through **thematic analysis**, I narrowed them down to three key themes that I deemed to be the most important (and which were themes that I knew I could write a lot about). You will have a lot of data and it is often tempting to want to include absolutely everything, but I have learned that it is better to include fewer points and go into more detail about them. I was lucky that I had research projects set as assignments during my first and second year of study, so I had learned previously that including absolutely everything is not the best way to go. These previous assignments better prepared me for my dissertation.

Scarlett

Access the **online resources** to hear our panellists' video reflections on this theme.

You can read about our panellists' backgrounds and research experiences on page xxvi.

most of the data you accumulate' (Wolcott 1990a: 35). You have to accept that a lot of the rich data you obtain will have to be discarded. If you do not do this, you will probably lose the sense of an argument in your work and your account of your findings might seem too descriptive and not sufficiently analytical. This is why it is important to use research questions or aims as a focus and to relate your findings back to them. For the same reason, it is also important to keep in mind the theoretical ideas and the literature that have influenced your thinking and will also have shaped your research questions.

Whichever research strategy you have used, if your research project is on a larger scale—if, for example, it is for an MPhil or PhD degree—you will probably need to present your results in more than one chapter. If this is the case, you should indicate which research questions or aims you will address in each chapter and provide some signposts about what will be included. In each chapter's conclusion, you should make clear what your results have shown and highlight any links with the other results chapter(s).

Discussion

In the discussion, you should reflect on the implications of your findings for the research questions or aims that have driven your research. In other words, how do your results help to address your research area? If you have specified hypotheses, the discussion will revolve around whether the hypotheses have been confirmed or not. If they have not been confirmed, you might speculate about some possible reasons for and implications of this. There are many ways to structure this section, but often it is best to simply use your research questions or aims as subheadings and address them directly. If your literature review has also been structured along similar lines, this should make it relatively easy to link your findings with existing research.

Conclusion

Like the conclusion of an essay, the conclusion of your write-up is where you should draw together the main ideas from your findings. This section should cover the following elements.

- *The argument so far.* A conclusion is not the same as a summary, but summarizing your argument so far at the start of your conclusion can help to emphasize the significance of what you have done. This means relating your findings and your discussion of them to your research questions or aims.
- *The implications of your findings for your research questions or aims.* Why are your findings important? Do they support or challenge previous research or theory? What might be the policy implications of your findings?
- *Any limitations of your research.* Reflecting on potential limitations of your research, with the benefit of hindsight, is a good way of demonstrating to readers (and examiners) that you are aware of any deficiencies in your work. You can frame this positively with phrases such as 'If this study were to be repeated then a higher response rate could be achieved through a face-to-face survey.'
- *Areas of further research.* Do your findings suggest any other areas of research? In other words, do they prompt any questions that you would need to conduct further research in order to answer?

You should avoid engaging in speculations that take you too far away from your data or that cannot be substantiated by it, and avoid introducing issues or ideas that you have not previously mentioned. Nothing in the conclusion should come as a surprise to the reader.

Appendices

In your appendices you might want to include such things as your questionnaire, coding frame, observation schedule, letters you sent to members of the sample, and letters you sent to and received from gatekeepers if you had to secure the cooperation of an organization. You might also include data that you have summarized in your results chapter so that a reader can review it if they want to.

References

The references section should include all references cited in the text. For the format of this section you should follow the guidance provided by your department. The most common format is usually a variation of the Harvard method (see Chapter 5), such as the one used in this book.

25.4 Writing up quantitative, qualitative, and mixed methods research

In this section, we explore three research-based articles that have been published in journals to see what lessons we can learn from them when writing up. The first article is based on **quantitative research**, the second on qualitative research, and the third on mixed methods research. To get the most out of this section, we suggest that you have the original full articles open as you read through this chapter so that you can see the whole of each piece of work.

We noted in Section 25.3 that the presentation and content of write-ups can vary slightly between institutions, departments, and individual research projects, and we can also see some variation between write-ups based on quantitative and qualitative research. There are slight differences between the ways that practitioners of the two research strategies (and mixed methods approaches) tend to write up their work, some of which you will notice in the example journal articles that we consider. We have chosen these three articles firstly because their topics are likely to be interesting and engaging to most social science students, across disciplines, and secondly because they clearly demonstrate some features that are often seen as desirable for that type of research in terms of presentation and structure. However, we are not presenting these articles as being perfect models to replicate, and because they are just three individual studies, you should not take them to represent all quantitative, qualitative, or mixed methods write-ups. It is also important to note that these articles are written for academic journals and are not written up in the same manner as, for example, a final-year dissertation. Even so, there are plenty of examples of good practice in them that apply regardless of the type of academic output.

Writing up quantitative research

We will look at how quantitative research tends to be written up by examining an article that was published in *Sociology*, the official journal of the British Sociological Association, but that deals with issues that cut across the social sciences. The article was subject to blind refereeing, meaning that it will have been read by two or three other academics, who will have commented on it and given the journal editor(s) their view about its merits and therefore whether it is worthy of publication. Usually, the referees suggest areas that need revising, and the journal's editors will expect the author (or authors) to respond to that feedback. Revised versions of articles are usually sent back to the referees for further comment, and this process may result in the author(s) having to revise the draft again. It may even result in rejection. Therefore, a published article is not just the end product of a research process, it is also the outcome of a feedback process. The fact that it has been accepted for publication does not mean that it is perfect, but the refereeing process indicates that it has certain crucial qualities and has met the standard of the journal.

An example of quantitative research writing

The article 'Towards an Ethical Framework for Publishing Twitter Data in Social Research: Taking into Account Users' Views, Online Context and Algorithmic Estimation' by Williams et al. (2017b) looks at how Twitter users feel about their data being used for research, drawing on data from an online survey of 564 Twitter users in the UK.

Like all journal articles, this one has an abstract. Its main content is structured as follows.

1. Introduction
2. Context
3. Ethics in social media research
4. Methods and measures
5. Findings
6. Discussion
7. Conclusion

Let's consider each section of the article.

Introduction

The opening three sentences of the introduction attempt to grab our attention, to give a clear indication of the article's focus, and to highlight the gap in knowledge that it is going to address. This is what the authors write:

> The recent surge in social media uptake and the programmatic availability of vast amounts of 'public' online interactional data to researchers have created fundamental methodological and technical challenges and opportunities for social science. These challenges have been discussed methodologically, conceptually and technically (see Burnap et al., 2015b; Edwards et al., 2013; Ruppert et al., 2013; Savage and Burrows, 2009; Sloan et al., 2013; Williams et al., 2013, 2017). However, there is an additional dimension that has received limited engagement in the sociology literature: the challenge of ethics (see Beninger et al., 2014; Metcalf and Crawford, 2016; Townsend and Wallace, 2016; Williams, 2015).
>
> (Williams et al. 2017b: 1150)

In just over 100 words, the authors have set out what the article is about and its significance. Let's look at what each sentence achieves.

- The first sentence sets the scene by identifying the context in which the research is based.
- The second sentence summarizes the key work in this area so far by referencing seven key studies.
- The third sentence suggests that there is a problem with the work so far—a gap that needs to be filled. In this sentence, the authors are moving towards a rationale (or argument) for their article. They use four other references to support their assertion that the gap exists.

So, by the end of the third sentence, the reader knows what the article is about and why the authors feel that their work will make a valuable contribution to the literature on this subject. The introduction closes by telling us exactly what the paper is going to do (signposting) and the argument that is being made:

> This article presents an analysis of Twitter users' perceptions of research conducted in three settings (university, government and commercial), focusing on expectations of informed consent and the provision [of] anonymity in publishing user content. The central arguments of the article are that ethical considerations in social media research must take account of users' expectations, the effect of context collapse and online disinhibition on the behaviours of

> users, and the functioning of algorithms in generating potentially sensitive personal information.
>
> (Williams et al. 2017b: 1150)

The clarity of purpose is essential here because the paper does not set out specific research questions; it just states its intentions (aims) and what it is going to investigate. In our walk-through of the main components of a social science write-up we noted that the introduction should outline the research questions or aims (see under 'Introduction'), and you will often come across articles like this one in which the question is not clearly stated in favour of a statement of what the paper is going to do. As we have said, the Williams et al. study and the other examples we consider in this section are not presented as ideals, and it is worth reflecting on whether a specific research question (rather than what could be called a research 'aim' or 'objective') would have made the article clearer. Thinking deeply 25.1 explores this in more depth.

Context

Having identified the need for the research in the introduction, by pointing to a gap in the existing literature, in this section the authors build the case further and develop their argument. They discuss the huge volume of data being produced online and the relationship between online and offline life. The argument they present is that, if we accept that the online and offline worlds are intrinsically connected and that the amount of online data being produced is significant, then this data offers an important opportunity to study the social world. They then move on to discuss the range of online platforms that could be studied and explain why they focus on Twitter in this paper.

One thing to note particularly in this section is the way in which the authors use the literature to support their argument. Sometimes they make an important point that is supported by multiple sources, for example 'The impact of the increase in social interaction via the machine interface on sociality has been discussed for some time

THINKING DEEPLY 25.1
Where are the research questions?

Considering how important we have said that research questions are through this book, you might be surprised to see that the Williams et al. (2017b) study does not appear to have any. Although it would have been simpler for us to examine a quantitative study that follows the standard structure, the reality is that you will often come across this phenomenon in the academic literature. So why are the research questions not stated? Does this mean this study did not have any?

The reality is that this study did have research questions—several, in fact. We know this because Luke, one of the authors of this textbook, was a co-author of the paper. The questions included:

RQ1) How concerned are Twitter users about their data being used by researchers?

RQ2) Do levels of concern differ depending on who is conducting the research?

RQ3) What are Twitter user expectations regarding anonymity and consent if their data are used in research?

All three of these questions are implicit in the study, were part of its design, and shaped every stage of the research process. So why did the authors choose not to state them explicitly in the article?

Sometimes, stating research questions and hypotheses can lead to quite a dry paper, even though they make an article easier to structure and write. In this paper the authors chose to begin instead with a clearly stated research objective and argument (specified at the end of the introduction), using this as a rhetorical technique to get straight to the point about a topic that they present as urgent and in need of attention. This is a risky strategy and you might well think that although it perhaps makes for a *better* read, explicitly specifying research questions and hypotheses would have made for a *simpler* read. Because of this, we would always recommend that students present their research questions explicitly where appropriate.

The message to take from this is that although we can provide guidelines as to how best to write up your work, in practice there is considerable variation and sometimes you (in consultation with your supervisor) will need to decide what is going to work best for your research.

(Beer, 2009; Lash, 2001, 2007)' (Williams et al. 2017b: 1151). At other times they focus on the work of a single study, for example 'Tinati et al. (2014) propose that social media in general, and specifically Twitter, offer potential for exploring empirical work that begins to unpack new social relations that are orientated around digital subjects and objects' (Williams et al. 2017b: 1151). Whichever approach they use, you will notice that they are *making the literature work for them* rather than being led by it. In other words, they are not simply summarizing what other people have written—they are using the work of others to advance their argument in a clear and persuasive way.

Ethics in social media research

When you look at this section you can see that its purpose is to summarize the current ethical guidance in the area of social media research, consider the legal implications, and review the academic literature in this area. In this section the authors identify four key ethical areas that are relevant for this study:

- the ethical standards of learned societies;
- the legal considerations in relation to data protection (now GDPR);
- the use of algorithms to classify users based on their behaviour and the content they produce; and
- what was known about public attitudes towards social media data before the study was conducted.

The authors are setting the scene and establishing the current thinking in each of these domains. Where appropriate, they are also identifying gaps in current knowledge—notably in the final section, where they state 'To date no academic research has statistically modelled the predictors of the views of users towards the use of their Twitter posts in various settings' (Williams et al. 2017b: 1154).

Methods and measures

The authors choose to split this section into three parts. The first part, 'Data and Modelling', discusses how the researchers collected their data, how they identified their sample, and what the impact of these methods might be. It discusses the use of non-probability sampling and justifies this choice with reference to the methodological literature. It also contains some technical details of the statistical modelling the authors used. The key thing to note is that the methodological considerations are all transparent and justified. The sections on 'Dependent Measures' and 'Independent Measures' list the questions that were asked to respondents and what the response options were (the variables). The authors use a table (Table 1) to clearly summarize this information, which is a common way of presenting quantitative data in articles. It is also very efficient and easy to read—imagine if you had to include all of that information in written form and how much space it would take up.

Findings

Although the paper might seem quite technical and there are a lot of results, this is where the authors pull out the most interesting findings. Rather than simply reporting what is in the table, the authors interpret the data for readers in line with their argument. For example, in Table 2 they look at how certain characteristics predict levels of concern about using Twitter data, comparing responses for university, government, and commercial settings. This is a complicated table that includes multiple statistical models, but the authors make the content accessible to non-technical readers by interpreting the results, for example: 'Lesbian, gay and bisexual (LGB) respondents were more likely to express concern over their Twitter posts being used in government . . . and commercial settings . . . compared to heterosexual respondents' (Williams et al. 2017b: 1157).

Discussion

In 25.3 we noted that sometimes the findings and discussion of them are combined into a single 'Results' (or similarly named) section. Here, there are separate 'Findings' and 'Discussion' sections, and you will have noticed that the authors are very efficient at simply reporting what their data shows in the findings section. It is in the discussion that they situate their findings within the wider context and reflect on the implications for their (not explicitly stated) research questions. They begin with a broad summary of what they have found:

> While the survey showed a general lack of concern from users over their posts being used for research purposes (with university research attracting least concern), 80 per cent of respondents expected to be asked for their consent ahead of their Twitter content being published, and over 90 per cent stated they expected anonymity in publication (in particular female and BME tweeters and those posting personal photographs).
>
> (Williams et al. 2017b: 1159)

The authors then link this to a similar finding using data from a Eurobarometer survey (a series of public opinion surveys that are regularly conducted in European Union member states) published in 2011. The authors use this to strengthen the findings of their study. In the second paragraph the authors point out that, although Twitter data is considered to be in the public sphere and therefore available as a resource for research, they have found that users of Twitter have a very different view of how their data should be treated. Once this problem has been stated, the authors move on to link their findings with existing literature and to explore the issue in more depth. The final part of the discussion provides some recommendations for researchers and ethics committees regarding the use of Twitter data, as well as a very clear framework (presented as a flowchart, which we include in Chapter 6—see Figure 6.1) to help with decisions around reproducing tweets in published work.

Conclusion

In this final section the authors begin by summarizing the problem:

> Researchers are now able to freely harvest social data at a hitherto unrealised scale and speed through public social media APIs. Codes of ethical conduct that were first written over half a century ago are being relied upon to guide the collection, analysis and representation of digital data. The result has been a rush to have a go without the benefit of the full picture.
>
> (Williams et al. 2017b: 1164)

They go on to point out that although the terms of service of social media platforms allow (and even promote) certain behaviours, we as social scientists should 'interpret and engage with the terms of service through the lens of social science research that implies a more reflexive ethical approach' (Williams et al. 2017b: 1164). They deliver a clear concluding message: that although the data is in the public domain, this study demonstrates that Twitter users feel differently, and ethical practice in the social sciences means that we have a duty to take their views into account. Finally, the authors offer four potential avenues of future research to build on their work.

Lessons

What lessons can we learn about writing up quantitative research from this article and other existing articles based on such research?

- The *introduction* should be powerful and try to grab the reader's attention straight away.
  - The *opening statements* should act as signposts to what the article is about and identify the gap in knowledge that your research is addressing.
  - The *research questions or aims* should be specified clearly and early on. Occasionally research questions are not stated explicitly, as in the Williams et al. (2017b) example, but we would strongly recommend that you do state them in your student research project.
  - Quantitative studies are concerned with the relationship between variables, and it may be beneficial to state explicitly what you expect these relationships to be (see Key concept 7.1 on hypotheses). While the hypotheses are not explicitly stated in the Williams et al. (2017b) example, the use of dependent and independent measures shows that the authors were testing for relationships between key variables.
  - The *argument* being made should be expressed clearly, and progressed throughout the write-up.
- The *research methods* used, and the reasons for these decisions, should be set out with clear explanations of how data was collected, what the sampling strategy was, and any limitations that might arise from this. The Williams et al. (2017b) study reports the variables (survey measures) and responses, alongside some useful **descriptive statistics** in Table 1 that show the reader who is in the sample and summarize the distribution of answers to the survey questions asked (although you might have to decide which survey **items** to present, as you might not have room to include every item).
- On a more general note, quantitative data can be *summarized* in a variety of ways. In the paper we discuss here, the authors used tables to present a lot of information at once, but you may also use graphs or diagrams.
- The key messages from the *findings* should be drawn out and explained in language that a non-technical reader could understand. They should then be linked back to the wider context, whether in a single 'Results' section or a separate 'Discussion'.
- The *conclusion* should not contain any new information. In our example here, it very briefly restates the problem and then summarizes the implication of this research on future practice, while suggesting areas that future research might explore.

Writing up qualitative research

Now we will look at an example of a journal article based on qualitative research. Again, we are not presenting this as an ideal or representative example, but as one that exhibits some features that are often seen as desirable in terms of presentation and structure.

An example of qualitative research writing

The article 'Holding Court: The Social Regulation of Masculinity in University Pickup Basketball' (Rogers 2019) uses the idea of 'inclusive masculinity' to explore how a group of racially diverse strangers are able to play basketball together in public arenas. The study is based on empirical data that the researcher collected using semi-structured interviews and participant observation. It was published in the *Journal of Contemporary Ethnography*, a leading interdisciplinary journal for research studies that use ethnographic methods.

The structure is as follows.

1. Introduction
2. Pickup Basketball
3. Methodology
4. Findings
5. Discussion
6. Conclusion

The structure is not dissimilar to the one used for the Williams et al. (2017b) study and it is one that is fairly typical for an empirical paper:

> Introduction → Literature review → Research design/ methods → Results → Discussion → Conclusions

Indeed, this layout is often used with both quantitative and qualitative research strategies. As we did with the Williams et al. article, we will examine the writing in terms of the article's structure.

Introduction

The introduction is made up of five paragraphs. Collectively, these paragraphs provide an immediate sense of what the article is about and where its focus lies. We can look again at what each paragraph achieves.

- The first paragraph is made up of six short sentences. Together, they outline the idea of 'hegemonic masculinity'—where physical strength, aggression, stoicism, and heterosexuality are defining characteristics.
- The second paragraph then outlines two empirical studies where this idea has been explored, highlighting that it has been examined in 'numerous studies'. This is a clear attempt to situate the paper within a wider body of knowledge.
- The third paragraph then narrows the focus to demonstrate how hegemonic masculinity has also been commonly explored in sports cultures.
- The fourth paragraph then begins to develop a 'knowledge gap' by suggesting that these forms of masculinity are being challenged in some areas by a more progressive performance of manhood that also emphasizes inclusivity. The author notes that this has been termed 'inclusive masculinity' and, again, that some authors have begun to explore how it is performed in three non-sporting contexts.
- The fifth and final paragraph is made up of three sentences. The first highlights how it is not yet clear how such an 'inclusive masculinity' might be realized in contexts that are 'more racially diverse, less governed by formal over sight, and less collegial by nature' (Rogers 2019: 733). The second sentence is a statement that confirms that this study will look at an area that conforms to these three conditions—pickup basketball. The final sentence then very briefly outlines why it is useful to explore arenas that might have previously been thought to be subject to toxic gender performances.

After what is a fairly short introduction, the reader has a clear idea of the rationale for research—that is to say what the research is about, and why it is interesting to look at the issue. It is interesting to note that this introduction has a funnel-like structure. It begins with 'the big idea', before slowly reducing it down until it finally introduces the specific context in which the study will take place. It is also interesting that although the title of the article is largely based around basketball—both 'holding court' and 'pickup basketball' are clear references to the game—the theoretical framing of the article itself is actually around that of 'inclusive masculinity'. This is largely because masculinity is the theoretical lens through which basketball will be viewed, and the game itself is part of a wider process within society.

Pickup Basketball

The section titled 'Pickup Basketball' serves as a short review of the game of 'pickup' basketball. In part, this section is needed because the author cannot assume that the reader will be familiar with the variant of the game—which involves the tacit organization of strangers into teams of revolving competitors. As the author highlights, '[t]o the uninitiated, pickup basketball courts are likely to appear chaotic and intimidating' (Rogers 2019: 733). This section is typical of ethnographies, due to the highly contextualized nature of ethnographic fieldwork, and the author uses it to helpfully describe the game in a concise and accessible manner.

Methodology

In this section, the author outlines

- the overarching approach to the study (ethnomethodology);
- an introduction to the data-collection methods (participant observation and semi-structured interviewing);
- a description of the ethnographic research process, including detail on the scale of data collection and how field notes were written;
- an overview of the sample, the number of people interviewed, the context in which the interviews took place, and a note about data saturation; and
- some reflection on the process of data collection that explores the role of identity on qualitative data.

Collectively, the methodology section enables the reader to understand the process of the research, and given the detail the author provides, the study would be broadly replicable. However, it is interesting to note that there is no detail on the process of analysis or the role of ethics in the research process. This constrains transparency somewhat, as it is not clear how the author analysed the data or how the study negotiated any ethical issues.

Findings

This section of the paper begins with a clear, confident statement about the overarching finding of the study: that while pickup basketball does provide an environment where aspects of traditional patriarchal hegemony still flourish, other norms of the pickup basketball court serve to promote harmony and inclusivity. The author then organizes the findings around two headings: evoking masculinity and regulating masculinity. These headings broadly reflect the author's introductory argument. The first demonstrates how more traditional forms of masculinity are performed within pickup basketball, and the second then details how those performances are constrained and negotiated to produce more inclusive forms of masculinity. The material under the second heading is further divided into a series of sub-headings that include segregation by skill level, semiformal adjudication, diffusing acts, sanctions, and community spirit. In each case, an introductory paragraph describes what is implied by the sub-heading in more detail—sometimes with reference to wider concepts—and this is followed by evidence for that assertion. For instance, the sub-heading 'community spirit' begins with a recognition that the positive role of solidarity for groups—later elaborated as 'shared identity, common goals, communal accountability' (2019: 742)—reaches back to the sociology of Émile Durkheim. The author then proceeds to demonstrate how this is achieved in practice on the pickup court—primarily through a sense of being both a basketball player and a member of the university.

For all of the three themes there is considerable use of passages from both field notes and the interview transcripts. For example, the subsection of community spirit uses the words of Lamar, 'an African American freshman [first-year student] at University B':

> You just have to realize where you are, at the end of the day. Nobody wants to lose, [but] some people out here, they're on scholarships and you don't want to lose those types of things over a pickup game. It doesn't really mean anything.
>
> (quoted in Rogers 2019: 742)

Thinking deeply 25.2 looks in greater detail into the use of verbatim quotations in social science publications.

Elsewhere, Rogers draws more on his field notes to describe interactions that were of interest and to provide evidence for overarching points. For example, in the section on semiformal adjudication he notes how pickup courts lack a formal referee. This can mean that there is the potential for conflict where 'foul' calls are disputed, so players use a system of 'shoot for it' to resolve disagreements about disputed foul calls.

Discussion

This section outlines the findings in the context of related literature. In this case, the author uses the Bourdieusian concepts of 'field', 'capital', and 'doxa', alongside Anderson's work on 'the Code of the Street', to show how there is a 'code of the courts' in pickup basketball. In other words, the author demonstrates the significance of their findings in relation to wider theoretical issues. There are also three sub-headings: respect others; different players require different treatment; and the enjoyment of the group is paramount. These are the key 'codes of the court'.

Conclusion

In this section, the author returns to many of the ideas and themes that informed their research rationale. For example, at one point they assess the implications of their findings for some of the main concepts that drove the investigation, such as the notion of a reflexive quasi-subject:

> In university pickup basketball, my research reveals a space that is racially diverse, almost exclusively male, unsupervised, and adversarial by design, yet ordered by an inclusive brand of masculinity. It is unclear whether the players are conscious of their gender expression, or if

THINKING DEEPLY 25.2
How verbatim quotations are used in write-ups

A number of qualitative methods generate data in the form of quotations, and researchers take different approaches to how and whether they include these verbatim quotations in their write-ups.

In a few cases, researchers will simply attempt to summarize the results without using quotations. This approach is more likely where the orientation of the paper is more theoretical in scope. However, many qualitative researchers include quotations in passing as they write, using them to reinforce or illustrate points they are making about the themes they have extracted from their data. This is especially likely if the results are being reported in a narrative style that attempts to 'tell the story' of the data. Researchers can also present quotations more formally, occasionally in tables. This technique is often used to summarize content more effectively or to give the paper a more formal style. Some researchers may also use tables because they think it gives less of a sense that the quotations are anecdotal or 'cherry-picked' to support the authors' argument.

At the other end of the spectrum, there are also qualitative researchers who choose to present qualitative data using more literary formats, perhaps as a poem or a piece of drama. According to Pickering and Kara (2017), these more creative methods are a response to continuing ethical concerns about what they term 'representational practice'—essentially how researchers represent 'others' in their research. In conventional research, researchers retain interpretative authority over their participants. They choose what to represent and how to represent it. This includes which quotes to use and which to leave out. However, Pickering and Kara note that those representations can have an impact on those who participated in the original research. In these terms, the presentation of research is an expression of power. Some researchers, therefore, are developing an ethics of engagement to better relate to their participants and their communities. This can involve working with participants to produce more inclusive forms of dissemination, such as poems, plays, song, and dance.

With this in mind, it is worth noting Corden and Sainsbury's (2006) recommendations that researchers should decide which approach they want to use and why, and that they should be able to justify the choice made if necessary. They conducted research into qualitative researchers' use of quotations and found that researchers use verbatim quotations for interview transcripts for a variety of reasons, such as to illustrate a point; to give voice to participants; to provide evidence; or to deepen readers' understanding. When Corden and Sainsbury examined a wide range of publications in the social policy field, they found a wide variety of approaches to the use of quotations. There was a lot of variation in how the people quoted were referred to, and in terms of editing conventions, such as the removal of 'er', 'erm', and false starts, as well whether pauses or laughter were indicated.

> instead they are regulating their conduct in service of other concerns like school spirit or the desire to avoid costly discipline. It is also unclear whether these norms might be found in pickup basketball settings that lack the formal structure and community of a university. Regardless, to scholars advocating a more nuanced and tolerant version of American masculinity, these findings should be encouraging.
>
> (Rogers 2019: 745)

In their final paragraph the author makes clear what they regard as the principal contribution of their research, which revolves around the notion that 'dominance-based machismo may eventually lose its grip on gender hegemony' (Rogers 2019: 745)—and that the study provides further evidence of that trend.

Lessons

Let's consider the lessons we can learn from this article, and other existing articles, about writing up qualitative research.

- The *introduction* should grab the reader's attention straight away.
  - It should feature strong *opening sentences* that give a clear indication of the nature and content of the article.
  - It should clearly set out the *rationale* of the research, identifying why the research is interesting and necessary, with some indication about what has been said about it in the literature.
  - It should justify the research by demonstrating a 'gap' in that literature.

- It should specify the aims and objectives of the research, even if these are relatively open-ended compared to those of most quantitative research.

- The *research design and methods* section(s) should described these elements and, where appropriate, justify their use. This will generally involve an outline of the research strategy, the research design, the sample, data collection, analysis, and ethics. However, it is often the case that qualitative studies will need to be described according to the requirements of the particular study in question. This will often mean giving greater weight to those issues that were significant to the research process.
- The *findings* section should present and discuss these in relation to the aims and objectives of the research. It should clearly outline links with specific items in the literature, and where appropriate should use wider concepts to illuminate the data.
- The *discussion* and *conclusion* should elaborate on the significance of the results in light of the aims of the research and the wider literature. They should also explore the implications of the investigation for the theoretical issues that will have guided the article's opening sections, and finish by providing a clear and succinct statement of the main theoretical contributions that the article has made.

Writing up mixed methods research

Interest in mixed methods research is steadily gaining momentum, but it has few set writing conventions, so even if we wanted to present an ideal example of a mixed methods journal article here, it would be very hard to identify one. To some extent, a mixed methods write-up borrows some of the conventions associated with writing up quantitative and qualitative research in terms of needing to start out with a research focus (in the sense of a research problem and/or some research questions). Creswell and Tashakkori (2007: 108), the former editors of the *Journal of Mixed Methods Research*, have suggested that 'good original/empirical mixed methods articles' should be:

- 'well-developed in both quantitative and qualitative components' (2007: 108); and
- 'more than reporting two distinct "strands" of quantitative and qualitative research; these studies must also integrate, link, or connect these "strands" in some way' (2007: 108).

They actually add a third feature of good mixed methods articles—that they should contribute to the literature on mixed methods research in some way. This seems to be quite a high expectation for many writers and researchers, although it could be argued that any mixed methods study that reflects on what insight the methodological approach has offered is making a contribution that can be read by the wider academic community. We suggest that you focus on the other two features.

The first feature implies that the quantitative and qualitative components of a mixed methods article should at the very least be well constructed. This means that mixed methods research should conform to both quantitative and qualitative research criteria. In terms of writing, for each of the components it should be clear what the research questions or aims were, how the sampling was done, what the data-collection technique(s) was or were, and how the data were analysed.

The second feature implies that a good mixed methods article will be greater than the sum of its parts—in other words, that the elements will be more effective when combined and interacting with each other than they would be if used separately. This addresses a tendency that some writers have identified (e.g. Bryman 2007; O'Cathain et al. 2007) for some mixed methods researchers not to link their two sets of findings, which means that they cannot get the maximum value from the research strategy. As Creswell and Tashakkori put it:

> The expectation is that, by the end of the manuscript, conclusions gleaned from the two strands are integrated to provide a fuller understanding of the phenomenon under study. Integration might be in the form of comparing, contrasting, building on, or embedding one type of conclusion with the other.
>
> (2007: 108)

Researchers are likely to find it easier to express the value of their use of mixed methods if they clearly state their rationale for including both quantitative and qualitative components in their overall research strategy. We discussed the reasons for conducting mixed methods research in Chapter 24 (especially Thinking deeply 24.1).

Creswell and Plano Clark (2018: 275–6) provide some more useful advice for writing up mixed methods research, especially in relation to its structure. They suggest that a mixed methods journal article should be structured along the following lines.

- *Introduction*. This could include a statement of the research problem or issue; an examination of the literature on the problem/issue; an examination of the problems with the existing literature, which might include indicating why a mixed methods approach would be beneficial (perhaps because much of the previous research is based mainly on just quantitative or qualitative research); and the specific research questions.

- *Literature review.* Although they say that this is optional, every social science journal article will review some previous work in the area of interest. Sometimes this is through a section titled 'Literature review' or, as in the Williams et al. (2017b) example above, a review of the literature might be spread across multiple sections (in that case, the literature was discussed in the 'Introduction', 'Context', and 'Ethics in Social Media Research' sections).
- *Methods.* This could include an indication of the rationale for the mixed methods approach; the type of mixed methods design being used (see Figure 24.2); data-collection and data-analysis methods; and indications of how the **validity** of the data can be judged.
- *Results.* This section reports the quantitative and qualitative findings in addition to the results of integrating both types of data; Creswell and Plano Clark (2018) suggest using figures or tables to help with presenting results, if possible, and trying to present integrated analysis jointly.
- *Discussion.* This section summarizes and explains the qualitative, quantitative, and integrated results; relates them to the literature; draws attention to any limitations of the investigation; possibly suggests areas of future research; and states the contributions of the study to the wider academic debate.

In terms of the overall structure, Creswell and Plano Clark's (2018) suggestions are very similar to those we would give (and have given—see 'Writing up quantitative research' and 'Writing up qualitative research') for an article based on quantitative or qualitative research. Where these recommendations differ is in the need to outline the mixed methods nature of the research and to bring the two sets of findings together—see Tips and skills 25.2.

An example of mixed methods writing

Many of these features can be seen in a study called 'Back on Track: A Longitudinal Mixed Methods Study on the Rehabilitation of Young Adult Cancer Survivors' by Hauken et al. (2019). The research was conducted in Norway and this article was published in the *Journal of Mixed Methods Research*. While—as we have emphasized throughout this section—we are not suggesting that it is perfect or represents the only way to write up mixed methods research, we have chosen it because of its good structure and clarity. As a reader it can sometimes be difficult to work out how mixed methods studies have been conducted unless the author takes great care to explain what both the quantitative and qualitative strategies were and what particular research design was adopted. This paper is a good example of how the writer can provide this detail.

The article is structured in the following way (excluding the abstract).

1. Introduction (it is not labelled as such, but it precedes the next section)
2. Previous Research
3. Theoretical Framework

TIPS AND SKILLS 25.2

In a mixed methods write-up, do not separate your quantitative from your qualitative findings

As we have just discussed, some researchers fail to get the most out of the mixed methods strategy because they do not link their two sets of findings. The same problem is common in student research projects. Some students who conduct mixed methods investigations treat their quantitative and qualitative findings as entirely separate. In PhD theses and master's dissertations, this can often result in separate chapters with labels like 'survey findings' and 'qualitative interview findings'. This may not be a problem if the writer then integrates the two (or more) sets of findings in the discussion sections or chapters. The Creswell and Tashakkori (2007) reflections on features of good mixed methods articles suggests that if you do not integrate your findings, you will limit the success and efficacy of your study.

4. Aim
5. Method and Materials
6. Results
7. Discussion
8. Conclusion

Introduction

It's interesting to note that this section doesn't have a subheading of 'Introduction', but this is clearly its purpose. The authors waste no time or words in getting straight to the point:

> This study focuses on the residential rehabilitation of young adult cancer survivors (YACS). Here, YACS are defined as young adults between 18 and 35 years of age who have completed primary cancer treatment (Feuerstein, 2007). Since YACS' special needs regarding survivorship are poorly understood (Institute of Medicine, 2013) and cancer rehabilitation is viewed as an evolving and complex process requiring time and effort (Davis, 2006), we applied a longitudinal mixed methods approach in the evaluation of the rehabilitation program. Here, qualitative and quantitative approaches are combined with longitudinal research in the context of one study in order to provide a nuanced picture of YACS' rehabilitation process over time as well as the outcomes of the program (Creswell & Plano Clark, 2011; Plano Clark et al., 2014). This may assist to increase the understanding of YACS' rehabilitation needs, processes, and outcomes, which may be important for improving survivorship care for YACS. Thus, this study adds to the mixed methods literature as an example of how a longitudinal mixed methods approach can yield an enriched understanding of both the rehabilitation process and outcomes when evaluating complex interventions in cancer rehabilitation.
>
> (Hauken et al. 2019: 339–40)

This opening passage achieves the following things:

- it defines the population of interest (who the study is concerned with);
- it identifies a gap in the understanding;
- it identifies itself as a mixed methods study *and* provides a rationale for a mixed methods approach; and
- it highlights the contribution of this work to the wider mixed methods literature.

By the end of this section we know quite a lot about the research, and this has been communicated in a very succinct and clear way.

Previous Research

In the 'Previous Research' section the authors review the existing literature and locate their study within a wider context. They begin by outlining the current understanding around the prevalence and nature of cancer in young adults, moving swiftly on to the issue faced by survivors. In the second paragraph the authors review the state of research on cancer rehabilitation, and in the third paragraph they criticize previous evaluation programmes (for example those using randomized control trials) and argue that mixed methods studies could be valuable in this area. Justifying the need for their study, they first identify potential for mixed methods studies in this area:

> the mixed methods approach is viewed as an upcoming approach for evaluating complex interventions, including evaluation of both processes and several outcome responses for capturing effects (Curry, Nembhard, & Bradley, 2009; Kroll & Morris, 2009).
>
> (Hauken et al. 2019: 340)

They then point out that few studies of this kind have looked at cancer rehabilitation (justifying this statement with reference to two other studies). This highlights the need for more work in this area. Rather cleverly, the authors then go on to discuss three mixed methods studies in a closely related area to highlight the potential for this method. They draw this conclusion:

> Supported by these studies, mixed methods seem to corroborate results, capture the complexity of the phenomenon studied, and [enrich] the interpretation of one type of result by using another . . . type (Creswell & Plano Clark, 2011; Kroll & Morris, 2009; Plano Clark et al., 2014).
>
> (Hauken et al. 2019: 340–1)

They then point out that they could not find any mixed methods studies that evaluated complex cancer rehabilitation interventions. In this way, they have demonstrated the power and potential of mixed methods in this area while still maintaining that there is a gap to be filled by their research.

Theoretical Framework

This is a short section in which the authors clarify how they are defining quality of life (QOL). It is very important to make sure that readers understand what the researcher means by the conceptual terms they use. Even if the reader disagrees with the definition, at least the concept has been properly defined.

Aim

Short subsections can be quite effective when you want to grab the attention of the reader. Here, the authors clearly state the aim of the study and set out their research question:

> The overall aim of this study is to develop an enriched understanding of both the rehabilitation process and outcomes in evaluating a complex rehabilitation program for YACS using a longitudinal mixed methods approach. The study addresses the following research question: Will participation in a complex rehabilitation program tailored for YACS improve their QOL outcomes and how do they describe their rehabilitation process over time?
>
> (Hauken et al. 2019: 341)

Methods and Materials

This section is split into six subsections.

1. Intervention—this sets out the five elements of the intervention programmes. (Notice also that the authors make reference to academic literature in this section. As we have stressed, this is not something that should be limited to the literature review.)
2. Research Design—an incredibly important section for a mixed methods study. The authors describe the nature of the prospective **convergent design** (a longitudinal parallel version of it) and tell us what it might add to our understanding of the phenomenon being studied.
3. Recruitment, Eligibility Criteria, and Participants—this explains who was eligible, and who the authors selected for the study. They also summarize the key demographic and medical characteristics of the study population.
4. Data Collection—Here, the authors set out the data-collection strategies for both the qualitative and quantitative approaches and the measures they used. They deal with the two elements separately, which makes it easier for readers to understand. (When we talk about not separating qualitative and quantitative components we are generally referring to results, findings, and discussions. It makes sense to split the two approaches when describing how you collected your data.)
5. Data Analysis—Again, this deals with quantitative and qualitative components separately, describing the analytical approach taken for each. However, after the separate descriptions the authors explain how the data were merged and analysed using the convergent parallel design.
6. Ethics—A short but important section explaining who approved the study and how the authors recorded the participants' consent.

Results

The quantitative results in Table 4 are very detailed, but you don't need to understand the intricacies of the analysis to appreciate the clear way in which the authors have written this part up. The first subsection on 'Baseline Results' starts with a summary of the quantitative analysis by providing a summary of the findings that the authors want to draw our attention to; then they link this to the relevant qualitative data using the four themes.

The next two subsections on 'The Rehabilitation Process' and 'Rehabilitation Outcomes' follow a similar pattern of integration, and Table 5 demonstrates how the qualitative and quantitative findings relate to each other. The key thing to note here is that the authors have not presented the quantitative and qualitative analysis as separate results sections. We can also see that the authors are not linking their results back to the literature at this point—they have chosen to focus on summarizing what they found, leaving the linking work for the discussion section.

Discussion

The discussion is split into four subsections, the fourth of which is specifically focused on the methodological implications of the study and its contribution to the literature on mixed methods, as recommended by Creswell and Tashakkori (2007). You will notice how smoothly the authors integrate their findings with previous work, for example:

> In line with previous research (Albritton et al., 2006; Institute of Medicine, 2013), the participants reported a range of physical and psychological late effects, naming fatigue as their primary issue. Katz et al. (2007) state that impairment in one or several dimensions of QOL may negatively influence overall QOL, as well as the other dimensions. Conforming [*sic*] this, YACS scored low overall in QOL and in RF [role function], SF [social function], physical capacity, and participation.
>
> (Hauken et al. 2019: 351)

The authors situate their study within the wider academic literature, highlighting where their findings are aligned to previous work and what their study adds. The final section makes some important observations about the difficulty of evaluating complex interventions using a longitudinal mixed methods approach and the issue of funding. The authors reflect on key issues, such as the implications of sample size, how **generalizable** their findings might be, and how to balance objectivity and active involvement. On this latter point the authors discuss the strategies they used to try to achieve this balance. They finish with a list of factors that demonstrate the feasibility and advantages of studying this topic using their chosen mixed methods approach.

Conclusion

After an extensive discussion, the conclusion is quite short and focuses on what the study contributes to existing knowledge. It ends with a strong statement on the value of the methodological approach:

> The findings demonstrate the strengths of applying a longitudinal mixed methods approach to the evaluation of a complex rehabilitation program for YACS by providing a comprehensive insight into YACS' rehabilitation needs, the development of the rehabilitation process as well as its outcomes. Thus, this study represents a promising starting point for cancer rehabilitation research tailored to YACS, and for the use of longitudinal mixed methods in cancer rehabilitation research. Further research is therefore highly warranted.
>
> (Hauken et al. 2019: 357)

This paragraph restates the mixed methods nature of the study and what insight the strategy has offered within the study, using the article as a platform to call for further research in this area.

Lessons

Let's consider the key lessons to be learned from this article and other articles reporting on mixed methods research.

- The *introduction* should clearly state the study's aims and research questions. The opening statements should summarize the problem and the rationale for the study clearly and succinctly, including the rationale for using mixed methods rather than a quantitative or qualitative approach.
- Either in the literature review or the equivalent section ('Previous Research', in the case of Hauken et al.'s 2019 study), the case should be clearly made for the work by situating it in the existing *academic literature* and explaining what it adds to the conversation about the issue.
- A clear and neat *structure* with lots of signposting is particularly important in a mixed methods write-up, to help the reader understand the researcher's logic, processes, and findings. In Hauken et al. (2019) the authors use subheadings to great effect, most notably in the 'Method and Materials' section.
- In terms of *research methods*, the data-collection and analysis strategies should be clearly explained. Unlike in discussions of findings, in this section it often works best to deal with qualitative and quantitative approaches separately.
- The *results* should integrate the quantitative and qualitative data. If there is a separate discussion section, the results should focus on reporting findings only. Because of the complexity of reporting mixed methods studies, you might find it easier to separate the *results* and *discussion* sections when writing up your own work.
- The *discussion* should link the findings back to the literature and reflect on the implications of the study design and methodological choices.
- The *conclusion* can be relatively brief if the discussion has been extensive. It should summarize the findings and demonstrate the strength of, and value added by, the use of a mixed methods approach.

KEY POINTS

- Good writing is probably just as important as good research practice. In fact, it is best thought of as a *part of* good research practice.
- The components and order of components of social research write-ups vary between institutions, disciplines, and individual research projects, but there are some core elements that are almost always included, in a particular order.

- A clear structure and a clear statement of your research aims and/or questions are important components of writing up research.
- Examining writing strategies shows us that social scientists do more than simply report findings: they want to get their points across in a persuasive way. For this reason, it is important to bear in mind the significance of your writing style and strategy when you write an essay or dissertation—as well as whether it conforms with your institution's guidance on academic writing.
- It is crucial that you have a clear argument running through your report of your work.
- Write-ups for quantitative, qualitative, and mixed methods research vary slightly in content and style, but the same broad principles apply.

QUESTIONS FOR REVIEW

1. Why is it important to consider the ways in which social research is written up?
2. Why is it important to be clear about your main argument when writing up your findings?
3. Why is signposting a good idea?
4. Read a different article based on quantitative research in a journal. Is it consistent with the article by Williams et al. (2017b)?
5. What is meant by 'rhetorical strategy'? Why might rhetorical strategies be important in relation to writing up social research?
6. Read a different article based on qualitative research in a journal. To what extent are its characteristics consistent with the article by Rogers (2019)?
7. If you were writing up the results of a qualitative interview study you had undertaken, what would your approach be to using (or not using) verbatim quotations from your transcripts?
8. Read a different article based on mixed methods research in a journal. To what extent are its characteristics consistent with the one by Hauken et al. (2019)?
9. How far does the article you have looked up succeed in integrating the quantitative and the qualitative findings?
10. What similarities and differences do you think there are between writing academic journal articles and writing up a student project?

ONLINE RESOURCES

www.oup.com/he/srm6e

You can find our notes on the answers to these questions within this chapter's **online resources**, together with:

- *audio/video comments* on this topic from our 'Learn from experience' panellists;
- *audio discussion from the authors* on why it is important to consider the ways in which social research is written up (review question 1);
- *self-test questions* for further knowledge-checking;
- a *flashcard glossary* to help you recall key terms; and
- a *Student Researcher's Toolkit* containing practical materials and resources to help you conduct your own research project.

GLOSSARY

Terms with an entry elsewhere in the Glossary are in colour.

Abductive reasoning, abduction A form of reasoning with strong ties to induction that grounds social-scientific accounts of social worlds in the perspectives and meanings of participants in those social worlds.

Action research An approach in which the action researcher and a client collaborate in the diagnosis of a problem and in the development of a solution based on the diagnosis.

Adjacency pair In conversation analysis, this term describes the tendency for certain kinds of activity in talk to be characterized by linked phases.

***Ad libitum* sample/sampling** A sampling approach in structured observation whereby the researcher records whatever is happening at the moment that observation is due to occur.

Alternative hypothesis A hypothesis that there is a relationship between two variables. Compare with null hypothesis.

Analytic generalization An approach to generalization often used by qualitative researchers where they use findings from a study to develop theoretical constructs that may be applicable in other contexts.

Analytic induction An approach to the analysis of qualitative data in which the researcher seeks universal explanations of phenomena by pursuing the collection of data until they stop finding cases that are inconsistent with their hypothetical explanation of a phenomenon (deviant or negative cases).

A priori sample/sampling An approach to sampling where the criteria for selection are established from the start of the research project and remain unchanged throughout.

Arithmetic mean ($\bar{x}$) Also known simply as the 'mean', this is what in everyday terms we call the 'average'—namely, the total sum of a set of values divided by the number of values.

Asynchronous online interview or focus group An online interview or focus group in which the communications between participants are not in real time, so that there may be long spaces of time between interviewers' questions and participants' replies and, in the case of focus groups, between participants' contributions to the discussion. Compare with synchronous online interview or focus group.

Attached email survey A survey in which respondents are sent a questionnaire, which is received as an attachment by email. Compare with embedded email survey.

Audit trail A term borrowed from accounting. When applied to social research, it means that the researcher keeps records of key decisions in the research process and maintains an evidence base to ensure that their main findings and concepts are fully supported.

Autobiographical research An approach to social research that examines the construction of life histories that are directed toward the self.

Bar chart A visual representation of data that uses bars to represent the count, percentage, or proportion of each category of a variable.

Behaviour sample/sampling A sampling approach in structured observation whereby an entire group is watched and the observer records who was involved in a particular kind of behaviour.

Big Data Extremely large sources of data, such as social media, that are not immediately amenable to conventional ways of analysing them.

Biographical research A range of qualitative approaches that are concerned with the construction of life stories. Biographical methods include the life history method and narrative analysis.

Bivariate analysis The examination of the relationship between two variables, as in contingency tables or correlation.

CACA Abbreviation of computer-assisted content analysis.

CAPI Abbreviation of computer-assisted personal interviewing.

CAQDAS Abbreviation of computer-assisted qualitative data analysis software.

CATI Abbreviation of computer-assisted telephone interviewing.

Case study A research design that involves the detailed and intensive analysis of a single case, where a 'case' could be an individual, group, or organization. The term is sometimes extended to include the study of just two or three cases for comparative purposes. However, the more common term for the examination of two or more cases is multiple-case study.

Case-to-case transfer An approach to generalization in qualitative research in which findings in one particular context are directly applicable in another.

Categorical variable A variable that takes on values that are names or labels, as opposed to numerical values. Nominal variables and ordinal variables are both types of categorical variable.

Category 1. In social science research, categories are the different modes or values that a variable can take. For example, the variable 'reason for gym use' could be banded into the categories 'relaxation', 'fitness', 'weight loss', and 'other'. 2. In grounded theory, a category occupies a space between a researcher's initial understanding of their data, which they develop during the coding process, and a theory. The researcher groups codes into concepts as they perceive connections between different codes, and can then group concepts into categories. Thus, a category has an intermediate position in terms of abstraction between coding and a theory. See also core category.

Causal, causality A causal connection between variables means that a variation in one variable causes variation in another. A researcher may have a concern with establishing causality rather than showing mere relationships between variables.

Cell The point in a table, such as a contingency table, where the rows and columns intersect.

Census The enumeration of an entire population. Unlike a sample, which comprises a count of some units in a population, a census relates to all units in a population. Thus, if a postal questionnaire is mailed to every person in a town or to all members of a profession, the research should be characterized as a census of that population.

Chi-square test Chi-square (χ^2) is a test of statistical significance that is most commonly employed to establish how confident we can be that the findings displayed in a contingency table can be generalized from a probability sample to a population.

Closed-ended question A question in an interview schedule or self-completion questionnaire that presents the respondent with a set of possible answers to choose from; such questions can be pre-coded. Also called 'fixed-choice question'. Compare with open-ended question.

Cluster sample/sampling A sampling procedure in which the researcher first samples areas (known as 'clusters') and then samples units from these clusters, usually using a probability sampling method. For example, a researcher might randomly select five voting districts within a city—five clusters—and then randomly select 30 individuals to be surveyed within each district.

Code, coding In quantitative research, codes are numbers that are assigned to data about people, or other units of analysis, when the data are not themselves numerical. Coding allows the information to be statistically processed. For example, in questionnaire-based research, the answer 'strongly agree' might be assigned the number 5. When answers are textual, as with an open-ended question, respondents' answers must be grouped into categories and those categories are then coded. In qualitative research, coding is a method of analysing textual data by generating an index of terms or labels based on the researcher's ongoing interpretation of the data. Qualitative coding is particularly associated with grounded theory.

Coding frame A listing of the codes that the researcher uses in their analysis of data. In relation to a structured interview schedule or questionnaire, the coding frame will delineate the categories used in connection with the answers to each question. A coding frame is particularly crucial in relation to the coding of open-ended questions. With closed-ended questions, the coding frame is essentially incorporated into the pre-given answer choices, so the term pre-coded is often used to describe such questions.

Coding manual In content analysis, this is the statement of instructions to coders that outlines all the possible categories for each dimension they are coding.

Coding schedule In content analysis, this is the form onto which the coder will enter all the data relating to an item they are coding.

Coefficient In a mathematical equation, a coefficient is a mathematical constant by which a variable is multiplied.

Coefficient of determination The proportion of the variance in the dependent variable that is predictable from the independent variable(s).

Comparative design A research design that involves the comparison of two or more cases in order to illuminate existing theory, or to generate new theoretical insights, based on contrasting findings uncovered through the comparison.

Comparative keyword analysis A method for the conjoint qualitative and quantitative analysis of large amounts of text.

Computer-assisted content analysis (CACA) Software that facilitates quantitative content analysis by counting the frequency of words or phrases in a body of text. It offers considerable advantages over manual methods, notably that it eliminates problems of human bias and cognitive limitations.

Computer-assisted personal interviewing (CAPI) A face-to-face survey interview in which the interviewer reads out questions as they appear on a computer and keys in respondents' answers. The software automates the use of filter questions to skip over items that do not apply to the individual interviewee.

Computer-assisted qualitative data analysis software (CAQDAS) Software designed for use in qualitative research to process and analyse textual materials.

Computer-assisted telephone interviewing (CATI) A survey interview carried out over the telephone in which the interviewer reads out questions as they appear on a computer and keys in respondents' answers. The software automates the use of filter questions to skip over items that do not apply to the individual interviewee.

Concept A name given to a grouping of phenomena that organizes observations and ideas by virtue of their possessing common features. In grounded theory, a concept is a key building block in the construction of a theory.

Concurrent validity One of the main approaches to establishing measurement validity. It involves relating a measure to a criterion on which cases (for example people) are known to differ and that is relevant to the concept in question.

Confidence interval In probability sampling, the range of values that is likely to obtain the true value of a parameter as it exists in the population from which the sample was taken.

Confounding variable A variable that is related to each of two other variables in a way that produces the appearance of a relationship between the two variables. Such a relationship is a spurious relationship.

Connotation, connotative A term used in semiotics to refer to the principal and most manifest meaning of a sign. Compare with denotation.

Constant An attribute in terms of which cases do not differ. Compare with variable.

Constant comparison A central tool of grounded theory that involves constantly comparing new data with existing data, concepts, and categories. It also involves comparing categories with each other and categories with concepts.

Constructionism, constructionist An ontological position that asserts that social phenomena and their meanings are continually being accomplished by social actors. Also called 'constructivism'. Constructionism is antithetical to objectivism.

Constructivism, constructivist Alternative term for constructionism.

Construct validity An assessment of the measurement validity of a measure that tests hypotheses that have been deduced from a theory that is relevant to the underlying concept. If the findings are consistent with the theory, this enhances confidence in the validity of the measure.

Content analysis An approach to the analysis of documents and texts that seeks to quantify their content in terms of predetermined categories and in a systematic and replicable manner. The term is sometimes used in connection with qualitative research as well: see qualitative content analysis.

Contingency table A table, comprising rows and columns, that shows the relationship between two variables. Usually, at least one of the variables is a nominal variable. Each cell in the table shows how often the categories of each of the two variables intersect, usually also showing a percentage.

Contingent sample/sampling An approach to sampling in which the criteria for selecting units evolve during the course of data collection and analysis.

Continuous recording A procedure in structured observation whereby observation occurs for extended periods so that the observer can carefully record the frequency and duration of certain types of behaviour.

Contrived observation A type of observation research where the observer actively intervenes to alter the situation in order to observe the effects of that intervention.

Control group In an experiment, the group who are not exposed to a certain treatment, in contrast to the experimental group, who are exposed to that treatment.

Convenience sample/sampling A sample that is selected because of its availability to the researcher. It is a form of non-probability sample.

Convergent design A mixed methods research design that involves collecting quantitative and qualitative data simultaneously and comparing and/or merging the resulting analyses to form an integrated analysis. This design is usually associated with triangulation.

Convergent validity An assessment of the measurement validity of a measure that compares it to another measure of the same concept that has been generated from a different method.

Conversation analysis The fine-grained analysis of spoken interaction in naturally occurring situations. The talk is recorded and transcribed so that detailed analyses can be carried out. The analysis is concerned with uncovering the underlying structures of talk in interaction and with how people achieve order through spoken interaction. Conversation analysis is grounded in ethnomethodology.

Core category In grounded theory and other forms of qualitative analysis, this is a key category that acts as an overarching motif, bringing together other categories that revolve around it.

Correlation An analysis of relationships between interval/ratio variables and/or ordinal variables that seeks to assess the strength and direction of the relationship between them. Pearson's *r* and Spearman's rho are both methods for assessing the level of correlation between variables.

Correlation coefficient A measure of the strength and direction of the relationship between two variables.

Covert research A term frequently used in connection with ethnographic research in which the researcher does not reveal their true identity. Such research violates the ethical principle of informed consent.

Cramér's *V* A method for assessing the strength of the relationship between two variables, at least one of which has more than two categories.

Creative research A fluid term applied to a range of approaches that aim to develop both the process and dissemination of research beyond its traditional disciplinary and communicative boundaries. It can include arts-based methods, poetry, theatre, and various visual mediums. It has also been applied to certain forms of mixed methods research, technology-enhanced research, and decolonizing methodologies.

Criterion validity How well scores on one measure of a concept predict scores on another measure.

Critical discourse analysis A form of discourse analysis that emphasizes the role of language as a power resource that is related to ideology and socio-cultural change. It draws in particular on the work of Michel Foucault.

Critical realism A realist epistemology that asserts that the study of the social world should be concerned with the identification of the structures that generate that world. Critical realism is 'critical' because its practitioners aim to identify structures in order to change them, so that inequalities and injustices may be counteracted. Unlike a positivist epistemology, critical realism accepts that the structures that are identified may not be amenable to the senses. Thus, whereas positivism is empiricist, critical realism is not.

Cross-sectional design A research design that involves the collection of data on a sample of cases at a single point in time in order to quantify the data in connection with two or more variables (usually many more than two), which the researcher then examines to detect patterns of association. Compare with longitudinal research.

Data saturation The principle that the researcher should continue sampling cases until no new insights are apparent in the data. See also theoretical saturation.

Deductive, deduction An approach to the relationship between theory and research in which the practitioner conducts research with reference to hypotheses and ideas that have been inferred from theory. Compare with inductive.

Denotation, denotative A term used in semiotics to refer to the meanings of a sign, as observed in the social context within which it operates, that are supplementary to and less immediately apparent than its connotation.

Dependent variable A variable that is causally influenced by another variable. See also independent variable.

Descriptive statistics Statistical tools used to describe data and their characteristics.

Diary A term that, in the context of social research methods, can mean different things. We can distinguish three types of diary: diaries written or completed at the behest of a researcher; personal diaries that can be analysed as personal documents, but that were produced spontaneously; and diaries written by social researchers as a log of their activities and reflections.

Dichotomous variable A variable with just two categories.

Dimension In the context of social science theories, dimensions are the aspects of a concept in which different individuals or cases may vary.

Discourse analysis An approach to the analysis of talk and other forms of discourse that emphasizes the ways in which versions of reality are accomplished through language. See also critical discourse analysis.

Distribution of values The entire data relating to a variable. For example, the ages of all members of a sample represent the distribution of values for that variable, age, in that sample.

Ecological fallacy The error of assuming that we can draw inferences about individuals from aggregate data.

Ecological validity An assessment of the extent to which social-scientific findings are relevant and applicable to people's everyday, natural social settings.

Embedded email survey A social survey in which respondents are sent an email that contains a questionnaire. Compare with attached email survey.

Empiricism, empiricist An approach to the study of reality that suggests that only knowledge gained through experience and the senses is acceptable.

Epistemology, epistemological A theory of knowledge, or what can be known. In this book, we mainly use the term to refer to a stance on what should pass as acceptable knowledge. Among these stances are positivism, realism, and interpretivism.

Eta (η) A test of the strength of the relationship between two variables. The independent variable must be a nominal variable and the dependent variable must be an interval variable or ratio variable. The resulting level of correlation will always be a positive number.

Ethnographic content analysis Alternative term for qualitative content analysis.

Ethnography, ethnographer Like participant observation, a research method in which the fieldworker is immersed in a social setting for an extended period of time, observing behaviour, listening to conversations both between others and with the fieldworker, and asking questions. However, the term has a more inclusive sense than participant observation, which emphasizes the observational component. The term 'an ethnography' can also refer to the written output of ethnographic research.

Ethnomethodology A sociological perspective concerned with the way in which social order is accomplished through talk and interaction. It provides the intellectual foundations of conversation analysis.

Evaluation research Research that is concerned with the evaluation of real-life interventions in the social world: for example, evaluating the success of a government programme.

Event sampling Alternative term for experience sampling.

Experience sampling Research methods that seek to capture people's affective states and/or behaviour at certain points in time. The researcher specifies these points in time, and asks participants to record such things as what they are doing or how they are feeling at each point. Also called 'event sampling'.

Experiment, experimental A research design that rules out alternative causal explanations of research findings (that is, it has internal validity) by having these features: (a) an experimental group, which is exposed to a treatment, and a control group, which is not, and (b) random assignment of sample members to the two groups. Instead of a control group, an experiment may comprise a further group (or groups) that are exposed to other treatments.

Experimental group In an experiment, the group who, unlike a control group, is exposed to a certain treatment.

Explanatory sequential design A mixed methods research design that involves first collecting and analysing quantitative data, and then collecting and analysing qualitative data in order to elaborate or explain the quantitative findings.

Exploratory sequential design A mixed methods research design that involves first collecting and analysing qualitative data and then collecting quantitative data.

External validity An assessment of the extent to which the results of a study can be generalized beyond the specific research context in which it was conducted.

Face validity An assessment of how well an indicator reflects the content of the concept in question.

Facilitator In focus group research, an alternative term for moderator.

Feminism, feminist A philosophical perspective that focuses on, and seeks to highlight, the disadvantages experienced by women and other marginalized groups as a result of patriarchal society.

Field notes A detailed chronicle compiled by an ethnographer of events, conversations, and behaviour, noted as they occur, and the researcher's initial reflections on them.

Field stimulation A form of structured observation in which the researcher directly intervenes in and/or manipulates a social setting in order to observe what happens as a consequence of that intervention.

File drawer problem This occurs when researchers experience difficulty publishing their findings because their research found that the independent variable does not have the expected effect, or that the variables they examined are unrelated. It is often suggested that such findings are then simply filed away in a drawer. The file drawer problem can produce bias when we want to summarize a field of research and especially when we conduct a systematic review (in particular a meta-analysis).

Filter question In survey research, a question that is constructed so that on the basis of their replies, some respondents will answer another question to which the filter question is linked, whereas others will skip to a later question. For example, the filter question might ask respondents whether they have driven while intoxicated, but will only ask about the number of times that has happened to those respondents who reply 'Yes'; other respondents (those who have answered 'No') will skip to a later question.

Focal sample/sampling A sampling approach in structured observation whereby a sampled individual is observed for a set period of time. The observer records all examples of whatever forms of behaviour are of interest.

Focus group A form of group interview in which there are several participants (in addition to the moderator); in the questions that the researcher asks, there is an emphasis on a fairly tightly defined topic, and the researcher focuses on interaction within the group and the joint construction of meaning.

Formal theory A collection of categories and concepts that help to describe, explain, or understand a range of empirical instances. Formal theory can be distinguished from substantive theory because formal theory is more abstract in nature, rather than relating to a single substantive area.

Foucauldian discourse analysis A form of discourse analysis influenced by the work of Michel Foucault. It is usually directed toward the investigation of how power is expressed through language and associated practices.

Frequency table A table that displays the number and/or percentage of units (for example, people) in different categories of a variable.

Functionalism The perspective that different institutions in society have functions, and that these parts are interconnected.

Gatekeeper Someone who controls or negotiates access to a group, setting, or organization that a researcher wants to study.

Generalization, generalizability A concern with the external validity of research findings.

Grounded theory An iterative approach to the analysis of qualitative data that aims to generate theory out of research data by achieving a close fit between the two.

Hermeneutics A term drawn from theology, which, when imported into the social sciences, is concerned with the theory and method of the interpretation of human action. It emphasizes the need to understand social phenomena from the perspective of the social actor.

Histogram A bar chart used to represent continuous variables, such as interval or ratio variables.

Hypothesis An informed speculation, which is set up to be tested, about the possible relationship between two or more variables.

Independent variable A variable that has a causal impact on another variable (that is, on a dependent variable).

Index Alternative term for scale.

Indicator A measure that is employed to refer to a concept when no direct measure of that concept is available.

Inductive, induction An approach to the relationship between theory and research in which the researcher uses the research results to generate theory. Compare with deductive.

Inferential statistics Tools for making inferences (estimates or predictions) about a population based on the analysis of data from a random sample of that population. They are used in tests of statistical significance and this process is referred to as statistical inference.

Inferential validity An assessment of whether the inferences and conclusions that arise from a research project are warranted, given the manner in which the study was conducted.

Infographic A representation of data or other information in a graphic format designed to make it easily understandable.

Informant-driven sample/sampling A variant of snowball sampling sometimes seen in ethnographic studies in which participants and events of interest are based on information provided by an informant or a gatekeeper.

Informed consent A key principle in social research ethics. It implies that prospective research participants should be given as much information as might be needed to make an informed decision about whether or not they want to participate in a study.

Internal reliability The degree to which the indicators that make up a scale are consistent.

Internal validity An assessment of the soundness of research findings that suggest a causal relationship between two or more variables.

Interpretative repertoire A collection of linguistic resources that are drawn upon in order to characterize and assess actions and events.

Interpretivism, interpretivist An epistemological position that requires the social scientist to grasp the subjective meaning of social action.

Inter-rater reliability The degree to which two or more individuals agree about the coding of an item. Inter-rater reliability is likely to be an issue in content analysis, in structured observation, and when coding answers to open-ended questions in research based on questionnaires or structured interviews.

Intersectionality The idea that every person occupies numerous positions within different social categories (including gender, social class, sexuality, and race) and that these intersect to influence their experience of the social world.

Intertextuality In critical discourse analysis, the interconnections of meanings that exist between texts and the contexts in which they were produced and received.

Interval variable A variable where the distances between the categories are identical across its range of categories.

Intervening variable A variable that is affected by another variable and that in turn has a causal impact on another variable. Taking an intervening variable into account often facilitates the understanding of the relationship between two variables. Also called a 'mediating variable'.

Interview guide A rather vague term that can refer to the brief list of areas to be covered in unstructured interviewing, which a researcher uses as memory prompts, or to the somewhat more structured list of issues to be addressed or questions to be asked in semi-structured interviewing.

Interview schedule A collection of questions designed to be asked by an interviewer. An interview schedule is always used in a structured interview.

Intra-rater reliability The degree to which an individual differs over time in the coding of an item. Intra-rater reliability is likely to be an issue in content analysis, in structured observation, and when coding answers to open-ended questions in research based on questionnaires or structured interviews.

Item This term is used in survey research based on questionnaires and structured interviews. It refers to a statement to which the respondent is expected to respond in terms of a predetermined format (for example, by indicating their level of agreement or disagreement). A Likert scale is made up of several items. In effect, an item is a question on a questionnaire or interview schedule, but the term 'item' is preferred as an item can be in the form of a statement rather than a question, so that there is no question mark.

Item non-response A survey respondent's failure to respond to an item in the survey, resulting in missing data. Compare with unit non-response.

Key informant Someone who offers the researcher, usually in the context of conducting an ethnography, perceptive information about the social setting, important events, and individuals.

Levels of measurement The relationship among the values that are assigned to the attributes for a variable.

Life history interview Similar to the oral history interview, but the aim of this type of unstructured interview is to glean information on the entire biography of the respondent.

Life history method A type of biographical research that emphasizes the inner experience of an individual and its connections with changing events and phases throughout their life course. It usually involves life history interviews and the use of personal documents as data.

Likert scale A widely used format developed by Rensis Likert for asking attitude questions. Respondents are typically asked their degree of agreement with a series of statements that together form a multiple-indicator or multiple-item measure. The scale is intended to measure the intensity of respondents' feelings or opinions about an issue.

Line graph A chart displaying bivariate data as a series of data points connected by straight line segments, with the positions of the points reflecting values on the *X* and *Y* axes of the chart.

Literature review A critical summary of previous research work related to your research area. See also narrative review and systematic review.

Longitudinal research A research design in which data are collected on a sample (of people, documents, etc.) on at least two occasions. Compare with cross-sectional design.

Maximum variation sample/sampling A purposive sampling approach that aims to ensure as wide a variation as possible in the dimension(s) of interest.

Mean The shortened name for the arithmetic mean.

Measurement validity The degree to which a measure of a concept truly reflects that concept. See also concurrent validity, construct validity, convergent validity, criterion validity, face validity, and predictive validity.

Measure of central tendency A statistic, such as the arithmetic mean, median, or mode, that summarizes a distribution of values.

Measure of dispersion A statistic, such as the range or standard deviation, that summarizes the amount of variation in a distribution of values.

Median The mid-point in a distribution of values.

Mediating variable Alternative term for intervening variable.

Member validation Alternative term for respondent validation.

Memo A note written by the researcher to accompany the process of qualitative analysis, particularly in the context of grounded theory.

Meta-analysis A form of systematic review that involves summarizing the results of a large number of quantitative studies and conducting various analytical tests to show whether or not a particular variable has an effect across the studies.

Meta-ethnography A form of systematic review that is used to achieve interpretative synthesis of qualitative research studies and other secondary sources, thus providing a counterpart to meta-analysis in quantitative research.

Micro-ethnography A short form of ethnographic study that a researcher can use to study a very tightly defined topic.

Missing data Data that are not available for a particular case—for example, when a respondent in survey research does not answer a question. These are referred to as 'missing values' in SPSS. The term item non-response is often used to refer to unanswered survey questions.

Mixed methods research A term that is increasingly employed to describe research that combines both quantitative research and qualitative research. It can also describe research that combines just quantitative methods or just qualitative methods (a strategy also known as multi-method research). However, in recent times, it has taken on this more specific meaning of combining quantitative and qualitative research methods.

Mixed mode survey A survey that offers respondents more than one method of answering questionnaires, such as when postal questionnaire respondents are given the option of completing the questionnaire online.

Mode The value that occurs most frequently in a distribution of values. (Note that this term can also refer to the type of research instrument being used—for example the particular mode of survey employed.)

Moderated relationship A relationship between two variables is said to be moderated when it holds for one category of a third variable but not for another category or other categories.

Moderator The person who guides the questioning and discussion of a focus group. Also called a 'facilitator'.

Moderatum generalization An approach to sampling in qualitative research in which findings from one study can be instructive, if not exhaustively so, of other contexts.

Multiple-case study A case study research design in which the researcher examines two or more cases in detail, usually but not necessarily to compare the findings deriving from the cases. See also comparative design.

Multiple-indicator measure A measure that employs more than one indicator to measure a concept.

Multiple-item measure A measure that is made up of more than one item.

Multi-method research A research project that uses more than one research method or source of data within the same research design. Increasingly, this term is used interchangeably with mixed methods research, but generally mixed methods involve both quantitative and qualitative approaches.

Multi-sited ethnography A form of ethnographic research that takes place in more than one geographical location. It places an emphasis on exploring the connections and relationships from ethnographic site to site, as well as the differences between them.

Multivariate analysis The examination of relationships between three or more variables.

Narrative analysis An approach to the elicitation and analysis of data that is sensitive to the sense of temporal sequence that people, as tellers of stories about their lives or events around them, detect in their lives and surrounding episodes and inject into their accounts.

Narrative research An approach to social research that attempts to explore how human experience is represented through textual, oral, and visual narratives.

Narrative review An approach to a literature review that is less focused than a systematic review and seeks to arrive at a critical interpretation of the literature that it covers.

Naturalism, naturalist A confusing term that has at least three distinct meanings: a commitment to adopting the principles of natural-scientific method; being true to the nature of the phenomenon being investigated; and a style of research that seeks to minimize the intrusion of artificial methods of data collection.

Negative relationship A relationship between two variables whereby as one increases the other decreases.

Netnography A form of ethnography that studies online or largely online communities. It has mainly been used in the fields of marketing and retailing.

Node A term used in the qualitative statistical software package NVivo to refer to the place where all material relating to a particular code is collected.

Nominal variable A variable that comprises categories that cannot be rank-ordered. Compare with interval, ordinal, and ratio variables.

Non-manipulable variable A variable that cannot readily be manipulated, either for practical or for ethical reasons, and that therefore cannot be employed as an independent variable in an experiment.

Non-probability sample A sample that has not been selected using a random sampling method. Essentially, this implies that some units in the population are more likely to be selected than others. Examples are convenience samples, purposive samples, and snowball samples.

Non-response See item non-response and unit non-response.

Non-sampling error Differences between the population and the sample that arise either from deficiencies in the sampling approach, such as an inadequate sampling frame or unit non-response, or from problems such as poor question wording, poor interviewing, or flawed processing of data.

Non-sequential sampling An approach to sampling in which the sample is established at the start of the research and does not change.

Normal distribution The tendency for data points to cluster around a central value in a predictable and symmetric manner.

Null hypothesis A hypothesis of no relationship between two variables. Compare with alternative hypothesis.

NVivo A statistical software package that facilitates the management and analysis of qualitative data.

Objectivism, objectivist An ontological position that asserts that social phenomena and their meanings have an existence that is independent of social actors. Compare with constructionism.

Observation research A form of research in which a researcher directly observes their subjects or participants in a natural setting, which avoids the problem of participants inaccurately reporting their behaviour. There are many observation approaches, both qualitative and quantitative.

Observation schedule A device used in structured observation that specifies the categories of behaviour that are to be observed and how behaviour should be allocated to those categories.

Official documents The administrative records associated with and produced by bureaucracies and organizations.

Official statistics Statistics compiled by, or on behalf of, state agencies in the course of conducting their business.

Online survey A very general term for any social survey conducted online. It includes the attached email survey and the embedded email survey, as well as surveys conducted using software packages designed for the purpose.

Ontology, ontological In the social sciences, a theory of the nature of social entities. See objectivism and constructionism.

Open-ended question A question employed in an interview schedule or self-completion questionnaire that does not present the respondent with a fixed set of possible answers to choose from but instead allows them to answer in their own words. Compare with closed-ended question.

Operational definition The definition of a concept in terms of the operations to be carried out when measuring it.

Operationalization A term originally used in physics to refer to the operations by which a concept (such as temperature or velocity) is measured.

Operationism, operationalism A doctrine, mainly associated with physics, that emphasizes the search for operational definitions of concepts.

Optimizing In survey research, a cognitive process that respondents may engage in that involves maximizing the amount of effort they put into answering a question, in order to arrive at the best possible answer. Compare with satisficing.

Oral history interview A largely unstructured interview in which the respondent is asked to recall events from their past and to reflect on them.

Ordinal variable A variable whose categories can be rank ordered (as in the case of interval and ratio variables), but where the distances between the categories are not equal across the range.

Outlier An extreme value in a distribution of values. If a variable has an extreme value—either very high or very low—the arithmetic mean and the range will be distorted by it.

Overt research Ethnographic research in which the researcher is open about their true identity and the purpose of their research.

Paradigm A term deriving from the history of science, where it was used to describe a cluster of beliefs and principles that influence what scientists should study, how they should do their research, and how they should interpret the results.

Participant observation Research in which the fieldworker is immersed in a social setting for an extended period of time, observing behaviour, listening to what is said in conversations both between others and with the fieldworker, and asking questions. Participant observation usually includes interviewing key informants and studying documents and, as such, is difficult to distinguish from ethnography. In this book, 'participant observation' is employed to refer to the specifically observational aspect of ethnography.

Participatory research Forms of collective inquiry that variously emphasize participation and/or action—hence the term 'participatory action research' (or PAR). The driving purpose of the research is to equalize the power differentials in the research process and attempt to promote change, often in local settings.

Pearson's *r* A measure of the strength and direction of the relationship between two interval/ratio variables.

Personal documents Documents such as diaries, letters, and autobiographies that are not written for an official purpose. They provide first-person accounts of the writer's life and events within it.

Phenomenology A philosophy that is concerned with the question of how individuals make sense of the world around them and how in particular the philosopher should bracket out preconceptions concerning their grasp of that world.

Phi Phi (Φ) is a method for assessing the strength of the relationship between two dichotomous variables.

Photo-elicitation Typically, a visual research method that involves getting interviewees to discuss one or more photographs in the course of an interview. The photograph(s) may be extant or may have been taken by the interviewee for the purpose of the research.

Pie chart A graphic used to present the categories of data as parts of a circle or slices of a pie.

Pilot A small-scale preliminary study conducted to test research instruments, for example survey questions, before undertaking a full-scale research project.

Population The universe of units from which a sample is to be selected.

Positive relationship A relationship between two variables whereby as one increases the other increases as well.

Positivism, positivist An epistemological position that advocates the application of the methods of the natural sciences to the study of social reality and beyond.

Postal questionnaire A form of self-completion questionnaire that is sent to respondents by postal mail and usually returned by them the same way.

Postmodernism A philosophical movement that displays a distaste for master-narratives and for a realist orientation. In the context of research methodology, postmodernists display a preference for qualitative methods and a concern with the modes of representation of research findings.

Pragmatism A philosophical movement that acknowledges the importance of an outcome to a problem or argument rather than the process through which the argument is made. 'Truth' becomes more about what works for a particular set of consequences or goals.

Pre-coded question On a questionnaire or interview schedule, this is a closed-ended question where a numerical code has been pre-assigned to each possible response. This practice removes the need for the application of a coding frame to the question after it has been answered.

Predictive validity An assessment of the measurement validity of a measure of a concept that uses a future benchmark as a criterion: when the benchmark is reached, the previously used measure can be compared with it to see how accurately it predicted the result.

Preference organization A term used in conversation analysis to refer to a sequence of talk in which particular responses are organized in terms of implied preference.

Probability sample/sampling A sample that has been selected using random sampling and in which each unit in the population has a known probability of being selected. Cluster sampling, simple random sampling, and systematic sampling are examples of probability sampling.

Properties In grounded theory and other forms of qualitative analysis, properties are characteristics or attributes that describe and help constitute an analytical category.

Purposive sample/sampling A form of non-probability sample in which the researcher aims to sample cases or participants in a strategic way, so that those sampled are relevant to the research questions that are being posed.

Qualitative content analysis An approach to documents that emphasizes the role of the investigator in the construction of the meaning of, and in, texts. There is an emphasis on allowing categories to emerge out of data and on recognizing the significance of the context in which an item being analysed (and the categories derived from it) appeared. Also called 'ethnographic content analysis'.

Qualitative research Research that emphasizes words rather than quantification in the collection and analysis of data. As a research strategy it is inductive, constructionist, and interpretivist, but qualitative researchers do not always subscribe to all three of these features. Compare with quantitative research.

Quantification rhetoric A term used in discourse analysis to refer to the way a writer or speaker supports or refutes claims using numerical statements.

Quantitative research Quantitative research usually emphasizes quantification in the collection and analysis of data. As a research strategy it is deductive and objectivist and incorporates a natural science model of the research process (in particular, one influenced by positivism), but quantitative researchers do not always subscribe to all three of these features. Compare with qualitative research.

Quasi-experiment A research design that is close to being an experiment but that does not meet the requirements fully and therefore does not exhibit complete internal validity.

Queer methodologies A multi-faceted term that is broadly informed by queer theory and queer studies. With overarching aims that question the sexual construction of the social, and the empirical emphasis on 'the observable', queer methodologies critically examine what 'we' know, and how 'we' think we know it.

Questionnaire A collection of questions administered to respondents. When used on its own, the term usually denotes a self-completion questionnaire.

Quota sample/sampling A sample in which participants are non-randomly sampled from a population in terms of the relative proportions of people in different categories. It is a type of non-probability sample.

R A widely used statistical software package that allows quantitative data to be managed and analysed. Other packages include SPSS, Stata, and SAS.

Random assignment In experiments, the random allocation of research participants to the experimental group and the control group.

Random digit dialling (RDD) A method of sampling, usually for a computer-assisted telephone interview survey, whereby telephone numbers are randomly generated.

Randomized controlled trial A study that meets the criteria of a true experiment. The term is used in fields such as the health sciences in which the goal is to test the effectiveness of an intervention, such as a clinical intervention.

Random sample/sampling A sample in which the inclusion of a unit of a population occurs entirely by chance.

Range The difference between the maximum and the minimum value in a distribution of values associated with an interval or ratio variable.

Ratio variable An interval variable with a true zero point.

RDD Abbreviation of **r**andom **d**igit **d**ialling.

Reactivity, reactive effect The response of research participants to the fact that they know they are being studied. Reactivity is expected to result in untypical behaviour.

Realism, realist An epistemological position that acknowledges a reality, independent of the senses, that is accessible to the researcher's tools and theoretical speculations. It implies that the categories created by scientists refer to real objects in the natural or social worlds. See also critical realism.

Reflexivity, reflexive In research methodology, a reflectiveness among social researchers about the implications, for the knowledge that they generate about the social world, of their methods, values, biases, decisions, and mere presence in the very situations they investigate.

Relationship In statistical analysis, a relationship represents an association between two variables whereby the variation in one variable coincides with variation in another variable. See also negative relationship, positive relationship, and spurious relationship.

Reliability The degree to which a measure of a concept is stable. See also internal reliability.

Repair mechanism In conversation analysis, attempts that people make in conversation to preserve turn-taking in adjacency pairs.

Replication, replicability The degree to which the results of a study can be reproduced by following the same research process.

Representative sample A sample that reflects the population accurately, so that it is a microcosm of the population.

Research design In this book, we use this term to refer to a framework or structure within which a researcher collects and analyses their data. A choice of research design reflects decisions about the priority being given to a range of dimensions of the research process (such as causality and generalization) and is influenced by the kind of research question that is posed.

Research method A tool, such as a survey, a structured interview, or a focus group, that a researcher uses to explore an area of interest by gathering information (data) that they then analyse.

Research question An explicit statement, in the form of a question, of what it is that a researcher intends to find out about. A research question not only influences the scope of an investigation but also how the research will be conducted and what research strategy and research design will be chosen.

Research strategy In this book, we use this term to refer to a general orientation to the conduct of social research (see quantitative research and qualitative research).

Respondent validation A process whereby a researcher gives a report of their findings to the people who were the subjects of their research, and requests feedback on that account. Also called 'member validation'.

Response set In survey research, the tendency among some people, when answering multiple-indicator measures, to reply in the same way to each item.

Rhetoric, rhetorical A concern, in writing or speaking, with appeals to convince or persuade the reader or audience.

Sample, sampling In social science research, the sample is usually the segment of the population that is selected for research. The method of selection may be based on probability sampling or non-probability sampling principles.

Sampling bias A distortion in the representativeness of a sample arising from some members of the sampling frame standing little or no chance of being selected for inclusion in the sample.

Sampling error Differences between a random sample and the population from which it is selected.

Sampling frame The listing of all units in the population from which a sample is selected.

SAS A widely used statistical software package that allows quantitative data to be managed and analysed. Other packages include SPSS, R, and Stata.

Satisficing A cognitive process involved in answering survey questions that involves minimizing the amount of effort involved. The respondent does not expend enough effort to arrive at the best possible answer. Compare with optimizing.

Scale A multiple-indicator measure in which the score a person gives for each component indicator is used to provide a composite score for that person. Also called an 'index'.

Scan sampling A sampling approach in structured observation whereby an entire group of individuals is scanned at regular intervals and the behaviour of all of them is recorded at each occasion.

Scatter diagram A type of graph where one value of an observation is plotted against another. It provides a visual representation of whether, and how, variables might be related to each other. Each axis represents the value of an observation, with points placed on the graph where those values intersect in individual cases.

Secondary analysis The analysis of data by researchers who will probably not have been involved in the collection of those data, and for purposes that may not have been envisaged by those responsible for the data collection. Secondary analysis may involve the analysis of either quantitative data or qualitative data.

Self-completion questionnaire A questionnaire that the respondent answers without the help or intervention of an interviewer. Also called a 'self-administered questionnaire'.

Semiotics The study or science of signs. It is an approach to the analysis of documents and other phenomena that emphasizes the importance of seeking out the deeper meaning of those phenomena. A semiotic approach is concerned to uncover the processes of meaning production and how signs are designed to have an effect upon actual and prospective consumers of those signs.

Semi-structured interview A term that covers a wide range of types of interview. It typically refers to a context in which the interviewer has a series of questions that are in the general form of an interview guide but where the interviewer is able to vary the sequence of questions. The questions are frequently somewhat more general in their frame of reference than those typically found in a structured interview schedule. Also, the interviewer usually has some latitude to ask further questions in response to what they see as significant replies.

Sensitizing concept A term devised by Herbert Blumer to refer to a preference for treating a concept as a guide in an investigation, so that it points in a general way to what is relevant or important. This position contrasts with the idea of an operational definition, in which the meaning of a concept is fixed in advance of carrying out an investigation.

Sentiment analysis The process of computationally finding and categorizing attitudes and opinions communicated by the author of a text, to identify whether their attitudes and opinions about something are neutral, negative, or positive.

Sequential sampling An approach to sampling in which units are selected according to their relevance to an emergent criterion during the course of a study.

Sign A term employed in semiotics. A sign is made up of a signifier (the manifestation of a sign) and the signified (that idea or deeper meaning to which the signifier refers).

Simple observation The passive and unobtrusive observation of behaviour.

Simple random sample A sample in which each unit has been selected entirely by chance. Each unit of the population has a known and equal probability of inclusion in the sample.

Snowball sample A non-probability sample in which the researcher makes initial contact with a small group of people who are relevant to the research topic and then uses these contacts to establish contacts with others.

Social desirability bias A distortion of data that is caused by participants responding to data collection exercises, for example surveys or focus groups, in ways that conform to their perceptions of socially acceptable beliefs or behaviour.

Spearman's rho (ρ) A measure of the strength and direction of the relationship between two ordinal variables.

SPSS Short for **S**tatistical **P**ackage for the **S**ocial **S**ciences, a widely used computer program that allows quantitative data to be managed and analysed. Other packages include R, SAS, and Stata.

Spurious relationship A relationship between two variables is said to be spurious if it is being produced by the impact of a third variable (often referred to as a confounding variable) on each of the two variables that form the spurious relationship. When the third variable is controlled, the relationship disappears.

Standard deviation A measure of dispersion around the arithmetic mean.

Standard error of the mean An estimate of the amount that a sample's arithmetic mean is likely to differ from the population mean.

Standardized interview A research interview, usually in the context of survey research, in which all respondents are asked exactly the same questions in the same order with the aid of a formal interview schedule. Also called a structured interview.

Stata A widely used statistical software package that allows quantitative data to be managed and analysed. Other packages include SPSS, R, and SAS.

Statistical inference The process of making inferences (estimates or predictions) about a population based on the analysis of data from a random sample of that population. See statistical significance.

Statistical significance A test of statistical significance allows the analyst to estimate how confident they can be that the results deriving from a study based on a randomly selected sample are generalizable to the population from which the sample was drawn. Such a test does not allow the researcher to infer that the findings are of substantive importance. The chi-square test is an example of this kind of test. The process of using a test of statistical significance to generalize from a sample to a population is known as statistical inference.

Stratified random sample A sample in which units are randomly sampled from a population that has been divided into categories (strata).

Structured interview An interview, usually in the context of survey research, in which all respondents are asked exactly the same questions in the same order with the aid of a formal interview schedule.

Structured observation A technique in which the researcher employs explicitly formulated rules for the observation and recording of behaviour. The rules inform observers about what they should look for and how they should record behaviour. Also called 'systematic observation'.

Substantive theory A term often used in relation to qualitative data analysis, particularly in respect to grounded theory, it refers to a collection of categories and concepts that help to describe, explain, or understand a particular substantive issue. A distinction is often made between substantive theory and formal theory.

Survey, survey research A cross-sectional research design in which data are collected, by self-completion questionnaire or by structured interview, on a sample of cases drawn from a wider population in order to collect a body of quantitative or quantifiable data in connection with a number of variables, which are then examined to detect patterns of relationships between variables.

Symbolic interactionism A theoretical perspective in sociology and social psychology that views social interaction as taking place in terms of the meanings that actors attach to action and things.

Synchronous online interview or focus group An online interview or focus group in which the communications between participants are in real time, so that there will be only brief time lapses between interviewers' questions and participants' replies and, in the case of focus groups, between participants' contributions to the discussion. Compare with asynchronous online interview or focus group.

Systematic observation Alternative term for structured observation.

Systematic review A review of the literature in a research domain that aims to provide an account of the literature that is comprehensive, capable of replication, and transparent in its approach. Systematic reviews pay close attention to assessing the quality of research in deciding whether a study should be included or not. Meta-analysis and meta-ethnography are both forms of systematic review.

Systematic sample A probability sampling method in which units are selected from a sampling frame according to fixed intervals, such as every fifth unit.

Test of statistical significance See statistical significance.

Text A term that is used either in the conventional sense of a written work or, in more recent years, to refer to a wide range of phenomena. For example, in arriving at a thick description, Clifford Geertz refers to treating culture as a text.

Thematic analysis A term used in connection with the analysis of qualitative data to refer to the extraction of key themes in one's data. It is a rather diffuse approach with few generally agreed principles for defining core themes in data.

Thematic synthesis Essentially, the application of thematic analysis to the synthesis of a set of qualitative studies in an area to arrive at an overall sense of what they show.

Theoretical sample/sampling A term used mainly in grounded theory to refer to purposive sampling carried out so that emerging theoretical considerations guide the selection of cases and/or research participants. Theoretical sampling is supposed to continue until a point of theoretical saturation is reached.

Theoretical saturation In grounded theory, the point when emerging concepts have been fully explored and no new theoretical insights are being generated. See also theoretical sampling.

Theory A group of ideas that aim to explain something, in this case the social world. The term is typically meant as an explanation of observed regularities.

Thick description A term devised by Clifford Geertz to refer to detailed accounts of a social setting that can form the basis for the creation of general statements about a culture and its significance in people's social lives.

Time sampling In structured observation, a sampling method that involves using a criterion for deciding when observations will occur.

Transcribing Preparing a textual version of a recorded interview or focus group session or, in conversation analysis, of naturally occurring conversation. Transcription can sometimes be facilitated by using automated voice-recognition software.

Transcription, transcript The textual version of a recorded interview or focus group session or, in conversation analysis, of naturally occurring conversation.

Triangulation The use of more than one method or source of data in the study of a social phenomenon so that findings may be cross-checked.

Trustworthiness A set of criteria advocated by some writers for assessing the quality of qualitative research.

Turn-taking The notion from conversation analysis that order in everyday conversation is achieved through orderly taking of turns.

Unit, unit of analysis The entity that you are analysing. For example, a unit in your sample could be an individual, a group, an artefact (report, photo, newspaper, blog), or a geographical entity (city, state, region, country).

Unit non-response A source of non-sampling error that occurs whenever some members of a sample—some units—refuse to cooperate, cannot be contacted, or for some reason cannot supply the required data. Sometimes simply referred to as 'non-response'. Compare with item non-response.

Univariate analysis The analysis of a single variable at a time.

Unobtrusive method A method of data collection that removes the potential for reactivity (a person's responses or behaviour being affected by the knowledge that they are participating in a study) by ensuring that the observer is not involved in the interactions or setting being studied.

Unstructured interview An interview in which the interviewer typically has only a list of topics or issues, often called an interview guide, that they will aim to cover. The style of questioning is usually very informal. The phrasing and sequencing of questions will vary from interview to interview.

Validity An assessment of the integrity of the conclusions that are generated from a piece of research. There are different aspects of validity. See, in particular, measurement validity, internal validity, external validity, and ecological validity. When used on its own, validity is usually taken to refer to measurement validity.

Variable An attribute in terms of which cases vary. See also dependent variable and independent variable. Compare with constant.

Vignette A hypothetical scenario of a situation presented to an interviewee, which they are invited to respond to or answer questions about.

Weighting The process of making statistical adjustments to survey data after they have been collected in order to improve accuracy: for example, adjustments to take account of non-response and/or unequal probability of respondents selecting a particular answer.

REFERENCES

Abawi, O., Welling, M. S., van den Eynde, E., van Rossum, E. F. C., Halberstadt, J., van den Akker, E. L. T., and van der Voorn, B. (2020). 'COVID-19 Related Anxiety in Children and Adolescents with Severe Obesity: A Mixed-Methods Study', *Clinical Obesity*, 10(6).

Abbas, A., Ashwin, P., and McLean, M. (2016). 'The Influence of Curricula Content on English Sociology Students' Transformations: The Case of Feminist Knowledge', *Teaching in Higher Education*, 21(4): 442–56.

Abramova, O., Baumann, A., Krasnova, H., and Lessmann, S. (2017). 'To Phub or Not to Phub: Understanding Off-Task Smartphone Usage and Its Consequences in the Academic Environment', Proceedings of the 25th European Conference on Information Systems (ECIS), Guimarães, Portugal, 5–10 June.

Abrams, K. M., Wang, Z., Song, Y. J., and Galindo-Gonzalez, S. (2015). 'Data Richness Trade-Offs Between Face-to-Face, Online Audiovisual, and Online Text-Only Focus Groups', *Social Science Computer Review*, 33(1): 80–96.

Ackroyd, S. (2009). 'Research Designs for Realist Research', in D. Buchanan and A. Bryman (eds), *Handbook of Organizational Research Methods*. London: Sage.

Adler, P. A. (1985). *Wheeling and Dealing: An Ethnography of an Upper-Level Drug Dealing and Smuggling Community*. New York: Columbia University Press.

Adler, P. A., and Adler, P. (1987). *Membership Roles in Field Research*. Sage University Paper Series on Qualitative Research Methods, 6. Newbury Park, CA: Sage.

Adler, P. A., and Adler, P. (2008). 'Of Rhetoric and Representation: The Four Faces of Ethnography', *Sociological Quarterly*, 49: 1–30.

Adler, P. A., and Adler, P. (2009). 'Using a Gestalt Perspective to Analyze Children's Worlds', in A. J. Puddephatt, W. Shaffir, and S. W. Kleinknecht (eds), *Ethnographies Revisited: Constructing Theory in the Field*. London: Routledge.

Adler, P. A., and Adler, P. (2012). Contribution to S. E. Baker and R. Edwards (eds), *How Many Qualitative Interviews is Enough? Expert Voices and Early Career Reflections on Sampling and Cases in Qualitative Research*. National Centre for Research Methods Review Paper, http://eprints.ncrm.ac.uk/2273/ (accessed 27 February 2021).

Ahuvia, A. (2001). 'Traditional, Interpretive, and Reception Based Content Analyses: Improving the Ability of Content Analysis to Address Issues of Pragmatic and Theoretical Concern', *Social Indicators Research*, 54(2): 139–72.

Akard, T., Wray, S., and Gilmer, M. (2015). 'Facebook Ads Recruit Parents of Children with Cancer for an Online Survey of Web-Based Research Preferences', *Cancer Nursing*, 38(2): 155–61.

Akerlof, K., Maibach, E. W., Fitzgerald, D., and Cedeno, A. Y. (2013). 'Do People "Personally Experience" Global Warming, and if so How, and Does it Matter?', *Global Environmental Change*, 23: 81–91.

Alaszewski, A. (2018). 'Diaries', in L. M. Given (ed.), *The SAGE Encyclopaedia of Research Methods*. London: Sage.

Alatinga, K. A., and Williams, J. J. (2019). 'Mixed Methods Research for Health Policy Development in Africa: The Case of Identifying Very Poor Households for Health Insurance Premium Exemptions in Ghana', *Journal of Mixed Methods Research*, 13(1): 69–84.

Al-Hindi, K. F., and Kawabata, H. (2002). 'Toward a More Fully Reflexive Feminist Geography', in P. Moss (ed.), *Feminist Geography in Practice: Research and Methods*. Oxford: Blackwell, 103–15.

Allison, G. T. (1971). *Essence of Decision: Explaining the Cuban Missile Crisis*. Boston: Little, Brown.

Altheide, D. L. (1980). 'Leaving the Newsroom', in W. Shaffir, R. A. Stebbins, and A. Turowetz (eds), *Fieldwork Experience: Qualitative Approaches to Social Research*. New York: St Martin's Press.

Altheide, D. L., and Schneider, C. J. (2013). *Qualitative Media Analysis*, 2nd edn. Los Angeles: Sage.

Alvesson, M., and Kärreman, D. (2000). 'Varieties of Discourse: On the Study of Organization through Discourse Analysis', *Human Relations*, 53(9): 1125–49.

Alwin, D., Baumgartner, E., and Beattie, B. (2018). 'Number of Response Categories and Reliability in Attitude Measurement', *Journal of Survey Statistics and Methodology*, 6(2): 212–39.

Amrhein, V., Greenland, S., and McShane, B. (2019). 'Scientists Rise Up Against Statistical Significance', *Nature*, 567: 305–9.

Anderson, A., Baker, F., and Robinson, D. (2017). 'Precautionary Savings, Retirement Planning and Misperceptions of Financial Literacy', *Journal of Financial Economics*, 126(2): 383–98.

Anderson, B. (2016). 'Laundry, Energy and Time: Insights from 20 Years of Time-Use Diary Data in the United Kingdom', *Energy Research and Social Science*, 22: 125–36.

Anderson, E. (1978). *A Place on the Corner*. Chicago: University of Chicago Press.

Anderson, E. (2006). 'Jelly's Place: An Ethnographic Memoir', in D. Hobbs and R. Wright (eds), *The SAGE Handbook of Fieldwork*. London: Sage.

Andrade, L. L. de (2000). 'Negotiating from the Inside: Constructing Racial and Ethnic Identity in Qualitative Research', *Journal of Contemporary Ethnography*, 29(3): 268–90.

Antonucci, L. (2016). *Student Lives in Crisis: Deepening Inequality in Times of Austerity*. Bristol, UK: Policy Press.

Anzaldúa, G. (1987). *Borderlands/la frontera*, vol. 3. San Francisco: aunt lute books.

Aresi, G., Cleveland, M. J., Vieno, A., Beccaria, F., Turrisi, R., and Marta, E. (2020). 'A Mixed Methods Cross-Cultural Study to Compare Youth Drinking Cultures in Italy and the USA', *Applied Psychology: Health and Well-Being*, 12(1): 231–55.

Armstrong, D., Gosling, A., Weinman, J., and Marteau, T. (1997). 'The Place of Inter-Rater Reliability in Qualitative Research: An Empirical Study', *Sociology*, 31: 597–606.

Armstrong, G. (1993). 'Like that Desmond Morris?', in D. Hobbs and T. May (eds), *Interpreting the Field: Accounts of Ethnography*. Oxford: Clarendon Press.

Aronson, E., and Carlsmith, J. M. (1968). 'Experimentation in Social Psychology', in G. Lindzey and E. Aronson (eds), *The Handbook of Social Psychology*. Reading, MA: Addison-Wesley.

Asch, S. E. (1951). 'Effect of Group Pressure upon the Modification and Distortion of Judgments', in H. Guetzkow (ed.), *Groups, Leadership and Men*. Pittsburgh, PA: Carnegie Press.

Askins, K. (2016). 'Emotional Citizenry: Everyday Geographies of Befriending, Belonging and Intercultural Encounter', *Transactions of the Institute of British Geographers*, 41(4): 515–27.

Athey, N., Boyd, N., and Cohen, E. (2017). 'Becoming a Medical Marijuana User: Reflections on Becker's Trilogy—Learning Techniques, Experiencing Effects, and Perceiving Those Effects as Enjoyable', *Contemporary Drug Problems*, 44(3): 212–31.

Atkinson, P. (1981). *The Clinical Experience*. Farnborough, UK: Gower.

Atkinson, P. (1990). *The Ethnographic Imagination: Textual Constructions of Society*. London: Routledge.

Atkinson, P. (2006). *Everyday Arias: An Operatic Ethnography*. Oxford: AltaMira.

Atkinson, P., and Coffey, A. (2011). 'Analysing Documentary Realities', in D. Silverman (ed.), *Qualitative Research: Issues of Theory, Method and Practice*, 3rd edn. London: Sage.

Atkinson, P., and Delamont, S. (2006). 'Rescuing Narrative from Qualitative Research', *Narrative Inquiry*, 16(1): 164–72.

Atkinson, P., Coffey, A., and Delamont, S. (2003). *Key Themes in Qualitative Research: Continuities and Changes*. Walnut Creek, CA: AltaMira.

Atkinson, R. (1998). *The Life Story Interview*. Beverly Hills, CA: Sage.

Atkinson, R. (2004). 'Life Story Interview', in M. S. Lewis-Beck, A. Bryman, and T. F. Liao (eds), *The Sage Encyclopedia of Social Science Research Methods*. Thousand Oaks, CA: Sage.

Atrey, S. (2019). *Intersectional Discrimination*. Oxford: Oxford University Press.

Attride-Stirling, J. (2001). 'Thematic Networks: An Analytic Tool for Qualitative Research', *Qualitative Research*, 1: 385–404.

Badcock, P., Kent, P., Smith, A., Simpson, J., Pennay, D., Rissel, C., de Visser, R., Grulich, A., and Richters, J. (2017). 'Differences between Landline and Mobile Phone Users in Sexual Behaviour Research', *Archives of Sexual Behavior*, 46(6): 1711–21.

Badenes-Ribera, L., Frias-Navarro, D., Bonilla-Campos, A., Pons-Salvador, G., and Monterde-i-Bort, H. (2015). 'Intimate Partner Violence in Self-Identified Lesbians: A Meta-analysis of its Prevalence', *Sexuality Research and Social Policy*, 12(1): 47–59.

Bahr, H. M., Caplow, T., and Chadwick, B. A. (1983). 'Middletown III: Problems of Replication, Longitudinal Measurement, and Triangulation', *Annual Review of Sociology*, 9: 243–64.

Bailey, A., Giangola, L., and Boykoff, M. T. (2014). 'How Grammatical Choice Shapes Media Representations of Climate (Un)certainty', *Environmental Communication*, 8: 197–215.

Baird, A. (2018). 'Becoming the Baddest: Masculine Trajectories of Gang Violence in Medellín', *Estudios Socio-Jurídicos*, 20(2): 9–48.

Ball, S. J. (1981). *Beachside Comprehensive: A Case Study of Secondary Schooling*. Cambridge: Cambridge University Press.

Bampton, R., and Cowton, C. J. (2002). 'The E-Interview', *Forum: Qualitative Social Research*, 3(2), www.qualitative-research.net/index.php/fqs/article/view/848/1842 (accessed 27 February 2021).

Banks, J. (2012). 'Edging Your Bets: Advantage Play, Gambling, Crime and Victimisation', *Crime Media Culture*, 9: 171–87.

Banks, J. (2014). 'Online Gambling, Advantage Play, Reflexivity and Virtual Ethnography', in K. Lumsden and A. Winter (eds), *Reflexivity in Criminological Research: Experiences with the Powerful and the Powerless*. Basingstoke, UK: Palgrave Macmillan.

Banks, M., and Zeitlyn, D. (2015). *Visual Methods in Social Research*, 2nd edn. London: SAGE.

Bansak, K., Hainmueller, J., and Hangartner, D. (2016). 'How Economic, Humanitarian, and Religious Concerns Shape European Attitudes toward Asylum Seekers', *Science*, 354(6309): 217–22.

Barbour, R. (2007). *Doing Focus Groups*. London: Sage.

Barbour, R. S. (2014). 'Analysing Focus Groups', in U. Flick (ed.), *The SAGE Handbook of Qualitative Data Analysis*. London: Sage, 313–26.

Barge, S., and Gehlbach, H. (2012). 'Using the Theory of Satisficing to Evaluate the Quality of Survey Data', *Research in Higher Education*, 53(2): 182–200.

Barnard-Wills, D. (2016). *Surveillance and Identity: Discourse, Subjectivity and the State*. London: Routledge.

Barter, C., and Renold, E. (1999). 'The Use of Vignettes in Qualitative Research', *Social Research Update*, 25, https://sru.soc.surrey.ac.uk/SRU25.html.

Bauman, Z. (1978). *Hermeneutics and Social Science: Approaches to Understanding*. London: Hutchison.

Baumgartner, J. C., and Morris, J. S. (2010). 'MyFaceTube Politics: Social Networking Web Sites and Political Engagement of Young Adults', *Social Science Computer Review*, 28: 24–44.

Bazeley, P. (2013). *Qualitative Data Analysis: Practical Strategies*. London: Sage.

Beardsworth, A. (1980). 'Analysing Press Content: Some Technical and Methodological Issues', in H. Christian (ed.),

Sociology of Journalism and the Press. Keele, UK: Keele University Press.

Beardsworth, A., Bryman, A., Ford, J., and Keil, T. (n.d.). '"The Dark Figure" in Statistics of Unemployment and Vacancies: Some Sociological Implications', discussion paper, Department of Social Sciences, Loughborough University.

Becker, H. S. (1958). 'Problems of Inference and Proof in Participant Observation', *American Sociological Review*, 23: 652–60.

Becker, H. S. (1963). *Outsiders: Studies in the Sociology of Deviance*. New York: Free Press.

Becker, H. S. (1967). 'Whose Side are We On?', *Social Problems*, 14: 239–47.

Becker, H. S. (1974). 'Photography and Sociology', *Studies in Visual Communication*, 1(1): 3–26.

Becker, H. S. (1982). 'Culture: A Sociological View', *Yale Review*, 71: 513–27.

Becker, H. S. (1986). *Writing for Social Scientists: How to Start and Finish Your Thesis, Book, or Article*. Chicago: University of Chicago Press.

Becker, H. S., and Geer, B. (1957). 'Participant Observation and Interviewing: A Comparison', *Human Organization*, 16: 28–32.

Becker, L. A. (n.d.) *Effect Size Calculators*, https://lbecker.uccs.edu/ (accessed 27 November 2020).

Becker, S., Bryman, A., and Sempik, J. (2006). *Defining 'Quality' in Social Policy Research: Views, Perceptions and a Framework for Discussion*. Lavenham, UK: Social Policy Association, www.social-policy.org.uk/downloads/defining%20quality%20in%20social%20policy%20research.pdf (accessed 27 February 2021).

Becker, S., Sempik, J., and Bryman, A. (2010). 'Advocates, Agnostics and Adversaries: Researchers' Perceptions of Service User Involvement in Social Policy Research', *Social Policy and Society*, 9: 355–66.

Belk, R. W., Sherry, J. F., and Wallendorf, M. (1988). 'A Naturalistic Inquiry into Buyer and Seller Behavior at a Swap Meet', *Journal of Consumer Research*, 14: 449–70.

Bell, C. (1969). 'A Note on Participant Observation', *Sociology*, 3: 417–18.

Bell, C., and Newby, H. (1977). *Doing Sociological Research*. London: George Allen & Unwin.

bell hooks (1989). *Talking Back: Thinking Feminist, Thinking Black*. Boston: South End Press.

Bengtsson, M., Berglund, T., and Oskarson, M. (2013). 'Class and Ideological Orientations Revisited: An Exploration of Class-Based Mechanisms', *British Journal of Sociology*, 64: 691–716.

Beninger, K., Fry, A., Jago, N., Lepps, H., Nass, L., and Silvester, H. (2014). *Research Using Social Media: Users' Views*. London: NatCen, www.natcen.ac.uk/media/282288/p0639-research-using-social-media-report-final-190214.pdf (accessed 1 March 2021).

Benson, M. (2011). *The British in Rural France: Lifestyle Migration and the Ongoing Quest for a Better Way of Life*. Manchester, UK: Manchester University Press.

Benson, M., and Jackson, E. (2013). 'Place-Making and Place Maintenance: Performativity, Place and Belonging among the Middle Classes', *Sociology*, 47: 793–809.

Benson, M., and Lewis, C. (2019). 'Brexit, British People of Colour in the EU-27 and Everyday Racism in Britain and Europe', *Ethnic and Racial Studies*, 42(13): 2211–28.

Berelson, B. (1952). *Content Analysis in Communication Research*. New York: Free Press.

Beresford, P. (2019). 'Public Participation in Health and Social Care: Exploring the Co-production of Knowledge', *Frontiers in Sociology*, 3: 41.

Bernhard, L., and Kriesi, H. (2019). 'Populism In Election Times: A Comparative Analysis of 11 Countries in Western Europe', *West European Politics*, 49(6): 1188–208.

Berthoud, R. (2000). 'Introduction: The Dynamics of Social Change', in R. Berthoud and J. Gershuny (eds), *Seven Years in the Lives of British Families: Evidence on the Dynamics of Social Change from the British Household Panel Survey*. Bristol, UK: Policy Press.

Beullens, K., and Schepers, A. (2013). 'Display of Alcohol Use on Facebook: A Content Analysis', *Cyberpsychology, Behavior, and Social Networking*, 16: 497–503.

Bharti, S., Vachha, B., Pradhan, R., Babu, K., and Jena, S. (2016). 'Sarcastic Sentiment Detection in Tweets Streamed in Real Time: A Big Data Approach', *Digital Communications and Networks*, 2(3): 108–21.

Bhaskar, R. (1989). *Reclaiming Reality: A Critical Introduction to Contemporary Philosophy*. London: Verso.

Bianchi, A., Biffignandi, S., and Lynn, P. (2016). 'Web-CAPI Sequential Mixed-Mode Design in a Longitudinal Survey: Effects on Participation Rates, Sample Composition and Costs'. Economic and Social Research Council *Understanding Society* Working Paper Series no. 2016–08, www.understandingsociety.ac.uk/sites/default/files/downloads/working-papers/2016-08.pdf (accessed 27 February 2021).

Bickerstaff, K., Lorenzoni, I., Pidgeon, N., Poortinga, W., and Simmons, P. (2008). 'Framing the Energy Debate in the UK: Nuclear Power, Radioactive Waste and Climate Change Mitigation', *Public Understanding of Science*, 17: 145–69.

Billig, M. (1992). *Talking of the Royal Family*. London: Routledge.

Billig, M. (1996). *Arguing and Thinking: A Rhetorical Approach to Social Psychology*. Cambridge: Cambridge University Press.

Billig, M. (2013). *Learn to Write Badly: How to Succeed in the Social Sciences*. Cambridge: Cambridge University Press.

Birt, L., Scott, S., Cavers, D., Campbell, C., and Walter, F. (2016). 'Member Checking: A Tool to Enhance Trustworthiness or Merely a Nod to Validation?' *Qualitative Health Research*, 26(13): 1802–11.

Bisdee, D., Daly, T., and Price, D. (2013). 'Behind Closed Doors: Older Couples and the Gendered Management of Household Money', *Social Policy and Society*, 12: 163–74.

Black, A., Burns, N., Mair, F., and O'Donnell, K. (2018). 'Migration and the Media in the UK: The Effect on Healthcare Access for Asylum Seekers and Refugees', *European Journal of Public Health*, 28 (suppl. 1, May), https://doi.org/10.1093/eurpub/cky047.081.

Blaikie, A. (2001). 'Photographs in the Cultural Account: Contested Narratives and Collective Memory in the Scottish Islands', *Sociological Review*, 49: 345–67.

Blaikie, N. (2004). 'Abduction', in M. S. Lewis-Beck, A. Bryman, and T. F. Liao (eds), *The Sage Encyclopedia of Social Science Research Methods*. Thousand Oaks, CA: Sage.

Blaikie, N., and Priest, J. (2019). *Designing Social Research: The Logic of Anticipation*. Cambridge: Polity Press.

Blair, J., Czaja, R., and Blair, E. (2014). *Designing Surveys: A Guide to Decisions and Procedures*. London: Sage.

Blatchford, P. (2005). 'A Multi-Method Approach to the Study of School Size Differences', *International Journal of Social Research Methodology*, 8: 195–205.

Blatchford, P., Bassett, P., Brown, P., and Webster, R. (2009). 'The Effect of Support Staff on Pupil Engagement and Individual Attention', *British Educational Research Journal*, 36: 661–86.

Blatchford, P., Chan, K. W., Galton, M., Lai, K. C., and Lee, J. C. (2016). *Class Size: Eastern and Western Perspectives*. Abingdon, UK: Routledge.

Blatchford, P., Edmonds, S., and Martin, C. (2003). 'Class Size, Pupil Attentiveness and Peer Relations', *British Journal of Educational Psychology*, 73: 15–36.

Blauner, R. (1964). *Alienation and Freedom*. Chicago: University of Chicago Press.

Bligh, M. C., and Kohles, J. C. (2014). 'Comparing Leaders Across Contexts, Culture, and Time: Computerized Content Analysis of Leader–Follower Communications', *Leadership*, 10: 142–59.

Bligh, M. C., Kohles, J. C., and Meindl, J. R. (2004). 'Charisma under Crisis: Presidential Leadership, Rhetoric, and Media Responses Before and After the September 11th Terrorist Attacks', *Leadership Quarterly*, 15: 211–39.

Blommaert, L., Coenders, M., and van Tubergen, F. (2014). 'Ethnic Discrimination in Recruitment and Decision Makers' Features: Evidence from Laboratory Experiment and Survey Data using a Student Sample', *Social Indicators Research*, 116: 731–54.

Bloor, M. (1997). 'Addressing Social Problems through Qualitative Research', in D. Silverman (ed.), *Qualitative Research: Theory, Method and Practice*. London: Sage.

Bloor, M. (2002). 'No Longer Dying for a Living: Collective Responses to Injury Risks in South Wales Mining Communities, 1900–47', *Sociology*, 36: 89–105.

Bloor, M., Frankland, S., Thomas, M., and Robson, K. (2001). *Focus Groups in Social Research*. London: Sage.

Blumer, H. (1954). 'What is Wrong with Social Theory?', *American Sociological Review*, 19: 3–10.

Blumer, H. (1956). 'Sociological Analysis and the "Variable"', *American Sociological Review*, 21: 683–90.

Blumer, H. (1962). 'Society as Symbolic Interaction', in A. M. Rose (ed.), *Human Behavior and Social Processes*. London: Routledge & Kegan Paul.

Bobbitt-Zeher, D. (2011). 'Connecting Gender Stereotypes, Institutional Policies, and Gender Composition of Workplace', *Gender and Society*, 25: 764–86.

Bock, A., Isermann, H., and Knieper, T. (2011). 'Quantitative Content Analysis of the Visual', in E. Margolis and L. Pauwels (eds.), *The SAGE Handbook of Visual Research Methods*. London: SAGE, 265–82.

Bock, J. J. (2018). 'Migrants in the Mountains: Shifting Borders and Contested Crisis Experiences in Rural Germany', *Sociology*, 52(3): 569–86.

Boepple, L., and Thompson, J. K. (2014). 'A Content Analysis of Healthy Living Blogs: Evidence of Content Thematically Consistent with Dysfunctional Eating Attitudes and Behaviors', *International Journal of Eating Disorders*, 47: 362–7.

Bogdan, R., and Taylor, S. J. (1975). *Introduction to Qualitative Research Methods: A Phenomenological Approach to the Social Sciences*. New York: Wiley.

Booker, C., Kelly, Y., and Sacker, A. (2018). 'Gender Differences in the Associations Between Age Trends of Social Media Interaction and Well-Being Among 10–15 Year Olds in the UK'. *BMC Public Health*, 18 (article no. 321), https://doi.org/10.1186/s12889-018-5220-4.

Bors, D. (2018). *Data Analysis for the Social Sciences: Integrating Theory and Practice*. London: Sage.

Bosnjak, M., Neubarth, W., Couper, M. P., Bandilla, W., and Kaczmirek, L. (2008). 'Prenotification in Web-Based Access Panel Surveys: The Influence of Mobile Text Messaging Versus E-mail on Response Rates and Sample Composition', *Social Science Computer Review*, 26: 213–23.

boyd, d (2014). *It's Complicated: Social Lives of Networked Teens*. New Haven, CT: Yale University Press.

Braekman, E., Berete, F., Charafeddine, R., Demarest, S., Drieskens, S., Gisle, L., Molenberghs, G., Tafforeau, J., Van der Heyden, J., and Van Hal, G. (2018). 'Measurement Agreement of the Self-Administered Questionnaire of the Belgian Health Interview Survey: Paper-and-Pencil versus Web-Based Mode', *PLoS ONE*, 13(5): e0197434.

Brandtzaeg, P. (2017). 'Facebook is No "Great Equalizer": A Big Data Approach to Gender Differences in Civic Engagement Across Countries', *Social Science Computer Review*, 35(1): 103–25.

Brannen, J., and Nilsen, A. (2006). 'From Fatherhood to Fathering: Tradition and Change Among British Fathers in Four-Generation Families', *Sociology*, 40: 335–52.

Brannen, J., Lewis, S., Nilsen, A., and Smithson, J. (eds) (2002). *Young Europeans, Work and Family: Futures in Transition*. London: Routledge.

Brannen, J., O'Connell, R., and Mooney, A. (2013). 'Families, Meals, and Synchronicity: Eating Together in British Dual Earner Families', *Community, Work and Family*, 16: 417–34.

Braun, V., and Clarke, V. (2006). 'Using Thematic Analysis in Psychology', *Qualitative Research in Psychology*, 3: 77–101.

Braun, V., and Clarke, V. (2013). *Successful Qualitative Research: A Practical Guide for Beginners*. London: Sage.

Brayfield, A., and Rothe, H. (1951). 'An Index of Job Satisfaction', *Journal of Applied Psychology*, 35: 307–11.

Bregoli, I. (2013). 'Effects of DMO Coordination on Destination Brand Identity: A Mixed-Method Study of the City of Edinburgh', *Journal of Travel Research*, 52: 212–24.

Brewster, Z. W., and Lynn, M. (2014). 'Black–White Earnings Gap among Restaurant Servers: A Replication, Extension, and Exploration of Consumer Racial Discrimination in Tipping', *Sociological Inquiry*, 84: 545–69.

Brick, J., and Williams, D. (2013). 'Explaining Rising Nonresponse Rates in Cross-Sectional Surveys', *Annals of the American Academy of Political and Social Science*, 645(1): 36–59.

Bridgman, P. W. (1927). *The Logic of Modern Physics*. New York: Macmillan.

Briggs, C. L. (1986). *Learning How to Ask: A Sociolinguistic Appraisal of the Role of the Interview in Social Science Research*. Cambridge: Cambridge University Press.

British Academy. (2015). *Count Us In: Quantitative Skills for a New Generation*. London: British Academy.

Britton, J. (2018). 'Muslim Men, Racialised Masculinities and Personal Life', *Sociology*, 53(1): 36–51.

Brooks, R., and Waters, J. (2015). 'The Hidden Internationalism of Elite English Schools', *Sociology*, 49: 212–28.

Brotsky, S. R., and Giles, D. (2007). 'Inside the "Pro-Ana" Community: A Covert Online Participant Observation', *Eating Disorders*, 15: 93–109.

Brown, D. (2003). *The Da Vinci Code*. New York: Doubleday.

Bruce, C. S. (1994). 'Research Students' Early Experiences of the Dissertation Literature Review', *Studies in Higher Education*, 19: 217–29.

Brüggen, E., and Willems, P. (2009). 'A Critical Comparison of Offline Focus Groups, Online Focus Groups and E-Delphi', *International Journal of Market Research*, 51: 363–81.

Bryant, A., and Charmaz, K. (eds) (2019). *The Sage Handbook of Current Developments in Grounded Theory*. London: Sage.

Bryman, A. (1974). 'Sociology of Religion and Sociology of Elites', *Archives de sciences sociales des religions*, 38: 109–21.

Bryman, A. (1988a). *Quantity and Quality in Social Research*. London: Routledge.

Bryman, A. (1988b). *Doing Research in Organizations*. London: Routledge.

Bryman, A. (1994). 'The Mead/Freeman Controversy: Some Implications for Qualitative Researchers', in R. G. Burgess and C. Pole (eds), *Issues in Quantitative Research*, Studies in Qualitative Methodology, vol. 4. Greenwich, CT: JAI Press.

Bryman, A. (1995). *Disney and his Worlds*. London: Routledge.

Bryman, A. (1999). 'Global Disney', in P. Taylor and D. Slater (eds), *The American Century*. Oxford: Blackwell.

Bryman, A. (2003). 'McDonald's as a Disneyized Institution: Global Implications', *American Behavioral Scientist*, 47: 154–67.

Bryman, A. (2004). *The Disneyization of Society*. London: Sage.

Bryman, A. (2006a). 'Integrating Quantitative and Qualitative Research: How is it Done?', *Qualitative Research*, 6(1): 97–113.

Bryman, A. (2006b). 'Paradigm Peace and the Implications for Quality', *International Journal of Social Research Methodology*, 9: 111–26.

Bryman, A. (2007). 'Effective Leadership in Higher Education: A Literature Review', *Studies in Higher Education*, 32: 693–710.

Bryman, A. (2008). 'Why Do Researchers Integrate/Combine/Mesh/Blend/Mix/Merge/Fuse Quantitative and Qualitative Research?', in M. M. Bergman (ed.), *Advances in Mixed Methods Research*. London: Sage.

Bryman, A. (2012). Contribution to S. E. Baker and R. Edwards (eds), *How Many Qualitative Interviews is Enough? Expert Voices and Early Career Reflections on Sampling and Cases in Qualitative Research*. National Centre for Research Methods Review Paper, http://eprints.ncrm.ac.uk/2273/ (accessed 27 February 2021).

Bryman, A. (2014). 'June 1989 and Beyond: Julia Brannen's Contribution to Mixed Methods Research', *International Journal of Social Research Methodology*, 17: 121–31.

Bryman, A., and Burgess, R. G. (1994a). 'Developments in Qualitative Data Analysis: An Introduction', in A. Bryman and R. G. Burgess (eds), *Analyzing Qualitative Data*. London: Routledge.

Bryman, A., and Burgess, R. G. (1994b). 'Reflections on Qualitative Data Analysis', in A. Bryman and R. G. Burgess (eds), *Analyzing Qualitative Data*. London: Routledge.

Bryman, A., and Burgess, R. G. (1999). 'Introduction: Qualitative Research Methodology—A Review', in A. Bryman and R. G. Burgess (eds), *Qualitative Research*. London: Sage.

Bryman, A., and Cramer, D. (2011). *Quantitative Data Analysis with IBM SPSS 17, 18 and 19: A Guide for Social Scientists*. London: Routledge.

Bryman, A., Becker, S., and Sempik, J. (2008). 'Quality Criteria for Quantitative, Qualitative and Mixed Methods Research: The View from Social Policy', *International Journal of Social Research Methodology*, 11: 261–76.

Buckle, A., and Farrington, D. P. (1984). 'An Observational Study of Shoplifting', *British Journal of Criminology*, 24: 63–73.

Buckton, C., Patterson, C., Hyseni, L., Katikireddi, S., Lloyd-Williams, F., Elliott-Green, A., Capewell, S., and Hilton, S. (2018). 'The Palatability of Sugar-Sweetened Beverage Taxation: A Content Analysis of Newspaper Coverage of the UK Sugar Debate', *PLoS ONE*, 13(12): e0207576.

Bulmer, M. (1979). 'Concepts in the Analysis of Qualitative Data', *Sociological Review*, 27: 651–77.

Bulmer, M. (1982). 'The Merits and Demerits of Covert Participant Observation', in M. Bulmer (ed.), *Social Research Ethics*. London: Macmillan.

Burawoy, M. (1979). *Manufacturing Consent*. Chicago: University of Chicago Press.

Burawoy, M. (2003). 'Revisits: An Outline of a Theory of Reflexive Ethnography', *American Sociological Review*, 68: 645–79.

Burger, J. M. (2009). 'Replicating Milgram: Would People Still Obey Today?', *American Psychologist*, 64: 1–11.

Burgess, R. G. (1983). *Inside Comprehensive Education: A Study of Bishop McGregor School*. London: Methuen.

Burgess, R. G. (1984). *In the Field*. London: Allen & Unwin.

Búriková, Z., and Miller, D. (2010). *Au Pair*. Cambridge: Polity.

Burnap, P., Gibson, R., Sloan, L., Southern, R., and Williams, M. (2016). '140 Characters to Victory? Using Twitter to Predict the UK 2015 General Election', *Electoral Studies*, 41: 230–3.

Butcher, B. (1994). 'Sampling Methods: An Overview and Review', *Survey Methods Centre Newsletter*, 15: 4–8.

Butler, A. E., Copnell, B., and Hall, H. (2018). 'The Development of Theoretical Sampling in Practice', *Collegian*, 25(5): 561–6.

Butler, T., and Robson, G. (2001). 'Social Capital, Gentrification and Neighbourhood Change in London: A Comparison of Three South London Neighbourhoods', *Urban Studies*, 38: 2145–62.

Cahill, M., Robinson, K., Pettigrew, J., Galvin, R., and Stanley, M. (2018). 'Qualitative Synthesis: A Guide to Conducting a

Meta-ethnography', *British Journal of Occupational Therapy*, 81(3): 129–37.

Calder, B. J. (1977). 'Focus Groups and the Nature of Qualitative Marketing Research', *Journal of Marketing Research*, 14: 353–64.

Callaghan, G., and Thompson, P. (2002). '"We Recruit Attitude": The Selection and Shaping of Routine Call Centre Labour', *Journal of Management Studies*, 39: 233–54.

Calvey, D. (2019). 'The Everyday World of Bouncers: A Rehabilitated Role for Covert Ethnography', *Qualitative Research*, 19(3): 247–62.

Camerer, C. F. (1997). 'Taxi Drivers and Beauty Contests', *Engineering and Science*, 60: 11–19.

Campbell, D. T. (1957). 'Factors Relevant to the Validity of Experiments in Social Settings', *Psychological Bulletin*, 54: 297–312.

Campbell, N., Ali, F., Finlay, A., and Salek, S. (2015). 'Equivalence of Electronic and Paper-Based Patient-Reported Outcome Measures', *Quality of Life Research*, 24(8): 1949–61.

Caretta, M. A., and Vacchelli, E. (2015). 'Re-thinking the Boundaries of the Focus Group: A Reflexive Analysis on the Use and Legitimacy of Group Methodologies in Qualitative Research', *Sociological Research Online*, 20(4): 58–70.

Carson, A., Chabot, C., Greyson, D., Shannon, K., Duff, P., and Shoveller, J. (2017). 'A Narrative Analysis of the Birth Stories of Early-Age Mothers', *Sociology of Health & Illness*, 39(6): 816–31.

Carter-Harris, L., Bartlett Ellis, R., Warrick, A., and Rawl, S. (2016). 'Beyond Traditional Newspaper Advertisement: Leveraging Facebook-Targeted Advertisement to Recruit Long-Term Smokers for Research', *Journal of Medical Internet Research*, 18(6), e117.

Cassidy, R. (2014). '"A Place for Men to Come and Do Their Thing": Constructing Masculinities in Betting Shops in London', *British Journal of Sociology*, 65: 170–91.

Catterall, M., and Maclaran, P. (1997). 'Focus Group Data and Qualitative Analysis Programs: Coding the Moving Picture as well as Snapshots', *Sociological Research Online*, 2, www.socresonline.org.uk/2/1/6 (accessed 27 February 2021).

Cavendish, R. (1982). *Women on the Line*. London: Routledge & Kegan Paul.

Cerulo, K. A. (2014). 'Reassessing the Problem: Response to Jerolmack and Khan', *Sociological Methods and Research*, 43: 219–26.

Chambliss, D., and Schutt, R. (2019). *Making Sense of the Social World: Methods of Investigation*. London: Sage.

Charlton, T., Coles, D., Panting, C., and Hannan, A. (1999). 'Behaviour of Nursery Class Children before and after the Availability of Broadcast Television: A Naturalistic Study of Two Cohorts in a Remote Community', *Journal of Social Behavior and Personality*, 14: 315–24.

Charlton, T., Gunter, B., and Coles, D. (1998). 'Broadcast Television as a Cause of Aggression? Recent Findings from a Naturalistic Study', *Emotional and Behavioural Difficulties*, 3: 5–13.

Charmaz, K. (1983). 'The Grounded Theory Method: An Explication and Interpretation', in R. M. Emerson (ed.), *Contemporary Field Research: A Collection of Readings*. Boston: Little, Brown.

Charmaz, K. (2000). 'Grounded Theory: Objectivist and Constructivist Methods', in N. K. Denzin and Y. S. Lincoln (eds), *Handbook of Qualitative Research*, 2nd edn. Thousand Oaks, CA: Sage.

Charmaz, K. (2002). 'Qualitative Interviewing and Grounded Theory Analysis', in J. F. Gubrium and J. A. Holstein (eds), *Handbook of Interview Research: Context and Method*. Thousand Oaks, CA: Sage.

Charmaz, K. (2004). 'Grounded Theory', in M. S. Lewis-Beck, A. Bryman, and T. F. Liao (eds), *The Sage Encyclopedia of Social Science Research Methods*. Thousand Oaks, CA: Sage.

Charmaz, K. (2006). *Constructing Grounded Theory: A Practical Guide through Qualitative Analysis*. London: Sage.

Chavez, Christina (2008). 'Conceptualising from the Inside: Advantages, Implications and Demands on Insider Positionality', *Qualitative Report*, 13(3): 474–94.

Chin, M. G., Fisak, B., Jr, and Sims, V. K. (2002). 'Development of the Attitudes toward Vegetarianism Scale', *Anthrozoös*, 15: 333–42.

Christensen, D. H., and Dahl, C. M. (1997). 'Rethinking Research Dichotomies', *Family and Consumer Sciences Research Journal*, 25(3): 269–85.

Cicourel, A. V. (1964). *Method and Measurement in Sociology*. New York: Free Press.

Cicourel, A. V. (1968). *The Social Organization of Juvenile Justice*. New York: Wiley.

Cicourel, A. V. (1982). 'Interviews, Surveys, and the Problem of Ecological Validity', *American Sociologist*, 17: 11–20.

Clairborn, W. L. (1969). 'Expectancy Effects in the Classroom: A Failure to Replicate', *Journal of Educational Psychology*, 60: 377–83.

Clark, A. (2013). 'Haunted by Images? Ethical Moments and Anxieties in Visual Research', *Methodological Innovations Online*, 8(2): 68–81, https://journals.sagepub.com/doi/10.4256/mio.2013.014 (accessed 28 February 2021).

Clark, A., and Emmel, N. (2010). 'Realities Toolkit #13: Using Walking Interviews', http://eprints.ncrm.ac.uk/800/1/2009_connected_lives_methods_emmel_clark.pdf (accessed 27 February 2021).

Clark, T. (2008). '"We're Over-Researched Here!" Exploring Accounts of Research Fatigue within Qualitative Research Engagements', *Sociology*, 42(5): 953–70.

Clark, T. (2019). '"Normal Happy Girl" Interrupted: An Auto/biographical Analysis of Myra Hindley's Public Confession', *Deviant Behavior*, https://doi.org/10.1080/01639625.2019.1689047.

Clark, T., and Foster, L. (2017). '"I'm Not a Natural Mathematician": Inquiry-Based Learning, Constructive Alignment and Introductory Quantitative Social Science', *Teaching Public Administration*, 35(3): 260–79.

Clark, T., Foster, L., and Bryman, A. (2019). *How to Do Your Dissertation or Social Science Research Project*. Oxford: Oxford University Press.

Clarke, V., and Braun, V. (2013). 'Teaching Thematic Analysis', *The Psychologist*, 26: 120–3.

Clayman, S., and Gill, V. T. (2004). 'Conversation Analysis', in M. Hardy and A. Bryman (eds), *Handbook of Data Analysis*. London: Sage.

Clifford, J., and Marcus, G. E. (eds.) (1986). *Writing Culture: The Poetics and Politics of Ethnography*. School of American Research Advanced Seminar. Oakland, CA: University of California Press.

Cloward, R. A., and Ohlin, L. E. (1960). *Delinquency and Opportunity: A Theory of Delinquent Gangs*. New York: Free Press.

Cobanoglu, C., Ward, B., and Moreo, P. J. (2001). 'A Comparison of Mail, Fax and Web-Based Survey Methods', *International Journal of Market Research*, 43: 441–52.

Coenen, M., Stamm, T. A., Stucki, G., and Cieza, A. (2012). 'Individual Interviews and Focus Groups in Patients with Rheumatoid Arthritis: A Comparison of Two Qualitative Methods', *Quality of Life Research*, 21(2): 359–70.

Coffey, A. (1999). *The Ethnographic Self: Fieldwork and the Representation of Reality*. London: Sage.

Coffey, A. (2014). 'Analysing Documents', in U. Flick (ed.), *The SAGE Handbook of Qualitative Data Analysis*. London: Sage, 367–80.

Coffey, A., and Atkinson, P. (1996). *Making Sense of Qualitative Data: Complementary Research Strategies*. Thousand Oaks, CA: Sage.

Coffey, A., Holbrook, B., and Atkinson, P. (1994). 'Qualitative Data Analysis: Technologies and Representations', *Sociological Research Online*, 2, www.socresonline.org.uk/1/1/4.html (accessed 28 February 2021).

Cohen, L., Manion, L., and Morrison, K. (2017). *Research Methods in Education*, 8th edn. Abingdon, UK: Routledge.

Cohen, R. S. (2010). 'When It Pays to be Friendly: Employment Relationships and Emotional Labour in Hairstyling', *Sociological Review*, 58: 197–218.

Cohen, S. (1972). *Folk Devils and Moral Panics*. London: MacGibbon and Kee.

Colditz, J. B., Welling, J., Smith, N. A., James, A. E., and Primack, B. A. (2019). 'World Vaping Day: Contextualizing Vaping Culture in Online Social Media Using a Mixed Methods Approach', *Journal of Mixed Methods Research*, 13(2), 196–215, https://doi.org/10.1177/1558689817702753.

Coleman, C., and Moynihan, J. (1996). *Understanding Crime Data: Haunted by the Dark Figure*. Buckingham, UK: Open University Press.

Coleman, J. S. (1958). 'Relational Analysis: The Study of Social Organization with Survey Methods', *Human Organization*, 16: 28–36.

Collins, M. (1997). 'Interviewer Variability: A Review of the Problem', *Journal of the Market Research Society*, 39: 67–84.

Collins, P. (2015). 'Osborne's Brave New Britain is a Pipe Dream', *The Times*, 16 January, www.thetimes.co.uk/tto/opinion/columnists/article4324673.ece (accessed 12 October 2020).

Collins, P. H. (1990). 'Black Feminist Thought in the Matrix of Domination', in P. H. Collins (ed.), *Black Feminist Thought: Knowledge, Consciousness, and the Politics of Empowerment*. Boston: Unwin Hyman, 221–38.

Collins, R. (1994). *Four Sociological Traditions*, rev. edn. New York: Oxford University Press.

Connelly, R., Gayle, V., and Lambert, P. S. (2016). 'Ethnicity and Ethnic Group Measures in Social Survey Research', *Methodological Innovations* 9, https://doi.org/10.1177/2059799116642885.

Converse, P. D., Wolfe, E. W., Huang, X., and Oswald, F. L. (2008). 'Response Rates for Mixed-Mode Surveys Using Mail and E-Mail/Web', *American Journal of Evaluation*, 29: 99–107.

Cook, T. D., and Campbell, D. T. (1979). *Quasi-Experimentation: Design and Analysis for Field Settings*. Boston: Houghton Mifflin.

Cooper, H. (2016). *Research Synthesis and Meta-Analysis: A Step-by-Step Approach*. London: Sage.

Corbin, J., and Strauss, A. (2015). *Basics of Qualitative Research: Techniques and Procedures for Developing Grounded Theory*, 4th edn. Los Angeles: Sage.

Corden, A., and Sainsbury, R. (2006). *Using Verbatim Quotations in Reporting Qualitative Social Research: Researchers' Views*. York, UK: Social Policy Research Unit, University of York, www.york.ac.uk/inst/spru/pubs/pdf/verbquotresearch.pdf (accessed 28 February 2021).

Cortazzi, M. (2001). 'Narrative Analysis in Ethnography', in P. Atkinson, A. Coffey, S. Delamont, J. Lofland, and L. Lofland (eds), *Handbook of Ethnography*. London: Sage.

Corti, L. (1993). 'Using Diaries in Social Research', *Social Research Update*, 2, http://sru.soc.surrey.ac.uk/SRU2.html (accessed 28 February 2021).

Couper, M. P. (2000). 'Web Surveys: A Review of Issues and Approaches', *Public Opinion Quarterly*, 64: 464–94.

Couper, M. P. (2008). *Designing Effective Web Surveys*. Cambridge: Cambridge University Press.

Couper, M. P., Traugott, M. W., and Lamias, M. J. (2001). 'Web Survey Design and Administration', *Public Opinion Quarterly*, 65: 230–53.

Cowls, J., and Bright, J. (2017). 'International Hyperlinks in Online News Media', in N. Brügger and R. Schroeder (eds), *The Web as History*. London: UCL Press, 101–16.

Crawford, S. D., Couper, M. P., and Lamias, M. J. (2001). 'Web Surveys: Perceptions of Burden', *Social Science Computer Review*, 19: 146–62.

Crenshaw, K. (1989). 'Demarginalizing the Intersection of Race and Sex', *University of Chicago Legal Forum*, 1989(1/Article 8): 139–67.

Crenshaw, K. (1991). 'Mapping the Margins: Intersectionality, Identity Politics, and Violence Against Women of Color', *Stanford Law Review*, 43(6): 1241–99.

Creswell, J. W., and Plano Clark, V. L. (2011). *Designing and Conducting Mixed Methods Research*, 2nd edn. Thousand Oaks, CA: Sage.

Creswell, J. W., and Plano Clark, V. L. (2018). *Designing and Conducting Mixed Methods Research—International Student Edition*, 3rd edn. Thousand Oaks, CA: Sage.

Creswell, J. W., and Tashakkori, A. (2007). 'Developing Publishable Mixed Methods Manuscripts', *Journal of Mixed Methods Research*, 1: 107–11.

Croll, P. (1986). *Systematic Classroom Observation*. London: Falmer.

Crompton, R., and Birkelund, G. (2000). 'Employment and Caring in British and Norwegian Banking', *Work, Employment and Society*, 14: 331–52.

Crook, C., and Light, P. (2002). 'Virtual Society and the Cultural Practice of Study', in S. Woolgar (ed.), *Virtual Society? Technology, Cyberbole, Reality*. Oxford: Oxford University Press.

Curasi, C. F. (2001). 'A Critical Exploration of Face-to-Face Interviewing vs Computer-Mediated Interviewing', *International Journal of Market Research*, 43: 361–75.

Curtice, J. (2016). 'A Question of Culture or Economics? Public Attitudes to the European Union in Britain', *Political Quarterly*, 87: 209–18.

Cyr, J. (2016). 'The Pitfalls and Promise of Focus Groups as a Data Collection Method', *Sociological Methods & Research*, 45(2): 231–59.

Dacin, M. T., Munir, K., and Tracey, P. (2010). 'Formal Dining at Cambridge Colleges: Linking Ritual Performance and Institutional Maintenance', *Academy of Management Journal*, 53: 1393–418.

Dai, N. T., Free, C., and Gendron, Y. (2019). 'Interview-Based Research in Accounting 2000–2014: Informal Norms, Translation and Vibrancy', *Management Accounting Research*, 42: 26–38.

Dale, A., Arber, S., and Proctor, M. (1988). *Doing Secondary Analysis*. London: Unwin Hyman.

Davidson, J., Paulus, T., and Jackson, K. (2016). 'Speculating on the Future of Digital Tools for Qualitative Research', *Qualitative Inquiry*, 22(7): 606–10.

Davis, K., Randall, D. P., Ambrose, A., and Orand, M. (2015). '"I Was Bullied Too": Stories of Bullying and Coping in an Online Community', *Information, Communication and Society*, 18: 357–75.

de Bruijne, M., and Wijnant, A. (2014). 'Improving Response Rates and Questionnaire Design for Mobile Web Surveys', *Public Opinion Quarterly*, 78(4): 951–62.

de Certeau, M. (1984). *The Practice of Everyday Life*. Berkeley: University of California Press.

De Leeuw, E. D., and Hox, J. P. (2015). 'Survey Mode and Mode Effects', in U. Engel, B. Jann, P. Lynch, A. Scherpenzeel, and P. Sturgis (eds), *Improving Survey Methods: Lessons from Recent Research*. New York: Routledge.

de Rada, V., and Domínguez, J. (2015). 'The Quality of Responses to Grid Questions as used in Web Questionnaires (Compared with Paper Questionnaires)', *International Journal of Social Research Methodology*, 18(4): 337–48.

De Vaus, D. (2013). *Surveys in Social Research*. London: Routledge.

De Vries, R. (2018). *Critical Statistics: Seeing Beyond the Headlines*. Basingstoke, UK: Palgrave.

Deacon, D. (2007). 'Yesterday's Papers and Today's Technology: Digital Newspaper Archives and "Push Button" Content Analysis', *European Journal of Communication*, 22: 5–25.

Deacon, D., Fenton, N., and Bryman, A. (1999). 'From Inception to Reception: The Natural History of a News Item', *Media, Culture and Society*, 21: 5–31.

Deakin, H., and Wakefield, K. (2014). 'Skype Interviewing: Reflections of Two PhD Researchers', *Qualitative Research*, 14(5): 603–16.

Delamont, S., and Atkinson, P. (2004). 'Qualitative Research and the Postmodern Turn', in C. Hardy and A. Bryman (eds), *Handbook of Data Analysis*. London: Sage.

Delamont, S., and Hamilton, D. (1984). 'Revisiting Classroom Research: A Continuing Cautionary Tale', in S. Delamont (ed.), *Readings on Interaction in the Classroom*. London: Methuen.

Demasi, M. A. (2019). 'Facts as Social Action in Political Debates about the European Union', *Political Psychology*, 40(1): 3–20.

Demetry, D. (2013). 'Regimes of Meaning: The Intersection of Space and Time in Kitchen Cultures', *Journal of Contemporary Ethnography*, 42: 576–607.

Denscombe, M. (2006). 'Web-Based Questionnaires and the Mode Effect: An Evaluation Based on Completion Rates and Data Contents of Near-Identical Questionnaires Delivered in Different Modes', *Social Science Computer Review*, 24: 246–54.

Denzin, N. K. (1968). 'On the Ethics of Disguised Observation', *Social Problems*, 15: 502–4.

Denzin, N. K. (1970). *The Research Act in Sociology*. Chicago: Aldine.

Denzin, N. K., and Lincoln, Y. S. (1994). 'Introduction: Entering the Field of Qualitative Research', in N. K. Denzin and Y. S. Lincoln (eds), *Handbook of Qualitative Research*. Thousand Oaks, CA: Sage.

Denzin, N. K., and Lincoln, Y. S. (2000). *Handbook of Qualitative Research*, 2nd edn. Thousand Oaks, CA: Sage.

Denzin, N. K., and Lincoln, Y. S. (2005a). *Handbook of Qualitative Research*, 3rd edn. Thousand Oaks, CA: Sage.

Denzin, N. K., and Lincoln, Y. S. (2005b). 'Introduction: The Discipline and Practice of Qualitative Research', in N. K. Denzin and Y. S. Lincoln (eds), *Handbook of Qualitative Research*, 3rd edn. Thousand Oaks, CA: Sage.

Denzin, N. K., and Lincoln, Y. S. (2011). 'Preface', in N. K. Denzin and Y. S. Lincoln (eds), *Handbook of Qualitative Research*, 4th edn. Los Angeles: Sage.

Department of Health [UK] (2005). *Research Governance Framework for Health and Social Care*. London: Department of Health.

Derrick, B., and White, P. (2017). 'Comparing Two Samples from an Individual Likert Question', *International Journal of Mathematics and Statistics*, 18(3): 1–13.

DeVault, M. L., and Gross, G. (2012). 'Feminist Qualitative Interviewing: Experience, Talk, and Knowledge', in S. N. Hesse-Biber (ed.), *Handbook of Feminist Research: Theory and Praxis*, 2nd edn. Thousand Oaks, CA: Sage, 173–97.

Díaz de Rada, V. D., and Domínguez-Álvarez, J. A. (2013). 'Response Quality of Self-Administered Questionnaires: A Comparison Between Paper and Web Questionnaires', *Social Science Computer Review*, 32: 256–69.

Diener, E., and Crandall, R. (1978). *Ethics in Social and Behavioral Research*. Chicago: University of Chicago Press.

Diener, E., Inglehart, R., and Tay, L. (2013). 'Theory and Validity of Life Satisfaction Scales', *Social Indicators Research*, 112: 497–527.

Diersch, N., and Walther, E. (2016). 'The Impact of Question Format, Context, and Content on Survey Answers in Early and Late Adolescence', *Journal of Official Statistics*, 32(2): 307–28.

Dillman, D. A., Smyth, J. D., and Christian, L. M. (2014). *Internet, Phone, Mail, and Mixed-Mode Surveys: The Tailored Design Method*, 4th edn. Hoboken, NJ: Wiley.

Dingwall, R. (1980). 'Ethics and Ethnography', *Sociological Review*, 28: 871–91.

Ditton, J. (1977). *Part-Time Crime: An Ethnography of Fiddling and Pilferage*. London: Macmillan.

Dixon-Woods, M., Angell, E., Ashcroft, R., and Bryman, A. (2007). 'Written Work: The Social Functions of Research Ethics Committee Letters', *Social Science and Medicine*, 65: 792–802.

Dommeyer, C. J., and Moriarty, E. (2000). 'Comparison of Two Forms of an E-Mail Survey: Embedded vs Attached', *International Journal of Market Research*, 42: 39–50.

Döring, N., Reif, A., and Poeschl, S. (2016). 'How Gender-Stereotypical are Selfies? A Content Analysis and Comparison with Magazine Adverts', *Computers in Human Behavior*, 55(B): 955–62.

Douglas, J. D. (1967). *The Social Meanings of Suicide*. Princeton: Princeton University Press.

Douglas, J. D. (1976). *Investigative Social Research: Individual and Team Field Research*. Beverly Hills, CA: Sage.

Drabble, L., Trocki, K. F., Salcedo, B., Walker, P. C., and Korcha, R. A. (2016). 'Conducting Qualitative Interviews by Telephone: Lessons Learned from a Study of Alcohol Use among Sexual Minority and Heterosexual Women', *Qualitative Social Work*, 15(1): 118–33.

Drdová, L., and Saxonberg, S. (2020). 'Dilemmas of a Subculture: An Analysis of BDSM Blogs about *Fifty Shades of Grey*', *Sexualities*, 23(5–6): 987–1008.

Durkheim, E. (1938/1895). *The Rules of Sociological Method*, trans. S. A. Solavay and J. H. Mueller. New York: Free Press.

Durkheim, E. (1952/1897). *Suicide: A Study In Sociology*, trans. J. A. Spaulding and G. Simpson. London: Routledge & Kegan Paul.

Dwyer, S. C., and Buckle, J. L. (2009). 'The Space Between: On Being an Insider–Outsider in Qualitative Research', *International Journal of Qualitative Methods*, 8(1): 54–63.

Eaton, M. A. (2018). 'Manifesting Spirits: Paranormal Investigation and the Narrative Development of a Haunting', *Journal of Contemporary Ethnography*, 48(2): 155–82.

Edmiston, D. (2018). 'The Poor "Sociological Imagination" of the Rich: Explaining Attitudinal Divergence towards Welfare, Inequality, and Redistribution', *Social Policy & Administration*, 52(5): 983–97.

Edwards, A. M., Housley, W., Williams, M. L., Sloan, L., and Williams, M. D. (2013). 'Digital Social Research, Social Media and the Sociological Imagination: Surrogacy, Augmentation and Re-orientation', *International Journal of Social Research Methodology* 16(3): 245–60, 10.1080/13645579.2013.774185

Eisenhardt, K. M. (1989). 'Building Theories from Case Study Research', *Academy of Management Review*, 14: 532–50.

Elias, N. (2000). *The Civilising Process: Sociogenetic and Psychogenetic Investigations*. Oxford: Blackwell.

Elliott, C., and Ellingworth, D. (1997). 'Assessing the Representativeness of the 1992 British Crime Survey: The Impact of Sampling Error and Response Biases', *Sociological Research Online*, 2(4), www.socresonline.org.uk/2/4/3.html (accessed 1 March 2021).

Elliott, H. (1997). 'The Use of Diaries in Sociological Research on Health Experience', *Sociological Research Online*, 2(2), www.socresonline.org.uk/2/2/7.html (accessed 1 March 2021).

Elliott, V. (2018). 'Thinking about the Coding Process in Qualitative Data Analysis', *Qualitative Report*, 23(11): 2850–61, https://nsuworks.nova.edu/tqr/vol23/iss11/14.

Ellis, C., and Bochner, A. (2000). 'Autoethnography, Personal Narrative, Reflexivity: Researcher as Subject', in N. K. Denzin and Y. S. Lincoln (eds), *Handbook of Qualitative Research*, 2nd edn. Thousand Oaks, CA: Sage, 733–68.

Emerson, R. M. (1987). 'Four Ways to Improve the Craft of Fieldwork', *Journal of Contemporary Ethnography*, 16: 69–89.

Erel, U., Reynolds, T., and Kaptani, E. (2017). 'Participatory Theatre for Transformative Social Research', *Qualitative Research*, 17(3): 302–12.

Erikson, K. T. (1967). 'A Comment on Disguised Observation in Sociology', *Social Problems*, 14: 366–73.

Ernst, F. A. (2014). *Ethnographic Fieldwork: Conducting Close-Proximity Research on Mexican Organized Crime*. SAGE Research Methods Cases Part 1, https://dx.doi.org/10.4135/978144627305013504182.

Ertesvag, S. K., Sammons, P., and Blossing, U. (2020). 'Integrating Data in a Complex Mixed-Methods Classroom Interaction Study', *British Educational Research Journal*, 10.1002/berj.3678.

Eschleman, K. J., Bowling, N. A., Michel, J. S., and Burns, G. N. (2014). 'Perceived Intent of Supervisor as a Moderator Between Abusive Supervision and Counterproductive Work Behaviours', *Work and Stress*, 28: 362–75.

Evans, A., Elford, J., and Wiggins, R. D. (2008). 'Using the Internet in Qualitative Research', in C. Willig and W. Stainton Rogers (eds), *SAGE Handbook of Qualitative Methods in Psychology*. London: Sage.

Fairclough, N. (1995). *Critical Discourse Analysis: The Critical Study of Language*. London: Longman.

Faraday, A., and Plummer, K. (1979). 'Doing Life Histories', *Sociological Review*, 27: 773–98.

Farkas, J., Schou, J., and Neumayer, C. (2018). 'Cloaked Facebook Pages: Exploring Fake Islamist Propaganda in Social Media', *New Media & Society*, 20(5): 1850–67.

Farnsworth, J., and Boon, B. (2010). 'Analysing Group Dynamics Within the Focus Group', *Qualitative Research*, 10(5): 605–24.

Faulk, N., and Crist, E. (2020). 'A Mixed-Methods Study of Library Communication with Online Students and Faculty Members', *College & Research Libraries,* 81(3): 361–77.

Fenton, N., Bryman, A., and Deacon, D. (1998). *Mediating Social Science*. London: Sage.

Ferguson, H. (2016). 'What Social Workers Do in Performing Child Protection Work: Evidence from Research into Face-to-Face Practice', *Child & Family Social Work*, 21(3): 283–94.

Festinger, L., Riecken, H. W., and Schachter, S. (1956). *When Prophecy Fails*. New York: Harper & Row.

Fetters, M.D. (2020). *The Mixed Methods Research Workbook: Activities for Designing, Implementing, and Publishing Projects: 7*. Los Angeles: SAGE.

Field, A. (2017). *Discovering Statistics Using IBM SPSS Statistics*. London: Sage.

Fielding, N. (1982). 'Observational Research on the National Front', in M. Bulmer (ed.), *Social Research Ethics*. London: Macmillan.

Filmer, P., Phillipson, M., Silverman, D., and Walsh, D. (1972). *New Directions in Sociological Theory*. London: Collier-Macmillan.

Finch, J. (1987). 'The Vignette Technique in Survey Research', *Sociology*, 21: 105–14.

Fink, K. (2018). 'Opening the Government's Black Boxes: Freedom of Information and Algorithmic Accountability', *Information, Communication & Society*, 21(10): 1453–71.

Fish, R. (2017). *A Feminist Ethnography of Secure Wards for Women with Learning Disabilities: Locked Away*. London: Routledge.

Fisher, K., and Layte, R. (2004). 'Measuring Work-Life Balance using Time Diary Data', *Electronic International Journal of Time Use Research*, 1: 1–13, www.eijtur.org/pdf/volumes/eIJTUR-1-1-3_Fisher_Layte.pdf (accessed 1 March 2021).

Flanders, N. (1970). *Analyzing Teacher Behavior*. Reading, MA: Addison-Wesley.

Fletcher, J. (1966). *Situation Ethics*. London: SCM.

Flick, U. (ed.) (2014). *SAGE Handbook of Qualitative Data Analysis*. London: Sage.

Flick, U. (2018). *An Introduction to Qualitative Research*. London: Sage.

Flyvbjerg, B. (2003). 'Five Misunderstandings about Case Study Research', in C. Seale, G. Gobo, J. F. Gubrium, and D. Silverman (eds), *Qualitative Research Practice*. London: Sage.

Fosnacht, K., Sarraf, S., Howe, E., and Peck, L. (2017). 'How Important are High Response Rates for College Surveys?', *Review of Higher Education*, 40(2): 245–65.

Foster, L., Diamond, I., and Jefferies, J. (2014). *Beginning Statistics: An Introduction for Social Scientists*. London: Sage.

Foster, L., and Gunn, A. (2017). Special Issue on Social Science Research Methods Education, *Teaching Public Administration*, 35(3), 237–40.

Foster, L., and Heneghan, M. (2018). 'Pensions Planning in the UK: A Gendered Challenge', *Critical Social Policy*, 38(2): 345–66.

Foucault, M. (1977). *Discipline and Punish*. Harmondsworth, UK: Penguin.

Foucault, M. (1991). *The Foucault Effect: Studies in Governmentality*. Chicago: University of Chicago Press.

Foucault, M. (1998). *The Will to Knowledge*. London: Penguin.

Foucault, M. (2009). *Security, Territory, Population: Lectures at the Collège de France, 1977–1978*. New York: Picador.

Fowler, F. J. (2013). *Survey Research Methods*, 5th edn. London: Sage.

Fowler, F. J., and Mangione, T. W. (1990). *Standardized Survey Interviewing: Minimizing Interviewer-Related Error*. Beverly Hills, CA: Sage.

Fox, B. H., and Jennings, W. G. (2014). 'How to Write a Methodology and Results Section for Empirical Research', *Journal of Criminal Justice Education*, 25: 137–56.

Fox, J., and Fogelman, K. (1990). 'New Possibilities for Longitudinal Studies of Intergenerational Factors in Child Health and Development', in D. Magnusson and L. R. Bergman (eds), *Data Quality in Longitudinal Research*. Cambridge: Cambridge University Press.

Frean, A. (1998). 'Children Read More after Arrival of TV', *The Times*, 29 April: 7.

Fredriksson, P., Öckert, B., and Oosterbeck, H. (2013). 'Long-Term Effects of Class Size', *Quarterly Journal of Economics*, 128(1): 249–85.

Freese, J., and Peterson, D. (2017). 'Replication in Social Science', *Annual Review of Sociology*, 43: 147–65.

Frey, J. H. (2004). 'Telephone Surveys', in M. S. Lewis-Beck, A. Bryman, and T. F. Liao (eds), *The Sage Encyclopedia of Social Science Research Methods*. Thousand Oaks, CA: Sage.

Fricker, R. (2008). 'Sampling Methods for Web and E-mail Surveys', in N. Fielding, R. M. Lee, and G. Blank (eds), *The Sage Handbook of Online Research Methods*. London: Sage, 195–216.

Gallaher, C. M., and WrinklerPrins, A. M. G. A. (2016). 'Effective Use of Mixed Methods in African Livelihoods Research', *African Geographical Review*, 35(1), 83–93.

Gambetta, D., and Hamill, H. (2005). *Streetwise: How Taxi Drivers Establish their Customers' Trustworthiness*. New York: Russell Sage Foundation.

Gambling Commission (2017). Gambling Participation in 2016: Behaviour, Awareness and Attitudes, www.gamblingcommission.gov.uk/PDF/survey-data/Gambling-participation-in-2016-behaviour-awareness-and-attitudes.pdf (accessed 27 November 2020).

Gans, H. J. (1962). *The Urban Villagers*. New York: Free Press.

Gans, H. J. (1968). 'The Participant-Observer as Human Being: Observations on the Personal Aspects of Field Work', in H. S. Becker (ed.), *Institutions and the Person: Papers Presented to Everett C. Hughes*. Chicago: Aldine.

Garcia, A. C., Standlee, A. I., Bechkoff, J., and Cui, Y. (2009). 'Ethnographic Approaches to the Internet and Computer-Mediated Communication', *Journal of Contemporary Ethnography*, 38 (1): 52–84.

Garfinkel, H. (1967). *Studies in Ethnomethodology*. Englewood Cliffs, NJ: Prentice-Hall.

Garthwaite, K. (2016). 'Stigma, Shame and "People Like Us": An Ethnographic Study of Foodbank Use in the UK', *Journal of Poverty and Social Justice*, 24(3): 277–89.

Geertz, C. (1973a). 'Thick Description: Toward an Interpretive Theory of Culture', in C. Geertz, *The Interpretation of Cultures*. New York: Basic Books.

Geertz, C. (1973b). 'Deep Play: Notes on the Balinese Cockfight', in C. Geertz, *The Interpretation of Cultures*. New York: Basic Books.

Geertz, C. (1983). *Local Knowledge*. New York: Basic Books.

Gershuny, J., and Sullivan, O. (2014). 'Household Structure and Housework: Assessing the Contributions of All Household Members, with a Focus on Children and Youths', *Review of Economics of the Household*, 12: 7–27.

Gerson, K., and Horowitz, R. (2002). 'Observation and Interviewing: Options and Choices', in T. May (ed.), *Qualitative Research in Action*. London: Sage.

Gibson, L. (2010). 'Realities Toolkit #09: Using Email Interviews', http://eprints.ncrm.ac.uk/1303/1/09-toolkit-email-interviews.pdf (accessed 1 March 2021).

Gibson, N. (2004). 'Action Research', in M. S. Lewis-Beck, A. Bryman, and T. F. Liao (eds), *The Sage Encyclopedia of Social Science Research Methods*. Thousand Oaks, CA: Sage.

Gicevic, S., Aftosmes-Tobio, A., Manganello, J., Ganter, C., Simon, C., Newlan, S., and Davison, K. (2016). 'Parenting and Childhood Obesity Research: A Quantitative Content Analysis of Published Research 2009–2015', *Pediatric Obesity*, 17(8): 724–34.

Gilbert, G. N., and Mulkay, M. (1984). *Opening Pandora's Box: A Sociological Analysis of Scientists' Discourse*. Cambridge: Cambridge University Press.

Gill, R. (1996). 'Discourse Analysis: Practical Implementation', in J. T. E. Richardson (ed.), *Handbook of Qualitative Research Methods for Psychology and the Social Sciences*. Leicester, UK: BPS Books.

Gill, R. (2000). 'Discourse Analysis', in M. W. Bauer and G. Gaskell (eds), *Qualitative Researching with Text, Image and Sound*. London: Sage.

Gioia, D. A., Corley, K. G., and Hamilton, A. L. (2012). 'Seeking Qualitative Rigor in Inductive Research: Notes on the Gioia Methodology', *Organizational Research Methods*, 16: 15–31.

Giordano, C., Piras, S., Boschini, M., and Falasconi, L. (2018). 'Are Questionnaires a Reliable Method to Measure Food Waste? A Pilot Study on Italian Households', *British Food Journal*, 120(12): 2885–97.

Giulianotti, R. (1995). 'Participant Observation and Research into Football Hooliganism: Reflections on the Problems of Entrée and Everyday Risks', *Sociology of Sport Journal*, 12: 1–20.

Glaser, B. G. (1992). *Basics of Grounded Theory Analysis*. Mill Valley, CA: Sociology Press.

Glaser, B. G., and Strauss, A. L. (1967). *The Discovery of Grounded Theory: Strategies for Qualitative Research*. Chicago: Aldine.

Glucksmann, M. (1994). 'The Work of Knowledge and the Knowledge of Women's Work', in M. Maynard and J. Purvis (eds), *Researching Women's Lives from a Feminist Perspective*. London: Taylor & Francis.

Gnambs, T., and Kaspar, K. (2015). 'Disclosure of Sensitive Behaviors Across Self-Administered Survey Modes: A Meta-analysis', *Behavior Research Methods*, 47(4): 1237–59.

Goffman, A. (2009). 'On the Run: Wanted Men in a Philadelphia Ghetto', *American Sociological Review*, 74: 339–57.

Goffman, A. (2014). *On the Run: Fugitive Life in an American City*. Chicago: University of Chicago Press.

Goffman, E. (1956). *The Presentation of Self in Everyday Life*. New York: Doubleday.

Goffman, E. (1979). *Gender Advertisements*. New York: Harper and Row.

Gold, R. L. (1958). 'Roles in Sociological Fieldwork', *Social Forces*, 36: 217–23.

Goldthorpe, J. H., Lockwood, D., Bechhofer, F., and Platt, J. (1968). *The Affluent Worker: Industrial Attitudes and Behaviour*. Cambridge: Cambridge University Press.

Goode, E. (1996). 'The Ethics of Deception in Social Research: A Case Study', *Qualitative Sociology*, 19: 11–33.

Goodings, L., Brown, S. D., and Parker, M. (2013). 'Organising Images of Futures-Past: Remembering the Apollo Moon Landings', *International Journal of Management Concepts and Philosophy*, 7: 263–83.

Gottdiener, M. (1982). 'Disneyland: A Utopian Urban Space', *Urban Life*, 11: 139–62.

Gottdiener, M. (1997). *The Theming of America: Dreams, Visions and Commercial Spaces*. Boulder, CO: Westview Press.

Goulding, C. (2009). 'Grounded Theory Perspectives in Organizational Research', in D. A. Buchanan and A. Bryman (eds), *The SAGE Handbook of Organizational Research Methods*. London: SAGE.

Gouldner, A. (1968). 'The Sociologist as Partisan', *American Sociologist*, 3: 103–16.

Grant, D., Hardy, C., Oswick, C., and Putnam, L. L. (2004). 'Introduction: Organizational Discourse: Exploring the Field', in D. Grant, C. Hardy, C. Oswick, and L. Putnam (eds), *The SAGE Handbook of Organizational Discourse*. London: Sage.

Grassian, D. T. (2020). 'The Dietary Behaviors of Participants in UK-Based Meat Reduction and Vegan Campaigns—A Longitudinal, Mixed-Methods Study', *Appetite*, 154, doi: 10.1016/j.appet.2020.104788.

Grazian, D. (2003). *Blue Chicago: The Search for Authenticity in Urban Blues Clubs*. Chicago: University of Chicago Press.

Greaves, F., Laverty, A. A., Cano, D. R., Moilanen, K., Pulman, S., Darzi, A., and Millett, C. (2014). 'Tweets about Hospital Quality: A Mixed Methods Study', *BMJ Quality and Safety*, doi: 10.1136/bmjqs-2014–002875.

Green, J., Steinbach, R., and Datta, J. (2012). 'The Travelling Citizen: Emergent Discourses of Moral Mobility in a Study of Cycling in London', *Sociology*, 46: 272–89.

Greene, J. C. (1994). 'Qualitative Program Evaluation: Practice and Promise', in N. K. Denzin and Y. S. Lincoln (eds), *Handbook of Qualitative Research*. Thousand Oaks, CA: Sage.

Greene, J. C. (2000). 'Understanding Social Programs through Evaluation', in N. K. Denzin and Y. S. Lincoln (eds), *Handbook of Qualitative Research*, 2nd edn. Thousand Oaks, CA: Sage.

Greenland, S., Senn, S., Rothman, K., Carlin, J., Poole, C., Goodman, S., and Altman, D. (2016). 'Statistical Tests, *P* Values, Confidence Intervals, and Power: A Guide to Misinterpretations', *European Journal of Epidemiology*, 31(4): 337–50.

Grele, R. J. (1998). 'Movement Without Aim: Methodological and Theoretical Problems in Oral History', in R. Perks and A. Thomson (eds), *The History Reader*. London: Routledge.

Grogan, S., Gill, S., Brownbridge, K., Kilgariff, S., and Whalley, A. (2013). 'Dress Fit and Body Image: A Thematic Analysis of Women's Accounts During and After Trying on Clothes', *Body Image*, 10: 380–8.

Groves, R. M., Fowler, F. J., Couper, M. P., Lepkowski, J. M., Singer, E., and Tourangeau, R. (2009). *Survey Methodology*, 2nd edn. Hoboken, NJ: Wiley.

Guba, E. G. (1985). 'The Context of Emergent Paradigm Research', in Y. S. Lincoln (ed.), *Organization Theory and Inquiry: The Paradigm Revolution*. Beverly Hills, CA: Sage.

Guba, E. G., and Lincoln, Y. S. (1994). 'Competing Paradigms in Qualitative Research', in N. K. Denzin and Y. S. Lincoln (eds), *Handbook of Qualitative Research*. Thousand Oaks, CA: Sage.

Guégen, N., and Jacob, C. (2012). 'Lipstick and Tipping Behavior: When Red Lipstick Enhance Waitresses Tips', *International Journal of Hospitality Management*, 31: 1333–5.

Guest, G., Bunce, A., and Johnson, L. (2006). 'How Many Interviews are Enough? An Experiment with Data Saturation and Variability', *Field Methods*, 18: 59–82.

Guest, G., Namey, E., and McKenna, K. (2017a). 'How Many Focus Groups are Enough? Building an Evidence Base for Nonprobability Sample Sizes', *Field Methods*, 29(1): 3–22.

Guest, G., Namey, E., Taylor, J., Eley, N., and McKenna, K. (2017b). 'Comparing Focus Groups and Individual Interviews: Findings from a Randomized Study', *International Journal of Social Research Methodology*, 20(6): 693–708.

Gullifer, J. M., and Tyson, G. A. (2014). 'Who Has Read the Policy on Plagiarism? Unpacking Students' Understanding of Plagiarism', *Studies in Higher Education*, 39: 1202–18.

Gunderman, R., and Kane, L. (2013). 'A Study in Deception: Psychology's Sickness', *The Atlantic*, 8 April, www.theatlantic.com/health/archive/2013/04/a-study-in-deception-psychologys-sickness/274739/.

Gunn, E., and Naper, A. (2016). 'Social Media Incumbent Advantage: Barack Obama and Mitt Romney's Tweets in the 2012 US Presidential Election Campaign', in A. Bruns, G. Enli, E. Skogerbo, and A. Larsson (eds), *The Routledge Companion to Social Media and Politics*. London: Routledge, 364–78.

Guschwan, M. (2017). 'Ethnography and the Italian Ultrà', *Sport in Society*, 21(6): 977–92, 10.1080/17430437.2017.1300400.

Gusterson, H. (1996). *Nuclear Rites: A Weapons Laboratory at the End of the Cold War*. Berkeley: University of California Press.

Gwet, K. (2014). *Handbook of Inter-rater Reliability: The Definitive Guide to Measuring the Extent of Agreement Among Raters*. Gaithersburg, MD: Advanced Analytics.

Halder, A., Molyneaux, J., Luby, S., and Ram, P. (2013). 'Impact of Duration of Structured Observations on Measurement of Handwashing Behaviour at Critical Times', *BMC Public Health*, 13: 705.

Halford, S. (2018). 'The Ethical Disruptions of Social Media Data: Tales from the Field', in K. Woodfield (ed), *The Ethics of Online Research*. Bingley, UK: Emerald, 13–26.

Halfpenny, P. (1979). 'The Analysis of Qualitative Data', *Sociological Review*, 27: 799–825.

Halkier, B. (2011). 'Methodological Practicalities in Analytical Generalization', *Qualitative Inquiry*, 17(9): 787–97.

Hall, W. S., and Guthrie, L. F. (1981). 'Cultural and Situational Variation in Language Function and Use—Methods and Procedures for Research', in J. L. Green and C. Wallatt (eds), *Ethnography and Language in Educational Settings*. Norwood, NJ: Ablex.

Hallett, R. E., and Barber, K. (2014). 'Ethnographic Research in a Cyber Era', *Journal of Contemporary Ethnography*, 43: 306–30.

Hammersley, M. (1989). *The Dilemma of Qualitative Method: Herbert Blumer and the Chicago Tradition*. London: Routledge.

Hammersley, M. (1992a). 'By What Criteria should Ethnographic Research be Judged?', in M. Hammersley, *What's Wrong with Ethnography?* London: Routledge.

Hammersley, M. (1992b). 'Deconstructing the Qualitative-Quantitative Divide', in M. Hammersley, *What's Wrong with Ethnography?* London: Routledge.

Hammersley, M. (2011). *Methodology: Who Needs It?* London: Sage.

Hammersley, M. (2018). 'What is Ethnography? Can It Survive? Should It?', *Ethnography and Education*, 13(1): 1–17.

Hammersley, M., and Atkinson, P. (1995). *Ethnography: Principles in Practice*, 2nd edn. London: Routledge.

Hammersley, M., and Atkinson, P. (2019). *Ethnography: Principles in Practice*, 4th edn. London: Routledge.

Hammersley, M., and Gomm, R. (2000). 'Bias in Social Research', in M. Hammersley (ed.), *Taking Sides in Social Research: Essays in Partisanship and Bias*. London: Routledge.

Hammond, P. (1964). *Sociologists at Work*. New York: Basic Books.

Hand, M. (2017). 'Visuality in Social Media: Researching Images, Circulations and Practices', in L. Sloan and A. Quan-Haase (eds), *The SAGE Handbook of Social Media Research Methods*. London: Sage, 215–31.

Hantrais, L. (1996). 'Comparative Research Methods', *Social Research Update*, 13, http://sru.soc.surrey.ac.uk/SRU13.html (accessed 1 March 2021).

Haraway, D. (2003). 'Situated Knowledges: The Science Question in Feminism and the Privilege of Partial Perspective', in Y. S. Lincoln and N. K. Denzin (eds), *Turning Points in Qualitative Research: Tying Knots in a Handkerchief*. Lanham, MD: AltaMira, 21–46.

Hardie-Bick, J. (2011). 'Skydiving and the Metaphorical Edge', in D. Hobbs (ed.), *Ethnography in Context*, vol. 3. London: Sage.

Hardie-Bick, J., and Bonner, P. (2016). 'Experiencing Flow, Enjoyment and Risk in Skydiving and Climbing', *Ethnography*, 17(3): 369–87.

Hardie-Bick, J., and Scott, S. (2017). 'Tales from the Drop Zone: Roles, Risks and Dramaturgical Dilemmas', *Qualitative Research*, 17(2): 246–59.

Harding, S. G. (1986). *The Science Question in Feminism*. Ithaca, NY: Cornell University Press.

Hardy, M., and Bryman, A. (2004). 'Introduction: Common Threads among Techniques of Data Analysis', in M. Hardy and A. Bryman (eds), *Handbook of Data Analysis*. London: Sage.

Hargittai, E., and Karaoglu, G. (2018). 'Biases of Online Political Polls: Who Participates?', *Socius: Sociological Research for a Dynamic World*, 4(2): 1–7.

Harper, D. (2002). 'Talking about Pictures: A Case for Photo Elicitation', *Visual Studies*, 17: 13–26.

Harrison, N., and McCaig, C. (2015). 'An Ecological Fallacy in Higher Education Policy: The Use, Overuse and Misuse of "Low Participation Neighbourhoods"', *Journal of Further and Higher Education*, 39(6): 793–817.

Hartsock, N. C. (1983). *Money, Sex, and Power: Toward a Feminist Historical Materialism* (p. 247). New York: Longman.

Hauken, M. A., Larsen, T. M. B., and Holsen, I. (2019). '"Back on Track": A Longitudinal Mixed Methods Study on the Rehabilitation of Young Adult Cancer Survivors', *Journal of Mixed Methods Research*, 13(3), 339–60, https://doi.org/10.1177/1558689817698553.

Hauser, O., Linos, E., and Rogers, T. (2017). 'Innovation with Field Experiments: Studying Organizational Behaviors in Actual Organizations', *Research in Organizational Behavior*, 37: 185–98.

Healy, K., and Moody, J. (2014). 'Data Visualisation in Sociology', *Annual Review of Sociology*, 40: 105–28.

Heap, J. L., and Roth, P. A. (1973). 'On Phenomenological Sociology', *American Sociological Review*, 38: 354–67.

Heath, S., Davies, K., Edwards, G., and Scicluna, R. (2017). *Shared Housing, Shared Lives: Everyday Experiences Across the Lifecourse*. Abingdon, UK: Routledge.

Heerwegh, D., and Loosveldt, G. (2008). 'Face-to-Face versus Web Surveying in a High Internet-Coverage Population: Differences in Response Quality', *Public Opinion Quarterly*, 72: 836–46.

Henwood, K., Shirani, F., and Finn, M. (2011). '"So you Think we've Moved, Changed, the Representation's got More What?" Methodological and Analytical Reflections on Visual (Photo-Elicitation) Methods Used in the Men-as-Fathers Study', in P. Reavey (ed.), *Visual Methods in Psychology: Using and Interpreting Images in Qualitative Research*. London: Psychology Press.

Herbell, K., and Zauszniewski, J. (2018). 'Facebook or Twitter? Effective Recruitment Strategies for Family Caregivers', *Applied Nursing Research*, 41(6): 1–4.

Heritage, J. (1984). *Garfinkel and Ethnomethodology*. Cambridge: Polity.

Heritage, J. (1987). 'Ethnomethodology', in A. Giddens and J. H. Turner (eds), *Social Theory Today*. Cambridge: Polity.

Hesse-Biber, S. N. (ed.) (2013). *Feminist Research Practice: A Primer*. London: Sage.

Hester, S. (2016). 'Answering Questions Instead of Telling Stories: Everyday Breaching in a Family Meal', *Journal of Pragmatics*, 102, 54–66.

Hewson, C., and Laurent, D. (2008). 'Research Design and Tools for Internet Research', in N. Fielding, R. M. Lee, and G. Blank (eds), *The SAGE Handbook of Online Research Methods*. London: Sage.

Heyvaert, M., Hannes, K., and Onghena, P. (2016). *Using Mixed Methods Research Synthesis for Literature Reviews: The Mixed Methods Research Synthesis Approach*, vol. 4. London: Sage.

Hill, K., and Davis, A. (2018). *Making Ends Meet Below the Minimum Income Standard: Families' Experiences Over Time*. Centre for Research in Social Policy Working Paper 662, www.lboro.ac.uk/media/wwwlboroacuk/content/crsp/downloads/reports/Making%20Ends%20Meet%20Below%20the%20MIS%20families%20experiences%20over%20time.pdf.

Hill, K., Davis, A., Hirsch, D., and Marshall, L. (2016). *Falling Short: The Experiences of Families Below the Minimum Income Standard*. Joseph Rowntree Foundation, www.jrf.org.uk/report/falling-short-experiences-families-below-minimum-income-standard.

Hine, C. (2000). *Virtual Ethnography*. London: Sage.

Hine, C. (2008). 'Virtual Ethnography: Models, Varieties, Affordances', in N. Fielding, R. M. Lee, and G. Blank (eds), *The SAGE Handbook of Online Research Methods*. London: Sage.

Hine, C. (2014). 'Headlice Eradication as Everyday Engagement with Science: An Analysis of Online Parenting Discussions', *Public Understanding of Science*, 23: 574–91.

Hirsch, J. (1981). *Family Photographs*. New York: Oxford University Press.

Hobbs, D. (1988). *Doing the Business: Entrepreneurship, the Working Class and Detectives in the East End of London*. Oxford: Oxford University Press.

Hochschild, A. R. (1983). *The Managed Heart*. Berkeley and Los Angeles: University of California Press.

Hodges, L. (1998). 'The Making of a National Portrait', *The Times Higher Education Supplement*, 20 February: 22–3.

Hoefnagels, M. (2017). *Research Design: The Logic of Social Inquiry*. London: Routledge.

Hofmans, J., Gelens, J., and Theuns, P. (2014). 'Enjoyment as a Mediator in the Relationship Between Task Characteristics and Work Effort: An Experience Sampling Study', *European Journal of Work and Organizational Psychology*, 23: 693–705.

Holbrook, A. L., Green, M. C., and Krosnick, J. A. (2003). 'Telephone versus Face-to-Face Interviewing of National Probability Samples with Long Questionnaires: Comparisons of Respondent Satisficing and Social Desirability Response Bias', *Public Opinion Quarterly*, 67: 79–125.

Holdaway, S. (1982). '"An Inside Job": A Case Study of Covert Research on the Police', in M. Bulmer (ed.), *Social Research Ethics*. London: Macmillan.

Holdaway, S. (1983). *Inside the British Police: A Force at Work*. Oxford: Blackwell.

Holsti, O. R. (1969). *Content Analysis for the Social Sciences and Humanities*. Reading, MA: Addison-Wesley.

Homan, R. (1991). *The Ethics of Social Research*. London: Longman.

Homan, R., and Bulmer, M. (1982). 'On the Merits of Covert Methods: A Dialogue', in M. Bulmer (ed.), *Social Research Ethics*. London: Macmillan.

Hood, J. C. (2007). 'Orthodoxy vs. Power: The Defining Traits of Grounded Theory', in A. Bryant and K. Charmaz (eds), *The SAGE Handbook of Grounded Theory*. Los Angeles: Sage.

Hordosy, R., and Clark, T. (2019), 'Student Budgets and Widening Participation: Comparative Experiences of Finance in Low and Higher Income Undergraduates at a Northern Red Brick University', *Social Policy and Administration*, 53(5): 761–75.

Hu, J. (2020). 'Horizontal or Vertical? The Effects of Visual Orientation of Categorical Response Options on Survey Responses in Web Surveys', *Social Science Computer Review*, 38(6): 779–92.

Huberman, A. M., and Miles, M. B. (1994). 'Data Management and Analysis Methods', in N. K. Denzin and Y. S. Lincoln (eds), *Handbook of Qualitative Research*. Thousand Oaks, CA: Sage.

Hughes, C., and Cohen, R. L. (eds). (2013). *Feminism Counts: Quantitative Methods and Researching Gender*. Abingdon, UK: Routledge.

Hughes, G. (2000). 'Understanding the Politics of Criminological Research', in V. Jupp, P. Davies, and P. Francis (eds), *Doing Criminological Research*. London: Sage.

Hughes, J. A. (1990). *The Philosophy of Social Research*, 2nd edn. Harlow, UK: Longman.

Humphreys, L. (1970). *Tearoom Trade: Impersonal Sex in Public Places*. Chicago: Aldine.

Humphreys, L., Gill, P., and Krishnamurthy, B. (2014). 'Twitter: A Content Analysis of Personal Information', *Information, Communication and Society*, 17: 843–57.

Humphreys, M., and Watson, T. (2009). 'Ethnographic Practices: From "Writing-up Ethnographic Research" to "Writing Ethnography"', in S. Ybema, D. Yanow, H. Wels, and F. Kamsteeg (eds), *Organizational Ethnography: Studying the Complexities of Everyday Life*. London: Sage.

Hutchby, I., and Wooffitt, R. (1998). *Conversation Analysis*. Cambridge: Polity.

Iacono, V. L., Symonds, P., and Brown, D. H. (2016). 'Skype as a Tool for Qualitative Research Interviews', *Sociological Research Online*, 21(2): 1–12.

Ibrahim, Q. (2018). 'Social Work Education in Arab Universities and Educators' Perceptions', *Social Work Education*, 37(1): 78–91.

Irvine, A. (2011). 'Duration, Dominance and Depth in Telephone and Face-to-Face Interviews: A Comparative Exploration', *International Journal of Qualitative Methods*, 10(3): 202–20.

Irvine, A., Drew, P., and Sainsbury, R. (2013). '"Am I Not Answering Your Questions Properly?" Clarification, Adequacy and Responsiveness in Semi-Structured Telephone and Face-to-Face Interviews', *Qualitative Research*, 13: 87–106.

Israel, M., and Hay, I. (2004). *Research Ethics for Social Scientists*. London: Sage.

Jack, I. (2010). 'Five Boys: The Story of a Picture', *Intelligent Life* (spring) [not available at time of this writing].

Jackson, K., Paulus, T., and Woolf, N. H. (2018). 'The Walking Dead Genealogy: Unsubstantiated Criticisms of Qualitative Data Analysis Software (QDAS) and the Failure to Put Them to Rest', *Qualitative Report*, 23(13): 74–91.

Jackson, W. (2020). 'Researching the Policed: Critical Ethnography and the Study of Protest Policing', *Policing and Society*, 30(2): 169–85, doi: 10.1080/10439463.2019.1593982.

Jæger, M. (2019). 'Hello Beautiful? The Effect of Interviewer Physical Attractiveness on Cooperation Rates and Survey Responses', *Sociological Methods and Research*, 48(1): 156–84.

James, N. (2016). 'Using Email Interviews in Qualitative Educational Research: Creating Space to Think and Time to Talk', *International Journal of Qualitative Studies in Education*, 29(2): 150–63.

Jamieson, J. (2000). 'Negotiating Danger in Fieldwork on Crime: A Researcher's Tale', in G. Lee-Treweek and S. Linkogle (eds), *Danger in the Field: Risk and Ethics in Social Research*. London: Routledge.

Jangi, M., Ferandez-de-Las-Penas, C., Tara, M., Moghbeli, F., Ghaderi, F., and Javanshir, K. (2018). 'A Systematic Review on Reminder Systems in Physical Therapy', *Caspian Journal of Internal Medicine*, 9(1): 7–15.

Janis, I. L. (1982). *Groupthink: Psychological Studies of Policy Decisions and Fiascos*, 2nd edn. Boston: Houghton-Mifflin.

Janmaat, J., and Keating, A. (2019). 'Are Today's Youth More Tolerant? Trends in Tolerance among Young People in Britain', *Ethnicities*, 19(1): 44–65.

Jefferson, G. (2004). 'Glossary of Transcript Symbols with an Introduction', in G. H. Lerner (ed.), *Conversation Analysis: Studies from the First Generation*. Amsterdam: John Benjamins, 13–31.

Jenkins, N., Bloor, M., Fischer, J., Berney, L., and Neale, J. (2010). 'Putting it in Context: the Use of Vignettes in Qualitative Interviewing', *Qualitative Research*, 10: 175–98.

Jensen, E., and Laurie, C. (2016). *Doing Real Research: A Practical Guide to Social Research*. London: Sage.

Jerolmack, C., and Khan, S. (2014). 'Talk is Cheap: Ethnography and the Attitudinal Fallacy', *Sociological Methods and Research*, 43: 178–209.

Jessee, S. (2017). '"Don't Know" Responses, Personality, and the Measurement of Political Knowledge', *Political Science Research and Methods*, 5(4): 711–31.

John, I. D. (1992). 'Statistics as Rhetoric in Psychology', *Australian Psychologist*, 27: 144–9.

John, P., and Jennings, W. (2010). 'Punctuations and Turning Points in British Politics: The Policy Agenda of the Queen's Speech, 1940–2005', *British Journal of Political Science*, 40: 561–86.

Johnston, M. (2017). 'Secondary Data Analysis: A Method of which the Time Has Come', *Qualitative and Quantitative Methods in Libraries*, 3(3): 619–26.

Jones, I. R., Leontowitsch, M., and Higgs, P. (2010). 'The Experience of Retirement in Secondary Modernity: Generational Habitus among Retired Senior Managers', *Sociology*, 44: 103–20.

Judge, M., and Wilson, A. (2018). 'Dual-Process Motivational Model of Attitudes toward Vegetarians and Vegans', *European Journal of Social Psychology*, 49(1): 169–78.

Kahan, D., McKenzie, T., and Khatri, A. (2019). 'U.S. Charter Schools Neglect Promoting Physical Activity: Content Analysis of Nationally Representative Elementary Charter School Websites', *Preventative Medicine Reports*, 14.

Kalton, G. (2019). 'Developments in Survey Research over the Past 60 Years: A Personal Perspective', *International Statistical Review*, 87(S1): S10–30.

Kamin, L. J. (1974). *The Science and Politics of IQ*. New York: Wiley.

Kaminska, O., and Foulsham, T. (2013). *Understanding Sources of Social Desirability Bias in Different Modes: Evidence from Eye-Tracking* (Report No. 2013–04). Colchester, UK: Institute for Social and Economic Research, University of Essex.

Kamp, K., Herbell, K., Magginis, W., Berry, D., and Given, B. (2019). 'Facebook Recruitment and the Protection of Human Subjects', *Western Journal of Nursing Research*, 41(9): 1270–81.

Kandola, B. (2012). 'Focus Groups', in G. Symon and C. Cassell (eds), *Qualitative Organizational Research: Core Methods and Current Challenges*. Los Angeles: Sage.

Kang, M. (1997). 'The Portrayal of Women's Images in Magazine Advertisements: Goffman's Gender Analysis Revisited', *Sex Roles*, 37(11–12): 979–96.

Kapidzic, S., and Herring, S. C. (2015) 'Race, Gender, and Self-Presentation in Teen Profile Photographs', *New Media and Society*, 17: 958–76.

Kaplan, D. (2004). *SAGE Handbook of Quantitative Methodology for the Social Sciences*. London: Sage.

Kapsis, R. E. (1989). 'Reputation Building and the Film Art World: The Case of Alfred Hitchcock', *Sociological Quarterly*, 30: 15–35.

Kara, H. (2015). *Creative Research Methods in the Social Sciences: A Practical Guide*. Bristol, UK: Policy Press.

Katz, J. (1982). *Poor People's Lawyers in Transition*. New Brunswick, NJ: Rutgers University Press.

Kavanagh, J., Campbell, F., Harden, A., and Thomas, J. (2012). 'Mixed Methods Synthesis: A Worked Example', in K. Hannes and C. Lockwood (eds), *Synthesizing Qualitative Research: Choosing the Right Approach*. Chichester, UK: Wiley.

Kellogg, K. C. (2009). 'Operating Room: Relational Spaces and Microinstitutional Change in Surgery', *American Journal of Sociology*, 115: 657–711.

Kellogg, K. C. (2011). *Challenging Operations: Medical Reform and Resistance in Surgery*. Chicago: University of Chicago Press.

Kendrick, K. H., and Holler, J. (2017). 'Gaze Direction Signals Response Preference in Conversation', *Research on Language and Social Interaction*, 50(1): 12–32.

Kentikelenis, A., Stubbs, T., and King, L. (2016). 'IMF Conditionality and Development Policy Space, 1985–2014', *Review of International Political Economy*, 23(4): 543–82.

Khan, S. (2011). *Privilege: The Making of an Adolescent Elite at St. Paul's School*. Princeton, NJ: Princeton Univesity Press.

Khan, S. (2014). 'The Science of Everyday Life', in S. Khan and D. R. Fisher (eds), *The Practice of Research: How Social Scientists Answer Their Questions*. New York: Oxford University Press.

Kibuchi, E., Sturgis, P., Durrant, G., and Maslovskaya, O. (2018). *Do Interviewers Moderate the Effect of Monetary Incentives on Response Rates in Household Interview Surveys?* NCRM Working Paper. Southampton, UK: National Centre for Research Methods.

Kidd, P. S., and Parshall, M. B. (2000). 'Getting the Focus and the Group: Enhancing Analytical Rigor in Focus Group Research', *Qualitative Health Research*, 10(3): 293–308.

Kimmel, A. J. (1988). *Ethics and Values in Applied Social Research*. Newbury Park, CA: Sage.

Kirk, J., and Miller, M. L. (1986). *Reliability and Validity in Qualitative Research*. Newbury Park, CA: Sage.

Kitchin, R. (2014). 'Big Data, New Epistemologies and Paradigm Shifts', *Big Data and Society*, 1(1).

Kitchin, R., and McArdle, G. (2016). 'What makes Big Data, Big Data? Exploring the Ontological Characteristics of 26 Datasets', *Big Data and Society*, 3(1).

Kitzinger, J. (1994). 'The Methodology of Focus Groups: The Importance of Interaction between Research Participants', *Sociology of Health and Illness*, 16: 103–21.

Kivits, J. (2005). 'Online Interviewing and the Research Relationship', in C. Hine (ed.), *Virtual Methods: Issues in Social Research on the Internet*. Oxford: Berg.

Knepper, P. (2018). 'Laughing at Lombroso: Positivism and Criminal Anthropology in Historical Perspective', *Handbook of the History and Philosophy of Criminology*, 51.

Kozinets, R. V. (2002). 'The Field behind the Screen: Using Netnography for Marketing Research in Online Communities', *Journal of Marketing Research*, 39: 61–72.

Kozinets, R. V. (2010). *Netnography: Doing Ethnographic Research Online*. London: Sage.

Kramer, A. D. I., Guillory, J. E., and Hancock, J. T. (2014). 'Experimental Evidence of Massive-scale Emotional Contagion through Social Networks', *Proceedings of the National Academy of Sciences of the United States of America*, 111: 8788–90, 10.1073/pnas.1320040111.

Krause, M., and Kowalski, A. (2013). 'Reflexive Habits: Dating and Rationalized Conduct in New York and Berlin', *Sociological Review*, 61: 21–40.

Kress, G., and Van Leeuwen, T. (2001). *Multimodal Discourse: The Modes and Media of Contemporary Communication*. London: Arnold.

Krippendorff, K. (2018). *Content Analysis: An Introduction to Its Methodology*. London: Sage.

Krosnick, J. (2018). 'Improving Question Design to Maximize Reliability and Validity', in D. Vannette and J. Krosnick (eds), *The Palgrave Handbook of Survey Research*. Basingstoke, UK: Palgrave, 95–101.

Krosnick, J. A. (1999). 'Survey Research', *Annual Review of Psychology*, 50: 537–67.

Krosnick, J. A., Holbrook, A. L., Berent, M. K., Carson, R. T., Hanemann, W. M., Kopp, R. J., Mitchell, R. C., Presser, S., Ruud, P. A., Smith, V. K., Moody, W. R., Green, M. C., and Conaway, M. (2002). 'The Impact of "No Opinion" Response Options on Data Quality: Non-Attitude Reduction or an Invitation to Satisfice?', *Public Opinion Quarterly*, 66: 371–403.

Kross, E., Verduyn, P., Demiralp, E., Park, J., Lee, D. S., Lin, N., Shablack, H., Jonides, J., and Ybarra, O. (2013). 'Facebook Use Predicts Declines in Subjective Well-Being in Young Adults', *PLOS One*, 8, www.plosone.org/article/info%3Adoi%2F10.1371%2Fjournal.pone.0069841 (accessed 1 March 2021).

Krueger, R. A. (1998). *Moderating Focus Groups*. Thousand Oaks, CA: Sage.

Krumpal, I. (2013). 'Determinants of Social Desirability Bias in Sensitive Surveys: A Literature Review', *Quality and Quantity*, 47(4): 2025–47.

Kuhn, T. S. (1970). *The Structure of Scientific Revolutions*, 2nd edn. Chicago: University of Chicago Press.

Kvale, S. (1996). *InterViews: An Introduction to Qualitative Research Interviewing*. Thousand Oaks, CA: Sage.

Lafleur, J. M., and Mescoli, E. (2018). 'Creating Undocumented EU Migrants through Welfare: A Conceptualization of Undeserving and Precarious Citizenship', *Sociology*, 52(3): 480–96.

Lamont, M., and Swidler, A. (2014). 'Methodological Pluralism and the Possibilities and Limits of Interviewing', *Qualitative Sociology*, 37(2): 153–71.

La Pelle, N. (2004). 'Simplifying Qualitative Data Analysis using General Purpose Software Tools', *Field Methods*, 16(1): 85–108.

LaPiere, R. T. (1934). 'Attitudes vs. Actions', *Social Forces*, 13: 230–7.

Laub, J. H., and Sampson, R. J. (2004). 'Strategies for Bridging the Quantitative and Qualitative Divide: Studying Crime over the Life Course', *Research in Human Development*, 1: 81–99.

Laub, J. H., and Sampson, R. J. (2019). 'Life-course and Developmental Criminology: Looking Back, Moving Forward—ASC Division of Developmental and Life-Course Criminology Inaugural David P. Farrington Lecture, 2017', *Journal of Developmental and Life-Course Criminology*, 6: 158–71.

Laurie, H., and Gershuny, J. (2000). 'Couples, Work and Money', in R. Berthoud and J. Gershuny (eds), *Seven Years in the Lives of British Families: Evidence on the Dynamics of Social Change from the British Household Panel Survey*. Bristol, UK: Policy Press.

Lavrakas, P. (ed.) (2008). *Encyclopedia of Survey Research Methods*. London: Sage.

Layder, D. (1993). *New Strategies in Social Research*. Cambridge: Polity.

Lazarsfeld, P. (1958). 'Evidence and Inference in Social Research', *Daedalus*, 87: 99–130.

Le Blanc, A. M. (2017). 'Disruptive Meaning-Making: Qualitative Data Analysis Software and Postmodern Pastiche', *Qualitative Inquiry*, 23(10): 789–98.

LeCompte, M. D., and Goetz, J. P. (1982). 'Problems of Reliability and Validity in Ethnographic Research', *Review of Educational Research*, 52: 31–60.

Ledford, C. J., and Anderson, L. N. (2013). 'Online Social Networking in Discussions of Risk: The CAUSE Model in a Content Analysis of Facebook', *Health, Risk and Society*, 15: 251–64.

Lee, R. M. (2000). *Unobtrusive Methods in Social Research*. Buckingham, UK: Open University Press.

Lee, R. M., and Fielding, N. G. (1991). 'Computing for Qualitative Research: Options, Problems and Potential', in N. G. Fielding and R. M. Lee (eds), *Using Computers in Qualitative Research*. London: Sage.

Lenzner, T. (2012). 'Effects of Survey Question Comprehensibility on Response Quality', *Field Methods*, 24: 409–28.

Letherby, G., Scott, J., and Williams, M. (2012). *Objectivity and Subjectivity in Social Research*. London: Sage.

Lewis, O. (1961). *The Children of Sánchez*. New York: Vintage.

Li, J., Ohlbrecht, H., Pollmann-Schult, M., and Habib, F. E. (2020). 'Parents' Nonstandard Work Schedules and Children's Social and Emotional Wellbeing: A Mixed-Methods Analysis in Germany'. *Zeitschrift für Familienforschung/ Journal of Family Research*, 32(2).

Lieberman, J. D., Koetzle, D., and Sakiyama, M. (2013). 'Police Departments' Use of Facebook: Patterns and Policy Issues', *Policy Quarterly*, 16: 438–62.

Liebling, A. (2001). 'Whose Side Are We On? Theory, Practice and Allegiances in Prisons Research', *British Journal of Criminology*, 41: 472–84.

Liebow, E. (1967). *Tally's Corner*. Boston: Little, Brown.

Lijadi, A. A., and van Schalkwyk, G. J. (2015). 'Online Facebook Focus Group Research of Hard-to-Reach Participants', *International Journal of Qualitative Methods*, 14(5): 1609406915621383.

Likert, R. (1932). 'A Technique for the Measurement of Attitudes', *Archives of Psychology*, 140: 1–55.

Lincoln, Y. S., and Denzin, N. K. (2005). 'Epilogue: The Eighth and Ninth Moments—Qualitative Research in/and the Fractured Future', in N. K. Denzin and Y. S. Lincoln (eds), *Handbook of Qualitative Research*, 3rd edn. Thousand Oaks, CA: Sage.

Lincoln, Y. S., and Guba, E. (1985). *Naturalistic Inquiry*. Beverly Hills, CA: Sage.

Lindesmith, A. R. (1947). *Opiate Addiction*. Bloomington, IN: Principia Press.

Linvill, D. L., and Warren, P. L. (2020). 'Troll Factories: Manufacturing Specialized Disinformation on Twitter', *Political Communication*, 37(4): 1–21.

Livingstone, S. (2019). 'Audiences in an Age of Datafication: Critical Questions for Media Research', *Television & New Media*, 20(2): 170–83.

Livingstone, S., Kirwil, L., Ponte, C., and Staksrud, E. (2014). 'In Their Own Words: What Bothers Children Online', *European Journal of Communication*, 29: 271–88.

Lloyd, A. (2012). 'Working to Live, Not Living to Work: Work, Leisure and Youth Identity among Call Centre Workers in North East England', *Current Sociology*, 60: 619–35.

Locke, K. (1996). 'Rewriting *The Discovery of Grounded Theory* after 25 Years?', *Journal of Management Inquiry*, 5: 239–45.

Lofland, J., and Lofland, L. (1995). *Analyzing Social Settings: A Guide to Qualitative Observation and Analysis*, 3rd edn. Belmont, CA: Wadsworth.

Longhi, S. (2020). 'A Longitudinal Analysis of Ethnic Unemployment Differentials in the UK', *Journal of Ethnic and Migration Studies*, 46(5): 879–92, 10.1080/1369183X.2018.1539254.

Longhurst, R. (2009). 'Embodied Knowing', in R. Kitchin and N. Thrift (eds), *International Encyclopedia of Human Geography*. Oxford: Elsevier, 429–33.

Lumsden, K., and Black, A. (2018). 'Austerity Policing, Emotional Labour and the Boundaries of Police Work: An Ethnography of a Police Force Control Room in England', *British Journal of Criminology*, 58(3): 606–23.

Lynch, M. (2000). 'Against Reflexivity as an Academic Virtue and Source of Privileged Knowledge', *Theory, Culture and Society*, 17: 26–54.

Lynd, R. S., and Lynd, H. M. (1929). *Middletown: A Study in Contemporary American Culture*. New York: Harcourt, Brace.

Lynd, R. S., and Lynd, H. M. (1937). *Middletown in Transition: A Study in Cultural Conflicts*. New York: Harcourt, Brace.

Lynn, M., Sturman, M., Ganley, C., Adams, E., Douglas, M., and McNeil, J. (2008). 'Consumer Racial Discrimination in Tipping: A Replication and Extension', *Journal of Applied Social Psychology*, 38(4): 1045–60.

Lynn, P., and Borkowska, M. (2018). 'Some Indicators of Sample Representativeness and Attrition Bias for BHPS and *Understanding Society*', Economic and Social Research Council *Understanding Society* Working Paper Series no. 2018–01, www.understandingsociety.ac.uk/research/publications/524851.

Lynn, P., and Kaminska, O. (2012). 'The Impact of Mobile Phones on Survey Measurement Error', *Public Opinion Quarterly*, 77: 586–605.

Macgilchrist, F., and Van Hout, T. (2011). 'Ethnographic Discourse Analysis and Social Science', *Forum: Qualitative Sozialforschung/Forum: Qualitative Social Research*, 12(1/January).

MacInnes, J. (2017). *An Introduction to Secondary Data Analysis with IBM SPSS Statistics*. London: Sage.

MacInnes, J., Breeze, M., de Haro, M., Kandlik, M., and Karels, M. (2016). *Measuring Up: International Case Studies on the Teaching of Quantitative Methods in the Social Sciences*. London: British Academy.

MacKay, J., Moore, J., and Huntingford, F. (2016). 'Characterizing the Data in Online Companion-Dog Obituaries to Assess their Usefulness as a Source of Information about Human–Animal Bonds', *Anthrozoös*, 29(3): 431–40.

Macnaghten, P., and Jacobs, M. (1997). 'Public Identification with Sustainable Development: Investigating Cultural Barriers to Participation', *Global Environmental Change*, 7: 5–24.

MacPherson, W. (1999). *The Stephen Lawrence Inquiry: Report of an Inquiry by Sir Willam MacPherson*. United Kingdom: Stationery Office.

Madriz, M. (2000). 'Focus Groups in Feminist Research', in N. K. Denzin and Y. S. Lincoln (eds), *Handbook of Qualitative Research*, 2nd edn. Thousand Oaks, CA: Sage.

Mahfoud, Z., Ghandour, L., Ghandour, B., Mokdad, A., and Sibai, A. (2015). 'Cell Phone and Face-to-Face Interview Responses in Population-based Surveys: How Do They Compare?', *Field Methods*, 27(1): 39–54.

Maitlis, S., and Lawrence, T. B. (2007). 'Triggers and Enablers of Sensegiving in Organizations', *Academy of Management Journal*, 50: 57–84.

Malinowski, B. (1967). *A Diary in the Strict Sense of the Term*. London: Routledge & Kegan Paul.

Malsch, B., and Salterio, S. E. (2016). '"Doing Good Field Research": Assessing the Quality of Audit Field Research', *Auditing: A Journal of Practice & Theory*, 35(1): 1–22.

Malterud, K., Siersma, V. D., and Guassora, A. D. (2015). 'Sample Size in Qualitative Interview Studies: Guided by Information Power', *Qualitative Health Research*, 26(13): 1753–60.

Manfreda, K. L., Bosnjak, M., Berzelak, J., Haas, I., and Vehovar, V. (2008). 'Web Surveys versus Other Survey Modes: A Meta-Analysis Comparing Response Rates', *International Journal of Market Research*, 50: 79–104.

Mann, C., and Stewart, F. (2000). *Internet Communication and Qualitative Research: A Handbook for Researching Online*. London: Sage.

Manokha, I. (2018). 'Surveillance: The DNA of Platform Capital—The Case of Cambridge Analytica Put into Perspective', *Theory and Event*, 24(4): 891–913.

Marcus, G., and Fisher, M. J. (1986). *Anthropology as Cultural Critique*. Chicago: University of Chicago Press.

Markham, A. (1998). *Life Online: Researching the Real Experience in Virtual Space*. London and Walnut Creek, CA: AltaMira Press.

Marsh, C. (1982). *The Survey Method: The Contribution of Surveys to Sociological Explanation*. London: Allen & Unwin.

Marsh, C., and Scarbrough, E. (1990). 'Testing Nine Hypotheses about Quota Sampling', *Journal of the Market Research Society*, 32: 485–506.

Marshall, C., and Rossman, G. (2016). *Designing Qualitative Research*. 6th edn. London: Sage.

Marshall, G., Newby, H., and Vogler, C. (1988). *Social Class in Modern Britain*. London: Unwin Hyman.

Martin, P., and Bateson, P. (2007). *Measuring Behaviour: An Introductory Guide*, 3rd edn. Cambridge: Cambridge University Press.

Mason, J. (1996). *Qualitative Researching*. London: Sage.

Mason, J. (2002). 'Qualitative Interviewing: Asking, Listening, Interpreting', in T. May (ed.), *Qualitative Research in Action*. London: Sage.

Mason, J. (2017). *Qualitative Interviewing*. London: Sage.

Mason, M. (2010). 'Sample Size and Saturation in PhD Studies Using Qualitative Interviews', *Forum: Qualitative Sozialforschung/Forum: Qualitative Social Research*, 11(3), article 8, www.qualitative-research.net/index.php/fqs/article/view/1428/3027 (accessed 1 March 2021).

Mason, W. (2018). '"Swagger": Urban Youth Culture, Consumption and Social Positioning', *Sociology*, 52(6): 1117–33.

Mason, W., Mirza, N., and Webb, C. (2018). *Using the Framework Method to Analyze Mixed-Methods Case Studies*. London: Sage.

Mason, W., Morris, K., Webb, C., Daniels, B., Featherstone, B., Bywaters, P., Mirza, N., Hooper, J., Brady, G., Bunting, L., and Scourfield, J. (2020). 'Toward Full Integration of Quantitative and Qualitative Methods in Case Study Research: Insights From Investigating Child Welfare Inequalities', *Journal of Mixed Methods Research*, 14(2): 164–83, https://doi.org/10.1177/1558689819857972.

Masterman, M. (1970). 'The Nature of a Paradigm', in I. Lakatos and A. Musgrave (eds), *Criticism and the Growth of Knowledge*. Cambridge: Cambridge University Press.

Matthews, K. L., Baird, M., and Duchesne, G. (2018). 'Using Online Meeting Software to Facilitate Geographically Dispersed Focus Groups for Health Workforce Research', *Qualitative Health Research*, 28(10): 1621–8.

Mattley, C. (2006). 'Aural Sex: The Politics and Moral Dilemmas of Studying the Social Construction of Fantasy', in D. Hobbs and R. Wright (eds), *The SAGE Handbook of Fieldwork*. London: Sage.

Mattsson, C., Hammarén, N., and Odenbring, Y. (2016). 'Youth "At Risk": A Critical Discourse Analysis of the European Commission's Radicalisation Awareness Network Collection of Approaches and Practices Used in Education', *Power and Education*, 8(3): 251–65.

Mawhinney, L., and Rinke, C. R. (2018). 'I Just Feel so Guilty: The Role of Emotions in Former Urban Teachers' Career Paths', *Urban Education*, 53(9): 1079–101.

Mayhew, P. (2000). 'Researching the State of Crime: Local, National, and International Victim Surveys', in R. D. King and E. Wincup (eds), *Doing Research on Crime and Justice*. Oxford: Oxford University Press.

Mays, N., Pope, C., and Popay, J. (2005). 'Systematically Reviewing Qualitative and Quantitative Evidence to Inform Management and Policy-Making in the Health Field', *Journal of Health Services Research and Policy*, 10 (Supplement 1): S6–20.

Mazmanian, M., Orlikowski, W. J., and Yates, J. (2013). 'The Autonomy Paradox: The Implications of Mobile Email Devices for Knowledge Professionals', *Organization Science*, 24: 1337–57.

McCabe, S. E. (2004). 'Comparison of Mail and Web Surveys in Collecting Illicit Drug Use Data: A Randomized Experiment', *Journal of Drug Education*, 34: 61–73.

McCall, L. (2005). 'The Complexity of Intersectionality', *Signs*, 30(3): 1771–800.

McCall, M. J. (1984). 'Structured Field Observation', *Annual Review of Sociology*, 10: 263–82.

McCrudden, M. T., and McTigue, E. M. (2019). 'Implementing Integration in an Explanatory Sequential Mixed Methods Study of Belief Bias About Climate Change With High School Students', *Journal of Mixed Methods Research*, 13(3): 381–400, https://doi.org/10.1177/1558689818762576.

McDonald, P., Townsend, K., and Waterhouse, J. (2009). 'Wrong Way, Go Back! Negotiating Access in Industry-Based Research', in K. Townsend and J. Burgess (eds), *Method in the Madness: Research Stories you Won't Read in Textbooks*. Oxford: Chandos.

McKeever, L. (2006). 'Online Plagiarism Detection Services: Saviour or Scourge?', *Assessment and Evaluation in Higher Education*, 31: 155–65.

McKernan, B. (2015). 'The Meaning of a Game: Stereotypes, Video Game Commentary and Color-Blind Racism', *American Journal of Cultural Sociology*, 3(2): 224–53.

McKernan, B. (2018). *Studying the Racial Stories We Tell Ourselves while Playing Games: The Value of Narrative Analysis in Cultural Sociology*. London: Sage.

Mead, M. (1928). *Coming of Age in Samoa*. New York: Morrow.

Mears, A. (2011). *Pricing Beauty: The Making of a Fashion Model*. Berkeley: University of California Press.

Medway, R. L., and Fulton, J. (2012). 'When More Gets You Less: A Meta-analysis of the Effect of Concurrent Web Options on Mail Survey Response Rates', *Public Opinion Quarterly*, 76: 733–46.

Mellahi, K., and Harris, L. (2016). 'Response Rates in Business and Management Research: An Overview of Current Practice and Suggestions for Future Directions', *British Journal of Management*, 27(2): 426–37.

Merryweather, D. (2010). 'Using Focus Group Research in Exploring the Relationships between Youth, Risk and Social Position', *Sociological Research Online*, 15(1): 11–23.

Merton, R. (1972). 'Insiders and Outsiders: A Chapter in the Sociology of Knowledge', *American Journal of Sociology*, 78(1), 9–47.

Merton, R. K. (1967). *On Theoretical Sociology*. New York: Free Press.

Merton, R. K., Fiske, M., and Kendall, P. L. (1956). *The Focused Interview: A Manual of Problems and Procedures*. New York: Free Press.

Mervis, J. (2020). 'Researchers Finally Get Access to Data on Facebook's Role in Political Discourse', *Science*, 13 February, www.sciencemag.org/news/2020/02/researchers-finally-get-access-data-facebook-s-role-political-discourse (accessed 21 July 2020).

Messing, J., Campbell, J., Wilson, J., Brown, S., and Patchell, B. (2017). 'The Lethality Screen: The Predictive Validity of an Intimate Partner Violence Risk Assessment for Use by First Responders', *Journal of Interpersonal Violence*, 32(2): 205–26.

Meterko, M., Restuccia, J. D., Stolzmann, K., Mohr, D., Brennan, C., Glasgow, J., and Kaboli, P. (2015). 'Response Rates, Nonresponse Bias, and Data Quality: Results from a National Survey of Senior Healthcare Leaders', *Public Opinion Quarterly*, 79(1): 130–44.

Meyer, B., Mok, W., and Sullivan, J. (2015). 'Household Surveys in Crisis', *Journal of Economic Perspectives*, 29(4): 199–226.

Midgley, C. (1998). 'TV Violence has Little Impact on Children, Study Finds', *The Times*, 12 January: 5.

Mies, M. (1993). 'Towards a Methodology for Feminist Research', in M. Hammersley (ed.), *Social Research: Philosophy, Politics and Practice*. London: Sage.

Miles, M. B. (1979). 'Qualitative Data as an Attractive Nuisance', *Administrative Science Quarterly*, 24: 590–601.

Miles, M. B., Huberman, A. M., and Saldaña, J. (2019). *Qualitative Data Analysis: A Methods Sourcebook*. London: Sage.

Milgram, S. (1963). 'A Behavioral Study of Obedience', *Journal of Abnormal and Social Psychology*, 67: 371–8.

Miller, R. L. (2000). *Researching Life Stories and Family Histories*. London: Sage.

Millward, P. (2009). 'Glasgow Rangers Supporters in the City of Manchester: The Degeneration of a "Fan Party" into a "Hooligan Riot"', *International Review for the Sociology of Sport*, 44(4): 381–98.

Minson, J., VanEpps, E., Yip, J., and Schweitzer, M. (2018). 'Eliciting the Truth, the Whole Truth, and Nothing But the Truth: The Effect of Question Phrasing on Deception', *Organizational Behavior and Human Decision Processes*, 147: 76–93.

Mintzberg, H. (1973). *The Nature of Managerial Work*. New York: Harper & Row.

Mishler, E. G. (1986). *Research Interviewing: Context and Narrative*. Cambridge, MA: Harvard University Press.

Miske, O., Schweitzer, N., and Horne, Z. (2019). 'What Information Shapes and Shifts People's Attitudes about Capital Punishment?' Proceedings of the 41st Annual Conference of the Cognitive Science Society.

Mitchell, J. C. (1983). 'Case and Situation Analysis', *Sociological Review*, 31: 186–211.

Mkono, M., and Markwell, K. (2014). 'The Application of Netnography in Tourism Studies', *Annals of Tourism Research*, 48: 289–91.

Mohanty, C. T. (1984). 'Under Western Eyes: Feminist Scholarship and Colonial Discourses', *Ground Report*, 19 February, 333–58.

Moore, T., McKee, K., and McCoughlin, P. (2015). 'Online Focus Groups and Qualitative Research in the Social Sciences: Their Merits and Limitations in a Study of Housing and Youth', *People, Place and Policy*, 9(1): 17–28.

Moran-Ellis, J., Alexander, V. D., Cronin, A., Dickinson, M., Fielding, J., Sleney, J., and Thomas, H. (2006). 'Triangulation and Integration: Processes, Claims and Implications', *Qualitative Research*, 6(1): 45–59.

Morgan, D. L. (1998a). *Planning Focus Groups*. Thousand Oaks, CA: Sage.

Morgan, D. L. (1998b). 'Practical Strategies for Combining Qualitative and Quantitative Methods: Applications for Health Research', *Qualitative Health Research*, 8: 362–76.

Morgan, D. L. (2002). 'Focus Group Interviewing', in J. F. Gubrium and J. A. Holstein (eds), *Handbook of Interview Research: Context and Method*. Thousand Oaks, CA: Sage.

Morgan, D. L. (2010). 'Reconsidering the Role of Interaction in Analyzing and Reporting Focus Groups', *Qualitative Health Research*, 20: 718–22.

Morgan, D. L., and Hoffman, K. (2018). 'A System for Coding the Interaction in Focus Groups and Dyadic Interviews', *Qualitative Report*, 23(3): 519–31.

Morgan, D. L., and Spanish, M. T. (1985). 'Social Interaction and the Cognitive Organization of Health-Relevant Behaviour', *Sociology of Health and Illness*, 7: 401–22.

Morgan, G., and Smircich, L. (1980). 'The Case for Qualitative Research', *Academy of Management Review*, 5: 491–500.

Morgan, M., Gibbs, S., Maxwell, K., and Britten, N. (2002). 'Hearing Children's Voices: Methodological Issues in Conducting Focus Groups with Children aged 7–11 years', *Qualitative Research*, 2(1): 5–20.

Morgan, R. (2000). 'The Politics of Criminological Research', in R. D. King and E. Wincup (eds), *Doing Research on Crime and Justice*. Oxford: Oxford University Press.

Morley, D. (1980). *The 'Nationwide' Audience: Structure and Decoding*. London: British Film Institute.

Morris, N., and Cravens Pickens, J. D. (2017). '"I'm Not a Gadget": A Grounded Theory on Unplugging', *American Journal of Family Therapy*, 45(5): 264–82.

Morse, J. M. (2004). 'Sampling in Qualitative Research', in M. S. Lewis-Beck, A. Bryman, and T. F. Liao (eds), *The Sage Encyclopedia of Social Science Research Methods*. Thousand Oaks, CA: Sage.

Moser, C. A., and Kalton, G. (1971). *Survey Methods in Social Investigation*. London: Heinemann.

Mühlböck, M., Steiber, N., and Kittel, B. (2017). 'Less Supervision, More Satisficing? Comparing Completely Self-Administered Web-Surveys and Interviews Under Controlled Conditions', *Statistics, Politics and Policy*, 8(1): 13–28.

Mullan, K., and Chatzitheochari, S. (2019). 'Changing Times Together? A Time-Diary Analysis of Family Time in the Digital Age in the United Kingdom', *Journal of Marriage and Family*, 81(4): 795–811.

Müller, K. (2017). 'Reframing the Aura: Digital Photography in Ancestral Worship', *Museum Anthropology*, 40(1): 65–78.

Munday, J. (2006). 'Identity in Focus: The Use of Focus Groups to Study the Construction of Collective Identity', *Sociology*, 40: 89–105.

Musa, I., Seymour, J., Narayanasamy, M., Wada, T., and Conroy, S. (2015). 'A Survey of Older Peoples' Attitudes towards Advance Care Planning', *Age and Ageing*, 44(3): 371–6.

Naab, T., Karnowski, V., and Schlütz, D. (2019). 'Reporting Mobile Social Media Use: How Survey and Experience Sampling Measures Differ', *Communication Methods and Measures*, 13(2): 126–47.

Näher, A-F., and Krumpal, I. (2012). 'Asking Sensitive Questions: The Impact of Forgiving Wording and Question Context on Social Desirability Bias', *Quality and Quantity*, 46(5): 1601–16.

Nash, C. J. (2016). *Queer Methods and Methodologies: Intersecting Queer Theories and Social Science Research*. London: Routledge, https://doi.org/10.4324/9781315603223 (open access).

National Centre for Social Research [UK] (2019). 'British Social Attitudes 36: Technical Details', www.bsa.natcen.ac.uk/media/39290/7_bsa36_technical-details.pdf (accessed 20 March 2021).

National Student Survey [UK] (2020). www.officeforstudents.org.uk/publications/the-national-student-survey-consistency-controversy-and-change/ (accessed 13 March 2020).

Natow, R. S. (2020). 'The Use of Triangulation in Qualitative Studies Employing Elite Interviews', *Qualitative Research*, 20(2): 160–73.

Nelson, L. K. (2017). 'Computational Grounded Theory: A Methodological Framework', *Sociological Methods & Research*, 49(1): 3–42, https://doi.org/10.1177/0049124117729703.

Neuendorf, K. (2016). *The Content Analysis Guidebook*. Thousand Oaks, CA: Sage.

Neuman, W. (2013). *Social Research Methods: Qualitative and Quantitative Approaches*. Harlow, UK: Pearson.

Nichols, K. (2016). 'Moving Beyond Ideas of Laddism: Conceptualising "Mischievous Masculinities" as a New Way of Understanding Everyday Sexism and Gender Relations', *Journal of Gender Studies*, 27(1): 73–85.

Noblit, G. W., and Hare, R. D. (1988). *Meta-Ethnography: Synthesizing Qualitative Studies*. Newbury Park, CA: Sage.

Nosowska, G., McKee, K., and Dahlberg, L. (2014). 'Using Structured Observation and Content Analysis to Explore the Presence of Older People in Public Fora in Developing Countries', *Journal of Aging Research*, article ID 860612.

Nowicka, M., and Ryan, L. (2015). 'Beyond Insiders and Outsiders in Migration Research: Rejecting A Priori Commonalities'. Introduction to FQS Thematic Section 'Researcher, Migrant, Woman: Methodological Implications of Multiple Positionalities in Migration Studies'. *Forum: Qualitative Sozialforschung/Forum: Qualitative Social Research*, 16(2/May).

Noy, C. (2008). 'Sampling Knowledge: The Hermeneutics of Snowball Sampling in Qualitative Research', *International Journal of Social Research Methodology*, 11: 327–44.

Noyes, J., Booth, A., Cargo, M., Flemming, K., Garside, R., Hannes, K., Harden, A., Harris, J., Lewin, S., Pantoja, T., and Thomas, J. (2017). 'Cochrane Qualitative and Implementation Methods Group Guidance Series—Paper 1: Introduction', *Journal of Clinical Epidemiology*, 97: 35–8.

Nyberg, D. (2009). 'Computers, Customer Service Operatives, and Cyborgs: Intra-Actions in Call Centres', *Organization Studies*, 30: 1181–99.

Oakley, A. (1981). 'Interviewing Women: A Contradiction in Terms', in H. Roberts (ed.), *Doing Feminist Research*. London: Routledge & Kegan Paul.

Oakley, A. (1998). 'Gender, Methodology and People's Ways of Knowing: Some Problems with Feminism and the Paradigm Debate in Social Science', *Sociology*, 32: 707–31.

O'Boyle, Timothy (2019). 'Protecting Self-Image: The Rationalization of Cheating in an International Billiard League', *Deviant Behavior*, 40(8): 1020–30, doi: 10.1080/01639625.2018.1456717.

O'Brien, K. (2010). 'Inside "Doorwork": Gendering the Security Gaze', in R. Ryan-Flood and R. Gill (eds), *Secrecy and Silence in the Research Process: Feminist Reflections*. London: Routledge.

O'Cathain, A. (2010). 'Assessing the Quality of Mixed Methods Research: Toward a Comprehensive Framework', in A. Tashakkori and C. Teddlie (eds), *SAGE Handbook of Mixed Methods in Social and Behavioral Research*, 2nd edn. Los Angeles: Sage.

O'Cathain, A., Murphy, E., and Nicholl, J. (2007). 'Integration and Publication as Indicators of "Yield" from Mixed Methods Studies', *Journal of Mixed Methods Research*, 1: 147–63.

O'Cathain, A., Murphy, E., and Nicholl, J. (2008). 'The Quality of Mixed Methods Studies in Health Services Research', *Journal of Health Services Research & Policy*, 13: 92–8.

O'Connor, H., and Madge, C. (2001). 'Cyber-Mothers: Online Synchronous Interviewing using Conferencing Software', *Sociological Research Online*, 5(4), www.socresonline.org.uk/9/2/hine.html (accessed 1 March 2021).

Office for National Statistics [UK] (2019a). *The National Statistics Socio-economic Classification (NS-SEC)*, www.ons.gov.uk/methodology/classificationsandstandards/otherclassifications/thenationalstatisticssocioeconomicclassificationnssecrebasedonsoc2010 (accessed 1 December 2020).

Office for National Statistics [UK] (2019b). *What is the Difference between Sex and Gender?*, www.ons.gov.uk/economy/environmentalaccounts/articles/whatisthedifferencebetweensexandgender/2019-02-21 (accessed 15 July 2020).

Office for National Statistics [UK] (2020). *User Guide to Crime Statistics for England and Wales*, www.ons.gov.uk/peoplepopulationandcommunity/crimeandjustice/methodologies/userguidetocrimestatisticsforenglandandwales.

O'Grady, C., Dahm, M. R., Roger, P., and Yates, L. (2014). 'Trust, Talk and the Dictaphone: Tracing the Discursive Accomplishment of Trust in a Surgical Consultation', *Discourse and Society*, 25: 65–83.

O'Kane, P., Smith, A., and Lerman, M. P. (2019). 'Building Transparency and Trustworthiness in Inductive Research through Computer-Aided Qualitative Data Analysis Software', *Organizational Research Methods*, 24(1): 104–39.

Okely, J. (1994). 'Thinking Through Fieldwork', in A. Bryman and R. G. Burgess (eds), *Analyzing Qualitative Data*. London: Routledge.

Olesen, B. R., and Nordentoft, H. M. (2013). 'Walking the Talk? A Micro-sociological Approach to the Co-production of Knowledge and Power in Action Research', *International Journal of Action Research*, 9(1): 67–94.

Olson, K., and Smyth, J. D. (2014). 'Accuracy of Within-Household Selection in Web and Mail Surveys of the General Population', *Field Methods*, 26: 56–69.

Oltmann, S. (2016). 'Qualitative Interviews: A Methodological Discussion of the Interviewer and Respondent Contexts', *Forum: Qualitative Social Research*, 17(2): 1–16.

Oncini, F. (2018). 'The Holy Gram: Strategy and Tactics in the Primary School Canteen', *Journal of Contemporary Ethnography*, 47(5): 640–70.

O'Neill, M., and Roberts, B. (2019). *Walking Methods: Research on the Move*. London: Routledge.

Onwuegbuzie, A. J., and Collins, K. M. T. (2007). 'A Typology of Mixed Methods Sampling Designs in Social Sciences Research', *Qualitative Report*, 12(2): 281–316, https://doi.org/10.46743/2160-3715/2007.1638 (accessed 1 March 2021).

Onwuegbuzie, A. J., and Leech, N. L. (2010). 'Generalization Practices in Qualitative Research: A Mixed Methods Case Study', *Quality and Quantity*, 44: 881–92.

Onwuegbuzie, A. J., Dickinson, W. B., Leech, N. L., and Zoran, A. G. (2009). 'A Qualitative Framework for Collecting and Analyzing Data in Focus Group Research', *International Journal of Qualitative Methods*, 8(3): 1–21.

Oppenheim, A. N. (2008). *Questionnaire Design, Interviewing and Attitude Measurement*, 3rd edn. London: Pinter.

O'Reilly, K. (2000). *The British on the Costa del Sol: Transnational Identities and Local Communities*. London: Routledge.

O'Reilly, K. A. (2010). *Service Undone: A Grounded Theory of Strategically Constructed Silos and their Impact on Customer-Company Interactions from the Perspective of Retail Employees*. Doctoral dissertation, Utah State University, http://digitalcommons.usu.edu/etd/669 (accessed 1 March 2021).

O'Reilly, K. A., Paper, D., and Marx, S. (2012). 'Demystifying Grounded Theory for Business Research', *Organizational Research Methods*, 15: 247–62.

O'Reilly, M., and Parker, N. (2013). '"Unsatisfactory Saturation": A Critical Exploration of the Notion of Saturated Sample Sizes in Qualitative Research', *Qualitative Research*, 13(2): 190–7.

O'Reilly, M., Dixon-Woods, M., Angell, E., Ashcroft, R., and Bryman, A. (2009). 'Doing Accountability: A Discourse Analysis of Research Ethics Committee Letters', *Sociology of Health and Illness*, 31: 246–61.

Ostrov, J., and Hart, E. (2013). 'Observational Methods', in T. Little (ed.), *The Oxford Handbook of Quantitative Methods in Psychology*, vol. 1. Oxford: Oxford University Press.

Ozgur, C., Dou, M., Li, Y., and Rogers, G. (2017). 'Selection of Statistical Software for Data Scientists and Teachers', *Journal of Modern Applied Statistical Methods*, 16(1): 753–74.

Padilla, J., and Leighton, J. (2017). 'Cognitive Interviewing and Think Aloud Methods', in B. Zumbo and A. Hubley (eds), *Understanding and Investigating Response Processes in Validation Research*. New York: Springer.

Pahl, J. (1990). 'Household Spending, Personal Spending and the Control of Money in Marriage', *Sociology*, 24: 119–38.

Palys, T. (2008). 'Purposive Sampling', in L. M. Given (ed.), *The Sage Encyclopedia of Qualitative Research Methods*, vol. 2. Thousand Oaks, CA: Sage.

Park, C. (2003). 'In Other (People's) Words: Plagiarism by University Students—Literature and Lessons', *Assessment and Evaluation in Higher Education*, 28: 471–88.

Parker, M. (2000). *Organizational Culture and Identity*. London: Sage.

Pasquandrea, S. (2014). '"They Might Read a Fly Speck": Musical Literacy as a Discursive Resource in Louis Armstrong's Autobiographies', *Social Semiotics*, 24: 514–29.

Paterson, B. L. (2012). '"It Looks Great But How Do I Know if it Fits?": An Introduction to Meta-Synthesis Research', in K. Hannes and C. Lockwood (eds), *Synthesizing Qualitative Research: Choosing the Right Approach*. Chichester, UK: Wiley.

Patton, M. Q. (1990). *Qualitative Evaluation and Research Methods*, 2nd edn. Beverly Hills, CA: Sage.

Patton, M. Q. (2015). *Qualitative Evaluation and Research Methods*, 4th edn. Thousand Oaks, CA: Sage.

Paulus, T. M., Lester, J. N., and Britt, V. G. (2013). 'Constructing Hopes and Fears Around Technology: A Discourse Analysis of Introductory Research Methods Texts', *Qualitative Inquiry*, 19(9): 639–51.

Paulus, T., Warren, A., and Lester, J. N. (2016). 'Applying Conversation Analysis Methods to Online Talk: A Literature Review', *Discourse, Context & Media*, 12: 1–10.

Pearson, G. (2009). 'The Researcher as Hooligan: Where "Participant" Observation Means Breaking the Law', *International Journal of Social Research Methodology*, 12: 243–55.

Pearson, G. (2012). *An Ethnography of Football Fans: Cans, Cops and Carnivals*. Manchester, UK: Manchester University Press.

Pedersen, M. J., and Nielsen, C. V. (2016). 'Improving Survey Response Rates in Online Panels: Effects of Low-Cost Incentives and Cost-Free Text Appeal Interventions', *Social Science Computer Review*, 34(2): 229–43.

Peek, L., and Fothergill, A. (2009). 'Using Focus Groups: Lessons from Studying Daycare Centers, 9/11, and Hurricane Katrina', *Qualitative Research*, 9: 31–59.

Pehrson, S., Stambulova, N. B., and Olsson, K. (2017). 'Revisiting the Empirical Model "Phases in the Junior-to-Senior Transition of Swedish Ice Hockey Players": External Validation through Focus Groups and Interviews', *International Journal of Sports Science & Coaching*, 12(6): 747–61.

Penn, R., Rose, M., and Rubery, J. (1994). *Skill and Occupational Change*. Oxford: Oxford University Press.

Peräkylä, A. (1997). 'Reliability and Validity in Research Based on Transcripts', in D. Silverman (ed.), *Qualitative Research: Theory, Method and Practice*. London: Sage.

Pettigrew, A. (1997). 'What is a Processual Analysis?', *Scandinavian Journal of Management*, 13: 337–48.

Pew Research Center (2019). Social Media Fact Sheet, www.pewinternet.org/fact-sheet/social-media/ (accessed 1 March 2021).

Pezzella, F., Fetzer, M., and Keller, T. (2019). 'The Dark Figure of Hate Crime Underreporting', *American Behavioral Scientist*, https://doi.org/10.1177/0002764218823844.

Pheko, M. M. (2018). 'Autoethnography and Cognitive Adaptation: Two Powerful Buffers Against the Negative Consequences of Workplace Bullying and Academic Mobbing', *International Journal of Qualitative Studies on Health and Well-Being*, 13(1): 1459134.

Phelps Moultrie, J., Magee, P. A., and Paredes Scribner, S. M. (2017). 'Talk About a Racial Eclipse: Narratives of Institutional Evasion in an Urban School–University Partnership', *Journal of Cases in Educational Leadership*, 20(1): 6–21.

Phillips, N., and Hardy, C. (2002). *Discourse Analysis: Investigating Processes of Social Construction*. Thousand Oaks, CA: Sage.

Phoenix, A. (2006). 'Interrogating Intersectionality: Productive Ways of Theorising Multiple Positioning'. *Kvinder, køn & forskning*, 2–3.

Phoenix, C., Smith, P., and Sparkes, A. C. (2010). 'Narrative Analysis in Aging Studies: A Typology for Consideration', *Journal of Aging Studies*, 24: 1–11.

Pickering, L., and Kara, H. (2017). 'Presenting and Representing Others: Towards an Ethics of Engagement', *International Journal of Social Research Methodology*, 20(3): 299–309.

Pinch, T., and Clark, C. (1986). 'The Hard Sell: "Patter Merchanting" and the Strategic (Re)production and Local Management of Economic Reasoning in the Sales Routines of Market Pitchers', *Sociology*, 20: 169–91.

Pink, S. (2004). 'Visual Methods', in C. Seale, G. Gobo, J. F. Gubrium, and D. Silverman (eds), *Qualitative Research Practice*. London: Sage.

Pink, S. (2015). *Doing Sensory Ethnography*. London: Sage.

Pink, S. (2020). *Doing Visual Ethnography*, 4th edn. London: Sage.

Piper, N. (2015). 'Jamie Oliver and Cultural Intermediation', *Food, Culture & Society*, 18(2): 245–64.

Piza, E., Welsh, B., Farrington, D., and Thomas, A. (2019). 'CCTV Surveillance for Crime Prevention: A 40-Year Systematic Review with Meta-analysis', *Criminology and Public Policy*, 18(1): 135–59, https://onlinelibrary.wiley.com/doi/full/10.1111/1745-9133.12419.

Platell, M., Martin, K., Fisher, C., and Cook, A. (2020). 'Comparing Adolescent and Service Provider Perceptions on the Barriers to Mental Health Service Use: A Sequential Mixed Methods Approach', *Children and Youth Services Review*, 115, 105101, https://doi.org/10.1016/j.childyouth.2020.105101.

Platt, J. (1981). 'The Social Construction of "Positivism" and its Significance in British Sociology, 1950–80', in P. Abrams, R. Deem, J. Finch, and P. Rock (eds), *Practice and Progress: British Sociology 1950–1980*. London: George Allen & Unwin.

Platt, J. (1984). '*The Affluent Worker* Revisited', in C. Bell and H. Roberts (eds), *Social Researching: Politics, Problems, Practice*. London: Routledge & Kegan Paul.

Platt, J. (1986). 'Functionalism and the Survey: The Relation of Theory and Method', *Sociological Review*, 34: 501–36.

Platt, J. (1996). *A History of Sociological Research Methods in America 1920–1960*. Cambridge: Cambridge University Press.

Plummer, K. (1983). *Documents of Life: An Introduction to the Problems and Literature of a Humanistic Method*. London: Allen & Unwin.

Plummer, K. (2001). 'The Call of Life Stories in Ethnographic Research', in P. Atkinson, A. Coffey, S. Delamont, J. Lofland, and L. Lofland (eds), *Handbook of Ethnography*. London: Sage.

Polsky, N. (1967). *Hustlers, Beats and Others*. Chicago: Aldine.

Poortinga, W., Bickerstaff, K., Langford, I., Niewöhner, J., and Pidgeon, N. (2004). 'The British 2001 Foot and Mouth Crisis: A Comparative Study of Public Risk Perceptions, Trust and Beliefs about Government Policy in Two Communities', *Journal of Risk Research*, 7: 73–90.

Potter, J. (1996). *Representing Reality: Discourse, Rhetoric and Social Construction*. London: Sage.

Potter, J. (1997). 'Discourse Analysis as a Way of Analysing Naturally Occurring Talk', in D. Silverman (ed.), *Qualitative Research: Theory, Method and Practice*. London: Sage.

Potter, J. (2004). 'Discourse Analysis', in M. Hardy and A. Bryman (eds), *Handbook of Data Analysis*. London: Sage.

Potter, J., and Hepburn, A. (2012). 'Discourse Analysis', in S. Becker, A. Bryman, and H. Ferguson (eds), *Understanding Research: Methods and Approaches for Social Work and Social Policy*. Bristol, UK: Policy Press.

Potter, J., and Hepburn, A. (2019). 'Shaming Interrogatives: Admonishments, the Social Psychology of Emotion, and Discursive Practices of Behaviour Modification in Family Mealtimes', *British Journal of Social Psychology*, 59(2): 347–64.

Potter, J., and Wetherell, M. (1987). *Discourse and Social Psychology: Beyond Attitudes and Behaviour*. London: Sage.

Potter, J., and Wetherell, M. (1994). 'Analyzing Discourse', in A. Bryman and R. G. Burgess (eds), *Analyzing Qualitative Data*. London: Routledge.

Potter, J., Wetherell, M., and Chitty, A. (1991). 'Quantification Rhetoric: Cancer on Television', *Discourse and Society*, 2: 333–65.

Poulton, E. (2012). '"If You Had Balls, You'd Be One of Us!" Doing Gendered Research: Methodological Reflections on Being a Female Academic Researcher in the Hyper-Masculine Subculture of "Football Hooliganism"', *Sociological Research Online*, 17: 4, www.socresonline.org.uk/17/4/4.html (accessed 1 March 2021).

Prada, M., Rodrigues D., Garrido, M., Lopesa, D., Cavalheiro, B., and Gaspar, R. (2018). 'Motives, Frequency and Attitudes Toward Emoji and Emoticon Use', *Telematics and Informatics*, 35(7): 1925–34.

Pratt, M. G. (2008). 'Fitting Oval Pegs into Round Holes: Tensions in Evaluating and Publishing Qualitative Research in Top-Tier North American Journals', *Organizational Research Methods*, 11: 481–509.

Preisendörfer, P., and Wolter, F. (2014). 'Who Is Telling the Truth? A Validation Study on Determinants of Response Behavior in Surveys', *Public Opinion Quarterly*, 78: 126–46.

Proksch, S.-O., and Slapin, J. B. (2010). 'Position Taking in European Parliament Speeches', *British Journal of Political Science*, 40: 587–611.

Psathas, G. (1995). *Conversation Analysis: The Study of Talk-in-Interaction*. Thousand Oaks, CA: Sage.

Puigvert, L., Valls, R., Garcia Yeste, C., Aguilar, C., & Merrill, B. (2019). 'Resistance to and Transformations of Gender-Based Violence in Spanish Universities: A Communicative Evaluation of Social Impact', *Journal of Mixed Methods Research*, 13(3): 361–80, https://doi.org/10.1177/1558689817731170.

Punch, M. (1979). *Policing the Inner City: A Study of Amsterdam's Warmoesstraat*. London: Macmillan.

Punch, M. (1994). 'Politics and Ethics in Qualitative Research', in N. K. Denzin and Y. S. Lincoln (eds), *Handbook of Qualitative Research*. Thousand Oaks, CA: Sage.

Rada, V., and Martín, V. (2014). 'Random Route and Quota Sampling: Do They Offer Any Advantage over Probability Sampling Methods?', *Open Journal of Statistics*, 4(5): 391–401.

Radley, A., and Chamberlain, K. (2001). 'Health Psychology and the Study of the Case: From Method to Analytic Concern', *Social Science and Medicine*, 53: 321–32.

Raskind, I. G., Shelton, R. C., Comeau, D. L., Cooper, H. L., Griffith, D. M., and Kegler, M. C. (2019). 'A Review of Qualitative Data Analysis Practices in Health Education and Health Behavior Research', *Health Education & Behavior*, 46(1): 32–9.

Ravn, S. (2018). '"I Would Never Start a Fight but . . .": Young Masculinities, Perceptions of Violence, and Symbolic Boundary Work in Focus Groups', *Men and Masculinities*, 21(2): 291–309.

Rayburn, R. L., and Guittar, N. A. (2013). '"This is Where You Are Supposed to Be": How Homeless Individuals Cope with Stigma', *Sociological Spectrum*, 33: 159–74.

Reason, P., and Rowan, J. (1981). *Human Inquiry: A Sourcebook of New Paradigm Research*. New York: John Wiley & Sons.

Reed, M. (2000). 'The Limits of Discourse Analysis in Organizational Analysis', *Organization*, 7: 524–30.

Rees, R., Caird, J., Dickson, K., Vigurs, C., and Thomas, J. (2013). *The Views of Young People in the UK About Obesity, Body Size, Shape and Weight: A Systematic Review*. London: EPPI-Centre, Social Science Research Unit, Institute of Education, University of London.

Reiner, R. (2000). 'Police Research', in R. D. King and E. Wincup (eds), *Doing Research on Crime and Justice*. Oxford: Oxford University Press.

Reinharz, S. (1992). *Feminist Methods in Social Research*. New York: Oxford University Press.

Reisner, S. L., Randazzo, R. K., White Hughto, J. M., Peitzmeier, S., DuBois, L. Z., Pardee, D. J., Marrow, E., McLean, S., and Potter, J. (2018). 'Sensitive Health Topics with Underserved Patient Populations: Methodological Considerations for Online Focus Group Discussions', *Qualitative Health Research*, 28(10): 1658–73.

Revilla, M. A., Saris, W. E., and Krosnick, J. A. (2014). 'Choosing the Number of Categories in Agree–Disagree Scales', *Sociological Methods and Research*, 43: 73–97.

Rhodes, R. A., and Tiernan, A. (2015). 'Focus Groups and Prime Ministers' Chiefs of Staff', *Journal of Organizational Ethnography*, 4(2): 208–22.

Riessman, C. K. (1993). *Narrative Analysis*. Newbury Park, CA: Sage.

Riessman, C. K. (2004). 'Narrative Interviewing', in M. S. Lewis-Beck, A. Bryman, and T. F. Liao (eds), *The Sage Encyclopedia of Social Science Research Methods*. Thousand Oaks, CA: Sage.

Riessman, C. K. (2008). *Narrative Methods for the Human Sciences*. Thousand Oaks, CA: Sage.

Riffe, D., Lacy, S., and Fico, F. (2014). *Analysing Media Messages: Using Quantitative Content Analysis in Research*. London: Routledge.

Ritchie, J., Spencer, L., and O'Connor, W. (2003). 'Carrying out Qualitative Analysis', in J. Ritchie and J. Lewis (eds), *Qualitative Research Practice: A Guide for Social Science Students and Researchers*. London: Sage.

Ritzer, G. (1975). 'Sociology: A Multiple Paradigm Science', *American Sociologist*, 10: 156–67.

Rivera, J. (2019). 'When Attaining the Best Sample is Out of Reach: Nonprobability Alternatives when Engaging in Public Administration Research', *Journal of Public Affairs Education*, 25(3): 314–42.

Robinson, S., and Leonard, K. (2019). *Designing Quality Survey Questions*. London: Sage.

Röder, A., and Mühlau, P. (2014). 'Are They Acculturating? Europe's Immigrants and Gender Egalitarianism', *Social Forces*, 92: 899–928.

Rogers, N. (2019). 'Holding Court: The Social Regulation of Masculinity in University Pickup Basketball', *Journal of Contemporary Ethnography*, 48(6): 731–49, doi: 10.1177/0891241619827369.

Rojek, C. (1995). *Decentring Leisure: Rethinking Leisure Theory*. London: Sage.

Rorty, R. (1979). *Philosophy and the Mirror of Nature*. Princeton: Princeton University Press.

Rose, G. (2016). *Visual Methodologies: An Introduction to Researching with Visual Materials*, 4th edn. London: Sage.

Rosenfeld, M. (2017). 'Marriage, Choice, and Couplehood in the Age of the Internet', *Sociological Science*, 4: 90–510.

Rosenhan, D. L. (1973). 'On Being Sane in Insane Places', *Science*, 179: 350–8.

Rosenthal, R., and Jacobson, L. (1968). *Pygmalion in the Classroom: Teacher Expectation and Pupils' Intellectual Development*. New York: Holt, Rinehart & Winston.

Rosnow, R. L., and Rosenthal, R. (1997). *People Studying People: Artifacts and Ethics in Behavioral Research*. New York: W. H. Freeman.

Roulston, K., deMarrais, K., and Lewis, J. (2003). 'Learning to Interview in the Social Sciences', *Qualitative Inquiry*, 9: 643–68.

Rowan, K. (2016). '"Who Are You in This Body?" Identifying Demons and the Path to Deliverance in a London Pentecostal Church', *Language in Society*, 45(2): 247.

Rubinstein, J. (1973). *City Police*. New York: Ballantine.

Rübsamen, N., Akmatov, M., Castell, S., Karch, A., and Mikolajczyk, T. (2017). 'Comparison of Response Patterns in Different Survey Designs: A Longitudinal Panel with Mixed-Mode and Online-Only Design', *Emerging Themes in Epidemiology*, 14:4.

Ryan, G. W., and Bernard, H. R. (2003). 'Techniques to Identify Themes', *Field Methods*, 15: 85–109.

Ryan, L. (2015). '"Inside" and "Outside" of What or Where? Researching Migration through Multi-Positionalities', *Forum: Qualitative Sozialforschung/Forum: Qualitative Social Research*, 16(2).

Ryan, L., Kofman, E., and Aaron, P. (2011). 'Insiders and Outsiders: Working with Peer Researchers in Researching Muslim Communities', *International Journal of Social Research Methodology*, 14(1): 49–60.

Ryan, S. (2009). 'On the "Mop-Floor": Researching Employment Relations in the Hidden World of Commercial Cleaning', in K. Townsend and J. Burgess (eds), *Method in the Madness: Research Stories you Won't Read in Textbooks*. Oxford: Chandos.

Sacks, H., Schegloff, E. A., and Jefferson, G. (1974). 'A Simplest Systematics for the Organization of Turn-Taking in Conversation', *Language*, 50: 696–735.

Salancik, G. R. (1979). 'Field Stimulations for Organizational Behavior Research', *Administrative Science Quarterly*, 24: 638–49.

Saldaña, J. (2021). *The Coding Manual for Qualitative Researchers*, 3rd edn. London: Sage.

Salkind, N., and Fry, B. (2019). *Statistics for People Who (Think They) Hate Statistics*. London: Sage.

Sallaz, J. J. (2009). *The Labor of Luck: Casino Capitalism in the United States and South Africa*. Berkeley: University of California Press.

Sammons, P., and Davis, S. (2017). 'Mixed Methods Approaches and their Application in Educational Research', in D. Wyse, N. Selwyn, and E. Smith (eds), *The BERA/SAGE Handbook of Educational Research*, vol. 2. London: SAGE, doi: 10.4135/9781473983953.n24.

Sampson, H., and Thomas, M. (2003). 'Lone Researchers at Sea: Gender, Risk and Responsibility', *Qualitative Research*, 3: 165–89.

Samuel, R. (1976). 'Oral History and Local History', *History Workshop Journal*, 1: 191–208.

Sanders, C. R. (2009). 'Colorful Writing: Conducting and Living with a Tattoo Ethnography', in A. J. Puddephatt, W. Shaffir, and S. W. Kleinknecht (eds), *Ethnographies Revisited: Constructing Theory in the Field*. London: Routledge.

Sandoval, C. (2000). 'US Third World Feminism: Differential Social Movement', in C. Sandoval, *Methodology of the Oppressed*. Minneapolis, MN: University of Minnesota Press, 40–63.

Sanjek, R. (1990). 'A Vocabulary for Fieldnotes', in R. Sanjek (ed.), *Fieldnotes: The Making of Anthropology*. Ithaca, NY: Cornell University Press.

Sarsby, J. (1984). 'The Fieldwork Experience', in R. F. Ellen (ed.), *Ethnographic Research: A Guide to General Conduct*. London: Academic Press.

Savage, M. (2010). *Identities and Social Change in Britain since 1940: The Politics of Method*. Oxford: Oxford University Press.

Savage, M. (2016). 'The Fall and Rise of Class Analysis in British Sociology, 1950–2016', *Tempo Social*, 28(2): 57–72.

Savage, M., and Burrows, R. (2007). 'The Coming Crisis of Empirical Sociology', *Sociology*, 41: 885–99.

Savage, M., Devine, F., Cunningham, N., Taylor, M., Li, Y., Hjellbrekke, J., Le Roux, B., Friedman, S., and Miles, A. (2013). 'A New Model of Social Class? Findings from the BBC's Great British Class Survey Experiment', *Sociology*, 47(2): 219–50, https://doi.org/10.1177/0038038513481128.

Schaeffer, N. (2017). 'Survey Interviewing: Departures from the Script', in D. L. Vannette and J. A. Krosnick (eds), *The Palgrave Handbook of Survey Research*. Basingstoke, UK: Palgrave, 109–19.

Schaeffer, N. C., Dykema, J., and Maynard, D. W. (2010). 'Interviewers and Interviewing', in P. V. Marsden and J. D. Wright (eds), *Handbook of Survey Research*, 2nd edn. Bingley, UK: Emerald.

Schegloff, E. A. (1997). 'Whose Text? Whose Context?', *Discourse and Society*, 8: 165–87.

Scheper-Hughes, N. (2004). 'Parts Unknown: Undercover Ethnography of the Organs-Trafficking Underworld', *Ethnography*, 5: 29–73.

Schneider, C. J. (2016). 'Police Presentational Strategies on Twitter in Canada', *Policing and Society*, 26(2): 129–47, doi: 10.1080/10439463.2014.922085.

Schneider, C. J., and Trottier, D. (2012). 'The 2011 Vancouver Riot and the Role of Facebook in Crowd-Sourced Policing', *BC Studies*, 175: 57–72.

Schneider, S. M., and Foot, K. A. (2004). 'The Web as an Object of Study', *New Media and Society*, 6: 114–22.

Schreier, M. (2014). 'Ways of Doing Qualitative Content Analysis: Disentangling Terms and Terminologies', *Forum: Qualitative Sozialforschung/Forum: Qualitative Social Research*, 15(1/January).

Schrøder, K. C. (2019). 'Audience Reception Research in a Post-broadcasting Digital Age', *Television & New Media*, 20(2): 155–69.

Schuman, H., and Presser, S. (1981). *Questions and Answers in Attitude Surveys: Experiments on Question Form, Wording, and Context*. San Diego, CA: Academic Press.

Schutz, A. (1962). *Collected Papers I: The Problem of Social Reality*. The Hague: Martinus Nijhof.

Schwartz-Shea, P., and Yanow, D. (2012). *Interpretive Research Design: Concepts and Processes*. New York: Routledge.

Scott, J. (1990). *A Matter of Record*. Cambridge: Polity.

Scourfield, J., Colombo, G., Burnap, P., Evans, R., Jacob, N., Williams, M., and Caul, S. (2019). 'The Number and Characteristics of Newspaper and Twitter Reports on Suicides and Road Traffic Deaths in Young People', *Archives of Suicide Research*, 23(3): 507–22.

Seale, C. (1999). *The Quality of Qualitative Research*. London: Sage.

Seale, C., Charteris-Black, J., MacFarlane, A., and McPherson, A. (2010). 'Interviews and Internet Forums: A Comparison of Two Sources of Qualitative Data', *Qualitative Health Research*, 20: 595–606.

Seale, C., Ziebland, S., and Charteris-Black, J. (2006). 'Gender, Cancer Experience and Internet Use: A Comparative Keyword Analysis of Interviews and Online Cancer Support Groups', *Social Science and Medicine*, 62: 2577–90.

Sebo, P., Maisonneuve, H., Cerutti, B., Fournier, J., Senn, N., and Haller, D. (2017). 'Rates, Delays, and Completeness of General Practitioners' Responses to a Postal Versus Web-Based Survey: A Randomized Trial', *Journal of Medical Internet Research*, 19(3): e83.

Seeman, M. (1959). 'On the Meaning of Alienation', *American Sociological Review*, 24: 783–91.

Seitz, S. (2015). 'Pixilated Partnerships—Overcoming Obstacles in Qualitative Interviews via Skype: A Research Note', *Qualitative Research*, 16(2): 229–35.

Sempik, J., Becker, S., and Bryman, A. (2007). 'The Quality of Research Evidence in Social Policy: Consensus and Dissension among Researchers', *Evidence and Policy*, 3: 407–23.

Shadish, W. R., Cook, T. D., and Campbell, D. T. (2002). *Experimental and Quasi-experimental Design for Generalized Causal Inference*. Boston: Houghton Mifflin.

Shah, A. P., and Gu, Y. (2020). 'A Mixed-Methods Approach to Identifying Sexual Assault Concerns on a University Campus', *Journal of Aggression Maltreatment & Trauma*, 29(6): 643–60, doi: 10.1080/10926771.2020.1734707.

Shapiro, S., and Humphreys, L. (2013). 'Exploring Old and New Media: Comparing Military Blogs to Civil War Letters', *New Media and Society*, 15: 1151–67.

Sharma, G. (2017). 'Pros And Cons Of Different Sampling Techniques', *International Journal of Applied Research*, 3(7): 749–52.

Shaw, C. R. (1930). *The Jack-Roller*. Chicago: University of Chicago Press.

Sheehan, K., and Hoy, M. G. (1999). 'Using E-Mail to Survey Internet Users in the United States: Methodology and Assessment', *Journal of Computer-Mediated Communication*, 4(3), https://onlinelibrary.wiley.com/doi/full/10.1111/j.1083-6101.1999.tb00101.x (accessed 20 March 2021).

Sheffield Fairness Commission (2013). *Making Sheffield Fairer*, www.sheffield.gov.uk/content/dam/sheffield/docs/your-city-council/our-plans,-policies-and-performance/Fairness%20Commission%20Report.pdf (accessed 15 July 2020).

Sheller, M., and Urry, J. (2006). 'The New Mobilities Paradigm', *Environment and Planning A*, 38: 207–26.

Shepherd, J., Garcia, J., Oliver, S., Harden, A., Rees, R., Brunton, G., and Oakley, A. (2002). *Barriers to, and Facilitators of the Health of Young People: A Systematic Review of Evidence on Young People's Views and on the Interventions in Mental Health, Physical Activity and Healthy Eating*. Vol. 2: Complete Report. London: EPPI-Centre, Social Science Research Unit, Institute of Education, University of London. https://eppi.ioe.ac.uk/cms/Portals/0/PDF%20reviews%20and%20summaries/Vol%202_Web.pdf?ver=2006-03-02-124349-650.

Shepherd, J., Harden, A., Rees, R., Brunton, G., Garcia, J., Oliver, S., and Oakley, A. (2006). 'Young People and Healthy Eating: A Systematic Review of Research on Barriers and Facilitators', *Health Education Review*, 21: 239–57.

Shuy, R. W. (2002). 'In-Person versus Telephone Interviewing', in J. F. Gubrium and J. A. Holstein (eds), *Handbook of Interview Research: Context and Method*. Thousand Oaks, CA: Sage.

Siegel, M., Johnson, R. M., Tyagi, K., Power, K., Lohsen, M. C., Ayers, A. J., and Jernigan, D. H. (2013). 'Alcohol Brand References in U.S. Popular Music, 2009–2011', *Substance Use and Misuse*, 48: 1475–84.

Sillince, J. A. A., and Brown, A. D. (2009). 'Multiple Organizational Identities and Legitimacy: The Rhetoric of Police Websites', *Human Relations*, 62: 1829–56.

Silva, E. B., and Wright, D. (2005). 'The Judgment of Taste and Social Position in Focus Group Research', *Sociologia e ricerca sociale*, 76–7: 241–53.

Silva, E. B., and Wright, D. (2008). 'Researching Cultural Capital: Complexities in Mixing Methods', *Methodological Innovations Online*, 2(3): 50–62, doi: 10.4256/mio.2008.0005 (accessed 1 March 2021).

Silverman, D. (1984). 'Going Private: Ceremonial Forms in a Private Oncology Clinic', *Sociology*, 18: 191–204.

Silverman, D. (1985). *Qualitative Methodology and Sociology: Describing the Social World*. Aldershot, UK: Gower.

Silverman, D. (2015). *Interpreting Qualitative Data*. London: Sage.

Silverman, D. (2017). *Doing Qualitative Research: A Practical Handbook*, 5th edn. London: Sage.

Simmel, G. (1908). *Soziologie: Untersuchungen über die Formen der Vergesellschaftung*. Leipzig: Duncker & Humblot.

Simon, H. (1960). *Administrative Behavior: A Study of Decision-Making Processes in Administrative Organizations*, 2nd edn. New York: Macmillan.

Singer, E. (2003). 'Exploring the Meaning of Consent: Participation in Research and Beliefs about Risks and Benefits', *Journal of Official Statistics*, 19: 273–85.

Singer, E., and Couper, M. (2017). 'Some Methodological Uses of Responses to Open Questions and Other Verbatim Comments in Quantitative Surveys', *Methods, Data and Analyses*, 11(2): 115–34.

Singh, S., and Wassenaar, D. (2016). 'Contextualising the Role of the Gatekeeper in Social Science Research', *South African Journal of Bioethics and Law*, 9(1): 42, doi: 10.7196/SAJBL.2016.v9i1.465.

Sink, A., and Mastro, D. (2017). 'Depictions of Gender on Primetime Television: A Quantitative Content Analysis', *Mass Communication and Society*, 20(1): 3–22, 10.1080/15205436.2016.1212243.

Sinyor, M., Schaffer, A., Hull, I., and Peisah, C. (2015). 'Last Wills and Testaments in a Large Sample of Suicide Notes: Implications for Testamentary Capacity', *British Journal of Psychiatry*, 206(1): 72–6.

Skeggs, B. (1994). 'Situating the Production of Feminist Ethnography', in M. Maynard and J. Purvis (eds), *Researching Women's Lives from a Feminist Perspective*. London: Taylor & Francis.

Skeggs, B. (1997). *Formations of Class and Gender*. London: Sage.

Skeggs, B. (2001). 'Feminist Ethnography', in P. Atkinson, A. Coffey, S. Delamont, J. Lofland, and L. Lofland (eds), *Handbook of Ethnography*. London: Sage.

Skoglund, R. I. (2019). 'When "Words Do Not Work": Intervening in Children's Conflicts in Kindergarten', *International Research in Early Childhood Education*, 9(1): 23–38.

Sleijpen, M., Boeije, H. R., Kleber, R. J., and Mooren, T. (2016). 'Between Power and Powerlessness: A Meta-ethnography of Sources of Resilience in Young Refugees', *Ethnicity & Health*, 21(2): 158–80.

Sloan, L. (2017). 'Who Tweets in the United Kingdom? Profiling the Twitter Population Using the British Social Attitudes Survey 2015', *Social Media and Society*, 3(1): 1–11, https://doi.org/10.1177/2056305117698981.

Sloan, L., Jessop, C., Al Baghal, T., and Williams, M. (2019). 'Linking Survey And Twitter Data: Informed Consent, Disclosure, Security and Archiving', *Journal of Empirical Research on Human Research Ethics*, 15(1–2): 63–76, 10.1177/1556264619853447.

Smithson, J., and Brannen, J. (2002). 'Qualitative Methodology in Cross-National Research', in J. Brannen, S. Lewis, A. Nilsen, and J. Smithson (eds), *Young Europeans, Work and Family: Futures in Transition*. London: Routledge.

Smyth, J. D., Dillman, D. A., Christian, L. M., and McBride, N. (2009). 'Open-Ended Questions in Web Surveys: Can Increasing the Size of Answer Spaces and Providing Extra Verbal Instructions Improve Response Quality?', *Public Opinion Quarterly*, 73: 325–37.

Smyth, J. D., Dillman, D. A., Christian, L. M., and Stern, M. J. (2006). 'Comparing Check-All and Forced-Choice Question Formats in Web Surveys', *Public Opinion Quarterly*, 70: 66–77.

Smyth, J., and Olson, K. (2015). 'Recording What the Respondent Says: Does Question Format Matter?' paper presented at the 2015 Annual Conference of the American Association for Public Opinion Research, Hollywood, FL.

Snee, H. (2013). 'Framing the Other: Cosmopolitanism and the Representation of Difference in Overseas Gap Year Narratives', *British Journal of Sociology*, 64: 142–62.

Snyder, N., and Glueck, W. F. (1980). 'How Managers Plan: The Analysis of Managers' Activities', *Long Range Planning*, 13: 70–6.

So, K. K. F., Oh, H., and Min, S. (2018). 'Motivations and Constraints of Airbnb Consumers: Findings from a Mixed-Methods Approach', *Tourism Management*, 67: 224–36, doi: 10.1016/j.tourman.2018.01.009.

Solheim, J., Rege, M., and McTigue, E. (2017). 'Study Protocol: "Two Teachers": A Randomized Controlled Trial Investigating Individual and Complementary Effects of Teacher–Student Ratio in Literacy Instruction and Professional Development for Teachers', *International Journal of Educational Research*, 86: 122–30.

Spratto, E., and Bandalos, D. (2020). 'Attitudinal Survey Characteristics Impacting Participant Responses', *Journal of Experimental Education*, 88(4): 620–42.

Sprokkereef, A., Larkin, E., Pole, C. J., and Burgess, R. G. (1995). 'The Data, the Team, and the Ethnography', in R. G. Burgess (ed.), *Computing and Qualitative Research*, Studies in Qualitative Methodology, vol. 5. Greenwich, CT: JAI Press, 81–103.

Stacey, J. (1988). 'Can there Be a Feminist Ethnography?', *Women's International Studies Forum*, 11: 21–7.

Stacey, M. (1960). *Tradition and Change: A Study of Banbury*. London: Oxford University Press.

Stake, R. E. (1995). *The Art of Case Study Research*. Thousand Oaks, CA: Sage.

Stanley, L., and Temple, B. (1995). 'Doing the Business? Evaluating Software Packages to Aid the Analysis of Qualitative Data Sets', in R. G. Burgess (ed.), *Computing and Qualitative Research*, Studies in Qualitative Methodology, vol. 5. Greenwich, CT: JAI Press, 169–97.

Stauff, M. (2018). 'The Assertive Image: Referentiality and Reflexivity in Sports Photography', *Historical Social Research/Historische Sozialforschung*, 43(2): 53–71.

Steele, S., Ruskin, G., McKee, M., and Stuckler, D. (2019). '"Always Read the Small Print": A Case Study of Commercial Research Funding, Disclosure and Agreements with Coca-Cola', *Journal of Public Health Policy*, 40: 273–85, https://doi.org/10.1057/s41271-019-00170-9.

Stewart, K., and Williams, M. (2005). 'Researching Online Populations: The Use of Online Focus Groups for Social Research', *Qualitative Research*, 5: 395–416.

Stoddart, M., Haluza-DeLay, R., and Tindall, D. (2016). 'Canadian News Media Coverage of Climate Change: Historical Trajectories, Dominant Frames, and International Comparisons', *Society and Natural Resources*, 29(2): 218–32.

Strauss, A. (1987). *Qualitative Analysis for Social Scientists*. New York: Cambridge University Press.

Strauss, A., and Corbin, J. M. (1990). *Basics of Qualitative Research: Grounded Theory Procedures and Techniques*. Newbury Park, CA: Sage.

Strauss, A., and Corbin, J. M. (1998). *Basics of Qualitative Research: Techniques and Procedures for Developing Grounded Theory*. Thousand Oaks, CA: Sage.

Strauss, A., Schatzman, L., Ehrich, D., Bucher, R., and Sabshin, M. (1973). 'The Hospital and its Negotiated Order', in G. Salaman and K. Thompson (eds), *People and Organizations*. London: Longman.

Streiner, D. L., and Sidani, S. (2010). *When Research Goes Off the Rails: Why it Happens and What You Can Do About It*. New York: Guilford.

Stroobant, J., De Dobbelaer, R., and Raeymaeckers, K. (2018). 'Tracing the Sources: A Comparative Content Analysis of Belgian Health News', *Journalism Practice*, 12(3): 344–61.

Sturges, J. E., and Hanrahan, K. J. (2004). 'Comparing Telephone and Face-to-Face Qualitative Interviewing: A Research Note', *Qualitative Research*, 4: 107–18.

Sturgis, P., Brunton-Smith, I., Kuha, J., and Jackson, J. (2014a). 'Ethnic Diversity, Segregation and the Social Cohesion of Neighbourhoods in London', *Ethnic and Racial Studies*, 37: 1286–309.

Sturgis, P., Roberts, C., and Smith, P. (2014b). 'Middle Alternatives Revisited: How the Neither/Nor Response Acts as a Way of Saying "I Don't Know?"', *Sociological Methods and Research*, 43: 15–38.

Sudman, S., and Bradburn, N. M. (1982). *Asking Questions: A Practical Guide to Questionnaire Design*. San Francisco: Jossey-Bass.

Surra, C. A., and Ridley, C. A. (1991). 'Multiple Perspectives on Interaction: Participants, Peers, and Observers', in B. M. Montgomery and S. Duck (eds), *Studying Interpersonal Interaction*. New York: Guilford Press, 35–55.

Sutton, R. I., and Rafaeli, A. (1988). 'Untangling the Relationship between Displayed Emotions and Organizational Sales: The Case of Convenience Stores', *Academy of Management Journal*, 31: 461–87.

Swain, J. (2004). 'The Resources and Strategies that 10–11-Year-Old Boys Use to Construct Masculinities in the School Setting', *British Educational Research Journal*, 30: 167–85.

Sweet, C. (2001). 'Designing and Conducting Virtual Focus Groups', *Qualitative Market Research*, 4: 130–5.

Synnot, A., Hill, S., Summers, M., and Taylor, M. (2014). 'Comparing Face-to-Face and Online Qualitative Research with People with Multiple Sclerosis', *Qualitative Health Research*, 24(3): 431–8.

Tabachnick, B., and Fidell, L. (2018). *Using Multivariate Statistics*. London: Pearson.

Tadajewski, M. (2016). 'Focus Groups: History, Epistemology and Non-individualistic Consumer Research', *Consumption Markets & Culture*, 19(4): 319–45.

Tarr, J. (2013). Overly Honest Social Science? The Value of Acknowledging Bias, Subjectivity and the Messiness of Research, https://blogs.lse.ac.uk/impactofsocialsciences/2013/03/13/overly-honest-social-science/.

Tashakkori, A., and Teddlie, C. (eds) (2010). *Handbook of Mixed Methods in Social and Behavioral Research*, 2nd edn. Los Angeles: Sage.

Taylor, J., Lamont, A., and Murray, M. (2018). 'Talking about Sunbed Tanning in Online Discussion Forums: Assertions and Arguments', *Psychology & Health*, 33(4): 518–36.

Tcherni, M., Davies, A., Lopes, G., and Lizotte, A. (2016). 'The Dark Figure of Online Property Crime: Is Cyberspace Hiding a Crime Wave?', *Justice Quarterly*, 33(5): 890–911.

Teddlie, C., and Yu, F. (2007). 'Mixed Methods Sampling: A Typology with Examples', *Journal of Mixed Methods Research*, 1: 77–100.

Thelwall, M. (2017). 'Sentiment Analysis', in L. Sloan and A. Quan-Haase (eds), *The SAGE Handbook of Social Media Research Methods*. London: Sage.

Thomas, D. R. (2006). 'A General Inductive Approach for Analyzing Qualitative Evaluation Data', *American Journal of Evaluation*, 27: 237–46.

Thomas, G., Fisher, R., Whitmarsh, L., Milfont, T., and Poortinga, W. (2018). 'The Impact of Parenthood on Environmental Attitudes and Behaviour: A Longitudinal Investigation of the Legacy Hypothesis', *Population and Environment*, 39(3): 261–76.

Thomas, J., and Harden, A. (2008). 'Methods for the Thematic Synthesis of Qualitative Research in Systematic Reviews', *BMC Medical Research Methodology*, 8, www.ncbi.nlm.nih.gov/pmc/articles/PMC2478656/pdf/1471-2288-8-45.pdf (accessed 1 March 2021).

Thomas, J., Harden, A., and Newman, M. (2012). 'Synthesis: Combining Results Systematically and Appropriately', in D. Gough, S. Oliver, and J. Thomas (eds), *An Introduction to Systematic Reviews*. London: Sage.

Thompson, C., Lewis, D., Greenhalgh, T., Taylor, S., and Cummins, S. (2013). 'A Health and Social Legacy for East London: Narratives of "Problem" and "Solution" Around London 2012', *Sociological Research Online*, 18(1), www.socresonline.org.uk/18/2/1.html (accessed 1 March 2021).

Thornberg, R. (2018). 'School Bullying and Fitting into the Peer Landscape: A Grounded Theory Field Study', *British Journal of Sociology of Education*, 39(1): 144–58.

Thornberg, R., and Charmaz, K. (2014). 'Grounded Theory and Theoretical Coding', in U. Flick (ed.), *SAGE Handbook of Qualitative Data Analysis*. London: Sage.

Timulak, L. (2014). 'Qualitative Meta-Analysis', in U. Flick (ed.), *SAGE Handbook of Qualitative Data Analysis*. London: Sage.

Tinati, R., Halford, S., Carr, L., and Pope, C. (2014). 'Big Data: Methodological Challenges and Approaches for Sociological Analysis', *Sociology*, 48: 663–81.

Tourangeau, R., and Smith, T. W. (1996). 'Asking Sensitive Questions: The Impact of Data Collection Mode, Question Format, and Question Context', *Public Opinion Quarterly*, 60: 275–304.

Tourangeau, R., and Yan, T. (2007). 'Sensitive Questions in Surveys', *Psychological Bulletin*, 133: 859–83.

Tourangeau, R., Conrad, F. G., and Couper, M. P. (2013). *The Science of Web Surveys*. Oxford: Oxford University Press.

Townsend, K., and Burgess, J. (eds) (2009). *Method in the Madness: Research Stories you won't Read in Textbooks*. Oxford: Chandos.

Tracy, S. J. (2010). 'Qualitative Quality: Eight "Big Tent" Criteria for Excellent Qualitative Research', *Qualitative Inquiry*, 16: 837–51.

Tranfield, D., Denyer, D., and Smart, P. (2003). 'Towards a Methodology for Developing Evidence-Informed Management Knowledge by Means of Systematic Review', *British Journal of Management*, 14: 207–22.

Trouille, D., and Tavory, I. (2016). 'Shadowing: Warrants for Intersituational Variation in Ethnography', *Sociological Methods & Research*, 48(3): 534–60.

Trow, M. (1957). 'Comment on "Participant Observation and Interviewing: A Comparison"', *Human Organization*, 16: 33–5.

Tufte, E. (1983). *Visual Display of Quantitative Information*. Cheshire, CT: Graphic Press.

Turner, V. W., and Bruner, E. (eds.) (1986). *The Anthropology of Experience*. Chicago: University of Illinois Press.

Tuinman M., Lehmann, V., and Hagedoorn, M. (2018). 'Do Single People Want to Date a Cancer Survivor? A Vignette Study', *PLoS ONE*, 13(3).

Turnbull, C. (1973). *The Mountain People*. London: Cape.

Tuttas, C. A. (2014). 'Lessons Learned using Web Conference Technology for Online Focus Group Interviews', *Qualitative Health Research*, 25(1): 122–33.

Twine, F. W. (2006). 'Visual Ethnography and Racial Theory: Family Photographs as Archives of Interracial Intimacies', *Ethnic and Racial Studies*, 29: 487–511.

Twine, R. (2017). 'Materially Constituting a Sustainable Food Transition: The Case of Vegan Eating Practice', *Sociology*, 52(1): 166–81.

Twitter (2019). 'Display Requirements: Tweets', https://developer.twitter.com/en/developer-terms/display-requirements.html.

Tyrer, S., and Heyman, B. (2016). 'Sampling in Epidemiological Research: Issues, Hazards and Pitfalls', *British Journal of Psychology Bulletin*, 40(2): 57–60.

Uekusa, S. (2019). 'Surfing with Bourdieu! A Qualitative Analysis of the Fluid Power Relations among Surfers in the Line-Ups', *Journal of Contemporary Ethnography*, 48(4): 538–62, https://doi.org/10.1177/0891241618802879.

Underhill, C., and Olmsted, M. G. (2003). 'An Experimental Comparison of Computer-Mediated and Face-to-Face Focus Groups', *Social Science Computer Review*, 21: 506–12.

Underwood, M. (2017). 'Exploring the Social Lives of Image and Performance Enhancing Drugs: An Online Ethnography of the Zyzz Fandom of Recreational Bodybuilders', *International Journal of Drug Policy*, 39: 78–85.

Uprichard, E., and Dawney, L. (2019). 'Data Diffraction: Challenging Data Integration in Mixed Methods Research', *Journal of Mixed Methods Research*, 13(1): 19–32, doi: 10.1177/1558689816674650.

Upton, A. (2011). 'In Testing Times: Conducting an Ethnographic Study of Animal Rights Protestors', *Sociological Research Online*, 16, www.socresonline.org.uk/16/4/1.html (accessed 1 March 2021).

Vacchelli, E. (2018). *Embodied Research in Migration Studies: Using Creative and Participatory Approaches*. Bristol, UK: Policy Press.

van Bezouw, M. J., Garyfallou, A., Oană, I. E., and Rojon, S. (2019). 'A Methodology for Cross-National Comparative Focus Group Research: Illustrations from Discussions about Political Protest', *Quality & Quantity*, 53(6): 2719–39.

Vancea, M., Shore, J., and Utzet, M. (2019). 'Role of Employment-Related Inequalities in Young Adults' Life Satisfaction: A Comparative Study in Five European Welfare State Regimes', *Scandinavian Journal of Public Health*, 47(3): 357–65.

van Dijk, T. A. (1997). 'Discourse as Interaction in Society', in T. A. van Dijk (ed.), *Discourse as Social Interaction*, Discourse Studies: A Multidisciplinary Introduction, vol. 2. Newbury Park, CA: Sage.

Van Maanen, J. (1978). 'On Watching the Watchers', in P. Manning and J. Van Maanen (eds), *Policing: The View from the Street*. Santa Monica, CA: Goodyear.

Van Maanen, J. (1988). *Tales of the Field: On Writing Ethnography*. Chicago: University of Chicago Press.

Van Maanen, J. (1991a). 'Playing Back the Tape: Early Days in the Field', in W. B. Shaffir and R. A. Stebbins (eds), *Experiencing Fieldwork: An Inside View of Qualitative Research*. Newbury Park, CA: Sage.

Van Maanen, J. (1991b). 'The Smile Factory: Work at Disneyland', in P. J. Frost, L. F. Moore, M. R. Louis, C. C. Lundberg, and J. Martin (eds), *Reframing Organizational Culture*. Newbury Park, CA: Sage.

Van Maanen, J. (2010). 'A Song for my Supper: More Tales of the Field', *Organizational Research Methods*, 13: 240–55.

Van Maanen, J. (2011). *Tales of the Field: On Writing Ethnography*, 2nd edn. Chicago: University of Chicago Press.

Van Maanen, J., and Kolb, D. (1985). 'The Professional Apprentice: Observations on Fieldwork Roles in Two Organizational Settings', *Research in the Sociology of Organizations*, 4: 1–33.

Van Selm, M., and Jankowski, N. W. (2006). 'Conducting Online Surveys', *Quality and Quantity*, 40(3): 435–56.

Vasquez, J. M., and Wetzel, C. (2009). 'Tradition and the Invention of Racial Selves: Symbolic Boundaries, Collective Authenticity, and Contemporary Struggles for Racial Equality', *Ethnic and Racial Studies*, 32: 1557–75.

Vaughan, D. (1996). *The Challenger Launch Decision: Risky Technology, Culture, and Deviance at NASA*. Chicago: University of Chicago Press.

Vaughan, D. (2004). 'Theorizing Disaster: Analogy, Historical Ethnography, and the *Challenger* Accident', *Ethnography*, 5: 315–47.

Vaughan, D. (2006). 'The Social Shaping of Commission Reports', *Sociological Forum*, 21: 291–306.

Venkatesh, S. (2008). *Gang Leader for a Day: A Rogue Sociologist Crosses the Line*. London: Allen Lane.

Verhagen, S., Hasmi, L., Drukker, M., van Os, J., and Delespaul, P. (2016). 'Use of the Experience Sampling Method in the Context of Clinical Trials', *Evidence Based Mental Health*, 19(3): 86–9.

Vincent, J., Kian, E. M., Pedersen, P. M., Kutz, A., and Hill, J. S. (2010). 'England Expects: English Newspapers' Narratives about the English Football Team in the 2006 World Cup', *International Review of the Sociology of Sport*, 45: 199–223.

Voas, D. (2014). 'Towards a Sociology of Attitudes', *Sociological Research Online*, 19, www.socresonline.org.uk/19/1/12.html (accessed 1 March 2021).

Vogl, S. (2013). 'Telephone versus Face-to-Face Interviews: Mode Effect in Semi-structured Interviews with Children', *Sociological Methodology*, 43(1): 133–77.

Vogt, W. (ed.) (2011). *Sage Quantitative Research Methods*. London: Sage.

Wacquant, L. (2004). *Body and Soul: Notebooks of an Apprentice Boxer*. Oxford: Oxford University Press.

Wacquant, L. (2009). 'Habitus as Topic and Tool: Reflections on Becoming a Prize Fighter', in A. J. Puddephatt, W. Shaffir, and S. W. Kleinknecht (eds), *Ethnographies Revisited: Constructing Theory in the Field*. London: Routledge.

Wagg, S. (2010). 'Cristiano Meets Mr Spleen: Global Football Celebrity, Mythic Manchester and the Portuguese Diaspora', *Sport in Society*, 13: 919–34.

Wagg, S. (2017). 'Leisure and "the Civilising Process"', in K. Spracklen, B. Lashua, E. Sharpe, and S. Swain (eds), *The Palgrave Handbook of Leisure Theory*. Basingstoke, UK: Palgrave.

Walby, S., and Towers, J. (2017). 'Measuring Violence to End Violence: Mainstreaming Gender', *Journal of Gender-Based Violence*, 1(1): 11–31.

Walker, J. (2010). 'Measuring Plagiarism: Researching What Students Do, Not What They Say', *Studies in Higher Education*, 35: 41–59.

Walsh, I., Holton, J. A., Bailyn, L., Fernandez, W., Levian, N., and Glaser, B. (2015). 'What Grounded Theory is . . . A Critically Reflective Conversation Among Scholars', *Organizational Research Methods*, 18(4): 581–99, 10.1177/1094428114565028.

Walters, R. (2020). 'Relinquishing Control in Focus Groups: The Use of Activities in Feminist Research with Young People to Improve Moderator Performance', *Qualitative Research*, 20(4): 361–77.

Wansink, B., Mukund, A., and Weislogel, A. (2016). 'Food Art Does Not Reflect Reality: A Quantitative Content Analysis of Meals in Popular Paintings', *SAGE Open*, 6(3): 1–10.

Warr, D. J. (2005). '"It Was Fun . . . But We Don't Usually Talk about These Things": Analyzing Sociable Interaction in Focus Groups', *Qualitative Inquiry*, 11: 200–25.

Warren, C. A. B. (2002). 'Qualitative Interviewing', in J. F. Gubrium and J. A. Holstein (eds), *Handbook of Interview Research: Context and Method*. Thousand Oaks, CA: Sage.

Warren, L. (2018). 'Representing Self-Representing Ageing', in A. Walker (ed), *The New Dynamics of Ageing*, vol 2. Bristol, UK: Policy Press, 219–42.

Warwick, D. P. (1982). 'Tearoom Trade: Means and End in Social Research', in M. Bulmer (ed.), *Social Research Ethics: An Examination of the Merits of Covert Participant Observation*. London: Macmillan, 38–58.

Wästerfors, D., and Åkerström, M. (2016). 'Case History Discourse: A Rhetoric of Troublesome Youngsters and Faceless Treatment', *European Journal of Social Work*, 19(6): 871–86.

Waters, J. (2015). 'Snowball Sampling: A Cautionary Tale Involving a Study of Older Drug Users', *International Journal of Social Research Methodology*, 18(4): 367–80.

Watson, A., Ward, J., and Fair, J. (2018). 'Staging Atmosphere: Collective Emotional Labour on the Film Set', *Social & Cultural Geography*, https://doi.org/10.1080/14649365.2018.1551563.

Watson, N., and Wilkins, R. (2011). 'Experimental Change from Paper-Based Interviewing to Computer-Assisted Interviewing in the HILDA Survey', HILDA Discussion Paper Series No. 2/11, Melbourne Institute of Applied Economic and Social Research, University of Melbourne.

Watts, L. (2008). 'The Art and Craft of Train Travel', *Social and Cultural Geography*, 9: 711–26.

Weaver, A., and Atkinson, P. (1994). *Microcomputing and Qualitative Data Analysis*. Aldershot, UK: Avebury.

Webb, E. J., Campbell, D. T., Schwartz, R. D., and Sechrest, L. (1966). *Unobtrusive Measures: Nonreactive Measures in the Social Sciences*. Chicago: Rand McNally.

Weber, M. (1947). *The Theory of Social and Economic Organization*, trans A. M. Henderson and T. Parsons. New York: Free Press.

Weinmann, T., Thomas, S., Brilmayer, S., Heinrich, S., and Radon, K. (2012). 'Testing Skype as an Interview Method in Epidemiologic Research: Response and Feasibility', *International Journal of Public Health*, 57: 959–61.

West, B., and Blom, A. (2017). 'Explaining Interviewer Effects: A Research Synthesis', *Journal of Survey Statistics and Methodology*, 5(2): 175–211.

Westmarland, L. (2001). 'Blowing the Whistle on Police Violence: Ethics, Research and Ethnography', *British Journal of Criminology*, 41: 523–35.

Wetherell, M. (1998). 'Positioning and Interpretative Repertoires: Conversation Analysis and Post-Structuralism in Dialogue', *Discourse and Society*, 9: 387–412.

Whitaker, C., Stevelink, S., and Fear, N. (2017). 'The Use of Facebook in Recruiting Participants for Health Research Purposes: A Systematic Review', *Journal of Medical Internet Research*, 19(8): e290.

White, P. (2017). *Developing Research Questions*, 2nd edn. London: Palgrave.

Whyte, W. F. (1955). *Street Corner Society*, 2nd edn. Chicago: University of Chicago Press.

Widdicombe, S. (1993). 'Autobiography and Change: Rhetoric and Authenticity of "Gothic" Style', in E. Burman and I. Parker (eds), *Discourse Analytic Research: Readings and Repertoires of Text*. London: Routledge.

Wikipedia (n.d., a). 'List of Hoaxes on Wikipedia', https://en.wikipedia.org/wiki/Wikipedia:List_of_hoaxes_on_Wikipedia (accessed 20 March 2021).

Wikipedia (n.d., b). 'Wikipedia: Size Comparisons', https://en.wikipedia.org/wiki/Wikipedia:Size_comparisons (accessed 20 March 2020).

Wilkinson, J. (2009). 'Staff and Student Perceptions of Plagiarism and Cheating', *International Journal of Teaching and Learning in Higher Education*, 20: 98–105.

Wilkinson, S. (1998). 'Focus Groups in Feminist Research: Power, Interaction, and the Co-Production of Meaning', *Women's Studies International Forum*, 21: 111–25.

Wilkinson, S. (1999). 'Focus Group Methodology: A Review', *International Journal of Social Research Methodology*, 1: 181–203.

Wilkinson, S., and Kitzinger, C. (2008). 'Conversation Analysis', in C. Willig and W. Stainton-Rogers (eds), *SAGE Handbook of Qualitative Research in Psychology*. London: Sage.

Williams, H. M., Topping, A., Coomarasamy, A., and Jones, L. L. (2020). 'Men and Miscarriage: A Systematic Review and Thematic Synthesis', *Qualitative Health Research*, 30(1): 133–45.

Williams, M. D. (2000). 'Interpretivism and Generalisation', *Sociology*, 34: 209–24.

Williams, M. D., Sloan, L., Cheung, S. Y., Sutton, C., Stevens, S., and Runham, L. (2016). 'Can't Count or Won't Count? Embedding Quantitative Methods in Substantive Sociology Curricula: A Quasi-experiment', *Sociology*, 50(3): 435–52, 10.1177/0038038515587652.

Williams, M. L. (2016). 'Guardians Upon High: An Application of Routine Activities Theory to Online Identity Theft in Europe at The Country and Individual Level', *British Journal of Criminology*, 56(1): 21–48, 10.1093/bjc/azv011.

Williams, M. L., and Burnap, P. (2016). 'Cyberhate on Social Media in the Aftermath of Woolwich: A Case Study in Computational Criminology and Big Data', *British Journal of Criminology*, 56(2): 211–38, 10.1093/bjc/azv059.

Williams, M. L., Burnap, P., and Sloan, L. (2017a). 'Crime Sensing with Big Data: The Affordances and Limitations of Using Open Source Communications to Estimate Crime Patterns', *British Journal of Criminology*, 57(2): 320–40, 10.1093/bjc/azw031.

Williams, M. L., Burnap, P., and Sloan, L. (2017b). 'Towards an Ethical Framework for Publishing Twitter Data in Social Research: Taking into Account Users' Views, Online Context and Algorithmic Estimation', *Sociology*, 51(6): 1149–68, 10.1177/0038038517708140.

Williams, S., Clausen, M. G., Robertson, A., Peacock, S., and McPherson, K. (2012). 'Methodological Reflections on the Use of Asynchronous Online Focus Groups in Health Research', *International Journal of Qualitative Methods*, 11(4): 368–83.

Willis, R. (2018). 'Observations Online: Finding the Ethical Boundaries of Facebook Research', *Research Ethics*, 15(1): 1–17.

Wilson, J. Q., and Kelling, G. L. (1982). 'The Police and Neighbourhood Safety: Broken Windows', *Atlantic Monthly*, 127: 29–38.

Wilson, J. Z. (2008). *Prison: Cultural Memory and Dark Tourism*. New York: Peter Lang.

Windsong, E. A. (2016). 'Incorporating Intersectionality into Research Design: An Example using Qualitative Interviews', *International Journal of Social Research Methodology*, 21(2): 135–47, doi: 10.1080/13645579.2016.1268361.

Wingfield, A. H. (2009). 'Racializing the Glass Escalator: Reconsidering Men's Experiences with Women's Work', *Gender & Society*, 23(1): 5–26.

Winkle-Wagner, R., Kelly, B. T., Luedke, C. L., and Reavis, T. B. (2019). 'Authentically Me: Examining Expectations that are Placed upon Black Women in College', *American Educational Research Journal*, 56(2): 407–43.

Winlow, S., Hobbs, D., Lister, S., and Hadfield, P. (2001). 'Get Ready to Duck: Bouncers and the Realities of Ethnographic Research on Violent Groups', *British Journal of Criminology*, 41: 536–48.

Wolcott, H. F. (1990a). *Writing up Qualitative Research*. Newbury Park, CA: Sage.

Wolcott, H. F. (1990b). 'Making a Study "More Ethnographic"', *Journal of Contemporary Ethnography*, 19: 44–72.

Wolf, D. R. (1991). 'High Risk Methodology: Reflections on Leaving an Outlaw Society', in W. B. Shaffir and R. A. Stebbins (eds), *Experiencing Fieldwork: An Inside View of Qualitative Research*. Newbury Park, CA: Sage.

Wolfinger, N. H. (2002). 'On Writing Field Notes: Collection Strategies and Background Expectancies', *Qualitative Research*, 2: 85–95.

Wolkowitz, C. (2012). '*Flesh and Stone* Revisited: The Body Work Landscape of South Florida', *Sociological Research Online*, 17, www.socresonline.org.uk/17/2/26.html (accessed 1 March 2021).

Wood, K., Patterson, C., Katikireddi, S. V., and Hilton, S. (2014). 'Harms to "Others" from Alcohol Consumption in the Minimum Unit Pricing Policy Debate: A Qualitative Content Analysis of UK Newspapers (2005–12)', *Addiction*, 109: 578–84.

Wood, R. T., and Williams, R. J. (2007). '"How Much Money Do You Spend on Gambling?" The Comparative Validity of Question Wordings to Assess Gambling Expenditure', *International Journal of Social Research Methodology*, 10: 63–77.

Woodfield, K. (ed.) (2018). *The Ethics of Online Research*, vol. 2. Advances in Research Ethics and Integrity. Bingley, UK: Emerald.

Woodfield, K., and Iphofen, R. (2018). 'Introduction to Volume 2: The Ethics of Online Research', in K. Woodfield (ed.), *The Ethics of Online Research*. Bingley, UK: Emerald, 1–12.

Woods, M., Macklin, R., and Lewis, G. K. (2016). 'Researcher Reflexivity: Exploring the Impacts of CAQDAS Use', *International Journal of Social Research Methodology*, 19(4): 385–403.

Woodthorpe, K. (2011). 'Researching Death: Methodological Reflections on the Management of Critical Distance', *International Journal of Social Research Methodology*, 14(2): 99–109.

Wright, C., Nyberg, D., and Grant, D. (2012). '"Hippies on the Third Floor": Climate Change, Narrative Identity and the Micro-Politics of Corporate Environmentalism', *Organization Studies*, 33: 1451–75.

Wright, C. J., Darko, N., Standen, P. J., and Patel, T. G. (2010). 'Visual Research Methods: Using Cameras to Empower Socially Excluded Youth', *Sociology*, 44: 541–58.

Wu, M.-Y., and Pearce, P. L. (2014). 'Appraising Netnography: Towards Insights about new Markets in the Digital Tourist Era', *Current Issues in Tourism*, 17: 463–74.

Yang, K., and Banamah, A. (2013). 'Quota Sampling as an Alternative to Probability Sampling? An Experimental

Study', *Sociological Research Online*, 19, www.socresonline.org.uk/19/1/29.html (accessed 1 March 2021).

Yeager, D. S., Krosnick, J. A., Chang, L., Javitz, H. S., Levendusky, M. S., Simpser, A., and Wang, R. (2011). 'Comparing the Accuracy of RDD Telephone Surveys and Internet Surveys with Probability and Non-Probability Samples', *Public Opinion Quarterly*, 75: 709–47.

Yin, R. K. (2009). *Case Study Research: Design and Methods*, 4th edn. Los Angeles: Sage.

Yin, R. K. (2017). *Case Study Research and Applications: Design and Methods*, 6th edn. Los Angeles: Sage.

Young, N., and Dugas, E. (2011). 'Representations of Climate Change in Canadian National Print Media: The Banalization of Global Warming', *Canadian Review of Sociology*, 48: 1–22.

Zempi, I. (2017). 'Researching Victimisation using Auto-ethnography: Wearing the Muslim Veil in Public', *Methodological Innovations*, 10(1): 2059799117720617.

Zhang, B., Mildenberger, M., Howe, P., Marlon, J., Rosenthal, S., and Leiserowitz, A. (2020). 'Quota Sampling using Facebook Advertisements', *Political Science Research and Methods*, 8(3): 558–64.

Zhang, C., and Conrad, F. (2018). 'Intervening to Reduce Satisficing Behaviors in Web Surveys: Evidence from Two Experiments on How it Works', *Social Science Computer Review*, 36(1): 57–81.

Zhang, X., Kuchinke, L., Woud, M., Velten, J., and Margraf, J. (2017). 'Survey Method Matters: Online/Offline Questionnaires and Face-to-Face or Telephone Interviews Differ', *Computers in Human Behavior*, 71: 172–80.

Zhang, Y., and Shaw, J. D. (2012). 'Publishing in *AMJ*—Part 5: Crafting the Methods and Results', *Academy of Management Journal*, 55: 8–12.

Zickar, M. J., and Carter, N. T. (2010). 'Reconnecting with the Spirit of Workplace Ethnography: A Historical Review', *Organizational Research Methods*, 13: 304–19.

Znaniecki, F. (1934). *The Method of Sociology*. New York: Farrar & Rinehart.

ZuWallack, R. (2009). 'Piloting Data Collection via Cell Phones: Results, Experiences, and Lessons Learned', *Field Methods*, 21: 388–406.

NAME INDEX

Note: Tables and figures are indicated by an italic *t* and *f* following the page number.

A

B

C

SUBJECT INDEX

Note: Tables and figures are indicated by an italic *t* and *f* following the page number.

J

K

L

M

N

O

R

S

T